Practical Predictive Analytics and ⬚⬚⬚⬚⬚⬚ ⬚ Systems for Medicine

This book is dedicated to the Guest Tutorial Authors,
in gratitude for all their expertise and hard work
in providing the central part of this book.

Practical Predictive Analytics and Decisioning Systems for Medicine

Informatics Accuracy and Cost-Effectiveness for Healthcare Administration and Delivery Including Medical Research

Linda A. Winters-Miner, PhD

Pat S. Bolding, MD

Joseph M. Hilbe, JD, PhD

Mitchell Goldstein, MD

Thomas Hill, PhD

Robert Nisbet, PhD

Nephi Walton, MS, MD

Gary D. Miner, PhD

Guest Chapter Authors:

Gerard Britton, JD, MS
Eric W. Brown, PhD
John W. Cromwell, MD
Darrell Dean, DO, MPH, CHCQM, FAIHQ
Jacek Jakubowski, PhD
Sven Koch, RN, PhD
Martin S. Kohn, MD, MS, FACEP, FACPE

Leslaw Kulach, MSc
Piotr Murawski, MSc
Chris Papesh, MBA
Vladimir Rastunkov, PhD
Danny W. Stout, PhD
Christopher L. Wasden, EdD

AMSTERDAM • BOSTON • HEIDELBERG • LONDON • NEW YORK • OXFORD • PARIS
SAN DIEGO • SAN FRANCISCO • SINGAPORE • SYDNEY • TOKYO

Academic Press is an imprint of Elsevier

Academic Press is an imprint of Elsevier
32 Jamestown Road, London NW1 7BY, UK
525 B Street, Suite 1800, San Diego, CA 92101-4495, USA
225 Wyman Street, Waltham, MA 02451, USA
The Boulevard, Langford Lane, Kidlington, Oxford OX5 1GB, UK

British Library Cataloguing-in-Publication Data
A catalogue record for this book is available from the British Library

Library of Congress Cataloging-in-Publication Data
A catalog record for this book is available from the Library of Congress

ISBN: 978-0-12-810062-2

For information on all Academic Press publications
visit our website at http://store.elsevier.com/

Working together
to grow libraries in
developing countries

www.elsevier.com • www.bookaid.org

Transferred to Digital Printing in 2016

Contents

Prologue to Part 1

Part 1
Historical Perspective and the Issues of Concern for Healthcare Delivery in the 21st Century

1. History of Predictive Analytics in Medicine and Health Care

2. Why did We Write This Book?

14. Patient-Directed Health Care

Prologue to Part 1, Chapter 15

15. Prediction in Medicine — The Data Mining Algorithms of Predictive Analytics

Prologue to Part 3

Part 3
Practical Solutions and Advanced Topics in Administration and Delivery of Health Care Including Practical Predictive Analytics for Medicine

Foreword by Thomas H. Davenport

I am pleased that you have purchased or picked up this book, because it covers one of the most important topics in health care and human society overall. What is more important than using data and scientific evidence to improve health care? As the many authors demonstrate throughout this volume, their topic has implications for not only our personal health, but also our finances, our happiness, and our legacy as a country and society.

Still, I suspect as you gaze upon this hefty tome you might find it a little overwhelming. Even if you're an expert in the field of healthcare informatics and analytics, there is likely to be much in this book that you don't know about. You may even feel that the term "practical predictive analytics" is something of an oxymoron.

However, dear reader, do not be dissuaded from diving into this book because of these concerns. First, the authors of most chapters are careful to define their terminology and stay away from highly technical expositions. An educated layperson can learn much from the book, and experts will have no problem with the great majority of chapters. The tone is relatively light in most chapters (at least, given the very serious subject), and there are even a few cartoons!

Secondly, the topics and terms are highly related. The reader comes to understand the relationships between and among various types of healthcare analytics, informatics, and tools and approaches for medical decision-making. Upon reading several chapters I realized, for example, that "predictive analytics" and "personalized medicine" are two sides of the same coin. These are two terms that I'd been familiar with for a while, but I never thought about their close relationship. Predictive analytics is simply the way we achieve personalized medicine; we are predicting how a particular patient will respond to a medicine or treatment, given that person's genotype and phenotype. It follows that the personalization of medicine is a probabilistic activity just like any other form of predictive analytics.

Thirdly, the book's chapters are replete with examples, and two entire parts — the second with tutorials, and the third with case studies — contain rich detail on how these ideas can be implemented in particular settings. I found the case studies particularly useful because they include factors that go well beyond the theory of predictive analysis in that particular domain. Many address issues such as culture, resistance by doctors and other practitioners, regulatory constraints, and other aspects of the institutional context in which predictive analytics are applied to health care.

Finally, you may find the volume of content in the book to be rather intimidating, as did I. However, I realized that the notions of personalization and prediction have relevance in navigating this book as well. Not all the content and chapters will be of equal interest to all readers. In a perfect world, we'd have a predictive analytics-based "configurator" that would tailor the content to each individual reader. Short of that, however, the Contents list can serve as your content personalization engine. I encourage you to use it aggressively.

In fact, I confess not to have perused all of the chapters herein, but I have checked out most of them. I can safely assure that they represent a high level of content quality on this most important of topics. Healthcare professionals, quantitative analysts, and anyone interested in the future of medicine will be consulting it for many years to come.

Thomas H. Davenport
President's Distinguished Professor, Babson College;
Fellow, MIT Center for Digital Business;

Co-founder and Director of Research,
International Institute for Analytics.

Foreword by James Taylor

Those of us working in analytics and decision management have long regarded medicine as a prime target area. Like many industries, medicine is seeing an explosion in available data as medical records are digitized, medical equipment monitors patients in real time, and medical research is provided in machine-readable formats. If these data can be effectively applied to make better decisions, then lives as well as money can be saved. Applying predictive analytics and decision management to diagnosis, treatment selection, cost management, fraud detection, and more will result in consistent, effective, cost-efficient medical outcomes. These decisions will be based not only on medical research and the skills of medical professionals, but also on the analysis of an extensive and rapidly growing body of data. A book on predictive analytics and decisioning systems in medicine, then, is both timely and necessary.

This book provides an introduction to both the healthcare industry and the predictive analytic process. It discusses the ongoing digitization of electronic medical records and how to use these systems, as well as the regulatory and research framework within which medicine operates today. A wide-ranging collection of examples shows the potential for predictive analytics and decisioning, while dozens of tutorial examples walk through real-world uses of predictive analytics in medicine. Critically, throughout the book, the authors keep the reader focused on the need to use data to improve decision-making, not just to make predictions.

There is a deep, across-the-board need for predictive analytics and more advanced decisioning systems in health care. This book offers a comprehensive look at the challenges, opportunities, techniques, and technologies.

James Taylor
CEO Decision Management Solutions

Author of Decision Management Systems: A Practical Guide
to Using Business Rules and Predictive Analytics *(IBM Press, 2011).*

Foreword by John Halamka

At Beth Israel Deaconess Medical Center in Boston, I oversee 3 petabytes of healthcare data. Big Data is no longer "big," since I can easily store, protect, and curate multiple petabytes growing at 25% per year. My challenge is turning data into information, knowledge, and wisdom.

Providing analytics and decision support to clinicians depends on good data, the appropriate business intelligence tools, and actionable visualizations. This book is a primer and roadmap for the entire process of supporting care with predictive analytics.

It includes an important discussion of healthcare data capture, highlighting variations in data quality and the usefulness of data gathered by different people in different workflows. Case studies illustrate how data can change care, getting the right care to the right patients at the right time.

The book also captures major trends, such as mobile technologies to gather patient-generated data and provide alerts/reminders to providers. It includes emerging technologies such as the transformation of unstructured data to structured data using natural language processing and inference such as IBM's Watson.

Healthcare IT industry pundits believe the next 5 years will belong to social networking, mobile, analytics, and cloud technologies. This book provides practical advice that helps navigate many of these trends as we all work to implement healthcare reform, supported by predictive analytics.

John Halamka, MD, MS
*Professor of Medicine and Chief Information Officer at the Beth Israel Deaconess Medical Center,
Chief Information Officer and Dean for Technology at Harvard Medical School,
Chairman of the New England Health Electronic Data Interchange Network (NEHEN),
CEO of MA-SHARE (the Regional Health Information Organization),
Chair of the US Healthcare Information Technology Standards Panel (HITSP),
and member of the Board of the Open Source Electronic Health Record Agent*

Author of The Best of CP/M Software *(Longman, 1984);* Real World Unix *(Longman, 1984);*
and Espionage in the Silicon Valley *(Longman, 1985)*, and of the blog
Geekdoctor: Life as a Healthcare CIO *(http://geekdoctor.blogspot.com/).*

Preface

Everyone is fascinated by predictions; everybody wants to know the future. Some people go to psychics, some go to mystics, others go to philosophers, to soothsayers, to television commentators, to a *Nostradamus* quatrain, or even to the ancient Incas. Recently, a new source of predictions has risen in our perceptions – Predictive Analytics.

What is different about predictive analytics, compared with the many other claims of future knowledge? Predictive analytics is based on relatively objective analyses of past data, following the principle that the best guide to the future is the past. All other predictions of the future are based on highly subjective (maybe even fraudulent) systems that their practitioners claim are predictive of (or at least relevant to) the future.

Why is this distinction so important?

First, it is impossible to know the future with certainty. Even those future events that we believe are absolutely certain can be thwarted from some previously unknown influence. We can't know everything in the present, and we certainly can't know anything for certain in the future.

Secondly, predictive analytics can expose new events that might happen in the future. The most intelligent approach to preparing for future events is to study past events, and be prepared for them to happen again. But, what if new events happen in the future? No other system can predict new events, with any degree of credibility.

Thirdly, predictive analytics allows different people to look at the same information, predict new events in the future, and compare their findings. These predictions can be analyzed according to their assumptions, methods, and outcome probabilities to decide which outcome is the best prediction of the future, even if we can't know for certain.

MODERN MEDICINE: AN EXERCISE IN PREDICTION AND PREPARATION

Modern medical treatment is composed of two general activities: (1) diagnosis, and (2) treatment. Both of these activities involve predictions. In the past, some medical practitioners based their predictions on naturopathic and nutrition philosophies. More modern practitioners base their predictions on results from the pharmaceutical industry's clinical trials. Some practitioners may trust the government to digest all of the information and clinical trial outcomes, and mandate the acceptable course of action. Other practitioners, such as medical researchers, just want to do it themselves, creating their own knowledge.

This book is based on the premise that the future becomes evident (as far as we can know it) by careful analysis of patterns in past data. This past evidence can provide trajectories of change in medical conditions and outcomes. For example, a tree that bends toward the sun at its apogee in the sky during the active growing season will continue to grow in that direction; that is the way living things in the world work. We can mark the starting point of growth, measure the angle and rate of tree growth, and (barring some catastrophic event) we can calculate where the top of the tree will be in 20 years, and how much wood it will provide if harvested.

Topol (2012) maintained that the starting point for human responses is the individual genome; from that point, our medical lives can be predicted. In this book, we will show how genomic information can be analyzed to predict a bewildering variety of medical outcomes.

Regardless of the starting point, we must follow some methodologies for analysis of past evidence in order to make predictions of any future medical outcome – but, these methodologies must all be compatible with each other. A recent issue of the *AARP Bulletin* posed this rather startling observation:

> *If home building were like health care, carpenters, electricians, and plumbers each would work with different blueprints, each with very little coordination...*

(AARP, 2012)

The resulting building constructed with such a disorganized methodology would not be very useful, nor would it persist for very long. But our health care system is like that! Many patients find their healthcare systems rather opaque, disorganized, and hard to navigate in order to produce acceptable outcomes. This situation in American health care must change.

WASTED COSTS IN AMERICAN HEALTHCARE SYSTEMS

Our healthcare system is not only disorganized and inefficient; it is also very costly, and a significant amount of the cost is wasted (AARP, 2012). Some of these wasted costs include:

- $210 billion — Unnecessary services
- $190 billion — Insurance overheads and bureaucratic costs
- $130 billion — Preventable errors/mistakes
- $105 billion — Excessive prices
- $75 billion — Fraud
- $55 billion — Missed prevention opportunities.

This book provides many useful methodologies that can be orchestrated to work together in future medical decision systems for building consistent medical outcomes without major cost wastage. This book also provides many tools for use by medical practitioners to make accurate predictions. The focus of these predictions is on anything related to medical or health care. You might be a practicing physician seeking correct and accurate medical outcomes, or you might be a hospital staff member who must demonstrate safety to the accreditation organizations, or you might be an analyst in a healthcare insurance organization who wants to predict the frequency and severity of loss risk. For all of those activities (and many more), *Practical Predictive Analytics and Decisioning Systems for Medicine* provides the data and the step-by-step tutorials that will put power into the hands of practitioners.

REFERENCES

AARP, 2012. Caring for the caregiver. AARP Bull. 53, 9.

Topol, E., 2012. The Creative Destruction of Medicine: How the Digital Revolution Will Create Better Health Care. Basic Books, New York, NY.

About the Authors

Linda A. Winters-Miner, Ph.D., earned her bachelor's and master's degrees at University of Kansas, her doctorate at the University of Minnesota, and completed post-doctoral studies in psychiatric epidemiology at the University of Iowa. While she, with her husband Gary Miner, raised their children, Becky and Matt, she spent most of her career as an educator, in teacher education and statistics and research design. She spent nearly two years as a site coordinator for a major (Coxnex) drug trial. For 23 years, Miner directed academic programs for Southern Nazarene University—Tulsa. Her program direction included three undergraduate programs in business and psychology and three graduate programs in management, business administration, and health care administration. She has authored or co-authored numerous articles and books including with Gary and others, and the first book concerning the genetics of Alzheimer's: *Alzheimer's disease: Molecular genetics, clinical perspectives and promising new research*. Linda authored some of the tutorials in the first two predictive analytic books published in 2009 and 2012 by Elsevier. At present, she teaches both undergraduate statistics & research at SNU-Tulsa, teaches statistics and predictive analytics for the IHI Family Practice Medical Residency program in Tulsa, and also teaches predictive analytics online, including healthcare predictive analytics, for both the University of California—Irvine and University of California—San Diego.

Pat Bolding, M.D., F.A.A.F.P. is a practicing board certified family physician. He has used an EMR (Electronic Medical Record) since his residency training in the mid 1980 s — at the time it was the "pioneering" Technicon Medical Information System. Later, as the CEO of a large family practice group (which also hosted a 30-resident training program), he led the selection and implementation of several EMR systems, beginning with the text-based Medic Autochart then Misys EMR and finally the A4-Healthmatics system. In 2007, he joined a multi-specialty group practice/integrated delivery system where he serves on the EMR committee that oversaw the implementation of the NextGen ambulatory EMR. More recently he was a member of the search committee that chose the Epic system to replace NextGen. He is a frequent speaker on health/medical topics and has a special interest in evidence-based medicine. He is an adjunct faculty member of Southern Nazarene University, teaching in the Health Care MBA program.

Thomas Hill, Ph.D., received his Vordiplom in psychology from Kiel University in Germany and earned an M.S. in industrial psychology and a Ph.D. in psychology and quantitative methods from the University of Kansas. He was associate professor (and then research professor) at the University of Tulsa from 1984 to 2009, where he taught data analysis and data mining courses. He also has been vice president for Research and Development and then the Analytic Solutions section at StatSoft Inc., where he has been involved for over 20 years in the development of data analysis, data and text mining algorithms, and the delivery of analytic solutions. Dr. Hill joined Dell through Dell's acquisition of StatSoft (www.StatSoft.com) in April 2014, and he is currently the Executive Director for Analytics at Dell's Information Management Group. Dr. Hill has received numerous academic grants and awards from the National Science Foundation, the National Institute of Health, the Center for Innovation

Management, the Electric Power Research Institute, and other institutions. He has completed diverse consulting projects with companies from practically all industries and has worked with the leading financial services, insurance, manufacturing, pharmaceutical, retailing, and other companies in the United States and internationally on identifying and refining effective data mining and predictive modeling solutions for diverse applications. Dr. Hill has published widely on innovative applications for data mining and predictive analytics. He is the author (with Paul Lewicki, 2005) of *Statistics: Methods and Applications*, the *Electronic Statistics Textbook* (a popular on-line resource on statistics and data mining), a co-author of *Practical Text Mining and Statistical Analysis for Non-Structured Text Data Applications* (2012); he is also a contributing author to the popular *Handbook of Statistical Analysis and Data Mining Applications* (2009).

Bob Nisbet, Ph.D. was trained initially in Ecology and Ecosystems Analysis. He has over 30 years experience in complex systems analysis and modeling, most recently as a Researcher (University of California, Santa Barbara). In business, he pioneered the design and development of configurable data mining applications for retail sales forecasting, and Churn, Propensity-to-buy, and Customer Acquisition in Telecommunications, Insurance, Banking, and Credit industries. In addition to data mining, he has expertise in data warehousing technology for Extract, Transform, and Load (ETL) operations, Business Intelligence reporting, and data quality analyses. He is lead author of the *Handbook of Statistical Analysis & Data Mining Applications* (Elsevier Academic Press, 2009), and a co-author of *Practical Text Mining* (Elsevier Academic Press, 2012). Currently, he serves as an Instructor in the University of California, Irvine Predictive Analytics Certification Program, teaches online courses in Effective Data preparation, and Introduction to Predictive Analytics.

Mitchell Goldstein, M.D., attended the University of Miami's Honor Program in Medical Education under an Isaac B. Singer full tuition scholarship, completed his pediatric residency training at the University of California, Los Angeles, and finished his Neonatal Perinatal Medicine training at the University of California, Irvine in 1994. Dr. Goldstein is board certified in both Pediatrics and Neonatal Perinatal Medicine. He is an Associate Professor of Pediatrics at Loma Linda University Children's Hospital and Emeritus medical director of the Neonatal Intensive Care Unit at Citrus Valley in West Covina, CA. He has been in clinical practice for 20 years. At the various places he has worked, Dr. Goldstein has become fluent in a multitude of EMRs including EPIC, Cerner, and Meditech. As a member of the Department Deputies Users Group at Loma Linda University Hospital, Dr. Goldstein participates in an ongoing EMR improvement process. Dr. Goldstein is a past president of the Perinatal Advisory Council, Legislation, Advocacy and Consultation (PACLAC) as well as a past president of the National Perinatal Association (NPA). Dr. Goldstein is the twice recipient of the annual Jack Haven Emerson Award presented to the physician with the most promising study involving innovative pulmonary research and the 2013 recipient of the National Perinatal Association Stanley Graven lifetime achievement award presented for his ongoing commitment to the advancement of neonatal and perinatal health issues. He is the editor of PACLAC's Neonatal Guidelines of Care as well as the Principal author of both the National Perinatal Association's 2011 Best Practice Checklist – Oxygen Management for Preterm Infants and Respiratory Syncytial Virus (RSV) Prophylaxis 2012 Guidelines. Dr. Goldstein serves on the editorial board of the Journal of Perinatology as well as Neonatology Today, has represented the NPA to the American Academy of Pediatrics (AAP) perinatal section, and is a moderator of NICU-NET, a neonatal listserv. He is an executive board member and is on the nominations committee for the Section on Advances in Therapeutics & Technology (SOATT) of the AAP. Dr. Goldstein chaired the NPA National Conferences in 2004, 2008 and 2011 and continues to be active in conference planning as the CME Continuing Medical Education (CME) chair for PACLAC. His research interests include the development of non-invasive monitoring techniques, evaluation of signal propagation during high frequency ventilation, and data mining techniques for improving quality of care. Dr. Goldstein has also been a vocal advocate for RSV prophylaxis and "right" sizing technology for the needs of neonates. Dr. Goldstein's recent publications have included "Critical Complex Congenital Heart Disease (CCHD)" which was dual published in *Neonatology Today* and *Congenital Cardiology Today*, the "Late Preterm Guidelines of Care" published in the *Journal of Perinatology*, and "How Do We COPE with CPOE" published in *Neonatology Today*.

Joseph M. Hilbe, J.D., Ph.D., is an emeritus professor at the University of Hawaii, an adjunct professor of statistics at Arizona State University, and a Solar System Ambassador with NASA/Jet Propulsion Laboratory, Caltech. An elected Fellow of the American Statistical Association and elected member of the International Statistical Institute, Dr. Hilbe is currently President of the International Astrostatistics Association, is a full member of the American Astronomical Society, and Chairs the Statistics in Sports section of the American Statistical Association. He has authored fifteen books in statistical modeling, and over 200 book chapters, encyclopedia entries, journal articles, and published statistical software, and is currently on the editorial board of seven academic journals. During the 1990 s, Dr. Hilbe was on the founding executive committee of the ASA Section on Health Policy Statistics, and served in various capacities in the health research industry, including: CEO of National Health Economics and Research Corp.; Director of Research at Transitional Hospitals Corp, a national chain of long term hospitals; Senior Statistician of NRMI-2, Genentech's National Registry for Myocardial Infarctions; lead biostatistical consultant, Hoffman-La Roche's National Canadian Registry for Cardiovascular Disease; and was Senior Statistical Consultant for HCFA's Medicare Infrastructure Project.

Nephi Walton, M.S., Ph.D. earned his MD from the University of Utah School of Medicine and a Masters degree in Biomedical Informatics from the University of Utah Department of Biomedical Informatics where he was a National Library of Medicine fellow. His Masters work was focused on data mining and predictive analytics of viral epidemics and their impact on hospitals. He was the winner of the 2009 AMIA Data Mining Competition and has published papers and co-authored books on data mining and predictive analytics. During his time at the University of Utah he spent several years studying genetic epidemiology of autoimmune disease and the application of analytical methods to determining genetic risk for disease, a work that continues today. His work has included several interactive medical education products. He founded a company called Brainspin that continues this work and has won international awards for innovative design in this area. He is currently a combined Pediatrics/Genetics fellow at Washington University where he is pursuing several research interests including the application of predictive analytics models to genomic data and integration of genomic data into the medical record. He continues to work with the University of Utah and Intermountain Healthcare to further his work in viral prediction models and hospital census prediction and resource allocation models.

Dr. Gary Miner received a B.S. from Hamline University, St. Paul, MN, with biology, chemistry, and education majors; an M.S. in zoology and population genetics from the University of Wyoming; and a Ph.D. in biochemical genetics from the University of Kansas as the recipient of a NASA pre-doctoral fellowship. He pursued additional National Institutes of Health postdoctoral studies at the University of Minnesota and University of Iowa, eventually becoming immersed in the study of affective disorders and Alzheimer's disease. In 1985, he and his wife, Dr. Linda Winters-Miner, founded the Familial Alzheimer's Disease Research Foundation, which became a leading force in organizing both local and international scientific meetings, bringing together all the leaders in the field of genetics of Alzheimer's from several countries, resulting in the first major book on the genetics of Alzheimer's disease. In the mid-1990 s, Dr. Miner turned his data analysis interests to the business world, joining the team at StatSoft and deciding to specialize in data mining. He started developing what eventually became the *Handbook of Statistical Analysis and Data Mining Applications* (co-authored with Drs. Robert A. Nisbet and John Elder), which received the 2009 American Publishers Award for Professional and Scholarly Excellence (PROSE). Their follow-up collaboration, *Practical Text Mining and Statistical Analysis for Non-structured Text Data Applications*, also received a PROSE award in February of 2013.

Overall, Dr. Miner's career has focused on medicine and health issues, so serving as the 'project director' for *Practical Predictive Analytics of Medicine* fit his knowledge and skills perfectly. Gary also serves as VP & Scientific Director of Healthcare Predictive Analytics Corp; as Merit Reviewer for Patient Centered Outcomes Research Institute that awards grants for predictive analytics research into the comparative effectiveness and heterogeneous treatment effects of medical interventions including drugs among different genetic groups of patients; additionally he teaches on-line classes in 'Introduction to Predictive Analytics', 'Text Analytics', and 'Risk Analytics' for the University of California-Irvine, and other classes in medical predictive analytics for the University of California-San Diego. He spends most of his time in his primary role as Senior Analyst-Healthcare Applications Specialist for Dell's Information Management Group, Dell Software (through Dell's acquisition of StatSoft in April 2014).

Acknowledgments

The eight co-authors express gratitude to many for the tremendous efforts towards the completion of this book.

The guest authors of chapters added their unique expertise through their efforts; for this we owe a debt of gratitude.

The guest authors of the tutorials and case studies added the lifeblood of the book — these tutorials provide the exemplars of methodologies; to these people we owe another debt of gratitude.

The editorial expertise of the Elsevier staff is greatly appreciated: thanks to Catherine A. Van Der Laan, in the Waltham, Massachusetts Elsevier office who took over the main editorial responsibilities halfway through the process; and then Melissa Read (of Perth, Australia) and Susan Armitage (of London, UK), who expertly took over project management and copy-editing for the typesetter — without them, and their continual diplomatic prodding of Gary and Linda Miner, this book would never have stayed on schedule.

Finally, the authors acknowledge and thank their families, who sacrificed time with their loved ones and offered their support throughout the two-and-a-half years during which this book was "in process."

Guest Authors

Gerard Britton, JD, MS, CEO, Topiary Discovery LLC, Jersey City, NJ, USA — Chapter 18.

Eric W. Brown, PhD, Director, Watson Technologies, IBM Research Yorktown Heights, New York, USA — Chapter 25.

John W. Cromwell, MD, University of Iowa Medical School, Iowa City, IA, USA — Chapter 24.

Darrell Dean, DO, MPH, CHCQM, FAIHQ, Medical Director for Clinical and Operational Performance Improvement — Floyd Medical Center, Rome, GA, USA — parts of Chapter 11.

Jacek Jakubowski, PhD, StatSoft Polska, AGH University, Krakow, Poland — Chapter 23.

Sven Koch, RN, PhD, University of Heidelberg, Heidelberg, Germany — parts of Chapter 16.

Martin S. Kohn, MD, MS, FACEP, FACPE, Chief Medical Scientist, Jointly Health, San Juan Capistrano, CA, USA — Chapter 25.

Leslaw Kulach, MSc, StatSoft Polska, Krakow, Poland — Chapter 23.

Piotr Murawski, MSc, Military Institute of Medicine, Warsaw, Poland — Chapter 23.

Chris Papesh, MBA, Papesh Consulting, and founder CEO of HCPA (Health Care Predictive Analytics), Las Vegas, NV, USA — Chapter 6; parts of Chapter 4; parts of Chapter 26.

Vladimir Rastunkov, PhD, StatSoft Inc., Tulsa, OK, USA — parts of Chapter 15.

Danny Stout, PhD, University of Oklahoma School of Medicine, Oklahoma City, OK, USA; and StatSoft Inc., Tulsa, OK, USA — parts of Chapter 15; parts of Chapter 22.

Christopher L. Wasden, EdD; Professor of Innovation; Executive Director, Sorenson Center for Discovery and Innovation; Associate Executive Director, Center for Medical Innovation; and David Eccles School of Business, University of Utah, Salt Lake City, UT, USA — Chapter 17.

Software Instructions

This book uses the Statistica software and access to it will ensure that you are able to follow along with the instructions in the Tutorials that use Dell Statistica.

At the website below, please enter the information requested of you and Dell will contact you with instructions to download *Dell Statistica*.

http://booksite.elsevier.com/9780124116436

Additionally, there is a folder of datasets located on this website. (You may notice in various places throughout the book that this website is referred to as 'The Companion Web Site').

Some of the tutorials use SAS-Enterprise Miner or R-Rattle; this software is not provided on this book's Companion Web site, but you can use a search engine to find the R website and download what you need; in fact in the tutorial using R-Rattle, instructions are provided on how to do this. If you do not have SAS-Enterprise Miner available to you, you could try to follow the instructions of the SAS tutorial by doing the equivalent processes in Dell Statistica. (However, the authors recommend that you only do this after doing a couple of the Dell Statistica tutorials so that you have learned your way around handling this software).

Introduction

At the end of 2013, a lot of turmoil developed in the US surrounding implementation of the Patient Protection and Affordable Care Act (ACA). As newspaper headlines at the time illustrated, the American political landscape was chaotic and many people were rather unsettled about the issues around how to organize effective and fair health insurance.

At the same time, new predictive analytics technologies that have fundamentally transformed practically all aspects of life — from CRM (customer relationship management) to general insurance, risk management, demand forecasting, or manufacturing — are only beginning to find applications in health care. It is likely that the impact and benefits of these technologies, once fully applied to optimize the overall performance of the healthcare system, will be as important for the overall quality of health care as structural and legislative reforms of the system. In fact, new developments in predictive analytics and statistical learning will be key to sustainable and successful healthcare reforms.

Significant changes in health care will have to happen. Healthcare costs have been skyrocketing, insurance premiums are increasing rapidly, and the existing healthcare system — like other industries — will have to adjust to leverage new technologies. This situation is reminiscent of the famous Far Side cartoon of the dinosaur convention by Gary Larson (Figure I.1).

Chapter 1 tells the story of King Solon of Ancient Greece, who instituted the *seisachtheia*, or the "shaking off of burdens" of the poor. This law was designed to address an inequality in 6th Century BC Greece, where a bankrupt person would become a slave to his rich creditors. In addition to losing their personal freedom, these newly poor people were excluded from healthcare treatment by physicians, who catered only to the rich. This is not unlike medical bankruptcies taking place in the modern world today, where people are tied to the often onerous debt caused by the extraordinary costs of their health care. One of the results of the *seisachtheia* was formation of the Hippocratic Corpus of medical documents by Hippocrates, which became the standard source of healthcare information for over 2,000 years. Something like the *seisachtheia* is needed in 21st Century American health care — relief from a system that seems to put people into virtual slavery, tying them down with burdensome debt and denying them liberty, the pursuit of happiness, and their lifelong dreams. A new Hippocratic Corpus could be developed using existing technology to link data in a seamless fashion, and create a standard source of healthcare data and actionable information.

Technology exists to create such a new-age Hippocratic Corpus, supporting what we might do with medical data. Technological advancements, however, have far outstripped our ability to analyze and make useful the data in the currently available formats. If the ACA (or its modification, possibly) is able to bring about a digital form of the Hippocratic Corpus of stored medical knowledge, it will be the beginning of a digital "Golden Age" in medicine and health care.

Currently, our ability to track, and make useful, medical information across the array of institutions and specialist physicians is limited severely by the fragmentation of the healthcare system. Much medical case-specific information is still in medical records that line the shelves of physicians' offices in paper format. The new and growing capability of our analytical technology combined with the severe lack of case-specific medical data renders our medical establishment as an amnesiac with an enormously high IQ (a powerful non-linear analytical system — our predictive analytical technology), but lacking all five senses, and providing little data to analyze.

In this book, we seek to break that logjam (at least conceptually) by showing readers what can be done using new predictive analytical capabilities with available healthcare data, and lead by examples (tutorials) of ways to "get 'er done" (as Larry the Cable Guy is fond of saying). What we can't do in this book is design the changes in storage systems, security systems, delivery systems, and legal systems (e.g., HIPAA) necessary to make it happen. Those changes will come. All we can do is set the stage with chapters on general concepts of medical decision systems, and present some practical tutorials designed to "grease the skids" for change to happen.

Evidence Based Medicine (EBM) is an important new paradigm that has not exerted much impact yet. Unlike Evidence Based Guidelines, EBM starts with guidelines and updates them using new information generated by clinical trials, medical journals, academic medical centers, government health institutes, and other authoritative sources of medical knowledge.

"The picture's pretty bleak, gentlemen. ... The
world's climates are changing, the mammals
are taking over, and we all have a brain
about the size of a walnut."

FIGURE I.1   The Dinosaur Convention cartoon by Gary Larson.

One of the biggest challenges to EBM implementation is the set of limitations associated with the "gold standard" of randomized control trials, including high cost, length of time, and often significant bias; the enormous problem of the lack of access to unpublished (possibly suppressed) data; and the issues of using results that are not applicable very often to the individual patient under treatment. Many practicing physicians realize how little good evidence we have for diagnosis and treatment of patients. If patients knew how much their physicians don't know, they might not want to see them. We need desperately to know the right test, and the right treatment, for the right patient at the right time. The goal of this book is to explain the enormous power of current technology in the search for evidence, which avoids those problems, and can provide timely, relevant, and practical information to use in the clinic and at the bedside.

The approach of this book is to present a background for the use of predictive analytics in health care, and provide practical tutorials to show how to perform important new tasks in medicine and health care, including the following.

1. *Gain new insights into disease pathways and progression.*
   Predictive analytics technology can provide new information and relationships between diseases and specific patient characteristics. The progression of the disease can be predicted for various treatments. This capability can provide unprecedented choice of treatments for patients by permitting optimization of the analysis of their data to enable the answering of existing questions, project the course of disease progression, generate new insights, and present new questions to analyze.
2. *Discover new knowledge and insights in real-life, not just in test tube cultures.*
   It is one thing to learn new things about diseases in the laboratory, but pathogens may act differently in the outside world. This new knowledge can lead to the discovery of root causes of diseases, and guide treatment of the real problem — not just the laboratory expression of it.
3. *Accelerate the pace of medical science.*
   New technology increases the rate at which new information can be discovered. The faster we can learn new things about diseases and their treatments, the quicker and more effectively we can cure them.
4. *Develop a new paradigm of personalized medical diagnosis and treatment.*
   We must shift our approach from treating the disease to treating the patient. This focus on the particular characteristics of the patient and the individual expression of the disease will lead to treatments optimized closely to the patient, and not just to population averages. The patient can play a vital role in health care.

ORGANIZATION OF THIS BOOK — WHY WE DID IT THIS WAY

When encountering the vast power of predictive analytics in medicine for the first time, the temptation is to seize upon a technique and want to try it out immediately. We recognize this great urge, and, rather than squelch it, we want to channel it through to fruition in responsible analysis.

Part 1

Part I of the book really has two sub-parts:

1. Background to healthcare — structure and organizations from which the data needed for effective predictive analytic modeling and decisioning can be obtained
2. The Predictive Analytic process itself.

Part 1 — First Sub-Part

Chapters 1—14 present an introduction to all (or many) of the aspects of health care, including methods like EMR, and organizations such as HIMSS that are part of the medical healthcare landscape. These serve as a very important background to predictive analytics, as it is from these "institutions" that the data are produced for needed effective data analysis. Throughout Chapters 1—14, the authors allude to the primary principles and practices of predictive analytics to prepare you to do it yourself ... responsibly. The tendency for analysts to go off "half-cocked" in using a new body of techniques will be minimized, if they read these chapters first. Chapter 1 presents the historical background for this book, and it also justifies the notion ensconced in the Affordable Care Act (ACA) to convert medical record to digital format, and make them available to all responsible parties to guide diagnosis and treatment of medical ailments. Chapter 2 presents many of the other reasons we wrote this book, builds the foundation of reasons for the application of information on past cases to the diagnosis of current cases, and presents some disturbing facts about medical research in America today. Chapter 3 explores the rich landscape of medical informatics to set the stage of how this powerful technology can revolutionize medical treatment in the future. Chapters 4—8 describe the standards, the regulatory structure, and the basis for electronic medical records (EMRs). Chapters 10—14 present features of the proper milieu in which EMRs are gathered and used.

Part 1 — Second Sub-Part

Finally, Chapter 15 gets to the "nuts and bolts" of predictive analytics. It introduces readers to the many powerful predictive analytical (data mining and text mining) techniques that can be employed to gather useful information from mountains of EMRs and other health data.

Part 2

After building a proper foundation for understanding and performing (at least simple) predictive analytical operations with medical data, tutorials and case studies are presented to permit readers to see how predictive analytical techniques can be employed in various analysis and prediction scenarios.

Part 3

The last part of the book, Chapters 16—26, describes some examples of how predictive analytics can be used in administration and the delivery of health care. These include Chapter 16, which summarizes how nurses can use predictive analytics; it is not the exclusive area of researchers and physicians, and Chapter 23, which shows an excellent example of how predictive analytics is applied to the entire organization and operations of the Military Institute of Poland. The success in Poland illustrates the downside of American regulatory constraints; they can get in the way of effective integration of new practices into health care. And this success suggests not that American regulatory structures should be abandoned, but rather that they must be redesigned to capitalize on the powerful capabilities of the new technology of predictive analytics in medicine and health care.

Prologue to Part 1

This book comprises three basic areas:

1. Context and opportunities
2. Practice
3. Theory.

Part 1 is primarily concerned with the first area.

Chapters 1–14 (basic area number one) acquaint the reader with the many facets of health care and explain the various aspects and organizations that, directly or indirectly, affect how medical and healthcare data are captured. These chapters offer the perspectives of history, including where we are at present and where we might be heading. The reader can become grounded in the context of medical research by examining the history, the organizations that arose, the arising needs from our cultural milieu, the attempts at answers to those needs, and where those answers may have fallen short.

Predictive analytics requires data, and good data. It is the task of the data miner to secure those data just as though they were gold. However, data mining is not enough. Predictive analytic methods seek to anticipate good outcomes, and good outcomes for individuals. Predictive models are only as good as the data that are processed by the models. Chapters 1–14 demonstrate the flow of data through history, including the laws that were meant to inhibit and those that were meant to increase the flow. We as researchers must know our context in order to apply our predictive analytic art to the canvas of individual outcomes.

In summary, data ("good data") are essential to the precision of predictive analytics. Good data are necessary for unleashing effective models from which excellent decisions can be made.

You, the reader, may wonder why we did not start this book with discussions of predictive analytic algorithms, and predictive analytic models and decisioning. But good decisioning can only come after good modeling, and neither of these can be obtained if one does not have good data as a starting point.

Linda A. Winters-Miner PhD and Gary D. Miner, PhD,

> Linda A. Winters-Miner and Gary D. Miner are co-developers of the structure, table of contents, organization, and effective learning formats of not only this book but also the other two books in this "mini-series": Handbook of Statistical Analysis and Data Mining Applications (2009) and Practical Text Mining and Statistical Analysis for Non-Structured Text Data Applications (2012).

Part 1

Historical Perspective and the Issues of Concern for Healthcare Delivery in the 21st Century

Chapter 1

History of Predictive Analytics in Medicine and Health Care

Chapter Outline

PREAMBLE

The underlying purpose of predictive analytics in medicine is to predict and direct decision-making in diagnosis and treatment. The central element in this decision-making process is the availability of medical information to serve it. The original medium of this information was the mind of the physician. However, quite early in history, some of this medical head knowledge was committed to writing. The purpose of this chapter is to trace the history of written forms of information storage, to serve as a foundation for the present conversion of it into digital form.

BACKGROUND

The underlying purpose of predictive analytics in medicine is to predict and direct decision-making in diagnosis and treatment of medical and health-related conditions. For the purposes of presenting the history of predictive analytics in medicine, I decided to recount the history of the core of analytical operations – medical information. Therefore, I defined the relevant historical context rather broadly to include all forms of storage and preservation of medical and healthcare information, beginning with written forms.

In the process of researching the history of written medical documentation for the purposes of diagnosis and treatment, I found many examples in history of the mandate of royal leaders (kings and emperors) to gather together current medical and health-related information, and make it available for diagnosis and treatment of common people. This process began among the early Pharaohs of Egypt and the Kings of the Ancient Middle East. But the greatest contribution by far was made by King Solon of Greece, when he commissioned Hippocrates to gather together jealously guarded texts from many independent Greek physicians to form the Hippocratic Corpus of medical documents. This corpus was expanded by the Greek physician Galen, under the commission of the Roman Emperor Commodus, thus creating the body of medical knowledge that remained the standard for almost 2000 years. The processes of maintaining it, however, was neither simple nor direct.

King Chosroes I of Persia supported the Nestorians (a heretical Christian sect), branded as heretics and banished from the Christian church of the Holy Roman Empire. The Nestorians fled eastward and were embraced by Chosroes (and Islam), because both believed that Jesus Christ was not the Son of God but only a prophet. The Nestorians helped to found the university at Jundi Shapur, and to translate the Greek Hippocratic Corpus into Arabic. This great interest of Chosroes preserved the Greek medical texts through the Middle Ages, when many of the Greek and Roman texts were destroyed. The Arabian works were translated into Latin during the Reformation, beginning with Erasmus in 1525, and remained as the standard in medical treatment until the rise of modern medicine at the beginning of the 20th century.

Despite the massive problem with sign-up for the insurance exchanges through the US government website in 2013, and regardless of your political stance today, one thing becomes quite clear in this history of medicine. It is that Obama and his mandate of conversion to digital medical records (in the Affordable Care Act of 2009) is simply following in the footsteps of many rulers in history to collect medical information into an available format (digital now, rather than written) to facilitate diagnosis and treatment of the common people of the day.

INTRODUCTION

The goal of this chapter is to provide a foundation in the history of medical practice for the development of decision tools that guide the determination of correct diagnosis and treatment of human ailments. In general terms, these tools can be classified as:

I. *Bodies of knowledge* that govern the nature of medical diagnosis and treatment
II. *Analytical approaches and decision systems* that integrate diverse knowledge elements and direct the formation of accepted medical practices.

These two tool types are related, in that the decision systems are based on existing bodies of knowledge available to the physician. In Part 1 of this chapter we will discuss the various types of bodies of knowledge in the history of medicine, and see how they affected the quality and appropriateness of medical treatment. In Part 2, we will discuss various ways that information resident in the bodies of knowledge has been combined, stored, analyzed, and used to express predictions of diagnosis and treatment. Prior to the invention of the computer, analysis and decision-making processes were performed entirely in the most powerful non-linear processing engine in the universe, the human brain — the brain of the physician. Here, we will discuss how computers enable us to build and process complex mathematical predictive algorithms, and deploy them in medical decision systems. We will focus on computers and medical databases, and the development of best practice documents among specialties in Personalized Medicine.

The reason for considering the development of bodies of written medical information in this digital age is to highlight the various types of bodies of medical knowledge and show how they have been used in the past, and to provide guidance for using future medical information in digital form. Bodies of written knowledge are of two types: (1) subject-related documents; and (2) case-related documents. Both of these sources of medical knowledge serve as major components of the knowledge infrastructure of modern medical practice. Proper discussion of medical decision systems today (and in the future) must include an understanding of all of the components of the system of medical practice on which they are built. In addition, discussion of the history of the development of the current medical practice system can yield valuable insights to help us meet the technical and political challenges of today. One such insight provided by the study of medical history is the relationship between past royal decrees and the collection of medical documents together into comprehensive bodies of information for the sake of diagnosis and treatment of all people in a society. This insight is particularly relevant to the challenge by current legislation that requires the digitizing of physician medical case records to form an electronic health record (EHR).

The availability of EHRs and digital medical knowledge databases will provide the foundation required by analytical medical decision and management systems of today and in the future. The overall goal of this book (described more fully in the Introduction to this volume) is to show how to use advanced analytics to build and use a medical decision system that draws upon all available digital sources of information to increase the effectiveness of medical diagnosis and treatment.

PART 1: DEVELOPMENT OF BODIES OF MEDICAL KNOWLEDGE

The process of determining the appropriate treatment is conditioned by the training of the physician in medical school plus his or her evaluation of the aspects of the case in relation to:

- Personal experience
- Personal judgment
- Written and/or digital records of medical and healthcare information from previous cases.

Personal experience and personal judgment have always been important factors affecting the success of medical diagnosis and treatment; they must be kept central to the practice of medicine. The third aspect, development and use of records of medical and healthcare information, forms the foundation of responsible medical practice to all members of a society. The various methods and tools used to integrate these three aspects of medical practice characterize the entire history of medical practice.

The recognition of the need to collect and maintain written medical records extends back to the dawn of recorded history. We will confine our discussion to cultures in the West and Middle East. Medicine in Far Eastern cultures developed almost independently from that in the West and Middle East, until medical practices and technology were imported from the West in the 20th century.

From the very beginning, medical diagnosis and treatment have been essentially prediction problems. Individual treatment specialists in primitive cultures (e.g., medicine men/women) learned to perform their responsibilities from experience and word-of-mouth. There was very little cooperation among them, and sometimes there was animosity. This medical practice environment generated a wide variation in the nature, quality, and availability of techniques in medical practice, and difficulty in the training of new specialists. Five examples are given to show how rulers in ancient cultures have managed these problems with medical care in the past. These examples provide insights into how societal forces generated royal responses to the problems in medical care, how the responses were expressed in specific cultures, and how they can guide us in our response to the challenges in medical and health care that we face in our society today. Our approach to this daunting task will include discussion of the following topics:

1. Earliest medical records in ancient cultures
2. Classification of medical practices in ancient and modern cultures
3. Medical practice documents in major ancient world cultures of Europe and the Middle East
4. Summary of royal decrees of medical documentation in ancient cultures
5. Effect of the Middle Ages on medical documentation
6. Rebirth of interest in medical documentation during the Renaissance.

EARLIEST MEDICAL RECORDS IN ANCIENT CULTURES

There is some controversy about the identification of the earliest manuscript of medical treatments. Many scholars point to the Code of Hammurabi ($\sim$1700 BC), containing accounts of various surgery procedures, recommended fees for service, and penalties for malpractice (Sigerist, 1951). But there are earlier Sumerian cuneiform texts that date to the reign of King Ur III (*ca.* 2100 BC) in the early Babylonian Empire, which contain instructions for medical treatments, without diagnostic information, designed to be used by experts. There are earlier records of spells and incantations among the Pyramid texts, caused to be written by King (Pharaoh) Unas on the walls of his pyramid; he was the last king of the Fifth Dynasty in Egypt ($\sim$2300 BC). The text includes many religious spells and incantations aimed at assuring the well-being of the Pharaoh in the after-life. Some evidence exists (if it is valid) that a very early Pyramid text (the Hearst Medical Papyrus, dated about 2500–2000 BC) contained some references to medical treatment (Reisner, 1905). This text mentions the Egyptian god Thoth, who gave the Egyptian physicians healing arts. Herodotus (484–425 BC) collected many documents of Egyptian medical practice, which he called "Hermetic books," because he identified the Egyptian god Thoth with the Greek god Hermes (Dawson, 2010). Clemens Alexandrinus (AD 215) collected 42 such

Hermetic books on anatomy, illnesses, eye diseases, gynecology, drugs, and surgical instruments (Alexandrinus, AD 215). If any of these Hermetic books existed, none survives (Sigerist, 1951).

CLASSIFICATION OF MEDICAL PRACTICES IN ANCIENT AND MODERN CULTURES

Development of medical practice appears to follow a similar pattern in all cultures studied (Sigerist, 1951). The earliest phase of medical practice in a given culture presumes supernatural causes and prescribes spiritual treatments for ailments and diseases (supernaturalistic medicine). The second phase abandons (at least partially) the supernatural medicine approach and accepts the naturalistic medicine approach, in which causes for ailments and diseases are sought among natural causes that can be studied in the natural world. The final phase is scientific medicine, based on accumulated medical informational documents, and results of scientific tests. Most cultures follow the pattern shown in Figure 1.1.

Even though this development trend describes the long-term trend in a culture, it is often the case that these approaches may be practiced at the same time by different segments of the culture (Sigerist, 1951). This was the case for supernaturalistic medicine and naturalistic medicine in Egypt and Mesopotamia. We find elements of naturalistic medicine along with scientific medicine in practice in many cultures today, even in the United States in the form of homeopathic medicine and conventional medicine.

Supernaturalistic Medicine ➡ Naturalistic Medicine ➡ Scientific Medicine

FIGURE 1.1   The normal course of development of medical treatments in many cultures.

MEDICAL PRACTICE DOCUMENTS IN MAJOR ANCIENT WORLD CULTURES OF EUROPE AND THE MIDDLE EAST

Medicine of some sort has been practiced in every ancient culture. In this chapter, we will confine the discussion to the developments of medical practice documents in Europe and the Middle East:

- Egypt
- Mesopotamia
- Greece
- Ancient Rome
- Arabia.

Some naturalistic medical texts were written in China *ca.* AD 600 (Unschuld, 1985), and in India even earlier than that (Sigerist, 1951), but these texts do not appear to represent ideas and relationships to predictive analytics that are not reflected in documents from countries of Europe and the Middle East.

Egypt

Many pyramids in Egypt contain hieroglyphic scripts with medical content, the earliest of which appear on tombs of the Fifth Dynasty, in about 2300 BC (Faulkner, 1969). These scripts contain many incantations and spells designed to help the Pharaoh in his after-life. Concepts of detailed examination, diagnosis, and prognosis (medical treatment) may have arisen in very early Egypt. The Edwin Smith Surgical Papyrus (*ca.* 1700 BC; see Figure 1.2) contains very detailed descriptions of 48 medical cases involving head and body wounds, sprains, and tumors. Serving as the founder of Egyptology, Breasted (1967) claimed that the Edwin Smith document is composed of a copy of an earlier document dating back to 3000−2500 BC in the form of 69 explanatory notes on the original document. If this document existed, it would be the earliest medical record of surgical information.

The Ebers Papyrus of 1550 BC is the largest among the most ancient Egyptian medical documents known (Bryan, 1930). It contains over 700 spells and incantations for turning away evil, disease-causing demons. The Hearst Medical Papyrus is thought to date back to 2000 BC or beyond (Reisner, 1905), but some controversy exists about the date.

According to Sigerist (1951), other known Egyptian medical papyri included:

- Kahum Papyrus (1900 BC) − On Gynacology and pregnancy
- London Papyrus (1350) − On recipes and incantations

FIGURE 1.2   Edwin Smith papyrus. *Reproduced with permission from: http://designblog.nzeldes.com/2011/03/hats-off-to-ancient-egyptian-medicine/*

- Berlin Papyrus (1350 BC) — On medical tests, pregnancy and fertility
- Chester Beaty Papyrus (1250 BC) — Drug recipes and diseases.

Herodotus identified the Egyptian god Thoth (mentioned in the Hearst Papyrus) with the Greek god Hermes, the god of healing. We know of many of these works through the writings of Herodotus and Clement of Alexandria. They referred to them as the Corpus Hermiticum, or the Hermetic books. Six of the 42 Hermetic books were on medical subjects of physiology, male and female diseases, anatomy, drugs, and instruments (Zeller, 1886).

Thus it appears that naturalistic and supernaturalistic medicine were practiced side by side in Ancient Egypt, as in Mesopotamia and Greece (see below).

Mesopotamia

The earliest medical text in Mesopotamia (associated with King Ur III, *ca.* 2100 BC) contained instructions for treatments of patients without diagnostic information, intended for use by experts only (Oppenheim, 1962). It is unclear whether the Babylonians were the first to document the concepts of detailed examination, diagnosis, and prognosis (medical treatment), or whether they just imported them from the Egyptians. In either case, enough medical knowledge was accumulated by the Middle Babylonian period (1532−1000 BC) to support separate texts for diagnosis and treatment.

During his reign at the end of this period, King Adad-apla-iddina (1068−1047 BC) decreed that existing medical records be collected to form a corpus of 40 tablets, referred to as the *Diagnostic Handbook*. Some of these tablets in the handbook listed treatments based on the number of days the patient had been sick (Tablets 15 and 16) and the pulse rate (Tablet 21). This and other similar numerical information used to compose diagnoses may represent the first bioinformatics "models" in medicine. We can see this same integration of medicine and numbers in the *Sakikku*, a large medical treatise of about 40 tablets divided into 5 parts (Neugebaur, 1957). Part II enumerates symptoms of diseases according to color, temperature, and movements of body parts. Part III describes treatments that were prescribed as a function of numerical information from observations described in Part II, combined with specific information about the disease course, phase, and amelioration/aggregation relative to the time of day.

Sumerians used a symbol for "not" in the place of zero, as a placeholder in their sexigecimal number system based on 16, rather than 10 (Kaplan, 2000). For example, the number 2013 was represented by a string of symbols for 2, followed by the symbols for "not," 1 and 3. They did not understand the concept of zero (that came later from the Moors in 11th century Europe), but they could do geometry with this system. There is evidence to suggest that they understood the geometry of the Pythagorean Theorem 1000 years before Pythagoras (Oppenheim, 1962; Kaplan, 2000). Evidence of this rather sophisticated number system combined with their detailed medical knowledge suggests that diagnoses based on the *Sakikku* were quantitative. To that extent, one of the roots of predictive analytics in medicine extends back to ancient Babylonia.

A vast collection of over 30,000 clay tablets was found in Nineveh and gathered into a library by Ashurbanipal, successor to King Sennacherib (Polastron, 2007). Over 700 of these tablets contained medical information. The tablets were distributed in many rooms according to a classification methodology. This library was the not the first if its kind, but it is the first known collection having most of the attributes of a modern library (Johnson, 1970) This collection was a great interest of Ashurbanipal; he was not above conquest to obtain new additions to it. To this extent, we can view that his collection arose from a royal mandate, and it serves as a second example of the collection of medical texts by royal decree.

The Babylonian medical tradition continued in practice until about 200 BC, after which it dropped out of awareness of medical practitioners. This decline of the Babylonian medical tradition in Asia Minor was contemporary with the rise of the Hippocratic Corpus in ancient Greece. Maybe these two events were related.

Greece

Medicine in Pre-Classical Greece

The cultural mindset and world-view in place can greatly affect the course of development of concepts and practices in a culture, sometimes in multiple directions. We can see two good examples of this human response phenomenon in the development of medical practice in the Greek history (and another one in Rome — see below). Beginning in about 600 BC, medicine became organized around two centers of the same supernaturalistic world-view: (1) the temple cult worship of the god-man Asclepius (a man who was "elevated" to the status of a god); and (2) the philosophy of the man Pythagoras.

1. Asclepius was a demi-god in Greek mythology, son of the god Apollo and a mortal mother, Coronis. He became the god of medicine, and his followers held that aliments and diseases could be healed by prayers and sacrifices, particularly in the temples erected for that purpose. Homer included a man named Asclepius in his story of the Iliad, as a physician to wounded men at the battle of Troy. In later years, he became "elevated" to the status of a god.
2. Pythagoras strived to create a balance among opposing forces acting on people. He quantified these forces with numbers, and analyzed these numbers (in terms of arithmetic) to guide medical treatments in terms of numbers. One of his treatments was to prescribe harmonic frequencies and music to treat human conditions. He invented instruments, and with the use of sound and vibration he was able to bring an individual's attention to the awareness of their Divine Nature in order to facilitate the healing process. Pythagorus was a "Renaissance man," in that his ideas ruled Philosophy, Mathematics, and Music, as well as Medicine, throughout the "Golden Age" of Greece ($\sim$550–300 BC).

Both of these forms of supernaturalistic medicine were practiced contemporaneously in Greece beginning about 600 BC and extending to about 450 BC, when a new approach was introduced by Empedocles via his philosophy (Sigerist, 1951). The previous belief system based on the philosophy of Parmenides held that the senses are not reliable, and that medical diagnosis and treatment should be found in supernaturalistic practices. Empedocles disagreed by stating that our senses are indeed a reliable guide to truth. He introduced the concept that all things were composed of four elements: Earth, Air, Fire, and Water. This belief was the first example of "atomistic" thinking in the Greek culture. This burgeoning culture permitted such philosophical disagreement, and the stage was set for Hippocrates (460–370 BC), who formulated the principle of the "true mixture of elements." These elements (he called them "humors") were black bile, yellow bile, phlegm, and blood. They were different from the four elements of Empedocles, but they followed the same philosophy of atomism (Empedocles) and balance (Pythagorus). Hippocrates believed that ailments and disease were caused by the wrong balance of the four humors; therefore, he sought medical treatments that restored the balance of humors to form the "true" mixture for human health. Naturalistic medicine had arrived in ancient Greece.

The result of this philosophical disagreement and the medical practices that it induced relegated supernaturalistic medical practice to the Asclepian temple, and Hippocratic practices to outside the temple (Sigerist, 1951). Thus, in Classical Greece, supernaturalistic medicine was practiced almost side by side with naturalistic medicine, following two very different world-views. We see reflections of this same tension today between homeopathic (or holistic) medicine practiced in a world-view dominated by modern scientific medicine, which developed from the naturalistic medicine on which homeopathic medicine is based. This similarity between ancient Greece and modern America of simultaneous practices arising from different world-views supports Solomon's claim that "...there is nothing new under the sun" (*Eccl.* 1:9).

At this point, you may be wondering how all of this relates to the history of predictive analytics. The reason is related to the biggest problem with early Greek medicine, even in its naturalistic state − its fragmentation, the lack of standardization, and the "cure" of both. Many early Greek medical texts included much biological and medical information and described treatments for ailments and diseases, but they were scattered throughout the country in many different locations under the control of different physicians. Similarly, most medical treatment information today is scattered in the offices of individual physicians. The solution to the problem in ancient Greece (see below) followed that in Mesopotamia, and it pre-shadows the solution to the modern problem in the USA mandated by the Affordable Care Act (ACA) in 2010. This solution involved the collection and standardization of medical information, which became the basis for responsible medical practice in Classical Greece; it may become so in America. If it is true that those who ignore the mistakes of the past are bound to repeat them (actually a misquote of a work by George Santayana), then it is logical to expect that some solutions to present problems can be found in history. This is true of the history of Mesopotamia, and Greece. It came about in ancient Greece in the following manner.

There was a serious problem in Athens, one of the two dominant city-states in the 5th century BC (along with Sparta). The then current form of democracy generated serious inequities among the people, resulting an environment of strong social unrest. They elected Solon, a statesman and poet, as king, to restructure the early democracy of Athens to reduce these inequities, and bring a measure of civil peace to the city-states. At that time, repressive laws forced the poor into slavery to the rich. Solon designed an economic program called the *seisachteia* ("shaking off of burdens") to release the lower classes from the burden of debt to those in the wealthy classes (Hammond, 1961). By canceling and reducing debts and abolishing a system of mortgage which had turned many poor landowners into virtual slaves, Solon significantly reduced the huge social and economic gap between the rich and the poor − the source of the social unrest. His concern to elevate the miserable state of the poor led Solon to decree that all medical texts be gathered together into one corpus, making them available to everyone, including the poor. This job was commissioned to the physician Hippocrates.

Hippocrates and Classical Greece

Hippocrates organized existing medical texts (and wrote some of them) in an attempt to integrate the previous philosophical concepts of Empedocles (the four elements), Philistion (the body is separate from the soul, and must be treated as such), and Diogenes (the soul, or the *pneuma*, is the vehicle of life; Wellmann, 1901) (see Figure 1.3). This group of

FIGURE 1.3 Roman coin of the first century AD from the island of Cos (birthplace of Hippocrates) showing his bust as of about 377 BC. (see why this Roman coin is important in the discussion of Roman medicine below). *Source: British Museum, **Coins and Medals catalogue number: GC18p216.216.***

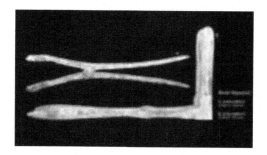

FIGURE 1.4 Rectal specula of the type used by Hippocrates. *Reproduced with permission from: www.hsl.virginia.edu/historical/artifacts/roman_surgical/*

documents included detailed discussions of brain, lungs, heart, liver, and blood, together with recommended treatments, and became known as the *Hippocratic Corpus* (about 400 BC). The corpus was composed of about 60 documents, and it represented the first widely distributed and integrated repository of medical information in the world that contained guides to diagnoses and treatments of ailments and diseases. A previous example of this sort of repository in the form of the Babylonian *Sakikku* documents written on clay tablets and stored in a royal library, was relatively inaccessible to common people.

Specific volumes of the Hippocratic Corpus were devoted to the four humors: black bile, yellow bile, phlegm, and blood. In this regard, Hippocrates followed the general approach of Empedocles, explaining medical illnesses as an imbalance between the four basic elements, but the elements in medicine were the four humors. Other volumes covered information and treatment regarding fractures, head wounds, gynecology, epidemics, obstetrics, ophthalmology, the heart, the veins, and bones. Hippocrates also used tools. He mentions using a rectal speculum (Figure 1.4) to observe a rectal fistula (Volume iii, p. 331).

Particularly relevant to the history of predictive analytics is that this repository of knowledge and practices arose largely due to concern for the poor in Greece (as it did in Mesopotamia). We see a reflection of this concern today in the current controversy over access to health information and health care in America. Evidently, our concern today is not purely a modern phenomenon — its roots extend back to ancient Greece and even to the cradle of civilization in Mesopotamia.

Ancient Rome

By winning the Second Punic War in 201 with the victory over Hannibal of Carthage, Rome was transformed from a relatively loose confederacy into a permanent, expansionary war machine (Muhlberger, 1998; www.nipissingu.ca/department/history/muhlberger/2055/l33anc.htm). One result of this unification was a push to declare war on Macedon. Why do that? Rome was very busy with consolidation of its new territory in Gaul (Spain and France), and rebuilding Italy after devastation of the war with Hannibal. Two reasons were offered by Eckstein (1987): (1) Rome was just coming to the aid of one of its allies being attacked by King Philip V of Macedon (even though it appears that Rome's emissaries engineered it); and (2) Rome had become a conscious imperialistic power in the Mediterranean world, and lusted for conquest of Greece. Muhlberger (1998) claims that these two theories tend to divide those who like the Romans from those who don't.

For whatever reason, Greece was conquered in a short space of about 60 years, and the existing social structure of Greece crumbled and became largely Roman. Along with this transformation, much of Greek medical literature and art was pushed aside and ignored. This purge included the Hippocratic Corpus, because early Romans believed that divination was the way to cure illnesses. In other words, they were stuck on supernaturalistic medicine. Then, along came Claudius Galen.

Galen

Claudius Galen (AD 131−201) (Figure 1.5) was a Greek physician from Pergamum, who went to Rome, and then studied at the famous medical school in Alexandria, Egypt. He was trained in the medicine of Hippocrates, and he revived interest in the Hippocratic Corpus (Sigerist, 1951). He stressed clinical observation of patients, during which he examined patients very closely to make his diagnosis and prescribe what he thought was the appropriate treatment. In his practice, he accepted the Hippocratic view that disease was the result of an imbalance between the four humors, and developed treatments aimed at restoring the "normal" balance among these humors. Galen adopted many of the medical

FIGURE 1.5   Bust of Galen. *Reproduced with permission from the US Library of Congress.*

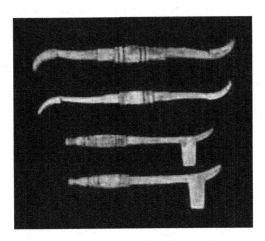

FIGURE 1.6   Various bone levers in use at the time of Galen. *Reproduced with permission from: www.hsl.virginia.edu/historical/artifacts/roman_surgical/*

instruments described by Hippocrates. Figure 1.6 shows some bone levers that may have been used to lever fractured bone into place.

Jealousy by Galen's rivals, and prejudice against Greeks among the Romans, caused him to flee Rome in AD 166, but he returned at the request of the Emperor Commodus. Because he served as the personal physician to Commodus, and later to Septimus Severus, he could work freely. The tide of imperial opinion turned so strongly back to Hippocrates and his work that a coin was minted with his portrait (see Figure 1.3); on the reverse side is shown the serpent entwined staff of Asclepius, which many centuries later was incorporated into the symbol of the American Medical Association and the logo of the World Health Organization. Mintage of this coin demonstrates the change in attitude of the Romans toward Greek medicine, fueled by Galen's success under the imperial aegis. We can view this revival of interest in the Hippocratic Corpus as the fourth example of a royal mandate for the collection and dissemination of medical documents for the benefit of the people.

Galen continued to add to the Hippocratic Corpus by writing many books and treatises himself. He was affected greatly by prominent Greek philosophers, including Aristotle and Plato. He took aspects from each Greek school of thought and combined them with his original thinking. In this manner, Galen viewed medical practice as interdisciplinary. This attitude is seen clearly delineated in his book, "The Best Physician is also a Philosopher." In this regard, Galen presaged the approach of modern scientists and thinkers, in which important ideas of many schools of thought are combined to help explain complex systems in the world (see Nisbet *et al.*, 2009). The books that he collected and wrote were still being used in the Middle Ages and, for many medical students, they were the primary source of information on medicine, particularly in the Arab world (Swain, 1996).

The Roman poet Horace quipped that *"Graecia capta ferum victorem cepit et artis intulit agresti Latio"* ("Greece, the captive, took captive her savage conqueror and brought her arts into rustic Rome" — Horace, *ca.* 14 BC, Epistles 2.1.156–157). What did Horace mean by that statement? The most common interpretation is that even the Romans realized that while Rome vanquished Greece militarily, Greece captivated the great interest of "rustic" Romans in the arts and sciences, and in the process "civilized" her. It might be said that Greece was the cradle of Western civilization, and that Rome was simply the vehicle that brought it into all of Europe over the roads built by the Romans. One of the most influential men in that process was Galen the physician. It may not be an overstatement to say that Galen brought Rome (and hence all of Europe) out of supernaturalism and into naturalistic medicine almost single-handedly, and the direct effect of his work on the practice of medicine persisted until the 20th century AD. The spirit of Hippocrates lives on in the Hippocratic Oath taken by every physician before entering into practice in America.

Arabia

The development of Arabian medicine is closely related to the history of Islam. In 622, Mohammed united the warring tribes of Arabia through a common religious and social system (Shanks and Al-Kalai, 1984). Medicine of the early Islamic and Umayyad period (661–750) was largely supernaturalistic, which included three principal treatments: (1) administration of honey; (2) blood-letting through collection in a cup; and (3) cautery (sealing blood vessels with fire).

A rather curious sequence of events happened in the Eastern Orthodox Christian church, which brought Greek and Roman medicine into the Arab world and maintained it until the 16th century:

1. As Bishop of Constantinople, Nestorius denied that Mary was the Mother of God, and was excommunicated at the Council at Ephesus in 431. Nestorius died shortly thereafter, but his followers fled east and founded the Nestorian Church, several medical schools, and a Nestorian center at Nisibis in Arabia.
2. The Persians at Nisibis warmly embraced the schools and the Nestorian center, and King Chosroes I founded the university at Jundi Shapur, which combined Indian philosophy with the Greek medicine brought by the Nestorians in their school. This action can be considered as another example of collection of medical documents by royal decree, but the purpose was for education, not the provision of medical care to the poor.
3. With the defeat of Heraclius, Emperor of the Eastern Roman Empire, the Arabs expanded their empire under the Umayyad Caliphate. This became an age of reawakening of Greek arts and medicine, and ushered in a second golden age of Greek culture.

Even though (or maybe because) Nestorius was branded as a heretic by the Eastern Orthodox Church, Nestorians were accepted in the Arab world as a Christian sect. Several other Christian men and families were also instrumental in the vending of Greek medical arts to the Arab world. Eight generations of the Christian Syriac-speaking Bakhtishu' family served as court physicians to the caliphs in Baghdad from about AD 770 to 1050 (Savage-Smith, 1994). These men were instrumental in translating Greek medical texts into Arabic. During this period, the Baghdad House of Wisdom (*Bayt al-Hikmah*) was founded to encourage the collection (in the form of a library) and translation of Greek works into Arabic. The most prodigious scholar in this library was Hunayn ibn Ishaq al-'Ibadi, another Syriac-speaking Christian, who translated almost all of the Greek medical works, half of Aristotle's works, and even the Jewish Septuagint. Arabs of the Golden Age of Arab culture were not at all adverse to Jewish and Christians literature existing in their midst, and they appear to have even promoted translations of it. Ishaq also included 95 Syriac and 34 Arabic versions of Galen's works. Figure 1.7 shows two pages of Ishaq's Arabic translation of Galen's introductory treatise on the skeletal system. Note that this book and other books up to the invention of the printing press were handwritten. Today, it is difficult for us to imagine the monumental impact of the printing press on the dissemination of knowledge throughout the world.

The importance of Arabian medicine lies not in its originality (which it does not have), but in that it was the vehicle that faithfully preserved the knowledge and arts of the Greeks by translating them into Arabic through Syriac versions. A major consequence of these translations is the preservation of the content of the Greek manuscripts. During the Renaissance, European scholars had no access to the original Greek texts, and so they translated the Arabic source into Latin, the European scholarly language of the day. The availability of the Hippocratic Corpus and other Greek medical documents in the Latin language made them readily available to Western scholars. It is interesting to note that this process was facilitated in the Arab world largely by Christians, who vended the preserved Greek medical and scientific works to Christian Europe, thus paving the way for the development of modern science and medicine.

FIGURE 1.7 A very rare copy of Hunayn ibn Ishaq's Arabic translation of Galen's introductory treatise on the skeletal system, *On Bones for Beginners*, known in Latin as *De ossibus ad tirones*, NLM MS P26, open at folios 62b—63a, the beginning of the treatise. *Reproduced with permission from the National Library of Medicine.*

SUMMARY OF ROYAL DECREES OF MEDICAL DOCUMENTATION IN ANCIENT CULTURES

Because of the tension among individual medical treatment specialists in ancient cultures, and the lack of uniformity among them, many ancient rulers sought to codify, standardize, and disseminate medical information in the form of written records to aid in medical diagnosis and treatment for all people in their societies. Many of these official documents exist today, and together they form the context in which modern medical records developed. These standardized documents were mandated by past rulers, because they would not have been developed apart from official mandates (*cf.* the previous discussion of Kings Adad-apla-iddina and Ashurbanipal in Mesopotamia, King Solon in early Greece, Commodus Caesar in Rome, and King Chosroes I of Persia).

From this viewpoint, we can understand some of the force behind the laws of modern countries that enable the collection and standardization of medical records in one place (e.g., the National Health Service of the UK in 1948; and in the United States, the Medicare Act of 1965 and the Affordable Care Act (ACA) of 2010. In addition, this historical context might lead us to believe that further centralization and standardization of medical and healthcare information in the USA is inevitable. This shadow of this inevitability lies particularly heavy on many physicians in the USA today, who must convert their written medical records to digital format during the next several years (a provision of the ACA) or lose increasingly large proportions of their Medicare reimbursements. Some medical specialties (e.g., dermatology) require handwritten figures of the body to be included in physicians' notes, documenting locations of skin problems. While these diagrams do not currently exist in electronic clinical data entry programs, they could be created by graphics routines that permit annotation of locations of past treatments — but these graphic routines may be slow in the development of software programs to implement digital record-keeping.

Due to the cost of digitizing and the initial lack of required software features available (i.e., graphics), some physicians will choose to delay document conversion and incur the cost of reduced Medicare reimbursements. Others who can do it will "bite the bullet" and do it as expeditiously as possible. But all practicing physicians will do it, eventually, as costs decline and the richness of software features increases. This conclusion is formed simply by the recognition that the realities of human nature and our need for medical care will interplay with the political and pragmatic realities in today's society in ways similar to those that occurred in other societies in the past. Technology that controls how it is done changes over time; human nature and basic human needs do not.

One of the themes of this book is the need to maintain current levels of personalized medicine AND provide electronic health records (EHRs) for use in diagnosis and treatment by all physicians. Only in this way can we leverage the power of predictive analytics to guide diagnosis and treatment across the entire landscape of medical practice in America. Certainly, it will be traumatic to convert all physician written records to digital format, but is can, and indeed must, be done. That is the modern expression of the pattern we can see in history of rulers mandating the collection and standardization of medical records at many times in the past.

Despite significant differences between the Democratic and Republican agendas on domestic affairs in American politics, it is clear that it is the Democratic political force that is driving this conversion. It appears that the administrations of Lyndon B. Johnson (the Medicare Act) and Barack Obama (the ACA) are just following in the footsteps of many ancient rulers to standardize bodies of medical information and medical care, and make benefits based on them available to all citizens.

EFFECTS OF THE MIDDLE AGES ON MEDICAL DOCUMENTATION

Between the fall of Rome (in 476, according to Gibbon, 1906) and the Renaissance (beginning in the 14th century), the development of medical knowledge came to a halt and was kept alive primarily in Arabia. In Europe, much of the knowledge of the Greeks and Romans was lost. The reason appears to be that Europeans (and particularly the early Britons) despised Rome, and destroyed or covered up anything pertaining to Rome — even Greek culture and knowledge promoted by Rome after Commodus. This disparagement and destruction of all things Roman after the fall of Rome paralleled the destruction by early Romans of all things of Greece after its conquest. Only in the Arab world were Greek and Roman medical documents preserved (see above). This situation prevailed for almost 1,000 years, up to the Renaissance.

REBIRTH OF INTEREST IN MEDICAL DOCUMENTATION DURING THE RENAISSANCE

The Renaissance was marked by two pivotal events that served to begin the breakdown of the stasis and the mindset controlled by the thinking of the Middle Ages: (1) the printing press, and (2) the Reformation (Eisenstein, 1991).

The Printing Press

The use of movable type was invented in China in 1048, but the concept of movable type did not surface in Europe until Gutenberg combined that concept with the screw press (Figure 1.8). This kind of press was used previously for wine and olive pressing, but Gutenberg was the first to adapt that technology to printing.

FIGURE 1.8   Johannes Gutenberg and his printing press. *Reproduced with permission from: Michael Halbert, Inkart.com.*

Thomas Carlyle (1836) quipped in his novel, *Sartor Resartus*, that "He who first shortened the labor of copyists by device of movable types was disbanding hired armies, and cashiering most kings and senates, and creating a whole new democratic world: he had invented the art of printing."

The effect of growing prosperity in the 15th century promoted the rise of literacy. Combined with the spread of Renaissance thinking, increased literacy moved many people to want to read. The invention of the printing press by Gutenberg in 1440 permitted the dissemination of new ideas quickly and accurately in written form, and permitted this expanding body of readers the opportunity to learn and adopt new ideas of the Renaissance.

The Protestant Reformation

The breakdown of the absolute control of religious and philosophical thinking in Europe by Luther and Calvin led to the introduction of new ideas into society. Luther and Calvin returned the Church to the primacy of the Bible. All doctrines of the Catholic Church were rejected unless sanctioned directly by the Bible, and the purity of the Bible was based on Arab translations of the Greek Texts, retranslated back into Greek. This awakening of interest in the Greek language prompted a parallel response in medical science (Porter, 1997).

The combination of the printing press, the consequent rapid spread of Renaissance thinking, and new ideas fueled by the Reformation generated a social climate that encouraged an increasing body of scientific and medical inquiry. Erasmus (1466−1536) drew upon both of these pivotal events to lead Europe back to the Greek medical works of Hippocrates and Galen.

Erasmus

Erasmus was a former monk who left his monastery to lead European scholarship for more than three decades, and established Greek as the standard for literary and theological studies (Porter, 1997). He translated the Arabian versions to produce the first modern Greek edition of the Hippocratic Corpus of books in 1525. The Reformation, dawning at the same time, spurred Erasmus to throw off the constraints of the Church that taught men to avoid invading the "sanctity" of the human body in the study of anatomy. The huge success of the reintroduction of Galen's medical works fueled Renaissance natural philosophers to become more inquisitive about human bodies. Thus, the stage was set by the availability of the printing press, and the loosened ties to the Church, for Erasmus to turn inquisitive minds towards a renewed interest in human anatomy.

Human Anatomy

The recovered Greek Texts supported the idea that ancient medicine was the right approach, and that scholars were the rightful guardians and interpreters of it (Porter, 1997).

Andreas Vesalius (1514−1564)

Vesalius was a Flemish anatomist who dissected the bodies of executed prisoners (human vivisection was still taboo at that time). He wrote many books on anatomy, including *De humani corporis fabrica* ("On the fabric of the human body"; see Figure 1.9). Despite his respect for ancient Greek medicine, his detailed drawings helped to correct some misconceptions of Galen and the Greek physicians, who dissected only animal bodies (Porter, 1997).

Thanks to the printing press, and published information about discoveries made by people such as Vesalius, it was very difficult for the established Catholic church to stop the spread of this "heretical" information, having been severely weakened by the Reformation. The *Fabrica* laid the foundation that guided studies of human anatomy based on direct observation, rather than analogies from animal dissection. This new approach, the practice of "anatomizing," became a common concept in medicine for several centuries (Porter, 1997).

William Harvey (1578−1657)

William Harvey was an English physician known for his complete description of the systematic circulation of blood by the heart. Blood circulation was known in the Arab world via the work of Ibn-al-Nafis (1213−1288) of Damascus, but his description was short and incomplete compared to that of Harvey (Porter, 1997).

FIGURE 1.9 From Andreas Vesalius' *De humani corporis fabrica* ("On the fabric of the human body"), Basel, Switzerland, 1555 (2nd edition). *Reproduced with permission from the Huntington Library Collections, San Marino, CA.*

MEDICAL DOCUMENTATION SINCE THE ENLIGHTENMENT

Subsequent to the Renaissance and the Reformation spurring new thinking of scholars about the world around us, many medical documents have been written on almost every conceivable aspect of medical science. This body of documents has become the source of information and basis for training of physicians in medical schools. However, it was difficult to absorb and incorporate the sheer volume of documents produced in the 18th and 19th centuries into medical practice. The variety of cases presented to the physician defied rigid characterization in publication in medical documents. These two challenges to physicians led to the development of medical case documentation standards, beginning in the 18th century, and to the development of medical databases in the 20th century. A short history of case medical documentation is presented below. Discussion of medical databases will be presented in Part 2 of this chapter.

Medical Case Documentation

Both Hippocrates and Galen recorded information on specific medical cases, but they were used only as examples of general principles and practices. These accounts of specific cases were recorded primarily for the purpose of strengthening the reputation and acceptance of specific physicians, rather than objectively reported for the sake of the case (Lloyd, 2006). Strangely enough, the earliest record of medical case documentation in the modern age comes from astrology, in the writings of Simon Forman's casebooks (Cook, 2001). These writings were intended to record the 10,079 consultations between March 16, 1596 and September 5, 1603. These casebooks contained detailed information about clients, and the advice given to them based on astrological relationships. At least 90% of the questions were about health and disease.

The early casebooks functioned as an important step in the development of modern medical records for individuals. Unfortunately, the individual case histories became resident on the physician's bookshelves, and were seldom gathered together for use by others. The modern development of the EMR concept has one foot anchored in early casebooks, and the other anchored in the physician's record library.

The Development of the US National Library of Medicine

As early as 1818, the Surgeon General of the US Army began to collect books for use in his work (Miles, 1984). This collection grew, and became known as the Library of the Surgeon General's Office. The library continued to expand

FIGURE 1.10 Slips of paper bearing citations for the Current List of Medical Literature being shingled by Hertha E. Bishop. *Reproduced with permission from: Miles (1984).*

until it contained over 17,000 volumes when, in 1872, the Surgeon General of the Army, John Shaw Billings, opened it to the public as the National Library of Medicine, becoming its director in 1883 (Miles, 1984). The library was awarded a building of its own on the Capitol Mall in 1886. The original goal of the library under the Surgeon General of the Army was to collect every medical document formally published in America in the form of books and pamphlet; that goal has continued through to the modern form of the library as the National Library of Medicine (NLM).

After World War II the library modernized, particularly under the directorship of Frank Bradway Rogers, who was trained in library science. Library organization became more hierarchical and academic in its focus on classification and cataloguing. In 1975, Rogers was awarded the honorary degree of Doctor of Science by the University of Toledo (Miles, 1984). Beginning in 1950, the library forged strong relationships with the American Medical Association (AMA) and received over 75,000 journal copies and publications from it. This huge influx of documents exacerbated the problem of cataloguing and indexing to produce the yearly *Index-Catalogue*. A simple listing of all publications (the *Current List of Medical Literature*) was to take its place; however, various supplements were published until 1961, when the final supplement to the *Index-Catalogue* contained 579,566 author titles, 538,509 book titles, and 2,566,066 article titles.

The *Current List* was produced by the "shingle" method developed in the Department of Agriculture. Indexers scanned articles, and transferred author and subject names to forms, which were passed to typists, who annotated each article with author names and subjects on separate slips of paper. These slips of paper were alphabetized and pasted onto a larger paper in an overlapping fashion (like shingles on a house) to form author and subject pages (Figure 1.10). The pages were accumulated for a month, and composed into the *Current Index*.

The challenge was to find a way to reduce the massive work necessary to shingle each publication of the *Current List*. This approach was abandoned in favor of a new punch-card method that involved sorting mechanically by machines. Use of punch cards utilizing the new Holorith code led directly to the development of computers, as described below.

PART 2: ANALYTICAL AND DECISION SYSTEMS IN MEDICINE AND HEALTH CARE

In the latter half of the 20th century, two themes developed in medicine that have yet to be integrated:

1. Computers and medical databases
2. Development of best practice documents among specialties in personalized medicine.

COMPUTERS AND MEDICAL DATABASES

Prior to the advent of the computer, storage of information was in print format. Computers permitted the electronic expression of information, allowing storage of data for a period of time. This storage was accomplished initially by magnetic cores or drums. With the invention of the Winchester 30-30 hard drive in 1956, storage volumes and storage times increased significantly; they have increased exponentially ever since.

One of the earliest movements away from storage of information in text form was the invention of the punch card, in which textual information (including numbers) was coded into a series of holes in a paper card. The code was designed by Holorith in 1889 (Randell, 1982). The Director of the Army Surgeon General's Library, John S. Billings, recommended that the US Census Bureau should store the 1890 Census information with punch cards, using the Holorith code, giving birth to the Holorith Company (Collen, 2012).

Thomas Watson took control of the Holorith Company in 1924, and renamed it International Business Machines (IBM), to focus on *Informatics* (coined by IBM), information science, and data communication (Augarten, 1984). The stage was set for the computer revolution, notwithstanding Thomas Watson Sr's reluctance to go there.

The Electronic Numeric Integrator and Calculator (ENIAC) was developed during World War II to help track ordinance trajectories (Rosen, 1969). Shortly after the war, this technology was adapted to peacetime uses in the form of UNIVAC to store the 1950 Census data. It didn't take long for IBM get in on the act by developing the IBM 701 (1952) and the IBM 704 (1954) to support the Korean War effort (Blum 1983). This effort led to the development of the Formula Translation language (FORTRAN), which became the primary computer programming language for scientific purposes until the 1990s.

Medical science and computer storage and retrieval capabilities came together with the development of the Massachusetts Utility Multi-Programming System (MUMPS) at the Massachusetts General Hospital in 1967. MUMPS has become the most common programming language for medical computer applications (Barnett *et al.*, 1981).

Medical Databases

One of the first medical databases was written in MUMPS at the Beth Israel Hospital in Boston (Bleich, 1969). This system used the hospital clinical database as a knowledge base, input data about a patient's acid—base balance, and recommended appropriate treatments. This system was particularly noteworthy because it was built for the express purpose of determining appropriate treatments. By the 1980s, medical knowledge bases were relatively common in specific institutions (Collen, 2012). One of particular mention was Infernet, at the University of California, San Francisco. Infernet was composed of a cardiac medical knowledge base and a Bayesian algorithm to infer the proper treatment of the cardiac patient. This system was a forerunner of things to come in the 21st century.

Medical Literature Databases

Printed documents were also collected by every US medical school to form libraries. These libraries were linked together in 1965 by the National Network of Libraries of Medicine (NN/LM), coordinated by the National Library of Medicine. The NN/LM provides access to biomedical information not available in the NLM. This combined library system allows interlibrary loan, and currently provides online access to many digitized medical documents.

MEDLINE (Medical Literature Analysis and Retrieval System) is a bibliographic database of biomedical and life sciences, which includes citations for articles from scientific journals of medicine, health care, biochemistry, biology, and microbiological evolution, accessible through the PubMed search interface from the NLM (www.ncbi.nlm.nih.gov/pubmed/). PubMed includes lists of books as well as the journal articles of MEDLINE. The current push by Google to digitize many of the world's works of literature (including previous important medical books) may be a harbinger of the future, when most printed documents may be available online. When this happens, the NN/LM with MEDLINE and PubMed will comprise the largest online medical database in the world.

BEST PRACTICE GUIDELINES

This proliferation of medical research documents in printed and electronic form has made it rather difficult for a physician to keep up with developments in a given medical specialty. Many medical specialty groups have sought to solve this problem by developing and issuing evidence-based best practice guidelines. These weighty documents suggest that care can be provided to patients, based on rigorous science and medical experts whose judgment is not motivated in any way by self-interest (Brawley and Goldberg, 2011). Worldwide, over 300 organizations have issued over 2,300 guidelines in their respective specialties. Grilli *et al.* (2000) reported that in the processes used to prepare 431 guideline documents, 67% did not describe the participants (patients and physicians), and 88% of the process documents did not provide adequate literature citations to support the guideline recommendations. Only 5% of the documents met these criteria.

Many of the guidelines are written by the US Preventive Services Task Force (USPSTF), an independent panel that advises the US government. Brawley and Goldberg (2011) cite recent USPSTF recommendations on breast cancer screening, where radiologists were specifically excluded from the group who wrote the guidelines. This exclusion was entirely proper; those physicians who benefit directly from the services rendered should be consulted for their input, but they should not be included in the specification of best practice guidelines. For many best practice guidelines, this is not so (Brawley and Goldberg, 2011).

Previous to 2009, the USPSTF strongly recommended that all women over the age of 50 have regular mammograms. In 2009 the USPTF changed its opinion, based on more recent studies. However, both bodies of studies ignored the 40% of women in their fifties and sixties who do not get mammograms, which includes about 5,000 lives lost to breast cancer (Brawley and Goldberg, 2011). The latter authors recommend that some of the effort spent in developing guidelines should be redirected to research to find better tests for breast cancer. The same recommendation might apply to all medical specialties with guidelines.

Best practice guidelines appear to be an attempt to collapse the sometimes widely varying opinions on medical practice available in the literature to form rather simplistic recommendations, and to replace intuition and common sense with evidence based on science (Brawley and Goldberg, 2011). This perception does not mean that we should not *include* evidence-based conclusions to guide best practices; rather, we must find ways to integrate evidence-based medical knowledge with intuition and experience. And we must find better tests and treatments, rather than spend a lot of time on collapsing large quantities of medical research (which may vary widely) into simplistic guidelines.

Guidelines of the American Academy of Neurology

One of the best set of guidelines was developed by the American Academy of Neurology (AAN), which provides at least suggestions for integrating evidence-based data and subjective judgments. Table 1.1 shows a set of guidelines for the treatment, by anticonvulsants, of painful diabetic neuropathy (PDN).

Notice the verbs "offered" and "considered." The introductory statement ("If clinically appropriate") applies to guidelines supported by all levels of evidence. These qualifiers suggest that the physician might consider these guidelines as inputs for the formation of treatment decisions, along with clinical observations and intuitive judgment provided by training and past experience. This is the right way to use guidelines documents in medical treatment.

TABLE 1.1 ANN Guidelines for the Treatment of Painful Diabetic Neuropathy*

Level of evidence	Treatment guidelines
Strong evidence	If clinically appropriate, Drug A should be offered
Moderate evidence	Drug B and Drug C should be considered
Moderate evidence	Drug D, Drug E, and Drug F should not be considered
Insufficient evidence	There is insufficient evidence to support use of Drug G
Clinical context	Although Drug H may be effective, it is potentially teratogenic, and should be avoided in diabetic women of child-bearing age

Specifications of the actual drug names are omitted.
Reproduced with permission from the American Academy of Neurology, www.aan.com.

POSTSCRIPT

Despite the significant problems with implementing the insurance exchanges mandated by the ACA in 2010, as mentioned earlier the Obama administration appears to be following in the footsteps of many rulers in the past to provide medical information for the diagnosis and treatment of common people. This discussion of the history of written and digital medical knowledge bases forms the foundation for discussions in the rest of the chapters of this book about how to analyze this impending flood of digital medical information with predictive analytics and analytical decision systems.

REFERENCES

Augarten, S., 1984. Bit by Bit: An Illustrated History of Computers. Ticknor & Fields, New York, NY.

Barnett, G.O., Souder, D., Beaman, P., Hupp, J., 1981. MUMPS — an evolutionary commentary. Comput. Biomed. Res. 14, 112—118.

Bleich, H.L., 1969. Computer evaluation of acid—base disorders. J. Clin. Invest. 48, 1689—1996.

Blum, B., 1983. Mainframe, minis, and micros; past, present and future. MEDCOMP. 1, 40—48.

Brawley, O., Goldberg, P., 2011. How we do Harm: A Doctor Breaks Ranks About Being Sick in America. St Martin's Press, New York, NY.

Breasted, J.H., 1967. Ancient Records of Egypt: Historical Documents from the Earliest Times to the Persian Conquest. University of Chicago Press, Chicago, IL.

Bryan, C.P., 1930. The Papyrus Ebers. Geoffrey Bles, London, UK. Available at: http://oilib.uchicago.edu/books/bryan_the_papyrus_ebers_1930.pdf.

Carlyle, T., 1836. Sartus Resartus. Available at: www.gutenberg.org/files/1051/1051-h/1051-h.htm\.

Collen, M.F., 2012. Computer Medical Databases: The First Six Decades (1950—2010). Springer, New York, NY.

Cook, J., 2001. Dr Simon Forman: A Most Notorious Physician. Chatto & Windus, London, UK.

Dawson, W.R., 2010. Herodotus as a Medical Writer. Bull. Inst. Classical Studies. 33, 87—96.

Eckstein, A.M., 1987. Senate and General: Individual Decision-Making and Roman Foreign Relations, 264—194 BC. University of California Press, Berkeley, CA.

Eisenstein, E.L., 1991. The Printing Press as an Agent of Change: Communications and Cultural Transformations in Early-Modern Europe, vol. 1. Cambridge University Press, Cambridge, UK.

Faulkner, R.O., 1969. The Ancient Egyptian Pyramid Texts. Oxford University reprint, Oxford, UK.

Gibbon, E., 1906. Decline and Fall of the Roman Empire, 12-volume edition, John Bagnell Bury (Ed.). Fred de Fau and Company, New York, NY.

Grilli, R., Magrini, N., Penne, A., Mura, G., Liberati, A., 2000. Practice guidelines developed by specialty societies: the need for a critical appraisal. Lancet. 355 (9198), 103—106.

Hammond, N.G.L., 1961. Land Tenure in Attica and Solon's Seisachtheia. J. Hellenistic Studies. 81, 76—98.

Johnson, E.D., 1970. History of Libraries in the Western World. The Scarecrow Press, Metuchen, NJ.

Kaplan, R., 2000. The Nothing That Is: A Natural History of Zero. Oxford University Press, Oxford, UK.

Lloyd, G.E.R., 2006. Principles and Practices in Ancient Greek and Chinese Science. Variorum, Ashgate, Burlington, VT.

Miles, W., 1984. A History of the National Library of Medicine. National Institutes of Health, Washington, DC.

Muhlberger, S., 1998. The Roman Conquest of Greece. Class Syllabus for History 2055 (Ancient Civilizations). Nipissing University, Ontario, Canada. Available at: (www.nipissingu.ca/department/history/muhlberger/2055/l33anc.htm).

Neugebaur, O., 1957. Exact Sciences in Antiquity. Brown University Press, Providence, RI, pp. 35—36.

Nisbet, R., Elder, J., Miner, G., 2009. Handbook of Statistical Analysis & Data Mining Applications. Academic Press, Burlington, MA.

Oppenheim, A.L., 1962. Mesopotamian Medicine. Bull. Hist. Med. XXXVI, 99—108.

Polastron, L.X., 2007. Books On Fire: The Tumultuous Story of the World's Great Libraries. Thames & Hudson Ltd, London, UK, pp. 2—3.

Porter, R., 1997. The Greatest Benefit to Mankind: A Medical History of Humanity. W.W. Norton & Co., New York, NY.

Randell, B. (Ed.), 1982. The Origins of Digital Computers, Selected Papers. 3rd ed. Springer-Verlag, New York, NY.

Reisner, G.A., 1905. The Hearst Medical Papyrus. J.C. Hinrichs, Zurich, Switzerland.

Rosen, S., 1969. Electronic computers: a historical survey. Comput. Surv. 1, 7—36.

Savage-Smith, E., 1994. Islamic Culture and the Medical Arts. National Library of Medicine, Bethesda, MD.

Shanks, N.J., Al-Kalai, D., 1984. Arabian medicine in the Middle Ages. J. Royal Soc. Med. 77 (1), 60—65.

Sigerist, H., 1951. A History of Medicine. Oxford University Press, Oxford, UK.

Swain, W. 1996. Galen. In: Hellenism and Empire: Language, Classicism, and Power in the Greek World, AD 50—250. Clarendon Press, Oxford, UK, pp. 357—379.

Unschuld, P.U., 1985. Medicine in China: A History of Ideas. University of California, Berkeley, CA.

Wellmann, M., 1901. Die Fragmente der sikelischen Arzte Akron, Philistion mtd des Diokles von Karystos. Weidmann, Berlin.

Zeller, E., 1886. Outlines of the History of Greek Philosophy. Longmans, Green, London, UK. Available at: ia700300.us.archive.org\outlineofthe-his00zelluoft.pdf.

Chapter 2

Why did We Write This Book?

Chapter Outline

PREAMBLE

In Chapter 1 we presented the history of medical documentation, showing five cases where past rulers mandated the collection of medical documents for the benefit of diagnosis and treatment of the common people. The challenge before medical professionals in the past was extracting relevant information from these medical records and applying it properly to guide treatment and diagnosis of individual cases. This chapter builds the foundation of reasons for the application of information on past cases to the diagnosis of current cases, and presents some disturbing facts about medical research in America today.

INTRODUCTION

It is interesting to trace the historical development of medical research. In doing so, though, we are faced with some problems concerning medical research in America today.

Before noting current problems of medical research, we should ask, what drives people to do research in the first place? The answer is contained in one word — disease. The word is so descriptive. It speaks of dis-ease. We are not at ease, and we want to be. The major driver of medical research is the quest to learn what makes people feel better and live longer. Another driver is curiosity. We want to know what conditions lead to certain outcomes, and how causative

Practical Predictive Analytics and Decisioning Systems for Medicine. DOI: http://dx.doi.org/10.1016/B978-0-12-411643-6.00002-8

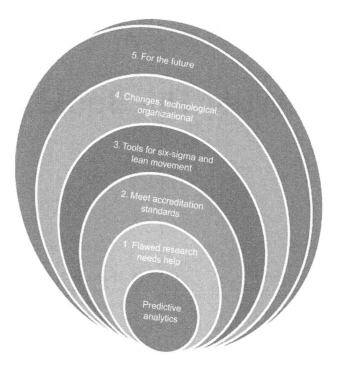

FIGURE 2.1 Organization of reasons for writing this book.

factors are related to, and what may predict, outcomes. This kind of natural patterning is what is called the "unsupervised learning" of cluster analysis and other exploratory techniques (Siegel, 2013). From clusters, we can find interesting relationships and can guess their causation. Guessing leads to hypothesis testing. Testing leads to discovery.

The remainder of this chapter details some of the reasons we decided to write this book, including one of the greatest drivers of all — the urge to predict the future, and particular the desire to predict to individuals. Figure 2.1 shows the organization of our reasons.

REASON 1: CURRENT PROBLEMS IN MEDICAL RESEARCH

Inaccuracies in Published Research Papers

In the summer of 2011, the *Wall Street Journal* reported that there were only 87 *retractions* in medical journals published during the period 2001 to 2005, whereas from 2006 to 2010 there were 436 retractions (Naik, 2011). The denominators were not given, so it was not possible to determine percentages. Nonetheless, a possible five-fold increase does seem exorbitant. In contrast, during the same time periods the numbers actually declined in two basic science journals, *Nature* and *Science*. Moreover, there were zero retractions in the *Astrophysical Journal* during both time periods. If the number of retractions is not serious enough, retractions often come long after the article has been published, and the retractions are often relegated to the final pages of journals, where they may not be seen (Collier, 2011).

Consequently, flawed studies may be retracted, but those flawed studies continue to "live" in the memory of readers and in the literature reviews of other researchers (Neale *et al.*, 2010). Varnell and colleagues (2004) examined articles from various medical journals, in which *only 15% of the articles appeared to use appropriate statistical procedures.* These were articles not retracted! Results of a similar study by Murray and co-workers (2008) fared slightly better, but even so, *over half* of those studies were flawed, and all of them were published in refereed journals. In addition to being flawed, some of the retracted studies were fabricated — i.e., the data were faked. That is a very disturbing revelation. One wonders how many studies have used fabricated data where this has not been discovered. Retraction rates have continued to climb in the past decade, though a portion of the increase may be due to a "higher level of scrutiny" due to Internet programs that identify unoriginality (plagiarism) (Steen *et al.*, 2013). In addition, the authors mentioned that journals are re-examining past articles using those same programs, which can increase the rates of retractions. The same study noted that the average months until retractions have decreased. There may be a downward trend of late (possibly because authors now know that plagiarism may be picked up easily). However, flawed research continues to be published. Predictive analytics have the potential of increasing the quality of research by developing accurate models.

What is happening in medical research to cause such a high incidence of flaws in studies? Are people generally uninformed about statistical procedures and research design? Are academics so driven to publish that they would fabricate data? Whatever the reasons, changes need to be made in medical research. Learning, predictive algorithms provide a positive change for medical research.

Improving Medical Research				
Discover Inaccuracies and Reduce High Retraction Rates	Determine Design Flaws	Discover Misuse of P Values – Gap Analysis	Provide more Research Education to Practitioners	Move from Traditional Statistical Models to Newer Predictive Analytics

Design Problems in Research Studies

Design problems account for some of the problems in medical research. For example, a fairly common design flaw is made when the researchers engage in randomizing groups in trials (GRT), rather than randomizing individuals to treatment groups (RT) or randomized clinical trials (RCT), as a convenient practice. A researcher might randomly assign the practices of physicians to treatment, thus randomizing the physicians rather than individuals within practices. There is a problem inherent in such designs. The individuals within each group may be relatively homogeneous in ways that could create biases, such as socioeconomic status, and ethnicity. The failure to randomize individuals can cause statistical differences not connected with the intervention. Hence, the predictive power of such studies may be overstated.

Another example of flawed design is conducting *multiple statistical analyses* on the same data, without adjusting the *P* value. Often, one can find studies with a table of t-tests, all using $P < 0.05$ as the critical probability. The reason that such a practice is not good is the following (taken from Miner, 2007):

The reason is that when we do more than one test in a hypothesis test we could be committing what Newsom (2007) called a "family wise" error. Each time we perform a test, the probability of a Type I error increases. (A Type I error is the probability of rejecting the null hypothesis when we should not.) The equation for determining the error is $\alpha_{FVE} \leq 1 - (1 - \alpha_{EC})^{C}$ (Newsom, 2007, para. 1). The α_{FVE} is the family wise error and the α_{EC} is the P level that is being used for the problem at hand. The exponent c is the number of comparisons being made.

Suppose one wanted to compare three means. One usually would run a three group ANOVA at the 0.05 level of significance and then conduct a post hoc *analysis. If running multiple t-tests then the equation would yield an alpha of: $\alpha_{FVE} \leq 1 - (1 - 0.05)^3 \leq 1 - 0.857^3 \leq 0.1426$.*

Therefore, if we were to make the three comparisons using multiple independent t-tests, the 0.05 level that we thought we were using would actually be 0.1426. If we used more groups, see what would happen to the P (alpha) level:

Number of comparisons	New alpha level
3	0.1426
4	0.1855
5	0.2262
6	0.2649
7	0.3017
8	0.3366

As one can see, the chances of finding a "significant" difference increase erroneously with each new contrast and the level of significance is not what we think. The ANOVA with post hoc procedures avoids this problem. The probability level of 0.05 stays at 0.05. (see also Chapter 9, p. 16).

Another problem is that traditional (confirmatory) statistics using P values are static methods that describe existing information, when instead we need models that "learn" and improve with new, and perhaps changing, information. The recommendations presented in this book often involve statistical learning theory algorithms, in which the predictive models evolve from the data and are refined in the presence of new data. Of course, if the model is a good one, it may not need to be refined for quite a time. As situations change, models need to be refined, if they no longer predict accurately.

The In His Image Family Medicine Residency Program (IHI) works through an outpatient clinic at the St John Medical Center in Tulsa, OK. While serving as research consultants for second-year IHI medical residents, two of the authors of this book found that residents were quite capable in applying findings from published articles to support topics of their studies. They had great respect for evidence-based research and for using decision rules or the "gold" standards. They did not, however, seem as well-versed in the traditional statistical analyses that produced the rules, or in the more modern techniques of predictive analyses.

- **Note**: One other problem can exist in predictive analytics even for those familiar with predictive techniques. Basically, one should divide the data into training and testing samples. The training data are meant to be used for exploratory analyses and developing what might be the best predictive models. The testing data, or holdout sample, are to be used for confirmatory analysis. Once the one predictive model has been determined, the model is used on the testing data to see how well the model predicts on the untouched data. At times, researchers use several models on the testing data. The testing data then, in essence, revert to training data and the analysis becomes an exploratory process, and not confirmatory as the researcher may think. In any predictive exercise, multiple tests on the same data should be considered exploratory. To be confirmatory, *the final model decision (alone) should be used on the testing data*. Many of the tutorials in this book are exploratory because the data are too few to divide. The reader should keep in mind that the tutorials are only to learn how to do the procedures, and many times the "findings," if any, should be considered as tentative or as hypotheses only.

A possible lack of research expertise begs the question of what residents were being taught in medical school concerning research design and data analysis. Walid (2010) found that 63% of the medical programs examined did not stress research at all. This means that up to 63% of doctors may have not been trained in methods of researching new treatments. Not teaching research methods would have violated the standards of the Accreditation Council for Graduate Medical Education (ACGME) (2011), which specified that resident MDs and DOs should be engaged in research and scholarly activities. This book may help in the research education of physicians.

A "Framework" for Determining Research Gaps

In response to design problems in medical research, Robinson and colleagues (2011) developed a "framework for determining research gaps" (p. vi) based on research in many organizations, such as the Agency for Healthcare Research and Quality (AHRQ). This framework revolved around two issues: (1) *identifying biases*, and (2) recognizing that certain *elements of vital information were missing in many research designs*. From this framework, Robinson *et al.* developed a grading system for research — a systematic effort to evaluate and suggest research that would be useful in the development of medical school curricula. It is hoped that efforts such as this will yield an increased emphasis on research within medical schools.

It was interesting to note that the Accreditation Council recommended that research activities should move from the top down (accreditation agency to practice). In spite of the recommendation of the Accreditation Council, Owczarzak and Dickson-Gomez (2011) warned that such initiatives may not be successful unless developed by front-line practitioners. In the IHI program described above, the front-line attending physicians worked closely with the second-year residents, and served as positive role models for them. Because of the stresses placed on residents, it is doubtful that they would have engaged in research without the push and involvement of the senior faculty at the point of care. The residents were definitely more influenced by their front-line attending physicians than they were by accreditation boards.

This book is aimed at encouraging practitioners (physicians, nurses, healthcare administrators, research assistants, and other care givers) to develop more of the skills required for successful predictive research, rather than the traditional analysis methods. Population statistics depend on normal distributions and are cumbersome when predicting to individuals. What is needed is learning Bayesian techniques of predictive analytics, demonstrated in this book. The instructive power of the *tutorials* (in the middle section of this book) comes from enabling those practitioners to analyze their own data using newer and more powerful predictive techniques.

REASON 2: PRACTICAL ASSISTANCE IS NEEDED TO INSURE SUCCESS FOR THE NEW INITIATIVES AND ACCREDITATION STANDARDS

Aid in Achieving Accreditation Standards		
Patient Protection & Accountable Care Act	The Joint Commission	Standards Organizations: HIMSS, Leapfrog Group, IHI, QIO, AHQA, PCORI

The success of methodology accelerants from accreditation standards testifies that the landscape of health care is changing. Examples of these accelerants include Six Sigma, accountable care organizations, types of payments, root cause analysis, meaningful use, coding issues, accreditation organizations, the Affordable Care Act, and evidence-based medicine (EBM; currently focused on large population-based studies). An initial concern with EBM was that the practice of medicine would no longer be an art in which individual patients were considered unique. The fear was that lists of procedures covering only the typical symptoms would be addressed, and complicated cases would no longer be served. Some criticized the use of EBM's mega-trials and the insistence that "bigger is better." Studies were thought by some EBM proponents to be somehow more significant if thousands of cases were involved. Instead, Hickey and Roberts (2011) recommended Bayesian techniques which use learning models. This book allows the researcher to conduct research in many ways. Some may use huge data warehouses, while also developing learning models in analyses. Others may use EBM data for tailoring treatments to individual patients by predicting specific outcomes.

There is no doubt that accrediting agencies do have an impact upon local research efforts. We can see the potential for this effect building, as a result of recent legislation. The *Patient Protection and Affordable Care Act* (ACA) (2011), signed into law by President Obama on March 23, 2010, included new requirements for accrediting agencies. On June 28, 2012, the Supreme Court upheld the law. The original 906-page document was massive and tedious to read — yet the medical community had not only to read it, but also to understand the document, because the law affected how much practitioners would be paid. Two of the nine "subtopics" in the Obama bill directly related to the need for this book:

- "Improving the quality and efficiency of health care"; and
- "Improving access to innovative medical therapies" (Responsible Reform for the Middle Class, 2011).

The authors of this book hoped that the ACA law would move consumers to become more informed about outcomes related to different medical treatments in the care of their health. In addition, it was hoped that the law would insure that doctors would be reimbursed according to patient outcomes. In this way, doctors would become more patient-centric in their thinking. Ideally, Medicare would reimburse for excellence in care, and those data would become available (transparent) to analyze outcomes. As a result of the law, we hoped to see more research into quality treatments that led to good results. Ideally, ACA would force accreditation organizations to revamp their standards to reflect requirements related to the law. In the best case scenario, this law would support metrics and methodologies associated with modern, more accurate predictive analytics.

The Joint Commission

Because standardization equates to community trust, accredited healthcare organizations can advertise that they have been recognized as providers of quality patient care. (In Chapter 10, Dr Mitchel Goldstein presents The Joint Commission (TJC) in more detail.)

TJC is the most recognized not-for-profit national accrediting organization (Joint Commission, 2012). The TJC has accredited over 19,000 healthcare entities throughout the United States. On its website, the Commission lists accreditation standards for:

- Ambulatory health care
- Behavioral health care
- Critical access hospitals

- Home care, hospitals
- Laboratory services
- Long-term care.

The Commission's mission statement is: "To continuously improve health care for the public, in collaboration with other stakeholders, by evaluating health care organizations and inspiring them to excel in providing safe and effective care of the highest quality and value" (Joint Commission, 2012). As TJC makes changes, it publishes prepublication changes (Joint Commission, 2011a). In Figure 2.2 is listed the prepublication statement under Standard IC.02.04.01, "Influenza Vaccination for Licensed Independent Practitioners and Staff," in the hospital link (Joint Commission, 2011b).

The standards may be purchased from TJC website. Woven within all the standards are the requirements for proof of standards, such as number 6 in Figure 2.2: "The hospital has a written description of the methodology used to determine influenza vaccination rates." When the accreditation team arrives, directions are given for methods of determining the denominator and the numerator for the rate provided by the hospital. Obviously, analytical process programs like Six Sigma (see Chapter 11) would apply as the hospital attempts to improve its required quality standards. For example, standard number 4 (in Figure 2.2) states that "The hospital includes in its infection control plan the goal of improving influenza vaccination rates" (Joint Commission, 2012). Chapter 12, Lean Hospital Examples, provides more information on The Joint Commission and its 2013 report, listing top-performing hospitals according to a specific set of standards set by The Joint Commission.

Standard IC.02.04.01
Influenza Vaccination for Licensed Independent Practitioners and Staff
Hospital Accreditation Program

IC.02.04.01

The hospital offers vaccination against influenza to licensed independent practitioners and staff.
Note: This standard is applicable to staff and licensed independent practitioners only when care, treatment, or services are provided on-site. When care, treatment, or services are provided off-site, such as with telemedicine or telephone consultation, this standard is not applicable to off-site staff and licensed independent practitioners.

Elements of Performance for IC.02.04.01	MOS	Tier	Score
1. The hospital establishes an annual influenza vaccination program that is offered to licensed independent practitioners and staff.		4	A
2. The hospital educates licensed independent practitioners and staff about, at a minimum, the influenza vaccine; non-vaccine control and prevention measures; and the diagnosis, transmission, and impact of influenza. (See also HR.01.04.01, EP 4)	Ⓜ	4	C
3. The hospital provides influenza vaccination at sites and times accessible to licensed independent practitioners and staff.		4	A
Ⓓ 4. The hospital includes in its infection control plan the goal of improving influenza vaccination rates. (For more information, refer to Standard IC.01.04.01)		4	A
Ⓓ 5. The hospital sets incremental influenza vaccination goals, consistent with achieving the 90% rate established in the national influenza initiatives for 2020. Note: The U.S. Department of Health and Human Services' Action Plan to Prevent Healthcare-Associated Infections is located at: http://www.hhs.gov/ash/initiatives/hai/tier2_flu.html.		4	A
Ⓓ 6. The hospital has a written description of the methodology used to determine influenza vaccination rates. (See IC.02.04.01, EP 1) Note: The National Quality Forum (NQF) Measure Submission and Evaluation Worksheet 5.0 provides recommendations for the numerator and denominator on the performance measure for NQF #0431 INFLUENZA VACCINATION COVERAGE AMONG HEALTHCARE PERSONNEL. See: http://www.qualityforum.org/WorkArea/linkit.aspx?LinkIdentifier=id&ItemID=68275 The Joint Commission recommends that organizations use the Centers for Disease Control and Prevention (CDC) and the NQF proposed performance measure to calculate influenza vaccination rates for staff and licensed independent practitioners. The CDC/NQF measure, however, does not include all contracted staff. Therefore, The Joint Commission recommends that organizations also track influenza vaccination rates for all individuals providing care, treatment, and services through a contract, since contracted individuals also transmit influenza.		4	A

FIGURE 2.2 Prepublication Hospital Standards. *Source: Joint Commission (2012).*

Other Standards Organizations in Health Care

The Healthcare Information and Management Systems Society (HIMSS) is a broad-based not-for-profit organization that concentrates on "optimal use" of IT. Chapter 4 is devoted to this highly influential group.

The Leapfrog Group is one such model for process analysis and control (Birkmeyer and Dimick, 2004; The Leapfrog Group, 2012). The Leapfrog Group's initial three recommended quality and safety practices have the potential to save up to 65,341 lives and prevent between 567,000 and 907,600 medication errors each year. Birkmeyer and colleagues (2001) predicted many lives saved because of Leapfrog initiatives. The first three initiatives were Computerized Physician Order Entry, Intensive Care Unit Physician Staffing, and Evidence-Based Hospital Referral (The Leapfrog Group, 2012).

The Institute for Healthcare Improvement (2012) is another quality healthcare group that works not only in the United States but also abroad. One is able to sign up at no cost and benefit from many wonderful educational assistance programs for hospitals, individuals, and schools.

Quality Improvement Organizations (QIOs) (2013) are private not-for-profit organizations based in each state. They contract with Centers for Medicare and Medicaid Services (CMS), are dedicated to improving quality, and review medical care given to Medicare patients.

The American Health Quality Association (AHQA) (2013), a not-for-profit educational organization, is the main association for the QIOs and provides a means of communication and collaboration for the QIOs. AHQA provides expertise and helps to develop quality projects for medical delivery systems.

The Patient Centered Outcomes Research Institute (PCORI) (2013) is funded under the Affordable Care Act (ACA), and in the future $1−2 from every person signed up for the ACA will be sent to PCORI. In this way, PCORI will become a major influence in quality in health care in the United States. The group contracts with research proposals for healthcare quality improvement and increased transparency. Healthcare entities may apply, and applications are reviewed in a very democratic process by scientists, stakeholders (drug companies, device manufacturers, etc.), and patient representatives (patients and/or patient advocates). Patient-centeredness is at the heart of the organization, and predictive analytics are encouraged that improve individual outcomes.

In all of the above, shifts in focus toward patient outcomes will occur in predictive analytic research. This book will help researchers in their efforts at using new learning models for data analysis.

REASON 3: TO MEET THE STANDARDS, HEALTHCARE ORGANIZATIONS NEED PRACTICAL ASSISTANCE AND TOOLS WITH IMPLEMENTING LEAN SYSTEMS

Examples of Problems that Highlight the Need for "Lean" and Predictive Tools

On the *Today* show of May 22, 2012, Dr Nancy Snyderman discussed the new recommendation from the US Preventive Service Task Force warning that the PSA blood test should not be used (Snyderman, 2012). She reported that the Preventive Service Task Force had conducted a large population study and determined that the PSA test was not associated with saving lives, compared to doing nothing. In fact, the test was so sensitive that upwards of 80% of the positive results were false. However, anecdotally there were examples of individuals being saved because of a PSA reading. The American Urological Society's president voiced his concern at the announcement, and declared the recommendation a "disservice to American men" (Marshall, 2012). Urologists are aware that the PSA test has a problem with false positives and should be used as a screening tool. The PSA test has not been effective in saving lives in large population studies; however, for men who have a history of prostate cancer in their families, the test can be used in conjunction with other tests to save individual lives. Here, we have a great example of the need for a predictive analytic tool for individually diagnosing prostate cancer. To see all sides of the PSA screening issue, readers are directed to the National Cancer Institute website (National Cancer Institute, 2012).

Provide Implementation Tools		
Six Sigma and Biomedical Informatics	Mistakes, Misdiagnoses and Root Cause Analysis	Use Quality Control Techniques from Business

Another issue is the question of what to do with mistakes. Without research, mistakes will happen. Even with research, mistakes will happen. It is what the medical community does with a mistake that makes all the difference. Needed are tools and organizations that aid in the *continuous improvement* movement. There is a natural tendency to want to cover up mistakes (Makary, 2012). The medical community is no different. Not disclosing mistakes in medicine is a natural inclination, because mistakes lead often to malpractice suits, which sometimes result in terminations among healthcare staff. According to Makary (2012), physicians are reluctant to "turn in" incompetent colleagues for reasons of internal politics and career paths. In addition, malpractice suits are associated with physician burnout and depression (Balch *et al.*, 2011), so it is natural to want to ignore mistakes. Rather than sweeping mistakes out of sight, it would be so much better in the long run to search for the causes of mistakes and eliminate them.

The following anonymous example comes from a purported actual incident, and serves as an example of the need for root causes. A patient died while in a delicate computer-assisted operation. The hospital assumed that the problem resulting in the patient's death was a systems problem (Kaplan, 2012). The hospital in this example was concerned with root causes (a form of predictive analytics) that would involve all stakeholders. It seemed that, at a crucial point in the operation, the computer screen froze and the surgeon could not properly operate. It took too long to get the technology to work again, and the patient died. The hospital called in one of the IT personnel to attend the post mortem meeting. In the process of discussion, participants discovered that the computer was never powered off, which would have cleared its RAM memory. Over time, the computer's memory filled, causing the screen to freeze. It would have been a simple thing to do, but the computer had been allowed to hibernate time after time. Mistakes do happen, but root cause analysis can minimize the incidence of mistakes and diminish the seriousness of their impact, and prevent recurrence. As a result of this incident, the computer subsequently was turned off after each use.

Misdiagnoses

This author is well acquainted with diagnostic errors. Her father died of lung cancer. His physician diagnosed his cough as "walking pneumonia" for over 6 months. When the "rare, small celled, aggressive" cancer was finally recognized as some kind of cancer, even then a biopsy was not done and the wrong kind of therapy was initiated. Her dad died four months later while taking the second course of treatment — the chemotherapy he should have had initially. He was too weakened, and the chemo killed him. This author's mother died of a brain infection because her doctor, an internist specializing in infectious diseases, failed to recognize the source of her headache and of the rash over her body when she visited him — even though he had been treating her for a lung infection for weeks. This author's brother died of prostate cancer after his urologist said his problem was urinary. His prostate was of normal size and his PSA was normal. By the time the diagnosis was discovered, the cancer was advanced and inoperable. Only in the latter couple of months of his life did the physicians reanalyze his original biopsy and discover that he had a second cancer — the same small celled, aggressive cancer that our dad had, only outside his lungs. That cancer had not been treated over the course of the year and a half that he lived with the disease.

About 98,000 preventable deaths occur due to misdiagnoses in the United States every year, according to Hernandez *et al.* (2010). Another estimate is up to 160,000 patients per year (Landro, 2013). The authors of the Hernandez *et al.* study surveyed physicians' knowledge of the most common misdiagnoses. Hernandez and colleagues emailed 551 surveys and received a 33% return. Pulmonary embolism is the most common medical misdiagnosis (relative incidence), and 40% of the physicians got that answer right. The most common (total incidence) misdiagnosis was infection, and only 7% of the physicians knew that. Physicians seemed more cognizant of the misdiagnosis that most often leads to litigation, which is breast cancer; 58% of the physicians knew that. Unless there is a lawsuit, diagnostic errors are not often brought to light.

ACA aims to remedy the situation, as it requires coordination among multiple providers (Landro, 2013). Perhaps this will happen, but, more importantly, the Institute of Medicine will study the impact of diagnostic errors on United States health care, according to that same article. Chapter 14, Patient-Directed Health Care, discusses what patients can do to avoid a misdiagnosis.

The problem of misdiagnoses is an example of a great opportunity for predictive analytics for lean tools such as searching for root cause analysis of diagnostic errors. Root cause analysis of medical mishaps is one of the main requirements of accreditation/lean standards. What is needed by a healthcare entity is a reporting system that does not penalize members. Penalties for mistakes destroy trust and communication. Trust and open communication are needed to support quality initiatives. There is a need for improving effectiveness of root cause analysis training so that support is built into the system (Bowie *et al.*, 2013). Support does not mean hiding errors and staying silent while patients are unknowingly walking into risk because an incompetent physician is in a position of power and can stall the career of a whistleblower (Makary, 2012). All stakeholders must be considered in implementing a collaborative model for policy procedures required for certification (Abdelhak *et al.*, 2012; Chapter 9). The stakeholders should include all persons in the system, including patients as well as the healthcare providers. In addition, transparency in hospital outcomes will help to warn patients — as when Dr Mark Chassin, then health commissioner of New York State, decided to make public the heart-surgery death rates (Makary, 2012). In addition, he mathematically adjusted the death rates by the complexity of the cases. Such transparency certainly would diminish any felt need for covering up incompetence. Improvement would surely follow. Again, there would be a need for root cause analysis. With efforts such as the above, no longer would incompetence be so easy to hide from public view (Makary, 2012). Retraining and culling would ensue.

Another example of the need for predictive analytics in lean processes is cited by Cuda-Kroen (2012), concerning the consequences of organ donation and the need to consider all of the stakeholders associated with a given operation (Cuda-Kroen, 2012). Cuda-Kroen warned that people who donate kidneys may have major complications that are not outlined to them before surgery. The reason that donors are not informed of these complications is that doctors don't know what to tell them. There have been few if any systematic follow-up studies concerning the consequences of donating a kidney from the point of view of the donor. Truly, all the stakeholders are not considered in this case. Researchers need to start thinking in new ways in order to capture all of the data necessary to inform all stakeholders (donors and recipients) of the possible complications of any operation. Predictive analytics might be able to determine which individuals might experience complications. Donors would become better informed, before an operation, in making their decision about whether or not to donate.

In addition to providing insights into possible adverse outcomes, predictive analytics gives us the ability to predict a target outcome. One such target outcome could be to reduce complications, as in the kidney donor example above. Another target outcome could be the reduction in mortality rates associated with a medical procedure. And predictive analytics might be able to inform a patient regarding the chances of complete recovery, with which hospital, which physician, and given their personal complications. Relevant factors could be collected for each person, and used as predictors of specific target outcomes. Predictors can even be text-based, such as case-reviewing contact notes.

Additional target outcomes that could be used for prediction studies include:

- Conformance rates to certain measures to gold standards of care, or appropriate use of prophylactic antibiotics, or appropriateness of orders
- Favorable outcomes required by accrediting agencies, using data from the National Physician Data Base (NPDB) or from the National Trauma Data Base (NTDB) and other national databases which are available at a fee for research purposes
- Gaps in the flow of communication
- Optimum timeliness of patients becoming admitted
- Costs (predicted by physician behaviors)
- Patient response, based on IT trouble tickets
- Complication rates
- Blood infection rates
- Other indices of patient safety.

Alkhoury and Courtney (2011) published a study using NTDB data in which trauma center designations (Levels I and II) were compared using many variables, such as length of stay (LOS), intensive care LOS, ventilator days, and mortality. The authors could have used predictive analytic methods to analyze and predict these variables as targets.

Six Sigma and Biomedical Informatics

Later in, Chapter 11, we explain more thoroughly the concepts of Six Sigma. Chapter 12 provides examples of healthcare initiatives and Chapter 3 explains biomedical informatics, but in this chapter we define them very simply. In addition we will also simply define ISO. Six Sigma basically is used for ideas concerned with systematic, statistically driven improvements for products, and is often used by manufacturing. The processes include measuring baselines, establishing goals, and moving toward those goals. Six Sigma originated as companies aimed for perfection of production such that six standard deviations would fit on each side of the mean between upper and lower tolerances. ISO stands for the International Standardization Organization, which sets industry standards. Starting in the 1940s, ISO now comprises over 100 national and international organizations. The basic ideal for both Six Sigma and the ISO standardization bodies is quality control. The aim is to continuously increase quality (ISO 9000 and ISO 9001, 2012).

The Joint Commission (2012, discussed above) for accreditation of healthcare organizations incorporates standards from the various ISO certification requirements, depending on organization type. ISO 9001 has international applications as well (ISO 9000 and ISO 9001, 2012). The principles are quite intuitive, focusing on customers (patients). ISO provides positive leadership that involves everyone at all levels of the organization to follow a process approach to increasing efficacy and efficiency systematically and continuously.

In addition to favorable outcomes, predictive analytics help to identify best practices to achieve those outcomes. Once identified, processes should be standardized around those practices for treating *individual patients*. A model for possible predictive analytics might involve the following (see also Tutorial J1, *Predicting Survival or Mortality for Patients with Disseminated Intravascular Coagulation and/or Critical Illnesses*). Some patients develop deep vein thrombosis and pulmonary embolism (DVT/ PE) after an operation. A surgical team might want to find out what patient conditions lead to this outcome. These conditions could be used as input variables to build a predictive model, which could then predict which patients would have a relatively high risk of this adverse outcome. Data could be collected over many cases or, as in Tutorial J1, from chart reviews, and a process control investigation (a predictive analytics activity could be conducted).

Another example for predictive analytic activity might be examining wait times to see which are "out of statistical control" or "special cases." Variables of such a study could be subjected to process analysis, using various statistical operations shown in the graphs of Figure 2.3. These graphs can be used to see that there are out-of-control areas. The spikes are instances in which quality may be out of control, and they identify special cases. Thus, process control decision rules may be needed.

The goal of this kind of analysis would be to find factors that adversely increase the wait times. The following are prediction approaches from business and industry that may be used for medical outcomes (Miner, 2005):

- *Static analysis* (using data as they are to complete the data mining sequence and find the best model for prediction). Static analyses use the traditional kinds of statistical analyses in hypothesis testing.
- *Dynamic*, in which the dependent variable is related to predictor variables associated with "1 to n" cases prior to the dependent variable in time sequence. The effect of these predictor variables on the dependent variable is thus "lagged" by one or more time periods. For more information, refer to Nisbet *et al.* (2009; Ch. 16).
- *Transformation* (examining runs and changes). Transformative models are learning models and use Bayesian statistical techniques.

Six Sigma concepts tend to overlap with predictive models. As a branch of Six Sigma, biomedical informatics aids in the discovery of problems and helps determine solutions to the problems by conducting root cause analyses. Some of the goals of Six Sigma in health care are:

- Increasing effectiveness
- Developing more efficient processes
- Increasing patient-centeredness.

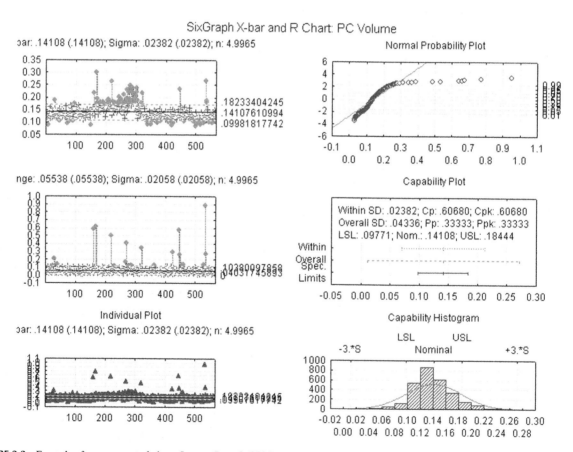

FIGURE 2.3   Example of process control chart. *Source: Statsoft (2004).*

With greater patient-centeredness, it is hoped that health care will be more equitable, timelier, safer, and more accessible to all. In order to achieve these goals, data must become available from all agencies and practitioners of biomedical Informatics. Data access is the lifeblood of healthcare administration. Those data must be made available for mandated government/accreditation purposes as well. Agencies must be provided access to data and to appropriate analytical results. The availability of these data will benefit nursing informatics (integrates elements of computer science, cognitive science, information science, and nursing), and it will also be very important in healthcare reform in the USA (McGonigle and Mastrian, 2009). All of these enhancements of the available data base consisting of data transparency, integration of ideas from many disciplines, and the root cause analysis (in the Six Sigma process) will provide fuel to processes resulting in *continuous improvement by discovering problems, aiding in the generation of possible solutions, and in the evaluation of those solutions as they relate to patient care.*

REASON 4: RESEARCH INTO TECHNOLOGICAL/ORGANIZATIONAL/PAYMENT CHANGES WILL BE NECESSARY

All of these new initiatives will require significant organizational change. Not all people in organizations affected by this change are pleased with this prospect. Researchers could examine all the ways in which society benefits or is threatened by the changes. They could focus on discovering which factors predict the most benefits, and to whom they apply. Certainly the requirements by the Office of the National Coordinator for Health Information Technology (ONC) will add complexity because of the many systems that exist today in healthcare entities (Lenert and Sundwall, 2012). Both the way in which the data are reported (electronic medical records — EMRs) and the kinds of devices used for data storage and sharing will impact our culture and bring about significant change. Predictive methods will be required to sort out the necessary processes and changes from the unnecessary.

Aid in Researching Changes				
Understand Organizational and Cultural Change Concepts	Address Resistance to Change	Determine Changes in Need for Transparency and Privacy	Examine the Roles of Regulations versus Innovation	Determine New Coding, EMR, Technology Changes Needed

Push Back in the Face of Change

Critics of changes in governmental regulations and accreditation guidelines related to access to data on technological devices could express concern that the devices and electronic records of doctors might become vulnerable to threats from hackers, such that privacy could be compromised. They might feel, for example, cloud storage security should be a chief consideration before data can be transparent (Paul *et al.*, 2012).

Informed Consent and Transparency

Regardless, the movement has already begun to ascertain informed consent of patients through patient portals. When patients sign up for their individual portals, they will be asked to fill out informed consents so that the data may be made transparent for research. Increased transparency will not only allow for more individualized research and fewer errors as mentioned above, but also reveal problem areas in systems and employees. Patients giving consent to use their data for research will stimulate projects, particularly prospective studies.

Possible Loss of Innovation Due to Changes

Critics of tight standards and the mandates of the ACA might feel the electronic-related requirements are expensive. Small medical practices may not be able to afford the modifications related to the requirements. Other critics may fear that the excise tax the US government plans to charge on all newly-conceived devices will reduce the variety of devices made, causing further reduction in the number of jobs available in medicine, and leading ultimately to increased costs of manufactured devices. Those concerns may be tempered, however, by promises of big savings to healthcare entities (Rajendran, 2013). In either case, predictive analytics can reduce costs by exposing specific areas where the costly resources are most needed, including the costs for storage and security of information. Innovation may, indeed, be limited, and, as a society, we need to decide how restrictive we want to be.

Smart organizations do not limit innovation but rather should encourage it; however, those organizations also need to be smart in how they bring about innovation. Normative mechanisms are not only powerful; organizations also gain legitimacy by appearing to have those long-accepted norms. Organizations must be isomorphic in many respects in order to be recognized as legitimate by the public and by its constituents (Arndt and Bigelow, 2000). Innovative organizations have to be cautious of changing so much that they are no longer perceived as legitimate. The authors recommended prospective impression management to combat the loss of legitimacy in innovative change, and such practices should be considered by healthcare organizations wishing to make fundamental changes. Arndt and Bigelow (2000) described "defensive impression management" (p. 504): "First, the organizations offered accounts that excused change and justified restructuring as appropriate. Second the organizations offered disclaimers about the new structure. Third, they concealed that they were innovators with respect to the diversified corporate structure." This study by Arndt and Bigelow (2000) might be a good one to review when an organization wishes to make innovative changes in its structure, especially in the face of constraining regulations.

Confusion in Coding and Payments Caused by Changes

Critics feared also that the expansion of coding (in accordance with CPT/ICD-10 guidelines that took effect on January 1, 2012) would cause confusion, because the training required would not be completed quickly. There are examples that illustrate this confusion even before the new codes were in effect. One of the authors experienced an insurance company denying some physician charges when the physician's office used the old (still in effect) codes, while the insurance company had started using the new codes. The insurance company assumed all the charges arose from an emergency, when the charges were related to a simple office visit. Such confusion and mismatched coding could cause unknown and undetermined biases in stored data until the transition were totally completed. Researchers accessing the databases might not be sure that the data truly represented reality, or, worse, they could assume that the data represented reality when in fact they did not. If biases like these occur in databases, they could adversely affect predictive analytic accuracies. Researchers must understand how to recognize bias, and know how to clean data to remove biases. In some of the tutorials of this book the reader will find data cleaning processes and/or the new automated Data Health Check Summary node in STATISTICA which automates data cleaning, which can be used in finding biases.

Chapter 14 discusses payment models. As an introduction, some are also discussed here. Capitation or bundled methods for reimbursement may cause physicians to skimp on care to save money (Kornfeld, 2011). Berenson and Rich (2010) found most of the current forms of payment to be inadequate for various reasons. The capitation model directing that physicians be paid at some interval for each patient may reward industriousness, but it can cause under-care of patients. In a strict capitation model, it was argued that complex cases were avoided and the preferred cases followed the norm; Hennig-Schmidt and colleagues (2011) concurred. Such a reward system could lead naturally to under-care, especially for patients with co-morbidities (co-occurring ailments). Also, researchers might prefer to investigate only easy-to-treat ailments, while avoiding difficult ones, because more patients can be seen in less time. This response pattern of physicians is sometimes referred to as "picking the low-hanging fruit." It may be argued, however, that by using predictive techniques physicians can become more efficient in practice, thus increasing excellence in practice, and increasing net revenue at the same time, while even considering complex cases. In other words, "complex" may not be so when using predictive analytics.

Chernew (2011) advocated a kind of bundling reimbursement system, in which a pay-for-performance element is included. The old fee for service (FFS) model has many problems, which include differences in charges and the coding systems that complicate its application. Chernew felt that physicians might want a bundling system at this point because bundling would allow for savings if systems were made more efficient. If bundling is used, then predictive analytics could be quite useful.

With the new CPT/ICD-10 guidelines in place and with new EMR systems all happening at once, it is possible that physicians might start choosing other occupations, leaving medical practice increasingly in the hands of physician assistants and nurse practitioners. Some hospitals have felt the cost pinch already, and have moved to having third-party contractors evaluate payments. This situation can lead, for example, to refusal to pay for a hip operation ordered by the physician, because an external stabilization device was not tried first. Despite the recommendation of this device by the reimbursement contractor, the physician should be able to make the decision about what procedure is best for a particular patient. However, the check sheets depending on "best evidence" (see the Virginia Mason Hospital example in Chapter 12) may not allow them to do so. On the other hand, such external checks and balances might be necessary to prevent physicians from adding more operations to their docket simply for monetary gain.

Overall, the use of predictive analytics to determine patient-centered treatments may increase access to necessary treatments, could save money, and optimally could allocate scarce treatment resources. Predictive analytics can generate decision rules "learned" through analysis of enhanced data sources, so that resources can be allocated on an individual basis, rather than resorting to an approach in which one process is "fit" to all. Patients themselves may even use predictive analytics as they take charge of their own health care, as discussed in Chapter 14.

Technology Difficulties

Meeting the requirements of accreditation mandates is another issue of concern. At present, data are kept in EMR systems that are institution-based, and they do not "speak" to one another. At the time of this writing, there were over 1,700 EMR systems in use across the United States (see Chapter 5). These and closed-architecture databases can be inconsistent, and unavailable to a physician or a group of physicians who switch their practices to a different location or hospital. It may be that the only way to move data between systems is in the form of flat files of comma-separated-values (CSVs), and these files may be unusable in the new system. New mandates associated with incompatibilities like these may trigger new information products able to translate and move data from one system to another. We are on the brink of major breakthroughs in predicting appropriate diagnoses and treatments, and the integration of data available through transparent and open architectures. At the time of this writing, however, the number of EMR systems is mind-boggling and finding a way to standardize is out of sight.

Organizational Culture

Some clinicians are quite wary of the new regulations, believing that the accountable care organizations (ACOs) will be run by non-physicians, when they should be run by the physicians who work directly with the patients. One organization that has expressed concern is the Association of American Physicians and Surgeons (AAPS) (2012). Some physicians advocate that only catastrophic illness should be billed to insurance carriers, and that patients should pay doctors directly for routine care. A variant of this model is already in place in the Concierge model of medical practice, in which patients pay a yearly fee for routine treatment (MDVIP, 2013).

Some physicians may fear that government and/or accreditation mandates could diminish their abilities to practice the art of medicine. Some of these doubting physicians call for *practice-based* as opposed to *evidence-based* medicine (Association of American Physicians and Surgeons, 2012). If the government mandates quality management systems, the critics reason that the quality measures cannot be trusted. The argument for practice-based medicine is based on the fact that the clinician knows the patient and can tailor the treatment to the idiosyncrasies of the particular individual, without regard to the norms of treatment. Practice-based medicine, it was thought, would listen more to the patient and the patient's response to treatment, rather than to the patient responses expected by the regulating organization. Ideally, there would be no conflict between practice-based medicine and the ideals of regulating organizations. *Predictive analytics for individuals can help to bridge the gaps between these two philosophies and add science to practice-based treatments.*

In the worst-case scenario, the act of ignoring research by regulating organizations will cause physicians to remain uninformed, especially so if the physician has severed ties with reimbursement organizations that keep up with research trends. An extreme case of the results of this ignorance is provided by the practice of Dr. Doctor Bliss (yes, his first name), physician to President James Garfield (Millard, 2011). Bliss did not listen to the research of Joseph Lister on applications of the Germ Theory to medical sanitation, believing that he, the clinician, knew best, and that invisible germs did not exist. Consequently, he probed Garfield's wounds with his dirty, bare fingers, causing Garfield to die of massive infection rather than from the bullet wound.

Today, society thinks medicine is steeped in the scientific method, and that Bliss's type of egotistical bungling cannot happen. Yet we find many retractions of medical research; could mistakes like this happen today? At this time, we really do not know the extent of misdiagnoses, but certainly the numbers are more than have been documented (Landro, 2013). Research recommendations followed by physicians today could be negated by tomorrow's findings. If practitioners trust "gold standard" research which happens to be flawed, then the situation is no better than in Bliss's day; much of medicine may be controlled by misconceptions reminiscent more of voodoo and superstition than of scientific research. The commentary on medical research by Freedman (2010) compiled a list of many of the possible flaws in medical research, including both conscious and unconscious flaws. He mentioned John Ioannidis, professor of a small group of Greek research critics, who wrote an excellent article on why most published research articles are false (Ioannidis, 2005). According to Freedman, and likely agreed to by Ioannidis, "there is an intellectual conflict of interest that pressures researchers to find whatever it is that is most likely to get them funded" (Freedman, 2010, p. 5). Some of the contradictions Friedman presented included:

> ... that mammograms, colonoscopies, and PSA tests are far less useful cancer-detection tools than we had been told; or when widely prescribed antidepressants such as Prozac, Zoloft, and Paxil were revealed to be no more effective than a placebo for most cases of depression; or when we learned that staying out of the sun entirely can actually increase cancer risks; or when we were told that the advice to drink lots of water during intense exercise was potentially fatal...
>
> (Freedman, 2010, p. 4).

Population Studies Versus Patient-Focused Care

Should we focus heath care on population-based metrics, as promoted by evidence-based medicine (EBM), or focus on the needs of individuals? This book examines that false dichotomy, and proposes integrating the two.

Based on the discussion above, the US medical care system, including its systems of payment, does seem to be in a state of disorder. For those who can afford private payment the US system can be the best in the world, but for those without the means of payment medical care is a nightmare that can ruin lives physically, financially, or both. However, one thing is certain. Problems in medical research and healthcare delivery represent opportunities for generating creative options to fix those problems. One of the most promising of these options is the opportunity to design better models of healthcare practices and payment systems. In a Frontline television special highlighting health care around the world, the healthcare system in Taiwan was described as a hybrid system that works. The United States could follow this model in the future (see video in Frontline, 2012). It remains to be seen how health care will change in the future. Medicare is increasing in costs, particularly for chronic diseases of the elderly, and the proportion of elderly is increasing (Erdem *et al.*, 2013). The ACA may not be able to halt the increases in costs, especially if younger, healthier people refuse to sign up, which seemed to be true in the beginning of the rollout. According to the Erdem *et al.* (2013) study, chronic kidney disease is one of the costliest diseases, which might be why certain Medicare-managed health organizations may not require a physical for signing, but do require that a person is not in the end stages of renal disease. How we will pay for the increases for all those needing care remains to be seen. Additionally, if physicians decide to "get out of medicine" then we will not have enough physicians to provide the medical care.

Regardless of the method of payment, however, it seems reasonable that as research demonstrates evidence-based practices and accurate models that can predict individual treatment, more effective treatment practices will follow. Research may ultimately favor EBM and Six Sigma processes. For example, a hospital analyzing a value stream in the clinical pathway of a particular type of operation might reveal overlapping functions among administrative and clinical personnel. Lean processes might dictate streamlining positions in an effort to save both time and money, as any redundancies might have added to the amount of time that patients were spending in the hospital. Or at the clinic level, a feature selection of data surrounding ankle breaks versus ankle sprains might reveal that only two questions of the Ottawa Guidelines for Acute Ankle Injury, rather than six, are required for a physician to determine with 95% accuracy whether or not an X-ray is needed (Watson *et al.*, 2011).

If it is granted that medical research is both desirable and necessary, then it follows that the best, most up-to-date methods for analysis should be used. Medical researchers should have the most powerful and accurate predictive analytics available at their disposal. This book will help researchers become better tooled for the job.

REASON 5: PRACTICAL REAL WORLD EXAMPLES ARE NEEDED THAT BRIDGE INTO A PHENOMENAL FUTURE

Exploratory Statistics/Individualized Statistics/Predictive Statistics

Suggestions for practical predictive analytic uses might be such as the following:

- How many days should we allow the average person to stay in the hospital after a hysterectomy? What factors predict the necessity for a particular patient to stay longer so as not to readmit?
- What is the gold standard treatment for renal cell carcinoma? How may those standards be used to individualize treatment?

- How much should insurance pay if there is a treatment that works best for a majority of people who have the disease? When should that payment be increased for a particular individual?
- If Medicare will pay for 180 days of care by a hospice, then what admission criteria should we use for the majority of cases to insure that those patients will not need care for more than 180 days? Making such a statement sounds crude until we realize that if a hospice cannot turn out someone who has been there for 256 days and Medicare stops paying at 180 days, the hospice cannot survive if it must serve many patients who will require more than the allotted time.
- What are the evidence-based decision rules for imaging scheduling for migraine patients?

Bridge to the Future		
Practical Examples Lean/ Quality Examples	Teaching Predictive Analytic Tools	Building the Future of Medicine, from genomics and mobile apps to hospital rooms of the future

Whatever might help develop standards of care, whatever might improve processes, and whatever will increase quality of care, decreasing costs and adding efficiency are areas for potential research.

Quality Medical Care Examples

When an organization decides to take the initiative to move toward quality improvement, prompted by its own desire or the requirements of the accrediting bodies, excellent medical practices can result. For example, one of the most famous quality hospitals, the Virginia Mason Hospital in Seattle, had some serious organizational attitudes that needed to be overcome to increase the quality of health care (see Chapter 12 for more information).

These outdated attitudes included the notion that the physician should be the central figure in medical delivery. Physicians were used to having all the perks, such as offices with windows looking outside, while placing patient rooms in the interiors without anything interesting to look at. Another notion was that a long delays between scheduling of appointments and treatment meant that the physician had a thriving practice. A third attitude consisted of the notion that phones in private practices should be answered by operators who were not medically trained. *By putting patients first in all attitudes*, all practices were examined from the patient's point of view so that wait times for appointments as long as 47 days were trimmed to the very day of the initial call. By plotting patient routes with blue yarn on a cardboard map of the complex (value streaming), new procedures and locations of services were put in place that helped to generate this drastic reduction in outpatient wait-time for treatment.

Practical Predictive Analytics for the Lean Movement

Predictive analytics can be extremely useful for generating accurate and timely decisions for hospitals' (1) healthcare administration; (2) healthcare delivery; and (3) basic medical research. Additional topics ripe for predictive analytics and which will be dealt with in this volume are:

- Operationalizing regulations − such as OASIS data for home health, National Quality Measures Clearinghouse
- Developing models for risk-standardization of readmission rates for various hospitalizations
- Evaluating the effectiveness of curricula such, as the IHI Open School Institute (Institute for Healthcare Improvement, 2012)
- Successful implementation of recommendations for Primary Care and Prevention (PCP) developed by Virginia Mason and the Virginia Mason Clinical Guidelines Committee
- Providing examples of Quality Hospitals' (e.g., Virginia Mason and others) patient experience as perfect within a hospital that has been honing its processes around the patients (again, see Chapter 12)
- Resolving issues surrounding the mandate for standardizing and sharing of data form health care entities
- Demonstrating examples of metrics that can be practiced on the front lines of medical practice
- Discussing the ideas of flawed medical research appearing in reputable medical journals
- Adapting to and implementing the phases of Meaningful Use

- Integration of those recording systems with process control (EMR and Six Sigma), such as conducting value stream analyses of the clinical pathways
- Mistake prevention — elimination of waste (processing waste), elimination of repetitive processes, elimination of "wait time," and related enhanced processes.

Education and Tools

Other compelling reasons for this book are integrally related to the cultural/political milieu in which these professionals practice and research, such as whether one is working in a hospital that believes in lean practices, open communication, and discovering root causes, or not. Helping others learn predictive analytic techniques is the overarching reason we wrote this book, and it is our desire to help those who would like to see their systems improve. Predictive analytics can help in all aspects of the challenges of medicine today.

It is hoped that predictive analytics can allow the medical community to develop decision rules *for individuals*, to effectively narrow the scope and number of treatments, which will save lives and optimize the use of scarce resources. The reader will certainly be interested in Chapters 13 and 14, concerning personalized medicine and patient-directed medicine, respectively. We might use predictive analytics to answer important questions like:

- Which patient will likely develop disseminated intravascular coagulation (DIV) after an operation?
- Which antidepressant will work for Jonathon?
- Which will be better for Harry; starting with chemotherapy or radiation?
- How many days will Joyce need to be in the hospital in order to make sure he or she does not return within 60 days?
- As a patient, what works best for me? How can I reduce my own costs?

Predictive analytics moves decision-making from deciding the gold standards for populations to predicting specific care for individuals.

Back to the Future

The answer to the question concerning why have we written this book certainly contains all of the reasons discussed above. In addition, we are on the event horizon for an explosion in medicine — genomics, care models, personalized medicine, patient-controlled medicine, medical machines and technological body art, nano-technology, and a future that we cannot even imagine at this time. All will be supported by predictive analytics. A good example is the emergence of genetic testing for individuals (see Chapters 13 and 14). At this time, people who send off for their genetic profiles may be told, for example, "You have the genetic potential to develop cystic fibrosis, which could be next month, next year, when you are 60 years old, or never" (Marcus, 2013, p. D1). Such a statement could bring more worry than if the person never knew his or her genetic potential. Physicians would have to keep watch for symptoms, which could increase costs. PA could reveal more to patients — perhaps relative risks using decision rules from weight of evidence, of when, under what circumstances, and perhaps how to avoid the disorder altogether.

It is interesting that medicine is returning to decisioning that includes weight of evidence (WoE). Decades ago, authors were advocating the use of weight of evidence in making diagnoses (De Dombal *et al.*, 1974; Cohen, 1980; Raines *et al.*, 2000; Weed, 2005). Raines *et al.* stated that the method was first developed in medicine in which the evidence consisted of symptomatology and the hypothesis was that the patient had the disease. Each of the symptoms had a pair of weights calculated for each of the symptoms depending upon the level of association with the disease in a large population of patients. The accumulation of the weights became the weight of evidence (p. 45). It is thought medicine is going back to the future, but now medicine has the opportunity to predict to individuals.

What would we like this book to accomplish?

- We want to stimulate research and analysis methods that will help people get well.
- We want to provide tools for evaluating innovations in genomics and technology.
- We want to help physicians and medical researchers learn to apply predictive analytics.
- We want to promote predictive analytics, because these approaches are so inherently interesting — searching for patterns and making predictions are fascinating in and of themselves.
- We want to promote clustering and other methods of exploratory research, which help to determine decision rules for best practices as applied to *populations and individuals*.
- We want to focus on developing standards of care across the board.

In summary, the reasons for writing this book can be classified according to:

- Finding solutions, and making decisions
- Promoting exploratory research for the future
- Promoting predictive research
- Medical research related to governmental regulations and accreditation guidelines.

This book will demonstrate *practical solutions drawn from predictive analytics methodologies*, which allow practitioners at all levels to:

- Make timely decisions concerning patient-centered medical delivery
- Build accurate models to optimize processes in health care administration and healthcare delivery.

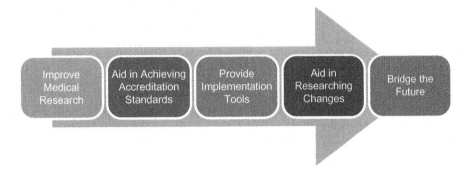

POSTSCRIPT

These reasons compose the potential landscape of applications of predictive analytics in medicine and health care. Chapter 3 (Biomedical Informatics) builds the common methodological infrastructure for analyzing patient-centered information for medical decisioning and optimization of operations in a healthcare organization. These methods are followed to build models on information from past cases to predict diagnosis and treatment for specific new cases. In this way, the promise of predictive analytics can be realized in all areas of health care in the future.

REFERENCES

Abdelhak, M., Grostick, S., Hanken, M.A., 2012. Health Information: Management of a Strategic Resource. fourth ed. Elsevier, St Louis, MO.

Accreditation Council for Graduate Medical Education, 2011. Common program requirements. <www.acgme.org/acwebsite/home/common_program_requirements_07012011.pdf>.

Alkhoury, F., Courtney, J., 2011. Outcomes after severe head injury: a National Trauma Data Bank-based comparison of Level I and Level II trauma centers. Am. Surg. 77 (3), 277–280.

American Health Quality Association, 2013. About AHQA. <www.ahqa.org/about-ahqa/ > Retrieved November 12, 2013.

Arndt, M., Bigelow, B., 2000. Presenting structural innovation in an Institutional Environment: Hospitals' use of impression management. Adm. Sci. Q. 45 (3), 494–522.

Association of American Physicians and Surgeons, 2012. Issues. <www.aapsonline.org/index.php/issues/>.

Balch, C.M., Oreskovich, M.R., Dyrbye, L.N., Colaiano, J.M., Satele, D.V., Sloan, J.A., Shanafelt, T.D., 2011. Personal consequences of malpractice lawsuits on American surgeons. J. Am. Coll. Surg. 213 (5), 657–667.

Berenson, R.A., Rich, E.C., 2010. US approaches to physician payment: the deconstruction of primary care. J. Gen. Intern. Med. 25 (6), 613–618.

Birkmeyer, J., Dimick, J., 2004. Potential benefits of the new Leapfrog standards: effect of process and outcomes measures. Surgery. 135 (6), 569–575.

Birkmeyer, J., Finlayson, E., Birkmeyer, C., 2001. Volume standards for high-risk surgical procedures: potential benefits of the Leapfrog initiative. Surgery. 130 (3), 415–422.

Bowie, P., Skinner, J., de Wet, C., 2013. Training health care professionals in root cause analysis: a cross-sectional study of post-training experiences, benefits and attitudes. BMC Health Serv. Res. 13 (1), 1–10.

Chernew, M.E., 2011. Why physicians should like bundled payment. Health Serv. Res. 46 (6Pt1), 1693–1697.

Cohen, J.L., 1980. Bayesianism versus Baconianism in the evaluation of medical diagnoses. Br. J. Philos. Sci. 31 (1), 45–62.

Collier, R., 2011. Shedding light on retractions. CMAJ. 183 (7), E385–E386.

Cuda-Kroen, G., 2012. Organ donation has consequences some donors aren't prepared for <www.npr.org/blogs/health/2012/07/02/155979681/organ-donation-has-consequences-some-donors-arent-prepared-for/>.

De Dombal, F.T., Leaper, D.J., Horrocks, J.C., Staniland, J.R., McCann., A.P., 1974. Human and computer-aided diagnosis of abdominal pain: further report with emphasis on performance of clinicians. Br. Med. J. 1 (5904), 376−380.

Erdem, E., Prada, S.I., Haffer, S.C., 2013. Medicare payments: how much do chronic conditions matter? MMRR. 3 (2), E1−E14.

Freedman, D.H., 2010. Lies, damned lies, and medical science. Atlantic Monthly. 306 (4), 76.

Frontline, 2012. Sick around America. Video found at: <www.pbs.org/wgbh/pages/frontline/sickaroundamerica/view/ >, Retrieved June 10, 2012.

Hennig-Schmidt, H., Selten, R., Wiesen, D., 2011. How payment systems affect physicians' provision behaviour − an experimental investigation. J. Health Econ. 30 (4), 637−646.

Hernandez, M.B., McDonald, C.L., Gofman, Y., Trevil, R., Bray, N., Hasty, R., et al., 2010. Physician familiarity with the most common misdiagnoses: implications for clinical practice and continuing medical education. Internet J. Med. Educ. 1 (2), 6.

Hickey, S., Roberts, H., 2011. Tarnished gold: the sickness of evidence-based medicine. CreateSpace.

Institute for Healthcare Improvement, 2012. Knowledge Center. <www.ihi.org/knowledge/Pages/default.aspx/ > Retrieved June 1, 2012.

Ioannidis, J.A., 2005. Why most published research findings are false. PloS Med. 2 (8), 696−701.

ISO 9000 AND ISO 9001, 2012, Plain English introduction. <www.praxiom.com/iso-intro.htm/>, Retrieved May 28, 2012.

Joint Commission, 2011a. Prepublication standard IC.02.04.01: Influenza vaccination for licensed independent practitioners and staff (November 21, 2011). www.jointcommission.org/influenza_vaccination_prepublication/ Retrieved January 2, 2012.

Joint Commission, 2011b. Improving America's hospitals: The Joint Commission's Annual Report on Quality and Safety 2011 (September 13, 2011). <www.jointcommission.org/2011_annual_report/>. Retrieved January 2, 2012.

Joint Commission, 2012. Our Mission. <www.jointcommission.org/about_us/about_the_joint_commission_main.aspx/>. Retrieved January 2, 2012.

Kaplan, G.S., 2012. Waste not: the management imperative for healthcare. J. Healthc. Manag. 57 (3), 160−166.

Kornfeld, R., 2011. Five ways ACOs infringe upon quality in patient care (October 28, 2011). <http://americasmedicalsociety.com/5-ways-acos-infringe-upon-quality-in-patient-care/>. Retrieved December 21, 2011.

Landro, L., 2013. The Biggest Mistakes Doctors Make. The Wall Street Journal, New York, NY, November 18, R1.

Lenert, L., Sundwall, D.N., 2012. Public health surveillance and meaningful use regulations: a crisis of opportunity. Am. J. Public Health. 102 (3), e1−e7.

Makary, M., 2012. Unaccountable: What Hospitals Won't Tell You and How Transparency Can Revolutionize Health Care. Bloomsbury Press, New York, NY.

Marcus, A.D., 2013. Genetic Testing Leaves More Patients Living in Limbo. The Wall Street Journal, New York, NY, November 19, D1.

Marshall, E., 2012. Prostate cancer test gets a failing grade. Science. http://news.sciencemag.org/2012/05/prostate-cancer-test-gets-failing-grade?ref=hp.

McGonigle, D., Mastrian, K., 2009. Nursing Informatics and the Foundation of Knowledge. Jones and Bartlett Publishers, Sudbury, MA.

MDVIP, 2013. Live healthy with a private doctor. <www.mdvip.com/> (Retrieved 2013).

Millard, C., 2011. Destiny of the Republic: A Tale of Madness, Medicine and the Murder of a President. Doubleday, New York, NY.

Miner, L.A., 2005. Visual Data Mining Case Study: Midwest Manufacturing Company. Paper presented at International Statistical Institute, Sydney, Australia.

Miner, L.A., 2007. Basic Statistical Analysis: An Online Text for Southern Nazarene University. Right-Brain, Inc, Tulsa, OK.

Murray, D.M., Pals, S.L., Blitstein, J.L., Alfano, C.M., Lehman, J., 2008. Design and analysis of group randomized trials in cancer: a review of current practices. J. Natl. Cancer Inst. 100 (7), 483−491.

Naik, G., 2011. Mistakes in scientific studies surge. Wall St. J. − Eastern Ed. A1−A12.

National Cancer Institute, 2012. Prostate-Specific Antigen (PSA) Test. www.cancer.gov/cancertopics/factsheet/detection/PSA.

Neale, A., Dailey, R.K., Abrams, J., 2010. Analysis of citations to biomedical articles affected by scientific misconduct. Sci. Eng. Ethics. 16 (2), 251−261.

Newsom, 2007. Post-hoc Tests. <www.upa.pdx.edu/IOA/newsom/da1/ho_posthoc.doc/>, Retrieved August 3, 2007.

Nisbet, R., Elder, J., Miner, G., 2009. Handbook of Statistical Analysis and Data Mining Applications. Elsevier, New York, NY.

Owczarzak, J., Dickson-Gomez, J., 2011. Providers' perceptions of and receptivity toward evidence-based HIV prevention interventions. AIDS Educ. Prev. 23 (2), 105−117.

Patient Centered Outcomes Research Institute, 2013. About us. <www.pcori.org/about-us/landing/>, Retrieved November 12, 2013.

Patient Protection and Affordable Care Act, Pub. L. No: 111−148, 124 Stat. 119, 2011. Retrieved December 31, 2011, from <www.gpo.gov/fdsys/pkg/PLAW-111publ148/pdf/PLAW- 111publ148.pdf/>.

Paul, R., Talreja, M., Sahu, A., Singh, K., 2012. Security issues in Cloud computing. Int. J. Comput. Sci. Eng. 4 (11), 1863−1867.

Quality Improvement Organizations, 2013. Outreach and quality improvement organizations. <www.cms.gov/Medicare/Quality-Initiatives-Patient-Assessment-Instruments/QualityImprovementOrgs/index.html?redirect = QualityImprovementOrgs/>, Retrieved November 12, 2013.

Raines, G.L., Bonham-Carter, G.F., Kemp, L., 2000. Predictive Probabilistic Modeling: Using Arcview GIS. ArcUser, www.esri.com.

Rajendran, J., 2013. What CFOs should know before venturing into the cloud. Healthc. Financ. Manag. 67 (5), 40.

Responsible Reform for the Middle Class: The Patient Protection and Affordable Care Act detailed summary. Retrieved December 31, 2011 from <http://dpc.senate.gov/healthreformbill/healthbill04.pdf/>.

Robinson, K.A., Saldanha, I.J., Mckoy, N.A., 2011. Development of a framework to identify research gaps from systematic reviews. J. Clin. Epidemiol. 64 (12), 1325−1330.

Siegel, E., 2013. Predictive Analytics: The Power to Predict Who Will Click, Buy, Lie or Die. Wiley & Sons, Hoboken, NJ.

Snyderman, N., 2012. New Recommendations for Prostate Cancer: Most Men Now Advised to Skip PSA Screening. Today Show. <www.nbcuniversalarchives.com/nbcuni/clip/51A01087_019.do/>.

StatSoft, 2004. STATISTICA Example from Sample Data Bases. StatSoft, Inc., Tulsa, OK.

Steen, R., Casadevall, A., Fang, F.C., 2013. Why has the Number of Scientific Retractions Increased? PLOS ONE. 8 (7), 1–9.

The Leapfrog Group, 2012. About Leapfrog. <www.leapfroggroup.org/about_leapfrog/>.

Varnell, S.P., Murray, D.M., Janega, J.B., Biltstein, J.L., 2004. Design and analysis of group randomized trials: a review of recent practices. Am. J. Public Health. 94 (3), 393.

Walid, M., 2010. Research productivity of OBGYN residency programs in USA. WebmedCentral Obstet. Gynaecol. 21 (8), WMC00475.

Watson, D., Rylander, E., Miner, L.A., Miner, G.D., 2011. Ottawa guidelines for ankle X-rays; An incidence Study at Family Medical Care. Paper presented at the 29th Annual Scientific Assembly and Retreat, IHI Family Medical Residency Program, Western Hills, OK.

Weed, D.L., 2005. Weight of evidence: a review of concept and methods. Risk Anal. 25 (6), 1545–1557.

Chapter 3

Biomedical Informatics

Chapter Outline

PREAMBLE

In the past, healthcare decision-making guided by previous medical information repositories (e.g., the Hippocratic Corpus) was primarily reactive in nature, in that information and experience were marshaled to diagnose and treat existing illnesses and disabilities. In this chapter, we begin to set the stage (as it were) for proactive decisioning in medicine and health care, facilitated by the construction of analytical models to predict future states, rather than react to existing healthcare conditions.

THE RISE OF PREDICTIVE ANALYTICS IN HEALTH CARE

Everyone likes the concept of gazing into a crystal ball to learn what will happen in the future. Chapter 1 discusses an important element of the history of medicine and health care in the Middle Ages, which was centered on mystical seers who vended medical advice. In fact, the concept of the medical casebook arose among those seers, seeking to document the many cases they advised. In our modern age science has replaced the crystal ball, but has been based largely upon what happened in the past, generating responses that are reactive to those events rather than proactive. Science can "look" into the future to the extent that it extends trends or events that have happened in the past; the problem is finding a way to view *new* information in a future context. However, gaining new insights from old data requires the complicated analysis of many interacting factors in medicine and health care to generate likely scenarios that might happen in

Practical Predictive Analytics and Decisioning Systems for Medicine. DOI: http://dx.doi.org/10.1016/B978-0-12-411643-6.00003-X

the future. This goal has eluded physicians, who are trapped by the perceptions of their own minds. Now, we have a way to do this — with computers.

The computer has revolutionized medicine and made possible many advances that have had a tremendous impact on health care and the life expectancy of humans. The computer is becoming an indispensible tool in the practice of health care as it becomes more advanced, and as the volume of information in health care increases exponentially. The American Medical Informatics Association (AMIA) has formally defined biomedical informatics as:

the interdisciplinary field that studies and pursues the effective uses of biomedical data, information, and knowledge for scientific inquiry, problem solving and decision making, motivated by efforts to improve human health.

(www.amia.org).

Predictive analytics plays a key role in these efforts, and becomes even more important as we advance in this field.

In the 2002 movie *Minority Report*, Tom Cruise plays a cop who keeps his city crime-free by catching murderers before they have a chance to commit a crime. In principle, this is the next level in law enforcement. This notion makes a good story because it plucks at the heartstrings of many people who are very interested to change what might happen in the future. The police in *Minority Report* depended on reports of special "precog" people who were able to "see" what the future would be, if events or actors in the present were left unchanged. How very much like the seers in the Middle Ages were the precogs of the film. The job of the police was to make the changes necessary to avoid the undesirable future (e.g., arrest the criminal before he commits the crime). We want to take analogous actions regarding our medical health care. Our challenge is to find some means of precognition in the technology of the present to provide some insights about what might happen in the future. We can't change the future in such a direct manner as did the police in *Minority Report*, but we can change what might happen in the future if we can predict with reasonable accuracy what it is that might happen. This is the realm of predictive analytics.

Health care is entering an era of development that is very similar in principle to the theme in the film *Minority Report*. The theme developing in health care is focused on using predictive analytics to follow a more proactive approach to the diagnosis and treatment of disease. Homicide is also a health statistic; therefore, the theme followed in *Minority Report* is of great interest to healthcare practitioners, at least in principle. In the Public Health Informatics section of this chapter, you will learn that the methodologies of predictive analytics are quite different from the way the "precog" people were used to "read" the future in *Minority Report*. In contrast, health care is leveraging the predictive power of artificial intelligence tools to predict probabilities, rather than certainties — but these probabilities can be high enough and accurate enough to have significant effects on prevention of adverse consequences (e.g., sickness and death).

MOVING FROM REACTIVE TO PROACTIVE RESPONSE IN HEALTH CARE

In the past, medicine was primarily a reactive field. When we are faced with a disease, we treat it; if the pain gets worse, we alleviate it; when someone stops breathing, we resuscitate him. One of the aims of predictive analytics in health care is to diagnose problems at an early stage of development (or even before they occur at all), before they have had a chance to take a toll on the human body. However, the role of predictive analytics does not stop once the individual develops the disease. Another aim of predictive analytics is to guide in selecting and tailoring treatments for individuals by predicting the course of events that is likely to occur with every treatment option that is available. Of course, these concepts apply not only to individuals but also to populations, and by using predictive analytics we can foresee public health threats and take the necessary steps to lessen their burden or prevent them from happening at all.

MEDICINE AND BIG DATA

Biomedical informatics involves developing techniques to efficiently process and analyze the data, producing summative results that can then be used to improve health outcomes. One of the biggest challenges in biomedical informatics today is developing techniques and tools to process the immense amount of data generated in health care today. The amount of biomedical data available today is tremendous, and it is growing exponentially; it is becoming one of the most important sources of "Big Data" (data volumes measured in terabytes and petabytes). The critical importance of it is defined in terms of life and death of many people. Vast amounts of biomedical data are being accumulated in many forms, such as free text, radiographs, photos, gene sequences, microarrays, vital signs, and lab values. We can produce, transmit, and store more of this data than ever before, and our capacities to store it and our abilities to analyze it are increasing at staggering rates. For example, the cost of 1 MB of data storage in 1995 was over 4,000 times the cost the same amount of storage in 2012, and the processing speed of the our desktop computers for analyzing it has increased about 30 times (from 100 MHz to over 3,000 MHz) since 1995. The bottleneck we face now is the limitation in our ability to process and synthesize these large volumes of data.

When working with such large volumes of data, the likelihood of finding associations occurring somewhere in the data set simply by chance is quite high, and the process of finding the true meaning behind data becomes extremely difficult, if not seemingly impossible. Imagine the immense number of calculations required by your brain just to perform an action as simple as throwing a wad of paper into a trash can. Light hits color sensors in your retina, which detect color, brightness, and depth. These signals are sent to the visual cortex (together with other parts of the brain), which processes every "pixel" of the digital image they form and identifies every object in your field of vision. After the trash can is identified as the target in your visual field (and the distance to it estimated), sensory signals from your hand are transmitted to your brain, providing information about the weight, consistency, and form of the wad of paper. The brain processes millions of pattern elements in your memory formed by similar signals caused by experiences in the past to calculate the force necessary to make the wad of paper follow the correct trajectory to the trash can. These signals and calculations are then combined to activate muscle groups, which receive visual, vestibular, proprioceptive, and tactile sensory input from thousands of neurons in the arm, shoulder, and hand to coordinate a smooth muscular action to propel the wad of paper to the trash can. Your nervous system is trained to do this through years of experience with inputs from your various sensory organs. All of these inputs must be combined together and coordinated in very complex ways to perform this apparently simple task. The time required to learn how to perform this action can be substantial, and the more experience the individual has in doing it, the smoother and more accurate is the toss. You will not get it on the first try, but each toss will get closer and closer to hitting the trash can, as your brain processes new information from each experience. This process is very similar in principle to the way predictive analytics tools learn to recognize patterns in data, example by example (i.e., row by row in the data file).

Although predictive analytics techniques are not as advanced as are analytical processes in the human brain, the capabilities of these techniques are growing continuously. They work on principles similar to those that control learning processes in the brain. Historical data are provided to the predictive analytics tool, functioning as cases (or experiences) in the past that are used to build a pattern, which is composed into an analytical model. The more historical data (or "experience") that are processed in the building (or training) of the model, the better it will perform. As time passes and new data become available, they can be added to the training data set, and the model can be retrained. So, as each year passes, your model can become increasingly accurate, as additional experience is available for the training process.

With the advent of meaningful use (see Chapter 9), there are considerable financial incentives for healthcare organizations to utilize their data stores to improve patient outcomes. Predictive analytics will play a key role in meeting the goals associated with the concept of meaningful use. This chapter will give a brief overview of the biomedical informatics field, and how predictive analytics can be applied to some of the key areas of informatics. The goal of this chapter is to create a stepping stone to inspire users of informatics technology to apply predictive analytics to their field in innovative and creative ways. This inspiration may lead them to create tools to improve health care and take on projects that will make a difference in health care and, ultimately, in people's lives.

AN APPROACH TO PREDICTIVE ANALYTICS PROJECTS

There are limitless possibilities when deciding on a predictive analytics project. Predictive analytics is well established in many areas of business, including customer relationship management (CRM), fraud detection, and sales forecasting, and, more recently, online retail, where retailers add offerings on the first web page, based on your own personal preferences as shown by what you looked at or purchased in the past, where you live, your gender, and your age. Individuals each have a personalized storefront showcasing the products they are most likely to buy, based on predictions of their likely purchases. Predictive analytics are also used to manage employees and schedule their shifts automatically based on the times buyer traffic is most likely to be the highest. For example, there appears to be a jump in traffic at a Jamba Juice as temperatures rise (Bellcross, 2012). In the airline industry predictive analytics are used to schedule flights, and Wall Street uses these technologies extensively to manage the buying and selling of stock. It is always important to consider how and where technologies are already being deployed before deploying them in our respective fields, in order to learn from what has already been done.

In health care we can do similar things, including:

- Catering treatments based on how a patient will respond optimally
- Offering additional services that a patient is likely to need and watching for additional symptoms or conditions that a patient is likely to develop
- Scheduling of nurses, doctors and other staff to match predicted patient volumes
- Efficient purchase and storage of medical supplies according to predicted demand.

The Predictive Analytics Process in Health Care

Regardless of the purpose for which predictive analytics is used, the same process of steps can be followed in the project. Figure 3.1 shows these key steps required to tackle a predictive analytics project in medicine and health care. The focus of this methodology is on the directed path of operations that move the researcher from hypothesis to solution. There are some feedback loops, which represent elements of the learning process, but the flow of operations leads to the desired end point – predictions that can be incorporated into medical decision-making. Following this methodology section are discussions of some key areas in bioinformatics where predictive analytics are being applied. There are innumerable examples in these areas, and those discussed are merely examples selected to inspire innovative thinking and encourage you to initiate projects of your own involving predictive analytics.

Process Steps

Step 1: Problem Definition

Define a problem/situation for which advanced notice will change your course of action and steps can be taken to change an outcome. Initially, choose problems that will have a relatively large impact, but also for which you will have significant domain support in solving. Once you identify a problem, you may even break it up into parts and tackle a

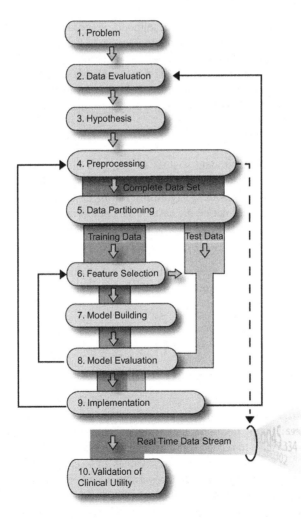

FIGURE 3.1   A predictive analytics process flow chart with feedback loops between Model Evaluation and Preprocessing-Feature Selection, and an overall iteration loop between Implementation and Data Evaluation. Copyright © 2013 Nephi Walton.

smaller piece of it before taking on the whole challenge. For example, you may be faced with the challenge to predict census at a children's hospital. There are many possible factors that can affect hospital census; therefore, one of the first tasks in solving this problem is to look at factors that have the largest impact on census. The general problem of hospital census could be broken down into various causes of admission, and it might be that the biggest driver of admissions is respiratory disease, primarily bronchiolitis. The causes of bronchiolitis could be further defined in terms of causal factors, the most likely of which could be RSV (respiratory syncytial virus). Consequently, the defined problem could be to predict an RSV outbreak.

Step 2: Identify Available Data Sources

Hospitals have a large store of data; however, ensure that you do not limit study to data that currently exist in the hospital. Other valuable data sources include:

- External causal data, like data on adverse weather conditions, which might drive people indoors, thereby promoting the transmission of viruses which can develop into disease outbreaks.
- Information available from local clinics and urgent care facilities, such as an increase in respiratory complaints, which can be related to an increase in positive respiratory viral tests, or an increase in emergency room visits.
- Secondary data, such as a spike in medication purchases at retail stores, which can be related to the defined problem. Other secondary data might include changes in television viewing patterns when children stay home from school, or an increase in web searches for respiratory symptoms.

You can also exercise your creativity, and do some research in the medical literature to identify other secondary sources of available data.

After the data sources have been identified, consider the likelihood of access to data from each one. For example, even though data for retail medication purchases are available, gaining access to that data can be quite difficult and expensive. You may decide to confine yourself initially to only those data sources that are readily available and can be accessed within your budget, but be careful not to limit yourself to just those available data sources related to known associations, because a major part of the predictive analytics process is the discovery of complex relationships that were previously unknown. Preliminary analysis might identify other useful data which were previously unrecognized.

Step 3: Formulate a Hypothesis

After you have identified the group of available data sources to use, you must formulate an hypothesis. Following the previous example, your hypothesis might be that you can predict RSV outbreaks with meteorological variables and positive viral test counts as inputs to a neural network modeling algorithm. In this case, the specific hypothesis is defined in terms of the methods proposed to test it. But that need not be the case — the appropriate methodology can be selected later.

Step 4: Data Preprocessing

Cleaning and preparing data for predictive analytical modeling can take from 70% to 90% of the total project time to complete; make your plans accordingly. Data preprocessing includes:

- Integration of data sets from multiple sources
- Filling of missing data elements with imputed values
- Deleting records and variables that are unusable for modeling
- Derivation of new variables to use as predictors
- Modifications in the data structure of the input data set (e.g., balancing data sets with rare targets)
- Data normalization and/or discretization.

Data formats and consistencies must be checked, and corrected where necessary. For example, testing of the same lab value, such as the level of thyroid stimulating hormone, may show different values and ranges of normal depending on the lab where it was processed. You might have to recode some variables, and derive other variables that you suspect might be predictive of the target outcome. Predictive analysis requires values in *every* row of *every* variable, or the modeling algorithm may ignore the entire row! Finally, you may need to normalize and or discretize the data to achieve better performance with your model. Discretizing means to create a separate variable for each unique value in a categorical variable (e.g., A, B, C). Remember the principle "garbage in = garbage out," and make sure your data are clean and consistent.

Step 5: Data Set Design

After the data set has been prepared at the data element level, you must perform several operations on the data set as a whole. These operations include the following.

- *Data set partitioning.* It is important to hold out a portion of your data for evaluating the accuracy of your model after it is built. Many predictive analytics algorithms will divide the input data set into two sub-sets used for training the testing model over many iterations through the data set. The *training set* is input to the algorithms, which evaluates the relative predictive weights associated with each variable (for neural nets), or the selected cut-points in the construction of a decision tree. These parameters are used to compose the predictive model, which is used to predict the target outcome for data in the testing set after the first iteration. The predicted values are compared with the actual values for each record in the testing data set, and an overall error is calculated. One of training parameters of the algorithm is modified slightly, based on the overall error, and the training data are input to the algorithm again. This process may go through hundreds of iterations until a specified threshold is reached (measured in terms of number of iterations performed, or a selected minimum error is reached).

  Thus, both the training and testing sets of data are used in the training operation. Evaluation of the accuracy should be performed on a data set not used in the training operation in any way. That means that you should create a *third* partition (the validation data set) in the data partitioning process, for use in calculating prediction accuracy. Don't base prediction accuracy on the training set, or even on the testing set, because your model may be over-trained for the specific training set, and it might fail significantly on any new data set. Some algorithms create all three data sets for you, most other algorithms create only training and testing data sets, and some algorithms don't partition input data sets at all — they depend on you to do the partitioning explicitly. Therefore, know your modeling algorithm!

- *Balancing of data sets with rare targets.* When an infant between the ages of 2 and 3 months presents to the emergency department with a fever, there is an approximately 7% chance that the fever is the result of a serious bacterial infection (Hui *et al.*, 2012). This is a relatively rare event, so only 7% of the data records will have Target value = 1, indicating a serious bacterial infection, and 93% will have a Target value = 0, indicating another cause — likely a more benign viral infection. It is very easy for a modeling algorithm to build a model that is 93% accurate, just by predicting all the rows as Target = 0; however, that model doesn't help you predict the infants that are at high risk for a serious bacterial illness. In order to do that, you must force the algorithms to focus more on the 7% of the records with the target value of 1, and less on the remaining 93%. There are three ways to do that:
- Delete enough records with Target = 0 to equal the number of records with Target = 1
- Duplicate enough records with Target = 1 to equal the number of records with Target = 0
- Calculate the ones-complement of the proportion of Target = 1 records (1 − proportion of Target = 1 records), and use that number as a weight to submit to the modeling algorithm, and treat Target = 0 records analogously.

Step 6: Feature Selection

In this step, we apply the principle of Occam's razor, which is essentially that if you have two competing theories that make exactly the same predictions, the simpler one is better. This is particularly important in predictive analytics with machine learning, because having too many features can lead to overfitting. A feature is the name given to a transformed variable. When a model is overfitted, it is conformed very closely to the training data set, including the noise in it (meaningless or inaccurate data that have no correlation to the outcome). As a result, the model may show very poor performance on any new data it encounters. There are a number of feature selection algorithms specific to the particular methods employed in machine learning. Each of these techniques can help you select only the features with the highest correlation to your outcome, and can improve your model's performance. Aside from the problem of overfitting, it makes no sense to use more data points if you can get equal or better results with a simpler model.

There is a caveat, however, that must be considered in the choice to use feature selection. Performing feature selection on your entire data set may bias your results, so make sure that you partition the data set before performing feature selection. If you are going to validate your model on a separate independent data set, then partitioning a third data set is not necessary. When using an independent data set, make sure it comes from the same population as the training and testing data partitions. Patient populations can differ markedly at different locations (e.g., Salt Lake City, UT, versus Detroit, MI), which may introduce a significant bias to your results.

Step 7: Model Building

This is where things get exciting and sometimes frustrating. There are many different predictive analytics algorithms that can be used to build your model. There are many predictive analytics software packages available currently, which contain a broad choice of modeling algorithms. Your choice may depend on your background, operating system, and budget. Popular among the choices of these packages are the following:

STATISTICA	www.statsoft.com/
IBM Modeler	www-01.ibm.com/software/analytics/spss/
Weka	www.cs.waikato.ac.nz/ml/weka/
SAS-EM	www.sas.com/
Orange	http://ax5.com/antonio/orangesnns/
R with RATTLE	www.r-project.org/
RapidMiner	http://rapid-i.com/content/view/181/190/
KNIME	www.knime.org/
Angoss	www.angoss.com/

Some of the modeling algorithms include logistic regression models, time series models, decision trees, artificial neural networks (ANNs), support vector machines (SVMs), naïve Bayes (NB), and k-nearest neighbors (KNN). If time and budget allow, it may be useful to try several different methods and compare their results.

Ensembles of different modeling algorithms may produce more accurate models than possible with any of the constituent algorithms. Most predictive analytics packages have modeling options that permit the design of ensemble models. It is recommended that several different ensembles be tried, before selecting the single algorithm (or group of them) that works best on your data set.

Step 8: Model Evaluation

After a predictive analytic model is created, that is not the end of the story. The model needs to be "evaluated" for reliability, sensitivity, and specificity. This model may have been created from small-sized datasets. Any model needs to be evaluated, but especially when the patient numbers that produced the model are small. This can be done using several methods, such as:

- Use of both a TRAINING and TESTING set of the data; if both sub-sets of data provide about the same accuracy, then the model may be a good one – but it still needs further evaluation.
- Use of a hold-out sample, where part of the dataset is "held out" in a random manner, with the rest being used as the TRAIN and TEST sets. Then, after the model is created, the hold-out sample is run against the model to see if the same accuracy scores are obtained and the individual scores seem reasonable.
- Use of V-fold cross-validation; this is a process where the dataset is sub-sampled numerous times (10 times is commonly used in real practice); if the accuracy scores of the V-fold cross-validation are about the same as for the train, test, and hold-out samples, then the model is probably quite robust.

The above list is not exclusive, as there are additional measures that can be taken to evaluate the model.

Step 9: Model Implementation

After the model is built and has been evaluated favorably, it can be deployed and tested in the operational systems where it will be used. This step in predictive analytics can be extremely difficult, because it may require interfacing with other systems, and collecting and analyzing current data on a daily basis, rather than working on an isolated dump of historical data. Don't put too much effort into integrating your model into the clinical workflow permanently, until you have completed Step 10 below. The deployed model cannot be used until it is proved to provide some clinical utility.

Step 10: Validation of Clinical Utility

You may spend a significant amount of time working on a prediction algorithm to predict admissions for the ER, only to find that there are no interventions that the hospital is willing or able to take to improve the outcome. You could build a very powerful predictive modeling solution, with no problem to solve. This is like designing a product that nobody wants to buy. The ability to deploy the model should be evaluated up front before you start the project. Make sure as you look at the outcome of your predictions that there are actual interventions that can take place based on the results. To prove your model makes a difference with the intervention, you must have some way to compare it to existing methods and demonstrate that your predictions actually improve health care.

The next operation could be labeled as Step 11: Re-evaluate, add more data, and rebuild the model. As emphasized earlier, a given model is not the end of analytical modeling; it is just one step along the way. Models "age" as new data become available. You might be able to improve model performance significantly by adding more data reflecting local demographic or societal changes. For example, you might be able significantly to improve the accuracy of a hospital census model by adding new inputs from seven different viral outbreak models. You can also build similar models using different variables, and combine their results to come up with a better estimate. Make sure, and remember, that as every year goes by, you have another year's worth of data for training your model. You could retrain monthly or even weekly, if you like.

MEANINGFUL USE

The term "meaningful use" is difficult to define. In practice, it covers a broad range of topics within the use of the electronic health record (EHR). Predictive analytics plays a critical role in meaningful use however this broad topic required its own chapter. Please see Chapter 9 for further discussion.

TRANSLATIONAL BIOINFORMATICS

There are a number of papers available in the literature on the use of predictive analytics in medical research, but its value can only be realized when predictions are used expressed in a form that can used successfully to impact patient care. This process is defined by AMIA as translational bioinformatics, to include:

> the development of storage, analytic, and interpretive methods to optimize the transformation of increasingly voluminous biomedical data, and genomic data, into proactive, predictive, preventive, and participatory health. Translational bioinformatics includes research on the development of novel techniques for the integration of biological and clinical data and the evolution of clinical informatics methodology to encompass biological observations. The end product of translational bioinformatics is newly found knowledge from these integrative efforts that can be disseminated to a variety of stakeholders, including biomedical scientists, clinicians, and patients.

(www.amia.org/applications-informatics/translational-bioinformatics).

The "Tricorder" medical device used in the *Star Trek* TV and film productions is not a far-fetched idea in bioinformatics; similar tools may be in use in the not too distant future. This device is used in these dramas to scan the human body, provide information about its health, and make a quick diagnosis and prognosis of treatment. The human body is a complex system controlled by a complex group of interacting biological signals, of which we are becoming increasingly aware. The actions and reactions of our body are the best indicators of what is happening in the body. However, this voluminous cascade of signals can be difficult to interpret. The decision of when and where to collect these signals is problematic in itself. When your body confronts an invader organism, signals are propagated to the white blood cells that indicate the nature of the invader and where it is, and trigger the appropriate response to defend the body against the threat. If we can sense and record these signals early, we might be able to prevent a healthcare disaster. In addition to the uses of these signals as data inputs, relationships between disease and other factors (e.g., genes, proteins, and adverse healthcare events) can be combined to build powerful predictive models useful in treating the disease. The process of building such predictive models and expressing the outcomes in terms useful for diagnosis and treatment of disease is the central goal of translational bioinformatics.

CLINICAL DECISION SUPPORT SYSTEMS

CDSSs are integrated analysis and deployment systems designed to facilitate decision-making in patient health care. They combine information about the current patients with information about past diagnoses and treatments stored in a database to provide feedback or recommendations that will aid in decision-making process at the point of care. The Healthcare Information and Management Systems Society (HIMSS) expands this definition to include patients as recipients of information, to permit patients to be active participants in their care. The definition of clinical decision support according to the HIMSS is:

> a process for enhancing health-related decisions and actions with pertinent, organized clinical knowledge and patient information to improve health and healthcare delivery. Information recipients can include patients, clinicians and others involved in patient care delivery; information delivered can include general clinical knowledge and guidance, intelligently processed

patient data, or a mixture of both; and information delivery formats can be drawn from a rich palette of options that includes data and order entry facilitators, filtered data displays, reference information, alerts, and others.

(www.himss.org/library/clinical-decision-support).

Therefore, CDSSs and HIMMS represent alternate expressions of translational biomedical informatics, which takes the results of scientific research to the bedside, to directly impact patient care.

CDSSs are separated by Plato's Problem; the gap between knowledge and experience. Clinical knowledge is a *cognitive* understanding of a set of known clinical rules and principles, based on medical literature, which guide our decision-making processes. Experience is an *acquired* understanding of medical outcomes gained through years of practice applying various outcomes related to various particular conditions, the majority of which cannot be learned sufficiently through reading and acquiring cognitive knowledge. This important distinction arises because there is an immense number of medical subjects in the literature that could be researched and taught. In addition, there are so many variables in the medical decision-making process that outcomes based on knowledge versus those based on experience are often discordant. It is practically impossible to teach physicians all of the knowledge acquired by experience, because the environmental variables are constantly changing so the body and nature of our experiences evolve through time, reflecting particular outcomes under specific conditions. Cognitive knowledge, however, is always associated with a limited scope of outcomes that are out of date, by necessity — there is a time-lag between subject outcomes and the reporting of them. For example, this distinction could come sharply into focus when choosing a physician to remove your kidney in surgery: would you choose one who has mastered a surgical textbook, or one who has the experience of 300 successful operations?

CDSSs can be classified into two types of systems:

- Knowledge-based support systems that are defined by a well-established set of rules that guide decisions, based on the interpretation of the medical conditions judged in the medical literature to be the best practice.
- Non-knowledge based systems that do not use a set of defined *a priori* rules, but instead use artificial intelligence algorithms to induce the rules through machine learning methods, allowing the system to learn from hundreds or even thousands of encounters, rebuilding the "model" set of rules as environmental variables change. These systems can be based on neural networks, genetic algorithms, support vector machines, decision trees, or any other machine learning technology, which "learns" to recognize patterns in data sets case by case.

Hybrid CDSSs

Hybrid CDSSs have been developed to allow the end user to synthesize the results from both knowledge and clinical experience, and make a clinical decision based on the results of both. (examples in the literature include Santelices *et al.*, 2010).

In such a hybrid system, multiple predicted outcomes are posed for the physician, based on data input from knowledge and experience bases, and furnished with associated probabilities to permit the selection of the appropriate decision. As we continue to learn more about cognitive science, and distil this knowledge into principles, we can apply them to improve these "intelligent" systems to help us make the best clinical decisions possible at the time. This practice of continuous incorporation of patient data, cognitive knowledge, and clinical experience is referred to often as "rapid learning." Rapid learning approaches that continuously update the CDSS as new data become available provide an ability to create decision models that adapt to the availability of new treatments, interventions, and metrics (variables) that can be input to the modeling process. This paradigm is shown in Figure 3.2.

Many CDSSs provide information on drug interactions and can generate allergy alerts. These alerts, however, are very basic, and do not include any information on many other factors, such as dose, time of administration, and the context in which the medications are given. Consequently, many physicians discount these warnings. On a given work day, it is very common for a physician to dismiss dozens of these warnings, as he or she prescribes medications in the hospital. In some instances physicians become so used to ignoring these warnings that they may accidentally disregard an important one. It is time to make these alerts more "intelligent," by using predictive analytics to predict levels at which problems occur, and to set thresholds to control when alerts will be generated. In addition, these alerts should provide information about the effectiveness of the drug for the given clinical scenario, and suggest more effective options, if a suboptimal treatment is selected. Such a system could include analysis of a patient's antibiotic prescription history before presenting a list of drugs for choice, or checking its database for any information about the susceptibility of the patient to a bacterial invasion if the chosen antibiotic does not provide broad enough coverage.

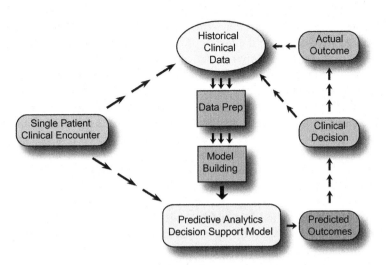

FIGURE 3.2 Illustration of the pathways in a hybrid CDSS (Clinical Decision Support System); these have been developed to allow the end user to synthesize the results from both knowledge and clinical experience, and make a clinical decision based on the results of both. Copyright © 2013 Nephi Walton.

CONSUMER HEALTH INFORMATICS

The AMIA definition of consumer health informatics is:

> *the field devoted to informatics from multiple consumer or patient views.*
>
> (www.amia.org/applications-informatics/consumer-health-informatics).

The focus is shifted from the problem resolution to understanding by the consumers of the nature of the problems, and the availability of various solutions to fix them. This new focus centers on information structures and programs that empower consumers to manage their own health. These programs can be classified into the following three groups.

1. Patient-Focused Informatics:
   - Predicting various elective procedures associated with a given treatment
   - Predicting the level and type of information required to support a given treatment
   - Predicting treatment schedules, based on patient symptoms and basic measurements
   - Recommending various interventions to be made or precautions to be delivered to prevent future ailments.
2. Health Literacy:
   - Presenting selected Internet resources to increase patient understanding of the nature of health problems, and their recommended treatments. Patients will access the Internet anyway, and therefore it is important to direct them to responsible websites, and screen out those that are inappropriate or present questionable information.
3. Consumer Education.

This shift in the focus of medical informatics addresses the need for healthcare information perceived by consumers by providing a means for them to acquire it responsibly. Most importantly, this new focus in informatics integrates consumers' preferences into health information systems. Consumer informatics stands at the crossroads of other informatics disciplines, such as nursing informatics, public health, health promotion, health education, library science, and communication science. From this central position, consumer informatics can function as a clearing house and a provider of valuable consumer-related information to other informatics disciplines.

DIRECT-TO-CONSUMER GENETIC TESTING

Related to consumer informatics, direct-to-consumer (DTC) genetic testing is a rapidly growing new industry in which DNA samples are accepted directly from consumers who then in turn receive a report from the analysis of the DNA that gives them information about their risk of developing certain diseases. There has been considerable debate about having such options available to consumers directly, because their lack of domain knowledge and inability to understand the report in the medical context may cause unnecessary worry and stress in individuals whose genetic make-up indicates an increased risk of certain diseases. This stress can cause some people to fall prey to (or even seek) relief from opportunistic marketing schemes that offer unproven treatments, cures, or preventative options for a disease. Some of the companies that offer these genetic testing services have recognized this problem, and offer genetic counseling to anyone who uses their service. Nonetheless, there are ethical concerns about this practice by responsible physicians, who question whether these tests have any positive effect on the health of the population and consider that they might have an overall negative psychological effect. There is certainly a beneficial place in medicine for genetic tests, when they are properly administered. For example, testing for mutations in the *BRCA1* and *BRCA2* genes can be done by responsible healthcare professionals. People with mutations in these genes may have a very high risk of disease, and can take preventative measures (such as prophylactic mastectomy) that have been proven to decrease mortality. Most of the thousands of other markers that are tested in DTC genetic testing are genetic variants that have minimal impact on the disease. In order to assign any practical meaning to these markers, they must be analyzed in context with the other information, such as family history, other genetic markers, and patient characteristics. There is a considerable need for research on the effects of DTC genetic testing and the benefits and harms that can arise from it. Predictive analytics can play a significant role in this field by including many more variables in the analysis, such as diet, activity, total disease burden, and environmental factors, to build more powerful predictive models and more accurate assessments of risk. In addition to providing a risk of disease, models could be built and deployed that show the predicted decrease in risk with behavioral modifications, dietary changes, or use of certain medications. Currently the future of this industry is very uncertain and many of the major players have halted their business secondary to pressure from the FDA, which has shut down 23andMe, the biggest player in the market. The FDA had intervened prior to shutting down 23andMe when Pathway Genomics attempted to sell DTC genetic testing kits at Walgreens (Darnovsky and Cussins, 2014). It is hard to determine at this point whether it will soon be possible to walk into a Wal-Mart and obtain your genetic sequence; the technology for sequencing is certainly in place, but the proper interpretation of the results and the infrastructure to manage this information is not. Whether or not this industry survives, the same principles and use of predictive analytics models could certainly be deployed with testing ordered for a patient by a physician.

USE OF PREDICTIVE ANALYTICS TO AVOID AN UNDESIRABLE FUTURE

Tools designed to predict future health must be used in the proper context. It is well known that health improvements are associated with changes in diet, demographic variables, exercise, and even education level. The opportunity to use a computer to explore various options and outcomes related to modifications of certain factors in their lives could potentially lead to people making appropriate changes in their lives. Charles Dickens presented a set of similar situations to Ebenezer Scrooge in *A Christmas Carol*. Instead of using a computer armed with predictive analytics programs (which, of course, didn't exist then!), he faced the old miser with the Ghosts of Christmas Past, Present, and Future. He used those literary vehicles to show Scrooge how decisions and events in the past led to his present circumstances, and how, if left unchecked, they would lead inevitably to a undesirable future. Scrooge was shocked! That response led him change his present actions, in the hope of avoiding what he was convinced would happen otherwise in the future. We can bundle those "ghosts" into a predictive analytical system to bring to reality the Victorian dream (and that, indeed, of everyone) to change some scary things that otherwise might happen in the future.

CONSUMER HEALTH KIOSKS

How would you like to walk up to a kiosk at a mall or drug store and be able to get a prescription, in the same way as you can get money at an ATM? That day is not far away. In addition to prescribing medications, these kiosks could offer on-the-spot lab testing and vitals measurement, or reassure you that your symptoms are not life threatening. Predictive analytics will be used in these systems to predict the outcome or severity of a problem, based on the available information compared against past visits. The kiosk may even be able to tell you to see a health provider, and recommend that you rush to the emergency room, or do nothing and just wait for time and nature to fix the problem.

PATIENT MONITORING SYSTEMS

A patient may be hospitalized when there is a significant risk that he or she may take a turn for the worse. Therefore, it is important to keep the patient in a controlled and monitored environment, where plenty of healthcare professionals are available should the need arise. These patients are monitored according to the level of risk assigned to the patient. For example, various levels of risk might direct that patient vitals be monitored every hour, every four hours, every eight hours, or even continuously. These measurements are necessary in order to assess the status of patient stability, and assure that there have been no changes related to the monitored values. Most hospitals have devised scoring systems to assess the patient's status and needs in order to ensure receipt of the proper level of care. For example, patient status may indicate whether a patient can be watched on the general floor or must be transferred to the intensive care unit (ICU). Despite the use of these monitoring systems, patients can become unstable very quickly and they may not be in the appropriate hospital location to receive the adequate level of care for their new condition. An intern might be presenting a patient to the attending physician outside the room, and a nurse might call out a code for an emergency response because the patient's blood pressure has dropped precipitously in a period of seconds, and the patient has stopped breathing. Instances like these beg the following questions:

- Was there something that could have been done sooner?
  — Probably there was, but staff limitations precluded it
- Could we have picked up a signal of the impending crisis quicker and taken action to prevent a near collapse and long stay in the ICU?
  — Yes, if the nurse could be dedicated full-time to the room.
- What went wrong in this instance — was the patient not properly assessed?

The assessment may have been correct at the time it was made, but patient status can change very quickly.

- Why not measure vitals more often on every patient?

The answers to all of these question are related to limitations in cost and resources. The more monitoring a patient receives, the more time and resources must be dedicated to that patient. This is why a stay on the general hospital ward is much less expensive than a stay in the ICU. Another common question is:

We have continuous monitoring systems available; why not apply them to every patient?

This would be a bad idea for many reasons, one of which is that the more equipment is hooked up to a patient, the more you restrict that patient's actions. This restriction may require the patient to stay in bed, which is often counterproductive during rehabilitation. Another reason is the excessive cost and time you will must spend contending with incidental findings and errors on monitoring devices. Because not all signals from monitoring devices are intelligently processed, they often produce erroneous measurements. It is very common in pediatrics to be called to a room to assess a patient with a low oxygen saturation, only to find the sensor dangling from the hand, or that the patient was moving so much that the machine was not picking up a good signal. Even with good signals, there is a broad range of normal responses and you are liable to encounter values that appear to be outliers if you monitor constantly. One particularly annoying event that physicians are commonly called to attend is the incidence of bradycardia during sleep. This condition can be completely normal, and it must be assessed in the context of the given problem and the medications the patient is taking. It is standard practice in medicine that unnecessary lab work is to be avoided, not just because of the added cost but also because there is a 5% chance that you may spend hundreds or thousands of dollars chasing an "abnormal" lab value (based on the mean and standard deviation of the entire population) that is completely normal for this person.

In pediatrics, the commonly used Patient Early Warning Score (PEWS) is a perfect example of an opportunity for predictive analytics to generate significant improvements in patient monitoring operations. When a pediatric patient receives a very low PEWS score (or two consecutive moderately low scores), the patient is assessed for transfer to the ICU. When low scores occur, the transfer order is written, and the ICU staff are called and they do the transfer assessment. Based on the judgment of the ICU staff, the transfer either happens or the physicians are reassured that transfer is unnecessary. While this system works reasonably well in most cases, physicians may find that they must occasionally write PEWS exception orders to keep the patients on the floor despite these low scores. Why does this happen? Many other variables are not considered in the system; assessment is based on population-based metrics, and not on all characteristics of the individual case. Physicians must compensate for this weakness in the PEWS system by over-riding it. Predictive analytics can be used to create models that can learn from experience, and apply all the appropriate patient characteristics to make a more accurate assessment.

ICUs have electronic systems to collect high-frequency measurements and closely monitor critically ill patients. In most instances, these measurements are stored in large databases, combined with information provided by other EHR systems. This situation is a prime opportunity for the design of predictive analytics projects, which compare the results from such systems to existing patient scoring systems and prognostic models. Early work on artificial intelligence in the ICU had focused on knowledge-driven techniques, as described in CDSSs above. More recently there has been research on data-driven methods, or experience-based artificial intelligence models. There is ample opportunity right now to implement predictive analytics systems in the ICU. It is the prime time to take advantage of the vast data stores that are available in today's ICUs, and start accounting for other characteristics of the patient that are not assessed in standard scoring methods.

Current predictions are derived from the analysis of raw signals from various monitors in the ICU. One of the key problems in these systems is the significant amount of noise in the monitors. The signals from these monitors can be affected by patient transport, patient movement, bad wiring, poor connections, and device failures, to name a few. Noise must be filtered out of signals before accurate predictions can be made. Many devices have signals that can be used in correlation with measurements to determine if the measurements are correct, such as the waveform on a pulse oximetry monitor. Some algorithms can filter out much of the noise, and thus clarify any valid signal (or the lack of it). Several of the challenges in making predictions in the ICU involve determining the points in time at which to make the measurements, and selection of the granularity or resolution of data on which to make predictions, considering the fact that different monitors capture information at different time resolutions. Physicians must also take into account interventions (e.g., medications given), and the status of the patient (such as bradycardia during sleep, and the rise in blood pressure when a child is screaming).

The major challenge for current medical devices in the ICU is their relative lack of accuracy and portability. Medical devices are evolving along with informatics technology, and more accurate devices will be developed. These devices will become smaller, less sensitive to movement, and less prone to errors, allowing the patient to have more mobility. This mobility will permit more frequent measurements, even permitting some patients to move away from the ICU for a period of time. As these devices evolve, predictive analytics can be progressively incorporated into them, allowing us to sense signals that may alert us to an impending crisis requiring intervention before it's too late. The majority of predictive modeling technology in use currently in ICUs is based on analytical techniques developed for classification and regression (numerical estimation), which consider measurements of variables in a time sequence as independent variables. Information can be extracted from these variables to permit modeling of a target outcome, based on changes in these variables over time. Classical time-series analysis considers only the signal present in the outcome, not the predictive signals present in the time sequence variables. (See Nisbet *et al.*, 2009, for a discussion of this subject.) These time sequence analyses have been very successful in medical informatics (e.g., for the prediction of the next diabetic episode).

Apart from accuracy and portability, another of the challenges of implementing systems in the ICU is that you are dealing literally with life and death situations, in which the stakes are high and there is little room for error. Models must have a high level of accuracy and high discriminative performance to be acceptable for use in this setting. Such models should be used not as a "crutch" to replace judgment, but as an additional aid to support it. When these models are validated against actual improvements in patient care, and reduction in mortality, they may replace older methods — but not until then. Because of the challenges in this new field of technology in the ICU, there are few such systems that have been deployed there. Although many proof-of-concept studies have been carried out, few systems have been validated. This is an area that is ripe for the use of predictive analytics to affect patient care directly and significantly.

PUBLIC HEALTH INFORMATICS

Public Health Informatics is defined as:

> *the application of informatics in areas of public health, including surveillance, reporting, and health promotion.*
> (www.amia.org/applications-informatics/public-health-informatics)

In this discipline, the focus is shifted from individuals to groups of people, and may include many other fields that can have an effect on the health of a population. Some examples of this broad list of fields include:

- *Weather* — cold and rainy weather may cause many people to stay in enclosed spaces during periods of cold or rain. This behavior may contribute to viral outbreaks in winter months.
- *Safety features* — the design of cars, buildings, and toys may affect the general public health of the nation.
- *Architecture and layout of streets* — the way in which people are forced to move in towns and cities may contribute to accidents, congestion, which affects depression, and the general state of human wellness in the vicinity.
- *Food cost and growing methods* — in large respect, we are what we eat, and the type and amounts of foods that people eat can affect public health in large geographical areas. The price of food can drive people to eat food that is not nutritious and may contribute to obesity
- *Food and sanitation standards* — local outbreaks of disease reduce the general state of public health.
- *Social programs* — Great pubic interest has been generated about the health effects of obesity, diabetes, and sexually transmitted diseases.

All of these areas of public health provide rich sources of data for use in predictive analytics, which can provide valuable insights to programs aimed at increasing the general state of wellness in our society. Even the mining of social networks can provide data for the use of predictive analytics to compare public health problems and status of different geographical areas.

Public health departments tend always to be strapped for cash, so it is important to predict areas with the biggest problems and prioritize the allocation of resources to those areas with the largest potential impacts. Insurance companies have begun to share their predictive analytics with healthcare providers so they can apply appropriate interventions to cut their costs. It may be possible to build to build similar relationships between insurance companies and departments of public health in areas where large numbers of insured individuals are concentrated.

Mining of social media is a growing phenomenon in our society. The data available from Twitter, Facebook, and LinkedIn provide a vast source of information about subjects that people love to share with others, particularly health-related issues. People are becoming increasingly connected through social media; it is hard to find someone who doesn't have a mobile device that can upload their photos, thoughts, and whereabouts into the social data cloud. This huge source of data could be tapped with predictive analytics to take the "pulse" of the general status of public health in society, and suggest where it is headed. Patterns of medically related complaints can be mined at various times to provide insights about changes in patterns of disease outbreak, obesity, mental health problems, and educational needs. Social media can provide information about the health-related interventions that are working, or indicators that show an increase in wellness.

This pulse of society can be related to geographical area by using GPS coordinates, and applied for prioritizing areas of high violence. Some police departments (e.g., in Memphis and Chicago) do this now to optimize the allocation of squad car and surveillance resources. These measures can be extended with predictive analytics to expose factors that encourage a high incidence of crime in an area. Analyses like these can be orchestrated to "diagnose" a development of conditions that might promote social unrest, depression, or other psychological conditions, and can help to design intervention measures to promote public health.

In recent years, an emphasis on disease prevention has arisen to complement a prior focus on diagnosis and treatment. It is difficult (if not impossible) for a physician to discuss every preventative strategy for any disease that may befall patients, during the short time allotted to a typical office visit. Through the use of predictive analytics we can analyze large populations of people to quantify risks related to public health, and help physicians to develop intervention programs for those patients at highest risk of some ailment or medical condition.

Large companies have very significant financial incentives to prevent injuries. Some companies monitor the incidence of workplace injuries and collect other data related to safety, and provide reports and real-time alerts to permit timely intervention to prevent injury. Some large companies have used predictive analytics to reduce injury incidence rates by more than 60%, which in turn has led to increased productivity and decreased workers' compensation fees (Schultz, 2012). A research group from Carnegie Mellon University (CMU) was able to build models that can predict the number of injuries at a worksite with 80−97% accuracy rates (Schultz, 2012).

Biosurveillance is a huge area in public health primarily stemming from national security interests and the threat of biological weapons. Several syndromic surveillance systems have been installed to detect outbreaks at local and national levels (Kaydos-Daniels *et al.*, 2013). Purchases of medication at large retailers are measured to assess signals of sickness. These same techniques can be used to aid in hospital management and implementing public health measures when a disease outbreak is predicated, which increases public awareness and hinders the spread of disease. This is one of the more mature areas of predictive analytics, although there is still a significant amount of work to be done.

Food-borne illness has been reported in the news media several times in the past few years, and recently a meningitis outbreak caused by a contaminated injectable steroid medication has shown that even drugs can carry illness. Predictive analytics can and will play an important role in predicting where the outbreak is likely to spread, and how it can be contained.

These are just a few of the applications of predictive analytics in public health. However, public health problems also generally involve large populations with lots of data, and are ideally suited to predictive analytics. This is an exciting field with endless possibilities of creating tools that will have a large impact.

MEDICAL IMAGING

Image mining is a relatively new, but growing area of predictive analytics. Images can be 2D, 3D, static, or moving (4D). Tools using these technologies are available for:

- Screening people for retinal macular degeneration
- Predicting cardiovascular events by using ultrasound flow imaging to measure pressures, velocities, and turbulence of flow related to the likelihood of future events

- Finding various problems on images consisting of billions of pixels, representing enormous amounts of special data
- CT lymph node analysis to support staging for cancer screening.

Soon we will be able to use complex image analysis predictive models, replacing more invasive means such as biopsies or removal of lymph nodes for tissues for staging cancer studies. We will be able to design surgeries and cater treatments without any invasive procedures.

Face recognition and other biometrics (e.g., eye scanning) are well-established as components in security systems. One of the most mature technologies using image analysis is recognition of specific information in images. Similar tools are being used for cell recognition and identifying nuclei and other organelles and their features to classify tissue samples. These morphological features are often indicative of what is happening to the organism as a whole. Information from these types of image analyses can be combined with physiological information to provide rich new variable combinations to use in building predictive models.

CLINICAL RESEARCH INFORMATICS

According to the AMIA:

Clinical Research Informatics involves the use of informatics in the discovery and management of new knowledge relating to health and disease. It includes management of information related to clinical trials and also involves informatics related to secondary research use of clinical data. Clinical research informatics and translational bioinformatics are the primary domains related to informatics activities to support translational research.

(www.amia.org/applications-informatics/clinical-research-informatics).

Clinical trials for new medications are expensive, often running into hundreds of millions of dollars. At the beginning of a trial, you should know how many patients you will be able to get, and how many are likely to drop out. Insufficient recruits can stall the start of a trial, causing severe delays and increasing costs, and drop-outs can affect reliability of results. Yet thousands of trials have been done, and there is an immense amount of information about these trials that is available for use. We can mine these data to increase the likelihood of better outcomes before we start such trials. Knowing what happened in the past in similar trials, we can optimize the study design before any money is invested, or cancel the trial if the preliminary results appear similar to those obtained previously.

INTELLIGENT SEARCH ENGINES

Researching a topic in PubMed (or any other online medical literature source) can be quite time consuming and difficult. Intelligent searching tools can use predictive analytics to present query results of keyword searches based on the context of the search string. One approach to doing this, semantic mapping, can be incorporated into search engines to present various strands of meaning for keywords, and permit researchers to search for what they mean, rather than just what they have entered literally into the search string. These alternate search paths can give researchers more pertinent and even rather obscure results that are important but would have been missed otherwise.

When people want to learn about a medical condition or a treatment, they rely on large search engines such as Google to find answers to their questions. Even though Google has improved over time, there still may be a significant amount of misinformation presented on the website, even on the first page of results. Researching a topic takes time and effort, even with comprehensive web sites like PubMed. This is particularly true for the average consumer who does not necessarily understand the terminology or context in the articles they find.

Information can be dangerous. It can lead people to spend excessive amounts of money on unproven treatments, and to neglect getting appropriate medical care, which sometimes leads to death. We could use predictive analytics to analyze Internet search phrases in the context of demographics, location, and search history to provide more "intelligent" search results, and report the level of understanding of the result topic by the medical community. Google is already doing some of this, but there are still significant dangers in following a Google search of information related to disease treatment. For example, criminals can take advantage of people with incurable diseases by offering the only "cures" available.

PERSONALIZED MEDICINE

Personalized medicine is a field that has huge potential for the use of prediction and association analyses. Specific treatments can be catered, based on past experience with other patients. Using exome or full genome analysis, it will soon be possible to predict how patients will respond to various drug and therapies. Personalized medicine systems can include information from image analysis, lab data, demographics, history of adherence to treatment, financial status, physiological signals, and other data sources to cater the best treatment to the patient based on predicted probabilities. This topic will be further discussed in Chapter 13.

HOSPITAL OPTIMIZATION

Hospital staffing, particularly nurse staffing, is a major issue in many hospitals today. A shortage of nurses can have a very detrimental effect on patient outcomes, while having too many nurses on shift adds unnecessary healthcare expense, which translates directly to higher patient costs. By predicting hospital census, the scheduling of nurses with predictive analytics technology can function to increase scheduling efficiency in during times of high need, while eliminating unnecessary shifts. Intelligent scheduling can also be applied to optimize availability, utilization, and storage of resources. Certain supplies or medications related to outbreaks must be available when an outbreak hits, but many of these supplies have relatively short shelf lives, which can be managed by just-in-time replenishment systems. On the other hand, having too great a quantity of supplies with short self lives can unnecessarily increase the operating expenses necessary to maintain them. Many staffing tools are available that use predictive analytics in the general business world; however, in medicine the stakes are higher and the processes and relationships to staffing are very complex. This is an area that is ripe for analytics, and there are many technologies common in the business world that can be applied to the world of health care.

As described in the public health section above, many businesses are looking at safety measures that can be recorded in order to predict accidents, and businesses have been successful in using these measures to predict and thereby prevent accidents from happening in the work place. In the hospital, accidents, mistakes, or changes in processes can have an even more dramatic impact, particularly in such high-stakes areas as ICUs. Incidence of morbidity and mortality can be greatly reduced by modeling outcomes with various hospital measures, and comparing them with actual outcomes, while increasing patient satisfaction at the same time. This is a very broad and important area where predictive analytics can be applied to significantly improve the quality and success of health care.

CHALLENGES

The extent of the space and the cost necessary to store biomedical data have been significant issues in the past, but these issues are becoming increasingly pressing and important now, as very large amounts of data are generated by existing medical systems. The prospect of storing all of the information in the entire genome of an individual is daunting enough (3 gigabytes in the Human Genome Project), but when related epigenetic effects (changes in gene expression without changes in the DNA nucleotide sequence) and temporal effects related to each gene are considered, the storage volume required for each person becomes truly gigantic (possibly, several terabytes). When you consider the data storage requirements for all of the people in a hospital census, which turns over many times during a given year, the storage volume may increase into petabytes. And that is just for one hospital for one year! We are on the brink of a monumental explosion in data volume in medicine and health care. The creation of advanced compression methods and algorithms to store and retrieve such information efficiently becomes paramount.

Privacy and security are also major concerns in the storage and use of any data about individuals. Since the passage of the American Health Insurance Portability and Accountability Act (HIPAA) in 2003, health providers must make sure that all medical records and related information (e.g., billing records) conform to a set of standards of documentation, handling, and privacy. But these standards are rather broad, and each state can choose the way that information is protected and made available to individuals. The problem is that there is a wide latitude among the states in regulation of patient health information. For example, Meingast and colleagues (2006) reported that Alabama had no general statute restricting the disclosure of patient information, while California has extensive regulations of such disclosures. This wide variability in disclosure regulations among the states provides a high probability of leakage and misuse of patient healthcare information during transmission across state lines. This problem is exponentially worsening as patient information becomes available in electronic format. It appears that we are still in the "Wild West" of information regulation in medicine and health care.

Meingast *et al.* (2006) pose some questions that remain today, even in the wake of the Patient Protections and Affordable Care Act of 2010:

- Who owns the data?
- How much data should be stored?

- Where should data be stored?
- To whom should these data be disclosed?
- Where should the data be stored, who owns the data, to whom should this data be disclosed without the patient's consent? (Unanswered questions abound regarding this area.)
- How should the data be secured?

The authors suggest some solutions to these problems, which are still relevant today:

- Define clear specifications for role-based access to healthcare data, in which different rules apply to people in different usage roles
- Define new HIPAA regulations to standardize how healthcare data can be used and transmitted between states
- Instigate rules to govern patient privacy in home monitoring programs
- Initiate policies and rules defining how data can be acquired for predictive analytical purposes, and who can have this access.

Other sources of health-related data can be sourced from the Internet, which raises the question of whether or not it is ethical to use this information without an individual's permission. In one case, a medical student happened to look at the Facebook page of a certain patient, and determined that the patient might be in a high-risk situation at home. This information led to an intervention, which could have saved the patient's life. Regardless of the happy ending, this example left lingering doubts about the propriety of such actions.

There is a considerable lack of consistency in terminology and measurements between medical practices and labs, and even within the same hospital. It is very hard to analyze data compiled from these sources, and we are still quite far from a universal standard in terminology and measurement. To make things more difficult, many of the measures in medicine are extremely subjective; you could easily get four different answers from four different physicians if you asked them to characterize a murmur, for example. You also have to take into consideration the temporal aspect of a measurement and the context in which it happened, which are not always recorded. We must anticipate significant challenges in these areas at the beginning of any predictive analytical project.

There is some suggestion that predictive analytics tools used in patient care, specifically CDSSs, should be regulated similarly to medical devices, requiring stringent acceptance, commissioning, and quality assurance. The CDSS would have to be validated on local datasets before approval. This can be problematic for rapid learning CDSSs, because they change constantly as information is gathered from patients. Methods to regulate and thereby ensure patient safety without losing the advantage of rapid learning will need to be addressed. Interestingly, emerging from the ACA Act is PCOR (Patient Centered Outcomes Research), a non-profit "contract-research" agency that is committed to developing transparent networks of medical data among healthcare organizations, including hospitals, clinics, and individual doctors. One goal of this is to produce CER (comparative effectiveness research) to "really" determine which treatments and drugs and medical devices are working for both "groups of patients" (grouped by age, race, sex, and other grouping factors, including genetic predisposition) and "individual patients" (primarily determined by DNA profiles plus other attributes). To do this will require that HIPAA laws and other regulatory processes, whether FDA or elsewhere, are worked through so that they will not be inhibitory to the development of accurate diagnostic and treatment methods. Only predictive analytics (PA) modeling can produce the accuracy that is needed for these efforts (traditional statistical P-value Fisherian statistics, for the most part, only work for "groups" or "means" of population groups; modern PA can pinpoint both groups and, more importantly, individuals). Predictive analytic modeling and decisioning is the only method that is currently available to make accurate predictions and prescriptions for individuals. Unfortunately, very little of this is being done; it is currently estimated by some that 99% of statisticians are still using traditional statistics and have not yet been able to grasp the value of data mining, text mining, and predictive analytic modeling.

SUMMARY

This is a very exciting time for predictive analytics in biomedical informatics. It is at the forefront of medical research, as we transition from reacting to disease to proactively preventing it. Predictive analytics is in its infancy in this field, and though many studies show predictions using small single-source data sets, there are few that are based on large amounts of clinical data available from many sources, such as images, lab values, physiological signals, genetics, and other patient demographics and characteristics. There are even fewer predictive analytics projects that have been incorporated into clinical practice. This situation provides abundant opportunities in almost every area of informatics for predictive analytics, and there is ample opportunity to use these tools to make a lasting difference in health care.

POSTSCRIPT

One of the challenges of medical informatics is the provision of means of effective communication of healthcare information to various organizations in forms that can be used. A collateral aspect of this communication is the coordination of its such use among organizations for various purposes. The primary organization that facilitates this communication and coordination of healthcare information is the Healthcare Information Management Systems Society (HIMSS). Chapter 4 will focus on this organization, together with other organizations similar to it.

REFERENCES

Bellcross, C.A., 2012. A Part-Time Life, as Hours Shrink and Shift. The New York Times.

Darnovsky, M., Cussins, J., 2014. FDA halts 23andMe personal genetic tests. What might this mean for the future of direct-to-consumer testing? MLO Med. Lab. Obs. 46 (3), 33.

Hui, C., Neto, G., Tsertsvadze, A., Yazdi, F., Tricco, A.C, Tsouros, S., et al., 2012. Diagnosis and Management of Febrile Infants (0−3 Months). Agency for Healthcare Research and Quality, Rockville, MD (Evidence Report/Technology Assessments, No. 205.) Introduction.

Kaydos-Daniels, S.C.I., Rojas Smith, L., Farris, T.R., 2013. Biosurveillance in outbreak investigations. Biosecur. Bioterror. 11 (1), 20−28.

Meingast, M., Roosta, T., Sastr, S., 2006. Security and Privacy Issues with Health Care Information Technology. Proceedings of the 28th IEEE EMBS Annual International Conference, New York, NY.

Nisbet, R., Elder, J.I.V., Miner., G.D., 2009. Handbook of Statistical Analysis and Data Mining Applications. Elsevier/Academic Press, New York, NY.

Schultz, G., 2012. Using Advanced Analytics to Predict and Prevent Workplace Injuries. Occup. Health Saf. 81 (7), 88, 90−91. Available at: http://ohsonline.com/Articles/2012/07/01/Using-Advanced-Analytics-to-Predict-and-Prevent-Workplace-Injuries.aspx.

FURTHER READING

Bellcross, C.A., Page, P.Z., Meaney-Delman, D., 2012. Direct-to-consumer personal genome testing and cancer risk prediction. Cancer J. 18 (4), 293−302.

Cai, H., Cui, C., Tian, H., Zhang, M., Li, L., 2012. A novel approach to segment and classify regional lymph nodes on computed tomography images. Comput. Math. Methods Med. 2012, 145926.

Cheng, S.K., Dietrich, M.S., Dilts, D.M., 2011. Predicting accrual achievement: monitoring accrual milestones of NCI-CTEP-sponsored clinical trials. Clin. Cancer Res. 17 (7), 1947−1955.

Güiza, F., Van Eyck, J., Meyfroidt, G., 2012. Predictive data mining on monitoring data from the intensive care unit. J. Clin. Monit. Comput. 27 (4), 449−453.

Isariyawongse, B.K., Kattan, M.W., 2012. Prediction tools in surgical oncology. Surg Oncol Clin. N. Am. 21 (3), 439−447, viii−ix.

Kamel Boulos, M.N., Sanfilippo, A.P., Corley, C.D., Wheeler, S., 2010. Social Web mining and exploitation for serious applications: Technosocial Predictive Analytics and related technologies for public health, environmental and national security surveillance. Comput. Methods Programs Biomed. 100 (1), 16−23.

Lambin, P., van Stiphout, R.G., Starmans, M.H., Rios-Velazquez, E., Nalbantov, G., Aerts, H.J., et al., 2013. Predicting outcomes in radiation oncology-multifactorial decision support systems. Nat. Rev. Clin. Oncol. 10 (1), 27−40.

Osheroff, J.A., Teich, J.M., Levic, D., Saldana, L., Velasco, F.T., Sittig, D.F., et al., 2012. Improving Outcomes with Clinical Decision Support: An Implementer's Guide. second ed. Scottsdale Institute, AMIA, AMDIS and SHM, Chicago, IL.

Phan, J.H., Quo, C.F., Cheng, C., Wang, M.D., 2012. Multiscale integration of -omic, imaging, and clinical data in biomedical informatics. IEEE Rev. Biomed. Eng. 5, 74−87.

Santelices, L., Wang, Y., Severyn, D., Druzdzel, M., Kormos, R., Antaki, J., 2010. Developing a hybrid decision support model for optimal ventricular assist device weaning. Ann. Thorac. Surg. 90 (3), 713−720.

Zheng, Y., Hijazi, M.H., Coenen, F., 2012. Automated "disease/no disease" grading of age-related macular degeneration by an image mining approach. Invest. Ophthalmol. Vis. Sci.pii: iovs.12-9576v1.

Chapter 4

HIMSS and Organizations That Develop HIT Standards

Chapter Outline

PREAMBLE

Communication and cooperation among healthcare organizations are not sufficient alone to assure that quality healthcare information can be made available and used effectively for diagnosis and treatment of medical conditions. This information must be of a consistent high quality and be commensurable (using a common system of measurement) across all subject areas. The same need was recognized in industrial and manufacturing organizations early in the 20th century, which gave rise to the American National Standards Institute (ANSI). Rather than set up a separate standards organization for healthcare information, HIMSS developed a strategic partnership with ANSI to control the quality and commensurability of healthcare data. This chapter describes the development and the nature of that strategic partnership.

INTRODUCTION

It seems obvious that health care could be improved if all the healthcare entities coordinated and communicated better; communication would improve if health information technologies (HIT) were standardized around best practices. There are organizations dedicated to improved communication and improved healthcare technology, including the Healthcare Information and Management Systems Society (HMISS), the American National Standards Institute (ANSI), and the Office of the National Coordinator for Health Information (ONC). Whereas the ANSI and ONC are standards organizations, the HIMSS not-for-profit organization is broader and concentrates on "optimal use" of IT. HIMSS has over 50,000 international members, who for the most part work in healthcare fields. HIMSS enjoys the membership of

Practical Predictive Analytics and Decisioning Systems for Medicine. DOI: http://dx.doi.org/10.1016/B978-0-12-411643-6.00004-1

not-for-profit organizations and corporate members, totaling over 770 organizations (HIMSS, 2013). HIMSS identified the four pillars for IT:

1. Improved quality
2. Improved safety
3. Increased cost-effectiveness
4. Increased access to care.

Introduction to the Strategic Partners

We must go back to 1916 to properly review the history of standardizing groups. In 1916, engineers started the United Engineering Foundation (UEF), which in the next 2 years morphed into ANSI (the American National Standards Institute). HIMSS originated in 1961 as the Hospitals Management Systems Society (HMSS), and then later that year became the Healthcare Information and Managements Systems Society (HIMSS). Since its founding, HIMSS has functioned as a strategic partner with ANSI. HIMSS functions solely as a volunteer organization, while the ANSI standards group includes members from public (governmental) organizations along with volunteers. The goals of HIMSS revolve around the improvement of healthcare through the use of information technology (HIMSS, 2013). ANSI's purpose is to enhance the global competitiveness of United States' business. ANSI increases competitiveness through the use of "voluntary consensus standards and conformity of assessment systems" (ANSI, 2013, p. 1). ANSI espouses among its goals optimizing marketability while maintaining public safety. These goals include concepts of "openness, balance, due process, and consensus" (ANSI, 2010, 2012). ANSI (2012) provides a concise historical video.

After the Second World War ended, industries shifted quickly back to private production. However, the rise of new technology initiated by the war effort brought new challenges to industries in the Western world, the greatest of which was the need for consistent safety, reliability, and quality among new products. In 1946, delegates from 25 countries met in London to facilitate the development of an international standards organization, which spawned the International Organization for Standardization (ISO) in 1947. ISO develops general standards for industrial production, such as the ISO 9000 series of industrial protocols. Following this lead, many Standards Developing Organizations (SDOs) were formed to develop standards for specific industries. ISO serves as the repository for the SDO manufacturing standards for each industry. The SDOs are viewed as ISO subsidiary groups focused on increasing product quality and safety in their respective industries. As product quality and safety increased, so did the potential for growth in quality of life for those who owned the products and services. Companies that used these standards also saw increased profits. People liked purchasing goods and services that worked well and that lasted a long time. The use of standards increased brand loyalty.

Similarly to consumers of industrial products, consumers of medical services want an improved quality of life also, and they expect their healthcare practitioners to provide quality health care. HIMSS functions as the primary SDO for health care, providing standards for health care and other services to increase quality and lower costs of healthcare provision.

While participation in these standards groups is voluntary, the standards produced were not. As ANSI (2010) deftly pointed out, compliance is obligatory once these standards become established. If the federal government decided that a group of standards was necessary, or if accrediting bodies deemed it so, then the standards were not to be voluntarily implemented. The term "voluntary" meant that participation in the organization is not mandatory, and that the original suggestions for standards were volunteered by those most closely associated with the standards. These volunteers could be interested organizations, members, professionals in the field, and members of professional organizations who provide the quality measures. The volunteers believed that standards were designed optimally by those who had special training, expertise, and experience in the field to which the standards pertained. For example, engineering standards are developed primarily by engineers and engineering groups, and accounting standards are developed primarily by accountants. Therefore, while the specific standards are developed by industry-specific standards organizations, compliance with them is administered by a combination of those organizations and government entities.

Many standards groups have been formed in the healthcare industry. Various groups tend to influence one another, and each is composed of subgroups, each designated by a string of acronyms; together, they present more acronyms than the average person would like to hear. Several groups stand out from the rest as having a great influence on data operations used by their information technology. One such organization is the public organization that emerged from the United States Department of Health & Human Services – the Office of the National Coordinator for Health Information (ONC). The National Coordinator was established by President George W. Bush in 2004, aimed at providing interoperability in EHR (electronic health records) within 10 years. President Bush wanted the electronic systems to talk to one another. That 10-year interval would have ended in 2014. There were to be exchanges, portals, planning, standards, certifications, sharing, health information products such as electronic prescriptions, and a public—private partnership. ONC was to provide guidance for the nationwide implementation of health information technology. Both President Bush's and President Obama's initiatives intend to propel health care forward by the use of technology:

> *Health information technology (IT) has come to occupy a unique position in health care policy: both President George W. Bush and President Barack Obama have articulated bold goals for health IT. Both presidents called for sweeping adoption of electronic health records (EHRs) within a decade — a torrential rate in a glacial industry. Both have framed health IT as a linchpin of health care reform, acknowledging that this will disrupt the status quo and existing interests. Both presidents recognize the need for strong federal participation in health IT. Both presidents have exhibited personal leadership over health IT strategy. There are few other health policy topics that enjoy such similar attention and continuity across otherwise very different presidencies.*

(Brailer, 2013, p. 1).

In 2012, ONC selected ANSI as the Approved Accreditor for health information, to house the permanent certification program. ANSI was selected also as the accreditation body for organizations that sought to set up certification programs for electronic health records technology. In the Permanent Certification Program link, we find the statement in the first paragraph:

> *The ONC Health Information Technology (HIT) Certification Program, formerly known as the Permanent Certification Program (PCP), is the second part of ONC's two-part approach to establish a transparent and objective certification process, following the Temporary Certification Program (TCP).*

RELATIONSHIP BETWEEN ANSI, HIMSS, AND ONC

Within this hierarchy of acronyms among healthcare standards organizations, ANSI is concerned with standards from a variety of fields, including health care. HIMSS is a standards organization within the ISO framework concerned with health care, and it exists in the private sector. ONC is a governmental entity concerned with healthcare interoperability among these organizations at the standards setting and compliance levels. These organizations may compete with one another to some extent, however transparently to the perception of the public, but they refer to one another, and cooperate in their efforts to move the medical community towards consistent standards.

ORGANIZATIONS CONNECTED TO OR INFLUENCED BY HIMSS

Organizations that are supported by, housed within, and/or associated with HIMSS include:

- American Medical Informatics Association (AMIA)
- Electronic Health Record (EHR) Association
- Radiological Society of North America (RSNA)
- Alliance for Nursing Informatics (ANI)
- American Medical Association (AMA)
- IHI (Institute for Healthcare Improvement) Open School.

Many other organizations are either sponsors of or are sponsored by HIMSS, including some hospitals, clinics, nursing groups, international informatics bodies, pharmaceutical groups, and government agencies; many others are involved indirectly with HIMSS. HIMSS is a very influential organization in health care, encouraging quality in all aspects of the healthcare field.

GOALS, ISSUES, AND IDEALS OF HIMSS

The four "pillars" of HIMSS are expressed as broad goals to improve quality, safety, cost-effectiveness, and access to care. Implicit in the goals of HIMSS is the need to address issues that could be considered within ISO, such as quality initiatives, standards, gap analysis, interoperability, integration, use of common terminology, and informatics issues, such as data structure and interchange protocols. The focus of the HIMSS goals is to share information seamlessly and securely among healthcare providers, and to support business policies and promote research studies to increase optimization of healthcare effectiveness and efficacy, and reduction in costs.

The basic driver of the goals and standards initiatives is the idea that good use of information technology increases benefit as much as the bad use of information technology increases the potential for harm. One chief objective of HIMSS is the development of standards by which governmental initiatives may be carried out through technology. The organization helps in the understanding of initiatives such as meaningful use. As each stage is rolled out, HIMSS provides what is needed for compliance, such as the recommendations by HIMSS task forces. An example is the task force for standards published in 2008 (HIMSS, 2012a).

ICD-10

Florence Nightingale was an early proponent of the ideal of a standardized and consistent disease classification for statistical and research purposes. She introduced the polar area diagram to visualize data (Figure 4.1), in which she shows how a simple mortality classification system can be presented visually (Cohen, 1984).

Many classification methodologies and attempts to apply them have been developed and refined over the years by practice and research studies. The resulting body of information has accumulated in the form of vast databases and methodologies in use currently. This information is awkward and difficult to apply by researchers in scientific studies, and for coders trying to obtain reimbursements. Standardization and ease of use of a disease classification system are crucial elements for both types of use, and for anyone attempting to conduct predictive analytics. Analysis of the "wrong thing" can give only wrong results.

To aid in standardization of disease classification, the International Classification of Diseases (ICD) provides a common language for healthcare delivery, worldwide. Practitioners require that diseases be classified properly to provide adequate healthcare services to their patients, and to guide future research properly. The ICD and other medical coding structures developed from the reporting requirements for Public Health disease and cause-of-death reporting in the UK, USA, and EU. The vast store of health information is useless without a consistent, well-defined disease classification system. This classification system is used also by insurance providers as the basis for payment of loss claims.

The tenth edition of the ICD classification system (ICD-10) was initiated in the 1990s, and is the latest version of a series of classification systems extending back even further. ICD-10 comprises three volumes of names, descriptions,

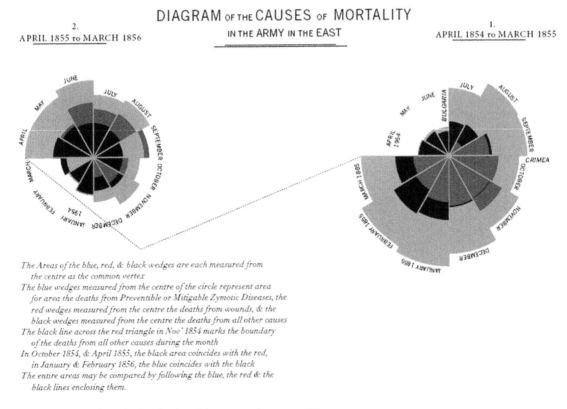

FIGURE 4.1   Florence Nightingale's visualization of the causes of army mortalities.

and codes for diseases. ICD-10 is in use commonly in other countries, but the United States has lagged in its acceptance of it. The reason for the delay is that the US versions have added a breadth of information to the categories. It is important that the United States adopts the new ICD-10 language for medical diagnoses and inpatient procedures, because the new version was mandated by Health and Human Services.

The previous ICD classification version (ICD-9, created in the mid-1970s) comprised about 17,000 codes to express the enormity of the classification problem in health care. ICD-10, however, has over 141,000 codes. The number of codes for inpatients alone swelled from 13,500 to about 69,000. Adoption of the ICD-10 will exert enormous strains on organization training programs. The huge effort to compose this labyrinth of codes into insurance forms to support claims payment may be viewed as a nightmare by healthcare staff. The Task Force for ICD-10 must ease the transition required in training programs and coding system use. These serious issues in training and coding have delayed the transition to ICD-10 by about a year, and it is scheduled to be completed by October 1, 2014 (CMS, 2013). It is likely that continuing challenges in this transition will delay its completion even more.

In view of this monumental task, the ICD-10 Task Force proposed major goals for 2013 (HIMSS, 2012b) and pilot testing of the guidelines to minimize the "guesswork" related to the guidelines (this article is no longer available on the website). While piloting, HIMSS intends to develop scenarios that can be used by healthcare entities trying to implement ICD-10:

1. Acceleration and validation of vendor readiness
2. Standardized testing for determining competency and for inter-rater reliability
3. Education
4. Coding and clinical documentation improvement (CCDI).

HIMSS ATTEMPTS TO HELP

In the face of the serious problem posed by the transition to the new codes, HIMSS came to the rescue by developing code mapping tools for users to move from ICD-9 to ICD-10. HIMSS provides translation mechanisms and programs for clinicians and others to learn how to implement the new coding rules (Figure 4.2).

In order to perform the code translation for reimbursement purposes, HIMSS had to map ICD-10 codes to ICD-9 codes to make them backwards-compatible with the old codes (Kohn, 2013). HIMSS is very interested in computer-assisted coding systems (CAC), which use symbolic and statistically based codes. Conversion tools may be developed by using various business intelligence tools. In large hospitals and hospital chains, responsibilities for code conversion may be assigned to informatics specialists, nurses, and even MDs.

HIMSS has made projections of coding needs in the years of 2013 and 2014, shown in Figure 4.3 (Kohn, 2013).

The need for coders may increase or decrease, depending on the success of transition efforts, and the resultant changes in timeline. As productivity decreases (presumably due to the complexity of the new code system), more coders will be needed. Fewer coders will be needed as the new system is learned.

FIGURE 4.2   An HIMSS training session. *Source: HIMSS (2012b).*

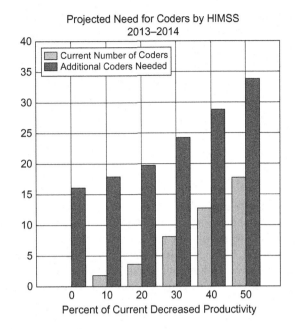

FIGURE 4.3 Projected numbers of coders needed. *Source: Kohn (2013).*

STANDARDIZATION IN CODING

The Certified Coders Association (CCA) is the accreditation body for coders, which provides coding standards for healthcare organizations. The coders are tasked with analyzing medical documents and assigning codes for healthcare providers, according to the CCA standards. The codes must be standardized, to assure that insurance companies can reimburse claims properly, to enable insurance companies to track trends (map equivalencies in outcome reports) across different providers. There are multitudes of claims forms and many abbreviations used; thus, there is an abundant risk of making mistakes. When coders use standardized codes and practices, mistakes will be minimized and proper reimbursements will be maximized. Such standardization is a great benefit in research studies, to facilitate the proper comparison and evaluation of results.

CARE CONTINUUM ALLIANCE (ANOTHER CCA) AND HEALTH OUTCOME DATA

The Care Continuum Alliance started out in 1999 as the Disease Management Association of America (DMAA). One purpose of that CCA is to generate reports on health outcome data. The CCA concentrates on population studies for wellness and the meaningful management of care across programs. As Lewis (2012) pointed out, the recommendations made by the CCA may artificially increase good outcomes, because of CCA methods of counting patients and depending on whether the patients are designated as chronic or non-chronic. Lewis (2012) was also critical of how averages were determined:

> *The fifth-grade arithmetic app on your Smartphone doesn't include a "compromise" feature that automatically averages two completely different solutions to the same problem.*

This complaint referred to the CCA's statement that its guidelines are based on a "consensus model" rather than on sound mathematics. He attributed this problem to the making of rules by the "voluntary nature of the committee." Everyone is able to offer opinions as to how the math is figured, and the "average" is selected. This approach is like trying to average a long jump between two rocks on a raging river with a short jump to the third rock, to predict how far to jump to the fourth rock. Following that approach, you are likely to fall into the river, and be swept away.

Lewis (2012) describes one study in which people with an illness were not counted until a person had a huge expense, followed by recovery. It is easy to see why there could be a reduction in costs the next year that is not related to intervention — but the cost reduction is attributed to the intervention anyway. *When* and *how* people are counted can make a huge difference in how the outcome is interpreted. Reporting agencies seek to show good results, and attribute them to better disease management. Data manipulations like this are orchestrated to further the researcher's advantage, and they not only produce biased results but also bolster the common attitude that statisticians can say anything they want to with data. Standard definitions and reporting practices should lead to more consistent outcomes, and, perhaps, the consensus model should be laid aside.

Links to the CCA (Alliance) are found on the HIMSS website. One such link described the "5 components of population health" that the CCA presented to Congress in Washington DC (CCA, 2012a) at its Population Health Innovations Showcase:

- Population identification
- Assessment
- Stratification
- Engagement/intervention
- Outcomes measurement.

During the past 7 years, the Care Continuum Alliance has focused on identifying best practices, developing definitions, and establishing measure sets and methodologies around each of those five components.

Lewis (2012) maintained that the major premise of the CCA guidelines (consensus) is simply wrong. Rather than relying on consensus, he claimed that the CCA guidelines should be based on sound mathematics. His claim implies that you cannot base healthcare treatment on both consensus and sound science. What if the consensus is in error? On the CCA homepage, under the research tab (CCA, 2012b), consensus is listed in conjunction with sound science to guide healthcare management:

The Outcomes Guidelines Report Volume 5, available as a free downloadable PDF, represents the latest product of a research initiative launched in 2006 to bring consensus, transparency and sound science to measuring clinical and financial outcomes in wellness and care management. It refines earlier work and adds new guidance on more broadly defined population health management programs.

(CCA, 2012b, p. 1).

HIMSS WEBSITE

The HIMSS website is resplendent with resources and materials. HIMSS publishes books, prepares newsletters for members, offers subgroup memberships, reports governmental news, publishes papers, and serves as a repository for a vast amount of data concerning health outcomes. One interesting example concerned St. John Medical Center, a hospital in Tulsa (Dindigal, 2012). The use of health business intelligence (HBI) purportedly resulted in St. John's reducing the number of transfusions associated with negative reactions by 18%, and reducing the total number of transfusions to an even greater extent (22%). The effect of these reductions was to reduce costs by $1.4 million annually, and to lessen the incidence of errors. There was no explanation of the results, however, that could show how the patients were entered or withdrawn from the analysis. This is an example of how important the experimental design is for avoiding methodology pitfalls in data analysis. According to Lewis (2012), the most common form of the "before and after fallacy" is committed when investigators use the same population before and after an intervention in medicine that includes a certain proportion of people who get better regardless of the intervention. Therefore Lewis observes that patients with a characteristic that is rather extreme on the first measurement tend to be closer to the mean of that characteristic on the second measurement. And, counterintuitively, if a characteristic is extreme on the second measurement, it will have been relatively close to the mean on the first measurement. Finally, people who are of low cost originally would not have made it into the study group at all. We must be particularly aware of this phenomenon of "regression to the mean" when designing scientific experiments and interpreting data.

Dindigal (2012) described some communication problems in hospitals related to the lack of interoperability of systems based on "makeshift databases." Problems of this sort are likely to continue for some time, even in face of the government mandate that systems must "talk" to one another. It is not clear whether or not Dindigal committed any before-and-after errors described by Lewis (2012), but he did mention many of the difficulties associated with obtaining and analyzing good data, implying that his data were handled appropriately.

Much data is available on the Internet today, and particularly enticing is the availability of data stored in data "clouds." These data are stored on clusters of computer servers located in diverse places in the world. The ease of access and the uncontrolled nature of many of these clouds presents issues related to data security and "shuffling" similar to those in the airline industry. Management of cloud data is similar in principle to that of an airline which overbooks flights because it has been determined that a certain percentage of flyers opt out at the last moment. If they overbook, then they can shuffle the customers to empty seats, which satisfies customers and ensures that the planes are full to maximize profitability. Sometimes, however, everyone shows up, and the airline must resolve the booking problem by trying to entice flyers to choose another flight, packaged with the offer of free tickets and, occasionally, overnight accommodations. These issues happen also in scheduling server use in data clouds. The problem for data processing is that moving (shuffling) of data to other servers creates data security issues that do not occur in the airline industry. Cloud servers have varying degrees of security, and sensitive personal health data could fall into the wrong hands. HIMSS is starting to collect data and make it available to investigators for research. Other agencies will be following suit, if they are not already doing so. As large amounts of healthcare data move to the data clouds, access and security could be compromised significantly. These potential problems associated with data access and security must be solved before healthcare data can become available to qualified investigators to fulfill the promise of the Affordable Care Act.

HIMSS ANALYTICS

HIMSS Analytics is a non-profit international subsidiary organization of HIMSS. The database used originated in 2004, when it absorbed the Dorenfest IHDS + Database® (HIMSS Analytics, 2013). The mission of the group is to provide quality data for decision-makers to make good predictions with healthcare information. They provide high quality consulting and solutions for marketing, strategic planning, and healthcare information technology system design. The group is run by a board of directors, and it provides domestic and international services to public and private hospitals and healthcare providers. Sample data sets are available from the HIMSS Analytics website. One example screen found on the HIMSS Analytics website is shown in Figure 4.4. The site is constantly changing, so other resources will be seen in the future.

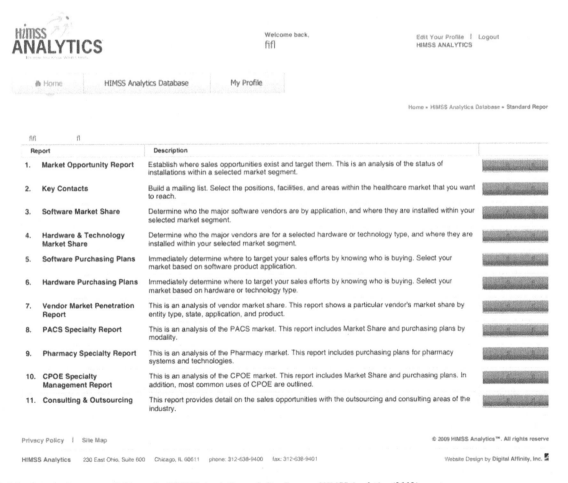

FIGURE 4.4 Sample data set available on the HIMSS Analytics website. *Source: HIMSS Analytics (2012).*

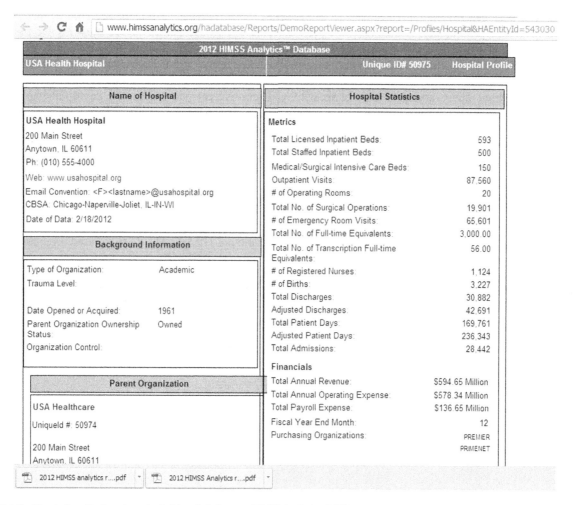

FIGURE 4.5 Hospital profile for a hypothetical hospital. *Source: HIMSS Analytics (2012).*

Clicking on another tab on the website led to a different example, shown in Figure 4.5.
The HIMSS Analytics® Database contains:

- Data from more than 5,300 hospitals
- Healthcare provider software, hardware, and infrastructure portfolios
- Market share data for over 130 software applications and technologies
- Contact information for 190,000 + IT and "C-Suite" decision-makers within acute, subacute, ambulatory, and home-health organizations
- Market segmentation and sizing statistics to evaluate opportunities across the USA
- Healthcare provider software and hardware purchasing plan information
- Identification of hospitals with major capital building projects
- A geo-mapping feature to provide an optional graphical representation of standard report data.

Note that these data sets are owned by HIMSS, and they are *not* likely to be available to investigators outside HIMSS Analytics. HIMSS Analytics staff can use these data sets to support their own PA studies (Chris Papesh, personal communication, March 30, 2013). According to Papesh, the HIMSS Analytics Database contains only high-level comparative hospital data and details about what types of systems are in use at various hospitals. This information is useful to health IT vendors and consulting firms or hospitals considering buying new clinical or business software. It does not appear that these data include patient information useful for predictive analysis of individualized healthcare information.

PROGRESS OF HIMSS

HIMSS has made significant progress in achieving better communication and coordination in the 50 years that the organization has been in existence, but there continue to be significant challenges for improvement in service quality and interoperability. Because HIMSS is a self-established advisory organization, similar groups might listen to HIMSS to gain ideas and insights, but there are no "teeth" in the suggestions made by HIMSS.

Compliance

It is certainly true that HIMSS is committed to moving health care in the direction of higher quality services; however, there remains much room for improvement of compliance with existing guidelines. Goldhill (2013) stated that over 100,000 Americans die of hospital acquired (nosocomial) infections per year, including his father. He cited that these preventable deaths were more than five times the number of people who were murdered each year by all other means. We spend much time and energy talking about gun control in our society today, but the failure to wash hands between patients is just as lethal (in total effect) as any automatic weapon. Infection death is not heralded very much in the daily news.

Technological interoperability is a worthy goal, but predictive analytics may generate solutions that lead us to problems associated with simple safety compliance, rather than information technology compliance. A big part of our response to these problems can include personal response patterns that contribute to health, and avoidance of facilities where these behaviors are not part of the culture of caring. In essence, these personal response patterns might help to define the concept of meaningful use at the individual level. In this way, the practice of predictive analytics for individuals within the context of personal meaningful use might become the true key to healthcare services improvement, rather than solving interoperability issues. In support of this notion, Goldhill (2013) pointed out that most of the increases in longevity in the USA have come about because people are not dying from heart disease as they did in the past. The reduction in deaths from heart disease has not come from increases in healthcare efficacy as much as from cessation of smoking, increases in exercise, and changes in diet quality. The last problem to overcome is the excess quantity of food consumed. If people in our society were moved to eat less, we would be in much better shape, individually and socially.

During the past 50 years, we have become very proficient in developing the technologies that *should* unite us; instead, we find just the opposite has occurred in many cases. Instead of progressing in a linear, organized, regulated fashion, entrepreneurs jump in wherever their expertise resides. As Papesh (personal communication, March 30, 2013) noted:

> Given the push in the USA to be extremely "free market" in healthcare, we have many vendors racing for the dollars, often with poor quality and uncoordinated Health IT solutions that do not exchange information well.

The lack of coordination has not been caused by a lack of effort on the part of organizations such as HIMSS. Indeed, politics, world events, and economic anomalies have intervened, as well as the competition for market share among electronic medical record (EMR) companies (HIMSS, 2012c). The result has been a lack of interoperability among competing groups in the midst of greater computing power. Various groups in varying specializations vie for certifications, and each specialty needs its own standards. A principal goal of interoperability has eluded HIMSS, as of the date of this book. HIMSS has tried to assist organizations to comply with the government initiatives, and has tried to establish standards among likely thousands of divergent entities. But progress has not been easy.

Interoperability

Interoperability has been a goal of HIMSS for a long time, but the achievement of it is very elusive. The term implies both information transmission and information reception in a form that can be used. While there is a difference between interoperability and health information exchange (HIE), the two concepts are often used synonymously (Fridsma, 2013). The difference between these two concepts is analogous to the difference between writing a message in one language and sending that message to someone who speaks a different language. The message may have been exchanged, but the person to whom the message is given will not be able to use the information. HIE can be achieved fairly easily by emailing the information to another organization; however, interoperability implies exchange *and* use of the information. After some form of HIE occurs, it is necessary to translate the message (or interpret the meaning of the data) after exchange, in order for the information to be used.

Many difficulties complicate the achievement of interoperability. Historically, the federal government merely suggested that interoperability be a goal, and gave incentives for development of standards. As noted earlier, George W. Bush created the Office of the National Coordinator for Health Information Technology (ONC), and goals specified by Bush's appointed head, Dr. David Brailer (MD), included:

- to interconnect providers
- to personalize health care.

Under ideal conditions, these lofty goals would bring efficacy and cost-effectiveness to health care. The goals were not mandated, however, and the resulting efforts were merely voluntarily performed by various healthcare entities. Later, the goals were mandated and the term "meaningful" was added.

Once mandated, the idea occurred to enterprising IT specialists that they could make money helping practices and hospitals with meaningful use and efforts at electronic coordination. Consultants with separate but "useful" programs went forth to sell their systems. EMR connectivity was like the Wild West, with many groups competing for clinic/hospital adoptions. Among these many competing groups, there just was no effective coordination. Many companies produced diverse IT solutions, which did not work together or even coexist well each other —even though there were many attempts to make them do so. The problem was that the entrepreneurs were not focused on interoperability and centralization; these were just an afterthought. For example, messages on charts were sent from one location to another, transferring to other IT packages, and then sent back to "update" the EMR. Time required to translate notes from one system to another increased, mistakes were made, and morbidity and mortality increased as a result.

Under President Obama, the attitude of government regulations became more insistent, and the concept of "voluntary" became mandatory under the law. Since the Supreme Court upheld the Affordable Care Act, medical service organizations have had to demonstrate transparency while upholding security and privacy even without the existence of corroborating standards for electronic health records (HIMSS, 2012a). In practice, however, this task is not easily achievable. It may take years to achieve such a sweeping change within healthcare agencies.

The current lack of standards in electronic medical and health records begs the question, "Who will set the standards?" HIMSS has espoused interoperability standards for 12 years or more (HIMSS, 2012d), and hospitals and clinics have tried to move to electronic record keeping during that time. ONC has now determined that ANSI will be the official group to produce the permanent standards.

Using its own analytical process, HIMSS has determined the progress toward the seven step EMR adoption model for both the USA and Canada. Table 4.1 shows the relative adoption rates in US and Canadian organizations.

Figure 4.6 shows the percent of installations of major vendors that have installed EMR systems.

Table 4.1 leaves out some important hospitals, such as VA hospitals, and the open source VistA EMR system that serves about 250 hospitals. This chart also does not show international hospitals. Kaiser hospitals use Epic, which has a broad base outside of Kaiser hospitals as well. Kaiser has 40 hospitals that serve over 8 million patients. However, the point is that there are many systems available for EMR.

LONG-RANGE PROBLEMS AND OPPORTUNITIES

The adoption of EMR technology and the standards controlling it requires a coordination effort among all parts of the organization, and follow-through in planning programs must be performed. Information technology "feudalism" is a long-standing practice, in which individual "fiefdoms" control and sequester their own data, and much duplication of effort results in many instances of "reinventing the wheel." A quick search online can identify over 400 EMR packages and vendors. The standard operating procedure of these vendors is to maximize the profit from the section of turf that they have carved out of the large market. Many vendors store their data in a cloud; Google is joining this effort (Pelino, 2008). Their patients can access their personal electronic health records in the cloud, and can "share" this information with their doctors. Personalized information storage could be the answer to personalized medicine. Our cars, our office chairs, and our toilets will be able to take our vitals and send the data to our medical files, which may or may not be shared with our doctors. A television commercial for Cisco (a networking company) describes a scenario where the accident victim's motorcycle helmet calls for emergency medical services, which are then coordinated, down to the ambulance arrival, approvals of the insurance plan, diversion to the hospital that is best equipped to handle the injury, and, for good measure, coordinated traffic lights for the ambulance on the way to the hospital. This subject will be expanded in the patient-directed medicine chapter (Chapter 14) of this book.

Personalized information storage can become a source of confusion and miscommunication. Even if information is sent to doctors, they may not be able to read it unless they have the facilities to receive the information. Currently,

TABLE 4.1 US and Canada EMR Adoption Model

Stage	Cumulative Capabilities	2012 Final	2013 Q1
EMR Adoption Model^{SM}			
Stage 7	Complete EMR; CCD transactions to share data; Data warehousing; Data continuity with ED, ambulatory, OP	1.9%	1.9%
Stage 6	Physician documentation (structured templates), full CDSS (variance & compliance), full R-PACS	8.2%	9.1%
Stage 5	Closed loop medication administration	14.0%	16.3%
Stage 4	CPOE, Clinical Decision Support (clinical protocols)	14.2%	14.4%
Stage 3	Nursing/clinical documentation (flow sheets), CDSS (error checking), PACS available outside Radiology	38.3%	36.3%
Stage 2	CDR, Controlled Medical Vocabulary, CDS, may have Document Imaging; HIE capable	10.7%	10.1%
Stage 1	Ancillaries − Lab, Rad, Pharmacy − All Installed	4.3%	4.2%
Stage 0	All Three Ancillaries Not Installed	8.4%	7.8%
Canada EMR Adoption Model^{SM}			
Stage 7	Complete EMR; CCD transactions to share data; Data warehousing; Data continuity with ED, ambulatory, OP	0.0%	0.0%
Stage 6	Physician documentation (structured templates), full CDSS (variance & compliance), full R-PACS	0.5%	0.5%
Stage 5	Closed loop medication administration	0.3%	0.3%
Stage 4	CPOE, Clinical Decision Support (clinical protocols)	2.3%	2.2%
Stage 3	Nursing/clinical documentation (flow sheets), CDSS (error checking), PACS available outside Radiology	33.8%	33.6%
Stage 2	CDR, Controlled Medical Vocabulary, CDS, may have Document Imaging; HIE capable	25.3%	26.9%
Stage 1	Ancillaries − Lab, Rad, Pharmacy − All Installed	14.8%	14.8%
Stage 0	All Three Ancillaries Not Installed	23.0%	21.7%
		$N = 640$	$N = 640$

Source: Data from HIMSS Analytics^{TM} Database © 2013

Vendor Name	Total Installations	Percent of Installations
• Meditech	1212	25.5%
• Cerner	606	12.8%
• McKesson	573	12.1%
• Epic Systems	413	8.7%
• Siemens Healthcare	397	8.4%
• CPSI	392	8.3%
• Healthcare Management Systems	347	7.3%
• Self-developed	273	5.8%
• Healthland	223	4.7%
• Eclipsys (Bought by Allscripts)	185	3.9%

FIGURE 4.6 Ranking of hospital EMR installations by vendor. *Source: HIMSS Analytics (2013).*

physicians are already inundated with data; this situation will get even worse with the problems that come with the increased access anticipated under the Obama health plan. Without the proper algorithms, information systems interfaces, and standards, practitioners may be unable to process the data, even if their systems can communicate with other electronic systems.

SOME QUESTIONS

Does lack of communication between all the healthcare entities make sense to the average person needing health care? Does it make sense that the oncologist does not talk with the primary care physician, or with the urologist, all of whom have valuable data to share? Does it make sense that a loved one died when a nurse gave an unscheduled dose, because a nurse on a previous shift gave the dose and entered the event on his EMR, but the next nurse gave a second dose, thinking that the first dose had not been given, because the updating process was taking a long time moving through non-cooperating systems? Can this situation be considered meaningful use in any way? How can predictive analytics help with such problems?

Predictive analytic researchers may be able to predict the time it takes EMRs to update, and to alleviate some other problems within the healthcare organization. Predictive analysts can crunch much of the data which inundate physicians, and distill information which is most important for proper health care. Perhaps we can influence the IT "fiefdoms" to talk with one another to facilitate some of these analyses. Analysis of the 100,000 Americans who die each year might be able to show what proportion of the loss is caused by issues related to interoperability. If we could show that a reduction in inoperability is related to a decline in lives lost, it might drive change. A very important driver of this change will be the monetary incentive to achieve this outcome.

Larsen (2012) maintained that in 2014 "all EHR technology must be certified to the 2014 criteria, whether the eligible provider or hospital is qualifying for incentives under Stage 1 or Stage 2 of Meaningful Use." According to Larsen, once the permanent criteria take effect, these points are worth consideration:

1. *By ONC's accounting, 40% of the certification requirements are unchanged from 2011, and are eligible for gap certification (certification of a previously certified EHR system);*
2. *Over 60% of the criteria are new, which will require new test methods and likely EHR system upgrades;*
3. *Of special note is the requirement that eight certified EHR medication-related functions demonstrate safety-enhanced design. This will be a challenging certification criterion to develop and administer.*

(Larsen, 2012).

It will be interesting to witness the compliance rate with these requirements, especially given the fact that new people must be hired and trained to code, in order to develop and administer the changes. At least there will not be the concern about what the final rule set will be.

THE CHALLENGE

A major challenge during the immediate future will be to identify those high priority issues related to HIMSS that could be resolved by the use of predictive analytics and the adoption of ANSI standards. Very few providers and hospitals have complied with the Office of National Coordinator (ONC) and Centers for Medicare and Medicaid Services (CMS).

HIMSS continues to provide a wealth of ideas for researchers using predictive analytics. The areas for research opportunities involve reporting, analyzing, monitoring, and predicting. The challenge is to "improve and optimize decisions and performance."

POSTSCRIPT

The operations of HIMSS developed the four pillars for IT: (1) improved quality; (2) improved safety; (3) increased cost-effectiveness; and (4) increased access to care. While HIMSS was effective in developing an appreciation for the need for these four pillars, a US Government organization was required to coordinate the dissemination of this information and incorporation of it into the IT structures of healthcare organizations. This organization (The Office of National Coordinator for Health Information Technology — ONC) set up the regulatory structure that mandated what information should be disseminated, and how it should be done. A future challenge is to identify high priority issues related to HIMSS and ANSI standards that can be resolved by predictive analytics studies. An ongoing challenge, however, is the design of proper formats for storing electronic medical information. Chapter 5 describes the necessary features of electronic medical records.

REFERENCES

ANSI, 2010. American National Standards Institute Overview of the US Standardization System: Voluntary Consensus Standards and Conformity Assessment Activities. <http://publicaa.ansi.org/sites/apdl/Documents/News%20and%20Publications/Brochures/U.S.StandardsSystemOverview_Third_Edition.pdf/>, retrieved November 30, 2012.

ANSI, 2012. A Historical Overview. <www.ansi.org/about_ansi/introduction/history.aspx?menuid = 1#.UMeVP4PBE9Y/>, retrieved December 11, 2012.

ANSI, 2013. ANSI: American National Standards Institute. <www.ansi.org/about_ansi/introduction/introduction.aspx/>, retrieved August 27, 2013.

Brailer, D.J., 2013. Presidential leadership and health information technology. http://content.healthaffairs.org/content/28/2/w392.full, retrieved August 27, 2013.

CCA, 2012a. CCA takes its 5 "components" of population health to DC. July 11, 2012. <www.govhealthit.com/news/cca-takes-its-5-components-population-health-dc/>, retrieved December 16, 2012.

CCA, 2012b. Care Continuum Alliance Homepage: Research Tab. <www.carecontinuumalliance.org/OGR5_user_agreement.asp/>, retrieved December 16, 2012.

CMS, 2013. Centers for Medicare and Medicaid Services. <www.cms.gov/>, retrieved August 26, 2013.)

Cohen, B.I., 1984. "Florence Nightingale". Scientific American. 250 (3), 128−137.

Dindigal, P., 2012. Healthcare Business Intelligence: Saving lives through enhanced information. <www.himss.org/content/files/Satyam021109.pdf/>, retrieved December 15, 2012.

Fridsma, D., 2013. Interoperability vs HIE: Words matter. Healthc. IT News.29.

Goldhill, D., 2013. Catastrophic Care: How American Health Care Killed My Father − and How We Can Fix It. Alfred A. Knopf, New York, NY.

HIMSS, 2012a. Standards. <www.himss.org/content/files/standards101/Standards_101.pdf/>, retrieved December 9, 2012.

HIMSS, 2012b. Transforming healthcare through IT. <www.himss.org/>, retrieved December 9, 2012 [Note: this article is no longer available on the website].

HIMSS, 2012c. Analysis of healthcare IT standards development initiative. <www.himss.org/asp/topics_focusdynamic.asp?faid = 673/>, retrieved December 2, 2012.

HIMSS, 2012d. Interoperability & standards toolkit. <www.himss.org/asp/topics_toolkit_InteroperabilityStandards.asp/>, retrieved December 9, 2012.

HIMSS, 2013. About Healthcare Information and Management Systems Society. <www.himss.org/AboutHIMSS/index.aspx?navItemNumber = 17402/>, retrieved August 27, 2013.

HIMSS Analytics, 2012. <www.himssanalytics.org/home/index.aspx/>.

HIMSS Analytics, 2013. History. <www.himssanalytics.org/about/history.aspx/>, retrieved August 28, 2013.

Kohn, D., 2013. Extreme Makeover − ICD 10 Code Edition: Demystifying the conversion toolkit, <www.slideshare.net/daksystcons/himss-2012-14180631#btnNext/>, retrieved March 30, 2013.

Larsen, E., 2012. Some observations on ONC's 2014 edition. <http://blog.himss.org/2012/03/07/some-observations-on-the-onc-nprm-from-himss12-and-hitsc-meeting/>

Lewis, A., 2012. Why Nobody Believes the Numbers. John Wiley & Sons, Hoboken, NJ.

Pelino, D., 2008. Hospitals have collected mountains of patient and clinical data − now what? Healthc. Financ. Manage. 62 (9), 142−144.

Chapter 5

Electronic Medical Records: Analytics' Best Hope

Chapter Outline

NOTE: EMR (electronic medical records) and EHR (electronic health records) terminology is used interchangeably in some of the literature, yet others define EMR and EHR precisely, with different, but overlapping, functions; this difference is discussed in Chapter 26).

PREAMBLE

In 1865, it was recognized that we need better means for storing and retrieving medical information; this is still true today. Also still true today is the critical need for appropriate data input techniques; it is at this point that most electronic medical record systems fail. This chapter presents the current state of development of electronic medical records.

INTRODUCTION

As early as 1965 it was recognized that "the need for better means of recording and retrieving data for medical records has become increasingly apparent" (Baird and Garfunkel, 1965). For the most part, that statement is as relevant today as it was then. The article goes on to describe a project at St. Christopher's Hospital for Children in Philadelphia, in which certain elements of the medical charts were "recorded via electronic data processing equipment, and then transcribed for the patients' charts." The data were entered via "mark—sense" cards, which were manually coded, and then fed into a machine to place a punch in the appropriate column. The card could then be read by a computer, the data tabulated, and reports produced. Many advantages were appreciated by users, including legible notes, chronological summaries, statistical reports, and control of utilization of drugs and lab tests. Ultimately, the project was ended due primarily to cost factors. The authors concluded that the ability to provide information in "real time" via a computer "will be associated with considerable expense, with administrative difficulties, and with a need for intensive educational effort." After reading this article almost 50 years later, a present-day physician or administrator who has had any significant experience with electronic medical systems feels a sense of *déjà vu* (or "paramnesia," using the medical term).

Practical Predictive Analytics and Decisioning Systems for Medicine. DOI: http://dx.doi.org/10.1016/B978-0-12-411643-6.00005-3

In 1968, Dr. G. Octo Barnett, head of the Massachusetts General Laboratory of Computer Science, reviewed the state of the art of computer applications in medicine (Barnett, 1968). He observed that little progress had been made in the "vital area of medical practice, information processing . . .," and that "early interest in bringing the revolution in computer technology to bear on medical practice was plagued with over-enthusiasm, naiveté and unrealistic expectations." One of his conclusions was "the chief limiting factor is inadequate input techniques." He added, "The most significant advances in this area will therefore result from innovations in methods of capturing medical record information."

Many frustrated doctors would agree that we are still waiting for those advances.

This sentiment is reflected in a recent article by Jha (2011), where the author writes, "Currently, the EHR remains a tool with vast potential, but a limited set of current capabilities." A report from The Institute of Medicine describes the US healthcare system as exceedingly complex and inefficient due primarily to its inability to capture clinical, process, and financial data in a way that allows for appropriate analysis (Kohn *et al.*, 2000). There is no lack of data! The problem is that most of it resides currently in paper charts in individual offices or hospitals, or in electronic medical record systems that do not have the capability to communicate with any other systems. We need a way to obtain or translate this data into a structured format (discrete data elements) which can then be used for the appropriate analysis. The primary tool to accomplish this is the electronic medical record (EMR).

Most of the codified data exists currently in the form of claims data gathered by insurance companies or government payers. This information can be quite extensive, including provider visits, diagnoses, pharmacy utilization, lab, X-ray, home health, and any other billable ancillary services, including hospitalization. Analysis of these data can paint a holistic picture of patients' interactions with the healthcare system, and reveal a lot about their overall health status; however, they lack specifics. Coupled with more specific elements contained in the EMR, such as vital signs, lab values, imaging reports, medical history, family history, and personal habits (smoking, exercise, occupation), a detailed and more complete picture is revealed. The potential of data analytics is to aggregate and analyze this body of data to paint a coherent picture of the patient in a way that has not been possible before, which can lead to diagnoses not considered previously.

This potential was introduced in general in earlier chapters. In order to realize this potential, within the goals of improved quality, lower cost, and greater accessibility, a successful healthcare system is directly dependent on providing the right information at the right time for the right analysis. A well-implemented, usable, interoperable EHR is critical for this to happen. And indeed it must happen, because

The complexity of modern medicine exceeds the inherent limitations of the unaided human mind.

(David Eddy, 1990).

In Chapter 1, we saw that the collection of medical records in written format has been mandated by at least five rulers during the past 7,000 years. Each of these rulers recognized that these records must be provided to all medical practitioners in a convenient format consistent with the state of communications abilities at the time. The only such format available in the past was written documents. We see the same need today, only the quantity has changed (from relatively little to a vast quantity), and the format required today is digital rather than written. Not only does this digital format permit efficient storage and retrieval of this vast quantity of healthcare information, but it also provides the necessary input for a rapidly expanding analytical capability developing throughout our civilization. To understand how this information can be leveraged to aid diagnosis and treatment programs in health care, we can begin with a discussion of the elemental structure of this information — the EMR.

WHAT IS AN EMR?

In simplest terms, an EMR is a digital reproduction of the information commonly found in a paper medical chart. It is usually locally housed (or remotely hosted but controlled) by the provider or institution, and it may have a degree of interoperability with other electronic systems (e.g., lab, billing) within the institution. This describes the vast majority of systems in use today.

Similar to but broader in scope than the EMR, the electronic health record (EHR), as defined by HIMSS, is a historical electronic record (historical instances of patient health treatment information) generated by one or more encounters in any care delivery setting. Included in this information are patient demographics, progress notes, problems, medications, vital signs, past medical history, immunizations, laboratory data, and radiology reports. The EHR automates and streamlines the clinician's workflow. The EHR has the ability to generate a complete record of a clinical patient encounter. Included in the EHR are other supporting care-related activities gathered either directly or indirectly via some interface, including systems for evidence-based decision support, quality management, and outcomes reporting.

For the rest of this chapter, we will use the broader term of EHR to include both concepts of EMR and EHR.

In 2003, in response to a request from the US Department of Health and Human Services, the Institute of Medicine (2003) published a report titled "Key Capabilities of an Electronic Health Record System," which defined the ideal core functionalities of EHR systems:

- Health information and data: Problem lists, medication lists, allergies, past medical and surgical history, family history
- Results management: Lab results, X-ray results, consultation correspondence
- Order entry/management: Computerized entry of medications, tests, consultations and other services
- Decision support: Alerts for drug allergies or interactions, reminders for needed services including screenings and immunizations, treatment algorithms
- Electronic communication and connectivity: Secure communication with patients and other caregivers
- Patient support: Patient access to their medical records, access to educational material
- Administrative processes: Provision of scheduling and billing functions or integration with dedicated systems
- Reporting and population health management: Use of standard data structures to facilitate quality improvement efforts and external reporting requirements.

The report included additional detail based on each of four care settings: (1) hospitals, (2) ambulatory clinics, (3) nursing homes, and (4) care elsewhere in the community.

The potential benefits of EHR systems include:

- Real-time on-site and remote access to patient information
- Electronic prescription ordering with automatic checking for drug interactions
- Electronic ordering and posting of lab results with some simple analysis, including trending of values
- Enhanced charge capture through communication with the billing system
- Clinical decision support, which could prevent or minimize errors in treatment, and provide reminders for needed lab immunizations or other procedures
- Clearance of space used previously for paper medical records
- Decreased or eliminated need for transcription of information
- Provision of reports to facilitate quality improvement
- Provision of legible notes
- Provision of valuable data for research on population health and other studies.

A BIT (OF A "BYTE") OF HISTORY ...

The concept of an electronic record has been known for many years. In 1945, an engineer named Vannevar Bush coined the term "memex" for:

> *a device in which an individual stores all his books, records, and communications, and which is mechanized so that it may be consulted with exceeding speed and flexibility. It is an enlarged intimate supplement to his memory.*
>
> (Bush, 1945).

The essential feature of this device was the use of "associative indexing" described as "the process of tying two items together" (Bush, 1945). This is the basic premise of what later came to be known as hypertext, which formed the basis of the World Wide Web and the relational computer database which is the foundation of the EHR. He proceeds to describe (somewhat presciently) a medical scenario in which "The physician, puzzled by a patient's reactions, strikes the trail established in studying an earlier similar case, and runs rapidly through analogous case histories, with side references to the classics for the pertinent anatomy and histology" (Bush, 1945).

An associated bit of history: Vannevar Bush (/væniːvɑr/van-NEE-var; March 11, 1890–June 28, 1974) was an American engineer, inventor, and science administrator whose most important contribution was as head of the US Office of Scientific Research and Development (OSRD) during the Second World War, through which almost all wartime military R&D was carried out.

Beginning in the early 1960s, several key developments occurred on the road to development of the electronic health record.

In 1962, IBM and Akron Children's Hospital collaborated to develop one of the first automated medical record systems. Lohr (2012) describes a familiar scenario, in which Roger Sherman, the hospital's administrator, said, "If we can mechanize much of this routine clerical work, our doctors and nurses will be able to spend more of their time using their professional training to give more direct and attentive care to patients." Some of the touted benefits of this system included the monitoring of drug dosages and prevention of potential drug interactions.

Dr. Lawrence Weed (1968) introduced the concept of the problem-oriented medical record (POMR), in which he systematized the written medical record in a logical, structured manner that promoted better communication of patient information. His system centered on individual problems independently, with associated history, clinical findings, lab results, assessment, and plan. This method of documentation became widely accepted, and a form of it is commonly referred to as the SOAP (Subjective, Objective, Assessment, Plan) note, which is the standard method of chart documentation today. His idea, however, was not widely accepted initially in the medical community because "the notion of structuring a present illness, a medical history, or a physical examination [was considered] tampering with the art of medicine" (Schultz,1988). Hurst (1971) remarked that "the logic system [Weed's POMR] and display of it prepares the student and physician for the computer world that is coming to our rescue."

Later, Dr. Weed led a team at the University of Vermont in the development of a problem oriented medical information system known as PROMIS which was based on the problem oriented medical record structure. The project was funded by the US government and was used on medical and gynecological wards at the University of Vermont. The system utilized touch-screen terminals and realized a degree of success until its government funding ended.

In 1968, the defense contractor Lockheed Corporation partnered with El Camino Hospital in Mountain View, California, to demonstrate the application of military technology database technology to society in general (Shortliffe, 2013). Engineers studied the operational flow of data in the hospital, and coded a system for computer replication of the workflow. The project went live in 1973 using an IBM mainframe computer. It was known initially as the Lockheed System and was later commercialized as the Technicon system, which was acquired eventually by Eclipsys (which later merged with Allscripts). In the mid-1980s this system was used for physician order entry (CPOE), utilizing a light pen to make selections from a screen; nurses used it for charting (from the current author's personal experience).

A significant milestone in the development of the EHR was reached in the late 1960s with the invention of a programming language called the Massachusetts General Hospital Utility Multi-Programming System (MUMPS) (Wikipedia.org, 2013), developed by the Massachusetts General Hospital (MGH) Laboratory of Computer Science specifically for use in healthcare systems. It was offered for general use with a no-cost license, was adopted by many commercial companies, and is still the most widely used programming language for medical applications. In 1971, the MGH laboratory team developed one of the most widely used ambulatory medical records systems, known as COSTAR (Computer Stored Ambulatory Record). The COSTAR license is in the public domain, and is still in use at many institutions.

The Regenstrief Medical Record System was developed at the Regenstrief Institute of Indianapolis in 1972, and was the first to implement clinical decision support (CDS). It uses rule-based reminders to provide real-time feedback to physicians while they are entering information into the system.

From the 1980s to the present, there has been a proliferation of electronic medical record systems. Many of the current EMR systems evolved from computerized practice management (billing) systems, which predated EMRs. As more EMR systems became available in the market, many companies added very basic documentation capabilities in order to be able to provide a "complete" solution for doctors' offices, either for use in stand-alone mode, or for integration with their existing systems. As a result, many of today's EMRs are designed more for charge capture and administrative functions than for clinical documentation.

Today there are literally hundreds of different EMR products with widely differing interfaces and functionality (over 1,700 vendors, to be exact, have surfaced since the Rand Report of 2005; not all of these are in business today). Many of these systems are "niche" products, dedicated to specific functions (e.g., Pharmacy, Radiology, ER, PT/Rehab, ICU). It is difficult to compare one system to another directly, even though interoperability appears to be the intended design of Meaningful Use mandates. Many of the more established companies do not even provide online demonstrations without the presence of a salesperson. There is no direct interoperability between systems, and most have their own proprietary data structures. This can pose a problem or even be a deterrent to changing products due to the very real potential for losing all or significant amounts of patient data accumulated in the current system because they may not be portable to the new system.

WHY AREN'T WE THERE YET?

Vaitheeswaran (2010) cites that:

American health care is one of the last great industries to remain largely undisrupted by the information-technology (IT) revolution of the past few decades.

The long-recognized need and the numerous potential benefits associated with electronic records beg the question: *why are we not much further along functionally than many of the early demonstration projects?* It is obvious that, from a technological standpoint, tremendous advances in computer capabilities have occurred, but the application in health care lags far behind that in other industries, such as banking and air travel, where data standards were established long ago, allowing for a seamless flow of data between organizational entities. Moore's Law states that computer processing chip performance doubles about every 18 months (beginning in 1958 with the invention of the integrated circuit), thereby increasing computing power at an ever-increasing pace. Software design tends to lag behind processor capabilities. Even so, many industries continue to push ahead with new capabilities and applications; not so in health care, where most current applications can run adequately only on computer platforms from years ago.

There are many reasons why there has not been more widespread adoption of information technology in health care, including cost, usability, disruption of workflow, and lack of interoperability.

Cost

EHR systems require a considerable initial investment for various hardware components (less so in a cloud-based setting) and necessary software to run them. In addition, there are significant ongoing licensing and maintenance fees. Another significant but very necessary cost is training for the physicians and staff. Often this cost is significantly underestimated; however, adequate training is a key element of successful implementation and ultimate adoption of the system. Another major cost is the loss of revenue from decreased production (i.e., patient care) during implementation and frequently for weeks or months later (if not forever). In the current predominant fee-for-service business model, it is often difficult to justify this expenditure without a demonstrable increase in productivity. Many EHR vendors claim that revenue is significantly increased because with easier and faster documentation the coding is more accurate and a doctor can see more patients, frequently resulting in a higher billing rate. While the coding enhancement is a common outcome, seeing more patients is not.

Usability

Recent surveys have shown decreasing user satisfaction, due largely to poor interface design. Often, EHR documentation takes more time than writing or (certainly) dictation. Without a great deal of customization, the user must adapt the workflow to the system; this may be inefficient and is always stressful. Customizing is costly, and always introduces the risk of "breaking" some component, or causing incompatibility with software upgrades (often, upgrades wipe out customized routines). Historically, the most satisfied users tend to be those using a system that has been highly customized to their workflow. More recently, vendors have been discouraging customization for these reasons and striving to keep the ongoing costs lower. Current EHR systems were designed more to digitize data and capture charges (business functions) than to document medical care functions. Clearly, there is a great need to generate some significant breakthroughs in interface design. One such promising technology is natural language processing (NLP), which is essentially voice recognition coupled with artificial intelligence. This innovation analyzes the context of words and phrases in the unstructured text of dictated notes, and extracts pertinent information (data elements) which can be used to populate specific data fields in a patient record.

One of the key measures of usability is the number of "clicks" required to complete a task. In fact, at some of the large health-related IT meetings, a popular session is a "click-off" contest in which representatives of several EHR vendors are on stage with their system running and projected onto a screen. Simultaneously, they are given a typical patient visit scenario to document in real time before an audience.

Another major usability issue has to do with physicians who work in more than one hospital. This could require learning how to use multiple EHRs in different formats in different offices or hospitals.

The user interface can directly affect the accuracy of the data entered. A key component of documentation is choosing the appropriate codes for the diagnoses and procedures performed during a patient visit, using the International Classification of Diseases, 9th revision, Clinical Modification (ICD-9-CM, 2013) and Current Procedural Terminology (2013). The codes are used to communicate the severity of illness or the patient's condition, and reflect any related health problems. The more specific the code is, the more accurately it reflects the patient's condition. Precision in coding, however, can be very time consuming, and it can take more time to choose and apply the correct codes than is spent in addressing the problem of the patient. The ICD-9 system contains approximately 16,000 codes with specificity of up to two decimal places. The soon to be implemented ICD-10 system comprises 66,000 codes with even more specificity. From a data analysis perspective this degree of specificity is highly desirable (even necessary), while to the busy clinician it can slow the workflow significantly. The workaround is to use a very general high-level code sufficient for billing purposes, but which sacrifices details about the patient's condition. Fortunately, there are add-on programs to help facilitate the more appropriate code selection.

User interface design in any software system can help to navigate the user through a labyrinth of options and codes, or it can pose significant obstacles to doing anything correctly. Mace (2012) quipped recently:

> *Software is a funny thing. Done well, it anticipates the needs of human beings, or other software, and responds in flexible, flowing harmony. Done poorly, software epitomizes everything wrong with modern society: impersonal, inflexible, regimented, mundane, boring, even maddening.*

Disruption of Workflow

The introduction of an EHR always requires a change in well-established (though not necessarily efficient) work habits. Early in the pre-implementation phase, these workflows should be studied and optimized. There is nothing worse than computerizing inefficient processes. There should be a degree of "mutual adaptation" in which the system and the user each make some changes to achieve the goal of optimal usability. It can be a taskmaster or helpmate. A useful question to ask physicians using an EHR is, *"Are you working for it . . . or is it working for you?"* Early in the implementation of any system, a certain "critical mass" of information must be input before the output can be helpful. If that critical point does not come, there is obviously a problem with the particular EHR, or with the implementation plan. With most EHRs, users have a simultaneous love−hate relationship . . . they love being able to access the information quickly from almost anywhere, and hate having to input information into the system. Obviously, required technological changes like this are very stressful for the entire staff.

> *There is nothing so useless as doing efficiently that which should not be done at all.*
>
> (Peter F. Drucker, management author, educator).

Lack of Interoperability

One of the keys to successful cost containment, and quality improvement in healthcare reform, is the ability to share patient data regardless of where services were performed. The lack of shared data has become an especially difficult barrier to cross. A key limiting factor is the general resistance to establishing a unique patient identification code caused by concerns about patient privacy and confidentiality. Adding to the public concern are the frequent reports of hackers breaking into databases of major institutions (e.g., banks, businesses, hospitals) which have sophisticated security systems designed to prevent such occurrences. System vendors have little incentive to facilitate information sharing, because proprietary data structures can be a key deterrent to discourage clients from changing to another EHR. Usually, there are no assurances from (or cooperation by) a current vendor to help in transferring data to a new system in a usable format. Optimally, cooperative data transfer should be included in negotiations for the purchase of any new EHR system, to prepare for the future event of moving to another system. It is not common for hospitals to have much interest in sharing data, because duplicate testing results in additional revenue in a fee-for-service environment. Also, hospitals may consider their data to be proprietary and by keeping control of their data make it less likely that patients or doctors will go to a competing institution. *(However, this is being changed by the Patient Centered Outcomes Research Institute [PCORI], a new research granting agency, which is giving grants/contracts for medical institutions to develop networks of data that are transparent and available for qualified predictive analytic research aimed at more accurate diagnosis, less costly health care, and other goals [www.pcori.org]. PCORI will be discussed more thoroughly in Chapter 13.)*

Lack of a common syntax is another reason for the lack of interoperability. Medical terminology is essentially multilingual, replete with multiple terms used for similar conditions, and stored in data structures in different formats. Unless truly universal semantic taxonomies are developed (permitting data to be exchanged directly), data interchange will require some sort of translation or mapping system to move data between systems. Currently, there is much interest in developing health information exchanges (HIEs), which are systems designed to facilitate patient data exchange between healthcare provider organizations. Many pilot HIEs are being developed at the state and regional levels, most of which are supported by government funding. Even if these exchanges are enabled to function properly, there is no compelling business model to support their continuing operation.

The Health Information Technology for Economic and Clinical Health (HITECH) Act passed by the US Congress in 2009 allowed for $30 billion to provide incentives to hospitals and physician groups to adopt EMRs and for HIE development. Qualifying physicians can receive up to $44,000 over 5 years, starting in 2012, after which there is a penalty of pay reduction from Medicare for failing to install an EHR. To qualify for an incentive payment, physicians must demonstrate that the EMR is being used to meet specific government objectives described in the category of "meaningful use" (see Chapter 9 for further information). Since most of the current EMR systems did not offer many of the meaningful use functions, this requirement stimulated vendors to develop these new capabilities as quickly as possible to take advantage of the new "buying frenzy."

FERRARIS AND COUNTRY ROADS

As a result of the stimulus, there has been a rapid and progressive adoption of EMRs by physician groups and hospitals. In 2009, approximately 22% of office-based physicians were using at least a basic EMR. By the end of 2012, that number was estimated to be as high as 60%. By contrast, in 2009 only 7.6% of hospitals were using even a basic EHR system, while only 1.5% were using a comprehensive system. But the adoption rate is changing rapidly for hospitals, too. Some have argued that this is a backwards approach, because much of the usefulness is lacking without the capability to share information with other systems. Physicians will have shiny new EHRs with no roads on which to drive them. The emphasis should have been on developing a data "interstate" highway infrastructure before building the EHR. Not surprisingly, amidst the "gold rush" to get the stimulus dollars to purchase EHRs, there is a growing sense of "buyer's remorse." The sales pitch is, *"If you just get an EHR system ... any system ... your life will be blissful. Developers claim that you can see more patients, increase your income, and go home earlier with all documentation done."* However, for many, this scenario is far from reality. It is likely to result in a significant number of system changes in the near future (already at 25−30% of EHR installations), or even reversion to paper. Sadly, some patients, and also insurers and Medicare officials, have accused doctors of "upcoding" (resulting in higher charges) after installing EHRs; they assume that doctors are just "checking boxes" for work not actually performed. Often, however, increased income is one aspect of the sales pitch that is realized in primary care. Coding levels (i.e., charges) for patient visits are determined by a complex set of rules with both objective and subjective components. More time can be spent in assigning the appropriate specific diagnostic codes and procedure code than in taking care of the patient. As a result, lower level codes are selected often to guard against these charges. Some audits have shown that manual under-coding occurs up to 25−30% of the time. The EHR system, however, keeps track of the coding rules in the background (rather than in the doctor's head), tallies the points as coding elements are selected, and automatically assigns the appropriate code.

In attempting to arrive at the truth, I have applied everywhere for information, but in scarcely an instance have I been able to obtain hospital records fit for any purpose of comparison.

Florence Nightingale's Notes on Nursing (Skretkowicz, 1993).

Due to the significant differences in functionality and user interfaces of the many systems, it is difficult to generalize about their benefits. When an article is published touting the benefits or successes that a group or hospital has experienced with a particular system, those claims may apply only in that specific setting with that specific software: "If you've seen one EMR ... you've seen one EMR" (Pat Bolding, 2013).

Many of the older legacy systems are based on outdated programming structures, which make changes or adding functions difficult by "tacking on" some extra code somewhat arbitrarily (especially in response to external requirements like "meaningful use"). Not surprisingly, these kinds of add-ons don't work very well, and can cause problems with the rest of the system. New entrants into the market (and there are many) have the advantage of utilizing more modern programming architecture and hardware. They can start from scratch in system development without having to drag along the "ball and chain" of the legacy systems. And since they don't have much of an installed base to support, it is much easier for them to make modifications to the program.

This current market situation, however, does present a dilemma for the potential buyer. The older company is likely to have a significant installed base of customers (but an older, possibly less functional product), and is much more likely to remain in business to provide support in the future. Some estimate that the turnover rate for new companies entering the market is as high as 20−25% a year. In addition, it is difficult to verify that the "de-install" rate (the number of institutions changing systems) is as high as it is claimed to be at 30% a year. Understandably, medical groups or hospitals are reluctant to make a system change after investing a great deal of time and money in the present system, even if it is viewed as not helpful to or even counterproductive to the organization. Surveys show, however, that most organizations find satisfaction only in their second or third system. This situation may be due largely to the benefit of being armed with practical knowledge and realistic expectations of the performance of the new system, after experiencing the problems and shortcomings of previous systems. In selecting the initial EHR, customers are at a disadvantage because they really don't know what to look for or even what questions to ask; they are literally at the mercy of the salesperson. Larger hospitals or hospital systems or groups of doctors will hire an independent consulting firm (such as Deloitte or PwC or Gartner) to assist them in selecting a complex software system, including EHR systems. This highly competitive industry is fraught with inaccurate representations of system capabilities, often with the promise that any desired feature will be in the "next upgrade." So, for the smaller clinics and hospitals, the bottom line is that you really don't know what you're getting ... until you've got it!

To mitigate the difficult task of choosing the "right" EHR, larger physician groups or hospitals (where the cost can be multiple millions of dollars), having more resources, often engage consultants who are knowledgeable about the industry to help with the selection process. Ideally, they would go through a formal RFP (request for proposal) process and hire the best technology advisors, select the best software for their needs (or build custom software or custom extensions), hire the best implementation firm (usually through a formal RFP process), and hire the right professionals to manage the implementation project.

Despite the problems and inadequacies of current EHR systems, there are some success stories. Two prominent examples often promoted are Kaiser Permanente and the US Veterans Administration system. A key distinguishing characteristic of these institutions is that they both have "captive" populations (or closed systems) and to a large degree operate outside the health system at large.

1. Kaiser is the largest US integrated managed care consortium. Kaiser is based in California, and owns most of its facilities (hospitals, clinics, ancillaries). Because its network is so large, patients can receive the vast majority of any healthcare needs within the Kaiser "universe." It uses a version of the Epic EHR throughout its healthcare system, which provides tight integration between facilities and providers. Because Kaiser is both the insurer and clinical provider, all patient information on claims and clinical procedures is readily available wherever a patient is seen; their current medical information is readily available in any Kaiser facility. This integration has helped to improve outcomes in disease management, and increased overall quality of healthcare scores.

2. The Veterans Administration has the largest healthcare system in the USA, with 7.8 million patients, 153 hospitals, 765 outpatient clinics, and 230 veterans centers. Many patients, who may have multiple medical problems, can be seen at several different locations, which in the past would have required frequent file transmissions, or voluminous faxes (sometimes, no records at all were sent). The VA EHR system, known as VistA (Veterans Health Information Systems and Technology Architecture) was developed over many years, beginning in the early 1970s. VistA uses Open Source, which means that it is available at no cost, and has resulted in adoption of versions at some hospitals in the US and elsewhere in the world. Use of the system with its extensive clinical decision support has resulted in significant improvement in several quality measures, including length of stay, preventive services, immunization rates, and medication errors. Similarly to Kaiser, healthcare scores in many areas are superior to similar measures in the private sector and Medicare.

The experiences of Kaiser and the VA, however, are not necessarily transferable to the general US healthcare system. One reason for this difficulty is that the closed structure of the Kaiser and VA systems provides more control over standards and protocols, compared to the general healthcare system. Also, there is a greater incentive to control costs and keep members healthy, because they must operate within fixed budget constraints (as opposed to fee-for-service, where more service means more income). Certainly, there are other examples of EHR successes, but results are inconsistent.

Factors that seem to increase the likelihood of successful EHR implementation include:

- Having one or more influential champions among the medical staff
- Judicious hardware selection to ensure acceptable system performance
- Requirement and provision of adequate training
- Interoperability with other systems
- Income support for physicians during implementation (when productivity usually decreases for a period of time)
- Having a user-friendly interface
- A culture that embraces the need for an EHR
- Readily available user support/assistance.

It is clear that we have a long way to go before we arrive at the destination of having a fully integrated and interoperative EHR culture in health care. Therefore, if EHR is analytics best hope (as claimed in the title of this chapter), and considering the current state of affairs in EHR use, there remains only hope for a future where analytics provides the foundation for development of higher quality health care. Clearly, there are major barriers yet to overcome, including total cost of ownership, improved interfaces, interoperability, and privacy and security issues. But change is definitely underway, and perhaps we are in the early stages of what Topol (2012) claims will result in the "Creative Destruction of Medicine." We can hope, however, that continued development of EHR systems, and their successful operation in healthcare organizations, will permit us to navigate successfully between the "Scylla and Charybdis" of destructive mis-application of EHR technology, and no application at all. However, the move of most hospitals in the USA (and over-seas in advanced economies) to using EHR systems is laying the framework for the coming decade of digital and mobile health care, with predictive analytics making sound use of the digital data to improve health outcomes.

Postscript Added By This Book's Project Manager And One Of The Guest Authors With Some Replies From The Primary Author

This is added with the goal of helping healthcare providers (whether large or smaller hospitals or clinics) to gain a better under-standing of EHR systems, and how best to go about deciding on a system that will work.

Guest Author:

My perspective on the EHR implementations, gained from working as a manager for Oracle/PeopleSoft and Big 5—KPMG con-sulting, and working for the University of California and Carnegie Mellon University managing administrative systems, has been centered on very large implementations of software solutions; for example, if a large hospital (or group of hospitals such as Kaiser) plans to invest in a major EHR system, like Epic, it needs to go through a formal RFP process and hire the best technol-ogy advisors, select the best software for its needs (or build custom software or custom extensions) and hire the best implemen-tation firm (usually through a formal RFP process), and hire the right professionals to manage the implementation project. Other large hospitals face a similar challenge to implement an EHR system. Large business firms face the same challenges to imple-ment complex enterprise-wide software systems.

An effective, efficient, and accurate EHR system is a large investment (the cost of implementing Epic may exceed $500 mil-lion for a large hospital). It is the responsibility of the management of the hospital (CEO and CIO, and also getting leading doc-tors involved) to implement the EHR system effectively; some do and some do not. Unless the hospital management and lead doctors are like children in a candy store, they do not rely on the unverified comments of software salesman before investing $100 million or $500 million.

Primary Author Response:

Regarding the purchase/implementation process, my content in Chapter 5 is slanted towards the ambulatory side (vs. hospital), which is where the majority of the activity has been (and still is my experience), and I agree about what SHOULD be the pro-cess. But I am sure you have seen examples where physician groups, hospitals, and healthcare systems have relied on internal IT people (bad idea) to make the decisions, or used outside consultants and still the choice was not a good fit. A KLAS survey from mid-2012 showed that up to 50% of surveyed groups or hospitals (mostly larger) were considering replacing their system. For example, the system I work for (a large regional center with a hospital and 350 multispecialty physician groups) is 1 year into the planning phase of implementing Epic next May (that will be the sixth EMR I have used). When I arrived 5 years ago, they had just signed with another EHR system (the first EMR system for this medical group), but after asking a few questions I knew they had bought the sales pitch, even though consultants had been involved. As you said, getting the right system is a challenge, even when done "right."

Guest Author Reply:

I am optimistic that the major investments in implementing EHR systems in major hospitals and hospital systems will pay off: we *will* have digital health data and can begin to apply predictive and prescriptive analytics to improve health care in the USA. Other advanced economies in our global world have high levels of EHR use in both hospitals and medical practices. I agree that in many medical practices in the USA effective EMR implementations have been lagging, despite incentives. I would expect that medical practice groups with solid EMR systems will rent out the IT systems, or larger hospital chains and HIE organizations will be reaching out to share base integrated EHR systems with regional physician groups. The Federal (and private insurance) incentives and penalties may drive more physicians to consolidate medical practices to share advanced integrated EHR systems. Ambulatory medical practice implementation of EHR systems is different than the hospital path. It appears that most mid-size and larger hospitals and hospital groups will have implemented enterprise EHR systems by mid-2014. While the sheer numbers of doctor practices may slant the number of EHR implementations towards physician practices, many billions of dollars more have been invested or are currently being invested in hospital EHR systems. Many larger physician practices have also imple-mented EHR systems.

The meaningful use provisions and ACO incentive are providing more revenue to practices that manage by improved perfor-mance measures, but also the incentives effectively require the use of advanced integrated EHR systems. In large states, such as New York and California, HIE organizations are working towards effective integration (the ability to share medical files between doctors, hospitals, and testing firms) of hospitals and medical practices. I would expect within the next 2–5 years to see effective HIE integration across the USA. I have attended local HIE and HIMSS meetings on HIE implementation. We may see effective HIE organizations across most states by 2015 or 2016. The process of integrating regional and national hospitals and local medical practices, in a secure manner, just takes some time. Excellent progress has been made in both EHR implementations and HIE integration in the past 5 years.

Given that the US does not have a national health service, and that we have a very fragmented healthcare industry, I am positive that we have made major progress over the past 5 years in implementing EHR systems and HIE steps towards providing integration of health records.

Principal "Project Manager" Author Response:

In 2005, the Rand Corporation (www.rand.org/news/press/2005/09/14.html; http://content.healthaffairs.org/content/24/5/1103. abstract?sid = 1cafe17a-bfe4-4fb5-8110-6d2d57f236a5) did a study that recommended that EMR be utilized in healthcare settings, suggesting that it would save money — maybe even $81 billion annually — in healthcare costs. In 2010 another Rand Report on HER use indicated that its adoption had only had a "limited effect" on healthcare costs (www.rand.org/news/press/ 2010/12/23.html). In February 2013 a second major Rand Corporation EHR study reported that, instead of saving money, the annual cost of medical care has grown by over $800 billion with the implementation of EMR since 2005 (www.rand.org/pubs/ external_publications/EP201000136.html; www.informationweek.com/healthcare/electronic-health-records/rand-health-it-no-bargain-yet/d/d-id/1108063?; www.nytimes.com/2013/01/11/business/electronic-records-systems-have-not-reduced-health-costs-report-says.html?_r = 0). To make matters worse, over 1,700 different vendors of EMR software systems have sprung up; why do you think this happened?

Analysis by others of the 2013 Rand Report provided statements such as the following:

The recent (Rand) analysis was sharply critical of the commercial systems now in place, many of which are hard to use and do not allow doctors and patients to share medical information across systems. "We could be getting much more if we could take the time to do a little more planning and to set more standards," said Marc Probst, CIO for Intermountain Healthcare, a large health system in Salt Lake City that developed its own EMR system and is cited by RAND as an example of how the technology can help improve care and reduce costs.

(From www.nytimes.com/2013/01/11/business/electronic-records-systems-have-not-reduced-health-costs-report-says.html?_r = 0)

It is interesting that some of the EHR systems and their vendors' services have been so bad in some medical organizations that several lawsuits have been filed. Of the over 1,700 EMR systems vendors, among the top five are EPIC, Cerner, and Allscripts. Both Allscripts and Cerner have had lawsuits filed against them for failed services — for example, in 2010 against Cerner and in 2012 against Allscripts, as reported in the (January 10, 2013; www.nytimes.com/2013/01/11/business/electronic-records-systems-have-not-reduced-health-costs-report-says.html?pagewanted = 2&_r = 0).

It is also interesting that the 2005 Rand Report was supported by vendors of the EMR industry (financed primarily by GE and Cerner: www.healthcareitnews.com/blog/rand-report-are-healthcare-and-health-it-dysfunctional-relationship).

The 2013 Rand Report was done independently, with no funding from EMR vendors.

A recent (October 13, 2013) Rand Report stated that there are serious concerns associated with electronic health records (EHRs) hindering physicians' job satisfaction (www.rand.org/pubs/research_reports/RR439.html; www.advisory.com/Daily-Briefing/2013/10/10/RAND-EHRs-may-be-making-some-doctors-miserable); this is probably an understatement, as I think we all know doctors who have left the field in the past few years because of these and other similar complicating factors, including greater difficulty in dealing with insurance concerns, and other medical doctors have gone to "cash only" or "pre-paid yearly care" systems.

Various 2013 Rand Reports made differing statements that could be interpreted as something to the effect that obviously a mistake was made in studying the EMR/healthcare use process fully back in their 2005 report, and that the EMR process may be "needed to be started all over again from scratch" (www.rand.org/news/press/2013/01/07.html; www.washingtonpost.com/ blogs/wonkblog/wp/2013/01/11/why-electronic-health-records-failed/; http://beforeitsnews.com/healthcare/2013/01/ehrs-are-dead-long-live-ehrs-2444810.html).

Obviously, the proposed effects of EMR as projected by the 2005 Rand Report have not happened; instead almost the opposite has occurred, as seen in Figures 5.1 and 5.2.

Doctors have not adopted EMR as the 2005 Rand Study predicted; most recent studies indicate that only 50% of doctors have digitized their records, with the hospitals falling far behind at about 30% (even though the mandates by Meaningful Use Phases I, II, and III stated that these should be in effect by January 2014). Even the doctors who opted for EMR were very frustrated in their use, with 75% stating major frustration with interoperability (e.g., the ability to connect with hospitals and other doctor's practices) (October, 2012: http://bipartisanpolicy.org/news/press-releases/2012/10/bipartisan-policy-center-calls-collaborative-action-accelerate).

Some, including one of the authors of this book, feel that none of the current "for profit" vendor's EMR/EHR systems is really successful, none meeting the mandates of meaningful use; others agree with this assessment, as in the following quotation:

"There is not one successful EHR system in the whole world," Waegemann said in an interview, because he believes **true interoperability** *and* **patient-centeredness** *have not been priorities; "We have been focusing too much on documentation for the purpose of reimbursement," Waegemann said.*

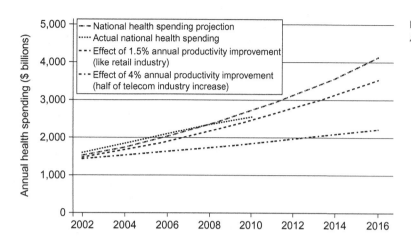

FIGURE 5.1   Effects on EMRs on US healthcare costs. *Source: Kliff (2013).*

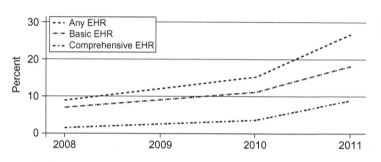

FIGURE 5.2   Percentage of US doctors adopting EMRs, 2008–2011. *Source: Kliff (2013).*

(C. Peter Waegemann, 2013, of the Medical Records Institute; in: www.healthcareitnews.com/news/stage-3-ehrs-draw-critics).

Major corporations, from GE to others, along with hospitals, have invested large quantities of money and resources into the current EMRs, but I really think the most-cost effective measure, from the ultimate payer, the patient, would be to start all over again, to build cost-effective/efficient EHRs which could literally save each doctor in the USA "hours per day" from what is going on currently. It could be done; but with so many different "political" factions involved, and billions of dollars already spent, will this advance happen? Some think it will (http://blog.himss.org/2012/02/23/himss-statement-on-release-of-meaningful-use-stage-2/):

If America is any indicator, the sky is the limit when it comes to potential gains from health IT. According to the Institute of Medicine, the US currently wastes more than $750 billion per year on unnecessary or inefficient health-care services, excessive administrative costs, high prices, medical fraud, and missed opportunities for prevention. Properly applied, health IT can improve health care in all of these dimensions. The payoff will be worth it. Indeed, as with the adoption of IT elsewhere, we may soon wonder how health care could have been delivered any other way.

(www.rand.org/commentary/2013/02/26/PS.html).

The Veterans Affairs Medical System has actually achieved a saving using its open-source (free) VistA EMR system (officially called "VistA") (of course US taxpayers paid for this at a cost of about $8 billion, as I understand it; however, VistA also has had a voluntary component, almost worldwide, in WorldVistA, which is an open-source free EMR system [http://en.wikipedia.org/wiki/VistA]). VistaA has shown 99.9% accuracy in its drug prescription processes, and greater accuracy in other things like medical diagnosis, and fewer medical errors, compared to a non-EMR medical system (*Business Week*, 2006).

The Veterans Affairs Health Administration (VHA) oversees the largest medical system in the United States. The VHA provides care to over 8 million veterans, employs 180,000 medical personnel, and operates 163 hospitals, over 800 clinics, and 135 nursing homes throughout continental USA, Alaska, and Hawaii *on a single electronic healthcare information network*. Nearly 25% of the nation's population is potentially eligible for VA benefits (US Department of Veteran Affairs, 2009).

Over 60% of all physicians trained in the USA rotate through the VHA on clinical electives, making VistA the most familiar and widely used EHR in the USA. Nearly half of all US hospitals that have a complete (inpatient/outpatient) enterprise-wide implementation of an EHR are VA hospitals using VistA (http://linuxmednews.com/1238189242; Jha *et al.*, 2009).

The Department of Veteran Affairs estimates it saved just over $3 billion in unnecessary healthcare costs in the 6 years after it adopted electronic medical records system-wide (Byrne et al., 2010; *this reference is full of data and well worth reading for those with a need to know more about the VA system*).

So if the US Veterans Affairs can make an EMR system that saves unnecessary medical tests, and thus reduces total healthcare costs, it seems that the private sector could do this also. More on the VistA and open-source EMR systems are discussed in Chapter 6.

POSTSCRIPT

The US Department of Veterans Affairs has been able to create an open-source EMR system that minimizes unnecessary medical tests, and thereby reduces the total healthcare costs; it seems that the private sector could do this also. More information is presented about VistA and other open-source EMR systems in Chapter 6.

REFERENCES

Arnst, C., 2006. The best medical care in the US. How Veterans Affairs transformed itself – and what it means for the rest of us. Business Week. 17 July, 50–56.

Baird, H.W., Garfunkel, J.M., 1965. Electronic data processing of medical records. N. Engl. J. Med. 272 (23), 1211–1215.

Barnett, G.O., 1968. Computers in patient care. N. Engl. J. Med. 279 (24), 1321–1327.

Bush, V., 1945. As we may think. The Atlantic. Retrieved from <www.theatlantic.com/magazine/archive/1945/07/as-we-may-think/303881/>.

Byrne, C.M., Mercincavage, L.M., Pan, E.C., Vincent, A.G., Johnston, D.S., Middleton, B., 2010. The value from investments in health information technology at the U.S. Department Of Veterans Affairs. Health Affairs. 29 (4), 629–638.

Eddy, D.M., 1990. Clinical decision making: from theory to practice. JAMA. 270, 520–526.

Hurst, J.W., 1971. Ten reasons why Lawrence Reed was right. N. Engl. J. Med. 284 (1), 51–52.

Institute of Medicine, 2003. Key Capabilities of an Electronic Health Record System Letter Report, <http://books.nap.edu/html/ehr/NI000427.pdf/>.

International Classification of Diseases, Ninth Revision, Clinical Modification (ICD-9-CM): National Center for Health Statistics, 2013. Website: www.cdc.gov/nchs/icd/icd9cm.htm

Jha, A.K., 2011. The promise of electronic records. Around the corner or down the road? [Editorial]. J. Am. Med. Assoc. 306 (8), 880–884.

Jha, A.K., DesRoches, C.M., Campbell, E.G., Donelan, K., Rao, S.R., Ferris, T.G., et al., 2009. Use of Electronic Health Records in US Hospitals. N. Engl. J. Med. 360, 1628–1638.

Kliff, S. 2013. Why electronic health records failed. Washington Post Wonkblog. Available at: http://www.washingtonpost.com/blogs/wonkblog/wp/2013/01/11/why-electronic-health-records-failed/.

Kohn, L.T., Corrigan, J.M., Donaldson, M.S. (Eds.), 2000. To Err is Human. National Academy Press, Washington, DC.

Lohr, S., 2012. The miracle of digital health records, 50 years ago. The New York Times. Available at: http://bits.blogs.nytimes.com/2012/02/17/the-miracle-of-digital-health-records-50-years-ago/

Mace, S., 2012. A call for intuitive EMRs. HealthLeaders Media, July 24. Retrieved from www.healthleadersmedia.com/page-4/TEC-282650/A-Call-for-Intuitive-EMRs.

Schultz J., 1988. A history of the PROMIS technology: An effective human interface. From A History of Personal Workstations. New York, NY, pp. 44–46. Available from: <www.campwoodsw.com/mentorwizard/>.

Shortliffe, T., n.d. Informatics – meaningful use. American College of Physician Executives – Health Information Technology. Accessed at: http://net.acpe.org/interact/HIT/MeaningfulUse/TranscriptionShortliffe.pdf (November 21, 2013).

Skretkowicz, V., 1993. Florence Nightingale's Notes on Nursing: the first version and edition. The Library. 15 (1), 24–46.

Topol, E., 2012. The Creative Destruction of Medicine. Basic Books, New York, NY.

US Department of Veteran Affairs, 2009. Facts about the Department of Veterans Affairs. Available at: http://www.va.gov/opa/publications/factsheets/fs_department_of_veterans_affairs.pdf.

Vaitheeswaran, V., 2010, November 22. A very big HIT. America's health industry is preparing for a $30 billion splurge on information technology. The World in 2011. The Economist Newspaper Limited.

Weed, L., 1968. Medical records that guide and teach. N. Engl. J. Med. 278 (12), 652–657.

Wikipedia.org. 2013. Mumps. Available at: http://en.wikipedia.org/wiki/MUMPS.

BIBLIOGRAPHY OF ADDITIONAL REFERENCES ON THE TOPIC OF MEDICAL RECORDS

Barnett, G.O., 1987. History of the development of medical information systems at the Laboratory of Computer Science at Massachusetts General Hospital. History of Medical Informatics. 1987, 43–49.

Bennett, K.J., Steen, C., 2010. Electronic medical record customization and the impact upon chart completion rates. Family Med. 42 (5), 338–342.

Bitton, A., Flier, L.A., Jha, A.K., 2012. Health information technology in the era of care delivery reform. To what end? J. Am. Med. Assoc. 307 (24), 2593–2594.

Blumenthal, D., Tavenner, M., 2010. The "meaningful use" regulation for electronic health records. N. Eng. J. Med. 363 (6), 501–504.

D'Avolio, L.W., 2009. Electronic medical records at a crossroads, impetus for change or missed opportunity? J. Am. Med. Assoc. 302 (10), 1109–1111.

Gill, J.M., 2009. EMRs for improving quality of care: Promise and pitfalls. Family Med. 41 (7), 513–515.

Grant, E., 2012. The promise of big data. Harvard Public Health, Spring/Summer.

Greenemeier, L., 2009, December 1. Will electronic medical records improve health care? Scientific American.

Gur-Arie, M., 2012. Why everything you know about EHR design is probably wrong. The Health Care Blog. Retrieved from <http://thehealthcare-blog.com/blog/2012/11/01/why-everything-you-know-about-ehr-design-is-probably-wrong/>.

Hardesty, L., 2012, October 21. Mining physicians' notes for medical insights. MIT News Office.

Himmelstein, D.U., Wright, A., Woolhandler, S., 2010. Hospital computing and the costs and quality of care: a National study. Am. J. Med. 123 (1), 40–46.

Holroyd-Leduc, J.M., Lorenzetti, D., Straus, S.E., Sykes, L., Quan, H., 2011. The impact of the electronic medical record on structure, process, and outcomes within primary care: a systematic review of the evidence. J. Am. Med. Inf. Assoc. 18, 732–737.

Hurtado, M., Swift, E.K., Corrigan, J.M. (Eds.), 2001. Envisioning the National Health Care Quality report. National Academy Press, Washington, DC.

Jones, S.S., Heaton, P.S., Rudin, R.R., Schneider, E.C., 2012. Unraveling the IT productivity paradox – lessons for health care. N. Engl. J. Med. 366 (24), 2243–2245.

Klompas, J., McVetta, J., Lazarus, R., Eggleston, E., Haney, G., Kruskal, B.A., et al., 2012. Integrating clinical practice and public health surveillance using electronic medical record systems. Am. J. Prevent. Med. 42 (6 Suppl. 2), S154–S162.

Kohane, I.S., Drazen, J.M., Campion, E.W., 2012. A glimpse of the next 100 years in medicine. [Editorial]. N. Engl. J. Med. 367 (26), 2538–2539.

Lin, K.W., 2012. Do electronic health records improve processes and outcomes of preventive care? [Editorial]. Am. Family Physician Web site.< www.aafp.org/afp.

Mandl, K.D., Kohane, I.S., 2012. Escaping the EHR trap – The future of health IT. N. Engl. J. Med. 366 (24), 2240–2242.

Mehta, N.B., Partin, M.H., 2007. Electronic health records: a primer for practicing physicians. Cleveland Clinic J. Med. 74 (11), 826–830.

MITRE Corporation, 2006. Electronic Health Records Overview. National Institutes of Health National Center for Research Resources. MITRE Center for Enterprise Modernization, McLean, VA.

Shekelle, P.G, Morton, S.C, Keeler, E.B., 2006. Costs and Benefits of Health Information Technology. Evidence Report/Technology Assessment No. 132. (Prepared by the Southern California Evidence-based Practice Center under Contract No. 290-02-0003.) AHRQ Publication No. 06-E006. Agency for Healthcare Research and Quality, Rockville, MD.

Trachtenbarg, D.E., 2007. EHRs fix everything – and nine other myths. Family Practice Management. Retrieved from

Tuli, K., 2009. Book review of the innovator's prescription: A disruptive solution for health care. N. Engl. J. Med. 360 (19), 2038–2039.

Wang, C.J., Huang, A.T., 2012. Integrating technology into health care. What will it take? J. Am. Med. Assoc. 307 (6), 569–570.

Zang, J., 2009. VA hospitals as digital pioneers. Wall Street J. <http://online.wsj.com/article/SB10001424052970204488304574428750133812262.html>.

Chapter 6

Open-Source EMR and Decision Management Systems

Chapter Outline

PREAMBLE

Are open-source electronic medical record (EMR) systems appropriate for use by healthcare organizations? All of the open-source EMR systems described in this chapter assume that the answer to this question is "Yes." Reasons for this conclusion are presented and discussed below, along with summaries of a number of open-source EMR systems in use today. Each healthcare organization must evaluate the pros and cons of adoption of open-source EMR systems, and judge whether or not features of specific EMR packages suit the needs of the organization. The chapter will provide the "grist" for the decision "mill" for choosing the EMR package that is suited best to the organization.

INTRODUCTION

The United Nations World Health Organization (WHO) has documented an increasing trend in epidemics of chronic disease, including heart disease, strokes, cancer, and diabetes, in many nations of the world. Many less developed countries, such as India, face epidemics of communicable diseases such as tuberculosis (TB); they also face severe problems with HIV-AIDS and respiratory disease, as well as child and maternal health problems. Some people believe that every doctor and healthcare provider caring for a patient anywhere in the world should have access to modern medical information systems. They reason that doctors and nurses need patient medical information, and software support to help provide the best prevention and medical care possible. In response to this perceived need, volunteer doctors, nurses, and developers, with the support of foundations, governments, and the World Health Organization, have formed open-source software communities to create electronic medical record EMR systems.

Over the past 40 years, open-source EMR systems have been among the leading systems in the development and evolution of medical record systems. The focus in this chapter is on free and open-source medical software systems and their potential to develop global EMR systems that are integrated with predictive analytic models and advanced decision management systems. The term "free" software means there is no charge for its use. The term "open source"

Practical Predictive Analytics and Decisioning Systems for Medicine. DOI: http://dx.doi.org/10.1016/B978-0-12-411643-6.00006-5

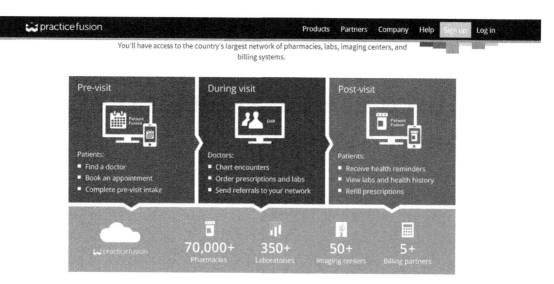

FIGURE 6.1   An example of an EMR display screen. Courtesy of PracticeFusion.com.

means that you have access to the source code: most open-source software is also free software. Some free software products do not provide access to the source code.

While some of the goals of the open-source EMR development are directed towards improving healthcare delivery in less developed nations, advances in open-source EMR systems can contribute to the development and adoption of consistent worldwide standards for the application of predictive analytics and decision management to EMR systems. Some people think that software should be free, and that the source code should be open to all programmers to see, study, change, and improve, and to build into other software products. Others doubt that quality software can be developed in a volunteer community of users and developers.

The discussion in this chapter will not include software that is free but not open source, such as the Practice Fusion EMR system. The source code for this package and others like it is not available. Companies like this give away the software package, but then sell advertising or research usage of clinical data captured. Such EMR systems are more similar to proprietary software systems, and the source code is not freely available to build and to enhance with predictive analytic and decision management systems.

High quality open-source software can be produced and will be widely used, as evidenced by the popularity of the Linux operating system, Apache web server, and MySQL database. Usage of open-source software is common in major organizations and software companies, such as Oracle and IBM (see Figure 6.1).

WHY CHOOSE AN OPEN-SOURCE EMR SOFTWARE APPLICATION?

It can be argued that only commercial software vendors can provide the level of testing and validation necessary to support efficient utilization of software applications for business and industrial use. The validity of that argument is drawn into question by the success of the Linux and MySQL applications common in many businesses and industries today. Even in the EMR field, comprehensive open-source hospital systems like WorldVistA (see below) have been developed with the close cooperation of the Veterans Administration. The success of VistA (and several other open-source EMR applications) has demonstrated that reliable open-source software can be developed and supported at a tiny fraction of the cost of commercial solutions. Some reasons for selecting open-source EMR solutions include:

1. The high cost of commercial EMR systems
2. The ability to maintain control, rather than ceding healthcare operations to a software vendor
3. The complexity of operations, tight schedules, and the need for specific customizations in healthcare organizations require considerable software configuration
4. Provision of implementation services for open-source EMR software by companies like Medsphere (www.medshpere.com)
5. Open-source software is used commonly in other commercial applications:
   a. Linux is used in a large number of industries
   b. MySQL is used in many businesses.

VistA — THE VETERANS ADMINISTRATION SYSTEM THAT STARTED IT ALL

The Veterans Health Information Systems and Technology Architecture (VistA) system is a leading EMR system developed over the past four decades by United States government employees, and it has been made available as open-source software available to hospitals and clinics globally. Hospitals in Mexico, Egypt, and the Philippines have implemented versions of VistA. The website associated with this system (www.WorldVista.org) presents comprehensive information, support documentation, and software downloads, and a history of the VistA EMR software project. The Department of Veterans Affairs (VA) teams designed the VistA system to serve VA patients in the United States. Approximately 6 million patients per year receive care in 153 VA hospitals, 773 community-based outpatient clinics, and 260 Vet Centers — one of the largest networks of hospitals and healthcare clinics in America (Department of Veterans Affairs, 2009).

The Healthcare Information and Management System Society (HIMSS) is the professional IT organization for the hospital and healthcare industries, and performs an ongoing analysis of advanced EMR systems. HIMSS ranks the VA VistA system among the most advanced and integrated EMR system implementations among American hospitals. The VA VistA system has won a number of awards, and has a comprehensive set of clinical features, but lacks a billing module because the VA does not bill its patients. VistA includes a medication bar-coding system, and VA procedures and systems have established high patient safety standards, and provide statistics on treatment results. Several open-source versions of VistA are available, including WorldVistA and OpenVistA. Besides the VA Federal system of hospitals, a number of American and overseas hospitals have implemented the open-source versions of VistA.

VistA is built upon the MUMPS (Massachusetts General Hospital Utility Multi-Programming System) technical architecture (see Chapter 5). MUMPS is a programming language with a built-in database, created in the 1960s, originally for use in the healthcare industry. Hospitals planning to implement versions of VistA have trouble finding MUMPS programmers. Some critics of the VistA system say that the VA Health System should replace the open-source VistA system with a modern proprietary software EMR system, such as Epic; however, many of the major EMR vendor systems, including Epic, are also built on the MUMPS programming language and architecture. MUMPS is very fast and is still used in high-speed and high-volume banking applications, as well as many healthcare systems.

In May 2013, an article posted to the Internet described the progress of the VA teams in incorporating predictive analytics into their clinical delivery practices (Peduli, 2013):

> *Veterans Affairs Drives Data Mining*
>
> *As of early this year, the Department of Veterans Affairs' Veterans Health Administration (VHA) had in its arsenal some 30 million veteran records, with accessible data including 3.2 billion clinical orders, 1.8 billion prescriptions and 2 billion clinical text notes (with a growth rate of 100,000 per day) ...*
>
> *In the yet-to-be-scheduled 24-month pilot, VHA will deploy advanced algorithms to sift through its Veterans Health Information Systems and Technology Architecture (VistA) EHR system. The goal is to use clinical reasoning and prediction systems — including advanced natural language processing (NLP) techniques and machine learning — to aid diagnoses, identify negative drug interactions and evaluate treatment decisions.*

FIVE OF THE BEST OPEN-SOURCE EMR SYSTEMS FOR MEDICAL PRACTICES

Several open-source EMR systems are targeted for medical practices and clinics. Highlighted below are a few of the leading open-source EMR systems that can be used globally and have the potential to support analytic models.

The OSCAR EMR System

OSCAR is the only widely-deployed open-source EMR system used in Canada. OSCAR is an acronym for Open-Source Clinical Application Resource. OSCAR was designed by doctors for doctors, for use in medical offices and by a variety of other frontline healthcare professionals in Canada and other countries. OSCAR was developed in 2001 by the Department of Family Medicine at McMaster University in Hamilton, ON, Canada (oscarcanada.org, 2001). The primary objective of the OSCAR system development was to produce a state-of the-art web-based EMR to support diverse academic and clinical functions. OSCAR has been implemented in large and small clinics across the country, primarily in the Ontario and BC areas. An increasing number of companies provide services to support server installation, maintenance, and user training and support (see Figure 6.2).

FIGURE 6.2 The OSCAR users group meeting in Vancouver, BC in 2008. *Source: www.oscarcanada.org/about-oscar.*

The user base is growing rapidly in Canada and a few other countries:

- There was a 75% increase in yearly OSCAR implementations in 2008.
- As of May 2009, OSCAR had a user base of 700–800 clinician users across BC, Alberta, Ontario, Quebec, and PEI.
- By 2011, installations included well over 1,000 physicians.
- By early 2012, the total number of users approached 700 in BC alone.

OpenEMR

OpenEMR is an open-source electronic medical record and a practice management application suite that includes patient billing and a patient portal. The www.open-emr.org/ website describes the OpenEMR community and provides full documentation, demos, and software downloads. OpenEMR is certified by:

- The US Federal Centers for Medicare and Medicaid Services (CMS) to participate in the medical practice reimbursement program for EMR systems that are implemented in accordance with the "Meaningful Use" standards and reporting requirements
- ONC Health Information Technology.

OpenEMR (Figure 6.3) enables medical practices to organize, populate, and maintain information effectively on all aspects of their patient visits, as well as supporting practice records and billing transactions. It provides comprehensive management of patient information, and is integrated with local health information exchange (HIE) networks to connect with lab and hospital data and speed referrals and prescriptions electronically. OpenEMR blends all the functions required to manage information on most aspects of a medical practice into an intuitive and user-friendly graphical interface.

OpenEMR is based on an open-source project, and therefore advances quickly via the development and contribution of new features by its supporting global community, which includes many physicians and developers.

In September 2012, InfoWorld gave OpenEMR the "Bossie Award" for the best open-source software 3 (Borck, 2012):

OpenEMR

This well-established app for small healthcare practitioners is an easily customized PHP/MySQL stack packed with features for managing medical practices. OpenEMR has everything from electronic medical records management to scheduling, billing, and reporting. One of the most impressive features is the onboard rules engine, which can generate alerts and workflows based on real-time clinical data like patient vitals, prescriptions, and lab results. The project team has been busy this year releasing performance enhancements, a virtual appliance, support for 19 languages, and a mobile front end to calendar and appointment schedule.

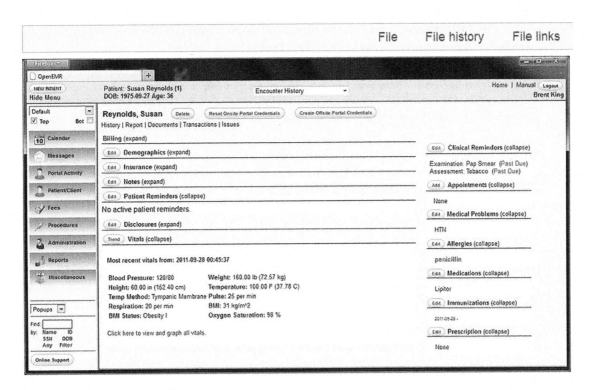

FIGURE 6.3 The OpenEMR Patient Summary screen.

OpenEMR GLOBAL PROJECTS

Peace Corps

The Peace Corps (PC) plans to deploy a comprehensive PC electronic medical record (PC-EMR) system to serve its volunteers stationed in 77 developing countries in fiscal 2013. Many of the developing countries in Africa and Asia where Peace Corp volunteers work have low-bandwidth connections to the Internet. In the field, Peace Corps staff will use the PC-EMR system on a laptop or mobile device. They will record basic medical information and synchronize it to OpenEMR, an open-source EMR and practice management system (Mosquera, 2013).

OpenMRS by Partners in Health

Partners in Health (PIH) is an international non-governmental health organization, based in Boston, that operates clinics and healthcare programs focused on helping the poor in developing countries to have access to modern scientific health care and preventive care. As a non-profit charity, PIH has focused on health challenges among the poorest nations and populations and operated successful programs and clinics in rural villages in Haiti, South America, Russia, and Africa.

Mission of Partners in Health

Partners in Health strives to bring the benefits of modern medical science to those most in need of them. Partnering with Harvard University and other institutions and research hospitals, PIH teams draw on the resources of the world's leading medical and academic institutions. PIH team members have focused on improving health systems in the world's poorest and sickest communities.

Since 2000, the challenge of making HIV and TB treatment available in poor countries has led to a new emphasis on improving healthcare delivery and prevention. PIH health programs focus on utilizing modern technology as a means to improve clinical care and program management.

In 2001, Partners in Health designed and deployed its first web-based electronic medical record (EMR) system. PIH's initial EMR system was implemented to manage the treatment of patients with multidrug-resistant tuberculosis (MDR-TB) at PIH's sister organization in Peru, Socios En Salud (SES). Later, the Medical Informatics team adapted this EMR to support PIH's HIV treatment programs in rural Haiti. In both countries, the original PIH EMR has proved to be a valuable clinical and program management tool. (Partners in Helath, 2013).

OpenMRS captures information that is used to track patient care and clinical outcomes in PIH clinics. Doctors, nurses and support staff analyze [and] aggregate results and forecast drug inventory needs, and generate required reports for funding agencies. PIH teams designed OpenMRS to function when not connected to a network, using an application that allows data to be entered and viewed when the Internet is unavailable. Later OpenMRS synchronizes the data when the connection is restored.

In 2004, PIH took advantage of an exciting opportunity to partner and refine its EMR, creating a new open-source version that is flexible, scalable, and adaptable. The first ideas and prototype of OpenMRS were conceived by Paul Biondich and Burke Mamlin from the Regenstrief Institute at the University of Indiana; the Regenstrief Institute has been a pioneer in developing medical informatics systems. The collaborative EMR product is a project called OpenMRS (Open Medical Records System) that combines the EMR systems and prototypes developed independently by PIH and Regenstrief teams and other contributors, including the South African Medical Research Council. Many other partners and developers around the world have contributed to the OpenMRS software code. The PIH Medical Informatics team began the development of OpenMRS in late 2004, and in 2006 the new OpenMRS system was deployed in a clinic in Rwinkwavu, Rwanda. It runs on Linux, Windows, or Apple systems. The system was developed by a worldwide community of volunteers from many different backgrounds, including technology, health care, and international development.

OpenMRS is now used in over 23 countries in the developing world (Figure 6.4). Several African nations have implemented the District Health Information System (DHIS) — a highly flexible, open-source health management information system and data warehouse to track countrywide health statistics, integrated with OpenMRS.

OpenMRS is built as open-source software, which enables the system to be used widely by organizations and sites with limited funding. OpenMRS can be downloaded for free by anyone who wishes to use the system. The system is based on international HL7 open standards for medical data exchange, allowing the exchange of patient data with other medical information systems. OpenMRS does not require expert programming to add new forms or to add new diseases. Data stored in OpenMRS is coded using a "concept dictionary," representing all the possible data items that can be collected. This greatly simplifies linking to existing international medical coding systems like ICD-10.

Like the original PIH-EMR, OpenMRS retains offline data entry and local area network features, but has the clear advantages of a Java-based Internet system. Finally, OpenMRS provides tools for data analysis, reporting, and patient viewing within a single integrated system, and it has integration with the DHIS data warehousing system.

Major OpenMRS PROJECTS

Using OpenMRS since 2009, the PIH Medical Informatics team has made significant progress in the development of new form-based tools and reporting tools to allow non-programmers to report outcomes and other important data for HIV/AIDS, TB, and other diseases. In Rwanda, PIH teams have also developed tools in primary care and chronic disease management, including heart disease.

FIGURE 6.4   Data officers undertook monthly training in software features, medical terminology and new data quality tools.

The OpenMRS MDR-TB module, to track the treatment of patients with multidrug-resistant tuberculosis (MDR-TB), is now running in several countries. New OpenMRS research data management tools were implemented to track clinical research beginning in 2009 for a large NIH-funded study of MDR-TB transmission.

With support from the Canadian Government's International Development Research Centre (IDRC), the OpenMRS team launched a mentor-driven training program: initial courses were provided in Rwanda for 10 Rwandan computer science graduates. PIH is working with the Rwandan government on its plan to roll out OpenMRS to 250 clinics in Rwanda, to support HIV treatment, primary care, and other clinical problems (source: www.pih.org/pages/who-we-are/).

Funding

The PIH Medical Informatics team has received grant funding support from the Rockefeller Foundation, the International Development Research Center (IDRC), the World Health Organization (WHO), and the US Federal Centers for Disease Control and Prevention (CDC). PIH has received past funding from the Bill and Melinda Gates Foundation for its healthcare improvement and prevention programs.

PIH and OpenMRS INFORMATICS PUBLICATIONS

PIH Medical Informatics team members have published 25 peer-reviewed papers and given many presentations at international health conferences. Furthermore, PIH team members are leaders in the evaluation of medical information systems in developing countries (Partners in Health, 2013).

Raxa Project

Based upon the OpenMRS EMR system, the Raxa JSS EMR open-source software project was scheduled to be implemented during 2013 at the Jan Swasthya Sahyog (JSS), a healthcare clinic non-governmental organization (NGO) in a rural, underserved community in India. The open-source Raxa system is a health information management system designed to provide decision support to health workers, and improve patients' access to their own personal health information (www.raxa.org/). Key objectives and functionality for Raxa include the following:

- Designed with a low-literacy population in mind: JSS patients in rural India
- Includes voice recognition and speech processing capabilities
- Designed to meet the requirements of rural clinics and hospitals in India and less developed countries
- Creates a secure, web-based application, user interface
- Uses the OpenMRS system as the foundation for the overall system
- The ability to be easily enhanced and updated remotely
- Replaces paper records, including X-rays, which fade and degrade with digital records
- Storage of digital health information in a local, encrypted server
- System backs up to a secure location using cloud computing technology
- Provides artificial intelligence, clinical decision support, and analytics to physicians and nurses
- Use of SMS cell phone alerts for medications, outpatient and surgical appointments, as well as follow-up notifications and two-way communication (use MOTECH open-source features).
- Raxa uses Apache v2.0 licensing, and is available for free download. The Raxa team hopes that health systems and individual providers, clinics, and rural hospitals around the world will find value in adapting Raxa to their needs.

As of early 2014, portions have been piloted at clinics, although the website does not indicate that the full system is operational (https://github.com/Raxa/Raxa-JSS).

MOTECH in Ghana

With core grant funding from the Bill and Melinda Gates Foundation, the Grameen Foundation has launched an initiative to determine how best to use mobile phones to improve the health care of pregnant women and babies in Ghana. Pregnant women can register to receive local-language voice messages: SMS messages provide advice for healthy pregnancy, while community health workers use cell phones to record health services provided. Targeted messages and alerts are sent to pregnant women and health workers when scheduled care has been missed; follow-up is required.

The open-source Mobile Technology for Community Health (MOTECH) Suite provides a set of services encompassing the five key functional mobile health (mHealth) areas:

1. Behavior change & demand generation
2. Managing patient data
3. Improving worker performance
4. Last-mile supply chain
5. Patient adherence.

MOTECH provides a set of field-tested services to ease mHealth deployments:

- CommCare makes interactions between patients and health workers more effective and provides workforce management
- MOTECH Core allows SMS messaging to patients and connections to other systems determined by a robust, rules-based system
- OpenLMIS and CommTrack provide reporting and notifications for supply chain logistics
- InSTEDD tools speed deployment efforts to connect with mobile operators.

MOTECH has been integrated with OpenMRS, one of the most popular open-source enterprise electronic medical record (EMR) system platforms used in developing countries. MOTECH has been implemented in several developing nations to improve healthcare delivery: in India and Africa, for child and maternal care, and for TB and HIV regimen adherence.

GLOBAL OPEN-SOURCE EMR SYSTEMS AND THE FUTURE OF ANALYTICS

Considering the expected fast growth of predictive analytics to serve less developed countries, open-source software EMR systems constitute a key element in the implementation of these solutions. The combination of predictive analytics with EMR systems is an exciting prospect, which can be built quickly upon the solid foundation of open-source healthcare EMR systems. Open-source systems can share data quickly over global locations without intellectual property (IP) limitations. Examples of widespread adoption of open-source EMR applications include the following:

1. OpenEMR for medical practices was selected by the Peace Corps and HP Program in Rural India; www.open-emr.org/
2. WorldVista for complex hospitals and clinics is used by more than 100 VA hospitals and clinics and has been implemented as an open-source hospital in Mexico and other countries; www.worldvista.org/
3. OpenMRS is used in Africa, and is WHO-UN funded; http://openmrs.org/
4. DHIS district system, integrated with OpenMRS, and Data warehouse http://dhis2.org/.

It is probable that open-source software tools will be soon incorporated into open-source EMR systems to produce effective predictive analytic models that will contribute to improving the health of the poorest populations and nations. These tools can include:

1. Business intelligence and reporting tools (e.g., Eclipse)
2. Data integration tools (e.g., Pentaho)
3. Predictive analytics tools (e.g., R, RapidMiner, and Rattle)
4. "Big Data" management tools (e.g., Hadoop).

POSTSCRIPT

Open-source EMR systems are becoming very popular in less developed countries of the world. In the USA, however, many commercial EMR systems are vying for dominance in healthcare organizations that have the financial flexibility to afford them. Given an EMR system for managing healthcare data, the next issue to address is how information resident in this data base can be leveraged to aid in medical diagnosis and treatment decisions. Chapter 7 discusses the concept of evidence-based medicine (EBM), which provides the framework in which digital information can be analyzed to provide case-specific decisions for guiding the development of accurate diagnoses and appropriate treatment regimes.

REFERENCES

Borck, J., 2012. The best open source applications. InfoWorld. Available at: <www.infoworld.com/slideshow/65165/bossie-awards-2012-the-best-open-source-applications-202530#slide21/>.

Department of Veterans Affairs., 2009. Fact sheet: facts about the Department of Veterans Affairs. <www.va.gov/opa/publications/factsheets/fs_department_of_veterans_affairs.pdf/>.

Mosquera, M., 2013. govhealthit.com: Government HealthIT, Peace corps plans EHR system in 2013. Available at: <www.govhealthit.com/news/peace-corps-plans-ehr-system-2013/>.

Oscarcanada.org., 2001. OSCAR project: brief overview. Available at: <www.oscarcanada.org/>.

Partners in Health., 2013. Electronic medical records. Retrieved from <http://www.pih.org/blog/university-hospitals-open-source-emr-a-model-for-evidence-based-health-care>.

Peduli, L., 2013. Veterans affairs drives data mining. Clinical Innovation and Technology . Available at: http://www.clinical-innovation.com/topics/analytics-quality/veterans-affairs-drives-data-mining.

Chapter 7

Evidence-Based Medicine

"I thought [evidence-based medicine] was silly. If medicine isn't based on evidence what is it based on?" — *focus group participant.*

(Ross *et al.*, 2009)

Chapter Outline

PREAMBLE

For thousands of years, traditional medical care was dependent upon the judgment and experience of the physician. The problem with this approach was that treatment varied widely, and it was largely unavailable to poor people. Collection of medical information into written documents helped to standardize treatments, and increase the general quality of health care. Even under this approach to health care, information from past cases was vended largely in the form of averages and trends among multiple cases. A superior approach is to customize medical diagnosis and treatment according to information specific to the case at hand. This approach is called evidence-based medicine (EBM). This chapter describes the elements of EBM, and how they can be marshaled to support predictive analytics, which will transform medical practice from reactive responses to existing conditions, to proactive measures to prevent medical conditions from occurring or becoming worse.

INTRODUCTION

Evidence-based medicine refers to the practice of medicine from the primary basis of empirical evidence gathered from cases in the past. It is distinguished from the historical practice of medicine primarily in its emphases on objective elements of decision-making (data, analyses, and conclusions), rather than subjective elements (intuition, judgment, and "informed" guesses). EBM appears to be the current "rage" in professional and regulatory circles to such an extent that historical medical practice based on "best" practices appears to be in danger of being shoved aside. The subjective role of the physician should not be discarded, though. Elements of objective data and subjective judgment should be combined into a holistic view of the medical reality the physician is attempting to diagnose and treat. This chapter will present the case that EBM is a necessary (and indeed the primary) basis for medical decision-making, but these objective elements must be combined with subjective judgment for the physician to treat the person, not just the disease or disability.

Practical Predictive Analytics and Decisioning Systems for Medicine. DOI: http://dx.doi.org/10.1016/B978-0-12-411643-6.00007-7

It is estimated that 30% of US healthcare spending — some $700 billion a year — is spent on tests, treatments, and procedures that provide little or no value (Beck, 2009).

GEODEMOGRAPHIC ELEMENTS OF MEDICAL TREATMENT

The *Dartmouth Atlas of Health Care* has demonstrated clearly that "geography is destiny" when it comes to health care: "The amount of care consumed by Americans is significantly dependent on where they live, on the capacity of the healthcare system where they live, and on the practice styles of local physicians" (Wennberg, 1998). The *Dartmouth Atlas* documents the wide geographic variation in the use of various treatments and diagnostic tests, and overall cost of care which is not explained by patient age, sex, or disease prevalence, suggesting that services are either over-utilized or under-utilized. Furthermore, results of some studies show that variation among specialists who work in the same group practice may be as great as variation among specialists across the entire state (IOM, 2013).

Most practicing physicians, when asked if they practice EB, respond that they always practice "evidence-based medicine"; however, the observed variation in practice suggests otherwise (Mayer, 2010, p. 17). According to Dr. David Eddy, professor of health policy and management at Duke University, "only about 15% of medical interventions are supported by solid scientific evidence" (Smith, 1991). This is partly because only 1 percent of the articles in medical journals are scientifically sound, and partly because many treatments have never been assessed at all (Smith, 1991, p. 798).

The Good Stewardship Working Group, as presented in the Archives of Internal Medicine (Kale *et al.*, 2011), presented the top five overused clinical activities in primary care as determined by consensus of a physician panel. These are commonly performed or ordered activities in primary care that were felt to provide little benefit to patients. The activities include:

1. Routine laboratory studies — complete blood count
2. Routine laboratory studies — urinalysis
3. Antibiotics for children with pharyngitis (non-strep)
4. Use of brand-name drugs (statins) for lowering cholesterol
5. Annual ECGs (electrocardiograms).

They estimated the annual cost to be almost $7 billion (Kale *et al.*, 2011).

Figure 7.1 illustrates (humorously) the rather "Wheel of Fortune" approach that appears to characterize cancer treatment in America.

According to a column in the *Wall Street Journal*, "Heart disease is among the most studied illnesses in all of medicine, yet just 11% of more than 2,700 recommendations approved by cardiologists for treating heart patients are supported by high quality scientific testing, according to new research" (Winslow, 2009).

A recent study by Prasad and colleagues (2013) reviewed 10 years of articles published in the prestigious *New England Journal of Medicine*, and concluded that about 40% of current medical practices may not be effective, 38%

FIGURE 7.1 The way many people treat non-evidence-based decision-making (Millenson, 2008).

only likely effective, and 22% inconclusive. A project sponsored by the *British Medical Journal* reviewed 3000 medical practices, finding that only about a third are effective and half were of unknown effectiveness (Prasad *et al.*, 2013). Medical textbooks are often outdated by the time they are published (or shortly thereafter). The medical literature has far exceeded an individual's capacity to assimilate relative information. As of 2005, approximately 10 million articles had been indexed in MEDLINE®, and 2 million new articles are published each year in 20,000 journals (Barker and Carter, 2005).

An oft-repeated anecdote during orientation for freshmen medical students (as was your author) — "Half of what you will learn in the next 4 years will be outdated by the time you graduate" — also speaks to the rapid change in medical information. (*Although that statement is likely largely true, the problem is we don't know which half is being referred to!*)

HOW CAN WE DEFINE THE NATURE AND BOUNDARIES OF EBM?

Clearly there is a systemic problem in health care!

As a way to address this obvious problem, a new paradigm in medical care evolved in the early 1990s. This new way of thinking was labeled "evidence-based medicine" (EBM).

According to Sackett *et al.* (1996), evidence-based medicine (EBM) is "the conscientious, explicit, and judicious use of the best evidence in making decisions about the care of individual patients." Stated another way, it is about applying the best evidence that can be found to the patient with a medical problem, resulting in the best possible care for each patient.

Another definition:

Evidence-based medicine is the use of mathematical estimates of the risk of benefit and harm, derived from high-quality research on population samples, to inform clinical decision-making in the diagnosis, investigation or management of individual patients.

(Greenhalgh, 2010, p. 1).

The defining feature of EBM, then, is the use of figures derived from research on populations to inform decisions about individuals (Greenhalgh, 2010, p. 1).

GENERAL PROBLEMS WITH EBM

Amid all the enthusiasm for EBM, there are legitimate concerns such as those pointed out by Feinstein and Horowitz (1997) in an article in the *American Journal of Medicine*. Some of the limitations include:

1. Published results based often on the "average randomized patient"
2. Lack of consideration of post-randomized events leading to modified treatment
3. Restriction of scope and quality of evidence gathered.

EVIDENCE-BASED MEDICINE AND ANALYTICS

So what does that have to do with analytics? Establishing evidence or proof of effectiveness (or lack thereof) for various treatments requires a great deal of data, gathered ideally through controlled prospective trials, systematic reviews, or *meta-analyses* (analyses of other analyses). Such trials are very expensive and often take years to complete. A good introduction to meta-analysis of clinical trials data is provided by DerSimonian and Laird (1986). A good recent example of meta-analysis is provided by Murray *et al.* (2008).

The emerging field of data analytics offers the possibility of *access* to and *analysis* of more data in a short period of time and, through the application of new analytical methods, provision of "evidence" of effectiveness of proposed treatments. Using data mining techniques, information can be assimilated from multiple sources (electronic medical records, labs, pharmacy, billing, radiology) and analyzed for patterns, trends, or correlations leading to reliable conclusions that can be applied easily to patient care. Unlike routine statistical analysis, which relies on structured, discrete data, analytics can use elements of "unstructured" data (such as free text), which is the state of most medical information. An excellent example of real-time analysis for clinical decision-making in the absence of traditional evidence is described by Frankovich *et al.* (2011), at Stanford, in which a treatment decision was synthesized utilizing their EMR system and data warehouse platform. In less than 4 hours they were able to analyze an "electronic cohort" to derive the best "evidence" for treating their patient.

The transition of data from refuse to riches has been key in the Big Data revolution of other industries.

(Murdoch and Detsky, 2013).

THE PATH TO EVIDENCE

Throughout most of history, medicine has been based primarily on observation, intuition, and anecdotes. The concept of the foundational methodology of evidence-based medicine, the *randomized controlled trial*, however, is not new.

The idea of a randomized trial extends back to the mid-17th century. Jan Baptista van Helmont, the Flemish physician and chemist, openly opposed the centuries-old practice of blood-letting for the treatment of most illness. In response to his critics, he proposed a clinical trial (some say a wager was involved) in which 200–500 poor people would be divided into two groups by casting lots (i.e., randomized). He would treat his patients without phlebotomy, while his critics would use as much blood-letting as they thought appropriate. The subsequent number of funerals would be the measure of success or failure (Magner, 1992). Apparently, this trial was never actually carried out.

It was another 100 years before the first recorded "comparative clinical trial" was performed in 1747 when the Royal Navy surgeon, James Lind, showed that scurvy could be prevented by consuming oranges or lemons. It was somewhat randomized, but not blinded. However, his findings were initially rejected by the Navy and would not be recognized as the cure for scurvy and widely implemented until over 40 years later.

Magner (1992) claimed that "Interestingly, blood letting contributed to the death of George Washington in 1799."

In 1836, Pierre Charles Alexander Louis (considered arguably as the father of epidemiology) conducted a trial to determine whether timing or amount of blood-letting for pneumonia made any difference to the duration of disease (Rangachari, 1997*)*. In this and other studies he introduced the concept of statistical analysis (often referred to as the "numerical method") to the evaluation of medical treatment. He concluded that blood-letting was of no value. Even though the results of his experiment were widely disseminated in the medical community in France and abroad (he was particularly popular with many American doctors), blood-letting continued to be the predominant treatment for a variety of conditions until the end of the century. Louis believed absolutely that data analysis was essential, writing that "a therapeutic agent cannot be employed with any discrimination or probability of success in a given case, unless its general efficacy, in analogous cases, has been previously ascertained", and thus, "without the aid of statistics nothing like real medicine is possible" (Rangachari, 1997).

Claude Bernard, a French physiologist and younger contemporary of Louis, praised the experiment:

We may be subject daily to the greatest illusions about the value of treatment, if we do not have recourse to comparative experiment. I shall recall only one recent example concerning the treatment of pneumonia. Comparative experiment showed, in fact, that treatment of pneumonia by bleeding, which was believed most efficacious, is a mere therapeutic illusion.

(Morabia, 2007; original source Bernard, 1865).

Bernard was an early proponent of evidence derived from comparative trials:

For comparative experiment is the sine qua non *of scientific experimental medicine; without it a physician walks at random and becomes the plaything of endless illusions. A physician, who tries a remedy and cures his patients, is inclined to believe that the cure is due to his treatment. Physicians often pride themselves on curing all their patients with a remedy that they use. But the first thing to ask them is whether they have tried doing nothing, i.e., not treating other patients; for how can they otherwise know whether the remedy or nature cured them?*

(Morabia, 2007).

The numerical method was highly controversial and met with a great deal of resistance. Criticism was strong and pointed: "The physician called to treat a sick man was not an actuary advising a company to accept or decline 'risks' but someone who dealt with a specific individual at a vulnerable moment." And, "they were not prepared to discard therapies validated by both tradition and their own experience on account of somebody else's numbers" (Rangachari, 1997).

The process of evaluating medical therapies continued to be largely anecdotal, based primarily on empirical observation and personal experience until the mid-1900s.

A pivotal event for modern clinical research occurred in 1948 with the publishing, in the UK, of the first double-blinded randomized controlled trial, which was designed by the British statistician Austin Bradford Hill. The study compared the treatment of pulmonary tuberculosis with streptomycin versus bed rest alone (Stolberg *et al.*, 2004). The trial succeeded in demonstrating both the effectiveness of the treatment for tuberculosis and the utility of the randomized controlled trial (Jones *et al.*, 2011). This achievement earned him the title "the father of modern clinical research," and ultimately established the randomized controlled trial as the gold standard for clinical research.

The first significant use of the randomized controlled trial in the United States was in 1954. This was the largest and most expensive medical experiment in human history. The trial was carried out to assess the effectiveness of the Salk vaccine as a protection against paralysis or death from poliomyelitis. Because the annual incidence of polio was 1 per 2,000, a very large population was necessary. Around 2 million children were enrolled at a cost of 5 million dollars. The experiment was a success in proving the effectiveness of the Salk vaccine and in helping to establish the randomized controlled trial as a viable clinical research method (Chen, 2003).

WHAT IS A RANDOMIZED CONTROLLED TRIAL?

The randomized controlled trial (RCT) has become the cornerstone for evidence-based medicine and clinical research in general. Some consider it to be the most important development in modern medicine, because the results are used to directly affect clinical practice. The RCT can be used to evaluate the effectiveness of treatments, including drugs, surgery, or other interventions, as well as diagnostic tests and screening programs. The power comes from randomization and "blinding." The randomization process is a formulaic method of creating groups of study participants who ideally are equivalent in every way except for the intervention under study. Proper randomization minimizes the number of variables that have to be considered and minimizes bias. Blinding, when possible, also minimizes bias and helps to limit subjective effects that could alter the outcome of the study. Most blinded studies are "double-blind," meaning that neither the participants nor any caregivers are aware of which intervention is being used.

Another essential foundational tool for EBM was introduced in the early 1970s with the publication of the book *Effectiveness and Efficiency: Random reflections on health services* by Dr. Archie Cochrane (1972). In the book, he demonstrated the value of systematic reviews of literature on a particular medical topic and made a rational argument for studying and applying the best evidence to a given clinical situation (Mayer, 2010). As interest in the concept of systematic reviews grew throughout the world, an Internet-based network of interested people was formed in 1992 and came to be known as "The Cochrane Collaboration." This is considered to be one of the top sources of information related to evidence-based medicine, through the preparation and publication of *Cochrane Reviews*. The Cochrane Collaboration website claims to have the largest collection of records of randomized controlled trials in the world (The Cochrane Collaboration, 2013).

In 1992, the Evidence-Based Medicine Working Group at McMaster University introduced EBM into medical education in a article in the *Journal of the American Medical Association* (Evidence-Based Medicine Working Group, 1992). This article contains a template for other programs to adopt, and, in support of its adoption, authors referred to EBM as a new paradigm developing in medical practice. This emerging practice de-emphasizes intuition, unsystematic clinical experience, and pathophysiological rationale as sufficient grounds for clinical decision-making, and stresses rather the examination of evidence from clinical research. This information must be gleaned from a literature search, and be composed into formal rules of application. EBM requires new skills to be developed in the physician regarding literature search and comparative analysis of evidence. The result will be clinical decisions based primarily on objective evidence, rather than subjective judgment. Intuition must still play a part in the decision regarding who applies evidence-based decisions, and when.

A new paradigm for medical practice is emerging. Evidence-based medicine de-emphasizes intuition, unsystematic clinical experience, and pathophysiologic rationale as sufficient grounds for clinical decision making and stresses the examination of evidence from clinical research. Evidence-based medicine requires new skills of the physician, including efficient literature searching and the application of formal rules of evidence evaluating the clinical literature.

(Evidence-Based Medicine Working Group, 1992, p. 2420)

While acknowledging the value and necessity of clinical experience and understanding of pathophysiology, this new paradigm in medical education places a significant emphasis on reading and interpreting medical literature from an evidence-based perspective. This emphasis requires a commitment to lifelong learning. In this regard, EBM is not unlike legal practice. As laws have extensive history and are very dynamic, so too is the evidence landscape of medicine. Physicians must be willing and able to prepare for a medical judgment (for diagnosis or treatment) in a similar fashion to how a lawyer prepares for a case in court. For EBM, however, the presiding judges are truth and effectiveness.

The article concludes:

Evidence-based medicine deals directly with the uncertainties of clinical medicine and has the potential for transforming the education and practice of the next generation of physicians.

(p. 2424).

And:

Evidence-based medicine will require new skills for the physician, skills that residency programs should be equipped to teach. While strategies for inculcating the principles of evidence-based medicine remain to be refined, initial experience has revealed a number of effective approaches. Incorporating these practices into postgraduate medical education and continuing to work on their further development will result in more rapid dissemination and integration of the new paradigm into medical practice.

(pp. 2424–25).

The concept of evidence based medicine rapidly became an integral component of the medical education curriculum: "Today, nearly all US medical schools report teaching evidence-based medicine as part of a required course, and the Accreditation Council for Graduate Medical Education (ACGME) has incorporated EBM into US residency training requirements" (Rysavy, 2013, p. 4).

The popularity of EBM rapidly spread throughout the medical world. In 1992, in PubMed, there were only two articles using the phrase "evidence-based medicine"; by 1997 there were more than 1,000 articles using the term. Likewise, a 2004 survey found 24 dedicated textbooks, 9 academic journals, and 62 Internet sites dedicated to the concept of EBM (Zimerman, 2013).

"Evidence-based" has even become a popular buzzword in other industries, with numerous articles citing the term in fields such as management, banking, leadership, architectural design, nutrition, therapy, education, and advertising.

IF NOT EVIDENCE BASED, THEN WHAT?

The new paradigm of EBM in medical care implies that much of medical decision-making in the past (and to a large degree what is still done today) is not based on evidence, but rather is based on non-objective methodologies (Greenhalgh, 2010) including:

1. *Decision-making by anecdote.* In this scenario, the clinician recalls how one or more other patients in the past have responded in a similar situation. Or the story could come from a colleague or medical school professor.
2. *Decision-making by collecting articles.* Here, the practitioner relies on information gleaned from a random collection of articles, often from a single recently published study.
3. *Decision-making by GOBSAT* (good old boys sat around a table). Often referred to as a "consensus statement" or "expert opinion." A group of respected experts gather for a sort of round table discussion expressing their own experiences and viewpoints, frequently spouting articles and studies off the top of their heads, and to the degree that there is overlapping agreement a declaration is made which may then become a protocol or guideline. A particular problem with this method is the vulnerability to bias and conflicts of interest.

In the absence of better data and evidence, these approaches are not necessarily unreasonable. However, evidence-based medicine seeks to bring more objective rationality to the decision-making process.

In a tongue-in-cheek manner, Isaacs and Fitzgerald (1999) presented alternatives to evidence-based medicine:

1. *Eminence-based medicine.* Experience trumps evidence. The more senior the colleague, the less importance he or she places on the need for anything as mundane as evidence. The white hair is the icon of this status.
2. *Vehemence-based medicine.* Volume is the key to convincing more timid colleagues.
3. *Eloquence-based medicine.* Sartorial elegance and verbal eloquence are powerful substitutes for evidence.
4. *Providence-based medicine.* If the caring practitioner has no idea of what to do next, the decision may be best left in the hands of the Almighty.
5. *Diffidence-based medicine.* Some doctors see a problem and look for an answer; others merely see a problem. The diffident doctor may do nothing from a sense of despair . . . .
6. *Nervousness-based medicine.* Fear of litigation is a powerful stimulus to over investigation and overtreatment. In an atmosphere of litigation phobia, the only bad test is the test you didn't think of ordering.
7. *Confidence-based medicine.* This is restricted to surgeons.

This list was delivered in the form of satire — but, as in much satire, there is an elements of truth in it.

THE EBM PROCESS

The implementation of EBM should follow a rational process. Mayer (2010) proposes an EBM process of six steps.

1. Craft a clinical question. Often called the PICO or PICOT formulation, this is the most important step, since it sets the stage for a successful answer to the clinical predicament. It includes four or sometimes five *elements*:
   - the patient
   - the intervention
   - the comparison
   - the outcome of interest
   - the timeframe.
2. Search the medical literature for those studies that are most likely to give the best evidence. This step requires good searching skills using medical informatics.
3. Find the study that is most able to answer this question. Determine the magnitude and precision of the final results.
4. Perform a critical appraisal of the study to determine the validity of the results. Look for sources of bias that may represent a fatal flaw in the study.
5. Determine how the results will help you in caring for your patient.
6. Finally, you should evaluate the results of applying the evidence to your patient or patient population.

Certainly, there were data, studies, and evidence prior to the era of evidence-based medicine. The difference is the rigorous analysis evidence-based medicine brings to the data with the recognition that all evidence is not equal. Indeed, many (if not most) of the studies published fail to meet any criteria for high quality (Ioannidis, 2005).

A central tenet of the EBM process is the grading of the evidence. In fact, the very backbone of EBM is the strength of the evidence, which is directly dependent on the quality of the data. There is overall general agreement on the relative strengths of data, as illustrated in the hierarchy of evidence graphic in Figure 7.2.

The strongest evidence comes from randomized controlled trials and systematic reviews including meta-analysis, while the weakest comes from single case studies (Hayes and Levine, 2011).

Evaluating the quality of a study is the most challenging task in the process, and several grading systems have been developed to assist. The first major US grading system was the US Preventive Services Task Force (USPSTF), published in 1989, which was based on a study's ability to eliminate bias and confounding factors (Gugiu and Gugiu, 2010). Its primary purpose is to assess the merits of preventive measures, including screening tests, counseling, immunizations, and preventive medications. It is widely used, and is constantly being updated. From the website:

> *The USPSTF is an independent panel of non-Federal experts in prevention and evidence-based medicine and is composed of primary care providers (such as internists, pediatricians, family physicians, gynecologists/obstetricians, nurses, and health behavior specialists).*

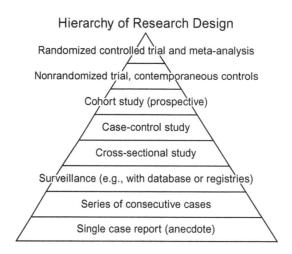

Hierarchy of Research Design

Randomized controlled trial and meta-analysis

Nonrandomized trial, contemporaneous controls

Cohort study (prospective)

Case-control study

Cross-sectional study

Surveillance (e.g., with database or registries)

Series of consecutive cases

Single case report (anecdote)

FIGURE 7.2 The relative strengths of data.

The USPSTF conducts scientific evidence reviews of a broad range of clinical preventive health care services (such as screening, counseling, and preventive medications) and develops recommendations for primary care clinicians and health systems. These recommendations are published in the form of "Recommendation Statements."

(http://www.uspreventiveservicestaskforce.org/index.html).

The most popular guideline for evaluating evidence is the Grades of Recommendation, Assessment, Development, and Evaluation (GRADE), published in 2005:

Of all the guidelines reviewed, the GRADE has the most sophisticated method for evaluating methodological quality. It not only includes a system for upgrading and downgrading studies but also possesses a method for assessing risk of bias ...

(Gugiu and Gugiu, 2010, p. 236).

EVIDENCE AT THE BEDSIDE

The ultimate goal of EBM, from an earlier stated definition, is to assist the practitioner in applying the best evidence that can be found to the patient with a medical problem, resulting in the best possible care for each patient. Unfortunately, even when there is broad agreement regarding the benefit of a studied treatment or test, the translation of evidence to action at the bedside has been a disappointing process. Studies indicate it takes an average of 17 years for new evidence to be used routinely at the bedside (Ortiz and Clancy, 2003).

There are many reasons why evidence is not used (Hayes and Levine, 2011):

1. Our affinity for new and "high-tech" tests and treatments
2. Lack of understanding about what constitutes high quality evidence
3. Financial and other conflicts of interest
4. Historical practice patterns and preferences
5. Definitive medicine
6. Market forces
7. Patient expectations.

Evidence not only indicates what interventions do work, but it also frequently demonstrates what does not work and perhaps should be abandoned. What initially appeared to be a plausible treatment or test that is used for many years may later be shown to be ineffective when appropriate studies are carried out. And, just as there is often reluctance to adopt new therapies as evidence indicates, there is possibly more reluctance to stop doing things that evidence indicates do not work and in fact may be harmful or cause overtreatment. Examples include performing Pap smears yearly on low-risk women, PSA testing for prostate cancer, use of cardiac stents in stable patients, and use of vertebroplasty for vertebral compression fractures.

When we meet a fact which contradicts a prevailing theory, we must accept the fact and abandon the theory, even when the theory is supported by great names and generally accepted.

Claude Bernard (1813−1878).

WHAT DO PATIENTS THINK?

While EBM is all the buzz in the healthcare world, surveys indicate the public at large is highly skeptical of the concept. Generally they have no real understanding of what it is and are confused by the implication that medical decisions are based on anything but evidence:

Whereas Washington, DC is abuzz with efforts to put science back in medicine, these consumers did not know it had ever left.

(Ross *et al.*, 2009).

A focus group study by Ross and colleagues revealed the significant language gap that exists between medical providers and patients with the healthcare dialect in general, including EBM. Respondents thought the term implied "a 'one-size-fits-all' approach that would undermine personalized medical care." And, although "Some found the term reassuring, associating it with rigorous and responsible medical treatment ... others viewed it as redundant and anxiety provoking because they assume that all medicine is anchored by research" (Ross *et al.*, 2009).

Another study, by Carman *et al.* (2010), found that there is a fundamental disconnect between the central tenets of evidence-based health care and the knowledge, values, and beliefs held by many consumers. Common terms like "medical evidence," "quality guidelines," and "quality standards" were "unfamiliar and confusing." Also, as in the previous study, there was an assumption that all providers based decisions on solid evidence. Other participant beliefs that were contrary to EBM fundamentals included:

1. All care meets minimum quality standards
2. Medical guidelines are inflexible
3. More care, and newer care, is better
4. More costly care is better.

Following from these beliefs, it is clear that patients may well interpret the application of evidence-based principles as a way to justify denying them necessary treatment. It is also clear that new approaches are needed to educate patients about the value and potential benefits of evidence-based medicine.

EVIDENCE-BASED MEDICINE VERSUS THE ART OF MEDICINE

Medicine is often described as an amalgam of art and science. The science of evidence-based medicine, with its mathematical rigors, can show us the effect of a given treatment on the average patient, while the art of medicine involves discerning whether that treatment would benefit the individual patient. Indeed, the application of evidence-based medicine is particularly challenging in patients with multiple chronic diseases. Randomized controlled trials are often not suitable for the realities of clinical practice, given patient heterogeneity, co-morbidities, and the use of multiple medications. In this scenario, with multiple variables, it is difficult or impossible to know if the results of a study would apply to a given patient (Vohra and Punja 2013).

In the clinic, the art of medicine is ideally applied using the best evidence available to make a "best guess" as to the most appropriate treatment for the patient, often involving trial and error, and hopefully minimizing the error.

PREDICTIVE ANALYTICS AND EBM

Returning to the earlier question regarding evidence-based medicine and predictive analytics, EBM is yet to be proven in itself as a better way to practice medicine. So far, there are no controlled trials proving the superiority of the EBM approach. It is plausible, however, to theorize that, using the tools of analytics, it may be possible to gather and analyze data in ways that allow more rapid and complete determination of the best evidence. Even so, there will still be the challenge of translating that knowledge to action at the bedside.

> Clinical decision-making has been described as "a balancing act, of art and science, intuition and analysis, gut instinct and evidence, experience and knowledge."

(Woolever, 2008).

POSTSCRIPT

With the prospect of the availability of a huge amount of digital medical data resulting from implementation of the Affordable Care Act (ACA), and the promise of significant benefits accruing from EBM, new coding standards had to be designed to handle these resources. This need resulted in the development of the ICD-10 standards, an upgrade to the previous ICD-9 standards followed previously. Chapter 8 describes these new standards, and relates them to the specific information requirements of predictive analytics.

REFERENCES

Barker, F., Carter, B., 2005. Synthesizing medical evidence: systematic reviews and meta-analyses. Neurosurg. Focus. 19 (4), 1.

Beck, M., 2009. Injecting Value Into Medical Decisions. Wall Street J. Retrieved from http://online.wsj.com/.

Bernard, C., 1865. Introduction à l'étude de la médecine expérimentale. Paris.

Carman, K.L., Maurer, M., Mathews Yegian, J., Dardess, P., McGee, J., Evers, M., et al., 2010. Evidence That Consumers Are Skeptical About Evidence-Based Health Care. Health Affairs. Accessed at <http://content.healthaffairs.org/content/early/2010/06/03/hlthaff.2009.0296.full.html/>.

Chen, T.T., 2003. History of statistical thinking in medicine. In: Lu, Y., Fang, J.-Q. (Eds.), Advanced Medical Statistics. World Scientific Publishing Co. Pte. Ltd, Singapore, Ch. 1.

Cochrane, A.L., 1972. Effectiveness and Efficiency: Random Reflections on Health Services. Nuffield Provincial Hospitals Trust, London, UK.

DerSimonian, R., Laird, N., 1986. Meta-analysis in clinical trials. Control. Clin. Trials. 7 (3), 177–188.

Evidence-Based Medicine Working Group, 1992. Evidence-Based Medicine – A New Approach to Teaching the Practice of Medicine. J. Am. Med. Assoc. 268 (17), 2420–2425.

Feinstein, A., Horwitz, R., 1997. Problems in the "Evidence" of "Evidence-Based Medicine". Am. J. Med. 103 (6), 529–535.

Frankovich, J., Longhurst, C.A., Sutherland, S.M., 2011. Evidence-based medicine in the EMR Era. N. Engl. J. Med. 365 (19), 1758–1759.

Greenhalgh, T., 2010. How to Read a Paper: The basics of evidence-based medicine. Fourth Ed. John Wiley & Sons Ltd, Chichester, UK.

Gugiu, P.C., Gugiu, M.R., 2010. A critical appraisal of standard guidelines for grading levels of evidence. Evaluation & the Health Professions. 33, 233–255.

Hayes, W.S., Levine, S.A., 2011. The Value of Evidence. Winifred S. Hayes, Inc, Accessed at www.hayesinc.com.

Ioannidis, J.P.A., 2005. Why most published research findings are false. PLoS Med. 2 (8), e124, Accessed at www.plosmedicine.org.

IOM (Institute of Medicine), 2013. Interim report of the Committee on Geographic Variation in Health Care Spending and Promotion of High-Value Care: Preliminary committee observations. National Academies PressInstitute of Medicine), 2013, Washington, DC.

Isaacs, D., Fitzgerald, D., 1999. Seven alternatives to evidence based medicine. Br. Med. J. 319, 18–25.

Jones, T.W., West, C.P., Newman, J.S., 2011. In Search of the facts: evidence-based medicine through the ages. J. Clin. Outcomes Manage. 18 (5), 205–210.

Kale, M.S., Bishop, T.F., Federman, A.D., Keyhani, S., 2011. Top 5 Lists Top $5 Billion. Arch. Int. Med. 171 (20), 1856–1858.

Magner, L.N., 1992. A History of Medicine. Marcel Dekker, Inc, New York, NY.

Mayer, D., 2010. Essential Evidence-Based Medicine. Second Ed. Cambridge University Press, New York, NY.

Millenson, M., 2008. Evidence of a Need for Change. Pacific Standard. Accessed from <www.psmag.com/health/evidence-of-a-need-for-change-4241/>.

Morabia, A., 2007. Claude Bernard, statistics, and comparative trials. JLL Bulletin: Commentaries on the history of treatment evaluation. Accessed at <www.jameslindlibrary.org/>.

Murdoch, T., Detsky, A., 2013. The inevitable application of big data to health care. J. Am. Med. Assoc. 309 (13), 1351.

Murray, D., Pals, S., Biltstein, J., Alfano, C., Lehman, J., 2008. Design and analysis of group-randomized trials in cancer: a review of current practices. J. Nat. Cancer Inst. 100 (7), 483–491.

Ortiz, E., Clancy, C.M., 2003. Use of Information Technology to improve the quality of health care in the United States. Health Serv. Res. 38 (2), xi–xxii.

Prasad, V., Vandross, A., Toomey, C., Cheung, M., Rho, J., Quinn, S., et al., 2013. A Decade of Reversal: an analysis of 146 contradicted medical practices. Mayo Clinic Proc. 88 (8), 790–798.

Rangachari, P.K., 1997. Evidence-based medicine: old French wine with a new Canadian label? J. R. Soc. Med. 90, 280–284.

Ross, M., Igus, T., Gomez, S., 2009. From our lips to whose ears? Consumer reaction to our current health care dialect. Permanente J. 13 (1), 8–16.

Rysavy, M., 2013. Evidence-based medicine: A Science of uncertainty and an art of probability. Virtual Mentor. 15 (1), 4–8.

Sackett, D.L., Rosenberg, W.M., Gray, J.A., Haynes, R.B., Richardson, W.S., 1996. "Evidence based medicine: what it is and what it isn't". Br. Med. J. 312, 71.

Smith, R., 1991. Where is the wisdom . . .? Br. Med. J. 303, 798–799.

Stolberg, H.O., Norman, G., Trop, I., 2004. Fundamentals of clinical research for radiologists: Randomized controlled trials. Am. J. Roentgenol. 183, 1539–1544.

The Cochrane Collaboration, 2013. Retrieved from www.cochrane.org/about-us.

Vohra, S., Punja, S., 2013. N-of-1 Trials: Individualized Medication Effectiveness Tests. Virtual Mentor. 15 (1), 42–45.

Wennberg, J.E., Dartmouth Atlas of Health Care Working Group, 1998. The Dartmouth Atlas of Health Care 1998. Center for the Evaluative Clinical Sciences, Dartmouth Medical School, Hanover, NH, p. 2.

Winslow, R., 2009. Study questions evidence behind heart therapies. Wall Street J. Retrieved from http://online.wsj.com/.

Woolever, D., 2008. The art and science of clinical decision making. Family Pract. Manag. 15, 31–36.

Zimerman, A.L., 2013. Evidence-based medicine: A short history of a modern medical movement. Virtual Mentor. 15 (1), 71–76.

Chapter 8

ICD-10

Chapter Outline

PREAMBLE

The phases of technical development in a science, as described in the Introduction to this book, began with descriptive studies, followed by classification studies, quantitative studies, and eventually, integrative studies, with periods of overlap between successive phases. While quantitative studies in medicine have begun, the classification phase continues in medicine and health care with the upgrading of the ICD-9 coding system to form the ICD-10 system of today. This chapter describes the development of this disease classification system, and explains how it relates to integrative studies performed with predictive analytics.

INTRODUCTION

Efforts to classify the causes of morbidity and mortality are not new. The first international classification, the International List of Causes of Death, was introduced by the International Statistical Institute (ISI) in 1893 at the ISI World Congress in Chicago. The International Classification of Diseases (ICD) has been revised a number of times and published in a series of editions to reflect advances in health and medical science over time (Weigel and Lewis, 1991; Bebbington, 1992; Innes *et al.*, 1997; Topaz *et al.*, 2013; WHO, 2013a).

RISE OF THE ICD

In 1948, the then-new World Health Organization (WHO) took over the scrutiny of the classification and published the 6th version of the ICD. Coincident with this transition, the ICD assumed its present name. ICD-6 was the first edition that incorporated morbidity (illness) as well as mortality. The WHO Nomenclature Regulations were adopted in 1967, and mandated that organizational member countries use the most current ICD revision to compile their mortality and morbidity statistics (Mulvihill, 2011; WHO, 2013a; Maguire, 2014).

Practical Predictive Analytics and Decisioning Systems for Medicine. DOI: http://dx.doi.org/10.1016/B978-0-12-411643-6.00008-9

The ICD is now in its tenth revision. ICD-10 was approved in 1990 by the Forty-third World Health Assembly (WHO, 2013a,b). There are well over 20,000 scientific articles that have cited ICD-10 metrics. ICD has been translated into 43 languages (WHO, 2013b). Approximately 120 countries worldwide use the classification to report their morbidity and mortality statistics. The ICD has become the global health information standard for mortality and morbidity statistics (Brouch, 2000; Innes *et al.*, 2000; Doll, 2005; Dimick, 2008; WHO, 2013c). The ICD is increasingly relevant not only in clinical care but also in research settings, and it has been used to define diseases processes and patterns. New applications have taken ICD-10 into the realm of healthcare management as well as outcomes research. Importantly, in the new paradigm of accountable care, it has been used to allocate resources effectively (Dimick, 2012a; Hartman *et al.*, 2012; Kostick, 2012). Mortality data are reported by more than 100 countries. As a major indicator of health outcomes, ICD-10 helps to monitor morbidity and mortality rates. These metrics can be used to gauge success in reaching Millennium Development Goals. Roughly 70% of the world's health expenditures are allocated using ICD reimbursement tools (NCBI, 1997; Bowman and Scichilone, 2013; WHO, 2013c).

WHY THE ICD?

These developments beg the question: What is the impetus to change from ICD-9 to ICD-10 coding? First, ICD-9 is based on old terminology, which in many cases is predicated on obsolete technology (Kloss, 2005; Schwend, 2007; Bowman, 2008). When technology changes, terminology cannot always keep pace (Dimick, 2012b,c). It would be absurd to expect that the authors of the original ICD would have had any concept of organ transplantation or artificial reproduction technologies (WHO, 2013a). From that perspective, the older schemata do not have room for the many upgrades to the system as technology ramps up. Change to a new scheme to describe new morbidity and mortality issues has been slow in implementation in the United States, possibly because of the large integrated nature of the healthcare system. In fact, the United States is one of the last countries to implement ICD-10 based revisions. Many of the other members of the international community (with smaller and less complicated systems?) have been on ICD-10 for over a decade. Staying with ICD-9, however, would limit the ability of the United States in sharing data internationally (AHIMA, 2005; Conn, 2006). ICD-10 includes better healthcare metrics, which facilitate data tracking and permit a more comprehensive view of history and treatments. This more complete and flexible system of data tracking can promote better decision-making in both clinical and financial areas, leading to more equitable reimbursements (Baldwin, 2010; Danzig, 2010).

ELEMENTS OF ICD DOCUMENTATION

Documentation begins at the very start of the patient visit. Vital required clinical information is obtained by nursing and other members of the clinical treatment team, in either written or electronic form, or in a hybrid of the two forms. Some of this documentation may be limited and some more detailed. ICD-10 does not change the rules for documentation, but it may require additional clinical information for requirements implicit in the ICD-10 description hierarchy. The ICD-9-CM rules were very specific; however, the codes have not kept up with the documentation requirements because they lack the necessary specificity, giving rise to the need for a new documentation hierarchy. By logical extension, the documentation requirements do synchronize well with the coding elements (Rihanek and DeVault, 2012; Rose, 2012; Viola, 2012; NICE, 2013a). It is hoped that the ICD-10 requirements will for the first time represent a clinical and systems classification system that meets both the intellectual and process requirements to keep up with the changes in medical technology, regulations, and charting requirements (Schwend, 2007; Goedert, 2008; Stausberg *et al.*, 2008; Barta, 2009; Kuehn, 2009; MGMA, 2009). Some future changes may not be anticipated, and formulation of an ICD-11 may become necessary.

From a clinical perspective, it is important to have a history and physical on admission of the patient to the hospital. For every clinical day at least one progress note is required, but there may be additional documentation that records a physician visit in the form of an encounter note. Many other types of notes may also be gathered, including:

- Operative or procedure notes
- Notes that document the interaction of various other ancillary services, including nursing, physical therapy, occupational therapy, and speech therapy notes
- Clinical notes from ancillary services such as pathology, dietary, and or pharmacy during the course of the hospitalization

- Ultimately, a discharge summary will be added, with recommendations for further follow-up, characterization of disability, and delineation of the hospitalization occurrences (Mulaik, 2011; Baldwin, 2012; Bryant, 2012; Clark *et al.*, 2012).

The challenge is to take the diagnoses in whatever form they have been recorded, identify co-morbidities (related illnesses) which may in turn lead to additional diagnoses, and identify causal factors. During stays in the hospital, complications must be identified; diagnoses must be characterized by their detailed anatomical location, sequelae (sequential effects), and degree of functional impairment. Any contribution of biologic and chemical agents should be identified and related to origin. Documentation for malignancies and other cancers must include the phase or stage of development, lymph node involvement, and any occurrence of lateralization or localization of the particular lesion. Any procedure, modification, palliation (treatment), or implant that is related to the original disease must be identified clearly, and related to the original lesion (AHIMA, 2012a; Rose, 2012; Viola, 2012; CMS, 2013; Guffey and Duchek, 2013).

THE ICD TIMETABLE

ICD-10 consists of three volumes in paper and electronic form. The first two volumes contain diagnosis code sets. The third volume contains procedure codes (WHO, 2013b,c). Currently, full ICD-10 coding is scheduled for implementation on October 1, 2014 (CMS, 2013). The transition to ICD-10 is required for everyone covered by the Health Insurance Portability Accountability Act (HIPAA), not just those who submit Medicare or Medicaid claims (Rode, 2010). The change to ICD-10, however, does not affect CPT (current procedural terminology) coding for outpatient procedures (Bendix, 2013; CMS, 2013). See Figure 8.1 for additional details.

CHANGES AHEAD FOR ICD-10 USERS

Healthcare providers, including payers, clearinghouses, and billers for their services, must be prepared for the transition to ICD-10. This process will require a change in standards used previously. Since January 1, 2012, all electronic transactions must use Version 5010 standards. Unlike the older Version 4010/4010 A standards, Version 5010 accommodates ICD-10 codes. ICD-10 diagnosis codes must be used for all services provided in the United States, and ICD-10 procedure codes must be used for all inpatient procedures (Weinstein, 2011; Williams, 2011). Claims with ICD-9 codes for services provided after the compliance deadline will no longer be reimbursed (Mulvihill, 2011).

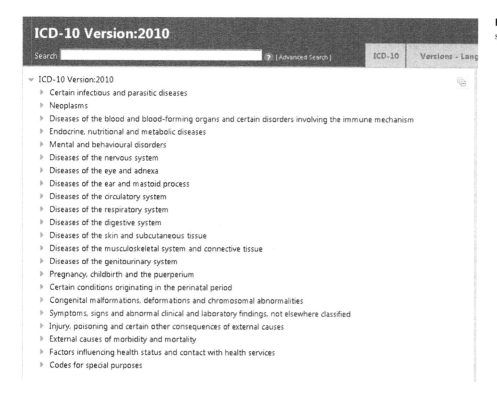

FIGURE 8.1 Initial classification screen in the ICD-10 application.

COMPARISON OF ICD-9 AND ICD-10

ICD-10 provides many capabilities that are more complete and more flexible for describing disease scenarios than those in ICD-9.

Increased Ability to Describe and Justify Treatment

ICD-10 is preferred over ICD-9 for its increased ability to substantiate the need for patient care or treatment. Because of enhanced descriptive terminology, ICD-10 is better able to provide statistics for morbidity and mortality rates. Additionally, these codes can be used to provide for documentation of medical necessity by translating the written terminology of medical procedures and physical exam findings into a universal common language, which must not only be used for medical billing purposes but also provide enhanced descriptive terms that better provide for diagnosis tracking and implementation of Big Data solutions for statistical analysis (Averill and Bowman, 2012; Clark, 2012; Rose, 2012).

The ICD-10 Descriptive Language is Much Richer

ICD-10 constitutes a more descriptive language than does ICD-9. The diagnosis must justify the care provided by the appropriate diagnostic fact documentation. Insurers will link or match the diagnosis code with the procedure or service code reported. If medical necessity is not met by the inclusion of the specific code, the insurance carrier or other payer may deny the service, or deem the service unnecessary or eligible for reduced reimbursement. By extension, if the diagnosis code does not match the appropriate facts, the insurer may also deny the service. Although this line of thought appears logical, the magnitude of studies ordered in the course of providing medical care might not always appear connected to explicit diagnosis code. For example, a patient entering the emergency room with a diagnosis code of leg pain may have had a chest X-ray, because his pain did not respond to initial treatment. Under ICD-10, the chest X-ray would be denied because the diagnosis code did not match the referring leg pain. Clinicians must be more cognizant of the linkages required to generate reimbursement. This new process provides enhanced emphasis on choosing the right code for the major diagnosis, and it also provides the auxiliary codes necessary to cover the necessary work-up (Bhuttar, 2011; Zeisset, 2011; Baldwin, 2012; Bryant, 2012; Viola, 2012; Zeisset and Bowman, 2012).

Prior to 1988, healthcare professionals used a written description of the encounter (whether it was an office visit, an ER visit, or an inpatient consultation) to provide a reason for the encounter on the insurance claim. These claims were non-standard by definition, because there was not a common language to describe the severity of the symptoms, location of the lesion, venue, or duration of physician time involved. This "Wild West" approach to diagnosis coding generated desperate payments and subjective denials. Moreover, this approach did not lend well to the calculation of actuarial data that could be used to standardize evidence, approach, and outcomes (ICD-10 Task Force, 1987; Weigel and Lewis, 1991; IHRIM, 1994; Prophet, 2002).

Facilitation of Mortality and Morbidity Analyses

ICD-10 standardized codes will allow the calculation of mortality, morbidity, and distribution of physician visits by a principal diagnosis. Healthcare costs can be calculated, provided price/performance of healthcare analyses are facilitated and complete. Healthcare quality metrics can be evaluated more accurately, permitting better predictions and planning for future healthcare needs. Enhanced statistical analysis portends improved patient safety, enhanced evidence for quality of care, and improved public health monitoring (Bebbington, 1992; NCBI, 1997; Langley and Chalmers, 1999; Pickett *et al.*, 1999).

IMPLICATIONS OF ICD-10 CHANGES

Greater Scalability and Extensibility Foster Information Sharing Among Institutions

One of the guiding principles of ICD-10 is that storage and retrieval of data must be quick and efficient. The analysis of healthcare information for evidenced-based decision-making is important in enhancing the transparency of data processing. By extension, this information can be scaled up easily for sharing and comparing healthcare information between hospitals, regions, different healthcare settings, and international settings as well. A very important data dimension added by ICD-10 is the temporal domain. Time stamps are added to each documented event, rendering them as time-based, rather than event-based, in organization. These enhancements enable the sharing of information and data comparisons looking across different periods of time. Also, comparisons can be made for various metrics for the same location across different time periods (Butler and Bonazelli, 2009; Giannangelo and Hyde, 2010). This form of data can facilitate time-series predictive analytical modeling by relating a given outcome to the state of a metric for a given patient at different times in the past. Analyses of this kind have been common in business data domains for a long time (e.g., retail). ICD-10 standards will provide the data structures to support this form of predictive analytics in medicine and health care in the future. This is indeed an exciting prospect.

More Specific Categories and Codes

In replacing ICD-9-CM with ICD-10-CM, providers will benefit from more specificity with increased numbers of categories and codes. ICD-10 will also, conversely, support the development of computer assisted coding. ICD-10 supports HIPAA provisions for transparency and standardization of the EMR (Watzlaf *et al.*, 2007; Conn, 2008; HHS, 2008a,b; Zender, 2008). ICD-10-CM has been synchronized and is consistent with the *Diagnostic and Statistical Manual of Mental Disorders* (DSM IV) as well as ICD-O-2, which have been used by cancer registry programs since 1995 (Willemse *et al.*, 2003; Bowman, 2005; Watzlaf *et al.*, 2007; HHS, 2008a).

Comparison of Codes

When ICD-9 and ICD-10 are compared, there are several differences in nomenclature that are immediately obvious. ICD-9-CM codes are three to five characters in length, while ICD-10-CM codes are three to seven characters in length. ICD-9-CM encompassed just in excess of 14,000 codes, but ICD-10-CM will have over 69,000 codes to start. Implicit in this coding redesign, ICD-10-CM will have increased flexibility for adding new codes when compared to ICD-9-CM. To accommodate this increase, where ICD-9-CM coding consists of a first character that could be alphanumeric (first character E or V or numeric), ICD-10-CM consists of a first character that can be alphanumeric, characters 2 and 3 that are numeric, and characters 4 through 7 that can be alphanumeric. By calculation, ICD-10-CM can potentially accommodate close to 375,000 codes. With the ability to code for numerous contingencies, ICD-10-CM can be very specific and detailed. Where ICD-9-CM lacked the ability to distinguish laterality, the ICD-10-CM language can distinguish between left- and right-sided diagnoses (CMS, 2013; Topaz *et al.*, 2013; WHO, 2013c).

ICD-10 CODES IN PRACTICE

The prospects for data analysis of these enhancements in ICD-10 are enticing. The ICD-9-CM coding system did not facilitate drill-down to important data elements, because it lacked specificity. The enhanced coding hierarchy of ICD-10 can improve accuracy and provide the necessary drill-down depth to allow improved data analysis. A common problem with ICD-9-CM was its inability to provide the specificity to allow proper codification of data for medical research and other applications where more exacting data collection was required. ICD-10-CM codes were designed to improve the ability to sharpen the precision for specifying a specific entity, location, duration, and severity, rendering it a valid research tool. Importantly, ICD-9-CM does not support interoperability and international data exchange, because it is not used in other countries. There is no clear translation tool to convert ICD-9-CM codes into valid ICD-10-CM nomenclature. ICD-10-CM is the new *lingua franca* (language of financial exchange) in medicine, and it will facilitate more accurate classification, and enhance interoperability and exchange with other countries.

As an example, consider a newborn infant diagnosed with omphalitis (an infection of the area around the site where the umbilical cord was previously attached) as an infection secondary to (a complication of) a tetanus infection. The ICD-9 section 771 codes refer to infections specific to the perinatal period. The ICD-9 code 771.3 for tetanus neonatorum (diseases specific to the neonate) includes tetanus omphalitis, although this is not immediately obvious from the header, and there is no way to track the incidence of omphalitis. ICD-9 has a number of these "stop-gap" solutions that do not figure well in the context of what should be a logical drill-down approach to finding the correct code. ICD-9 coding tends to be both cumbersome and time consuming to use for finding and utilizing the appropriate diagnostic code. ICD-10 is more than a simple refresh of the ICD-9 codes. The alphabetic index identifies this as P38.9, or omphalitis newborn. The more precise tabular index assigns A33 to tetanus. The correct code under ICD-10 is A33, and only the A33 code would be entered for this diagnosis.

For the normal infant born under the ICD-9 coding system, the V30–V39 codes have been assigned. If a baby is born in the hospital, "0" is added to the V30 code, such that the code reads V30.0. If the baby is born by via vaginal delivery, a fourth digit is added and the code becomes V30.00. If the baby is delivered by cesarean section, a "1" is added, and the code is V30.01. Codes V31–V37 deal with twins and other higher-level multiple deliveries (see list below). V38 does not exist, and V39 is an unspecified code that "has been reserved for future designation."

V30	Single Liveborn
V31	Twin Liveborn, Mate Liveborn
V32	Twin Liveborn, Mate Stillborn
V33	Twin Liveborn, unspecified
V34	Other Liveborn Multiple, Mates All Liveborn
V35	Other Liveborn Multiple, Mates All Stillborn
V36	Other Liveborn, Mates Live and Stillborn

Under ICD-10, the category Z38 codes according to the type and place of birth. Z38.0 refers to a single liveborn infant born in the hospital. Z38.00 indicates a single liveborn infant delivered vaginally. Z38.01 refers to a single liveborn infant delivered by cesarean section. In both cases, as with ICD-9, the first digit after the decimal point refers to the venue of delivery. In the ICD-10 system, however, the matrix is expanded to include additional specific descriptors that are more precise in describing both the type of delivery and place of birth. For example, Z38.2 indicates a single liveborn infant with an unspecified place of birth (Kostick, 2011).

In the case of a "broken arm," information required for treatment includes a characterization of the type of open fracture, whether or not there is growth-plate injury, the level of fracture displacement, and any joint involvement. Further metrics define the level of healing (or, for that matter, whether healing is in process), and subdivisions of fracture type. Under ICD-9 there are five codes for fracture of the distal or lower end of the radius, two codes for a Colles' fracture, two codes for a fracture of the lower end of the forearm, six codes for an undefined part of the radius, but no code for whether an open fracture is present. By comparison, ICD-10 has 318 codes for fractures involving the distal or lower end of the radius, which include 120 fractures of the distal or lower or unspecified part of the radius. This classification is further subdivided into 60 Gustilo class I or II codes, and 50 Gustilo IIIa, IIIb, and IIIc codes. Moreover, there are 48 separate codes each for Colles', Barton's, Smith's, radial styloid, and Galeazzi's fracture. Finally, there are 84 codes for fractures of the forearm that do not specify upper or proximal versus lower or distal. The need for enhancement of ICD-9 can be illustrated and put into context of the complete needs related to patient treatment. For example, a physician may see a patient in follow-up for non-union (failure to heal) of what was an open fracture of the right distal radius with an intra-articular extension and a minimal separation with nominal tissue damage. ICD-9-CM allows coding for "Other open fracture of the distal end of the radius," or 813.52. ICD-10-CM allows "Other intra-articular fracture of the lower end of the right radius, subsequent encounter, open fracture type I or II, and non-union," or S52571M. ICD-10-CM captures the narrative intent of the follow-up more adequately. By comparison, the ICD-9-CM code leaves much of the description undefined. Attempts to define the intent of the appointment with ICD-9-CM did not prove to be practical. ICD-9 only has 32 codes that are related to fractures of the radius, while ICD-10 has 1,731 (Dimick, 2008; Bryant, 2011; Zeisset, 2011; Comfort, 2012; Trustee, 2012).

ICD-10 CHANGES IN TERMINOLOGY

There are also terminology changes in ICD-10. ICD-9 refers to an amputation, where ICD-10 refers to a detachment. "Amniocentesis" is replaced by "drainage." "Debridement" now covers "excision," "extraction," "irrigation," and "extirpation." A "tracheostomy" is referred to as a "bypass." A "cesarean section" is now referenced as an "extraction of products of conception" (Schulz *et al.*, 1998; Barta, 2010; WHO, 2013c). Although some of these terms seem less specific than ICD-9 terms, it is clear that these descriptors point to use of a common terminology for other body locations or to accommodate additional procedures at the same site. Thus, a "bypass" might be used to refer to other locations in the body where the function of an organ, in our example the trachea, has been circumvented to achieve function (Bryant, 2011; WHO, 2013c).

IMPLEMENTATION ISSUES OF CHANGING TO ICD-10

In addition to meeting necessary compliance, ICD-10 will facilitate the clearer and more precise documentation codes, which will reduce ambiguity and allow more specific and objective design of insurance contracts covering medical claims. This should result in more appropriate payment for services, based on a realistic coding schemata rather than on group-based assumptions. This individualized treatment provides the additional specificity to allow for payments based on differences between physical findings, complexity, and laterality (i.e., the side of the body that the treatment occurs — right or left), rather than based on some similar procedure. In addition, more specific and unambiguous coding will facilitate better risk prediction, and improve actuarial understanding and development of appropriate risk management strategies. From an angle of resources management, these tools will lead to more effective detection of fraud, waste, and abuse, which are more difficult to document and track under ICD-9. Finally, and as supported by its international adaption, ICD-10 will allow more accurate understanding of population dynamics, and help with better understanding of the differences between diverse world patient populations (Bryant, 2011; WHO, 2013b,c).

WHAT LIES AHEAD FOR PAYERS AND PROVIDERS?

For Providers

All healthcare providers should (must?) develop an implementation plan that includes an assessment of their organization, delineating how it may be affected by the implementation of ICD-10. This plan should consider issues of schedule, cost, resources needed, and payments. This implementation plan should include a schedule of activities and tasks, and the dependencies between them. The cost of each task should be delineated clearly; having a timeline is crucial to the success of the plan. The cost of the implementation must be budgeted, within an overall financial analysis that includes collaborative efforts with intramural or extramural departments that provide provider billing services and software. Developers of software instruments must be required to put plans in place to ensure ongoing compliance with changes involved not only in the transition from ICD-9 to ICD-10, but also in subsequent modifications to the various code delimiters, and ultimately in transition to ICD-11 specifications. In situations where healthcare providers handle billing and software development internally, medical records, coding, clinical, IT, and finance staff must coordinate ICD-10 transition efforts (Butler *et al.*, 2011; Cook, 2011; Dimick, 2011; Jacobs, 2011; Morrissey, 2011; Weinstein, 2011).

For Payers

On the other side of the financial infrastructure, payers (i.e., insurance companies) must implement new payment policies to correspond to the new ICD-10 coding rules, which will vastly increase the possible payment scenarios. Software vendors that interface with payers must develop readiness plans and timelines for product development, testing, availability, and training to support ICD-10. There are many potential pitfalls ahead, as providers leverage the more complete inventory of ICD-10 codes to develop new reimbursement systems. One such pitfall to avoid is the problem of translation of the existing databases using ICD-9 codes to those required by ICD-10. Payers must develop translation tools that are cost-neutral across risk groups (Majerowicz, 2011). Importantly, the implementation plan should be in place prior to the transition (Bhuttar, 2011; Carolan, 2011; Cook, 2011; AHIMA, 2012b; CMS, 2013; Conn and Robeznieks, 2013). First the work must be planned, and then the plan must be worked. Attempts to implement ICD-10 without such a plan is a formula for disaster.

TRANSITION IS A JOINT EFFORT

Unless health information service (HIS) providers take a proactive role in assisting with the transition, claims will not be paid. Although there has been much consternation regarding the potential high cost of implementation, HIS products and services, including computerized physician order entry (CPOE) and electronic medical records (EMR), will become obsolete if steps are not taken to prepare for them (Jacobs, 2011; Conn and Robeznieks, 2013).

Based on continuing revisions to both ICD-9-CM and ICD-10 code, vendors, systems integrators, and educators requested a "code freeze" (DeVault, 2012). The last regular annual update to both ICD-9-CM and CD-10 was made on October 1, 2011. The ICD9-CM coordination and maintenance committee was to continue to meet twice a year during the freeze. As of October 1, 2012, there existed only a limited capacity for updates to both ICD-9-CM and ICD-10 code sets to capture new technology and new diseases (Mulaik, 2012; Barnhouse and Rudman, 2013; CMS, 2013). New updates to ICD-9-CM will phase out from October 1, 2013 — the original implementation date of ICD-10) (NICE, 2013b). From that date onward, updates will only be made with respect to ICD-10 code. ICD-9-CM will no longer be updated, as it will not be considered HIPAA compliant. As of October 1, 2014, there will be regular scheduled updates to ICD-10. Any codes that did not meet the criteria of being a new technology or new disease during the moratorium would be then presented for consideration in ICD-10 (Atkins *et al.*, 2012; Averill and Bowman, 2012; Dimick, 2012c).

The 11th version of ICD is currently under development through an international web-based collaborative process. The World Health Organization (WHO) has been recruiting interested parties to participate in the revision process through an online forum. It is hoped that subsequent revisions of ICD will be a classification system that will be more focused on user input and need. The 11th revision process is underway, and the final ICD-11 will be released in 2015. Through an online revision process and advances in information technology, the ICD-11 vetting process will be made available to interested providers. For the first time, peer-reviewed comments and input will be added through the "beta" revision period (Rief *et al.*, 2010; Eurosurveillance Editorial, 2012; Leon-Chisen, 2013). There is considerable concern in the United States and other nations that have yet to make the transition regarding the timetable for the transition to ICD-10, given the encroaching mandate for migration to ICD-11. It is hoped that ICD-11 in its final form will be easier to navigate, and it will include a clear and defined path for migration that was absent from the ICD-9 to ICD-10 transition (Leon-Chisen, 2013).

POSTSCRIPT

Notwithstanding the problems of transition from ICD-9 to ICSD-10, developers realize that classification is an ongoing problem. As we improve our medical instruments and our ability to combine more types and greater quantities of information in to disease management, our classification system must evolve to keep pace with changes in our understanding.

REFERENCES

AHIMA (American Health Information Management Association), 2005. US must adopt ICD-10-CM and ICD-10-PCS. J. AHIMA. 76 (26), 28.

AHIMA, 2012a. ICD-10 toolkit. New toolkit provides resources to assist with the ICD-10 transition. J. AHIMA. 83, 36−37.

AHIMA, 2012b. Expecting a bargain: HIM directors at risk of underestimating ICD-10 coder training costs. J. AHIMA. 83, 68.

Atkins, K., Burke, L., Dinh, A.K., Donahue, L.H., Endicott, M., Grebner, L.A., et al., 2012. Transitioning to ICD-10-CM/PCS in the classroom: countdown to 2014. J. AHIMA. 83, 68−73.

Averill, R., Bowman, S., 2012. There are critical reasons for not further delaying the implementation of the new ICD-10 coding system. J. AHIMA. 83, 42−48, quiz 49.

Baldwin, G., 2010. Is ICD-10 the industry's wake up calls? Health Data Manag. 18 (46−48), 50−52.

Baldwin, G., 2012. ICD 10: time to get serious. Health Data Manag. 20, 30−32, 34, 36 *passim*.

Barnhouse, T., Rudman, W., 2013. ICD-10-CM/PCS status check. J. AHIMA. 84, 38−40.

Barta, A., 2009. Differentiating procedure approach in ICD-10-PCS. Fifth character captures specificity. J. AHIMA. 80, 78−80, quiz 82.

Barta, A., 2010. Obstetric coding in ICD-10-CM/PCS. J. AHIMA. 81, 68−70, quiz 71.

Bebbington, P., 1992. Welcome to ICD-10. Soc. Psychiatry Psychiatr. Epidemiol. 27, 255−257.

Bendix, J., 2013. ICD-10: can physician groups stave off or delay implementation? As some physicians fight the mandate, payers and EHR vendors get ready. Med. Econ. 90 (15−16), 23−24.

Bhuttar, V.K., 2011. Crosswalk options for legacy systems. Implementing near-term tactical solutions for ICD-10. J. AHIMA. 82, 34−37.

Bowman, S., 2005. Coordinating SNOMED-CT and ICD-10. J. AHIMA. 76, 60−61.

Bowman, S., 2008. Why ICD-10 is worth the trouble. J. AHIMA. 79, 24−29, quiz 41−42.

Bowman, S., Scichilone, R., 2013. ICD-10-CM/PCS part of a global network of information standards. J. AHIMA. 84, 52−53.

Brouch, K., 2000. Where in the world is ICD-10? J. AHIMA. 71, 52−57.

Bryant, G. ICD-10 Implemenation Update for Revenue Cycle, <www.hfma-nca.org/documents/2011%20Spring%20Conference/March%2024/ Revenue%20Cycle/T-P3%20ICD-10%20Implementation%20Update_G%20Bryant%20pptx.pdf/> (2011).

Bryant, G., 2012. Engaging physicians in ICD-10 planning: the documentation link. J. AHIMA. 83, 54−55.

Butler, R., Bonazelli, J., 2009. Converting MS-DRGs to ICD-10-CM/PCS. Methods used, lessons learned. J. AHIMA. 80, 40−43.

Butler, R., Mills, R., Averill, R., 2011. Reading the fine print on ICD-10 conversions. Even highly automated conversions require review. J. AHIMA. 82, 28−31, quiz 32.

Carolan, K., 2011. An ICD-10 vendor checklist. Planning now makes for a smoother transition. J. AHIMA. 82, 26−28.

Clark, J.S., 2012. The facts about ICD-10-CM/PCS implementation. Implementation will improve the quality of patient care. J. AHIMA. 83, 42−43.

Clark, J.S., Eichelmann, T.A., Fuller, J.C., Hays, S., Lobdell, B.B, Mangat, N., et al., 2012. Electronic documentation templates support ICD-10-CM/ PCS implementation. J. AHIMA. 83, 66−71.

CMS. Centers for Medicare and Medicaid Services Homepage, <www.cms.gov/Medicare/Coding/ICD10/index.html?redirect = /icd10/> 2013.

Comfort, A., 2012. Coding open fractures in ICD-10-CM. J. AHIMA. 83, 64−66.

Conn, J., 2006. House passes IT bill. Deadline set for ICD-10 implementation. Mod. Healthc. 36, 12.

Conn, J., 2008. Ready or not ... HHS prepares for ICD-10; some say not so fast. Mod. Healthc. 38, 16.

Conn, J., Robeznieks, A., 2013. Code worry. Docs say ICD-10 implementation carries hefty cost. Mod. Healthc. 43, 14.

Cook, D.A., 2011. Coming soon: Medicaid EHR incentives and ICD-10 conversion. J. Med. Assoc. Ga. 100, 24.

Danzig, C., 2010. Billing & coding. ICD-10: experts fear executive attention lags. Hosp. Health Netw. 84, 19.

DeVault, K., 2012. Data management a hot topic at ICD-10 summit: top ten lists, documentation teams, and code freeze info among highlights. J. AHIMA. 83, 54–56.

Dimick, C., 2008. ICD-10 postcards. Canadians, Australians share experiences with ICD-10 implementation. J. AHIMA. 79, 33–35.

Dimick, C., 2011. Top 10 for ICD-10. Essential tasks for the first phase of the journey. J. AHIMA. 82, 38–41.

Dimick, C., 2012a. Welcome to ICD-10 university: lessons learned from the ICD-10 summit. J. AHIMA. 83, 38–41.

Dimick, C., 2012b. "Don't slow down": an ICD-10 summit wrap-up. J. AHIMA. 83 (52–56), 58.

Dimick, C., 2012c. ICD-10 delay impacts all sectors of healthcare: industry attempts to answer the question 'what now'? J. AHIMA. 83, 32–37.

Doll, B.A., 2005. Project Management 101. Skills for Leading and Working in Teams, Part 1. J. AHIMA. 76 (1), 62–63.

Eurosurveillance Editorial, 2012. WHO seeking input from health experts into ICD-11. Eurosurveillance: bulletin Européen sur les maladies transmissibles [European communicable disease bulletin]. 17 (20).

Giannangelo, K., Hyde, L., 2010. Retooling quality measures for ICD-10. J. AHIMA. 81, 56–57.

Goedert, J., 2008. Beware the challenges of ICD-10. Health Data Manag. 16, 10.

Guffey, S., Duchek, D., 2013. Preparing your practice for ICD-10. J. Med. Pract. Manag. 28, 303–305.

Hartman, K., Phillips, S.C., Sornberger, L., 2012. Computer-assisted coding at the Cleveland Clinic: a strategic solution. Addressing clinical documentation improvement, ICD-10-CM/PCS implementation, and more. J. AHIMA. 83, 24–28.

HHS (US Department of Health and Human Services), 2008a. HHS proposes adoption of ICD-10 code sets and updated electronic transaction standards. J. AHIM. 79, 10.

HHS (US Department of Health and Human Services), 2008b. Office of the Secretary. HIPAA administrative simplification: modification to medical data code set standards to adopt ICD-10-CM and ICD-10-PCS. Proposed Rule Federal Register. 73, 49795–49832.

ICD-10 Task Force, 1987. Report of the ICD-10 Task Force. Am. Med. Rec. Assoc. J. 58, 51–56.

IHRIM (Institute of Health Record Information and Management), 1994. ICD-10: making the changeover from ICD-9, in April 1995. IHRIM. 35, 6–7.

Innes, K., Hooper, J., Bramley, M., DahDah, P., 1997. Creation of a clinical classification. International statistical classification of diseases and related health problems – 10th revision, Australian modification (ICD-10-AM). Health Inf. Manag. 27, 31–38.

Innes, K., Peasley, K., Roberts, R., 2000. Ten down under: implementing ICD-10 in Australia. J. AHIMA. 71, 52–56.

Jacobs, J., 2011. What ICD-10 means for doctors: the 2013 coding update may lead to revenue loss if physicians are not prepared. Health Manag. Technol. 32, 31.

Kloss, L., 2005. The promise of ICD-10-CM. Health Manag. Technol. 26 (48), 47.

Kostick, K., 2011. From V codes to Z codes: transitioning to ICD-10 (updated). J. AHIMA. 82, 60–63.

Kostick, K.M., 2012. Coding diabetes mellitus in ICD-10-CM: improved coding for diabetes mellitus complements present medical science. J. AHIMA. 83, 56–58, quiz 59.

Kuehn, L., 2009. Preparing for ICD-10-CM in physician practices. J. AHIMA. 80, 26–29.

Langley, J.D., Chalmers, D.J., 1999. Coding the circumstances of injury: ICD-10 a step forward or backwards? Inj. Prev. 5, 247–253.

Leon-Chisen, N., 2013. If we procrastinate long enough, will ICD-11 be ready? Hosp. Health Netw. 87, 12.

Maguire, N., 2014. ICD-10-CM diagnosis coding. J. Med. Pract. Manag. 27, 393–394.

Majerowicz, A., 2011. Developing an ICD-10-CM/PCS coder training strategy. J. AHIMA. 82, 58–60.

MGMA (Medical Group Management Association), 2009. Final ICD-10 code sets, updated electronic transaction standards make big changes for physician groups. MGMA Connex. 9, 9–12.

Morrissey, J., 2011. Your ICD-10 to-do list. Hosp. Health Netw. 85 (24–28), 21.

Mulaik, M.W., 2011. ICD-10: physician documentation. Radiol. Manag. 33, 28.

Mulaik, M.W., 2012. ICD-10: updates and new codes. Radiol. Manag. 34, 31.

Mulvihill, L., 2011. The National transition from ICD-9 to ICD-10. J. Regist. Manag. 38, 100–101, quiz 108–109.

NCBI (National Center for Biotechnology Information), 1997. Implementation of the International Statistical Classification of Diseases and Related Health Problems, 10th Revision (ICD-10). Epidemiol. Bull. 18, 1–4.

NICE (National Institute for Health and Care Excellence), 2013a. ICD-10 means better documentation is a must. Hosp. Case Manag. 21, 113–114.

NICE (National Institute for Health and Care Excellence), 2013b. Ready to hit the pause button. Execs back call for another year's delay on ICD-10. Mod. Healthc. 43, 27–28.

Pickett, D., Berglund, D., Blum, A., Wing, L., 1999. A quick review of ICD-10-CM. J. AHIMA. 70, 99–100.

Prophet, S., 2002. ICD-10 on the horizon. J. AHIMA. 73, 36–38, 40–41; quiz 43–44.

Rief, W., Kaasa, S., Jensen, R., Perrot, S., Vlaeyen, J.W.S., Treede, R.-D., et al., 2010. The need to revise pain diagnoses in ICD-11. Pain. 149, 169–170 .

Rihanek, T., DeVault, K., 2012. Converting data to ICD-10 with GEMs: reference mapping tools will aid in system transition. J. AHIMA. 83, 42–43.

Rode, D., 2010. Navigating the perfect storm. HIM roles in steering through healthcare reform, ARRA, ICD-10, and HIPAA. J. AHIMA. 81 (18), 20.

Rose, A.D., 2012. Transitioning a physician practice to ICD-10. J. AHIMA. 83, 70–72.

Schulz, S., Zaiss, A., Brunner, R., Spinner, D., Klar, R., 1998. Conversion problems concerning automated mapping from ICD-10 to ICD-9. Methods Inf. Med. 37, 254–259.

Schwend, G., 2007. Expanding the code. The methodical switch from ICD-9-CM to ICD-10-CM will bring both challenges and rewards to healthcare. Health Manag. Technol. 28 (12), 14.

Stausberg, J., Lehmann, N., Kaczmarek, D., Stein, M., 2008. Reliability of diagnoses coding with ICD-10. Int. J. Med. Inform. 77, 50−57.

Topaz, M., Shafran-Topaz, L., Bowles, K.H., 2013. ICD-9 to ICD-10: evolution, revolution, and current debates in the United States. Persp. Health Inf. Manag. 10, 1d.

Trustee, 2012. 95.8% more procedure codes in ICD-10 than in ICD-9. Trustee: J. Hosp. Govern. Boards. 65, 36.

Viola, A., 2012. It's your move. Using gaming and simulation exercises in ICD-10 planning. J. AHIMA. 83, 38−39.

Watzlaf, V.J., Garvin, J.H., Moeini, S., Anania-Firouzan, P., 2007. The effectiveness of ICD-10-CM in capturing public health diseases. Persp. Health Inf. Manag. 4, 6.

Weigel, K.M., Lewis, C.A., 1991. Forum: In sickness and in health − the role of the ICD in the United States health care data and ICD-10. Top. Health Rec. Manag. 12, 70−82.

Weinstein, K., 2011. Is your practice management system ready? HIPAA 5010 and ICD-10 have implications for virtually every PM system. Health Manag. Technol. 32, 26.

Willemse, G.R., Van Yperen, T.A., Rispens, J., 2003. Reliability of the ICD-10 classification of adverse familial and environmental factors. J. Child Psychol. Psychiatr. 44, 202−213.

Williams, B., 2011. ICD-10/5010: move it or lose it! Tennessee Med. 104 (23−25), 27.

World Health Organization, 2013a. History of the development of the ICD, <www.who.int/classifications/icd/en/HistoryOfICD.pdf/>.

World Health Organization, 2013b. Home Page of the World Health Organization, <www.who.int>.

World Health Organization, 2013c. International Statistical Classification of Diseases and Related Health Problems 10th Revision, <http://apps.who.int/classifications/icd10/browse/2010/en/>.

Zeisset, A., Bowman, S., 2012. Strategies for ICD-10 implementation. Healthc. Financ. Manag. 66 (96−98), 100−102.

Zeisset, A., 2011. Coding injuries in ICD-10-CM. J. AHIMA. 82, 52−54, quiz 55.

Zender, A., 2008. ICD-10 in the big picture. J. AHIMA. 79, 100.

Chapter 9

"Meaningful Use" — The New Buzzword in Medicine

Chapter Outline

PREAMBLE

Chapter 9 moves the focus of our discussion to the level of over-arching issues (i.e., "meaningful use") governing the proper use of medical information. The term "meaningful use" has a different meaning for different people. This chapter explains some of these meanings, and relates them to the core need in medicine and health care for tools, methodologies, and treatments that are effective to guide decisions for accurate diagnosis and effective treatment.

INTRODUCTION

As it pertains to health care, meaningful use is the new nirvana. This term, "Meaningful Use," has been bantered around sufficiently frequently that we "think" we know what it means when we see it. Nevertheless, there is a dichotomy of thought as to what the best path is to achieve a "meaningful product" that embodies the use of the term. That said, most medical professionals are clear in their need to adapt to this new pathway but are less clear in terms of what this means for them for the near and distant future.

For example:

- Is it sufficient to accept the hospital's recommendation for a specific MIS (medical information system), HIS (health information system), or EMR (electronic medical record) product that will comply with meaningful use despite the fact that the software is not designed for the particulars of the office or specialty practice?
- What if the software vendor no longer meets certain objectives?
- Does the physician practice lose the opportunity to participate in certain incentive-based programs?
- Further down the line, will the physician be punished if the office uses software that no longer carries the "meaningful use" imprimatur?

There needs to be a defined path to achieve certain concrete objectives designed to meet the new mandates. Moreover, there needs to be a certain guarantee that compliance with this process will be remunerated in a manner that is neither arbitrary nor capricious.

The board of medical specialists now requires this type of "practice-based learning" to maintain board certification. Currently, this is one of several criteria that have roughly equal precedence. The concept of lifelong learning is implicit in this connection. The idea is that the physician will define certain projects or objectives in the course of his or her practice, and that these projects will drive improvement in outcomes. A number of clearinghouses have been defined to accept or reject the validity of the project and its objectives. Although the process is relatively new and not defined in the same way for all specialties, there will come a point in the near future where the adaption of meaningful use will not only be the gateway to better compliance as well as remuneration, but also an entry point for board certification. Hospital accreditation may ultimately be based on achieving a certain level of physician compliance with the process.

Hospital and physician collaboration is implicit in achieving these goals. Accountable care organizations (ACOs) will facilitate broad-based physician and hospital interactions across multiple specialties in geographical areas and will drive care efficiencies. Real effort has to be made to avoid disconnecting known referral patterns that function well for certain patient populations but not others. ACOs defined in the most general sense will eliminate specialty access in certain segments of the hospital population that may find themselves without access to a preferred referral location in the name of meaningful use. Certainly, incentive-based initiatives will compel earlier adaption and will leave those who opt out at a competitive disadvantage, but this must not come at the expense of losing out on quality-based initiatives that existed before meaningful use. The clear intent is to encourage a meaningful use of data and quality objectives that are based on real-world considerations that will drive improvements in healthcare delivery.

The requirements for meaningful use have been articulated by the national offices for Health and Human Services (HHS) (http://healhit.hhs.gov) as well as the Centers for Medicare and Medicaid Services (CMS) (www.cms.gov).

STAGE I OF "MEANINGFUL USE"

Meaningful use includes both a core set and a menu set of objectives that are specific to eligible professionals or eligible hospitals and critical access hospitals (CAHs). For eligible professionals, there are a total of 25 meaningful use objectives. To qualify for an incentive payment, 20 of these 25 objectives must be met. There are 15 required core objectives. The remaining 5 objectives may be chosen from the list of 10 menu set objectives.

For eligible hospitals and CAHs, there are a total of 24 meaningful use objectives. To qualify for an incentive payment, 19 of these 24 objectives must be met. There are 14 required core objectives. The remaining 5 objectives may be chosen from a list of 10 menu set objectives.

Stage II of meaningful use is expected to be implemented in 2013.

Stage III is expected to be implemented starting on January 1, 2014 and will extend into 2015 and, we expect, beyond to expand on the initial framework and also to be developed on the basis of future initiatives.

Interestingly, as of September 2013 many medical establishments had not even started the implementation of Stage I. However, the directive that Stage III will start in January 2014 is still mandated, meaning that those hospitals and clinics that have NOT started Stage I, or even Stage II, will have to start this by November 2013 and then immediately be "up and running to speed" with Stage III when January 2014 arrives, or the group will be penalized by not receiving financial reimbursements for their services (we are writing this in November, 2013, so we do not know yet exactly how this will play out during 2014 and beyond . . .).

MEANINGFUL USE GOALS FOR HOSPITALS

For hospitals, HHS has created a checklist of 14 *requirements* that must be met to achieve the first stage of "meaningful use." In addition, it has another list of 10 *choice* objectives, and the hospital must meet at least 5 of them.

The 14 Requirements (Hospitals Must Meet All of These)

1. *Use computerized provider order entry (CPOE) for prescriptions.*

   Computerized provider order entry is by no means easy to implement. From a public perspective, the hospital and physician unit are viewed as one and the same. In actuality, there are many often disparate needs between physicians and hospitals. Where one hospital system predominates it is easy for the hospital to call the shots, but in many locales physicians are part of provider groups that provide services at two or more hospital venues. If Patient

A is admitted to Hospital A, obtains prescriptions on discharge and tries to fill these prescriptions at another pharmacy in another hospital network (Hospital B) where the physician has privileges, then unless there is transparency between the two hospital networks Hospital B can be dinged for non-utilization of CPOE. The need for systems that are interactive and reciprocal cannot be overemphasized.

2. *Check for drug–drug and drug–allergy interactions.*

Drug–drug and drug–allergy interactions are the basis of significant hospital morbidity. Hospitals must address this by maintaining up-to-date databases of reactions of various compounds as well as patient allergies. Routing information regarding patient allergies between patient, patient charts, physician, and involved hospitals has never been easy. Medical identification bracelets are generally worn by patients with more severe allergic reactions and reactions to certain medications. However, the patient who arrives at the hospital disoriented without the proper identifying medic alert bracelet or other form of identification remains at risk.

3. *Maintain an up-to-date problem list of diagnoses.*

Databases are very good at maintaining lists of diagnoses. Physicians are less good at maintaining these lists and keeping them up to date. Although an IS system can give the appearance of good data, as the old adage goes: "garbage in and garbage out." Effective compliance requires collaboration between physician and hospital. Methods of effectively transferring information between providers and hospitals must be improved in order to reduce the effort and time involved in transferring information from the outpatient setting to the hospital environment at the point of patient admission. Although transparency is attractive, it is not the sole motivator for physician–database interaction. Financial incentives abound for using certain database solutions which may or may not integrate naturally with those selected by hospital networks. There is the continued danger of not resolving diagnoses or entering new emerging ones into the medical record because they were realized in the outpatient setting.

4. *Maintain an active medication list.*

This is perhaps the easiest of the requirements to meet. Physicians order the medications through CPOE, and the medications appear on the active medication list. This is not as straightforward in certain areas of the hospital where medications are supplied on an emergent basis, such as the emergency room, delivery room, or code situation. Granted, these represent exceptions rather than the general rule. Efforts to promote compliance should not come at the expense of immediate availability of these crucial medications.

5. *Maintain an active medication allergy list.*

Medication allergies are based on knowledge of a reaction and the extent of the reaction. A penicillin allergy that produces an anaphylactic reaction is no doubt more significant than one that produces a rash alone. It is significant that the physician provider as well as the hospital be aware of these in looking for alternative means of treatment. A history of a rash with penicillin may induce the physician to find a better medication within the same class; the risk of anaphylaxis may encourage the provider to steer clear of all related compounds.

6. *Record demographics on date of birth, language, gender, race, ethnicity, and date and preliminary cause of death.*

Demographics are important in recognizing trends and characterizing illness and disease states that are likely to cause mortality. In our multiethnic society, language, race, and ethnicity increasing blur. Class and disparity differences may be ultimately more important in recognizing trends in disease state and progress.

7. *Record and chart changes in height, weight, blood pressure and BMI. In children aged 2–20 years, growth charts must also be plotted.*

For most pediatricians, this is an interesting requirement. Although children grow continuously from birth to late adolescence and in some cases beyond 20 years of age, the range from 0–2 years is actually most important and requires the most vigilance. Disease states such as hypothyroidism and early nutritional deficiencies are often unmasked during the first months of life; if these are missed, the liability associated with this lack of follow-up can be devastating. It would appear the emphasis on growth missed the point.

8. *Record whether each patient (aged 13 and up) smokes.*

Smoking cessation has an important place in the improvement of health and health maintenance. Although cessation is not part of the mandate, recording whether a patient is a smoker has important implications for identifying the need for program development as well as targeting specific demographic areas where increased smoking prevalence is endemic. Certain smoking cessation programs have been tied to a "sin" tax on tobacco products. In other cases (California in particular), taxes on tobacco products have been used to shore up children's hospitals. Moreover, early identification allows for better prediction of needed resources 20–30 years down the road when these "precocious" teenagers begin to have health problems related to chronic tobacco exposures.

9. *Report hospital clinical quality measures (a separate list of requirements) to government authorities.*

Hospital clinical quality measures are a moving target. Leapfrog initiatives are most familiar on a national basis, but have limited scope for applicability. For example, the initial requirement for compliance for a hospital with an obstetrical focus was based on the administration of steroids for pregnant mothers in preterm labor. Although this is an important measure for the prevention of long-term morbidities, only roughly 10% of all babies will be born premature. If a hospital has 1,000 deliveries a month, this is a significant measure that can reduce long-term morbidities in a significant proportion of the hospital population. However, what if the hospital only has 100 deliveries a month and a significant number of the high-risk mothers are transferred or diverted to a higher level of care? In this situation only 4—5% of the anticipated deliveries may be born premature, with a potential impact of fewer than 50 patients per year. From a broader view, the smaller hospital may appear to be less successful by both percentage and absolute number of administrations; however, the applicable therapy may be given appropriately in all cases. As with all measures, care must be taken to identify the correct reporting mechanism. If all the members of an applicable class are identified and receive or are impacted by the same quality measures, the absolute number should be meaningless. Yet another indicator of quality is defined by the absolute number of babies that are in the neonatal intensive care unit on a daily basis. If this number is less than 15, the quality measure is not met. The emphasis is not just related to an evidence-based achievement of a desired measurement but also focuses on the achieving the desired outcome with the desired penetrance. In this context, there is the danger that a perfectly functional hospital setting might be dinged for its size and level of acuity. Quality measures must be broadly applicable and not discriminate against smaller venues serving a geographically remote patient base or meeting a specific need in an area of disparity.

10. *Implement one clinical decision support rule related to a high priority hospital condition along with the ability to track compliance with that rule.*

(This means identifying a serious problem, creating a way to solve it and tracking your success. An example could include reducing preventable readmissions to the hospital — see this book's Tutorials B and D for examples of predictive analytic models that can predict which individual patient is "at risk" for re-admission, thus allowing treatment methods to be followed to avoid a re-admission.)

Clinical decision support rules related to a high-priority hospital condition mirror the continuous quality improvement implicit in recertification for physician specialty medical boards. As insurers gravitate toward a model with decreased incentives toward bringing patients back into the hospital for follow-up, or for a diagnosis code related to a previous hospitalization, the emphasis is on getting the diagnosis right the first time, treating it, and insuring that the patient can get adequate treatment on an outpatient basis all while reducing the length of stay. The question of what is preventable needs more refinement. It is not sufficient to say that a quality indicator is not met because a readmission occurred. Certain diagnosis codes will have a higher readmit rate for diagnoses that may or may not be preventable. Others may be preventable in certain socioeconomic classes but not others. It is hard to treat congestive heart failure on an outpatient if the patient cannot afford the necessary medication, or if the preferred primary care location is the emergency room of the county hospital.

11. *Provide patients with an electronic copy of their health information (diagnostic test results, problem list, medication lists, medication allergies, discharge summary and procedures) upon request.*

This appears to be a simple requirement but is mired in complexity. What sort of electronic format satisfies this requirement?

Examples:

- Is it sufficient to hand the patient a PDF-formatted document that can be read on any platform, or do the same transactional requirements exist for HIPAA (Health Insurance Portability and Accountability Act, 1996) protections between hospitals?
- If the patient is the conduit, what happens if the patient loses the data and the information falls into the hands of someone who is not authorized to have access to the medical record?

Note: One of the current authors lives in a state where a network of hospitals, clinics, and individual physicians' offices has been put together into a consortium to provide this so-called Patient Portal. The overall process looks impressive on the flow chart diagram of this organization, yet the electronic portal is not working, at least for some of the medical organizations. How do we know this? The author is a patient in one of the large clinics of this consortium and, because the electronic patient portal is not working, when the author leaves the examining room he is handed a stack of xeroxed papers giving the entire history of his clinic records; some of the patients will try to hand this stack of papers back to the

(Continued)

(Continued)

doctor, saying "I do NOT want this!" What is the doctor to do? If the doctor takes the papers back, then the doctor/clinic is "at fault" in not complying with this directive, and is potentially subject to fines. Other patients take the stack of pages (which are *not* stapled together) and drop some of them as they exit the long hallways of this clinic; others drop pages in the parking lot on the way to their car; and who knows what happens to those patients that actually get all of the pages into their car? What happens after that? I know what I do with them: I either throw them in the waste basket, un-shredded, or occasionally file them away in my medical records.

However, the info on these is *not accurate* — why? They write them to "comply with regulations" and provide CODES which are *not* my diagnosis — why? To get more revenue from "different codes"? Or are the doctors and nurses just in a hurry to get all this information entered electronically, and thus make mistake, after mistake, after another mistake. *Summary:* My medical records are filled with "mistakes" not only in Dx, but also in medications, and sometimes contain information that we did not even discuss or was part of the patient—doctor session included in that day's "summary" — why?

Under the auspices of HIPAA compliance, if a physician or hospital inadvertently allows medical information to be stolen, fines begin at $25,000 per instance. Although necessary waivers could authorize the release of information to the patient, the burden of proof often falls to the physician to demonstrate that the information that passed into the wrong hands came not from a breach in office security or their careless handling of the medical record but from a chart that had been transferred to the patient. Until these transactional details are resolved, a simple request for information translates into potential liability. (Clearly, having a secure electronic portal system is much safer than the current method of "handing out pages of the patient's record," which is happening at many healthcare facilities.)

12. *Provide patients with an electronic copy of their discharge instructions at the time of discharge, upon request.*
    (*Note*: Again, if this is available; one of the current authors has asked for this repeatedly at the four different medical clinics, for different specialities, that he utilizes, and so far been told "We do not have this available!")
    The presumption here is future oriented. A plurality of patients, especially the elderly and the poor, still do not have access to electronic media. It is unreasonable to assume that an 80-year-old with chronic obstructive pulmonary disease will have the patience to learn to use a tablet or PDA to better access his care plan. Instructions inscribed on plain paper, while very retro in orientation, meet a critical need. Until we have a population that is broadly e-literate and electronic-device capable, this will largely be disregarded.

13. *Have the ability to exchange information (such as medications, allergies and test results) electronically with other doctors and facilities.*
    HL7 and other transaction-based systems are designed to produce the efficiencies that will allow physicians and hospital systems to exchange information across different HIS systems and hospital networks. Practically speaking, each HIS system is its own country with complex transactional rules and portability, but only at a price. Should a hospital try to change its *lingua franca*, the cost of implementation will always include a fee to import a certain amount of data from the past few years to the new system. As these systems are resource intensive and sometimes not on site, legacy HIS systems are poorly supported and implemented. Generally, once a hospital has made the transition, no more than 3 to 4 years of data are available to the treating physician, let alone the hospital to which the patient is referred. Before this measure can be implemented, various parameters need to be defined in terms of scope, number of years that the medical record needs to remain accessible electronically, and translational format.

14. *Protect electronic health information and patient privacy.*
    The protections of electronic health information and patient privacy are implicit in HIPAA, but patient privacy is often relative. The electronic health information must not be protected to the exclusion of care of the patient. This concept is often lost on well-meaning clerks and hospital administrators who fail to understand the basis for the transparency behind the original incentive. On the one hand, there are severe penalties for healthcare workers who violate privacy laws, even without malice or intent; on the other, there is the often contemptible self-reporting mechanism that promises leniency but causes institutional embarrassment and opens the door to patient-originated civil litigation.

The 10 *Choice* Objectives (Hospitals Must Meet 5 of These)

1. *Implement drug formulary checks.*
   (A drug formulary is a list of prescription drugs preferred by your health plan. Checking this list helps ensure you're not paying extra for an expensive drug when a cheaper one will treat your condition just as well.)

Drug formulary checks are routinely accomplished by group purchasing organizations (GPOs) at the hospital level. These GPOs are supposed to provide the best possible pharmaceuticals (or medical devices) at the best possible price. However, they operate with a federally sanctioned exemption from anti-kickback legislation. *There is rampant opportunity for formulary adjustment to favor a drug which nets the hospital better remuneration as opposed to one that has a better price performance for the patient.* The challenge is to implement a patient-oriented approach.

2. *Record advance directives for patients 65 years or older.*

Advance directives are intended to reduce the anxiety and unnecessary contemplation associated with end-of-life discussions. In a coordinated healthcare delivery system there is the potential to reduce cost associated with unnecessary procedures, lab tests, and hospitalizations where an aggressive effort to resuscitate is not indicated or desired. Many have criticized this approach as a potential precedent for the so named "Death Squads" implicit in the new healthcare plan. There is the danger that advance directives can be assigned where there is not agreement between healthcare provider, patient, and other vested parties. Outcomes such as length of stay can be favorably impacted by directives that impose less-intensive care algorithms, favoring earlier discharge or demise.

3. *Incorporate test results as "structured data" so they can be searched, collected and reported automatically by computer systems.*

Most hospitals and healthcare systems have already migrated most of their day-to-day medical record-keeping to a structured hospital information system. These structured data are often contained in a HIS proprietary format that may not be searchable by the physicians and other healthcare providers who have a vested interest in its implementation. The automatic reporting element may not necessarily be clinical-outcomes based and may focus instead on the economic features of one practice versus another, insinuating that less expensive care or care delivered with fewer tests may be preferred to evidence-based practice.

4. *Generate lists of patients by specific conditions to use for research, outreach, reduction of disparities and quality improvement.*

On the surface, the use of lists to generate evidence-based research seems logical. However, there is danger in using these lists to generate data that push in the direction of less favorable advanced directives. A diagnosis that is associated with a poor outcome on the basis of use of older technologies, less than perfect surgical technique or medical management, or a systems problem (e.g., nosocomial infection) can push in the wrong direction in the interests of improving outcomes. There is a danger in presuming that the best way to reduce infection is to not admit or care for patients who are likely to get these infections and thus increase disparity under the banner of quality improvement.

5. *Use EHRs to provide the appropriate education and resources to patients.*

EHRs have the potential to hold vast quantities of medically relevant health education and patient resources. The challenge is to make sure that these educational materials are relevant to the diagnosis and specific to the patient's condition. Although mastitis (inflammation of the breast tissue) is commonly associated with difficulties arising from lactation, a 60-year-old woman with mastitis has little use for information describing the positive benefits of breastfeeding. Physicians commonly have different ideas about the extent or nature of follow-up. Different but related procedures may have different aftercare expectations. Appropriate education and resources assume a basic understanding of certain medical procedures; in areas of disparity, EHRs may not cater to the lowest common denominator.

Maybe this is the place to make a distinction between EHRs and EMRs. These two terms, EHRs (electronic health records) and EMRs (electronic medical records), are used interchangeably by many people in the healthcare field. Yet others make a clear distinction, and state: *"While EHRs do everything EMRs do, EHRs are more complex."* This distinction, and the extra value of EHRs, is pointed out in the following.

One of the biggest benefits of the EHR is quick access to and transfer of medical records between parties who are caring for a particular patient. Many people are confused by the terms EMR and EHR and while some have used them interchangeably, the two are quite different. Electronic medical records (EMRs) are computerized versions of a patient's medical chart. This information is used by providers in their office and EMR programs can vary from practice to practice. EMRs are not designed to enable transfer of data electronically to other care providers and may even need to be manually printed for sharing.

EHRs are more complex. While EHRs do everything EMRs do, they are part of a network designed to share data universally with other participating parties no matter where in the country they are. Not being just an electronic patient record, an EHR requires users to examine and redesign office workflow and processes to maximize the efficiency of the system. Practice leaders must ensure staff training and coordination of system implementation with daily office duties and be prepared to work closely with the vendor who installs the system to correct any problems during startup.

Once established, information moves seamlessly with the patient from the doctor's office, to the hospital, to the nursing home and anywhere else as needed. This means a greater access to accurate patient information, plus improvements in patient safety and faster access to medical care.

Do EHRs Improve Communication and Care Between Patients and Physicians?

Since EHRs were formally launched in 2012, their benefit has been seen for patients across the lifespan. These improvements include:

- *Easier access to patient-specific medical data*
- *Drug interaction alerts for improved medication safety*
- *Drug refill reminders*
- *Alerts to remind physicians when lab results are ready*
- *Vaccination and screening reminders*
- *Access to data sets for patients with the same conditions (diabetes, hypertension, etc.)*
- *Identification of trends in the patient history without searching through the entire chart*
- *Streamlined patient care and more time for providers to spend with the patient.*

Financial Benefits of EHR Implementation

The Centers for Medicare and Medicaid Services (CMS) has developed an incentive program for medical providers to encourage the implementation of EHRs. Rolled into a program known as meaningful use, CMS has developed standards that participants in the program must meet for reimbursement. This could mean up to $44,000 a year for physicians who treat Medicare patients, and more than $62,000 annually for providers whose practice volume is 30 percent Medicaid patients. Providers who participate in the program have a set timeframe to demonstrate that they are using their EMRs "meaningfully" (such as electronic prescription use and responsible information sharing) or could face a reduction in reimbursement starting in 2015 [see also Figure 9.1].

[From*: The Data Behind Electronic Health Records; http://publichealthonline.gwu.edu/ data-behind-electronic-health-records/; July 23, 2013;* © *2013 School of Public Health and Health Services, George Washington University.*]

Some of the performance results that should be generated because of use of EHRs are listed below. But are the expected results, as defined below in points 6–10, being realized as of early 2014? At this point we would have to say

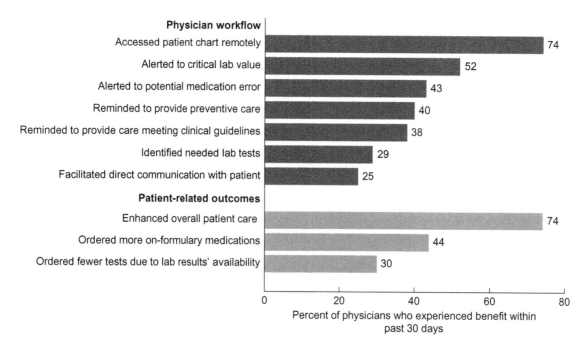

FIGURE 9.1   How do EHRs benefit public health? The graph above shows the percentage of physicians whose electronic health records provided selected benefits (United States, 2011).

an absolute "No," for the most part, because the intercommunication among different EHRs (i.e., their "transparency") has not been worked out, even though this is one of the mandated "bullet points" of Meaningful Use Stage I.

6. *When a patient is transferred from another doctor or hospital, perform medication reconciliation to make sure all of the patient's drugs are listed and are correct.*

   Medical reconciliation is simply matching admit medications with those that are prescribed on discharge or transfer. Hospital formularies that are not compliant with outpatient therapy or drug shortages *can produce results that can be reconciled but are not in the best interests of the patient.* If a hospital does not have availability of a particular medication on admission, there is a danger that the medication will never be reconciled. The reconciliation process needs to extend beyond the simple admit/discharge mindset and must accommodate the pre-admit medications as well as the forced substitutions that occur during hospitalization prior to the patient discharge and reunification with the original medication regimen.

7. *When a patient is transferred to another doctor or hospital, provide a summary of the patient's care.*

   This simple act should be obvious. Before the institution of HIPAA, consent was implicit with the transfer of the patient from one hospital to another. Now, there are separate consents for medical records, insurance, and acknowledgments of patient privacy that must all be secured prior to authorization of transfer of patient care summaries. Even if all the consents are extant, lack of data transfer beyond the initial summary results in broadly increased costs to patients and plan providers. Essentially if the patient transfers from one hospital to another with an expensive send-out test pending, there is no assurance that the result will ever make it to the patient's chart. The receiving hospital physician will not be able to retrieve the information because the patient identifier is not the same as that of the referring hospital. The referring hospital physician may fear the very act of accessing the electronic medical record because he feels that this act may trigger compliance oversight since there is no active relationship with the patient. *As a result, duplicative labwork, "reinventing the wheel," has become the order of the day.*

8. *Be able to submit immunization records electronically to the appropriate government agencies.*

   Submission of immunization records to the appropriate government agencies will require a more cohesive effort at the national level. Although progress has been made towards computerizing existing paper immunization cards and proprietary hospital systems, beyond certain rare immunizations *there is no unified governmental agency to receive routine immunization data.*

9. *Be able to submit reportable lab results electronically to the appropriate government agencies.*

   (State and local governments specify which lab results are reportable in each location. For example, in some states doctors must report positive HIV tests.)

   In different geographic locations, different diseases are reportable. These mechanisms are dependent on extensive state and local networks as well as adequate reporting mechanisms at the level of the local hospital or public health clinic. In areas of the greatest need, areas of disparity, reporting mechanisms parallel the accessibility to health care. In the poorest areas of New York, reporting mechanisms can be secured because of the relative short distance to access some of the more sophisticated care in the nation; in rural Mississippi, despite comparable disparity, access is imperiled by lack of availability of local resources. *A mechanism to assure uniform reporting is still lacking.*

10. *Be able to submit "syndromic surveillance" data electronically to public health agencies.*

    (Syndromic surveillance means doctors and health agencies monitor patient symptoms so they will know if there is an outbreak of disease.)

    Syndromic surveillance is largely the purview of the Centers for Disease Control in Atlanta. Manually reporting to the county or state health department is the usual mechanism by which information is transferred to the CDC. Broad strides in the pattern detection of influenza outbreaks has helped stave off epidemics such as H1N1 in 2007−2008, which many had predicted would be comparable in scope to the 1918 influenza outbreak. Electronic surveillance is a step above, and requires the implementation of clinic-based systems that can capture information that might otherwise be lost on a triage sheet. A patient actually has to access services in order to trigger reporting. *If an emergency room is triaging all patients who walk in with influenza syndromes to go home without intervention, the incidence and severity of an epidemic can be compromised.*

MEANINGFUL USE GOALS FOR DOCTORS

The Department of Health and Human Services has a list of *requirements* that individual doctors must meet to achieve meaningful use. These requirements are similar to those for the hospitals, but differ in terms of their scope and applicability. Doctors must meet their 15 requirements plus 5 of the 10 *choice* objectives.

The 15 Requirements (Doctors Must Meet All of These)

1. *Use computerized provider order entry (CPOE) for prescriptions.*

    CPOE is a mixed bag for physicians. Clearly, a proper implementation of CPOE can greatly reduce the possibility of medical error. Error-checking is system dependent, and some health information systems do a better job than others. The generic patient does not fit extremes of weight or age. In the case of neonates, most formularies have been scaled beyond usefulness. Error-checking is a matter of guesswork since most of the doses are too small for exacting dose calculation when placed in so-called smart pumps that are incapable of delivering the desired dose in the desired time interval.

2. *Check for drug—drug and drug—allergy interactions.*

    Checking for drug—drug interactions requires access to a common drug database. Most HIS systems excel at determining whether one drug has the potential for interaction with another drug. Drug allergy interaction reporting and checking are dependent on the extent to which the physician understands the drug allergy. A penicillin rash and penicillin-derived anaphylaxis are completely different reactions to the same substance; but both are likely to turn up as a drug—allergy interaction, often without a qualifier. If a patient is *in extremis* and requires a drug that might produce an innocuous rash but the physician substitutes a less effective alternative because of a perceived allergic reaction, this requirement has produced a less desirable outcome.

3. *Maintain an up-to-date problem list of diagnoses.*

    An up-to-date problem list has been a staple of the physician note since the mid-1970s. The idea of a problem-oriented medical record standardized the concept that a set group of diagnoses could be used to focus care along the line of medical problems and in turn utilized to provide better care pathways. Ultimately, these are foci of the new mandates. If we know what diagnoses are most common and we know their expected outcomes, we can reduce the cost of health care by finding the most efficient practices that produce the best outcomes at the best possible cost. ICD-9 and ICD-10 will further hone and refine the problem list by refining what is meant by "pneumonia." The problem is that the maintenance of these diagnosis codes is very time intensive. A simple admission for a well baby may require no more than one or two diagnoses. An intensive care admission of a patient with renal failure, respiratory failure, and cardiac compromise is much more time consuming since the additional diagnoses of hyperkalemia, hypotension, and pneumonia must also be entered. Physicians are increasingly moving from interacting with their patients at the bedside to using tablets and workstations at the charting station.

4. *Generate and transmit permissible prescriptions electronically (eRx).*

    Fraudulent prescriptions have long plagued the medical community. By the time the error is realized, it is often too late to stop the unintended dispensing of a highly addictive narcotic or medication that can be used to formulate a more addictive, recreational drug. Methods that have evolved to produce better compliance have included triplicate forms for narcotic use as well as registered prescriptions tied to a known serial number. Both methods were flawed and led to further abuses, including the theft of these *carte blanche* documents, under the guise that they were so secure that they would not be questioned. Physicians could be held criminally responsible for inadvertent loss of these forms. Many physicians still have a considerable investment in lock boxes for these triplicate prescriptions. With the change to electronically submitted prescriptions, multiple efficiencies improved. Physicians no longer have to worry that patients will lose their prescriptions on the way to the pharmacy, and the pharmacy can transmit a token that guarantees their receipt of the intended medication. Issues of illegible physician handwriting are no longer a problem. Linked pharmacies can transmit prescription information to their affiliates so that a patient can replace a prescription even while traveling, without having to contact the physician. Still, however, there are issues. Physicians are not always able to use the same electronic prescription service with all of the hospitals where they care for patients; some classes and more sophisticated prescription medication forms are not covered by these services; and if a patient decides to change pharmacy because of cost, convenience, or another reason, the ease of taking the paper prescription to an "out of network" pharmacy might not exist. *(It is interesting to note that one of the first EMR/EHR systems, the free open source VistA-EHR, has a 99.9% accuracy rate in e-drug prescriptions. Why do we not have this same accuracy from the numerous systems — actually over 1,700 EMR/EHR for-profit vendor systems — that have developed since 2006?)*

5. *Maintain an active medication list.*

    The active medication list has always been a difficult part of medical practice. A patient can choose to see one or many different subspecialists and receive prescriptions from all of them. Medications from a broken arm 10 years ago can suddenly surface as the patient attempts to treat excess pain economically. Some patients may be forthcoming; others may be less likely to divulge the multitude of different therapeutic paths that they may be following simultaneously; and most patients simply cannot remember all the medications they have taken over a lifetime, one of the reasons being the "odd sounding scientific names" that are given to most medications — these names and doses just do not stick in patients' minds. Thus the only accurate way to meet this mandate is to have an e-system that requires entry before a prescription can be dispensed to the patient. The challenge outside of the hospital is for the physician to integrate all of these many disparate sources into one common document that is reflective of the actual therapy.

6. *Maintain an active medication allergy list.*

Medication allergies are often self-reported by the patient to the physician in the outpatient setting. These have to be corroborated against actual symptomatology. Certainly, the physician in the outpatient setting will have different challenges than in the hospital setting, but the severity of the reaction must be maintained as well as the type and class of the medication involved. To be absolutely accurate, this goal can only be obtained by scientific testing with each patient.

For one of the authors of this book, an "allergic reaction" to a blood pressure medication took 5 years to diagnose, using three specialists: (1) the family medical doctor, who prescribed the medication; (2) the allergist to whom the family medical doctor referred the patient (the allergist's initial diagnosis being that some sort of "unusual COPD was going on") — but eventually, in addition to the lung infections, three different types of skin eruptions occurred; (3) the dermatologist who was then brought into the picture, who confirmed that there were several different types of "skin eruptions" occurring. At this point, 5 years into the process, the lung infections and skin eruptions were becoming more common, so all three doctors decided that the most likely culprit was the BP medication, namely Benicar HTC — so to "scientifically" determine this, the author went off the Benicar HTC and within 1 month most of the skin eruptions had resolved, and by 6 months were fully resolved. By the end of a year, the "unique COPD" diagnosis could no longer be accepted, as the lung infections had disappeared, the COPD medications were not needed, and the lung function tests were the best ever. Returning to use of Benicar HTC for a short period of time brought back these symptoms. Thus this "double check" pretty well proved the allergy.

In the meantime, this author had been treated for 5 years for a Dx that really did not exist; the Dx had to be revised; yet the "new diagnosis" is "couched" in the medical records, presumably so that the doctor/clinic can justify prescribing the meds and treatments over the 5-year period, being reimbursed from insurance, without suffering a penalty because of mis-diagnosis and treatment. (The author, the patient, laughs out loud as he reads the reams of paper records that are handed to him at each visit; if the electronic patient portal, where the patient could also enter data such as day-by-day responses to medications, etc., were functioning correctly this patient would be able to "set the record straight," and really provide much more scientific information from which a good prediction model and thus a better prescription could have been made. But this is the thesis of this book: when these electronic procedures are perfected, all of us patients will realize these goals; and this is happening very rapidly around us, even if we do not realize it. For example, the minute-by-minute monitoring of blood pressure, heart rhythms, etc. from mobile phones via mobile apps is happening right now in certain parts of the USA, and will be "invading" and covering all of us within just a few years, if not months ... so there is "hope on the horizon ..."

So, in reality, how much effort is needed to accurately determine if an individual patient is "really" allergic to any specific medication? To do so takes clear and clean scientific process. But this is happening: see FutureMed (http://futuremed2020.com/) and the efforts of Singularity University (http://singularityu.org/; www.ted.com/talks/ray_kurzweil_announces_singularity_university.html; http://singularity.org/; http://singularityu.org/overview/).

7. *Record demographics on date of birth, language, gender, race, and ethnicity.*

These are common elements of the physician chart in the office setting. Various physician practice management software solutions exist to record this information. Some of the more sophisticated ones link with the hospital information system and can pull as well as push demographic information as the information becomes available.

8. *Record and chart changes in height, weight, blood pressure, and BMI. In children and adolescents aged 2−20 years, growth charts must also be plotted.*

This requirement for vital sign and morphometric tracking is very similar to the hospital requirement. As noted above, a pediatric physician is more likely to have up-to-date information regarding patients less than 2 years of age because of the importance of tracking possible disease states in this category of patient. *This is one area where the requirement does not go far enough in requiring vital information.*

9. *Record whether each patient (aged 13 and up) smokes.*

In their office, most pediatricians and family physicians make an exceptional effort to deter their younger patients from smoking. *Here again, however, the requirement is not sufficiently broad to capture the lower end of the spectrum.* Especially in areas of disparity, it is not too unusual to find a pediatric patient with a 5−10 pack-year history of smoking (number of packs per day × years) by age 13 years.

10. *Report ambulatory clinical quality measures (a separate list of requirements) to government authorities.*

    Quality measures are tools by which we can assess various healthcare outcomes. Most ambulatory tools focus on the ability of current practices to address certain National Quality Forum (NQF) aims. The early goals include adherence to chronic medications, statin therapy for individuals with coronary artery disease, adherence to chronic medication for diabetics, monthly monitoring for patients who are on anticoagulants, and monitoring for patients who are on anticoagulants and who may be taking antibiotics at the same time, as well as adherence to antipsychotic medication regiments for patients with schizophrenia.

11. *Implement one clinical decision support rule related to a high priority hospital condition along with the ability to track compliance with that rule.*

    Physicians are required to develop a clinical decision support rule for enhancing health care. While the decision regarding the appropriate clinical decision support rule is largely left to the physician (in fact, CMS will not issue guidance on the choice of this rule), previous requirements for drug–drug and drug–allergy interactions may not be used. However, the implementation of a process that best meets a physician workflow and is tailored to the demographics of the patient population will qualify. A measure designed to reduce prescription error by incorporating certain practice-based strategies may satisfy this requirement.

12. *Provide patients with an electronic copy of their health information (diagnostic test results, problem list, medication lists, medication allergies, discharge summary and procedures) upon request.*

    The provision of this requirement is dependent on patient computer literacy as well as portability and security of the document. A patient who requests this information must have the means to receive it. A USB drive, while convenient, represents an open invitation to HIPAA compliance issues if it is not adequately secured. This security, necessary for the reliable transport of information, must also prevent patient information from being altered, so that the information can be reliably interpreted by another provider.

    (*Note*: Again, although mandated, this requirement seems to be the last one to be implemented; at least in certain areas of the USA where some of the authors live this e-Patient Portal just does not yet exist, even though the flow charts of the medical organizations may clearly have it as part of their diagram illustrating how they are meeting Meaningful Use stages . . .)

13. *Provide clinical summaries for patients for each office visit.*

    The objective of this parameter is to try to provide clinical summaries to patients for each office visit. In this area, the benchmark is for physicians to provide these summaries to more than 50% of all patients within a window of a three-day period. There is the expectation that this will include reasonable updates, including updates to the problem list, as well as medications that may have been prescribed or discontinued. Implicit in this mandate is the understanding that the physician should not demand a fee to provide this information.

14. *Have the ability to exchange information (such as medications, allergies, and test results) electronically with other doctors and facilities.*

    This measure requires the capability to transact critical clinical information from provider to provider. The measure of this capability tests the capacity of the physician's EHR to provide a certified transfer of key clinical data. *This capacity is often fraught with complications.* Although the attestation requires that this transaction is not a simulation and is between two distinct and separate entities, no cost ceiling is delineated. The nominal cost for a single transaction may rise exponentially when the physician has to deal with numerous different systems with different requirements among different providers with different information transfer capacities. Even within the context of the requirement, a successful test is not mandated. *An unsuccessful electronic exchange meets the requirement of the measure.*

15. *Protect electronic health information and patient privacy.*

    These privacy issues are already contained within HIPPA. Physicians are required to perform a security risk analysis, identify areas of risk, and correct these deficiencies according to established protocols. These updates might include updates to security software as well as change to the workflow process in the interest of expediting and eliminating deficiencies within the system. *There is no exemption made for this requirement.*

The 10 Additional *Choice* Objectives for Individual Physicians (5 of These Must Be Met to Achieve Compliance)

1. *Implement drug formulary checks.*

    (A drug formulary is a list of prescription drugs preferred by your health plan. Checking this list helps ensure you're not paying extra for an expensive drug when a cheaper one will treat your condition just as well.)

The physician implementation requires drug formulary checks. To include this as a choice objective, a physician must have access to at least one internal or external formulary during the period in which the report is generated. Physicians writing fewer than 100 prescriptions during the EHR reporting epoch are excluded from using this mechanism.

2. *Incorporate test results as "structured data" so they can be searched, collected, and reported automatically by computer systems.*

The incorporation of clinical test data into a physician EHR is not a simple task. This measure requires that 40% of the lab test data ordered by the physician be incorporated into the physician EHR as structured data that can be searched and compiled into useful outcomes-based research. Obviously, physicians who do not order studies that are reported in a simple positive/negative format or numeral data cannot participate in this measure.

3. *Generate lists of patients by specific conditions to use for research, outreach, reduction of disparities, and quality improvement.*

This measure requires the generation of lists of patients who have certain disorders that can be quantified in such a way that quality improvement can be achieved through the reduction of disparity through research, outreach, or an other mechanism. The measure requires that the physician generates at least one report listing patients with the specific condition. *There are no exclusion criteria for this measure.*

4. *Send patient reminders (to patients who want them) about prevention or follow-up care.*

Another option is for the physician to send reminder notifications for preventive and follow-up care. A 20% threshold is required for patients who are either younger than 5 or older than 65 years during a particular EHR reporting period. Although no minimum is specifically mentioned, a physician who has no patients in either age group is excluded from using this as evidence of compliance to meaningful use. There is an ability to exclude patients who opt out of notification as well as those who are not maintained using EHR technology implicit in this objective.

5. *Provide patients with electronic access to their health information (including lab results, problem list, medication lists, and allergies) within 4 business days.*

Patient electronic access is considered a cornerstone of meaningful use.

(*Note:* Yet, in the experience of some of the authors, this "cornerstone of meaningful use" is not being met, and seems to have been put at the bottom of the doctor's/hospital's/medical healthcare delivery systems priority list.)

The objective is met by providing lab results and other pertinent information to patients within 4 business days of the information being available to the physician. The criterion for this measure is met by 10% of the physician's patients having access to this information. It is left to the physician to stop certain information from being included in this mandate. Any physician whose practice does not create or produce information that can be disseminated by these mechanisms is excluded from this measure. Although this is a crucial issue, as the requirement for compliance is low, this has been deprioritized in favor of the more concrete mandates. Any increasingly erudite consumer base will ultimately force the issue and is already evident in certain models (e.g., Kaiser Permanente, 2014; Wellpoint, 2014).

6. *Use EHRs to provide the appropriate education and resources to patients.*

The challenge to find context-relevant information for patient education has long been an issue. EHR technology can be useful to identify meaningful resources that are not only patient specific but also appropriate to the patient's level of understanding. In turn, these resources have the potential to decrease unnecessary patient utilization by steering patients in the direction of additional pertinent experiences. The emphasis is placed on reducing the frequency with which a patient would see the same provider multiple times within the same EHR reporting period. The measure for this option is 10% of all unique patients seen by a physician. *There are no exclusion criteria.*

7. *When a patient is transferred from another doctor or hospital, perform medication reconciliation to make sure all of the patient's drugs are listed and are correct.*

In a manner not dissimilar to a hospital admission, a physician receiving a patient in referral from another provider should perform a medication reconciliation. Only patients who are included in the EHR are affected by this option. The measure requires that 50% of all transitions of care relating to patients who come from another provider have their medications electronically reconciled by the EHR. If a physician does not have a patient who transitions to his or her care during the reporting period, this criterion cannot be used.

8. *When a patient is transferred to another doctor or hospital, provide a summary of the patient's care.*

This meaningful use measure requires that the physician who transfers a patient from his or her care to another provider or care facility creates a summary of the care provided. Here, again, the measure requires a 50%

compliance, but there is no requirement that the summary be electronic. Physicians who do not transfer their patients to other physicians or facilities are excluded from this mechanism.

9. *Be able to submit reportable lab results electronically to the appropriate government agencies.*

(State and local governments specify which lab results are reportable in each location. For example, in some states doctors must report positive HIV tests.)

The capacity to submit meaningful lab results directly to governmental agencies is crucial to this competency. The measure requires at least one completed test of the EHR technology's capability to submit information. Here again, an unsuccessful test meets the criterion, but the physician is expected to initiate regular reporting if the test is successful. The expectation is that the test be conducted with actual information and not utilize fictitious data. Physicians who have no valid need to submit this information are excluded from this particular modality.

10. *Be able to submit "syndromic surveillance" data electronically to public health agencies.*

(Syndromic surveillance means doctors and health agencies monitor patient symptoms so they'll know if there's an outbreak of disease.)

This category requires the submission of electronic syndromic surveillance information to appropriate public health agencies in accordance with usual practice. The measure requires the submission of at least one test of reporting syndromic information. A successful test must also include follow-up information unless the public health agencies are not able to receive this information. Unsuccessful tests are considered valid under this measure, and simulated data are excluded. Physicians who do not generally report syndromic information are excluded from this option.

MEANINGFUL USE REQUIREMENTS OF STAGE I, STAGE II, AND STAGE III

The Meaningful Use regulations set by the CMS are being introduced in three stages over the course of 5 years (from 2011 to 2015).

- *Stage I (2011–2012)*

  This is the "start-up" phase. It sets the foundation for electronic data capture and information sharing by using Meaningful Use compliant systems, like DrFirst's Rcopia-MU.
- *Stage II (2013–2014)*

  This stage involves many of the same requirements of Stage I, but increased percentages of use. This increase in usage involves features like showing a greater number of patient data records, computerized physician order entries (CPOE) or more e-prescribing. Additionally, all Menu Options will become Core Objectives; and additional Objectives may be added.
- *Stage III (2015)*

  This stage, as with Stage II, continues to expand the use of electronic data capture and information sharing to levels of 80–90% on average. In addition, this stage will take into account future rules and decisions based upon knowledge gathered by the first two stages.

(www.drfirst.com/meaningful-use/meaningful-use-requirements.jsp).

(Stage III, as of this writing in late November, 2013, was mandated to start January 1, 2014 but was delayed until 2017 (Lowes, 2013)).

Requirements for Stage I of Meaningful Use

Medicare Providers

Meaningful Use objectives are organized into two sets — a "core" set and a "menu" set. These objectives must be met to obtain Meaningful Use incentive funds. While the *objectives* for Stage I of Meaningful Use are the same for an eligible professional or an eligible hospital or CAH, the *requirements* are slightly different for each.

Eligible professionals have 25 Meaningful Use objectives to meet. However, in order to qualify for Meaningful Use incentive payments, 20 of these 25 objectives must be met in accordance with the following rules:

- 15 required core objectives
- 5 objectives from the list of 10 menu set objectives.

Eligible hospitals and CAHs, by comparison, have 24 Meaningful Use objectives to meet. For them to qualify, 19 of these 24 objectives must be met in accordance with the following rules:

- 14 required core objectives
- 5 objectives from the list of 10 menu set objectives.

Medicaid Providers

For Stage I of the Meaningful Use incentives, eligible Medicaid providers must adopt, implement, or upgrade to a certified Meaningful Use system to qualify for the federal incentive payments.

Rcopia-MU Certified Modular EHR

There is a wide assortment of certified software available, but in order to achieve Meaningful Use you need a program like DrFirst's RcopiaMU Certified Modular EHR (www.drfirst.com/rcopia-mu-meaningful-use.jsp) that allows you to meet Meaningful Use regulations while growing your health IT at your own pace. Complete the Demo Form found on the above website to learn more about how DrFirst can help you achieve your Meaningful Use requirements.

POSTSCRIPT

For those readers who want to delve deeper into the Meaningful Use Stages and also see the "current status" of their implementation, the following site is the best government link to provide this information; and then from this link, you can click to other links, taking you to official government information on Meaningful Use Stage I, Stage II, and Stage III: www.cms.gov/Regulations-and-Guidance/Legislation/EHRIncentivePrograms/Meaningful_Use.html.

The focus on underlying issues of medical care continues in Chapters 10 and 12 in relation to hospital certification and optimization. The focus sharpens with Chapter 11 to emphasize the need to study actual root causes of medical and health conditions.

BIBLIOGRAPHY

Resources for further study, for those readers of this book that have a particular interest in the Meaningful Use topic.

Abbett, S.K., Bates, D.W., Kachalia, A., 2011. The meaningful use regulations in information technology: what do they mean for quality improvement in hospitals? Jt. Comm. J. Qual. Patient Saf. 37 (7), 289, 333–336.

Ahmed, A., Chandra, S., Herasevich, V., Gajic, O., Pickering, B.W., 2011. The effect of two different electronic health record user interfaces on intensive care provider task load, errors of cognition, and performance. Crit. Care Med. 39 (7), 1626–1634.

Amatayakul, M., 2011. Meaningful tips for achieving meaningful use. Healthc. Financ. Manag. 65 (10), 120–122.

American Optometric Association, 2011a. Practical hints on meaningful use. Optometry. 82 (12), 757–765.

American Optometric Association, 2011b. Attestation of core objectives for the meaningful use of electronic health records. Optometry. 82 (3), 181–190.

Baldwin, G., 2011. The long shadow of meaningful use. Health Data Manag. 19 (1), 46–48, 53-45.

Banas, C.A., Erskine, A.R., Sun, S., Retchin, S.M., 2011. Phased implementation of electronic health records through an office of clinical transformation. J. Am. Med. Inform. Assoc. 18 (5), 721–725.

Barton, A.J., 2011. The electronic health record and "meaningful use": implications for the clinical nurse specialist. Clin. Nurse Spec. 25 (1), 8–10.

Benin, A.L., Fenick, A., Herrin, J., Vitkauskas, G., Chen, J., Brandt, C., 2011. How good are the data? Feasible approach to validation of metrics of quality derived from an outpatient electronic health record. Am. J. Med. Qual. 26 (6), 441–451.

Benson, S., 2011. Meaningful use and clinical documentation. J. AHIMA. 82 (2), 36–37.

Bernd, D.L., Fine, P.S., 2011. Electronic medical records: a path forward. Front. Health Serv. Manag. 28 (1), 3–13.

Bertini, E., Tatu, A., Keim, D., 2011. Quality metrics in high-dimensional data visualization: an overview and systematization. IEEE Trans. Vis. Comput. Graph. 17 (12), 2203–2212.

Bloomrosen, M., Starren, J., Lorenzi, N.M., Ash, J.S., Patel, V.L., Shortliffe, E.H., 2011. Anticipating and addressing the unintended consequences of health IT and policy: a report from the AMIA 2009 Health Policy Meeting. J. Am. Med. Inform. Assoc. 18 (1), 82–90.

Blumenthal, D., 2011. Meaningful use: an assessment. An interview with David Blumenthal, M.D., National Coordinator for Health Information Technology, Office of the National Coordinator. Interview by Mark Hagland. Healthc. Inform. 28 (1), 40, 44.

Bolla, Y., 2011. Meaningful use 101. Nurs. Manag. 42 (8), 18–22.

Bormel, J., 2011. Problem lists are the keys to meaningful use. Put the big picture on your problem list. Health Manag. Technol. 32 (2), 40–41.

Buhler, M.F., 2011. Meaningful use incentive or unsound business practice. J. Okla. State Med. Assoc. 104 (4), 121–122.

Cebul, R.D., Love, T.E., Jain, A.K., Hebert, C.J., 2011. Electronic health records and quality of diabetes care. N. Engl. J. Med. 365 (9), 825–833.

Classen, D.C., Bates, D.W., 2011. Finding the meaning in meaningful use. N. Engl. J. Med. 365 (9), 855–858.

Coiera, E., 2011. Do we need a national electronic summary care record? Med. J. Aust. 194 (2), 90–92.

Collins, S.A., Vawdrey, D.K., Kukafka, R., Kuperman, G.J., 2011. Policies for patient access to clinical data via PHRs: current state and recommendations. J. Am. Med. Inform. Assoc. 18 (Suppl. 1), i2–i7.

Conde, C., 2011a. A good deal. Tex. Med. 107 (4), 43–47.

Conde, C., 2011b. High tech u. Tex. Med. 107 (7), 55–61.

Conn, J., 2011. "Age of meaningful use". HIMSS convention delivers with hot IT topics. Mod. Healthc. 41 (9), 12–13.

Crosson, J.C., Bazemore, A.W., Phillips Jr.R.L., 2011a. EHR implementation without meaningful use can lead to worse outcomes. Am. Fam. Physician. 84 (11), 1220.

Crosson, J.C., Etz, R.S., Wu, S., Straus, S.G., Eisenman, D., Bell, D.S., 2011b. Meaningful use of electronic prescribing in 5 exemplar primary care practices. Ann. Fam. Med. 9 (5), 392−397.

Das, S., Eisenberg, L.D., House, J.W., Lee, K.J., Lusk, R.P., Nielsen, D.R., et al., 2011. Meaningful use of electronic health records in otolaryngology: recommendations from the American Academy of Otolaryngology−Head and Neck Surgery Medical Informatics Committee. Otolaryngol. Head Neck Surg. 144 (2), 135−141.

de Brouwer, H., Stegeman, G.A., 2011. LEAN approach toward automated analysis and data processing of polymers using proton NMR spectroscopy. J. Lab. Autom. 16 (1), 1−16.

DesRoches, C.M., Miralles, P., Buerhaus, P., Hess, R., Donelan, K., 2011. Health information technology in the workplace: findings from a 2010 national survey of registered nurses. J. Nurs. Adm. 41 (9), 357−364.

Dimick, C., 2011. Meaningful use: notes from the journey. J. AHIMA. 82 (10), 24−30.

Dorr, D.A., Cohen, A.M., Williams, M.P., Hurdle, J., 2011. From simply inaccurate to complex and inaccurate: complexity in standards-based quality measures. AMIA Annu. Symp. Proc. 2011, 331−338.

Dykes, P.C., Dadamio, R.R., Goldsmith, D., Kim, H.-E., Ohashi, K., Saba, V.K., 2011. Leveraging standards to support patient-centric interdisciplinary plans of care. AMIA Annu. Symp. Proc. 2011, 356−363.

Dysvik, E., Sommerseth, R., Jacobsen, F.F., 2011. Living a meaningful life with chronic pain from a nursing perspective. Narrative approach to a case story. Int. J. Nurs. Pract. 17 (1), 36−42.

Eagle, D., Barr, T.R., 2011. Achieving meaningful use of electronic health records for the oncologist. Oncology (Williston Park). 25 (8), 684, 688, 690.

Elnahal, S.M., Joynt, K.E., Bristol, S.J., Jha, A.K., 2011. Electronic health record functions differ between best and worst hospitals. Am. J. Manag. Care. 17 (4), e121−e147.

Evans, J.R., Barker, R.A., 2011. Defining meaningful outcome measures in trials of disease-modifying therapies in Parkinson's disease. Expert Opin. Pharmacother. 12 (8), 1249−1258.

Fang, H., Peifer, K.L., Chen, J., Rizzo, J.A., 2011. Health information technology and physicians' perceptions of healthcare quality. Am. J. Manag. Care. 17 (3), e66−e70.

Fleming, N.S., Culler, S.D., McCorkle, R., Becker, E.R., Ballard, D.J., 2011. The financial and nonfinancial costs of implementing electronic health records in primary care practices. Health Aff. (Millwood). 30 (3), 481−489.

Friedman, A.N., Fadem, S.Z., 2011. Making measures count. Clin. J. Am. Soc. Nephrol. 6 (6), 1507−1511.

Gagliardi, F., 2011. Instance-based classifiers applied to medical databases: diagnosis and knowledge extraction. Artif. Intell. Med. 52 (3), 123−139.

Gibbings, T., Konigsbach, D., Reicher, M.A., 2011. Meaningful use in radiology. J. Am. Coll. Radiol. 8 (9), 657−660.

Goedert, J., 2011. Making the most of meaningful use. Health Data Manag. 19 (9), 36, 38, 40 *passim*.

Goel, M.S., Brown, T.L., Williams, A., Hasnain-Wynia, R., Thompson, J.A., Baker, D.W., 2011. Disparities in enrollment and use of an electronic patient portal. J. Gen. Intern. Med. 26 (10), 1112−1116.

Grantham, D., 2011. Meaningful use: "yes you can!" Behav. Healthc. 31 (4), 64−66, 69.

Guise, J.M., Viswanathan, M., 2011. Overview of best practices in conducting comparative-effectiveness reviews. Clin. Pharmacol. Ther. 90 (6), 876−882.

Hagland, M., 2011. Balancing act: Can CMIOs and CIOs make physician documentation work for everyone? Healthc. Inform. 28 (5), 8−10, 12, 14.

Henricks, W.H., 2011. "Meaningful use" of electronic health records and its relevance to laboratories and pathologists. J. Pathol. Inform. 2, 7.

Hess, C.T., 2011. Your meaningful use and international classification of diseases, 10th revision checklists. Adv. Skin Wound Care. 24 (9), 440.

Hilts, M.E., 2011. CIOs report on one of their busiest years: Healthcare CIOs have their hands full with meaningful-use missions and other priorities. But their pockets are fuller, too, with a growing compensation and healthy bonuses. Health Manag. Technol. 32 (9), 6−8, 10.

Hoffman, S., Podgurski, A., 2011. Meaningful use and certification of health information technology: what about safety? J. Law Med. Ethics. 39 (Suppl. 1), 77−80.

Holmes, C., 2011. The problem list beyond meaningful use. Part I: The problems with problem lists. J. AHIMA. 82 (2), 30−33, quiz 34.

How do we get to meaningful use? Elsevier's Special Edition, Nanotechnology: Introducing the Future. Volume 32, issues 3 & 4. Available at: www.journals.elsevier.com/technovation/special-issues/.

Hussain, A.A., 2011. Meaningful use of information technology: a local perspective. Ann. Intern. Med. 154 (10), 690−692.

Jain, S.H., Seidman, J., Blumenthal, D., 2011. Meaningful use: the authors reply. Health Aff. (Millwood). 30 (1), 182.

Joch, A., 2011. Information technology. Meaningful use funding: When should you apply? Hosp. Health Netw. 85 (5), 11−12.

Johnson, K.H., Bergren, M.D., 2011. Meaningful use of school health data. J. Sch. Nurs. 27 (2), 102−110.

Joiner, K.A., Castellanos, N., Wartman, S.A., 2011. Resource allocation in academic health centers: creating common metrics. Acad. Med. 86 (9), 1084−1092.

Jones, J.B., Shah, N.R., Bruce, C.A., Stewart, W.F., 2011. Meaningful use in practice using patient-specific risk in an electronic health record for shared decision making. Am. J. Prev. Med. 40 (5 Suppl. 2), S179−S186.

Jones, S.S., Friedberg, M.W., Schneider, E.C., 2011a. Health information exchange, health information technology use, and hospital readmission rates. AMIA Annu. Symp. Proc. 2011, 644−653.

Jones, S.S., Heaton, P., Friedberg, M.W., Schneider, E.C., 2011b. Today's "meaningful use" standard for medication orders by hospitals may save few lives; later stages may do mo. Health Aff. (Millwood). 30 (10), 2005−2012.

Kaiser Permanente, 2014. <http://en.wikipedia.org/wiki/Kaiser_Permanente/>, last retrieved May 10, 2014).

Kallem, C., 2011. Transforming clinical quality measures for EHR use. NQF refines emeasures for use in EHRs and meaningful use program. J. AHIMA. 82 (11), 52−53.

Karmali, K., Grobovsky, L., Levy, J., Keatings, M., 2011. Enhancing cultural competence for improved access to quality care. Healthc. Q. 14 (Spec. No. 3), 52−57.

Kazzaz, D., 2011. Meaningful use: the glass half full. Md. Med. 12 (1), 25−26.

Ketchersid, T., 2011. Health information technology: driving adoption. Nephrol. News Issues. 25 (10), 30−31.

Khorasani, R., 2011. CMS incentive payments for meaningful use of health care IT for radiologists: will they fund the needed change? J. Am. Coll. Radiol. 8 (2), 139−140.

Klimek, J., van Terheyden, N., Brient, P., Servais, C., Bellini, E., Hitchcock, R., et al., 2011. How do we get to meaningful use? Health Manag. Technol. 32 (5), 12−15, 31.

Kohler, F., Xu, J., Silva-Withmory, C., Arockiam, J., 2011. Feasibility of using a checklist based on the international classification of functioning, disability and health as an outcome measure in individuals following lower limb amputation. Prosthet. Orthot. Int. 35 (3), 294−301.

Kuperman, G.J., 2011. Health-information exchange: why are we doing it, and what are we doing? J. Am. Med. Inform. Assoc. 18 (5), 678−682.

Lai, M., Kheterpal, S., 2011. Creating a real return-on-investment for information system implementation: life after HITECH. Anesthesiol. Clin. 29 (3), 413−438.

Lee, K.J., Smith, R.M., 2011. EHR/EMR: "Meaningful use," stimulus money, and the Serenity Prayer. Ear Nose Throat J. 90 (2), E25.

Leftwich, R.B., 2011. EHR update: progress on meaningful use requirements. Tenn. Med. 104 (9), 36−37.

Lovis, C., Ball, M., Boyer, C., Elkin, P.L., Ishikawa, K., Jaffe, C., et al., 2011. Hospital and Health Information Systems − Current Perspectives. Contribution of the IMIA Health Information Systems Working Group. Yearb. Med. Inform. 6 (1), 73−82.

Lowes, R., 2013. CMS Delays Stage 3 Meaningful Use Until 2017. Medscape News.www.medscape.com/viewarticle/817443 (retrieved May 10, 2014).

Madison, L.G., Phillip, W.R., 2011. A case study of user assessment of a corrections electronic health record. Perspect. Health Inf. Manag. 8, 1b.

Mayhew, A., Cano, S., Scott, E., Eagle, M., Bushby, K., Muntoni, F., 2011. Moving towards meaningful measurement: Rasch analysis of the North Star Ambulatory Assessment in Duchenne muscular dystrophy. Dev. Med. Child Neurol. 53 (6), 535−542.

McCartney, P.R., 2011. Meaningful use and certified electronic health records. MCN Am. J. Matern. Child Nurs. 36 (2), 137.

MGMA Government Affairs Department, 2011. 7 tips for meaningful EHR use. MGMA Connex. 11 (6), 29.

Mostashari, F., 2011. Moving forward on meaningful use. The ONC's Farzad Mostashari, MD, offers his perspectives on the road ahead. Interview by Mark Hagla. Healthc. Inform. 28 (3), 51−52.

Murphy, J., 2011. Hitech programs supporting the journey to meaningful use of EHRS. Comput. Inform. Nurs. 29 (2), 130−131.

Nanji, K.C., Rothschild, J.M., Salzberg, C., Keohane, C.A., Zigmont, K., Devita, J., et al., 2011. Errors associated with outpatient computerized prescribing systems. J. Am. Med. Inform. Assoc. 18 (6), 767−773.

Nilsson, P., Andersson, H.I., Ejlertsson, G., Blomqvist, K., 2011. How to make a workplace health promotion questionnaire process applicable, meaningful and sustainable. J. Nurs. Manag. 19 (7), 906−914.

Noah, P., 2011. Implementing electronic documentation. Crit. Care Nurs. Q. 34 (3), 208−212.

O'Neill, S.M., Hempel, S., Lim, Y.-W., Danz, M.S., Foy, R., Suttorp, M.J., et al., 2011. Identifying continuous quality improvement publications: what makes an improvement intervention 'CQI'? BMJ Qual. Saf. 20 (12), 1011−1019.

Ortolon, K., 2011. Quality as a revenue stream. Tex. Med. 107 (4), 55−58.

Osten, J., 2011. Leave no money on the table. Healthc. Financ. Manag. 65 (3), 88−90.

Pallin, D.J., Sullivan, A.F., Espinola, J.A., Landman, A.B., Camargo Jr.C.A., 2011. Increasing adoption of computerized provider order entry, and persistent regional disparities, in US emergency departments. Ann. Emerg. Med. 58 (6), 543−550.e543.

Patel, M., Chait, M., 2011. Retroactive adjustment of perceived time. Cognition. 119 (1), 125−130.

Patterson, P., 2011. Meaningful use: what it means for ORs. OR Manager. 27 (7), 13−16.

Rao, S.R., Desroches, C.M., Donelan, K., Campbell, E.G., Miralles, P.D., Jha, A.K., 2011. Electronic health records in small physician practices: availability, use, and perceived benefits. J. Am. Med. Inform. Assoc. 18 (3), 271−275.

Raths, D., 2011a. Business intelligence effort get a boost. The meaningful use framework highlights the value of data warehouses and BI tools. Healthc. Inform. 28 (1), 18, 20, 22−23.

Raths, D., 2011b. The wake-up call. Healthcare reform's value-based purchasing model has as much impact as meaningful use requirements on how hospitals support ambulatory practices. Healthc. Inform. 28 (3), 26, 28.

Raths, D., 2011c. The new frontier. With prodding from meaningful use requirements, providers are starting to think about the type of tools they will need to engage patients and caregivers. Healthc. Inform. 28 (3), 40, 42−43.

Rudin, R.S., Salzberg, C.A., Szolovits, P., Volk, L.A., Simon, S.R., Bates, D.W., 2011. Care transitions as opportunities for clinicians to use data exchange services: how often do they occur? J. Am. Med. Inform. Assoc. 18 (6), 853−858.

Samal, L., Linder, J.A., Lipsitz, S.R., Hicks, L.S., 2011. Electronic health records, clinical decision support, and blood pressure control. Am. J. Manag. Care. 17 (9), 626−632.

Sockolow, P.S., Adelsberger, M.C., Bowles, K.H., 2011. Identifying Certification Criteria for Home Care EHR Meaningful Use. AMIA Annu. Symp. Proc. 2011, 1280−1289.

Strom, B.L., Schinnar, R., 2011. Center for Education and Research on Therapeutics. Evaluating health information technology's clinical effects. LDI Issue Brief. 16 (4), 1−4.

Tenforde, M., Jain, A., Hickner, J., 2011. The value of personal health records for chronic disease management: what do we know? Fam. Med. 43 (5), 351−354.

Tjia, J., Field, T.S., Fischer, S.H., Gagne, S.J., Peterson, D.J., Garber, L.D., et al., 2011. Quality measurement of medication monitoring in the "meaningful use" era. Am. J. Manag. Care. 17 (9), 633−637.

Turgeon, L., 2011. More meaning for meaningful use? MLO Med. Lab. Obs. 43 (6), 8.

Tzeng, H.-M., 2011. Using multiple data sources to answer patient safety-related research questions in hospital inpatient settings: a discursive paper using inpatient falls as an example. J. Clin. Nurs. 20 (23−24), 3276−3284.

Wellpoint. Improving your health. www.wellpoint.com/PW_D014810.html, last retrieved May 10, 2014.

Wieland, J.B., 2011. OIG targets meaningful use. MLO Med. Lab. Obs. 43 (4), 38.

Woolf, S.H., Braveman, P., 2011. Where health disparities begin: the role of social and economic determinants − and why current policies may make matters worse. Health Aff. (Millwood). 30 (10), 1852−1859.

Yu, P.P., 2011. Why meaningful use matters. J. Oncol. Pract. 7 (4), 206−209.

Zarlengo, R., 2011. Meaningful use for the pediatrician. Med. Health R. I. 94 (7), 209−210.

Zusman, E.E., 2011. Meeting meaningful use objectives for Electronic Health Record implementation. Neurosurgery. 69 (2), N24−N26.

Chapter 10

The Joint Commission

Formerly the Joint Commission on Accreditation of Healthcare
Organizations (JCAHO)

Chapter Outline

PREAMBLE

This chapter raises the level of medical operations to the level of the hospital, as the center of medical treatment, rather than the physician's office. The central issue in hospital-centered care is the quality of the services provided by the hospital; high quality goods and services can become submerged in the "broader" issues of administrative operations and the need to "keep the lights on" in the facility. Certification of hospitals is the best way to keep quality central, and this is the task of the Joint Commission.

HISTORY OF THE JOINT COMMISSION

Ernest Codman was a Boston surgeon who practiced in the early part of the 20th century. He was an acknowledged advocate of hospital reform, a pioneer in the field of outcomes management in patient care, and the first American physician to track patients' outcomes past their initial hospitalizations in a systematic manner. Using "end result cards," Dr. Codman kept basic demographic data on every patient. Diagnosis, treatment, and outcome were codified. Each patient was tracked for at least 12 months to determine long-term outcomes. The "end results system" created an opportunity to identify clinical misadventures. These clinical misadventures would be used as the basis for improving the care of future patients by focusing attention on process improvement. Dr. Codman felt that both clinical information and process improvement should be made public so that patients could make an informed choice of physicians and hospitals. These efforts contributed to the founding of the American College of Surgeons Hospital Standardization Program (Pearre, 1955; McCleary, 1977; Roberts *et al.*, 1987). The Joint Commission on Accreditation of Hospitals (JCAH) was created by merging the Hospital Standardization Program with like quality measures contributed by the American College of Physicians (ACP), the American Hospital Association (AHA), and the American Medical Association (AMA) (Pearre, 1955; Roberts *et al.*, 1987).

From its founding in 1951, the Joint Commission on Accreditation of Hospitals developed processes that were largely targeted towards developing the metrics for the certification process and analysis of what constituted grounds for corrective action (*Joint Accreditation Commission is proposed*, 1951; *Bylaws of the Joint Commission*, 1952). In 1965 the federal government selected the organization's accreditation process as the one that would be used to qualify a hospital for the Medicare Conditions of Participation (i.e., accreditation at the federal level) (*Joint Accreditation Commission is proposed*,

Practical Predictive Analytics and Decisioning Systems for Medicine. DOI: http://dx.doi.org/10.1016/B978-0-12-411643-6.00010-7

1951; *Bylaws of the Joint Commission*, 1952; *Joint Commission accredits 199 hospitals*, 1953; *Accreditation of hospitals*, 1955; *Joint Commission on Accreditation of Hospitals*, 1955; Carroll, 1971). Although this process had been in place for 45 years, as of July 15, 2010, Section 125 of the Medicare Improvements for Patients and Providers Act of 2008 (MIPPA) changed the certifying agency to the Centers for Medicaid and Medicare Services (CMS). During the transition period, a methodology involving corporation between the two agencies was worked out to avoid a delay or mismanagement of the accreditation process (Card and Lehmann, 1987; *Medicare and Medicaid programs*, 1993; Jost, 1994).

At the time of its first inception, the Joint Commission (TJC) was known as the Joint Commission on Accreditation of Hospitals (JCAH). Subsequently, the TJC was known as the Joint Commission on Accreditation of Healthcare Organizations (JCAHO). It was only more recently that the organization transitioned to its current identity as the Joint Commission (*Joint Accreditation Commission is proposed*, 1951; *Bylaws of the Joint Commission*, 1952; Tousignaut, 1977; McCleary, 1977; *Joint Commission: who, when, why?*, 1998; Franko, 2002). The organization is currently based in Oakbrook Terrace, Illinois, but maintains a virtual presence across the United States through numerous satellite networks of reviewers. The organization mission statement defines the TJC's function as "to continuously improve health care for the public, in collaboration with other stakeholders, by evaluating health care organizations and inspiring them to excel in providing safe and effective care of the highest quality and value" (Rich, 1996; Flanagan, 1997).

THE JOINT COMMISSION INTERNATIONAL

In 1997, the Joint Commission International (JCI) was established as a division of Joint Commission Resources, Inc. (JCR), a non-profit arm of the Joint Commission. The JCI provides international healthcare accreditation services to hospitals around the world and brings income into the US-based parent organization. This not-for-profit private corporation currently accredits hospitals in Asia, Europe, the Middle East and South America, and is seeking to expand its business further (Donahue and van Ostenberg, 2000). The JCI extends the Joint Commission's mission of encouraging improvement in the quality of patient care internationally by evaluating healthcare organizations, public health agencies, and health ministries worldwide. By evaluating, improving, and enhancing patient care as well as patient safety, international health organizations may seek accreditation. Through international recognition, publications, and education programs, JCI accreditation provides similar reassurance to a commitment to high quality of care (Ente, 1999; Donahue and van Ostenberg, 2000).

The JCI also provides a number of educational programs. Information regarding these "Practicums" including costs, is available on their website (www.jointcommissioninternational.org/; Figure 10.1). The JCI publishes hospital surveys, with an average fee of approximately $50,000 for a full hospital survey (Donahue and Yen, 1997; Bohigas, 1998; *Joint*

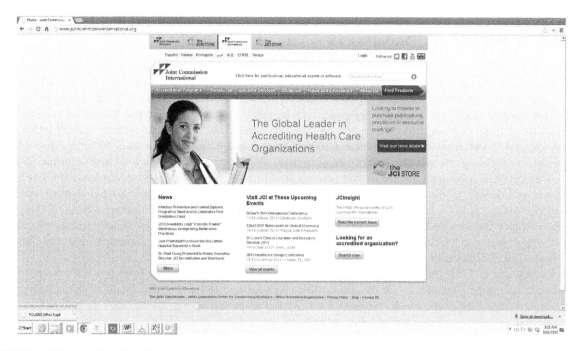

FIGURE 10.1 Web page of the Joint Commission.

Commission to offer international accreditation services, 1998; Donahue and van Ostenberg, 2000; *Announcing the new Joint Commission International Center for Patient Safety*, 2005). Reimbursement for surveyors' travel, accommodations, and other incidentals is required in addition to the survey fee. Additional consulting may be necessary and is not included in the survey cost, but may be required for a hospital to be successful in the accreditation process (Rhea, 2008; Inal, 2009, Karaarslan, 2009; *Joint Commission International aims to improve health care*, 2012; Day *et al.*, 2013).

JOINT COMMISSION ACCREDITATION

Under the auspices of TJC, all healthcare organizations are surveyed on a 3-year accreditation cycle; laboratories and other health related process entities are reviewed every 2 years. Individualized hospital results are not released to the public. Whether the organization passed accreditation, the date that accreditation was awarded or revoked, and any cited deficiencies are published. A specified level of compliance to most applicable standards is necessary to achieve accreditation (Snyder and Westerfield, 1997; Boylan and Westra, 1998).

In its present form, TJC is a non-profit tax-exempt 501(c) corporation that is responsible for the accreditation of well over 20,000 healthcare entities primarily in the United States (*Joint Commission Accreditation reaches 20,000 mark*, 2013). There is a 32-member board of commissioners that includes clinicians (nurses and physicians), employers, labor representatives, quality experts, consumer advocates, and educators that helps guide TJC and provides oversight in a medical environment that is by nature diverse, as well as direction in public policy, business, and consumer interaction. In large part, Joint Commission accreditation is a requirement of licensure at the state level. Federal reimbursement programs such as Medicaid mandate TJC certification as a condition of participation. Site inspections usually follow a triennial cycle, but these inspections may occur at any time. The prestigious Joint Commission Gold Seal of Approval is predicated on the results of an on-site survey by TJC every 3 years (laboratories, every 2 years) (Murray, 2012; *The Joint Commission announces top performers*, 2012; *Joint Commission accreditation reaches 20,000 mark*, 2013).

The results of both satisfactory and unsatisfactory surveys are available to the public on the Quality Check website (www.qualitycheck.org; Figure 10.2). In addition, Quality Check consists of a number of resources from TJC regarding accredited organizations as well as other programs. National Patient Safety Goal compliance, National Quality Improvement, Centers for Medicare & Medicaid Services' mortality and readmission measures, TJC's top performers on Key Quality Measures Goals performance, patient satisfaction information, accreditation/certification approvals, and other

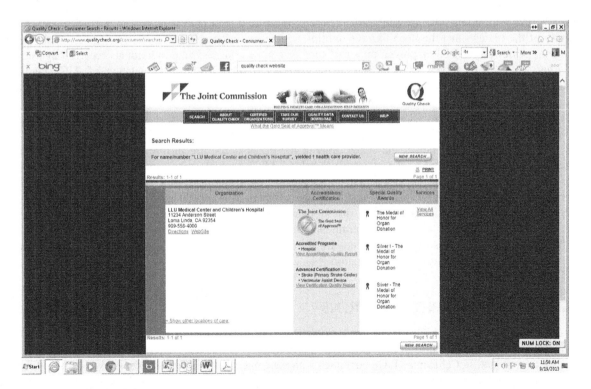

FIGURE 10.2 Quality Check website.

award information can be located on this website. Since its inauguration in 1996, the Quality Check website has helped TJC meet its obligation to the public in providing comparative data regarding accredited institutions. Consumers can:

- Search for accredited and certified organizations
- Find organizations by type of service provided within a geographical area
- Download free hospital performance measure results
- Print a list of Joint Commission certified disease-specific care and healthcare staffing programs.

The most controversial component of TJC's accreditation process is the unannounced full survey. Surveys take place 18 to 39 months after the previous site visit. These surveys are a key component of the accreditation process. "Unannounced" means the organization does not receive an advance notice of its survey date. These unannounced surveys began on January 1, 2006. Formerly, TJC's practice had been to give healthcare organizations some warning regarding the timing of inspections, and two leading newspapers raised concerns regarding the validity of these inspections. The *Washington Post* reported that nearly all of those hospitals that are inspected ultimately are accredited. The *Boston Globe* observed that TJC "has long been dominated by representatives of the industries it inspects," throwing into question whether advance notification would give these organizations excessive warning regarding areas that TJC intended to target in its inspections (Jost, 1994). The unannounced surveys have in large part been a response to these criticisms. However, the JCI still gives ample notice to its planned hospital inspections at international venues.

Preparing for a Survey

The preparation process for a survey is nerve-racking for the healthcare facility as well as its staff. Often, hospitals will conduct mock surveys off-cycle to identify any real or perceived deficiencies prior to the actual site visit. It is essential that either the hospital compliance officer or some other designated individual be well versed on the current standards, policies, and procedures relative to the current expectations of TJC. Further, there must be a process in place to achieve expedited improvement or palliation of any area found to be out of compliance. The initial survey recognizes standards that have been in place for at least 4 months prior to the first evaluation. Subsequent surveys are based on evidence of practice and intent during the entire 3-year period of accreditation. Stop-gap measures placed into effect shortly before a survey or after a long delay when a deficiency was clearly noted are not credited to the institution and may be grounds for remediation (Rich, 1996).

The surveyors selected by TJC are generally experts in their field who are employed by TJC. Because of the sporadic nature of the reviews and the need to have multiple specialists in geographically relevant areas of the country, a number of the reviewers may be employed on a part-time or contract basis. These individuals receive ongoing training regarding the changes in survey expectations, must maintain a high level of knowledge of TJC standards and performance-related criteria, and be available to travel to various healthcare organizations to evaluate their facilities and practice performance.

Preparation for a Joint Commission survey is very time- and resource-intensive for all healthcare organizations. Academic medical centers as well as small community hospitals spend a considerable amount of money preparing for surveys. Questions exist as to whether the stated aims of the organization are in line with what is actually surveyed. Evidenced-based medicine is cited as the main driver behind TJC's regulatory requirements; however, there is sparse evidence that meeting these requirements actually improves hospital metrics. Some data have suggested that despite improved "outcome measures," TJC survey outcome improvements have been associated with problems in quality improvement despite high cost and increasingly strict requirements. Although TJC regulates and certifies the healthcare industry, there is no independent agency or governmental organization that has oversight of TJC. The metrics for selection of the specific quality measures (and not others) have not been made public and are not completely clear. The evidence-based reasoning for continued accreditation is an evolving process.

OTHER REGULATORY ORGANIZATIONS

It is important to recognize that TJC is not the only organization that regulates healthcare practices in the United States. While the public respects the validity of its assessment, a number of states have alternative organizations involved in performance assessment. In California, TJC cooperates with state agencies in a "joint process" which is codified in the California health and safety code to provide accreditation. A TJC survey is not required for licensure in Wisconsin, Pennsylvania, and Oklahoma (Flanagan, 1997).

There are also other healthcare accreditation organizations in the USA unrelated to the Joint Commission (Donahue and van Ostenberg, 2000). On September 26, 2008, the Centers for Medicare and Medicaid Services (CMS) granted deeming authority for hospitals to DNV Healthcare Inc. (a division of Det Norske Veritas [DNV]). DNV is a Norwegian company that has had business interests in the USA dating from before 1900. DNV Healthcare is the leading accreditor of US hospitals integrating ISO 9001 quality compliance with the Medicare Conditions of Participation, and may represent TJC's leading competitor in the USA. DNV states that it uses continuous quality improvement (CQI) to produce a "we are always prepared, always improving" as opposed to a "hurry up and get ready" mentality in client healthcare facilities.

JOINT COMMISSION STANDARDS

The Joint Commission has published standards in a number of different areas of healthcare delivery:

- Ambulatory Health Care (CAMAC) (*CMS continues to recognize Joint Commission*, 2009)
- Behavioral Health Care (CAMBHC) (Hanold *et al.*, 1997)
- Critical Assess Hospitals (CAMCAH)
- Disease-Specific Care (DSC)
- Health Care Staffing Services (HCSS)
- Home Care (CAMHC) (Malloy, 1990)
- Hospitals (CAMH)
- Laboratory Services (CAMLAB) (*Joint Commission on Accreditation of Healthcare Organizations*, 1995)
- Nursing and Rehabilitation Center (CAMLTC)
- Office-Based Surgery (CAMOBS).

Performance measurement and accountability measures for hospitals were introduced in 1997 using the Joint Commission's Outcomes Research Yields eXcellence (ORYX) initiative. This initiative was designed to integrate outcomes as well as other performance measurement data into the process of accreditation. In turn, ORYX supports Joint Commission accredited organizations through its measurement requirements for quality improvement efforts. A metric of performance validation and measurement calibration are necessary to establish the credibility and veracity of any evaluation. For health care, this activity is of paramount importance. Further modification to the performance and accountability measures were adapted in June, 2010, to help hospitals develop preparation tools for performance measures in the healthcare environment. These measures have been divided into both accountability and non-accountability categories. Accountability measures are most important, and these are evaluated according to four distinct criteria. Research, proximity, accuracy, and adverse effects tracking have been found to produce the most gains and positive impact in patient outcomes when hospitals demonstrate improvement in areas related to these objectives. Further, TJC hopes to continue to develop accountability measures for its ORYX initiatives. An 85% average compliance goal must be met in accordance with an element of performance 1 to reach the baseline accreditation criteria for TJC institutions (Weber, 1999; *Ready to answer ORYX data questions?*, 2000).

TJC also publishes a series of critical events in its "Sentinel Event Alert." According to TJC, the alert "identifies specific types of sentinel and adverse events and high risk conditions, describes their common underlying causes, and recommends steps to reduce risk and prevent future occurrences." Hospitals and other vested organizations may use these alerts to identify and improve processes in their infrastructure that can put them at risk for one of these events (*Special report on sentinel events*, 1998; Bressler, 2000; *Citing reports of alarm-related deaths*, 2013). These may facilitate a root cause analysis which generally will show a lack of or failure to comply with policies and procedures that were designed to prevent the specific event, problems with hierarchical relations (an inability to address or raise the issue to a level of importance to a higher-level practitioner), failure to communicate, or inadequate education or orientation of staff (*The Joint Commission: four key root causes loom large in sentinel event data*, 2012). In order to ameliorate this problem, a "culture of safety" must be created where individuals at any level of involvement are empowered to identify issues without fear of retribution. Procedures must be created for responding to or logging processes which fail to produce the desired result. These are codified as "sentinel events." The meaning of what a "sentinel event" entails should be communicated organization-wide. Regardless of previous events, each "sentinel event" must have its own root cause analysis. Support systems must be made available and easy to access for hospital staff who have reported the occurrence, to create a "safety culture" without fear of retribution. To the extent that it affects them, patients must be accorded the right to take part in decisions regarding their care. To that extent, patients must be informed about untoward events that produced outcomes which were unintended and thereby reportable under sentinel event review to TJC.

Sentinel events rising to the level of national concern are presented in TJC's Sentinel Event Alert. This is a complimentary publication of TJC that is provided to the public domain regarding these specific issues, the scope of the problem, potential problems that are tied into the performance of staff or the local safety culture, and solutions that incorporate existing protocol with new innovative technologies that have the potential to reduce the occurrence further (Chassin and Loeb, 2013).

One such example is the risk of unintended retained foreign objects (URFOs). These URFOs are a major contributor to morbidity and mortality, and have been implicated in increasing the cost and complexity of care when they occur. TJC identified specific situations when this issue was more likely to occur (e.g., an urgent or emergent procedure, or when the procedure intent or direction changed intraoperatively), but further criticized existing protocols as being inadequate to prevent up to 22% of all URFOs reported to TJC (*New Joint Commission Report warns*, 2002; *Preventing unintended retained foreign objects*, 2013). To demonstrate process improvement, TJC cited real improvements achieved by vested healthcare facilities and suggested higher reliability counting solutions, intraoperative procedures involving multiple counts, and even the use of novel technologies or concepts to achieve still higher compliance with an ideal of zero defects. Moreover, it is emphasized that these URFOs continue to be reported to TJC as reviewable events and that the patient be involved in the process, especially when further investigation and remediation is indicated (Judson *et al.*, 2013; *Preventing unintended retained foreign objects*, 2013).

NATIONAL PATIENT SAFETY GOALS

The Joint Commission established its National Patient Safety Goals (NPSGs) program in 2002 (*Patient safety alert*, 2002; *Joint Commission announces national patient safety goals*, 2003). The NPSGs were created to help organizations accredited by TJC to focus on specific high priority areas of national concern with respect to patient safety. These first NPSGs were implemented on January 1, 2003.

One of the more important NPSGs was a concerted effort to avoid the use of abbreviations that were confusing or potentially misleading. In 2004, TJC released its list of unapproved abbreviations. This list is posted prominently in many hospitals, and is the basis for eliminating "shortcuts" that are potential causes of medical error (see Table 10.1) (The Joint Commission, 2004).

The Joint Commission's National Patient Safety Goals (NPSGs) promote specific improvements in patient safety (*Joint Commission mission statement revised*, 2000). Problematic areas in health care and healthcare delivery are targeted. Evidence- and expert-based solutions to these problems are proposed. A system design that is well structured is vital to the delivery of safe, high quality health care (*CMS continues to recognize Joint Commission*, 2009; Main, 2009; *A look at The Joint Commission*, 2011; *Robust process improvement*, 2011). As such, the Goals are oriented towards applying system-wide solutions, as opposed to focusing on minutiae. Through NPSGs, the Joint Commission promulgates major changes in patient safety in healthcare entities worldwide. Recent NPSGs include targeting the spread of infection due to multidrug-resistant organisms, catheter-related bloodstream infections (CRBSIs), patient handoff, and surgical site infections (SSIs). Patient involvement in and input regarding safety efforts are an essential part of the NPSGs (*Joint Commission paints detailed picture*, 2009; *The Joint Commission to include patient satisfaction data*, 2009; Ernst, 2010; *Joint Commission anticipates more discussion*, 2010; McKinney, 2010; *The Joint Commission moving to link accountability to accreditation*, 2010). The Universal Protocol with its associated identifiers to reduce surgical errors and existing regulations on medication reconciliation has been refocused, based on input to the Joint Commission (*Announcing the new Joint Commission International Center for Patient Safety*, 2005; *Joint Commission calls for changes*, 2005; Weinstock, 2009).

The Goals were developed by a panel of well-recognized patient safety experts. These experts, who comprise the Patient Safety Advisory Group, help guide the Joint Commission on the initiation, development, and updating of the NPSGs. The Patient Safety Advisory Group is comprised of nurses, physicians, allied health professionals, pharmacists, risk managers, and clinical specialists, as well as others with experience in patient safety issues in a vast array of healthcare settings (*Joint Commission announces national patient safety goals*, 2003; Traynor, 2010). The Patient Safety Advisory Group collaborates and works with the Joint Commission staff to recognize patient safety issues of the highest priority. The Patient Safety Advisory Group is also responsible for helping the Joint Commission recognize the best path for dealing with these issues (*Joint Commission mission statement revised*, 2000; *Joint Commission announces national patient safety goals*, 2003; *Announcing the new Joint Commission International Center for Patient Safety*, 2005; *The Joint Commission announces the 2009 National Patient Safety Goals*, 2008; Weinstock, 2009; Scott and Gerardi, 2011). The Joint Commission works collaboratively with the Patient Safety Advisory Group on not only NPSGs but also Sentinel Event Alerts, standards/survey processes, performance measures, educational materials, and

TABLE 10.1 Official "Do Not Use" List (2004)*

Do not use	Potential problem	Use instead
U, u (unit)	Mistaken for "0" (zero), the number "4" (four) or "cc"	Write "unit"
IU (International Unit)	Mistaken for IV (intravenous) or the number 10 (ten)	Write "International unit"
Q.D., QD, q.d., qd (daily)	Mistaken for each other	Write "daily"
Q.O.D., QOD, q.o.d., qod (every other day)	Period after the Q mistaken for "I" and the "O" mistaken for "I"	Write "every other day"
Trailing zero (X.0 mg) Lack of leading zero (.X mg)	Decimal point is missed	Write X mg Write 0.X mg
MS	Can mean morphine sulfate or magnesium sulfate	Write "morphine sulfate" or "magnesium sulfate"
MSO_4 and $MgSO_4$	Confused for one another	Write "morphine sulfate" or "magnesium sulfate"

*National Patient Safety Goals (NPSGs) including a list of medical abbreviations that were confusing or potentially misleading; this table was presented in 2004.

establishment of outcome goals (Chassin, 2008; Masica *et al.*, 2009; Singleton, 2009; *Joint Commission Annual Report on Quality and Safety*, 2010; Samet, 2012). TJC asks for input from practitioners and providers as well as provider organizations, purchasers of value-based services, consumer groups, and other advocates before designating what are the highest priority safety issues and the most logical course of action to address these issues. TJC then evaluates where the issue has the greatest application and will refine the focus of the NPSG to a specific accreditation program if it determines that the goal is specific to a certain program (*Hospitals make progress on quality*, 2007; DerGurahian, 2008; Samet, 2012).

One example of this process is the new NPSG on clinical alarm safety (*Joint Commission releases sentinel event alert*, 2013). Although most monitors, ventilators, IV pumps, and other patient tracking devices have built-in safeguards, a broad safety initiative was lacking in the development of specific requirements for the industry. TJC has approved implementation of the goal in a two-phase process in 2014 and 2016. The new NPSG on clinical alarm safety (NPSG.06.01.01), approved in June 2013, will be applicable for both general care hospitals and critical access hospitals. In phase one, beginning January 1, 2014, hospitals will need to identify and prioritize alarm safety across their entire enterprise (*Clinical alarms goal remains intact*, 2003; Kreimer, 2011; *Citing reports of alarm-related deaths*, 2013; *Joint Commission releases sentinel event alert*, 2013; Mitka, 2013). The alarms identified will initially be at the discretion of the institution, based on what is perceived as the highest priority for their patient population. In phase two, which begins on January 1, 2016, hospitals will be expected to develop and construct unique policies and procedures on alarm safety and educate staff across the organization on how to manage these alarms (Kreimer, 2011; *Citing reports of alarm-related deaths*, 2013; *Joint Commission releases sentinel event alert*, 2013). Phase two has not been finalized and may be changed to accommodate evidence from phase one enhancements, medical literature, and novel applications of best practice. The current plan involves making changes in the phase two requirements available to client hospitals through field review and *Perspectives*. The Emergency Care Research Institute (ECRI) and the Association for the Advancement of Medical Instrumentation (AAMI) have prioritized safety alarm management and the dispersal of alarm fatigue as an issue of national concern. TJC has corroborated these concerns and supports these efforts, which may be incorporated into phase two as these programs generate new data (Kreimer, 2011; *Citing reports of alarm-related deaths*, 2013; *Joint Commission releases sentinel event alert*, 2013).

There is an organized drive from industry which has lent support as well (Patient Safety Movement, 2013a). In January 2013, a consortium of medical device and pharmaceutical manufacturers, EMR and CPOE vendors, physicians, and other interested physicians and healthcare professions led by the Masimo Corporation convened to discussed additional applications of the NPSGs to the health systems that were affected by their deployment (http://patientsafetymovement.org/). Specifically, the summit focused on the promise of achieving "zero preventable deaths by 2020" (Moore, 1998; Patient Safety Movement, 2013b). Several well-defined NPSGs were highlighted, including the reduction of unnecessary blood transfusion, improved hand-off, anesthesia problems, wrong patient/wrong site surgeries, and interoperability. Summit attendees were asked to make a pledge to improve patient safety and to share data across platforms.

With disparate medical devices, EMRs and CPOE systems, and other systems-based data, comply with meaningful use but do not share data well between systems (*Citing reports of alarm-related deaths*, 2013). The summit appeared poised to solve the Tower of Babel issues that had long plagued healthcare settings by connecting people, ideas, and technology to confront the problem of over 200,000 preventable patient deaths in US hospitals each year (*Citing reports of alarm-related deaths*, 2013). By providing actionable ideas and innovations that transform the process of care, patient safety can be dramatically improved and patient preventable deaths can be eliminated. In July 2013, TJC signed on as a summit co-convener for 2014, effectively making interoperability with industry and transparency a sufficient and necessary partner in the effective management of NPSGs (Parl *et al.*, 2010; Patient Safety Movement, 2013a).

Information on safely managing alarm systems must be refined prior to incorporating these guidelines into the NPSG. New International Standardization Organization (ISO) specifications figure prominently in tracking these emerging alarm management issues. In addition, the Joint Commission published a Sentinel Event Alert on clinical alarm management in April 2013. The general format of the new NPSG was described, and the Alert also provided suggestions for the assessment and management of risks associated with alarms, as well as components of the alarm management that may require additional enhancements. TJC has two Take 5 podcasts and a PowerPoint presentation as well as a webinar on this subject (*Special report on sentinel events*, 1998; Bressler, 2000; *The Joint Commission: four key root causes loom large in sentinel event data*, 2012; *Citing reports of alarm-related deaths*, 2013; *Joint Commission releases sentinel event alert*, 2013).

More information on each of the NPSGs for TJC's program is available on TJC's website. Questions can be submitted to the Standards Interpretation Group through voicemail at (630) 792-5900, or via the Standards Online Question Submission Form (https://web.jointcommission.org/sigsubmission/sigonlineform.aspx) (*A look at The Joint Commission*, 2011; Chassin *et al.,* 2010; Chassin and Loeb, 2011, 2013).

POSTSCRIPT

The Joint Commission (TJC) focuses on quality and safety in patient care. There are, however, many other concerns operative at the level of the hospital and healthcare organization, the most important of which is efficiency of operations. Chapter 11 discusses strategies for creating "lean" hospitals, which provide efficient operations, in addition to issues of quality and safety in health care emphasized by TJC.

REFERENCES

Accreditation of hospitals, 1955. Some policies and actions of the joint commission in regard to who may do surgery, consultations, chiropodists, and many other matters. Ohio Med. 51, 168–170.

A look at The Joint Commission, 2011. Next stop, high reliability. Bull. Am. Coll. Surg. 96, 58–59.

Announcing the new Joint Commission International Center for Patient Safety, 2005. Joint Commission perspectives. Jt. Comm. Perspect. 25, 1–2.

Bohigas, L., 1998. Accreditation across borders: the introduction of Joint Commission accreditation in Spain. Jt. Comm. J. Qual. Improv. 24, 226–231.

Boylan, C.R., Westra, R., 1998. Meeting joint commission requirements for staff nurse competency. J. Nurs. Care Qual. 12, 44–48.

Bressler, H., 2000. The Sentinel Event policy: a response by the Joint Commission. J. Health Law. 33, 519–539.

Bylaws of the Joint Commission, 1952. On Accreditation of Hospitals. Bull. Am. Coll. Surg. 37, 238–244.

Card, W.F., Lehmann, R., 1987. An overview of the methodology used by the Joint Commission to evaluate Medicare-certified HMOs. Qual. Rev. Bull. 13, 415–417.

Carroll, W.W., 1971. Joint Commission myth – (and the reality). AORN J. 14, 37–41.

Chassin, M., 2008. Other voices. Quality, safety top New Joint Commission Chief's agenda. Interview by Matthew Weinstock. Hosp. Health Netw. 82 (16), 18.

Chassin, M., Conway, J.B., Umbdenstock, R.J., Dwyer, J., Langberg, M.L., Petasnick, W.D., 2010. Accreditation. Chassin and Joint Commission aim to inspire. Interview by Howard Larkin. Hosp. Health Netw. 84 (24–28), 22.

Chassin, M., Loeb, J., 2011. The ongoing quality improvement journey: Next stop, high reliability. Health Aff. 30 (4), .

Chassin, M., Loeb, J., 2013. High-reliability health care: getting there from here. Milbank Q. 91 (3), 31.

Citing reports of alarm-related deaths, 2013. The Joint Commission issues a sentinel event alert for hospitals to improve medical device alarm safety. ED Manag. 26 (Suppl.), 1–3.

Clinical alarms goal remains intact, 2003. Joint Commission expands 2004 goals. Biomed. Instrum. Technol. 37, 307.

CMS continues to recognize Joint Commission, 2009. Ambulatory surgical center accreditation. Joint Commission perspectives. Jt. Comm. Accredit. Healthc. Org. 29, 10.

Day, S.W., McKeon, L.M., Garcia, J., Wilimas, J.A., Carty, R.M., de Alarcon, P., et al., 2013. Use of Joint Commission International standards to evaluate and improve pediatric oncology nursing care in Guatemala. Pediatr. Blood Cancer. 60, 810–815.

DerGurahian, J., 2008. Future considerations. Joint Commission report: safety barriers persist. Mod. Healthcare. 38, 12.

Donahue, K.T., vanOstenberg, P., 2000. Joint Commission International accreditation: relationship to four models of evaluation. J. Int. Soc. Qual. Healthcare. 12, 243−246.

Donahue, K.T., Yen, J., 1997. Joint Commission International. Jt. Comm. J. Qual. Improv. 23, 71.

Ente, B.H., 1999. Joint Commission World Symposium on Improving Health Care Through Accreditation. Jt. Comm. J. Qual. Improv. 25, 602−613.

Ernst, D.J., 2010. The Joint Commission cuts key patient-safety measure. MLO: Med. Lab. Obs. 42, 48.

Flanagan, A., 1997. Ensuring health care quality: JCAHO's perspective. Joint Commission on Accreditation of Healthcare Organizations. Clin. Ther. 19, 1540−1544.

Franko, F.P., 2002. The important role of the Joint Commission. AORN J. 75, 1179−1182.

Hanold, L., Koss, R.G., McBeth, S., 1997. JCAHO standards and performance measurement systems. Joint Commission on Accreditation of Healthcare Organizations. Behav. Healthc. Tomorrow. 6, 39−40.

Hospitals make progress on quality, 2007. Safety goals, but can do better, Joint Commission says. Hosp. Health Netw. 81, 72.

Inal, T.C., 2009. Joint Commission International Accreditation for Clinical Laboratories: monitor, analyze and improve. Clin. Biochem. 42, 303.

Joint accreditation commission is proposed, 1951. Mod. Hosp. 76, 70.

Joint Commission, 1988. Who, when, why? Disch. Plann. Update. 8, 9−10.

Joint Commission accreditation reaches 20,000 mark, 2013. Bull. Am. Coll. Surg. 98, 68−69.

Joint Commission accredits 199 hospitals, 1953. Bull. Am. Coll. Surg. 38, 159.

Joint Commission announces national patient safety goals, 2003. J. pain palliat. care pharmacother. 17, 116−119.

Joint Commission Annual Report on Quality and Safety, 2010. Shows hospitals improving. Joint Commission perspectives. Jt. Comm. Accredit. Healthc. Org. 30 (1), 10−11.

Joint Commission anticipates more discussion, 2010. On physician. Joint Commission perspectives. Jt. Comm. Accredit. Healthc. Org. 30 (1), 3.

Joint Commission calls for changes, 2005. To improve patient safety. Biomed. Instrum. Technol.(Suppl.), 6−7.

Joint Commission International aims to improve health care, 2012. Delivery in developing countries. Joint Commission perspectives. Jt. Comm. Accredit. Healthc. Org. 32, 6.

Joint Commission mission statement revised, 2000. To include patient safety. Joint Commission perspectives. Jt. Comm. Accredit. Healthc. Org. 20, 5.

Joint Commission on Accreditation of Healthcare Organizations, 1995. Additional standards for surveying freestanding laboratories. 1994 Accreditation Manual for Pathology and Clinical Laboratory Services. Joint Commission perspectives. Jt. Comm. Accredit. Healthc. Org. 15, LSM1−LSM7.

Joint Commission on Accreditation of Hospitals, 1955. JAMA. 157, 1614−1615.

Joint Commission paints detailed picture, 2009. Of "hospital of the future". Healthc. Benchmarks Qual. Improv. 16, 25−28.

Joint Commission releases sentinel event alert, 2013. On alarm hazards. Health Devices. 42, 200.

Joint Commission to offer international accreditation services, 1998. Joint Commission perspectives. Jt. Comm. Accredit. Healthc. Org. 18 (1−2), 5.

Jost, T.S., 1994. Medicare and the Joint Commission on Accreditation of Healthcare Organizations: a healthy relationship? Law Contemp. Probl. 57, 15−45.

Judson, T., Howell, M.D., Guglielmi, C., Canacari, E., Sands, K.J., 2013. Miscount incidents: a novel approach to exploring risk factors for unintentionally retained surgical items. Jt. Comm. J. Qual. Patient Saf. 39 (10), 2.

Karaarslan, I., 2009. Joint Commission on International Accreditation workshop: Planning, development and provision of laboratory services. Clin. Biochem. 42, 284−287.

Kreimer, S., 2011. Quality & safety. Alarming: Joint Commission, FDA set to tackle alert fatigue. Hosp. Health Netw. 85, 18−19.

Main, E.K., 2009. New perinatal quality measures from the National Quality Forum, the Joint Commission and the Leapfrog Group. Curr. Opin. Obstet. Gynecol. 21, 532−540.

Malloy, J.A., 1990. Home care accreditation through Joint Commission on Accreditation of Healthcare Organizations. J. Intraven. Nurs. 13, 185−187.

Masica, A.L., Richter, K.M., Convery, P., Haydar, Z., 2009. Linking joint commission inpatient core measures and national patient safety goals with evidence. Proceedings (Bayl. Univ. Med. Cent.) 22, 103−111.

McCleary, D., 1977. Joint Commission on Accreditation of Hospitals − twenty-five years of promoting improved health care services. Am. J. Hosp. Pharm. 34, 951−954.

McKinney, M., 2010. Smoothing transitions. Joint Commission targets patient handoffs. Mod. Healthc. 40, 8−9.

Medicare and Medicaid programs, 1993. Recognition of the Joint Commission on Accreditation of Healthcare Organizations standards for home care organizations − HCFA. Final notice. Fed. Regist. 58, 35007−35017.

Mitka, M., 2013. Joint commission warns of alarm fatigue: Multitude of alarms from monitoring devices problematic. JAMA. 309, 2315−2316.

Moore Jr.J.D., 1998. Going public. Joint Commission launches radio ad campaign. Mod. Healthc. 28, 12.

Murray, K., 2012. Are you ready for The Joint Commission survey? Nurs. Manag. 44, 56.

New Joint Commission report warns, 2002. Sentinel events most likely in the ED. ED Manag. 14, 133−135.

Parl, F.F., O'Leary, M.F., Kaiser, A.B., Paulett, J.M., Statnikova, K., Shultz, E.K., 2010. Implementation of a closed-loop reporting system for critical values and clinical communication in compliance with goals of the joint commission. Clin. Chem. 56, 417−423.

Patient safety alert, 2002. Joint Commission issues patient safety goals. Healthc. Benchmarks Qual. Improv. 9 (Suppl.), 3−4.

Patient Safety Movement, 2013a. Homepage. <http://patientsafetymovement.org/>.

Patient Safety Movement, 2013b. Campaign Zero. <http://patientsafetymovement.org/pdf/CampaignZero%20-%20Patient%20Safety%20Checklists.pdf>.

Pearre, A.A., 1955. The history and organization of the Joint Commission on Accreditation of Hospitals. Md. State Med. J. 4, 698−700.

Preventing unintended retained foreign objects, 2013. The Joint Commission Sentinel Event Alert, 5.

Ready to answer ORYX data questions? 2000. Here's what Joint Commission will ask. ED Manag. 12, 37−42.

Rhea, S., 2008. Global project. Joint commission international starts quality, safety demo in three locations. Mod. Healthc. 38, 17.

Rich, D.S., 1996. Meeting Joint Commission requirements for competence assessment. Am. J. Health Syst. Pharm. 53, 726−729.

Roberts, J.S., Coale, J.G., Redman, R.R., 1987. A history of the Joint Commission on Accreditation of Hospitals. JAMA. 258, 936−940.

Robust process improvement, 2011. At The Joint Commission. Bull. Am. Coll. Surg. 96, 75.

Samet, D.H., 2012. The Joint Commission: an update on the environment of care and life safety challenges for 2011. J. Healthc. Prot. Manag. 28, 91−95.

Scott, C., Gerardi, D., 2011. A strategic approach for managing conflict in hospitals: responding to the Joint Commission leadership standard, Part 2. Jt. Comm. J. Qual. Patient Saf. 37, 70−80.

Singleton, K.A., 2009. A time for patient care to shine with Joint Commission National Patient Safety Goals. Medsurg. Nurs. 17, 372−373 (2008).

Snyder, R., Westerfield, J., 1997. From chaos to excellence: preparing for a successful Joint Commission survey. J. Nurs. Adm. 27, 10−13.

Special report on sentinel events, 1998. Joint Commission on Accreditation of Healthcare Organizations. Joint Commission perspectives. Jt. Comm. Accredit. Healthc. Org. 18 (19−33), 36−42.

The Joint Commission, 2004. Facts about the Official "Do Not Use" List, www.jointcommission.org/assets/1/18/Do_Not_Use_List.pdf

The Joint Commission, 2012. Four key root causes loom large in sentinel event data. ED Manag. 24, S3−S4.

The Joint Commission announces the 2009 National Patient Safety Goals and requirements, 2009. Joint Commission perspectives. Jt. Comm. Accredit. Healthc. Org. 28 (1), 11−15.

The Joint Commission announces top performers, 2012. On key quality measures. Joint Commission perspectives. Jt. Comm. Accredit. Healthc. Org. 32 (1), 3.

The Joint Commission moving to link accountability to accreditation, 2010. Hosp. Peer Rev. 35, 109−113.

The Joint Commission to include patient satisfaction data, 2009. On quality check. Joint Commission perspectives. Jt. Comm. Accredit. Healthc. Org. 29, 1.

Tousignaut, D.R., 1977. Joint Commission on Accreditation of Hospitals' 1977 standards for pharmaceutical services. Am. J. Hosp. Pharm. 34, 943−950.

Traynor, K., 2010. Joint Commission updates National Patient Safety Goals for. Am. J. Health Syst. Pharm. 66, 2062−2064.

Weber, D., 1999. Evolution of Joint Commission ORYX initiative. QRC Advis. 15, 9−12.

Weinstock, M., 2009. Joint Commission raises the bar on patient safety. New center will identify weaknesses and develop targeted solutions. Hosp. Health Netw. 83, 16−17.

Chapter 11

Root Cause Analysis, Six Sigma, and Overall Quality Control and Lean Concepts

The First Process to Bring Quality and Cost-Effectiveness to Medical Care Delivery

Chapter Outline

PREAMBLE

In 1996, the Institute of Medicine (IOM) launched a program to improve the quality of health in the nation. This focus led to the incorporation of the Six Sigma predictive analytical process developed in other industries. The combination of Six Sigma processing and Deming's emphasis on continuous quality improvement led to the development of the fishbone process model. The core element of the fishbone model is root cause analysis. This chapter presents a rich landscape of quality control issues in health care, with a focus on root cause analysis in hospitals.

INTRODUCTION

One cannot consider predictive analytics in medicine without examining quality and lean concepts. Maximizing processes and eliminating systematic waste are the goals of most accreditation organizations, and the basic concepts must be understood in order to be able to predict efficient and personalized outcomes. This chapter outlines basic concepts of quality and how they apply to health care.

Part 1 provides brief definitions of Six Sigma and Quality Control, Root-Cause Analysis, and Leapfrog, and then a brief history as they developed during the 1990s and early 2000s. The materials come from lecture materials entitled "Learning from Medical Errors and Turning them into Quality Improvements," by Mitchel Goldstein, MD. It presents these historical developments in "outline format" from his lectures, so that the reader can get a rapid overview of the historical development of quality.

Part 2 presents, in "prose format," the 2012–2014 thinking on quality improvement; this is followed by Part 3, which provides one medical doctor's personal journey in establishing a Quality Unit for a regional medical center.

PART 1: SIX SIGMA AND QUALITY CONTROL, ROOT CAUSE ANALYSIS, AND LEAPFROG AS THEY DEVELOPED DURING THE 1990s AND EARLY 2000s: LEARNING FROM MEDICAL ERRORS AND TURNING THEM INTO QUALITY IMPROVEMENTS

THE NEED FOR QUALITY: MEDICAL ERRORS

Epidemiology of Medical Errors

- Medical errors are associated with inexperienced clinicians, new procedures, extremes of age, complex care, and urgent care.
- In the United States, medical error is estimated to result in 44,000 to 98,000 unnecessary deaths each year, and 1,000,000 excess injuries.
- In a typical 100- to 300-bed hospital in the United States, excess costs of $1,000,000 to $3,000,000 per annum are due to excessive hospitalization and complications secondary to medication errors.

    (As per: http://en.wikipedia.org/wiki/Medical_error)

Approaches to Error

- Traditional response – to identify the responsible individual and find an "appropriate" punishment.
- Quality models produce new rules that add additional checks to the system to try to prevent further errors.
- Although errors are reduced, the potential for their occurrence remains unless root causes are found.
- Errors can be avoided by identifying problematic systems and simply avoiding these systems. For example, we can avoid vitamin K anaphylaxis associated with rapid IV administration by not administering it IV (this supposes that other methods of administration are equally effective).

DEFINITIONS

Statistical Process Control

- Statistical process control (SPC) is a method for achieving quality control in manufacturing processes.

- Walter A. Shewhart and W. Edwards Deming introduced these methods in to American industry during World War II to improve aircraft production; however, the principles were generally ignored in the United States until many years after World War II (Darr, 1994).
- Deming was also instrumental in introducing SPC techniques into post-war Japan, where his ideas were readily accepted.

Total Quality Management

- A newer model for improvement in medical care takes its origin from W. Edwards Deming in a model of total quality management (TQM).
- In this model, systems of care are evaluated for process issues that contribute to errors in care.
- Japanese manufacturers applied his techniques widely and experienced new international demand for Japanese products.

Deming's Principles

- Create constancy of purpose.
- Take the lead in adopting the new philosophy.
- Cease dependence on inspection to achieve quality.
- End the practice of awarding business on the basis of cheapest costs.
- Improve constantly.
- Institute training on the job.
- Institute leadership.
- Drive out fear.
- Break down barriers between departments.
- Eliminate slogans, exhortations, and targets.
- Eliminate management by numbers, and management by objective. Substitute leadership.
- Remove barriers to pride in workmanship.
- Institute education and self-improvement.
- Put everybody to work to accomplish the transformation.

Six Sigma

- DMAIC (Define, Measure, Analyze, Improve, and Control) — basic methodology to improve existing processes
  - Define out-of-tolerance range.
  - Measure key internal processes critical to quality.
  - Analyze why defects occur and explore opportunity for improvement.
  - Improve the process to stay within tolerance.
  - Control the process to stay within goals.
- DMADV (Define, Measure, Analyze, Design, Verify) — basic methodology of introducing new processes (initially introduced by Motorola).
  - Define the process and where it would fail to meet customer needs.
  - Measure and determine if the process meets customer needs.
  - Analyze the options to meet customer needs.
  - Design in changes to the process to meet customers' needs.
  - Verify the changes have met customer needs.

Cost—Benefit Analysis

- Process of weighing the total expected costs versus the total expected benefits.
- Monetary calculations of initial expense versus expected return.
- Monetary values may be assigned to less tangible effects such as risk, loss of reputation, market penetration, long-term strategy alignment, or malpractice risk.

Pareto Efficiency

- Movement from one alternative allocation to another that can make at least one individual better off, without making any other individual worse off is called a Pareto improvement or Pareto optimization.
- An allocation of resources is Pareto efficient or Pareto optimal when no further Pareto improvements can be made.

Kaldor-Hicks Efficiency

- Using Kaldor-Hicks efficiency, a more efficient outcome can leave some people worse off.
- An outcome is more efficient if those that are made better off could in theory compensate those that are made worse off and lead to a Pareto optimal outcome (i.e., no one worse off).
- Aggregation problems are associated with discrepancies such as the marginal value of money of rich and poor people.

Examples of Errors

- Wrong-site surgery, such as amputating the wrong limb.
- Giving the wrong drug (wrong patient, wrong chemical, wrong dose, wrong time, wrong route).
- Misdiagnosis.

METHODS TO IMPROVE SAFETY AND REDUCE ERROR

- Voluntary reporting of errors.
- Root cause analysis.
- Systems for ensuring review by experienced or specialist practitioners.

Root Cause Analysis

- Do all reasoning from solid evidence.
- Determine what influenced the consequences, i.e., determine the necessary and sufficient influences that explain the nature and the magnitude of the consequences.
- Establish tightly linked chains of influence.
- At every level of analysis determine the necessary and sufficient influences.
- Whenever feasible, drill down to root causes.
- There are always multiple root causes.

Ishikawa Diagram

(See Figure 11.1)

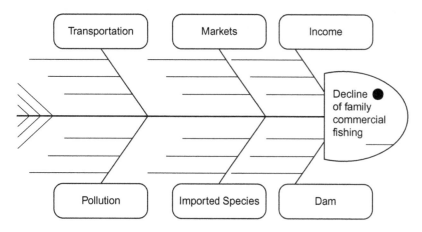

FIGURE 11.1 A typical Ishikawa diagram, also known as a "fishbone process."

- A graphical method for finding the most likely causes for an undesired effect.
- Because of its shape, it is also known as the fishbone diagram (cause-and-effect diagram or root cause analysis).

Apollo Process

- The Apollo process is a four-step method for incident investigation:
  1. Define the problem. What do we want to prevent from recurring? When and where did it occur? What is the significance of the problem?
  2. Analyze cause-and-effect relationships. Once the problem is defined, we need to understand the causes and how they interact with one another.
  3. Identify solutions. Solutions are specific actions that control causes.
  4. Implement the best solutions. The best solutions are those that prevent problem recurrence, are within our control, and meet our goals and objectives.

  For further details see http://apollorca.com/process/process.shtml.

Systems for Ensuring Review

- All staff to review all clinically significant discrepancies at monthly meetings.
- Radiologists review films within 12 hours as a quality control measure, and if a significant misinterpretation is found patients are asked to return.
- After initial improvements, the rate of false-negative errors fell from 3% (95% confidence interval 2.8−3.2%) to 1.2% (1.03−1.37%). After the processes were redesigned it fell further to 0.3% (0.26−0.34%).

  Further details can be found in Espinosa and Nolan (2000).

HISTORY OF QUALITY IN HEALTH CARE

Crossing the Quality Chasm: The IOM Health Care Quality Initiative

- In 1996, the Institute of Medicine (IOM) launched a concerted, ongoing effort focused on assessing and improving the nation's quality of care (http://www.iom.edu/focuson.asp?id = 8089).

Phase One: 1996−1999

The first phase of this Quality Initiative documented the serious and pervasive nature of the nation's overall quality problem, concluding that "the burden of harm conveyed by the collective impact of all of our health care quality problems is staggering" (Chassin *et al.*, 1998).

IOM Definition of Quality:

- The degree to which health services for individuals and populations increase the likelihood of desired health outcomes and are consistent with current professional knowledge.
- This phase built on an intensive review of the literature conducted by RAND to understand the scope of this issue (Schuster *et al.*, 1998).
- A framework was established that defined the nature of the problem as one of overuse, misuse, and underuse of healthcare services (Chassin *et al.*, 1998).

Phase Two: 1999−2001

The Committee on Quality of Health Care in America, laid out a vision for how the healthcare system and related policy environment must be radically transformed in order to close the chasm between what we know to be good quality care and what actually exists in practice.

Reports released during this phase:

- To Err is Human: Building a Safer Health System (IOM, 1999)
- Crossing the Quality Chasm: A New Health System for the 21st Century (National Research Council, 2001)
  - Stress that reform around the margins is inadequate to address system ills.

TABLE 11.1 Ten Rules for Care Delivery Redesign

Current Approach	New Rule
Care is based primarily on visits	Care is based on continuous healing relationships
Professional autonomy drives variability	Care is customized according to patient needs and values
Professionals control care	The patient is the source of control
Information is a record	Knowledge is shared and information flows freely
Decision-making is based on training and experience	Decision-making is evidence based
Do no harm is an individual responsibility	Safety is a system property
Secrecy is necessary	Transparency is necessary
The system reacts to needs	Needs are anticipated
Cost reduction is sought	Waste is continuously decreased
Preference is given to professional roles over the system	Cooperation among clinicians is a priority

Source: Table 3-1 in Crossing the Quality Chasm: A New Health System for the 21st Century (National Research Council, 2001).

- Placed a spotlight on how tens of thousands of Americans die each year from medical errors.
- Put the issue of patient safety and quality on the radar screen of public and private policy-makers.

Crossing the Quality Chasm: A New Health System for the 21st Century 2001):

- Describes broader quality issues.
- Defines six aims – care should be safe, effective, patient-centered, timely, efficient, and equitable.
- Provides 10 rules for care delivery redesign (Table 11.1).

Phase Three: 2001–Recent Present

- The focus is on operationalizing the vision of a future health system described in the Quality Chasm report.
- Many others are working to create a more patient-responsive 21st century health system, including clinicians/healthcare organizations, employers/consumers, foundations/research, government agencies, and quality organizations.
- This collection of efforts focuses reform at three different overlapping levels of the system: the environmental level, the level of the healthcare organization, and the interface between clinicians and patients.
- Recent and ongoing IOM efforts are multifaceted.

Fostering rapid advances in health care: learning from system demonstrations:

- Redesign primary care and care for those with chronic conditions
- Create an information and communications technology infrastructure, making health insurance coverage available and affordable at the state level
- Reform malpractice to make it patient-centered, safety focused, and non-judicial.

Redesigning care delivery:

- Restructure care delivery; and, at the behest of the Agency for Health Care Research and Quality, an IOM effort recommended 20 such priority areas for national action (IOM, 2003).
- At the Quality Chasm Summit (2004), leaders from exemplary communities and national organizations designed community-focused strategic plans to be implemented at the community level for a subset of the priority areas.
- Keeping Patients Safe: Transforming the Work Environment of Nurses (National Research Council, 2004a) identifies solutions to problems in hospital, nursing home, and other healthcare organization work environments that threaten patient safety through their effect on nursing care.
- The report's findings and recommendations address the related issues of management practices, workforce capability, work design, and organizational safety culture.

Furthering measurement and informed purchasing:

- Encouraged the federal government to take advantage of its position as purchaser, regulator, and provider of healthcare services to determine quality for the healthcare sector.
- Designed in concert with ideas laid out in the Quality Chasm report.

Reforming health professions education:

- Important implications for current and future health professionals.
- Health Professions Education: A Bridge to Quality (National Research Council, 2003a) encourages programs and institutions engaged in clinical education, recommending the implementation of a core set of competencies.
- Targets a mix of approaches including leveraging oversight organizations, fostering enhanced training environments, and initiating public reporting.
- Encouraging information technology implementation:
- Importance of a dramatically improved information technology infrastructure to support a 21st century health system.
- The Key Capabilities of an Electronic Health Record (National Research Council, 2003b) identifies eight care delivery functions that are essential for such records to promote greater safety, quality, and efficiency.

The eight core functions:

1. Health information and data
2. Result management
3. Order management
4. Decision support
5. Electronic communication and connectivity
6. Patient support
7. Administrative processes and reporting
8. Reporting and population health.

Patient Safety: Achieving a New Standard for Care (National Research Council, 2004b):

- Plan for development of data standards for collection, coding, and classification of patient safety information.
- Establishment of a national health information infrastructure, with ongoing promotion of data standards; status of current standards-setting activities in health data interchange, terminologies, and medical knowledge representation; and comprehensive patient safety programs in healthcare organizations.

Comprehensive Drug Safety

- The Institute of Medicine is mandated by Congress to "carry out a comprehensive study of drug safety."
- Identify quality issues in order to provide a blueprint for system-wide change.
- Develop a full understanding of drug safety and quality issues through an evidence-based review of literature, case studies, and analysis. This review will consider the nature and causes of medication errors, their impact on patients, the differences in causation, impact, and prevention across multiple dimensions of healthcare delivery — including patient populations, care settings, clinicians, and institutional cultures.
- Attempt to develop credible estimates of the incidence, severity, and costs of medication errors that can be useful in prioritizing resources for national quality improvement efforts and influencing national healthcare policy.
- Evaluate alternative approaches to reducing medication errors in terms of their efficacy, cost-effectiveness, appropriateness in different settings and circumstances, feasibility, institutional barriers to implementation, associated risks, and the quality of evidence supporting the approach.
- Provide guidance to consumers, providers, payers, and other key stakeholders on high priority strategies to achieve both short-term and long-term drug safety goals, to elucidate the goals and expected results of such initiatives and support the business case for them, and to identify critical success factors and key levers for achieving success.
- Assess the opportunities and key impediments to broad nationwide implementation of medication error reductions, and to provide guidance to policy-makers and government agencies (including the Food and Drug Administration, the Centers for Medicare and Medicaid Services, and the National Institutes of Health) in promoting a national agenda for medication error reduction.

- Develop an applied research agenda to evaluate the health and cost impacts of alternative interventions, and to assess collaborative public and private strategies for implementing the research agenda through AHRQ and other government agencies.

(Congress in the Medicare Modernization Act of 2003 (Section 107(c))

THE LEAPFROG INITIATIVE

Organizational Goals of the Leapfrog Group

The Leapfrog Group (Figure 11.2) is organized to help organizations that buy health care who are working to initiate breakthrough improvements in the safety, quality, and affordability of health care for Americans.

This is a non-mandated program aimed at mobilizing employer purchasing power to alert America's health industry that big leaps in healthcare safety, quality, and customer value will be recognized and rewarded.

Mission statement:

To trigger giant leaps forward in the safety, quality, and affordability of health care by:

- Supporting informed healthcare decisions by those who use and pay for health care.
- Promoting high-value health care through incentives and rewards.

Why Leapfrog?

- In 1998, a number of large employers discussed how they could work together to use the way they purchased health care to have an influence on its quality and affordability.
- There was dysfunction in the healthcare marketplace. Employers were spending billions of dollars on health care for their employees, with no validation of quality or comparison of healthcare providers.

Leapfrog link to the Institute of Medicine:

- A 1999 report by the Institute of Medicine gave the Leapfrog founders an initial focus — reducing preventable medical mistakes.
- More deaths occur in hospitals each year from preventable medical mistakes than there are from vehicle accidents, breast cancer, and AIDS.

"Leap" to new initiative:

- The report actually recommended that large employers provide more market reinforcement for the quality and safety of health care.
- Health organizations could take a "leap" forward with employees, retirees, and families by rewarding hospitals that implement improvements in quality and safety.
- Leapfrog receives support from its membership, the Business Roundtable, and the Robert Wood Johnson Foundation.

Potential for improvement:

- The Leapfrog Group's membership of Fortune 500 companies and other large private and public healthcare purchasers provides health benefits to more than 34 million Americans in all 50 states.
- Leapfrog members have agreed to base their purchase of health care on principles that encourage provider quality improvement and consumer involvement.

FIGURE 11.2 Overview of The Leapfrog Group.

Cost containment:

- The Leapfrog Group's initial three recommended quality and safety practices have the potential to save up to 65,341 lives and prevent between 567,000 and 907,600 medication errors each year (Birkmeyer and Dimick, 2004).
- Implementation could also save ~$41.5 billion annually.

Three concepts:
American health care remains far below obtainable levels of basic safety, quality, and customer value.

- The health industry would improve rapidly if purchasers recognized and rewarded superior safety and value.
- Voluntary adherence to purchasing principles by the largest employers would provide an impetus to encourage other purchasers to participate.
- These principles should not only champion value but focus on specific innovations offering "great leaps" to maximize media and consumer support and adoption by purchasers.

Leaps in Hospital Quality and Safety

The Leapfrog Group has identified and refined four hospital quality and safety practices that are the focus of its healthcare provider performance comparisons and hospital recognition and reward.

- The quality practices are:
  - Computer physician order entry.
  - Evidence-based hospital referral.
  - Intensive care unit (ICU) staffing by physicians experienced in critical care medicine.
  - The Leapfrog Safe Practices Score, based on the NQF-endorsed Safe Practices.

Computer physician order entry (CPOE):

- With CPOE systems, hospital staff enter medication orders via a computer linked to prescribing error prevention software.
- CPOE has been shown to reduce serious prescribing errors in hospitals by more than 50%.

Evidence-based hospital referral (EHR):

- Consumers and healthcare purchasers should choose hospitals with extensive experience and the best results with certain high-risk surgeries and conditions.
- By referring patients needing certain complex medical procedures to hospitals offering the best survival odds based on valid criteria — such as the number of times a hospital performs these procedures each year or other process or outcomes data — research indicates that a patient's risk of dying could be reduced by 40%.

ICU physician staffing (IPS):

- Staffing ICUs with doctors who have special training in critical care medicine, called "intensivists," has been shown to reduce the risk of patients dying in the ICU by 40%.
- Under Leapfrog initiatives, primary-care physician access to the ICU environment is limited.

The Leapfrog Safe Practices score:

- The National Quality Forum's 27 Safe Practices — The National Quality Forum-endorsed 30 Safe Practices cover a range of practices that, if utilized, would reduce the risk of harm in certain processes, systems, or environments of care.
- Included in the 30 practices are the original three Leapfrog leaps. For this new leap, added in April 2004, hospitals' progress on the remaining 27 safe practices was to be assessed.

Four Primary Criteria for Purchasing

- There is overwhelming scientific evidence that these quality and safety leaps will significantly reduce preventable medical mistakes.
- Their implementation by the health industry is feasible in the near term.
- Consumers can readily appreciate their value.
- Health plans, purchasers, or consumers can easily ascertain their presence or absence in selecting among healthcare providers.

Adherence to the following four purchasing principles:

- Educating and informing enrollees about the safety, quality, and affordability of health care and the importance of comparing the care that healthcare providers give. Initial emphasis on the Leapfrog safety and quality practices.
- Recognizing and rewarding healthcare providers for major advances in the safety, quality, and affordability of care.
- Holding health planners accountable for implementing the Leapfrog purchasing principles.
- Building the support of benefits consultants and brokers to use and advocate the Leapfrog purchasing principles with all of their clients.

Deadline to meet these Standards:

- Leapfrog purchasers are working with the provider community to arrive at aggressive but feasible target dates.
- Application of the purchasing principles and implementation of Leapfrog's quality practices takes time and a certain amount of effort and planning.

Timeline

- The Leapfrog Group began collecting data in June 2001 by querying urban and suburban hospitals in 6 regions, and has recently expanded from 23 to 28 regions
- In 2004, Leapfrog's 23 regions accounted for almost half of the US population and encompassed 1,664 urban, suburban, and rural hospitals.
- By 2005, 55% (692) of targeted hospitals had responded. More than 240 hospitals outside of the 23 regions had responded to the survey on their own initiative, without a formal request from Leapfrog.
- By 2013, more than 1,300 hospitals voluntarily participated in Leapfrog incentives.

PART 2: ROOT CAUSE ANALYSIS, SIX SIGMA AND QUALITY CONTROL, AND LEAN CONCEPTS IN HOSPITALS AND HEALTHCARE FACILITIES AS THEY EXIST IN 2013–2014

PART OUTLINE:

1. Six Sigma
2. Quality Control
3. Lean Concepts for Healthcare Delivery
4. Root Cause Analysis

SIX SIGMA

Six Sigma aims to achieve quality by reducing variation in processes. Six Sigma aims to reduce error rates such that six standard deviations around the mean of a process fit between the upper and lower tolerances. For example, a manufacturer producing lock barrels had to make sure the diameters of the barrels were right. If they were too large they would not fit the assembly of the lock, and if they were too small they also would not fit. The upper and lower control limits ideally include six standard deviations on each side of the mean to result in no more than 3.4 bad parts in 1,000,000 opportunities for error (99.9997% accuracy) (Harry and Crawford, 2004). Of course, that very stringent standard is often modified, depending upon the analysis of the process for a company. There is a curve of diminishing returns, and if the return on investment (ROI) is less with more precision, then less precision is tolerated until the ROI diminishes. (Finding that point of diminishing returns would be an opportunity for predictive analytics.) Harry and Crawford (2004) used an airline example. Baggage arrivals are on about a four sigma process, whereas passenger arrival (fatality rate) is on a six sigma process, and "To put that in perspective, a person is about 1,800 times more likely to get to his destination safely than his luggage is" (p. 8).

Early in the 20th century in the United States, more error was tolerated in production. If a company owned a majority of the market share, then if a production method produced 92% good parts and 8% bad parts, there was little concern. It was easier to do what had always been done and not modify systems. The bad parts were simply discarded or reworked. If a company has the market, then it does not have to worry too much about sending out bad parts, as long as it is making a comfortable or increasing profit. If energy was abundant, the companies did not care if energy was wasted. If air was plentiful, then a little pollution wouldn't hurt — it would simply blow away. If, on the other hand, other companies start competing with better products, as did Japan after World War II, with the help of D. Edward Deming, then suddenly American companies started losing market share. Japan was using Six Sigma methodology (interestingly, a US invention) and the United States was not (Carson and Carson, 1993). Scarcity of natural resources and governmental regulations further propelled companies to reduce waste and to streamline processes. One question, as we apply quality concepts to health care: what model has been used in the past, and what will constitute the future? And what happens if a government takes over health care?

Deming's famous 14 points are shown in Anderson *et al.* (1994, Table 1). Those 14 points emphasized continuous improvements in quality through excellence in leadership, training, and trust, and elimination of the fear of making mistakes, of quotas, and of barriers to quality. He ended by saying that transformation is everyone's job, from the top to the bottom of an organization.

Deming's principles became heavily used in American industry, and gradually the movement spread to other fields. In addition, Six Sigma has changed its focus from simply reducing errors to reducing costs, and finally to adding value (Harry and Crawford, 2004). Goals of the newest Six Sigma focus are to deliver the best product in a timely fashion, with the fewest errors and the least amount of resources, as the focus is on value. "For business purposes, value is defined as delivering a product or service to the right spot, at the right time, in the correct volume, and at the lowest possible cost" (Harry and Crawford, 2004, p. 8). This change in focus led to the total quality management movement of the 1980s in the United States.

QUALITY CONTROL

Total Quality Management (TQM) is sometimes used synonymously with Six Sigma because quality management generally combines the standardization of Six Sigma with the processes of DMAIC (defining, measuring, analyzing, improving, and controlling) (Chang, 2009). However, TQM and DMAIC are but two of the methodologies of Six Sigma. Levels of Six Sigma in terms of amount of training and in levels of savings to the company are generally green belt and black belt. Information on certification, levels, and amounts of money saved by an organization may be found on the Six Sigma website (Six Sigma, 2013). The various methodologies of Six Sigma may be found on the Six Sigma website as well. At this writing 18 methods were listed, including Kaisen and Lean. The various methodologies are also used synonymously with Six Sigma in the literature.

Quality attainment in medical settings, including hospitals, aims to provide a faster service while increasing quality care. If patients are seen in a timely fashion, with accurate diagnoses and treatments, then healing can begin sooner and costs can be saved. Faster and more accurate processes lead to serving more patients within a time interval and increasing income, while avoiding money suckers such as hiding and fixing errors, and paying out lawsuits. Faster and more accurate processes also mean increasing patient satisfaction and, even more important, helping people to live longer by increasing health.

Examples of Using Six Sigma in Health Care

Bao *et al.* (2013) attempted to use Six Sigma concepts to address the problem of "irrational" drug use in six hospitals in China. They reported that on many occasions people were dying not from their diseases but from inappropriate or erroneous uses of medications. They used the DMAIC process of Six Sigma to reduce the error rates from around 8% to about 4%.

Karr (2011) suggested changing the terminology, moving away from the term Six Sigma and toward terms such as best practices and Kaizen. Regardless of what it is called — Six Sigma, lean management, continuous progress, quality improvement, or quality attainment — increasing good process outcomes is desirable.

Scheeres (2012) talked about value stream maps for health care, and examined each step of the process through the eyes of the consumer (interesting use of term "consumer"). People used to be patients, now they are consumers. People used to be students; now they are customers (Scheeres, 2012, p. 26). Learning to Sort, Set in order, Sanitize, Standardize, and Sustain (the 5S system) an area free of clutter with a place for everything is easy and impactful. Kumar and Kwong (2011) used surveys for gap analysis to help identify areas ripe for analysis and revision.

Six Sigma has been used for a variety of targets, such as for increasing revenue in hospitals (Plonien, 2013), for patient satisfaction (Kerfoot, 2007), for patient flow (Roesler and Dydyk, 2007), and for patient safety (in this case, when the pharmacist earns a black belt in Six Sigma (Young, 2004).

LEAN CONCEPTS FOR HEALTH CARE: THE LEAN HOSPITAL AS A METHODOLOGY OF SIX SIGMA

Lean hospitals practice DMAIC. Lean clinics practice DMAIC. As processes are examined, inefficient and non-contributing processes are lopped off (surgically removed), resulting in a cleaner and leaner organization. Mazur *et al.* (2012) discussed implementation of lean processes in hospitals during their first year. The authors identified two major processes, single-loop and double-loop learning models, in "the detection and the elimination of error" (p. 11). First-loop issues are generally dealt with first. The first loop finds errors and attempts to correct them. The deep values or root issues are not dealt with initially. After the first and immediate issues (symptoms) have been solved and put into the "control" mode, the deep roots and values issues are dealt with. In the second loop, the hospital reflects about what its values are, directions in which it wants to move, and what those directions mean. The authors stated that it is important to help employees get to the second level of reflection because it is at that level that a deeper understanding and commitment to the lean process occurs.

The first task is to identify waste and then eliminate it. Identifying the waste exemplifies the first loop. Cookson *et al.* (2011) used the acronym WORMPIT to help them identify processes that needed to be examined. (WORMPIT stood for Waiting, Overproduction, Rework, Motion, Processing (as in over-processing), Inventory, and Transportation.) Thse researchers gave a good example of using such identification in creating a value stream map of patients entering the emergency room and everything that happened to the patients until they saw the physician. Members of the team observed patients as they went through the process. Exact times were noted, and Post-it notes were used to map all the steps. From the original eight steps, including steps of time-wasters, Cookson *et al.* were able to move to only five steps, as shown in Figure 11.3.

Unfortunately, in poor economic times some hospitals tended to abandon quality efforts – just when they actually needed them the most (Burton, 2011). Instead of dropping efforts, practicing continuous deployment is important even if new initiatives cannot be started because of lack of funds. Murphree *et al.* (2011) agreed, adding that even when a project finished, instead of dropping it the project should be moved into a "control" phase – which is another word for

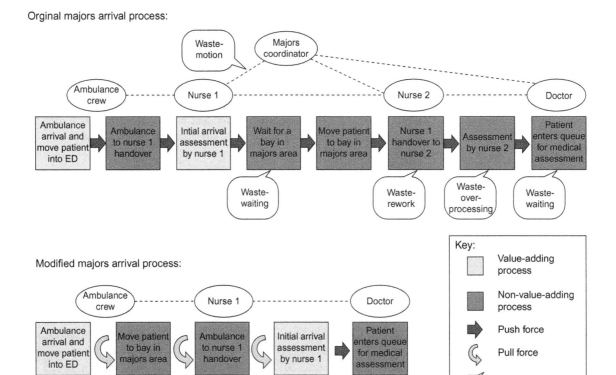

FIGURE 11.3 Lean value stream mapping. *Source: Figure 1 in Cookson* et al. *(2012, p. 27).*

continuous deployment. Six Sigma defines the last "C" in the acronym DMAIC (Define, Measure, Analyze, Improve, and Control) as "control" (not "close") (p. 44).

Many lessons can be learned from an institution that involved the entire organization in quality improvement, such as Mount Sinai in 2000 (Chassin, 2008). Such a large undertaking had to have top-down support, and it did, but the author warned that hospital settings are not exactly like manufacturing plants, and that top-down mandates do not always match the sub-system culture but that teamwork is needed. Deming no doubt would agree even for manufacturing facilities. Much time, effort, training, and money was no doubt given to such an undertaking, but in the end the efforts paid off. Many projects were undertaken in the data-driven environment. One thing they learned at Mount Sinai was to depend on data rather than on people's perceptions of how they thought things were going. They carefully measured base lines and then found the metrics that would insure reliability of measure. Use of control charts aided in their collection and analysis. Some of their improvements were a

28% reduction in excess dosing in patients with kidney dysfunction, 52 minute reduction in turnaround time, 700% improvement in tracking of patient controlled analgesics, 90 minute reduction in bed turnover time, 91% defect reduction in cardiac stents, AICD, pacemakers, 85% defect reduction in chemotherapy revenue capture, and 90% defect reduction in OB/GYN revenue enhancement.

(Chassin, 2008, pp. 51–52).

The latter three provided savings and revenue of over $7 million. Definitely, Six Sigma paid off for them in terms of money, but no doubt it also paid off in terms of increasing good patient outcomes. Chapter 12 discusses the many aspects of the lean hospital movement and provides excellent examples.

ROOT CAUSE ANALYSIS

Root Cause Analysis (RCA) is one of the tools used within Six Sigma (Six Sigma, 2013). The "five whys" is a method of discovering root causes. Continuously asking "why?" can help drive the discovery of reasons for errors (Connelly, 2012; iSix Sigma, 2013). The most fundamental reason for the failure or the error is the root cause (Dattilo and Constantino, 2006).

"The Five Whys" is a technique used many times when human interactions are involved in the processes from which the problem or error arose. For example, when the patient in Chapter 2 died because the computer froze, it was important to ask why it happened.

- Why did the patient die? Because the operation could not continue.
- Why could the operation not continue? Because the computer screen froze.
- Why did the computer screen freeze? Because the computer had not been powered down after many days of use.
- Why was the machine not powered down? Because those running the surgeries did not know the computer needed to be shut down, and it was faster simply to hibernate the machine.

After determining the root cause of the problem, the problem could be solved and someone was designated to power down the computer after operations. Problem discovery for healthcare systems often is more complex than in the previous example, in which many causes are found to interact with an event. Connelly (2012) suggests involvement of all stakeholders in an interdisciplinary team is important for drilling down to causes. The team needs to answer as to what happened, how it happened, why it happened, and what should be done to prevent a reoccurrence (p. 316).

Teams rather than individuals have become the focus for accreditation bodies, and a thorough analysis of root causes can often avoid sanctions, particularly for sentinel events such as the one described above in which the patient died (Dattilo and Constantino, 2006). Evidently the Joint Commission, formerly called the JCAHO, maintains a database of sentinel events, their tracking, and reviews. The JCAHO started the endeavor in 1995 and continues to today. Over 3,100 events had been collected as of 2005. What a treasure trove that database would be for medical data miners.

In the United Kingdom, the National Patient Safety Association set up a procedure for root cause analysis (Mengis and Nicolini, 2010) by focusing on questions. The questions are given in Table 11.2. Everyone is asked to answer the questions in writing so that a matrix of events may be constructed, and a time-line of events devised, and in order to identify all the factors involved. Further, a plan is devised so that the same problem will not happen in the future. The plan specifies responsibilities and times for those responsibilities to be carried out. The authors recommended solutions for common challenges to successful root cause analysis. For example, they emphasized that nurses should be trained in RCA so that they can be more assertive when the meetings take place.

Statistical procedures can certainly be a help in the entire process of RCA. Statistical feature selection and root cause analysis helps to find the patterns which can predict problems and assists in sorting through all the data generated

TABLE 11.2 The Root Cause Analysis Process

Question	Process
What happened?	Reporting the adverse event through the incident-reporting system and prioritizing, from "minor" to "major," by using an information technology or paper-based reporting system and risk-assessment matrix
How did it happen?	Drawing up a timeline for the incident based on clinical notes and statements of the staff involved by using or referring to narrative chronology, tabular timelines or time–person grids
Why did it happen?	Identifying contributory factors and root causes during investigation team meetings comprising staff with expert knowledge but no involvement in the incident by using or referring to the appropriate analytical or group-interaction tools
What should be done to prevent it from happening again?	Developing an action plan to identify the actions needed, when they should be made, and who should be responsible for carrying them out

Source: Mengis and Nicolini (2010, p. 18), adapted from National Patient Safety Agency (2004).

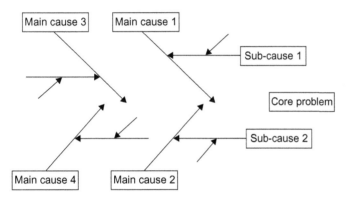

FIGURE 11.4 Another fishbone diagram. *Source: Li and Lee (2011, p. 279).*

by all the shareholders. It is wise to find those variables that actually predict, rather than those that people only think will predict. In other words, the team should brainstorm and collect all information from the clinical notes. Members might assume they know what the causes are, but feature selection can sometimes point out predictive relationships that were not thought of without the statistical analysis. A number of the tutorials in this text contain feature selection analyses.

Fishbone diagrams are used in root cause analysis to visually display the causes of a problem. The causes are arranged by their relative importance in bringing about an event. Li and Lee (2011) provided a thorough explanation of the fishbone process, and Figure 11.4 shows their fishbone diagram skeleton illustrating causes and sub-causes of a problem. The authors also mentioned that fishbone diagrams can be turned to positives, exploring paths to opportunities or to increasing good outcomes. In a reverse fishbone, all the items are stated positively and the outcome is value added.

Decision trees can also be used in graphical understanding of problem outcomes. Decision trees are generated using data and could easily be used in searching for root causes. Freitas (2011) demonstrated the use of decision trees for finding the best tests for patients, considering the costs involved (see Figure 11.5).

Root cause analysis, with all its many tools, is being used in many areas in health care, including the following.

- Considering nosocomial infections as seminal events requiring root cause analysis (Radtke, 2004). The hospital, in deciding whether an infection causes an unintended death, should consider the condition of the patient upon their entering the hospital.
- Certainly wrong-site surgery should undergo RCA (Dattilo and Constantino, 2006).
- Exploring the extra costs of phlebotomy (such as redraws) that may affect the bottom line (Nasir, 2013).
- Examining complications in plastic surgery, as in Rangaswamy's study on abdominoplasty (Rangaswamy, 2013). One photograph in the article showed a nasty infection of a patient who was described as a "medical tourist"

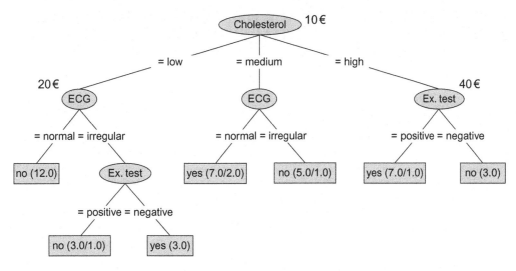

FIGURE 11.5 Cost-sensitive decision tree for cholesterol. *Source: Freitas (2011, p. 286).*

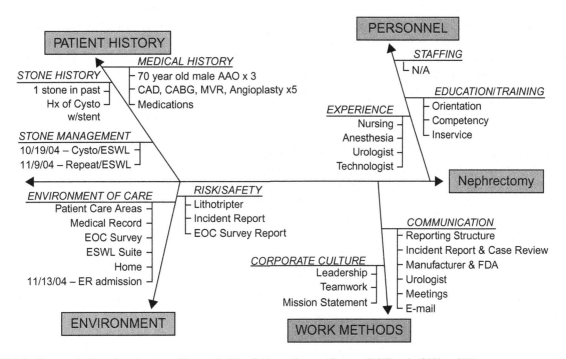

FIGURE 11.6 Cause and effect of nephrectomy illustrated with a fishbone diagram. *Source: Cahill* et al. *(2008, p. 251).*

(p. 370). The author pointed out that, to avoid possible necrotizing fasciitis, it is paramount that the patient has access to a qualified person or the surgeon for at least 10 days post-operation. (Chapter 14 discusses the current trend for people to obtain medical care and expensive surgeries in other countries. There should always be enough time for post-surgery infection control worked into a person's travel plans.)

- Cahill *et al.* (2008) reported RCA concerning a patient who died after his second kidney stone shock-wave operation. The patient died from bleeding 4 days after the second operation (see Tutorial J1, on disseminated intravascular coagulation, to learn more about bleeding after surgery). A CT scan revealed a fractured kidney. This event brought on an "intensive investigation by the Sentinel Event Committee" (p. 449). Figure 11.6 shows the fishbone analysis of the cause and effect elements.

PART 3: EXPERIENCES OF A DOCTOR WHO IMPLEMENTED A QUALITY CONTROL DEPARTMENT IN A HOSPITAL SYSTEM DURING THE 1990s — AN ERA WHEN QUALITY WAS ANYTHING BUT THE NORM

By Guest Author Darrell Dean, DO, MPH, CHCQM, FAIHQ; retired from position of Medical Director for Clinical & Operational Performance Improvement. Dr. Dean has also been the CME Surveyor for ACCME accreditation of hospitals for the Medical Association of Georgia. Previously, Dr. Dean was Internal Consultant for coding and documentation for Centrex Primary Care Network. He was also Associate Medical Director, Staff Physician, North Georgia Medical Association and serves as locum tenens for all 17 practice sites. He worked at the Georgia Department of Human Resources, Division of Public Health as the District Medical Director, Coosa Valley Health District. Dr. Dean received his Master of Public Health degree, Health Policy & Administration Track from Emory University, Rollins School of Public Health.

NOTE: This section is written by a physician who spent 10 years developing a quality improvement department in a regional medical center. It is presented here as a "personal story" so the reader can get a better glimpse of what a physician has to go through to implement such a quality program.

QUALITY IMPROVEMENT

General Introduction

There is no doubt in anyone's mind that there are quality problems in hospitals (and in all other healthcare facilities). The definition and priority of what those problems are and how to improve them is a topic of concern to multiple constituencies; the definition and priority assignment will depend on their position and beliefs as well as what they have to gain, or lose, as a result of the solutions that are chosen and implemented. An allied issue of significance is that the intricacies of this complex topic are monumental.

The information presented in this chapter is not designed to offer an overall solution, but to present an overview of one approach, which I coordinated over a 10-year period with some success, that may contribute to efforts to improve quality in other local facilities.

The concept of healthcare quality improvement has been discussed, written about, legislated, taught, discarded, debated, endorsed, and embraced. Quality improvement initiatives began to be seriously addressed in 2001, when the US Center for Medicare and Medicaid Services (CMMS) and the Joint Commission (TJC) developed and agreed upon the "Core Measures" that hospitals were incentivized to implement. The endeavor of hospitals trying to achieve greater reimbursement based on those quality measures was followed by intense efforts to achieve higher and higher compliance rates. There were planning, policies, and education, along with comparisons between and among hospitals to determine how to improve those rates. As a result, hospital scores improved; to be in the "top 10%" of hospitals in performance was everyone's goal. As a consequence, it became more difficult to get to that "top 10%" level. The positive results were improvement in care for the conditions enumerated by the required CMMS and TJC measures. The negative aspect was that other identifiable quality improvement issues were set aside.

As time has passed since the initiation of the CMMS and TJC Core Measures, a number of additional quality measures have been proposed and mandated by the federal government, insurance companies, and various "quality improvement organizations."

As a consequence of all this focus on quality deficiencies in health care, it is now common for hospitals to have quality departments and directors of quality. A further result is that there is a variety of software, books, journal articles, and seminars relating to improvements in healthcare quality and performance improvement. However, one size does NOT fit all. A simply designed and recommended program to solve quality problems is not likely to succeed in any specific healthcare facility. Instead, developing a process that takes into account the unique structure and functions of a healthcare entity, and designing well-planned approaches to solve specifically identified problems, with broad input and involvement from different departments and entities involved, is much more likely to be successful.

Definition of Healthcare Quality

If one is going to attempt to improve healthcare quality, it is important to understand what healthcare quality is. There are multiple definitions promulgated by various organizations and individuals.

The Institute of Medicine (IOM) has been the earliest healthcare quality improvement motivator, beginning with its book *To Err is Human* (National Research Council, 2001). The IOM definition of quality is "The degree to which health services for individuals and populations increase the likelihood of desired health outcomes and are consistent with current professional knowledge [the fewer errors will occur]." That is certainly comprehensive and conveys the correct concept. They followed up that initial report with the following "aims" of a high quality healthcare system with the following specific goals for health care:

- *Safe* — prevent injuries to patients caused by the care that is supposed to help them
- *Effective* — providing services based on scientific knowledge to all who could benefit, and refraining from providing services to those not likely to benefit (avoiding underuse and overuse)
- *Patient-centered* — providing care that is respectful of and responsive to individual patient preferences, needs, and values, and ensuring that patient values guide all clinical decisions
- *Timely* — reducing waits and sometimes harmful delays for both those who receive and those who give care
- *Efficient* — avoiding waste, in particular waste of equipment, supplies, ideas, and energy
- *Equitable* — providing care that does not vary in quality because of personal characteristics, such as gender, ethnicity, geographic location, and socioeconomic status.

Other organizations have definitions of healthcare quality that fits their particular niche in the overall scheme of health care.

There are two (or more) audiences to which an appropriate definition applies. Those are (1) providers of healthcare services, and (2) recipients or patients. Varied and more academic definitions fit the providers, and relate to evidence, technology, procedural competence, and meeting specifically accepted goals. Much simpler and practical definitions apply to the receivers (patients). The providers need to be cognizant of both, while the receivers need to be confident that they will have their concerns included and receive the care defined. The IOM definition does include the providers of healthcare services, but the definition for the receivers deserves to be separate from that for the providers.

A defining statement made by receivers of health care might be as follows:

Care for me in a way that respects me as an individual, that includes my participation in and understanding of decisions related to all illnesses and healthcare issues that I might face, and that includes consideration of my financial and educational level, as well as my goals for healthcare outcomes.

This statement simply reiterates what the IOM definition includes, but in simpler, more understandable words.

Healthcare providers, especially in hospitals — physicians, nurses, technicians, administrators, and all the other support staff — can contribute to appropriate outcomes in keeping with the IOM definition of quality. In order to do that, however, it is imperative to have a Quality Department that has the sole priority of monitoring and measuring the quality of the care provided. Operating with this understanding, processes, procedures, programs, and education can be developed and implemented through a Quality Department to raise the level of care. Even in the highest quality institutions there is always room for improvement, and the Quality Department's vigilance can provide that service.

The Quality Department in a Hospital

The Quality Department in a hospital needs to be an independent department reporting to the Chief Medical Officer (CMO). The Medical Director of Quality should be the Quality Department director, but the department needs, minimally, another person with a clinical background and both IT and personnel management expertise. This Quality Department assistant should be tasked with the administrative functions of the department to free the medical director to observe, develop policy, appoint quality-related committees, and prepare reports for the executive team, board of directors, medical staff, and other stakeholder audiences, as well as develop solid relationships with all of the medical staff members. Another significant task of the Medical Director of Quality is to communicate with the medical staff secretary, particularly with regard to issues related to medical staff applicants and their qualifications. A not uncommon issue for the medical staff secretary pertains to odd issues that arise, related to an applicant's past, which the typical application form or process may not cover. The secretary needs a physician that can help in addressing problems that arise. Although this may fall under the purview of the Chief Medical Officer, the CMO is often overwhelmed with other tasks such that some of the functions of that position do not get addressed in the desired timeframe. In my view, selecting physicians to add to a medical staff is very much related to quality of care in the hospital. Providing input to medical and surgical policy related to quality of care is another important function of a Medical Director of Quality. The Medical Director of Quality needs to be alert to additional duties required of physicians and the hospital director that may be unique to the specific hospital.

Issues Discovered

In the course of my 10 years as a Medical Director of Quality (actual title was Medical Director of Clinical and Operational Performance Improvement), there were quite a number of issues that came to my attention. My way of functioning was to become aware of the primary reasons for the occurrence of any practice that was causing, or could cause, harm to a patient, and then working to correct or improve the faulty practice. A specific policy at my hospital was developed to address the traditional attitude of punishing a hospital employee when an adverse event occurred. The only thing punishment accomplishes is to hide events in the future. This does no good for future patients. We promulgated a policy of identifying/reporting quality related problems and educating any involved person or persons so that the problem was prevented from happening in the future.

Learning about poor quality issues was an initial and ongoing step in identifying where I needed to devote my efforts. The following is a list of some of the issues addressed and on which resolution or improvement occurred:

- Improvement in performance on "core measures"
- Appropriate hand hygiene (nationally is at 40% – very poor)
- reduction in preventable mortality
- Identification of the main post-operative infections and development of prevention techniques
- Addressing other hospital-acquired infections, and their causes and prevention
- Reducing ventilator-acquired pneumonia cases
- Reducing urinary catheterizations and catheter-associated urinary tract infections
- Improving early sepsis identification and rapid initiation of treatment (especially in the Emergency Department (ED))
- Formation of an Antibiotic Stewardship Committee to address the inappropriate use of antibiotics
- Instigation of a major program to improve education of hospitalists, other medical staff and nurses in the newer methods of diabetes treatment (including use of basal-bolus insulin)
- Methods of reducing patient falls
- Improving the content of documentation generally (doctors, nurses, all other personnel), and legibility
- Improvement and understanding of ways to deal with urinary incontinence
- Education on the importance of teamwork
- Focus on other issues, including physician support and encouragement, appropriate physician behavior, nurse well-being, importance of effective communication.

The above are examples, not a comprehensive listing, of the projects undertaken over time.

The Quality Department is the repository of data from the clinical departments. The analysis of those data is one of the main avenues for identification of quality issues that need to be addressed. Those departments from which data need to be gathered include the following:

- Nursing
- Physicians (all disciplines)
- Laboratory
- Infection Control
- Respiratory
- Pharmacy
- Coding (including documentation information)
- Surgery
- Anesthesiology
- Emergency Department
- Psychiatry
- Social Services
- Coordinated Care
- Housekeeping
- Admission and Discharge
- Physical Therapy
- Rehabilitation
- Six Sigma (or other similar activities).

In addition to reviewing data, I was able to discover quality issues and promote quality performance by other, more traditional methods. The value of electronic medical record (EMR) systems cannot be denied, but personal interactions with physicians, nurses, and other personnel of various types should not be overlooked (and today can be included as "notes" in the EMR, and thus handled with *text analytics* as part of a quality control optimization system).

The following is a listing of job duties I undertook on a routine basis:

- Facilitation of the bimonthly Board Quality Committee meetings, which involved the following:
  - informing the members about quality issues/concerns/problems/programs/successes
  - preparing the agenda
  - reviewing the agenda with the Chairman prior to meetings
  - preparing and delivering information about quality topics relevant to the hospital
  - preparing the Board Quality Committee's report to the full hospital Board of Directors.
- Facilitation of the Clinical Advisory/Peer Review Committee's quarterly meeting (this multidisciplinary physician committee's role was to provide input about their quality concerns and the needs of the physicians relative to their practice in the hospital):
  - preparing the agenda for meetings and inviting speakers on topics relevant to the members concerns
  - reviewing and editing minutes of meetings
  - preparing presentations, as needed, of peer review issues as they arose.
- Appointing and leading quality teams to address quality issues that arose, based on data reviewed, internal chart reviews (based on information received), or internal research.
  1. Managing the peer review process by identifying and responding to suspected physician quality-of-care concerns reported to me by any of the various departments or individuals, following the medical staff's peer review policy
  2. Performing special projects, such as 2×2 mortality reviews, catheter-associated UTI review and others as needed, and preparing reports of the reviews for appropriate bodies
  3. Meeting with medical staff physicians as needed concerning quality or behavioral issues, or to discuss their performance or failure in order to address identified documentation or other requirements (such as use of order sets, legibility, required quality measures)
  4. Orienting new physicians and mid-levels to acquaint them with our specific quality measures, standard orders, unsafe abbreviations, expectations, etc.
  5. Performing a daily review of mortalities and evaluating the need, if any, for in-depth review to determine if the mortality was potentially preventable
  6. Performing a daily review of the surgery schedule to identify whether a procedure that might represent a quality issue was being addressed surgically, or whether a surgeon had scheduled a procedure for which he/she was not credentialed that was prohibited by policy (for example, tonsillectomy was not to be performed on a child under age 3 years, but must be referred to a facility that has Pediatric ICU).
- Attending the meetings of the Medical Care Evaluation Committee
- Attending all clinical department quarterly meetings and reporting on quality issues, if needed
- Attending Council meetings (General Surgery, Vascular Surgery, Cardiology, Emergency Care, Hospitalist), and providing quality perspective related to their speciality
- Helping to develop and participating in a Diabetes Task Force, formed to address the seriously inadequate treatment of hospitalized diabetes patients who were admitted either because of their diabetes or because of diabetes co-morbidity
- Attending monthly Operations Council meetings
- Attending monthly Hospital Board of Directors meetings
- Attending Medical Executive Committee meetings and reporting on quality initiatives, peer review cases and activities, and responding to questions from members
- Serving as Medical Director for the following:
  - Employee Health Department
  - Quality Department
  - Coordinated Care Department
  - Diabetes Foot Clinic, and serving as the Supervising Physician for the four Nurse Practitioners who worked in that clinic.
- Miscellaneous activities as follows:
  - chairing Utilization Review Committee
  - responding to problem calls from any department, unit, nurse, or physician to help resolve any issues that arose
  - assisting with medical record deficiency process (such as calling physicians or policy questions)

- being available to treat employee patients as needed
- consulting on coding issues and Coding Specialist queries as needed
- along with the hospital's Risk Manager, meeting with patient and/or family to discuss adverse outcomes that occurred while a person was hospitalized to help answer questions about the care provided and explain what occurred.

I list all of the above to illustrate the wide-ranging involvement of a physician who takes on the role of Medical Director of Performance Improvement (Quality). That is not to say that every hospital would require (or even encourage) the doctor in that position to assume responsibility for all of these duties. The point I am making is to demonstrate that the role of a full-time physician in that position includes keeping his/her ears open and cultivating positive relationships with hospital staff, medical staff, administration staff, and all others in order to be cognizant of as many of the quality issues as possible. Then steps can be taken to work collaboratively to find solutions to improve what needs attention.

Additional recommendations for a Medical Director of Quality are to participate in quality organizations, such as Institute of Healthcare Improvement (IHI), American Board of Quality Assurance, and Utilization Review Physicians. There are a number of other such organizations, and the importance of participation is to broaden one's knowledge and learn new ways of improvement and about new tools. Being aware of and reading about quality issues from other quality organizations is likewise valuable. Those organizations certainly include the CDC, SHEA, I and DSA, among others.

One dictum I have repeated often, and that I think is at least a partial answer to our current greatly increased healthcare costs, is: "The highest quality of medical care produces the lowest cost."

QUALITY OF CARE EXAMPLES

Example 11.1

I was meeting with a representative of a medical products manufacturing company, in October 2009. During our discussion about urinary catheterization kits, I mentioned the subject of prevention of catheter-associated urinary tract infections. Hospital acquired infections are a frequent and serious issue which hospital quality staff and teams work diligently to reduce. CA-UTI is said to be the most frequent of those infections. Having done a large number of urinary catheterizations — as an orderly during my college career, as a medical student, and more as a practicing physician with hospital privileges — during my decades of practice, I was well-versed on the procedure of urinary catheterization and its drawbacks. One of the methods of reducing such infections, based on CDC recommendations, as well as those of other quality organizations, was to use sterile technique when inserting catheters. I casually mentioned to the representative that there was no way sterile technique could be observed with the catheter kits currently available from manufacturers. He inquired as to what I would recommend to achieve the goal of using sterile technique. My recommendations included having much larger drapes, including a larger fenestrated drape with adhesive strips on one side to attach to the thighs of the patient and keep it in place during the procedure; two pairs of gloves, one outside the sterile section of the kit to be used during cleansing of the urethral meatus, and a separate pair to be donned after the sterile section of the kit was opened; a larger amount of lubricant than was typically provided; and a 16g Foley catheter already attached to the collection bag. In my opinion, these would be the minimum features of an acceptable kit. He said his company could produce kits with those features. They did produce those for our hospital. As a result of that conversation, shortly afterwards I was invited by the company to participate in a group of people from various hospitals across the United States and meet at company headquarters to come up with an improved catheter kit, incorporating my suggestions as well as including additional features suggested by the other participants. Ultimately those kits were manufactured, and they are now available across the USA.

Along with the improved catheter kits, I formed a multidisciplinary committee to address the issue of reducing catheter-associated urinary tract infections. That committee developed a multi-pronged program designed to accomplish the goal of reducing those infections.

Our first step was to develop a method of capturing the incidence of the infections. That was accomplished by reviewing billing data and noting cases that included documentation of a urinary tract infection and catheterization. One of the subsets of that data gathering was to look at the cases that were admitted through the Emergency Department and catheterized there prior to admission. That was a result of the impression by the team members that many catheters were inserted in that location.

The main additional features of our plan included the following:

- Education of physicians, nurses and nursing assistants on the issues related to catheter-associated infections.
- Training classes for nurses who did catheter insertions, with required annual competency evaluations.
- Development of a sticker to be placed in a progress note section that requested date of insertion, and a box to check (by physician) to indicate that catheter could be removed or left in place.
- Tracking of catheter days and number of infections.

After 3 months, our rate of catheter-associated urinary infections was reduced to zero. Although it did not stay at that level, it has continued to be lower than published rates.

Example 11.2

During an annual meeting in 2008 of non-profit hospitals, of which our hospital is a member, there was a presentation concerning preventable mortalities. At the time, as a result of my daily review of our hospital mortalities, I was becoming concerned about the issue. Because of my concern, our state organization of non-profit hospitals, which has a Quality Department, was engaged to come and do a chart review of recent mortalities. They reviewed the 50 most recent hospital deaths, and their results showed that our top five causes of mortality were due to cancer, cardiovascular disease, strokes, sepsis, and respiratory conditions. Other diagnoses leading to mortality included several different causes, but not a significant number.

As result of this review and revelation, further reviews of cases and data in our possession were conducted, especially of the top five causes of death. Cancer as a cause of death was not specifically addressed, since we concluded that, in most hospitalized cases, the death was unavoidable. We made the following specific efforts:

- Focused attention on the federally required core measures for acute myocardial infarction.
- Formed a multidisciplinary stroke committee and applied and received certification from the Joint Commission as Stroke Center of Excellence.
- Began a focused education effort for physicians (especially the Emergency Room physicians and hospitalists on early recognition and aggressive treatment).
- Provided education and sought input from the hospital's Respiratory Department and pulmonologists to identify gaps and needs of patients with chronic respiratory disease.
- Developed a protocol for early recognition of sepsis and specific education and provided this to Emergency Department physicians, stressing early identification and aggressive treatment of sepsis cases. In the event that sepsis could not be confirmed soon after admission, then the aggressive methods of treatment could safely be withdrawn.

While the above listing is not exhaustive and does not detail all that was done, it does provide a guide to some of the areas of focus that were utilized to reduce preventable deaths. Those efforts were successful over a several-year period, significantly reducing the preventable mortality rate in the hospital.

POSTSCRIPT

Once the root cause of an outcome is found, processes can be put in place in hospitals to assure efficiency of operation, which will work together to prevent negative outcomes in hospital treatments. Chapter 12 describes several approaches to development of this efficiency of operation, which can define the "lean hospital."

REFERENCES

Anderson, J.C., Rungtusanatham, M., Schroeder, R.G., 1994. A theory of quality management underlying the Deming management method. Acad. Manag. Rev. 19 (3), 472−509.

Bao, L., Chen, N., Shang, T., Fang, P., Xu, Z., Guo, W., et al., 2013. A multicenter study of the application of Six Sigma management in clinical rational drug use via pharmacist intervention. Turkish J. Med. Sci. 43 (3), 362−367.

Birkmeyer, J.D. and Dimick, J.B., 2004. The Leapfrog Group's Patient Safety Practices, 2003: The Potential Benefits of Universal Adoption. Available at: http://leapfroggroup.org/media/file/Leapfrog-Birkmeyer.pdf.

Burton, T.T., 2011. Improve how you improve. Indl. Eng. 43 (8), 48−53.

Cahill, K., Cruz, E., Guilbert, M., Oser, M., 2008. Root cause analysis following nephrectomy after Extracorporeal Shockwave Lithotripsy (ESWL). Urol. Nurs. 28 (6), 445−453.

Carson, P., Carson, K.D., 1993. Deming versus traditional management theorists on goal setting: can both be right? Bus. Horiz. 36 (5), 79.

Chang, J.L., 2009. Six sigma and TQM in Taiwan: an empirical study of discriminate analysis. Tot. Qual. Manag. Bus. Excell. 20 (3), 311−326.

Chassin, M.R., Galvin, R.W., The National Roundtable on Health Care Quality, 1998. The urgent need to improve health care quality Institute of Medicine National Roundtable on health care quality. JAMA. 280 (11), 1000−1005.

Chassin, R., 2008. The Six Sigma initiative at Mount Sinai Medical Center. Mt Sinai J. Med. 75 (1), 45−52.

Connelly, L.M., 2012. Root cause analysis. MedSurg. Nurs. 21 (5), 313−316.

Cookson, D., Read, C., Mukherjee, P., Cooke, M., 2011. Improving the quality of Emergency Department care by removing waste using Lean Value Stream mapping. Int. J. Clin. Leadersh. 17 (1), 25−30.

Darr, K., 1994. Eulogy to the master: W. Edward Deming. Hosp. Top. 2 (1), 4−5.

Dattilo, E., Constantino, R.E., 2006. Root cause analysis and nursing management responsibilities in wrong- site surgery. Dimens. Crit. Care Nurs. 25 (5), 221−225.

Espinosa, J.A., Nolan, T.W., 2000. Reducing errors made by emergency physicians in interpreting radiographs: longitudinal study. Br. Med. J. 320, 737−740.

Freitas, A., 2011. Building cost-sensitive decision trees for medical applications. AI Comm. 24 (3), 285−287.

Harry, M.J., Crawford, J., 2004. Six Sigma for the little guy. Mech. Eng. 126 (11), 8−10.

IOM (Institute of Medicine), 1999. In: Kohn, L.T., Corrigan, J.M., Donaldson, M.S. (Eds.), To Err is Human. National Academies PressInstitute of Medicine), 1999, Washington, DC.

IOM, 2003. In: Adams, K., Corrigan, J.M. (Eds.), Transforming Health Care Quality: Priority Areas for National Action. National Academies Press, Washington, DC.

iSix Sigma. Determine the root cause: The 5 whys. http://www.isixsigma.com/tools-templates/cause-effect/determine-root-cause-5-whys/>.

Karr, T., 2011. Determining what healthcare should be. Ind. Eng. 43 (9), 45−48.

Kerfoot, K., 2007. Patient satisfaction and high-reliability organizations: what's the connection? Urol. Nurs. 27 (6), 558−559.

Kumar, S., Kwong, A.M., 2011. Six Sigma tools in integrating internal operations of a retail pharmacy: a case study. Technol. Healthc. 19 (2), 115−133.

Li, S., Lee, L., 2011. Using fishbone analysis to improve the quality of proposals for science and technology programs. Res. Eval. 20 (4), 275−282.

Mazur, L., McCreery, J., Rothenberg, L., 2012. Facilitating lean learning and behaviors in hospitals during the early stages of lean implementation. Eng. Manag. J. 24 (1), 11−22.

Mengis, J., Nicolini, D., 2010. Root cause analysis in clinical adverse events. Nurs. Manag. UK. 16 (9), 16−20.

Murphree, P., Vath, R., Daigle, L., 2011. Sustaining lean Six Sigma projects in health care. Physician Executive. 37 (1), 44−48.

Nasir, A., 2013. Hidden phlebotomy expenses: exposing and eliminating excess costs. Med. Lab. Obs. 45 (8), 45−47.

National Patient Safety Agency, 2004. Root Cause Analysis Toolkit. www.msnpsa.nhs.uk/rcatoolkit/course/iindex.htm.

National Research Council, 2001. Crossing the quality chasm. A. New Health System for the 21st Century. Committee on the Quality of Health Care in America. National Academies Press, Washington, DC.

National Research Council, 2003a. In: Greiner, A.C., Knebel, E. (Eds.), Health Professions Education: A Bridge to Quality. The National Academies Press, Washington, DC.

National Research Council, 2003b. The Key Capabilities of an Electronic Health Record. The National Academies Press, Washington, DC.

National Research Council, 2004a. In: Page, A. (Ed.), Keeping Patients Safe: Transforming the Work Environment of Nurses. National Academies Press, Washington, DC.

National Research Council, 2004b. In: Aspden, P., Corrigan, J.M., Wolcott, J., Erickson, S.M. (Eds.), Patient Safety: Achieving a New Standard for Care. National Academies Press, Washington, DC.

Plonien, C., 2013. Six Sigma for revenue retrieval. Nurs. Econ. 31 (2), 90−98.

Radtke, K., 2004. Get to the root of sentinel events involving infection control. Nurs. Manag. 35 (6), 18−22.

Rangaswamy, M., 2013. Minimising complications in abdominoplasty: An approach based on the root cause analysis and focused preventive steps. Ind. J. Plast. Surg. 46 (2), 365−376.

Roesler, K., Dydyk, D., 2007. The oncology service line's use of Six Sigma in the Cowdery patient care center: creating standardized processes to improve patient flow, improving staff and patient satisfaction. Oncol. Nurs. Forum. 34 (2), 524.

Scheeres, D., 2012. My favorite things. Ind. Eng. 44 (6), 26.

Schuster, M.A. Reifel, J.L., and McGuigan, K., 1998. Assessment of the quality of cancer care: a review for the National Cancer Policy Board of the Institute of Medicine; <www.iom.edu/~/media/Files/Activity%20Files/Disease/NCPF/randfnl.pdf/>.

Six Sigma. Six Sigma Home page. <www.isixsigma.com/.

Young, D., 2004. Six Sigma black-belt pharmacist improves patient safety. Am. J. Health-Syst. Pharm. 61 (19), 1988−1996.

Chapter 12

Lean Hospital Examples

Chapter Outline

PREAMBLE

The Joint Commission (described in Chapter 10) rated hospitals in 2013. Many of the top-rated hospitals followed operational principles of Charles Deming and the Six Sigma process model, comprising the foundation of the practice of root cause analytical procedures (described in Chapter 11). These hospitals employed a number of these efficient management principles to create "lean" operations. Chapter 12 describes the lean operations of several of these hospitals and how they did it.

INTRODUCTION

Increasingly, hospitals are embracing lean concepts. They do so for many reasons — to ensure best practices, to avoid litigation, and for accreditations standards and better patient outcomes, because they see the principles working so well in industry for the bottom line, and because the current perception is that the best hospitals practice lean principles. These are but some of the reasons. Lean practices that incorporate predictive analytics have become the future of medicine. Nicholas (2012, p. 47) outlined lean principles succinctly, as seen in Figure 12.1.

Hospitals such as Kaiser Permanente, Virginia Mason, and the Henry Ford Hospital use what are called *Kaizen* or *lean* principles. These hospital organizations are discussed below as examples of lean hospitals. Additionally, the Joint Commission (see Chapter 10), which accredits hospitals, brought forth its 2013 report on quality and safety in October of 2013. It was interesting to see how these three organizations fared in that report, which for the first time named top-performing hospitals (The Joint Commission, 2013).

LEAN KAIZEN CONCEPTS

Kaizen means changing for the better (Nicholas, 2012), and cooperative concepts or "working together" emphasizes the importance of teams. "Changing for the better" includes:

- Noting sequences within systems (*value stream map[ping]* or *VSM*) — how do elements flow now?
- *Using 5S*, a filing system of tools that makes sure the right tool is at hand at the right time

Practical Predictive Analytics and Decisioning Systems for Medicine. DOI: http://dx.doi.org/10.1016/B978-0-12-411643-6.00012-0

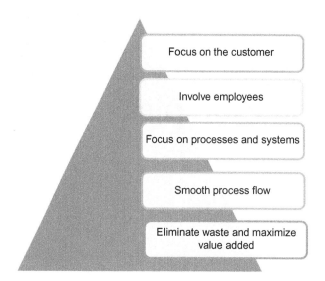

FIGURE 12.1 Lean principles. *Source: Nicholas (2012, p. 47).*

- *Standardizing* work — everyone does a process in the same way, and that process has been derived by gathering data to find the best process.
- *Producing, preparing, processing (3Ps)* — a high-level problem-solving method in which waste is eliminated by focusing on products and processes. The team generally will think of analogous examples from nature to help members think divergently. Many paths to the same end are generated, and then the most parsimonious path is decided upon, tested, and re-evaluated to determine optimal flow patterns (EPA, 2013).

For example, a lean team may be focusing on how the patients move around in a particular department. The team follows patients and maps their movements in the department, such as how long they wait at each place, the redundancies, backtracking, and so forth. The collection of the flow data becomes a value stream map (VSM). The VSM team analyzes the flow patterns to see if it can think of better arrangements of services to eliminate wasted movement and duplication. Optimized flow reduces time. Virginia Mason spent much effort on VSM (Kenny, 2011).

VSM is explained very well by Tapping and colleagues (2009). Certainly, predictive analytics (PA) could be coupled with any of the lean concepts for added power. PA is now being used by industry, and it could be used in health care in much the same way. Root cause analysis, for example, could be greatly aided by the use of feature selection. Any time an organization collects reliable data, those data could be used to predict. Motion studies, coupled with the 5S system of making sure all materials are sorted, at hand, and organized by need, could be used to predict time savings on new systems. Reading through Protzman *et al.* (2011) provides multitudinous ideas for predictive analytic projects. Figure 12.2 shows the 5S phases (Tapping *et al.*, 2009).

As stated in Chapter 11, the quality movement was initiated in the 1940s by W. Edwards Deming. Deming's influence aided post-war Japan in gaining its footing in the return journey to economic wealth. Certainly, Deming had to have influenced Ohno and others in the Kaizen movement adopted by Toyota (Toyota, 2013). There were distinctions in methods and philosophies between Deming and Ohno, but the push toward continuous improvement was shared. Inevitably, quality principles would flow into most organizations, beginning in manufacturing by engineers, but then into other businesses, health care, and education. In the 1960s Toyota applied for the Deming prize, putting into practice the TQM principles of Deming, and in 1965 Toyota won the prize (Toyota, 2013).

Kaplan (2012) displayed a "Wheel of Waste" which clearly specifies seven "wastes." Figure 12.3 shows this wheel, which Kaplan derived from the Kaizen training materials originally used by Toyota. The wheel of waste is also referred to as WORMPIT. If each of those areas could experience continuous improvements, it would likely help to transform the entire organization.

One may wonder at the terminology of Six Sigma, Lean, and Kaizen, and so forth. As Burton (2010) aptly stated, "These concepts are simply tools for making improvements." They are not magical, but rather are data-driven. He provided a schematic of how the concepts are integrated (Figure 12.4).

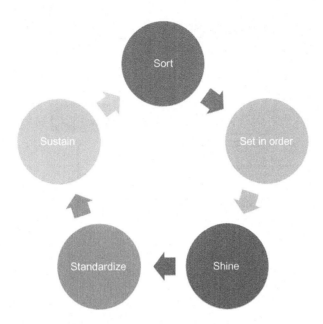

FIGURE 12.2   The 5S system. *Figure adapted from Tapping* et al. *(2009, p. 161).*

FIGURE 12.3   The seven types of waste. *Source: Kaplan (2012, p. 162).*

As Figure 12.4 demonstrates, the concepts flow into one another and, indeed, tools of the methods may be mixed together. Hospitals that are considered "lean" use whatever it takes to make progress and reduce waste while keeping the patient in mind as the chief customer. Interestingly, Kaiser Permanente tends to blend all methods (Rodak, 2012).

When lean concepts first started hitting hospitals at the turn of the millennium, Alan Mulally, at present the CEO of Ford Motor Company, had been in top leadership positions at Boeing, where he had used lean principles. Mullally's last position with Boeing was as head of commercial planes. He had worked at Boeing for 38 years before moving to Ford, where he also used lean principles such as "working together" (Hoffman, 2012). His leadership at Boeing achieved lean production. Mulally was also a major reason Boeing pulled up its nose after an economic dive. He joined Ford in 2006 as

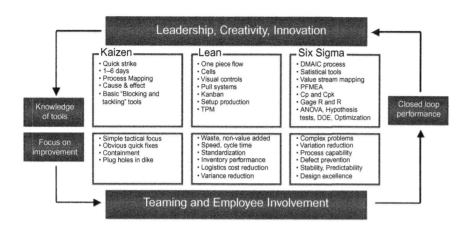

FIGURE 12.4 Leadership, creativity, and innovation in the lean movement in Kaizen, Lean, and Six Sigma, among other considerations. *Source: Burton (2010).*

CEO and Ford's stock steadily rose (Hoffman, 2012), also in part through use of lean concepts. (It should, however, be noted that Henry Ford was a very early creator of lean concepts when he opened his first plant using assembly lines and standard practices in 1913 [Strouse, 2008]). Mulally had been considered for a CEO position with Microsoft, although not everyone was enamored with the possibility (Jackson, 2013) because Mulally, critics felt, did not have a background in "Internet, cloud, and big data" (Ibid., p. 2). After many months of (presumed) negotiations, Mulally did not move to Microsoft but then resigned from Ford as of July 1, 2014 (Boudette *et al.*, 2014), to perhaps seek other board positions. At any rate, many would agree that Mulally left Ford in much better shape than its condition when he signed on.

HENRY FORD HOSPITALS

What is interesting about Mulally's career trajectory is that the Henry Ford Health System adopted a lean philosophy, taking its training from Henry Ford Production Systems (Zarbo, 2013). Zarbo announced the 2014 training sessions on the hospital website, for "physicians, nurses, technologists, pathologists, residents, directors, managers, administrators, quality and medical officers" (Zarbo, 2013, p. 1). In his announcement, Zarbo stated, "This approach to LEAN is based upon Deming's management principles of leading and practicing in a culture that uses manufacturing-based work rules and process improvement tools derived from the Toyota Production System" (p. 1). The sessions were also to focus on the problem-solving method PDCA (Plan, Do, Check, and Act). So, using an outside entity, health care improved for this example hospital.

When Virginia Mason Hospital decided it wanted to overhaul itself in 2001, it noticed Boeing's strides. Boeing had been using Toyota Motor Company as its model. Toyota was transformed by Taiichi Ohno, who developed many of the Kaizen methods (Kaplan, 2012). Interestingly, Ohno developed his ideas by observing supermarkets in the United States and seeing how the customers could select anything they wanted without delay.

Thus, two major hospitals were influenced by industry, and, in particular, by two motor companies.

THE JOINT COMMISSION ANNUAL REPORT, 2013

In October 2013, the Joint Commission (2013) published its annual report on the quality movement in hospitals across the United States. In that document all the increases in health outcome research were reported, and they were impressive. Over one-third of the hospitals made it into the category of "Top Performer on Key Quality Measures." Over 77% more hospitals than last year were within one standard of being a top performer. Hospitals are encouraged to share with one another their solutions for quality measures. Lean measures and quality are here to stay. With lean measures will come lower costs and better care for patients. The Joint Commission determines a composite score of all the quality measures, and for 2012 the hospitals achieved a 97.6% composite score. Figure 12.5 shows the percent of hospitals with composite scores higher than 95%.

Transparency Just Increased

For the first time the Joint Commission (TJC), in its yearly report, has named names for its top performers. One can find the names of the hospitals that made the top performance list by state. The list starts on page 40 in the Appendix. Previously, TJC referred to the top performers and announced how many, what percentage increased, and so on. This year, the list is spelled out. Of course, it is possible to find if a hospital is accredited by going to the quality website

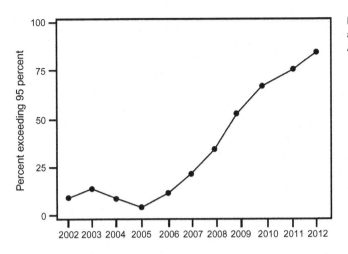

FIGURE 12.5 Graph of the number of hospitals reporting data accountability since the Joint Commission made this recommendation. *Source: The Joint Commission (2013, p. 12).*

(Quality Check, 2013). Increased transparency in this very important annual document by TJC should be a stimulus to the other hospitals, and no doubt many hospitals did make improvements in 2012 for the 2013 report but simply did not improve in enough categories to reach top performer level.

Although the Ford hospitals have won many awards, none was on this year's Joint Commission list of top performers, but Ford Hospital in Detroit did receive the Commission's Seal of Approval and special recognitions (Quality Check, 2013). Virginia Mason was also not on the list. This author found it very interesting to discover that in her hometown, a small community hospital, Lawrence Memorial Hospital, *is* on the list.

KAISER PERMANENTE MANAGED CARE ORGANIZATION

Kaiser Permanente (KP) is a managed care organization known for its excellence and integrated care for over 9 million members (Strandberg-Larsen *et al.*, 2010). Of its 37 hospitals, 27 were named as Top Performers by TJC — i.e., 73% of its medical centers (The Joint Commission, 2013). KP is referred to as "integrated" because it provides all patient services, from a primary care physician to hospitalization and pharmacy services. KP has a variety of health plans, from low to high premiums, depending on co-pays (Strandberg-Larsen *et al.*, 2010). KP seems to be highly responsive to the changing political climate of fall 2013. They said in a recent message to members,

> If federal and state governments intend to change the health care coverage rules and the composition of federal and state marketplaces in 2014, we hope those changes will be done thoughtfully and with all stakeholders involved, to obtain the best outcome. Our common goal should be to minimize any unintended effects, and avoid — as much as possible — further disruption for individuals and families who are already seeing significant change as a result of health care reform.
>
> We will continue to update our members and customers on how these changes will impact them as the details of this proposal and its implementation become clearer.

(KP.org, 2013).

KP HealthConnect is an integrated electronic health system using electronic medical records (EMRs). KP started HealthConnect in 2004, which documents across all its systems. The EMR also connects the patients to their own records. Furthermore, messages are sent between providers to increase the communication, coordination, and patient-centeredness (see Chapters 2 and 14 for a call for such systems) (Chen *et al.*, 2009).

KP studied other organizations and concluded that there were six proficiencies among top (lean) organizations (Rodak, 2012). These proficiencies were: "leadership alignment, knowledge of the system, measurement of improvement, sharing best practices, training, and involvement of the entire organization" (Rodak, 2012, p. 1). KP used an eclectic approach incorporating lean tools from all methods of improvement. According to Lisa Schilling, RN, MPH, vice president of healthcare performance improvement at Kaiser Permanente, "We don't want to teach people a new language around improvement; we want to teach [them] how to focus on designing care around the person so they can bring the tools [they need] to make that care better" (Rodak, 2012, p. 1). KP uses three themes in its approach: *learn*, *apply*, and *share*. KP learns what works and teaches the principles to everyone in the organization, from the bottom to the top. KP used experts in Six Sigma to help them apply "black belt" strategies in their application of quality improvement. Once they found methods that worked, they shared those methods with others in the organization.

VIRGINIA MASON HOSPITAL IN SEATTLE

One good example of a "lean hospital" effort is provided by Virginia Mason Medical Center, which began its Kaizen quest in 2001 (Kaplan, 2012). Kaizen means "continuously improving processes" (Kenny, 2011). Also associated with Kaizen is the idea of "working together," as mentioned above (Hoffman, 2012). In 2001, Virginia Mason decided to transform itself. At that time, it was losing money and was experiencing over 300 litigations per year. Leadership wanted to reinvent the way in which it delivered health care. One of the most transforming paradigms was the idea that patients should be the center of any medical facility (Kaplan, 2012). Taking care of the patients became reducing waste — for example, stop wasting patients' time, stop wasting patients' resources, and tighten processes to improve quality. The board and leaders of Virginia Mason met and developed what became the "strategic plan pyramid," which placed the patient at the top. Actually, for some of the physicians this new system was not what they wanted. Up to the transformation the hospital had operated around the physicians, not the patients. In the traditional, old way, patients waited for doctors, patients traveled around the hospital, back and forth at odd appointment intervals, and basically patients provided for the welfare of the provider. Everything turned over with the lean initiatives. Dedicated physicians, driven more by passion than their stock portfolio, were happy. Those few who could not let go of the old system, let go of the new system and left. The team approach and cooperation among members helped with problem-solving, reduction of error, and targeting effective treatments. Predictive analytics certainly could help with targeting effective treatments.

To standardize systems, Virginia Mason developed check sheets that were evidence-based and which were placed into computer programs when deciding what procedures were allowed for patients. For example, if a doctor thought a patient needed an MRI, the case was put through the check-sheet sequence developed from best practices models, and decision rules determined if the procedure would be used (Hoffman, 2012). Decision rules could certainly be aided by predictive analytics, using techniques such as decision trees and weight of evidence to help predict individual patient outcomes. Using the Kaizen process, three tools were highly useful — value streams, the 3Ps, and 5S.

Figure 12.6 shows Virginia Mason's Career Site, and one is struck by its statement to future employees:

Welcome to the future of health care. Where the patient is everything, and you are empowered to affect real change, right now. As part of our interdisciplinary team, you'll play an active role. And you'll be amazed how much more effective and enjoyable your career becomes without all the waste.

(Virginia Mason, 2013, p. 1).

FIGURE 12.6   Virginia Mason Careers website. *Source: Virginia Mason (2013).*

Although Virginia Mason was not listed as a top performer by the Joint Commission (2013), it should be noted that Leapfrog, an organization for patient safety, honored both Virginia Mason Medical Center and the University of Maryland Medical Center as "Leapfrog Top Hospitals of the Decade" (The Leapfrog Group, 2013). The Leapfrog Group "is a coalition of public and private purchasers of employee health benefits founded a decade ago to work for improvements in health care safety, quality and affordability" (The Leapfrog Group, 2013), and publishes a voluntary annual survey that covers all manner of safety and efficiency measures.

It is interesting that the University of Maryland Medical Center was also not listed in the Joint Commission's top performers in certain key indicators. One point the Leapfrog Group makes is that the participating hospitals value transparency. In lean processes, mistakes are not viewed as they have been traditionally in health care but are analyzed and used as opportunities for improving processes. Rather than determining an individual who is at fault, the team understands that when mistakes happen it is the system that failed and the team needs to correct the system.

EXAMPLES OF LEAN PROJECTS

Oncology: Infusion Therapy

Lean methodology was used to decrease the time for outpatient chemotherapy infusion (Belter *et al.*, 2012). The authors were able to *reduce the original 88 minutes to 68 minutes*. The result was that they could see more patients, and those patients were more satisfied. Figure 12.7 shows the value stream map of the pre-data.

The lean team completed what they called a "Genba walk," meaning that they went to each area of the value stream map and looked for "visible waste." Improvements in communication between the infusion center, the laboratory, and the pharmacy resulted in patients being able to *reduce by 15 minutes* the time of arrival before treatment.

Gaarde *et al.* (2007) also used lean principles to increase efficiency in an infusion clinic. They used a number of techniques after their initial (pre-intervention) observations. They created a "pod system" for the nurses so they would all be in one area. Keeping the nurses in one area meant that supplies and medications would be more readily available in their system. They reformatted their appointment scheduling and instituted an automated paging system to alert when medications had been prepared and were ready. *They reduced the amount of walking about on the part of nurses by 80%*, and *reduced patient wait time by 69%*. It can be imagined that the nurses were not quite as tired at night, and perhaps happier (though one wonders if they gained any weight by having their exercise reduced!). Patients would have been quite happy to have a reduced wait time. Cancer patients generally have other things they would like to do with their time than spending it in a hospital clinic with the possibility of germs all around them.

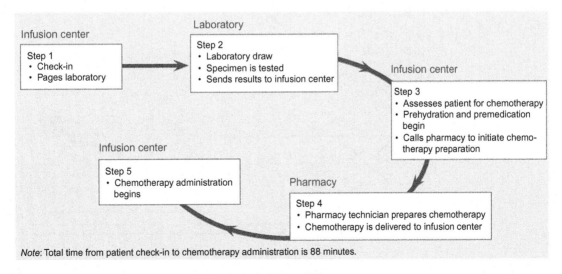

FIGURE 12.7   Example of a value stream map. *Source: Belter et al. (2012, p. 138).*

Cardiology

In the Netherlands, the Deventer Hospital cardiology department used Six Sigma methods following the DMAIC steps (explained in Chapter 11) of Define, Measure, Analyze, Improve, and Control (Schoonhoven *et al.*, 2011). The authors examined the overall resource efficiency (ORE), or "the number of patients per time unit divided by the potential capacity" (p. 390). The potential capacity was defined as the total time scheduled for the cardiologists divided by the processing time per patient (p. 390). To increase the ORE, they examined bottlenecks, conflicting scheduling of the facilities, arrival times, and missed appointments, as well as the variation in the processes used with each patient. They also produced the value stream map in Figure 12.8. The reader should look at the map in the original article, although it was not totally clear even there. However, this value stream map gives the reader some inkling of their flow charting. The authors noted that there was a full color map online, if one had access to the journal.

The authors were able to *improve their processes and reduce the time per patient*. In doing so, they were able to *increase revenues* to the outpatient clinic.

Reducing Patient Falls

Wilkes Barre General Hospital in Pennsylvania used Six Sigma to reduce the rate of falls in its 39-bed medical surgical unit (Veluswamy and Price, 2010). Veluswamy and Price used root cause analysis to discover fall patterns by examining the records of each fall of the past year and by walking around to inspect systems. They examined toileting procedures and mattress alarm systems (discovering that the mattresses had lost their alarm sensitivity). They also used a different alarm system and even placed alarms on chair and wheelchair seatbelts. Further, patients were evaluated by the physical therapy staff to alert the staff of those patients with increased likelihood of falling. They educated the staff and developed a no-fall campaign of posters and flyers. In the end, they *reduced the fall rate from 6.2 falls per 1,000 patient days to 2.06.*

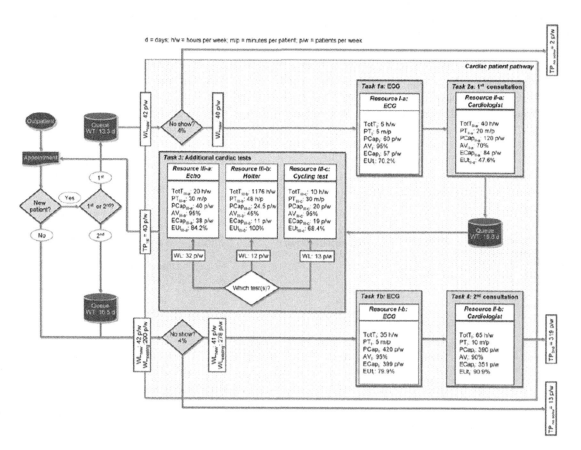

FIGURE 12.8 Value stream map. *Source: Schoonhoven* et al. *(2011, p. 392).*

Reducing Catheter-Associated Urinary Tract Infections

By using a root cause analysis to pinpoint the causes of contaminated samples for the lab, the lean team instituted a standardized process for urine collection, along with education, in the hospital's critical care unit (which started with approximately 20% contaminated samples). Contaminated samples produce false positives, increases in time, and re-sampling, which is also expensive. The standardized process that the hospital instituted provided the lab with a "test-ready" sample. This process change eliminated much re-sampling because the lab had been rejecting samples that were more than an hour old. With test-ready samples, the lab could work faster and reject fewer. By the end of the year, the contamination rate dropped from about 20% to under 6%.

Intravenous (IV) Laboratory Lean Project

L'Hommedieu and Kappeler (2010) used value stream mapping, process standardization, and just-in-time processing and delivery for the IV medication needs at a children's hospital. They retrospectively examined all IV orders for the past 30 days to determine what times the medication orders were changed, ordered, or discontinued, and found the times that were most vulnerable to change. They discovered, for example, that discontinuations were more likely to occur during physicians' hospital rounds.

Once they had predicted the best times for production and delivery, the lab was able to start saving money for the hospital to the tune of nearly $8,200 per week, or an *annual savings of about $426,000*. The Joint Commission, no doubt, was proud of them, and some should have earned black belts.

Emergency Room Application of Lean

As mentioned in Chapter 11, Cookson *et al.* (2011) uses value stream mapping to remove the WORMPIT in the Leicester (United Kingdom) Emergency Department. They added a concept of separating value streams, and likened it to a highway in which all the trucks drove in one lane and all the cars in another. The speed overall should increase. Honestly, this author is not sure about the truck lane, but overall, there should be increases in flow. Cookson *et al.* (2011) included a photo of the value stream mapping; Figure 12.9 shows this very complicated project.

Obviously, the processes *were* complicated. The authors noted that the process was not difficult, but that it did require the team to step out of its normal role and be what one can imagine in anthropological terms to be a participant-observer. It takes stepping out of one's role to be able to observe the system for waste. This team was able to *shave off 20 minutes* from patient arrival to nurse assessment. When one is in pain and dis-ease, those 20 minutes could seem like an eternity.

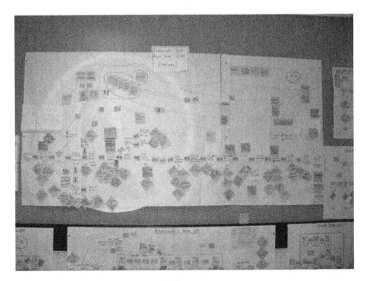

FIGURE 12.9 A very complicated value stream mapping. *Source: Cookson* et al. *(2011, p. 28).*

SUMMARY

In looking at examples of lean, it seems evident that the hospitals stepping out into the unfamiliar have made tremendous strides. They are richly rewarded by the accreditation agencies. These hospitals have found creative ways of cutting the waste, and will continue to do so in the future. Lean hospitals use the tools that have been found effective. Important to remember is the team aspect of lean management. Unless all stakeholders are valued and involved, disenfranchisement can follow. Further, making every second count can seem like a cattle call to patients. As one second-year resident said when learning some of the principles of predictive analytics, "Okay, so we can accurately predict based on selected variables, and then the time we spend with patients can move from 7 minutes to, say, 3 minutes. At that point, we'll be required to spend only 3 minutes on each patient. What kind of job is that?"

We must preserve humanity. People — patients and their physicians — are not machines. We as people need time to form relationships and enjoy each other at some level. We need humor and compassion and kindness. Patients will not maintain high levels of satisfaction if they are put through a system like machine parts. They also know, deep inside, that physicians are more likely to miss a diagnosis if they are watching the clock to make sure a standard of patients per hour is met and exceeded. Desjarlais-deKlerk and Wallace (2013) noted that when patients have a more personalized relationship with their doctors, they tend to have better outcomes. They analyzed interactions of two urban physicians and two rural physicians. The amount of time spent with the patients did not significantly differ (11 minutes per patient in the urban doctors; 12.5 minutes for the rural doctors). The rural doctors interacted with their patients on a much more personal level, and knew the patients outside the clinic (remember the TV series, *Northern Exposure*?) There was lots of joking, and talking about family members, not related to health. It appeared that there was a lot of trust, and that the doctors knew the patients in ways not related to the clinic, lab tests, or symptoms. Chapter 14 discusses the need for open communication between patients and physicians, especially for helping the physician to make good diagnoses. Given the problem of missed diagnoses that exists at present, cutting down on the time with patients may be contradictory to achieving the best outcomes. Parts for a car can be standardized with ease when manufacturers use lean methods and predictive analytics.

Again, patients are humans and not cars. PA should consider the amount of time and the quality of interactions between patients and doctors (the human side) as predictor variables when predicting correct diagnoses and good outcomes. *Predictive analytics done correctly in healthcare will maximize individualized medicine to achieve correct diagnoses, better health, and, when at all possible, life over death.*

POSTSCRIPT

Efficient operation for groups of patients in healthcare organizations is only one of several necessary elements of a high quality medical treatment system. Chapter 13 turns our attention to another necessary element — treatment of the individual. Groups of people don't get sick; individuals do. The design of efficient operations of healthcare organizations (i.e., hospitals) is certainly important, but it must be viewed only as the context within which to practice personalized medicine. Because the nature of human health care is so complicated and we know so relatively little about it, many individual maladies may appear as outliers, from the perspective of our group analyses. We must treat the outliers as normal operations in our healthcare system. Chapter 13 builds the foundation for accomplishing this goal.

REFERENCES

Belter, D., Halsey, J., Severtson, H., Fix, A., Michelfelder, L., Michalak, K., et al., 2012. Evaluation of outpatient oncology services using lean methodology. Oncol. Nurs. Forum. 39 (2), 136–140.

Boudette, N.E., Rogers, C., Lublin, J.S., 2014. Mulally's legacy: setting Ford on a stronger course as CEO prepares to retire, car maker is profitable and its vehicles are selling well. Available at: <http://online.wsj.com/news/articles/SB10001424052702304049904579515852823291232>, retrieved May 12, 2014.

Burton, T.T., 2010. Is this a Six sigma, Lean, or Kaizen project? <www.isixsigma.com/new-to-six-sigma/how-is-six-sigma-different/six-sigma-lean-or-kaizen-project/>.

Chen, C., Garrido, T., Chock, D., Okawa, G., Liang, L., 2009. The Kaiser Permanente Electronic Health Record: transforming and streamlining modalities of care. Health Aff. 28 (2), 323–333.

Cookson, D., Read, C., Mukherjee, P., Cooke, M., 2011. Improving the quality of Emergency Department care by removing waste using Lean Value Stream mapping. Int. J. Clin. Leader. 17 (1), 25–30.

Desjarlais-deKlerk, K., Wallace, J.E., 2013. Instrumental and socioemotional communications in doctor–patient interactions in urban and rural clinics. BMC Health Serv. Res. 13 (1), 261–268.

EPA, 2013. Lean thinking and methods. <www.epa.gov/lean/environment/methods/threep.htm>.

Gaarde, A., Utech, J., Devery, T., Singh, S., 2007. Application of lean principles positively impacts clinical efficiency in an ambulatory chemotherapy infusion suite. Oncol. Nurs. Forum. 34 (2), 498.

Hoffman, B.G., 2012. American icon: Alan Mulally and the flight to save Ford Motor Company. Random House, Inc, New York, NY.

Jackson, E., 2013. Why Alan Mulally would be a terrible choice as the next Microsoft CEO (30 September, 2013). <www.forbes.com/sites/ericjackson/2013/09/30/why-alan-mulally-would-be-a-terrible-choice-as-the-next-microsoft-ceo/>.

Kaplan, G.S., 2012. Waste not: the management imperative for healthcare. J. Healthc. Manag. 57 (3), 160–166.

Kenny, C., 2011. Transforming health care: Virginia Mason Medical Center's pursuit of the perfect patient experience. CRC Press, New York, NY.

KP.org, 2013. Kaiser Permanente comments on proposal to address coverage changes in 2013, <http://share.kaiserpermanente.org/article/kaiser-permanente-comments-on-proposal-to-address-coverage-changes-in-2014/> (retrieved November 16, 2013).

L'Hommedieu, T., Kappeler, K., 2010. Lean methodology in i.v. medication processes in a children's hospital. Am. J. Health Syst. Pharm. 67 (24), 2115–2118.

Nicholas, J., 2012. An integrated lean-methods approach to hospital facilities redesign. Hosp. Top. 90 (2), 47–55.

Norihiko, S., Ingrassia, P., 2013. Ford's Mulally won't dismiss Boeing, Microsoft speculation (October 18, 2013). <www.reuters.com/article/2013/10/18/us-ford-mulally-idUSBRE99H15P20131018>.

Protzman, C., Mayzell, G., Kerpchar, J., 2011. Leveraging lean in healthcare: transforming your enterprise into a high quality patient care delivery system. CRC Press, New York, NY.

Quality Check, 2013. The Joint Commission, Quality check: Find a health care organization. <www.qualitycheck.org/consumer/searchQCR.aspx>.

Rodak, S., 2012. Learn, apply, share: Kaiser Permanente's 3-step strategy for healthcare quality improvement (March 14, 2012). <www.beckershospitalreview.com/quality/learn-apply-share-kaiser-permanentes-3-step-strategy-for-healthcare-quality-improvement.html>.

Schoonhoven, M., Kemper, B.H., Brilleman, M.I., Does, R.M., 2011. Quality quandaries: streamlining the path to optimal care for cardiovascular patients. Qual. Eng. 23 (4), 388–394.

Strandberg-Larsen, M., Schiøtz, M.L., Silver, J.D., Frølich, A., Andersen, J.S., Graetz, I., et al., 2010. Is the Kaiser Permanente model superior in terms of clinical integration? A comparative study of Kaiser Permanente, Northern California and the Danish healthcare system. BMC Health Serv. Res. 2010. 10, 91.

Strouse, R., 2008. Adopting a lean approach. Eval. Eng. 47 (4), 56–60.

Tapping, D., Kozlowski, S., Archbold, L., Sperl, T., 2009. Value stream management for lean healthcare. MCS Media, Inc.

The Joint Commission, 2013. Improving America's hospitals: The Joint Commission's annual report on quality and safety. <www.jointcommission.org/assets/1/6/TJC_Annual_Report_2013.pdf>.

The Leapfrog Group, 2013. The Leapfrog Group announces top hospitals of the decade. <www.leapfroggroup.org/news/leapfrog_news/4784721>.

Toyota, 2013. History of Toyota, 1960–1969. <www.toyota-global.com/company/history_of_toyota/1960-1969.html> (retrieved November 7, 2013).

Veluswamy, R., Price, R., 2010. I've fallen and I can't get up: reducing the risk of patient falls. Physician Exec. 36 (3), 50–53.

Virginia Mason, 2013. Careers at Virginia Mason Medical Center <http://jobs.virginiamason.org/?utm_source = careersite> (retrieved November 11, 2013).

Zarbo, R., 2013. Henry Ford Health System Pathology and Laboratory Medicine: On site lean training: Henry Ford System Training Sessions. <www.henryford.com/body.cfm?id = 50135> (retrieved November 7, 2013).

Chapter 13

Personalized Medicine

P4 [Personalized; Preventive; Predictive; and Participatory] medicine will mandate that every sector of the public and private healthcare systems rewrite their business plans over the next 10 years.

In 10 or 15 years, with the fast decline in the cost of next-generation[genetic] sequencing, we will potentially have access to the complete[human] genome and [associated] medical, molecular, cellular, and environmental data for a growing fraction of the human population in both developed and developing countries. This will afford us an unparalleled opportunity to [use predictive analytics on] these data for [developing] the predictive medicine of the future.

(Paraphrased from: Lee Hood *et al.*, 2012).

Chapter Outline

Practical Predictive Analytics and Decisioning Systems for Medicine. DOI: http://dx.doi.org/10.1016/B978-0-12-411643-6.00013-2

PREAMBLE

In several ways, Chapter 13 is the pivotal chapter in this book. Previous chapters provided the background and history of medical information storage, and availability. Various systems of coding and quality control of data were presented. This chapter presents the full rationale for using this digital information for building "smart" decisioning systems.

WHAT IS PERSONALIZED MEDICINE?

The cartoon shown in Figure 13.1 is from a 1971 article on personalized medicine (Gibson, 1971). The author had used this term to describe having a personalized relationship with a physician rather than seeing a battery of specialists for each condition (Gibson, 1971). *This is the earliest article to appear in PubMed using the search term "personalized medicine."*

The article was written to express the fear of the medical communities' departure from personalized medicine into an era of subspecialists. It is ironic that the cartoon was meant to depict the medical communities moving *away* from a personalized format of medicine, and yet is very close to depicting personalized medicine as it is viewed today.

The first use of the term "personalized medicine" in its present meaning was on April 16, 1999. This use of the term appeared in the title of an article by Robert Langreth and Michael Waldholz published in the *Wall Street Journal*, entitled "New Era of Personalized Medicine — Targeting Drugs for Each Unique Genetic Profile" (Langreth and Waldholz, 1999). The article described the formation of the Single Nucleotide Polymorphism (SNP) Consortium. Its purpose was to create a comprehensive SNP map of the human genome, which would provide the subsequent possibility of being able to develop drugs specific to a person's genetic make-up. This article was later published in the scientific literature in the journal *The Oncologist* (Langreth and Waldholz, 1999; Jørgensen, 2009).

Today, personalized medicine has a very broad definition that spans a number of medical fields; however, the succinct definition could be stated as "the tailoring of a treatment to an individual based on their unique characteristics." The treatment may be a medication, an exercise, a diet, a surgical procedure, or any other therapeutic measure used within the field of medicine. The treatments may be tailored to the individual by using genetic markers or other biological markers, environmental information, behavioral information, demographic information, or any other information that might change the way the patient responds to the treatment. Using these factors, physicians can determine a type of

FIGURE 13.1   Cartoon: "Personalized Medicine". *Source: Gibson (1971).*

treatment, the duration of treatment, what dose to give, what kind of follow-up is needed, or who is most likely to have certain side effects. With this information in hand, the appropriate monitoring system can be assigned to each patient.

At this time, however, it is not economical or realistic to think that research can be done on each individual to discover and produce medications that are appropriate for use only with that person. The President's Council of Advisors on Science and Technology (PCAST) accepted the succinct definition of personalized medicine presented above. The Council went on to explain further:

> It [personalized medicine] does not literally mean the creation of drugs or medical devices that are unique to a patient, but rather the ability to classify individuals into sub-populations that differ in their susceptibility to a particular disease or their response to a specific treatment. Preventive and therapeutic interventions can then be concentrated on those who will benefit, sparing expense and side effects for those who will not.

(PCAST, 2008).

P4 Medicine

More recently, Dr. Leroy Hood of the Institute for Systems Biology termed personalized medicine "P4™ medicine" (Hood and Tian, 2012). He describes the four components of this medical approach with 4 Ps:

- *Personalized* — i.e., a medicine or treatment that takes into account a person's genetic or protein profile.
- *Preventive* — i.e., anticipating health problems and focusing on wellness, not disease.
- *Predictive* — i.e., directing appropriate treatment, and avoiding drug side effects.
- *Participatory* — i.e., empowering patients to take more responsibility for their health and care.

P5 to P6 Medicine

Others have gone on to define further the nature of personalized medicine, adding "Psychocognitive" and "Public" components to the 4 Ps:

- *Psychocognitive* aspects refer to how individuals act to prevent, cope with, and react to illness; decide about different therapeutic options; interact with healthcare providers; and adhere to treatment (Gorini and Pravettoni, 2011)
- *Public* refers to societal and population-based media formats that involve shared and open-source entities consisting of a combination of e-health, e-medicine, and telemedicine in which computers, "expert systems," and innovative online health communities play a central role in a patient's health (Bragazzi, 2013).

PERSONALIZED MEDICINE, GENOMICS, AND PHARMACOGENOMICS

The activity of personalized medicine is associated commonly with the application of pharmacological treatments to a person with a specific set of genes (a genotype). Personalized medical treatment expects that a given person will respond differently than another person because the two individuals have different sets of genes which cause different responses. The study of the specific nature of responses to drugs by people of different genetic complements is called *pharmacogenomics*.

Genetics and pharmacogenomics were included as components of personalized medicine when it was first described. While both of these components are crucial elements of personalized medicine, it encompasses much more, including many environmental (non-genetic) processes that occur within the human body, or impact the human body from external influences. The advances in genetics over the past decade have been breathtaking. Medical science has learned that the expression of genes within each individual determines that individual's ability to fight off or contract disease, and governs how they will respond to medications and treatments.

Modern gene sequencing technology can map entire genomes at far faster rates and at lower prices than previous generations of this technology. The technology has led to an onslaught of genetic data, which has raised many new possibilities as well as substantial problems — not least of which is the lack of a suitable infrastructure within medicine to support and process this large amount of information. This situation is changing rapidly, however, and in the near future individual genotypes will be considered a vital part of everyone's medical record.

Pharmacogenomic studies have led to the development of drug therapies designed (targeted) for specific genetic complements. Many of these targeted drugs have been approved by the FDA for the treatment of disease, and many more are in the development stages. Among these targeted drugs, those designed to treat cancer, specific single gene loci genetic diseases, and infectious disease are among the most prominent treatments in use. Increasingly smaller sub-sets (groupings) of diseases are being identified and targeted with focused pharmacological therapies that are designed to work at the molecular level for that specific group of diseases (Charlab and Zhang, 2013).

Pharmacogenomics is an important application of genomic sequencing. It is well known that the same drug may have a different effect on different individuals due both to their personal genomic background and to their environmental living habits (Heller, 2013). Genetic information can be used to assign drug doses as well as reduce side effects. For example, differences in genetic complements (genomes) are known to affect patients' responses to antipsychotic drugs (Emmett *et al.*, 2014). Based on pharmacogenomic trials, genetic tests for four drugs are routinely used before the drugs are administered to patients: the antiviral drug (for HIV) abacavir (Ziagen™), and the chemotherapy drugs trastuzumab (Herceptin™), mercaptopurine (Purinethol™), and irinotecan (Camptosar®). These tests are used prior to administration for different reasons; for example, people with a certain genetic make-up experience very bad side effects from the drug abacavir. In contrast, trastuzamab does not have any effect on treatment unless the patient has the correct genetic profile (www.genome.gov/27530645).

Differences Among Us

When considering personalized medicine, many people relate it to our genetic make-up; however, this is only a small part of the differences among us that determine how we will respond to treatments. Two people, such as identical twins, can have identical genetic make-up, but if the genes are not expressed equally there will be different results. The science that describes the control of gene expression is *epigenetics*. Epigenetics is an umbrella term that covers effects of many DNA regulatory systems, including DNA methylation, histone modification, nucleosome location, and noncoding RNA. Our genes can be considered as a set of instructions, and our epigenetic "markers" determine how those instructions are carried out. Many of these epigenetic effects related to environment influences are heritable. Therefore, what you eat, drink, and do today may affect your great-grandchildren in the future (Vanhees *et al.*, 2014).

Differences Go Beyond Our Body and Into Our Environment

How we respond to treatment is also affected by the things we do, what we have access to, and things we touch or eat. For example, certain medications are not as effective when taken with certain foods, or some people may have limited access to certain types of food. The sociodemographic status of the individual may also affect the outcome of a treatment, based on the access they have to care. Appropriate education can affect the manner and regularity with which patients will take a medication. For people who forget to take daily medications, prescription of a drug to be taken once per week might be a better choice, even though it might not be as effective as a daily dose. Certain foods we eat habitually can change our bodies, and those changes can affect our genetic expressions, resulting in a different response to medications. The toxins, allergens, weather, and infections to which we are exposed in our environment can affect the state of our health, development of a disease, and response to treatments. These are just a few examples of the many variables that can affect our bodies and overall health.

Changes from Birth to Death

A very distinct series of genetic transcription events take place after conception, which control the development of a functional human being. These processes change over time through distinct causal pathways. The genes that are expressed in a four-celled embryo are not the same as those expressed when we are sitting in a kindergarten class learning to read. Yet, all humans go through the same development phases: *in utero* development, infant to toddler, prepubescent to pubertal child. During each stage, important developmental milestones are achieved though distinct biological processes that determine our future functional human nature. With respect to intrinsic nature, human beings can be viewed as having a preprogrammed pathway that governs growth and development. However, the expression of this governing influence on the developmental milestones and the timeline of progress through the developmental phases are variable, depending on age and environmental influences.

Under normal conditions, the distinct series of gene expressions control growth and maturity stages, although tragic events or errors in gene transcription along the way may cause death before all stages are completed. It is also possible that aging and death itself are to a degree a result of preprogrammed effects determined by gene transcription. This idea has been debated for years and is often discredited; the prevailing view remains that aging occurs as a result of the accumulation of molecular damage over time, which leads to functional and physiological decline. Single gene alterations have been shown to delay aging in model organisms, although it is thought these changes do so by improving maintenance and repair functions that slow down damage accumulation. A growing body of evidence, however, indicates that specific genetic instructions drive aging in model organisms (de Magalhães, 2012). Regardless of the mechanism, everyone goes through aging differently, and lifespan is variable even between individuals with identical genetics. Science does show there are multiple cellular signals and genetic markers that can be used to enhance tracking of the aging process and help to predict the time of death. The ability to measure these signals and predict some of these changes may lessen the burden of aging, and may prolong life.

Ancestry and Disease

Historically, most disease-causing mutations and predispositions have been passed down through successive human generations. As personalized medicine becomes more prominent in our generation, the genetic and medical history in our ancestry becomes much more relevant. This information is important, because we are likely to have the same mutations and therefore the same disease types and responses to treatment as those whose genes we share. These ancestral clues discovered through disease social networks will be important in the definition of disease in the future (Ramos *et al.*, 2013).

It Is Not About Just Our Genome

Personalized medicine expands beyond our own genome into the genome of microorganisms that inhabit our bodies. Our microbiome refers to the collective genomes of the microorganisms that reside within our bodies. These include bacteria, viruses, and microbial eukaryotes. There are 100 times more genes in our microbiome than in our own DNA. Many of these organisms are beneficial and even necessary for human health; others cause problems, and all of them affect our health. Some people have called the microbiome an "organ" because it interacts closely with the rest of the body and has considerable effects on our health. An increasing number of human diseases are being examined for correlative or causative associations with the microbiome, including, but not limited to, autoimmune disorders, cardiovascular disease, asthma, periodontal disease, obesity, and even some cancers (Cho and Blaser, 2012; Liu *et al.*, 2012; Weinstock, 2012).

CHANGING THE DEFINITION OF DISEASES

In 2006, the GAIT (Glucosamine/Chondroitin Arthritis Trial) trial consisted of a randomized controlled trial of the efficacy of glucosamine and chondroitin sulfate for painful knee osteoarthritis. At the American College of Rheumatology (ACR) meeting in November 2006, a debate was conducted on this subject (The Great Debate, 2006). Two groups of scientists argued for and against the efficacy of the drugs in treatment, using the same drug trial data from the GAIT study. Both groups considered different aspects and different sub-groups of the clinical drug trial. One side was convinced of efficacy of the drugs demonstrated in the trial data and also by personal experience; the other was not. On the surface, it might appear that both groups could not be right, yet both groups were composed of highly educated physicians using the same scientific data to debate a clinical question — but they arrived at different conclusions. It is quite likely that both groups may have been right; they just considered different groups of people in the trial data (Clegg *et al.*, 2006).

Medical practice depends upon large studies of very heterogeneous groups of people to determine the most effective medications. The groups are gathered on the basis of similar symptoms, while the molecular or genetic bases of their disease may be entirely different. It is not uncommon for diseases with completely different molecular bases to be grouped together solely on the presentation of similar physical symptoms. When diseases are grouped in this way it is very difficult to find a treatment that works for everyone, because each disease is a different problem. When this approach is used, the disease is not cured; only the symptoms are alleviated. As more is learned about these diseases and how to further characterize disease processes on a molecular level, physicians and medical scientists need to rethink the definition of disease and further group diseases in order to treat each one more appropriately.

This transition in characterizing disease has started already with the treatment of many types of cancer. Molecular sub-typing of breast cancer has now become standard practice before treatment (Bastien *et al.*, 2012). It is likely that medical science will look back at the way these tumors were treated previously as rather barbaric compared to the precise therapies of the future. Physicians will no longer apply the shotgun approach to curing disease, but instead will use precision — personalized medicine — to treat the each disease in the most effective way.

The National Research Council (NRC) recognized this need and formed a committee to explore the feasibility and need for a new taxonomy of human disease based on molecular data. The results of the meeting of this committee were published in a report entitled "Toward Precision Medicine: Building a Knowledge Network for Biomedical Research and a New Taxonomy of Disease" (NRC, 2011). This report suggested the need for an information system, which the committee termed a "Knowledge Network of Disease". This network would integrate information from researchers on causes of disease with clinical information, thus allowing researchers, healthcare providers, and the public to share and update this information in real time. The system would be based on an "Information Commons," or data repository, that links layers of molecular data, medical histories, socioeconomic information, environmental information, and health outcomes to *individual patients*. The data in the Information Commons would be updated regularly by the research community and from entries in the medical records of participating patients.

Creation of such a knowledge network would have a tremendous impact on health care; it would be a gold mine, and not only for data mining and predictive analytics for model development to predict the best way to treat an individual patient. Access to these large data sets and the latest research data can enable scientists to formulate and test hypotheses more easily and quickly, to understand disease pathophysiology and assign treatments. These predictive analytic models could segregate patients further by individual characteristics (including genotypes) to create personalized treatment plans for patients. In addition, this process would define disease sub-types more accurately, which then would be included in the new taxonomies of disease. *The NRC (2011) report concluded that widespread data sharing is an essential component to the creation of new disease taxonomy because of the amount of data that are necessary to redefine a disorder and create a subtype.*

In order for such a knowledge network to be put in place, HIPAA (Health Insurance Portability and Accountability Act, 1996) regulations would have to be modified to allow individual data (rather than just aggregated data) to be utilized for research and analysis. Only by using each individual's data can these reliable models for scoring new patients be developed. This can happen only through a combination of events, including individual patient's consent, de-identification of data/case, shared networks of data using the same format, and security controls to prevent misuse of data. Such changes in HIPAA must happen before any money is spent in developing these knowledge networks. The Patient Centered Outcomes Research Institute was created by healthcare regulators to study the effectiveness of treatments among individuals and groups (PCORI, 2013).

Data in these knowledge networks should be open for multiple researchers to mine, allowing researchers from different backgrounds and perspectives to add valuable insight into the disease process, thus ensuring the best results. In addition, an efficient validation process must be developed to incorporate information from the disease knowledge network into a new taxonomy of disease. Such validation includes assuring reproducibility and clinical utility of a process prior to incorporating it into clinical use. This project would be a substantial undertaking, but the benefits would be tremendous.

Although the costs of creating this network would be substantial, the potential cost savings over time are likely to make the project self-sustaining in the long term. The steps required to undertake such a project are outlined in the report (NRC, 2011), and one entity to make this happen is now functioning (PCORI, 2013); this was funded initially by a large appropriation coming out of the Health Reform Laws. Continued funding will be provided by a fee of $2/year per person who signs up for the Health Reform Insurance plan. Under this perpetual funding plan, predictive models based on individual information can continue to be enhanced in the future.

SYSTEMS BIOLOGY

Systems biology is the study of the components, interactions, and dynamics of a biological system. In the past, most medical research was done on individual genes or proteins, without a complete understanding of the biological system of which they are a part. Advances in technology are increasing our ability to conduct research and ask questions in the context of biological systems. A good analogy can be seen in the structure and function of an automobile. An individual part, such as the alternator, can be studied in relationship to its ability to generate electricity. This approach does not provide very useful information unless we look at the alternator in the context of the whole car. A car can function well without an alternator, but it will stop functioning over time as the battery loses energy without an energy generator to replace it. A cursory analysis of the problem separate from other components of the system might lead to the conclusion that the car isn't running because the battery has failed. The battery might be charged with an external charger, but it will fail again in the future. Our failure to make a long-term correction to the problem is based on our focus on a single element of a complex system, without an understanding of the other components that make it work properly. In contrast, an understanding of the interconnection and dynamics between the battery and the alternator may show that the cause of the problem is that the alternator which charges the battery doesn't work. This conclusion might lead to a further conclusion that the belt which drives the alternator might be broken. This analogy of the automobile battery can be applied to many biological problems. For example, an association might be discovered between a bodily dysfunction, the lack of a protein (the "battery") related to it, and the gene (the "alternator") that generates it. Exclusive focus on the protein without consideration of its place in the biological system may obscure the true cause of the disease. Even if we had the knowledge that the alternator exists, it would be difficult to figure out that the alternator caused the car to stop running because we could remove the alternator completely from the car and yet, with a fully charged battery, the car would still run for a considerable amount of time. It is only over time that the effects of the non-functioning alternator would become apparent. We must understand the system in order to correct the problem in the best (most accurate) way. Studying the effect in the context of the biological system will permit physicians to devise long-term solutions to problems, rather than continuing to treat symptoms as they arise.

There are four key properties of systems that must be understood in order to understand how any system (including biological systems) works:

1. The structures or parts that compromise the system
2. The system design
3. The system dynamics, or how the system behaves
4. The control mechanisms of the system.

If we can understand these key elements we can do a better job to model disease systems, and test hypotheses in intelligent and focused ways.

The study of biological systems requires teams and large collaborations of experts on each component involved in the system. Only by the formation of these collaborations, and using the latest technology to lay out the design, structure, and function of these networks, can the speed of scientific research be increased significantly, and focused to find solutions to problems in an efficient manner. This potential has begun to be realized in our society, and only recently have the tools necessary to drive research with a systems approach become available.

Predictive analytics with decisioning capabilities can and will play a crucial role in this process, creating predictions of system behavior that can be tested, validated, and placed into action by making treatment decisions for individual patients. It is crucial to create predictions of interventions needed at key positions in the system, in order to target accurately the pharmacological therapies appropriate for an individual. The only alternative is to follow the current medical treatment model in trying various therapies one at a time, over a period of time, until one is found to work. In addition to predicting appropriate pharmacological therapies, this systems-level understanding of the treatment can also provide clues to the understanding and prediction of side effects. The systems approach enables physicians to combine complex signals from several compartments of biological systems to create predictive models for accurate diagnosis of the disease, deploying the best treatment, and predicting accurately the best outcome.

Systems biology is still in its early stages and we have not yet realized its full potential. The potential benefits of this approach are tremendous and there is a potential to revolutionize health care and our understanding and treatment of human disease (Kitano, 2002).

EFFICACY OF CURRENT METHODS – WHY WE NEED PERSONALIZED MEDICINE

Evidence-based medicine (EBM) remains the current goal for treatment in our medical system. In Chapter 7, however, evidence is presented to support the case that physicians in the USA like to think that they are using the best of EBM in their practices, but the evidence they appeal to is based on the efficacy of a therapy on a large heterogeneous group of people, which will no longer suffice as the basis for treatment standards. Physicians can no longer provide treatment based on the mean of the population while ignoring the outliers; instead, they must base their treatment decisions on characteristic groups whose individual characteristics control their response to therapy. Many of the medications used widely (e.g., antidepressants) are barely more effective than a placebo when evaluated in large studies; similar results are seen with homeopathic medications. Yet many people have positive responses with these medications, while others do not. This diversity of responses "muddies the waters," making it difficult for the physician to prescribe the appropriate medication or treatment. If medical researchers and physicians were to break down these sample populations into sub-groups, it is likely that ensuing studies would find similarities among people with similar responses, thus allowing physicians to redefine and break down the phenotype of the disease. The use of K-Means and E-Means clustering techniques is one way to find these sub-groups of patients who respond similarly (this subject is discussed and illustrated with cluster diagrams in Chapter 22, and a clear example from the University of Iowa Surgery Department is given in Tutorial D).

PREDICTIVE ANALYTICS IN PERSONALIZED MEDICINE

Personalized medicine presents a tremendous opportunity to develop systems for predictive analytics coupled with decisioning systems. There are so many complex relationships and variables involved in the regulation of human health that, even when all the principles or relationships behind disease mechanisms are clearly understood, there will continue to be a need to refine the predictive analytics models as additional scientific knowledge is discovered and environmental changes occur over time. To further illustrate this dynamic, refer to the example discussed in Chapter 3 in which a wad of paper is thrown into a trash can, or consider a basketball thrown into a hoop. The physics that regulates the flight of the paper or the basketball is understood clearly, and the amount of force necessary to make sure the object cast falls into the goal can be judged closely — but there is a large combination of environmental variables that can affect the direction of flight and the amount of force required; therefore, a static model would be impractical. Too many influences would affect the flight of the object, and it would be impossible to build a model built for every possible situation ahead of time.

THE FUTURE: PREDICTIVE AND PRESCRIPTIVE MEDICINE

Much of the medical practice in the past has been focused on reacting to problems, rather than anticipating them. Such "reactive" medicine must be replaced by *predictive and prescriptive* medicine. This is not a new concept; even Hippocrates recognized its value in ancient Greece, long before we knew anything about DNA. Hippocrates said: "He will manage the cure best, who foresees what is to happen from the present condition of the patient" (Adams, 1849). Yet, over 2,000 years later, we are only beginning to realize the full potential of that maxim, and we are just starting to practice predictive medicine. Our conventional view of medicine focuses primarily on symptoms, which are the late manifestations of disease. Most medical practice today neglects molecular signals that may serve as harbingers hours, days, months, or even years before the onset of a disease. Often, conventional medicine also ignores underlying mechanisms of the symptoms and treats only what is physically discernible at the time the patient presents.

The future of medical practice must be focused on predicting and thereby preventing disease, rather than reacting to symptoms after the disease has already taken its toll. The human body is composed of many complex interacting systems. These systems send signals at every level in order to communicate with each other. Currently, we have the abilities to process and interpret these signals effectively; in fact, these abilities are increasing daily as medical scientists acquire new and faster technologies (e.g., "smart phone" applications). These new technologies can provide a richer landscape of data and analytical methods for building better predictive models for use in providing a near real-time scoring for individual patients for diagnosis and treatment decision-making. The human can be viewed as a complex system of "factories" communicating and shipping things around the body. Modern medicine, however, does not pay attention to this system of factories, and without this holistic treatment of such a complex system medical treatments may cause it to become unregulated, which may overload some of the systems and cause them to fail. This rather *ad hoc* approach to medicine is contrasted with the highly controlled function of an actual commercial factory, where quality control workers monitor constantly all the processes that occur in the factory. If some factory process has a problem or begins operating outside of its normal range, the appropriate corrective action can be taken immediately to prevent product failures. In medicine, these failures represent misdiagnoses, improper treatments, and even death. If physicians are able and willing to harness the messages from all of these bodily systems, they will be able to correct the problems in these systems before they become overloaded, permitting the maintenance of equilibrium among systems. In the future (and actually this is beginning to happen already — see, for example, FutureMed/Singularity University, 2013), we will be able to monitor each of our organ systems through a variety of biological signatures that will tell us the current state of the organ. By analyzing the signatures of the bodily organs and systems (e.g., the circulatory system), doctors can locate the problems and begin an intervention before there are any clinical manifestations. In this way, medicine will no longer be reactive, attempting to rebuild a "factory" that has already become highly unstable and fraught with failures; instead, medicine can become proactive and maintain systems in the human body in a healthy equilibrium. This situation has been in place in many of the commercial industries of the world for nearly 20 years, and it is time that it also happens in medicine, medical research, and healthcare delivery.

Application of Predictive Analytics and Decisioning in Predictive and Prescriptive Medicine

There are at least four medical measures that can utilize predictive analytics to maintain our bodies in a healthy state of equilibrium:

1. Determining or predicting risk of disease, and predicting best preventative measures to follow to prevent disease.

2. Monitoring health for failing organs and systems, followed by applying early interventions before the body gets out of balance.
3. Detecting disease early, to head it off before the patient develops clinical symptoms.
4. Predicting what our needs are, psychologically, physically, and nutritionally, and applying the appropriate therapies, nutrition, etc. to meet those needs.

When physicians and patients work together as a team to apply these measures, making interventions, as needed, patient bodily systems can be maintained in a healthy equilibrium (see Figure 13.2).

Another area for the application of predictive analytics to healthcare delivery is to assist in the recovery of a biological system when the human body falls out of equilibrium. When this occurs, through aging, disease, or lack of sufficient nutritional, psychological, or physical support, predictive models can provide information to help move the system back into equilibrium. The nature of this equilibrium is dynamic, not static. The optimum level of any part of a complex biological system changes over time, and control systems in them must adjust to these changes. Predictive models must focus on solutions to move the functioning of the body back to the proper level for a given time, and this level is a "moving target." Therefore, predictive modeling must be part of an adaptive process in which the current state of the optimum solution keeps pace with the changing needs of the body.

Definitions of homeostasis will vary at different points in the human lifespan, and different interventions will be required at different stages of life. A good example is our diets. Very few people can eat high-caloric junk foods like they may have done as teenagers and still maintain a healthy weight. Bodily metabolic rates change with age and opportunities for exercise may diminish, but if the caloric intake does not change then the body increases in weight. Predictive models can facilitate accurate diagnoses, provide valuable input for the prescription of appropriate therapy for the individual, monitor the response to therapy, and adjust therapy as appropriate. The opportunities also include the use of patient data in intensive care units or other hospital settings, and predicting disastrous events in advance, thus allowing preventive measures to be taken before the events occur.

The time is right for the shift to predictive–prescriptive personalized medicine. Considerable advancements in the processing of very large data volumes ("Big Data") provide us with an unprecedented ability to both understand and monitor the complexities in the function of the human body. This ability, in conjunction with powerful analytical tools available today, positions us at the beginning of an exciting era in which predictive analytics will play a substantial role in improving human health.

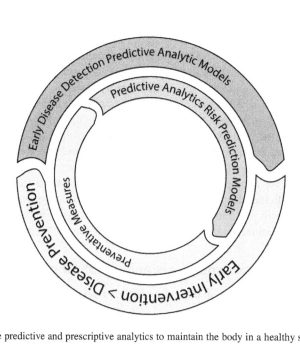

FIGURE 13.2 Four areas that can use predictive and prescriptive analytics to maintain the body in a healthy state. Copyright © 2013 Nephi Walton.

THE DIVERSITY OF AVAILABLE HEALTHCARE DATA

There are multiple types of data that can be used to build predictive analytics models in medicine and health care. It is likely that the best models will incorporate multiple data sources. Each data source provides a perspective on the pattern sought by the modeling software. Individual perspectives can be combined by the mathematical algorithms in a fashion analogous to the way the human brain composes the perception of depth from the separate images of the same objects viewed at slightly different angles. Mathematical algorithms can sense patterns in the combined data set that may not have been clearly defined in any single data set. Combining data from multiple sources of genetic and environment information will enable the modeling algorithms to predict the best outcome and prescribe the best intervention for a given individual.

This individual-centric approach in medical diagnosis and treatment considers factors like a person's ability to adhere to the necessary treatment when prescribing the best therapy. The use of predictive analytic numeric and text data-mining capabilities combined with the abundance and diversity of data sources available provides medicine and health care with the greatest likelihood of making a good prediction and providing an effective treatment. The best models will incorporate the best variables from among the vast array of data sources that relate to the incidence and treatment of a disease. The result is that hundreds or even thousands of variables may be analyzed using various feature selection techniques to generate the "shortlist" of variables for building the model (see Chapters 15, on data-mining algorithms, and Chapter 22, on decisioning systems, where the use of feature selection techniques is discussed). This shortlist of variables is much more likely to produce a better model than will a larger list. The predictive accuracy of successive models may increase as the number of important variables decreases, as successive feature selection operations occur — at least up to a point. Beyond this "sweet spot" the predictive accuracy will decrease as the number of variables increases. Adding further variables beyond this point functions only to add "noise" to the data set, which depreciates the accuracy of the model. This effect is likely to become increasingly important as additional open networks of healthcare data become available. For example, as effects of the PCORI efforts accumulate (PCORI, 2013), it is likely that the number of variables readily available to medical practitioners will increase greatly within the next 2 to 3 years.

Diversity of Data Types Available

Many types of data are available for building predictive analytical models. The most important of these types include:

1. Phenotypic data
2. Clinical information
3. Real-time physiological data
4. Imaging data
5. Genomic data
6. Transcriptomics data
7. Epigenomics data
8. Proteomics data
9. Glycomics data
10. Metabolomics data
11. Metagenomics data
12. Nutrigenomics data
13. Behavioral measures data
14. Socioeconomic status data
15. Personal activity monitoring data
16. Climatological data
17. Environmental data.

1. Phenotypic Data

This is where it all starts. We recognize traits that appear to be different from the standard population, and when these traits are problematic we call it a syndrome or disease. This is how disease has been defined for centuries. Unless there is a physical, mental, or psychiatric—psychological manifestation, we don't consider a "defect" such as a genetic mutation to be a disease. Many "defects" have evolved as a means of adaptation to the environment, and offer some advantages; therefore, they are not viewed as defects but rather as beneficial new characteristics. When this happens, the common perception of the norm changes. The usual types of genetic mutations are very different from those that are imputed to cause the super powers of characters cast in the *X-Men* movies. Instead, most mutations are "deleterious" in that they reduce the general state of health or vigor of the organism. A few mutations can be viewed as beneficial (or "good") for the organism. These beneficial mutations are favored in the process of natural selection because they provide some advantage in coping with competition or changing environmental conditions.

Although there are a few scattered traits that appear to be controlled by a single gene (such as eye color or hair color), for most diseases many different genes can be involved. For example, arthritis can be viewed as a single disease with many different manifestations. These manifestations are characterized by which joints are affected, how early the disease first appears in an individual, what medications the disease responds to, the amount of bone deformity caused, the amount of pain, the durations of pain, and related symptoms such as heart disease. The combination of these physical or physiological manifestations with a particular disease is called the "phenotype." In the past, medicine was defined in terms of the phenotype of the disease. Medicine, however, is moving more toward defining disease by the "genotype."

Definition of the phenotype is very problematic. Defining a phenotype can be a difficult task because there are overlapping characteristics among phenotypes in a single individual, or among different individuals who have varying levels of expression of disease. This situation is complicated further by environmental interactions and disorders caused by multiple genes. Once the phenotype is defined, however, searching for it from the clinical information based on this definition may require an extensive review of medical records, requiring the employment of text-mining methods to increase the speed of retrieval. The phenotype is often included in clinical information, but unfortunately is often hidden in current healthcare documentation practices in large bodies of non-standard free-form text, from which it must be derived. The medical record systems (in the USA) are being pushed to achieve much greater accuracy by the provisions of the Meaningful Use Stage I, Stage II, and Stage III directives, all of which come into effect during the year 2014. As this process evolves, the effort to define and derive the phenotype from medical records will become easier and more standardized. Unfortunately, current medical science uses a diversity of terms and expressions often to describe the same things, the choice of which is based on the experience, training, and location of service of an individual doctor or nurse.

2. Clinical Information

Clinical information includes the total documentation for the patient encounter in the hospital or clinic. It is from this vast array of information that the phenotype is derived. Information includes the physician's notes and patient's history; it also includes routine measurements such as height, weight, blood pressure, temperature, heart rate, respiratory rate, and other miscellaneous lab metrics. These metrics include all of the observations made by the physician, nurse, and other healthcare staff each time a patient is seen, and any measurements taken during that patient visit. Additionally, it includes much of the information discussed below. It is likely that, over the next 1–5 years, the clinical medical record will incorporate even more information, including genomic, epigenetic, and proteomic data, as the structure of Electronic Medical Records (EMRs) is refined.

3. Real-Time Physiological Data

In a hospital, patients are subjected to a barrage of measurements – particularly in intensive care units, where they are connected to continuous monitoring devices. These devices enable nurses or physicians to make an immediate intervention if a crisis arises, such as shock, heart failure, or respiratory failure. Monitoring systems like these help to save lives in hospitals, and are necessary parts of any hospital system. Many times, however, monitoring may not happen at the most opportune time using the best available resources. By the time that a nurse notices a sudden drop in blood pressure or heart rate, the damage may have occurred already. Many of these events may be predicted ahead of time, in real-time, by models which evaluate subtle changes in these physiological measurements compared against an extensive historical record, to make predictions sufficiently ahead of time to prepare an appropriate intervention before significant damage occurs. Unfortunately, the current situation is that much or all of the data gathered in real-time monitoring are discarded. If the data were retained in the medical record, they could serve as a rich source for building predictive analytics models to forecast such things as:

- Predicting a patient's response to treatment
- Predicting deterioration or adverse events

- Predicting transfer to the PICU (Patient Intensive Care Unit)
- Predicting a patient's return to a particular ICU after being transferred to a regular ward bed
- Predicting return to the hospital after being discharged.

4. Imaging Data

Various forms of imaging are used to make diagnoses, and to monitor patients' disease and recovery. Imaging capabilities of medical instruments are improving rapidly, allowing physicians to use less-invasive methods and high-resolution pictures to monitor what is happening in the body, often in real time. These imaging modalities include:

- CT scans
- X-rays
- Ultrasound
- Magnetic resonance imaging (MRI)
- Functional magnetic resonance imaging (f-MRI)
- Nuclear medicine
- Positron emission tomography (PET)
- Photoacoustic imaging
- Breast thermography
- Echocardiography
- Microscopy.

It is reasonable that these images may contain signals that might indicate where the disease is headed, and that they can be used to diagnose and track progression of disease to allow physicians and nurses to react sooner and to a better effect before a problem progresses. Currently, the interpretation of these images requires a trained human eye. The eye of a trained radiologist is a complex image-analysis organ that can quickly summarize the image in its entirety. The brain of the radiologist contains a vast clinical knowledge base that is associated closely with what is seen in these images, as a result of many years of training while staring at these images in the context of human disease.

Despite this close linkage between the image perception and the magnificent and powerful computer of the brain behind the eyes, it is not possible to analyze the image pixel by pixel to sense very subtle of changes in the perception. This limitation becomes ever more apparent as the spatial resolution of these images increases with advances in technology. New techniques are being developed to analyze electronically and quantify pathology on these images (Angell et al., 2013; Budin et al., 2013; Heidrich et al., 2013; Song and Lee, 2013). As these techniques mature, there will be ample opportunity to mine this vast amount of imaging data and perform analyses that are not possible using only human judgment. Data derived from common image characteristics (modalities) are currently being used for predicting prognoses in cancer and cardiovascular disease. Additionally, even obesity is being diagnosed more accurately and managed more effectively using these methods (Gallagher et al., 2008). All of these imaging modalities show great potential for future predictive and prescriptive personalized medicine (Brizel, 2011).

5. Genomic Data

The cost of genome sequencing has decreased significantly over the past few years. In 2003, the cost of sequencing a human genome was $2.7 billion; this price dropped to $1,000 dollars in 2014. Although we have achieved a low cost for sequencing it still costs thousands of dollars to interpret the resulting data and make it meaningful. The decrease in cost and time required to sequence a genome will promote its use in health care, and provide a huge amount of data for analytical modeling. Genetic data form the backbone of personalized medicine and pharmacogenomics.

DNA – The Centerpiece of Heredity and Bodily Differences

Genetic information is encoded in the DNA (deoxyribonucleic acid) molecule, described by Watson and Crick in 1952. DNA is a double-stranded molecule, with the two strands coiled in the form of a helix (Figure 13.3). The molecule is organized in two long chains of nucleotides, composed of pairs of deoxyribose sugar and high-energy phosphate groups connected by pairs of nucleobases – guanine (G), adenine (A), thymine (T), and cytosine (C), Adenine always pairs with thymine, and guanine always pairs with cytosine. A specific sequence of paired nucleobases of a given length of nucleotides is called a gene. The DNA molecule is tightly coiled into a long structure called a chromosome. Humans have 46 chromosomes in two groups, one group inherited from the mother and one from the father.

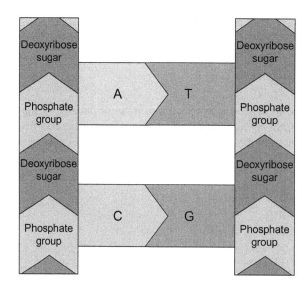

FIGURE 13.3   Structure of the DNA molecule; this shows the connection of multiple nucleotides, each one of which is composed of a deoxyribose sugar, a high-energy phosphate group, and a nucleobase. *Source: DNAspecialtitle.blogspot.com.*

Genes function to encode specific proteins; some of these proteins function as enzymes, which act as catalysts in various chemical reactions in the body, and other function as structural "building blocks" or function in other ways. If the specific sequence of nucleobases is disrupted by some chemical or physical disturbance, the gene will fail to encode the protein properly, and the function of that gene will be lost (or at least partially lost). This process is called a mutation. For example, dietary proteins (proteins that are eaten as food) are broken down into smaller molecules like phenylalanine, which in turn should be broken down into tyrosine, a reaction catalyzed by the enzyme phenylalanine hydroxylase. A single gene controls the production of phenylalanine hydroxylase, and if that gene is damaged or missing in the chromosome, the enzyme cannot be produced. This disease is called phenylketonuria (PKU). Symptoms of PKU are severe mental retardation and spastic movements.

Many bodily process are affected by multiple genes, and therefore a disruption in one of the genes may lead only to a decrease in the protein products, rather than a complete lack of the protein.

The combined sequence of these nucleotides among all of the 46 chromosomes composes the genotype of an individual. The genotype, in combination with the unique environment of an individual, is what determines a person's phenotype. The expression of the phenotype composes the physical, physiological, psychological, psychiatric, and spiritual characteristics of an individual. There are about 3 billion bases in human DNA, and more than 99% of them are the same in all people. This information is the combination of genetic sequences passed on from both parents, with the origin of each piece of the total sequence alternating from one parent or the other in a nearly random fashion, leading to the unique characterization of each individual. This unique characterization is caused by just the 1% difference in the genetic sequence. Sometimes, however, this very small genetic difference causes very large differences among individuals; small changes in DNA sequence can have large effects. Larger genetic differences will have even larger effects. For example, mice and men differ only in about 15% of their DNA; this means that men and mice are 85% identical (National Human Genome Research Institute, 2010).

DNA Replication and Mutation

The genetic system has the ability to make copies of the DNA molecules. This process is called replication. Many molecule types are necessary for this process, including several types of ribonucleic acid (RNA), and the enzyme DNA polymerase. Each strand of DNA in a double helix can serve as a pattern, or template, for duplicating the sequence of nucleotides. This critical process takes place when cells divide, ensuring that the resulting cells have the same DNA as the undivided cell. A gene mutation is defined as "a permanent change in the DNA sequence that makes up a gene." The large majority of the DNA in cells of all organs and tissues in a body is the same. Some differences do arise, though, through processes of mutation.

Somatic Mutations

Somatic mutations occur in body cells (not germinal cells, which control heredity) when some external agent (e.g., a chemical) disrupts the sequence in a gene by breaking the nucleobase bonds directly or interfering with the normal replication process. The effects of these mutations are persistent in all cells replicated from them in the body. Sometimes these mutations are benign, but they can be the source of cancer, and they may be implicated in other diseases (Poduri *et al.*, 2013). Somatic mutations are not passed on to future generations.

Germline Mutations

Mutations in the sexual cells of organisms (seeds in plants; gonads in animals) are inheritable. The mutations that are inherited are called germline mutations, and these are what confer the inheritance of human disease through subsequent generations (Genetics Home Reference, 2013). These germline mutations can happen during the recombination process in cell division in the sexual cells. The mutations are passed on via the egg or the sperm cell, which are combined to form a new DNA of the child. Once these mutations are established in the sexual cells, they can then be passed on to future generations. Some mutations will produce harmful or fatal results while others will produce no effect, an effect that is benign, or, in rare cases, an effect that is beneficial.

There are several types of genetic mutations that can occur from the rearrangement, deletion, or repetition of the nucleobases A, G, C, and T that form the DNA strands. When these changes happen, the resulting proteins that are produced by the gene sequence may be defective, may have a new or altered function, or may not be made at all. These mutations can have a wide range of effects, with some making no difference at all, or having a minimal effect, while others can be fatal. There are thousands of mutations that have been linked to human disease, physical characteristics, drug response, and other physiological properties.

Genetic testing for disease has become increasingly sophisticated and also more easily available. This testing was originally very laborious and expensive, and therefore only small sequences of DNA were examined. Today, the entire genome can be sequenced at varying resolutions. The most common genetic studies in the past few years have been based on SNPs, or single-nucleotide polymorphisms (pronounced "snip," or "snips" for plural). SNPs are DNA sequence variations in a single nucleotide in the genome that differs between different people and covers a small span of the DNA strand. Using these relatively common variations, it is possible to detect medium to large genomic lesions. Genome-wide association studies (GWAS) involve the genotyping of hundreds of thousands or millions of SNPs which are then analyzed in relation to a particular disease or phenotype using hypothesis-free agnostic approaches. GWAS have shown considerable success in mapping susceptibility loci for common diseases. As of September 14, 2013, the National Human Genome Research Institute's GWAS catalog listed 1,701 publications identifying 11,495 SNPs with association with one or more of over 900 different phenotypes (Hindorff *et al.*, 2013). The associations that have been identified by GWAS have identified relationships with many genes that previously would not have been thought to be good candidates as causes for particular diseases or phenotypes. Thus, GWAS have added greatly to our knowledge about genes and processes involved in human disease. While the variants discovered have contributed significantly to knowledge of the disease processes, they have made only small contributions to medicine's ability to make predictions of an individual's risk for developing a particular disease; this is because the effect size of most variants is very small and most diseases are extremely complex, involving multiple genes and other complex factors. The variants identified by GWAS explain only a small proportion of the total genetic variance involved in most disorders.

Meta-analysis of GWAS involves combining the results of several GWAS studies to increase the power of the analysis with the goal of finding more statistically significant associations and novel genetic associations. This approach has become very popular for the discovery of new genetic loci for common diseases. A large number of the genetic risk variants discovered recently have come from large-scale meta-analyses of GWAS studies (Evangelou and Ioannidis, 2013; Wagner, 2013).

Although GWAS have the advantage of lower cost and speed of analysis, one of their weaknesses is that they are designed only to look at common variants based on the SNPs that are analyzed, and thus skip large portions of the genome. Only recently has it been possible to perform genetic analysis economically at single nucleotide resolution, using whole-exome sequencing and whole genome sequencing. The exome is the expressed genome, which means that part of the genome is transcribed and then translated into proteins. These newer sequencing approaches have the potential to explain some of the missing heritability from GWAS analyses of diseases. The significance of the areas of the genome not expressed (referred to as introns) is not entirely clear; this "junk" DNA likely plays an important role in our physical being and definitely plays a role in the DNA structure and therefore the expression of DNA

(Hesselberth, 2013). Time and cost can be saved by sequencing only the expressed portion of the genome; however, the remainder of the genome is still being studied and is also thought to have some significance for normal functioning and disease processes (Katsanis and Katsanis, 2013).

The exome only represents about 1% of the entire human genome but holds 85% of the mutations identified in inherited diseases. There is still some advantage to whole genome sequencing, a process which takes into account every nucleotide in the genome. However, at this time it is still impractical for most laboratories to perform whole genome sequencing because of the extensive analysis required for the substantially larger set of information gathered combined with the cost and time required to perform the sequencing. The advances in exome and whole genome sequencing have brought about considerable excitement but also significant challenges, particularly in analysis and interpretation of these exceptionally large data sets (Pavlopoulos *et al.*, 2013; Wang *et al.*, 2013).

Finding *single* genes to define or determine the origin of complex disease is usually not possible, even with whole genome and whole exome sequencing. Most diseases involve complex interactions between multiple genes, other molecular factors, and the environment. This explains how disease can be passed down through families and skip generations. Because of the complexity of most diseases, robust disease prediction models must be based on multiple genes and include a multitude of other molecular and environmental variables, as outlined in this chapter. The focus of most genomic medicine has been on disease; with increased availability it will become further integrated into primary medical care, playing a critical role in assessment and promotion of wellness and health. Combining a genetic analysis with basic clinical indicators such as blood pressure, body mass index, glucose, and cholesterol measures would give the primary care physician a detailed personalized plan to prevent disease in patients at risk. The use of genomic data for prevention and wellness is on the 10-year agenda for the United States Department of Health and Human Services Healthy People 2020 health promotion program (Healthy People 2020, 2013a,b; Patel *et al.*, 2013; Wade *et al.*, 2013).

The ability to combine genetic information with clinical data is crucial for health care and predictive analytics. Clearly, full integration of this ability into clinical practice is needed in the future. However, before a complete clinical integration can happen, data sets are vitally necessary for building predictive models that can be used for diagnosis and treatment in clinical medicine. This need has been recognized, and several initiatives are in place now for gathering these data for analytical modeling and research. Three notable examples of such efforts are:

1. The *Personal Genome Project* (PGP) (Personal Genome Project, 2005, 2013).
2. The *Electronic Medical Records and Genomics Network* (eMERGE) (eMERGE, 2013 —www.genome.gov/ 27540473).
3. The *Patient Centered Outcomes Research Institute* (PCORI, 2013).

The Personal Genome Project

The Personal Genome Project (PGP) is a non-profit public repository of integrated genomic, environmental, and health data sets, whose goal is to make a wide spectrum of data about humans accessible to researchers and clinical practitioners to increase our knowledge of the human body and improve human health. This project functions to sequence all 3 billion base pairs of the DNA of individuals participating in the project, and then combines this information with their medical records and environmental exposures, and finally compares it with their phenotypic traits. This project uses open-source, open-access, and open-consent frameworks. This means that there are no constraints placed on the usage of the data. Contributors of DNA each have their own interface, which enables them to continue to contribute additional information over their lifetime from various sources, including:

- Historical (longitudinal) records of status
- Medical and social history
- Environmental exposures
- Nutrition
- Lifestyle
- Physical measurements
- Blood chemistry
- Presence or absence of microbes and viruses
- Other pertinent data.

These data are freely available to researchers and are a valuable resource for data mining and predictive analytics (www.personalgenomes.org/).

The Electronic Medical Records and Genomics (eMERGE) Network

The Electronic Medical Records and Genomics (eMERGE) Network is a national consortium organized by the National Human Genome Research Institute to combine DNA biorepositories information with electronic medical record (EMR) systems for large-scale, high-throughput genetic research. There are several academic medical centers across the US that participate in this network. The eMERGE model does not require active recruitment for the study or gathering of samples because it uses cases and controls from various EMR systems, for which genetic samples have already been collected as specimens, thus saving time and money. This network uses these data not only for genetic research, but also to help develop some other frameworks and guidelines related to genomic medicine in the areas of ethics, legal issues, privacy, and community engagement (http://emerge.mc.vanderbilt.edu/; Katsanis and Katsanis, 2013).

The Patient Centered Outcomes Research Institute (PCORI)

The Patient Centered Outcomes Research Institute (PCORI) is a new non-profit research institute mandated by the ACA (Accountable Care Act) Health Reform Laws, funded by seed money from the national government, and to be sustained by $2 per person per year signed up for national healthcare coverage. One of the primary goals of PCORI is to develop regional and national database networks of patient data with the goal of developing accurate predictive and prescriptive models for more accurate diagnosis and treatment of diseases on an individual basis (PCORI, 2013).

Large biorepositories and community sharing of health-related information will become a major part of health care and research in the near future, especially regarding rare diseases for which pooled resources and aggregation of data from affected individuals in the country and world are required to generate enough cases to study the disease effectively. We are at the onset of an exciting era in genomics that will present significant computational, scientific, legal, and ethical challenges. This large-scale integration of healthcare data in the future has only just begun today.

6. Transcriptomics Data

Transcriptomics data are generated by the measurement of gene expression profiles with microarrays. The genes encoded in each cell affect the phenotype only if they are expressed. The first step in gene expression is transcription of DNA into RNA. Often, cellular mechanisms can suppress the expression of genes, and this suppression might occur only under certain conditions. Gene expression profiles provide a measure of the activity of the genes in our body. This process is very complex, as millions of genes are transcribed in different locations in our bodies at the same time.

Even though the DNA in each location of the body is the same, expression of the genes along the DNA backbone may differ significantly in different locations, because these locations (e.g., the brain and the heart) exert different influences on gene expression. These differences in gene expression provide for the different functions required in these locations. If that landscape of gene expression were not complicated enough, each cell in our body may be transcribing differently. For example while an individual's brain and heart have the same genetic backbone, the genes that are actively being transcribed at each site are very different because these organs obviously have very different functions and don't necessarily use the same parts of the genome to execute their functions. To further complicate things, expression of genes is affected by physiological and environmental conditions, which can cause a wide variation in expression, depending on when the sample is taken. In summary, gene expression profiles vary over time, across different physiological and other environmental conditions, and also based on the location within the body. Therefore, the total bodily landscape of transcriptions (the transcriptome) consists of all DNA transcription molecules (i.e., messenger RNA [mRNA], transfer RNA [tRNA], small nuclear RNA [snRNA], ribosomal RNA [rRNA], and other non-coding RNA) produced in the transcription process at a specific developmental stage or physiological condition. These measurements are useful for studying diseases with focal pathological findings where expression can be measured in areas of change, such as with cancer or multiple sclerosis (Sánchez-Pla *et al.*, 2012).

7. Epigenomics Data

The genetic information encoded in DNA is not the only thing inheritable in the human body. Through epigenetics, other factors can create heritable changes in our molecular make-up; some of these include development conditions (i.e., *in utero*), environmental chemicals, drugs, aging, and diet. These factors can cause changes in the chromatin material (histones) that is wrapped around the double-helix DNA chain to form the chromosome. These changes in chromatin are caused primarily by the addition of a methyl group to the histone that is provided by one of the modifying factors listed above. DNA methylation can affect the expression of the DNA genes, and these changes are heritable, even though the DNA base sequence is not changed. Epigenetic mechanisms play important roles in gene expression, DNA repair, and recombination. Epigenetic features are tied to specific locations on our genome and can be inherited; however, they can also be modified or erased in response to molecular signaling during development, or by environmental effects. Similarly to changes in the base sequence of DNA, these epigenetic mechanisms can cause significant problems. Some defects in epigenetic regulation have been linked to human disease, including developmental defects, metabolic disorders, and cancer. Additionally, epigenetic mechanisms can be associated with other diseases, including (but not limited to) psychiatric disorders, diabetes, and asthma.

Epigenetic control of gene expression is centered primarily on the association of DNA with chromatin. This organization begins with 147 base pairs of DNA wrapped around eight different histone proteins. This assembly of DNA and histones is referred to as a nucleosome. The resultant nucleosomes are packaged tightly together into compact fibers known as chromatin. It is through this complex structure that epigenetic regulation occurs, where areas with less chromatin and hence more DNA exposed for translation are expressed, and also areas more tightly bound are silenced or not expressed. Epigenetic regulation occurs primarily through four mechanisms:

1. The first mechanism is the post-translational modification of histone proteins; modifying these proteins, which form the core of the nucleosome, alters the local chromatin conformation. Changes in chromatin compaction affect the accessibility of genes for transcription. Genes in loosely packed regions, referred to as euchromatin, are more actively expressed, and those in more tightly packed regions, called heterochromatin, are where the gene is not expressed.

2. The second mechanism is through direct DNA modification. DNA modification, specifically methylation of cytosine, is crucial for many genetic processes, including DNA imprinting, X-chromosome inactivation, and long-range silencing of genomic regions. DNA methylation is a general marker of gene silencing, and it prevents transcription by interfering with transcription factor binding. Other modified forms of cytosine, outside of methylation, have more recently been discovered. DNA methylation is typically associated with tightly condensed chromatin.

3. The third mechanism involves non-coding RNA molecules interacting with specific target mRNAs and triggering a cascade of events resulting in specific mRNA degradation and thus preventing transcription. Acting in concert with the previously described aspects of the epigenetic machinery, non-coding RNAs contribute to the regulation of these processes.

4. The fourth mechanism involves packaging the chromatin into a higher-order structure within the cell nucleus. Chromatin accessibility and nucleosome positioning within this higher order package is also an important epigenetic mechanism. It is more common to find elements that regulate gene expression in regions of the genome that are more accessible in the higher-order packaging.

These epigenetic mechanisms often work together to regulate DNA expression. For example, small non-coding RNA molecules can participate in directing DNA methylation. Additionally, enhancer elements in accessible regions can even encode for small non-coding RNA molecules themselves. In summary, epigenetic features primarily control DNA expression through allowing or disallowing transcriptional machinery access to DNA.

This sophisticated regulation of DNA transcription plays a critical role in many cellular processes. It is crucial in determining the type of cell (heart cell, brain cell, blood cell, skin cell, etc.) a cell will become in early development as we progress from a single fertilized cell into a complex organism. It is also an important mechanism in turning on or off genes that promote or inhibit cancer.

The epigenome includes the entirety of these epigenetic features throughout the genome. Compared to the more static genome, the epigenome is very dynamic and will differ depending on the tissue type, the person's age and types of exposures, and many other factors, some yet to be discovered. This diversity of effects renders the study of the epigenome in relation to human disease much more complicated than studying the genome. The genome has a common set of DNA molecules that is fairly constant in all the cells in the body. In contrast, the epigenome must be studied in the right tissue at the right time and under the right conditions, because it can easily change based on these factors. Despite its complexity, knowledge of the epigenome is crucial to understanding human disease; therefore, significant efforts are underway to further study and better define the human epigenome.

To address the complexity of the human epigenome, the National Institutes of Health (NIH) launched the Roadmap Epigenomics Project in 2007. One of the goals of this project is to create a series of epigenome reference maps, available to the public. These maps include a wide array of cell lines and cell and tissue types from individuals at various developmental stages, and with various diseases and health states. The National Center for Biotechnology Information Epigenomics database was created as a repository for these data. The data consist of DNA methylation patterns, histone modifications, chromatin accessibility, and small RNA transcripts. The website for this project is at www.roadmapepigenomics.org. More information, data, and tools for epigenomics can also be found on the NCBI website (Capell and Berger, 2013; Epigenomics, 2013; Fingerman *et al.*, 2013).

8. Proteomics Data

Following the genomic and transcriptomic processes in genetic studies, the next step is the formation of proteins, called proteomics. There are many molecular mechanisms that can modify the shape and function of these proteins. The science of proteomics consists of quantifying these proteins, in an effort to understand their physiological functions in the body. The composition of proteomic processes (the proteome) varies based on the type of cell, its location, and its environment, and can change over time. Different genes are expressed in different types of cells, so the proteins expressed in different cells can vary widely depending on the body organ, tissue, or location.

Cells are extremely complex and contain a large number of molecules that interact both within the cell and outside the cell, enabling cells to function, communicate, and perform the necessary functions to sustain life. One of the primary goals of science is to understand how these cells function and communicate. The central dogma of molecular biology describes the flow of molecular information from DNA as it is transcribed into RNA, and then translated to form proteins. Although this three-step sequence is largely true, the complete process is far more complex. There are many mechanisms by which proteins are created or modified that are not directed by information in the DNA. Some examples of these mechanisms are epigenetic marks, alternative splicing, non-coding RNAs, protein–protein interactions, and post-translational modifications. Given the independence and many possible modifications that are possible outside the central dogma, it could be argued that analysis of proteins as the key functional entities of the cell forms the principal level of information required to understand how cells function.

The very characteristics that give proteomics an advantage over genomics and transcriptomics in understanding cell function also complicate the study of proteins. Global protein analysis is a significant analytical challenge, considering the diversity of proteins throughout the body, the complex number of modifications, and the variety of ways that they can be modified. Proteins are primarily measured with mass spectrometry, although other methods are also used. These technologies have advanced significantly during recent years. A decade ago, the sequencing and identification of an individual protein was a significant challenge. Today, the identification and quantification of nearly all proteins is now achievable in a single experiment. These advances are referred to as next-generation proteomics, and reflect the comprehensive coverage of DNA and RNA species by next-generation nucleic-acid sequencing methods. The huge amount of data that can now be generated has created a desperate need for computational tools to organize and mine the data (Altelaar *et al.*, 2013).

9. Glycomics Data

Glycomics is the comprehensive assessment of glycans or sugars. Glycans are important building blocks of the four major biomolecules of life — carbohydrates, nucleic acids, lipids, and proteins. They are involved in virtually every pathophysiological condition in medicine. The analysis of these biomolecules gives medical science a better understanding of human physiology (Wells and Hart, 2013). Glycosylation is the covalent attachment of glycans to proteins or lipids. Glycosylation is the most abundant post-translational modification of proteins. It is also the modification that provides the most structural diversity. Greater than 50% of the entire human proteome is modified with glycans. Glycosylation plays a critical role in many biological processes that affect human health, including cell recognition and cell-to-cell communication (Li *et al.*, 2013). Both cell recognition and cell-to-cell communication are critical in embryo development, immunity, autoimmune diseases, cancer, and other human diseases. Glycosylation is determined by both genetics and environmental factors, so some elements of disorders related to glycosylation are inherited but environmental effects also play a role both directly and through mediation of epigenetic mechanisms. Glycans are analyzed with liquid chromatography, mass spectrometry, and capillary electrophoresis. Both quantitative and qualitative changes in glycan structures have been found in many complex diseases, including cancer (Zoldoš *et al.*, 2013).

10. Metabolomics Data

Metabolism is the set of processes inside the cell that produce energy and cellular building blocks such as amino acids, nucleotides, and lipids. These building blocks and the biochemical intermediate products generated during their production and utilization are referred to as metabolites. Examples of metabolites are amino acids, organic acids, sugars, fatty acids, lipids, steroids, small peptides, and vitamins. Metabolomics is the study of the complete set of metabolites of low or intermediate molecular weight reflecting the physiological, developmental or pathologic state of the cell, tissue, organ, or organism. Although the way scientists conceive concepts in this field now is relatively new, even the ancient Greeks believed the concept that changes in tissue and biologic fluids could be early signs of pathology and might indicate disease. In 1506, Ullrich Pinder described the possible medical value of the smell, color, and taste of urine; all of these characteristics of urine are the result of the metabolites contained therein (Syggelou *et al.*, 2012). Metabolite levels are a product of the sum effect of genetics, transcription, post-transcriptional regulation, and environmental processes. The measurement of cell status, health, and activity defines the physiological phenotype of the cell and its health at any given moment in time. Metabolomics is focused on comprehensive profiling of metabolites from cells and bio-fluids. While the genotype is relatively static, metabolomics reflects the dynamic nature of biologic systems in response to the environment and their interaction with other systems. Thus it is possible to use these measures to determine the effects on the body of hormones, drugs, food, chemicals, and any other environmental exposures.

Metabolomic studies are performed on biological fluids such as urine, plasma, cerebrospinal fluid, maternal milk, or saliva, or on tissue samples from various organs in the body. For example, urine can be obtained very easily, and it contains a significant amount of information on the overall metabolic state of an individual. The unique biochemical composition of urine is affected by a complex combination of the effects of genotype, physiologic conditions, disease state, environment, nutrition, and drug or toxic elements ingested. Analysis of urine could allow for prediction of disease progression, early detection of disease, and monitoring of a patient's disease progression, treatment response, or recovery.

Soon, it may be possible to develop personalized treatment regimens based on the current metabolic status of the patient, based on their static genotype, and computer readouts of the current state of their body at that moment. This facility expands the boundaries of personalized medicine to encompass any changes in these variables up to the second the patient presents. A primary goal of medicine is the creation of individualized treatment regimens that are optimized for a patient's metabolic status.

Metabolomics has an advantage over some of the other "omics" in that there is a smaller set of variables to analyze. Compared to more than 20,000 genes in genomics (disregarding the millions of possible mutations in those genes), more than 80,000 transcripts measured in transcriptomics, and the greater than 10,000,000 proteins measured in proteomics, metabolomics is concerned with less than 3,000 metabolites. This relatively small number of variables gives us a much more manageable set of data, and the measurements are a result of the activity of the other "omics" that contain a greater number of variables. These metabolites are involved in the major biochemical pathways in the human body, including glycolysis, Krebs cycle, and lipid metabolism. They are involved in signal pathways as transmitters and hormones, and they can measure specific pathological biochemical processes, such as oxidative stress. These measures provide a real-time measurement of the status of these pathways and systems (Syggelou *et al.*, 2012).

Metabolomics has perhaps had the greatest impact in cancer research, allowing researchers to apply a cellular phenotype to cancer cells in an effort to understand more completely the processes that occur within cancer cells. Metabolites are used currently in cancer for tumor staging and assessment of treatment efficacy (Vermeersch and Styczynski, 2013). While metabolomics has a large impact on cancer research, it is growing in importance in the study of many other diseases, including multiple sclerosis, asthma, Alzheimer's, and infertility (Gomez-Casati *et al.*, 2013). There is an increasing use of metabolomics in the monitoring of neonatal disorders, growth, and development (Fanos *et al.*, 2013).

11. Metagenomics Data

We have a world within ourselves in the form of our microbiome. The human body is inhabited by millions of organisms living in communities working together with our own cellular environment, sometimes to our benefit and other times to our detriment. Each of these microorganisms has its own genetic make-up, which can have a substantial effect on how we function and how our body reacts to or even develops disease. The human microbiome is a complex assemblage of the microbes inhabiting many sites in the human body. The components of this microbiome include bacteria, viruses, and fungi. Today's technology allows for in-depth sequencing and analysis of these communities and their members. In the foreseeable future, measuring microbiota composition could become standard clinical practice, as it may become diagnostic for some diseases or indicate increased susceptibility to others. The microbiota of a number of disease states are being examined and it is possible that we can improve or maybe even cure some disease states just by modifying the microbiome (Eloe-Fadrosh and Rasko, 2013). The microbiome has been implicated as having an effect in many diseases, including rheumatoid arthritis, autism, asthma, and cancer.

One of the most striking examples of recent studies of the microbiome was carried out on a number of pairs of twins, where one twin was obese and the other was thin. The fecal microbiota from the twins were transplanted into mice. The mice that received the fecal microbiota from the obese twin had increased obesity, while those with microbiota from the lean twin remained lean. This should not give us the excuse to get off the treadmill and blame all our fat on bugs in our digestive system, but it certainly can give us a better understanding of the potential impact of the microbiome and how much it truly does influence our health (Ridaura *et al.*, 2013).

The NIH has recognized the importance of the microbiome in human health and disease by founding the Human Microbiome Project (HMP). The aim of the HMP is

to characterize the microbial communities found at several different sites on the human body, including nasal passages, oral cavities, skin, gastrointestinal tract, and urogenital tract, and to analyze the role of these microbes in human health and disease.

Information and data are available at http://commonfund.nih.gov/hmp/ (Human Microbiome Project, 2013).

12. Nutrigenomics Data

We are what we eat! This statement is literally true, for we get the building blocks for our body's development from the foods we ingest. Each of these foods has a unique genetic composition , and each interacts differently with our body. Nutrigenomics is "the science of the effect of genetic variation on dietary response and the role of nutrients and bioactive food compounds in gene expression" (Fenech *et al.*, 2011). What we eat can directly affect gene transcription and therefore can affect overall human health and phenotype. The response to nutrients is based on the body's genetic make-up, and how the body metabolizes and interacts with these nutrients. Because the health effects of nutrition are based on the body's genetic composition, different people with different ethnicities require different types of nutrition. It is possible, therefore, that better health outcomes can be achieved through customizing nutritional intake to be consistent with the genetic composition of the body. Because dietary factors are important controllers of human health, it is not difficult to expect certain effects of McDonald's versus the Mediterranean diet, but predictions are much more complex and can be hard to make (Fenech *et al.*, 2011).

13. Behavioral Measures Data

One of the most important aspects of success of treatment and preventive measures is the patient's behavior in regard to the intervention. Will they take the medication as prescribed? Will they avoid the things that prevent recurrence? Will they make changes in their exercise or diet that prevent disease? Will they avoid risks? The answers to these and many other questions can often be answered by analyzing aspects of patient behavior. Patient behavior is often predicted using the Theory of Planned Behavior (TPB) model (Ajzen, 1991), which attempts to take into account the many variables that can affect a patient's behavior and determine whether the patient will comply with an intervention. This test is included often in clinical data. However, on a larger scale for research purposes, it can be extrapolated to consider what and where we eat, how much we exercise, what type of job we have, how much stress we are under, how many friends we have, and how we interact with other human beings. All of these factors have effects on our physiology and overall physical and mental health. One of the assumptions of the TPB model is that a given behavior is a function of attitude, intention, and beliefs. Such measures have been used in many health studies to predict behavior-related health outcomes, such as adherence to medication in HIV patients (Jones *et al.*, 2012). Some of the important variables in TPB models include: descriptive norms, subjective norms, self-identity, self-efficacy, locus of control, behavioral control, anticipated regret, desires and emotions, moral norms and anticipated affect, social cognition properties, prototypes and willingness, conscientiousness, and goals and their properties.

The variations of the deployed TPB models acknowledge the complexity of factors underlying the ultimate behavioral choice, but nevertheless they assume that the behavior is predicted by some combination of social cognitive factors about the behavior. Each variable that is added to the model may increase incrementally the predictive power of the TPB model, but may also introduce some unexplained variance with each predictor. Meta-analyses have shown that beliefs and attitudes in the TPB model predict 39% of the behavioral intention and 27% of the actual behavior, with notably stronger prediction when behavior is based on self-reports. In order to close the gap between behavioral intention and actual behavior, Gollwitzer and Sheeran (2006) proposed the addition of implementation intention.

14. Socioeconomic Status Data

Socioeconomic status (SES) is a composite measure of an individual's economic and sociological standing. It is a complex assessment measured in a variety of ways that account for a person's work experience and economic and social position in relation to others, based on income, education, and occupation. Socioeconomic status has been a powerful determinant of health; as a general rule, wealthy people tend to be in better health than people of poorer status (Erreygers, 2013). There appears to be a significant impact of socioeconomic status on a multitude of diseases, including:

- Cardiovascular disease (Gershon *et al.*, 2012)
- Respiratory disease (Bashinskaya *et al.*, 2012)
- Mental health-related disorders (Businelle *et al.*, 2013).

Some of the metrics of socioeconomic status include:

- Highest level of education attained
- Education of parents
- Current occupation
- Net income
- Household income
- Wealth (assets, capital)
- Other related variables.

People are usually separated into groups based on these metrics, from least advantaged to most advantaged, or low, medium, or high SES (Galobardes *et al.*, 2006). There are many complex factors in the relationship between socioeconomic status and health. People with relatively few resources may not have very good access to care services, or even transportation to get health care. They may not have the time to focus on their health, or sufficient education to realize the impact that certain elements have on their health. Priorities can vary also; one person might be trying to maintain good health, while another person is a single mother trying to maintain a family with a minimum wage job. The stress related to a person's socioeconomic status alone may impact his or her health (Businelle *et al.*, 2013). Regardless of the mechanism, there is a strong association between SES and health. Many studies with many different diseases have found profound implications of socioeconomic status for disease (Bashinskaya *et al.*, 2012; Gershon *et al.*, 2012).

15. Personal Activity Monitoring Data

Devices that measure human movements have existed for centuries. Leonardo da Vinci was perhaps the first to conceptualize the pedometer; his design was a device worn at the waist with a long lever affixed to the thigh with a ratchet-and-gear mechanism that recorded the number of steps taken during walking. Needless to say, the design has been improved over time, and now pedometers record more than steps (e.g., pulse rate), and some are so tiny as to fit into a watch or smaller device. Perhaps the more striking feature of today's devices (and the most important for the purposes of this book) is their ability to track and store this information over time. These devices have been used extensively for physical activity research, allowing for objective measurement of physical activity beyond what has been learned through questionnaires. They are used now for comparing a population's overall physical activity, and then targeting interventions at those individuals with decreased physical activity who have a predicted higher risk of adverse outcomes associated with decreased physical activity and obesity.

Some of these data are in the public domain and can be used to produce predictive analytic models. The US government began using an accelerometer in the National Health and Nutrition Examination Survey (CDC, 2013) in 2003−2004. Interestingly, use of this technology found that less than 5% of US adults met the national physical activity by pedometer, in contrast to 45−51% meeting the requirement by survey. There may be some inaccuracies in the measurement of this activity, but much of the discrepancy is probably also related to an individual's overestimation of actual physical activity; thus the true value probably lies between 5% and 51%. As the technology in physical-activity monitors advances, these measures will become more accurate. Research has shown that individuals who show less activity on these devices are at increased risk of developing obesity, hypertension, dyslipidemia, and insulin resistance. There is strong evidence that, despite its limitations, a wearable monitor can provide a more valid assessment of physical activity than can a physical activity questionnaire.

Some of the newer applications of wearable monitors provide monitoring of sedentary behaviors and sleep. A sedentary activity, as defined by the Sedentary Behavior Research Network, is "any waking behavior characterized by an energy expenditure <1.5 metabolic equivalents (METs) while in a sitting or reclining posture." Sleep is defined and tracked differently using other devices. Some adults who engage in excessive sedentary behaviors have an increase in cardio-metabolic risk factors (Bassett, 2012). In fact, one study using questionnaire data showed that time spent in two sedentary behaviors, car driving and TV watching, are highly correlated with mortality from a variety of direct causes. Significant associations have been observed between sedentary time and waist circumference, triglycerides, HDL, resting blood pressure, plasma glucose, metabolic risk, and death (Bassett, 2012). Lack of proper sleep has been associated with diabetes, cardiovascular disease, poor immunity, mood disorders, obesity, and hypertension. By tracking this information it may be possible to predict future disease.

Personal activity monitors are now available from many companies, including Bodymedia, Nike, Fitbit, Basis, Motorola, Jawbone, Striiv, and Larklife; these devices are readily available and easily obtainable by consumers, usually directly via online ordering. These devices produce a considerable amount of data on human activity that has been missed by older methods; thus science now has the ability to mine these data to build predictive models and improve human health. Aside from personal tracking devices, there are a number of apps for mobile devices that allow tracking of activity and also calories expended; some examples of these include LoseIt, MyFitnessPal, FatSecret. MyNetDiary, and RunKeeper. As these technologies and apps improve, they will allow individuals to monitor intake and activity more accurately, and will become a goldmine of information for data mining and predictive analytics.

16. Climatological Data

Weather patterns have effects on health in a number of ways. Certain illnesses are more prevalent during certain weather conditions. Additionally, weather affects not only the time spent outdoors but also the amount of time spent indoors, with increased exposure to other people. Weather conditions also affect an individual's amount of physical activity (at least for most people). Climate change is thought to have had an effect on both the incidence and global patterns of human disease. Climate-related environmental variables have been associated with cardiovascular disease, respiratory diseases, mental illness, and infections (see Figure 13.4). The abundance and distribution in populations of infectious organisms in our ecosystems is dependent on climate, and infections related to these organisms account for approximately 60% of human pathogenic illnesses (Bengis *et al.*, 2004). Climate has considerable affect on respiratory diseases which may exhibit exacerbated symptoms based on environmental conditions — for example, asthma, where the pollen concentration in the air is dependent on weather, weather changes, pollutants trapped by inversions, and other factors (Redshaw *et al.*, 2013). Climate can play an important role in predicting disease, especially communicable disease, where weather predictions may be combined with an individual's genetic and "omic" profile to predict an oncoming disease or infection. The availability of accurate predictive and prescriptive models will allow physicians (and even individuals who monitor themselves) to manage infections effectively when these weather conditions are present.

FIGURE 13.4 Climatic conditions causing non-communicable illnesses, and associated pharmaceutical treatments. Reproduced from Redshaw *et al.*, 2013.

17. Environmental Data

Environmental data encompass all that the body comes in contact with, both externally and internally, including chemicals, food, weather, force, toxins, sensations, smells, sounds, and visualizations. Anything outside our physical body that can be introduced to the inside or affect the inside of our bodies can be an environmental stimulus. These environmental stimuli may not all be physical things; they may also be situational, such as in the case of stress or stressful situations. The environment regulates the amount of oxygen delivered to our lungs based on elevation, the particles that are in the air, environmental interactions, the disease to which we are exposed, the amount of sunlight, and even things like the gravitational force on our bodies. Besides these geographical environmental variables, there are many variables that impact us daily and affect our health, including chemicals, diet, lifestyle, physical and psychological stress, and infectious agents. All of these exposures can have an effect on our health and disease processes. New technologies and methodologies for assessing human exposures are being developed, which will provide opportunities to expand our knowledge base and provide useful data for building predictive models for human disease (Weis *et al.*, 2005; Ng *et al.*, 2013).

ALL THE OTHER "OMICS"

In this chapter we have covered many of the core "omics" in use today that will play important roles in predictive analytics in health care, but we certainly have not addressed all of them. There are a number of sub-omics, such as the methylome as a subset of the epigenome or the spliceome as part of the transcriptome. Other "omics" are emerging and several others exist already or are being defined at the time of this publication. Other notable "omics" that will likely play important roles in predictive analytic models, include toxicoproteomics and autoantibodyomics. Toxicoproteomics is the study of proteins expressed in response to chemical and environmental exposures, which is a part of the larger field of toxicogenomics (Wetmore and Merrick, 2004). The autoantibodyome is the compete profile of autoantibodies developed by an individual, which will be critical in the predictive management of autoimmune disease (Chen *et al.*, 2012). All of these and other forthcoming "omics" will play important roles, and they will be important in the future for building build predictive models for disease prevention and health.

THE FUTURE

It is anticipated that "omics" data and other standard health measurements will be combined to become an important part of personalized health care. This information can not only provide risk information on diseases for individuals, but also serve as a real-time monitor of the physiological state of a body in the form of an integrative Personal Omics Profile (iPOP). The iPOP has been discussed now in several papers, and a proof of concept was performed by Chen *et al.* (2012). A major aspect of the iPOP is its contribution to the building of accurate predictive models of disease risk. Longitudinal (historical) documentation of an iPOP can guide prevention and intervention to prevent disease processes, and provide detailed information for personalized treatment. A schematic of the implementation of iPOP is shown in Figure 13.5. This technology would be especially helpful for complex diseases such as autism, Alzheimer's, and autoimmune disorders where multiple factors contribute to the disease and the associated morbidity. The iPOP is modular, allowing the addition and incorporation of new biological measurements as they become available. This modular design does not require the maturation of all the "omics" fields in order to start using this technology. The integration of such technology into standard healthcare practices is an exciting prospect (Chen and Snyder, 2013; Li-Pook-Than and Snyder, 2013).

The future of health care can be related to the development of missiles in warfare. Early missiles had a predetermined target at which they were aimed — but any changes in conditions around them could set them off course, causing them to miss their target. Modern intelligent missiles still have a planned trajectory, and a target at which they are aimed, but they can adjust the trajectory and the target, following signals from sensors regarding their current conditions or problems that arise in flight. These adjustments have to be based on the predicted flight path, because the speed of the missile puts it in a position far from the location where the data were collected. So all interventions must be made on a predicted trajectory. This is very similar to the path personalized medicine will take in the future. This basis for determining the predicted "trajectory" of health care for an individual will begin with genetic profiling done at birth, taking into consideration the parents' disease states and "omic" profiles. This predicted healthcare trajectory will produce a risk score to guide the nature and timing of interventions to achieve the best possible outcome. Thus, our "omic" profile will then be monitored at set points in time to help guide the choice of preventive measures, and, if needed,

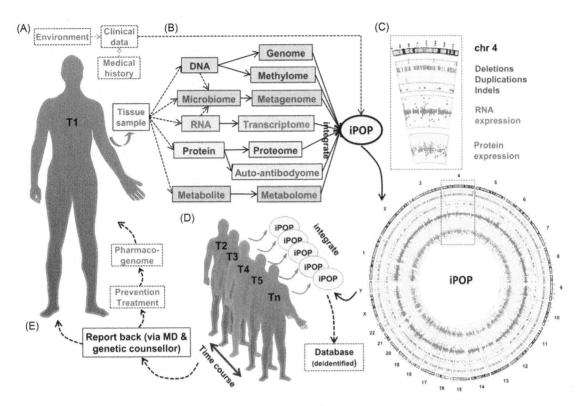

FIGURE 13.5 Integrative Personal Omics Profile (iPOP). Schematic representing the implementation of iPOP for personalized medicine.
(A) Participant tissue sample (e.g., PBMC) is collected, while environment (diet, exercise, etc.), medical history, and clinical data are recorded. T1 is the first time point.
(B) Selected omic analysis involved in a sample iPOP study (Chen *et al.*, 2012).
(C) Sample Circos plot (Krzywinski *et al.*, 2009) of DNA (outer ring), RNA (middle ring), and protein (inner ring) data matching to chromosomes.
(D) iPOP performed and integrated at multiple time points: T2, T3, T4 (viral infected), and T5 up to Tn states, including disease state(s). Gray and green forms represent a relatively healthy individual and a disease state, respectively.
(E) Report data back to genetic counselor and medical practitioner with better informed choices for prevention and/or treatment (matched with pharmacogenetic data), if needed.

From Li-Pook-Than and Snyder (2013).

interventions made in order to fend off or to prevent disease. By maintaining the trajectory, we can minimize the risk of disease and maintain our bodies in a healthy equilibrium.

Figure 13.6 shows a conceptual interface of a possible risk scoring system for disease. The vertical dashed bars/lines represent population-based risk matched for age and gender. The gray areas represent individual calculated risk of an individual, based on genetic makeup and background information, and the gray bars' length indicates the confidence interval. The red and green bars represent the risk, based on the individual's iPOP at the time of testing. The bars are red if the risk has been elevated above their baseline, and green if it has decreased. The orientation of the arrows shows the direction they are headed based on their last iPOP assessment. The length of the arrows indicates the confidence interval. The diseases shown in Figure 13.6 are the top 10 causes of mortality in the United States. Many of these diseases could theoretically be able to be subdivided into specific types of each disease. For example, clicking on the plus sign to the right of cancer would display a list of variety of cancers with similar scores. Some of the items on the list would rely on environmental and behavioral measures, rather than upon "omic" data. For example, accidents are more likely to happen with people who have risky behaviors, although there are some genetic associations linked to risk taking that increase the likelihood of accident. An increased risk of suicide could be related to life stressors and current depressed mood, but it may be related substantially also to the presence or absence of the genes involved in major depressive disorder. The increased risk of influenza could be secondary in its effect to not having received a flu shot before the beginning of the flu season. Many measures will be required to create effective predictive models that can help maintain a healthy equilibrium.

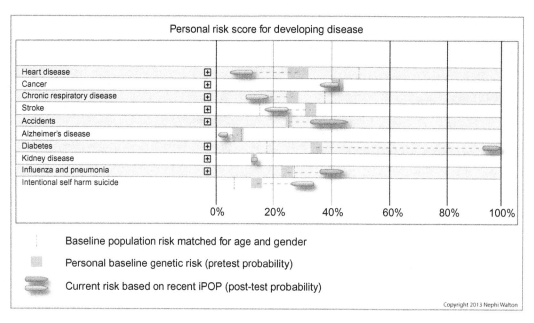

FIGURE 13.6   Personal risk score for developing disease. © *2013 Nephi Walton.*

Challenges

We face many challenges as we integrate predictive modeling into personalized health care. Some of these challenges raise questions to which we have no answers at present.

Challenge 1

A new infrastructure must be created for health care. As personalized medicine based on individual characteristics becomes the norm, healthcare providers and pharmacists must be educated about these measures and how to prescribe and manage patients in a less standard manner. This transition will also require additional education in the use of complicated tools to help manage this information. The structure of electronic medical record systems in their present configuration cannot incorporate or manage even genetic information, let alone integrate all the other variables such as metabolomics, epigenetics, and transcriptomics.

Challenge 2

Who will pay for gene sequencing of every individual for healthcare purposes? Granted, the cost of genotyping is declining rapidly, but is still relatively expensive, and even patients with significant genetic features and disabilities often have difficulty getting insurance companies to pay for testing. Considering the difficulties in gaining approval for testing of sick people, it is hard to imagine convincing insurance companies to pay for a relatively expensive test on an otherwise healthy individual. One argument for these tests might be that the genetic information could save money through preventive care. The problem with using that argument is that it opens up the possibility that insurance companies might raise prices or deny coverage based on genetic information.

Challenge 3

Who will regulate predictive models that directly affect patient care? How will these models be tested for clinical use? The possibility of FDA regulation for these models is a consideration, but it raises some serious concerns. If the FDA becomes involved with predictive modeling, will the costs of testing and regulation drive up the prices? Probably it will. In addition, can we expect the FDA to be able to interpret and integrate predictive modeling properly in its deliberations? Probably we cannot, at least in the near future. Serious questions are already being raised about the regulation of genetic testing, in the wake of new offerings by many companies to provide genetic testing services directly to consumers. These and many other questions regarding genetic testing remain open as we enter this era of predictive medicine.

Challenge 4

What effects will predictions of health outcome have on an individual's mental health and general overall daily anxiety levels? Knowing that there is a certain probability of developing a debilitating disease could have a significant impact on an individual's mental state. Patient response to genetic risk assessments is highly variable, depending on disease and a number of other issues. Strategies have been developed to present this information effectively, but more research is needed in this area as it develops (Lautenbach *et al.*, 2013).

Challenge 5

Does the ability to predict someone's health outcome change his or her behavior? For years, it has been known that the effects of smoking cause cancer and cardiovascular disease, and contribute to a myriad of other diseases. Yet people continue to smoke. Diet and exercise can also reduce a person's health burden significantly on a number of different fronts, yet the rate of obesity continues to rise in America. Millions of people smoke cigarettes, millions are overweight, and millions have high cholesterol. Regardless of the many warnings in schools and the media that these practices are associated with high risks of serious diseases, many people continue the practices. We are bombarded constantly regarding the benefits of healthy diet and exercise, yet we continue to get fatter, and maintain unhealthy diets. Early evidence from studies in this area suggest that genetic risk has a minimal effect on behavior, and has questionable effectiveness in motivating changes in behavior (Henrikson *et al.*, 2009). Based on this information, significant effort must be made to create plans for effective interventions, in order for personalized medicine to be effective in its truest form. Despite the possibility that people may not change their behavior, predicting risk does give the physician an advantage for prescribing the proper medications for people on the edge of disorders such as diabetes or hypertension. Strong predictions by these models might induce the physician to prescribe drugs earlier than otherwise. Currently, we do not have information to determine when or how genetic risk information might motivate healthy behavior. Identifying the settings in which genetic risk can motivate healthy behavior and identifying which people are likely to respond to this information are important goals for predictive analytics (Henrikson *et al.*, 2009).

Challenge 6

With the possibility of building clinical risk prediction models also comes the possibility of legal liability. There has been little if any litigation that addresses the use of risk prediction models. However, as they become more widely used, the prospect of a legal liability and lawsuits will only increase. There is, however, an existing body of litigation on family history and genetics that would have some relevance to the use of risk prediction models. The possibility of a "bad prediction" is a legal concept that presents some complexity, and it is very difficult to judge its significance at this early stage of the implementation of predictive analytic risk models. Outside of blatant misuse or absolute failure to use a required risk prediction model, there is very little legal guidance to avoid the risk for medical liability (Black *et al.*, 2012).

Challenge 7

Many of the biological (body) specimens that are required for full "omics" analysis are not acquired easily. More effective and less invasive methods of gathering this information will be required to get a good assessment of the "omics" of the body. For example, requiring a brain biopsy and undergoing general anesthesia at every check-up is not a likely possibility considering the risk, time, and cost involved, yet some markers of neurological disease using today's technology would require this information.

Challenge 8

The technology required for personalized medicine is certainly not perfect, and many refinements and further developments are needed. For example, despite the hype about the value of whole genome and whole exome sequencing, these tests still have an error rate above 1%. This might not sound like much, but when you consider the billions of nucleotides involved, this 1% error rate becomes quite significant in its effect on diagnosis and treatments. Significant improvements have been made recently in computing ability and Big Data storage capacities, but we are still not where we need to be to process the huge amount of information these new "omics" technologies can provide. For example, data on just 200 patients can consume petabytes (a million gigabytes, or 1,000 terabytes) of data storage (Chen *et al.*, 2012).

Challenge 9

It is likely that the implementation of the iPOP into daily practice will modify the role of the physician, and require the added services of genetic counselors to assist patients in making their medical choices. Consideration must be given for creating a model for this type of interaction, and for determining how this process will fit into our healthcare delivery and reimbursement systems.

Challenge 10

The scientific disciplines covered by personalized predictive medicine are numerous, and the tremendous amount of data and computing power required to employ them is unprecedented. New devices and techniques must be developed to collect and analyze these data. The complete implementation of personalized predictive medicine will require the concerted work of teams of scientists and engineers from many fields, along with guidance from ethical and legal professionals to develop guidelines for implementing this technology. The task is daunting, but also very exciting.

POSTSCRIPT

Chapter 13 ends with presentation of a number of challenges in medical information for merging group-based medical treatment with personalized medical care. No solutions are given to these challenges; for the large part, no solutions yet exist. The stage is set in the next two chapters for developing solutions to meet those challenges in patient-directed health care (Chapter 14), using appropriate analytical algorithms introduced in Chapter 15. Then, we move into the tutorials — the heart of this book.

REFERENCES

Adams, F., 1849. The Genuine Works of Hippocrates. W. Wood & Company, New York, NY.

Ajzen, I., 1991. The theory of planned behaviour. Org. Behav. Hum. Decis. Process. 50, 179−211.

Altelaar, A.F., Munoz, J., Heck, A.J., 2013. Next-generation proteomics: towards an integrative view of proteome dynamics. Nat. Rev. Genet. 14 (1), 35−48.

Angell, H.K., Gray, N., Womack, C., Pritchard, D.I., Wilkinson, R.W., Cumberbatch, M., 2013. Digital pattern recognition-based image analysis quantifies immune infiltrates in distinct tissue regions of colorectal cancer and identifies a metastatic phenotype. Br. J. Cancer. 109 (6), 1618−1624.

Bashinskaya, B., Nahed, B.V., Walcott, B.P., Coumans, J.V., Onuma, O.K., 2012. Socioeconomic status correlates with the prevalence of advanced coronary artery disease in the United States. PLoS ONE. 7 (9), e46314.

Bassett, D.R., 2012. Device-based monitoring in physical activity and public health research. Physiol. Meas. 33 (11), 1769−1783.

Bastien, R.R.L., Rodríguez-Lescure, A., Ebbert, M.T.W., Prat, A., Munárriz, B., Rowe, L., et al., 2012. PAM50 breast cancer subtyping by RT-qPCR and concordance with standard clinical molecular markers. BMC Med. Genomics. 5, 44.

Bengis, R.G., Leighton, F.A., Fischer, J.R., Artois, M., Morner, T., Tate, C.M., 2004. The role of wildlife in emerging and re-emerging zoonoses. Rev. Sci. Technol. OIE. 23, 497−511.

Black, L., Knoppers, B.M., Avard, D., Simard, J., 2012. Legal liability and the uncertain nature of risk prediction: the case of breast cancer risk prediction models. Public Health Genomics. 15 (6), 335−340.

Bragazzi, N.L., 2013. From P0 to P6 medicine, a model of highly participatory, narrative, interactive, and "augmented" medicine: some considerations on Salvatore Iaconesi's clinical story. Patient Prefer. Adherence. 7, 353−359.

Brizel, D.M., 2011. Head and neck cancer as a model for advances in imaging prognosis, early assessment, and posttherapy evaluation. Cancer J. 17 (3), 159−165.

Budin, F., Hoogstoel, M., Reynolds, P., Grauer, M., O'Leary-Moore, S.K., Oguz, I., 2013. Fully automated rodent brain MR image processing pipeline on a Midas server: from acquired images to region-based statistics. Front. Neuroinform. 7, 15.

Businelle, M.S., Mills, B.A., Chartier, K.G., Kendzor, D.E., Reingle, J.M., Shuval, K., 2013. Do stressful events account for the link between socioeconomic status and mental health? J. Public Health (Oxf). June (13), 1741−3842.

Capell, B.C., Berger, S.L., 2013. Genome-wide epigenetics. J. Invest. Dermatol. 133 (6), e9.

CDC, 2013. <www.cdc.gov/nchs/nhanes.htm>.

Charlab, R., Zhang, L., 2013. Pharmacogenomics: historical perspective and current status. Methods Mol. Biol. 1015, 3−22.

Chen, R., Snyder, M., 2013. Promise of personalized omics to precision medicine. Wiley Interdiscip. Rev. Syst. Biol. Med. 5 (1), 73−82.

Chen, R., Mias, G.I., Li-Pook-Than, J., Jiang, L., Lam, H.Y., Chen, R., et al., 2012. Personal omics profiling reveals dynamic molecular and medical phenotypes. Cell. 148 (6), 1293−1307.

Cho, I., Blaser, M.J., 2012. The human microbiome: at the interface of health and disease. Nat. Rev. Genet. 13 (4), 260−270.

Clegg, D.O., Reda, D.J., Harris, C.L., Klein, M.A., O'Dell, J.R., Hooper, M.M., et al., 2006. Glucosamine, chondroitin sulfate, and the two in combination for painful knee osteoarthritis. N. Engl. J. Med. 354 (8), 795−808.

de Magalhães, J.P., 2012. Programmatic features of aging originating in development: aging mechanisms beyond molecular damage? FASEB J. 26 (12), 4821−4826.

Eloe-Fadrosh, E.A., Rasko, D.A., 2013. The human microbiome: from symbiosis to pathogenesis. Annu. Rev. Med. 64, 145−163.

eMERGE (Electronic Medical Records and Genomics Network), 2013. Available at: <www.genome.gov/27540473>.

Emmett, M.R., Kroes, R.A., Moskal, J.R., Conrad, C.A., Priebe, W., Laezza, F., et al., 2014. Integrative biological analysis for neuropsychopharmacology. Neuropsychopharmacology. 39 (1), 5−23.

Epigenomics, 2013. <www.ncbi.nlm.nih.gov/epigenomics/>.

Erreygers, G., 2013. A dual Atkinson measure of socioeconomic inequality of health. Health Econ. 22 (4), 466−479.

Evangelou, E., Ioannidis, J.P., 2013. Meta-analysis methods for genome-wide association studies and beyond. Nat. Rev. Genet. 14 (6), 379−389.

Fanos, V., Antonucci, R., Atzori, L., 2013. Metabolomics in the developing infant. Curr. Opin. Pediatr. 25 (5), 604.

Fenech, M., El-Sohemy, A., Cahill, L., Ferguson, L.R., 2011. Nutrigenetics and nutrigenomics: viewpoints on the current status and applications in nutrition research and practice. J. Nutrigenet. Nutrigenomics. 4 (2), 69−89.

Fingerman, I.M., Zhang, X., Ratzat, W., Husain, N., Cohen, R.F., Schuler, G.D., 2013. NCBI epigenomics: what's new for 2013. Nucleic Acids Res. 41 (D1), D221−D225.

FutureMed/Singularity University, 2013. <http://singularityu.org/2012/11/01/futuremed-scheduled-for-february-4-9-2013-at-singularity-university/>; <http://singularityu.org/tag/futuremed/>.

Gallagher, D., Shaheen, I., Zafar, K., 2008. State-of-the-art measurements in human body composition: a moving frontier of clinical importance. Int. J. Body Compos. Res. 6 (4), 141−148 (Author manuscript available in PMC 2011, January 11).

Galobardes, B., Shaw, M., Lawlor, D.A., Lynch, J.W., Davey Smith, G., 2006. Indicators of socioeconomic position. J. Epidemiol. Community Health. 60, 95−101.

Genetics Home Reference, NIH, 2013. <http://ghr.nlm.nih.gov>.

Gershon, A.S., Dolmage, T.E., Stephenson, A., Jackson, B., 2012. Chronic obstructive pulmonary disease and socioeconomic status: a systematic review. COPD. 9 (3), 216−226.

Gibson, W.M., 1971. Can personalized medicine survive? Can. Fam. Physician. 17 (8), 29−88.

Gollwitzer, P.M., Sheeran, P., 2006. Implementation intentions and goal achievement: a meta-analysis of effects and processes. Adv. Exp. Soc. Psychol. 38, 69−119.

Gomez-Casati, D.F., Zanor, M.I., Busi, M.V., 2013. Metabolomics in plants and humans: applications in the prevention and diagnosis of diseases. Biomed. Res. Int. 2013, 792527.

Gorini, A., Pravettoni, G., 2011. P5 medicine: a plus for a personalized approach to oncology. Nat. Rev. Clin. Oncol. 8 (7), 444.

Healthy People 2020, 2013a. <www.healthypeople.gov/2020/>.

Healthy People 2020, 2013b. Framework: the vision, mission, and goals of Healthy People 2020. <www.healthypeople.gov> (accessed 19.09.13.).

Heidrich, A., Schmidt, J., Zimmermann, J., Saluz, H.P., 2013. Automated segmentation and object classification of CT images: application to *in vivo* molecular imaging of avian embryos. Int. J. Biomed. Imaging. 2013, 508474.

Heller, F., 2013. Genetics/genomics and drug effects. Acta Clin. Belg. 68 (2), 77−80.

Henrikson, N.B., Bowen, D., Burke, W., 2009. Does genomic risk information motivate people to change their behavior? Genome Med. 1 (4), 37.

Hesselberth, J.R., 2013. Lives that introns lead after splicing. Wiley Interdiscip. Rev. RNA. 6, 677−691.

Hindorff, L.A., MacArthur, J., Morales, J., Junkins, H.A., Hall, P.N., Klemm, A.K., et al., 2013. National Human Genome Research Institute. A Catalog of Published Genome-Wide Association Studies. <www.genome.gov/gwastudies> (accessed 14.09.13.).

Hood, L., Tian, Q., 2012. Systems approaches to biology and disease enable translational systems medicine. Genomics Proteomics Bioinformatics. 10 (4), 181−185.

Hood, L., Balling, R., Auffray, C., 2012. Revolutionizing medicine in the 21st century through systems approaches. Biotechnol. J. 7 (8), 992−1001.

Human Microbiome Project, 2013. <http://commonfund.nih.gov/hmp/>.

Jones, G., Hawkins, K., Mullin, R., Nepusz, T., Naughton, D.P., Sheeran, P., et al., 2012. Understanding how adherence goals promote adherence behaviours: a repeated measure observational study with HIV seropositive patients. BMC Public Health. 12, 587.

Jørgensen, J.T., 2009. New era of personalized medicine: a 10-year anniversary. Oncologist. 14 (5), 557−558.

Katsanis, S.H., Katsanis, N., 2013. Molecular genetic testing and the future of clinical genomics. Nat. Rev. Genet. 14 (6), 415−426.

Kitano, H., 2002. Systems biology: a brief overview. Science. 295 (5560), 1662−1664.

Krzywinski, M., Schein, J., Birol, I., Connors, J., Gascoyne, R., Horsman, D., et al., 2009. Circos: an information aesthetic for comparative genomics. Genome Res. 19, 1639−1645.

Kuhl, P.K., Coffey-Corina, S., Padden, D., Munson, J., Estes, A., Dawson, G., 2013. Brain responses to words in 2-year-olds with autism predict developmental outcomes at age 6. PLoS ONE. 8 (5), e64967.

Langreth, R., Waldholz, M., 1999. New era of personalized medicine: targeting drugs for each unique genetic profile. Oncologist. 4 (5), 426−427.

Lautenbach, D.M., Christensen, K.D., Sparks, J.A., Green, R.C., 2013. Communicating genetic risk information for common disorders in the era of genomic medicine. Annu. Rev. Genomics Hum. Genet. 14, 491−513.

Li, F., Glinskii, O.V., Glinsky, V.V., 2013. Glycobioinformatics: current strategies and tools for data mining in MS-based glycoproteomics. Proteomics. 13 (2), 341−354.

Li-Pook-Than, J., Snyder, M., 2013. iPOP goes the world: integrated personalized Omics profiling and the road toward improved health care. Chem. Biol. 20 (5), 660−666.

Liu, B., Faller, L.L., Klitgord, N., Mazumdar, V., Ghodsi, M., Sommer, D.D., et al., 2012. Deep sequencing of the oral microbiome reveals signatures of periodontal disease. PLoS ONE. 7 (6), e37919.

National Human Genome Research Institute, 2010. <www.genome.gov/10001345>.

National Research Council (US) Committee on a Framework for Developing a New Taxonomy of Disease, 2011. Toward Precision Medicine: Building a Knowledge Network for Biomedical Research and a New Taxonomy of Disease. National Academies Press, Washington (DC).

Ng, S.C., Bernstein, C.N., Vatn, M.H., Lakatos, P.L., Loftus Jr.E.V., Tysk, C., et al., 2013. Epidemiology and Natural History Task Force of the International Organization of Inflammatory Bowel Disease (IOIBD). Geographical variability and environmental risk factors in inflammatory bowel disease. Gut. 62 (4), 630–649.

Patel, C.J., Sivadas, A., Tabassum, R., Preeprem, T., Zhao, J., Arafat, D., et al., 2013. Whole genome sequencing in support of wellness and health maintenance. Genome Med. 5 (6), 58.

Pavlopoulos, G.A., Oulas, A., Iacucci, E., Sifrim, A., Moreau, Y., Schneider, R., et al., 2013. Unraveling genomic variation from next generation sequencing data. BioData Min. 6 (1), 13.

PCORI, 2013. Patient Centered Outcomes Research Institute. <www.pcori.org/>.

Personal Genome Project, 2005, 2013. <www.personalgenomes.org/>.

Poduri, A., Evrony, G.D., Cai, X., Walsh, C.A., 2013. Somatic mutation, genomic variation, and neurological disease. Science. 341 (6141), 1237758.

President's Council of Advisors on Science and Technology, 2008. Priorities for personalized medicine: report of the President's Council of Advisors on Science and Technology. September 2008. OCLC Digital Archive. <www.ostp.gov/galleries/PCAST/pcast_report_v2.pdf> on December 9, 2008.

Ramos, E., Doumatey, A., Elkahloun, A.G., Shriner, D., Huang, H., Chen, G., et al., 2013. Pharmacogenomics, ancestry and clinical decision making for global populations. Pharmacogenomics J. July (9), . Available from: http://dx.doi.org/doi:10.1038/tpj.2013.24.

Redshaw, C.H., Stahl-Timmins, W.M., Fleming, L.E., Davidson, I., Depledge, M.H., 2013. Potential changes in disease patterns and pharmaceutical use in response to climate change. J. Toxicol. Environ. Health B. Crit. Rev. 16 (5), 285–320.

Ridaura, V.K., Faith, J.J., Rey, F.E., Cheng, J., Duncan, A.E., Kau, A.L., et al., 2013. Gut microbiota from twins discordant for obesity modulate metabolism in mice. Science. 341 (6150), 1241214.

Sánchez-Pla, A., Reverter, F., Ruíz de Villa, M.C., Comabella, M., 2012. Transcriptomics: mRNA and alternative splicing. J. Neuroimmunol. 248 (1–2), 23–31.

Song, J.W., Lee, J.H., 2013. New morphological features for grading pancreatic ductal adenocarcinomas. Biomed. Res. Int. 2013, 175271.

Syggelou, A., Iacovidou, N., Atzori, L., Xanthos, T., Fanos, V., 2012. Metabolomics in the developing human being. Pediatr. Clin. North Am. 59 (5), 1039–1058.

The Great Debate, 2006. Perspectives on Glucosamine and Chondroitin Sulfate. Moderator: Marc C. Hochberg, MD, MPH; University of Maryland, Baltimore, MD.

Vanhees, K., Vonhögen, I.G., van Schooten, F.J., Godschalk, R.W., 2014. You are what you eat, and so are your children: the impact of micronutrients on the epigenetic programming of offspring. Cell Mol. Life Sci. 71 (2), 271–285.

Vermeersch, K.A., Styczynski, M.P., 2013. Applications of metabolomics in cancer research. J. Carcinog. 12, 9.

Wade, C.H., Tarini, B.A., Wilfond, B.S., 2013. Growing up in the genomic era: implications of whole-genome sequencing for children, families, and pediatric practice. Annu. Rev. Genomics Hum. Genet. 14, 535–555.

Wagner, M.J., 2013. Rare-variant genome-wide association studies: a new frontier in genetic analysis of complex traits. Pharmacogenomics. 14 (4), 413–424.

Wang, Z., Liu, X., Yang, B.Z., Gelernter, J., 2013. The role and challenges of exome sequencing in studies of human diseases. Front. Genet. 4, 160.

Weinstock, G.M., 2012. Genomic approaches to studying the human microbiota. Nature. 489 (7415), 250–256.

Weis, B.K., Balshaw, D., Barr, J.R., Brown, D., Ellisman, M., Lioy, P., et al., 2005. Personalized exposure assessment: promising approaches for human environmental health research. Environ. Health Perspect. 113 (7), 840–848.

Wells, L., Hart, G.W., 2013. Glycomics: building upon proteomics to advance glycosciences. Mol. Cell. Proteomics. 12 (4), 833–835.

Wetmore, B.A., Merrick, B.A., 2004. Toxicoproteomics: proteomics applied to toxicology and pathology. Toxicol. Pathol. 32 (6), 619–642.

Zoldoš, V., Horvat, T., Lauc, G., 2013. Glycomics meets genomics, epigenomics and other high throughput omics for system biology studies. Curr. Opin. Chem. Biol. 17 (1), 34–40.

Chapter 14

Patient-Directed Health Care

In health care, all of us are spending insane amounts of money. Yet the system makes us feel like paupers, as if we should be grateful for whatever we get.

(Goldhill, 2013)

Chapter Outline

PREAMBLE

A modern application of the proverb "Physician heal thyself" (Luke 4:23) points to a subtle shift in medical care, particularly with the resource of the Internet to use as a source of information. Treating one's self is not just for physicians; it is for the rest of us too. A dermatologist in Monterey, CA, told a patient that he didn't know much about a particular skin malady, and recommended that the patient consult the Internet to learn about it (www.yelp.com/biz/rheim-james-md-monterey). Is that bad advice? We think not. Doctors can't know everything. The patient has a responsibility to enter into personal medical care. That is the subject of this chapter.

THE EMPOWERED PATIENT

On May 14, 2013, *Today Show* hosts announced that Angelina Jolie had elected to undergo a prophylactic double mastectomy. Her genetic tests had revealed that she would have an 87% chance of developing breast cancer and a 50% chance of developing ovarian cancer. With this information, she chose to have the surgeries that both removed and reconstructed her breasts. Dr. Nancy Snyderman called Jolie's procedure an example of personalized medicine. Jolie's surgery was also an example of patient-directed medicine.

Practical Predictive Analytics and Decisioning Systems for Medicine. DOI: http://dx.doi.org/10.1016/B978-0-12-411643-6.00014-4

Chapter 13 discusses personalized medicine that is patient-centered. There is certainly overlap between these two chapters, but there are distinctions. Patient-centered (personalized) medicine views the patient from the point of view of the provider. Providers attempt to increase patient satisfaction and good medical outcomes. Patient-driven health care views the patient from the patient's point of view. How can patients take more responsibility for their own health care, and what predictive analytic studies might be useful in their taking more responsibility?

PATIENT DEFINED

Enter the word "patient" into a Google search string, and these definitions emerge:

- Adjective: able to wait without becoming annoyed or anxious
- Noun: a person receiving or registered to receive medical treatment
- Synonyms: (adjective) uncomplaining, long-suffering, enduring, tolerant.

Traditionally, patients have waited; they sit in waiting rooms, waiting for the medical people to dispense medicine to them. Patients are long-suffering, enduring pain, waiting for someone else to serve them, to save them. Patients assume that the doctors know best. Most patients do what doctors tell them to do, otherwise they might fear that they could die. Formerly passive patients may sense that the time has come to step out of that waiting role. Many patients are beginning to "wake up" and take more control of their medical destinies. This trend begs a number of questions, such as:

- What are the limits and constraints of patient-directed medicine?
- What are some of its possibilities?
- What do patients look like when they are sharing in the responsibilities and when they are directing their own care?
- How are patients changing the ways in which medicine is practiced?
- How could they better direct their own health care rather than leaving that to others?

This chapter focuses on patient-directed medicine from six basic conceptual perspectives (see Figure 14.1).

Included in each conceptual perspective of Figure 14.1 are both an examination of the existing research and suggestions for predictive analytic research. The six areas do, naturally, overlap, but we will examine them separately as much as possible. These six perspectives can be expressed in the form of concept questions:

- *Empowerment and Involvement* – How might patients be empowered to become more involved with their medical care?

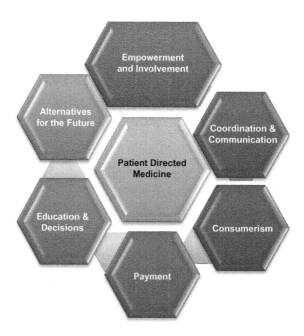

FIGURE 14.1 Six conceptual perspectives for patient-directed medicine.

- *Coordination & Communication* – How can patients increase coordination and communication among their doctors to effect better outcomes?
- *Consumerism* – How are patients using cost comparisons and shopping resources to reduce healthcare costs?
- *Payment* – How do patients pay for health care? What are their choices?
- *Education & Decisions* – How might doctors educate patients and how might patients educate themselves to interact intelligently, and be prepared better to make crucial decisions?
- *Alternatives for the Future* – What are the future alternatives and new models of health care for patients?

Rather than simply looking at what medical professionals can do for patients, this chapter looks at what patients might do for themselves, and at possible areas for predictive analytic research, as identified in boxes.

CONCEPT 1: EMPOWERMENT AND INVOLVEMENT – HOW CAN PATIENTS BE EMPOWERED TO BECOME MORE INVOLVED WITH THEIR MEDICAL CARE?

Involvement and empowerment are closely related. If a patient feels no personal power, that person is less likely to become involved in decision-making, regardless of attempts to the contrary on the part of the medical community. With positive personal power, the patient will be more apt to demand participation, even if the system does not encourage it. The best situation is developed when both patient and physician believe that patients should participate in their own health care as much as possible. Some aspects of this topic are listed below.

Patient Involvement

Cvengros *et al.* (2009) noted that there were inconsistencies in various studies concerning the importance of patient involvement in achieving good outcomes. In some studies patient involvement seemed to add to good outcomes, and in others it was not so. Cvengros *et al.* hypothesized that congruence between physicians and patients was most important for increasing good outcomes. The authors thought that the mismatches were what was driving the inconsistencies in the literature. They called congruence "symmetry." Admittedly, they had many limitations that affected the generalizability of their study, but it certainly provides some variables to test in a predictive analytic (PA) study. Matching characteristics between physician and patient might be examined concerning:

1. Desire for information sharing
2. Decision-making
3. Behavioral involvement
4. Emotional support needed and given
5. Patient satisfaction measures needed and provided.

Hindrances to Patient Involvement

Another literature review stated that empowerment was identified as a key factor in improving health care (Davis *et al.*, 2007). In the article, the authors stated that the United Kingdom National Patient Safety Agency identified that international indicators of patient involvement were key factors in improving health services, and particularly in improving safety. They identified factors that contributed to higher rates of involvement in patient health care (factors predicting high involvement):

1. *Demographics*: being younger, female, and highly educated.
2. *Emotions and coping*: having active coping skills (high resilience).
3. *Severity of illness*: varied by individual (and a variable that might be more conducive to personalized PA, rather than population analysis) – some people wanted to get more involved the sicker they got, while others wanted someone else to take over.
4. *Illness symptoms*: again, an area of individualized response on variables such as individual response to symptoms, type of treatment, and individually perceived impact of participation on outcome.
5. *Prior experience and beliefs about those incidents*: how the individual considered previous experiences with the medical community would impact on the individual's willingness or demands to participate.
6. *Knowledge and beliefs of the attending physician*: how the physician believes patient involvement will help or hinder. For example, in the Davis *et al.* (2007) study, 58% of the physicians thought that patients were somewhat often

or very often partially responsible for medical errors that were committed. Generally, physicians viewed patient involvement positively. However, if matching patients is important, then PA studies might examine congruence and not simply physician preferences.

7. *Physician—patient interactions.* When interactions were positive, patient involvement was higher. When physician—patient interactions were negative, patient involvement was not encouraged and was lower.

Intuitively, it seems that positive interactions, positive self-esteem, knowledge, and patient involvement in decision-making (as much as is feasible) would all score positively for assuring good medical outcomes.

Some evidence that supports this hypothesis includes:

- *Patient involvement in therapy.* Arnetz *et al.* (2004) noted that, in physical therapy, better outcomes accompanied goal-setting that involved both therapist and patient.
- *Patient involvement in medication compliance.* Later, Arnetz *et al.* (2010) looked at cardiac patients from 11 Swedish hospitals. The patients were given questionnaires on their cardiovascular symptoms, their medication compliance, their participation in cardiac rehabilitation, and their achievement of secondary preventive goals (Ibid., p. 298). The authors conducted follow-ups on the patients 6—10 weeks after their hospitalizations for myocardial infarction. There was no consistency between involvement and all final outcomes. Some associations *were* found between more involvement and fewer cardiovascular symptoms upon follow-up. Other outcomes were non-significant.

A study of the conversations between physicians and patients in the exam room highlighted the involvement or lack thereof that tends to occur. Patients expect their doctors to diagnose, but do not want them to make the wrong diagnosis (Gill *et al.*, 2010). The authors spoke of pre-emptive resistance in which the patient had already decided on possible diagnoses, explaining symptoms that agreed with those diagnoses, and then provided counter-examples when the physicians suggested something else. Meanwhile, the physicians were trying to collect data, make hypotheses, and come up with a good diagnosis. The study showed the dynamic interactions that occur in a situation like this. The authors wondered if the patients might exert undue influence on the physicians, causing imprecision in diagnosis. On the other hand, they maintained that such interactions might broaden the possibilities that the doctor might consider.

Videotaped patient—doctor interviews could be the basis of an interesting predictive study of these interactions. In the event of a correct diagnosis, data could be collected to compare patients with active participation and those who were less vocal and more passive.

Articles related to the collaborative nature of the patient/physician relationship include the following.

- *Patient self-treatment can derail physicians' quest for the truth.* Gill *et al.* (2010, p. 16) seemed to cast patients in a role of those not knowing anything, but who made guesses which succeeded only in throwing doctors off of correct paths of diagnosis. They reported that patients were appealing to "categories of knowledge that are legitimately theirs as lay members of society," and presented to their physicians diagnostic possibilities that were "well-known and common sense." The effect of this interaction on the physician was to derail a more scientific process of collecting patient data and forming hypotheses.
- *Patient interactions can be positive.* Cocksedge and May's (2005) study contrasted with that of Gill *et al.* (2010). Rather than thinking that patients were taking their doctors in a wrong direction, Cocksedge and May (2005) suggested that doctors should listen *more* to the involved patients and that patient cues are missed frequently. (This study will be addressed again below in the Coordination of Care and Communication section.)
- *Importance of patient autonomy.* Who should be the one to decide when the patient is incompetent or underage? Dworkin (2003) provided much legal expertise on patient autonomy, explaining the rights of parents to make decisions for their children. Also included in this study was much information on patient autonomy in general. Dworkin told of an old, evidently well-known lawsuit against a surgeon who did not awaken the patient from anesthesia before completing the same operation on her right ear as had been done on the left ear. The patient sued.
- *End-of-life situations.* Likewise, end-of-life choices have special legal considerations (Dworkin, 2003).

- *Privacy concerns can hinder research.* Informed consent and HIPAA (Health Insurance Portability and Accountability, 1996) laws increase patient autonomy, control over self-information, and participation. However, those very privacy provisions can frustrate well-intentioned predictive research.

Patient involvement is generally crucial during the end-of-life period. Patients and the families of patients generally want to be informed and involved, at least in the United States. Other countries may differ. Aspects of end-of-life issues include the following:

- Parents must be included in the decisions concerning their children, in terms of withdrawing or withholding treatment. There must be clear and timely communication and exchanges of information (Giannini *et al.*, 2008).
- Patients are quite vulnerable towards the end of life. They need support from their families. However, in this qualitative study of just six patients, there was not a clear model for support. Lind *et al.* (2013) believed that end-of-life decision-making would be a gray area for future research.
- Mo *et al.* (2012) also found no consistent pattern among patients in Korea, and recommended that information and decision-making should be individualized according to the needs, preferences, and culture of the patient.
- Legal euthanasia occurs in some other countries, such as in Belgium (Van Wesemael *et al.*, 2009). Decisions in those countries need specialized physicians who are called in to consult.
- Over time, knowledge of and planning to make advanced directives has increased, but actual creation of them has not (Cintron *et al.*, 2006).
- In the United States it is frequently assumed that patients need to know their diagnoses in order to take more control of their care. This view is not necessarily held worldwide. In some countries, doctors believe that patients should not be involved in the decision-making process. In Singapore many doctors believed that their patients were not capable of rational thought, because they were ill, and should not always be included in the diagnosis (Chan and Goh, 2000). Instead, family members were included, especially if the patient did not want, or was too incapacitated, to take the medical advice. A similar finding concerning the sharing of prognosis was uncovered in Kazakhstan by Shinkarenko *et al.* (2007). Physicians and patients preferred that the patient not be informed of a terminal illness diagnoses. Rather, the families were to be told the diagnosis.

Variables related to patients' involvement in their medical care might be very predictive in models, particularly those variables that match patient characteristics and environmental (physician/caregiving) variables. If this notion (termed the "symmetry hypothesis") turns out to be predictive, then patient-driven care should include the patient's responsibility in finding a physician that matches his or her personal characteristics. Need for symmetry might also require more skills in the physician for identifying the areas that might not correspond, and then attempting to ameliorate the physician's behaviors to match the characteristics of the patient. Such attempts might be good areas for research. Researchers could monitor physician listening behaviors for use in predictive studies.

Patient outcomes might be predicted from patient characteristics such as resiliency, locus of control, and personal efficacy. Another good study might examine this matching process in end-of-life decisions. Personalized medicine using predictive analysis would be especially useful in end-of-life decisions.

CONCEPT 2: COORDINATION OF CARE AND COMMUNICATION

Patient care depends upon good communication and coordination. Increased use of specialists has increased the opportunities for miscommunication or lack of communication among the specialists, the primary care physicians, and patients. Goldhill (2013) illustrated this situation very well with the example of his friend "Bill," a wealthy co-founder of an investment firm, who began having breathing problems during a ski trip. This event prompted a journey to specialists, who disagreed with one another and did not coordinate with each other. He saw four pulmonologists, a hematologist, and a cardiologist. Diagnoses from this suite of specialists included lymphoma, from which he was told he would die very soon; a congenital heart defect; and lung diseases of various kinds. Bill was shocked at the lack of coordination between doctors about their diagnoses, and how they communicated with him. The specialists seemed unable to think beyond their specialties, and they could not generate alternate diagnoses. Bill's wealth could not generate "more coordinated service." "It was shocking how much work he had to do himself, from hounding doctors for appointments, making sure their test results were communicated to other specialists, to wading through mountains of online data to determine the best treatment options" (Goldhill, 2013).

Note: Goldhill's case description brought back memories of helping to coordinate one of the first Alzheimer's drug trials in the late 1980s. Patient records were replete with instances of the older people taking medications that interacted negatively with one another [this was before pharmacies or hospitals kept track of patient–drug interactions]. Physicians who called the Alzheimer's clinic often said, "I never knew so-and-so was taking that!" Each patient had at least three or four physicians and each one prescribed different medications. Often the medications from one doctor caused symptoms that another doctor then unknowingly treated with a different, confounding medication. The need for coordination has a long history. The patients in the study were anything but self-directed. They and their caregivers were positively swamped with trying to cope with a most unfortunate disease. Those patients needed a medical advocate.

Certainly, disease type, severity of disease, and incapacitation level must be considered in any predictive model involving patient-directed medical care. The point at which a patient needs an advocate would be a good subject for research.

Initially, patients go to their doctors for medical advice. In the delivery of this advice, patients must listen to their doctors, and doctors must listen to their patients. Effective communication is a two-way street. A number of studies have pointed to various topics of importance in doctor–patient communication:

- *Physician tune-out.* Cocksedge and May (2005) analyzed doctor–patient consultations by examining non-verbal cues and behaviors, along with the verbal exchanges. The authors found that some physicians might simply tune out their patients' ideas by using the strategies listed in Table 14.1.
- *What patients want.* Two authors investigated what patients want and who they consider to be a good doctor; in a qualitative study, patients evaluated a physician as "good" if he or she listened to them (Kliems and Witt, 2011). In addition, patients can tell when their doctors assume what the problems are and jump to conclusions about a diagnosis without considering patient concerns (Cocksedge and May, 2005; Kliems and Witt, 2011).
- *Listen to what patients say.* According to Kliems and Witt (2011), German doctors spent 11–24 seconds in the introduction and 7.6 minutes interviewing the patient. Some health maintenance organizations (HMOs) in the United States require the physician to spend an average of 7–8 minutes per patient. According to National Public Radio, the average patient is allowed to speak for only 12–15 seconds before the physician interrupts (Varney, 2012).

Chapter 2 discussed the problem of misdiagnosis (*Wall Street Journal*, 2013a), which many patients do not consider when they visit their physicians. Figure 14.2 lists the steps patients can take to help prevent diagnostic errors. Patients should take the initiative to minimize diagnostic errors, if they value their own health. Patients must remember that physicians are human, and have limitations. They get tired, they must interact with many people, and, just like the rest of the world, they would like to get away and go home at the end of the day. At the end of a day, physicians can feel absolutely exhausted after providing care for so many people in their practice that day. Seldom do they have the luxury of spending hours (let alone days) with a team of junior colleagues debating various diagnoses (as is portrayed on the TV show, *House*!).

In research articles the key ingredient in good communication seems to be the primary care physician, in that the PCP is the hub of the communication wheel (Pham *et al.*, 2009). In the context of medical homes (explained below), family doctors will coordinate a team of specialists and medical practitioners to provide the required care for their

---

TABLE 14.1 Methods of Tuning Out the Patient

Tuning out strategies

- Deferring listening to another time
- Reassuring
- Changing the subject
- Interrupting
- Nodding appropriately but allowing the mind to wander
- Using body language (such as standing up, a closed posture)
- Reducing sympathy
- Being directive
- Making a plan

Source: Cocksedge and May (2005, p.1003).

What Patients Can Do | Steps you can take to prevent or detect diagnostic errors

TELL YOUR STORY WELL Communicate symptoms and timing carefully.	**DON'T ASSUME** no news is good news: Follow up if you don't hear back after a test or appointment.	**ASK YOUR DOCTOR** these questions: • Can you review my primary concerns and symptoms?	• Will the tests you are proposing change the treatment plan? • Are there findings or symptoms that don't fit your diagnosis?	• When should I expect to see my test results? • What resources can you recommend for me to learn more about the diagnosis?
KEEP ACCURATE RECORDS of symptoms and when they started.	**ENCOURAGE** your doctors to think broadly.	• How confident are you of the diagnosis?	• What else could it be?	
MAKE SURE YOU KNOW your test results.	**KNOW** that there may be uncertainty and that the initial diagnosis is only a working diagnosis.	• What further tests might be helpful to make you more confident?	• Can you facilitate a second opinion by providing me with my medical records?	Source: BMJ Quality & Safety The Wall Street Journal

FIGURE 14.2   What patients can do: steps you can take to prevent or detect diagnostic errors. **Source:** *Wall Street Journal, 2013a, p. R2.*

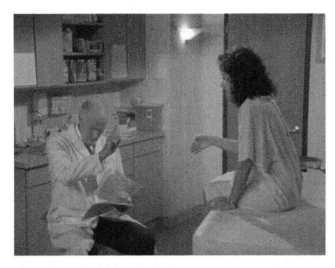

FIGURE 14.3   *The Difficult Patient* (Dr. van Nostrum and Elaine, 2008). Available to view at http://www.youtube.com/watch?v=ZJ2msARQsKU.

patients. Playing a more central role in medical practice will place even greater burdens on the schedules of primary care physicians (PCPs). Generally, PCPs have a high patient load and work long hours for much less pay than their specialist counterparts receive. They have a greatest responsibility for good communication, but have the least amount of time to do so. The direction of a patient's own care can become more difficult and more imperative because of the characteristics of his or her specific healthcare system. It is likely that patients will need to take more responsibility in facilitating communication and overcoming barriers in the future. Patients must ask questions, follow up interactions with physicians, and conduct research for themselves, as suggested in Figure 14.3. They will have to do so with great tact and skill, in order to avoid being considered a "difficult" patient. In the video *The Difficult Patient* (2008), the character, Elaine, reads in her own chart that at one time a nurse documented that she was "difficult." Elaine tried to contest the label, only to be judged by the physician as more difficult. To escape the label she engaged other physicians, only to find the pronouncement following her from practice to practice. Her rash remained untreated.

(The reader should spend a few minutes reviewing this important film. It is very humorous, but the reader should also reflect back on Chapter 2 in which this author shared her own personal story about family members who were misdiagnosed — especially her mother, who had a rash. The reader should also remember that the disorder most often misdiagnosed is infection.)

There are many barriers before PCPs that hinder them from becoming more involved with patient health care owing to the diversity of specialists involved. The following list describes some of these barriers.

● *Physician workload.* The first barrier is the sheer number of other physicians the PCP must coordinate. The authors observed that a PCP might deal with hundreds of other physicians in the treatment of his or her patients. The number of communications and the time to perform them will continue to be a barrier to effective coordination among specialists treating a patient. Patients can help by making sure messages are relayed properly between doctors. This might mean patients can transport reports personally to facilitate proper communications.

TABLE 14.2 Problems in Communication by Developmental Level

Challenges to care-getting	Childhood	Adolescence	Young adulthood	Midlife	Old age
Personal barriers	Trust limited to parents as protectors	Embarrassed to disclose symptoms	Fearful of appearing weak and needy	Conflict between generativity needs and care-getting	Threatened by dependency when asking for help
	Unskilled in articulating needs	Negotiation skills not fully developed	Help-seeking threatens independence	Illness-related loss of self-esteem limits help-seeking	Unassertive in communicating needs
Social barriers	Wants to limit parental distress	Fears stigma from peers	Job/family responsibilities inhibit care-getting	Job/family responsibilities inhibit care-getting	Patient may also be a caregiver
Barriers to getting medical care	Separation from parents during treatment	Only assent required for treatment	Lack of support from partner in dealing with healthcare system	Lack of support from partner in dealing with healthcare system	Co-morbidities interfere with getting responsive cancer care
Facilitators of care-getting	Skillful parental advocacy and support	Strong peer support	Emotional support from partner	Emotional support from family	Advocacy by family
	Supportive school environment	e-literacy; self-advocacy	e-literacy; self-advocacy	e-literacy; self-advocacy	Patient–physician–family partnership
Issues of access/availability to formal and informal care-getting	Lack of direct communication with healthcare providers	Conflict with parents may inhibit medical care-getting	Availability of partner or close friends	Availability of family members/friends/neighbors	Availability of spouse/adult child/friends/neighbors
	Older sibling availability	Peer "shield" availability	Parent/work role strain inhibits access	Parent/work role strain inhibits access	Access to physician

Source: Kahana *et al.* (2009).

- *Personal characteristics.* Personal characteristics of patients can become either barriers to or facilitators of good communication and coordination between medical providers and patients living with cancer (Kahana *et al.*, 2009). This study showed that negative self-evaluation and various disabilities were among those demographics and personal characteristics of patients that inhibited communication significantly. Widowed or divorced women were less likely to get help. If patients had relatively low income or chronic illness, they were even less likely to get coordinated medical help. On the other hand, the study showed that patients had better informal support systems if the family of origin had strong norms of family obligation (Ibid., p. 179).

  Another study agreed that personal characteristics of patients can either hinder or help communication (Kahana *et al.*, 2009). Proper communication was also facilitated when patients had access to various social resources to organize support. Optimism, resourcefulness, faith, prayer, and spirituality likewise facilitated communication. Kahana *et al.* (2009) also gave some advice for treatment of patients in wheelchairs, which insisted that doctors speak to the patient as well as to the person pushing the wheelchair. The patient should be able to talk with the doctor directly. The authors mentioned the value of marshaling resources on the Internet and social networks, such as Facebook, and on smart phones. Table 14.2, from Kahana *et al.* (2009), provides a guide to developmental, age-related issues related to caregiving, most of which represent problems in communication and coordination.

- *Less insurance leads to less care.* One study found that the child patients receiving the greatest amount of good coordination and communication were those with insurance, and those who were less ill than others in the study (Tippy *et al.*, 2005). There were no significant differences related to any other factor. This outcome is a strong indictment for the current medical community, and suggests that money may be an important factor in receiving adequate coordinated care and excellent communication patterns. Under various capitation plans, physicians are not rewarded for taking the more difficult cases because difficult diagnoses and treatment take more time.

Co-morbidities (health problems related to other health problems) also require more time, causing greater expense for their treatment. The type of insurance and payment types may impact communication by subtly influencing the physician, as mentioned above. For example, the physician may have time limits, and perhaps unreimbursed co-morbidities might not be discussed.

All of the barriers listed above are good candidates for future predictive analytics research in the area of patient-directed medicine. Predictive analytical models could be built to determine if good medical outcomes could be predicted by the degree of match between doctor and patient communication expectations. Education models for both patients and physicians might result from such research. Other studies might examine communication styles of physicians/support staff and interruptions as predictors of good outcomes.

- *Lack of patient-centered collaborative programs.* The medical home concept for integrated care is conceptually a good way to increase communication among all entities. Medical homes centered on patients have comprehensive service programs, and use teams of medical providers. According to the Patient-Centered Primary Care Collaborative (PCPCC, 2013), there are five elements of a medical home:
  1. Collaborative (patients and care providers form a team)
  2. Comprehensive (from prevention, to treatment of chronic illnesses; all-inclusive physical and mental)
  3. Coordinated (organized and active communication among entities)
  4. Accessible (better hours, shorter waiting times)
  5. Quality and safety (commitment through use of IT, informed decision-making).

  Medical homes expect that physicians will lead a team in which decisions result from a group effort guided by government mandated standards (Massina, 2013). The current role of the physician in medical homes must change from that of being totally responsible for diagnoses and treatments to one of partnering with patients and the rest of the medical team. The goal will be for more communication and coordination of care. Patients will be grouped into "homes" in an effort to provide consistent care over time. Physicians should experience some relief in burden, but ineffective electronic medical records (EMRs) could decline this relief, and physicians may experience more electronic "paperwork" to document all the required information.

The Integrated Healthcare Delivery System Model

Another model for increasing communication between the disparate parts of health care is the integrated healthcare delivery system (IHCDS) or health maintenance organization (HMO). Kaiser Permanente uses a form of this system (Bevan and Janus, 2011; Kaiser Permanente, 2013), integrating health plans, physicians, and medical teams to achieve positive outcomes for the patients. Kaiser Permanente incorporates sophisticated information technology to achieve smooth transitions between clinics, primary care, specialists, and hospitals, all with the patient at the center (Kaiser Permanente, 2013).

Bevan and Janus (2011) wondered why the IHCDS service model had not been used in the UK, and why it was not in more widespread use in the United States, considering that communication and coordination is reportedly increased by its use. In the UK, patients go to a general practitioner first, who then sends them to specialists as needed. Bevan and Janus thought that overall care would be better for patients in an IHCDS model. The IHCDS model is contrasted with medical homes and accountable care organizations in Figure 14.4. Note that communication and coordination are prime objectives.

In other countries, the more common use of EMR systems and treatment teams increases the efficiency and coordination of care (Schoen *et al.*, 2006); therefore, the trend in the United States towards referral to medical homes may be a very good move.

Examining the elements of the care-giving model, such as medical homes, ACO, or IHCDS, would be a good source of variables for predicting communication effectiveness and patient satisfaction.

CONCEPT 3: CONSUMERISM IN HEALTH CARE

We seem to be in a consumer-driven age. Advertising by doctors and hospitals has become the norm. Sometimes, patients are unduly influenced because of all the medical advertising they see. Direct-to-consumer advertising (DTCA) in medicine

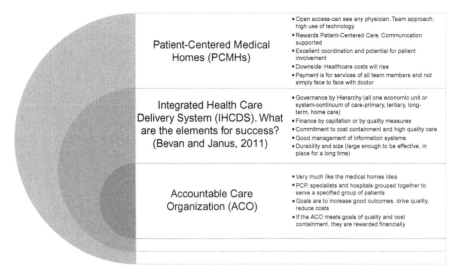

Patient-Centered Medical Homes (PCMHs)	• Open access-can see any physician. Team approach; high use of technology • Rewards Patient-Centered Care. Communication supported • Excellent coordination and potential for patient involvement • Downside: Healthcare costs will rise • Payment is for services of all team members and not simply face to face with doctor
Integrated Health Care Delivery System (IHCDS). What are the elements for success? (Bevan and Janus, 2011)	• Governance by Hierarchy (all one economic unit or system-continuum of care-primary, tertiary, long-term, home care) • Finance by capitation or by quality measures • Commitment to cost containment and high quality care • Good management of information systems • Durability and size (large enough to be effective, in place for a long time)
Accountable Care Organization (ACO)	• Very much like the medical homes idea • PCP, specialists and hospitals grouped together to serve a specified group of patients • Goals are to increase good outcomes, drive quality, reduce costs • If the ACO meets goals of quality and cost containment, they are rewarded financially

FIGURE 14.4 PCMH, IHCDS, and ACO comparisons.

FIGURE 14.5 Billboards today advertise all kinds of "Health Improvement Procedures"; doctors and specialist hospital groups compete with one another to get patients. **Source:** *Adapted by author from street billboard. Please note Gary Miner in photo.*

has greatly proliferated in the past 15 years, and its impact was thought at one time to be negative for patients (Lexchin, 1999; Mackert *et al.*, 2010). The media influence public perceptions, and when they align their products with medicine, scientific research, and clinical tests (or anything that even sounds scientific), it appears that the influence increases. A spokesperson in a white coat or even an actual physician in a commercial may command attention. "Diseases" that at one time were unheard of, such as dry eyes, erectile dysfunction, OAB (over-active bladder), or low T, are referred to commonly in the media, and the curatives are as familiar as gum or brands of orange juice. Billboards advertise operations as though they were cars, as in Figure 14.5 (adapted from a picture of an actual billboard − note one of the authors on the billboard!).

Gibson and Singh (2010) relayed one heartbreaking example of a young boy with pectus excavatum (funnel chest). His condition was relatively mild, and the condition inhibited his day-to-day activities only slightly. The boy was actually very healthy, but may have experienced a somewhat better quality of life if the problem had been fixed. His parents saw advertised on a billboard a new "less invasive" procedure to fix the problem. The advertisement seemed so enticing, indicating that the operation would fix the problem simply, and that it would be easy on the patient. At the initial visit, the surgeon gave the parents a single study showing impressive statistics; he also gave them other educational material on the condition. The parents were intelligent and well-educated; they had the ability to make good judgments. They elected to have their son's chest "fixed." They trusted what the doctor said, and they wanted to believe that the procedure would be easy on their son. The result, though, was catastrophic. Cascading problems and the unavailability of a senior surgeon on the weekend when the surgery was performed led to complications from a perforated duodenal ulcer that were fatal (Gibson and Singh, 2010).

On the other side of targeted advertising, physicians are often pressured by patients to prescribe the newest medicines advertised in the media. Pirisi (1999) found that some physicians feel pressured into prescribing the medications that prompt patients to visit them. Family physicians were more likely than internists to succumb to the wishes of the patients. The problem with this response pattern is that physicians know that patients value the prescription of the medicine, and so they treat the desire, not the medical need. A prescription in hand seems to validate the office visit, for some reason.

Television is a commonly used avenue for the marketing of medical devices and medication. Dramatic effects and hushed tones are often employed at the end of a glorious advertisement, along with music, to generate a feeling of relaxed interest in the viewer. Images of nature and restful bathtubs are used to couch possible side effects soothingly expressed in the background: disclaimers like "may cause shortness of breath, liver damage, increased chances of heart attack, stroke, and even death. If you experience any of these, please contact your doctor immediately." Some disclaimers state that "If you are pregnant or likely to become pregnant, you should not take ... ."; that disclaimer would apply to most women between the ages of 15 and 50, but they want very much to insulate the viewer from drawing that conclusion.

The following list presents some research studies related to advertising and consumerism.

- *Advertising does drive medical consumerism.* Datti and Carter (2006) found that advertising seemed clearly to influence patients to visit their physicians. Datti and Carter hypothesized that the older people would be more susceptible than younger people to direct-to-consumer advertising. Surprisingly, they did not find an effect of age in their findings. They did find, however, that about a third of all the people exposed to DTCA visited their doctors to ask for prescriptions of advertised medications — and about 69% of those received it. There were 2,601 people in the study. This means that about one-fourth of the people so exposed to the advertising received the advertised medicines — a boom for pharmaceutical companies.
- *People are consumer-oriented.* Salgo (2006) stressed that we tend to be consumer-oriented; we pay for goods and services, and we expect good results. Doctors are also beginning to view patients as consumers, or paying customers. There is a dark side to seeing patients as consumers, though. As physicians move more people through the healthcare system, they make more money (Salgo, 2006). It is not simply Medicare that requires physicians to see more patients in less time. The combined effect of this consumerism in health care is to move physicians toward the goal of making money, rather than caring for people.
- *Privacy of prescription data.* Gilbert (2011) cited a Supreme Court case (Sorrell *v* IMS Health) on the question of whether or not prescription histories could be being sold to drug companies, which could use predictive analytics (data mining) to predict which elements should be included in strong sales pitches to doctors who prescribe them. In the end, the law enacted to restrict the sales was found by the Supreme Court to violate the First Amendment of free speech. This sort of targeted marketing is used also by Internet social media and search engines to push medications. Facebook and Google are not the only data-miners among media, and it's not just patients who are targeted but physicians as well. In their own defense, drug companies claim that they do not want to waste doctors' time with talking about medicines of no interest to them. Data mining will be used by an increasing number of elements of our society in the future.

Predictive analytics (PA) tools can be used to save lives, time, and money. PA can also be used to serve pure profit motives, with the focus on the paying consumer. Fortenberry *et al.* (2010) found that billboards were effective in encouraging patients to frequent specific medical practices. They suggested billboard rotation frequency, revealed that the use of corner tabs was unproductive, and suggested ways that digital billboards could be used more effectively.

In the United States (and also in some other countries), people may go to their doctors with lists of orders for advertised medicines and Google searches of possible diagnoses. We are becoming consumer-oriented in our healthcare thinking, and we expect to be served; television, Facebook, and Twitter tell us what the "truth" is, and we want it! If you want to know which five foods should be eliminated to decrease belly fat, simply look at the right-hand side of the Facebook page in Figure 14.6.

Many people use Google to search for their symptoms, and are targeted from then on by Internet data miners.

A good PA study could be to gather information on what diagnoses patients have looked up before they visit their doctors, and then see if the final diagnosis could be predicted from them. Other studies could look at how the targeted marketing affects the patient/physician interactions and final diagnoses.

FIGURE 14.6 Ad from Facebook.

Some forms of advertising are rather indirect, and aren't perceived by the patient. Years ago physicians' office staff welcomed the drug reps who came in loaded with "goodies" of pens, note pads, and handy items that would be useful in an office, all with the company logo written on them. This practice is no longer allowed; however, the representatives still try to influence in any way possible. The pharmaceutical reps still make appointments with physicians to tell them about the latest advancement in medicines. Some medical practices will allow the sales reps to bring lunches for the entire staff. When introducing new appliances for operations, the reps will even go into the operating room to help the physician use the new device properly. The Federal "Sunshine Act" (enacted February 1, 2013) mandated that all physicians must start recording all payments and gifts received from medical device companies and pharmacies, beginning in August 2013 (Fisher, 2013). It would be interesting to use PA to determine the effects of the Sunshine Act on the purchases of devices and drugs.

A study could be done predicting device purchases from reps who either do or do not go in to the operation room, as was done by one undergraduate of Southern Nazarene University.	The results might be quite surprising. See Tutorial Z, in which the presence of device representatives did seem to influence sales.

Additional studies could use sales as an outcome and predict them from various drug rep attempts at advertising and helping physicians.

Perhaps advertising does increase awareness of possible medications — but how much does the public know about the clinical trials that are conducted to validate their use? Do people in the general public understand even the basics of the concept of a double-blind random design? Are those designs being used by drug companies? The answer is that most patients do not know how drug trials are conducted. Most people assume all medicines approved for use by the FDA have been rigorously researched and tested sufficiently to assure their safety and effectiveness. If patients knew that a new medicine had been tested for only 6 weeks (or even as long as 6 months or a year), would they be willing to take it? Do people conduct as much research prior to a knee replacement as is done commonly prior to a car replacement? Do people visit one car lot and believe everything the sales person says automatically? All of these questions beg the same answer: No! Patients should be equally concerned about finding the right knee replacement procedure (and surgeon to replace it) as they are about finding the right car to buy.

Patients must assume increasing responsibility to prevent illness, and to monitor costs and to be accountable for their own health. For non-emergency care, the patient who practices self-directed health care will be concerned about the cost of tests, and how many tests are run, and will investigate the latest research on the risks and benefits of various treatments. In other words, patients must become well-informed consumers of healthcare services.

Comparison shopping is another stratagem patients can practice to increase the quality of their health care and lower its cost. One area of comparison shopping is for imaging services. Many doctor clinics have imaging capacities, where this imaging could be done. Currently, the government law allows hospitals to charge more for diagnostic tests than it allows doctors to charge. Imaging at hospitals may be encouraged by hospitals, because it is much more lucrative than using a physician in his or her own office — for example, the cost for a shoulder MRI in Tulsa in 2013 ranged from a low of $600 to a high of $4,000 (New Choice Health, 2013). Patients should learn about the price differentials before they choose a relatively high-priced procedure. New Choice Health offers transparent cost comparisons in featured cities. Resources such as this one could assist patients seeking information on costs. Armed with this information, a patient could inform the PCP about it, who might be able to arrange for a test at the least expensive facility, and receive the same information. In the shoulder imaging example, the full cost of the cheapest alternative was less than the co-pay of some of the others. Many people use comparison shopping to minimize the cost of car repair; they should do so for their medical care also.

Areas of consumerism that could certainly be ripe for predictive studies:
1. Attitudes of patients and physicians toward new medicines
2. Public understanding of basic research design
3. How influenced are physicians by patient pressure?
4. Hospitals researching the influence on purchases of the presence of the company representatives during operations
5. Medical outcomes due to "direct to customer" advertising
6. Influence of customer price-shopping on services
7. A study of drug trials – lengths of time studies run, numbers of adverse events
8. One could even text mine the long pharmaceutical inserts in medications.

CONCEPT 4: PATIENT PAYMENT MODELS

Proper health care in the USA (and in some other countries) means having insurance so that we can visit a doctor for little or no out-of-pocket expense. Those with insurance are not charged as much for a given healthcare service as those without insurance. As Goldhill (2013) pointed out, we don't count the costs we pay in insurance premiums and monies we pay the government. We also do not count the costs we are deferring to the future in terms of national debt.

When asked, "Do you have health care?" we think insurance. We are frightened if we don't have "health care" and feel vulnerable, helpless, and exposed. For those who have no health insurance, the Affordable Care Act (ACA) came not a moment too soon. The huge downside of the ACA is that costs could increase for many with the addition of previously uninsured people. The outflow of this downside is that, as of late 2013, health insurance policies of millions of people have been cancelled, because that is the most effective way for insurance actuaries to flee the increased cost of covering people without previous health insurance. Technical problems with the ACA-mandated health insurance exchange sign-up system have prevented most of these people from getting new insurance policies. The result is that for the sake of covering many previously uninsured people, many more people have become uninsured. It is likely that this problem will be fixed quickly by the government, but the final cost will certainly be significantly higher than it was before for most people. All of the changes in healthcare delivery will impact how delivery is reimbursed. The changes will result from increased technology, and changes in how insurance will be offered, by the government and in the workplace (Flareau *et al.*, 2012). Patients will have to take an active role in sorting through options to become enlightened consumers.

Research topics on the importance of healthcare insurance include the following.

- *Uninsured people receive less treatment.* Doyle (2005), researching outcomes from automobile accidents, found that uninsured patients received 20% less treatment than did insured patients.
- *Reimbursement amount vs. number of patients.* In 2014, it is expected that people who are within 138% of the poverty level are to be eligible for Medicaid, under provisions of the ACA (APHA, 2013). It was assumed that all those people being added would lead to many more services provided. However, White (2012) found that the number of services was more closely tied to the amounts of insurance reimbursed per patient than to the number of patients. According to White, "either the use of managed care tools or the relatively low reimbursement rates, or both – may have limited the utilization effect of the coverage expansion" (Ibid., p. 978).
- *Length of enrollment can be important.* On the other hand, Howell and Trenholm (2006) compared outcome for undocumented children enrolled in an insurance program for a year with that for those who had just entered the program, and found that those who were enrolled longer were healthier.
- *Public vs. private insurance differences.* Einarsdóttir *et al.* (2013) studied babies from over 1,000 Australian women in public and private insurance groups, and found that babies in the public insurance group were more likely to have a lower Apgar score, and were given less specialized care, than were babies of mothers with private insurance. Thankfully, there was no difference in resuscitation rates. The authors were troubled by the increased risk of respiratory morbidity, even though infants of publicly insured women had a lower likelihood of admission to specialized care programs.

- *Importance of any form of health insurance.* McWilliams (2009) reviewed over 60 articles on the health effects of having or not having health insurance. As may be expected, people having insurance were healthier; based on this outcome, McWilliams argued for national health insurance for the United States.

It seems that some insurance is better than no insurance, but perhaps private insurance is best.

Burden of Health Care upon the Future

When people get sick most of them don't think about the enormous burden they are placing on future generations, caused by requested medical scans and/or procedures, unless they must pay for the procedures by themselves. Increases in technology and in medical diagnostic activity lead to increases in the use of them. Physicians may use new technology as a protection against litigation. Lawsuits increase costs, technology increases costs, and covering more people increases costs. The public seems to expect the level of medical treatment to increase, which leads to increasing costs, at rates far exceeding inflation, even when the rest of the economy suffers recession. The result is that medical costs continue to rise precipitously, apparently without question — as long as insurance pays for it.

Goldhill (2013) suggested that we can "follow the money" when discussing the impacts of healthcare costs. In US dollars (adjusted for inflation), the United States Hospital Insurance budget increased from $893 million in 1966 to $208,419 million (over 208 *billion*) in 2012 (Office of Management and Budget, 2013, Table 4.1). Thus, a 233-fold increase has occurred over the past 46 years. This rate of increase was not anticipated by those who made projections at the inception of the budget (Sanders, 1965, 1967; Myers, 1967, 1994).

According to the US Census (NPG, 2013; US Census Bureau, 2013), the US population increased from an estimated 198,712,056 in 1967 to 313,914,040 in 2012, and would climb even further to over 315,000,000 in 2013. The population ratio between 2013 and 1967 is about 1.58 (i.e., not even twice as large). These figures show that about $4.49 per person was budgeted for health care in 1967; this had risen to about $661.65 per person by 2013. According to the Bureau of Labor Statistics (2013), $1.00 in 1966 would be worth $7.18 in 2013. Multiplying the per person 1967 budget of $4.49 by 7.18 yields $32.23, which is what would be budgeted today to match the cost in 1967. In reality, though, what has happened is that healthcare costs have increased 20.53-fold (661.65/32.23) in 46 years (corrected for inflation).

A greater than 20-fold increase seems a bit exorbitant over a 46-year time period. If the current trend continues, who will be able to afford health insurance? Not very far into the future, it is likely that the only people able to afford health care in the United States will be the super wealthy. This prospect behooves us to become more involved in costs. We should determine which costs we should bear and which we should not. Should we expect insurance to cover the cost of band-aids, or only catastrophic events? Later in this chapter we will analyze alternate plans.

Mis-application of Treatment Increases Costs

Another factor of cost increase is the application of various treatments to the wrong people. Often, it is difficult for clinicians to know for certain if the intended treatment is appropriate — and they certainly don't want to err on the side of sending sick people away.

Predictive analytics can help by predicting more accurately when to use a high-priced technology. Thus, PA can help to keep costs down. Tutorial I describes a model that predicted the need for hospitalization for emergency patients complaining of chest pain. One model was 100% sensitive (correctly identified all of the patients that had a subsequent heart attack) but less specific (correctly identifying a portion of those who could go home). A different model was 100% specific and less sensitive. By combining both models, it was possible to correctly identify those who needed to be sent home and those who needed to be kept in, resulting in hospital savings (Alekseiv and Harris, 2013).

Many Insurance Plans — Few Differences

Insurance plans are many and diverse. Various coverage models that at one time were quite different in terms of structure and function now seem to be blending. All plans are created for cost containment and increases in quality, and their creators do not want to lose money.

The most basic categories of insurance are the *indemnity model* (traditionally Blue Cross/Blue Shield), and *managed care* (HMOs such as Kaiser and Humana). *Point of service* (POS) is a kind of hybrid between an HMO and the indemnity model. Figure 14.7 compares some of the choices that patients might have within each basic model. However, even the basic breakdown in Figure 14.7 does not differentiate the types completely. Within each type are subtypes, which tend to overlap with other models. Commonalities are more prevalent than differences among many insurance companies. Payment authorization often varies between companies; sometimes payment authorization can differ even within the same company.

One example of this distinction in the life of Kevin Dwyer was portrayed on the *Today Show* on July 16, 2013. Kevin was in the latter stages of cystic fibrosis. At 40 years of age, he was older than the average age of survival from the disease, but he continued to plan for his life, including his recent engagement. He and his sister, Martha, had researched all medications and drug trials, and had looked at interactions, mode of action, and so on. They were extremely well informed and self-directed. They found a new drug, Kayldeco, that they thought would work. Kevin and his doctor wrote to Kevin's insurance company. The drug was expensive ($25,000) per month. The drug company reviewer turned down Kevin's repeated requests (three appeals), stating that the drug was not approved by the FDA and was not deemed "medically necessary." What was so extraordinary about the story was that Kevin's sister also had the disease, at about the same stage, and had been approved for the drug. Kevin by this time was close to death, while Martha was seemingly quite well, as she had been on the drug for some time. Martha's company was the same as Kevin's. The two experienced the "luck of the draw" when their requests went to different reviewers. The *Today Show* was able to tell Kevin that he would be covered. The insurance company relented after at least two sources had reported on the discrepancy.

Workers in companies that supply employee insurance may not be given any choice of insurance plans, unless they seek their own insurance outside their companies. Employers may let employees choose between a PPO and HMO. Retirees used to having their places of work make insurance decisions can be shocked at the variety of choices open to them beyond the basic provisions of Medicare, Part B and Part D. Even Medicare can seem scary, with so many regulations and forms, and decisions to make. In addition, with the ACA, even more choices abound. Patients must become informed to make good choices for themselves.

In medical homes, the focus is moving back again to the PCP (Gottlieb, 2013). Under ObamaCare, specialists will have to lower their charges incrementally over the next decade for a total reduction of 16.7% for Medicare. During the same decade, it is projected that payments to PCPs will increase only about 1%. More emphasis and equity will be placed on the primary care physician. However, with lowered costs more people might decide to see specialists, if their plans allow.

PA studies could predict medical outcomes from variables of reimbursement decisions, types of insurance, and healthcare costs. Patient-driven health care is not simply a nicety but might even save one's life.

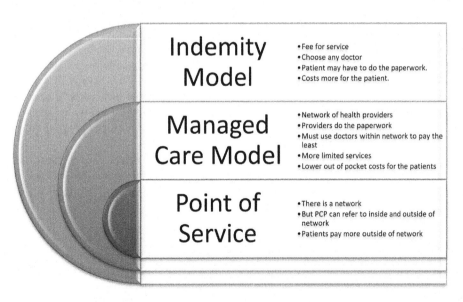

FIGURE 14.7 Models of insurance types.

CONCEPT 5: PATIENT EDUCATION AND PATIENT SELF-EDUCATION AND DECISIONS

How should patients behave when directing their health care? Researching medical conditions can be quite enlightening and interesting (and sometimes frightening), but one thing is certain: a patient cannot make informed healthcare decisions without knowledge about its elements. Genetic information will become increasingly important in self-directed health care. What is done with that information will be important also, and it will be very interesting.

Patients can conduct literature reviews before visiting their physicians. Most if not all state schools allow state residents to walk into the library and use the materials. Materials often include online databases that have huge amounts of articles on every subject. Although Wikipedia and Google have their strengths, there is nothing like visiting research journals for the most up-to-date information. A patient researcher might not be unduly influenced by the results of one favorable study if there are eight others that show no difference, or even adverse events. Perhaps patients should ask their doctors questions and then study some more. Patients could help keep their doctors informed of the latest research, especially that on rare diseases which busy physicians might not have time to read. Patients who have educated themselves with solid research would be in a better position to make decisions about their care.

Knowledge of the results of predictive analytic studies may help patients make better informed decisions for themselves. Sometimes they make their own decisions that differ from their physician's preferences for them. For example, Gill *et al.* (2010) conducted a study that is a good example of how patients can direct their own care when given information. This study consisted of 89 breast cancer patients, some of which were diagnosed using the Oncotype DX genetic test. Results from the test were fed into a predictive analytics model which was used to recommend chemotherapy and hormonal treatments. The model combined a genetics test, Oncotype DX, in concert with other variables, such as demographics, producing individual prediction scores for recurrence, helpful in deciding whether or not to select chemotherapy. If the score is low, the decision is easy and there should be no chemotherapy. A high score means chemotherapy. In the middle, though, one needs to use clinical judgment and hunches. The oncologists had recommended chemotherapy (and hormones) for 42 of the 89 patients when they did not know the results of the Oncotype DX test. After the results, they narrowed these down to just 23 patients that they thought needed chemotherapy. Most of the patients followed their doctor's advice; however, seven of the women in the study chose not to and opted for other treatments or observation.

The Gill *et al.* (2010) study did not address the reasons for the non-compliance. However, the new test did seem to reduce anxiety over choices for both doctors and patients, and the knowledge from the study did allow patients to make their own decisions, regardless of what their doctor recommended. Predictive analytics need not be 100% accurate to provide benefit in decision-making. The Gill *et al.* (2010) study is a good example of how patients really do direct their own care when they are in possession of information.

Patients can be extremely well-versed on the research in a disease or disorder. As previously stated, they can even bring information to a physician in a collaborative partnership which informs the physician. In contrast, physicians can also educate their patients in the office or even in seminars which they open up to the public. Such educational seminars can at the same time advertise the physician to the public (Van Doren and Blank, 1992).

Ultimately, patients are responsible for much of their own health, and they should educate themselves. Some conditions appear very unexpectedly, but others are suspected in advance – as was the case with Angelina Jolie, who knew her family history of breast cancer. Similarly, patients might know that a parent died early of heart disease, or that other members of the family developed Alzheimer's disease. Patients cannot remain simply ignorant of vital information relating to their health, but should meet the challenges that face them with whatever is possible to ameliorate the debilitating effects our genes have on our health and well-being.

Our current epidemic of obesity highlights the need for patient-directed health care. Information is needed both by patients and their care providers. Such information might be part of what physicians teach their patients, perhaps by using patient portals (discussed below). On the other hand, it may be necessary for patients to bring up the topic, becoming more involved.

Often doctors are reluctant to talk about weight with their patients. The reasons are unclear, but determining the reasons for reluctance to discuss one of the major health problems in the USA (as well as other countries) would be a great topic for a predictive analytic study in personalized medicine. The problem of obesity is complicated, but we need to know how much of the problem is related to lack of knowledge about food as the patient chooses what and how much to eat.

Information Concerning Obesity

Estimates are that up to 60% of the American public is either overweight or obese. Obesity in children is endemic and getting worse. If patients are to direct their own medical care, they really need to start with doing something about their choices leading to obesity. Obesity is quickly becoming the number one health issue in the United States, and in other countries as well. For example, obesity rates have grown in the United States from 12% in 1990 to 23% in 2005, to over 30% in 2013 (Menifield *et al.*, 2008; CDC, 2013) (see Figure 14.8).

By examining Figure 14.8, it is clear that the problem is not simply in the United States, although the USA has led the world in obesity. Recently, Mexico is said to have outstripped the United States (though people should probably keep their clothes on in both countries!) (CBS, 2013).

Education concerning nutrition and exercise may be needed, and, probably, the earlier the better. Variables for a study of obesity could be

knowledge of good nutrition, socio-economic status, dietary consumption, age, the availability of fitness facilities, employee

sponsored fitness and training facilities, insurance company sponsored fitness facilities, incentives to join health and fitness programs, Wellness programs, and life style choices (time spent watching television, engaging in low-level exercise, etc.)

(Menifield et al., 2008, p. 87)

Geographic locations of obesity might be predicted from factors such as how much nutrition education is emphasized in various parts of the country. Figure 14.9 shows the geographical distribution of obesity.

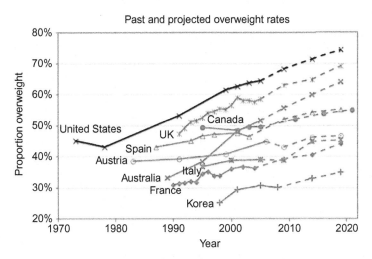

FIGURE 14.8 Projected rates of overweight over time (CBS, 2013).

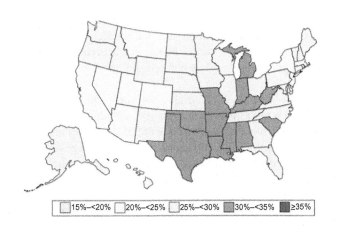

FIGURE 14.9   Prevalence of self-reported obesity among US adults (BRFSS, 2011). *Source: CDC (2013).*

Effects of obesity include the following.

- *Costs of obesity.* Obesity increases costs in health care and productivity. In 2011, costs attributable to obesity were about $73.1 billion for the United States (Yang and Nichols, 2011). Those costs included medical costs, loss of productivity while at work, and absenteeism. The Affordable Care Act (ACA) allows employers to reduce the healthcare premiums of the non-obese by as much as 30%.
- *Obesity contributes to the development of diseases.* Obesity is linked to many diseases and disorders, such as coronary heart disease, hypertension, type 2 diabetes, osteoarthritis and damage to load-bearing joints, gallstones, stroke, asthma, and high cholesterol (Bidgood and Buckroyd, 2005; Yang and Nichols, 2011). Are all people aware of these facts? Nutrition programs can also include the consequences of weight gain, in the same way that smoking education has informed children of the dangers of smoking.
- *Cascading effects of sleep with obesity.* As people enlarge, the incidence of sleep apnea increases − but sleep apnea does not necessarily cause obesity. Rather, there could exist sub-types of obesity, with excessive daytime sleepiness perhaps related to metabolic disturbances and stress (Vgontzas *et al.*, 2008). Short hours of sleep were associated with significant weight gain in a prospective weight study of 7,027 Finns (Lyytikäinen *et al.*, 2011). Further, sleep deprivation of only one night increased ghrelin ("feed me" hormone) levels (Schmid *et al.*, 2008). Schmid *et al.* cited other studies in which leptin ("don't feed me") levels decreased with longer periods of sleep deprivation.

People should be self-interested enough to take charge of their weight and live a lifestyle that supports good health. However, achieving weight loss and avoiding weight gain is more complicated than patients deciding to take charge. Patients and physicians need to stay abreast of the newest research in obesity, and researchers truly need to find answers. Education about the root causes of obesity could be quite helpful in avoiding it for those who are not yet obese, such as children.

Researchers tend to view obesity or any other disease from population statistics. Doctors traditionally look at patients' symptoms, and collection of the symptoms gives rise to diagnoses. By considering population statistics, physicians tend toward eliminating or reducing the symptoms without regard for the individual characteristics of the patient (Haiech and Kilhoffer, 2012). The patient does not occupy the central position with this paradigm. Patients taking charge of their own care can help physicians focus on the individual.

Haiech and Kilhoffer (2012) offered a new paradigm for education and personalized medicine. In this new paradigm the patient, rather than the symptoms, becomes the center of the physician's thoughts. Patient-centeredness can result in a complex integration of elements from the ecosystem, such as viral attack, xenobiotics, and individual genetic characteristics. PA studies allow finely tuned, homogeneous stratification of the patient populations in which the elements aid in the customization of treatment. The process truly *personalizes medicine* (Haiech and Kilhoffer, 2012, p. 299). Louca (2012) agreed that the potential of personalized medicine requires researchers to find new methods of data analysis, given the huge data streams of genomic data and the need for translating the findings into medical practice (p. 211). Truly personalized medicine creates more knowledge for and about the individual patient. With self-knowledge, the patient becomes more involved in care.

There are fundamentally two parts of predictive medicine: the first predicts what *subgroup* the patient will fall into, and the second uses *individualized characteristics* of the patient to help fine-tune treatment modalities. Involving the patient in collecting and analyzing his or her own data can accomplish the fine-tuning, so medicine becomes, as Haiech and Kilhoffer said, "truly personalized." Both the patient and the physician learn about the patient. Tutorials E and F center on weight management, demonstrating the use of predictive analytic methods. Tutorial E examines data from many patients, while Tutorial F comprises an *n* of 1, which allows an individual to self-educate in a way that is very new to the field.

Kravitz *et al.* (2008) outlined how such "*n* of 1" trials could be conducted using a random, double-blind design. Neal and Kerckhoffs (2010) presented a work flow for patient-specific modeling (PSM) used in tailoring treatments and optimizing for individual patients. Their blood-flow models were 3D, and patient specific. Imaging via magnetic resonance imaging (MRI), computed tomography (CT), ultrasound (US), and image processing was used to generate models of computational fluid dynamics. According to Kravitz *et al.*, by using their modeling methods and advanced predictive analytics other researchers have been able to predict aneurism ruptures (Kravitz et al., pp. 112−113) for individuals, such as abdominal aortic aneurysms and cerebral aneurysms.

Pravettoni and Gorini (2011) warned that in our efforts at individualizing predictions in genomic research, we should be careful not to leave out the psychocognitive aspects of the patients. Patients need to be empowered in the process, the knowledge from which will transform their lives.

Patients can educate themselves concerning triggers and behaviors, and predictive analytics can help the process. People find it difficult to lose weight and also to maintain weight loss. Likely there are methods for weight loss that work best in populations. Individuals working with their physicians might benefit from PA by gathering repeated data on their own individual patterns. Tutorials E and F exemplify the contrast of a group study and an individual study for predicting weight loss. Physicians and patients may collaborate through patient portals. The portals would collect the data available to both. Data from many individuals could be combined through those same portals. (Patient portals will be discussed next.)

Predictive analytics could be taught to patients through portals. Patient portals could also be equipped with short courses that patients could take to help them understand studies that they have read and to understand the information the physician supplies. Ideally, patients would learn some basic research methods and physicians would communicate transparently the numbers involved. Researchers could then assess the effectiveness of such efforts.

Patient Portals

More on patient portals will be covered in Concept 6, Alternatives and New Models. However, the topic of patient portals should also be considered in self-education, as mentioned above. Patient portals are electronic, Internet-based applications that allow patients access to their own information and educational resources. Clinics and hospitals are beginning to use patient portals. Although the efficacy of patient portals for increasing good outcomes has not yet been demonstrated, there is much hope that portals will empower patients and allow them to be more informed concerning their own care (Ammenwerth *et al.*, 2012).

Patient portals are potentially an excellent way for patients to educate themselves. Patients can see their information online. They can better direct their own health care with more information. They access test results, doctors' notes, and education concerning any condition. There might also be links to specific diseases and online research articles.

One such study used predictive analytics to find resources for burn patients in the Netherlands. Doupi and van der Lei (2002) explored importing information from patient profiles via EMR systems and then linking them to relevant HTML documents. This study was written over 11 years ago. By now, healthcare IT specialists should be much more able to achieve such results.

Beth Israel (see Concept 6), in setting up its patient portals, invited the doctors, PCPs, to participate (Walker *et al.*, 2011). Those PCPs that participated were able to withhold notes if they felt it would harm a patient, but for the most part the notes were shared by participating PCPs. Patients were enthusiastic about seeing their doctor's notes. Some physicians were enthusiastic and some were not. Most (61–81%) of the participating physicians thought the open notes were a good idea, but only 16–33% of non-participating physicians from the three sites agreed.

If physicians thought that patients would not understand their own medical information, there could also be links to statistical information and patients could educate themselves regarding terminology and research methods. One study recommended that statistics be taught to all children so that when children became adults, all patients would be able understand concepts such as absolute risks, mortality rates, and natural frequencies (Gigerenzer *et al.*, 2007). Mini courses comprising concepts such as those could be incorporated within patient portals so that patients could educate themselves.

PA might predict patient outcomes based on physician participation in sharing notes within patient portals. Effects of patient education on outcomes could also be researched.

Conclusion

A highly dynamic, involved, self-learning patient model contrasts brilliantly with the old view of the patient as recipient — a passive entity.

CONCEPT 6: ALTERNATIVES AND NEW MODELS

Insurance Companies Going International

If patients are not super wealthy and healthcare costs continue to rise as they have in the United States, in the near future they could find themselves shipped off to other countries by their healthcare providers (Gibson and Singh, 2010). Surprise!!

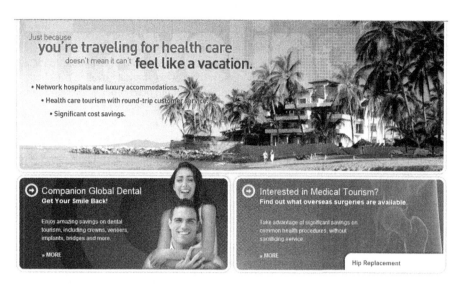

FIGURE 14.10 Come travel with us!! *Source: Blue Cross of South Carolina (2013).*

Companion Global Healthcare is a company connected at arm's length to Blue Cross and Blue Shield. Blue Cross of South Carolina (2013) invites its members to consider Companion Global Healthcare:

Members traveling abroad will receive:

- *Surgical services*
- *Travel arrangements, including flights and hotels*
- *VIP transfer services from airports to hospitals*
- *Passports and visas (if necessary)*
- *Coordination of medical services.*
  While abroad, members will also receive:

- *Hospitality services unavailable in many US hotels*
- *Choice of different room types − from private to deluxe accommodations*
- *International staff with on-site interpreter services for multiple languages*
- *Significant cost savings.*

(Blue Cross of South Carolina [2013], from the Global Healthcare website, enticing its members to consider international medicine.)

At Companionglobalhealthcare.com, the header reads "Just because you're traveling for health care doesn't mean it can't feel like a vacation" (Figure 14.10). Note the "hip replacement" tab at the bottom of the figure. Now, if people cannot afford to have their teeth whitened in the United States they can fly to India to have it done while they get their root canal treatment and crowns fitted as well. Prices generally include the airfare and accommodation. The only thing they might miss is their family and friends by their side.

Certainly, most people would prefer to receive medical care within their own hospital. However, people with incomes above $75,000 but no healthcare insurance might be interested in the savings that international care provides. (This assumes, of course that they have not signed up for Affordable Care and are accepting the penalty.) They might consider an international package for elective procedures. They might take charge and opt for international care. If enough people do their own research and determine that better care can be had elsewhere, why not? They could satisfy the urge to visit other countries at the same time. Where the situation might get dicey is when insurance companies require that patients *must* opt for international care when they are not given a choice.

Alternative Screenings

One company touts non-invasive diagnostic screening tests (Life Line Screening, 2013). Set up in churches, generally, asymptomatic "patients" are queued one at a time to receive the four or five tests that are given. They are later alerted to any abnormalities − information they may take to their doctors. One family doctor in Washington, DC (Common Sense, 2011) stated that the Life Line Screening tests are unproven. It is conceivable that this kind of searching out problems could cause more harm than good in that, given false positives, people could end up with unnecessary treatment.

On the other hand, Rasmussen *et al.* (2007) found that, in primary care, appropriate screening was very useful in prolonging life without any increase in total costs. Their randomized study followed patients for 6 years. It might be good for patients to suggest to their doctors that they be screened for cardiovascular disease. One of the screens in the Rasmussen study was BMI, and the physicians scheduled regular follow-up appointments helping patients to improve their cardiovascular risk odds. (Follow-ups with patients might be a good idea for weight loss as well. Normally, after telling a patient that he or she is obese, there is no follow-up. The situation might change, now that obesity is listed as a disease.)

In the future, rogue private companies might spring up to provide low-cost diagnostic alternatives to patients at the patients' request. Patients who are concerned or curious can find out for themselves — people already are using drugstore screenings for pregnancy, blood sugar levels, HIV and urinary tract infections, and high blood pressure; why not for strep, ultrasound, and so on? Patients could take care of routine problems and leave the more difficult diseases to the physicians.

An Alternative to Traditional Insurance

If patients are to take greater initiative in self-care, they will have to start thinking more like consumers and health insurance may need to change accordingly. As the days have rolled onward since the launch of Affordable Care, it has become fairly evident that changes will need to be made. As long as they perceive that someone else is paying the bills, patients often really don't care how much procedures cost. If they are paying themselves, then they might have a different attitude — they are not as excited about Affordable Care, and they might wish they could shop around more. Consumer-driven health plans (CDHPs) may be an answer (Goldhill, 2013). These plans would cover catastrophic events and would have high deductibles for day-to-day medical care, but also would have lower premiums. Those low premiums could be coupled with depositing the difference into health savings accounts (HSAs). To be useful, the government would have to allow tax-free funds to build up over time. There are caps on HSAs now. At this point people are able to select the level of care they desire for differential pricing. For many people, though, the rollout of the ACA has meant less care for more money.

In contrast, Goldhill pointed out that low premiums would allow more people to afford insurance and they would pay for themselves rather than increasing the burden on government funds. Generally, the lower-income people are younger and just starting out. They tend to be healthier and would not need to pay deductibles, since they wouldn't be accessing services as much. Goldhill did not discuss children, though. Health expenses for children are high, and perhaps plans should consider covering children regardless.

If the child issue were resolved, workers could start saving into an HSA as soon as they made advancements. The healthcare consumer would no doubt be interested in shopping around to find less expensive procedures and care, and that cost-comparison shopping should eventually reduce costs. In any event, it will be interesting to see how the USA solves the cost-of-healthcare problem.

Doctors Striking out on their Own

Doctors are increasingly refusing to take Medicare. By 2012, a total of 9,539 physicians were opting out of Medicare (Beck, 2013). They might start charging what Medicare pays and forego the insurance altogether. Some have begun making house calls now that they have extra time from no longer filling out all the required paperwork. Patients who opt for a CDHP plan as above would surely appreciate a concierge-type personal doctor. They would not have to rely on insurance either. Such arrangements might have an effect upon the ACA. In order for the ACA to work, all will need to be "on board," including healthy young people. Healthy young people might choose instead to take advantage of the concierge physician and CDHPs, despite the penalties for not signing up with the ACA. The ACA demands that everyone has insurance, but quite a number of young people, at the time of this writing, have found it less expensive to take a penalty rather than sign up (Weaver and Radnofsky, 2013).

A PA study might try to predict who will and will not sign up for insurance as the government requires, and as the penalties rise, and who will opt for other models, accepting the government's penalty.

Alternative Ways of Knowing about Ourselves

Genomic Predictions

As Chapter 13 tells us, gene research will become increasingly important for predictions in all diseases.

Note: Nearly 40 years ago, Dr. Gary Miner wanted to map genes and then track people over time to see what problems they would develop. He wanted to track all medical outcomes, such as illnesses, broken bones, and so on, so that he could make accurate predictions from a person's genetic make-up. He wrote a grant proposal to the NIH, for Alzheimer's disease as a prototype, and even devised an ingenious method to bridge the limitations of coordinating his analog equipment and digital computer. His grant was not funded, stating that his new ideas were not "the way in which research should go." Gary, as is typical of him, was ahead of his time.

The future is now, given predictive analytic techniques, as researchers are cataloguing genes, gathering warehouses of data, and making just such predictions as Gary imagined many years ago. (Refer to Chapter 13 for more information on genetic predictions.) Aspinall (2009) provides perspective:

> One hundred years ago, if a patient came in with lethargy, bruising, and night sweats, the best that the physician could say is you have a disease of the blood. Twenty years later we understood leukemia and lymphoma were different. Twenty years after that, we knew chronic, acute, indolent, and aggressive. What happened next created the initial work on personalized medicine — we can now quantify 90 or perhaps as many as 150 different genotypes for leukemia and lymphoma. What are the other areas that we might fruitfully participate?

(Aspinall, 2009, p. 527).

Angelina Jolie made her decision because of her genetic propensity. Of course we all have particular genetic endowments, and some of those genes supply us with likelihoods of diseases. Even given those endowments, to a large extent patients control their outcomes. They may know that they have a family history of heart disease. If so, they could control their diets and exercise in an effort to ameliorate the genetic potential. Equally, a negative decision also controls their fate. Patients could exert more precise control over their destinies by making proper modifications if their genes were mapped and if they knew what probabilities accompanied their futures. They would need support for that kind of infrastructure for data and information. Researchers would need to build a national database. Efforts at building a cooperative database and cooperative research efforts have already begun (LLerena *et al.*, 2007; Kawamoto *et al.*, 2009).

Complete gene mapping is very expensive at the time of this writing. Who will pay for that? At least drug companies cannot patent our specific genes, but they can patent their testing procedures and they can charge. On the other hand, personalized medicine can potentially save money by reducing the number of drugs that a patient needs (Aspinall, 2009). In addition, costs for gene testing have declined over time, and likely will become much more affordable in the future. As we learned in Chapter 13, genomic research holds great promise for determining possible outcomes. The website 23andMe (2013) offers gene testing, for only $99, for approximately 240 "health conditions and traits." Figure 14.11 is taken from their website. However, the fate of the company is in the hands of the FDA, as on November 25, 2013, a warning letter was sent to it stating that 23andMe had to discontinue its marketing (*Wall Street Journal*, 2013b). Many legal and ethical issues will result, no doubt.

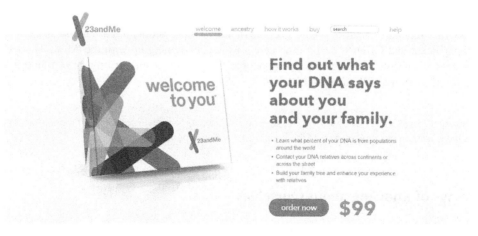

FIGURE 14.11 23andMe.com site. Courtesy of 23andMe.com

On Saturday, August 24, 2013, Gary and I were privileged to help host the family reunion following the Tulsa Alzheimer's walk. This family was one of the families we tested some 30 years ago (Miner *et al.*, 1989), and children of some of the members have about a 95% chance of inheriting their family's Alzheimer's gene. Some of the discussion revolved around getting life and long-term care insurance before taking the gene test. After the gene test, they knew that they would not be able to purchase insurance. Many issues are involved in gene testing, and one is the issue of who would be privy to the information.

Barring a genetic map, people can still examine family trees and note what diseases everyone had. By collecting their own data from their families, they can draw tentative conclusions about what fates await them − unless they consider lifestyle changes. Information on genetics could be another item of education posted in patient portals. People are already swabbing their cheeks and sending their DNA off to be analyzed for paternity, or to determine whether they are "part Native American," or where their ancestors came from; why not to get their partial or full gene maps? In addition to having information in portals, patients could get a gene map app for their phones to analyze their genome and predict future diseases in the privacy of their own homes or at a restaurant with friends. As mentioned in Chapter 2, there are some potential problems with knowing one's genome. The *Wall Street Journal* called the problem "patients living in limbo" (Marcus, 2013). If a person learns that he or she has a chance of acquiring a disorder or disease, what kind of chance is it? Are there percentages that are known? Is the test able to give some kind of timeframe? Are there environmental activities that can prevent the expression of the gene? Predictive analytics has the potential of moving people out of "limbo land."

Physicians might have individual patients track their own data and could engage in predictive analytics to help individuals discover what works and does not work in terms of therapies. Again, Tutorials E and F highlight the difference between a group analysis and an individual predictive analysis.

Personalized medicine using genomic information can streamline and personalize treatments, potentially saving money. The studies below emphasize personalization.

- *Diagnosing tumor types for individuals.* Baek *et al.* (2008) used microarray technology to analyze best practices for individuals to diagnose accurately and specifically for tumor types. They used predictive analytic methods such as boosted trees, and feature selection and cross-validation methods. Although it seemed they were not satisfied with the accuracy of the algorithms developed, they did feel hopeful that these methods could be trained to increase accuracy, and had "good potential for selecting gene sets" that could potentially benefit in prescribing specific and targeted treatments for individuals.

- *Using organizational charting for single nucleotide polymorphisms (SNPs) data.* Holger *et al.* (2008) suggested methods for organizing huge amounts of genetic data used in genetic personalized medicine. They used diabetes as a model and presented organizational charts. They also mentioned a very interesting website for formulating and organizing data, Galaxy (2013). An excellent short basic "101" tutorial, among others, is given at the Galaxy site (Galaxy, 2013). The site is free, and an account can be set up there in order to develop data sets. The tutorial demonstrates determining within one of the free data sets the highest number of SNPs on a particular exon. This was done by first generating an SNPs database, then an exons database, merging the two, and then using an algorithmic "tool" to count the number of SNPs on the particular exon.

- *Possibility of orphan drugs.* On the other hand, Friedman (2012) raised the thought that personalized medicine might actually increase the prices of medicine by essentially creating "orphan" drugs, which are those drugs that are needed by only a very small number of individuals. Orphan drugs are created by some companies for rare diseases. If personalized medicine determines subgroups that respond to medications differently, those predictive studies would, in essence, artificially create the orphan niches. Friedman feared either "mini monopolies" of pharmaceutical companies with the ability to command a high price, or, on the other side, and equally feared, governmental price regulation.

Patients and their doctors could access sites such as the Galaxy site in developing their own personalized studies.

- *Predictive analytics for patient decision-making.* In 2011, Dr. Diane Watson, then an Institute for Healthcare Improvement (IHI) second-year resident, researched ankle injuries and, using predictive analytics, found that two questions asked, instead of the six of the guidelines, would provide more predictability of whether someone needed an X-ray for an ankle injury than would the answers to all six (Watson *et al.*, 2011). Two questions were faster than six and the interpretation was smoother, with a better chance of being accurate. As mentioned above, Alekseiv and Harris (2013), also with IHI, provided their tutorial on a prediction study of who needed to be hospitalized after entering the ER with chest pain. With 100% sensitivity and 100% specificity by combining two predictive models, their study had the potential of saving up to 75% of the hospital costs (see Tutorial I).

Predicting individual outcomes is the essence of personalized medicine. As expected, researchers are finding ways to personalize medicine in genetics (Colombet *et al.*, 2004; Baek *et al.*, 2008; Galas and Hood, 2009; Blokzijl *et al.*, 2010). Evers *et al.* (2012) emphasized that such interdisciplinary and "translational" views of medicine are what is needed. They proposed that frameworks for personalized medicine should bridge all the clinical sciences, as well as the concepts of participatory health care which center on involved patients.

Such patient involvement in fine-tuning responses is possible when an individual tracks his or her own data over time. Self-tracking is what Kraft (2013) called the "quantified self." Kraft said that in order for patients to actually be a part of collecting their own data using apps of various kinds, physicians need to be incentivized to use such data. At present, most physicians are not compensated for answering emails or conducting Skype sessions. Physician incentives would ensure that patients' data were used, and then patients would become more involved in such efforts. Communication between patients and physicians exists when patients are included in such tasks and knowledge increases. Increased communication and involvement enhance the effectiveness of treatments.

Connectivity

Social media have the potential for increasing patient control. Data miners can use Twitter, Facebook, and Google searches to predict outbreaks of illnesses such as flu and colds. Patients can connect to others who have their symptoms to see what they have found out and how they have been treated. Support groups form spontaneously on the Internet for every disorder imaginable. Although physicians may dread our lists, we can also rule out certain disorders even before seeking medical help. There are other sources for connecting patients more directly with their care, and giving them more opportunities to have a say in their care. More and more hospitals and clinics are introducing computerized portals for patients to view and make additions.

A Facebook post influenced the Yoplait company to change its product (Yoplait, 2013) (see Figure 14.12).

FIGURE 14.12   Face page of Yoplait Youtube video.

Online Resources Connect Patients and Medical Personnel

Beth Israel Deaconess Medical Center (BIDMC, 2013), home of over 300 clinical trials, is committed to research and inpatient information/education. BIDMC boasts using all the "gold standards," but also boasts of conducting much research.

Computerized patient portals provided documents and reports from hospitals and clinicians. The BIDMC portals also provide reminders for patients and clinicians. These reports can remind the physicians of gold standards from evidence-based medicine, which can affect not only mortality but also financials. Reminders can help the patients take

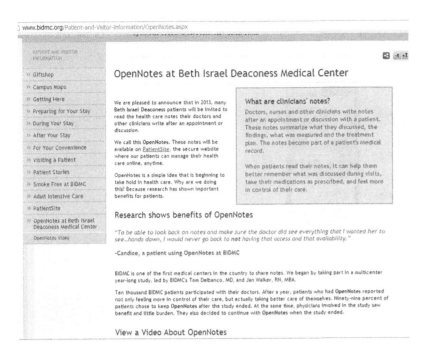

better care of themselves. Portals could be a means of incentivizing physicians to interact with patients and their data, as well as a means for collecting data for analysis — both for forecasting and for predictive analytics.

Also included could be ongoing research projects in which patients enter their own data (see Tutorial F, on individualized weight management). Data can be gathered and analyzed and sent to governmental agencies that require transparency. BIDMC (2013) not only sent data out but also brought them back again, plus additional data, using a structure, process, and outcome framework. The data gathered from HIMSS, the Hospital Consumer Assessment of Healthcare Providers, and the Systems (HCAHPS) survey were matched to their data by using CMS hospital identifiers (Angst *et al.*, 2012), and additional research was possible. Not only did the hospital use data for research but also included the patients in a very personal sense by using its patient portal called "Patientsite" (see Figure 14.13).

Patientsite (BIDMC, 2013) is an online portal for patients to manage their health care. Patients can view their records securely 24 hours a day. They may make amendments to those records and communicate with their doctors and other healthcare personnel. The site is available for PCs, tablets, and smart phones.

The site was to add "Open Notes" (BIDMCb, 2013), allowing patients to read and comment on whatever notes are shared among medical personnel. Figure 14.14 shows a screenshot taken on May 6, 2013.

Innovative Cleveland Clinic

Cleveland Clinic is known for innovation (producing the first face transplant surgery, for example). Cleveland Clinic has gone online with its patients (Monegain, 2013). Cleveland started its patient portal, MyChart, in June 2013, with plans to bring everything in patients' records securely to them by the end of 2013. Patients have access to lab reports, medication lists, summaries of visits, preventive care advice, X-ray reports, physician notes, and so on. One thing provided is a delay in results so that information may first be reported by the physician. In this way, patients will not have to find out they have a serious diagnosis via the Internet.

Body Computing

Dr. Leslie Saxon, USC cardiologist, presented a TED talk describing her Body Computing Conferences of 2008 and 2009 (Saxon, 2010). She defined the traditional model of patient/physician interaction or the "nurturing physician" image with these words:

I'm in a room with a patient that's anxious and that's unclothed and many don't come with their mothers. And if with their mothers their mothers are more nervous than they are. And [I'm] trying to impart some information to them in that very tense

FIGURE 14.14   Patientsite. A video is provided for patient instruction concerning the concept. *Source: BIDMCb (2013).*

environment and then locking that information up within me, who − very difficult to access. Never letting it [that information] go anywhere or vetting it or letting it get expressed, or get further iterated is a big mistake.

(Transcribed from TED talk).

   Saxon mentioned implantable defibrillators, fully networked, which increase sudden heart attack survival rates from 2% to 99%. Saxon has devised a number of electronic devices that allow a patient to broadcast information − for example, there are body tattoos that broadcast heart rates wirelessly into smartphone apps. Saxon clarified that technology, while seemingly cold and impersonal, actually allows for more compassionate care and better outcomes.

"Patients want their data" (Saxon, 2010) − so why not give them the data? If they have the data, why not make predictions that are individually personalized from those data?

Diagnosis Apps

The *Wall Street Journal* predicted the increased use on online symptom-checkers, and said that it was good for patients to search out possible diagnoses (Landro, 2013). The front page advertised the article with the title, "The Do-It-Yourself Diagnosis" (p. A1). It would not be a long step to assume that patients of the future will bring to their physicians lists of possible diagnoses and their reasons for ruling out some of them. Physicians themselves may rely on such online help when diagnosing patients. Making those programs available to patients, perhaps in a patient portal, might help the overworked physician. The patient may be better able to make thoughtful self-analysis of symptoms over time, as he or she is only concerned with one patient while the physician has hundreds to consider. The lists that the patients bring to their physicians could actually be helpful in improving diagnoses, with proper self-education.

   Patrick Soon-Shiong described his "medical information highway" that allows a patient's doctor to submit a patient's tissue to a site that quickly determines how the patient's mutated DNA is speaking to the cancer cells. This information is submitted to a huge database in the cloud. The doctor will then determine the specific nano-therapy for that individual (Fineman, 2013). Astounding as this revelation may be, more astounding is the idea of patients sending their own samples and receiving individualized treatment plans from the cloud.

Researchers could use diagnostic apps, body computing, and such-like in portals as predictor variables.

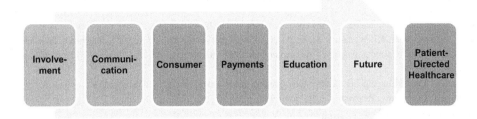

FIGURE 14.15 Smart healthcare is the responsibility of the patient.

CONCLUSION

Predictive analytics reaches all people. People encounter that long arm in every click as they surf the Internet. The appetite for data among data miners knows no boundary, and will only increase in the future. It is not surprising to realize that companies will now start monitoring employees via electronic devices measuring heretofore private domains, such as heart rates and measures of stress, as they say what to whom at meetings (*Wall Street Journal*, 2013b). Privacy issues are already a concern as we become ever more connected to monitoring devices. What social pressures will exist in the future to "voluntarily" submit to an employer's requests for data? For medical data? Who will decide? How will patients participate in the future? What will be the rules for participation? Will HIPAA disappear in the demand for data "for their own good"? These are questions that will confront people as they consider ethical dilemmas concerning an individual's privacy versus that individual's health, or individual privacy versus public health.

Patients in the future will have a greater responsibility for directing their own health care. All the areas mentioned above will impact patient-directed care, including patient empowerment and involvement, communication and coordination, education and self-education, consumerism, payment options, and, finally, all the new advances from genetics and technology. Certainly predictive analytics will have an important place, and researchers today are on the cusp of exciting applications. PA research in patient-directed medicine holds great promise for increasing good outcomes while reducing costs. PA also leaves us with a number of ethical issues that need to be addressed.

In the end, however, patients increasingly must depend upon themselves to be smart about their own health care (see Figure 14.15). They cannot simply trust that their doctors will always know what to do and will communicate with one another. Patients have to take responsibility for their *involvement*; need to be sure that *communication* goes in both directions; must become better *consumers*, especially where *costs and payments* are concerned; need to *educate* themselves to maintain health; and must actively gain awareness of *changes in technology now and in the future*. Patient-directed health care is a life and death matter, not to be taken lightly.

POSTSCRIPT

All the vast bewildering sources of data available to medical analysis beg the question: Do we have to know everything about everything medical? The answer is yes … and no. We don't have to know everything in each area of the data sources, but we should know how to use data from every source. Each source of information provides a unique perspective on patterns of medical interest. How those patterns are distinguished by graphical methods and data-mining algorithms is the subject of Chapter 15.

REFERENCES

23andMe, 2013. The leading health and ancestry DNA service. <www.23andme.com/?utm_source=google&utm_medium=cpc&utm_campaign=SearchBranded&utm_term=mid200&utm_content=23c_Search_Paid_Brand&cvosrc=ppc.google.23andme&matchtype=e&network=g&mobile=&searchntwk=1&content=&creative=29982265105&keyword=23andme&adposition=1t1&gclid=CK6F--_1p7oCFSNp7AodvxkAoQ>, retrieved October 27, 2013.

Alekseiv, S., Harris, A., 2013. Detection of stress induced ischemia in patients with chest pain after "rule-out ACS" protocol. Paper presented in his image scientific assemblage and retreat, 27 June, 2013.

Ammenwerth, E., Schnell-Inderst, P., Hoerbst, A., 2012. The impact of electronic patient portals on patient care: a systematic review of controlled trials. J. Med. Internet Res. 14 (6), 37.

Angst, C.M., Devaraj, S., D'Arcy, J., 2012. Dual role of IT-Assisted communication in patient care: a validated structure-process-outcome framework. J. Manag. Inf. Syst. 29 (2), 257–292.

APHA, 2013. American Public Health Association: Medicaid Expansion. <www.apha.org/advocacy/Health+Reform/ACAbasics/medicaid.htm>.

Arnetz, J., Winblad, U., Höglund, A., Lindahl, B., Spångberg, K., Wallentin, L., et al., 2010. Is patient involvement during hospitalization for acute myocardial infarction associated with post-discharge treatment outcome? An exploratory study. Health Expect. 13 (3), 298–311 (Academic Search Premier, EBSCOhost, viewed 11 July 2013).

Arnetz, J.E., Almin, I.I., Bergström, K.K., Franzén, Y.Y., Nilsson, H.H., 2004. Active patient involvement in the establishment of physical therapy goals: effects on treatment outcome and quality of care. Adv. Physiother. 6 (2), 50–69.

Aspinall, M., 2009. Personalized medicine and pathology. Arch. Pathol. Lab. Med. 133 (4), 527–531.

Baek, S., Moon, H., Ahn, H., Kodell, R.L., Lin, C., Chen, J.J., 2008. Identifying high-dimensional biomarkers for personalized medicine via variable importance ranking. J. Biopharm. Stat. 18 (5), 853–868.

Beck, M., 2013. More doctors steer clear of Medicare. Wall St. J. 247 (24), A1.

Bevan, G., Janus, K., 2011. Why hasn't integrated health care developed widely in the United States and not at all in England? J. Health Polit. Policy Law. 36 (1), 141–164.

Bidgood, J., Buckroyd, J., 2005. An exploration of obese adults' experience of attempting to lose weight and to maintain a reduced weight. Couns. Psychother. Res. 5 (3), 221–229.

BIDMC, 2013. Beth Israel Deaconess Medical Center: we never forget that before you are a patient you are a person. <www.bidmc.org/About-BIDMC.aspx>.

BIDMCb, 2013. Open notes. <www.bidmc.org/Patient-and-Visitor-Information/OpenNotes.aspx.

Blokzijl, A.A., Friedman, M.M., Pontén, F.F., Landegren, U.U., 2010. Profiling protein expression and interactions: proximity ligation as a tool for personalized medicine. J. Intern. Med. 268 (3), 232–245.

Blue Cross of South Carolina, 2013. Companion Global Healthcare: because it matters how you're treated. <www.southcarolinablues.com/members/discountsaddedvalues/companionglobalhealthcare.aspx>.

BRFSS, 2011. Methodologic Changes in the Behavioral Risk Factor Surveillance System in 2011 and Potential Effects on Prevalence Estimates. Available at: <http://www.cdc.gov/surveillancepractice/reports/brfss/brfss.html>.

Bureau of Labor Statistics, 2013. CPI Inflation Calculator. <www.bls.gov/data/inflation_calculator.htm>.

CBS, 2013. Mexico takes title of "Most Obese" from America. <www.cbsnews.com/8301-202_162-57592714/mexico-takes-title-of-most-obese-from-america/>, July 8.

CDC, 2013. Adult Obesity Facts, Centers for Disease Control. <www.cdc.gov/obesity/data/adult.html> (retrieved July 17, 2013).

Chan, D., Goh, L., 2000. The doctor–patient relationship: a survey of attitudes and practices of doctors in Singapore. Bioethics. 14 (1), 58.

Cintron, A., Phillips, R., Hamel, M., 2006. The effect of a web-based, patient-directed intervention on knowledge, discussion, and completion of a health care proxy. J. Palliat. Med. 9 (6), 1320–1328.

Cocksedge, S., May, C., 2005. The listening loop: a model of choice about cues within primary care consultations. Med. Educ. 39, 999–1005.

Colombet, I., Bura-Rivière, A., Chatila, R., Chatellier, G., Durieux, P., 2004. Personalized versus non-personalized computerized decision support system to increase therapeutic quality control of oral anticoagulant therapy: an alternating time series analysis. BMC Health Serv. Res. 4, 27–28.

Common Sense Family Doctor, 2011. Common sense thoughts on health and conservative medicine from a family doctor in Washington, DC: "Preventive health screenings" that are hardly a Life Line. <http://commonsensemd.blogspot.com/2011/02/preventive-health-screenings-that-are.html> (February 7, 2011).

Cvengros, J.A., Christensen, A.J., Cunningham, C., Hillis, S.L., Kaboli, P.J., 2009. Patient preference for and reports of provider behavior: impact of symmetry on patient outcomes. Health Psychol. 28 (6), 660–667.

Datti, B., Carter, M.W., 2006. The effect of direct-to-consumer advertising on prescription drug use by older adults. Drugs Aging. 23 (1), 71–81.

Davis, R.E., Jacklin, R., Sevdalis, N., Vincent, C.A., 2007. Patient involvement in patient safety: what factors influence patient participation and engagement? Health Expect. 10 (3), 259–267.

Doupi, P.P., van der Lei, J.J., 2002. Towards personalized Internet health information: the STEPPS architecture. Med. Inform. Internet Med. 27 (3), 139–151.

Doyle Jr.J.J., 2005. Health insurance, treatment and outcomes: using auto accidents as health shocks. Rev. Econ. Stat. 87 (2), 256–270.

Dworkin, R.B., 2003. Getting what we should from doctors: rethinking patient autonomy and the doctor–patient relationship. Health Matrix J. Law Med. 13 (2), 235.

Einarsdóttir, K., Haggar, F.A., Langridge, A.T., Gunnell, A.S., Leonard, H., Stanley, F.J., 2013. Neonatal outcomes after preterm birth by mothers' health insurance status at birth: a retrospective cohort study. BMC Health Serv. Res. 13 (1), 1–7.

Evers, A.M., Rovers, M.M., Kremer, J.M., Veltman, J.A., Schalken, J.A., Bloem, B.R., et al., 2012. An integrated framework of personalized medicine: from individual genomes to participatory health care. Croat. Med. J. 53 (4), 301–303.

Fineman, H., 2013. Meet Patrick Soon-Shiong, the LA billionaire reinventing your health care. <www.huffingtonpost.com/2013/12/01/patrick-soon-shiong_n_4351344.html> (December 1, 2013).

Fisher, N., 2013. The Sunshine Act is finally final. <www.forbes.com/sites/aroy/2013/02/11/the-sunshine-act-is-finally-final/> (February 11, 2013).

Flareau, B., Yale, K., Konschak, C., Bohn, J.M., 2012. Clinical Integration: A Roadmap to Accountable Care. Convurgent Publishing, LLC, Virginia Beach, VA.

Fortenberry Jr.J.L., Elrod, J.K., McGoldrick, P.J., 2010. Is billboard advertising beneficial for healthcare organizations? an investigation of efficacy and acceptability to patients. J. Healthc. Manag. 55 (2), 81–96.

Friedman, Y., 2012. Will personalized medicine be a driver for widespread price controls? J. Commer. Biotechnol. J. Commercial Biotechnol. 18 (3), 3–4.

Galas, D.J., Hood, L., 2009. Systems biology and emerging technologies will catalyze the transition from reactive medicine to predictive, personalized, preventive and participatory (P4) Medicine. Interdiscipl. Bio Cent. 1, 1–4.

Galaxy, 2013. Galaxy 101: The very first tutorial you need. <https://main.g2.bx.psu.edu/>.

Giannini, A., Messeri, A., Aprile, A., Casalone, C., Jankovic, M., Scarani, R., et al., 2008. End-of-life decisions in pediatric intensive care. Recommendations of the Italian Society of Neonatal and Pediatric Anesthesia and Intensive Care (SARNePI). Pediatr. Anesth. 18 (11), 1089–1095.

Gibson, R., Singh, J.P., 2010. The Treatment Trap. Ivan R. Dee, Chicago, IL.

Gigerenzer, G., Gaissmaier, W., Kurz-Milcke, E., Schwartz, L.M., Woloshin, S., 2007. Helping doctors and patients make sense of health statistics. Psychol. Sci. Public Interest (Wiley-Blackwell). 8 (2), 53–96.

Gilbert, S., 2011. Medicine that's a little too personalized. Hastings Cent. Rep. 41 (4), 49.

Gill, V., Pomerantz, A., Denvir, P., 2010. Pre-emptive resistance: patients' participation in diagnostic sense-making activities. Sociol. Health Illn. 32 (1), 1–20.

Goldhill, D., 2013. Catastrophic Care: How American Health Care Killed My Father — And How We can Fix it. Alfred A. Knoff, New York, NY.

Gottlieb, S., 2013. Doctors will have to take a pay cut under Obamacare. <www.forbes.com/sites/scottgottlieb/2013/06/28/doctors-will-have-to-take-a-pay-cut-under-obamacare/> (June 28, 2013).

Haiech, J., Kilhoffer, M.-C., 2012. Personalized medicine and education: the challenge. Croat. Med. J. 53 (4), 298–300.

Holger, M., Hogan, J., Kel, A., Kel-Margoulis, O., Schacherer, F., Voss, N., et al., 2008. Building a knowledge base for systems pathology. Brief Bioinform. 9 (6), 518–531.

Howell, E.M., Trenholm, C., 2006. The effect of new insurance coverage on the health status of low-income children in Santa Clara County. Health Serv. Res. 42 (2), 867–889.

Kahana, E., Kahana, B., Wykle, M., Kulle, D., 2009. Marshalling social support: a care-getting model for persons living with cancer. J. Fam. Soc. Work. 12 (2), 168–193.

Kaiser Permanente, 2013. Kaiser Permanente's Integrated Health Care Model. <http://mydoctor.kaiserpermanente.org/ncal/facilities/region/santarosa/area_master/about_us/health_care_model/>.

Kawamoto, K., Lobach, D.F., Willard, H.F., Ginsburg, G.S., 2009. A national clinical decision support infrastructure to enable the widespread and consistent practice of genomic and personalized medicine. BMC Med. Inform. Decis. Mak. 9 (1), 1–14.

Kliems, H., Witt, C.M., 2011. The good doctor: a qualitative study of german homeopathic physicians. J. Altern. Complement. Med. 17 (3), 265–270.

Kraft, D., 2013. Future med blog: interview of Dr Daniel Kraft by Quadia Web TV. <http://futuremed2020.com/blog/> (retrieved October 9, 2013).

Kravitz, R.L., Duan, N., Niedzinski, E.J., Hay, M., Subramanian, S.K., Weisner, T.S., 2008. What ever happened to N-of-1 trials? Insiders' Perspectives and a look to the future. Milbank Q. 86 (4), 533–555.

Landro, L., 2013. A better diagnosis. Wall St. J. 247 (19).

Lexchin, J.J., 1999. Direct-to-consumer advertising: impact on patient expectations regarding disease management. Dis. Manag. Health Outcomes. 5 (5), 273–283.

Life Line Screening, 2013. Life line screening: the power of prevention. <www.lifelinescreening.com/>.

Lind, R., Nortvedt, P., Lorem, G., Hevrøy, O., 2013. Family involvement in the end-of-life decisions of competent intensive care patients. Nurs. Ethics. 20 (1), 61–71.

LLerena, A., Michel, G., Jeannesson, E., Wong, S., Manolopoulos, V.G., Hockett, R., et al., 2007. Third Santorini conference pharmacogenomics workshop report: pharmacogenomics at the crossroads: what else than good science will be needed for the field to become part of Personalized Medicine? Clin. Chem. Lab. Med. 45 (7), 843–850.

Louca, S., 2012. Personalized medicine — a tailored health care system: challenges and opportunities. Croat. Med. J. 53 (3), 211–213.

Lyytikäinen, P., Rahkonen, O., Lahelma, E., Lallukka, T., 2011. Association of sleep duration with weight and weight gain: a prospective follow-up study. J. Sleep Res. 20 (2), 298–302.

Mackert, M., Eastin, M.S., Ball, J.G., 2010. Perceptions of direct-to-consumer prescription drug advertising among advanced practice nurses. J. Med. Mark. 10 (4), 352–365.

Marcus, A.D., 2013. Genetic testing leaves more patients living in limbo. Wall St. J. November 19, 2013, D1.

Massina, J., 2013. Obamacare transforms med school. <www.modernhealthcare.com/article/20130204/INFO/302049986>.

McWilliams, J., 2009. Health consequences of uninsurance among adults in the United States: recent evidence and implications. Milbank Q. 87 (2), 443–494.

Miner, G.D., Richter, R.W., Valentine, J.L., Miner, L.A. (Eds.), 1989. Alzheimer's Disease: Molecular Genetics, Clinical Perspectives and Promising New Research. Marcel Dekker, Inc., New York, NY.

Menifield, C.E., Doty, N., Fletcher, A., 2008. Obesity in America. ABNF J. 19 (3), 83–88.

Mo, H., Shin, D., Woo, J., Choi, J., Kang, J., Baik, Y., et al., 2012. Is patient autonomy a critical determinant of quality of life in Korea? End-of-life decision making from the perspective of the patient. Palliat. Med. 26 (3), 222–231.

Monegain, B., 2013, July. Cleveland Clinic gives patients access to their EMRs. Healthcare IT News, 10(7), HIMSS, 20.

Myers, R.J., 1967. What would "Medicare" cost? comment. Am. Risk Insur. Assoc. 34 (1), 141−147.

Myers, R.J., 1994. How Bad were the original actuarial estimates for Medicare's hospital insurance program? Actuary. February, 6−7.

NPG, 2013. Negative population growth: facts and figures. <www.npg.org/facts/us_historical_pops.htm>.

Neal, M., Kerckhoffs, R., 2010. Current progress in patient-specific modeling. Brief. Bioinform. 11 (1), 111−126.

New Choice Health, 2013. Your healthcare marketplace. <www.newchoicehealth.com/Home>.

Office of Management and Budget, 2013. Historical Tables. Table 2.4 Composition of social insurance and retirement receipts and of excise taxes: 1940−2018. <www.whitehouse.gov/omb/budget/Historicals> (retrieved 5 May, 2013).

PCPCC, 2013. About us: the leading national coalition dedicated to advancing the patient-centered medical home. <www.pcpcc.org/about>.

Pham, H.H., O'Malley, A.S., Bach, P.B., Saiontz-Martinez, C., Schrag, D., 2009. Primary care physicians' links to other physicians through medicare patients: the scope of care coordination. Ann. Intern. Med. 150 (4), 236-W:40.

Pirisi, A., 1999. Patient-directed drug advertising puts pressure on US doctors. Lancet. 354 (9193), 1887.

Pravettoni, G., Gorini, A., 2011. A P5 cancer medicine approach: why personalized medicine cannot ignore psychology. J. Eval. Clin. Pract. 17 (4), 594−596.

Rasmussen, S.R., Thomsen, J.L., Kilsmark, J., Hvenegaard, A., Engberg, M., Lauritzen, T., et al., 2007. Preventive health screenings and health consultations in primary care increase life expectancy without increasing costs. Scand. J. Public Health. 35 (4), 365−372.

Salgo, P., 2006. The doctor will see you for exactly seven minutes. <www.nytimes.com/2006/03/22/opinion/22salgo.html?_r=2&> (March 22, 2006).

Sanders, B.S., 1965. What would Medicare cost? J. Risk Insur. 32 (4), 579−594.

Sanders, B.S., 1967. What would Medicare cost? Author's reply. J. Risk Insur. 34 (1), 148−166.

Saxon, L., 2010. Body computing and network communications. <www.youtube.com/watch?v=bl9do6mGq1M> (August 18, 2010).

Schmid, S.M., Hallschmid, M., Jauch-Chara, K., Born, J., Schultes, B., 2008. A single night of sleep deprivation increases ghrelin levels and feelings of hunger in normal-weight healthy men. J. Sleep Res. 17 (3), 331−334.

Schoen, C., Osborn, R., Huynh, P.T., Doty, M., Peugh, J., Zapert, K., 2006. On the front lines of care: primary care doctors' office systems, experiences, and views in seven countries. Health Aff. 25 (6), w555−w571.

Shinkarenko, A., Shinkarenko, I. Miner, L.A., Miner, G.D., 2007, June. Truth telling about terminal diagnoses in Kazakhstan. Paper presented at the 25th Annual Scientific Assembly and Retreat, IHI Family Medical Residency Program, Western Hills.

Tippy, K., Meyer, K., Aronson, R., Wall, T., 2005. Characteristics of coordinated ongoing comprehensive care within a medical home in Maine. Matern. Child Health J. 9 (2 Suppl), S13−S21.

US Census Bureau, 2013. US Department of Commerce: US Census Bureau. <www.census.gov/#>.

Van Doren, D.C., Blank, K.M., 1992. Patient education: a potential marketing tool for the private physician. J. Health Care Mark. 12 (1), 71−77.

Van Wesemael, Y., Cohen, J., Onwuteaka-Philipsen, B.D., Bilsen, J., Distelmans, W., Deliens, L., 2009. Role and involvement of life end information forum physicians in euthanasia and other end-of-life care decisions in Flanders, Belgium. Health Serv. Res. 44 (6), 2180−2192.

Varney, S., 2012. What's Up, Doc? When Your Doctor Rushes Like The Road Runner. <www.npr.org/blogs/health/2012/05/24/153583423/whats-up-doc-when-your-doctor-rushes-like-the-road-runner> (May 24, 2012).

Vgontzas, A.N., Bixler, E.O., Chrousos, G.P., Pejovic, S., 2008. Obesity and sleep disturbances: meaningful sub-typing of obesity. Arch. Physiol. Biochem. 114 (4), 224−236.

Walker, J., Leveille, S.G., Ngo, N., Vodicka, E., Darer, J.D., Dhanireddy, S., et al., 2011. Inviting patients to read their doctors' notes: patients and doctors look ahead. Ann. Intern. Med. 155 (12), 811−819.

Wall Street Journal, 2013a. Journal Report Leadership: Information Technology Dow Jones and Company, pp. R1−R6 (October 21).

Wall Street Journal, 2013b. The FDA and Thee: regulators move to control 23andMe's new genetic tests. <http://online.wsj.com/news/articles/SB10001424052702304465604579220003539640102> (November 25, 2013).

Watson, D., Rylander, E., Miner, L.A., Miner, G.D., 2011, June. Ottawa guidelines for ankle X-rays; An incidence Study at Family Medical Care. Paper presented at the 29th Annual Scientific Assembly and Retreat, IHI Family Medical Residency Program, Western Hills, OK.

Weaver, C., Radnofsky, L., 2013. Health Website Woes Widen as Insurers Get Wrong Data. The Washington Post, October 17, 2013.

White, C., 2012. A comparison of two approaches to increasing access to care: expanding coverage versus increasing physician fees. Health Serv. Res. 47 (3 Pt 1), 963−983.

Yang, Y., Nichols, L.M., 2011. Obesity and health system reform: private vs. public responsibility. J. Law Med. Ethics. 39 (3), 380−386.

Yoplait, 2013. Sparked by a post. <www.youtube.com/watch?v=is_yJAo38M8>.

FURTHER READING

Allain, G., 2012. Personalized medicine. MLO Med. Lab. Obs. 44 (7), 54−58.

Brune, K., 2011. Culture change in long term care services: Eden-Greenhouse-Aging in the community. Educ. Gerontol. 37 (6), 506−525.

Chambers, J.A., Swanson, V., 2012. Stories of weight management: factors associated with successful and unsuccessful weight maintenance. Br. J. Health Psychol. 17 (2), 223−243.

Council, L., Geffken, D., Valeras, A., Orzano, A., Rechisky, A., Anderson, S., 2012. A medical home: changing the way patients and teams relate through patient-centered care plans. Fam. Syst. Health. 30 (3), 190−198.

Deakin, D., 2011. Personalized medicine. Oncology & Clinical Trials in the 21st Century. [Online article]. pp. 14−17. <http://www.pitt.edu/~anq5/trends.html>.

Epstein, R.S., Teagarden, J., 2010. Comparative effectiveness research and personalized medicine. Pharmacoeconomics. 28 (10), 905−913.

Fleck, L.M., 2010. Personalized medicine's ragged edge. Hastings Cent. Rep. 40 (5), 16.

Freeman, R., 2010. Personalized medicine and oncology: a commentary and key questions. J. Commer. Biotechnol. 16 (3), 197−200.

Gass, D.A., 2011. Impact of recent IP caselaw on biomarkers and personalized medicine. J. Commer. Biotechnol. 17 (2), 191−194.

Gilbert, S., 2010. Personalized cancer care in an age of anxiety. Hastings Cent. Rep. 40 (5), 18.

Gundert-Remy, U., Dimovski, A., Gajović, S., 2012. Personalized medicine − where do we stand? pouring some water into wine: a realistic perspective. Croat. Med. J. 53 (4), 314−320.

Hallin, K., Henriksson, P., Dalén, N., Kiessling, A., 2011. Effects of interprofessional education on patient perceived quality of care. Med. Teach. 33 (1), e22−e26.

Heyman, J.C., Sealy, Y.M., 2011. Physicians' involvement with the New York State health care proxy. Educ. Gerontol. 37 (8), 674−686.

Hindle, L.L., Carpenter, C.C., 2011. An exploration of the experiences and perceptions of people who have maintained weight loss. J. Hum. Nutr. Diet. 24 (4), 342−350.

Holland, D.J., Bradley, D.W., Khoury, J.M., 2005. Sending men the message about preventive care:an evaluation of communication strategies. Int. J. Mens Health. 4 (2), 97−114.

Kaufman, M.B., 2011. Meeting coverage. Decision-makers urged to put personalized medicine into action. Formulary. 46 (11), 502.

Korostishevsky, M.M., Cohen, Z.Z., Malkin, I.I., Ermakov, S.S., Yarenchuk, O.O., Livshits, G.G., 2010. Morphological and biochemical features of obesity are associated with mineralization genes' polymorphisms. Int. J. Obes. 34 (8), 1308−1318.

Krilich, C., 2011. Lessons learned at a patient-centered medical home. Physician Exec. 37 (2), 58−63.

Li, C.C., 2011. Personalized medicine − the promised land: are we there yet? Clin. Genet. 79 (5), 403−412.

Lindh, M., Hugo, J., 2005. Students' reflections on self-directed learning using patient studies in a masters programme in family medicine in South Africa. Educ. Prim. Care. 16 (4), 474−481.

Loftus, N., 2013. The Sunshine Act is finally final. <www.forbes.com/sites/aroy/2013/02/11/the-sunshine-act-is-finally-final/> (February 11, 2013).

Lubitz, S.A., Ellinor, P.T., 2012. Personalized medicine and atrial fibrillation: will it ever happen? BMC Med. 10 (1), 1−8.

Marsh, E., 2013. Reflections of a medical ex-practitioner. Wall St. J. (East Ed). A19.

McGinnis, J., 2010. Evidence-based medicine. Inf. Knowl. Syst. Manag. 8 (1−4), 145−157.

Needham, B.R., 2012. The truth about patient experience: what we can learn from other industries, and how three Ps can improve health outcomes, strengthen brands, and delight customers. J. Healthc. Manag. 57 (4), 255−263.

Raparia, K., Villa, C., DeCamp, M.M., Patel, J.D., Mehta, M.P., 2013. Molecular profiling in non-small cell lung cancer: a step toward personalized medicine. Arch. Pathol. Lab. Med. 137 (4), 481−491.

Redfern, J., Mckevitt, C., Wolfe, C.A., 2006. Risk management after stroke: the limits of a patient-centred approach. Health Risk Soc. 8 (2), 123−141.

Schilsky, R.L., 2010. Personalized medicine in oncology: the future is now. Nat. Rev. Drug Discov. 9 (5), 363−366.

Shahar, E., 2008. Does anyone know the road from a randomized trial to personalized medicine? a review of 'treating individuals. from randomized trials to personalised medicine,' Peter M. Rothwell. J. Eval. Clin. Pract. 14 (5), 726−731.

Sohn, S., 2011. Making personalized health care more precise: implications of neuroscientific findings. J. Neurosci. Psychol. Econ. 4 (1), 37−43.

Spiegelman, P., 2007. Retention recipe. Mark. Health Serv. 27 (2), 40.

The Difficult Patient, 2008. Dr. van Nostrum and Elaine. (Video).

Toiviainen, H.K., Vuorenkoski, L.H., Hemminki, E.K., 2010. Patient organizations in Finland: increasing numbers and great variation. Health Expect. 13 (3), 221−233.

Yurkiewicz, S., 2010. The prospects for personalized medicine. Hastings Cent. Rep. 40 (5), 14.

Prologue to Part 1, Chapter 15

This prologue is for a single chapter, Chapter 15 ... you will discover the reason why this chapter was "singled out" as you read below.

Chapter 15 is the real introduction to the "nuts and bolts" of predictive analytics for healthcare, medicine, and medical research. Topics discussed include graphics and simple visualization in medical predictive analytics; using data to predict important outcomes; the algorithms of true machine learning predictive analytics; using the right algorithm for the right purpose; using clustering for comparative effectiveness research; and heterogeneous treatment effect (HTE) analysis of drug and other treatment modalities. Additionally text analytics, dimension reduction, and link analysis are discussed as they apply to medical problems.

Rather than repeating here in Chapter 15 all of the details of predictive analytic methodology including data mining and text analytics, the reader who wants more detail can find it in the previous two books in this "mini-series":

- *Statistical Analysis & Data Mining Applications*, by Nisbet, R., Elder, J., and Miner, G. 2009. Elsevier/Academic Press, New York, NY.
- *Practical Text Mining and Statistical Analysis for Non-Structured Text Data Applications*, by Miner, G., Delen, D., Elder, J., Fast, A., Hill, T., and Nisbet, B. 2012. Elsevier/Academic Press, New York, NY.

Chapter 15

Prediction in Medicine — The Data Mining Algorithms of Predictive Analytics

Chapter Outline

PREAMBLE

There is a bewildering array of graphical methods and data mining algorithms available for use to distinguish relationships between various medical outcomes and the vast number of variables available in electronic health records (EHRs) and other medical records. This chapter describes major types of techniques in relationship to their strengths and weaknesses, and the best way to use them in medical informatics studies.

INTRODUCTION

The purpose of this chapter is to provide a general overview of the algorithms used in predictive analytics, specifically with regard to medical applications. This general overview does not go into the detail which has been expertly provided in other texts (Hill and Lewicki, 2007; Hastie *et al.*, 2009; Nisbet *et al.*, 2009), but gives an overview of the algorithms which are masterfully covered in those books.

Many of the chapters of this book discuss applications of modern predictive modeling techniques to predict risk, cluster symptoms, and patient outcomes. This chapter provides a summary of the typical algorithms and "tools" that are used to derive accurate and actionable information and predictions from data. The methods described here are used commonly in various domains where decisions can be improved by consulting historical data, leveraging the repeatable patterns found in those data that enable accurate predictions and insights. These methods and algorithms have transformed many business processes significantly — for example, by predicting credit risk more accurately, identifying probable fraud, or gauging customers' propensity to purchase certain goods or services. There is little doubt that these methods are transforming healthcare delivery, and the monitoring of its effectiveness.

The purpose of this chapter is to provide general overviews of different types of analytical approaches and algorithms used in these applications. Most of these methods are implemented in modern comprehensive analytics platforms and frameworks. In order to evaluate the suitability of certain algorithms and methods to solve certain problems, it is necessary to understand the nature of the computations that are performed by them; it is not necessary, however, to understand all details of the computations that are performed. The goal of this chapter is *not* to provide detailed formulas or discussions of algorithm implementation, but rather to present the logic, applicability, and strengths and weaknesses of different methods. References are provided for those who wish to understand the details of the computations used by these methods.

THE USE OF SIMPLE DESCRIPTIVE STATISTICS, GRAPHICS, AND VISUAL DATA MINING IN PREDICTIVE ANALYTICS

Prior to completing any data analysis project, the first step which should be taken is to understand the data that will be used in the analysis. This is as true for predictive analytics as it is for t-tests, multiple regression, and analysis of variance. Predictive analytics must be viewed through a lens which has insight into the problem at hand; without this insight, conclusions would be based upon suppositions and assumptions which could lead to unwelcome and even disastrous results. Therefore, before proceeding to discussions of the algorithms that compose the broad scope of predictive analytics, it will be most beneficial to review how simple descriptive statistics, graphics, and visual data mining can assist in understanding the basic distributions and relationships of the data that will be used in predictive modeling.

The Insight of Simple Descriptive Statistics

Of the wide variety of statistical tools that are available in the world of Business Intelligence, several of the most beneficial are tabulation and cross-tabulation of data, which are heavily relied upon to help understand data. This is true for traditional data analysis, and it is true also for predictive analytics. Through the use of simple frequency tables, insight can be gained about trends among the variables, relationships which may be shared among variables, and the nature of the data that will be utilized in further analysis.

The understanding imparted by the investigation of simple descriptive statistics is a necessary step in predictive analytics. Through this initial and often elementary investigation a unique understanding can be gained into the demographics of a patient population — for instance, changes in patient diagnoses, and even trends in areas of practice management. If through the review of patient diagnoses you see that your population of type II diabetics is steadily increasing, you can expect that you will see a higher increase of referrals for patient education, specialist appointments for podiatrists and ophthalmologists, and possibly emergency room visits. It is through the review of simple descriptive statistics that the relationships among these latter groups are related to the changes in a patient population.

Visual Data Mining

Not only are graphical summaries useful to review and investigate interesting patterns found in descriptive statistics; additional insights can also be gained through viewing this information in graphical form. The human ability to detect patterns or trends from visual summaries of data should not be underestimated, and often is one of the most useful ways to gain new insights. Visual inspection of graphics is sometimes called visual data mining. In particular, salient patterns can be detected when variables are broken down by meaningful dimensions, categorized across other variables of interest, or otherwise augmented. For example, you may want to view average patient characteristics such as body mass index (BMI) across various grouping variables such as surgical wound classifications.

- *Surgical wound classification and BMI.* To illustrate how simple graphs based on variables averaged across groups can yield important insights; consider the graph shown in Figure 15.1.

  The figure shows the mean BMI for a sample of patients who had surgery from January 1, 2011 through June 30, 2012. Surgical wound classifications utilize the degree of contamination present in a wound to predict the risk of postoperative infections. This provides valuable information related to outcomes for educational, economical, and clinical purposes; also, it improves health care quality and aids in reporting.

  It is apparent that patients with a higher average BMI have an increased occurrence of wound type class *Clean-Contaminated*. This type includes any wound open for drainage or reopened to remove wires or pins, or for other surgical reasons. While these are considered as clean wounds, they carry a higher potential for infection.

- *Heart rate and current procedural terminology (CPT) code groupings.* To illustrate the "power" of simple graphical summaries based on visual data mining results, in another example, consider the graph in Figure 15.2.

  The charts in Figure 15.2 were derived from 1,302 records of surgeries. The analyses leading to these results consisted of first classifying the CPT codes into groups by anatomy. The cases can then be analyzed, even in real time, to assign each surgery to one or more of these categories, without requiring the attending physician to make the determination and classification.

  The next step in this application can then consist simply of an analysis of any other variable of interest compared to these groupings. For example, it is apparent that higher heart rates are associated with groupings of Liver and Adrenal, while lower heart rates are associated with Breast. Further analysis can then be conducted on these groupings, if they are considered to be of interest or determined to be actionable. Again, simple graphical analyses and presentation of results can quickly identify important and actionable information.

One of the primary benefits of visual data mining is that interesting and important insights can be gained immediately through visual inspection of graphical representations of data. It can be much easier, and more efficient, to view a series of graphs representing data than to review analytical results from Random Forests, for purposes of preliminary review and initial understanding of data. Scatterplots, means plots, variability plots, and a wide range of other graphs are the mainstay of visual data mining, especially when categorized or viewed across other variables. As the age of Big Data progresses, however, innovative and interactive tools will continue to be created which aid in data visualization, assisting in the ability to detect patterns and trends in data through initial visual inspection. This initial inspection is invaluable in gaining information about variable distributions, value ranges, interactions, relationships among variables, and clusters of cases across variable ranges.

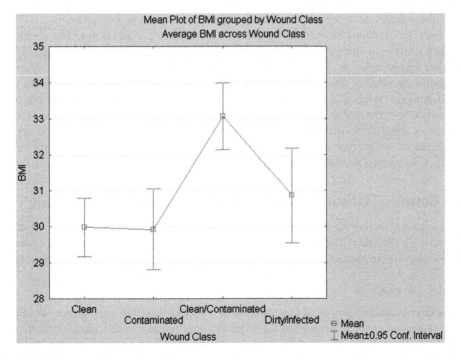

FIGURE 15.1 Mean plot of BMI grouped by wound class.

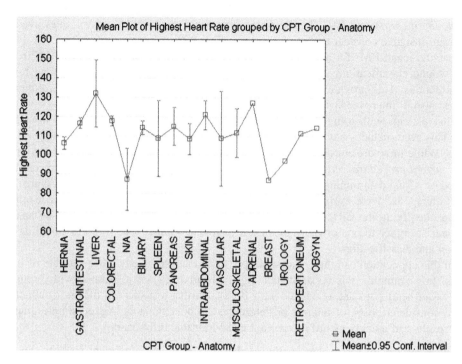

FIGURE 15.2 Average highest heart rate by CPT code groupings.

PREDICTIVE MODELING: USING DATA TO PREDICT IMPORTANT OUTCOMES

Predictive analytics, which includes data mining methods, are employed commonly to improve the level of predictability for outcomes of interest or key performance indicators (KPIs). At the most basic level, predictive modeling seeks an adequate model for an outcome variable as a function of a vector of predictors in the form of $y = f(x)$, where y is the outcome predicted from a vector of predictors. The task is to predict an outcome y based on a vector of values for predictor variables $x_1, x_2, \ldots, x_n$. For example, y could be a discrete outcome such as the American Society of Anesthesiologists (ASA) physical status classification, or fraudulent medical claim behavior, and the predictors x could consist of physical fitness scores or coded properties of the client chart, to name but a few.

Advances in technology over time have improved many algorithms to permit them to run on data sets very quickly, while completing such analyses would have taken days or even weeks just a few short years ago. These data sets are so large that they can no longer reside on a physical hard drive, but are now in distributed file systems or in the cloud. This is especially true in the medical field, where the size of databases grows exponentially over time.

In many medical domains, predictive modeling is now performed routinely in order to predict outcomes with models, which are subsequently optimized to improve various KPIs. Moreover, information can be extracted from unstructured data forms such as detailed physician notes, insurance claim narratives, or adjuster notes, and leveraged through text mining and alignment with other numerical data. Thus, additional opportunities are provided to enhance the accuracy of the predictive models, providing unmatched benefit to medical organizations or governmental institutions.

The Difference Between Statistical Models and General Predictive Modeling

Before proceeding to general overviews of the algorithms used in predictive analytics, it is necessary to review the differences that exist between statistical models that are considered traditional statistical analysis techniques, such as multiple regression and logistic regression, and those algorithms that are used in predictive analytics and data mining.

Traditional Statistical Analysis

The driving force behind traditional statistical data analysis is hypothesis testing and estimation of parameters. A good example is multiple regression (part of the general linear model in principle). In this analytical approach, the parameters of a model are estimated through the observed least squares approach. Those parameters are used in an equation which will then predict an outcome variable or response variable y as a linear function of the available predictors, or x, variables.

As the model is estimated, parameters are tested for statistical significance above a specified level. Statistical significance of parameters means that the effect on the model of input variables is evaluated to be greater than zero. Typically, only those parameters that are found in fact to be statistically significant are retained for the final model. What this means is that for those parameters which were not found to be statistically significant, the x values and associated parameters are set equal to zero.

In essence, statistical analysis of data usually amounts to testing specific *a priori* hypotheses about relationships of a particular type (e.g., linear relationships) between predictors and outcomes in a data sample. If the specific statistical models and hypotheses are mis-specified, then a predictor that *could* actually have important diagnostic value for the accurate prediction of an outcome might be missed.

Predictive Modeling Using General Approximators

The focus in predictive modeling and data mining is not on hypothesis testing, but rather on the detection of repeated patterns of values in the data that can be used to make accurate predictions of future outcomes. These specific predictive models or *machine learning* algorithms can typically detect relationships of any type between the outcome variables and the predictors, and approximate them closely to make accurate predictions. Hence, these types of learning algorithms are also sometimes called *general approximators*.

Some of the algorithms used for predictive modeling are such good approximators that efforts must be taken to make sure that they do not *overlearn* the data. Overlearning means that the algorithm is tuned closely to data patterns present in the data sample used to train a predictive model, but which do not represent the population at large. This situation results in relatively poor prediction accuracy using new observations. The risk presented by this potential problem is the reason why prediction accuracies are usually calculated based on data in a hold-out data set not used in any way to train the model.

The Algorithms of Predictive Modeling

Consistent with the general overview of the algorithms used in predictive analytics presented in this chapter, a deep-dive into the algorithms used in predictive models will not be provided. There is a variety of resources that can be readily accessed which can provide this information. Some references have previously been provided, and there are also free resources that can be accessed via the Internet, such as the *Electronic Statistics Textbook* at www.statsoft.com/textbook/, and associated YouTube tutorials at www.youtube.com/user/StatSoft. This chapter will cover a general overview of the different types of algorithms popularly used in predictive modeling, guidance for using those algorithms, and their associated benefits and disadvantages.

k-Nearest Neighbor and Similar Methods

A good example of an algorithm that is a general approximator for relationships among a set of data is the k-Nearest Neighbor algorithm. This algorithm makes no assumptions whatsoever regarding the relationships among the data, but instead uses the data alone to make new predictions with observed data; the model is inherent in the data, and it might even be said that the "data are the model." This algorithm finds exemplars among the observations that are most like the new data presented to the algorithm, and then assigns to the new data point the predicted value of the exemplar most similar to it.

Figure 15.3 shows an example of a classification solution using the k-Nearest Neighbor algorithm. In this data set there are two predictor variables, *Predictor 1* and *Predictor 2*. Existing observations in the learning data set are represented by circles and squares, Category A and Category B respectively, within the scatterplot. New observations are represented by triangles. The job of the k-Nearest Neighbor algorithm is to predict the Category (A or B) to which the triangle (new) data points belong.

Through visual inspection of the scatterplot, you can observe that positions of the triangles occur in groups of squares and circles that form rather homogeneous "neighborhoods" around the triangles. Intuitively, it is easy to make predictions of the proper classification of the new observations (triangles), based upon the majority shape of the plotted data points in these neighborhoods. While this classification example may appear easy, the task of finding a linear (line of best fit) solution for this example, or even a curvilinear solution, would be extremely difficult if not impossible, illustrating the utility of this specific general approximator algorithm.

The k-Nearest Neighbor algorithm is also known as a "memory-based learner." The general approach to modeling is analogous to the game of turning over a flash card to see a picture, turning it back over, and then trying to make predictions of which flash cards will turn up next, based upon your memory of where previous pictures were located in the

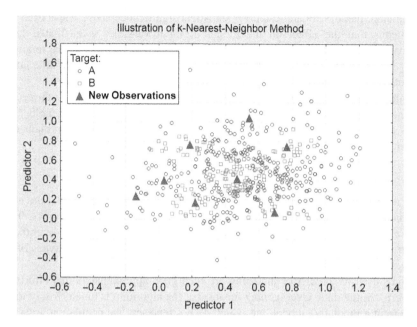

FIGURE 15.3   Classifying new observations using k-Nearest Neighbor method.

deck. The algorithm remembers where all of the observed data are located, and then makes predictions for new data based upon memory of where the observed data are located. For the practical implementation of this general approximator there are additional important considerations, such as:

- How "distance" in some similarity metric is calculated between the observed and predicted observations.
- How many neighbors to consider when making predictions.
- How to make the final prediction when you consider more than one nearest neighbor.

Benefits of the k-Nearest Neighbor Algorithm

The two primary benefits of the k-Nearest Neighbor algorithm are efficiency and flexibility. The algorithm is efficient in its simplicity, speed, and scalability. As described above, the mechanics of the algorithm are readily apparent, and it is simple to understand and implement. Because of the simplicity it is also very fast, and this speed makes it very easy to deploy on to very large, complicated data sets, making it scalable to data where other more complicated algorithms may experience difficulties. The flexibility in this algorithm is shown in its ability to handle data sets where the relationships are very complicated, unexplainable by either linear or curvilinear relationships.

Because of the ability of this algorithm to determine similarity among data, it is often used in replacing missing data. This does require appropriate preprocessing of variables used in the analysis, and also setting appropriate parameters for choosing which observations the algorithm will memorize to make new predictions on unseen data. Once this is done, however, it does a very good job of computing values or predictions for missing data. For example, the methods described in this book can be used to classify medical claims. This would be achieved by first having experts select typical "example claims" of interest which belong to a specific claim category, such as fraud, and then using those exemplars to automatically assign new claims to categories of interest.

Disadvantages of the k-Nearest Neighbor Algorithm

In some ways, this algorithm is not really a learning algorithm, but a memory-based "look-up." The predictor variables and learning sample (*exemplars*) must be chosen *a priori*. The algorithm then memorizes these data, and makes predictions based on that memory. The algorithm does not "learn" patterns in the data. Furthermore, once the learning sample is designated, it must be decided how many observations will be used for the nearest neighbors in making predictions for new data. In addition, this algorithm suffers from the curse of dimensionality (number of predictors), and prediction accuracy can suffer greatly when hundreds, if not thousands, of predictor variables are used, which is often the case in many data sets for which data mining algorithms are frequently employed. Some other data mining algorithms give insight into what variables are the most important in making new predictions. This facility is not available in the k-Nearest Neighbor algorithm, and thus constitutes a significant disadvantage.

Extensions to the Approach

The Support Vector Machine (SVM) algorithm is an extension to this approach that extends the k-Nearest Neighbor algorithm from a memory-based learner to an actual learning algorithm. Like the k-Nearest Neighbor algorithm, SVM assumes that the algorithm determines neighborhoods based upon observed data presented to the algorithm, from which predictions are made for new unseen data. SVMs take additional steps, however, by dividing the learning data into partitions. These partitions are created using lines or hyperplanes (composed of more than three dimensions), which are calculated from the learning data using vectors of each predictor variable to compose the dimensions of the hyperplane. SVMs are similar to other learning algorithms, particularly neural networks, but they are more closely aligned with the k-Nearest Neighbor algorithm in that neighborhoods are defined, and from the location of new data inside or around these neighborhoods predictions are made.

Recursive Partitioning Algorithms (Decision Trees)

One of the most prevalent algorithms utilized in predictive modeling is the recursive partitioning algorithm, also known as decision trees for the visual appearance of the output which is often generated. Like the k-Nearest Neighbor algorithm, recursive partitioning algorithms are rooted in a very simple concept. For example, think of a classification task of finding cells that are either malignant or benign. Consider a learning data set in which approximately 50% of the cases are malignant and 50% of the cases are benign. The first step in the processing of the recursive partitioning trees algorithm is to assess all the available predictors in the learning data set to identify the variable which will function best to split the data set into categories of malignant and benign, based upon the values in that predictor variable. The best split is defined as the split which will create the most pure sub-groups, or one group with mostly malignant cases and one group with mostly benign cases. This process is the first partition and it is followed recursively, in that all variables are all considered once again and the predictor which will create the most pure sub-groups from the first partition is chosen, thus creating more pure groups. As this recursive partitioning takes place, a "tree" is created in which all splits form two sub-groups, or a binary split.

This algorithm is not limited to just classification problems. In the case of regression problems, instead of basing the split on the purity of sub-groups the split is based on how dissimilar the means are in each group relative to their respective standard deviations. In the regression application of recursive partitioning trees, the goal is to find the greatest separation of values in the dependent variable based on recursive splits on a chosen predictor variable.

Example of a Simple Data Mining Application

Below you will find a relatively simple example of how to predict white blood cell (WBC) count, based on blood urea nitrogen (BUN) and weight in kilograms. A simple regression tree result may look like that shown in Figure 15.4.

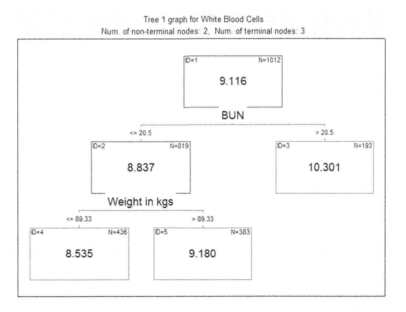

FIGURE 15.4 A simple regression tree model relating the weight and BUN to mean WBC.

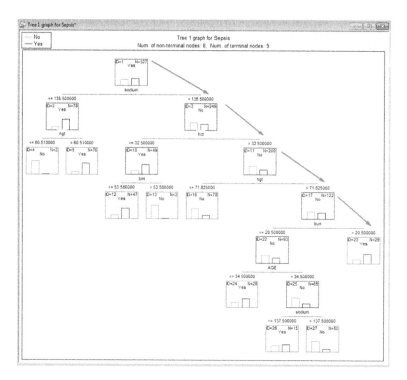

FIGURE 15.5   Decision tree model for predicting sepsis.

Notice that the average WBC across all patients in this sample is 9.116. If BUN is above 20.5, however, then the average WBC count of the sub-group of ($N = 193$) patients is 10.301, while those that have BUN below 20.5 have an average WBC count of 8.837. Furthermore, the $N = 819$ patients in the left node after the first split in Figure 15.4 can further be partitioned into two groups, one with $N = 383$ patients, who have a weight in kilograms above 89.33 and who have a WBC count of 9.180, and the other group with $N = 436$ patients and a weight below 89.33 kilograms who have an average WBC count of 8.535.

One of the primary advantages of recursive partitioning (or decision tree) algorithms is that analyses will result in relatively simple-to-interpret results of if−then "rules" for predicting the outcome of interest. An elaboration of this approach is shown in Figure 15.5, generated from the analysis of another medical problem.

Each box or "node" in the tree shown in Figure 15.5 contains two histo bars, indicating the relative frequencies of the *Yes* and *No* decisions (sepsis or no sepsis). Figure 15.5 also highlights a "path" or rule consisting of a combination of predictor values (in boxes ID = 3, ID = 11, ID = 17, and ID = 23) that will result in a likely *Yes* decision (i.e., likely for sepsis). Following this decision path, if a patient has *sodium* > 135.5, and *HCT* > 32.5, and the *HGT* is > 71.825, and *BUN* is > 20.5, then sepsis is very likely. This decision is made in one of the nine "terminal" nodes, beyond which there are no further splits (see node ID = 23, with $N = 29$). (NOTE: both boxes ID 16 and 17 are marked "No"; the reader may think that one should be marked "Yes," but this is not the case since the majority of cases in both 16 and 17 are "No.").

Implementations

Algorithms based on the partitioning of data into progressively more homogeneous sub-groups are described in detail by Hastie *et al.* (2009). Some other algorithms include C4.5, Classification and Regression Trees (CARTs), and Chi-square Automatic Interaction Detection (CHAID). They do differ in calculations, but all are consistent in their use of recursive partitioning to divide the sample data set into increasingly homogeneous sub-groups. There are slight differences between the binary tree described above and some of the other algorithms, such as allowing for multiple splits at a single step with CHAID instead of a binary split. Results of this algorithm include multiple sub-samples at each step, hence resulting in a wider tree instead of a taller tree.

Strengths of Recursive Partitioning Algorithms

Strengths of recursive partition algorithms include:

- The ability to model complex relationships in a simple format
- Interpretability of the results
- Flexibility of the algorithm.

Recursive partitioning algorithms have been applied successfully to model very complex relationships among variables, and they provide output that allows novice users to understand the complex relationships being modeled. Complex dependencies among variables (including multiple dependencies on a single variable) are handled easily in recursive partitioning algorithms. And, regardless of the complexity of the model, a simple, easy to use and interpret set of results is provided, which allows for understanding of how predictions are made using these results, or rules. The interpretability of results is vitally important for industries that require a certain amount of transparency in how predictions are made and how those predictions are used in subsequent applications. This is especially true for industries that are subject to governmental regulations and oversight. Finally, this algorithm has been shown to be very flexible. Using one adaptation of this algorithm, users can select predictors which are to be used for specific splits, and also specify how those splits are to be made. This flexibility is very useful in applications where specific constraints or regulatory compliance objectives have to be met, and prediction-accuracy goals must be met at the same time, or where specific predictors are deemed to be more "actionable" and useful than others. For example, a patient's blood pressure functioning as a predictor of risk may be controllable, whereas gender, age, or other demographic variables are not; thus, the latter variables may not be as useful for building actionable models of risk.

Weaknesses of Recursive Partitioning Algorithms

The problem of primary concern with recursive partitioning algorithms is that the solutions are sometimes "locally optimal solutions" rather than "globally optimal solutions." Put another way, a specific solution may be very good (accurate) but not necessarily the *best possible solution* given the data. This can impact the stability of the results. For example, imagine a case in which you are analyzing data with a recursive partitioning algorithm, and at some point in that analysis, two variables are presented to the algorithm which will exactly split the data into sub-samples of equal purity. Most software implementations will choose at random which variable to use for that split. It is important, however, to consider how this operation impacts the resulting tree. Because the usual goal is to build models with good predictive accuracy, rather than those with the absolute *best* accuracy, the random choice among the two splitting variables may not be a problem. However, this specific split may yield a locally optimal solution for this data sample, and not a globally optimal solution for the entire data universe. This effect occurs because specific splits higher up in the tree will affect the quality of splits further down the tree; thus any one tree will be only one of many possible trees that could be built, some of which may (or may not) provider better predictive accuracy. It is useful, therefore, to have diagnostics in software packages which help to investigate the impact of predictors and splits among those predictors, and which compensate for this shortcoming of recursive partitioning algorithms. On the other hand, this issue usually does not pose a big problem in practice because the practical concern is to leverage data for better predictions and decisions, and a "very good" solution can be tremendously useful and actually save lives, even if there may be one that is a little bit better. Furthermore, it is usually the case that the automation of multiple modeling algorithms to compete against each other will ensure that a near-optimal model will be discovered.

Early Stopping Techniques

Recursive partitioning algorithms do such a good job at learning the patterns among data that if no limitations were placed upon the algorithm, it could learn perfectly to express the patterns in a set of data presented to the algorithm; eventually, every single observation could be classified into its own terminal tree node. While this may be useful for understanding and making predictions on the data from which the algorithm is learning, it makes the algorithm prone to error because of overlearning when the final tree model is applied to new data different from the learning sample. A decision must be made about when the tree-growing procedure should stop in order to maximize generalizability of the analysis. Early stopping controls how large the trees are allowed to be grown, and resultantly the complexity of the rules being generated. Various stopping functions include specifying a minimum number of records in a parent or a child branch. Some implementations of recursive partitioning algorithms allow for methods of cross-validation, where trees and their rules are derived from repeatedly drawn learning samples and applied to repeatedly drawn (hold-out) samples. From this procedure, estimates of prediction errors can be derived which, in turn, guide decisions about when to stop the tree-building process.

Neural Networks

Neural network algorithms were modeled after how the neurons of the human brain work. There are billions of neurons in the human brain, which are connected to other neurons, with sometimes thousands of connections per neuron. The cells accumulate an incoming nerve signal until its strength exceeds a learned threshold, and then the cell "fires" a nerve impulse to the next cell in the network, following some linear or non-linear activation function. It is from this biological model that a class of algorithms called Artificial Neural Networks (ANNs) was developed. These ANN algorithms mimic the function of the cells in our brain. Input is received into the ANN algorithm through a series of data variables forming an input layer of "neurons." Each input neuron is connected to each of a number of a middle (or "hidden") layer of neurons, and then composed into one or several output neurons. If the inputs result in a signal of sufficient strength, the cell activation function passes on an appropriate signal. This is shown schematically in Figure 15.6.

Following the architecture of the diagram in Figure 15.6, data provided by the input neurons (variables) are recoded and transformed, using various functions associated with the neurons in the hidden layer. These values are analogous to statistical weights. Some functions include the identity function, a simple linear function, sigmoid function, and so on. These values become the presented values for the *hidden layer* neurons. Using an activation function, these values are then combined as appropriate and transmitted to the *output layer* of neurons (usually 1). This output value represents the solution to the non-linear relationship between the input variables and the output variable (the "target").

Succinctly, this can be thought of as a choreographed set of non-linear equations that allow for the connection of input parameters to one or more output values. The parameters of these non-linear equations, also known as the activation functions, are then estimated through a general function optimization algorithm with the purpose of minimizing prediction error of the response variable given the input data.

Benefits of Neural Networks Algorithms

In general, artificial neural networks can be used to model any relationship between an observed variable or group of variables, and an outcome variable or variables. The fact that ANNs function as general approximators of relationships means that they will usually provide a smooth response function. This has made ANN algorithms very popular for various engineering applications where a smooth predicted response is required. ANNs have been used successfully in medical research, with applications ranging from predicting disease dispersion over time to grouping medical data based on key characteristics such as pre-existing conditions.

A simple neural network

| Input | Hidden | Output |
| layer | layer | layer |

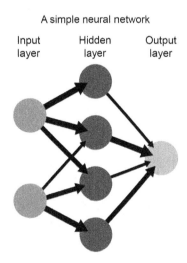

FIGURE 15.6 Simple schematic of an artificial neural network.

Disadvantages of Neural Networks Algorithms

Two primary disadvantages of neural network algorithms are:

- The large computing resources required for completing neural network analyses.
- Poor interpretability of results.

Because of the complexity of the tasks being achieved by neural networks, it is not surprising that neural networks require large computing resources. Models of simple to moderate complexity can take a significant amount of computer resources to generate a satisfactory solution. Therefore, a neural networks algorithm may not be the best choice for finding a modeling solution for a problem with a large number of predictors and observations. Also, it can be difficult, or sometimes impossible, to interpret the results to determine the important predictor variables for a prediction. Recursive partitioning algorithms follow a simple set of rules and logic that allows for interpretation of results, whereas there is no such simple set of rules or criteria generated by neural networks. While sensitivity analyses can reflect the relative importance of predictor variables in some ANNs, much more information about the structure of the model and its predictors is available for the interpretation of results from recursive partitioning algorithms.

Model Ensembles

The age-old adage claiming that two minds are better than one reflects the benefit of multiple perspectives on reality. That adage applies similarly to the use of algorithms in predictive analytics. One approach is to use multiple algorithms to approximate the relationships among the data, where each algorithm provides a different mathematical perspective of the patterns in the data set. Seni and Elder (2010) provide a resource which details the various methods for combining multiple algorithms to produce an ensemble of models. Just like in a musical ensemble, each instrument (algorithm) plays its own part. As an example, consider an analysis which predicts whether or not a patient is hypoglycemic. Five models can be built using a variety of algorithms, including recursive partitioning algorithms and neural networks, to predict the class for the patient. Some decision rule is invoked to combine the results of multiple algorithms. For categorical outputs, this decision rule is usually the majority vote. With the use of this decision rule, if three of the algorithms predict the hypoglycemic class and two algorithms predict the non-hypoglycemic class for a given record, the class is classified as hypoglycemic by majority vote. For regression problems with real number outputs, the mean of the predicted responses would be computed. Ensemble models are often found to have better predictive accuracy than individual algorithms making predictions on their own.

Choosing the Right Algorithm for the Right Analysis

It may appear that the proper choice of algorithm is dictated by the type of data being presented to it, particularly if the data include structured data (presented as records and fields) as well as unstructured data (i.e., text). However, in reality, this is not the case. Decisions concerning which algorithm to use for a given analysis should be made on the basis of interpretability of results, and whether or not predictions will be based on interpolations or extrapolations of input data.

Interpretable Models vs. "Black Box Models"

Following the approach described above, algorithms can be classified into one of two classes:

- Algorithms generating easily interpretable results.
- Algorithms generating results that are not easily interpretable.

The latter class of algorithms is sometimes called "black box" algorithms because their inner workings are not easily scrutinized. Recursive partitioning algorithms have a long history of providing results that are easy to interpret. This is one of the reasons why this class of algorithm has been found to be particularly useful in regulated industries, or industries with a need to understand the predictions being made by a model. Neural networks fall into the class of "black box" algorithms, which are popular due to their power at making accurate predictions rather than to the ease of interpretation of their results. For example, available data for a problem might include expected healthcare expenses based on patient age, gender, and overall physical conditioning, as well as physician text notes, which might include specific medical terms such as "heart disease." With a recursive partitioning algorithm or decisioning tree algorithm, it might be shown clearly that subsequent healthcare costs are more likely to grow based on the relationships among these variables. The results from analyses with neural networks would not lead to a clear and immediate understanding of how the prediction was made, even if the final models yielded highly accurate predictions.

Often, interpretability of results is not only a desire but a requirement that can have legal implications. For example, predictions of pricing for insurance policies or for credit ratings in insurance and financial applications are constrained by regulatory requirements regarding what information can and cannot be used to approve or deny applications, or to price insurance policies. This makes it critical for the selected models of insurance policy price or credit ratings to generate outputs which show clearly what variables were used to predict the risks or prices.

Interpolation and Extrapolation

In the medical field especially, there are instances where continuous "smooth" functions are needed. In these instances, with continuously sliding values of a specific input variable, a continuously changing output function is observed. For example, consider the case where the constant monitoring of blood sugar in a type I diabetic is controlled by the level of insulin delivered by an insulin pump, which was prescribed by the physician in charge of the case. The setting on the insulin pump determines the amount of insulin delivered for the respective blood sugar level in the patient. Obviously, it is important that there be a smooth and continuous response of the pump to deliver insulin, based on the level of sugar in the blood. A neural network model could certainly deliver this smooth response function. However, another case might be served better by a decision tree algorithm, which could predict one of three dosage levels of a new medication to reduce lipids in mildly hypercholesterolemic men and women. The decision tree model would only be able to output three distinct values: low dosage, medium dosage, and high dosage. This categorical (rather than continuous) output function might be appropriate for this specific study, but it would not serve well if a continuous output prediction of dosage was needed.

CLUSTERING: IDENTIFYING CLUSTERS OF SIMILAR CASES, AND OUTLIERS

The algorithms that have been discussed thus far are those specific to predictive modeling, where there is a known outcome or dependent variable. Following this approach, predictive models are built to predict the level of the dependent variable. For example, a model can be built using historical data of hospital readmissions to predict, for new cases, the expected probability of hospital readmission. Since this class of algorithm learns from an identified dependent variable, we can say that *supervised* learning algorithms are involved in that the accurate or inaccurate prediction is supervised by a set of known values in a variable with in the learning data set.

Another class of algorithms operates without known dependent variables, and these are referred to as *unsupervised* learning algorithms. In these cases, there is not a specific outcome variable of interest. Rather, the algorithm learns to recognize repeated patterns that are present in the data. Through this type of learning it is possible to identify important data clusters, stratifications in the data, and influential segments of the population. For example, medical claim fraud detection applications might operate on data describing the history of cases with known fraud, using supervised learning algorithms, but some cases of fraud are not identified by the analysis. In these cases, it may be useful to apply unsupervised learning or clustering algorithms to identify the types or "buckets" of cases predicted as non-fraud that are similar to each other. Those "buckets" or clusters and their characteristics can then be inspected to detect unusual combinations of input variables, or cases that cannot be easily assigned to any cluster and thus are somehow unusual given the other cases in the training data. This information can be used to modify the fraud probability scores for some customers predicted as non-fraud, which might cause the fraud detection system to flag these records as probable fraud.

Unsupervised learning, or clustering, usually involves algorithms that assign observations to clusters or buckets of data based on shared characteristics and qualities that are similar across all the input variables in the analyses. A variety of algorithms can be used for this purpose, with some of those algorithms described below.

Clustering Algorithms

There are three general classes of clustering algorithms:

- k-Means clustering (with and without expectation maximization)
- Hierarchical clustering
- Self-organizing maps (including Kohonen networks).

k-Means Clustering (and Expectation Maximization)

There are two primary goals in these algorithms: minimizing distances within a cluster, and maximizing distances between clusters (cluster centers). In order to differentiate between clusters of similar data in a data set, the algorithms

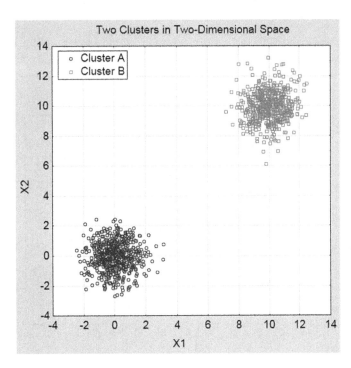

FIGURE 15.7   Two clusters of points in two-dimensional space.

first minimize the distances between the observations in a single cluster. Then, distances are maximized between clusters or cluster centers.

As an example, imagine a hypothetical case of two input dimensions X1 and X2, and two clusters of points: *Cluster A* and *Cluster B*. A scatterplot identifying the clusters is shown in Figure 15.7.

The clusters are easily identifiable by visual inspection as two clouds of points with a definable distance between the two clouds. The k-means clustering algorithm will also do what a visual inspection was able to; namely, correctly identify the points that belong to each cluster. This algorithm will accomplish this by following these steps:

1. Two points are chosen at random. These become the cluster centers.
2. All data are processed and individual data points are assigned to the closest cluster center. This can be done using different measures of distance, such as Euclidian distance.
3. New cluster centers are computed. These are the means of all cases assigned to each cluster center.
4. Steps 2 and 3 are repeated until there are no remaining points to be assigned to different clusters over consecutive iterations, or until some other convergence criterion is reached.

These four steps give a general summary of the logic in the processing of k-means clustering. The goal of this processing is to assign points to clusters over successive iterations so that convergence to an optimal solution is reached. Convergence occurs when there are no other optimal solutions where points within a cluster are closer together, and cluster centers are farther apart.

Distances and Probabilities (Expectation Maximization Clustering)

There are several methods followed to calculate distance in algorithms like k-means. One of the ways is to calculate the simple Euclidean distances between data points and their respective cluster centers, minimizing the distance between points within clusters and maximizing the distance to points of different clusters. To visualize this, an example is presented in Figure 15.8 that shows data points and the associated cluster center, which are multivariate normal in distribution (see the bar charts on the right side of the figure).

An alternate way to express the distance between data points is to calculate the probabilities of data points belonging to each of the cluster centers. In this case, the probability is also an expectation that a certain point within the data set can be expressed as belonging to this respective distribution. Therefore, the k-means algorithm can be used to maximize this expectation or the probability that the data point belongs to, or was sampled from, the population or cluster. This approach is called expectation maximization (EM).

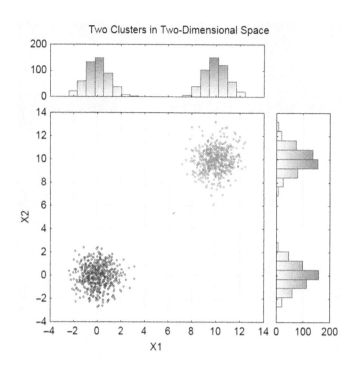

FIGURE 15.8 Normal distributions for two clusters separated in two-dimensional space.

Differences Between the k-Means and EM Algorithms

While the k-means and EM algorithms function basically in the same way, in that they assign points to clusters, there are some unique advantages to the EM algorithm. One such advantage is that assumptions which underlie multivariate normality do not need to be met in order to use the algorithm. Other types of data can be presented to the algorithm, including continuous variables from non-normal distributions, and also different distributions for discrete variables.

Strengths of k-Means and EM Algorithms

Both the k-means and EM algorithms are very efficient, in that they are very scalable and can be applied to large amounts of data. For example, clustering applications of medical claims data can result in huge amounts of data, and when unstructured (text) data are included the size of the data set can become exponentially larger. This extremely large amount of data is handled very well by the k-means and EM algorithms. Clusters of claims are identified which are similar to one another, and either distances or probabilities are computed for data points and their cluster centers using the clustering algorithm. The closer a data point is to the cluster center, the more typical it is for that group; the further away a data point is from a cluster center, the more atypical it is of that cluster. In this scenario, the distance becomes a measure of how typical or atypical a claim is to a certain cluster. If a claim is found to be close to the cluster center of a certain group, it is highly likely that it does belong to that group. If the data point is relatively far away from the cluster center, it is an indication that this claim may differ enough to justify further investigation to determine if this document might fit into existing types of claims, or if it represents a new type or grouping of claim.

Weaknesses of k-Means and EM Algorithms

One weakness of the k-means and EM algorithms centers around the question of how many clusters are actually present in the data set. For specific solutions using both the k-means and EM algorithms, the number of clusters in the data set must be specified before running the algorithm. The optimal number of clusters might not be known before the clustering operation is performed, but a number must be specified to the algorithm.

One way of dealing with this is to make a "good guess" at cluster number to start this process; subsequent to the first run you can do "what-if" runs, changing the cluster number until the model best fits the data.

There are methods available — such as v-fold cross-validation — that can help to estimate how many clusters exist within a data set. In this technique, different clustering solutions are computed with different numbers of clusters. Each cluster solution is built on a different combination of v − 1 sub-sets of the entire data set (e.g., v = 10 is a common choice), and the respective solution is applied to the remaining hold-out sub-set. Comparison of the average distances across all of the models and their respective hold-out data set will identify at what number of clusters the average distance does not change significantly as the number of cluster increases. This will allow you to see when the correct number of clusters has been identified.

Another ambiguity of the k-means and EM algorithms is that final results can be significantly impacted by the initial choice of cluster centers. If a particular number of clusters has been identified as a possible solution, it may not be the overall best solution for the set of data. It may be a locally optimal solution, rather than a globally optimal solution. Since this problem can have a significant effect on the final quality and usefulness of results from these algorithms, it is good practice to run an analysis multiple times with different choices for the initial cluster centers. If consecutive runs yield similar results, then it is likely that the respective cluster solution is robust with respect to the choice of initial cluster centers.

Hierarchical or Tree Clustering

Another popular clustering method is hierarchical clustering. The goal of this method is to build a hierarchical tree that expresses the distances between the items being clustered.

Figure 15.9 provides an example of such a tree, showing a hierarchical tree clustering solution for selected terms and synonyms used in a corpus of 76 articles related to genetics and migraine headaches. The graph is constructed as follows.

First, a data matrix is computed where each observation or case is a medical article, and where each column holds relative frequencies of terms used in the respective article. A distance matrix can be computed from these input data, which expresses the degree of co-occurrences of terms across documents. For example, you could compute correlations to express the similarity of co-occurrences of terms, and then rescale them so that the resulting coefficients denote distance rather than similarity. If two terms "Polymorphic" and "Genotype" co-occurred almost always across the document corpus (all of the articles), these could be interpreted to lie very "close" to each other in terms of distance, while two terms that almost never co-occur would be very "distant" from each other.

The hierarchical tree algorithm processes the distance matrix and combines the terms that are closest together (most similar). Subsequently, the distance matrix is updated to reflect the distance between the combined terms, and all other terms in the distance matrix. The process then repeats by choosing the next pair of items to join by finding the smallest distance between any two terms (or combined terms from a previous step). This process continues until all items are joined.

The y-axis in Figure 15.9 (labeled *Linkage Distance*) is the distance between individual terms (or combined terms) in the distance matrix at which the respective terms listed on the x-axis are merged into the body of the tree.

For example, consider the subset of the hierarchical cluster tree shown in Figure 15.10. Apparently, the terms *Genetics*, *Department*, *Study*, and *Associated* co-occur frequently in the corpus of articles. In retrospect, it is likely that the term *Genetics Department* should have been defined as a separate phrase. In this graph these terms are shown to be correlated, with relatively little distance between them. In contrast, the term *Aim* is not related to *Genetics* or to *Department*.

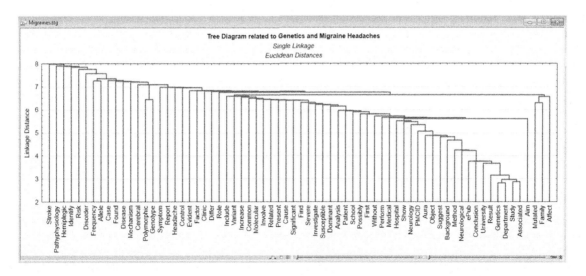

FIGURE 15.9 Hierarchical (tree) clustering of selected terms and synonyms used in articles related to genetics and migraine headaches.

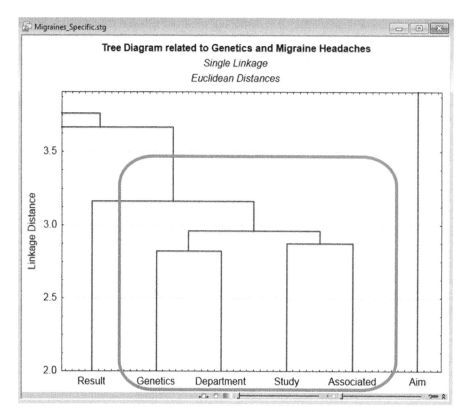

FIGURE 15.10 Small section of a hierarchical (tree) clustering solution.

Strengths of Hierarchical Tree Clustering Algorithms

The unique characteristic of this algorithm is that it permits an evaluation of how "items" (e.g., words or terms) co-occur across a number of rows or cases (e.g., documents).

Weaknesses of Hierarchical Tree Clustering Algorithms

The primary weakness of the hierarchical tree clustering algorithm is related to the requirement to compute a distance matrix of items that will be presented to the algorithm for clustering. This is not a problem with small data sets, but for large data sets with hundreds or hundreds of thousands of items this distance matrix between all items to be clustered becomes very large, requiring significant processing resources to generate it. A second weakness is related to the flexibility provided to the user to select different distance measures, different distances between items in a cluster, and different distances between clusters. The choice of different measures, such as Euclidean or squared Euclidean distances, will have an impact on the final clustering results. Further, the algorithm must compute the initial distance matrix for the items to be clustered, the distances between items and clusters, and/or distances between clusters. Computing this latter distance between clusters during the application of the clustering algorithm also introduces ambiguity and choices. For example, the distance between two clusters each consisting of two items can be defined as the smallest distance between any two items in the two clusters, the distance between the cluster centers or means, or the largest distance between any two items in the two clusters. These rules are also called linkage or amalgamation rules, and the specific choices made defining and computing distances will greatly impact the final composition of clusters.

Kohonen Networks or Self-Organizing Feature Maps

Neural network methods can also be used for clustering. As described earlier, in the context of predictive modeling techniques, neural networks fit systems of non-linear equations to data, to optimize the accuracy of prediction. In Kohonen networks, or self-organizing feature maps (SOFMs), the goal rather is to cluster observations into a "lattice" of "boxes" (clusters), to achieve maximum separation between the observations in different clusters. This "mapping" of observations to boxes in the lattice (clusters) is typically accomplished using non-linear activation functions.

In terms of interpretation, the results of Kohonen networks are very similar to those created via k-means clustering. Observations assigned to the same cluster tend to be more similar to each other than those in different clusters. However, Kohonen networks will typically use non-linear activation functions to achieve the assignment of observations to clusters.

Strengths and Weaknesses

The Kohonen or SOFMs algorithms are generally more computationally "expensive" than the k-means or EM clustering methods. This means that for very large data sets Kohonen networks may be impractical because of the computational effort involved to build the models. Because of the greater simplicity of k-means and EM clustering methods, the easier interpretation of results (identification of variables and variable values that define the respective cluster centers), and the better scalability to manage larger data problems, k-means clustering methods are probably most commonly applied in many real-world applications.

TEXT MINING ALGORITHMS

Text mining in the context of predictive modeling involves the process by which unstructured information — mostly text — can be turned into vectors of numbers, which can then be used to improve the predictive accuracy of models. There are many different approaches and use cases where unstructured text information is processed in some automated fashion to gain better insights about some specific corpus of text ranging from sentiment analysis of satisfaction surveys to patent searches in government repositories. An approach needs to be developed that will automatically transform unstructured data into actionable information. This actionable information will allow interested parties to gain better insight into the corpus of text under consideration. Some use cases could include sentiment analysis of tweets on Twitter about patient wait-time satisfaction, or even patent searches in government repositories. At some point during the process, the body of text will be transformed into vectors (rows) of numbers which can be processed with various statistical and data mining algorithms and methods (see, for example, Feldman and Sanger, 2007; Weiss *et al.*, 2010).

A common approach to incorporate text into predictive modeling projects is to apply so-called *statistical natural language processing* (SNLP) methods. This approach starts by counting words and phrases across documents, and calculates relative or otherwise transformed word frequencies as predictors in a model. For example, consider the combination of physicians' notes and comments with structured numeric indicators (i.e., in the form of tables) that is used to support a study of health risks. A physician may not record any specific symptoms of heart disease, but notes might be added as a reminder to look for such symptoms again during the next scheduled physical. Thus, while there are no formal data fields that are appropriate to record the physician's notes, this information can be used to increase the accuracy of subsequent health risk predictions (see, for example, Polon, 2011; Zasadil and Peele, 2012).

Text mining and clustering can be used in predictive modeling to uncover unexpected information. Known factors relevant to a diagnosis and treatment are encoded as fields in databases of most record-keeping systems. SNLP can enhance that information by detecting words, phrases, and word combinations that indicate something unusual or novel.

DIMENSION REDUCTION TECHNIQUES

The basic process in predictive modeling and clustering is to extract information from the available inputs that is relevant to the analytic problem at hand. In many applications there can be hundreds or thousands, or even more possible predictor variables, and the task is either how to extract from those predictor candidates those that are relevant, or how to reduce the predictor space to fewer underlying relevant dimensions. The latter problem is particularly relevant to statistical natural language processing. Recall that, in text mining applications, a common approach is to extract (relative) word and phrase counts for each document in a document corpus. In practice, this technique can yield over a thousand words or terms that are counted — i.e., generate a large number of predictor candidates for subsequent modeling based on those counts.

Latent Semantic Indexing

A common technique used to extract underlying dimensions of meaning (latent semantic dimension) from a body of text is latent semantic indexing (LSI). These dimensions are composed from a matrix of documents-by-word-counts that can serve to differentiate between all documents in a corpus. The extraction method is based on *singular value decomposition* (SVD), useful for feature extraction from large matrices, to identify the underlying latent dimensions that summarize most of the information contained in the data.

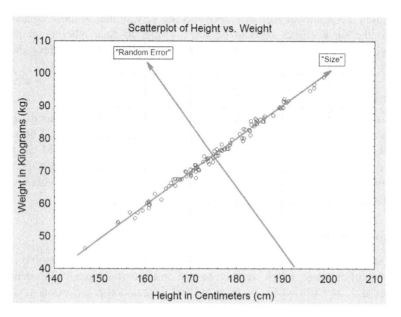

FIGURE 15.11 Rotation in two dimensions.

Singular value decomposition is similar to principal components analysis (PCA). Both techniques can be interpreted as strategies to rearrange the dimensions of the original input space (the variables) to a reduced space that summarizes most of the information contained in the original matrix. Figure 15.11 provides a simple example. Suppose you conducted a study to measure the height and weight of 100 persons, and created a scatterplot of the results; such a scatterplot might look like the one shown (along with additional annotations).

In short, it is evident that the variability across the individual observations in the study can be summarized with a simple new dimension, computed as the sum (or weighted sum) of the two dimensions *Height in Centimeters* and *Weight in Kilograms*. You might label that new dimension "Size" — i.e., the "essence" of the information contained in the two original variables can be summarized via the single label and derived new variable *Size*. This new variable contains most of the relevant information from the two original variables; it contains the relevant information to allow differentiation between the original observations (for example, to distinguish between "small people" and "large people").

SVD and PCA are very similar, but they operate on different data vectors entering into the computations. If the covariance matrix of each technique were modified to contain mean adjusted data vectors, both SVD and PCA would yield identical results. The end result of both techniques is the same: namely, a small number of dimensions which represents most of the information contained in a large number of original input variables.

Partial Least Squares

In some applications, the task is to reduce the dimensions of a high-dimensional input (or *X)* data set (by using a technique like SVD or PCA) when there are also one or more dependent or *Y* variables of interest. In those cases, *partial least squares* (PLS) can be a good option for feature extraction, i.e., to reduce the dimensionality of the input data. PLS, also known as *projection to latent structure*, was first utilized as a method for modeling in industrial applications in the 1960s, but the use of this technique was soon translated over to other industries and applications.

PLS is similar to multiple regression, in that it models the relationship of a number of predictor variables to a dependent variable, but PLS is different in that it also reduces the dimensions of the data set, yielding latent constructs or dimensions defined as linear combinations of the original variables. As discussed above, there may exist a large number of predictor variables for use in modeling, and it might be more efficient to represent this large number of predictor variables by a few latent constructs (linear combinations of the original variables) which contain most of the information available in the original variables.

The general idea of PLS is to construct a set of components that accounts for as much as possible of the total variation in the data set, while modeling the dependent *Y* variables in the process. Thus, the extraction of linear combinations or constructs proceeds in its processing subject to the underlying goal function to maximize the relationship between the input or *X* variables with the output or *Y* variables (see Figure 15.12).

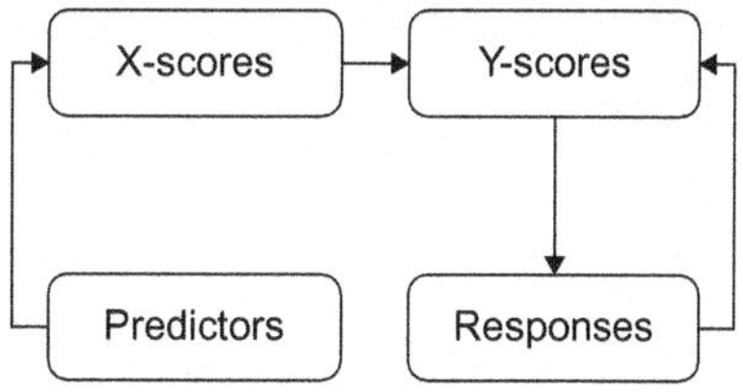

FIGURE 15.12 A schematic representation of the PLS model.

There are various efficient algorithms that accomplish these computations — see, for example, the NIPALS algorithm (Rannar *et al.*, 1994) or the SIMPLS algorithm (de Jong, 1993) — yielding *X* and *Y* scores for few dimensions from a much larger set of *Predictors* (*X*) and *Responses* (*Y*). These scores can then be used as input for subsequent modeling and clustering.

Feature Selection vs. Feature Extraction

SVD, PCA, and PLS are dimension reduction techniques, and use a large number of input variables in order to find a smaller number of latent constructs, which represent most of the information in the original input data. In this sense, a new set of features is extracted from the original data set. Hence, these methods can be thought of as feature extraction techniques.

While these techniques extract most of the information in the original data set, there is some information that is not represented, and in some instances this lost information can be important — for example, in cases like insurance fraud detection. Typically, there are only a few predictor variables among a large number of candidate predictors that are highly related to the probability of fraud. The predictive modeling algorithms rely on these variables to indicate the probability of fraud (see, for example, Francis, 2003). If these variables are used in an extraction technique, some of the valuable information contained in them can be lost. This will result in less-accurate models.

In such applications, it is more important to identify and select from among all available predictors those that have the greatest diagnostic value for the prediction or modeling task at hand. Thus, in this case the task is described better as *feature selection* (selecting specific predictors) rather than *feature extraction* (finding the underlying constructs or dimensions that large numbers of predictors have in common).

There are many approaches to successful feature selection. One approach is to cycle automatically through all predictor candidates one variable at a time, and use some statistic of association to decide whether or not each respective predictor shows any relationship to the dependent variable of interest. Then, choose those predictors that show the highest association.

When screening predictor candidates in this manner, it is important to avoid relying on simple linear correlation coefficients as the only indicator of association, because the final relationships of interest may not be linear. Therefore, it is common to rely on non-parametric statistics and techniques that are effective at identifying *any* relationship between a predictor and an outcome, regardless of the nature of the relationship.

Interaction Effects

Of course, when selecting predictors based on a review of associations one-variable-at-a-time, the most important relationships for predictive modeling purposes may be missed: namely, interaction effects. For example, if a specific predictor is relevant only for males older than 50, while it is not important or related to the outcome of interest in the opposite manner for females younger than 50, then that predictor may be missed. The reason is that it only plays an important role in the interaction also involving patients' *Age* and *Gender*. Some techniques have been created for analyzing genetic data in cancer studies, which have the capability to find interactions among predictor variables Ritchie *et al.* (2001).

There is no foolproof way to detect all possible interaction effects among large numbers of predictor candidates, short of explicitly testing the associations for all interaction effects. That, however, can involve millions of possibilities. In practice, recursive partitioning or tree methods, as reviewed earlier in this chapter, can be usefully applied to large numbers of predictor variables to identify important predictors and predictor interactions. To be clear, and as discussed above, recursive partitioning methods may not yield the very *best* solutions, or selection of predictor variables, but they usually will identify a *very good* selection of predictor variables that will enable useful and accurate subsequent modeling.

DETECTING THE INTERRELATIONSHIPS AND STRUCTURE OF DATA THROUGH ASSOCIATION AND LINK ANALYSIS

Millions of orders for medical tests are placed each day. There are times that the exams are ordered in a specific sequence, and there are times when the sequence is not as systematic. Some commonly ordered tests for patients with diabetes mellitus include eye examinations, foot examinations, kidney tests, and hemoglobin A1C tests. These tests are typically ordered together. Tests for a patient being prepared for a heart transplant are also organized at the same time. However, the order in which they are performed is vitally important. Association and link analysis algorithms seek out the relationships in transaction data sets like these, detecting both what transactions tend to happen in certain groups, and in what order those transactions occur.

Orders for individual tests described above exist in a database in the form of a single transaction. This transaction can exist on a computer on a local hard drive, or (as is happening with increasingly frequency) in a huge distributed file system where pieces of data are stored across multiple servers in order to accommodate the growing sizes of such databases. There are times when an order is placed for only a single test, such as a throat culture to detect strep throat. At other times tests are ordered in bulk, often in a specific sequence, such as tests preparing an individual for a heart transplant. When analyzing such data with algorithms for association and link analysis, rules are created which will identify what items co-occur with the greatest frequency.

A possible application of this type of analysis is to suggest a procedure or test that needs to be ordered, but was perhaps overlooked. In other instances, it may be possible that too many tests were ordered. While this may not occur very often, the benefits of association and link analysis in instances such as this can range from reducing costs of unnecessary medical tests through to saving human lives.

The Support and Confidence Statistics

There are two statistics commonly used in association and link analysis which describe the strength of the relationship: Support and Confidence. *Support* is the probability (relative frequency) of items or combinations of items occurring across all items. In a situation with two tests (*A* and *B*), Support is calculated as the relative frequency of tests *A* and *B* co-occurring. *Confidence* describes the conditional probability; for example, given test *A*, what is the probability of *B* also occurring in the same transaction?

The usefulness of these statistics is that they allow for the extraction of common and less-common rules from a transaction database. In some applications, the most common associations are of interest (e.g., best practices, most common sequence of medical symptoms); in other applications, the unusual or low-probability rules are of interest (e.g., in fraud detection). Note that different algorithms for association and link analysis also allow for the detection and extraction of simple association rules, as well as *sequential* rules to reflect the order in which specific items co-occur (e.g., to detect when test *A* precedes test *B*, and vice versa).

Applications of association and sequence analysis algorithms range from fraud detection to identifying best practices or recommendations. For example, the common suggestion systems as implemented at web-based retailers' sites are based on such algorithms, to identify up-sell opportunities for customers who purchased a specific product or service.

SUMMARY

This chapter provides an overview of common methods and algorithms in predictive modeling and data mining. While traditional statistical modeling techniques have relied on hypothesis testing around specific statistical prediction models, the predictive modeling algorithms now used commonly across various industries and domains rely on general pattern-recognition learning algorithms that can identify repeated patterns of any kind efficiently in historical data, and use those patterns to generate accurate predictions. While results and specific predictions stemming from the applications of such algorithms can sometimes be difficult to interpret, there are methods that can identify even very complex relationships and make them accessible to interpretation.

The common methods in data mining include supervised learning and predictive modeling, unsupervised learning and clustering, and various other specific analytic use cases such as text mining, feature selection and extraction, and the identification of associations and sequences of items (tests, procedures, medication) in transaction databases such as those describing the sequence of specific medical services provided to patients.

Taken together, these techniques have transformed domains from marketing, risk analysis, and management, through manufacturing, and they are poised to transform the effectiveness and efficiency of healthcare delivery in the future by identifying common patterns in the vast amount of available patient and medical information that is reliably associated with higher-quality and more desirable outcomes.

POSTSCRIPT

Chapters 1 through 15 compose Part I of this book, and they lay the foundation for medical researchers to use predictive analytical techniques to model various outcomes in their areas of responsibility. Now, we transition into Part II of the book, the tutorials section, to show how to use some of this technology to model various outcomes in medical informatics.

REFERENCES

de Jong, S., 1993. SIMPLS: an alternative approach to partial least squares regression. Chemom. Intell. Lab. Syst. 18, 251–263.

Feldman, R., Sanger, J., 2007. The Text Mining Handbook. Cambridge University Press, Cambridge, MA.

Francis, L., 2003. Martian Chronicles: Is MARS better than neural networks? March. Available from <www.data-mines.com>.

Hastie, T., Tibshirani, R., Friedman, J., 2009. The Elements of Statistical Learning: Data Mining, Inference, and Prediction. 2nd ed. Springer Series in Statistics, New York, NY.

Hill, T., Lewicki, P., 2007. Statistics Methods and Applications. StatSoft, Tulsa, OK (Also available as (Electronic Version): StatSoft, Inc. (2011). Electronic Statistics Textbook. Tulsa, OK: StatSoft. WEB: http://www.statsoft.com/textbook/.).

Nisbet, R., Elder, J., Miner, G., 2009. Handbook of Statistical Analysis and Data Mining Applications. Academic Press, New York, NY.

Polon, J., 2011. Text Mining Case Study: Text Mining for Health Insurance. Presentation delivered at the 2011 Society of Actuaries Health Meeting, Boston, MA.

Rannar, S., Lindgren, F., Geladi, P., Wold, S., 1994. A PLS Kernel algorithm for data sets with many variables and fewer objects. part 1: theory and algorithm. J. Chemom. 8, 111–125.

Ritchie, M., Hahn, L., Roodi, N., Bailey, R., DuPont, W., Parl, F., Moore, J., 2001. *Multifactor dimensionality reduction* reveals high-order interactions among estrogen-metabolism genes in sporadic breast cancer. Am. J. Hum. Genet. 69 (1), 138–147.

Seni, G., Elder, J., 2010. Ensemble Methods in Data Mining: Improving Accuracy Through Combining Predictions. Morgan and Claypool Publishers, Chicago, IL.

Weiss, S.M., Indurkhya, N., Zhang, T., 2010. Fundamentals of Predictive Text Mining. Springer, New York, NY.

Zasadil, S., Peele, P., 2012. Learning from Text Mining in Medical Care Management Notes. Paper presented at the 34th Annual Meeting of the Society for Medical Decision Making, Phoenix, AZ.

Prologue to Part 2

In Part 2 of this book we get into the core of effective learning — hands-on examples in the form of step-by-step tutorials and case studies:

- A. *Case studies*. Through these examples, you, the reader, can get a good idea of the parameters that need to be considered in various domains, and if you wish to create a simple data set yourself based on variables explained in the case study, you can also work through these types of examples. The reasons that data sets are not supplied for these case studies primarily reside in current HIPPA regulations.
- B. *Tutorials*. In effect, these are case studies with data. Using the data sets supplied in the accompanying Elsevier web page for this book, you can follow step-by-step and work through these examples so that you can gain the skills in using effective analytic and decisioning methods effectively. These tutorials are done in various predictive analytic software.

(For the STATISTICA tutorials, the software is available for download as a time-limited trial from the Elsevier Companion book website; for the other software examples you will need to have access to the software if commercial, or download the free software from its site where applicable — e.g., R and Rattle tutorials are examples of freeware/open source software.)

Part 2

Practical Step-by-Step Tutorials and Case Studies

Guest Tutorial Authors

Sergii Alekseiev, MD, IHI Family Practice Residency, Tulsa, OK, USA

Magid Amer, MD, MBBCh, FRCS, FRCP, FACP, semi-retired; formerly Professor of Medicine, Ohio State University, Columbus, OH, USA

David P. Armentrout, PhD, Faculty IHI Family Practice Residency Program, and Family Medical Care Clinics, Tulsa, OK, USA

Elizabeth Barancik, MS, University of California-Irvine, Irvine, CA, USA

Michael Cook, PhD, CFM, Kaiser Foundation Health Plan, Los Angeles, CA, USA

John W. Cromwell, MD, University of Iowa Hospitals & Clinics, Iowa City, IA, USA

Kenny Darrell, MS, Elder Research, Inc., Charlottesville, VA, USA

Christopher D. Farrar, PhD, Windrose Analytics, LLC, Columbus, OH, USA

Frank Hamilton, MD, IHI Family Practice Residency, Tulsa, OK, USA

Ambria Harris, DO, IHI Family Practice Residency, Tulsa, OK, USA

Welling Howell, BS, Wheatstone Analytics LLC, Pennington, NJ, USA

Jacek Jakubowski, PhD, StatSoft Polska, AGH University, Krakow, Poland

Amy Junghyun Lee, Department of Psychology, Brigham Young University-Hawaii, Laie, HI, USA

Mahmood H. Khichi, MD, FAAP, Warren Clinic PICU, Tulsa, OK, USA

Michał Kusy, MSc, StatSoft Polska, Krakow, Poland

Samrat Majumdar, MSc, University of Calcutta, Kolkata, India

Ronald Mellado Miller, PhD, Department of Psychology, Brigham Young University-Hawaii, Laie, HI, USA

John E. Meyers, PsyD, Concussion Clinic, Schofield Barracks, HI, USA

Grzegorz Migutb, MSc, StatSoft Polska, Krakow, Poland

Stephanie Moncada, MS, CVS Caremark Corporation, Chicago, IL USA

Wanda P. Parsons, MBA, MHA, Southern Nazarene University − Tulsa, OK, USA

Pamela Peele, PhD, UPMC Health Plan, Pittsburgh, PA, USA

Steve Petitt, MBA, CNB Marketing Research & Consulting, New York, NY, USA

Vladimir Rastunkov, PhD, StatSoft Inc., Tulsa, OK, USA

David Redfearn, PhD, Independent Consultant, Health Care Analytics, Las Vegas, NV, USA

Zachary W. Rupp, Department of Psychology, Brigham Young University-Hawaii, Laie , HI, USA

Edward Rylander, MD, IHI Family Practice Residency, Tulsa, OK, USA

Brian J. Smith, Hillcrest Medical Center, Tulsa, OK, USA

Danny W. Stout, PhD, University of Oklahoma School of Medicine, Oklahoma City, OK, USA; and StatSoft, Inc., Tulsa, OK, USA

Haranath Varanasi, MS, BTech, CMC Americas, TATA Group, Los Angeles, CA, USA

Matthew Wagner, PhD, Elder Research, Inc., Charlottesville, VA, USA

Chamont Wang, PhD, The College of New Jersey, NJ, USA

Charlene Wang, BS, HealthFirst Inc., Trenton, NJ, USA

Ralph Winters, BA, BS, EmblemHealth, Greater New York City, NY, USA

Ken Yale, DDS, JD, ActiveHealth Management, San Francisco, CA, USA

Scott Zasadil, PhD, UMPC Medical Plan, Pittsburgh, PA, USA

Tutorial A

Case Study: Imputing Medical Specialty Using Data Mining Models

David Redfearn, PhD

Chapter Ouline

BENDING THE CURVE

"Bending the Curve" refers to reducing the existing trend of rising healthcare costs in the United States, which has been running at a rate two or three times higher than inflation – a trend that is widely recognized as unsustainable. The United States is now spending nearly double what other industrialized nations spend on health care, without a corresponding improvement in outcomes.

As of 2008, American healthcare spending had surpassed $2.3 trillion – three times the $714 billion spent in 1990, and eight times the $253 billion spent in 1980. Furthermore, between 1999 and 2007 the share of the Gross Domestic Product (GCP) devoted to health care rose from 13.7% to 16.2%, making American health care one of the most expensive systems in the world.

Practical Predictive Analytics and Decisioning Systems for Medicine. DOI: http://dx.doi.org/10.1016/B978-0-12-411643-6.00016-8

A number of initiatives have been developed over the past decade to try to "bend" this cost curve by reducing the annual increases to a more manageable level (no-one reasonably expects to actually reduce costs). At the Federal level, the healthcare reform agenda has been set by the Patient Protection and Affordable Care Act, 1996 (PPACA), with goals of significantly expanding coverage, improving patient care, reining in costs, and reducing waste. These initiatives encompass payment and insurance reform (e.g., bundled payments/episodic payment models), healthcare innovation and technology reform (e.g., electronic medical records), and organization and operational reform (e.g., accountable care organizations, evidence-based medicine). One particular initiative, generally implemented by health insurance carriers, has been the development of "cost-efficient" networks of providers (primarily physicians and hospitals) that provide quality outcomes at reduced cost. These high-performance networks have had some success in the market, and have been implemented by most of the large for-profit (e.g., WellPoint, Aetna, United) and non-profit (Blue Cross/Blue Shield plans) carriers across the USA.

There are some specific technical requirements for these networks. One key issue — the central concern of this tutorial — is the accurate determination of physician medical specialty. It may be surprising to hear that this is not particularly easy, but physicians often report multiple medical specialties, and may choose a "primary" medical specialty for reasons largely unrelated to their actual practice characteristics. Primary medical specialties are used for printed and electronic provider directories, and many physicians choose less-specific specialties in order to attract more patients.

In the next section, we discuss the standard methodology for developing cost-efficient networks and why accuracy of medical specialty is so important.

IDENTIFYING COST-EFFICIENT PHYSICIANS AND NETWORKS

Cost-efficient physicians are identified by comparing their costs for treating their specific mix of patients to the average performance of their same medical specialty peers for the same case mix. These methods all use medical claim data submitted by physicians and hospitals and paid by insurance carriers (or government agencies). Physicians with average costs lower than expected (the peer group average) are considered "cost-efficient," while those with average costs higher than expected are considered "cost-inefficient." The trick here lies in making sure that the cost comparisons are "fair" to physicians. Doctors generally respond to any claim that they are too expensive by saying "But, my patients are sicker."

Physicians treat patients who vary widely in their underlying health status — the specific health conditions involved and the severity of illness — and physicians may vary in the average severity level of their patient panel. Accordingly, it is important to control for the patient severity case-mix for each physician. This is generally accomplished by using clinical models that group medical claims into clinically homogeneous "episodes of care." There are a number of commercial products available that build episodes of care. The most prominent commercial vendors are Optum/Symmetry (Episode Treatment Groups), Truven (Medical Episode Groups), Cave Consulting (Cave Episode Groups), and some new entrants such as the HCI3 Prometheus model. For purposes of these analyses, any of these models would work, as they all are designed to build clinically homogeneous and statistically stable episodes. We use the Symmetry ETG model for this analysis.

The Episode Treatment Group Model

The Episode Treatment Group (ETG) model was introduced in to the market in 1993 and is widely used in medical informatics. Episodes are created by collecting all inpatient, outpatient, ancillary, and drug services into mutually exclusive and exhaustive clinical categories. For individual patients, the ETG model recognizes and categorizes co-morbidities, complications, and treatments that affect the patient's clinical profile, healthcare utilization, and costs.

The ETG grouper first determines when a member becomes eligible for coverage based on enrollment information fed into the grouper. The claim input data is sorted into chronological order and the grouper then reviews each claim, building a treatment episode by identifying an anchor record and continuing to collect all clinically relevant information across time until an absence of treatment ("clean period") is detected, indicating that the episode has been completed.

As a practical matter, the grouper has to deal with both chronic and acute episodes of care. Acute episodes such as bronchitis have clear start and end points. Chronic episodes such as diabetes essentially last forever, and in practice are separated into annual components. In addition, patient eligibility gaps can affect whether it is possible to identify "complete" episodes of care — when a patient is not eligible for coverage, he or she can't generate the claim data needed for the grouper to determine the start and end of episodes.

The key features of ETG are anchor records, clusters, and non-anchor (ancillary and pharmacy) claim records. Anchor records are identified when the medical claim is submitted by a clinician for services related to the evaluation

TABLE A.1 Examples of Base ETGs

Code	ETG
130100	Aids
163000	Diabetes
164800	Obesity
317500	Carpal Tunnel
351700	Cataract
388100	Hypertension
438300	Acute Bronchitis
601100	Pregnancy with Delivery
666000	Acne
713102	Closed Fracture – Knee/Lower Leg
779400	Routine Exam

of a member's condition (so-called evaluation and management, or "E&M," services), or for surgical or related procedures. Claims submitted by a medical facility (for room and board, or emergency room services) may also create an anchor record.

The anchor record starts an episode of care. The ETG grouper evaluates every ancillary and pharmaceutical service against all existing episodes to determine the best fit and groups the claims into clusters, each with one anchor record. Clusters are then mapped into the appropriate episode of care, and each type of episode is assigned a base ETG number. There are a total of 524 base ETGs defined in the current model, each identified with a six-digit number.

Some examples of base ETGs are shown in Table A.1.

Once the base ETG has been established, the grouper examines the clinical data for complications, co-morbidities, or treatments (e.g., surgery or active management of neoplasms). The base ETG code is expanded to incorporate these additional classifications (the full classification system uses nine-digit numbers to identify these elaborated ETGs).

The base ETG classification is designed to be clinically homogeneous, but significant patient variation can remain. To address this issue, the model also calculates an ETG-specific risk score based on information from the complications and co-morbidities identified in the episode. The ETG risk scores are then rolled up into risk categories using multiple linear regression analyses to determine the impact of the severity scores on the overall costs for an episode. Separate models are estimated for each base ETG where severity adjustment was indicated. In addition to complications and co-morbidities, the models account for patient demographics (age/gender), and interactions between complications and interactions between co-morbidities. The result is that some ETGs may have up to four severity categories. The combination of base ETG and severity level yields a clinically homogeneous episode of care. Adding the severity levels to the base ETGs yields a total of 681 severity adjusted episodes.

This is a very large set of clinical categories, but, as we will see, modern data mining (DM) models can accept hundreds or even thousands of predictors, and tools are available to select a smaller number of "best" predictors for detailed analysis. And, of course, this summarization into episodes of care represents many fewer diagnostic categories than if raw ICD9 diagnostic codes were used — the ICD-9 system consists of tens of thousands of separate codes, not to mention the even more elaborate ICD-10 system coming in October 2014.

Episodes of care are patient-level concepts — each episode of care is uniquely attached to a patient. It is possible for a single patient to have multiple episodes running at the same time, and that acute episodes may recur in the analysis period. Episodes are usually built from 2 or 3 years of claim data; 1 year is the minimum time period to get useful information.

Building Episode Profiles for Physicians

In order to use the episode data as part of a physician cost-efficiency analysis, the episodes must be attached to a single physician. For many episodes, only a single physician is involved in providing care. In this case, the physician "responsible" for the patient care is unambiguous. However, for many episodes — particularly those involving complicated care and high cost — many physicians in different specialties may be involved. For example, there may be a primary care physician (PCP) managing overall care, with a specialist (e.g., Cardiology) providing special treatments, or even a surgeon (e.g., Thoracic Surgeon) performing surgery. This may all be part of the episode of care. The question becomes how to choose a single provider responsible for the episode, when many physicians are rendering care.

There are many different approaches to addressing this problem, but most analyses use service cost or patient contact measures to choose a single physician. For example, for medical episodes we might choose the physician with the most patient contact (the highest number of patient visits); for surgical episodes, we might choose the physician with the highest service costs in the episode (this tends to assign responsibility to a surgeon when a surgery is performed). Typically, we require that the selected physician accounts for a substantial proportion of total care; a minimum of 30% of costs or visits is often used. The point here is that the episode needs to be assigned to a single physician responsible for a preponderance of patient care and management.

After assigning a responsible physician to each episode, all the episodes can be rolled up to the physician level. Since physicians treat many different patients, a single physician may be responsible for many episodes (within and across patients); some physicians have several hundred episodes assigned. The patients whose episodes are assigned to a specific physician will vary in clinical characteristics and severity of illness. The overall mix of patients and episodes represents the case-mix for the physician — the relative frequency of specific ETGs and their associated severity. In general, the physician's average cost of care is calculated by taking an average of all their episode costs. Thus, this average cost represents a case-mix adjusted measure of cost, and directly accounts for the average illness burden of the physician's patient panel.

Building Episode Cost Norms

To evaluate a physician's cost-efficiency, we need a normative or "expected" cost for each ETG. Accordingly, episode data for the complete physician sample is used to calculate average costs for each separate ETG by physician specialty. Thus, for example, for ETG 388100 (Hypertension) we will have an average cost calculated separately for each physician specialty treating this condition — General Practitioners, Family Practitioners, Internal Medicine, Cardiologists, etc. Physicians generally insist that their performance be compared to same-specialty peers. In addition, this approach helps control for unmeasured differences in underlying patient severity. For example, diabetics treated by Endocrinologists are generally more severely ill than those treated by Family Practitioners.

The physician sample used to build the normative ETG costs should be comparable to the physician sample being evaluated, and generally this means physicians in the same geographical area and the same contracted network.

Calculating Physician Cost-Efficiency

For each physician being evaluated, each of their assigned episodes is compared to the normative episode cost (matched by ETG category) and an actual/expected cost ratio is calculated. When this ratio is greater than 1.0, the physician's cost is higher than expected; when the ratio is less than 1.0, the physician's cost is less than expected. When these individual cost-efficiency ratios are averaged (taking into account the distribution of ETGs assigned to the physician), the resulting value represents the overall cost-efficiency for the physician taking into account their specific patient mix of conditions and severity levels. Thus, the physician's patients may in fact be sicker than average, but he or she is being compared to expected costs that reflect the same elevated patient and severity mix.

WHY PHYSICIAN SPECIALTY IS IMPORTANT

It should be obvious from this discussion that we need to have an accurate characterization of physician specialty, both for the normative cost calculations and for the specific comparison of actual to expected costs. Average costs for a specific ETG may vary substantially across medical specialties. This may be because average patient severity varies across specialties (as was mentioned previously), or just because practice patterns differ across specialties (medical sub-specialties may provide more costly, and intensive care costing more than primary care physicians).

If we mischaracterize a physician specialty, the episode costs are going to be included in the wrong normative cost data and this can bias all the individual cost-efficiency comparisons. If a physician is matched to the wrong specialty norm, average costs may not be representative — and in fact the mix of high-frequency ETGs may not match well — so the normative cost data may be less reliable. If we make these mistakes, then the cost-efficiency measurement will be inaccurate.

Normally, we simply take the primary medical specialty reported by the physician. However, as noted previously, this specialty may not be representative of the physician's actual practice and case-mix. Physicians may provide more than one specialty — some provider database systems can accommodate many specialties for the same doctor. (The data we are using includes up to four separate medical specialties for a single physician.) Because the "primary" (e.g., first-listed) specialty is used for provider directories, it may be used more for "advertising" than to represent actual practice.

Physicians in many specialties may be "board certified" in that specialty (via special training and examinations). Physicians will generally seek board certification in their primary specialty, so choosing the first-listed board certified specialty can reduce error but it does not completely solve the problem. For example, a Gastroenterologist may be board certified in both Internal Medicine (listed first) and Gastroenterology (listed second), when their practice is confined to Gastroenterology.

We need to accurately identify the physician specialty to be used in the cost-efficiency calculations. Of course, you could just ask each physician for the specialty they want to use for the comparison; this may work for small physician networks. However, this will not be feasible for larger networks, which may consist of 50,000 or more individual doctors. Also, we don't expect a high volume of inaccurate specialties, and contacting every physician would therefore be a huge waste of resources in most cases.

USING ETG DATA TO IMPUTE SPECIALTY

ETGs and episodes of care assigned to a physician characterize the physician's medical practice — the types of patients and the types of illness they treat. Assuming that different specialties treat a distinctive mix of patients and conditions, it should be possible to analyze the episode data and use that information to "impute" the true specialty for the physician no matter what specialty they self-assign. That is the analytic task described here.

The situation is made difficult because of the substantial overlap that may exist between the practices of different specialties. An MD license is general and does not restrict the type of cases and patients a physician may treat. (An old joke is that a General Practitioner can perform brain surgery.)

For example, we would expect that General Practitioner and Family Practitioner specialties treat a very similar patient mix. On the other hand, we expect much less overlap between the Internal Medicine (IM) specialty and the key IM subspecialties (Pulmonology, Rheumatology, Gastroenterology, and Cardiology). Among these subspecialties, there should be little confusion between pulmonary, rheumatology, gastroenterology, and cardiac conditions and episodes.

One issue with using statistical DM techniques to build these kinds of models is that while the models can perform well (in a statistical sense), it can be difficult to understand "why" the models perform as they do. Accordingly, our evaluation includes a requirement of "face validity" — that is, we should be able to view the distribution of episodes and ETGs for the specialty categories defined by the models, and clearly see and understand why the models performed as they did. In cases where we need to reassign physician specialty for cost-efficiency profiling, we have to be able to explain that process to the physicians being evaluated. They have to see and understand why the reassignment makes sense. They will not accept a "Black Box" statistical model.

To make this analysis more comprehensive, we have chosen to run three separate tests of the DM models — and we have specific expectations for how the DM models will perform in each case:

1. *A physician sample consisting of Internal Medicine, Pulmonology, Rheumatology, Gastroenterology, and Cardiology specialties.* In this case, we expect the DM models to be able to assign the correct medical specialty to each physician — that is, the models should identify "IM" doctors who actually are practicing more like one of the subspecialties, or a subspecialty (e.g., Pulmonology) actually practicing more like a general Internist. We do not expect to have the subspecialties reassigned. For example, we do not expect Pulmonologists to be confused with Rheumatologists, or Gastroenterologists, or Cardiologists.
2. *A physician sample consisting of General Practitioner and Family Practitioner specialties.* In this case, we expect the practice patterns for these two specialties (e.g., the distribution of specific ETGs) to be essentially the same — that is, these specialties typically treat the same kinds of primary care conditions. We do not expect the DM models to be able to distinguish between these specialties.
3. *A physician sample consisting of Pediatric and General Surgery specialties.* In this case, we don't expect to see any confusion between the conditions and patients treated by each specialty. The distinguishing characteristics should be patient age and the presence of a surgical procedure — or conditions typically treated by surgical procedures. We would never expect pediatricians to call themselves surgeons, or vice versa (there are pediatric surgical subspecialties, but these physicians are not included in this physician sample.) In this case we expect DM models to separate these specialties perfectly, with no reassignments.

Accuracy of the Criterion Variable

Note that this example of model development is a bit unusual in the sense that the criterion used in model development (the medical specialty provided by the physician) is known to have significant errors — in fact, identifying those errors (and correcting them) is the primary purpose of the analysis. Normally, when we build predictive models, we develop the model where the criterion is known to be accurate. Say, for example, that we want to develop a clinical model that will predict the future costs for a sample of patients. However, to develop the model, we use retrospective data in which we know the actual costs for the member in the base period, and use the episode data as the predictor and the (actual) costs as the criterion. Once the model is developed, it can be used to predict future (as yet unknown) patient costs. In the current analysis, we don't know the "real" physician specialty for all physicians. We have a specialty assigned to every physician, but we don't know which of those assignments are correct.

When we actually build the data mining models, the software reports an error rate. This makes complete sense when the criterion is known to be accurate — the error rate represents the proportion of cases in which the criterion is not predicted accurately. However, in the current context, the "error rate" simply represents the proportion of physicians for which the model "reclassifies" their medical specialty — and the best measure of model "error" lies in how it performs across samples and time. We don't expect a large number of reassignments — most of the time the reported specialty will be accurate — but we want to flag the physicians practicing outside their reported specialty. Thus, we prefer low model error rates when we evaluate the models. This will be discussed further later in the chapter.

THE ANALYSIS SAMPLE

The episode and provider data used in this analysis come from a large Preferred Provider Network (approximately 75,000 physicians of all medical specialties) serving a membership of about 6 million individuals. The ETG data is derived from an analysis of 2 years of medical claims data (ending September 2012). Because of the delay in adjudicating claims, 3 months of claim runout is used to make sure complete paid claims data are available to build episodes. Version 7.6 of the ETG grouper was used to build the episodes.

The episodes were assigned to specific physicians based on highest cost (for surgical episodes) and most contact (for medical episodes). The physician specialty used as the criterion variable was the first-listed board certified specialty available, or if no board certification was available, the first-listed specialty (using information from the provider directory database and supplied by the physicians themselves). Up to four different specialties are available for each physician.

Physicians with less than 10 episodes assigned were excluded from the analysis. Given this low episode volume, it would be difficult for any model to accurately identify specialty.

The three analysis samples shown in Tables A.2–A.4 were used.

The source episode information was organized by physician, with each record representing a single episode for that physician. Table A.5 shows an example of what the source data looked like.

These data are summarized to the physician and base ETG level. The proportion column shows the proportion of the physician's episodes represented by the specific base ETG. (For an individual physician, these sum to 1.0.). The ETG proportion is the measure of the ETG mix for an individual physician. (It is best practice to scale the predictors so that predictors with greater numeric ranges dominate those in smaller numeric ranges; also, scaling can help avoid numerical difficulties during model calculation.)

TABLE A.2 Internal Medicine and Subspecialties

Specialty	Count	Percent
Pulmonology	424	4.61
Cardiology	1,193	12.99
Internal Medicine	6,543	71.22
Rheumatology	241	2.62
Gastroenterology	786	8.56
Total	9,187	100.00

TABLE A.3 General Practice/Family Practice

Specialty	Count	Percent
Family Practice	5,218	89.23
General Practice	630	10.77
Total	5,848	100.00

TABLE A.4 Pediatrics/General Surgery

Specialty	Count	Percent
Pediatrics	3,090	72.95
General Surgery	1,146	27.05
Total	4,236	100.00

TABLE A.5 Sample ETG data for Input to the Data Mining Models

Physician	Base ETG	ETG Proportion	Specialty
1	ETG164800_Obesity	0.0892857143	PL
1	ETG238800_Mooddisorder,depressed	0.0178571429	PL
1	ETG239800_Anxietydisorder/phobia	0.0178571429	PL
1	ETG240600_Otherpsych/behaviordisorder	0.0178571429	PL
1	ETG315000_InflamCNS,other	0.0178571429	PL
1	ETG316000_CVA	0.0178571429	PL
1	ETG316700_Otherhered/degenCNSdisorder	0.0178571429	PL
1	ETG318600_Otherneurologicaldiseases	0.0714285714	PL
1	ETG386500_Ischhrtdis	0.0178571429	PL
1	ETG386800_CHF	0.0178571429	PL
1	ETG386900_Cardiomyopathy	0.0178571429	PL
1	ETG388100_Hypertension	0.0535714286	PL
1	ETG403500_Chronicsinusitis	0.0357142857	PL
1	ETG404700_Congen&acqanomENT	0.0178571429	PL
1	ETG405300_OtherENTdisorders	0.482142857	PL
1	ETG438800_Asthma	0.0178571429	PL
1	ETG439300_COPD	0.0178571429	PL
1	ETG669001_Othminskintrau-foot/ankle	0.0178571429	PL
1	ETG712208_Jtdegen-back	0.0178571429	PL
1	ETG748100_Chromosomalanomalies	0.0178571429	PL
2	ETG163000_Diabetes	0.0303030303	CD

(Continued)

TABLE A.5 (Continued)

Physician	Base ETG	ETG Proportion	Specialty
2	ETG164700_Hyperlipidemia,other	0.0757575758	CD
2	ETG164800_Obesity	0.0303030303	CD
2	ETG386500_Ischhrtdis	0.227272727	CD
2	ETG386600_Pulmonaryhrtdisease	0.0454545455	CD
2	ETG386800_CHF	0.0454545455	CD
2	ETG386900_Cardiomyopathy	0.0454545455	CD
2	ETG387400_Valvulardisorder	0.121212121	CD
2	ETG387700_Othconductiondisorder	0.0454545455	CD
2	ETG387800_A-fib&flutter	0.0303030303	CD
2	ETG388100_Hypertension	0.257575758	CD
2	ETG439300_COPD	0.0454545455	CD

Data mining models expect the input data in a different format. To meet this requirement, the input data was "transposed" so that rows became columns (observations converted to variables). Figure A.1 illustrates what (a portion of) the resulting data table looks like.

Three additional variables were added for each physician in the analyses: average patient age (for their total patient population), "average" gender (Male coded as 1 and Female Coded as 2), and average patient risk.

The use of the patient-level risk variable requires further explanation. As has been described, the ETG model includes the option to assign a risk score and risk category to every episode – these risk scores are specific to an ETG. Each base ETG can have up to four different severity categories. Adding the severity levels to the ETG classifications increases the number of unique ETGs from 524 to 681. As we will see, many ETGs represent relatively rare conditions, and thus the frequency of occurrence for a specific physician is low. Adding the ETG-specific risk categories makes this situation worse. When the predictors used in the data mining analysis have very low variance they will generally not contribute to the prediction, and should be removed from the analysis since they only contribute "noise" to the model. Preliminary investigation showed that these "rare" ETGs dropped out of the analysis anyway, and using the base ETG categories reduced the predictors that had to be removed from the analyses. We discuss the procedures used to select key predictors for the data mining models in a subsequent section.

However, patient severity *is* an important factor in the physician case-mix. A separate patient-level risk score was available (the Verisk DxCG Model 18 Retrospective patient risk score). Note that this score is not episode-specific; it attempts to measure all the risk factors operating for the patient. Because this is a single value, it is easy to add to the analysis, and thus the DM models can incorporate overall patient risk in the predictions. For the DxCG risk score, 1.0 represents "average" patient risk (and cost) in their normative calibration sample, 2.0 indicates twice average risk and costs, etc. The assumption here is that average patient population severity may vary across specialties.

After the addition of the age, gender, and risk variables to the base ETGs, we had 421 predictor variables for the Internal Medicine analysis, 422 predictor variables for the Family Practice/General practice analysis, and 412 predictor variables for the Pediatrics/General Surgery analysis.

These data (along with the standard specialty code as the dependent variable) were the starting point of the analysis.

OVERVIEW OF THE DATA MINING PROCESS

In the first step in the process we need to prepare the data for modeling. This has already been described: choosing the default medical specialty information (the model dependent variable); obtaining the episode data assigned to physicians; adding patient age, gender, and average patient severity data (the model predictor variables); and formatting the data for analysis.

Physician	ETG163000_Diabetes	ETG164700_Hyperlipidemia, other	ETG164800_Obesity	ETG238800_Mooddisorder,depressed	ETG239800_Anxietydisorder/phobia	ETG240600_Otherpsych/behaviordisorder
1	0	0	0.0892857143	0.0178571429	0.0178571429	0.0178571429
2	0.0303030303	0.0757575758	0.0303030303	0	0	0

FIGURE A.1   Sample Data Input Format.

The second step involves identifying redundant variables. Often, multiple predictors can carry similar information (that is, they are highly correlated). In this step, a simple correlation test is applied to identify redundant inputs and remove them from further consideration for modeling.

The third step involves selecting key predictor variables, and is sometimes known as dimension reduction. While data mining models can handle large numbers of predictors, the analysis process is faster and easier to interpret with fewer predictors. The trick here is to identify key predictors without impacting the performance of the model. For example, starting with 400 predictors, we could cut this down to 10 predictors in the model — but the accuracy of the resulting model would also likely be reduced. There are specific "feature selection" procedures that can be used to do this selection, and this will be described in a later section of this tutorial.

The fourth step involves actually testing various data mining models on the data. There are a large number of different models that can be tested, and these models vary in how well they perform when run against a specific data set. What these procedures have in common is that they identify ("learn") specific patterns in the data one case at a time (much as a human being does). The traditional statistical assumptions (normality, uncorrelated errors) are not made or required. Thus, we don't have to be concerned with the internal calculations of the models; we can try different models and select the model with the best performance. For this analysis, we tested Support Vector Machine (SVM), MAR Splines, Boosted Trees, Random Forest, and Classification and Regression Tree (C&RT) models.

DATA MINING SOFTWARE

For this tutorial, we are using Statistica Data Miner (Version 12). This is a very powerful analysis system that supports the full range of data management and analysis procedures needed for this work. The software runs on Windows (XP, Win7, or Win8, in both 32-bit and 64-bit versions). The illustrations in this tutorial are screen shots from this software.

The Statistica DM software supports running these analyses in a variety of different ways — from almost completely automated "Data Mining Recipes" to standalone, manual setups. We have generally chosen manual setups and processing, but also accept procedure defaults in most cases.

DATA MINING STEP BY STEP

In this section of the tutorial, we work through the analysis of the IM specialties step-by-step so that every step and decision in the analysis is explicit.

Input Data

As described in the data preparation discussion, we create a table with the dependent variable (specialty) and all the predictors for each of the physicians in the analysis. You can see what this looks like for the Internal Medicine analysis in the screen shot shown in Figure A.2.

Figure A.2 consists of 423 variables and 9,187 rows (physicians).

Data: impute_im2013.sta* (423v by 9187c)

	1 Physician	2 spec	3 age_mean	4 gender_mean	5 ETG130600_Other infectdisease	6 ETG162200_Hypo-func tthyroidgland	7 ETG162400_Malneo thyroidgland	8 ETG164500_Nutritional deficiency	9 ETG164700_Hyperlipidemia other	10 ETG164800_Obesity
1	1	IM	56.1367041	1.58928839	0.00187265918	0.00561797753	0.00187265918	0.00187265918	0.00187265918	0.00561797753
2	2	IM	54.3303571	1.56357143	0.00892857143	0.0491071429	0	0.0133928571	0.00446428571	0.0178571429
3	3	IM	47.0869565	1.43478261	0	0.0434782609	0	0	0.0434782609	0.0434782609
4	4	IM	52.9766166	1.49217221	0.00587084149	0.0322896282	0	0.000978473581	0.0215264188	0.00293542074
5	5	IM	61.0944444	1.34444444	0.0111111111	0.0388888889	0	0.0166666667	0.0555555556	0
6	6	IM	70.9166667	1.61458333	0	0.0729166667	0	0.0104166667	0.03125	0
7	7	IM	63.4513889	1.57638889	0.00347222222	0.00347222222	0	0.0104166667	0	0.00694444444
8	8	IM	71.4772727	1.65909091	0.0227272727	0.0454545455	0	0.0454545455	0.0113636364	0.0113636364
9	9	IM	45.1646392	1.79381443	0.0206185567	0.24742268	0	0.00515463918	0.0103092784	0.0463917526
10	10	IM	56.8592593	1.33333333	0.00740740741	0.037037037	0	0.00740740741	0.0666666667	0.037037037
11	11	IM	47.5137615	1.58715596	0.00917431193	0.0137614679	0	0.0137614679	0.0779816514	0.0321100917
12	12	IM	57.5726496	1.64102564	0	0.0598290598	0	0.0256410256	0.0170940171	0.0256410256
13	13	IM	51.041958	1.48951049	0	0.013986014	0	0.013986014	0.041958042	0
14	14	IM	53.7358892	1.47390841	0.00425985091	0.0394036209	0.00319488818	0.0330138445	0.0340788072	0.0905218317
15	15	IM	68.9375	1.3125	0	0	0	0	0	0
16	16	IM	65.8159509	1.47862761	0	0.0306748466	0	0	0.0981595092	0
17	17	IM	49.5446429	1.6875	0	0	0	0	0	0.00446428571
18	18	IM	63.9456522	1.55978261	0.0108695652	0.0434782609	0	0	0.0760869565	0.00543478261
19	19	IM	39.9563882	1.51781327	0.00614250614	0.00614250614	0	0	0.00982800983	0.00614250614
20	20	IM	51.122449	1.36734694	0.0612244898	0.0204081633	0	0	0	0.0408163265

FIGURE A.2   Sample Data Input In Statistica.

Redundant Variables

In this step we identify redundant variables — that is, highly correlated predictors which carry very similar information. Some ETGs "go together" in practice (such as Diabetes and Diabetic Retinopathy), and this can show up in the ETG data in the analysis. You would not necessarily need to have both variables in the analysis to identify physicians who treat a high proportion of diabetics.

These redundant variables are easily identified by correlating all the predictors with each other, and scanning the resulting matrix of correlations for high values.

The specific question here is the criterion we use to identify redundant variables. In this case we have chosen a correlation of 0.71 or higher, indicating that two variables have 50% or more of their variation in common. This is a fairly arbitrary selection and could be adjusted up or down, but should probably be kept at a relatively high level so as to not exclude variables with some unique (possibly critical) predictive power.

We select Basic Statistics and Correlation matrices as shown in the dialog in Figure A.3.

The dialog for selecting the variables for the analysis is shown in Figure A.4.

We then run the correlation analysis by clicking on the Summary button (Figure A.5).

The resulting correlation matrix is then displayed (Figure A.6).

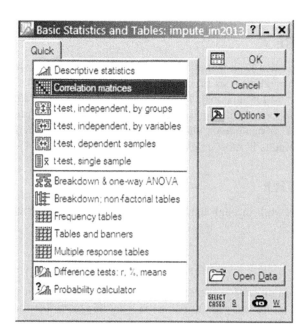

FIGURE A.3   Selecting Correlations as Method.

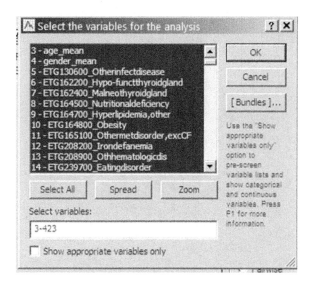

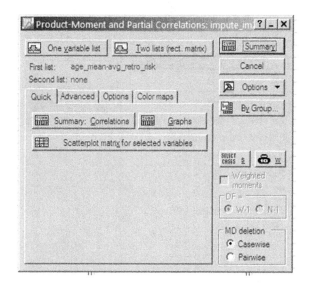

FIGURE A.4   Selecting Predictors for Analysis.

FIGURE A.5   Run Summary Analysis for Correlations.

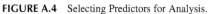

FIGURE A.6   Correlations Among Predictors.

An examination of the correlation matrix indicates that no correlation exceeds the $r = 0.71$ criterion − in fact, the highest observed correlation is 0.51. We conclude that there are no redundant predictors in the analysis, and thus all 421 predictors remain in the analysis at this point.

Selecting Key Predictors

There are many different possible methods to select key predictors − that is, predictors that are actually significantly (in both the statistical and non-statistical sense) related to the dependent variable (provider specialty). We have tested two different approaches for this analysis.

Perhaps the simplest approach is to simply calculate the variability (e.g., standard deviation or coefficient of variation) of each of the predictors. Variables with very little variation (in this particular context, ETGs with very low frequency) cannot relate to anything, and will not be a significant predictor of physician specialty.

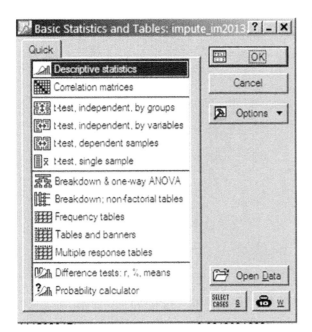

FIGURE A.7 Dialog to Retrieve Descriptive Statistics for Predictors.

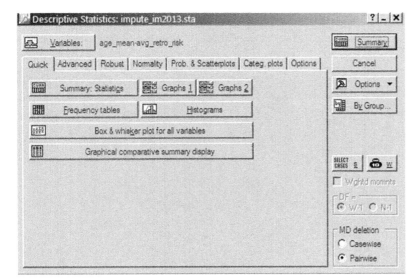

FIGURE A.8 Selecting Variables to Analyze.

This analysis is easily accomplished using the Statistica Basic Statistics Module (Figure A.7).

Clicking OK opens a dialog to select the variables for the analysis (Figure A.8).

Selecting the Advanced tab lets us specify the statistics we want to see (Figure A.9).

Here, we have selected Valid N, Mean, Standard Deviation, Coefficient of variation, and Minimum & maximum values. Clicking Summary runs the analysis (Figure A.10).

We can use either the Coefficient of Variation (Standard Deviation divided by Mean — sometimes known as relative standard deviation) or the Standard Deviation statistic itself for this analysis. We simply re-sort the data by CV or Standard Deviation, from Low to High, to identify the variables with little variation. For this example, we sorted by SD (ascending). The variables at the top of this listing are candidates for exclusion from the model (Figure A.11).

Feature Selection

As noted, we are trying to identify variables with enough variation to actually contribute to the prediction of the dependent variable — physician specialty. Statistica DM offers a procedure that can do this directly: Feature Selection.

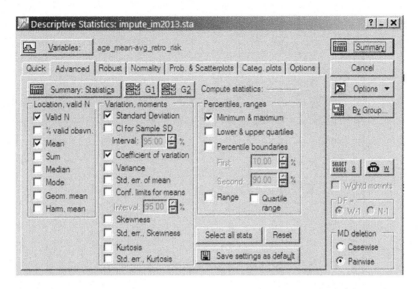

FIGURE A.9   Dialog to Select Descriptive Statistics.

Variable	Valid N	Mean	Minimum	Maximum	Std. Dev.	Coef.Var.
age_mean	9187	55.44688	7.775510	91.36364	8.872480	16.002
gender_mean	9187	1.54366	1.000000	2.00000	0.153336	9.933
ETG130600_Otherinfectdisease	9187	0.00491	0.000000	0.50526	0.014466	294.344
ETG162200_Hypo-functthyroidgland	9187	0.02667	0.000000	0.57025	0.041755	156.546
ETG162400_Malneothyroidgland	9187	0.00106	0.000000	0.58252	0.009913	935.575
ETG164500_Nutritionaldeficiency	9187	0.00723	0.000000	0.38346	0.018665	258.332
ETG164700_Hyperlipidemia.other	9187	0.03187	0.000000	0.72000	0.043010	134.974
ETG164800_Obesity	9187	0.01754	0.000000	0.79070	0.034130	194.570
ETG165100_Othermetdisorder.excCF	9187	0.01323	0.000000	0.44565	0.029750	224.796
ETG208200_Irondefanemia	9187	0.00436	0.000000	0.20755	0.013554	310.814
ETG208900_Otthhematologicdis	9187	0.00698	0.000000	0.40000	0.020750	297.394
ETG239700_Eatingdisorder	9187	0.00020	0.000000	0.14815	0.002881	1475.932
ETG239800_Anxietydisorder/phobia	9187	0.00881	0.000000	0.24359	0.016701	189.477
ETG271200_Acutealcoholintoxicati	9187	0.00061	0.000000	0.16667	0.005096	837.127
ETG350600_Inflameyedisease	9187	0.00080	0.000000	0.49740	0.006545	818.535
ETG386100_Hypertension	9187	0.15021	0.000000	0.83333	0.126004	83.885
ETG402200_Inflamoralcavity	9187	0.00037	0.000000	0.07143	0.002248	604.102
ETG403100_T&Aorpharyngitis	9187	0.01909	0.000000	0.54545	0.036390	190.671
ETG403300_Acutesinusitis	9187	0.01381	0.000000	0.31841	0.026699	193.391
ETG473100_Infectstom&esoph	9187	0.00442	0.000000	0.45098	0.013822	312.671
ETG473300_Inflamesophagus	9187	0.01376	0.000000	0.40000	0.031042	225.626
ETG473500_Gastritis.duodenitis	9187	0.00607	0.000000	0.50000	0.020473	337.171
ETG473800_Ulcer	9187	0.00303	0.000000	0.34483	0.012944	427.192
ETG474200_Nonmalneostom&esoph	9187	0.00060	0.000000	0.16667	0.004184	701.698
ETG474400_Traumastomoresoph	9187	0.00012	0.000000	0.10000	0.001657	1403.379
ETG474500_Anomalystomoresoph	9187	0.00090	0.000000	0.40741	0.008078	893.717
ETG474900_Diverticulitis/diverti	9187	0.01014	0.000000	0.43750	0.032779	323.168
ETG475000_Othinfectdiseaseintest	9187	0.00299	0.000000	0.18750	0.010271	343.100
ETG475200_Inflamintest&abdom	9187	0.00159	0.000000	0.15000	0.008201	516.724
ETG475300_Inflamboweldisease	9187	0.00764	0.000000	0.96774	0.028894	378.353
ETG475400_Malneolgintest	9187	0.00096	0.000000	0.24138	0.006287	653.963
ETG475600_Nonmalneosmintest&abdo	9187	0.00825	0.000000	0.69231	0.032926	399.321
ETG476100_Vasculardisintest&abdo	9187	0.00043	0.000000	0.10000	0.003555	827.058

FIGURE A.10   Descriptive Statistics Results.

The methods implemented in the Feature Selection and Variable Screening (FSL) module are specifically designed to handle extremely large sets of predictors. You can select a subset of predictors from a large list of candidate predictors without assuming that the relationships between the predictors and the dependent or outcome variables of interest are linear, or even monotone. Therefore, this module can serve as an ideal pre-processor for predictive data mining, used to select manageable sets of predictors that are likely related to the dependent (outcome) variables of interest,

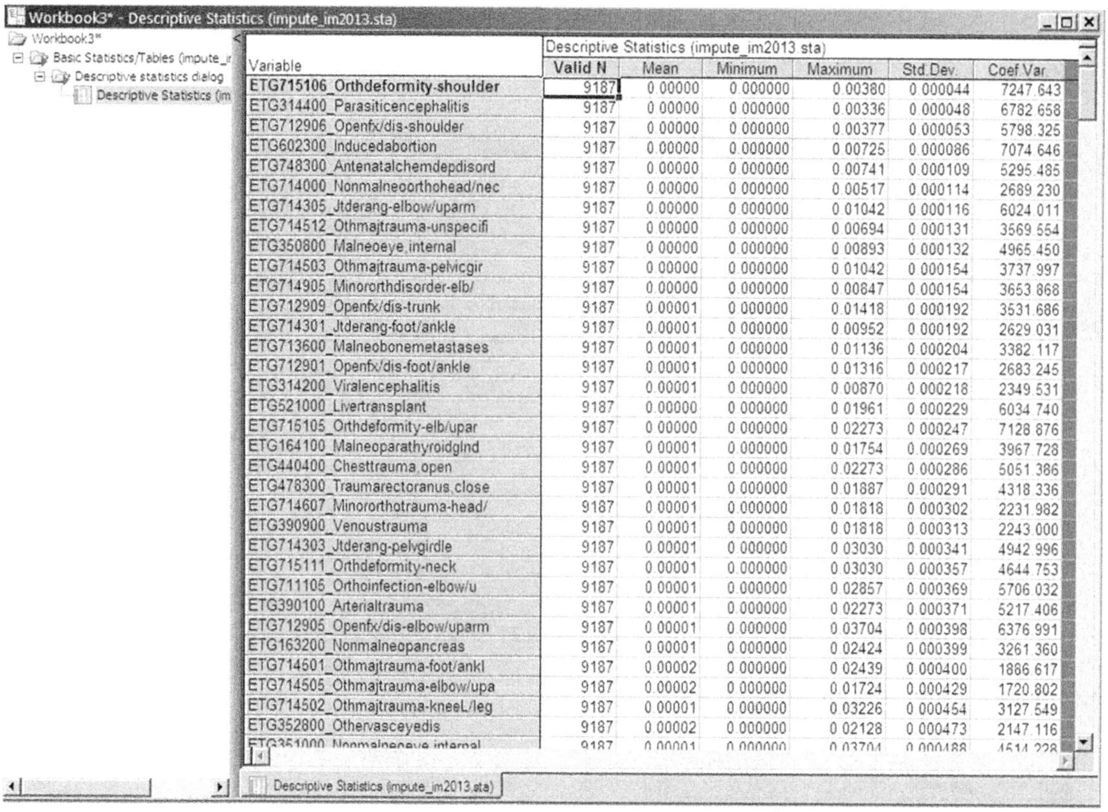

Descriptive Statistics (impute_im2013 sta)

Variable	Valid N	Mean	Minimum	Maximum	Std.Dev.	Coef.Var.
ETG715106_Orthdeformity-shoulder	9187	0.00000	0.000000	0.00380	0.000044	7247.643
ETG314400_Parasiticencephalitis	9187	0.00000	0.000000	0.00336	0.000048	6782.658
ETG712906_Openfx/dis-shoulder	9187	0.00000	0.000000	0.00377	0.000053	5798.325
ETG602300_Inducedabortion	9187	0.00000	0.000000	0.00725	0.000086	7074.646
ETG748300_Antenatalchemdepdisord	9187	0.00000	0.000000	0.00741	0.000109	5295.485
ETG714000_Nonmalneoorthohead/nec	9187	0.00000	0.000000	0.00517	0.000114	2689.230
ETG714305_Jtderang-elbow/uparm	9187	0.00000	0.000000	0.01042	0.000116	6024.011
ETG714512_Othmajtrauma-unspecifi	9187	0.00000	0.000000	0.00694	0.000131	3569.554
ETG350800_Malneoeye.internal	9187	0.00000	0.000000	0.00893	0.000132	4965.450
ETG714503_Othmajtrauma-pelvicgir	9187	0.00000	0.000000	0.01042	0.000154	3737.997
ETG714905_Minororthdisorder-elb/	9187	0.00000	0.000000	0.00847	0.000154	3653.868
ETG712909_Openfx/dis-trunk	9187	0.00001	0.000000	0.01418	0.000192	3531.686
ETG714301_Jtderang-foot/ankle	9187	0.00001	0.000000	0.00952	0.000192	2629.031
ETG713600_Malneobonemetastases	9187	0.00001	0.000000	0.01136	0.000204	3382.117
ETG712901_Openfx/dis-foot/ankle	9187	0.00001	0.000000	0.01316	0.000217	2683.245
ETG314200_Viralencephalitis	9187	0.00001	0.000000	0.00870	0.000218	2349.531
ETG521000_Livertransplant	9187	0.00000	0.000000	0.01961	0.000229	6034.740
ETG715105_Orthdeformity-elb/upar	9187	0.00001	0.000000	0.02273	0.000247	7128.876
ETG164100_Malneoparathyroidglnd	9187	0.00001	0.000000	0.01754	0.000269	3967.728
ETG440400_Chesttrauma.open	9187	0.00001	0.000000	0.02273	0.000286	5051.386
ETG478300_Traumarectoranus.close	9187	0.00001	0.000000	0.01887	0.000291	4318.336
ETG714607_Minororthotrauma-head/	9187	0.00001	0.000000	0.01818	0.000302	2231.982
ETG390900_Venoustrauma	9187	0.00001	0.000000	0.01818	0.000313	2243.000
ETG714303_Jtderang-pelvgirdle	9187	0.00001	0.000000	0.03030	0.000341	4942.996
ETG715111_Orthdeformity-neck	9187	0.00001	0.000000	0.03030	0.000357	4644.753
ETG711105_Orthoinfection-elbow/u	9187	0.00001	0.000000	0.02857	0.000369	5706.032
ETG390100_Arterialtrauma	9187	0.00001	0.000000	0.02273	0.000371	5217.406
ETG712905_Openfx/dis-elbow/uparm	9187	0.00001	0.000000	0.03704	0.000398	6376.991
ETG163200_Nonmalneopancreas	9187	0.00001	0.000000	0.02424	0.000399	3261.360
ETG714601_Othmajtrauma-foot/ankl	9187	0.00002	0.000000	0.02439	0.000400	1886.617
ETG714505_Othmajtrauma-elbow/upa	9187	0.00002	0.000000	0.01724	0.000429	1720.802
ETG714502_Othmajtrauma-kneeL/leg	9187	0.00001	0.000000	0.03226	0.000454	3127.549
ETG352800_Othervasceyedis	9187	0.00002	0.000000	0.02128	0.000473	2147.116
ETG351000_Nonmalneoeye.internal	9187	0.00001	0.000000	0.03704	0.000488	4514.228

Descriptive Statistics (impute_im2013.sta)

FIGURE A.11   Sorted Data.

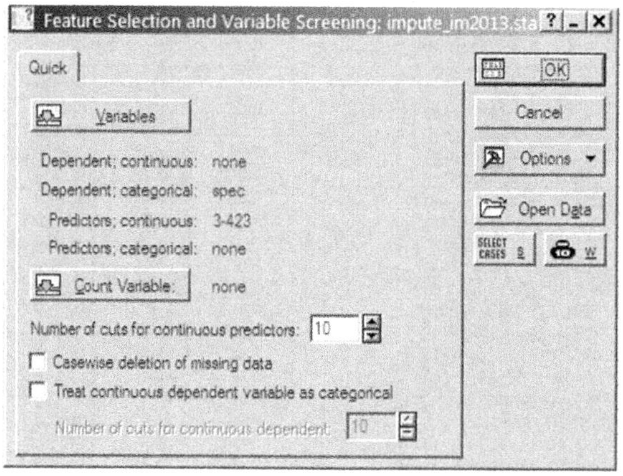

FIGURE A.12   Statistica Feature Selection Dialog.

The first step in this process is to open the Feature Selection dialog and select the variables in the analysis (Figure A.12). For this process, all 421 predictors are included in the analysis.

Note the parameter for "Number of cuts for continuous predictors." This is set to 10 by default. The program will divide the range of values for each continuous predictor into K intervals, and compute statistics based on the frequencies in those intervals for classification type problems, as we have here. The number of splits in the predictors can be set by the user. Note that if K is set to 2, we are assuming only linear relationships between the predictor and dependent variable. If K is set to 3, we could capture simple monotone or quadratic relationships. The default value of 10 is well suited to perform screening for practically all types of monotone or complex non-monotone relationships.

Clicking OK starts the analysis, and it runs in a few seconds. The results dialog then appears (Figure A.13).

There are two options here: we can select a specific number of "best" predictors (sorted by Chi-square values or p values), or we can define significance level and use that to select predictors. Selecting a significance level (e.g., $p < 0.01$) is helpful if we don't, *a priori*, know the number of optimal predictors.

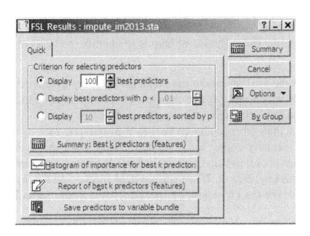

FIGURE A.13   Feature Selection Results Selection Dialog.

Best predictors for categor		
	Chi-square	p-value
ETG386500_Ischhrtdis	5547.711	0.00
ETG475600_Nonmalneosmintest&abdo	5376.331	0.00
ETG711400_Adultrheumatoidarthrit	5319.383	0.00
ETG475300_Inflamboweldisease	5031.744	0.00
ETG473300_Inflamesophagus	4938.691	0.00
ETG474900_Diverticulitis/diverti	4912.039	0.00
ETG387400_Valvulardisorder	4844.776	0.00
ETG477400_Hemorrhoids.simple	4722.578	0.00
ETG438800_Asthma	4639.078	0.00
ETG711700_Autoimrheumdiseaseexcl	4513.965	0.00
ETG476400_Irritablebowelsyndrome	4507.540	0.00
ETG711600_Lupus	4380.350	0.00
ETG478500_Othdiseaserectum/anus	4217.803	0.00
ETG387700_Othconductiondisorder	4016.205	0.00
ETG712204_Jtdegen-lowerarm	3920.466	0.00
ETG388100_Hypertension	3867.360	0.00
ETG387800_A-fib&flutter	3733.581	0.00
ETG439300_COPD	3676.146	0.00
ETG476900_Otherdiseaseintest&abd	3659.144	0.00
ETG666900_Psoriasis	3633.999	0.00
ETG711912_Majjtinfl-unspecified	3214.936	0.00
ETG712202_Jtdegen-kneeL/leg	3148.525	0.00
ETG439800_Otherinflamlungdisease	3139.881	0.00
ETG478000_Nonnalneorectoranus	2978.394	0.00
ETG405300_OtherENTdisorders	2930.266	0.00
ETG386900_Cardiomyopathy	2919.019	0.00
ETG164600_Gout	2763.603	0.00
ETG473800_Ulcer	2677.177	0.00
ETG473500_Gastritis.duodenitis	2602.428	0.00
avg_retro_risk	2571.623	0.00
ETG208200_Irondefanemia	2384.670	0.00
ETG711910_Majjtinfl-other	2344.360	0.00
ETG523200_Othhepatobiliarydiseas	2320.418	0.00
ETG437400_Bactlunginfection	2220.442	0.00
ETG474200_Nonmalneostom&esoph	2184.508	0.00

FIGURE A.14   100 "Best" Predictors After Feature Selection.

However, with a large sample size (in this case we are analyzing 9,187 observations) p values for many predictors will effectively be zero, and cannot be uniquely sorted. In fact, applying the p < 0.01 criterion for these data yields over 305 predictors. Accordingly, we ended up selecting the 100 best predictors sorted by Chi-square values. (We did a considerable amount of testing of model performance after varying the number of predictors in the model; details of this work are not reported here, but model performance did not vary significantly across a wide range of predictors − from the full set of 421 variables down to 100.)

Clicking on the Summary button generates the list of selected variables. These are the predictors used in subsequent analyses (Figure A.14).

TESTING THE DATA MINING MODELS

We now are prepared to test several different data mining models on the data. The intent here is to identify the best performing DM model. We use three different criteria:

1. The model "error rate" — that is, the proportion of physicians in the analysis where the predicted specialty is different from the starting specialty. To be conservative, we prefer models which make fewer changes. That is, we assume that the assigned specialty is accurate in most cases and does not need to be changed.
2. When we assign an IM specialty to a subspecialty, we expect that subspecialty to be listed in our provider data base. For example, each physician can have up to four listed specialty codes; the default selection is for the first-listed board-certified specialty. Many subspecialty physicians are board certified first in Internal Medicine, and then in their subspecialty; the first-listed IM specialty will be assigned by default. If we run the DM model and it reassigns this IM specialty to, say, Pulmonology, we would expect to see the Pulmonology specialty listed as the second, third, or fourth specialty for that physician.
3. The actual pattern of reassignments. The models should identify "IM" doctors who actually are practicing more like one of the subspecialties, or a subspecialty (e.g., Pulmonology) actually practicing more like a general Internist. We do not expect to have the subspecialties reassigned. For example, we do not expect Pulmonologists to be confused with Rheumatologists, or Gastroenterologists, or Cardiologists. We can actually examine the matrix of original and predicted specialties for each model to identify these patterns.

We have tested the following models: Support Vector Machine (SVM), MAR Splines, General Classification and Regression Trees (C&RT), Random Forests, and Boosted Trees. The intention here is to test a variety of different data mining models against our data. Model performance is related to source data characteristics, and we want a model that works well for our specific task.

Each model was run separately on the IM analysis data. As an example, we will show the steps involved in running the SVM model.

Running the SVM Model

The first step is to open our IM analysis data and select the SVM model. SVM is an option under Data Mining Machine Learning in the Statistica DM system (Figure A.15).

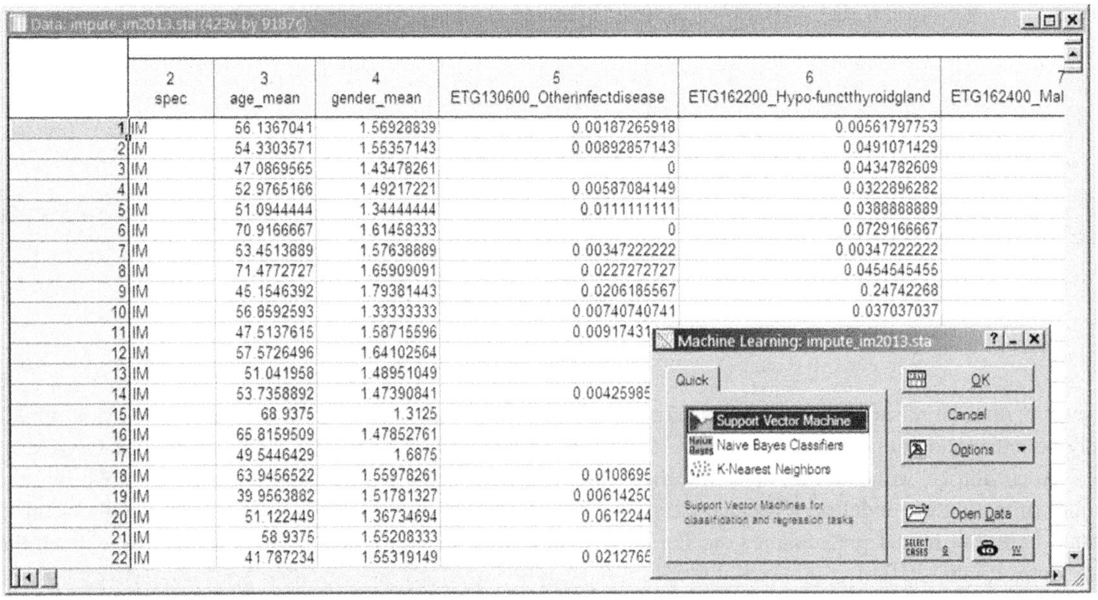

FIGURE A.15 Selecting SVM for the Data Mining Process.

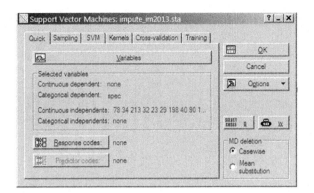

FIGURE A.16   Selecting Target and Predictor Variables.

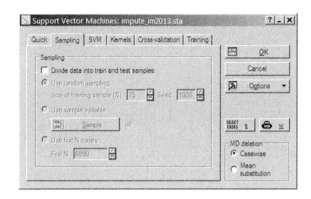

FIGURE A.17   Dialog to *De-Select* Training and Testing Samples.

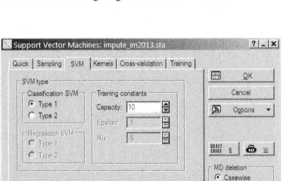

FIGURE A.18   Use SVM Defaults.

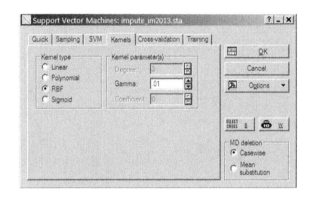

FIGURE A.19   Take Defaults for Kernel Options.

We select Support Vector Machine and open the setup dialogs. The first step is to select the target and predictor variables (Figure A.16). The target is (of course) the physician specialty code, and the predictors consist of the 100 predictors selected in the Feature Selection analysis (described previously).

Each tab of the SVM dialog allows adjustment to model defaults. The Sampling Tab, by default, separates the data into train and test samples (Figure A.17); this provides a check to the stability of the model. We have deselected this option for this analysis — we want to run the model on all the data, since we want the best predictions based on all the data. (We will examine the results of this option in a later discussion.)

The SVM Tab allows the user to select SVM Type, Training Constants, and how to handle missing data. We use the Classification and Capacity defaults unchanged (Figure A.18). We do not have any missing data in the input data, so the MD parameter has no effect on the analysis.

The Kernels Tab lets us select a Kernel type and the Gamma Kernel parameter (Figure A.19).

The Radial Basis Function (RBF) has been found to work well with most data, so we take the default. The Gamma of 0.01 is estimated by the software (1/number of inputs) and works well with our data.

The SVM model builds a set of "hyperplanes" that separate the input data into classes; the Gamma parameter controls the "flexibility" of the decision boundaries. For very small values of Gamma the decision boundary is nearly linear; higher values generally provide better model fit, but high values can result in overfitting.

The Cross-validation Tab allows the user to use v-fold cross-validation, which can help identify optimal model training parameters (Figure A.20). This is turned off by default, and we do not change this.

The Training Tab controls some key parameters for the training process as the model is built. The defaults are fine and are not changed (Figure A.21).

The model is now ready to run; clicking on OK starts the analysis process.

The first result screen shows the overall results of the analysis (Figure A.22). Note that the class accuracy of the model is 89.278% based on the training (that is, the complete) data sample. The "error rate" for the model is 10.722%. As we have mentioned previously, this is not an error rate in the traditional sense; it only says that the predicted

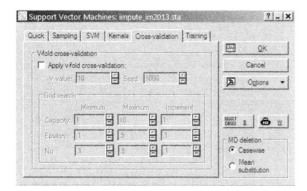

FIGURE A.20 Cross Validation Turned Off.

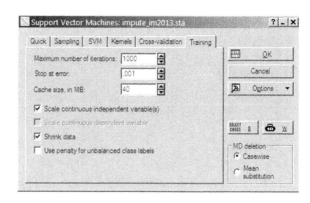

FIGURE A.21 Take Training Defaults.

FIGURE A.22 Basic Results of the SVM Analysis.

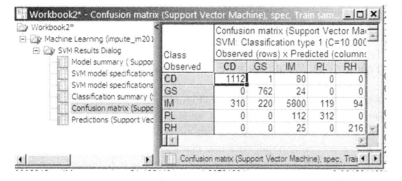

FIGURE A.23 SVM Confusion Matrix.

specialty was different from the original specialty for about 11% of the physicians in the analysis. Recall that we will select models with relatively low error rates.

To get more complete information about the model, we select the Summary, Model, Descriptive statistics, and Predictions options. This creates the output and stores it in separate sheets in an output workbook. There are two things we are particularly interested in: the "Confusion matrix" and the predictions.

The confusion matrix sheet shows the cross-tabulation of the original and predicted specialty generated by the model (Figure A.23). These will be the key data that we will examine for each model.

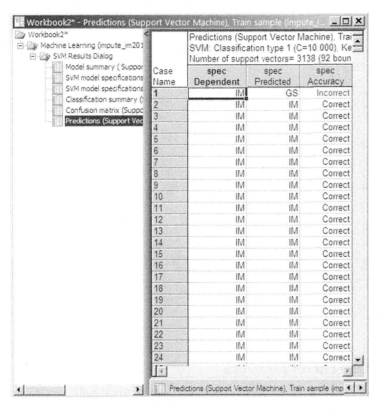

FIGURE A.24 SVM Specialty Predictions vs Reported by Physician.

The predictions sheet shows the original and predicted specialty for all 9,187 physicians in the analysis (Figure A.24). This information will be used later to document the differences in episode distribution for physicians with reassigned specialties.

Split-Sample Model Validation

Recall that the SVM procedure supports splitting the analysis data into separate training and testing samples. The model is developed on the training subset and validated against the testing sample. If the class accuracy is similar for both samples, we have increased confidence in the validity and generalizability of the SVM model.

To demonstrate this approach, we re-ran the SVM analysis using the split-sample method. We used the defaults provided: the training sample is a simple 75% random sample of the data (Figure A.25). All other SVM parameters were the same as used for the original analysis.

The results of this analysis are shown in Figure A.26.

As can be seen, the class accuracy values decrease slightly for the test sample, but model accuracy holds up very well. This gives us increased confidence that the SVM DM model is stable.

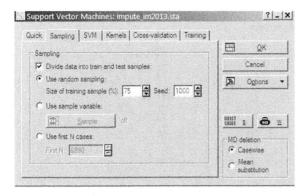

FIGURE A.25 SVM Retest Using Split Sample.

FIGURE A.26 SVM Results Using Split Sample.

COMPARING THE PERFORMANCE OF DIFFERENT MODELS

We ran the following models against the IM specialty data: Support Vector Machines (SVM), MAR Splines, General Classification and Regression Trees (C&RT), Random Forests, and Boosted Trees.

We first examine the Class Accuracy of the various models. These values are shown in Table A.6.

Clearly, the Support Vector Machine model has the best performance for these data; Boosted Trees is clearly the worst. (This substantial variation in performance is an indication of how some DM models are better fits for specific problems than others, and is not unusual. That is why it is prudent to test a variety of models against the data.)

Recall that the class "error" values simply represent the proportion of physician specialties where the predicted specialty differs from the observed specialty. It is useful to examine how the observed and predicted specialties vary for each model; we have specific expectations (criteria) for how the models should perform.

1. Because we expect specialty to be correct most of the time, we don't expect a high proportion of reassignment.
2. We expect some physicians with an Internal Medicine specialty to actually be practicing more like one of the subspecialties (Cardiology, Gastroenterology, Pulmonology, or Rheumatology).
3. We expect some subspecialty physicians to be practicing more like a general Internist, but we don't expect to have subspecialties reassigned. For example, we do not expect Pulmonologists to be confused with Rheumatologists, or Gastroenterologists, or Cardiologists.

TABLE A.6 Comparison Of Data Mining Model Accuracy

DM Model	Class Accuracy	Class Error
SVM	89.3%	11.7%
MARS	86.9%	13.1%
C&RT	86.3%	13.7%
Random Forest	86.1%	13.9%
Boosted Trees	61.9%	38.1%

SVM

The SVM model prediction meets all three of our criteria. First, most physicians in each specialty are not reassigned. (This is reflected in the high class accuracy score.) Some IM physicians are assigned a new subspecialty, but this proportion is relatively low. This confirms that most physicians in the analysis have an accurate specialty assigned and only a limited number of specialties need to be reassigned.

In addition, for the IM subspecialties (CD, Cardiology; GS, Gastroenterology; PL, Pulmonology; and RH, Rheumatology), the model generally assigns specialty either to the original subspecialty or to IM — there is only one case where specialty is reassigned between subspecialties (one cardiologist is reassigned to gastroenterology). As we indicated earlier, we do not expect this kind of confusion. The counts are shown in Table A.7.

TABLE A.7 SVM Model Specialty Reassignment

SVM	Class Predicted				
Class Observed	IM	CD	GS	PL	RH
IM	5800	310	220	119	94
CD	80	1112	1	0	0
GS	24	0	762	0	0
PL	112	0	0	312	0
RH	25	0	0	0	216

MARS

The MARS model shows a slightly higher proportion of reassigned specialties, and there are three cases of subspecialties being swapped: Cardiology to Gastroenterology, Pulmonology to Rheumatology, and Rheumatology to Pulmonology (Table A.8).

TABLE A.8 MARS Specialty Reassignment

MARS	Class Predicted				
Class Observed	IM	CD	GS	PL	RH
IM	5863	305	192	92	91
CD	137	1055	1	0	0
GS	163	0	633	0	0
PL	172	0	0	251	1
RH	58	0	0	1	182

C&RT

The C&RT model reassigns more IM specialties, and also some cases where one subspecialty is reassigned to another (Table A.9).

Random Forest

The Random Forest model shows only one case of one subspecialty being assigned to another subspecialty. However, this model also reassigns a much larger volume of subspecialties to the Internal Medicine specialty (Table A.10).

TABLE A.9 C&RT Specialty Reassignment

C&RT	Class Predicted				
Class Observed	IM	CD	GS	PL	RH
IM	**5517**	345	276	269	136
CD	142	**1049**	1	0	1
GS	39	0	**746**	1	0
PL	41	1	0	**381**	1
RH	6	1	0	3	**231**

TABLE A.10 Random Forest Specialty Reassignment

Random Forest	Class Predicted				
Class Observed	IM	CD	GS	PL	RH
IM	**6071**	238	200	4	30
CD	201	**991**	1	0	0
GS	91	0	**695**	0	0
PL	390	0	0	**34**	0
RH	128	0	0	0	**113**

Boosted Trees

This is the worst performing model tested – it reassigns a much larger proportion of physicians, and also reassigns many subspecialties to another subspecialty (Table A.11).

Thus, we have a set of four models that reclassify many physician specialties based on their patient and ETG case-mix. As was mentioned earlier, the SVM model has the lowest error rate, but this simply represents the number of physicians reassigned in the model. In this context the lower error rate indicates that the SVM model reclassifies a smaller number of specialties, but the reassignment has higher face validity since subspecialties are not reclassified to another subspecialty – only to the more general Internal Medicine specialty. This makes the most sense, given what we know about how physicians practice.

TABLE A.11 Boosted Trees Specialty Reassignment

Boosted Trees	Class Predicted				
Class Observed	IM	CD	GS	PL	RH
IM	**3397**	414	222	2352	158
CD	17	**1031**	1	143	1
GS	9	0	**638**	139	0
PL	26	6	0	**388**	4
RH	2	0	0	8	**231**

TABLE A.12 Reassignment To Specialty Reported By the Physician

SVM Reassignment	Total Reassigned Count	Count with Matching Specialty	Percent with Matching Specialty
IM→GS	220	201	95.45%
IM→CD	310	295	95.16%
IM→PL	119	113	94.96%
IM→RH	94	88	93.62%

ADDITIONAL PROVIDER INFORMATION

As mentioned earlier, we have up to four different reported medical specialties for each physician; this is self-reported data from the provider (physicians can provide any specialty or specialties they want, but Board Certification is validated before being accepted). We can re-examine the SVM model reassignment in this context: if the model predicts a different specialty, is that specialty one that has been self-reported for that physician (as a secondary specialty)?

For each of the IM physicians reassigned to a different subspecialty by the SVM model, we checked to see what other specialties had been supplied for that physician in the provider information database. Table A.12 shows the results of this analysis for each IM→Subspecialty assignment:

This is very reassuring — when the model suggests the physician is actually practicing outside his or her "primary" medical specialty, in almost every case the physician has included this specialty in the information provided. This is consistent with what we have assumed is happening when physicians self-report their specialties. For example, a physician may list Internal Medicine as his or her first specialty, but also list Gastroenterology as a second specialty. From the physician's point of view, there is no inconsistency here; IM board certification was received first, and the physician was subsequently certified in Gastroenterology and practices as a Gastroenterologist. The SVM model is detecting this practice pattern and suggesting the reassignment.

FACE VALIDITY OF THE SVM MODEL SPECIALTY REASSIGNMENT

Beyond the statistical accuracy of the DM models, we require that they have at least minimal face validity. In practice, this means that we need to be able to understand "why" the models made the specialty assignments that they did, and the reassignments need to be consistent with other information we have about the physician.

We have addressed this question by examining the highest frequency ETGs for each of the specialties — particularly the specialties reassigned by the SVM model. Thus, we should expect to see a different set of ETGs or difference relative frequencies of ETGs for the reassigned specialties.

INTERNAL MEDICINE REASSIGNMENT

For physicians classified as Internists, the DM model could accept that specialty, or reassign the physician to the appropriate IM subspecialty of Pulmonology, Cardiology, or Rheumatology. The figures below show the top 20 highest frequency ETGs for each sample: IM remaining IM, IM reassigned to Pulmonology (PL), IM reassigned to Gastroenterology (GS), IM reassigned to Cardiology (CD), and IM reassigned to Rheumatology (RH). We expect the highest frequency ETGs to be different for each of these samples.

IM REMAINING IM — ETG FREQUENCY

Internal Medicine specialists treat a wide variety of conditions (Figure A.27), with Hypertension, Diabetes, Hyperlipidemia, and Acute Bronchitis accounting for more than 25% of their case-mix. The high frequency of the Hypertension ETG will be key to the SVM model reclassification.

Data: IM_IM ETG Frequency.sta (1v by 418c)	
Category	**Frequency t:** **Percent**
388100Hypertension	14.54088
163000Diabetes	4.75470
164700Hyperlipidemia, other	4.06885
438300Acute bronchitis	4.06084
403100T&A or pharyngitis	3.92367
162200Hypo-funct thyroid gland	3.91705
403300Acute sinusitis	3.26282
438800Asthma	2.28744
587400Infect lower GU sys, not STD	2.15746
403200Allergic rhinitis	2.03050
403500Chronic sinusitis	1.61360
667800Oth skin inflam	1.56744
405300Other ENT disorders	1.55241
164800Obesity	1.53754
667200Minor bact skin infection	1.51401
238800Mood disorder, depressed	1.45225
402900Otitis media	1.42464
239600Anxiety disorder/ phobia	1.23453
634900Menstrual condition	1.19008
164500Nutritional deficiency	1.18551

FIGURE A.27 IM Remaining IM – ETG Frequency.

Data: IM_PL ETG Frequency.sta (1v by 223c)	
Category	**Frequency t:** **Percent**
438800Asthma	18.78486
405300Other ENT disorders	15.67837
439300COPD	11.83386
388100Hypertension	5.20038
437400Bact lung infection	3.79301
439800Other inflam lung disease	3.59564
164800Obesity	3.50124
403200Allergic rhinitis	2.91770
403500Chronic sinusitis	2.90912
441500Other pulmonary disorder	2.66884
438300Acute bronchitis	2.33416
318600Other neurological diseases	1.69913
386800CHF	1.65623
386500Isch hrt dis	1.18424
439700Occ & envir pulm disease	1.08985
163000Diabetes	1.01261
240600Other psych/behavior disorder	0.91822
162200Hypo-funct thyroid gland	0.88389
316000Cerebral vascular disease	0.80666
403300Acute sinusitis	0.75517

FIGURE A.28 IM Reclassified as Pulmonologists – ETG Frequency.

IM RECLASSIFIED AS PULMONOLOGIST – ETG FREQUENCY

Note that these physicians treat a high variety of Asthma, "Other ENT Disorders," and COPD (Figure A.28). Asthma represents almost 19% of their volume; for the Internal Medicine doctors, Asthma represents a little over 2% of their practice. Clearly, the SVM model is detecting these differences in relative frequency and assigning these physicians to the Pulmonology specialty.

IM RECLASSIFIED AS GASTROENTEROLOGIST – ETG FREQUENCY

Again, we see a very different distribution of ETGs – the highest frequency ETGs for these (reassigned) Gastroenterologists (Diverticulitis, Inflamed Esophagus, Irritable Bowel Syndrome, Non-Malignant Neoplasm of the Small Intestine, and Hemorrhoids; Figure A.29) do not appear in the top 20 ETGs for the Internal Medicine specialty. The SVM model is detecting these differences in making the reassignment.

IM RECLASSIFIED AS CARDIOLOGIST – ETG FREQUENCY

Here, the differences in ETG frequencies are somewhat different. The highest frequency ETG is for Hypertension (as is the case for Internal Medicine), but it represents almost 30% of the ETGs assigned to the (reassigned) Cardiologists – a rate twice as high as for IM. In addition, the other high frequency ETGs for the (reassigned) Cardiologists – Ischemic Heart Disease, Valvular Disorder, and Conduction Disorder (Figure A.30) – do not appear in the top 20 ETGs for IM. These are specific differences in the distribution of ETGs that are being detected by the SVM model.

IM RECLASSIFIED AS RHEUMATOLOGIST – ETG FREQUENCY

The highest frequency ETGs for the (reassigned) Rheumatologists – Rheumatoid Arthritis, Autoimmune Disease, Joint Degeneration, Lupus, and Psoriasis (Figure A.31) – do not appear in the top 20 for the IM specialty. These are all core diseases treated by Rheumatologists.

Data: IM_GS ETG Frequency.sta*	
	Frequency tal
Category	Percent
474900Diverticulitis/diverticulosis	9.637642
473300Inflam esophagus	8.444204
476400Irritable bowel syndrome	7.820443
475600Non mal neo sm intest & abdom	6.735172
477400Hemorrhoids, simple	6.634217
475300Inflam bowel disease	5.613845
521400Infectious hepatitis	5.375879
478500Oth disease rectum/anus	4.690824
476900Other disease intest & abdom	3.107986
388100Hypertension	3.007031
473500Gastritis, duodenitis	2.974581
208200Iron def anemia	2.094826
473100Infect stom & esoph	1.961421
473800Ulcer	1.961421
521800Cirrhosis	1.831621
523200Oth hepatobiliary disease	1.636921
165100Other met disorder, exc CF	1.467460
475000Oth infect disease intest/abd	1.153777
478000Non nal neo rect or anus	1.110510
476800Hiatal hernia	1.067244
164700Hyperlipidemia, other	1.009555
163000Diabetes	0.872544
522300Cholelithiasis	0.868938

FIGURE A.29 IM Reclassified As Gastroenterologist — ETG Frequency.

Data: Frequency table: etg (im_cd)*	
	Frequency t
Category	Percent
388100Hypertension	29.70704
386500Isch hrt dis	23.45252
387400Valvular disorder	7.87434
387700Oth conduction disorder	6.14343
164700Hyperlipidemia, other	5.52341
387800A-fib & flutter	4.45903
386800CHF	2.60411
386900Cardiomyopathy	2.05901
163000Diabetes	1.92208
162200Hypo-funct thyroid gland	1.56815
164800Obesity	1.47773
388300Cardiac congenital disorder	1.09021
316000Cerebral vascular disease	1.07213
389000Arterial inflammation	0.54511
389500Atherosclerosis	0.50636
438800Asthma	0.46502
386600Pulmonary hrt disease	0.45727
438300Acute bronchitis	0.37977
387100Heart failure, diastolic	0.37202
439300COPD	0.36427

FIGURE A.30 IM Reclassified as Cardiologist — ETG Frequency.

Data: IM_RH ETG Frequency.sta*	
	Frequency t
Category	Percent
711400Adult rheumatoid arthritis	17.82631
711700Autoim rheum disease exc lupus	7.92280
712202Jt degen -knee L/leg	5.28912
711600Lupus	4.54183
666900Psoriasis	4.46202
712204Jt degen -lower arm	4.42574
712000Osteoporosis	4.36770
712208Jt degen -back	4.08474
711910Maj jt infl -other	3.56236
711912Maj jt infl -unspecified	3.43902
164600Gout	2.98919
388100Hypertension	2.73525
389000Arterial inflammation	2.66996
712212Jt degen -unspecified	2.53210
712211Jt degen -neck	2.03874
667800Oth skin inflam	1.48734
714803Bursitis/tendonitis-pelv gird	1.33498
162200Hypo-funct thyroid gland	1.21164
714806Bursitis/tendonitis-shoulder	1.02300
238800Mood disorder, depressed	0.82711

FIGURE A.31 IM Reclassified as Rheumatologist — ETG Frequency.

Data: PL_IM ETG Frequency.sta	
	Frequency t
Category	Percent
388100Hypertension	12.20884
438800Asthma	10.85523
439300COPD	5.95939
405300Other ENT disorders	4.11356
438300Acute bronchitis	4.04325
403500Chronic sinusitis	3.68287
163000Diabetes	3.00606
164800Obesity	2.88301
437400Bact lung infection	2.75995
403200Allergic rhinitis	2.71601
164700Hyperlipidemia, other	2.07436
668200Non mal neo skin	2.03041
162200Hypo-funct thyroid gland	1.96009
403300Acute sinusitis	1.92494
386500Isch hrt dis	1.89857
318600Other neurological diseases	1.67883
439800Other inflam lung disease	1.65246
403100T&A or pharyngitis	1.53819
667800Oth skin inflam	1.51182
386800CHF	1.30087

FIGURE A.32 Pulmonologist Reclassified as IM — ETG Frequency.

SUBSPECIALTY REASSIGNMENT

Some of the physicians reporting a subspecialty (Pulmonology, Gastroenterology, Cardiology, and Rheumatology) are reassigned to IM by the model. In these cases, we expect the reassigned doctors to have an ETG distribution similar to the "standard" IM ETG distribution identified earlier. Figures A.32—A.35 show these distributions.

Data: GS_IM ETG Frequency.sta

Category	Frequency t: Percent
388100Hypertension	11.80374
164700Hyperlipidemia, other	4.69306
473300Inflam esophagus	3.65015
587400Infect lower GU sys, not STD	3.05760
163000Diabetes	2.89168
474900Diverticulitis/diverticulosis	2.77317
478500Oth disease rectum/anus	2.70206
477400Hemorrhoids, simple	2.58355
473500Gastritis, duodenitis	2.55985
475300Inflam bowel disease	2.46504
475600Non mal neo sm intest & abdom	2.44134
521400Infectious hepatitis	2.41763
476400Irritable bowel syndrome	2.37023
162200Hypo-funct thyroid gland	2.37023
438300Acute bronchitis	2.20431
403100T&A or pharyngitis	1.99099
473100Infect stom & esoph	1.49324
208900Oth hematologic dis	1.25622
208200Iron def anemia	1.23252
165100Other met disorder, exc CF	1.23252

FIGURE A.33 Gastroenterologists Reclassified as IM − ETG Frequency.

Data: CD_IM ETG Frequency.sta

Category	Frequency t: Percent
388100Hypertension	24.66741
386500Isch hrt dis	7.70510
164700Hyperlipidemia, other	6.50407
163000Diabetes	3.97265
387400Valvular disorder	3.82483
162200Hypo-funct thyroid gland	3.42757
164800Obesity	2.42979
316000Cerebral vascular disease	2.34664
387700Oth conduction disorder	2.30968
438300Acute bronchitis	1.82927
386800CHF	1.58906
387800A-fib & flutter	1.57058
388300Cardiac congenital disorder	1.26571
403100T&A or pharyngitis	1.17332
390600Varicose veins leg	1.14560
389500Atherosclerosis	1.13636
438800Asthma	1.00702
403500Chronic sinusitis	0.95159
712208Jt degen -back	0.95159
473500Gastritis, duodenitis	0.91463

FIGURE A.34 Cardiologists Reclassified as IM − ETG Frequency.

FIGURE A.35 Rheumatologists Reclassified As IM − ETG Frequency.

Data: RH_IM ETG Frequency.sta

Category	Frequency t: Percent
712000Osteoporosis	13.96063
388100Hypertension	7.69370
711400Adult rheumatoid arthritis	6.05021
712208Jt degen -back	5.16525
711700Autoim rheum disease exc lupus	4.65956
162200Hypo-funct thyroid gland	3.97327
712202Jt degen -knee L/leg	3.28698
208200Iron def anemia	2.72711
712212Jt degen -unspecified	2.51038
164600Gout	2.47426
711600Lupus	2.23948
666900Psoriasis	2.20336
438300Acute bronchitis	2.14918
712211Jt degen -neck	1.76991
403100T&A or pharyngitis	1.75185
164700Hyperlipidemia, other	1.66155
712204Jt degen -lower arm	1.55319
403300Acute sinusitis	1.26422
587400Infect lower GU sys, not STD	1.19198
711910Maj jt infl -other	1.15586

PULMONOLOGIST RECLASSIFIED AS IM − ETG FREQUENCY

While we see relatively high frequencies for Asthma and COPD, the most frequent ETG is Hypertension − the highest frequency IM ETG (Figure A.32). In addition, Diabetes, Obesity, and Ischemic Heart Disease also show up in the top 20 ETGs. The SVM model is apparently using these distinctions to reassign these physicians.

GASTROENTEROLOGIST RECLASSIFIED AS IM – ETG FREQUENCY

Hypertension is the highest frequency ETG for these physicians. In addition, Hyperlipidemia and Diabetes show up with relatively high frequency (Figure A.33).

CARDIOLOGIST RECLASSIFIED AS IM – ETG FREQUENCY

Almost 25% of the practice of these physicians concerns the treatment of Hypertension, the primary ETG for Internal Medicine specialists. In addition, Diabetes is relatively high frequency (Figure A.34).

RHEUMATOLOGIST RECLASSIFIED AS IM – ETG FREQUENCY

While Osteoporosis is the highest frequency ETG for these physicians, Hypertension still represents 7.6% of the practice (Figure A.35). This reassignment is more questionable, since so many orthopedic conditions are high frequency for these practices. The SVM model again seems to be focusing on the Hypertension ETG.

Further analysis of this group of physicians is probably needed before accepting this reclassification.

Overall DM Model Assignment – Discussion

We have used the SVM DM model to distinguish between physicians assigned to the IM specialty but actually practicing as a IM subspecialist (Pulmonologist, Cardiologist, or Rheumatologist), and to identify physicians assigned an IM subspecialty but actually practicing more like a general Internist.

Of the two different questions, the model clearly does the best job of identifying an IM physician actually practicing as a subspecialist. The DM model also does a decent job of identifying Pulmonologists, Cardiologists, Gastroenterologists, and Rheumatologists actually practicing as general Internists – with the Rheumatology reassignment harder to understand.

However, it is clear that the SVM model does have face validity – the reassigned specialties make sense and are credible. This is sufficient information to reassign the physician specialties for provider profiling – or perhaps just asking the reassigned physicians to confirm our results. (The relatively low volume of these reassigned physicians makes asking the physicians for their specialty more practical and feasible – much better than calling all 8,000 physicians.)

MODELS FOR GENERAL PRACTICE/FAMILY PRACTICE

Recall that we chose this physician sample because we expect the patient mix and practice patterns of General Practice and Family Practice physicians to be very similar. In that case, we don't expect the data mining models to do much reassignment of physician specialty. The result of the modeling is discussed below.

For this analysis, we ran the SVM model as a stand-alone procedure. We followed the same process used for the IM analysis. Importantly, we used feature selection to identify the 100 best predictors, and those predictors were used as input to the SVM model. The results of the SVM analysis are shown in Figure A.36.

Class accuracy for this model is 89.227, which is a very good performance. However, we also need to look at the cross-tabulation of the observed vs predicted specialties. This information is shown in Figure A.37.

We expected the Family Practice and General Practice physicians to have essentially the same case-mix, and the SVM model classification shows this. The model does not reassign any FP physicians; all GPs are reassigned to the Family Practice specialty. The model is saying that these two specialties have essentially the same practice patient mix.

Note that there are many more Family Practitioners than General Practitioners in the analysis (5,218 vs 630 physicians, respectively) so the "FP Case-Mix" is most heavily weighted in the analysis, and physician specialty is going to be mapped to this case mix.

Given these specialties treat the same kinds of medical conditions, the results of the analysis imply that the two specialties could be combined for norms and normative comparisons. The relative frequency of the ETGs in the norms will have only a small effect on the observed vs expected normative comparison.

FIGURE A.36   Results of SVM Analysis For GP and FP.

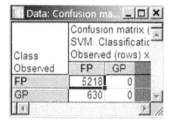

FIGURE A.37   SVM Reclassification of GP and FP.

FP vs GP vs IM

We performed one additional test of how the SVM model performs when analyzing primary care specialties: we ran an analysis of Family Practice, General Practice, and Internal Medicine specialties. In this case, we expected the model to be able to separate the IM from the GP and FP specialties.

For this analysis, we selected the 100 best predictors using the feature selection process. It is interesting that the first-listed (highest Chi-square value) is the patient risk score. We expect IM patients on average to be somewhat sicker − presenting more serious conditions.

The SVM model performs very well in this situation. The model summary is shown in Figure A.38. The model class accuracy is 94.117%.

We are also interested in the specific predicted specialties; these are shown in the Confusion matrix from the SVM model. These data are shown in Figure A.39.

For the FP and GP specialties, the model performs exactly the same as for the original analysis (when only FP and GP specialties were included): no Family Practitioners are reassigned, and all General Practitioners are reclassified as FP. Of the Internal Medicine specialties, 99 are reclassified as Family Practitioners; the remaining 6,444 remain IM.

Traditionally, GP, FP, and IM specialties are considered to be primary care specialties (pediatrics and OB/Gyn specialties are also generally included in this category). However, this analysis tells us that the IM specialty treats a different mix of patients. For provider profiling, we would not want to include all three specialties in the same norm.

MODELS FOR PEDIATRICS/GENERAL SURGERY

There should be very little confusion between the practice mix of Pediatricians and General Surgeons − beginning with the average patient ages for these two specialties. We expect the DM models to distinguish between these two specialties and do very little, if any, reassignment.

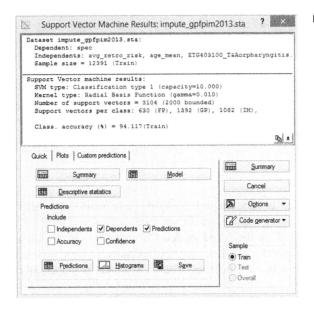

FIGURE A.38   SVM Analysis of GP, FP, and IM Specialties.

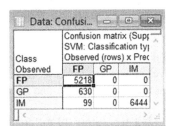

FIGURE A.39   SVM Model Reassignment In GP, FP, IM Analysis.

We used the stand-alone SVM model to analyze these data, and followed the same process used for the IM analysis. We used feature selection to identify the 100 best predictors, and used those predictors in the SVM analysis. The results of the analysis are shown in Figures A.40 and A.41 — first, the overall model class accuracy (which was 98.702); and second, the confusion matrix, which shows the reclassification output by the SVM model.

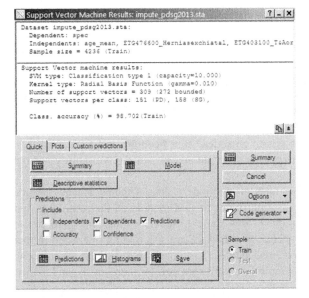

FIGURE A.40   SVM Model Analysis of Pediatrics and General Surgery.

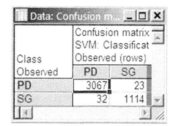

FIGURE A.41   SVM Model Reassignment of Pediatrics and General Surgery.

The class accuracy is very high (and in fact, the SVM model itself is very simple). This was (apparently) not a difficult classification problem (as we expected).

Of the 4,236 physicians in this analysis, only 55 were reassigned by the SVM model. Our suspicion is that these physicians are actually pediatric surgeons. There actually is a separate pediatric surgery specialty (which was not included in this analysis), but some pediatricians may do a higher volume of surgeries. The SVM model is (apparently) detecting this difference.

We could probably improve the model even more if we specifically flagged the episodes in which a surgery had been performed. Recall that the ETG model does include a "treatment" category which could be added to the model.

GENERAL COMMENTS

For this sample of specialties and physicians, the data mining models we tested can reliably distinguish differences in patient case-mix, and can be used to "reassign" physician specialties — so that normative comparisons will be more accurate and "fair." Thus, this kind of analysis can be used as part of a physician cost-efficiency analysis, and will improve the accuracy of the results.

It is also clear that some understanding of the underlying data is necessary — we couldn't just throw 40 different medical specialties into one analysis and expect the statistical models to distinguish among them all. We deliberately chose specific sets of specialties (e.g., Internal Medicine and its subspecialties of Pulmonology, Gastroenterology, Cardiology, and Rheumatology) in which we knew that confusion was possible.

In addition, we need to be cautious about interpreting and using these results, for a number of reasons.

First, these are only mathematically models — they are not "reality." They are complicated and hard to explain to physicians, who we don't expect to be statistical experts. That is why looking closely at the results in terms of actual distributions of episode of care, and trying to establish face validity for the models, is so important. Our analysis of the face validity of the models is reassuring.

Second, there is the fundamental question about the reliability of the data mining models. Normally, when developing data mining models, analysis data are split into "development" and "validation" samples. The model parameters are developed on the development sample and tested again the validation sample. Generally, error rates increase in the validation sample (and that is what we have observed in a separate analysis exploring this issue). However, we have argued that, given the fact that medical practice and patient case-mix vary substantially across time, we don't expect it to be possible to develop the model on one sample and then apply it (scoring new data) across time and physician samples. It is also clear that splitting the development and validation samples reduces the data volume available for model development, and this makes the models less robust. We have chosen an approach in which the models are regenerated for each sample (of physicians and episodes) as it becomes available, and then the model is applied to the same sample of data under analysis. A specific separate analysis of the "reliability" of the DM models is described below.

Third, there is the related problem of how to consider the "error" rates of the models. One of the advantages of data mining software such as Statistica Data Miner is that we can run different types of DM models on the same data and then pick the model with the lowest error rate for further examination. In this context, the error rates simply represent the number of physicians who are assigned to a different medical specialty — and we are specifically interested in that reassignment; the model "error" here is simply telling us that the original medical specialty is not accurate. We choose models with lower rates of "error" because we are interested in "simpler" models that can be more easily understood and explained (face validity).

TABLE A.13 SVM Model Reassignment For Two Different Time Periods

December 2011 Predictions	December 2010 Predictions				
	Pulmonology	Cardiology	Internal Medicine	Rheumatology	Row Totals
Pulmonology	402	0	22	0	424
Cardiology	0	1,336	31	0	1,367
Internal Medicine	27	45	5,735	9	5,816
Rheumatology	0	0	14	274	288
Column totals	429	1,381	5,802	283	7,895

TESTING MODEL RELIABILITY

We did not use the normal split-sample data mining approach for all these analyses, for the reasons discussed earlier. However, we *are* interested in how reliable these results are across time. Accordingly, we did a separate analysis to compare model results for the same physicians across two time periods.

For this analysis, we chose the IM (and IM subspecialties) and the SVM model. We created two analysis datasets. The first sample is based on 2 years of episode data ending December 2010; the second sample is based on 2 years of episode data ending December 2011. We took care to make sure that the same physicians were in both episode samples. Half of the episodes in these two analyses will be the same, and half will be different. (Both samples have in common episodes incurred in calendar 2010; episodes in calendar 2009 and episodes in calendar 2011 will be different.)

This approach represents an attempt to capture changes in physician patient (and ETG) case-mix across time; both changes in case-mix and changes in medical practice across 3 calendar years are going to exist in these two samples.

We ran the SVM model on both samples and examined the specialty predictions of the two models. If the SVM model is robust, then the specialty (re)assignments should be very similar for the two time periods. Table A.13 shows the results of this analysis.

For 148 physicians, the 2010 model and the 2011 model disagreed about specialty — an "error" rate of 1.87%. This indicates that the DM model classifications are accurate and stable — at least across the time period we analyzed here. This performance is good enough that we could argue that the model, once defined, could be used for a few years before needing to recalibrate the predictions.

Our suspicion is that the (very small) disagreement we see in this analysis is due to significant changes in the practice mix of the physicians reassigned. If that is in fact the case, then it would be better to simply rerun the DM analysis each year to make sure we capture those changes. But, it doesn't seem critical to do so.

POSTSCRIPT

We have argued that it is important to correctly characterize physician medical specialty for cost-efficiency analyses. The specialty assigned to the physician determines which normative data they will be compared to — and we know that average episode costs (for the same ETG) can vary by specialty.

In order to see what happens to cost-efficiency scores, we performed an additional analysis on the Internal Medicine and IM Subspecialty sample. We selected the SVM model, which seemed to be the best performing model, and identified all the physicians where the model suggested the medical specialty should be changed (that is, Cardiologists practicing as Internists, Internists practicing as Rheumatologists, etc.). We then reassigned the physician specialty for these physicians, and recalculated the cost-efficiency ratios using the new normative comparisons.

Recall that the calculated efficiency score is an observed (physician) to expected (specialty norm) ratio — ratios less than 1.0 indicate that the physician is relatively cost-efficient. Because of the underlying variability in these O/E scores, it is common practice to use statistical tests to measure the reliability of the measure. In this case, we calculate 95% confidence intervals around these O/E scores — the confidence interval takes into account both the volume of episode data and its inherent variability. We then examine the confidence intervals to determine whether we can reliably classify the physician as "cost-efficient" or "cost-inefficient." Thus, if the upper confidence interval is less than 1.0 we can say that we have a 95% confidence that the "true" O/E ratio is less than 1.0, and thus the physician is cost-efficient. If the lower

TABLE A.14 Changes In "Cost-Efficiency" Classification After Specialty Reassignment

Original Efficiency Flag	New Efficiency Flag			
	DK	N	Y	Total
DK	220	22	88	330
N	92	34	9	135
Y	33	2	74	109

confidence interval is greater than 1.0 we have a 95% confidence that the physician is cost-inefficient. When the confidence intervals span the 1.0 value, we can't reliably determine efficiency, and thus the classification is "Don't Know."

We use these classifications (Y, N, and DK) to see if using the corrected physician specialties changes efficiency classifications.

For this analysis, we had a total of 574 physicians with a new specialty assigned. The cross-tab Table A.14 shows how these classifications change.

In this analysis, a total of 246 out of 574 (42.9%) physicians change their efficiency scores after "correcting" their assigned medical specialty. In a few cases, "inefficient" physicians are now classified as "efficient," and vice versa. In most cases however, physicians move back and forth between the Don't Know classification and the efficient and inefficient classifications. Most change results from reclassifying Pulmonologists, and least for Cardiologists — but specialty changes have substantial impact for each of the IM and IM subspecialties.

It is clear that reassigning the medical specialty does make a substantial difference in how the physicians are classified. And recall that this efficiency classification has a real impact on physicians — it can affect whether they are able to participate in specific networks and it can affect reimbursement.

Given the considerable impact changing specialty can have on efficiency ratings, it would be prudent to actually contact the physicians where the model suggests a different specialty. We have seen that, for most cases, the reclassified physicians have already reported the new specialty (though not as their primary specialty), so this should not be controversial.

Note also that the DM models select a relatively small number of physicians for possible reassignment — we don't have to contact the entire physician panel. This saves time and effort.

Clearly, data mining has value in ensuring the validity and accuracy of provider cost-efficiency profiling.

Tutorial B

Case Study: Using Association Rules to Investigate Characteristics of Hospital Readmissions

Scott Zasadil, PhD and Pamela Peele, PhD

Chapter Outline

NOTE: This tutorial is presented as a case study, as the data set is proprietary. However, the final 16 variables selected for the data set used for this study are described in Table A.5 and a fictitious data set is shown in Figure A.1; thus, readers should be able to construct a similar data set (either fictitious or from real data) if they want to work through all of the steps of this tutorial.

OBJECTIVES/PURPOSE

A readmission within 30 days of a hospitalization is a commonly used quality measure of hospital care. Readmission (or readmit) rates allow us to understand how inpatient care for particular conditions may contribute to issues with post-discharge, medical stability, and recovery. According to recent estimates, nearly one out of every five Medicare patients is readmitted to the hospital within 30 days, and unplanned readmissions cost Medicare approximately $17.4 billion annually (Jencks *et al.*, 2009). Since 2011, the Centers for Medicare & Medicaid Services (CMS) have publicly reported the readmission rates of Medicare-certified hospitals for acute myocardial infarction, heart failure, and pneumonia. In addition, under Section 3025 of the Affordable Care Act, CMS is authorized to decrease Medicare payments to hospitals with higher than expected readmissions beginning in fiscal year 2013.

This increased focus on reducing unplanned 30-day readmissions has accelerated efforts to help hospitals and other interested healthcare stakeholders identify those patients who are at risk for post-discharge problems, and target improvements in discharge planning and aftercare processes. In this tutorial, we demonstrate how to use association rules or frequent pattern mining, a common data mining technique, to extract readmission risk factors from hospital admission data in a healthcare insurance claims database. We use StatSoft's STATISTICA Data Miner product to illustrate the steps involved in this technique.

Practical Predictive Analytics and Decisioning Systems for Medicine. DOI: http://dx.doi.org/10.1016/B978-0-12-411643-6.00017-X

COMMON READMISSION CONDITIONS

Tables B.1–B.3 provide an overview of the most common readmission conditions in Pennsylvania and among Medicare and Medicaid populations nationally. Table B.1 identifies the top 10 initial admission conditions leading to an all-cause 30-day readmission in Pennsylvania in 2010. The list includes a range of readmission rates, because the conditions are identified by the *total number* of readmissions for that condition and not the rate itself. For example, "Pregnancy and Related Disorders" has a low readmission rate (3.5%), but the sheer number of readmissions for this initial admission condition warrants its inclusion in the top-10 list.

TABLE B.1 Readmission Rates in Pennsylvania by Initial Admission Condition (Pennsylvania Healthcare Cost Containment Council, April 2012)

Initial admission condition	30-day readmission rate (%)
Heart Failure	24.3
Mental Health Disorder	13.3
Abnormal Heartbeat	12.9
Primary Cancer	17.7
Chronic Obstructive Pulmonary Disease (COPD)	20.2
Coronary Artery Disease and Chest Pain	11.3
Pneumonia	16.0
Septicemia	21.0
Pregnancy and Related Disorders	3.5
Intestinal Inflammation	13.9

TABLE B.2 Readmission Rates for Medicare Patients by Cause of Initial Hospitalization (Jencks et al., 2009)

Cause of initial hospitalization	30-day readmission rate	Proportion of all readmissions (%)
Medical		
All	21.0	77.6
Heart failure	26.9	7.6
Pneumonia	20.1	6.3
COPD	22.6	4.0
Psychoses	24.6	3.5
Gastrointestinal problems	19.2	3.1
Surgical		
All	15.6	22.4
Cardiac stent placement	14.5	1.6
Major hip or knee surgery	9.9	1.5
Other vascular surgery	23.9	1.4
Major bowel surgery	16.6	1.0
Other hip or femur surgery	17.9	0.8

TABLE B.3 Readmission Rates for Medicaid Patients by Major Diagnostic Condition (Jiang *et al.*, 2010)

Major diagnostic condition	30-day readmission rate	Proportion of all readmissions (%)
Pregnancy, Childbirth & Puerperium	3.8	21.7
Circulatory System	10.4	11.7
Mental	11.8	9.4
Respiratory System	11.4	8.4
Digestive System	10.3	7.5
Alcohol/Substance Abuse	13.0	6.6
Hepatobiliary System and Pancreas	12.3	4.7
Nervous System	9.5	4.6
Kidney & Urinary Tract	12.4	4.0
Musculoskeletal System & Connective Tissue	8.3	3.9
Endocrine, Nutritional & Metabolic	10.7	3.4
Skin, Subcutaneous Tissue & Breast	8.0	2.6
Female Reproductive System	6.4	2.0
Myeloproliferative & Poorly Differentiated Neoplasms	37.4	2.0
Blood, Blood Forming Organs & Immunological	14.1	1.6
Injuries, Poisonings & Toxic Effects of Drugs	8.4	1.6
Infection & Parasite	11.5	1.5
Ear, Nose, Mouth & Throat	7.2	0.9
Human Immunodeficiency Virus Infections	17.2	0.8
Factors Influencing Health Status & Other Contacts with Health Services	9.9	0.6
Male Reproductive System	7.2	0.2
Multiple Significant Trauma	7.9	0.2
Eye	6.9	0.1
Burns	6.1	0.1

Table B.2 identifies the most common causes of initial hospitalization that lead to a readmission within 30 days for Medicare patients nationally, and provides the proportion of these readmissions relative to all readmissions.

Table B.3 identifies the most common major diagnostic conditions that lead to a readmission within 30 days, and provides the proportion of these readmissions relative to all readmissions for the national Medicaid beneficiary population.

Examination of Tables B.1−B.3 shows that heart failure, pneumonia, gastrointestinal problems, and COPD are frequent causes of readmissions. Therefore, we should anticipate seeing these conditions in our subsequent analysis.

DATA SET

Our data source for this analysis contains 2 years of medical claims from all payers (i.e., Medicare, Medicaid, Medicare-Medicaid Eligible, Commercial, Children's Health Insurance Plans). All non-pregnancy, acute-care initial

TABLE B.4 Pre-Existing Chronic Conditions Occurring in at Least 10% of the Data Set

Pre-existing chronic conditions	Percentage in data set	30-day readmission rate (%)
ASTHMA – Asthma	14.4	16.0
COPD – Chronic Obstructive Pulmonary Disease	19.8	20.4
CHF – Congestive Heart Failure	14.0	24.5
CAD – Coronary Artery Disease	27.9	18.5
DM – Diabetes Mellitus	28.5	17.7
HTN – Hypertension	62.0	15.6
AF – Atrial Fibrillation	11.8	20.4
RENAL – Renal Disease	10.0	26.2
Overall		14.1

admissions from a set of 12 hospitals in southwestern Pennsylvania were identified. Our working data set comprises 29,937 admissions and all of the associated medical claims for individuals incurring the admissions for all medical services rendered during the 2 years of data capture.

Inclusion in this data set was subject to the following constraints:

1. 12 months continuous enrollment in the health plan preceding the first-observed admission to ensure sufficient medical claims history for capturing the patient's chronic conditions.
2. Enrolled for 30 days post-discharge without a readmission, or have a readmission before 30 days post-discharge. That is, either observe a readmission, in which case we have already observed the outcome of interest, or follow the patient long enough to guarantee that he or she is not readmitted.
3. Discharged to home rather than transferred to another acute care facility or to a nursing facility. Readmissions include those at *any* hospital, not just the admitting hospital or one of the 12 hospitals selected to identify the initial set of admissions.

Pre-existing chronic conditions will be used in constructing our association rules. Due to their rarity, infrequent chronic conditions are much less likely to contribute to any meaningful rule. In order to be included in this analysis, we will specify that any given chronic condition must be present in at least 10% of the data set. Table B.4 identifies the pre-existing chronic conditions that meet this constraint, and their associated 30-day readmission rates.

The data set is comprised of claims information coded by healthcare providers, using the International Classification of Diseases (ICD-9) coding system which contains 14,000 diagnosis codes and 3,900 surgical procedure codes. Since these codes are far too granular to be useful for our purposes, we map the universe of ICD-9 codes to higher-level diagnosis categories found in the Clinical Classifications Software (CCS) available from the Healthcare Cost and Utilization Project Healthcare Cost and Utilization Project (HCUP, 2012). This mapping allows us to collapse diagnoses and procedures into a smaller number of hierarchical and clinically meaningful categories. Table B.5 presents the resulting 16 categorical (string) variables now contained in the data set for constructing the association rules.

Note that:

1. The variable flags are coded with values, for example, as ("", "READMIT") instead of the more conventional (0, 1) as it makes the generated association rules easier to read.
2. The Level 1 CCS rollups for diagnoses and procedures contain the most general specification.
3. If no surgical operation was performed during the hospitalization, then CCS_Proc_1, CCS_Proc_2, and CCS_Proc_3 will be set to "N/A." Thus, we will be able to determine if the lack of a surgical procedure during hospitalization is a factor in readmissions.
4. In order to distinguish, for example, CCS_Dx_2 from CCS_Proc_2, the values of the CCS_Dx variables will be prefixed by "Dx_" and the values of the CCS_Proc variables will be prefixed by "Proc_". The association rules algorithm looks for frequent patterns in the set obtained by pooling together all values from all variables. Thus, it is important that a particular value be distinct among the set of all variables.

TABLE B.5 Categorical Variables for Constructing Association Rules

Variable	Description
READMIT	Readmission within 30 days flag
ASTHMA	Asthma condition flag
COPD	Chronic Obstructive Pulmonary Disease condition flag
CHF	Congestive Heart Failure condition flag
CAD	Coronary Artery Disease condition flag
DM	Diabetes Mellitus condition flag
HTN	Hypertension condition flag
AF	Atrial Fibrillation condition flag
RENAL	Renal Disease condition flag
CCS_Dx_1	Level 1 CCS rollup for primary ICD-9 diagnosis
CCS_Dx_2	Level 2 CCS rollup for primary ICD-9 diagnosis
CCS_Dx_3	Level 3 CCS rollup for primary ICD-9 diagnosis
CCS_Dx_4	Level 4 CCS rollup for primary ICD-9 diagnosis
CCS_Proc_1	Level 1 CCS rollup for primary ICD-9 procedure
CCS_Proc_2	Level 2 CCS rollup for primary ICD-9 procedure
CCS_Proc_3	Level 3 CCS rollup for primary ICD-9 procedure

Figure B.1 provides a portion of an artificial data set which is used for illustrative purposes. The highest level CCS rollup for ICD-9 is "18"; thus, the CCS diagnoses shown are bogus, non-existent diagnoses (e.g., CCS_Dx_2 = 91.4). These are displayed in place of any genuine diagnosis in order to ensure that no real patient is shown that can possibly have this combination.

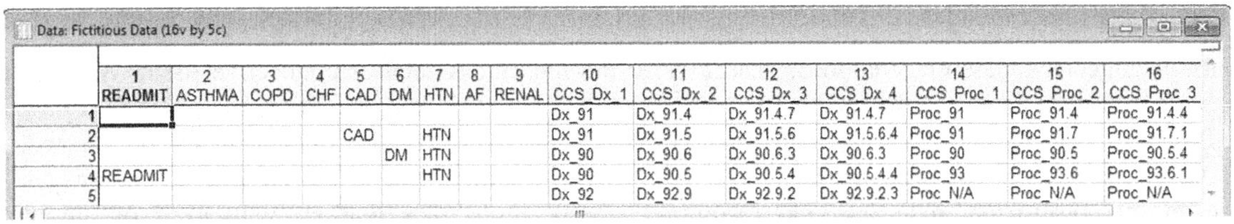

	1 READMIT	2 ASTHMA	3 COPD	4 CHF	5 CAD	6 DM	7 HTN	8 AF	9 RENAL	10 CCS_Dx_1	11 CCS_Dx_2	12 CCS_Dx_3	13 CCS_Dx_4	14 CCS_Proc_1	15 CCS_Proc_2	16 CCS_Proc_3
1										Dx_91	Dx_91.4	Dx_91.4.7	Dx_91.4.7	Proc_91	Proc_91.4	Proc_91.4.4
2					CAD		HTN			Dx_91	Dx_91.5	Dx_91.5.6	Dx_91.5.6.4	Proc_91	Proc_91.7	Proc_91.7.1
3						DM	HTN			Dx_90	Dx_90.6	Dx_90.6.3	Dx_90.6.3	Proc_90	Proc_90.5	Proc_90.5.4
4	READMIT						HTN			Dx_90	Dx_90.5	Dx_90.5.4	Dx_90.5.4.4	Proc_93	Proc_93.6	Proc_93.6.1
5										Dx_92	Dx_92.9	Dx_92.9.2	Dx_92.9.2.3	Proc_N/A	Proc_N/A	Proc_N/A

FIGURE B.1 Sample portion of a fictitious data set.

Even with aggregation of the ICD-9 codes into a smaller number of high-level CCS categories, we anticipate that most of the rules will apply to a small subset of the original data. Due to the scarcity of these rules within the whole set, spurious association rules may be produced. It is advisable to split the working data set into two mutually exclusive data sets: a training set and a testing set. The training set will be used to construct candidate association rules, and the test set will be used to test whether or not the rules can be shown to hold true in general. Each data set contains one-half of all patients in our working data set, with 14,966 admissions in the training set and 14,971 admissions in the test set. The sets are not the same size because a patient may be admitted multiple times over the 2-year time span.

ASSOCIATION RULE BASICS

Association rules reveal the relationship or correlation between sets of items in a data set. An association rule takes the following form: if *Body*, then *Head*, written *Body* ⇒ *Head*, where *Body* and *Head* stand for one or more categorical attributes. The goal is to discover joint *values* of the attributes that frequently occur together. Note that the implication simply means co-occurrence and not necessarily causality. A clear advantage of using association rules is the explicit specification of the rules that they generate.

The *support* or *coverage*, **supp**(*Body*⇒*Head*), for a particular association rule *Body*⇒*Head*, is defined as the proportion of total records that contain **both** *Body* and *Head*. The *confidence* or *accuracy*, **conf**(*Body*⇒*Head*), of the rule *Body*⇒*Head* is defined as the percentage of all records containing *Body* that also contain *Head*. Notice that the confidence is nothing more than the conditional probability that *Head* occurs, given that *Body* occurs.

In this tutorial, the categorical attributes are the primary diagnosis and procedure during the index (initial) hospitalization, whether or not the patient has a specified co-morbidity (e.g., diabetes mellitus) or was readmitted to a hospital within 30 days. Our intent is to discover rules where the *Head* is a 30-day readmission. The *Body* of the rule will be a grouping of inpatient diagnoses, procedures, and co-morbidities that are affiliated with a later readmission.

Association rules are commonly used for undirected data mining, as they reveal patterns in the data without a specified target. By focusing only on the subset of rules which have a *Head* of READMIT here we will be employing association rules in a quasi-directed manner. The application of association rules to other medical and healthcare topics has been described in papers by Brossette *et al.* (1998), Doddi *et al.* (2001), Ma *et al.* (2003), and Ordonez (2006).

DATA SUBSETS

Crucially important to this analysis is the support (proportion of instances) of a rule. Since association rules are built from a *minimum* value of support, "interesting" but less frequent rules will not be discovered if, relative to the entire set, they make up only a small fraction of the records. For example, we may discover that 23 out of 25 times a COPD patient admitted for a specific intestinal infection is later readmitted. Since this fraction of (chronic condition, primary diagnosis) pairings is so small with respect to the entire set, the association rules algorithm would never capture it due to its small support (23/29,937). However, restricted to a set containing only diseases of the digestive system, we have a better chance of finding this fraction of pairings as its support relative to this reduced set will be larger. We thus begin the analysis by considering subsets of the data that have the most potential for producing interesting rules.

Table B.6 identifies the four general conditions with the highest volume of admissions in our data set. We note that over 56% of admissions come from four general conditions:

1. Diseases of the circulatory system
2. Diseases of the respiratory system
3. Diseases of the digestive system
4. Diseases of the musculoskeletal & connective tissue system.

The fourth diagnosis class of conditions, "Diseases of the musculoskeletal & connective tissue system," accounts for 11.8% of the admissions, but the readmission rate is only 5.6%. This low readmission rate implies that the readmission flag, the *Head* of the association rules that we wish to discover, will be deficient in the set and will result in supports which are too low for our purposes. Thus, we will not investigate this fourth class of admissions and concentrate instead on constructing data sets and readmission association rules that go with each of the other three diagnoses.

To construct, for example, the "Diseases of the circulatory system" (CCS_Dx_1 = Dx_7) subset, go to the STATISTICA Data tab and select Subset (Figure B.2). This assumes that the complete data set is active.

Next, select Cases within the subset dialog and click OK (Figure B.3).

TABLE B.6 General Conditions with the Highest Volume of Admissions

CCS level 1	Description	Admission (%)	Readmission rate (%)
7	Diseases of the circulatory system	20.8	13.8
8	Diseases of the respiratory system	10.1	15.7
9	Diseases of the digestive system	13.4	15.3
13	Diseases of the musculoskeletal & connective tissue system	11.8	5.6

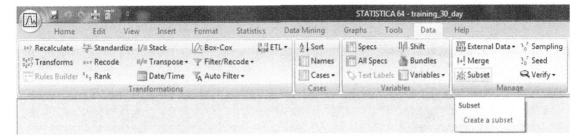

FIGURE B.2   Selecting subset from STATISTICA Data tab.

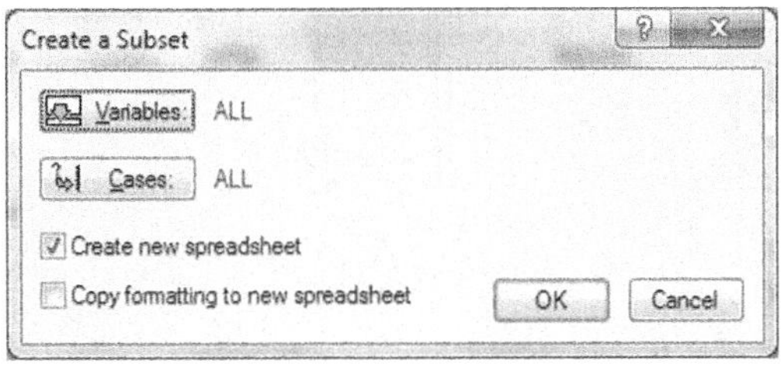

FIGURE B.3   Selecting cases within the subset dialog.

This will display a Case Selection Conditions dialog. Enable Selection Conditions and enter "Dx_7" in the Expression box and click OK (Figure B.4). Notice that we have to surround "Dx_7" by quotes, as CCS_Dx_1 is a string variable.

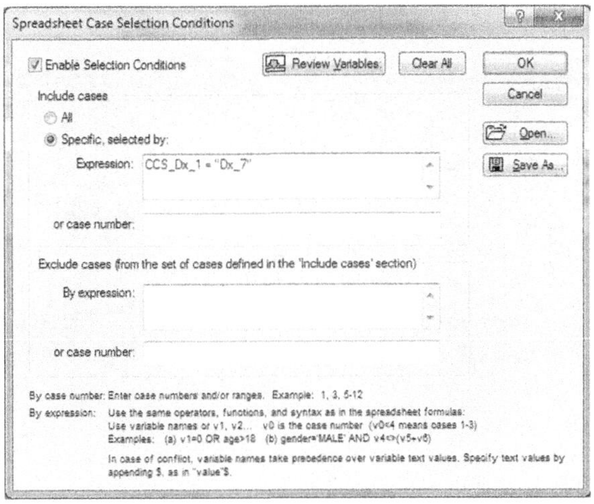

FIGURE B.4   Selecting case conditions.

GENERATION OF ASSOCIATION RULES

Our goal is to uncover associations among the chronic conditions, primary diagnosis, and primary procedure with readmission rates that are high enough to be useful. The overall readmission rate is 14.1%, and we want to find association rules linked to a readmission rate substantially above this level. As seen in Table B.4, by themselves, renal disease and congestive heart failure have readmission rates near 25%, so we will look for rules whose readmission rates exceed 25%. This level will also ensure that the number of rules which are found won't drown us in too much information.

To construct the association rules, begin by selecting the Association Rules module under the STATISTICA Data Mining tab (Figure B.5). The following figures (Figures B.6−B.10) illustrate the result of performing this operation while the data set is active. Alternatively, the user may select the Association Rules module and then navigate to the Open Data button in the Association Rules specification window.

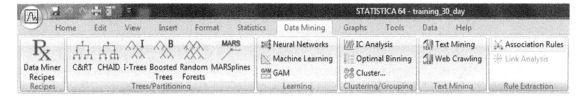

FIGURE B.5   Invoking the Association Rules module.

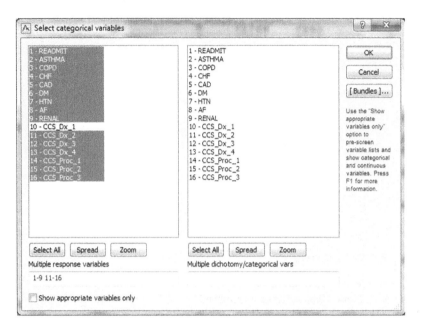

FIGURE B.6   Variable selection.

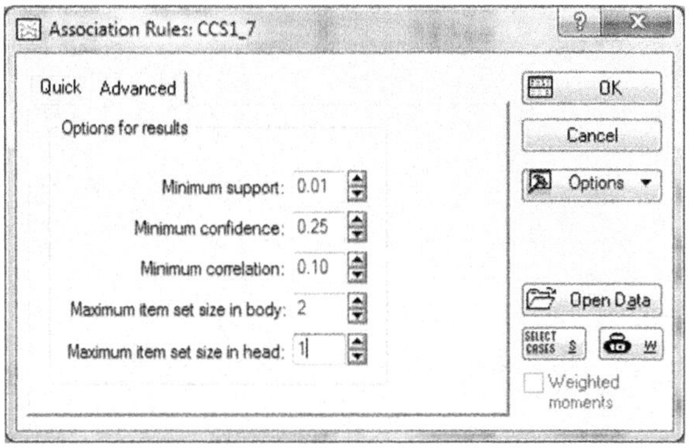

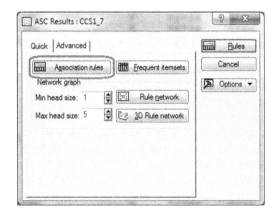

FIGURE B.7   Association rules specification.

FIGURE B.8   Selecting Association rules.

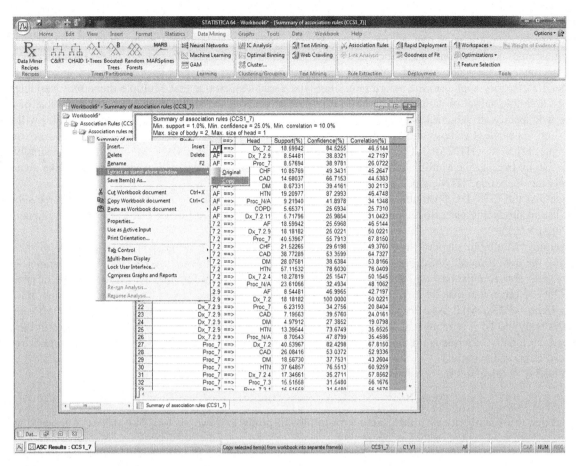

FIGURE B.9 Association rules set.

	1	2	3	4	5	6
	Body	**==>**	**Head**	**Support(%)**	**Confidence(%)**	**Correlation(%)**
471	AF, Dx_7.2.11	==>	READMIT	1.47767	25.8427	16.5502
555	Dx_7.2, RENAL	==>	READMIT	2.56987	25.3165	21.6024
968	ASTHMA, CHF	==>	READMIT	1.54192	34.7826	19.6136
978	ASTHMA, CAD	==>	READMIT	1.50980	26.8571	17.0543
988	ASTHMA, DM	==>	READMIT	1.41343	27.6730	16.7498
1039	ASTHMA, COPD	==>	READMIT	1.63829	29.3103	18.5588
1065	CHF, DM	==>	READMIT	3.75843	25.1613	26.0444
1084	CHF, RENAL	==>	READMIT	2.44137	29.5720	22.7563
1151	CHF, COPD	==>	READMIT	3.08384	27.3504	24.5965
1163	CHF, Dx_7.2.11	==>	READMIT	3.08384	28.7425	25.2147
1211	CAD, RENAL	==>	READMIT	2.66624	25.8567	22.2372
1451	DM, Dx_7.2.11	==>	READMIT	2.18439	25.0923	19.8280
1596	HTN, Dx_7.2.11	==>	READMIT	3.56569	25.0000	25.2864
1722	RENAL, COPD	==>	READMIT	1.50980	29.1925	17.7803
1731	RENAL, Dx_7.2.11	==>	READMIT	1.34918	26.7516	16.0899
1929	Proc_N/A, COPD	==>	READMIT	2.24863	26.2172	20.5635
1969	COPD, Dx_7.2.11	==>	READMIT	1.83103	28.6432	19.3956

Summary of association rules (CCS1_7)
Min. support = 1.0%, Min. confidence = 25.0%, Min. correlation = 10.0%
Max. size of body = 2, Max. size of head = 1

FIGURE B.10 Readmission association rules.

This will bring up a variable selection window (Figure B.6).

There are two variable types that can be entered: Multiple response, and multiple dichotomy. Multiple response variables can assume more than one value, such as a single variable which lists *all* diagnoses present on admission, not just the primary one. As the name suggests, Multiple dichotomy/Categorical variables have values that indicate whether or not a specific category applies to the record (e.g., flag-type variables). Notice that Multiple dichotomy variables can be viewed as a simple subset of variables of type Multiple response with the single response being the value of the flag. Here we will specify all variables as being Multiple response only, because the generated association rules will be more uniform and appear less verbose and confusing. Using Multiple dichotomy variables would result in rules containing, for example, HTN = = HTN (or HTN = = 1, if HTN was left coded as a 0, 1 flag). Multiple response simply outputs the value, so by treating the Multiple dichotomy variable as a multiple response with trivial responses, the above example simply has the value "HTN" appearing in the Association rules.

Notice that the CCS_Dx_1 variable is NOT selected, as it has already been utilized to create the three subsets that we will use in producing our association rules. Once the variables are entered, click OK to bring up the Specifications dialog (Figure B.7).

By setting "Minimum support" to 0.01, we require that any rule has to be present in at least 1% of the records. Examining the definition of confidence, we observe that for the situation of *Head* = READMIT, the *confidence is nothing more than the readmission rate* for that rule. Thus, here we are looking for rules which have a readmission rate of at least 25%. Notice also that we have set "Maximum item set size in head" to be 1. The *only* outcome that we care about is *Head* = READMIT. Also, because of the low anticipated value of the support, requesting a "Maximum item set size in body" to be 3 or more will likely generate only a few rules which actually have three items in the body of the rule. Additionally, if a rule is not interesting with a two-way interaction, then it is unlikely that a three-way interaction would be more insightful.

STATISTICA calculates the "cosine correlation" given by

$$\text{supp}(Body \Rightarrow Head)/(\text{sqrt}(\text{supp}(Body)) * \text{sqrt}(\text{supp}(Head)))$$

so named due to its similarity with the cosine term in the dot-product of two vectors. We will set this value at 0.10 to avoid discarding weak, but nevertheless interesting, rules.

Click OK and, when the results dialog is displayed upon completion, click Association rules (Figure B.8).

This will generate a STATISTICA Workbook containing the full set of association rules (Figure B.9). We are only interested in the subset which has *Head* = READMIT, so we will need to create a subset of these rules.

Within the Workbook, right click on Summary of association rules, Extract as stand-alone window, and select Copy. Produce a subset from this data set corresponding to Head = READMIT following the same steps as described in the "Data Subsets" section. Figure B.10 shows the results for diseases of the circulatory system as produced by the training set.

Not surprisingly, and as we anticipated in the Common Readmission Conditions section, the primary diagnosis of 7.2.11 – "Congestive heart failure" is implicated in a large number of readmissions. It is notable that, by itself, congestive heart failure has a readmission rate of 24.2%, just shy of being classified as a stand-alone rule. As Figure B.10 illustrates, congestive heart failure needs an interaction with a chronic condition in order to exceed the 25% threshold level that we have imposed. In addition, we note that a single record may apply to multiple rules. For example, a patient diagnosed with ASTHMA, CHF, and CAD would satisfy both the third and fourth rules in Figure B.10.

ADDING VARIABLES – LIFT

Lift (or Interest) is a commonly used and simple measure for evaluating association rules. The lift of an association rule, defined as **supp**(*Body* ⇒ *Head*)/(**supp**(*Body*)**supp**(*Head*)) or what is the same thing, **conf**(*Body* ⇒ *Head*)/**supp** (*Head*), measures how many times more often *Body* and *Head* appear together than would be expected if they were independent of each other. Values greater than 1 indicate that records which include *Body* tend to include *Head* more frequently than records that do not include *Body*.

Besides the lift, numerous other quantitities have been introduced to measure the predictive ability of an association rule. Useful descriptions of these other methods can be found in papers by Tan *et al.* (2004) and Azevedo and Jorge (2007).

In order to create a new column for the Lift in the set of rules, select the last column in the data set, right-click, and select Add Variables (Figure B.11).

In the Add Variables dialog, name the new variable Lift and specify the formula to use in the box at the bottom (Figure B.12). **Supp**(*Head*) is the proportion of observations in the training data set which contain READMIT. For the

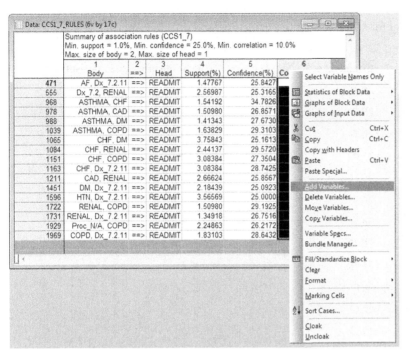

FIGURE B.11 Adding lift variable.

FIGURE B.12 Lift formula.

subset we created consisting of admissions for a disease of the circulatory system, we find **supp**(*Head*) = 0.139415. Also, **v5** is shorthand for the confidence (the fifth variable). Examining the definition of lift and using 0.01 to convert confidence from a percentage yields the indicated formula.

READMISSION RULES – 30 DAYS

The small support values ($<3.75\%$) found here may indicate the presence of spurious association rules. Therefore, we must validate them through direct application of our association rules on the hold-out test set and calculate the resulting readmission rates. Table B.7 provides the readmission rates in the test set for "Diseases of the circulatory system" after applying the association rules.

TABLE B.7 Readmission Rates in Test Set for "Diseases of the Circulatory System" After Applying Association Rules

Rule	Support	Confidence	Lift	Readmission rate in test set (%)
Dx_7.2 & RENAL	2.57	25.32	1.82	26.52
Dx_7.2.11 & AF	1.48	25.84	1.85	29.89
Dx_7.2.11 & CHF	3.08	28.74	2.06	26.49
Dx_7.2.11 & DM	2.18	25.09	1.80	24.26
Dx_7.2.11 & HTN	3.57	25.00	1.79	23.60
Dx_7.2.11 & RENAL	1.35	26.75	1.92	31.82
Dx_7.2.11 & COPD	1.83	28.64	2.05	24.86
Proc_N/A & COPD	2.25	26.22	1.88	20.58
ASTHMA & CHF	1.54	34.78	2.49	28.37
ASTHMA & CAD	1.51	26.86	1.92	23.47
ASTHMA & DM	1.41	27.67	1.98	18.95
ASTHMA & COPD	1.64	29.31	2.10	21.05
CHF & DM	3.76	25.16	1.80	23.33
CHF & RENAL	2.44	29.57	2.12	29.58
CHF & COPD	3.08	27.35	1.96	23.10
CAD & RENAL	2.67	25.86	1.85	25.60
RENAL & COPD	1.51	29.19	2.09	24.03

TABLE B.8 Final Association Rules for "Diseases of the Circulatory System"

Rule	Support	Confidence	Lift	Readmission rate in test set (%)
Dx_7.2 & RENAL	2.57	25.32	1.82	26.52
Dx_7.2.11 & RENAL	1.35	26.75	1.92	31.82
Dx_7.2.11 & AF	1.48	25.84	1.85	29.89
Dx_7.2.11 & CHF	3.08	28.74	2.06	26.49
RENAL & CHF	2.44	29.57	2.12	29.58
CHF & ASTHMA	1.54	34.78	2.49	28.37
CAD & RENAL	2.67	25.86	1.85	25.60

Using the results from the test set as the true merit of an association rule and keeping only rates >25%, Table B.8 provides our final set of rules for those admissions whose primary diagnosis is "Diseases of the circulatory system," with the identified diagnoses being described in Table B.9.

Two of the rules bear additional explanations:

1. Because the overall readmission rate for Renal Disease by itself is 26.2%, the last rule — CAD & RENAL, which has a readmission rate of only 25.6% — may appear as if it does not belong here. However, for the subset consisting of only circulatory system admissions, the readmission rate for Renal Disease is 23.2%. Thus, for this subset, the CAD & RENAL rule does indeed provide a slight increase in the readmission rate over its nominal value for RENAL by itself.

TABLE B.9 CCS Circulatory System Diagnosis

Diagnosis	Description
7.2	Diseases of the Heart
7.2.11	Congestive Heart Failure

TABLE B.10 Final Association Rules for "Diseases of the Respiratory System"

Rule	Support	Confidence	Lift	Readmission rate in test set (%)
Dx_8.1 & RENAL	1.20	28.13	1.80	30.91
Dx_8.1.1 & RENAL	1.13	30.91	1.98	35.90
Dx_8.2.3 & CHF	2.00	25.42	1.63	25.78
Proc_6 & COPD	1.00	25.42	1.63	30.00
Proc_16 & COPD	1.47	25.00	1.60	29.17
RENAL	2.53	25.85	1.66	28.89
CHF & RENAL	1.60	32.43	2.08	35.14
RENAL & CAD	1.67	26.04	1.67	27.27

TABLE B.11 CCS Respiratory System Diagnosis

Primary Diagnosis	Description
8.1.1	Pneumonia
8.1	Respiratory infections
8.2.3	Obstructive chronic bronchitis

2. Dx_7.2.11 represents a primary diagnosis of congestive heart failure. Thus the fourth rule, Dx_7.2.11 & CHF, simply represents a patient having CHF whose hospitalization is due to congestive heart failure itself rather than some other cause — say, a myocardial infarction.

We repeat this entire exercise with CCS Level 1 = 8, "Diseases of the respiratory system," and provide the results in Tables B.10 and B.11. In this case, the fourth and fifth rules involve the highest-level aggregation of the ICD-9 procedure codes and do not offer a great deal of insight. Therefore, we break these two rules into their more refined and descriptive, procedures. Table B.12 provides the results of this breakdown along with the percentage of cases that the more granular procedure applies to. Notice, however, that there is not enough support for these sub-procedures to qualify as a separate rule. It is only by grouping them together that we generate a sufficient number to exceed the minimum support threshold. For example Proc_6.4.2 & COPD has a mere 0.4 for its support. Table B.12 is merely provided so as to give some understanding of the underlying procedures which make up this rule.

Tables B.13−B.15 provide the final results for CCS Level 1 = 9, "Diseases of the digestive system." As before, detailed breakdowns for the diagnoses and procedures have been added, as the higher-level descriptions are too ambiguous and vague.

TABLE B.12 CCS Respiratory System Procedures for Patients *with COPD.*

Primary procedure	Description	Detailed procedure and percentage of cases
6	Operations on the respiratory system	6.4.2 – closed (endoscopic) biopsy of bronchus (37.5%)
		6.3 – thoracoscopic excision of lesion or tissue of lung (15%)
		6.9 – thoracoscopic decortication of lung (10.0%)
16	Miscellaneous diagnostic and therapeutic procedures	16.27.2 – continuous invasive mechanical ventilation for less than 96 consecutive hours (19.4%)
		16.2.2 – computed axial tomography of thorax (18.1%)

TABLE B.13 Final Association Rules for "Diseases of the Digestive System"

Rule	Support	Confidence	Lift	Readmission rate in test set (%)
Dx_9.8.2	1.25	36.23	2.41	52.46
Dx_9.4.4	1.10	48.89	3.25	30.56
Proc_7	1.45	38.67	2.57	32.43
Proc_7.12.3	1.00	41.67	2.77	36.96
RENAL	2.05	26.11	1.74	25.14
RENAL & DM	1.45	30.85	2.05	26.04
CHF	2.50	25.00	1.66	25.37
COPD & AF	1.10	30.14	2.00	25.93

TABLE B.14 CCS Digestive System Diagnosis

Primary diagnosis	Description	Detailed ICD-9 diagnosis and percentage of cases
9.8.2	Other liver diseases	Cirrhosis of liver (43.5%)
		Hepatic encephalopathy (31.9%)
9.4.4	Other disorders of stomach and duodenum	Angiodysplasia of stomach and duodenum with hemorrhage (33.3%)
		Persistent vomiting (24.4%)
		Acquired hypertrophic pyloric stenosis (15.5%)
		Gastroparesis (11.1%)

TABLE B.15 CCS Digestive System Procedures

Primary procedure	Description	Detailed procedure and percentage of cases
7.12.3	Venous catheterization	
7	Operations on the cardiovascular system	7.12.3 – venous catheterization (61.3%)
		7.16 – hemodialysis (16%)

The association rules that go with a digestive system diagnosis are clearly the most interesting. In contrast to the other two major disease systems, two diagnoses (9.8.2 and 9.4.4) do not need to be paired with a chronic condition in order to meet the threshold of 25% for the readmission rate. Also, the surgical procedure observed in these rules is a **circulatory** system procedure rather than a digestive system procedure.

Procedure 7.12.3, Venous Catheterization, describes the insertion of a long, thin tube into one of the large veins for purposes of delivering fluids or medications. One of its uses is for the purposes of intravenous feeding. This is a likely scenario, as this occurs in the context of the diseases of the digestive system data set.

Further examination of our sets of rules reveals that, in many cases, underlying chronic condition(s) drive readmissions — not the specific primary diagnosis. For example, the RENAL rule in Table B.13 ("Diseases of the digestive system") has a 30-day readmission rate of 25.1%. This undoubtedly reflects the fact that renal disease has a readmission rate of 26.2% for the entire data set. This set of patients just happened to be admitted for a digestive system disease, but their true cause of readmission was the renal disease.

READMISSION RULES — 180 DAYS

By changing the readmission timeframe to 180 days and requiring the patient to be either continuously enrolled for 180 days post-discharge or until a readmission occurs, the readmission rate increases to 31.2%. This will increase the support of those associations containing READMIT and will allow us to capture more readmission rules. Tables B.16—B.21 provide the new sets of rules for CCS Level 1 = 7, 8, and 9 using a confidence of 0.6 instead of 0.25, but keeping a support of 0.01, correlation of 0.10, maximum item set size in Body of 2, and maximum item set size in Head of 1.

We note that, even at 180 days, there is no substantial difference in the conditions associated with a readmission for an index diagnosis of "Diseases of the circulatory system." However, comparing the 30-day readmission rules with the 180-day readmission rules for "Diseases of the respiratory system" and "Diseases of the digestive system," we can see similarities and differences. For example, gastrointestinal hemorrhage clearly is important for 180-day readmissions but not for 30-day readmissions. It should be noted that a primary diagnosis of 8.6 — "Respiratory failure; insufficiency; arrest" appears in the 180-day rule set but just barely misses making the cut for the 30-day readmission set. For the 30-day set, 8.6 has a 27.1% readmission rate in the training set, but when this rule is applied to the test set we find a readmission rate of only 24.5%. Also, it should be noted that CHF, a circulatory disease, has a strong influence on the 180-day readmissions for the class of diseases of the respiratory system; 9 of the 13 rules (69%) include CHF. In contrast, only 25% of the 30-day rules contain a CHF.

In contrast to the 30-day rules, the 180-day rules for the respiratory system contain a few with fairly sizable support. For example, the rule CHF & HTN has a 180-day support of 11.5. These high values of support can be explained by the fact that at 180 days, there is an increased prevalence of readmissions. The 30-day support for the rule CHF & HTN turns out to be large, too, at 4.67. It does not appear in the list of 30-day association rules, as its confidence of 23.81 falls below the threshold value of 25 that we specified.

TABLE B.16 Final Association Rules for "Diseases of the Circulatory System" — 180-Day Readmission

Rule	Support	Confidence	Lift	Readmission rate in test set (%)
Dx_7.2.11 & ASTHMA	1.49	72.41	2.32	65.75
Dx_7.2.11 & RENAL	3.08	67.97	2.18	65.71
Dx_7.2.11 & COPD	3.86	66.87	2.14	62.58
RENAL & CHF	4.81	64.76	2.08	62.87
RENAL & COPD	3.26	72.44	2.32	60.77
RENAL & ASTHMA	1.52	72.88	2.34	60.00
ASTHMA & CHF	2.58	64.60	2.07	63.57

TABLE B.17 Final Association Rules for "Diseases of the Respiratory System" — 180-Day Readmissions

Rule	Support	Confidence	Lift	Readmission rate in test set (%)
Dx_8.6 & CHF	1.02	82.35	2.64	81.25
Dx_8.2 & CHF	5.19	62.83	2.01	65.52
Dx_8.2.3 & CHF	5.12	64.22	2.06	66.36
Dx_8.6.1 & CAD	1.24	77.27	2.48	62.50
Proc_16 & CHF	1.68	63.89	2.05	77.42
Proc_16.27 & CHF	1.32	81.82	2.62	81.82
Proc_16.27 & COPD	1.32	72.00	2.31	75.00
Proc_16.27 & CAD	1.32	81.82	2.62	63.64
Proc_16.27 & HTN	1.75	72.73	2.33	60.87
CHF & COPD	9.21	60.58	1.94	65.73
CHF & RENAL	3.29	72.58	2.33	65.52
CHF & HTN	11.48	60.62	1.94	63.85
CHF & DM	8.11	61.33	1.97	62.82

TABLE B.18 CCS Respiratory System Diagnosis — 180-Day Readmissions

Diagnosis	Description
8.2	Chronic obstructive pulmonary disease and bronchiectasis
8.2.3	Obstructive chronic bronchitis
8.6	Respiratory failure; insufficiency; arrest (adult)
8.6.1	Respiratory failure

TABLE B.19 CCS Respiratory System Procedures — 180-Day Readmissions

Procedure	Description
16	Miscellaneous diagnostic and therapeutic procedures
16.27	Respiratory intubation and mechanical ventilation

SUMMARY

This tutorial has demonstrated how to identify high readmission rate rules using association rules data mining on the initial admission diagnosis. Lowering the confidence will generate more rules, but at the expense of a lower readmission rate for these rules, making them less valuable for predicting which patients are at risk for readmission. Likewise,

TABLE B.20 Final Association Rules for "Diseases of the Digestive System" — 180-Day Readmissions

Rule	Support	Confidence	Lift	Readmission rate in test set (%)
Dx_9.10 & CHF	1.30	64.86	2.08	75.00
Dx_9.10.7 & CAD	1.25	62.16	1.99	65.31
Dx_9.8.2	1.79	60.00	1.92	74.00
RENAL & DM	2.76	64.56	2.07	64.63
RENAL & AF	1.35	71.43	2.29	63.89
RENAL & CHF	2.00	69.81	2.24	62.50

TABLE B.21 CCS Digestive System Diagnosis — 180-Day Readmissions. Results are for 9.10 *with CHF* and 9.10.7 *with CAD*

Diagnosis	Description	Detailed ICD-9 diagnosis and percentage of cases
9.8.2	Other liver diseases	9.8.2.1 – cirrhosis of liver without mention of alcohol (32.0%)
		9.8.2.2 – hepatic encephalopathy (26.0%)
		9.8.2.2 – other sequelae of chronic liver disease (12.0%)
9.10	Gastrointestinal hemorrhage	9.10.7 – hemorrhage of gastrointestinal tract, unspecified (81.3%)
9.10.7	Hemorrhage of gastrointestinal tract	9.10.7 – hemorrhage of gastrointestinal tract, unspecified (100.0%)

lowering the minimum support will generate additional rules, but these rules will be rarer and thus less useful. Because of the simplicity inherent in the association rules, this technique should provide valuable insights for hospitals and other healthcare stakeholders seeking to reduce higher than expected readmissions.

REFERENCES

Azevedo, P., Jorge, A., 2007. Comparing rule measures for predictive association rules. 18th European Conference on Machine Learning, pp. 510–517.

Brossette, S., Sprague, A., Hardin, M., Waites, K., Jones, W., Moder, S., 1998. Association rules and data mining in hospital infection control and public health surveillance. J. Am. Med. Inform. Assoc. 5 (4), 373–381.

Doddi, S., Marathe, A., Ravi, S., Torney, D., 2001. Discovery of association rules in medical data. Med. Inform. Internet Med. 26 (1), 25–33.

Healthcare Cost and Utilization Project (HCUP), 2012. 2012 HCUP Tools and Software. Agency for Healthcare Research and QualityHCUP), 2012, Rockville, MD. Available at: <www.hcup-us.ahrq.gov/tools_software.jsp>.

Jencks, S., Williams, M., Coleman, E., 2009. Rehospitalizations among patients in the Medicare fee-for-service program. N. Engl. J. Med. 360, 1418–1428.

Jiang, H.J., Wier, L.M, Potter, D.E.B., Burgess, J., 2010. Hospitalizations for potentially preventable vonditions among Medicare-Medicaid dual eligibles, 2008. HCUP Statistical Brief #96. Agency for Healthcare Research and Quality, Rockville, MD. Available at: <http://www.hcup-us.ahrq.gov/reports/statbriefs/sb96.pdf>.

Ma, L., Tsui, F., Hogan, W., Wagner, M., Ma, H., 2003. A framework for infection control surveillance using association rules. AMIA Annu. Symp. Proc. 410–414.

Ordonez, C., 2006. Association rule discovery with the train and test approach for heart disease prediction. IEEE Trans. Inform. Technol. Biomed. 10 (2), 334–343.

Pennsylvania Healthcare Cost Containment Council, 2012. Hospital Readmissions in Pennsylvania 2010. Available at: <www.pch4.org>.

Tan, P., Kumar, V., Srivastava, S., 2004. Selecting the Right Objective Measure for Association Analysis. Inform. Syst. 29, 293–313.

Tutorial C

Constructing Decision Trees for Medicare Claims Using R and Rattle

Ralph Winters, BA, BS

Chapter Outline

OBJECTIVE

This tutorial will demonstrate how to construct decision trees using Rattle, a data mining GUI which runs under open-source R. The data used will be the 2010 Chronic Conditions Public Use File (PUF), which contains data from 2010 Medicare claims. This aggregated file provides averages for various cost and/or utilization measures for the full Medicare population. For this example we will be using the presence of 11 chronic conditions with indicator variables (1 = condition present, 0 = condition not present) to predict the Gender of the beneficiaries (1 = Male, 2 = Female).

Variables

1. Alzheimer's Disease and Related Disorders or Senile Dementia
2. Cancer
3. Heart Failure
4. Chronic Kidney Disease

Practical Predictive Analytics and Decisioning Systems for Medicine. DOI: http://dx.doi.org/10.1016/B978-0-12-411643-6.00018-1

5. Chronic Obstructive Pulmonary Disease
6. Depression
7. Diabetes
8. Ischemic Heart Disease
9. Osteoporosis
10. Rheumatoid Arthritis/Osteoarthritis Arthritis
11. Stroke/Transient Ischemic Attack.

Three other variables will be considered for the model:

- Age (Ordinal) – beneficiary's age reported in six categories: (1) under 65; (2) 65–69; (3) 70–74; (4) 75–79; (5) 80–84; (6) 85 and above
- Average Prescriptions per Beneficiary (Part D = 12) – average number of prescriptions per beneficiary for beneficiaries enrolled in Medicare Part D for 12 months in the calendar year
- Count of Beneficiaries (Part D = 12) – count of beneficiaries enrolled in Medicare Part D for 12 months in the calendar year (used to weight the population).

ABOUT DECISION TREES

Decision trees have been around for a long time in predictive analytics and serve many uses: exploratory data analysis, variable selection, and, of course, prediction. They are easily interpretable by non-statisticians, and in many cases require little data preparation. Another advantage is that they handle missing values contained within the model.

ABOUT RATTLE

Rattle (http://rattle.togaware.com/) is a self-contained data mining application which runs completely within R. No knowledge of the R language is necessary, although it helps to know the basics of the language so that analyses can be customized.

DATA PREPARATION

Data were downloaded from the CMS site and imported into Excel. Suppressed records were deleted from the files, and the resulting file was output to the tab delimited file contained on the disk.

INSTALLING R

R must be installed before installing Rattle. Detailed instructions can be found at the R Home Page (www.r-project.org/).

INSTALLING RATTLE

Start the "R" program. The RGUI Window interface will appear (Figure C.1). Select Packages/Install Packages(s) from the menu. Select a CRAN Mirror for the location nearest you, and press OK. A list of packages will appear. Select "rattle" and press OK. During the installation you may be prompted to install additional R packages that are required to run Rattle.
   Additional information about installing Rattle can be found at the Rattle Home Page (rattle.togaware.com).

STARTING RATTLE AFTER INSTALLATION

1. Start the "R" program. The RGUI Window interface will appear. Select "Packages/Load Pages" from the menu. The "Select one" dialog will appear. Select "rattle" and press OK.
2. At the R Console command line, type **Rattle()** to start the Rattle GUI.

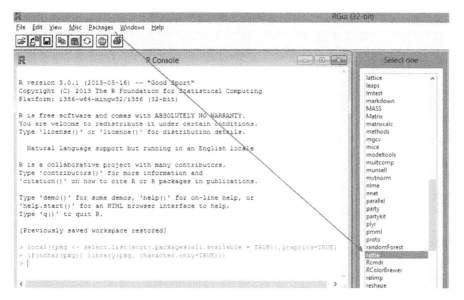

FIGURE C.1   R console.

THE RATTLE TAB BAR

The Rattle tab bar (Figure C.2) organizes the data mining activities via tabs.

1. The Data tab is used to import external data into the Analysis, and to set the variable roles. It is also used to partition the data into Training and Validation Data Sets. A Training Data Set is used to develop the predictive model. The Validation Data Set consists of data NOT used to build the model, and is used to measure how stable the model's performance is expected to be.
2. The Explore tab is used to obtain descriptive statistics about the variables; this includes means, standard deviations, and interactive plots of the data.
3. The Test tab includes two sample statistical tests, including correlation tests.
4. The Transform tab is used to transform or recode the format of one variable to another − e.g., character to numeric
5. The Cluster tab identifies groups with similar characteristics using k-means.
6. The Associate tab develops association rules among the variables.
7. The Model tab applies an assortment of different predictive models to the data, including regression, neural network, and decision tree based models.
8. The Evaluate tab assesses the performance of the models.
9. The Log tab keeps track of all modeling activity within Rattle, and allows you to repeat an analysis multiple times, or customize the behavior.

FIGURE C.2   The Rattle tab bar.

IMPORTING THE TUTORIAL TEXT FILE

1. From the Data tab, select the folders icon to the right of the filename box. In the Select A File dialog (Figure C.3), select the filter at the bottom right of the screen and change it to "TXT Files." Then navigate to "2010_Chronic_Conditions_PUF.txt" on the disk provided. After the file has been selected, click "Open."
2. The filename will then appear in the filename box. Enter "\t" in the Separator box to indicate that this is a tab-delimited file.

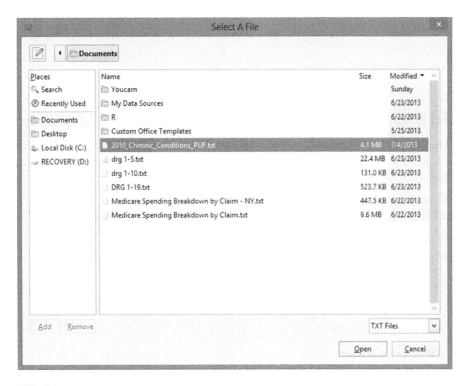

FIGURE C.3 Select A File dialog.

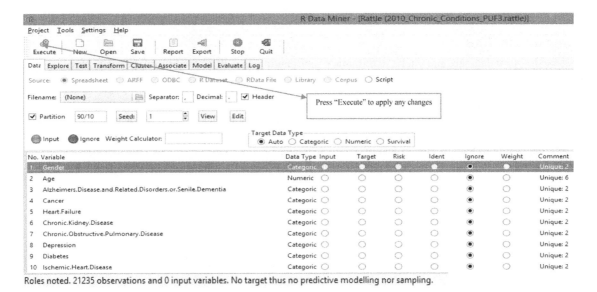

FIGURE C.4 Data menu.

3. You are now in the Rattle data menu (Figure C.4). Make sure the Header and Partition boxes are checked, and change the box to the right of "Partition" to 90/10/0. Set the Seed Parameter to 1. The data will be partitioned into a 90% training and a 10% test (validation) data set.
4. Press the *EXECUTE* button near the top left of the screen to apply the changes.
5. Place the cursor on any variable and select all of the variables (Ctrl-A). Then click the red IGNORE button.
6. All of the variables should be shown as Ignored (make sure you are in full-screen mode to see the radio buttons!). This will make it easier in the future to assign specific roles to the data.
7. Press the *EXECUTE* button near the top left of the screen again to apply the changes.

RATTLE DATA MENU

Please refer to Figure C.4.
Example C1: Predicting Gender

Setting the Variable Roles

Variable roles are used in Rattle to indicate which variables will be used as Input variables (or Predictors) and which variable is to be used as the target (or dependent) variable. Variables with an Ignore role do not enter into the analysis. Roles can be interchanged by clicking the radio buttons and pressing *EXECUTE*.

1. Select Gender (Variable 1) as the target variable, and Variables 2–13, and 55 as Input variables
2. Press *EXECUTE*, and the display changes to the roles assigned.

The Comment column will indicate more information about the variable, such as the number of unique levels (Figure C.5). This makes it easy to pinpoint any problems in the data – in this case, if Gender showed three unique levels we would probably need to investigate.

The bottom of the screen gives you more information about the role assignment. In our case, you should see this message displayed:

(Scroll down to see remaining variables)

Exploring the Data

The Explore data tab gives you more detailed information about the characteristics of each variable.

The Summary Analysis

1. Select the Explore data tab, and click the Summary radio button as well as the Summary check box
2. Press *EXECUTE*
3. Refer to Figure C.6 (summary statistics).

The Summary tab will give you basic frequencies and descriptive statistics about each of your variables. If you wish to probe further, there are other kinds of analysis you can perform, such as correlations or interactive plots of the data, by selecting the appropriate radio button and pressing *EXECUTE*.

In our case, we can see that there are missing values for X.Average.Prescriptions.per.Beneficiary. This will be a problem, since we intend to use it as a weighting variable, and weighting variables cannot contain missing values.

Roles noted. 21235 observations and 13 input variables. The target is Gender. Categoric 2. Classification models enabled.

No.	Variable	Data Type	Input	Target	Risk	Ident	Ignore	Weight	Comment
1	Gender	Categoric	○	●	○	○	○	○	Unique: 2
2	Age	Numeric	●	○	○	○	○	○	Unique: 6
3	Alzheimers.Disease.and.Related.Disorders.or.Senile.Dementia	Categoric	●	○	○	○	○	○	Unique: 2
4	Cancer	Categoric	●	○	○	○	○	○	Unique: 2
5	Heart.Failure	Categoric	●	○	○	○	○	○	Unique: 2
6	Chronic.Kidney.Disease	Categoric	●	○	○	○	○	○	Unique: 2
7	Chronic.Obstructive.Pulmonary.Disease	Categoric	●	○	○	○	○	○	Unique: 2
8	Depression	Categoric	●	○	○	○	○	○	Unique: 2
9	Diabetes	Categoric	●	○	○	○	○	○	Unique: 2
10	Ischemic.Heart.Disease	Categoric	●	○	○	○	○	○	Unique: 2
11	Osteoporosis	Categoric	●	○	○	○	○	○	Unique: 2
12	Rheumatoid.Arthritis.Osteoarthritis.Arthritis	Categoric	○	○	○	○	●	○	Unique: 2
13	Stroke.Transient.Ischemic.Attack	Categoric	○	●	●	●	●	●	Unique: 2

FIGURE C.5 Data menu after role assignment.

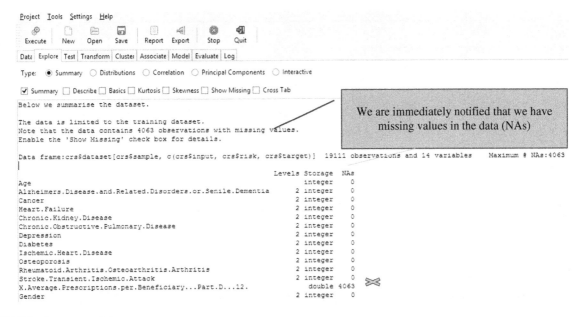

FIGURE C.6 Summary statistics.

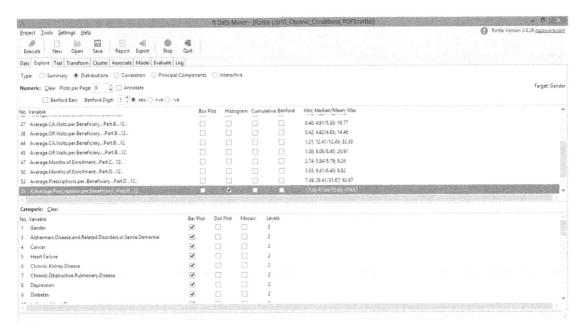

FIGURE C.7 Distributions selections.

The Distributions Analysis

1. Select the Distributions radio button under Type: (see Figure C.7)
2. Change Plots per Page to 9
3. Check the Histogram box for Variable 55 (top pane)
4. Check BarPlot for Variables 1–13 (bottom pane)
5. Press *EXECUTE*.

If there are more plots than fit on a page, the output spills over to multiple pages, and you will need to need to select the appropriate window in the R Console to view (Figure C.8).

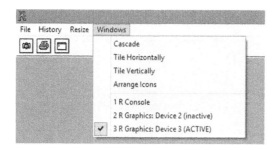

FIGURE C.8 Select chart window.

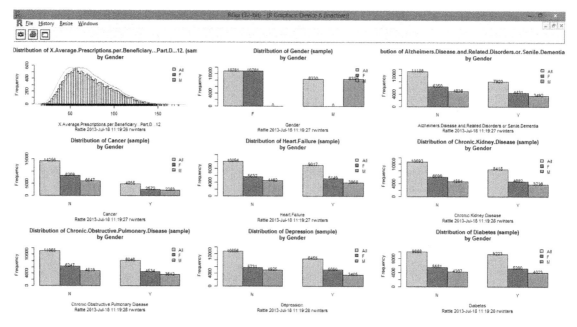

FIGURE C.9 Distribution plots.

Observe that variable 55 (X.Average.Prescriptions.per.Beneficiary) has an extremely left skewed distribution with a significant number of missing values (Figure C.9), and is unusable at this point. In the next section we will smooth out this variable.

Females outnumber males by a ratio of about 4 : 3. It is difficult to see if there is any difference in Gender by looking at the graphs, so we will keep all the variables in the model.

Create Weighting Variable

The CMS 2010 Chronic Conditions PUF is an aggregated file in which each record is a *profile* or *cell* defined by the characteristics of Medicare beneficiaries. The number of rows (or records) in this file represents the number of unique profiles in the Medicare population. Since this file is only supplied in aggregate form, we will use the Count of Beneficiaries (Part D = 12) [Variable 53] as a proxy for the number of beneficiaries for each row. This variable is chosen partly since the "Average Prescriptions per Beneficiary (Part D = 12)" will be considered to be included in the model.

The problem is that Variable 53 has been read as a character variable, when in fact it needs to be treated as a numeric variable. To perform this in Rattle, we will use the Transform tab.

1. Select the Transform tab
2. Select Variable 53 after scrolling down towards the end
3. Select Type: Recode as the Transform, select "As Numeric" (located *under* the line which begins with "Binning:")
4. Press *EXECUTE*.

This transform will convert a character variable to a NEW numeric Variable 56 and prefix the name with TNM_ (Transform to Numeric).

Note that column 2 of the output states that there are still missing values for Variable 56 (Figure C.10). This is a problem for a weight variable, since all observations need to have positive values. To accommodate this, we will replace all missing observations with zero.

1. From the Transform menu, select the Impute type, and select Zero/Missing as the imputation method (Figure C.11)
2. Press *EXECUTE*.

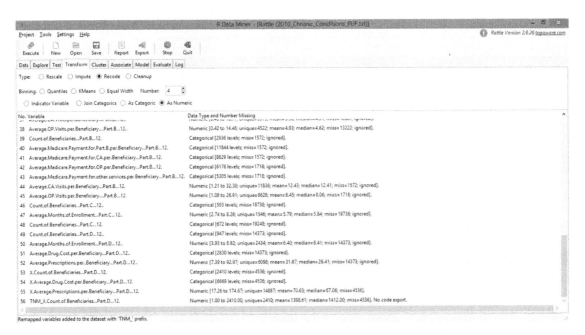

FIGURE C.10   Transform to numeric.

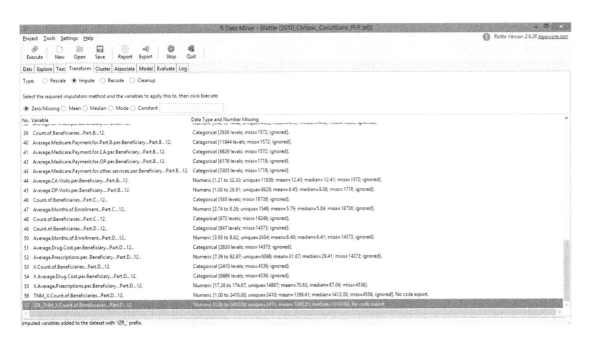

FIGURE C.11   Transform missing (NAs) to zero.

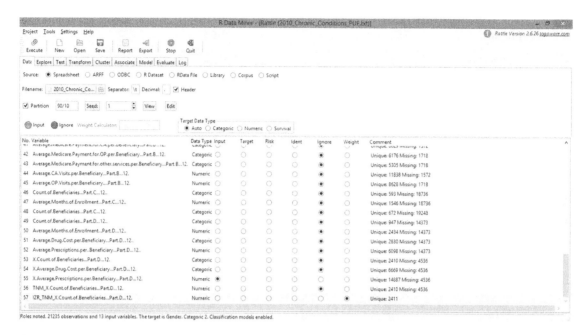

FIGURE C.12   All roles set.

This will create another new variable with the prefix IZR_ (insert zeros) with no missing (NA) values (Variable 57).

Setting the Weight Variable Role

1. Return to the data tab and select Variable 57 with the Weight role
2. Set Variable 56 to IGNORE
3. Press *EXECUTE*
4. Observe the message at the bottom of screen, that roles have been set (Figure C.12).

NOTE: As an alternate to replacing missing values with 0, we could have chosen to replace missing values with the mean, median, or mode of the sample, or simply delete observations from the analysis. This might have been done if we were using this variable as input; however, since it is used for weighting only, we are setting the weight to zero for all observations having no Medicare Part D Claims.

1. Return to the Explore tab
2. Set "Type:" to Distributions, Number of Plots per page to 4, and Check Histogram for Variable 57
3. Uncheck the other variables (unless you want to see them as well)
4. Press *EXECUTE* to display the histogram (Figure C.13).

Over 4,000 observations will not be included in the model (0 beneficiary count). This is due to the fact that we are only looking at the drug portion of Medicare (part D), and the other rows pertain to Parts A and B.

Running the Model

1. Navigate to the Model tab.
2. Set these parameters in the Model tab: Type = Tree, Algorithm = Traditional, Min Split = 1, Min Bucket = 1, Max Depth = 5 Complexity = 0.01
3. Insure that "Include Missing" is unchecked
4. Press *EXECUTE*, and the Decision Tree Model Summary will appear (Figures C.14 and C.15).

Rattle is using the part CART algorithm, which always starts at the root (all of the data), and then continues to split the data until it cannot split any more, or until MINSPLIT is achieved (asterisk appears on that line, and it is considered a terminal node). How a node is split depends upon the method chosen; however, for classification predictions the GINI method is the default. In lay terms, GINI will look at the "impurity" of a node and will calculate the probability of misclassifying an observation by classifying it according to the distribution of the classes at each node along the tree.

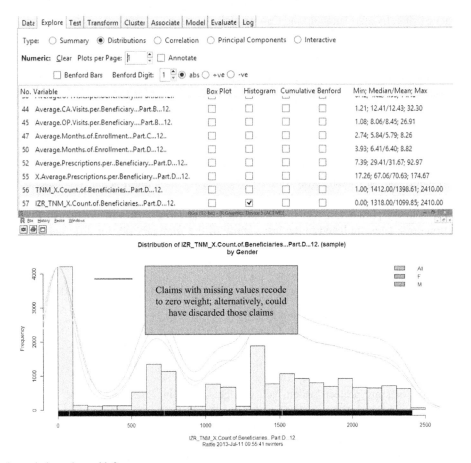

FIGURE C.13 Replace missing values with 0.

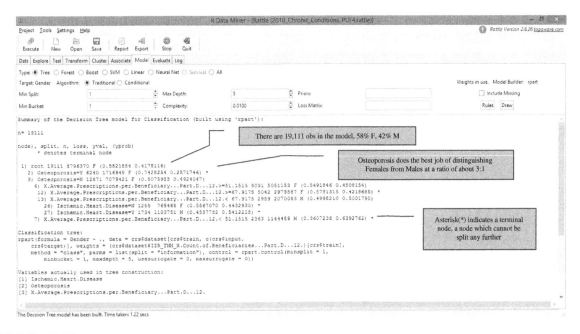

FIGURE C.14 Model output.

FIGURE C.15 Model output continued.

The way that splitting occurs depends upon how the model parameters are set on the page.

Min Split: This is the number of observations that must exist in a node before a split is attempted. We set this to 1 for illustration purposes; however, it is usually a larger number (20 is the default).

Min Bucket: This is the minimum number of observations that must be left in a Leaf after a split occurs. This is also set to 1 for illustration purposes, but some data miners like to set this to 30 so that it corresponds to a minimum sample size.

Max Depth: This corresponds to how large the tree grows. If a tree grows too large, it may become very complex and hard to understand, and may need to be "pruned." Setting the maximum depth to 5 produces a tree that is easy to understand and good for demo purposes.

Cp: This is the complexity parameter, which is used for tree pruning. We will set this to the default 0.01 in this example. Prediction error rates are listed in the last section of the summary out for different levels of Cp.

Saving the Model

This would be a good time to save the model, so when we exit Rattle, we can open the file and resume where we left off.

1. Press the Save icon and the Save Project Dialog box will pop up (Figure C.16)
2. For the name of a project, enter 2010_Chronic_Conditions_PUF5.rattle and press Save.

To open a previously saved model:

1. Click the Open icon
2. If you already have an existing project loaded, you will get a warning message that the new project will overwrite the existing project
3. If you will to process, press Yes and a file dialog box will open so that you may select an existing project to load.

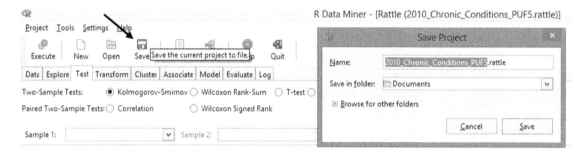

FIGURE C.16 Save project dialog.

Graphical View

As an alternative to the text summary output above, we can look at the classifications via a tree-based view. To obtain this, click "Draw" in the upper right-hand side of the display to obtain a visual display of the model. This is usually a much better way to initially view a model.

As you can see, each node is split into two paths, depending upon whether the condition listed under the "parent" node is true (YES), or not (NO). In our example tree (Figure C.17), we can see that the node hierarchy is five deep, after which the node splitting stops.

Each node contains the dominant (or majority) class (M or F), along with the classification percentage breakdown, and the percent of the total population contained in the specific node.

Looking at a Specific Node

The classification of Females, via the diagnosis of Osteoporosis, is prominently displayed in Node 2 (bottom left of diagram); 74% of those with Osteoporosis were females. To get to a classification of Male, the algorithm has to do a little more splitting work:

- Node 3 — 68% of the data consist of those with NO diagnosis of Osteoporosis, split as F/51%, M/49%
- Node 4 — All Females from Node 3 with an average no. of prescriptions $> = 51$
- Node 7 — All Males from Node 3 with Prescriptions <51.

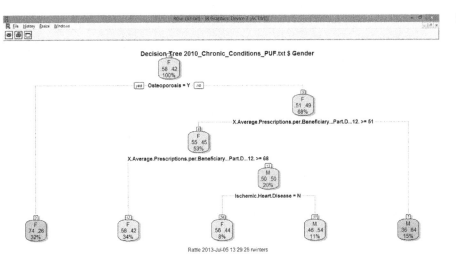

FIGURE C.17   Graphic model output.

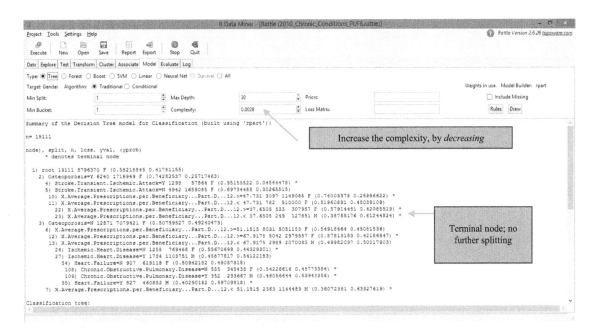

FIGURE C.18   Model output more detailed.

So, you may ask, where are the Males with Osteoporosis, and those with Prescriptions $>= 51$?

The answer to the second part is contained in Node 13. The logic from decision trees can sometimes be a bit convoluted. In this case it is Prescriptions $>= 51$ THEN Prescriptions <68. However, at this node level, there is only a 50% chance that the beneficiary will be Male.

For Males with Osteoporosis, we first have to change the Complexity parameter to a lower number (Figure C.18), and then press *EXECUTE*. This will lead to a more detailed tree (Figure C.19), although not necessarily a more significant one. *Note*: The second example of the tutorial will demonstrate some techniques for showing only certain branches of a tree, which makes the tree view more readable.

Evaluating the Model

Rattle offers several methods for model evaluations. An Error (or "Confusion") matrix tabulates the number of correct and incorrect (false positives and false negative) predictions vs the actual results. ROC charts plot true positive vs false

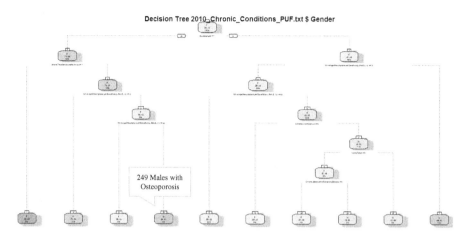

FIGURE C.19 Graphic tree complexity = 0.0028.

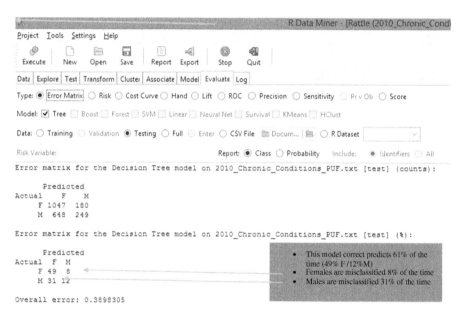

FIGURE C.20 Confusion matrix.

positive rates, and can be used, for example, to determine the cut-off value for a clinical test. By analyzing an ROC curve, a researcher can attempt to identify a point which minimizes false positive and false negatives.

To use the Error matrix method (Figure C.20):

1. Navigate back to the "R Data Miner [Rattle]" window
2. Select the Evaluate tab
3. Select Error Matrix as the evaluation method
4. Check Model = Tree, and Data = Testing
5. Press *EXECUTE.*

Other measures of accuracy can be chosen by selecting a different Type from the Evaluate tab. Figure C.21 shows the output from the "Hand" package. As you can see, the ROC curve for the model outperforms a random or trivial model (straight line). The point closest to the upper left-hand corner on the curve is the point which indicates approximately a 30% true positive rate vs a 15% false positive rate. This would typically be unacceptable for a clinical study, but might be acceptable for a research study.

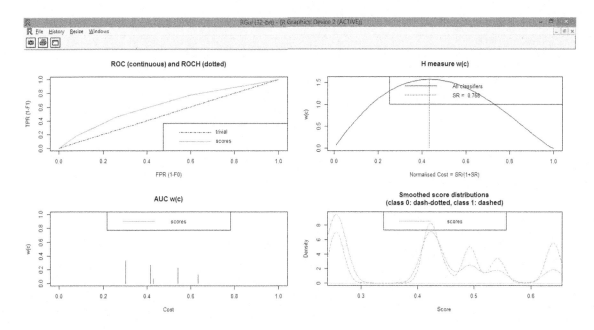

FIGURE C.21 "Hand" output.

Pruning the Tree

Often the tree size will get too large to be practical and it will be necessary to prune or cut off branches. We saw this earlier when we expanded the tree to include Males with Osteoporosis. If we were to view that tree, we would find it overly complex. Pruning a tree enables you to simplify the tree, and construct one that makes logical sense.

Interactive pruning of a tree can be performed by issuing R commands via a script or directly within the console.

1. Navigate to the R Console by clicking on the R Icon on the taskbar, and selecting "RGui - R Console" (Windows 8)
2. Copy the following text into the R Console immediately after the " > " prompt: PrunedTree <- prp(crs$rpart, snip = TRUE)$obj # interactively trim the tree fancyRpartPlot(PrunedTree, main = "Osteoporosis = Y cp = .0028")
3. The resulting classification tree appears, in edit mode (Figure C.22, pre-pruned tree). Click on a node text label, near the center of the label, and the branches will gray out, signifying that those node will be pruned from the tree (Figure C.23). Click the node again, and the nodes will reappear.
4. For our example, click on the X.Averag > = 51 node. All the branches below that node will become inactive.
5. Press the QUIT icon when you are done. The pruned decision tree will appear in the graphics window (Figure C.24).

EXAMPLE C2: PREDICTING AVERAGE DRUG COST FOR MEDICARE PART D

In this example we will use the "Conditional" target algorithm instead in the "Traditional (CART)" algorithm. According to some statisticians (Strobl *et al.*, 2007) CART algorithms have a selection bias towards variables which are continuous or have a higher number of categories. Therefore, a GINI split has a higher probability of selecting an optimal split point given a large number of categories, even though the split may not be informative. The "Conditional" algorithm separates the splitting from the inference by using Chi-square test statistics to test the association, only keeping the associations which are significant, and thus removing bias due to a large number of categories.

1. If you are starting the tutorial from here, open the saved project
2. Navigate to the Data menu
3. Set Variables 1−15 and 29−30 to the Input role
4. Set Variable 56 to the Weight role
5. Set all other roles to IGNORE
6. Press *EXECUTE*.

Do NOT set a target variable.

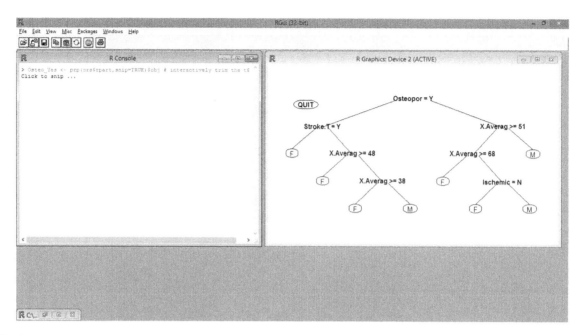

FIGURE C.22 Pre-pruned tree.

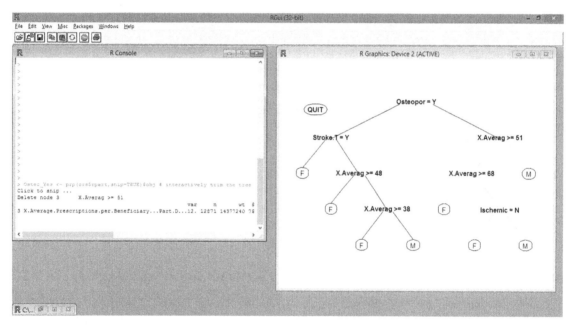

FIGURE C.23 Selecting branches.

Transforming Average Drug Per Beneficiary to a Target Variable

Variable 54 is another example of a variable which was imported as character that needs to be transformed prior to analysis.

1. Navigate to the Transform menu
2. Select 54 X.Average.Drug.Cost.per.Beneficiary
3. Select Type: Recode as the Transform, select "As Numeric" (located under the "Binning" line).
4. This transform will convert a character variable to a NEW numeric variable and prefix the name with TNM_X (Figure C.25).

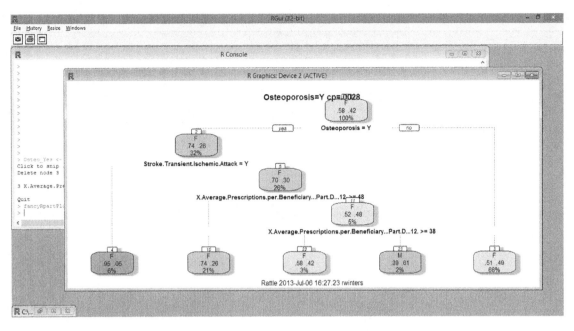

FIGURE C.24   Pruned tree.

FIGURE C.25   Character to numeric.

Delete Observations with Missing Values

Note that there are still over 4,000 missing values. Instead of changing imputed missing values to zero, this time we choose to delete missing values from the analysis data set.

From the Transform tab, select Variable 58.

1. Select Cleanup as the Transform type and "Delete Obs with Missing" as the type of cleanup
2. Press *EXECUTE* and then Yes (Figure C.26)
3. After the transform has been executed, note (at the bottom of the screen) that the mean, median, and unique values have remained unchanged, but now there are no missing values for the target variable (Figure C.27).

Bin the Variables

Rather than treat the target variable as numeric, we want to consider binning the target variable into three categories (High, Medium, and Low), or two categories (High, and Low).

1. Select Recode as the Transform Type, set Binning = Quantiles and number of bins equal to 3
2. Select Variable 58
3. Press *EXECUTE*

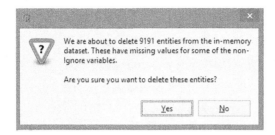

FIGURE C.26   Cleanup.

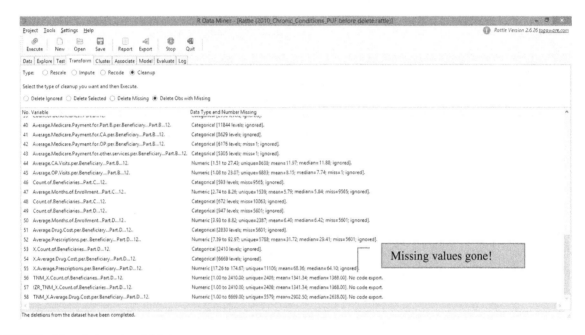

FIGURE C.27   After missing values deleted.

4. Set the number of bins equal to 2, and reselect Variable 58
5. Again, press EXECUTE (Figure C.28).

Exploring the Bins

To see how Rattle has binned Variable 54, navigate to the Explore tab.

1. Select Type = Distributions
2. Check the Bar Plot Box for Variables 59 and 60
3. Press EXECUTE (Figure C.29).

The ranges of the bins are usually represented in scientific notation. In Figure C.30, the category names have been annotated and the range expanded to standard notation within the box to make it easier to see (Figure C.30).

For both binning methods there are a more than adequate number of counts in each bin, so we will use the 3-bin variable as our target.

Navigate to the Data menu again (Figure C.31):

1. Set Variables 1–15 and 29–30 to the Input role
2. Set Variable 56 to the Weight role
3. Set BQ3_TNM.X.Average.Cost.per.Beneficiary to the Target role
4. Set all other variables to IGNORE

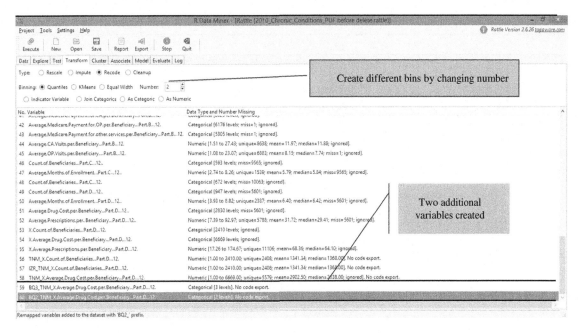

FIGURE C.28   Binning the variables.

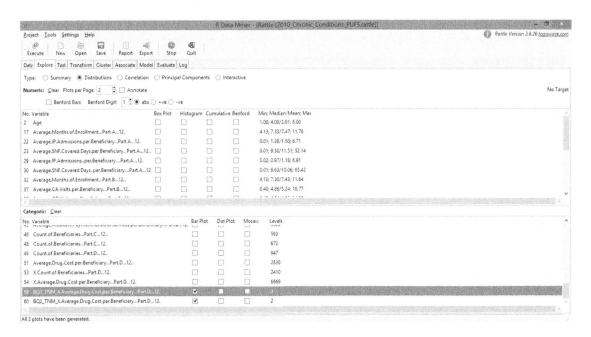

FIGURE C.29   Selecting the binned variables.

5. Check the Partition box and set the value to 90/10

6. Set Seed Parameter to 1

7. Press *EXECUTE*.

Running the Conditional Model

1. Navigate to the Model tab

2. Set Type to Tree

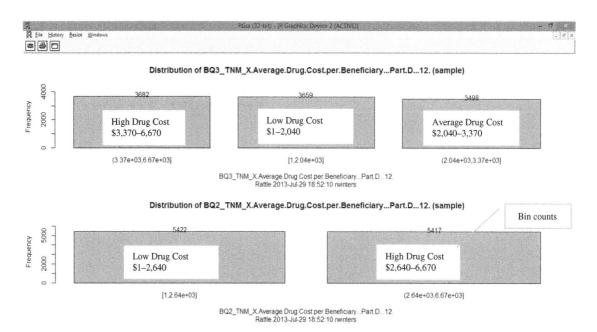

FIGURE C.30   Two or three bins.

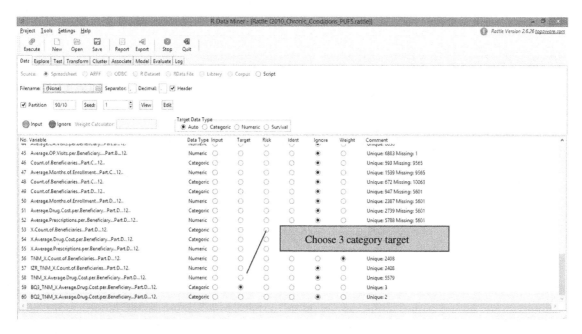

FIGURE C.31   Setting the target variable.

3. Set Algorithm to Conditional
4. Set Max Depth to 3
5. Set Min Split to 1
6. Set Max Bucket to 1
7. Press *EXECUTE*.

Notice the summary states that there are eight terminal nodes (Figure C.32). Eight nodes can fit comfortably on a page, so this example is good for illustration.

Press Draw in the upper right corner to plot the decision tree (Figure C.33).

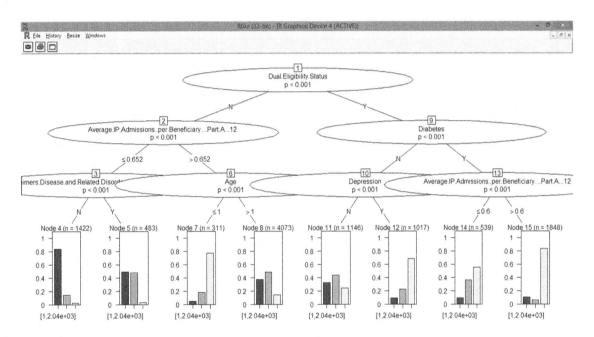

FIGURE C.32   Output from conditional model.

FIGURE C.33   Conditional model graph.

Notice that the output is different from the traditional plot. For each of the terminal nodes there is a bar graph, with each bar indicating the percent of that node which was classified into one of the three target classes. The bars are ordered from lowest cost to highest cost.

The highest bar in each terminal node represents the "majority class" − i.e., the best predictor for the terminal branch. There are two nodes with a class predictor of 80% or more: Node 4 and Node 15. Since a "Y" branch indicates the presence of that condition we will look at terminal Node 15, which consists of all "Y" paths. Follow Node 15 from the top. The logic states that this node contains all Dual Eligibility members (Node 9), with multiple chronic conditions including diabetes (Node 13), who were admitted >0.6 on average, in the last 12 months (Node 13). These members were predicted as having the highest probability of being in the highest drug cost group.

To see how the model performs as a whole, let's look at the Error (or Confusion) matrix (Figure C.34).

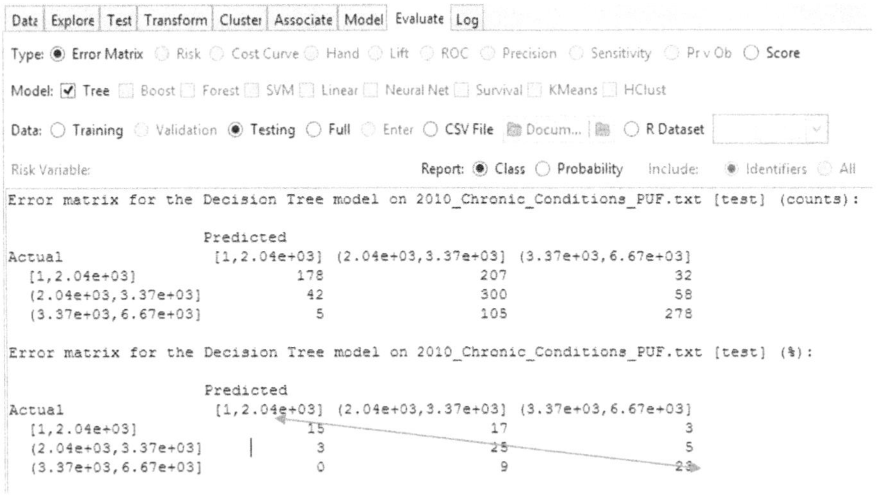

FIGURE C.34 Confusion matrix: three outcomes.

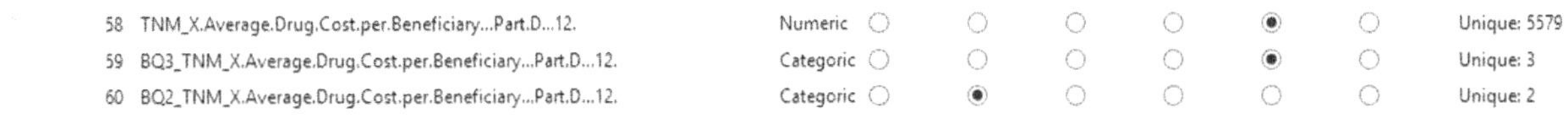

FIGURE C.35 Splitting using only two categories.

1. Navigate to the Evaluate tab
2. Select Error Matrix
3. Select Data: Testing
4. Press *EXECUTE*.

The Actual class that each observation was in is arranged, in columns, under the label "Actual"; the Predicted class is arranged as rows underneath the label "Predicted." The first matrix is the actual counts of the categorization and the second matrix is the percentage of each cell of the whole sample. The diagonal arrow represents the percentages of the sample where the prediction is equal to the actual outcome.

For the lowest cost group, 15% were correctly classified; 25% were correctly classified for the average cost group; and 23% were correctly classified for the high cost group. Therefore, the percentage correctly classified is 63%. Alternatively, it could be stated that the error rate is 37%. Randomly assigning a prediction to any of the three bins would be 33%, so we can see that this illustrative model has some prediction power.

Looking at the marginal columns can also tell us a great deal about the specific classifiers. For example, predicting the highest cost category correctly occurred 278 times, while it was classified incorrectly $32 + 58 = 90$ times. The weakest category is the middle category, which had more incorrect classifications (312) than correct classifications (300).

Since the middle category is weak, we will see if performing another split using only two categories improves the model:

1. Navigate to the Data tab and set Variable 60 (BQ2_...) to the Target role and Variable 59 (BQ3_ ....) to IGNORE.
2. Press *EXECUTE* (Figure C.35)
3. Navigate to the Model tab
4. Set Max Depth = 30 and Min Bucket = 1000
5. Press *EXECUTE* (Figure C.36).
   The Output indicates that there are 9 terminal nodes. We have given instructions to grow the tree to a maximum depth of 30 nodes. However, to allow display of the tree graph on one page, for tutorial purposes only, we have specified that the minimum number of nodes in any leaf will be 1,000.
6. Next, press the Draw icon.

In this example we have added an additional branch level consisting of Mode 5 (Figure C.37).

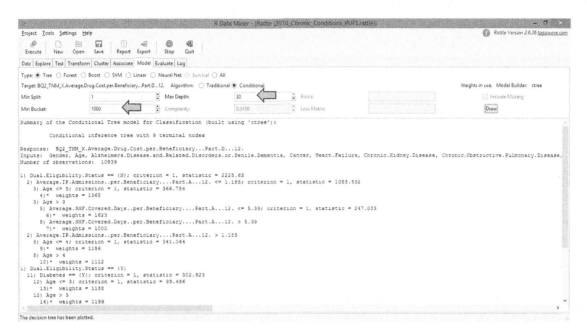

FIGURE C.36   Conditional model binary outcomes.

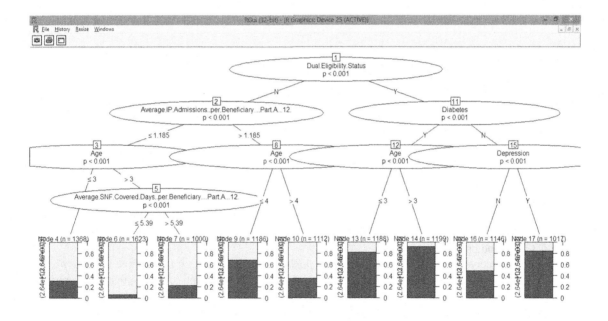

FIGURE C.37   Model conditional binary graph.

Model Performance

Error Matrix

1. Navigate to the Evaluate tab
2. Select Error Matrix
3. Press *EXECUTE*.

Note that the overall error rate is now 25%, which is an improvement over the three-outcomes model of 37%. The overall error rate could actually be improved further; however, in order to display the graphic tree on one page, we will keep it as is (Figure C.38).

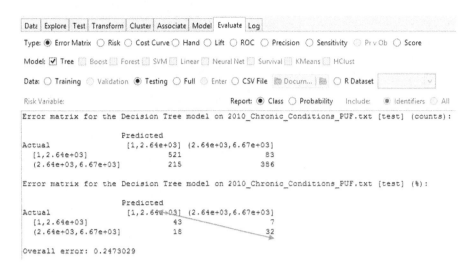

FIGURE C.38 Confusion matrix binary model.

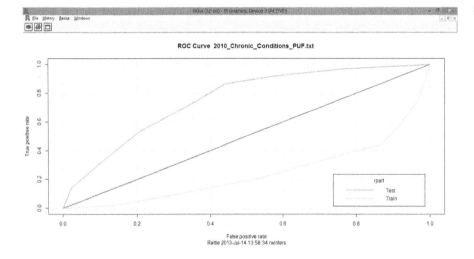

FIGURE C.39 ROC plot.

ROC Curve

A ROC Curve is an alternative method to judge the quality of a model.

Select ROC Curve and press *EXECUTE*.

ROC is plotted as a curve on an X–Y axis. The *false positive rate* is placed on the X axis; the *true positive rate* is placed on the Y axis. An ideal model will "hug" the upper left corner of the graph, meaning that on average it contains many true positives, and a minimum of false positives (Figure C.39). The area under the curve (AUC) is a model goodness-of-fit measure that compares it to a baseline 50% measure (the straight line). In our case, the AUC is 76% (Figure C.40). A random model (the straight line) would have an AUC of 50%, since it simply bisects the graph.

THE RATTLE LOG

Rattle keeps track of all R Commands issued in the log. This is done predominantly for model repeatability; however, it is interesting to be able to view the log to see what is happening behind the scenes in R.

1. Navigate to the Log tab
2. Select Tools/Export from the Action menu
3. Enter a filename in the pop-up box
4. Press Save.

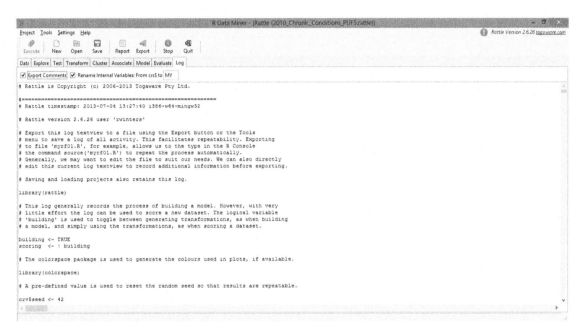

FIGURE C.40   ROC statistics.

FIGURE C.41   Options when saving the file.

Once a file is saved, you can open up the file as a script in R Console, and rerun the commands without using Rattle. Rattle provides two options when saving the file (Figure C.41):

1. *Export comments* − when checked, all of the comments are exported along with the R commands. When unchecked, only the R commands are exported.
2. *Rename internal variables from crs$ to*: − in this case, you supply a new name for the R objects. This is useful for cases in which you are running multiple models in R console.

CONCLUSION

R makes a great addition to your toolset for getting started with predictive analytics in health care.

Running Rattle on top of R is even better, since Rattle is completely menu driven, requires very little R coding, and follows good data mining practices. It is also a good entrée into the native R environment, where you might find additional predictive analytics capabilities which suit your needs.

REFERENCE

Strobl, C., Boulesteix, A.L., Augustin, T., 2007. Unbiased split selection for classification trees based on the Gini index. Comput. Stat. Data Anal. 52 (1), 483−501.

FURTHER READING

2010 Chronic Conditions Public Use File (PUF), n.d. Retrieved from <www.cms.gov/Research-Statistics-Data-and-Systems/Statistics-Trends-and-Reports/BSAPUFS/Downloads/2010_ChronicConditions_GenDoc.pdf>.
R Project Home Page, n.d. Retrieved from R Project Home Page: <www.r-project.org/>.
Rattle Home Page, n.d. Retrieved from <http://rattle.togaware.com/>.

Tutorial D

Predictive and Prescriptive Analytics for Optimal Decisioning: Hospital Readmission Risk Mitigation

Thomas Hill, PhD, Vladimir Rastunkov, PhD and John W. Cromwell, MD

Chapter Outline

EDITOR'S NOTE: This chapter is best described as a "combined case study and tutorial," or as an "advanced tutorial." This study assumes that the reader is familiar with the use of STATISTICA software and thus can perform some of the steps that are not explicitly provided. Therefore, for the new user of STATISTICA, it might be better to work through some of the other tutorials in this book before attempting to do all the steps needed to recreate this case study. (For those who want to do this, we suggest working through Tutorial M, on Schistosomiasis, and/or Tutorials F-1 and F-2, and G-3, on WoE and Automatic Binning, before doing this tutorial.) Alternatively, readers can read through this study and then decide which parts they can perform without studying other tutorials. The data set is provided on the companion web page of this book.

OVERVIEW

Traditional statistics and hypothesis testing were successfully used in medicine for decades, and some areas of statistics were developed specifically to address use cases and solve analytic problems in medicine and healthcare delivery (see, for example, Cox, 1972; Lee, 1980). However, advanced predictive analytics or data mining methods — such as neural networks and ensemble models (see Nisbet *et al.*, 2009) — were usually considered "black boxes," not useful for providing interpretable results and actionable information and guidance. These analytic approaches have thus not been routinely applied to analyze medical or patient-care data.

In this tutorial we will describe the advantages of general (non-statistical) predictive modeling methods and algorithms, discuss ways to derive useful interpretations and actionable guidance from results, and show how general prediction models can be combined and improved with decision rules to deliver an effective "decisioning" system — i.e., an automated system that will provide relevant risk assessment and predictions.

Practical Predictive Analytics and Decisioning Systems for Medicine. DOI: http://dx.doi.org/10.1016/B978-0-12-411643-6.00019-3

Statistical Data Analysis vs General Predictive (Pattern Recognition) Models

There are a number of important differences between traditional statistical analysis and modeling (e.g., multiple regression and logistic regression) compared to the general predictive modeling techniques that have been widely adopted across many domains over the past decade or so (see, for example, Breiman, 2001; also Miner *et al.*, 2012).

Statistical analysis and modeling is typically based on testing of hypotheses and the estimation of population parameters from samples, based on statistical/mathematical reasoning alone. For example, in multiple regression the parameters of a linear model are estimated that predict some outcome or response variable y as a linear function of the available predictor or x variables. Thus these traditional methods reflect the "mean" or average of a population, and have become the basis of Evidence-Based Medicine (EBM). They are often referred to by physicians as "best practices," but, unfortunately, do not provide predictions for an individual, although an individual that may be one or two standard deviations from the average may respond quite differently to medical treatments.

In contrast to statistical modeling, the algorithms for general predictive modeling use a much more pragmatic approach. Namely, data mining and general predictive modeling typically apply general learning or pattern recognition algorithms to extract from sample data repeatable patterns that allow for the most accurate predictions, regardless of the nature and complexity of the relationships between predictors and outcomes. These modern statistical learning theory methods thus make predictions for the "individual," not the mean of a population, and thus offer the best hope of making accurate predictions/prescriptions for the individual patient.

Example Data

Due to the Health Insurance Portability and Accountability Act of 1996 (HIPAA), the use of real healthcare data, even blinded to a high degree, is unlikely to be possible. For the purpose of this tutorial we've selected a different approach, by generating simulated data that have a format similar to that seen in the field. So all conclusions based on the data are for illustration purposes only, and do not contain any scientific information.

The preview of the data is shown in Figure D.1. The data description and statement of the problem are courtesy of Dr. John W. Cromwell.

The data set contains the following fields:

ID — unique identifier of the patient
Unplanned Readmission — binary variable that shows that specific patient was readmitted to the hospital (Unplanned Readmission = 1)
Age — continuous variable that contains the age of the patient
Surgeon ID — unique ID of the surgeon
EBL — Estimated blood loss
Apgar_Score — interval of the Apgar score of the patient
HMB_within_60_days — *beta*-hydroxy *beta*-methylbutyric acid measurement
ASA — physical status classification system
Gender — gender of the patient
WND_Class — wound contamination class
TrainTest — train and test samples identifier.

	1 ID	2 Unplanned Readmission	3 Age	4 Surgeon ID	5 EBL	6 Apgar_Score	7 HMB_within_60_days	8 ASA	9 Gender	10 WND_Class	11 TrainTest
1	758	0	29	3	3300	5-6	4.2	3	male	02	Test
2	708	0	26	2	1400	9-10	1.6	9	male	02	Test
3	229	1	32	1	3300	5-6	1.5	0	female	02	Test
4	248	1	37	3	1100	9-10	1	3	male	02	Test
5	531	0	22	2	500	5-6	0.2	3	male	02	Train
6	490	0	33	4	500	5-6	2.5	3	male	02	Train
7	634	0	25	4	200	9-10	0.9	3	female	02	Train
8	265	1	23	2	800	1-2	2.7	2	female	02	Test
9	655	0	28	2	3300	5-6	4.5	3	female	00	Train
10	848	0	26	2	800	9-10	3.3	2	male	02	Train

FIGURE D.1 Preview of the data simulated for this tutorial.

THE GOAL

The goal of this tutorial is to create an analytic flow that investigates predictors of readmission, builds an analytic model, combines model with expert-defined logic, and provides sensitivity analysis for the selected prediction. We'll use *STATISTICA* Workspace as the primary environment for implementation of this logic. The subsequent sections of this tutorial are devoted to specific steps of this process.

Step 1: Data Acquisition

STATISTICA Workspace is the environment for building analytic workflows and templates. It is often viewed as "graphical" programming environment: users construct workflows from a set of predefined nodes and use graphical user interfaces to modify node parameters as needed. Advanced users who have elementary programming skills in Visual Basic can additionally create their own nodes. The links between the nodes can be viewed as data flows from one node to another, whereas transformations and calculations happen within the nodes. The process starts from a data acquisition node. We create a new workspace from *File − New − Workspace*. Workspaces allow four primary channels for data input: (1) data configuration template predefined in *STATISTICA* Enterprise, (2) in-place database connection node, (3) embedded *STATISTICA* spreadsheet, and (4) import node (e.g., from MS Excel) or input-generator SVB node.

For the sake of simplicity in this tutorial we'll be using embedded *STATISTICA* spreadsheet node. By clicking the Data Source button we select the spreadsheet to be used in the workflow (Figure D.2).

The workflow is shown in Figure D.3.

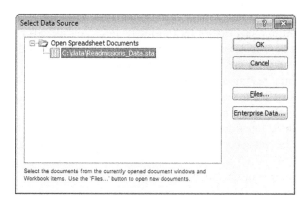

FIGURE D.2   Select Data Source dialog.

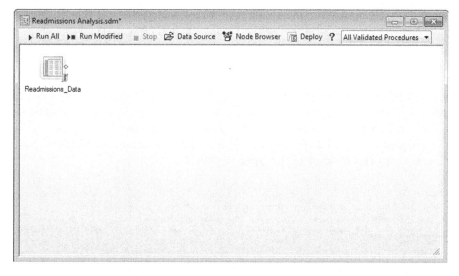

FIGURE D.3   Screenshot of the workspace.

Even though it is possible to change the size of the workspace area at any moment, it is recommended to reserve enough space to allocate analysis objects beforehand.

Step 2: Feature Selection and Predictor Coding

A first step in any analysis that can potentially involve hundreds of predictor candidates is to identify relevant predictors that are likely to provide diagnostic value for the prediction of the respective outcome of interest, such as the probability for hospital readmission after discharge. Specifically, an initial review of available predictor variables should focus on how different parameters impact the risk of readmission if considered by themselves.

Target Variable

In this example the variable *Unplanned Readmission* represents the target variable, describing whether or not the respective patient was readmitted to the hospital within 30 days following discharge (0, no readmission; 1, readmitted at least once). Our simulated data file contains only eight predictors. The real data may contain hundreds of variables that can be used as predictors, including Gender, Age, and others.

Feature Selection

One approach to screen a large number of predictor candidates is to apply general feature selection algorithms. For example, the *STATISTICA* Feature Selection and Variable Screening module (StatSoft, Inc., 2013) applies so-called recursive partitioning or tree algorithms (see Nisbet *et al.*, 2009) to all predictor variables to derive predictor importance, and to select a subset of k best and likely most useful predictors. The search will be performed predictor-by-predictor; i.e., this approach will perform a fast first-order (no-interactions considered) search of potential predictors of the outcome variable. Importance can be calculated using different statistics that reflect the degree to which different possible partitions of the values observed for a predictor under consideration will provide maximum differentiation between outcomes (e.g., maximum differential readmission rates).

Note that, even though it is a first-order search, predictors that contribute to significant interaction effects will likely still be detected, and identified in subsequent modeling.

The Feature Selection node can be found in *Data Mining − Tools − Feature Selection* (Figure D.4).

When the node is added to the workspace, we need to connect it to the data source and to click on the *Edit Parameters* control.

Feature Selection requires definition of the target and input variables (Figure D.5).

Next, we execute the workspace.

As shown on the screenshot in Figure D.6, the Feature Selection node has generated a downstream Reporting Document node that will accumulate all results. Importance Plot is the main result in this analysis, and is saved in Reporting Documents (Figure D.7).

We may look into dependence of the readmission rate on the surgeon ID that was identified with top importance by adding a 2D Box Plots node to the workspace (*Graphs − Common − Box*) (Figure D.8).

Note that we've selected unplanned readmission as a dependent variable and surgeon ID as independent (according to the coding selected unplanned readmission is equal to 1, so the average value of this variable will represent the readmission rate).

The two graphs are combined in Figure D.9. The insert in the upper-right corner demonstrates variation in the readmission rates for different surgeons. It should be considered as a coincidence that Surgeon ID has the highest importance score in our simulated data. In practice, however, a similar result was observed due to the fact that difficult patients were usually assigned to a specific surgeon − so this was not an indication of his or her skills, but rather an initial (upon assignment) expert classification of the group of patients.

FIGURE D.4 Feature Selection node location on the ribbon bar.

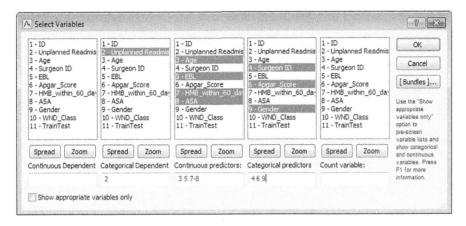

FIGURE D.5   Variables for the Feature Selection.

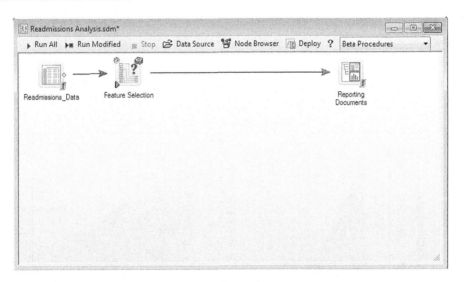

FIGURE D.6   Screenshot of the workspace.

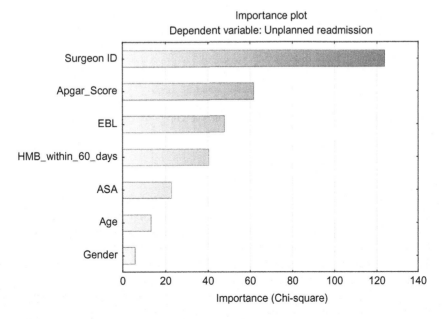

FIGURE D.7   Importance plot.

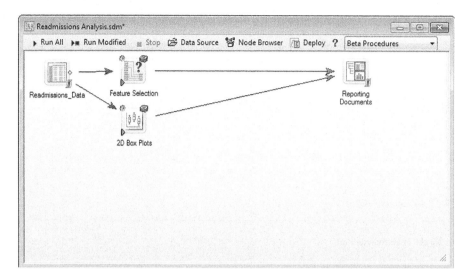

FIGURE D.8 Screenshot of the workspace.

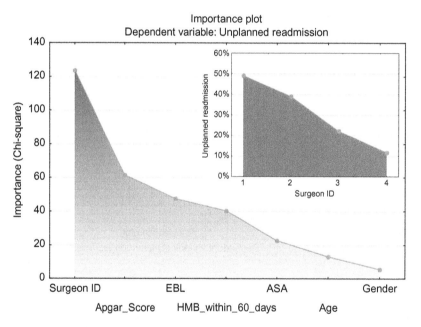

FIGURE D.9 Variable importance plot for readmission rate. Small insert in the upper right-hand corner shows average readmission rates by surgeon ID.

Predictor Coding, for more Interpretable Results

After selecting predictors that will likely provide the greatest power for predicting the outcome of interest (hospital readmission probability, in this case), they are often recoded into meaningful intervals (for continuous predictors) or combined categories (for discrete predictors). Thus, when the recommendations from final results are provided to decision-makers, they can be communicated in ways that are more easily understood.

For example, in this analysis a predictor variable EBL (estimated blood loss from the surgical procedure in milliliters) may be an important predictor of readmission risk. EBL is a continuous variable, and in order to derive simpler recommendations and rules describing the relationship between EBL and readmission risk it is useful to divide the range of values in this variable into intervals associated with different risk.

Weight-of-Evidence (WoE) Coding

In the case of risk-probability prediction, so-called optimal weight-of-evidence recoding can be very useful. Specifically, the weight of evidence (WoE) statistic for each (possible) binning of values in a continuous variable is calculated as follows (see also Siddiqi, 2006):

$$\text{WoE} = \left[\ln\left(\frac{\text{Distr ''Read\_Rela\_unplan} = 0''}{\text{Distr ''Read\_Rela\_unplan} = 1''} \right) \right] .100$$

The smaller the value of WoE for a specific binned group of observations, the higher is the percentage of readmissions in that group. The goal of WoE coding in risk modeling is to identify binning (interval boundaries) based on historical data, so that the observations in each interval are maximally uniform with respect to (readmission) risk, while the differences in (readmission) risk across the intervals (groups) are maximized.

Further, in order to arrive at more easily interpreted results, certain constraints can be applied to the binning algorithm — for example, to impose a linear risk function for the predictor over the consecutive bin intervals. Linear, quadratic, or higher-order polynomial constraints can be applied to the calculations of optimal predictor intervals (bins), to yield the largest differences in risk across the coded intervals while observing the respective constraint.

By recoding continuous predictors into binned intervals, or re-binning the categories of discrete predictor variables, the final results predicted from the application of general predictive modeling algorithms are often more easily communicated, providing clearer guidelines for specific interval boundaries that are associated with greater risk. In a sense, instead of using the original predictor values and metrics, predictions can then be communicated in terms of risk profiles and groups rather than more abstract specific values or often non-linear functions.

The data set used in this tutorial is already prepared and does not require binning. However, for reference purposes we'll point out that the Weight of Evidence node is located under *Data Mining — Tools — Weight of Evidence* (Figure D.10).

Once added to the workspace the node provides an interactive environment for working with the groups, applying various constraints (e.g., Monotone, One minimum or maximum, One minimum and one maximum for continuous variables), defining interactions, and customizing groups (Figure D.11). As the result the module generates a set of transformations from initial variables to weight-of-evidence codes. Those transformations are defined by the Rules node.

Step 3: Predictive Modeling and Interpreting Results

In this example, a general predictive modeling algorithm called stochastic gradient boosting trees (Friedman, 1999) will be used for modeling readmission probabilities. This method usually demonstrates excellent performance and robustness for classification and risk prediction tasks.

In classification problems it is important to understand the correct selection of prior probabilities. If classes have significantly different numbers of observations, equal priors are recommended (Classification tab of the Boosted Trees Specifications dialog). In our case, we add a Frequency tables node to calculate the percentage of cases with Unplanned Readmission = 1 (*Statistics — Basic Statistics — Frequency Tables*) (Figures D.12 and D.13).

Results indicate that unplanned readmission was seen in 30% of cases in this data set, so we'll use equal prior probabilities in this example.

In order to build the Boosted Trees model in *STATISTICA*, the following steps can be used. On the *Data Mining* tab we select *Boosted Trees* and *Boosted Classification Trees* (Figures D.14 and D.15).

We access parameters of the node, select variables, and identify different parameters of the analysis as shown on the screenshot in Figure D.16.

Next, on the advanced tab, we set the *Maximum n of nodes* to 7. This parameter represents the maximum complexity of each individual tree.

FIGURE D.10 Weight of Evidence node location on the ribbon bar.

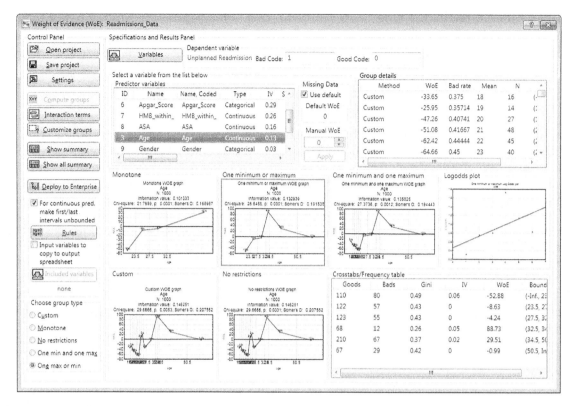

FIGURE D.11 Weight of Evidence node interface.

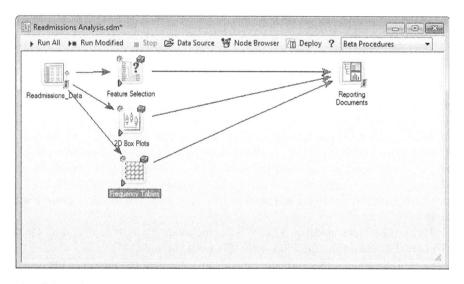

FIGURE D.12 Screenshot of the workspace.

	Frequency table: Unplanned Readmission			
Category	Count	Cumulative Count	Percent	**Cumulative Percent**
0	700	700	70	70
1	300	1000	30	100
Missing	0	1000	0	100

FIGURE D.13 Frequency table.

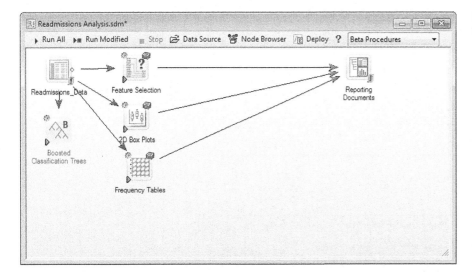

FIGURE D.14   Boosted Classification Trees location on the ribbon bar.

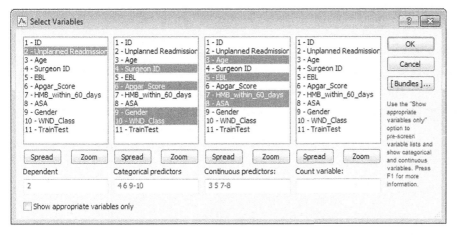

FIGURE D.15   Screenshot of the workspace.

FIGURE D.16   Variable Selection dialog.

For model quality assessment we need to generate results such as a classification matrix and lift chart. Consequently, we make the settings on the Classification tab as in Figure D.17.

Finally, on the Advanced tab we select the variable that will identify cases for the test sample. If the variable is not selected, the Test sample will be randomly assigned (Figure D.18).

When all settings are done (Figure D.19) we execute the workspace and move to the analysis of the results.

As the screenshot in Figure D.20 demonstrates, the Boosted Classification Trees node generates output for Reporting Documents, PMML Model, and Rapid Deployment nodes.

Note that the Boosted Trees is an iterative algorithm that is used to find the best solution. However, initialization of parameters is done in every run using randomization function. This means that results achieved in two consecutive runs or on different machines may not be identical.

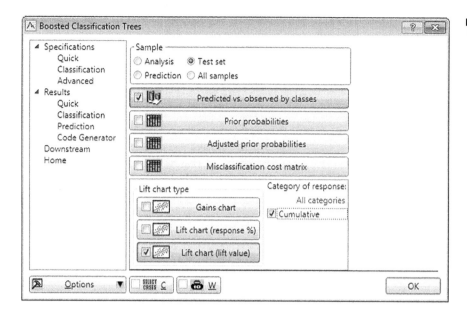

FIGURE D.17   Boosted Classification Trees node parameters.

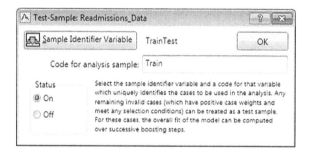

FIGURE D.18   Test-Sample variable selection dialog.

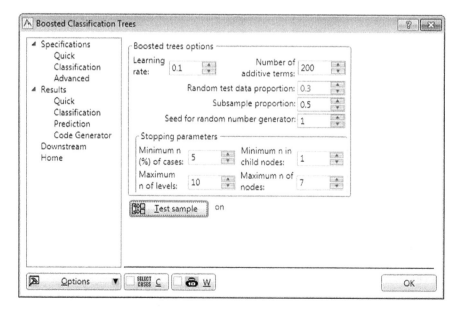

FIGURE D.19   Boosted Classification Trees node parameters.

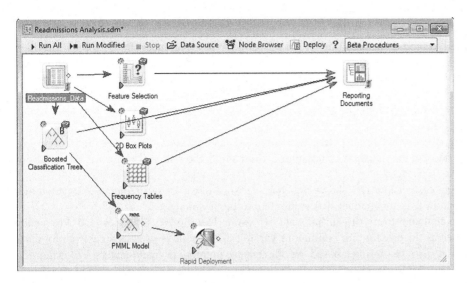

FIGURE D.20 Screenshot of the workspace.

Assessing the Quality of the Model: Lift Charts

The quality of models is usually characterized by lift charts. The value of lift is computed as the ratio of the readmission rate in a sample compared to the baseline readmission rate. Specifically, following best practices, the prediction model is applied to a hold-out sample of observations (not used for the model-building process itself), and then the top 10% of patients with the highest predicted readmission risk are selected. The actual readmission rates for those patients are then computed.

This process is repeated for the next 10% of patients in the hold-out samples, and so on, to construct an entire lift chart as shown in Figure D.21 (see also Nisbet *et al.*, 2009).

The base-rate for hospital readmission was approximately 33% in this test subset. The actual readmission rate is around 74.2%, or almost twice as high, when applying the model to a hold-out sample of patients (not used for the model-building process itself), and selecting the top 10% of patients in that sample with the highest predicted readmission risk.

Put another way, through the application of the predictive model patients can be identified with a predicted readmission risk nearly twice as high as that for the average patient.

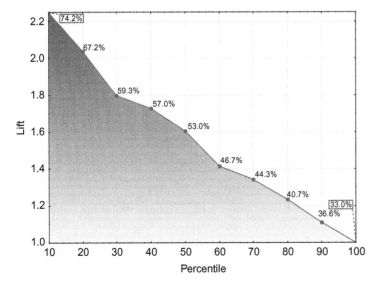

FIGURE D.21 Lift chart for test sample. Point labels show readmission rates in %.

Understanding the Implications of Results: What-If and Reason Scores

Once the model is built, it can be used to predict probabilities of readmission for new patients. Those probabilities then can be used to bring recommendations to professionals working with those patients. However, while the identification of higher-risk patients is important, it is equally important to know how to mitigate this risk, or what to do about it.

Reason scores are a way to explain the prediction of analytic models and to identify the root causes driving specific prediction. The term emerged in the risk-scoring domain, where a final score is computed as the sum of reason scores from multiple predictors (see Siddiqi, 2006).

In general, reason scores are computed as first-order partial derivatives of the considered parameter (probability of readmission, in our case). Thus, they address the question concerning by how much the risk will change if the values of a specific predictor variable changes or is changed.

For example, consider the following case. Table D.1 shows the characteristics of a patient predicted to have an elevated risk for hospital readmission (and in fact, this patient was readmitted to the hospital).

The values in parentheses are calculated from the initial data by using Descriptive Statistics and Frequency Tables nodes (the average value is used as the baseline for continuous variables; the mode is used as a baseline for categorical variables). The "baseline" can also be defined based on the expert opinion or meta-analysis of scientific publications.

In this tutorial we'll be looking at the increase or decrease in the predicted probability of readmission in response to changing one of the parameters to the baseline value. Positive differences in our case mean that the specified factor contributed towards the increase of readmission probability by x%; otherwise it decreased that probability by x% compared to baseline.

It is important to note that these values are not additive, as they are calculated under the assumption that all other variables except those under consideration are fixed at their values. Still, these values can be placed into a graph that provides an immediate "recommendation" of how changing a specific predictor value will affect likelihood of readmission.

As discussed above, we prepare the data set for further simulations (this process can be automated with SVB nodes, but this falls beyond the scope of this tutorial) (Figure D.22).

TABLE D.1 Characteristics of the Patient (Values in Parentheses Show Baseline)

Parameter name	Value	Parameter name	Value
Age	22 (33.544)	HMB_within_60_days	1.8 (2.976)
Surgeon ID	1 (4)	ASA	9 (2.828)
EBL	3300 (1714.9)	Gender	Male (Male)
Apgar_Score	7−8 (5−6)	WND_Class	02 (02)

Data: Scenarios 1 case.sta (9v by 10c)

	1 Age	2 Surgeon ID	3 EBL	4 Apgar_Score	5 HMB_within_60_days	6 ASA	7 Gender	8 WND_Class	9 Variable
1	22	1	3300	7-8	1.8	9	male	02	
2	33.544	4	1714.9	5-6	2.976	2.828	male	02	
3	33.544	1	3300	7-8	1.8	9	male	02	Age
4	22	4	3300	7-8	1.8	9	male	02	Surgeon ID
5	22	1	1714.9	7-8	1.8	9	male	02	EBL
6	22	1	3300	5-6	1.8	9	male	02	Apgar_Score
7	22	1	3300	7-8	2.976	9	male	02	HMB_within_60_days
8	22	1	3300	7-8	1.8	2.828	male	02	ASA
9	22	1	3300	7-8	1.8	9	male	02	Gender
10	22	1	3300	7-8	1.8	9	male	02	WND_Class

FIGURE D.22 Spreadsheet for sensitivity analysis.

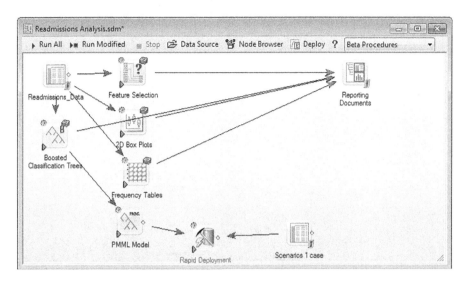

FIGURE D.23 Screenshot of the workspace.

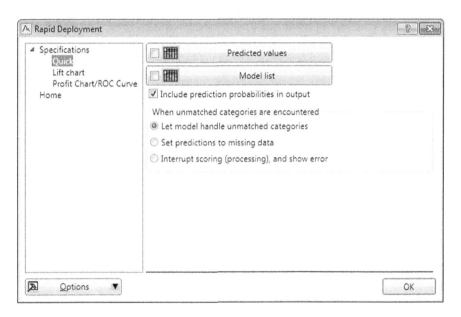

FIGURE D.24 Rapid Deployment node parameters.

The first row contains values of the case in question. The second row represents the "baseline" values. The rest of the rows represent copies of the case with the baseline value substituted instead one of the values. The name of the variable is recorded in the *Variable* column. In order to calculate predictions for all scenarios, we plug the data set into the workspace and connect it to the Rapid Deployment node (Figure D.23).

Before we run the Rapid Deployment node we need to include prediction probabilities in the output using the settings shown in Figure D.24.

Next, we execute the Rapid Deployment node and append predicted probabilities to the initial data set using *Concatenate Variables* node (*Data − Manage − Merge − Concatenate Variables*) (Figure D.25).

The result is shown as a spreadsheet in Figure D.26, or in the form of the calculated differences from the baseline (Figure D.27).

Figure D.28 shows that major contributing factors for the considered patient are Surgeon ID, EBL, and HMB_within_60_days.

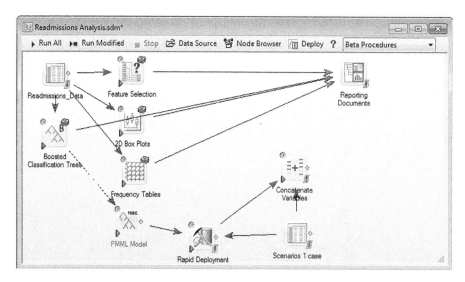

FIGURE D.25   Screenshot of the workspace.

	1 Age	2 Surgeon ID	3 EBL	4 Apgar_Score	5 HMB_within_60_days	6 ASA	7 Gender	8 WND_Class	9 Variable	10 BoostTreeModel
1	22	1	3300	7-8		1.8	9 male	02		0.858130
2	33.544	4	1714.9	5-6	2.976	2.828 male	02			0.059238
3	33.544	1	3300	7-8		1.8	9 male	02	Age	0.812519
4	22	4	3300	7-8		1.8	9 male	02	Surgeon ID	0.389945
5	22	1	1714.9	7-8		1.8	9 male	02	EBL	0.614272
6	22	1	3300	5-6		1.8	9 male	02	Apgar_Score	0.861380
7	22	1	3300	7-8	2.976		9 male	02	HMB_within_60_days	0.709434
8	22	1	3300	7-8		1.8	2.828 male	02	ASA	0.797643
9	22	1	3300	7-8		1.8	9 **male**	02	Gender	0.858130
10	22	1	3300	7-8		1.8	9 male	02	WND_Class	0.858130

Data: Concatenate Variables* (10v by 10c)
Summary of Deployment (Scenarios 1 case)

FIGURE D.26   Spreadsheet with predictions.

1 Variable	2 ΔP
Surgeon ID	54.6%
EBL	28.4%
HMB_within_60_days	17.3%
ASA	7.0%
Age	5.3%
Gender	0.0%
WND_Class	0.0%
Apgar_Score	-0.4%

FIGURE D.27   Sensitivities.

While the nature of why or how Surgeon ID impacts readmission risk may be complex (e.g., it could be a function of the severity of cases seen by different surgeons), this small example demonstrates that predictions derived from data mining methods can be explained in the same way as those from simpler statistical regression type models.

Step 4: Decision Management and Prescriptions

Decisioning logic that summarizes the rules guiding the decision-making process usually needs to be integrated with model predictions, for the following two reasons: (1) in order to associate statistical probabilities of certain conditions

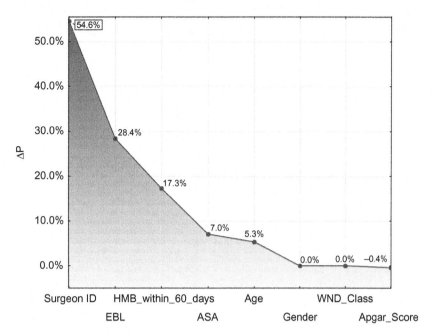

FIGURE D.28   Reason scores of different factors for patient with characteristics shown in Table D.1.

to specific prescriptions for the next "recommended" action; and (2) in order to augment analytic models with specific domain knowledge that is not captured by the analytic model.

In the previous steps we've described the workflow to build prediction for the readmission probability based on the model. Here, we'll discuss how predicted values can be combined with rules logic.

The section *Step 2. Feature Selection and Predictor Coding* described WoE coding as a data preparation step to bin the range of predictor values into intervals associated with different risk. Note that such data pre-processing and binning of predictors for maximum predictive power while maintaining simple interpretability can be incorporated into the scoring process as simple rules, via *if.. then.. elseif.. endif* statements.

In addition, by combining into such rules predicted risk probabilities and *a priori* expert knowledge about risk not captured in the analyses (e.g., because of lack of data), and linking it to action plans to mitigate risk, an effective automated decision support ("decisioning") system can be built.

For example, Figure D.29 shows part of a decisioning logic flow implementing the optimal binning for predictor EBL (estimated blood loss from the surgical procedure in milliliters), linking the specific interval boundaries for this predictor to specific action plans or Prescriptions (Prescription 1, Prescription 2, etc.). The right side of Figure D.29 shows how this logic is implemented in the STATISTICA Decisioning Platform.

The entire workflow that summarizes knowledge about the patients' readmission probabilities can now be used to score patients at the point of discharge, and to execute appropriate action plans to mitigate readmission risk. Again, it is important to note that these predictive analytic and decisioning system predictions can be made for "individual patients," thus providing the best possible care for the individual.

The rules can be implemented on the workflow as follows. First, we add a subset node to separate scenario of interest (*Data − Subset*) with the parameters shown in Figure D.30.

The node outputs a single case described above (Figure D.31).

Now we add the Rules node (*Data Mining − Deployment − Rules Builder*) with the set of rules as shown in Figure D.29 (Figure D.32).

The combined output can now be retrieved as shown in Figure D.33.

For new patients the above workspace can be simplified to model deployment nodes only, as shown in Figure D.34 (the workspace node can be copied and pasted from one workspace to another − for example, by using well-known Windows keys Ctrl + C and Ctrl + V).

In STATISTICA Enterprise, the workspace can become a reusable template and be deployed to the STATISTICA Enterprise metadata repository. This functionality is available for STATISTICA Enterprise users through the Deploy button.

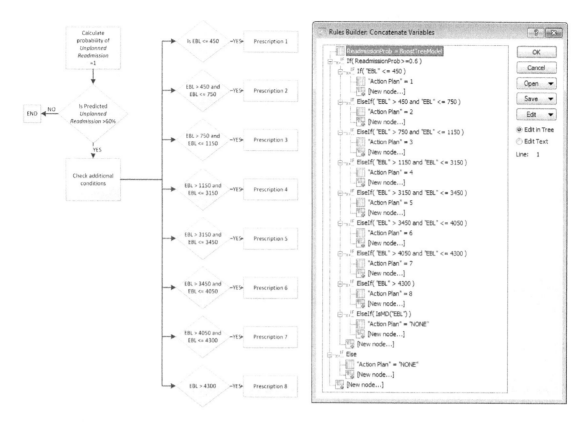

FIGURE D.29 Illustration of Rules logic and implementation in STATISTICA Rules Builder.

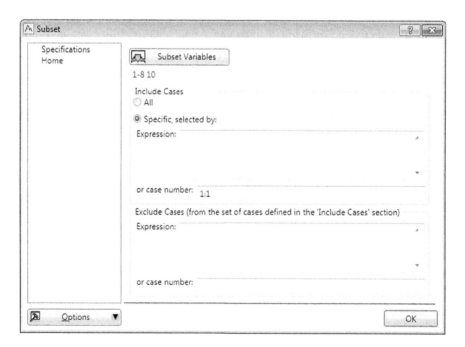

FIGURE D.30 Subset node parameters dialog.

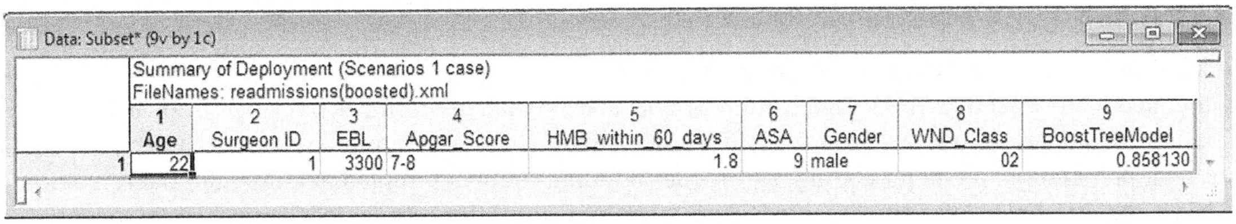

	Summary of Deployment (Scenarios 1 case) FileNames: readmissions(boosted).xml								
	1 Age	**2** Surgeon ID	**3** EBL	**4** Apgar_Score	**5** HMB_within_60_days	**6** ASA	**7** Gender	**8** WND_Class	**9** BoostTreeModel
1	22	1	3300	7-8	1.8	9	male	02	0.858130

Data: Subset* (9v by 1c)

FIGURE D.31   Spreadsheet with parameters for single case.

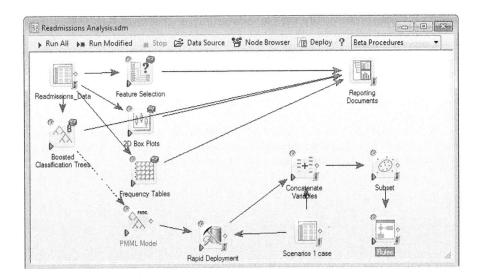

FIGURE D.32   Screenshot of the workspace.

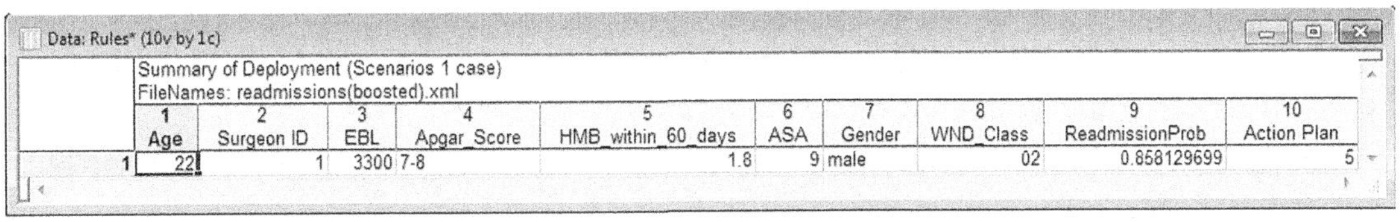

	Summary of Deployment (Scenarios 1 case) FileNames: readmissions(boosted).xml									
	1 Age	**2** Surgeon ID	**3** EBL	**4** Apgar_Score	**5** HMB_within_60_days	**6** ASA	**7** Gender	**8** WND_Class	**9** ReadmissionProb	**10** Action Plan
1	22	1	3300	7-8	1.8	9	male	02	0.858129699	5

Data: Rules* (10v by 1c)

FIGURE D.33   Final result. The spreadsheet contains probability predicted with analytic model and action plan assigned based on rules.

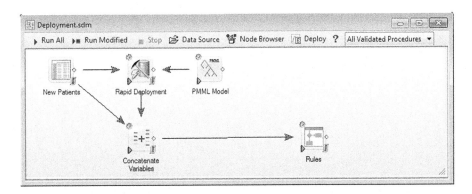

FIGURE D.34   Deployment workspace.

CONCLUSIONS

This tutorial provides an overview of how modern advanced predictive modeling and pattern recognition algorithms can be integrated with effective rules logic into a single decisioning platform, delivering actionable prescriptions to improve patient outcomes. Using an example data set describing hospital readmission risk in a sample of patients, all steps from data preparation, predictor coding, and model building to model implementation and interpretation were discussed. Using the example data set, the predictive modeling algorithms provided a prediction model that can be expected to successfully identify the top 10% of patients with a readmission risk almost twice as high compared to baseline risk. In addition, this tutorial described how results derived from complex modeling procedures can yield interpretable and actionable results that can be combined into action plans for mitigating risk ("prescriptive analytics").

REFERENCES

Breiman, L., 2001. Statistical modeling: the two cultures. Stat. Sci. 16 (3), 199–231.

Cox, D.R., 1972. Regression models and life tables. J. R. Stat. Soc. 34, 187–220.

Friedman, J.H., 1999. Stochastic Gradient Boosting. Stanford University, Stanford, CA.

Lee, E.T., 1980. Statistical Methods for Survival Data Analysis. Lifetime Learning, Belmont, CA.

Miner, G., Elder, J., Hill, T., Nisbet, R., Delen, D., Fast, A., 2012. Practical Text Mining and Statistical Analysis for Non-Structured Text Data Applications. Elsevier, New York, NY.

Nisbet, R., Elder, J., Miner, G., 2009. Handbook of Statistical Analysis and Data Mining Applications. Elsevier, New York, NY.

Siddiqi, N., 2006. Credit Risk Scorecards: Developing and Implementing Intelligent Credit Scoring. Wiley & Sons, New York, NY.

StatSoft, Inc., 2013. STATISTICA (data analysis software system), version 12. <www.statsoft.com>.

Tutorial E

Obesity — Group: Predicting Medicine and Conditions That Achieved the Greatest Weight Loss in a Group of Obese/Morbidly Obese Patients

Linda A. Winters-Miner, PhD

Chapter Outline

BACKGROUND

As stated in Chapter 14, obesity is a huge and growing problem in the United States and in other parts of the world. Obesity also increases risk for depression (Dong *et al.*, 2004; Murphy *et al.*, 2009; Wenjun *et al.*, 2010; Faith *et al.*, 2011; Zhao *et al.*, 2011; Chang and Yen, 2012). Afari *et al.* (2010) found in twin studies that both depression and obesity tend to be inherited; Bliss (2006) claimed to have found two alleles. Whether depression causes obesity or obesity causes depression, the two tend to be related. Stress, especially work-related, seems to be a factor in obesity (Nishitani and Sakakibara, 2006; Heinan and Darling, 2009; Duffy *et al.*, 2012). Being overtired and not getting enough rest was found to be related to stress (Obesity may be associated with lack of sleep, 2005; Overtime, overtired, and overweight; 2005; Nedeltcheva *et al.*, 2010).

Clinical guidelines exist for the treatment of obesity (Lau *et al.*, 2007), and there is evidence that if physicians use the guidelines and the 5As of patient counseling concerning obesity, there are increases in motivation on the part of patients (Jay *et al.*, 2010). The 5As stand for Assess risk, Advise change, Agree and collaborate, Assist in addressing barriers, and Arrange for follow-up. Physicians often, however, do not use either the guidelines or the 5As (Melamed *et al.*, 2009), even though they do tend to spend more time with obese patients, prescribing them more medications (Pearson *et al.*, 2009). Jay *et al.* (2009) found that the most competent physicians were the ones who readily dealt with obesity in their patients. Pediatricians evidently worked better with children than did general practitioners (Wethington *et al.*, 2011).

Workplaces could be one answer to the problems of obesity, by offering wellness portals for employees (Heinan and Darling, 2009) and by restructuring the workplace to encourage exercise (Perry, 2012).

THE TUTORIAL

The data set "Weight Data — Group" was used for an example in this tutorial. The data are fabricated and assume that 101 obese or morbidly obese people were included as cases. The following were recorded: weights, stress, sleep, items from the Beck Depression Inventory II, weight changes since last doctor visit, support person, support from physician/

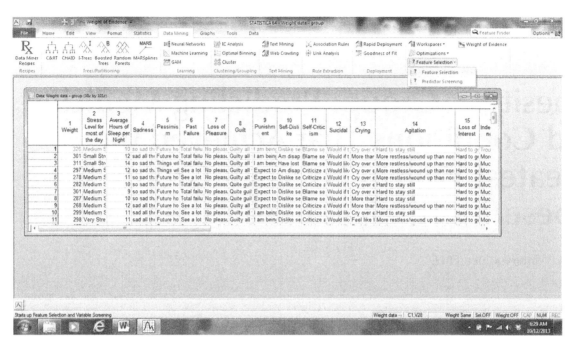

FIGURE E.1 The Data — Click on Feature Selection.

FIGURE E.2 Result Allowing One to Select Variables.

medical staff, times eating out, exercise time per day, number of servings of green vegetables, medication type, secondary medication, gender, ethnicity. This tutorial uses STATISTICA version 12, ribbon view.

Normally, one uses hold-out data when exploring a model. This tutorial shows only an exploratory phase. If there were more data, and if the data were real, the full data mining process would have been used. So, the reader needs to understand that all of the below could be included in working with training data. Once an apparently useful model was found, that model and that model alone would be used on the testing data (or the hold-out data). It is important to realize that one should not make anything more than speculative statements when working with training data.

First, do a feature selection to see which, if any, variables predict weight loss. Figure E.1 shows where to find the procedure.

Figure E.2 shows the resulting box where you can select variables.

We will predict the weight change category, Variable 28, from all other variables, except for any other weight variable. I also did not use the Beck total score (see Beck *et al.*, 1996) but wanted to see if any of the individual scores would predict weight change for this feature selection (see Figure E.3).

Click OK to obtain Figure E.4.

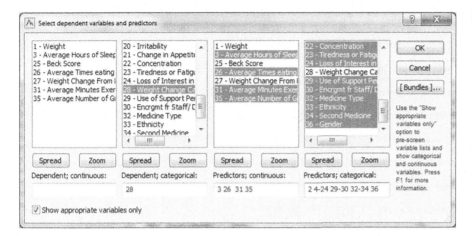

FIGURE E.3 Variables to Select.

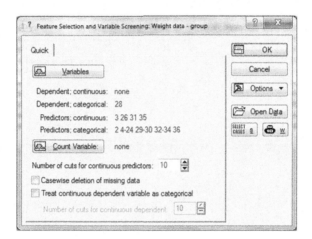

FIGURE E.4 Result – Click OK.

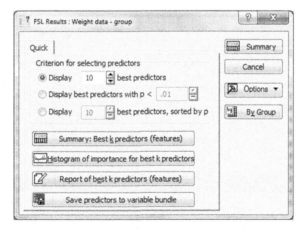

FIGURE E.5 Click on Histogram of Importance.

Now click OK to see Figure E.5.

One has the choice of how many variables to select as the bespredictors. The default is 10 which generally works well. Click on Histogram of importance for best k predictors, to see Figure E.6.

Interpreting an importance plot is fairly simple. The length of the bar shows the relative "importance" in predicting the dependent variable (in this case, the weight change category). The table does not show the direction of the

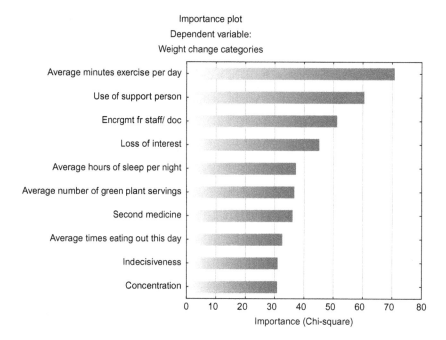

FIGURE E.6 Importance Plot.

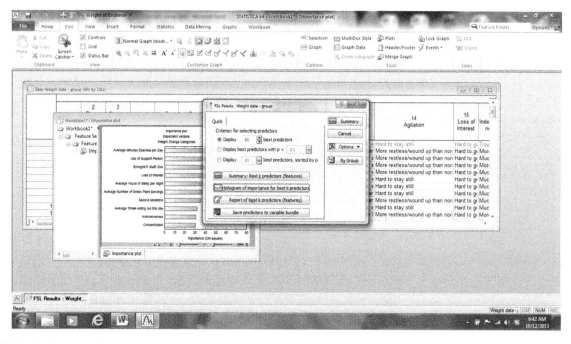

FIGURE E.7 FLS Tab and Click Cancel.

prediction. Other analyses would allow for that, such as an ANOVA. One cannot assume the direction of the prediction. I suggest that the cut-off point be set between the top four to seven.

Now, just to check, we will go back and try the total Beck score rather than the individual items. Click on the FSL Results tab at the bottom left of your tray to pull up the feature selection box as in Figure E.7.

Click on Cancel to get back to choosing the variables. Click Variables to choose new variables as in Figure E.8.

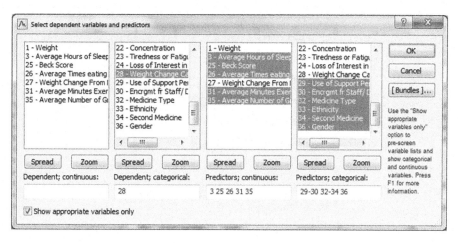

FIGURE E.8 New Variables.

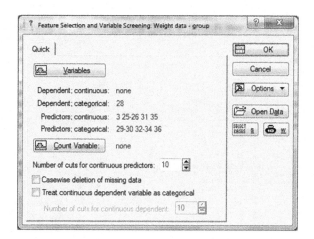

FIGURE E.9 Result of clicking OK.

Again click OK to see Figure E.9.

Click on the Importance plot to achieve Figure E.10.

To see the relationship for the Beck score, we can conduct a quick ANOVA.

Click on the Statistics tab and then ANOVA. Highlight One-Way ANOVA as in Figure E.11.

Click OK and then click on Variables to choose the ones we would like. Figure E.12 shows that we want the Beck score as our dependent variable and weight change category as the independent variable.

Click OK (Figure E.13) and then on All effects/Graphs (Figure E.14).

Click OK on Figure E.15.

Figure E.16 is a mean with confidence intervals graph.

The relationships were not significant, as the confidence intervals all overlap to a great extent (p = 0.187). It could be that there is no relationship between the Beck scores and the weight gains/losses, or perhaps other things are going on. There is significant depression in all of the weight groups, as none of the means go below about 29. Dealing with the depression, it seems, would be a primary goal of the physicians of these people. We might also look at the actual weight gain/loss scores with the Beck scores in a correlation. We'll next use a scatterplot, under the Graphs tab (Figure E.17).

Click on Variables when you see the dialog box in Figure E.18.

Select the Beck score for the X coordinate and the actual weight change (Variable 27) for the Y variable as in Figure E.19.

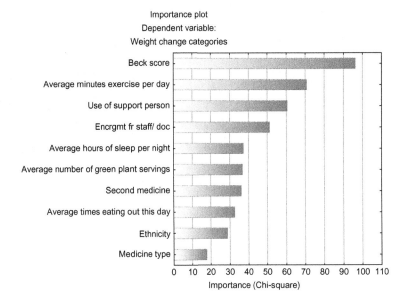

FIGURE E.10 New Importance plot.

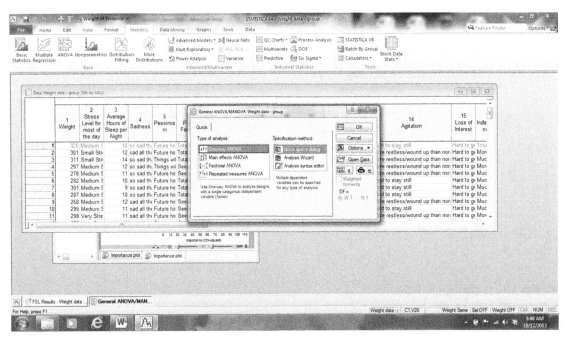

FIGURE E.11 Conduct ANOVA.

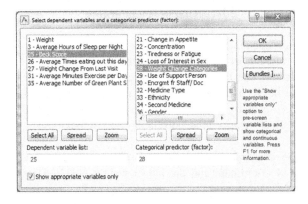

FIGURE E.12 Beck is Dependent and Weight Change is Independent Variable.

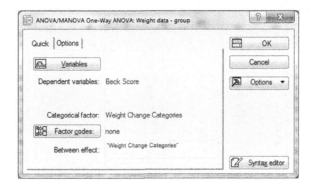

FIGURE E.13   Click OK.

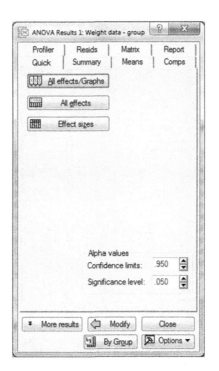

FIGURE E.14   Click All Effects.

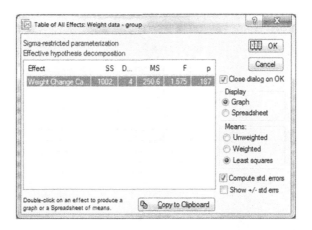

FIGURE E.15   Click OK.

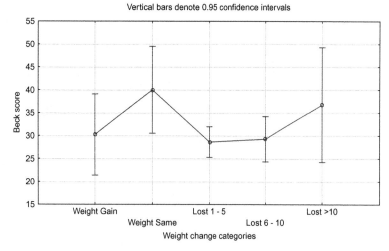

Weight change categories; LS means
Current effect: F(4, 96)=1.5753, p=.18711
Effective hypothesis decomposition
Vertical bars denote 0.95 confidence intervals

FIGURE E.16 Mean with Error Plot.

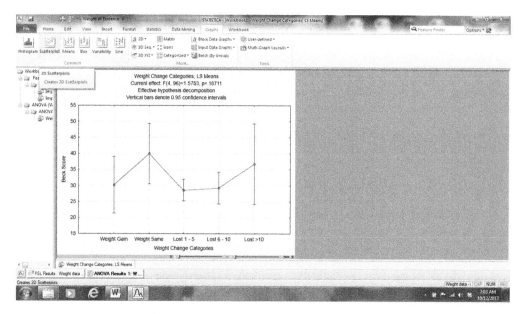

FIGURE E.17 Find Scatterplots.

FIGURE E.18 Click on Variables.

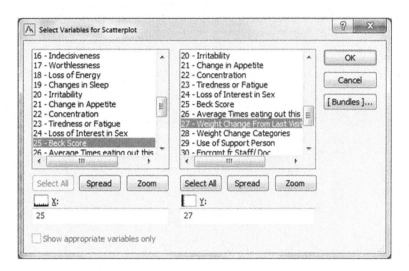

FIGURE E.19 Select Variables for Scatterplot.

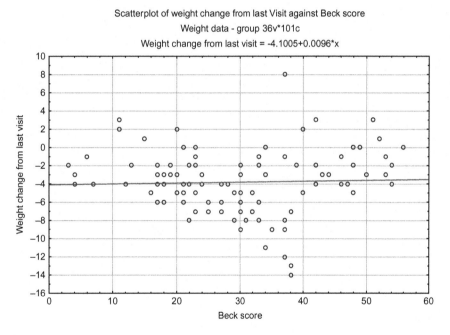

FIGURE E.20 Scatterplot.

Click OK and OK again to reveal Figure E.20.

We would be hard-pressed to see any relationship there. It is possible that there is a negative relationship until the Beck scores approach 35−40 resulting in a more positive relationship. This could be a curvilinear relationship that won't be picked up by linear stats. We will now go to the Data Mining Recipe to see if we can make predictions that do not depend on linear relationships.

Click on the FSL Results tab once again to see Figure E.21. Click on Report of best k predictors to see the list of predictors from the second feature selection that we did, which shows Figure E.22.

I went back to run the first feature selection again so I could get the best k predictors as in Figure E.23, for that analysis.

We can combine the variables for our project using these: 25 31 3 35 26 29 30 15 34 33 16 22 32.

Go to Data Mining and Data Mining Recipes as in Figure E.24.

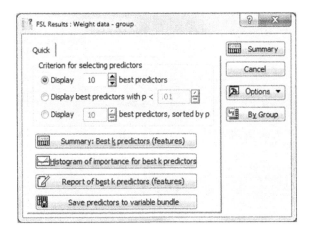

FIGURE E.21 Click FSL tab to get this back. Click Report of best K predictors.

BOX

Best predictors for categorical dependent var: Weight change categories

Best continuous predictors: 25 31 3 35 26

Best categorical predictors: 29 30 34 33 32

END BOX

FIGURE E.22 Output.

BOX

Best predictors for categorical dependent var: Weight change categories

Best continuous predictors: 31 3 35 26

Best categorical predictors: 29 30 15 34 16 22

END BOX

FIGURE E.23 Best k predictors from first feature selection.

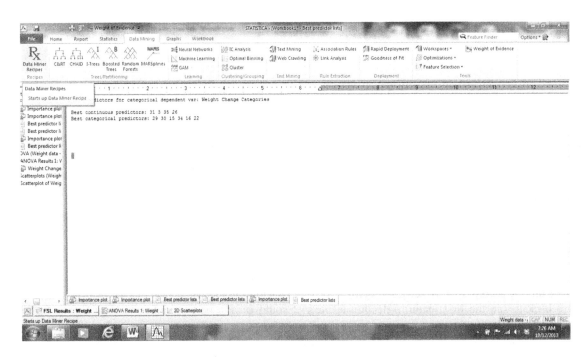

FIGURE E.24 Find Data Mining Recipes — Ribbon View.

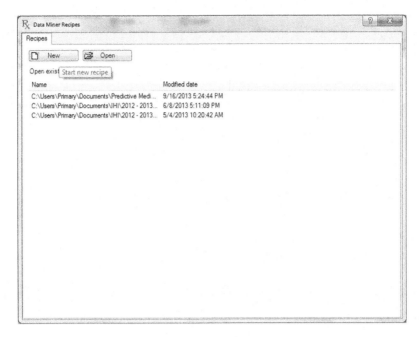

FIGURE E.25   Click New.

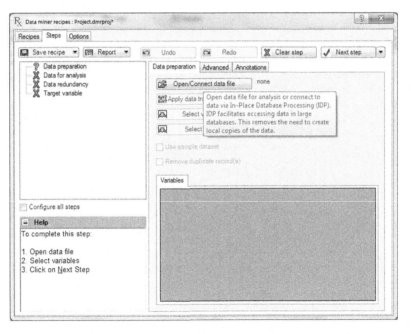

FIGURE E.26   Open the Data Set.

Click on Data Mining Recipes. In Figure E.25 click on New.

Then click to open the data set (Figure E.26).

Figure E.27 shows that the open data set may be inserted into the project. Click on the data set and OK.

Now the data set is selected and the Xs are red (Figure E.28).

Select the variables as in Figure E.29.

Click OK. Now we are ready to select the modules we would like to run. Figure E.30 shows where to click to "Configure all steps" at the bottom left. Click that and see that the Xs turn blue.

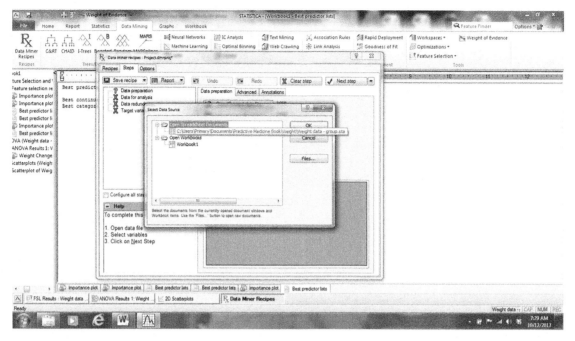

FIGURE E.27 Click on the correct data file and insert.

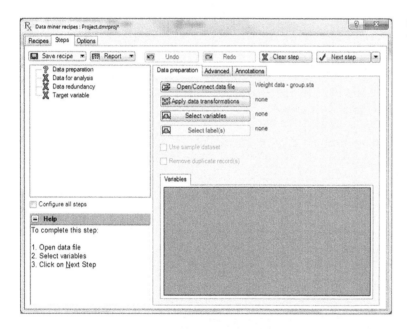

FIGURE E.28 Note the Xs are red. Click on select variables.

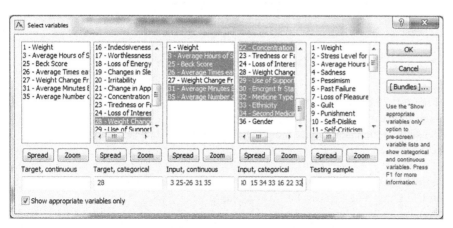

FIGURE E.29 Select the variables. Note that show appropriate variables only is selected.

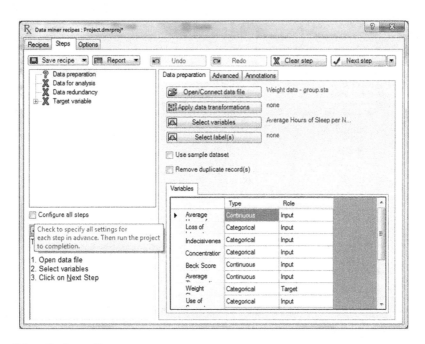

FIGURE E.30 Where to click on Configure all steps.

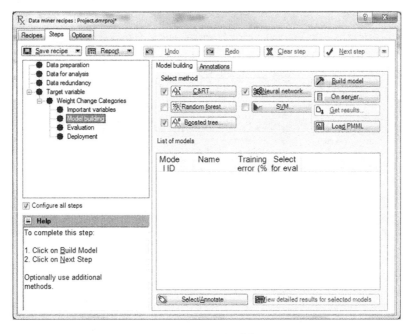

FIGURE E.31 Click and note that Xs turn to purple/blue dots. Click on Model building.

Figure E.31 shows clicking on "Target variable," and then on "Model building" to see that three models are selected by default.

We would like to add Random forest and Support vector machines (SVMs), so click those boxes to see Figure E.32.

Next, unclick Configure all steps to bring back the red Xs. In the upper right-hand corner of Figure E.33 click on the down arrow beside Next step so that you can run to completion. Click "Run to completion."

Allow the program to run (Figure E.34).

The first report is the overall accuracy of the models. In Figure E.35, we can see that SVM has the least amount of error in prediction.

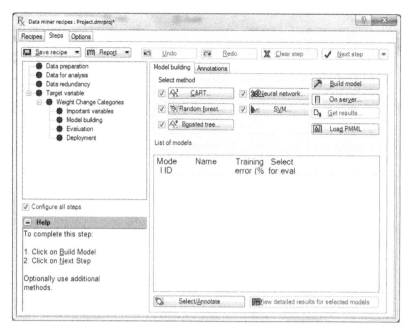

FIGURE E.32 Select Random forest and SVM as well.

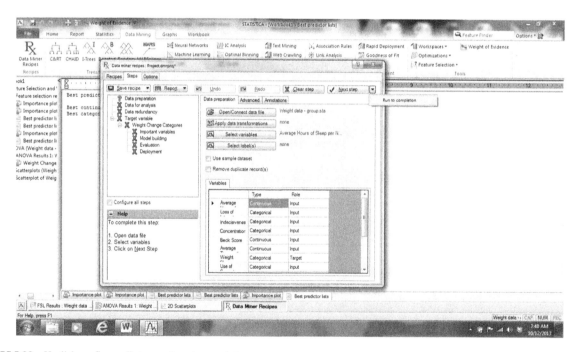

FIGURE E.33 Unclick configure all steps and run to completion.

Pull the edge of the screen so you can see the items to the left of the main screen as in Figure E.36.

Under Evaluation Summary, click on SVM to reveal the prediction scores (Figure E.37).

Looking at Figure E.38, we can see the percentages.

We can see from the figure that SVM correctly identified all of the gained weight category, 87.5% of the Lost 1−5 category, 100% of the Lost 6−10 category, and 80% of the Lost >10 category.

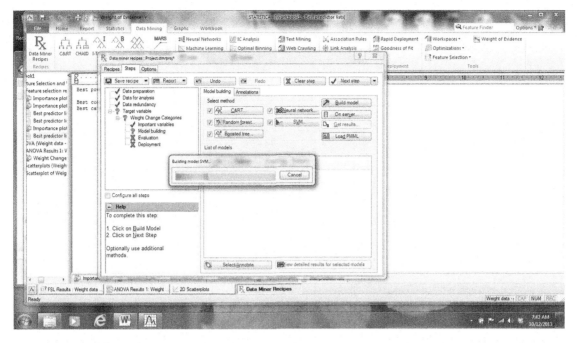

FIGURE E.34 Let it run.

		1	2	3
Model selected for deployment		4		
Model Evaluation Summary	ID		Name	Error rate (%)
		4	SVM	8.91
		5	Neural network	10.89
		1	C&RT	28.71
		3	Boosted trees	32.67
		2	Random forest	92.08
Table		Step options		
		Date and time	10/12/2013 7:43:32 AM	

FIGURE E.35 Model Accuracy – SVM had the least amount of error.

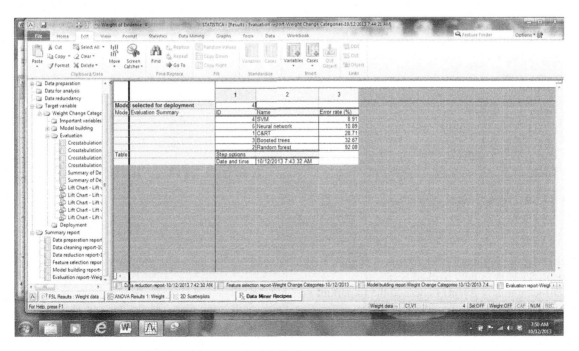

FIGURE E.36 Push the edge of the screen to the right to see what is behind.

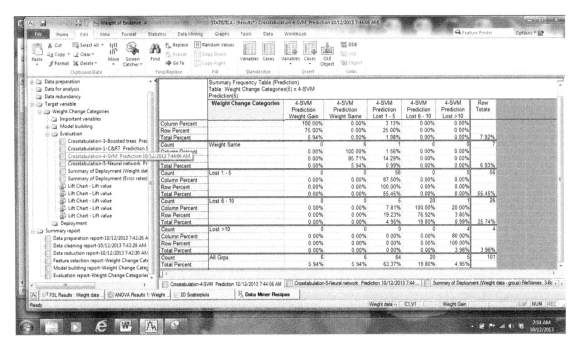

FIGURE E.37   Under Evaluation click on SVM.

	Summary Frequency Table (Prediction) Table: Weight Change Categories(5) x 4-SVM Prediction(5)					
	Weight Change Categories	4-SVM Prediction Weight Gain	4-SVM Prediction Weight Same	4-SVM Prediction Lost 1 - 5	4-SVM Prediction Lost 6 - 10	4-SVM Prediction Lost >10	Row Totals
Column Percent		100.00%	0.00%	3.13%	0.00%	0.00%	
Row Percent		75.00%	0.00%	25.00%	0.00%	0.00%	
Total Percent		5.94%	0.00%	1.98%	0.00%	0.00%	7.92%
Count	Weight Same	0	6	1	0	0	7
Column Percent		0.00%	100.00%	1.56%	0.00%	0.00%	
Row Percent		0.00%	85.71%	14.29%	0.00%	0.00%	
Total Percent		0.00%	5.94%	0.99%	0.00%	0.00%	6.93%
Count	Lost 1 - 5	0	0	56	0	0	56
Column Percent		0.00%	0.00%	87.50%	0.00%	0.00%	
Row Percent		0.00%	0.00%	100.00%	0.00%	0.00%	
Total Percent		0.00%	0.00%	55.45%	0.00%	0.00%	55.45%
Count	Lost 6 - 10	0	0	5	20	1	26
Column Percent		0.00%	0.00%	7.81%	100.00%	20.00%	
Row Percent		0.00%	0.00%	19.23%	76.92%	3.85%	
Total Percent		0.00%	0.00%	4.95%	19.80%	0.99%	25.74%
Count	Lost >10	0	0	0	0	4	4
Column Percent		0.00%	0.00%	0.00%	0.00%	80.00%	
Row Percent		0.00%	0.00%	0.00%	0.00%	100.00%	
Total Percent		0.00%	0.00%	0.00%	0.00%	3.96%	3.96%
Count	All Grps	6	6	64	20	5	101
Total Percent		5.94%	5.94%	63.37%	19.80%	4.95%	

FIGURE E.38   Note correct predictions percentages.

By clicking on Summary of Deployment (Figure E.39), one can see the incorrect and correct classifications made by each model. SVM definitely worked best.

Under the summary report, I checked the important variables once again (Figure E.40).

Again, we can look at the relationships by examining mean with error plots (easily derived though the ANOVA module, though one can also go to the graphing functions). One can use other variables related to the four categories;

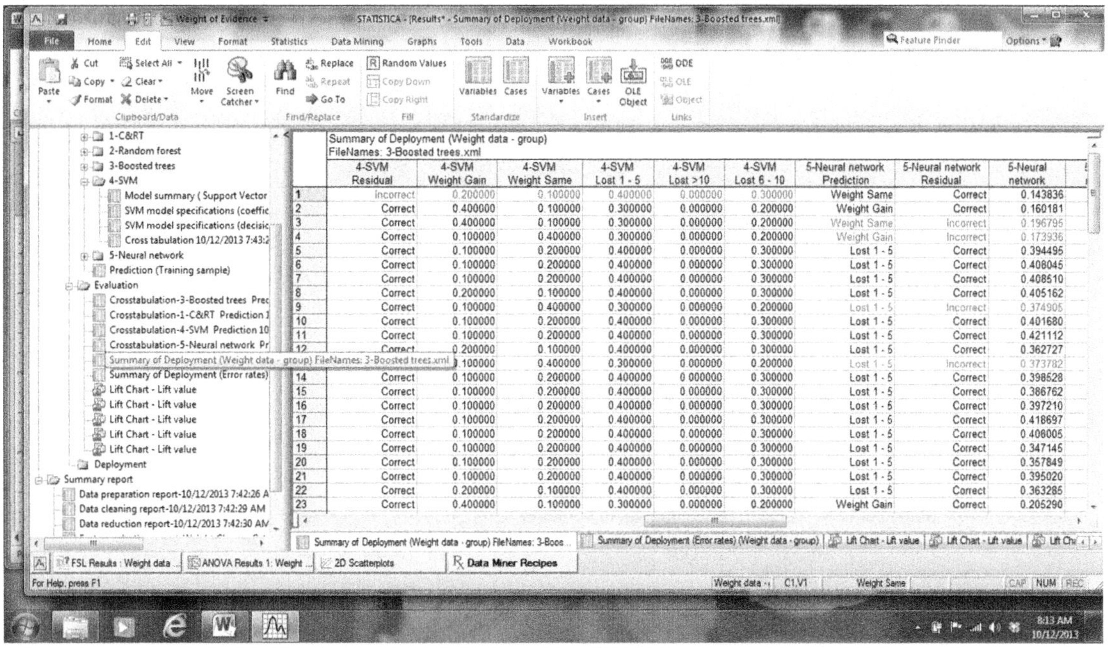

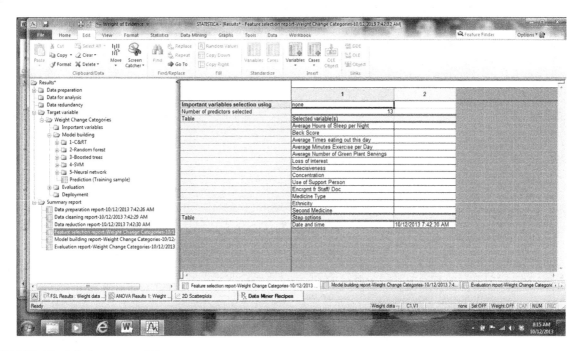

FIGURE E.39   Correct and incorrect identifications by model.

FIGURE E.40   Check for important variables.

for example, the actual weight change. For example, Figure E.41 is a shows graph of weight change by encouragement from the medical staff.

It seems that the more encouragement the patient received, the more weight was lost. Perhaps we need to look at the actual weight lost or gained in a data mining recipe. We may have lost crucial information by forming groups.

I repeated the steps above for a Data Mining Recipe, but this time used weight gained or lost as the dependent variable (Variable 27).

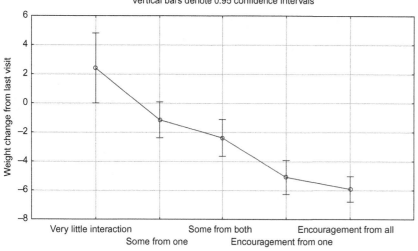

Encrgmt fr Staff/ Doc; LS Means
Current effect: F(4, 96)=19.419, p=.00000
Effective hypothesis decomposition
Vertical bars denote 0.95 confidence intervals

FIGURE E.41 Mean with Error Plot of Weight Change by Encouragement.

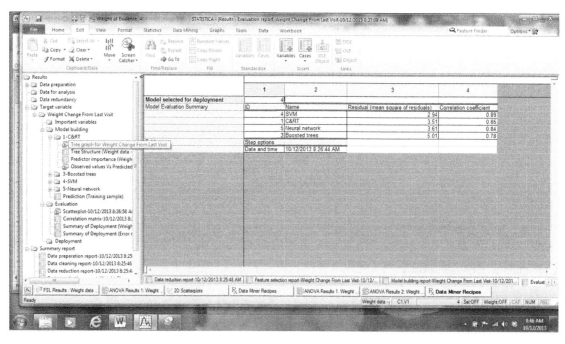

FIGURE E.42 Repeated model.

	1	2	3	4
Model selected for deployment	4			
Model Evaluation Summary	ID	Name	Residual (mean square of residuals)	Correlation coefficient
	4	SVM	2.94	0.89
	1	C&RT	3.51	0.85
	5	Neural network	3.61	0.84
	3	Boosted trees	5.01	0.78
Table	Step options			
	Date and time	10/12/2013 8:26:44 AM		

FIGURE E.43 Accessing C&RT.

Again, SVM seemed to be the best model, which yielded the highest correlation, as may be seen in Figure E.42.

It looks like C&RT is a close second, and this is still acceptable as it is easy to see the relationships in C&RT. Find the module by examining Figure E.43.

I clicked on the first option, as shown in Figure E.44.

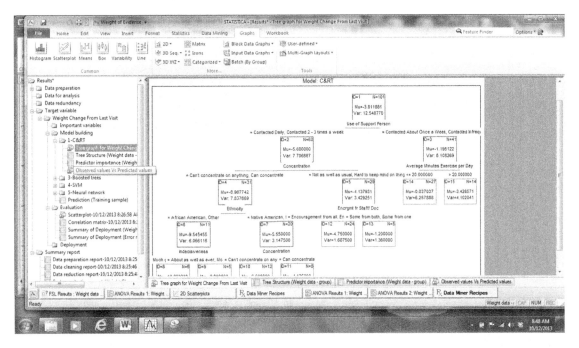

FIGURE E.44   Tree Graph.

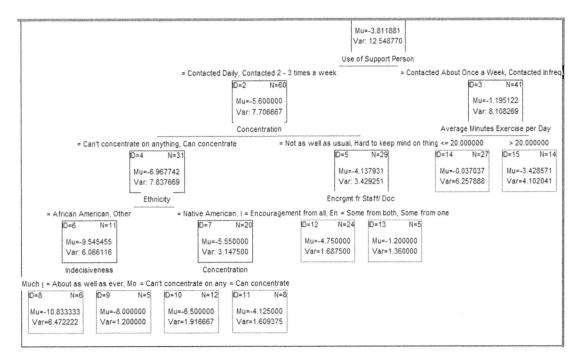

FIGURE E.45   Tree Graph in Better Detail.

Figure E.45 shows the tree graph in more detail.

One additional item was the desire to see if Depression could be predicted from any of the independent variables. A feature selection was completed using the Beck scores as the dependent variables and 1 3 31 for continuous variables and 32–34 36 2 for discrete variables as predictors. Figure E.46 shows the importance plot that was generated.

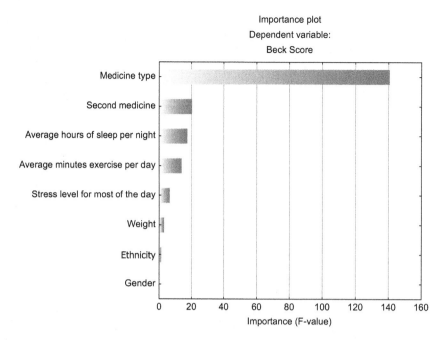

FIGURE E.46 Importance Plot.

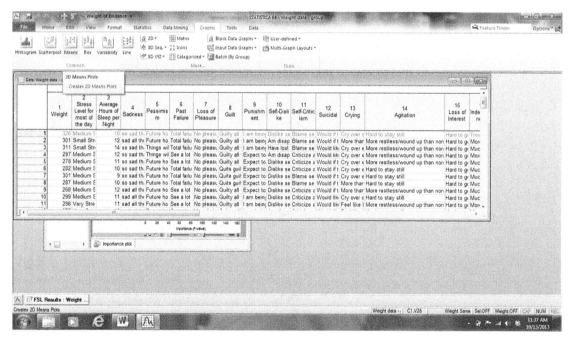

FIGURE E.47 Finding Mean with Error Plots.

Medicine type seemed to be the most predictive of depression scores. To see the relationship, I used a mean with error plot. Go to Graphs, and Means Plots as in Figure E.47.

Select the variables (Variable 25, Beck Score, as the dependent, and Variable 32, Medicine Type, as the independent or grouping variable), and click Multiple as in Figure E.48. Keep the defaults for a clean graph and click OK to see Figure E.49.

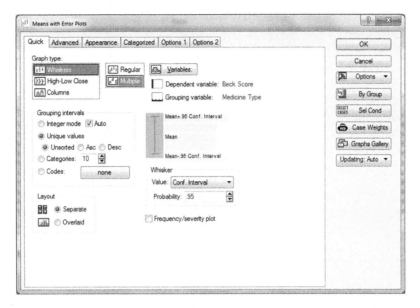

FIGURE E.48   What to Select.

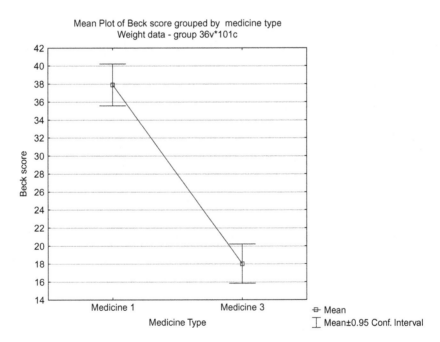

FIGURE E.49   Mean with Error Plot.

As front-line antidepressants go, Medicine 3 seemed the best as it achieved the lowest depression scores. Medicine 1 was not a placebo, but seemed to do no better than nothing. No doubt the recommendation would be to use Medicine 3 for depression.

At this point, one might want to go to the interactive models such as SVM in order to see if a more accurate model could be developed for predicting weight change.

Tutorial F1, a weight exercise for one individual (also fabricated data) will demonstrate how to set training and testing samples within the data miner recipes. Note in this data set, the one red case, case 1. That case is the fictitious participant for Tutorial F1. Tutorial F1 also uses fabricated data and is exploratory only.

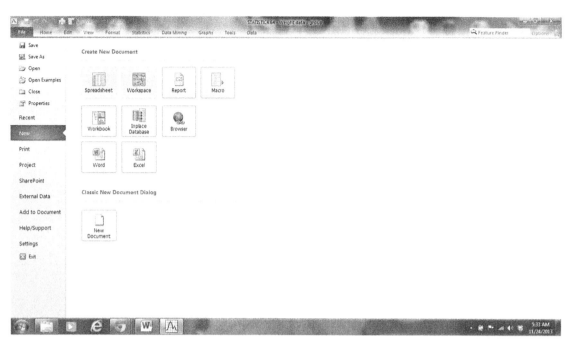

FIGURE E.50 File, New Workspace — then select Beta procedures.

Support Vector Machine (SVM)

In Figure E.50, go to File and then New Workspace. Select Beta Procedures.

Connect the data as in Figure E.51.

Select variables as in Figure E.52.

Go to Node Browser, All, and select Support Vector Machine (beta) as in Figure E.53.

The node will connect to the data. Double click on the node so you can edit the parameters.

I clicked All for each (Figure E.54).

I selected train and test and used the default of 75% for training (Figure E.55), and then selected the default (Figure E.56).

Unless you have a license that allows for code generation, unclick the code generators or the module will not work (Figure E.57).

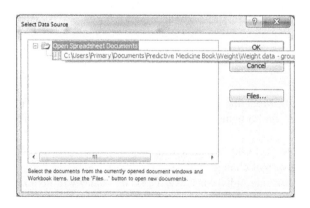

FIGURE E.51 Connect the data.

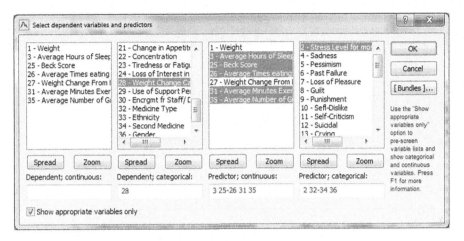

FIGURE E.52 Select the Variables.

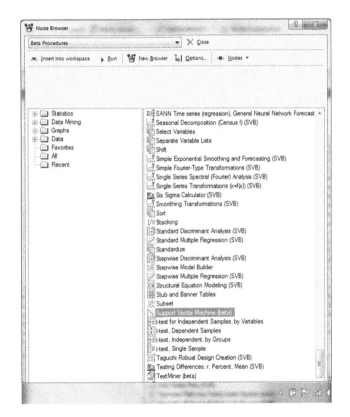

FIGURE E.53 Highlight the data then select support vector machine beta and insert into workspace.

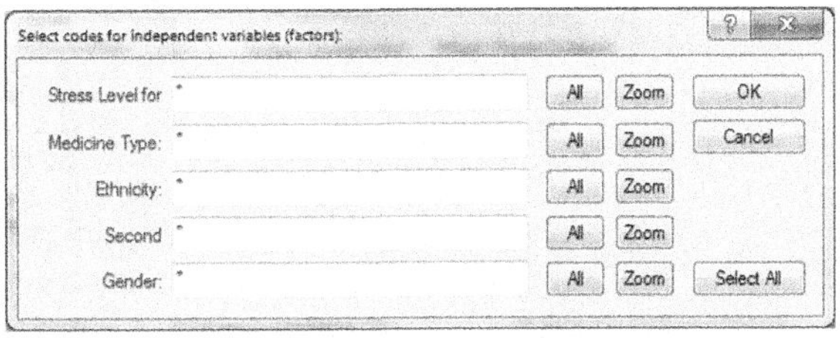

FIGURE E.54 Edit the parameters by double-clicking on the node. Select All for each.

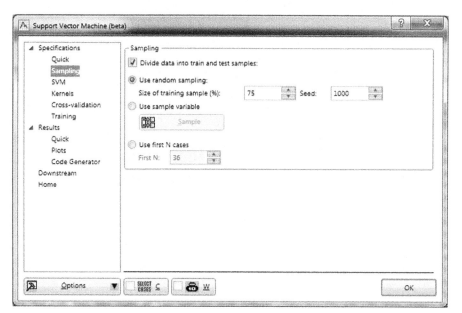

FIGURE E.55 Using the default for training and testing.

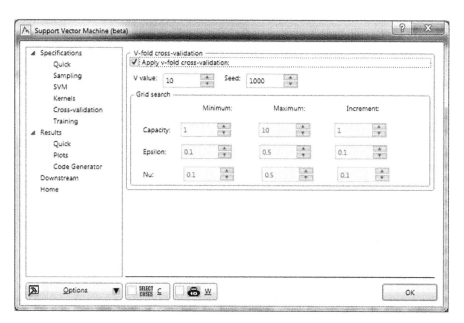

FIGURE E.56 Apply Cross-Validation.

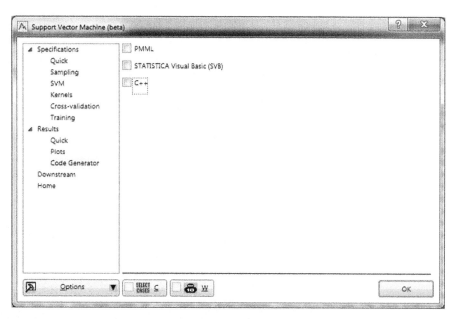

FIGURE E.57 Unclick code generation if clicked.

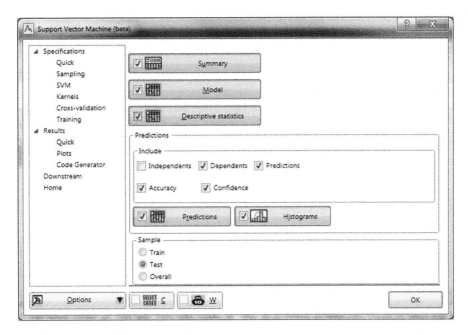

FIGURE E.58 Select the results you would like.

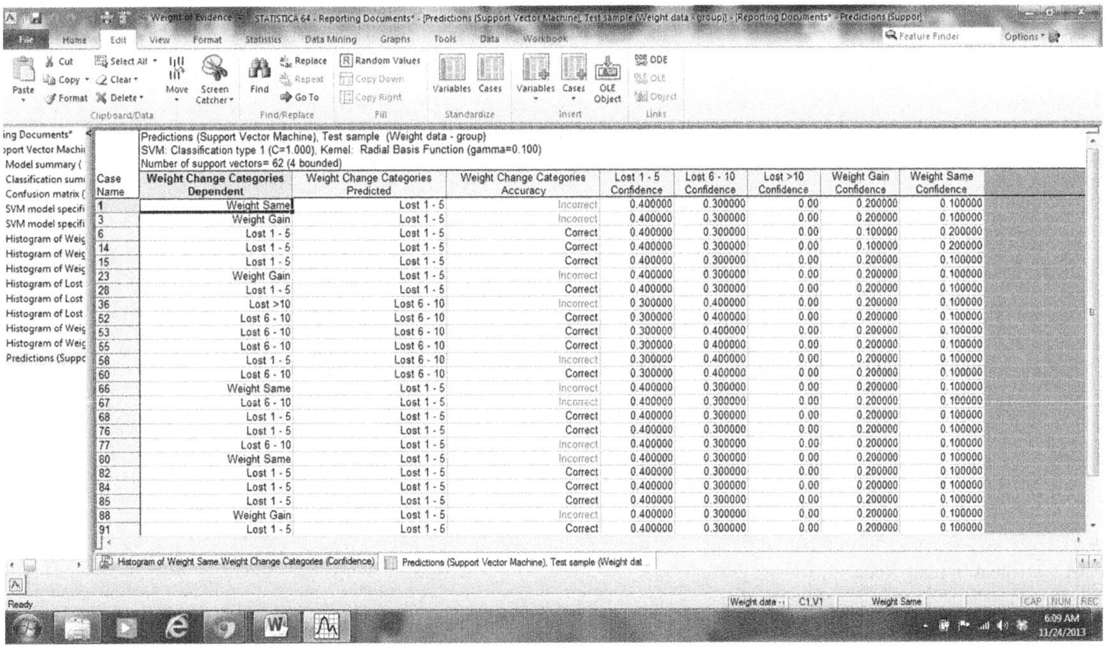

FIGURE E.59 The output did not look good.

Under Results, select what you would like (I selected those in Figure E.58).

Let the model run and open the reporting documents. This analysis did not look very good as almost half of the predictions of the test group were incorrect as in Figure E.59.

It might be that the binning of the weight change is not effective so I changed it to simply three categories: 1 weight loss, 2 stayed the same, 3 weight gain.

First I made the new category beside the old one and then deleted the old one so the variable numbers would stay the same as in Figure E.60.

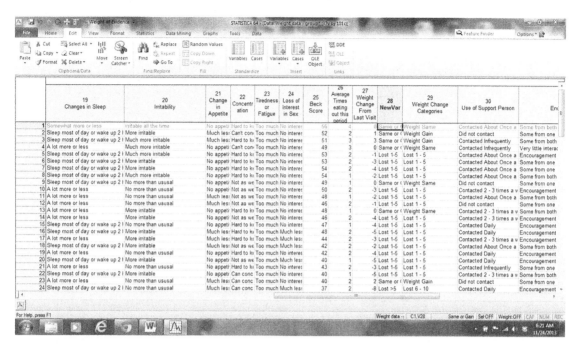

FIGURE E.60   Changed Weight Variable to Three Categories.

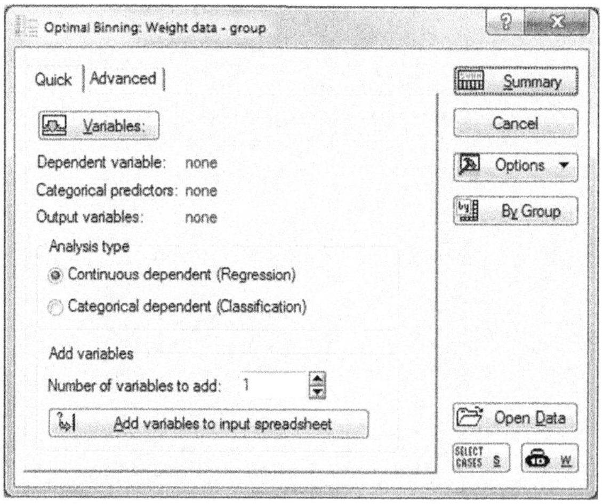

FIGURE E.61   Optimal Binning Node.

With the new target variable, I reran the analysis. One other thing I could have tried was the Optimal Binning node under Data Mining as in Figure E.61.

I decided to try my intuition instead. This time with the new data set-up, I went to the Data Mining tab and selected Machine Learning SVM (Figure E.62).

I selected variables as before (Figure E.63).

I decided to choose 70% for the training and 30% for testing. I saw that from the dropdown menu, under SVM, Type 1 was chosen as the default, which I kept, and also selected the cross-fold validation. This time, the predictions were a bit better, as in Figure E.64, and probably all that can be expected from fabricated data.

I also wanted to compare the interactive C&RT with coded design, and with V-fold validation, to see if it was possible to achieve a better classification matrix with a more interesting tree (Figures E.65, E.66).

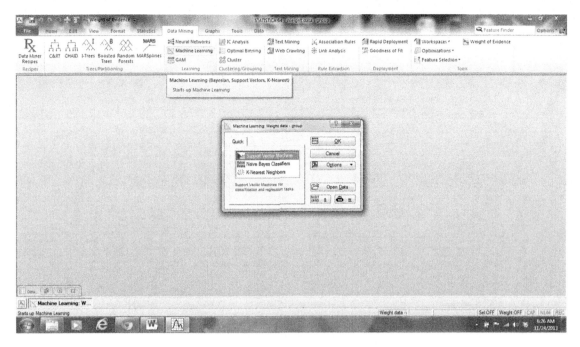

FIGURE E.62   Finding Support Vector Machines.

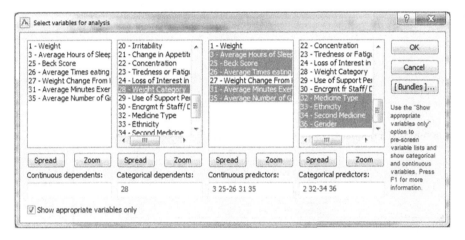

FIGURE E.63   Select Variables.

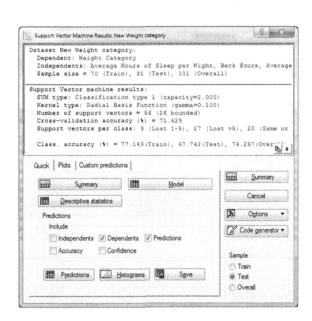

FIGURE E.64   Use 70%/30% and the v-fold. See new predictions.

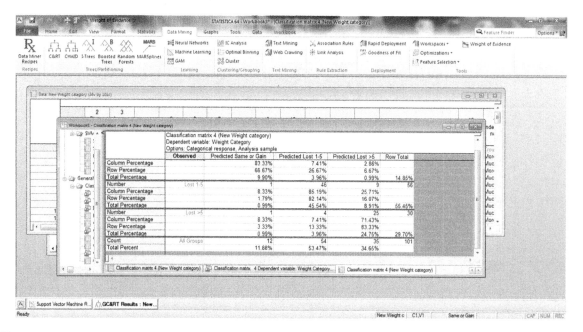

FIGURE E.65   C&RT.

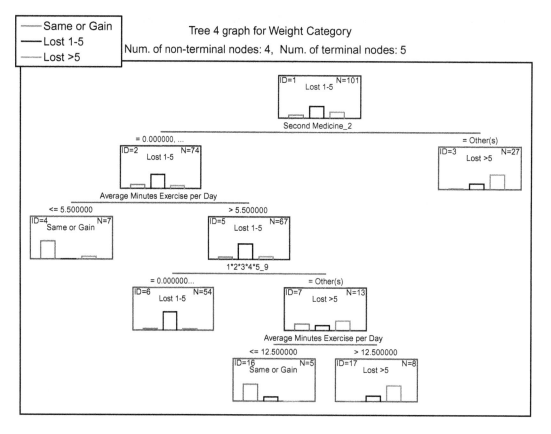

FIGURE E.66   Trees from C&RT.

Exercise may play a role when taking Medicine 2.

In data mining, it is assumed that the data have been cleaned either by hand or by using a program to help, such as STATISTICA's data health check. To data mine properly, one generally randomly divides the data set into training and testing data sets. The training data can be used for exploration, but even within training one should use training and testing samples, which are often options in data mining modules. There are many options for exploring data, and once what seems to be a good model has been found, that model is applied to the testing data. One may have a good model for a particular setting, but in order to test the model thoroughly and to generalize, testing data from other settings must be used to ascertain the validity and reliability of the model. Furthermore, accuracy of a model may change over time due to changes in the population and environment, and other changes, so the model should continually be tested and assessed over time.

REFERENCES

Afari, N., Noonan, C., Goldberg, J., Roy-Byrne, P., Schur, E., Golnari, G., et al., 2010. Depression and obesity: do shared genes explain the relationship? Depress. Anxiety. 27 (9), 799–806.

Beck, A.T., Steer, R.A., Brown, G.K., 1996. Beck Depression Inventory II. Available at: <http://Pearsonassessments.com>.

Bliss, R., 2006. Genetic variations affect obesity-related risks. Agric. Res. 54 (3), 5.

Chang, H., Yen, S.T., 2012. Association between obesity and depression: evidence from a longitudinal sample of the elderly in Taiwan. Aging Ment. Health. 16 (2), 173–180.

Dong, C.C., Sanchez, L.E., Price, R.A., 2004. Relationship of obesity to depression: a family-based study. Int. J. Obes. Relat. Metab. Disord. 28 (6), 790–795.

Duffy, S., Cohen, K., Choi, S., McCullagh, M., Noonan, D., 2012. Predictors of obesity in Michigan Operating Engineers. J. Community Health. 37 (3), 619–625.

Faith, M.S., Butryn, M.M., Wadden, T.A., Fabricatore, A.A., Nguyen, A.M., Heymsfield, S.B., 2011. Evidence for prospective associations among depression and obesity in population-based studies. Obes. Rev. 12, e438–e453.

Heinan, L., Darling, H., 2009. Addressing obesity in the workplace: the role of employers. Milbank Q. 87 (1), 101–122.

Jay, M., Kaylet, A., Ark, T., McMacken, M., Messito, M.J., Richter, R., et al., 2009. Physicians' attitudes about obesity and their associations with competency and specialty: a cross-sectional study. BMC Health Serv. Res. 9, 106–116.

Jay, M., Gillespie, C., Schlair, S., Sherman, S., Kalet, A., 2010. Physicians' use of the 5As in counseling obese patients: is the quality of counseling associated with patients' motivation and intention to lose weight? BMC Health Serv. Res. 10, 159–168.

Lau, D.W., Douketis, J.D., Morrison, K.M., Hramiak, I.M., Sharma, A.M., Ur, E., 2007. 2006 Canadian clinical practice guidelines on the management and prevention of obesity in adults and children [summary]. CMAJ. 176 (8), S1–S13.

Melamed, O.C., Nakar, S., Vinker, S., 2009. Suboptimal identification of obesity by family physicians. Am. J. Manag. Care. 15 (9), 619–624.

Murphy, J.M., Horton, N.J., Burke Jr.J.D., Monson, R.R., Laird, N.M., Lesage, A.A., et al., 2009. Obesity and weight gain in relation to depression: findings from the Stirling County Study. Int. J. Obes. 33 (3), 335–341.

Nedeltcheva, A.V., Kilkus, J.M., Imperial, J., Schoeller, D.A., Penev, P.D., 2010. Insufficient sleep undermines dietary efforts to reduce adiposity. Ann. Intern. Med. 153 (7), 435–441.

Nishitani, N.N., Sakakibara, H.H., 2006. Relationship of obesity to job stress and eating behavior in male Japanese workers. Int. J. Obes. 30 (3), 528–533.

Obesity may be associated with lack of sleep, 2005. Eat. Disord. Rev. 16 (2), 6.

Overtime, overtired, and overweight: workplace can affect weight gain, 2005. Eat. Disord. Rev. 16 (5), 4–5.

Pearson, W.S., Bhat-Schelbert, K., Ford, E.S., Mokdad, A.H., 2009. The impact of obesity on time spent with the provider and number of medications managed during office-based physician visits using a cross-sectional, national health survey. BMC Public Health. 9, 436–442.

Perry, L.S., 2012. Standing up: redesigning the workplace to address obesity. Prof. Saf. 57 (6), 77–84.

Wenjun, Z., Cruickshanks, K.J., Schubert, C.R., Nieto, F., Guan-Hua, H., Klein, B.K., et al., 2010. Obesity and depression symptoms in the Beaver Dam Offspring Study population. Depress. Anxiety. 27 (9), 846–851.

Wethington, H.R., Sherry, B., Polhamus, B., 2011. Physician practices related to use of BMI-for-age and counseling for childhood obesity prevention: a cross-sectional study. BMC Fam. Pract. 12 (1), 80–88.

Zhao, G., Ford, E., Li, C., Tsai, J., Dhingra, S., Balluz, L., 2011. Waist circumference, abdominal obesity, and depression among overweight and obese U.S. adults: National health and nutrition examination survey 2005–2006. BMC Psychiatry. 11 (1), 130–138.

Obesity — Individual: Predicting Best Treatment for an Individual from Portal Data at a Clinic

Linda A. Winters-Miner, PhD

Chapter Outline

INTRODUCTION

Weight of Evidence (WoE) is used if the researcher needs transparency in the predictive model. WoE allows one to view the binning rules being used for predicting outcomes. From WoE it is possible to predict the occurrence or probability of an event by combining evidence (preponderance of evidence) for predicting an outcome. WoE was used in the 1970s–1990s as an aid to diagnosis (De Dombal *et al.*, 1974; Cohen, 1980; Weed, 2005). Because the "rules" for binning can be known and even selected from options, the system becomes transparent. After the binning process with WoE further predictive analyses are completed. The signed metric of WoE indicates the power of some variable(s) to explain an outcome. If the sign is positive, then the outcome is more likely. If the sign is negative, the outcome is less likely. At the time it was initially used there were objections to using computers with weight of evidence, as the medical community often did not believe that a computer could predict as well as clinicians. However, as Cohen said, "This is exactly what one should expect if the computer is really supplied with just the same weight of evidence as the clinicians consciously or unconsciously obtain" (Cohen, 1980, p. 60).

In WoE, a bifurcated target variable is used. One value is "good" and one is "bad." The value of WoE is the ratio of relative frequency of "goods" to relative frequency of "bads." Generally, after using the STATISTICA node for WoE, one uses modeling such as logistic regression for a prediction model.

Such transparency might be needed by regulated industries which cannot use a more "black box" type of analysis, such as neural networks in which relationships are unseen. With WoE, one can explain exactly what rules are being used. WoE might also be used if variables are not normally distributed but when linear models are desired in the analysis. For this analysis, which, again, uses fabricated data, several analyses are illustrated.

This tutorial is a continuation of Tutorial E. The data are for one individual. The first entry of this individual is the same person as case number one (highlighted) for the group data, Weight data — Group.sta. The goal of this tutorial is to shed light on usefulness of methods for weight loss for this person, based on the person's own data. Which of the methods (predictor variables) will most likely lead to weight loss? The tutorial will be completed using two methods — first by using Weight of Evidence (WoE), and second by using a data mining recipe (C&RT). The WoE analysis will be the same as in Tutorial G, using a stepwise model. What is illustrated below is the WoE that is created when one decides to separate

Practical Predictive Analytics and Decisioning Systems for Medicine. DOI: http://dx.doi.org/10.1016/B978-0-12-411643-6.00021-1

a continuous variable into two groups by hunch, and then assume that new variable properly reflects the actual variable. A stark difference is presented between the two WoE procedures using the "hunched" variable and a data mining procedure using the continuous variable. Binning, if done carefully in data mining and using large amounts of data, can create a good process, especially if there is a hold-out sample used. As Danny Stout wrote:

WOE allows for easier interpretation of a model. Without WOE, if you have a model you can say that as medication goes up, weight goes down. However, you can't say at what dosages of medication weight goes up or down. If you use WOE to bin a predictor of medication you will get WOE codes for different levels of medication where you can easily interpret the chances of weight going up or down.

(Danny Stout, personal communication, October 28, 2013)

In the following two WoE examples the data are few, and even with a hold-out sample the process turned out not to be a good one for helping to explain the relationships. Information was lost. These examples do allow one to see how to conduct WoE using STATISTICA.

The data file, Weight data — Individual.sta, comprises 101 days of data for an individual trying to lose weight and trying to reduce depression. It was assumed for this exercise that the data were generated by the patient and uploaded on the clinician's portal. The variables included weight, mood and depression, amounts of exercise, number of times eating out, medication types, and the number of weeks until next doctor appointment. The patient was a 32-year-old Caucasian female. She was taking Medication 1 at the time the group data were being gathered by chart review.

Note for some users: Tutorial E, as does Exercise G3 of Tutorial G, uses version 12 of STATISTICA. If you had an earlier version of STATISTICA and installed version 12, version 12 will likely remember your old settings. You may need to complete a few steps in order to see some of the figures as they are presented in this tutorial. The special instructions have been placed at the end of Exercise G3, starting at p. 757 of Tutorial G. Otherwise, begin here.

BACKGROUND

Patient portals potentially produce more accuracy in diagnoses because physicians often make "contextual errors" during routine office exams (Weiner *et al.*, 2010). The Weiner *et al.* (2010) controlled study defined such errors as physicians missing cues to correct diagnoses and treatments. Actors were trained to present either "contextual" or "biomedical" cues that physicians might or might not pick up in the diagnosis. If a physician probed further, a more accurate diagnosis and/or treatment resulted. The "patients" were actors trained to maintain consistent scripts. For example, an "asthma patient" complaining that his medication was not working well might mention awakening at night coughing and wheezing, or that he had recently lost a job (two red flags). A physician probing for gastro-esophageal reflux disease in this case would be defined as a "biomedical" probe, while probing for the patient not taking medicine due to cost would be a "contextual" probe. Physicians missed about half of the contextual cues and about 40% of the biomedical cues. The authors pointed out that measuring compliance to treatment guidelines as "a quality indicator" is fairly straightforward as a measure. However, discovering if physicians are truly individualizing patient care is not easy to measure (Weiner *et al.*, 2010, p. 75). The authors emphasized the need for better indicators of individualizing patient care.

If constructed carefully, patient portals might help physicians catch the contextual and biomedical cues that are so often missed within the context of a short office visit. One such design resulted from the work of authors in Japan in which they predicted up to 5-year probabilities of diabetes complications (Ko *et al.*, 2010). Portal parameters provided those probabilities and the authors noted that patient—physician interactions increased. Their Joint Asia Diabetes Evaluation (JADE) Program "combined the concepts of risk stratification and protocol-driven care" (Ko *et al.*, 2010, p. 1). Figure F1.1 shows the flow that includes predictive analytics and data mining in their portal.

Patients potentially serve as a good source of their own data which physicians can use in personalizing treatments. Adamovich *et al.* (2005) developed a virtual reality program for post-stroke hand rehabilitation. This system allowed patients to locate remotely from the physician, and allowed for precise data collection concerning the muscle movements of the patient. It is conceivable that such a system could be connected to a portal and patients could receive virtually monitored physical therapy. The physician could later examine the data collected by the portal and fine-tune the model for that particular patient. Fine tuning could occur either in real time or after the fact. Figure F1.2 shows screenshots reported in the Adamovich *et al.* (2005) paper.

Obtaining patient information from the Internet demonstrates one other potential advantage. With the increased distance and perceived anonymity, patients may be less likely to provide an answer that is considered to be socially desirable (Langenbruch *et al.*, 2010). Langenbruch *et al.* (2010) gathered data on treatment of psoriasis and found that Internet patients were less satisfied with their treatment than those who responded to the same questions but from clinics. The

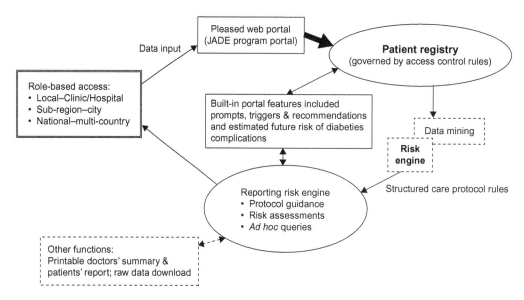

FIGURE F1.1 Logistics and components of the web-based electronic portal of the JADE Program.

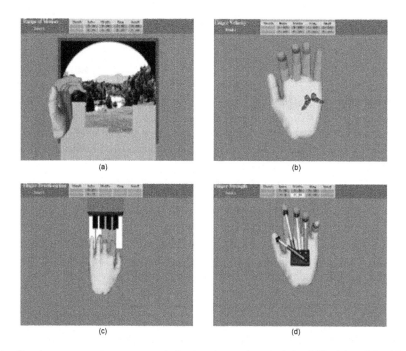

FIGURE F1.2 Screenshots of various movements: range, speed, fractionation, and strength (p. 163). *Adapted by Adamovich* et al. *(2005), from Boian* et al., *2002).*

authors thought that the differences in responses could be due to fundamental differences in the populations sampled, in that perhaps more disgruntled people responded to the online questions. They also thought that the differences could be due to the differences in anonymity. Anonymity allowed the patients to say what they really thought without being in the presence of their physicians. Portals would not be anonymous, but they do provide a distance from the physician which might allow for more revelation. At least there would not be the constant pressure of time to respond quickly that exists in physicians' offices. Perhaps responses could be more thought out, and more contextual and biomedical cues would be revealed. Once revealed, those cues might be more evident to the physicians.

This tutorial assumes that the patient entered data on a daily basis, and risk functions would then be conducted on behalf of the one patient rather than data from a group. The specific parameters that drive weight gain and loss for an individual might be different than for those using grouped data.

THE EXERCISE

Method 1: Weight of Evidence Using Individual Items for Beck Scores

With the Weight data – Individual.sta data set open, click on File and New as in Figure F1.3. Note that Variable 33 is the variable in question. It was created in this manner. The weight of the day before was used as the base for each new day. If the weight was 318 on one day and went to 317 on the next, the change was categorized as a loss. Then if the next day the weight were 317 again, the category was given "no change or gained." This process was used for each day and resulted in the binary variable, weight change, Variable 33.

Click on Workspace to achieve Figure F1.4 and then click on All Validated Procedures. Click OK.

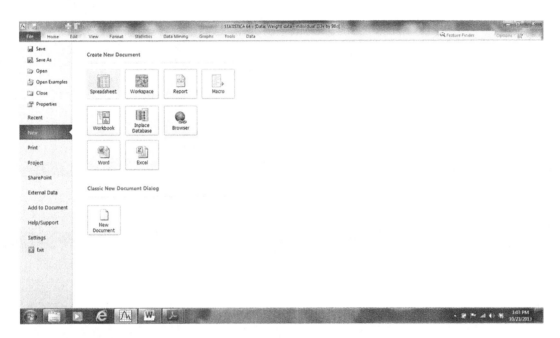

FIGURE F1.3   Open a new project.

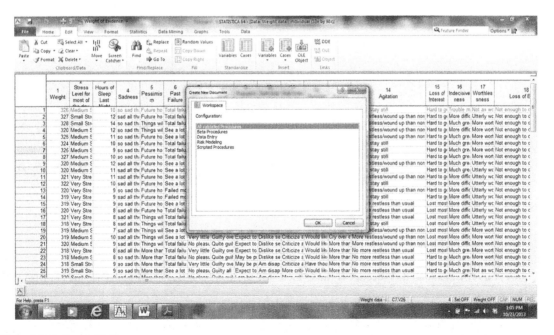

FIGURE F1.4   Select all procedures.

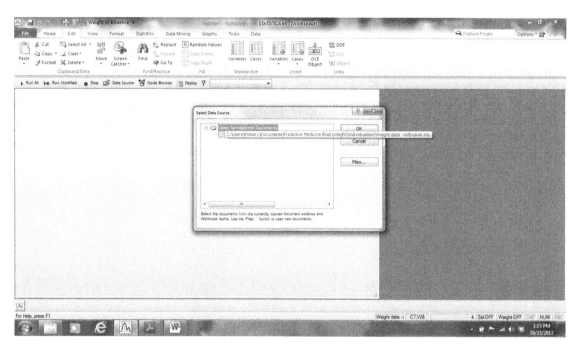

FIGURE F1.5 Connect data file.

FIGURE F1.6 Pull data over to the left.

Connect your data as in Figure F1.5.

Pull that data node over a bit so it's easy to work around (see Figure F1.6).

Again click on All Validated Procedures and then on Beta Procedures, which has the newest procedures (Figure F1.7).

Go to the Data Mining tab and click on Weight of Evidence (WoE) as in Figure F1.8.

Clicking on Weight of Evidence will drop the node directly into the workspace, as in Figure F1.9. I also pulled the node over a little for ease of use and then connected the data to the node by using the circle on the data (if one

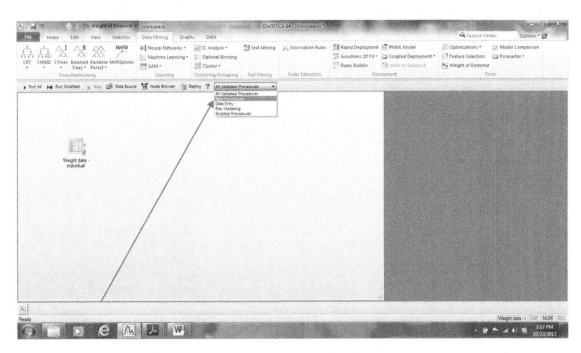

FIGURE F1.7   Select Beta Procedures.

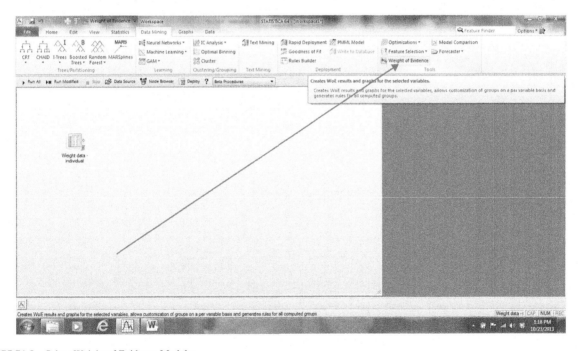

FIGURE F1.8   Select Weight of Evidence Module.

highlights the data first and then clicks on the WoE node, the node will automatically connect to the data and will be in the optimum position.)

Pull the arrow all the way to the WoE node and let go. Click on the little gear symbol (edit the parameters) on the upper left of the weight of evidence node to display Figure F1.10.

Select the variables as in Figure F1.11. WoE predicts two level outcomes, so we will predict (no change or weight gain) versus weight loss, Variable 33 from the other variables. Instead of using the Beck score, use the separate items to see if some combination of them might associate with weight loss.

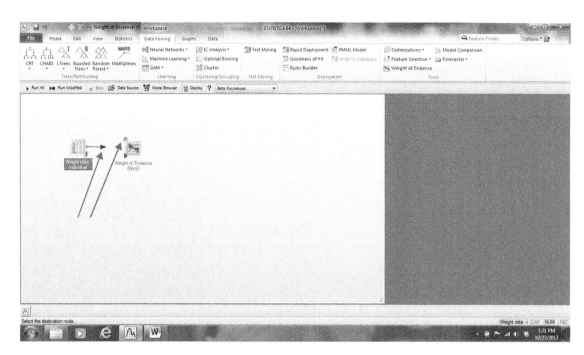

FIGURE F1.9 Connection of WoE to Data. Click on gear to Edit Parameters.

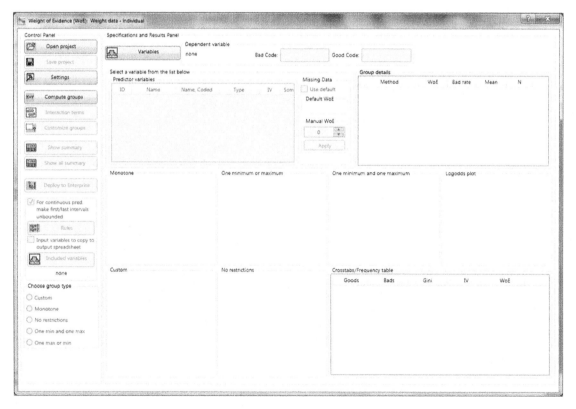

FIGURE F1.10 Resulting screen − click on variables to select.

Click OK. Double click in the box for "Bad Code" to display Figure F1.12.
Click on Zoom to find the code for no change or gained (Figure F1.13), highlight, and then OK.
Click OK again at Figure F1.14.

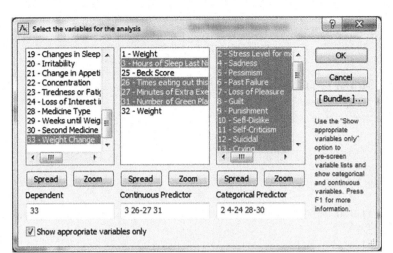

FIGURE F1.11 Select Variables.

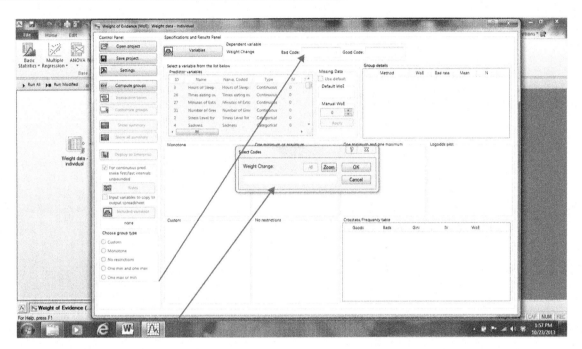

FIGURE F1.12 Click in "bad code" to get this box.

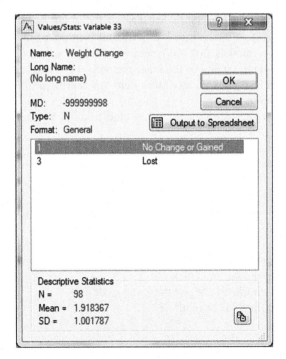

FIGURE F1.13 Select No Change or Gained for bad code.

FIGURE F1.14 Result.

FIGURE F1.15 Repeat process for Good Code. Select Lost for good code. Click OK.

Complete the same procedure for the Good code for the top half (See Figure F1.15).

Now click "Compute groups" as in Figure F1.16.

Allow the procedure to run as in Figure F1.17.

Figure F1.18 shows the results once the procedure runs. These results are for "Minutes of Extra Exercise."

Looking at the IV for minutes of exercise, which is 0.22, one sees that this variable is weakly related to the dependent variable. The red box around the most productive model, the default, is the solution we will use. If in possession of other knowledge about a variable, one could choose any of the other models that the researcher thought would be better. The crosstabs frequency table is given on the lower right. By clicking on any of the other methods we would see the resulting log odds plot and the crosstabs frequency table. We could also click on any other item and see the resulting boxes for that variable. Figure F1.19 chooses hours of sleep, for example.

Choosing different variables is one way of seeing the breaks in the values of the variables in predicting the propensity of high or low group.

Click on the red X to close the screen and Figure F1.20 shows that you can then embed to workspace.

As Figure F1.21 shows, we next run the WoE module by clicking on the little green arrowhead on the lower left of the box (Run to Node).

The module then produces the SVB Rules module (see Figure F1.22).

Move the rules node to the right for convenience, and connect the data to it by dragging over the red arrow. Click on the small diamond on the right middle section of the data box (Figure F1.23).

Right click on the rules node to edit the parameters (Figure F1.24).

Select the output variable in Figure F1.25 and click False on Output Error Variable. We will not use that error variable and, by clicking False, the variable will not be listed in the output data file. Click OK.

Figure F1.26 shows how to run the rules node. Click on the little green triangle below the Rules node.

Click on the little scroll on the output weight data file to see the document as in Figure F1.27.

FIGURE F1.16 Click on Compute Groups.

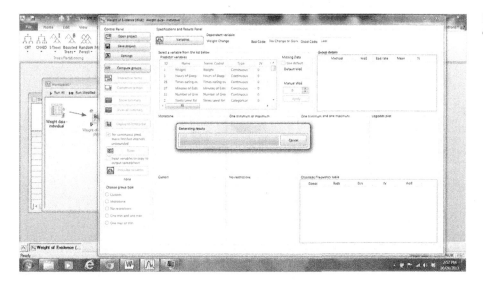

FIGURE F1.17 Let the program compute.

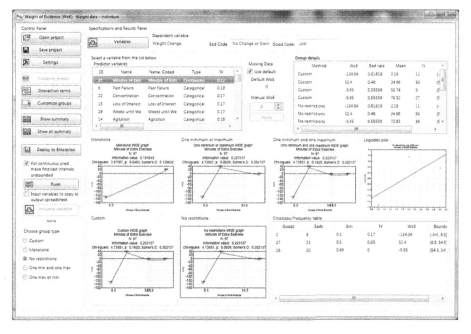

FIGURE F1.18 Shows results for Minutes of Extra Exercise.

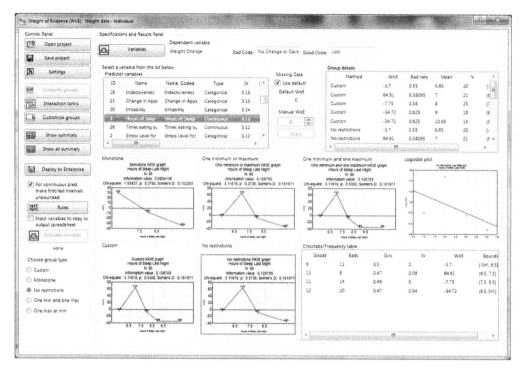

FIGURE F1.19   Highlighting hours of sleep.

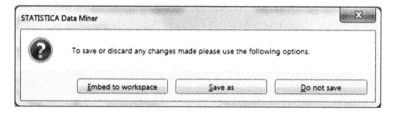

FIGURE F1.20   Embed to workspace.

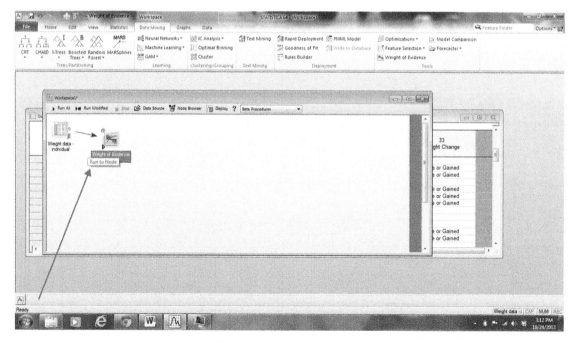

FIGURE F1.21   Shows running WoE module by clicking on the little green arrow on the lower left of the box (run to node).

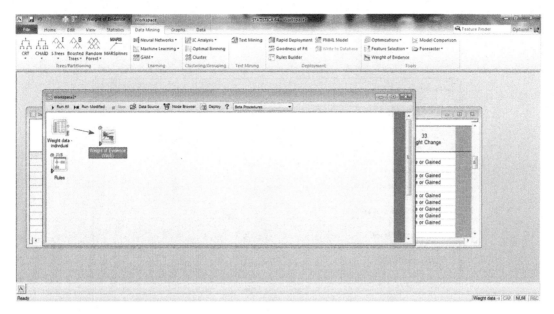

FIGURE F1.22 Resulting SVB Rules module.

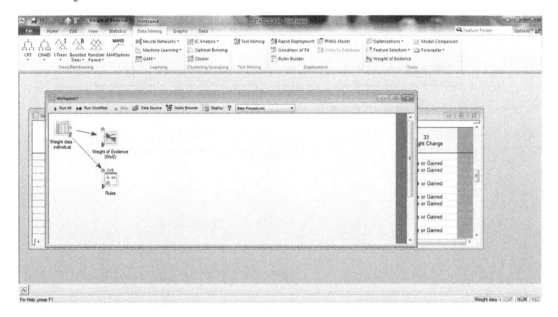

FIGURE F1.23 Move the rules node to the right for convenience, and connect the data to it by dragging over the red arrow.

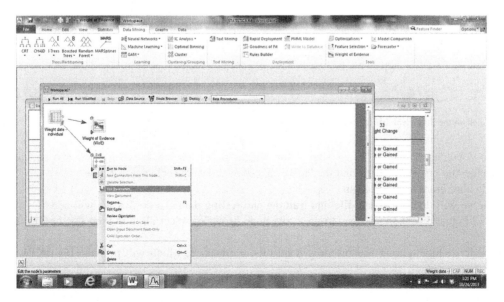

FIGURE F1.24 Right click on the rules node to edit the parameters.

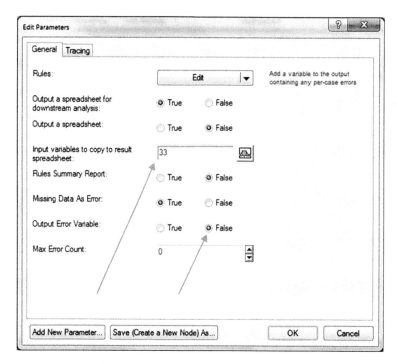

FIGURE F1.25 Select variable and click false on output error.

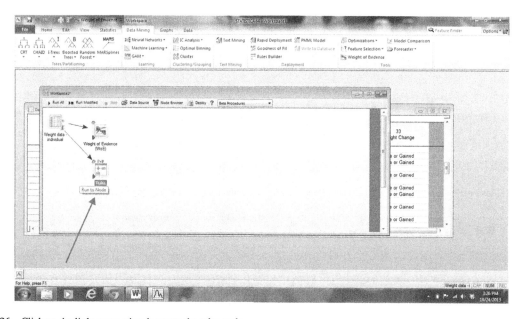

FIGURE F1.26 Click on the little green triangle to run the rules node.

Viewing the document in Figure F1.28 shows how the rules for sorting between good and bad outcomes having been applied to the "no change/gained" and the "lost weight" of the weight change variable.

Close the file and return to the analysis.

At this point we will divide the data file into training and testing data. To do this we will add "Define Training and Testing Sample." Figure F1.29 shows how to go to the node browser, select all, and then Define Training and Testing Sample.

Select the node by highlighting and inserting it into the workspace, which will produce Figure F1.30. Connect the arrow from the data.

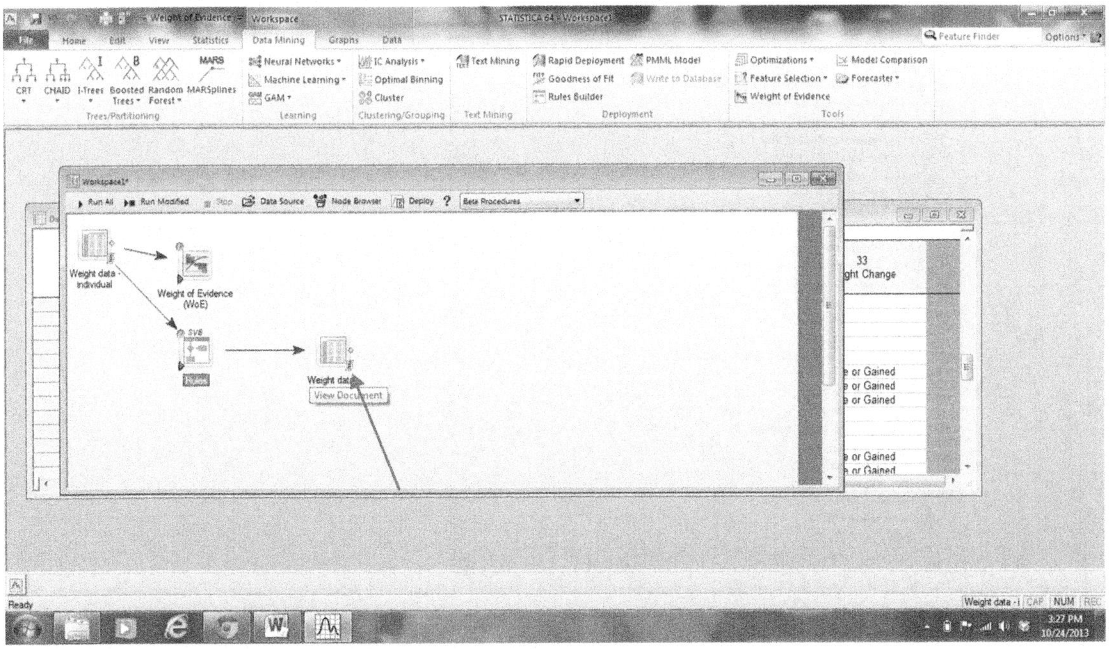

FIGURE F1.27 Click on little scroll for output document.

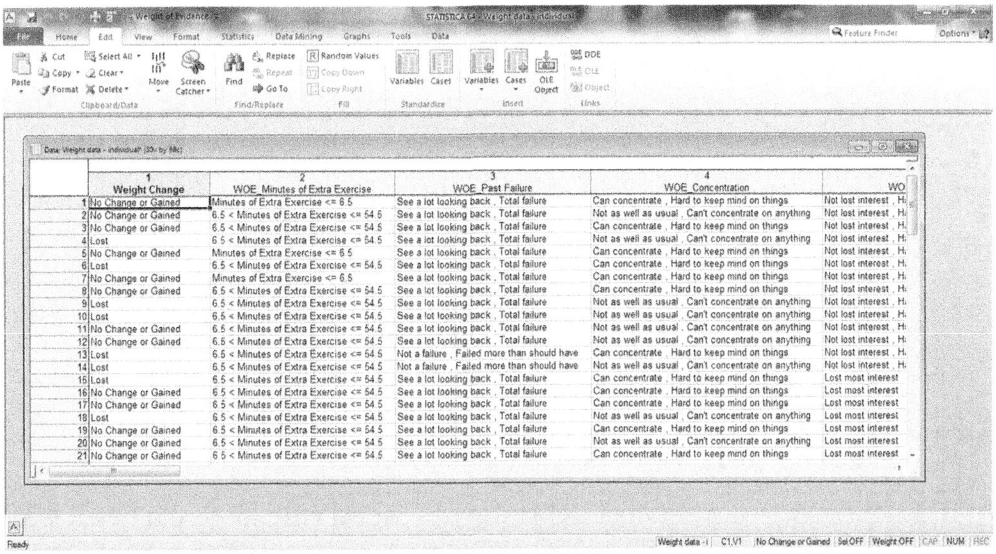

FIGURE F1.28 Shows the rules for sorting.

Again, if you highlighted the second Weight data — individual file in Figure F1.30 before selecting the node, when inserting, the node will automatically connect properly.

Double click on the Define Training and Testing node to produce Figure F1.31, at which point you can edit the parameters.

Change the name to Sample (with no space after the word Sample), X out the validation, and place 70% for training and 30% for testing (see Figure F1.32).

Click OK and then click on the lower left green arrowhead to run the program. View the document (click on the scroll) to see that now we have an additional variable in the data in Figure F1.33.

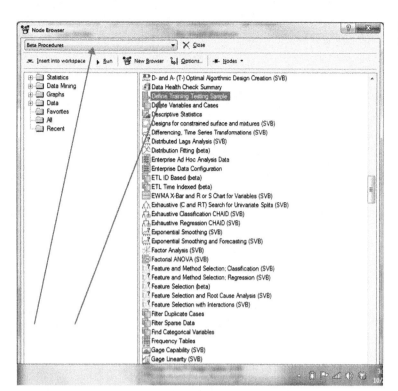

FIGURE F1.29 How to define training and testing sample.

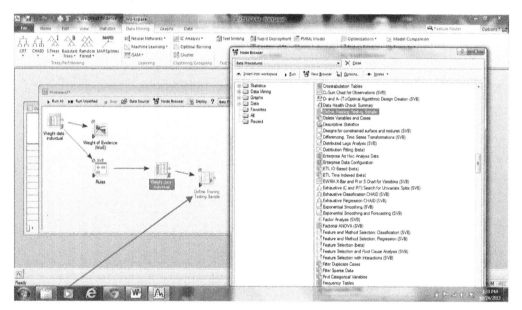

FIGURE F1.30 Shows the module inserted into the workspace.

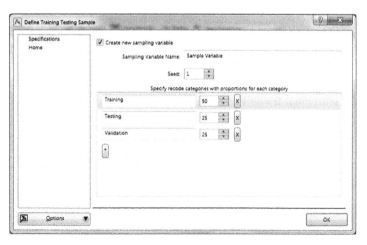

FIGURE F1.31 Double click the node to edit the parameters.

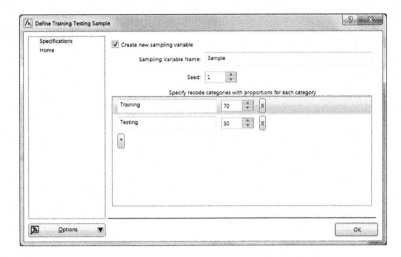

FIGURE F1.32   Change the name to Sample, (with no space after the word Sample), X out the validation, and choose 70% for training and 30% for testing.

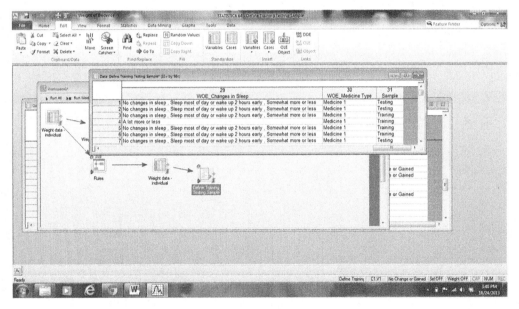

FIGURE F1.33   View the document to see that there is a new variable in the data.

Next, we will separate the two samples. *Make sure the Define Training Testing Sample module is highlighted.* Go to the node browser, select All, and then Subset (Figure F1.34). Insert into the workspace. Highlight the Define Training Testing Sample again, and insert Subset.

Figure F1.35 shows what the subset will look like connected to the define training and testing node.

Place two of these in the workspace as in Figure F1.36 (remember to highlight Training/Testing node each time a subset node is selected).

Right click on each subset and rename as in Figure F1.37.

Right click on the other one and rename this as testing as well.

Double click on each sample and specify what the samples will comprise, as in Figures F1.38 and F1.39. Note that the quote marks are important.

The resulting workspace should look like Figure F1.40. Run each of the subset nodes to create the samples.

Each subset was run in Figure F1.41. Open each of the documents and note the separation of cases. By clicking on the document symbol for each sample, we can see the cases that were selected for each sample.

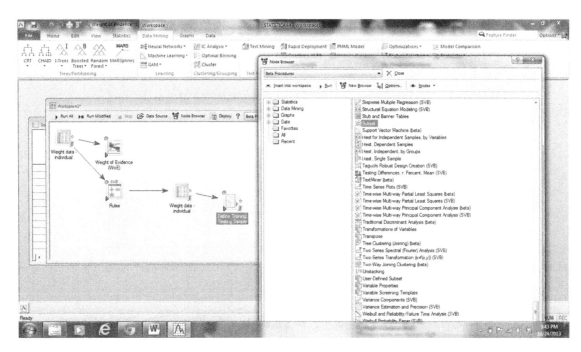

FIGURE F1.34 The "Define Training Testing Sample" node is highlighted so the selected procedure will connect with the node.

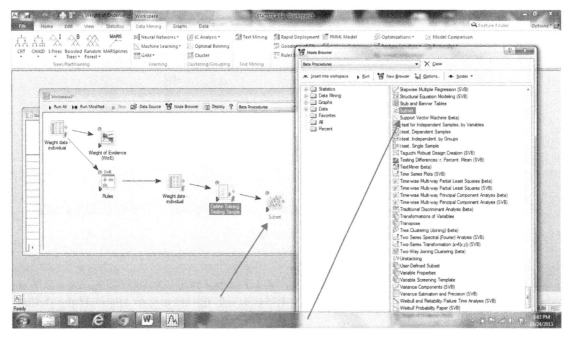

FIGURE F1.35 Click subset which is added.

We next insert a stepwise model builder for the training sample. *Highlight the training subset sample.* Go to Statistics, Advanced Models, and then Stepwise Model Builder as in Figure F1.42. Note that the Subset training is highlighted while selecting Stepwise Model Builder so that the stepwise model will attach to the Training Subset sample.

Figure F1.43 shows the result in the workspace.

Right click on the model builder to edit the parameters as in Figure F1.44.

Figure F1.45 shows the resulting screen.

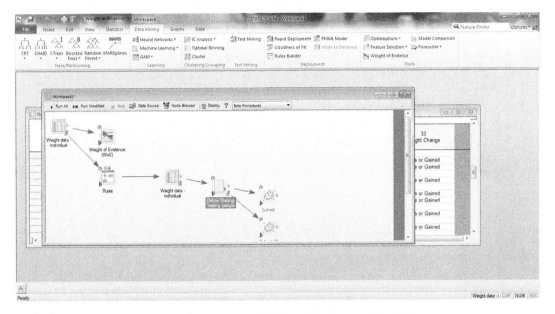

FIGURE F1.36 Place two of these in the workspace. Remember to highlight training/testing node each time.

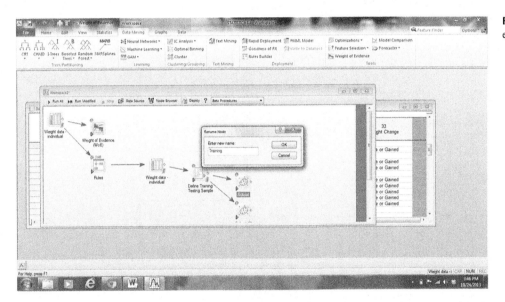

FIGURE F1.37 Right click on each subset and rename.

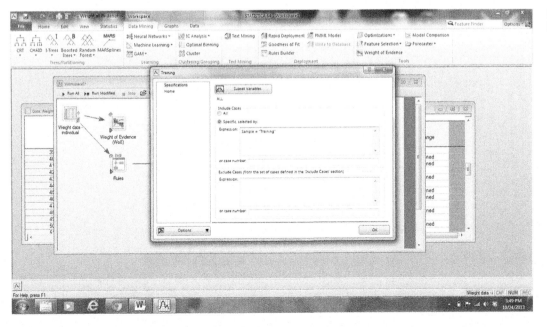

FIGURE F1.38 Specify sample.

FIGURE F1.39 Specify sample – quote marks are important for each!!

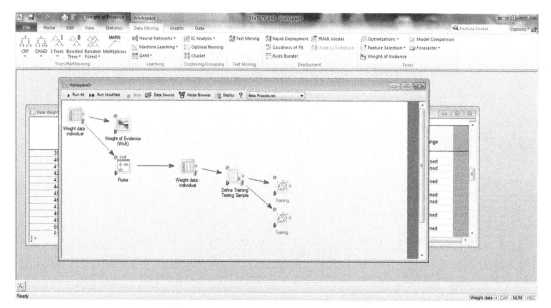

FIGURE F1.40 Resulting workspace.

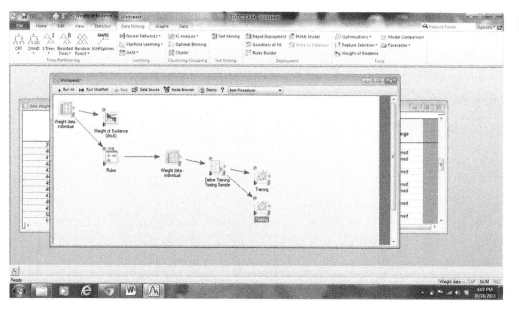

FIGURE F1.41 Subset workspace.

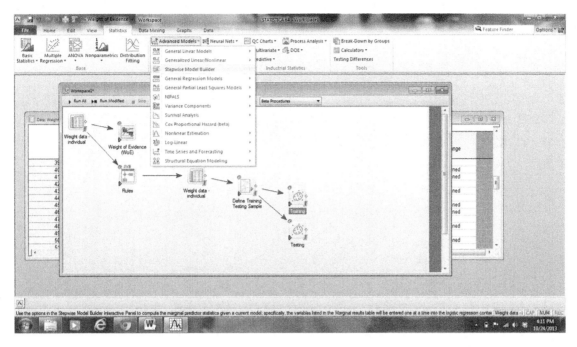

FIGURE F1.42   Go to Statistics, Advanced Models, and then Stepwise Model Builder.

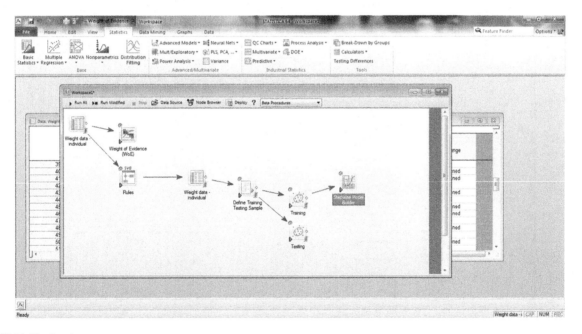

FIGURE F1.43   Result.

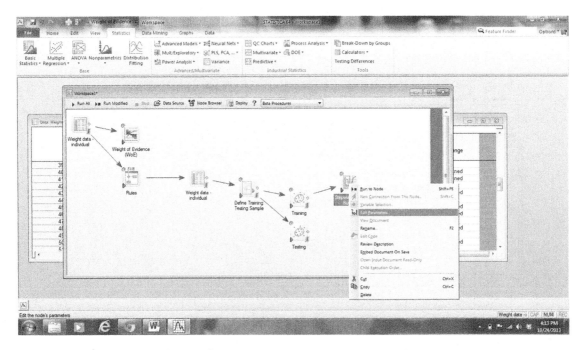

FIGURE F1.44 Right click on the model builder to edit the parameters.

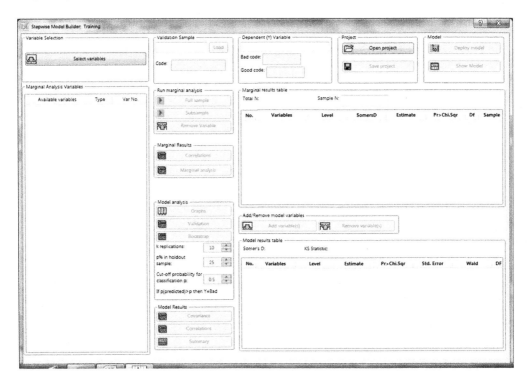

FIGURE F1.45 Resulting screen.

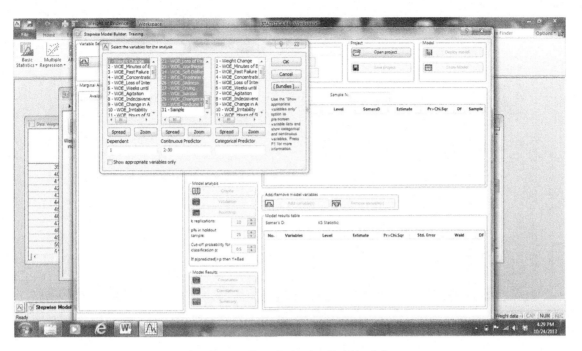

FIGURE F1.46   Variable selection — Unclick the box that says Show Appropriate Variables Only.

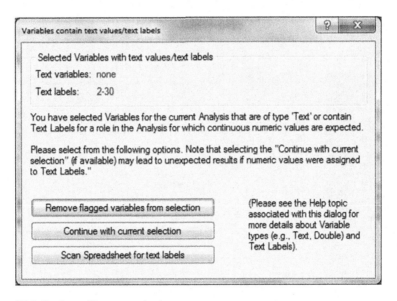

FIGURE F1.47   Don't worry. Click Continue with current selection.

Figure F1.46 demonstrates the variable selection. Unclick the box that says Show appropriate variables only, as we need to select our predictor variables in the continuous box, because they truly are continuous.

Click "continue with current selection" when Figure F1.47 shows up.

Again select the codes for good and bad as in Figure F1.48.

The resulting dialog box looks like that in Figure F1.49.

Now, click on "Run Full sample"; Figure F1.50 shows the result.

By clicking the Somers D we can line up the variables by strength and then add them into the model one by one. After each addition the model runs it is possible actually to select anything that might seem potentially useful when one examines the literature in the field. Figure F1.51 shows what happened when we arranged by Somers D. (I clicked Somers D twice and then highlighted the first one.)

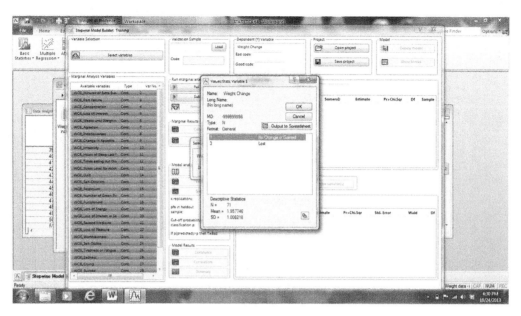

FIGURE F1.48   As before, select the codes for good and bad.

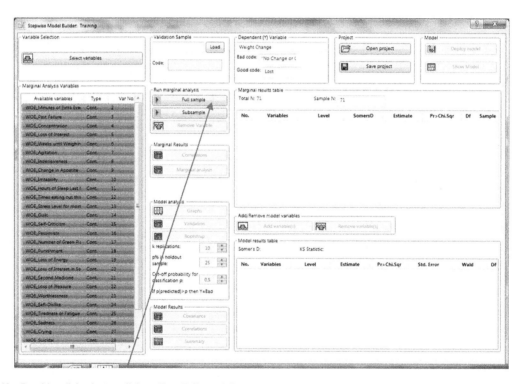

FIGURE F1.49   Resulting dialog box — click on "Run Full sample".

Figure F1.52 shows adding the highlighted variable.

Now we add the second variable. Note the red (significant) estimate before adding.

Figure F1.53 shows what happened to the model once we added the second variable, as well as how the addition changes the Somers D values of those remaining on the top portion.

Now, since we added a variable, the values of the other variables have changed. We can now add more and, after each addition, view the effects. Figure F1.54 shows Guilt about to be added.

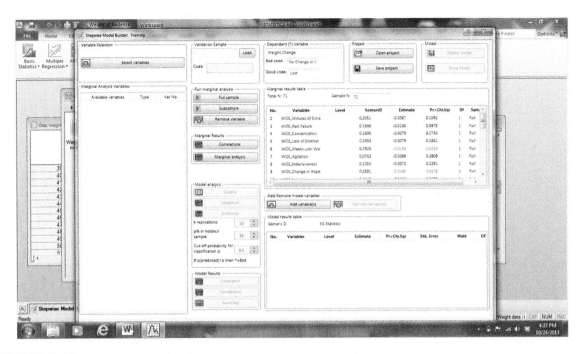

FIGURE F1.50 Result.

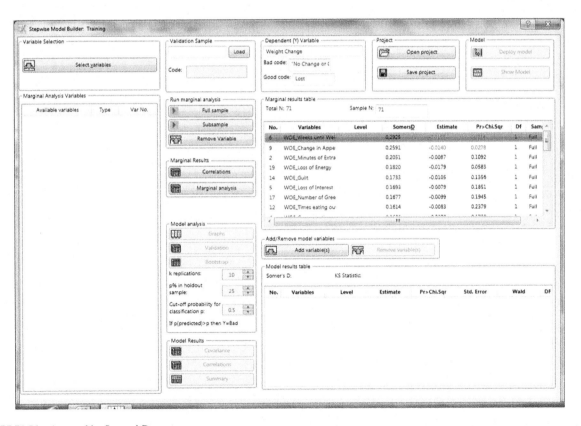

FIGURE F1.51 Arranged by Somers' D

FIGURE F1.52   Adding the highlighted variable.

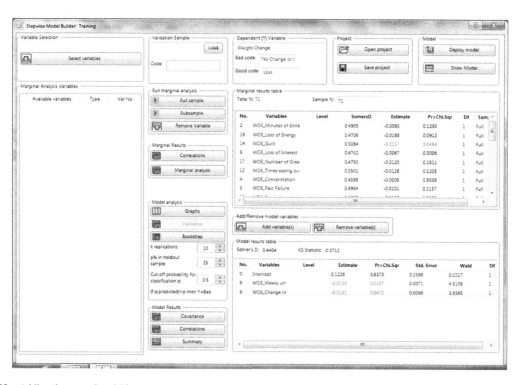

FIGURE F1.53   Adding the second variable.

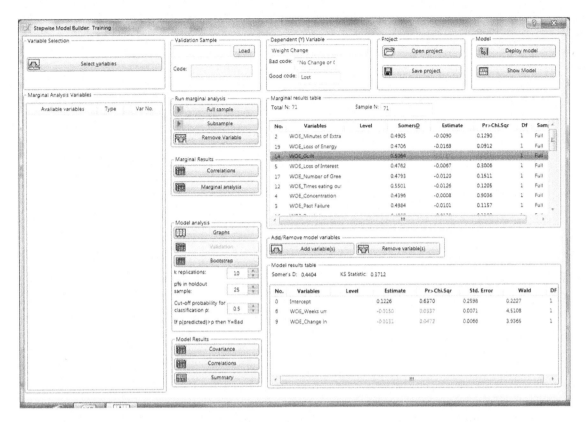

FIGURE F1.54   Guilt about to be added.

FIGURE F1.55   Red X out of the stepwise node and select Embed to workspace.

Now at this point we are simply working with the training data, and soon we will test our model on the training data. We might go ahead and add in a few more that the literature said might be important, or any others that we were interested in and had a hunch might be predictive. I decided to add in Sleep, Exercise, and Medicine type. If this were to be completed again, I might have used the Beck score instead of all the individual items. I lined up the Somers D once again and added Times eating out and Punishment. The model does not look very good at this point, but we'll go ahead. The data were fabricated, after all.

Now close (by clicking the red X in the upper right) out of the stepwise node and select Embed to workspace, as in Figure F1.55.

Run the node of the stepwise model builder to achieve the PMML Model and Rapid Deployment in Figure F1.56.

Drag the Rapid Deployment over to the Testing data, as in Figure F1.57.

Next, connect the Testing data to the Rapid Deployment, which will apply the PMML code to the data.

Figure F1.58 shows right clicking on the Rapid Deployment and editing the parameters to select the procedures for the output.

In Figure F1.59, we can see the parameters that can be edited.

Figure F1.60 shows the result of first selecting Lift chart in Figure F1.59 and then selecting Gains chart and Lift chart.

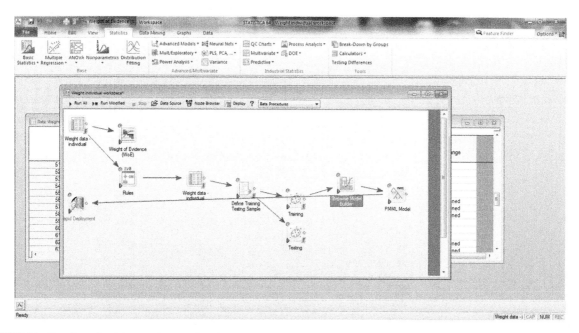

FIGURE F1.56 Run the node of the stepwise model builder.

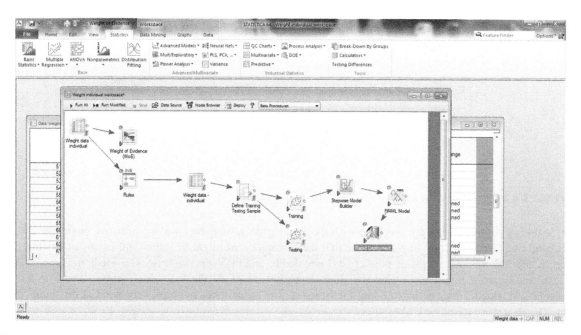

FIGURE F1.57 Drag the Rapid Deployment over to the Testing data.

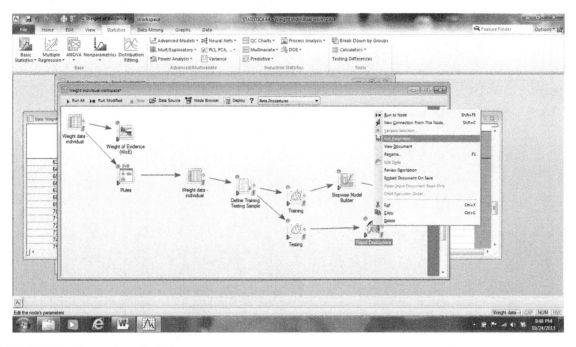

FIGURE F1.58   Select the procedures for the output.

FIGURE F1.59   Parameters that can be edited.

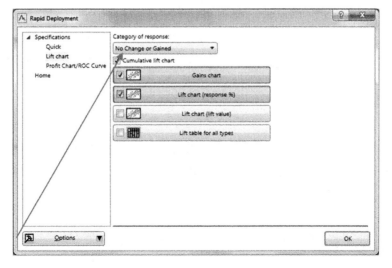

FIGURE F1.60   Selecting gains chart and lift chart. No Change or Gained is the category of the response.

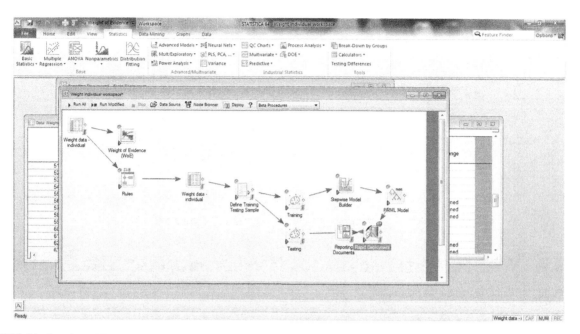

FIGURE F1.61   Run the rapid deployment node and note there are documents produced.

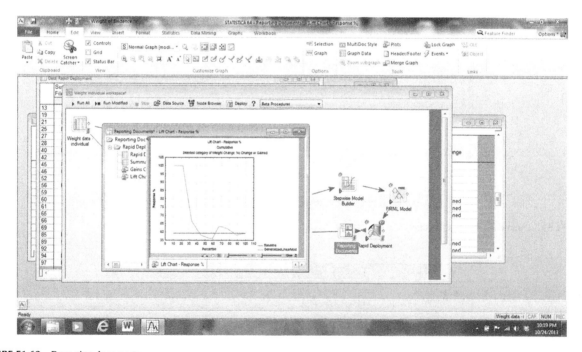

FIGURE F1.62   Reporting documents.

Note that in Figure F1.60 No Change or Gained is the category of the response for this analysis.

Click OK and then run the rapid deployment node. Note now there are documents to display (Figure F1.61).

Double click to examine the reporting documents as in Figure F1.62.

The Gains chart in Figure F1.63 indicates that our model did not predict much better than when not using the model.

In looking at the summary of the deployment in Figure F1.62, we see that the model accuracy was only 56%, which isn't any better than flipping a coin.

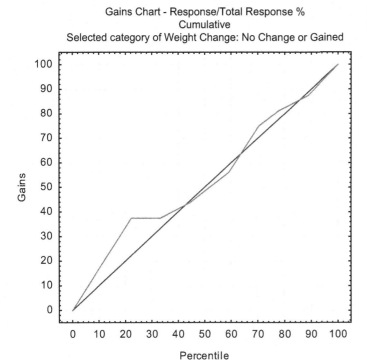

Gains Chart - Response/Total Response %
Cumulative
Selected category of Weight Change: No Change or Gained

FIGURE F1.63 Not a good gains chart!! Remember the data are made up. The process is what we need to learn.

Again, the data are fabricated, and so we might not expect to obtain a good model. The bifurcated variable was created from actual weights day to day. It might have been better to have used Gained or Lost based on that first weight instead. Information is lost when one moves from continuous data to categorical. Perhaps it would be more appropriate to use a naturally divided variable such as Died versus Lived, as in the DIC tutorial. Or it might be that using the individual questions from the Beck Depression Inventory rather than the total score was simply too unreliable. In the next illustration, I used the Beck scores rather than the individual questions that made up the Beck. However, in this illustration we clearly see that, by using WoE, the categorical items were transformed into continuous variables for the regression.

Method 2: Weight of Evidence using Beck Scores Rather than Individual Items

I repeated the above steps but used the Beck score instead of the individual items. Figures F1.64 through F1.105 show the progression.

Method 3: Using Weight (not Bifurcated) and Using Data Miner Recipe

Now, I decided to use predictive modeling but with a slightly different target. For this analysis I used the actual weight rather than the binary weight variable, and used the Beck scores rather than the individual items that made up the Beck score.

First, I conducted a feature selection as may be seen in Figure F1.106.

Select the variables after seeing Figure F1.107.

Select variables as in Figure F1.108.

Click OK and then OK again to arrive at Figure F1.109.

Click on the Histogram of importance for best k predictors to arrive at Figure F1.110.

Medicine type seemed most predictive, followed by the much less predictive Beck score and extra exercise. We might try only those variables, but we might also include the first six.

Click on "Data Miner Recipes" and then on "New" as in Figure F1.111.

Click on the Open/Connect data file (Figure F1.112).

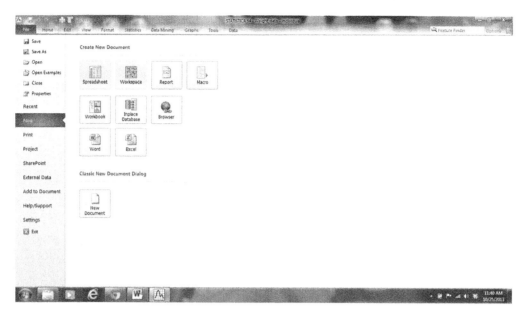

FIGURE F1.64 File new and open a new workspace.

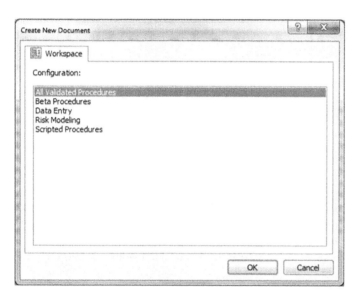

FIGURE F1.65 Select all validated procedures.

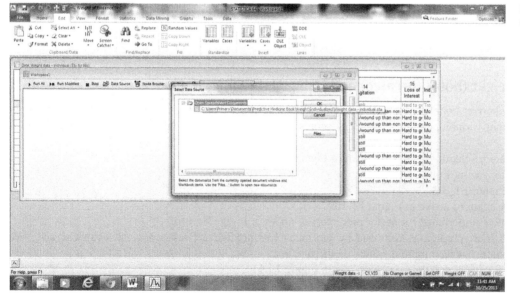

FIGURE F1.66 Connect the data.

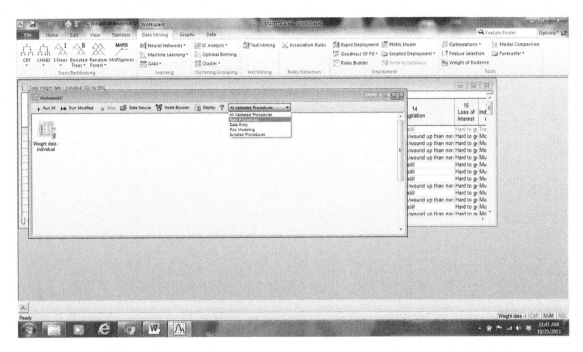

FIGURE F1.67   Select beta procedures.

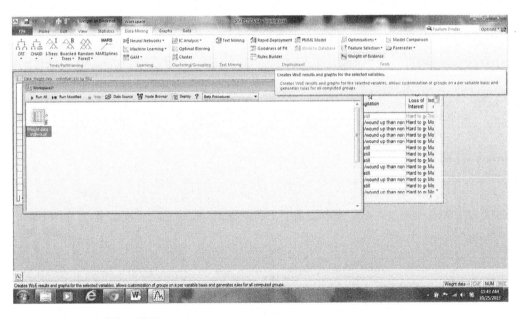

FIGURE F1.68   Highlight data and click on WoE.

FIGURE F1.69 Click to select variables.

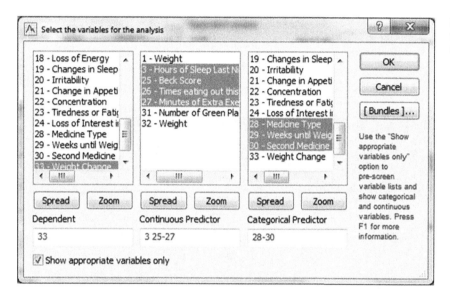

FIGURE F1.70 These variables were used — note Beck Score rather than all the items that comprised the Beck Score.

FIGURE F1.71 Define bad code.

FIGURE F1.72   Define good code.

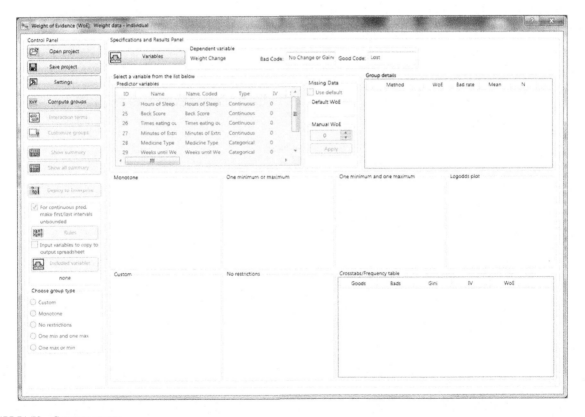

FIGURE F1.73   Compute groups.

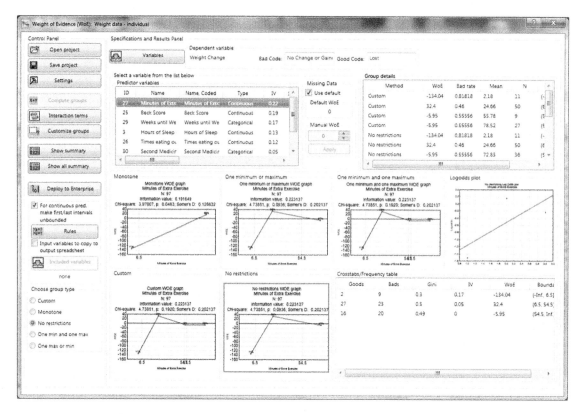

FIGURE F1.74 View output. First item, minutes of extra exercise, is highlighted.

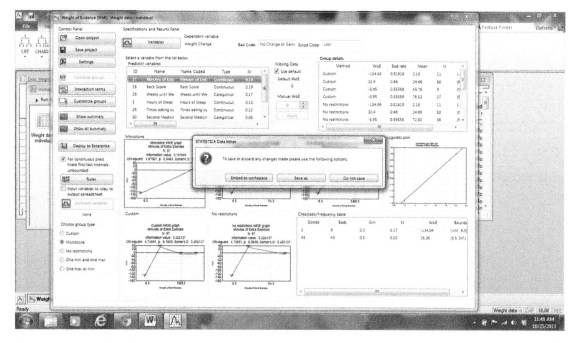

FIGURE F1.75 Close and embed to workspace.

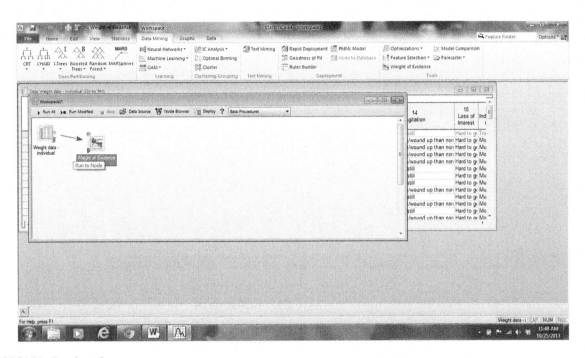

FIGURE F1.76   Run the node.

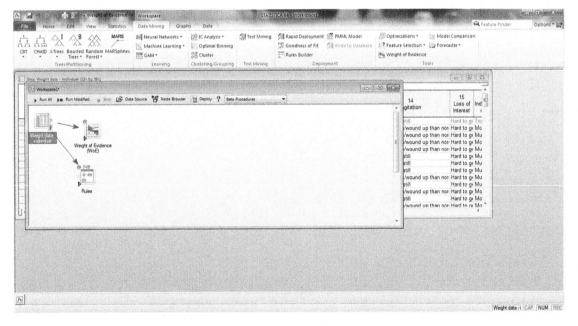

FIGURE F1.77   Note that rules are generated.

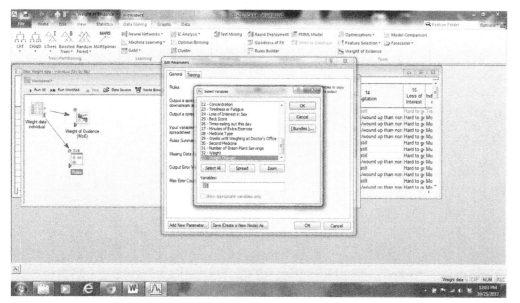

FIGURE F1.78 Double click and edit parameters. Select the target binary variable.

FIGURE F1.79 No need for Output Error Variable. Click to False. All else is the same. OK.

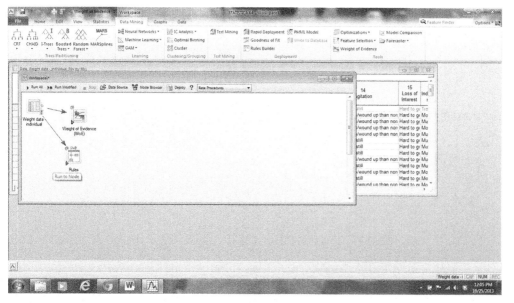

FIGURE F1.80 Run the node.

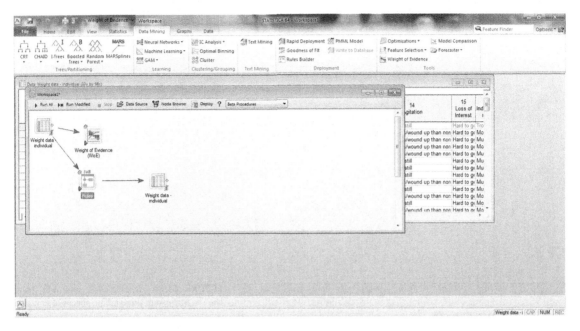

FIGURE F1.81 Note output.

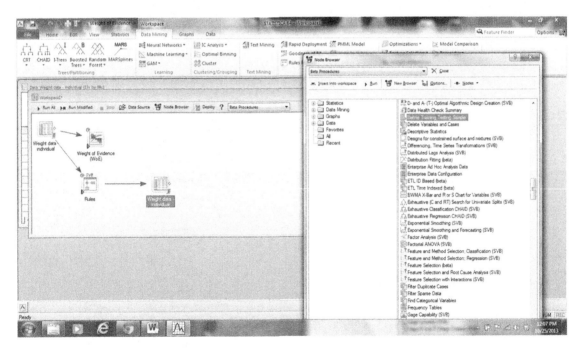

FIGURE F1.82 Define the training and testing samples.

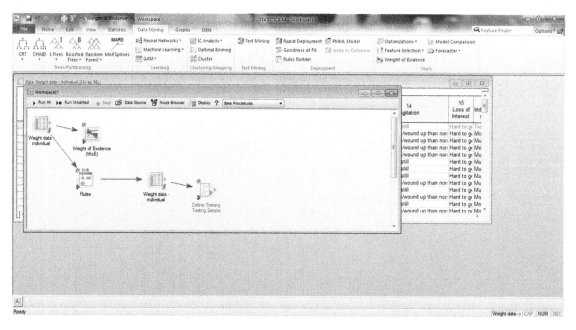

FIGURE F1.83
Node shows.

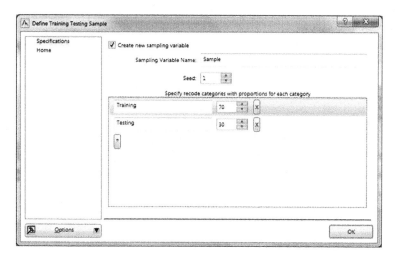

FIGURE F1.84 Double-click and edit parameters as shown. Make sure there are no spaces after Sample.

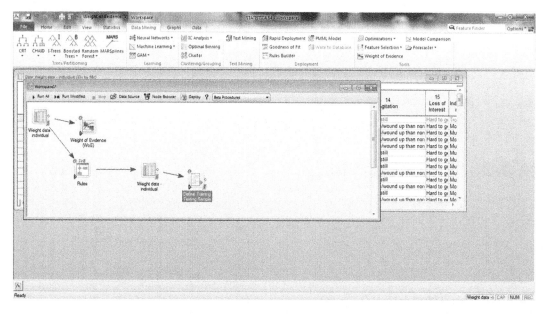

FIGURE F1.85 Run node.

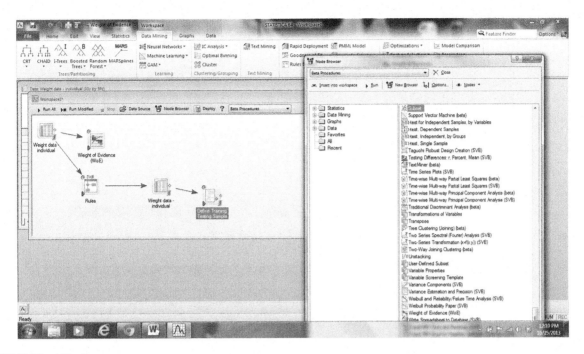

FIGURE F1.86 Add subsets.

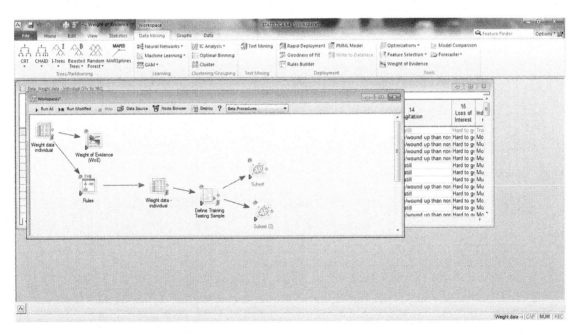

FIGURE F1.87 Notice subsets added to Training and Testing Sample node.

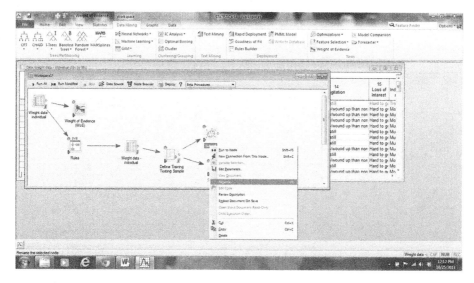

FIGURE F1.88 Rename subsets.

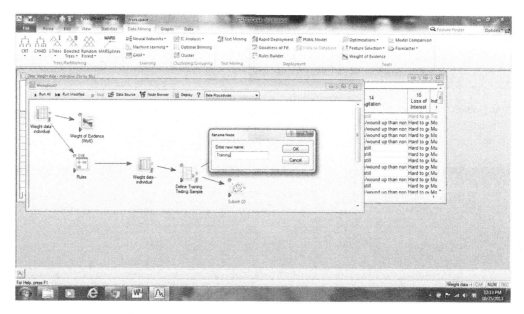

FIGURE F1.89 Rename subsets (Training and Testing).

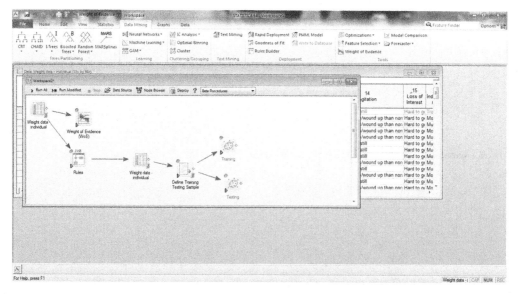

FIGURE F1.90 Note they are named.

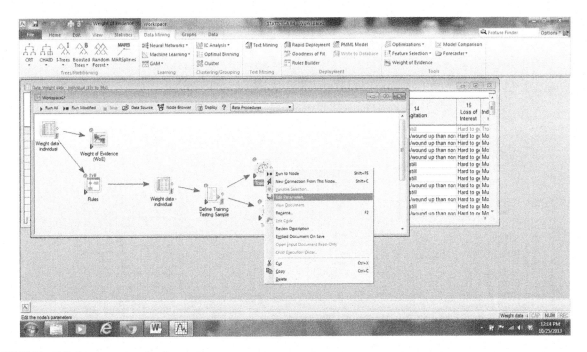

FIGURE F1.91 Edit the parameters of each.

FIGURE F1.92 Define Sample = "Training" so that the subset will be the training cases.

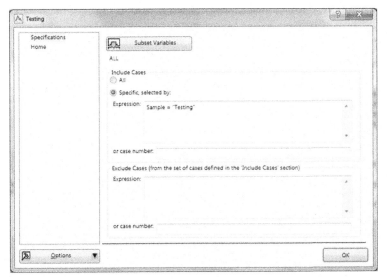

FIGURE F1.93 Define Sample = "Testing" so that the subset will comprise the testing cases.

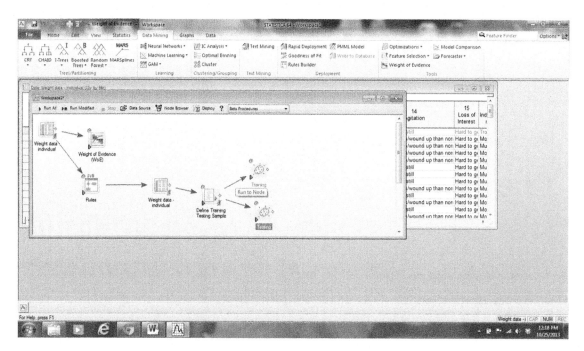

FIGURE F1.94   Run the nodes.

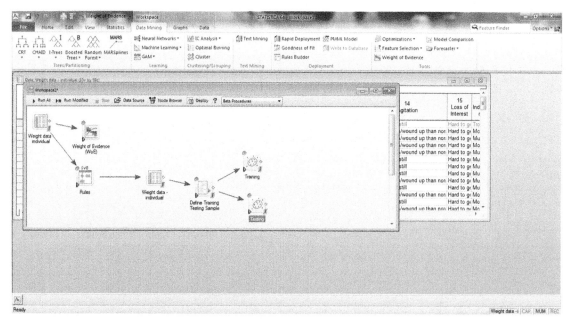

FIGURE F1.95   Note they look a bit different now.

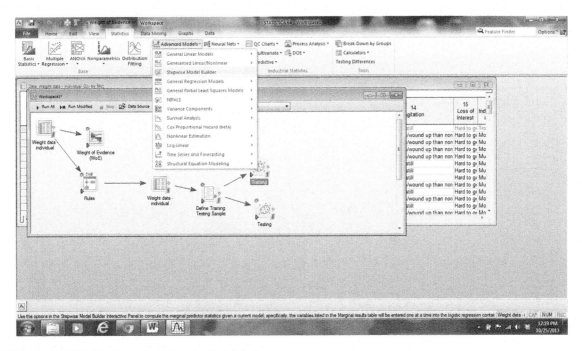

FIGURE F1.96   Highlight Training and add Stepwise Model Builder.

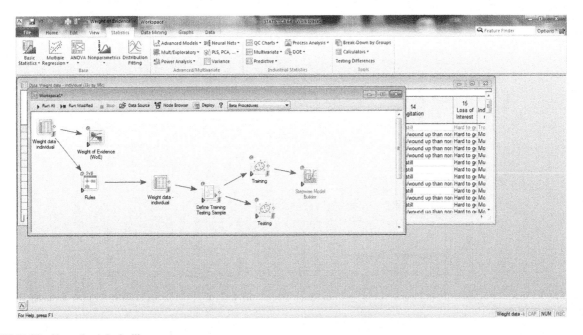

FIGURE F1.97   Note what it looks like.

FIGURE F1.98   Double click and edit the parameters.

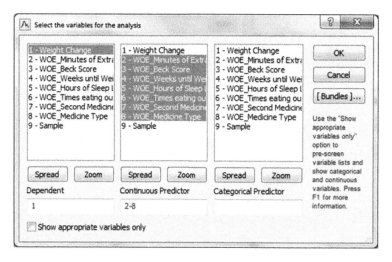

FIGURE F1.99   Select the variables as in Figure. Note we are now using only the Beck scores. Unclick the Show appropriate variables only, so that they will show in the proper column.

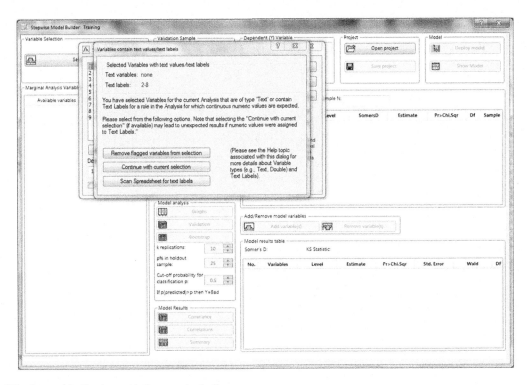

FIGURE F1.100   Ignore this. Continue with the current selection.

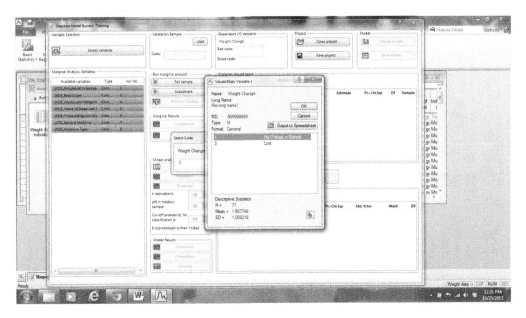

FIGURE F1.101   Define good and bad codes.

FIGURE F1.102 Run full sample.

FIGURE F1.103 Note the red outputs to add to the model.

FIGURE F1.104 The addition changes the ones left.

FIGURE F1.105 The addition of all of the variables still did not result in a better system.

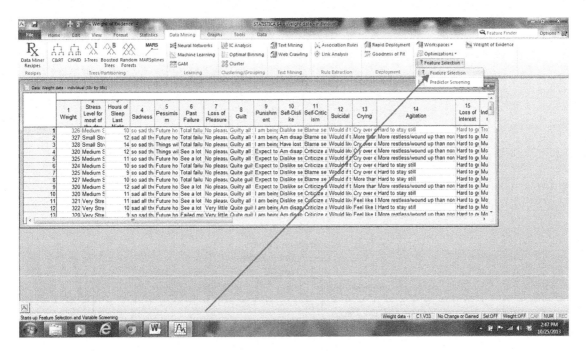

FIGURE F1.106 Select feature selection.

FIGURE F1.107 Select variables.

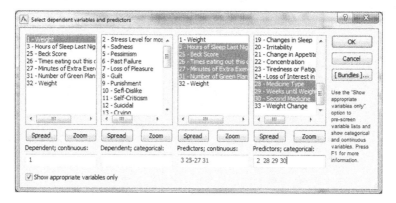

FIGURE F1.108   Variables selected.

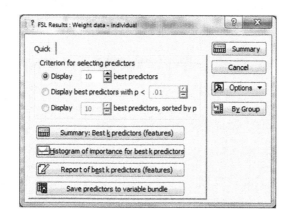

FIGURE F1.109   Click on the histogram.

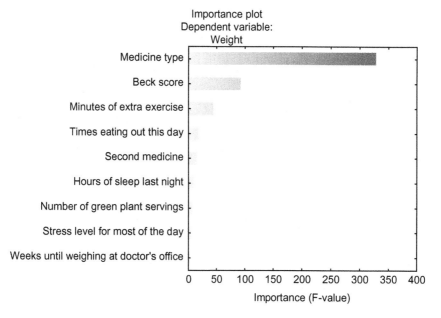

FIGURE F1.110   Importance Plot.

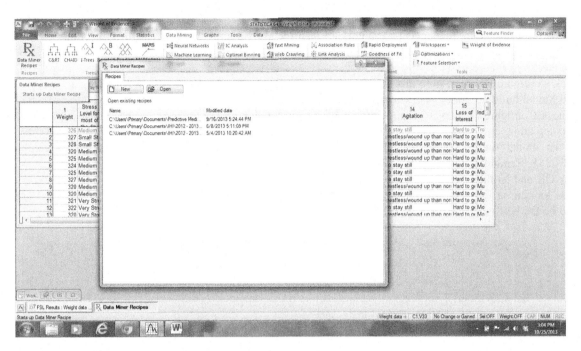

FIGURE F1.111   Click on "Data Miner Recipes" and then on "New."

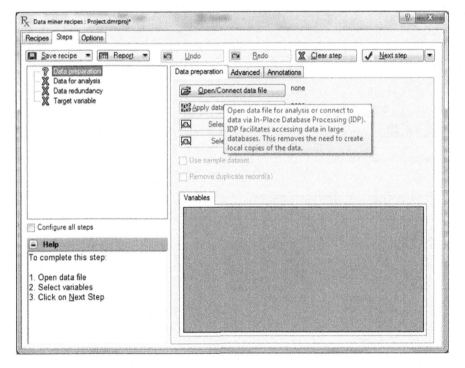

FIGURE F1.112   Click on the Open/Connect data file.

Select the data file and click OK (see Figure F1.113).

Make Weight the target (dependent variable) and then the six variables from the feature selection (variables 3, 25, 26, 27, 28, and 30) as in Figure F1.114. Then click OK.

Note the Xs in Figure F1.115.

Check Configure all steps; note that the Xs turn blue. In Figure F1.116, I have clicked on Target Variable, Weight, and then Model building. I then also selected Random forest and SVM.

Uncheck Configure all steps to change the Xs back to red. Click on the down arrow beside Next step and click on Run to completion, as in Figure F1.117.

Let the model run to completion and then look at the error rates on the various models. Note that, as in Figure F1.118, Random forest would not run.

Click OK and let the rest run.

When looking at the results in Figure F1.119, from this preliminary analysis, things look pretty good and C&RT seems to be the best model.

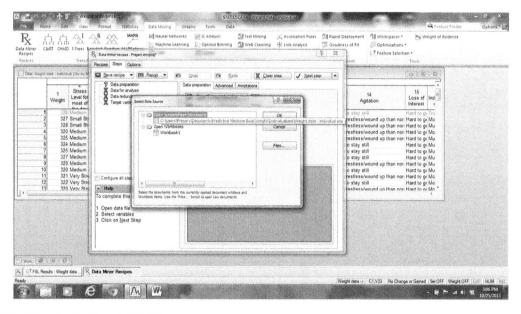

FIGURE F1.113 Select the data file and click OK.

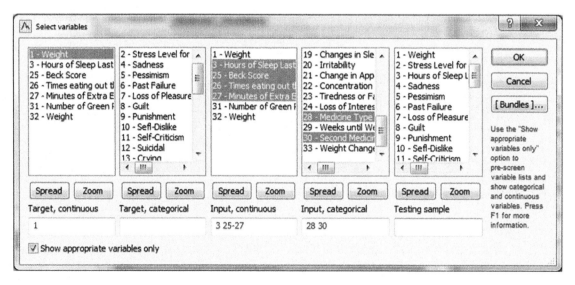

FIGURE F1.114 Select variables: Make Weight the target and use the six variables from the feature selection.

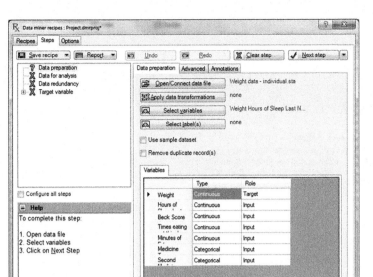

FIGURE F1.115 Note the red Xs.

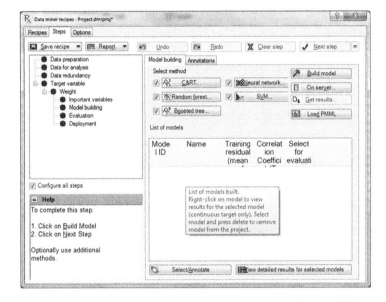

FIGURE F1.116 Check Configure all steps; note that the Xs turn blue. Also select Random Forest and SVM.

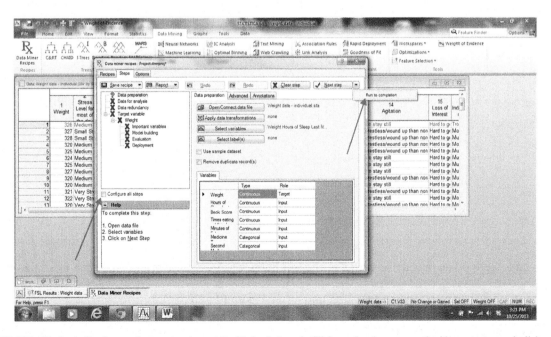

FIGURE F1.117 Uncheck Configure all steps to change the Xs back to red. Click on the down arrow beside next step and click on Run to completion.

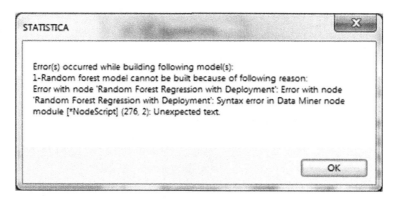

FIGURE F1.118 Don't panic. Random Forest would not run. Click OK and let the rest run.

Model selected for deployment		1		2	3	4
Model Evaluation Summary		ID		Name	Residual (mean square of residuals)	Correlation coefficient
		1		C&RT	8.98	0.98
		5		Neural network	10.35	0.97
		4		SVM	63.17	0.96
		3		Boosted trees	18.9	0.95
Table		Step options				
		Date and time		10/25/2013 3:22:42 PM		

FIGURE F1.119 C & RT seems to be the best model.

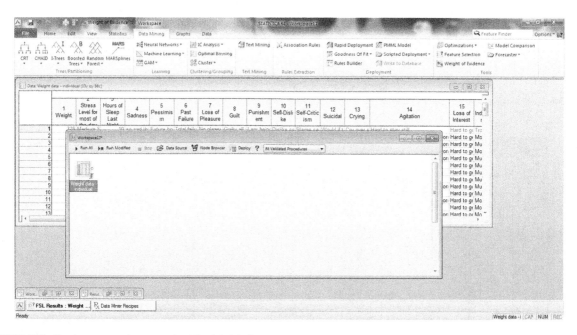

FIGURE F1.120 Create a new workspace, and put the data into it.

At this time, we'll do an interactive C&RT to see if it holds when we use a v-fold procedure in a more interactive module.

First create a new workspace, and put the data into it (see Figure F1.120).

Double click on the data to reveal Figure F1.121. Click to select the variables.

Select the variables as in Figure F1.122.

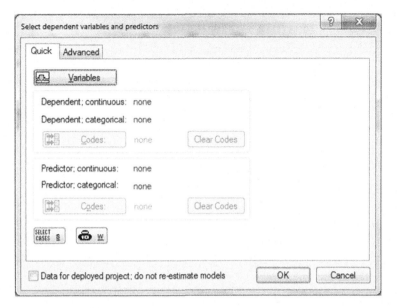

FIGURE F1.121   Double click on the data to reveal this. Click on variable to select.

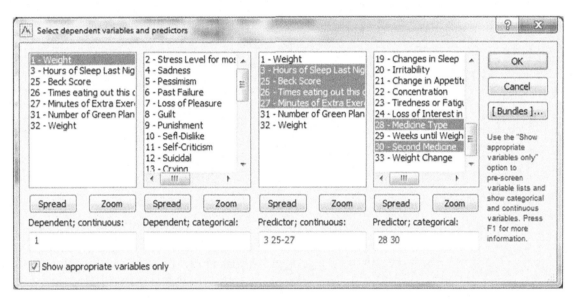

FIGURE F1.122   Select variables.

Click OK and OK again. With the data highlighted go to the node browser, find Data Mining, C&RT, and, finally, Standard Regression Trees (Figure F1.123).

Double click and enter the node into the workspace, which then connects to the data (Figure F1.124).

Double click on the C&RT node and edit the parameters. In Figure F1.125, select All results. Change the default to the desired n per node. For the size of the data set, I decided to set to 4 instead of 5 to see if the resulting tree graph will have several levels.

Under V-Fold Crossvalidation, click true, as in Figure F1.126.

Click OK when finished and go back to the node. Run the node and see the resulting tree graph (Figure F1.127) by clicking on it in the reporting documents.

Figure F1.128 shows the tree graph more closely.

In examining the importance plot in the C&RT, we see a similar pattern in Figure F1.129, with Beck score, Minutes of extra exercise, and Medicine type being very important for predicting weight.

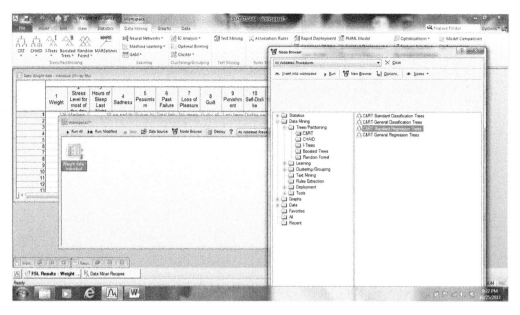

FIGURE F1.123   With the data highlighted go to the node browser, p0565 find Data Mining, C&RT, and, finally, Standard Regression Trees.

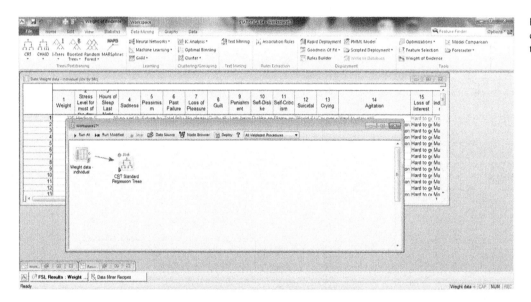

FIGURE F1.124 Double click and enter the node into the workspace.

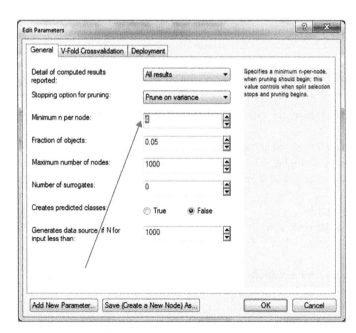

FIGURE F1.125 Double click on the C&RT node and edit the parameters. change desired n per node to 4.

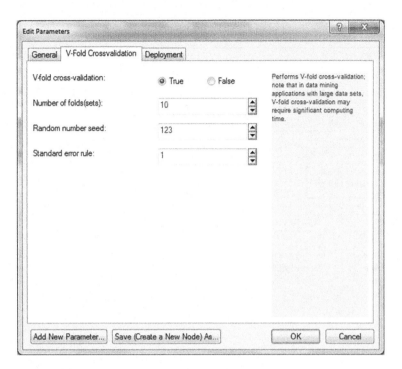

FIGURE F1.126   Under V-Fold Crossvalidation, click true.

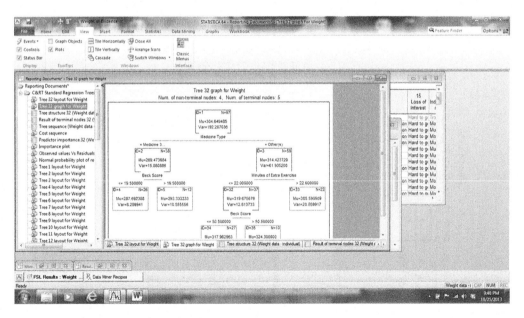

FIGURE F1.127   Resulting tree graph after running the node.

Examine Figure F1.127 to see that Medicine 3 was associated with lower weight. Further, if the Beck score was lower than 19.5, there was an association with lower weight. If the other medication was taken then exercise became important, with the break coming at 22 minutes. Finally, if the patient were to exercise for less than 22 minutes, her score on the Beck should be under 50 to be associated with the lower of the two weight means.

For this patient it appeared that weight would be lost if Medication 3 were given, and if depression were to be kept at a fairly low level. It is possible that the medication reduced depression, which caused the person to be more satisfied and thus not eat as much. It might be that the medication caused weight loss, which then caused depression to subside.

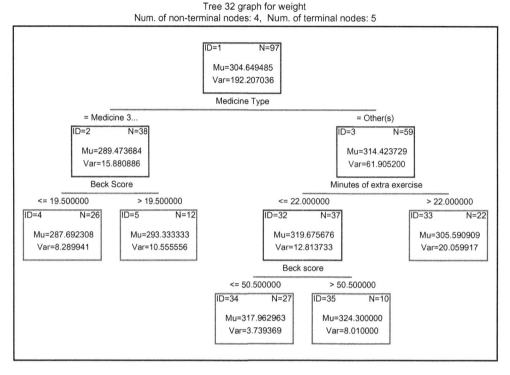

FIGURE F1.128   A closer look.

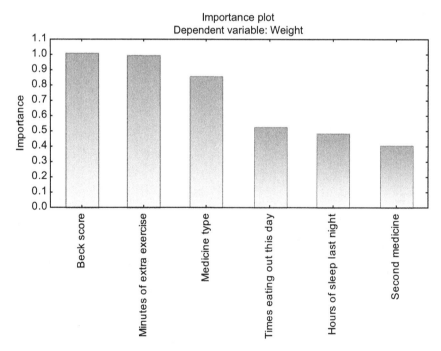

FIGURE F1.129   Importance Plot.

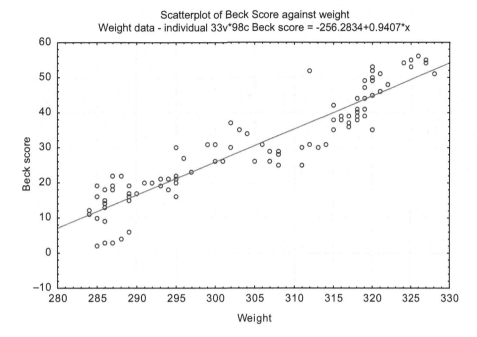

FIGURE F1.130 Positive correlation.

The correlation between weight and depression was positive and strong (Figure F1.130). However, we cannot assume causation with correlational findings.

Based on this analysis, it is likely that Medication 3 would be more helpful to this individual than Medication 1 (Medication 1 being the conclusion of the group data). For this individual, depression was associated with weight gain. Perhaps Medication 1 had an antidepressant effect.

Because the actual weight variable in the C&RT resulted in good predictive value, it seems clear that generating a dependent binary variable from an interval variable failed these data. Too much information was lost, the "hunch" binning procedure was not a good one, and the data were not plentiful enough to make good use of WoE. A natural binary variable such as in Tutorial J1 (Disseminated Intravascular Coagulation), in which the outcome was known to be either death or life, would be preferable.

The next tutorial, Tutorial F2, will demonstrate a method of binning the weight variable so that the binning might more accurately reflect the actual continuous variable. That new binned variable will be used in a WoE with several analyses attached to it, so the reader can get a better understanding of how the program can work.

REFERENCES

Adamovich, S.V., Merians, A.S., Boian, R., Lewis, J.A., Tremaine, M., Burdea, G.S., et al., 2005. A virtual reality-based exercise system for hand rehabilitation post-stroke. Presence: Teleoperators Virtual Environments. 14 (2), 161−174.

Boian, R., Sharma, A., Han, C., Merians, A.S., Burdea, G.,Adamovich, S., et al. 2002. Virtual reality-based post stroke rehabilitation. Proceedings of MMVR 2002 Conference, 64−70.

Cohen, J.L., 1980. Bayesianism versus Baconianism in the evaluation of medical diagnoses. Br. J. Philos. Sci. 31 (1), 45−62.

De Dombal, F.T., Leaper, D.J., Horrocks, J.C., Staniland, J.R., McCann., A.P., 1974. Human and computer-aided diagnosis of abdominal pain: Further report with emphasis on performance of clinicians. Br. Med. J. 1 (5904), 376−380.

Ko, G.T., Wing-Yee, S., Tong, P.C., Le Coguiec, F., Kerr, D., Lyubomirsky, G., et al., 2010. From design to implementation − The Joint Asia Diabetes Evaluation (JADE) Program: A descriptive report of an electronic web-based diabetes management program. BMC Med. Inf. Decis. Making. 10 (1), 26−35.

Langenbruch, A.K., Schäfer, I.I., Franzke, N.N., Augustin, M.M., 2010. Internet-supported gathering of treatment data and patient benefits in psoriasis. J. Eur. Acad. Dermatol. Venereol. 24 (5), 541−547.

Weed, D.L., 2005. Weight of evidence: a review of concept and methods. Risk Anal. 25 (6), 1545−1557.

Weiner, S.J., Schwartz, A., Weaver, F., Goldberg, J., Yudkowsky, R., Sharma, G., et al., 2010. Contextual errors and failures in individualizing patient care. Ann. Intern. Med. 153 (2), 69−75.

Tutorial F2

Obesity – Individual: Automatic Binning of Continuous Variables and WoE to Produce a Better Model Than the "Hand Binned" Stepwise Regression Model of Tutorial F1

Linda A. Winters-Miner, PhD

Chapter Outline

INTRODUCTION

This tutorial is a continuation of the individual weight data from Tutorial F1. This tutorial demonstrates the binning of a continuous variable, Weight, so that the variable can be better used in a WoE plus analysis. In addition, this tutorial demonstrates how to complete additional analyses and compare them in a lift chart. This tutorial assumes the reader has worked through tutorial F1.

THE EXERCISE

First open the data Weight data – Individual.sta. In the previous study, during the C&RT analysis we noted that medication was a good predictor of weight loss. Figure F2.1 shows the relationship in a mean with error plot.

 Obviously the person's weight was smaller when taking Medicine 3.

 It seems reasonable to bin the weight by the medication type, and that is what was done here.

 As before, open a new workspace as in Figure F2.2.

 Click on Workspace to achieve Figure F2.3 and then click on All Validated Procedures. Click OK.

 Connect your data as in Figure F2.4.

 Pull that data node over a bit so it's easy to work around (see Figure F2.5).

 Again click on All Validated Procedures and then on Beta Procedures, which has the newest procedures.

 Double click on the data to select the variables. Unclick the box that says Show appropriate variables only. Figure F2.6 shows the variable selection.

 Note, we are selecting Weight as the categorical predictor as though it was a categorical variable. Click OK.

 Click on Data Mining, and Optimal Binning to add to the workspace.

 Double click on the Optimal Binning node to edit the parameters. Figure F2.7 shows the default parameters.

Practical Predictive Analytics and Decisioning Systems for Medicine. DOI: http://dx.doi.org/10.1016/B978-0-12-411643-6.00022-3

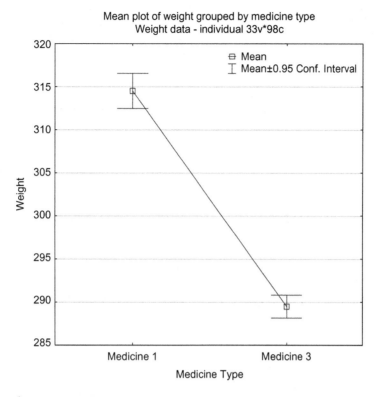

FIGURE F2.1 Mean with error plot.

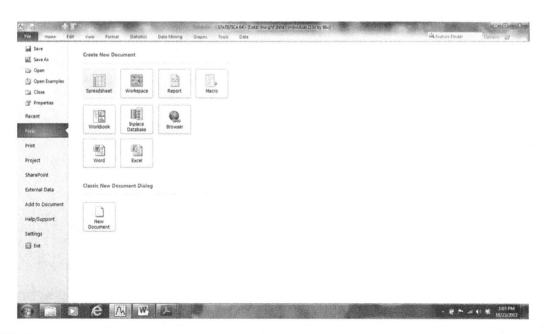

FIGURE F2.2 Open a new workspace.

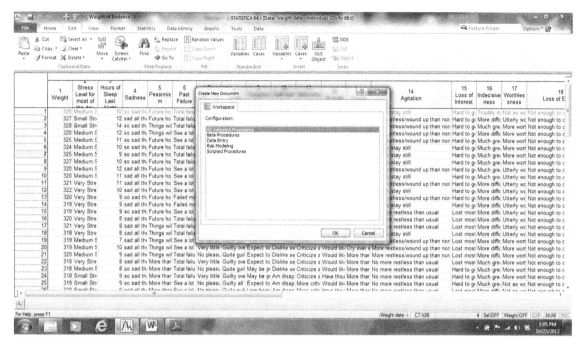

FIGURE F2.3   Click on All Validated Procedures. Click OK.

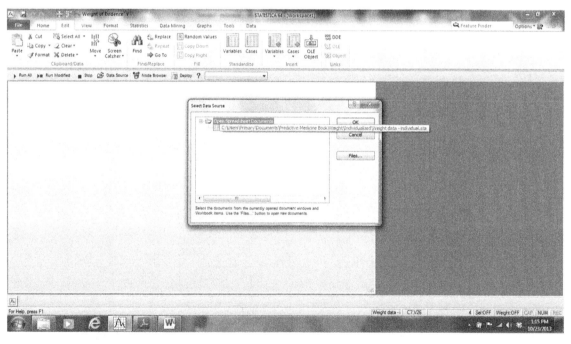

FIGURE F2.4   Connect the data.

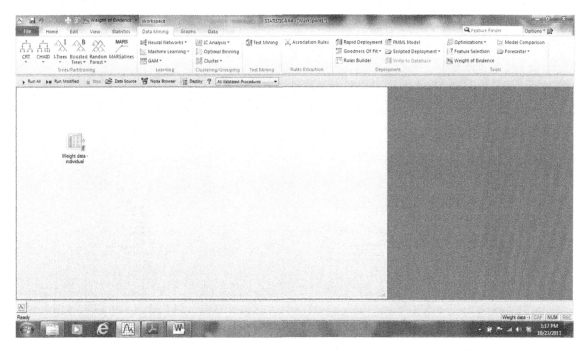

FIGURE F2.5   Pull that data node over a bit to provide more room.

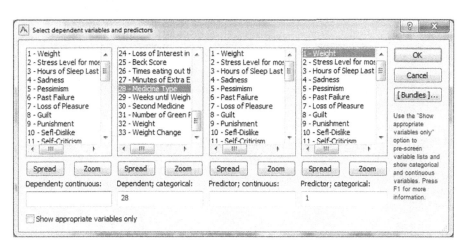

FIGURE F2.6 Select the variables. Uncheck the show appropriate variables so we can select weight as a categorical variable.

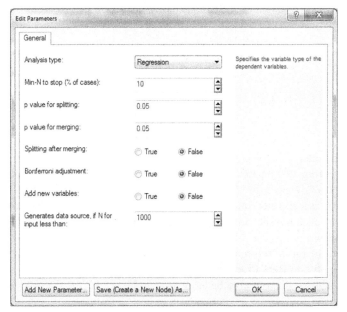

FIGURE F2.7   Double click on Optimal Binning node to edit the parameters. Click OK and run the node.

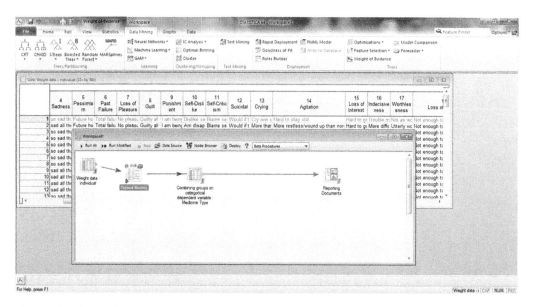

FIGURE F2.8   The running of the node.

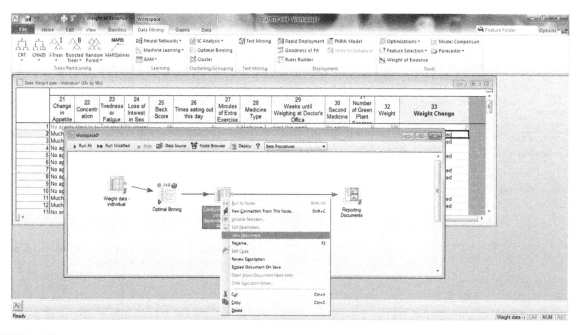

FIGURE F2.9   View the document.

Keep everything the same. Click OK and run the node.

Figure F2.8 shows the completion of the running of the node.

Note the data between the binning node and the reporting documents. View the document by right clicking on it (Figure F2.9).

Figure F2.10 shows that the Weight variable (1) has been transformed into a binary variable based on the medication type. Medicine Type, Variable 28, will no longer be used in analysis. Save the new data set as Weight binned.sta. Use this data set for the next analysis. Open Weight binned.sta.

Close out that workspace. It might be named and saved for future reference. Next, create a new workspace. Add the binned data to it. Click on All Validated Procedures and finally on Beta Procedures. Open WoE as in Figure F2.10.

Double click on the WoE module so that the variables and parameters may be entered as in Figure F2.11.

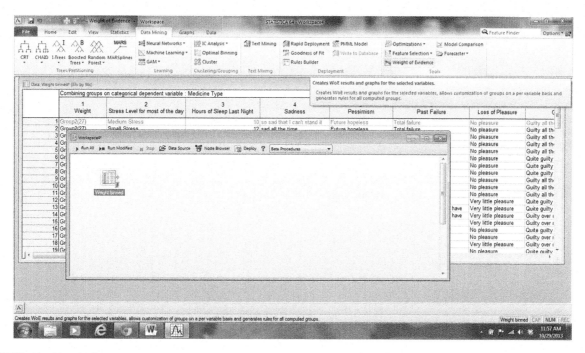

FIGURE F2.10 The Weight variable has been transformed into a binary variable based on the medication type.

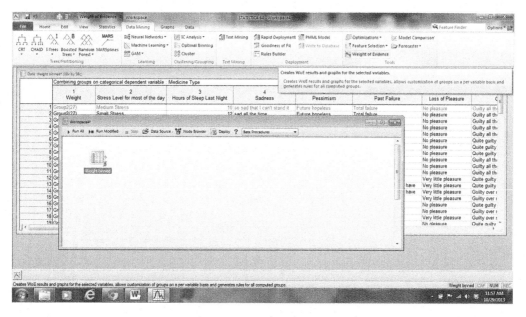

FIGURE F2.11 Double click on the WoE module so that the variables and parameters may be entered.

This time, I would like to see if any of the individual Beck items might be significant predictors in the regression model. First, the variables need to be transformed into continuous variables, so we use the WoE node in this way. Figure F2.12 shows the variables of interest.

Set the Good and Bad codes as in Figure F2.13. Because Group 2 is associated with the higher weights, Group 2 is the "bad" code.

Compute groups as in Figure F2.14.

I clicked on Show all summary after the groups computed, as in Figure F2.15.

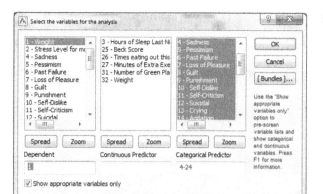

FIGURE F2.12 The variables of interest.

FIGURE F2.13 The variable stats help us to see which is bad and which is good. Set the good and bad codes from this.

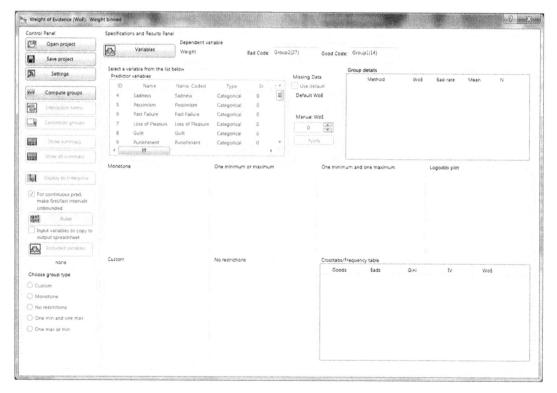

FIGURE F2.14 Compute groups.

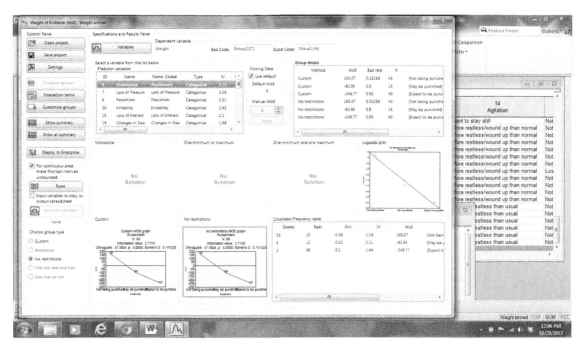

FIGURE F2.15   Show all summary.

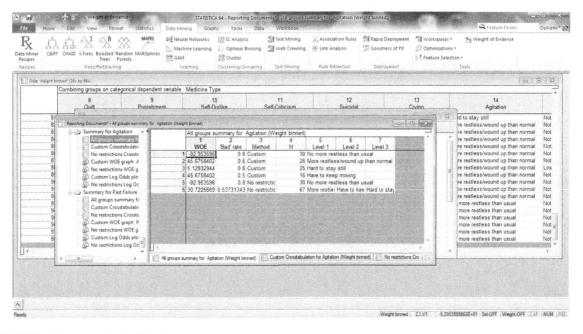

FIGURE F2.16   Close out and embed into the workspace.

Close out and embed into the workspace. Figure F2.16 shows the document for All groups summary for Agitation, the first variable displayed in the reporting documents.

Note the WoE scores. If the relative frequency of goods is less than the relative frequency of bads, the WoE value will be negative; if the relative frequency of goods is greater than the relative frequency of bads, the WoE value will be positive. This process transforms the variables to a common scale so they can be used in subsequent logistic regression analysis.

Close that file and run the WoE node, resulting in Figure F2.17.

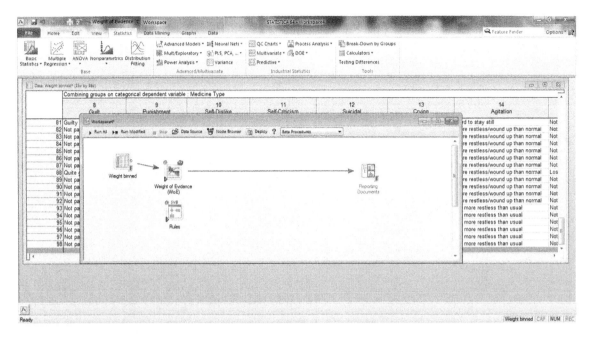

FIGURE F2.17   Run the WoE node.

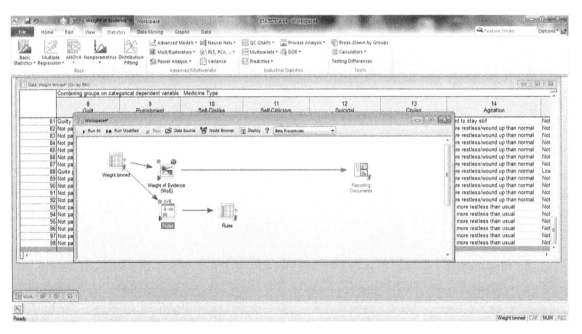

FIGURE F2.18   Connect the data and run the rules node.

Connect the data and run the rules node to achieve Figure F2.18.

Edit the parameters of the rules and add Weight as the dependent variable, as in Figure F2.19.

Run the Rules module to achieve the new data set in Figure F2.20.

If you like you can embed most of the elements of your workspace by right clicking and checking to embed on those items that are not already embedded (see Figure F2.21).

Next, highlight the data and click on Stepwise Model Builder from the Statistics tab (see Figure F2.22).

Double click on the model builder and edit the parameters as seen in Figure F2.23.

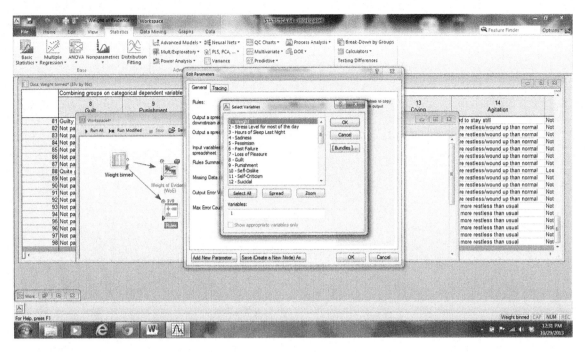

FIGURE F2.19   Edit the parameters of the rules and add Weight as the dependent variable.

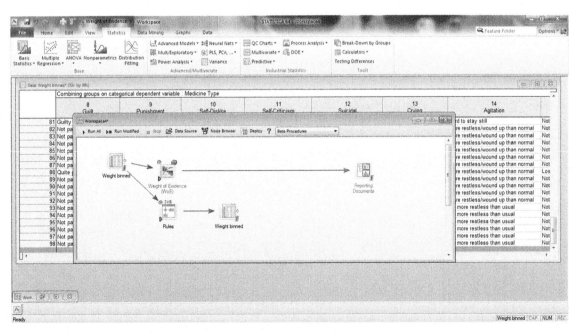

FIGURE F2.20   Run the Rules module.

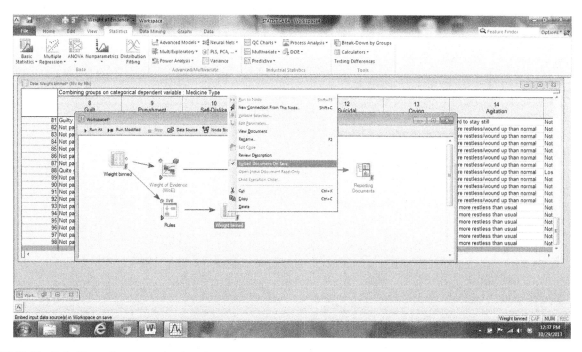

FIGURE F2.21 Embed items that are not already embedded.

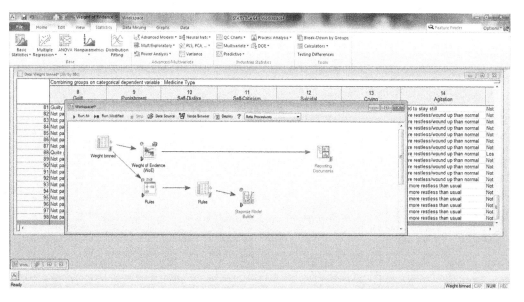

FIGURE F2.22 Highlight the data and click on the Stepwise model builder.

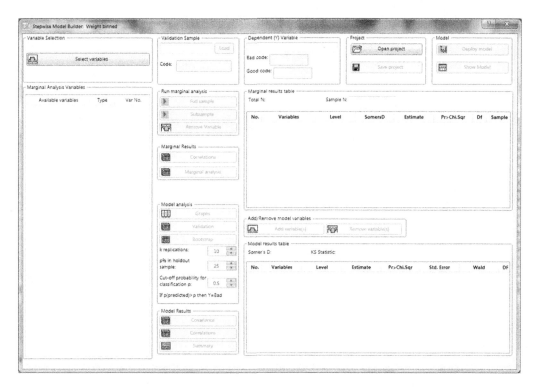

FIGURE F2.23   Double-click on the model builder and edit the parameters.

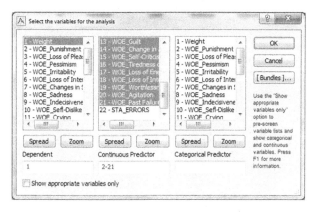

FIGURE F2.24   Start with the variables. Unclick the box that shows appropriate variables only. The items have been transformed and now work like continuous variables.

Start with the variables in Figure F2.24. Unclick the box that shows appropriate variables only. The items have been transformed and now work like continuous variables.

It will tell you that this is wrong, but ignore the warning and continue with the selection.

Next set your Good and Bad codes. In this case, Group 2 is associated with the higher weights and becomes the bad code.

Run the full sample as in Figure F2.25.

Now, we do seem to have some variables that will enter into the regression well (see Figure F2.26).

I decided to add the top six into the model (Figure F2.27).

As in Figure F2.28, I added two more to see what that would do to the model.

The Somer's D has now moved to 1.00 in Figure F2.29.

FIGURE F2.25 Ignore the subsequent warning and continue. Set your Good and Bad codes. Group 2 is set as bad. Run the full sample.

FIGURE F2.26 Now the variables will work.

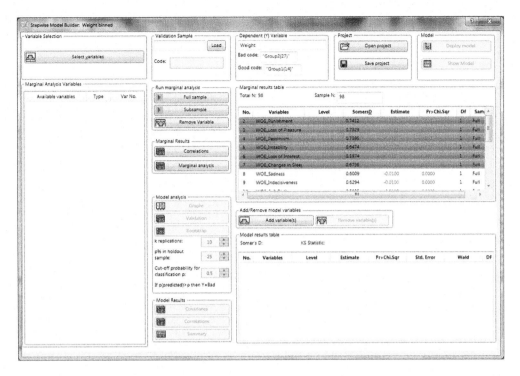

FIGURE F2.27   Here I added the top six into the model.

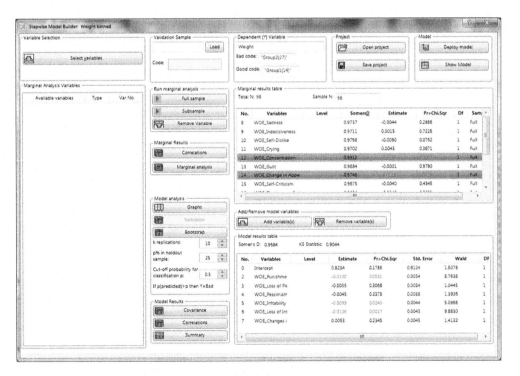

FIGURE F2.28   In this figure, I added two more to see what that would do to the model.

FIGURE F2.29 The Somers' D has now moved to 1.00.

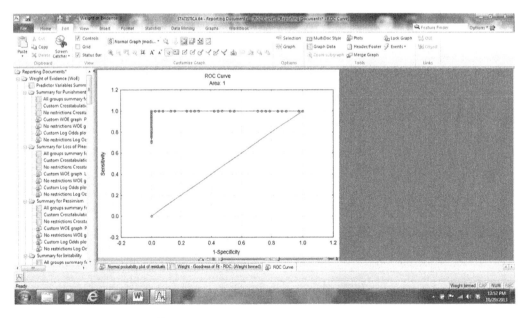

FIGURE F2.30 Lots of output in the workspace!!

I clicked on Summary, Covariance, Graphs, and Display model to see if those will be in the summary documents. Click the X and embed to workspace.

I clicked OK again for the "Warnings" box. Next I ran the stepwise model.

Indeed, I did get lots of output!! See Figure F2.30.

Go to the bottom area to see the summaries. I clicked on the Lift chart and saw Figure F2.31 for the model.

The sensitivity and specificity chart is also interesting (Figure F2.32).

Lift chart - Lift value
cumulative

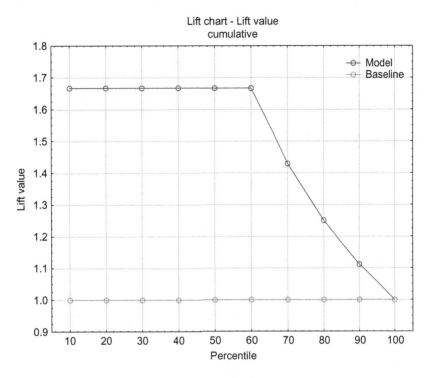

FIGURE F2.31   Lift Chart.

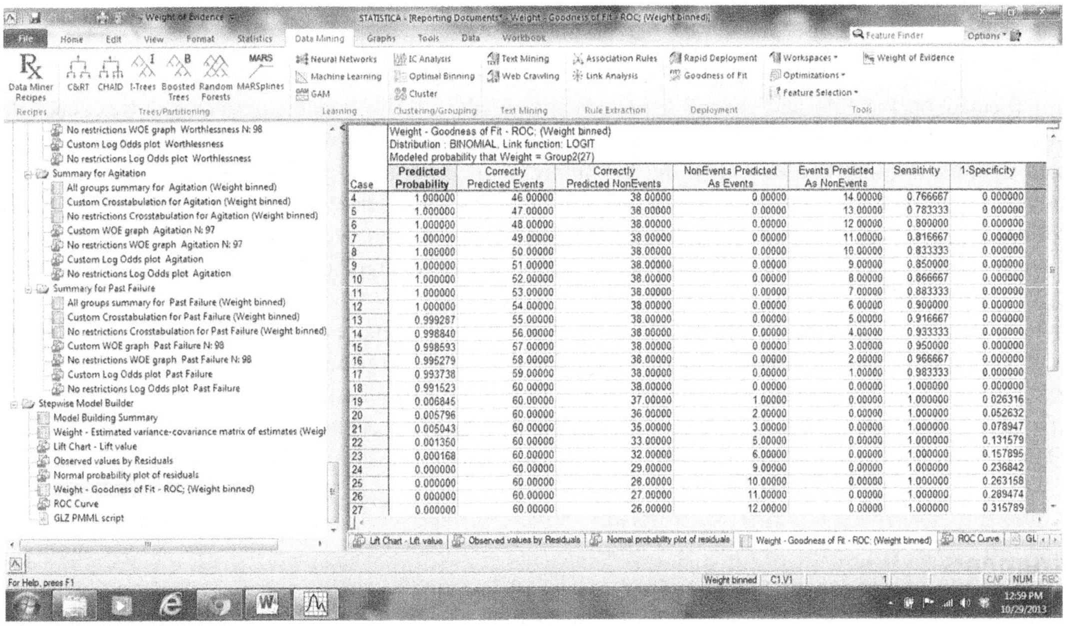

FIGURE F2.32   Sensitivity and Specificity Chart.

Clearly, binning the Weight variable by medication did, in fact, improve the regression model for the individual items in the Beck survey. Note that in Tutorial F1, using a hand-binned variable, the resulting prediction model, stepwise regression, was not a good one. It truly makes a difference if one can find a reasonable way to bin variables.

Resiliency Study for First and Second Year Medical Residents

David P. Armentrout, PhD, Linda A. Winters-Miner, PhD, and Danny W. Stout, PhD

Chapter Outline

INTRODUCTION

Data were collected on the first and second year residents of the In His Image International Residency Program in Tulsa, Oklahoma. Data were collected on three consecutive family medicine residency classes (10 residents per year), and repeated data on the first two classes at the beginning of their second year. The purpose for the data was to see what differences there might be between the first and second years. At the time of this writing we did not have full data for each resident, and would have to wait another year to gather the second year data for this year's first year residents. However, we had enough cases to demonstrate some potentially useful predictive analytics. We ended up with three exercises.

The first exercise used the data from the non-standardized instrument on resilience. The purpose of the first exercise was to see if we could predict first or second year from the components of the resilience instrument. The second exercise attempted to predict the total resources and the total drain scores from two published instruments, the 16PF and the Myers & Briggs (both described below). The third exercise demonstrates decisioning using weight of evidence (WoE), using the TSCS2, the 16PF, and the Myers & Briggs, in predicting the total resilience scores.

The Instruments

The data set (Resident Resiliency) contains four instruments as sources of information, besides the demographic variables for each resident. The first is a non-standardized instrument for resilience (Resilience Survey). The second source is the Tennessee Self-Concept Scale (TSCS2). The third source of data is Catell's 16PF instrument (Catell et al., 1957), which later formed the basis of the Big Five (Fazeli, 2012). Finally, the fourth instrument is the Myers & Briggs Type Indicator (Myers and McCaulley, 1985). The instruments are described below. In addition we gathered demographic information such as age, number of children, and so on.

Practical Predictive Analytics and Decisioning Systems for Medicine. DOI: http://dx.doi.org/10.1016/B978-0-12-411643-6.00023-5

Resilience Survey

A. As there is no standardizing population for this instrument, the scores are absolute, rather than statistical (percentile, standard score, etc.). The higher the score, the more of the sampled variable is present.

B. Survey divisions: the results are divided into two divisions, summative scores and individual resource scores.

C. Summative scores:

1. Total Resource **TotRsr**. The Total Resource score is the sum of all the resource scores, and as such provides an estimate of the overall emotional/spiritual resource available for a person's use when confronted with life stressors.

2. Total Drain **TotDrn**. People not only have positive patterns and behaviors that comprise an individual component of resilience; they also can have co-existing, negative patterns which mitigate the positives that are present. Consequently, each of the nine resource scales has two questions to sample these negative patterns, the sum of which constitutes the Total Drain Score.

3. Total Resilience **TotRsl**. The final summative score is Total Resilience, the combination of available resource and drain for each resilience factor. The higher the score, the more likely the respondent is to be successful in garnering, organizing, and implementing both internal and external resources to meet the demands and challenges of life stressors.

Resource Scores that comprise the Total Resource Scores are:

1. *SFC — Self Care*. The scores on this scale reflect the adequacy of the respondent's self-care. High scores on SFC suggest that the respondent is attuned to his or her physical, spiritual, and emotional needs and takes appropriate steps to take care of them on a consistent basis. People with high scores are also likely to have healthy interpersonal boundaries.

2. *SOC — Social Support*. There are multiple ways that relational connection buffers one from the impact of life stressors. Connection with others offers affirmation, reassurance, and comfort at the emotional level. At a sociological level, connection provides a sense of belonging, and an affirmation of structures and beliefs outside of the individual which contain meaning and values. At an intellectual/behavioral level, such connection provides an information exchange structure through which other's perceptions, information, and resources can be exchanged. High SOC scorers are more likely to have good networks of relationship and, when married, a strong and healthy relationship with their mate.

3. *PRD — Prediction*. Predictability in a person's life offers a platform of stability from which to operate. It affords the opportunity to process in advance, consider options, and incorporate planning, resource gathering, and/or the implementation of other strategies to manage, avoid, or attenuate the stressors they encounter in life. High scorers are most likely to have the ability to bring order into a chaotic situation or environment.

4. *CON — Control*. While PRD focuses on the organization and management of external factors, CON samples the sense of efficacy and or mastery of the individual. Designed to take dominion in his or her own life, control is a very important part of a person's core make-up. High scorers are more likely to have skill sets with which they are both aware and involved. The existence of skill sets and access to them provides support through creating a sense of capability in the presence of stress and environmental chaos.

5. *SPR — Spirituality*. Like social connection, there is a strong literature that consistently demonstrates the stress-buffering effects of a strong personal spirituality as opposed to mere religious activity. While the latter can be beneficial, it is the intimate spirituality or relationship with God, often called intrinsic religion or spirituality, that has been singled out and repeatedly documented for its ability to buffer a person from the negative impact of life stressors. High scores indicate an individual who experiences God as both personally relevant and intimately involved in his or her life.

6. *CHR — Character Elements*. The CHR scale estimates the availability of long-term life patterns that strengthen and simplify the respondent's life. These elements sample what are commonly thought of as virtues, such as integrity, honesty, and the like. The presence of these patterns provides automatic responses that increase resources, and add a buffer to the demands created by stressors, as well as a foundation to rebuild upon when life's assumptions are challenged and/or broken.

7. *PRS — Perspective*. Stressors have the ability to draw in or absorb the individual. The more absorbed into the stressor, the more "in-your-face" it is, the more a person's ability to respond is impaired. When absorbed by a stressor, its threats and demands are experienced more intensely and emergently. It is harder to identify what is

needed, let alone decide the required actions. Emotionality is increased with the loss of perspective, as are choices and appraisal which rely on more intellectual processes. The PRS buffering skills and resource reflect the ability to distance from the stressor sufficiently to garner resources, plan a strategy and implement responses, and provide for respite.

8. *FGV — Forgiveness*. The presence of significant anger, resentment, bitterness, and hatred creates an internal platform full of fissures, making it increasingly difficult to address stressors encountered. The larger, deeper, and more numerous the cracks are, the more the foundation from which the person lives is compromised. Active, ongoing, intentional forgiving is the primary tool we have for relieving and freeing ourselves from such an impediment. FGV provides an estimate of how much/well the forgiveness process is engaged.

9. *BIO — Biological*. The biological scale is a highly specific form of self-care and thus supplements the SFC scale, providing an estimate of how well respondents monitor and attend to their physiological needs. The physiological strength and health of a person is the platform from which he or she copes with the challenges of life, and includes physical health, exercise, balanced nutrition and healthy eating patterns, restoring sleep, and ability to regulate physiological arousal. High scorers are not particularly Olympic athletes; rather, they are likely to have a higher awareness of the importance of monitoring and addressing these needs.

TSCS2

The second source of data was the Tennessee Self-Concept Scale (Fitts, 1965; Bolton, 1979) and comprises the variables that start with TSCS2 (Variables 103 to 117). This scale measures personality characteristics (Bolton, 1979). The scores are:

- *self-concept: physical; moral; personal; family; social; academic/work*
- *supplementary: identity; satisfaction; behavior*
- *validity: inconsistent responding; self-criticism; faking good; response distribution*
- *summary: total self-concept; conflict.*

(NZCER, 2013)

Cattell 16PF Questionnaire

The third component of the data set comprised the personality variables of the Cattell 16PF Questionnaire (Catell *et al.*, 1957; Lebovits and Ostfeld, 1970). The 16PF has been well researched, and recently was used to identify excellence in nursing as predicted from the scale (Li *et al.*, 2013). The table below shows the variables listed in the data set.

118	Warmth (Reserved—Warmth)
119	Reasoning (Concrete—Abstract)
120	Emotional Stability (Reactive—Emotionally stable)
121	Dominance (Deferential—Dominant)
122	Liveliness (Serious—Lively)
123	Rule-Consciousness (Expedient—Rule conscious)
124	Social Boldness (Shy—Socially bold)
125	Sensitivity (Utilitarian—Sensitive)
126	Vigilance (Trusting—Vigilant)
127	Abstractedness (Grounded—Abstracted)
128	Privateness (Forthright—Private)
129	Apprehension (Self-assured—Apprehensive)
130	Openness to Change (Traditional—Open to change)
131	Self-Reliance (Group-oriented—Self-reliant)
132	Perfectionism (Tolerates disorder—Perfectionistic)
133	Tension (Relaxed—Tense)
134	Extraversion (Introverted—Extroverted)
135	Anxiety (Low anxiety—High anxiety)
136	Tough-Mindedness (Receptive—Tough-minded)
137	Independence (Accommodating—Independent)
138	Self-Control (Unrestrained—Self-control)

Myers & Briggs Type Indicator

Finally, the Myers & Briggs Type Indicator (Myers and McCaulley, 1985; McCaulley, 1990) comprises variables 139 to 146. McCaulley (1990) provides this description of the types.

> *The MBTI items are concerned with four bi-polar preferences; items force choices between two equally valuable poles of each preference to determine the relative preference of one over the other. The four preferences are as follows:*
>
> *Extraversion attitude (E) or Introversion attitude (1). In the extraverted attitude (E), persons seek engagement with the environment and give weight to events in the world around them. In the introverted attitude (I), persons seek engagement with their inner world and give weight to concepts and ideas to understand events.*
>
> *Sensing perception (S) or intuitive perception (N). When using sensing perception (S), persons are interested in what is real, immediate, practical, and observable by the senses. When using intuitive perception (N), persons are interested in future possibilities, implicit meanings, and symbolic or theoretical patterns suggested by insight.*
>
> *Thinking judgment (T) or Feeling judgment (F). When using thinking judgment (T), persons rationally decide through a process of logical analysis of causes and effects. When using feeling judgment (F), persons rationally decide by weighing the relative importance or value of competing alternatives.*
>
> *Judgment (J) or Perception (P). When the orientation toward the world uses judgment (J), persons enjoy moving quickly toward decisions and enjoy organizing, planning, and structuring. When the orientation to the world uses perception (P), persons enjoy being curious and open to changes, preferring to keep options open in case something better turns up.*
>
> (McCaulley, 1990, paras 11−15)

EXERCISE G1: PREDICTING YEAR FROM SURVEY QUESTIONS

David P. Armentrout, PhD, and Linda A. Winters-Miner, PhD

For this exercise we are using the traditional view of STATISTICA rather than the ribbon view. We are using STATISTICA version 12.

If we wanted to predict the year of a resident, likely we would simply ask. However, the following allows us an opportunity to see if we can predict year from a non-standardized survey instrument. Such a prediction would allow us to form hypotheses about what changes might occur between the first and second years.

The following variables could be used as predictor variables:

Resource items: 73, 76, 79, 82, 85, 88, 91, 94, 97
Drain scores: 74, 77, 80, 83, 86, 89, 92, 95, 98

Let's look at the Cronbach reliabilities for these.

Pull down statistics, Figure G.1.

Figure G.2 shows that we go to Multivariate Exploratory Techniques and select Reliability/Item Analysis.

We select the variables for each scale. Figure G.3 shows our selection of the positive resiliency items which may be seen in the variable selection box.

Click OK and then note what appears in Figure G.4.

Click the Advanced tab. Under Correlation matrix, select NO as in Figure G.5. Click OK.

Figure G.6 shows that the Cronbach alpha is 0.884. This is fairly good reliability.

Click on the Summary: Item-total statistics as in Figure G.7 to note what the alpha would be if items were removed. We kept the items.

Do the same for the total drain score, as in Figures G.8−G.10.

The drain score has an internal consistency of 0.86. The two scores which make up the total resiliency scores seem to have decent internal reliability.

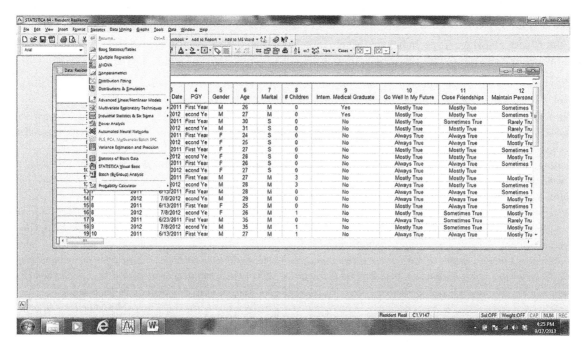

FIGURE G.1 Statistics Tab.

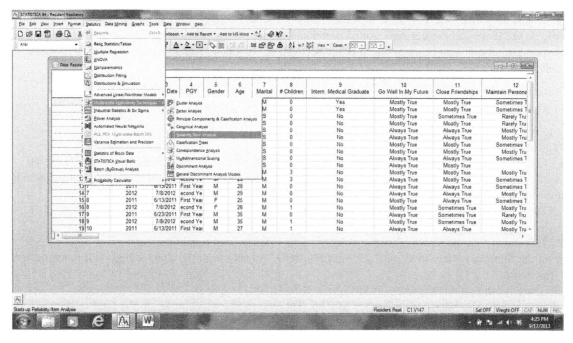

FIGURE G.2 Go to Multivariate Exploratory Techniques and select Reliability/Item analysis.

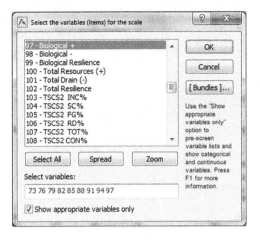

FIGURE G.3 Select Variables for Each Scale.

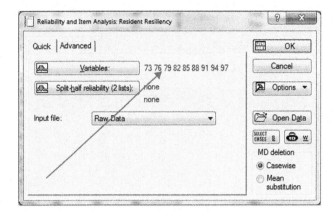

FIGURE G.4 Variables show up in the dialog box for Positive Resilience Items.

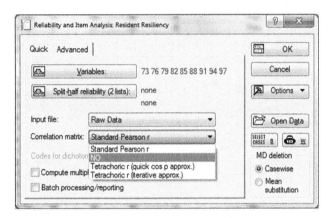

FIGURE G.5 Click the Advanced tab. Under Correlation matrix, select NO. Then click OK.

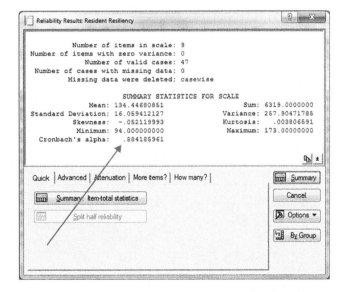

FIGURE G.6 Cronbach alpha.

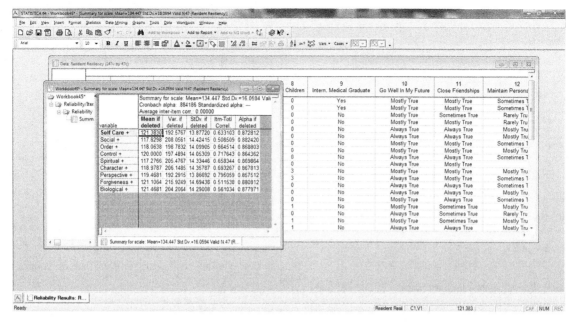

FIGURE G.7 Summary: Item-total statistics.

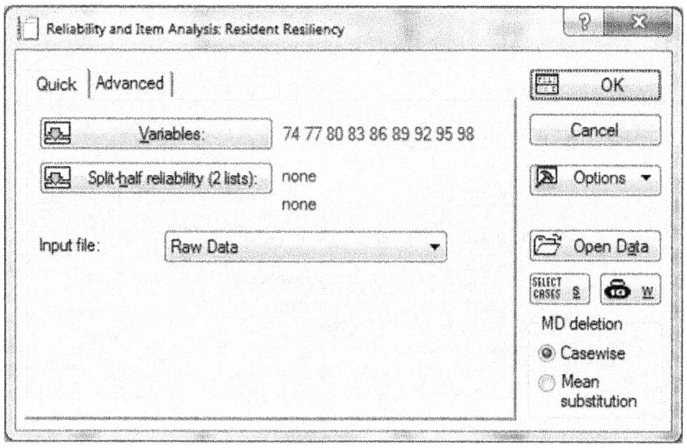

FIGURE G.8 Select variables for Total Drain Score.

FIGURE G.9 Cronbach alpha for Total Drain Score.

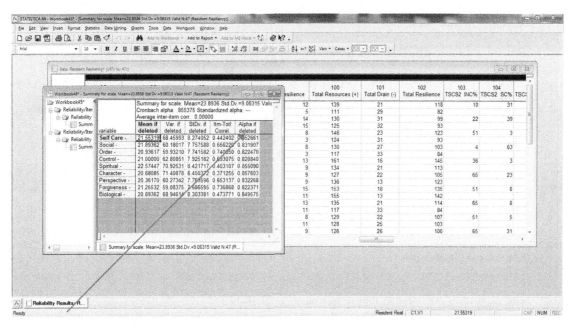

FIGURE G.10 Note affect of deleting variables on the Chronbach.

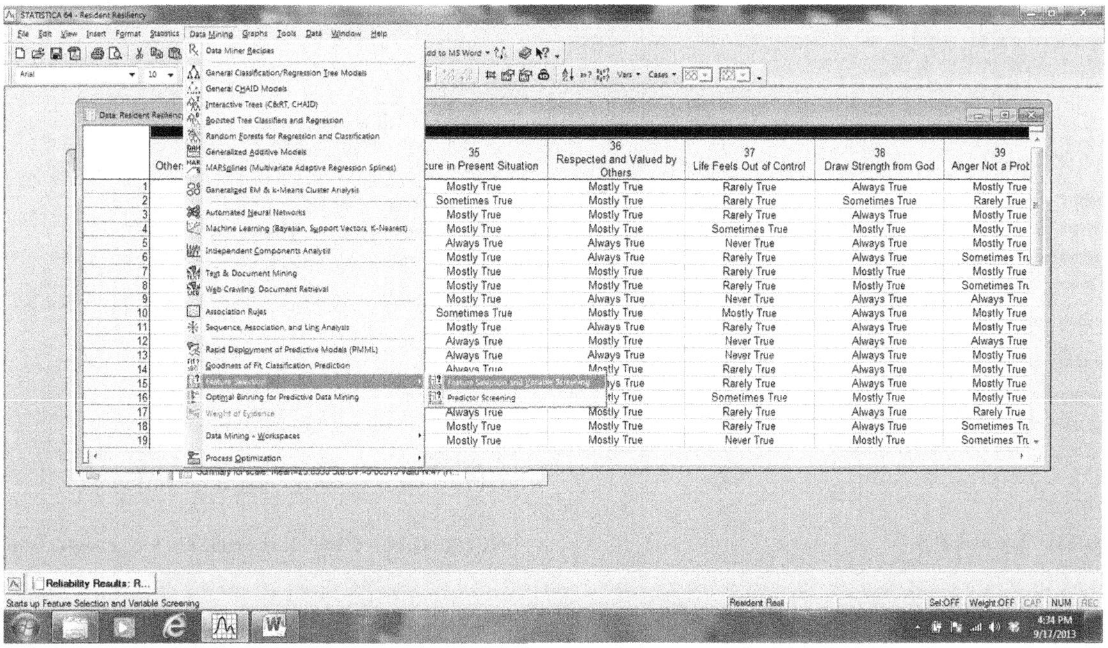

FIGURE G.11 Data mining pull-down menu.

To predict first year or second year, start with a feature selection to see which of the positive and negative items most predict year. Figure G.11 shows the area in the pull-down tab for Data Mining.

Figure G.12 shows how to select the variables. Note, "Show appropriate variables only" is checked at the bottom left. In this way, only those variables that are appropriate for continuous or discrete data are allowed in the selection. Our dependent (target) variable was PGY, or year: year 1 or year 2. In the continuous predictors box, we selected all the positive and negative variables.

After selecting the variables, click OK and Figure G.13 emerges.

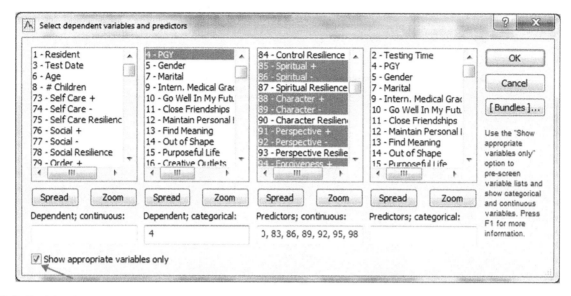

FIGURE G.12   Select the variables. Note the check mark on appropriate variables only.

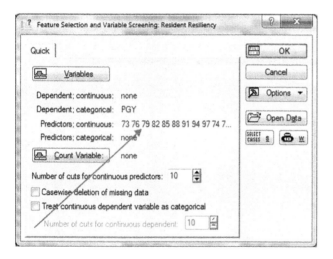

FIGURE G.13   Note variables.

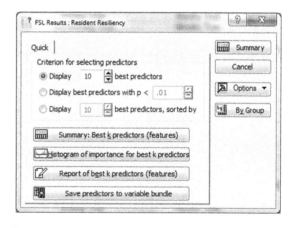

FIGURE G.14   Click OK in Figure G.13 to get result here.

Click OK and Figure G.14 emerges. Note that we can select the top 10 predictors by default, or we can change that number. We left it as the default. We could also select those predictors that had a probability level less than 0.01 or whatever level we wanted. We used the default, which is the Chi-square method. At this point it really makes no difference, as we are exploring and not concerned with performing an hypothesis test.

Click on the "Histogram of importance for best k predictors" tab to reveal Figure G.15.

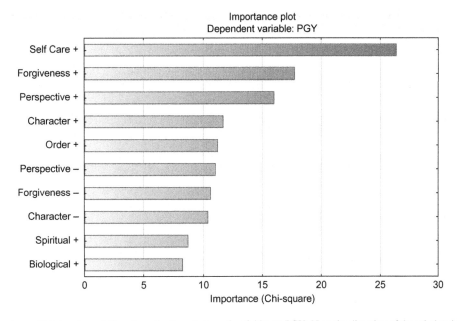

FIGURE G.15 Importance Plot showing relative strength of prediction of variables to PGY: Note the direction of the relationship is not given.

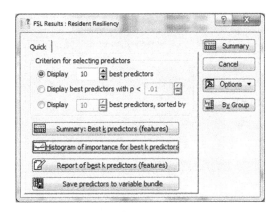

FIGURE G.16 Click on the first tab, Summary: Best k predictors.

Figure G.16 shows us how to look at the probabilities for these variables. Click on the first tab, "Summary: best k predictors."

Note that Figure G.17 shows the Chi-square values and the associated p values.

With the lowest two over 0.05, it seems pointless to go for more variables. We next clicked the "Report of best k predictors" in Figure G.18.

We find that the best continuous predictors by number were 73 94 91 88 79 92 95 89 85 97.

We might like to look for other variables that might separate the two groups, but the TSCS2, the 16PF, and the Myers & Briggs were given only to the first year residents. Items 5 through 9 might be used, however. Let's look at 5−9 in a feature selection. (See Figures G.19−G.22.)

Age seems a natural, since the second years typically would be older.

Let's look at the p values for these items (Figures G.23 and G.24).

None looks promising. It also makes sense (if you had observed this residency program over the years) that many babies are born across the 3 years. So we suspected the number of children might predict year. We might throw that variable into the mix, because the increase in children has not been formally documented, to these authors' knowledge. So we will try the following variables to see if we can accurately predict year, 1 or 2. The variables are 73 94 91 88 79 92 95 89 85 97 and 8 (children).

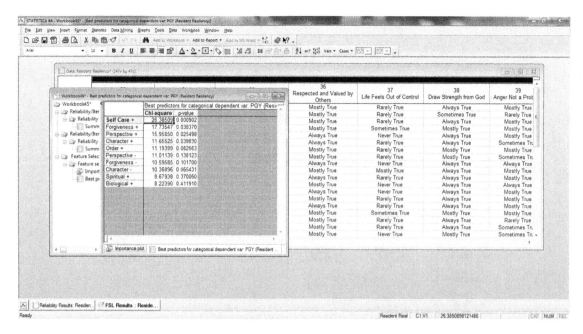

FIGURE G.17 Examining the probabilities.

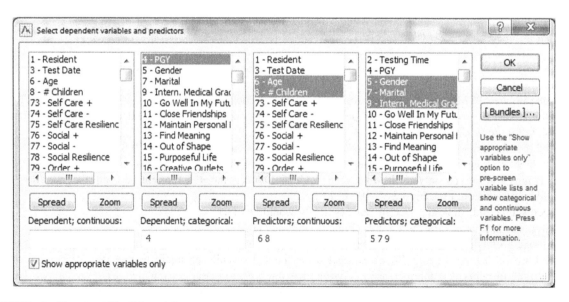

FIGURE G.18 See the items by clicking on Report of best k predictors.

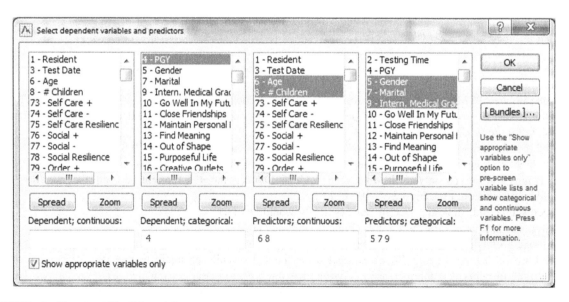

FIGURE G.19 Looking at variables 5 through 9.

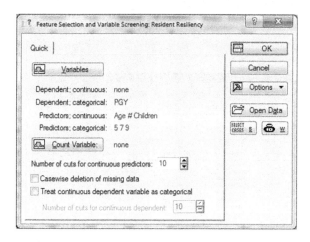

FIGURE G.20 Setting up the feature selection for variables 5–9, predicting PGY

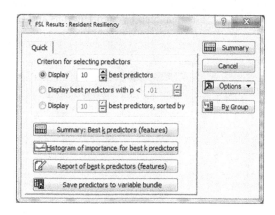

FIGURE G.21 Click on Histogram of importance for best k predictors.

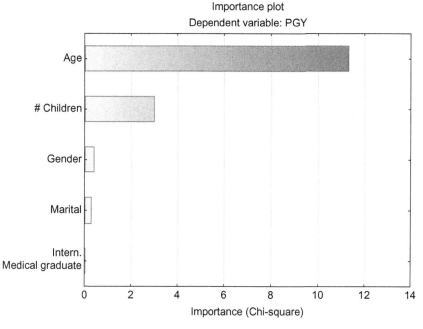

Importance plot
Dependent variable: PGY

FIGURE G.22 Of course age should be related in the importance plot. PGY 3 students tend to be older than PGY1. Note number of children might be slightly predictive.

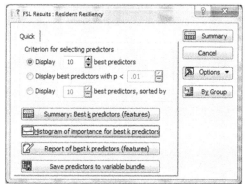

FIGURE G.23 Click summary best k predictors to see the probabilities.

	Best predictors for categorical dependent var	
	Chi-square	**p-value**
Age	11.30962	0.184765
# Children	2.99395	0.223806
Gender	0.40231	0.525900
Marital	0.28912	0.590785
Intern. Medical Graduate	0.03555	0.850456

FIGURE G.24 The result is not particularly good.

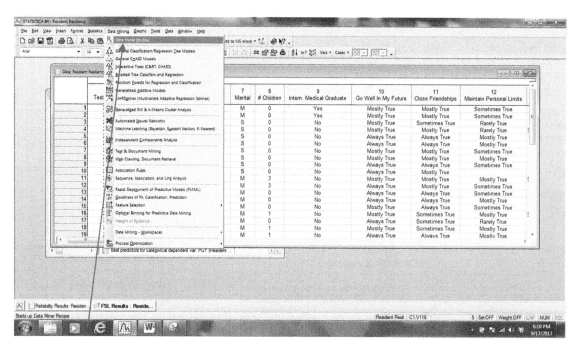

FIGURE G.25 Beginning a data mining project with the best variables.

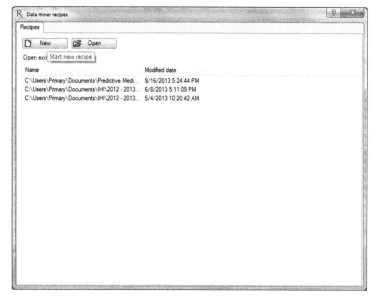

FIGURE G.26 Start new project.

First, open up the Data Miner recipe as in Figure G.25.

Click "Start new recipe" as Figure G.26 demonstrates.

Click the "New" button to show Figure G.27.

From Figure G.27 click on "Open/Connect data file"; Figure G.28 shows the resulting screen in which you will be able to see your file to highlight, and then click OK.

In Figure G.29, click on "Select variables" to reveal Figure G.30.

Figure G.30 allows selection of the appropriate variables. Note that "Show appropriate variables only" is checked. Enter the variables as shown below.

Click OK to reveal Figure G.31.

Check the box that says "Configure all steps." The change is reflected in Figure G.32.

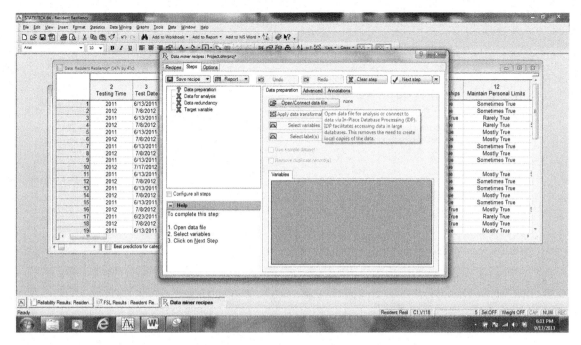

FIGURE G.27 Click new.

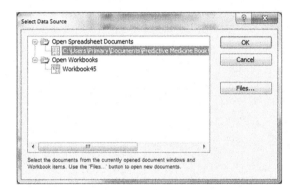

FIGURE G.28 Open/Connect data file.

FIGURE G.29 Select variables.

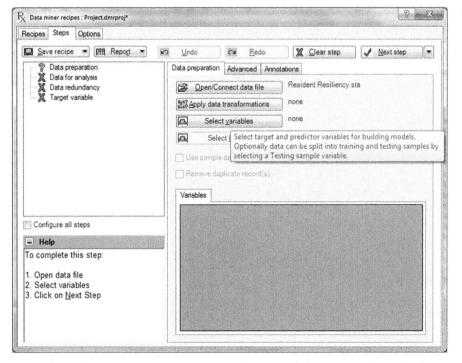

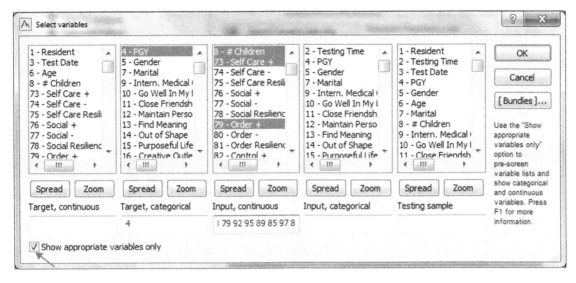

FIGURE G.30 Enter variables. Note that the "Show appropriate variables only" is checked.

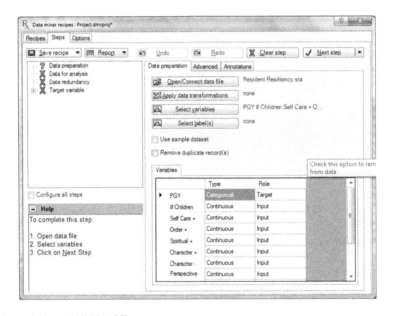

FIGURE G.31 After selecting variables and clicking OK.

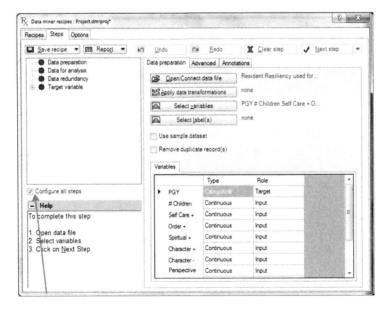

FIGURE G.32 Configure all steps — the red turns blue.

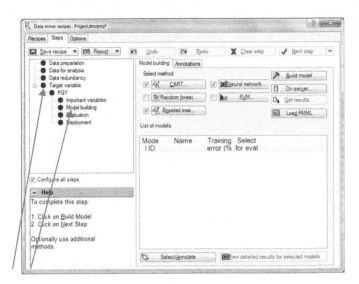

FIGURE G.33 Target Variable was opened and then Model Building. Three models are automatically checked.

FIGURE G.34 Also click on Random forest and SVM.

Note that now we can make changes to the modeling. In Figure G.33 the Target variable was opened, as was PGY. Click on "Model building". Note that three methods of predicting are checked by default: C&RT, Boosted tree, and Neural networks.

We also selected Random forest and SVM in Figure G.34.

Next uncheck "Configure all steps", which will bring back the red Xs. In the upper right, click on the arrow button to the right of "Next step" as in Figure G.35, and click on "Run to completion." Allow the model to run, which can take some time.

Figure G.36 provides the evaluation summary for the models. Note that Neural network has the least amount of error and Random forest has the greatest amount of error in predicting year of resident.

It was interesting that Neural network is the best predictor of year, with only 6.38% error. That means that the method would have correctly predicted about 94% of the time. This would be the model to use if we could not ask a resident his or her year, but could ask the questions on the survey that predicted.

We can examine the lift charts for first years in Figure G.37.

Figure G.38 shows the Lift Chart for second years.

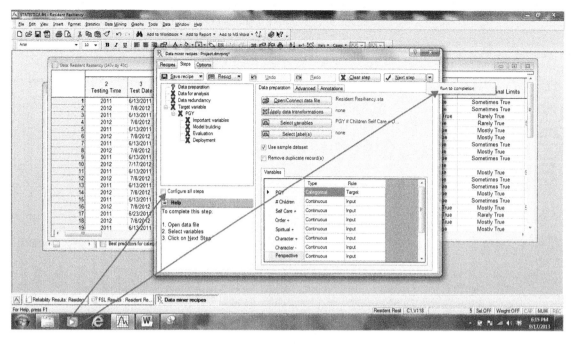

FIGURE G.35 Uncheck configure all steps, turning the Xs to red and click run to completion.

	1	2	3
Model selected for deployment	5		
Model Evaluation Summary	ID	Name	Error rate (%)
	5	Neural network	6.38
	4	SVM	10.64
	3	Boosted trees	27.66
	1	C&RT	29.79
	2	Random forest	34.04
Table	Step options		
	Date and time	9/17/2013 6:21:28 PM	

FIGURE G.36 Evaluation summary for the models

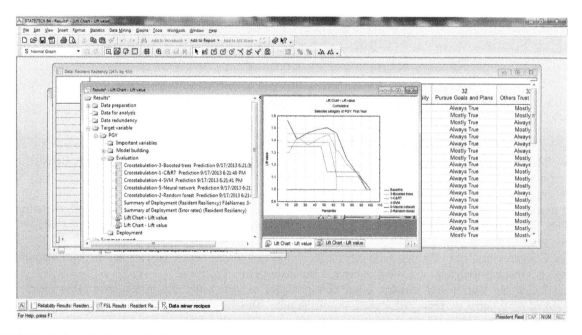

FIGURE G.37 Examine the lift charts for first years.

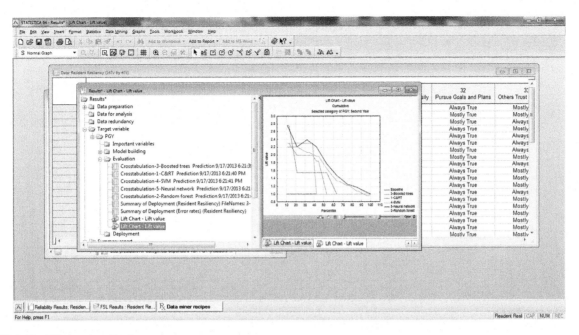

FIGURE G.38 Lift chart for second years.

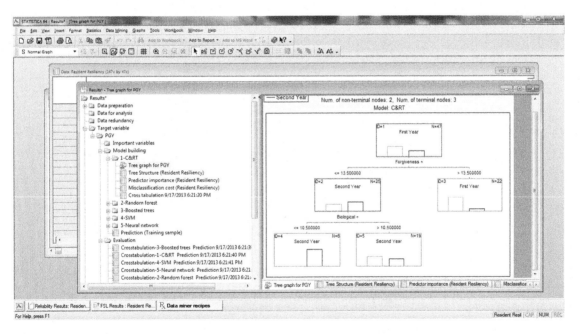

FIGURE G.39 C&RT

C&RT generally gives nice graphics for examining relationships, so we can go there next in Figure G.39, realizing, of course, that this model is wrong about a third of the time.

In that model the variables of forgiveness and biological components were identified as predicting but with about 30% error.

If we wanted to see how the variables we obtained from the first feature selection might predict year, we could have simply used "Mean with error plots" for the variables identified from feature selection. One does not always have to use full prediction algorithms.

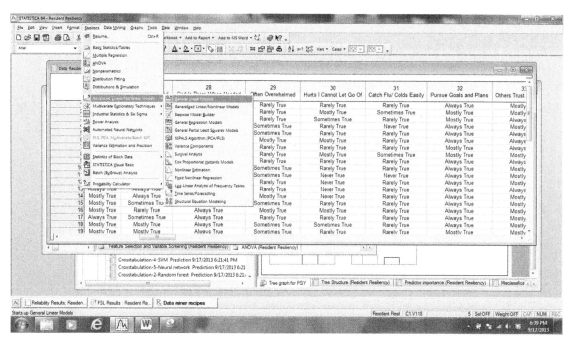

FIGURE G.40 Finding the mean with error plots using General Linear Models.

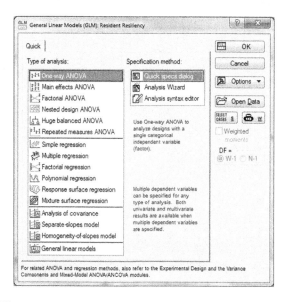

FIGURE G.41 Choose One-Way ANOVA.

Again here are the variables (so you can copy and paste them into the program):

73 94 91 88 79 92 95 89 85 97 8

We'll use them a few at a time so as not to have too much confusion in our graphs.

Figure G.40 shows how to find the mean with error plots using general linear modeling. Go to Statistics, Advanced Linear/Nonlinear Models, over to General Linear Models, and click.

Choose One-way ANOVA, as in Figure G.41.

Next, in Figure G.42 click on Variables to select the ones we want.

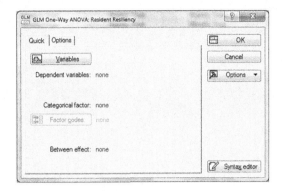

FIGURE G.42 Click on Variables.

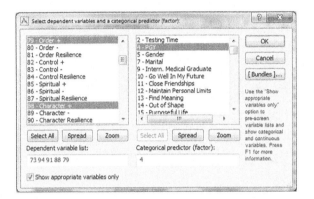

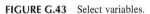

FIGURE G.43 Select variables.

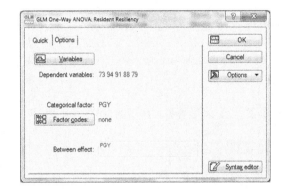

FIGURE G.44 Resulting screen

First we selected the positive resiliency items in the Dependent variables list and the PGY variable in the Categorical predictor box, as in Figure G.43. Note, we are only using the first five variables that showed up in original feature selection.

Figure G.44 shows the resulting screen.

Click OK to reveal Figure G.45.

Click the button that says, "All effects/Graphs." Then, in Figure G.46, click OK.

We highlighted all the variables in Figure G.47 in order to obtain a graph showing all relationships at once.

Figure G.48 displays the resulting graph.

Figure G.49 shows our workspace at this point.

None of these relationships was statistically significant, and in our exploration we are not particularly concerned with significance, but the trend seems evident. Let's check the next five variables, which are the negative items, and finally, number of children.

Back-up by selecting Modify as in Figure G.50.

Figure G.51 shows the screen after clicking "Modify." The first variables are still in there.

Click on Variables and put in the negative items. See Figure G.52 after clicking OK.

Figures G.53−G.55 demonstrate the repeated steps, and Figure G.56 shows the resulting graph. Again, none of the relationships is significant.

What is this? Something may have moved upward?? Oh, those are negatives. So there may have been slightly more challenge with respect to Perspective, Forgiveness, and Character. Hmmm …. It may be that negative Perspective and negative Forgiveness increase in Year 2, but the confidence intervals greatly overlap. Spiritual + and Biological + seem to decline somewhat, along with those revealed in the first graph (Figure G.48).

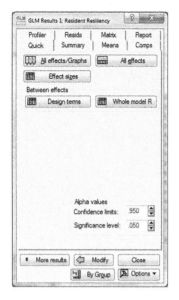

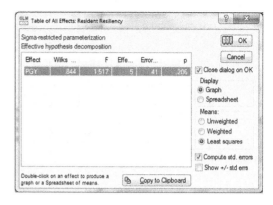

FIGURE G.46   Click OK.

FIGURE G.45   Click the button that says, "All effects/Graphs."

FIGURE G.47   Highlight all variables.

PGY; LS Means
Wilks' lambda = 0.84389, F (5, 41) = 1.5169, p = 0.20573
Effective hypothesis decomposition
Vertical bars denote 0.95 confidence intervals

FIGURE G.48   Resulting Mean With Error Plot.

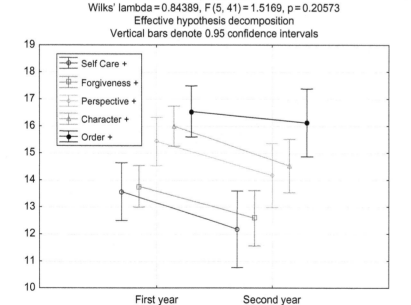

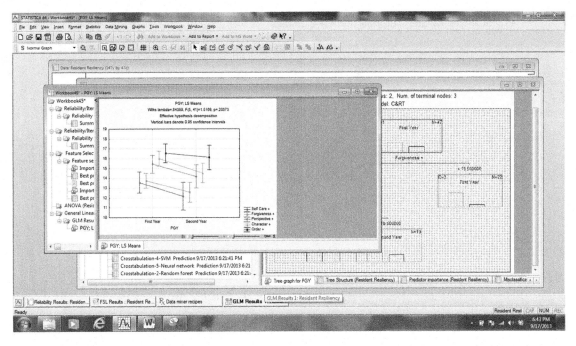

FIGURE G.49 Workspace at This Point.

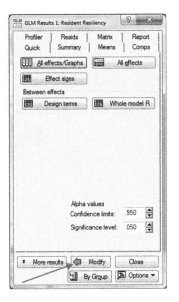

FIGURE G.50 Modify to back up.

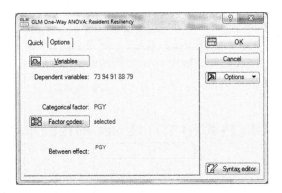

FIGURE G.51 Resulting Screen. Click on variables and put in the negative items.

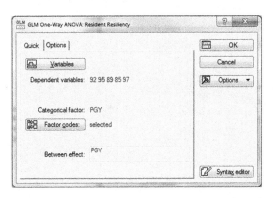

FIGURE G.52 Click OK

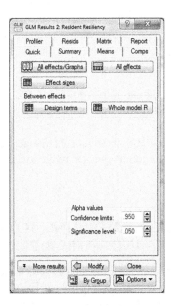

FIGURE G.53 Click on All effects/Graphs.

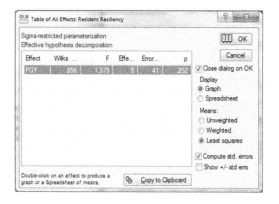

FIGURE G.54   Click OK.

FIGURE G.55   Highlight all variables.

FIGURE G.56   Resulting Mean with Error Plot.

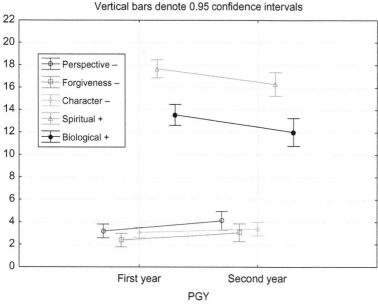

PGY; LS Means
Wilks' lambda = 0.85607, F (5, 41) = 1.3787, p = 0.25225
Effective hypothesis decomposition
Vertical bars denote 0.95 confidence intervals

Let's look at children in Figure G.57.

Well, not significant either, but it might be that there are increasing numbers of children as the years go by (Figure G.58).

Casual observation would substantiate this hypothesis. Perhaps there could be some causal relationships between the increases in children and the reduction of positive aspects of Resilience and the increase of negative aspects. One wonders.

EXERCISE G2: PREDICTING TOTAL POSITIVE RESOURCES AND TOTAL NEGATIVE DRAIN FROM 16PF AND MYERS & BRIGGS

David P. Armentrout, PhD, and Linda A. Winters-Miner, PhD

This tutorial is a continuation of Exercise G1 using the data set Resident Resiliency.sta. Now we will use two other instruments for our prediction, but we will use another view so you can get used to STATISTICA when it looks a bit different. Let us change to a ribbon view as shown in Figure G.59.

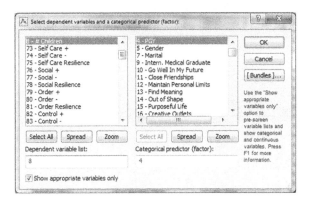

FIGURE G.57   Modify again and select #Children with PGY.

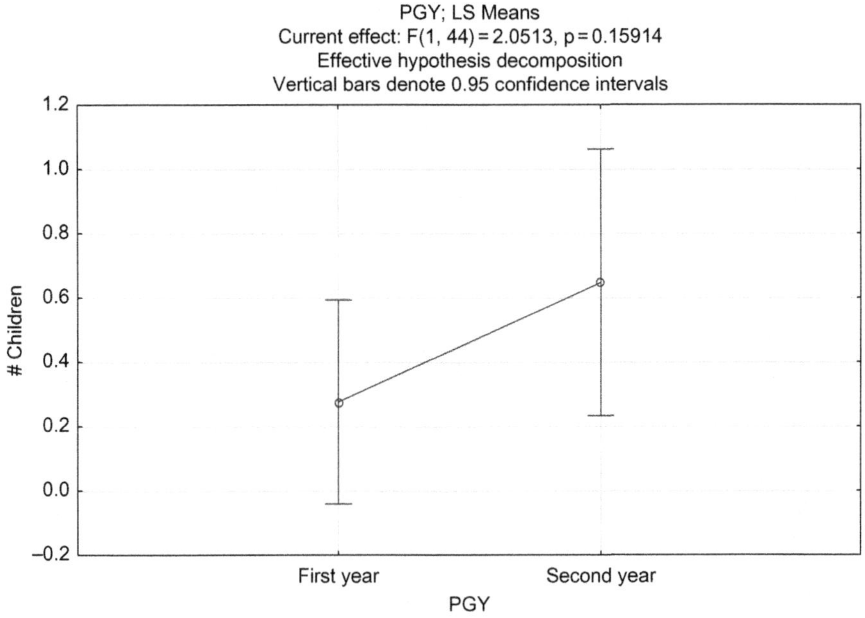

PGY; LS Means
Current effect: F(1, 44) = 2.0513, p = 0.15914
Effective hypothesis decomposition
Vertical bars denote 0.95 confidence intervals

FIGURE G.58   Hmmmm.

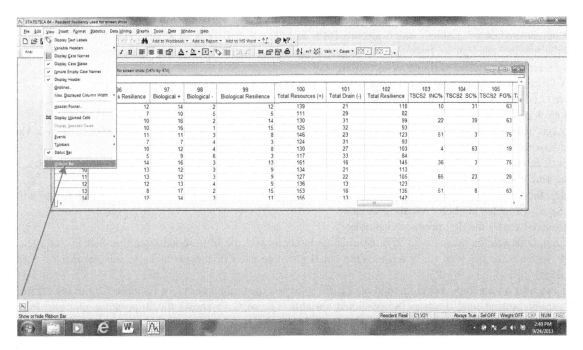

FIGURE G.59   Changing to Ribbon View under the View Tab.

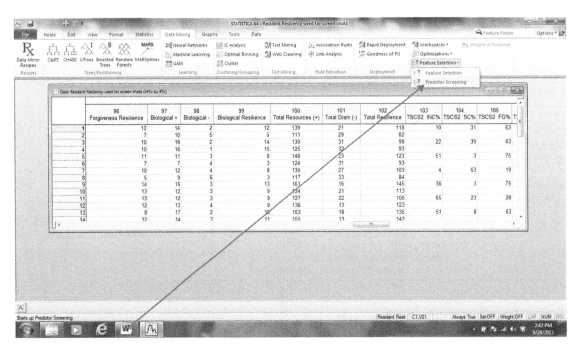

FIGURE G.60   Choose Prediction Selection.

It might be interesting to see if we can predict the positive and negative resources from the 16 personality variables (16PF) and from the Myers & Briggs scores. We will save using all three instruments until Exercise G3, when we use Weight of Evidence, Decisioning. At that time, we will also use the process of separating the data into training and testing sub-samples before completing the analysis. Training data will be used in formulating the model and then the testing data will be used to verify the model. In this tutorial, however, we again use all the data for the exercise.

In this Exercise G2 tutorial, we will predict the total of the negatives first (Total drain score 101), using feature selection, and then predict the positives by going straight to the data mining recipe.

First open the file and, under Statistics, click on Feature Selection. Figure G.60 shows where to find Feature Selection under the ribbon view. Click on the Data Mining tab and then on Feature Selection.

Click on Predictor Screening and select the variables. Figure G.61 shows the resulting screen.

Figure G.62 shows how to select 101 as the continuous dependent variable (the target) and Variables 118−146 as the continuous predictor variables, which are the 16PF and Myers & Briggs variables. The model in this form is the same as the feature selection we have used in the last analysis, but the output is somewhat different. Note that we might also have a binary dependent variable as an option.

Click OK and OK again. The model works as in Figure G.63.

Figure G.64 shows the Screening Results box.

First click on "Summary: Variable importance" to see the listing and the F values in Figure G.65.

Click on "Breakdown summary" to see the output in Figure G.66, to view the summary statistics of each variable to discover how the response changes across levels of the optimally binned predictor variable.

For a different view, as Figure G.67 shows, click on any one of the variables in the Select predictor box, and then click Box and Whisker plot (Figure G.68). We chose Variable Aprhnsn.

Finally, the Overlaid scatter plot (Figure G.69) with means can be used for continuous predictors to show the correlations. Select variables of choice, or all of them.

Figure G.70 shows the first predictor variable.

The diamonds are the means with 95% confidence intervals and the blue squares are the medians, at each level of the 16PF variable for the total drain scores. One could examine each of the variables in this manner to examine the relationships.

Next, we will return to the other method of feature selection (described above in Exercise G1) to see an importance plot of variables using total drain as the predicted variable. Figure G.71 shows the Importance plot and Figure G.72 shows the listing of important variables.

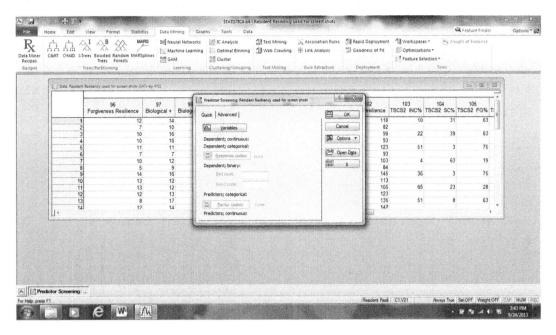

FIGURE G.61   Resulting Screen − click on Variables.

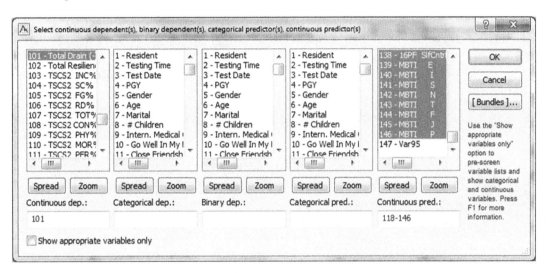

FIGURE G.62   Select Variables.

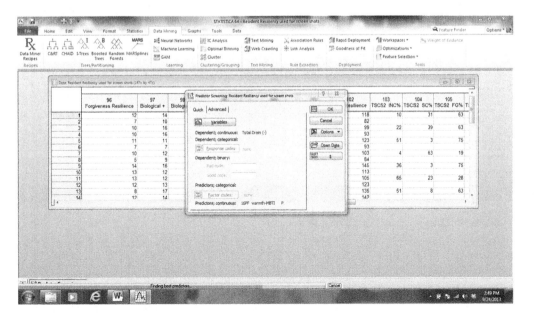

FIGURE G.63   Click OK.

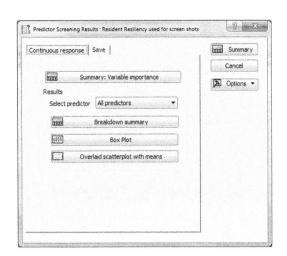

FIGURE G.64 Screening Results Box — Click on Summary: Variable Importance.

		Importance: Total Drain (-) (Resident Resilien		
		R-squared	F-statistic	Variable number
16PF	**Aprhnsn**	0.677096	10.06508	129
16PF	Anxty	0.645462	11.37857	135
16PF	EmoStab	0.599759	9.36558	120
MBTI	S	0.564245	4.96365	141
16PF	Tensn	0.521793	6.81966	133
MBTI	P	0.470801	5.56030	146
16PF	Domince	0.378651	8.22691	121
MBTI	F	0.368159	3.64173	144
MBTI	E	0.344240	7.08681	139
16PF	Vigilnce	0.291338	11.51110	126
MBTI	I	0.286462	11.24107	140
MBTI	N	0.267602	2.28361	142
16PF	Abstrtns	0.241403	8.91023	127
16PF	Livlinss	0.224361	8.09929	122
16PF	SocBldns	0.224361	8.09929	124
16PF	Extrvrsn	0.198791	6.94718	134
16PF	SlfRelnc	0.184064	6.31641	131
16PF	Indpndnc	0.125805	4.02947	137
MBTI	T	0.097580	3.02769	143
16PF	Senstvty	0.092244	2.84529	125
MBTI	J	0.088138	2.70641	145
16PF	RulCnscs	0.086021	2.63527	123
16PF	TghMdns	0.083105	2.53785	136
16PF	warmth	0.061168	0.31274	118
16PF	SlfCntrl	0.053513	1.58307	138
16PF	reasong	0.038409	1.11840	119
16PF	Datnss	0.028325	0.81621	128

FIGURE G.65 Variables, R-squared, and F values.

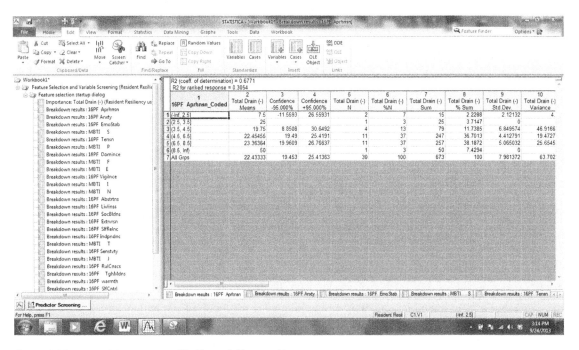

FIGURE G.66 Click on "Breakdown summary" in Figure G.64 to see this.

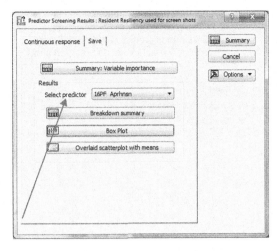

FIGURE G.67 Click on any one of the variables in the Select predictor box, and then click Box and Whisker plot

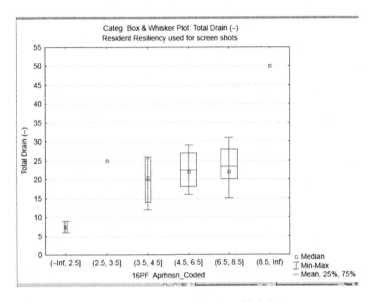

FIGURE G.68 Result for Variable Variable Aprhnsn. (Apprehension seemed to rise with drain.)

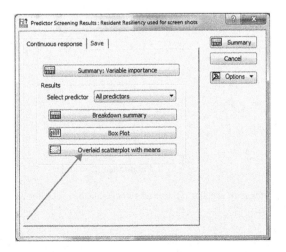

FIGURE G.69 Select Overlaid Scatter Plot.

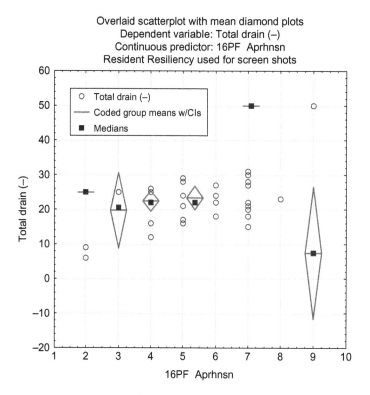

FIGURE G.70 Result.

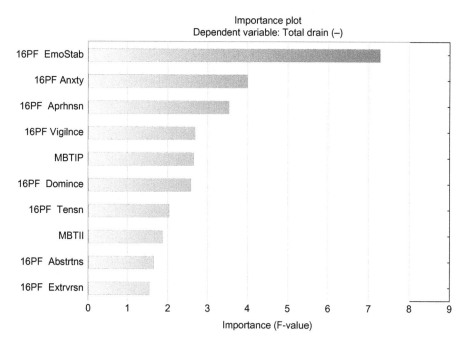

FIGURE G.71 Choosing the other method of feature selection. (Under data mining, feature selection and the first entry, feature selection.)

	Best predictors for continuous dependent	
	F-value	p-value
16PF EmoStab	7.282309	0.000283
16PF Anxty	3.999181	0.006913
16PF Aprhnsn	3.540781	0.012472
16PF Vigilnce	2.690570	0.045599
MBTI P	2.650806	0.037829
16PF Domince	2.584202	0.046139
16PF Tensn	2.034448	0.109745
MBTI I	1.877844	0.118119
16PF Abstrtns	1.654176	0.172695
16PF Extrvrsn	1.551636	0.211649

FIGURE G.72   Best Predictors.

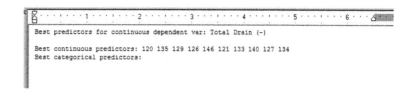

FIGURE G.73   Summary: Best k predictors.

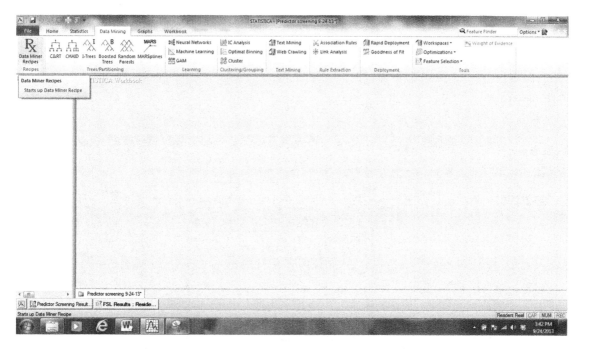

FIGURE G.74   Open a Data Mining Recipe.

Figure G.72 shows the p values (by clicking on "Summary: Best k predictors"). It looks like the first six could be important. We will select those from Figure G.73.

We will use variables 120 135 129 126 146 121 for our Data Miner Recipe, seen in Figure G.74.

Select "New" from the screen in Figure G.75.

Then click on the data and add them to the project (Figure G.76).

Figure G.77 shows the variables selected and also that the "Show appropriate variables only" box has been marked.

Click OK and then "Configure all steps," so that the blue dots show up. See Figure G.78.

Figure G.79 shows how to click on the target variable then on Model building to check off all the models.

Unclick "Configure all steps" and then click on "Run to completion" (Figure G.80).

Let the model run as in Figure G.81.

It looks like Random forest would not run (Figure G.82). Simply click OK and see what will run.

None of the models that ran gave good predictions. Figure G.83 shows that Boosted trees has the highest correlation. We might complete an interactive boosted trees. We might also add the number of children to see if we can get a better prediction. Or perhaps we should subtract some of the variables.

We ran the program again with only the top three variables (Figure G.84):

The improvement was only slight for Boosted trees. See Figure G.85.

It seems that the resiliency *drains* could not be predicted well from the 16 personality traits and the Myers & Briggs scores.

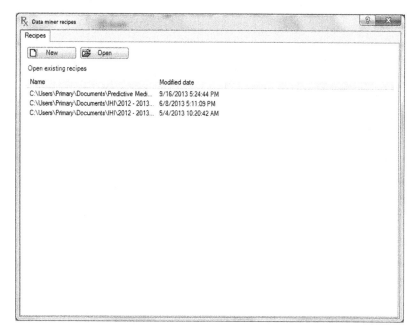

FIGURE G.75 Select New.

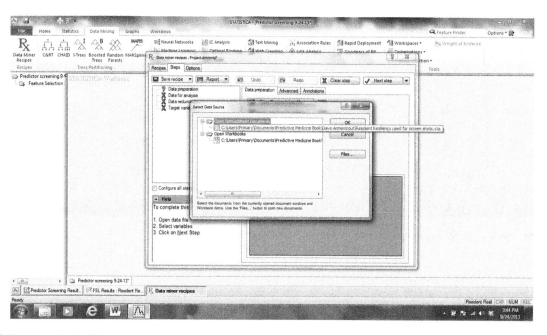

FIGURE G.76 Open the data file.

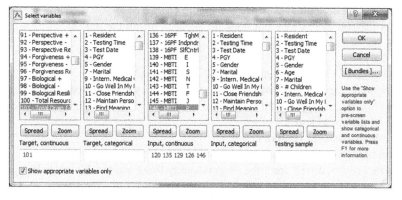

FIGURE G.77 Click on Variables and select variables.

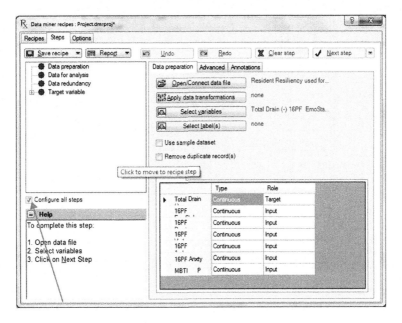

FIGURE G.78   Click Configure all steps.

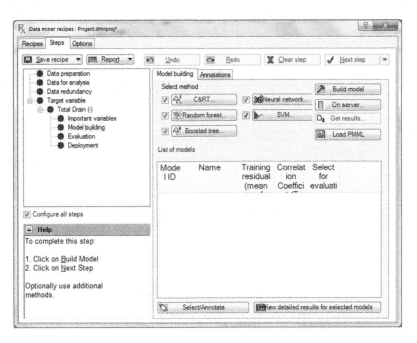

FIGURE G.79   Make sure all models are checked.

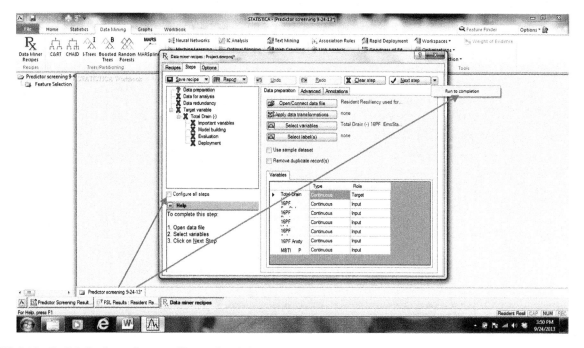

FIGURE G.80 Unclick Configure all steps and Run to Completion.

FIGURE G.81 Let the program run.

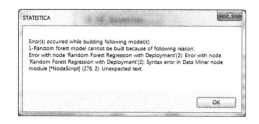

FIGURE G.82 Click OK if a model will not work.

Model selected for deployment	1	2	3	4
	3			
Model Evaluation Summary	ID	Name	Residual (mean square of residuals)	Correlation coefficient
	3	Boosted trees	55.47	0.56
	1	C&RT	78.65	
	5	Neural network	59.47	0.49
	4	SVM	67.6	0.41
Table	Step options			
	Date and time	9/24/2013 3:52:24 PM		

FIGURE G.83 Boosted trees has the highest correlation. Boosted trees interactively might be a good choice.

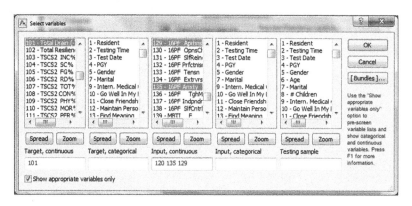

FIGURE G.84 Or perhaps we should subtract some of the variables.

	1		2	3	4
Model selected for deployment	2				
Model Evaluation Summary	ID		Name	Residual (mean square of residuals)	Correlation coefficient
		2	Boosted trees	52.03	0.58
		4	Neural network	62.04	0.46
		3	SVM	73.4	0.33
		1	C&RT	78.65	
Table	Step options				
	Date and time	9/24/2013 3:59:44 PM			

FIGURE G.85 Slight improvement for Boosted trees.

	1		2	3	4
Model selected for deployment	4				
Model Evaluation Summary	ID		Name	Residual (mean square of residuals)	Correlation coefficient
		4	SVM	193.38	0.5
		3	Boosted trees	234.71	0.47
		1	C&RT	196.48	0.47
		5	Neural network	203.36	0.46
Table	Step options				
	Date and time	9/24/2013 4:05:44 PM			

FIGURE G.86 Data Mining recipe predicting the positive resiliency scores from the personality traits and Myers & Briggs.

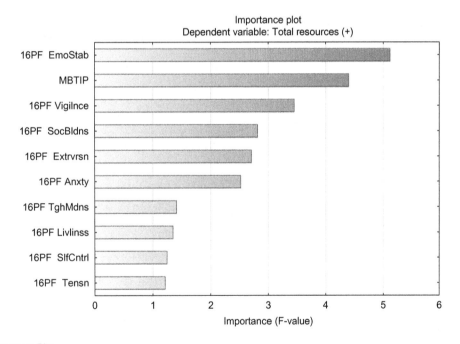

FIGURE G.87 Importance Plot.

Next we ran a Data Miner recipe predicting the *positive* resiliency scores from the personality traits and Myers & Briggs. Figure G.86 shows the Evaluation Summary. The output in Figure G.86 was run with all of the variables.

There is quite a bit of error in both systems. Using feature selection yielded Figure G.87.

We decided to run a simple correlation for the top two to see if those relationships approached significance. Figure G.88 shows where to find the Multiple Regression node.

Select variables in Figure G.89.

Click OK and OK. Figure G.90 shows that only Emotional Stability in the 16 personality variables correlated significantly with the total positive resiliency scores. Figure G.91 shows the scatterplot.

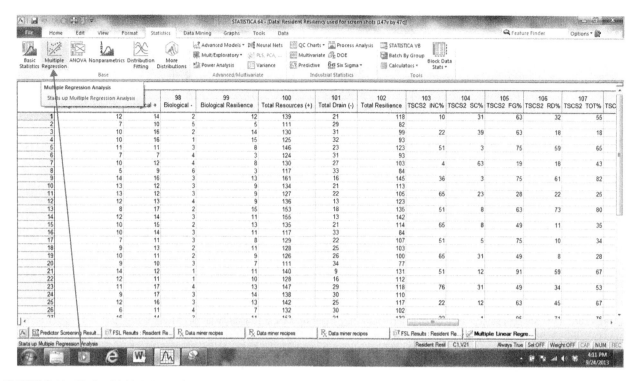

FIGURE G.88   Finding Multiple Regression Node.

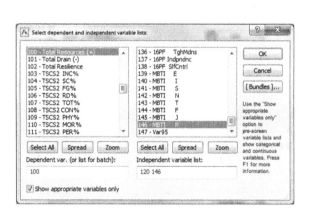

FIGURE G.89   Select the variables.

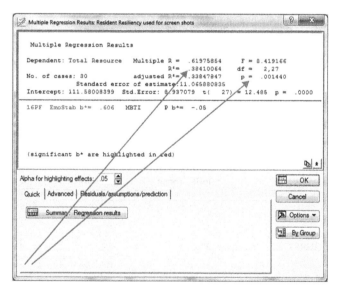

FIGURE G.90   Significant Correlation.

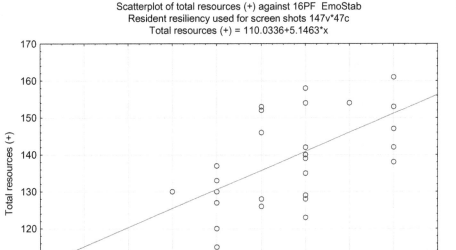

Scatterplot of total resources (+) against 16PF EmoStab
Resident resiliency used for screen shots 147v*47c
Total resources (+) = 110.0336+5.1463*x

FIGURE G.91   Scatterplot

It seemed that emotional stability predicted positive resiliency. We did not add the number of children to our analysis.

EXERCISE G3: PREDICTIVE ANALYTICS WITH DECISIONING: USING WEIGHT OF EVIDENCE

This exercise is the third and final of the G series. The data file PGY1.sta contains as cases the residents in their first year from the original file, Resident Resiliency.sta. We have only 30 cases in PGY1, but have conducted WoE, and even separated the file into two data sets; Training and Testing. Whether we would arrive at a good predictive model was questionable, but the exercise is instructive. In the future, with more data and examining other variables for the model, we might be able to improve our model.

(Note for some users: Exercise G3 uses version 12 of STATISTICA. If you had an earlier version of STATISTICA and installed version 12, version 12 will likely remember your old settings. You may need to complete a few steps in order to see some of the figures as they are presented in this tutorial. The special instructions have been placed in the Appendix at the end of this tutorial. Otherwise, begin here.)

With the PGY1.sta data set open, click on File and New as in Figure G.92.

Click on Workspace to achieve Figure G.93 and then click on All Validated Procedures.

Connect your data as in Figure G.94.

You might want to pull that PGY1 data node over a bit so it's easy to work around (see Figure G.95).

Again, click on All Validated Procedures and then on Beta Procedures, which has the newest procedures (Figure G.96).

Note that when you select the Beta Procedures, the top of the bar changes its selections (Figure G.97).

Go to the Data Mining tab and click on Weight of Evidence, as in Figure G.98.

Clicking on Weight of Evidence will drop the node directly into the workspace, as in Figure G.99.

Click on the little gear symbol on the upper left of the Weight of Evidence node to display Figure G.100.

Select the variables as in Figure G.101.

Click OK. Double click in the box for "Bad Code" to display (Figure G.102).

Click on Zoom to find the code for Bottom Half (Figure G.103), and then OK.

Click OK again at Figure G.104.

Complete the same procedure for the Good Code for the top half (see Figure G.105).

Now click "Compute groups" as in Figure G.106.

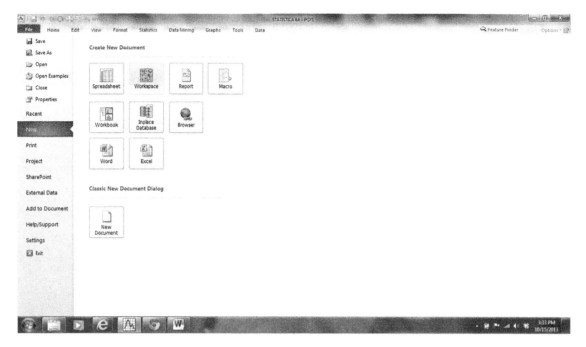

FIGURE G.92 Click on File and New.

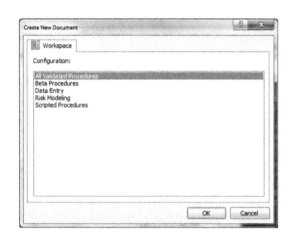

FIGURE G.93 Click All Validated Procedures.

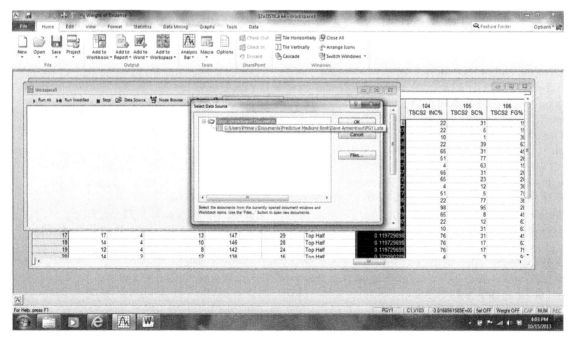

FIGURE G.94 Pull in the data.

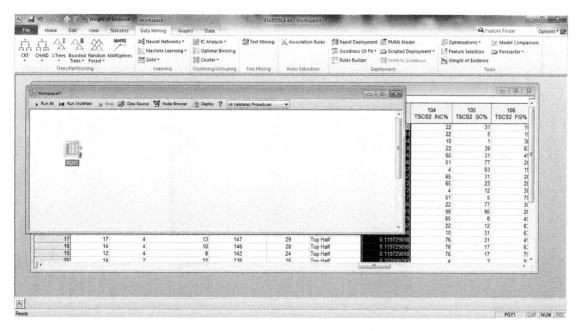

FIGURE G.95 Pull node to the left to make room.

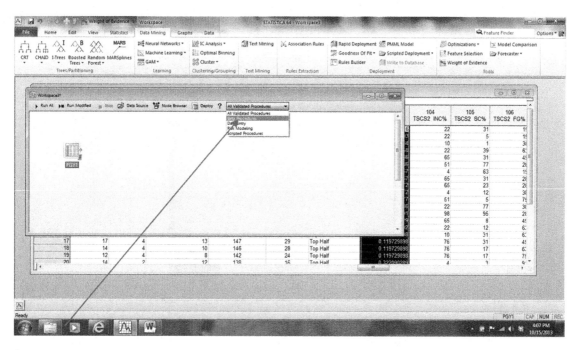

FIGURE G.96 Click on Beta Procedures.

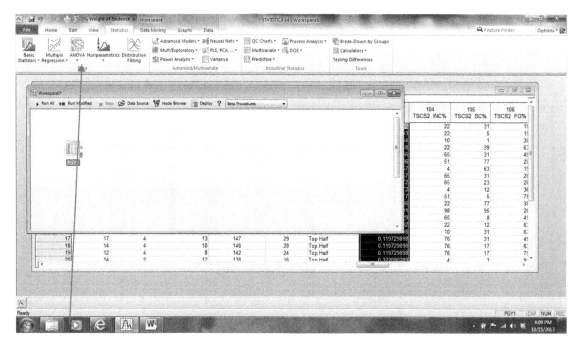

FIGURE G.97 Note - the top of the bar changes its selections.

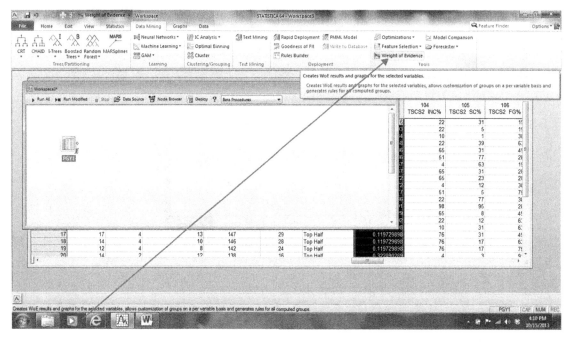

FIGURE G.98 Go to Data Mining tab and click on Weight of Evidence. Note that the data are highlighted.

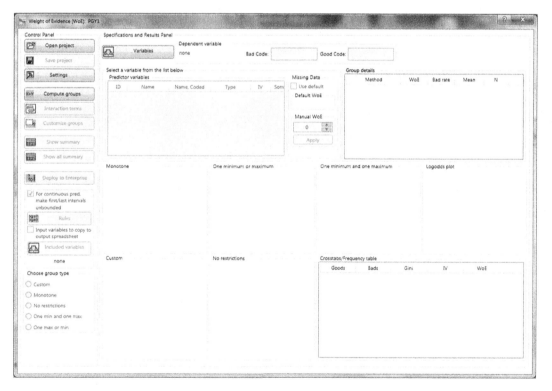

FIGURE G.99 Node drops into workspace and connects to data.

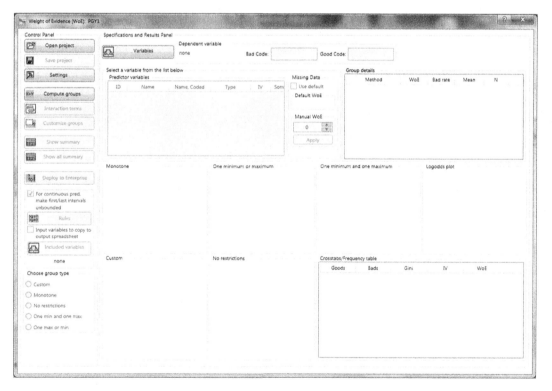

FIGURE G.100 Result of clicking on the little gear symbol on the upper left of the Weight of Evidence.

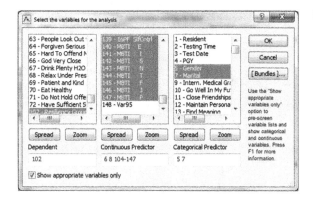

FIGURE G.101 Click on Variables and select the variables.

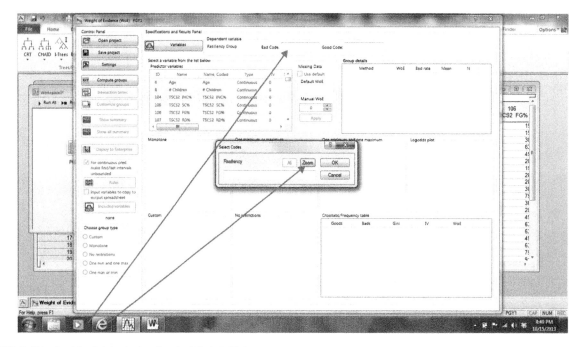

FIGURE G.102 Double click in the box for "Bad Code." Click on Zoom to select.

FIGURE G.103 Select Bottom Half for the Bad Code and click OK.

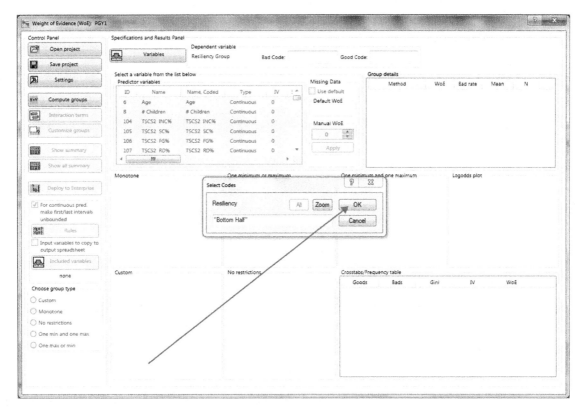

FIGURE G.104 Click OK again.

FIGURE G.105 Repeat the process but for the Good Code this time.

FIGURE G.106 Now click "Compute groups."

Allow the procedure to run as in Figure G.107.

Figure G.108 shows the results once the procedure has run. Note that there were some outputs that had no solution; this happened because of the small number of cases.

The red box around the most productive model, the default, is the solution we will use. Variable 105 is the one highlighted in Figure G.108. We could click on any other item and see the resulting boxes. Figure G.109 chooses Anxiety, for example. Choosing different variables is one way of seeing the breaks in the values of the variables in predicting the high or low group.

Click on the red X to close the screen and Figure G.110 shows that you can then Embed to workspace.

As Figure G.111 shows, we next run the WoE module by clicking on the little green arrow head on the lower left of the box.

The module then produces the SVB Rules module (see Figure G.112).

Move the Rules node to the right for convenience, and connect the data to it by dragging over the red arrow. Click on the small diamond on the right middle section of the PGY1 box (Figures G.113, G.114).

Right click on the Rules node to edit the parameters (Figure G.115).

Select the output variable in Figure G.116, and click False beside the Output Error Variable. We will not use that error variable and, by clicking False, the variable will not be listed in the output data file.

Figure G.117 shows how to run the Rules node.

Click on the little scroll on the bottom right of the output data file to see the document ("View Document"), as in Figure G.118.

Viewing the document in Figure G.119 shows how the rules have been applied to the bottom half and the top half of the output variable.

Close the file and return to the analysis.

At this point we will divide the data file into Training and Testing data. To do this we will add "Define Training Testing Sample." Figure G.120 shows how to go to the Node Browser, select All, and then Define Training Testing Sample.

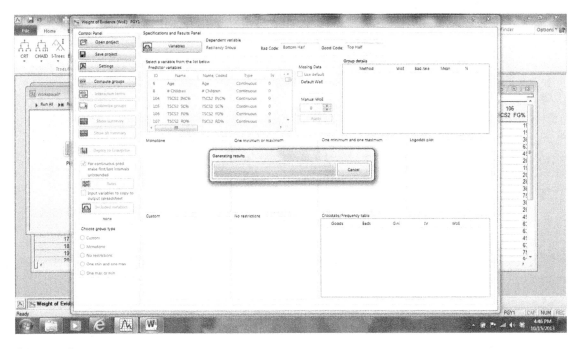

FIGURE G.107   Let it run.

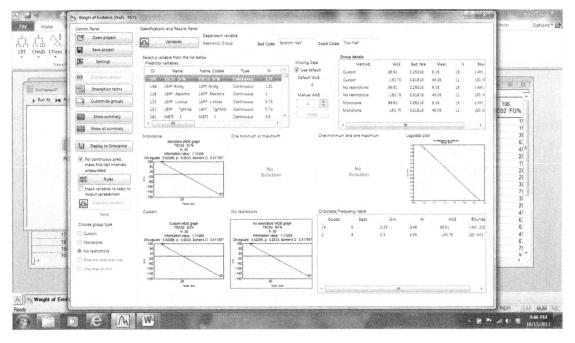

FIGURE G.108   Result: The red box around the most productive model, the default, is the solution we will use.

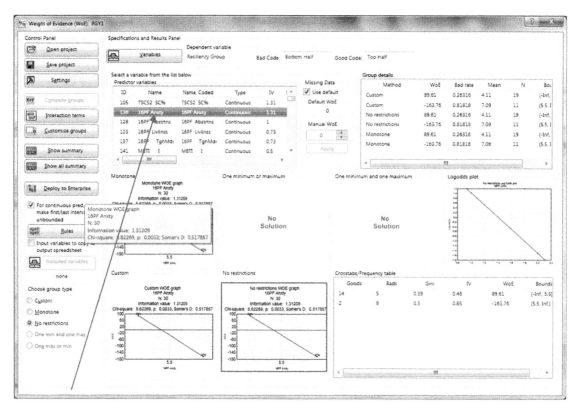

FIGURE G.109 Result of clicking on another variable: Anxiety.

FIGURE G.110 Embed to workspace

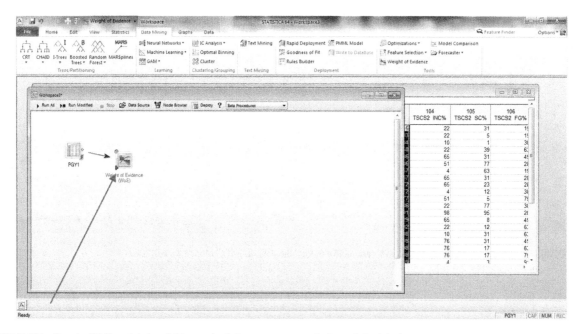

FIGURE G.111 Run the WoE module by clicking on the little green arrow on the lower left of the box.

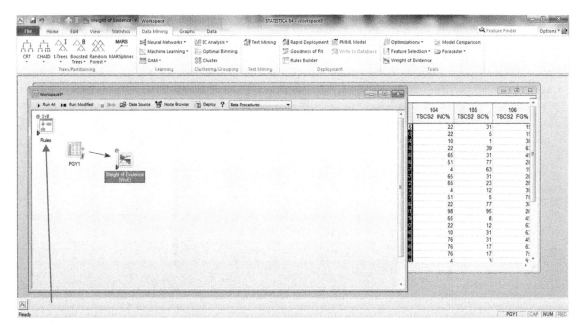

FIGURE G.112 Then produces the SVB Rules module.

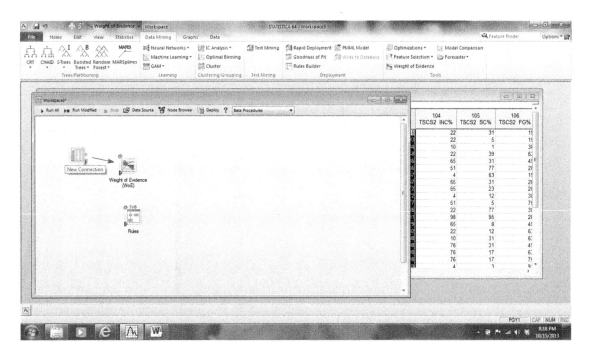

FIGURE G.113 Move the Rules node to the right for convenience, and connect the data to it by dragging over the red arrow.

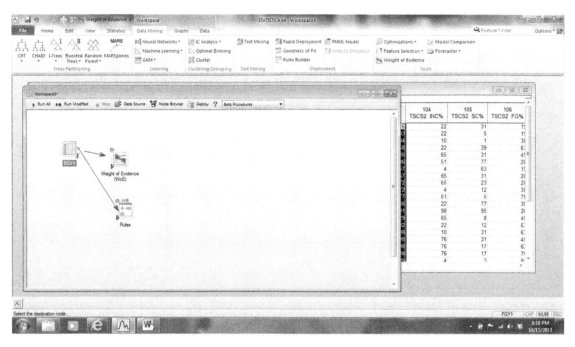

FIGURE G.114 Click on the small circle on the right middle section of the PGY1 box to get the red arrow.

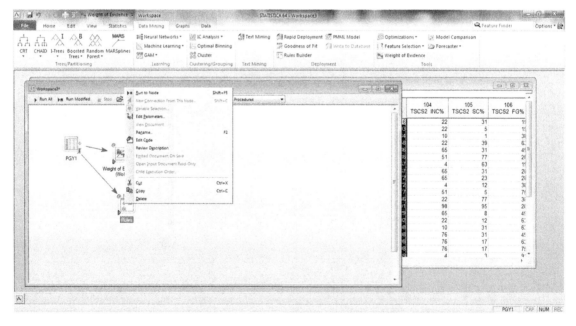

FIGURE G.115 Edit the Parameters.

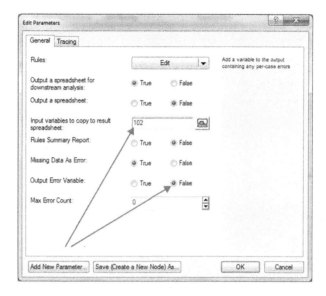

FIGURE G.116 Select the output variable and click False, beside the Output Error Variable.

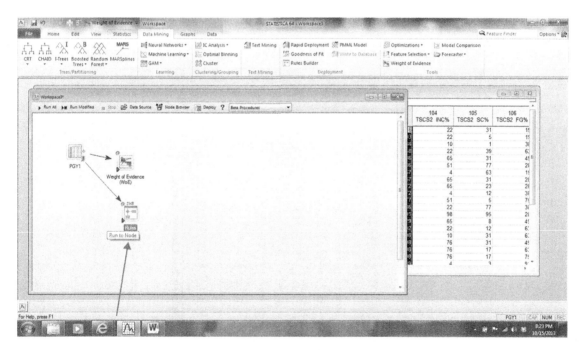

FIGURE G.117 Run the Rules node.

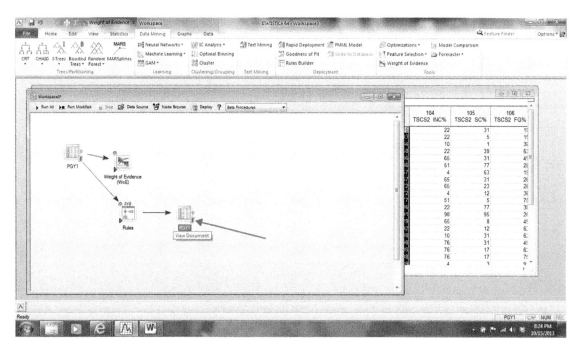

FIGURE G.118 Click on the little scroll to view document.

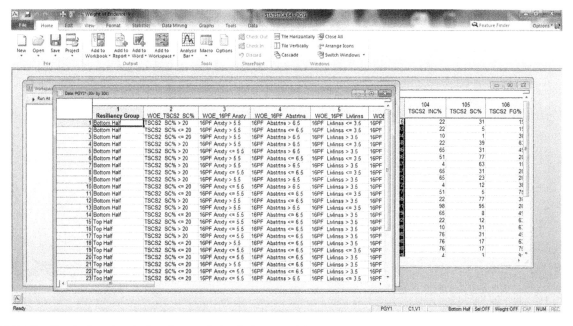

FIGURE G.119 Showing how the rules have been applied to the bottom and the top half of the output variable.

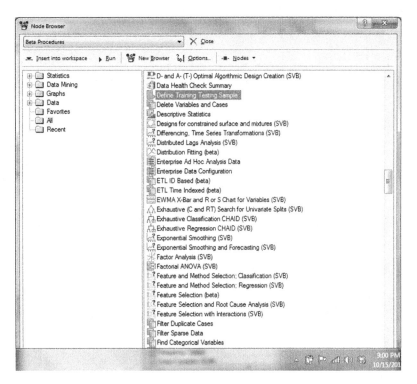

FIGURE G.120 Go to the Node Browser, select All, and then Define Training Testing Sample.

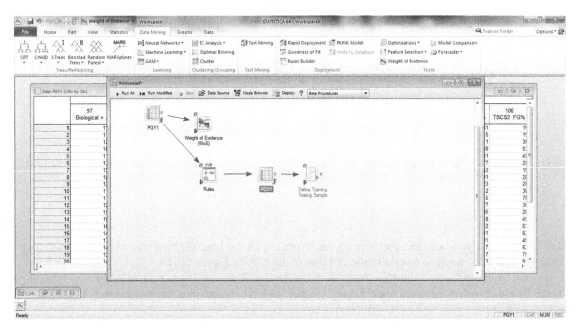

FIGURE G.121 Result. Double click on the Define Training Testing Sample node.

Select the node by highlighting it and inserting it into the workspace, which will produce Figure G.121. Connect the arrow from the data.

Double click on the Define Training Testing Sample node to produce Figure G.122, at which point you can edit the parameters.

Change the name to Sample (with no space after the word Sample), X out the Validation, and place 70% for Training and 30% for Testing (see Figure G.123).

FIGURE G.122   Edit the parameters.

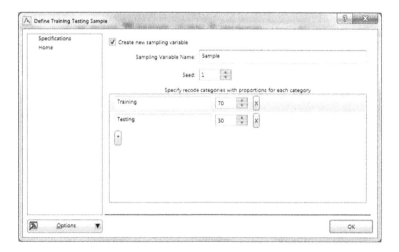

FIGURE G.123   Change the name to Sample (with no space after the word Sample), X out the Validation, and place 70% for training and 30% for testing.

Click OK. A green arrow becomes apparent on the lower left of the box; click on this to run the program. View the document to see that now we have an additional variable in the data in Figure G.124.

Next, we will separate the two samples. Make sure the Define Training Testing Sample module is highlighted. Go to the Node Browser, select All, and then Subset (Figure G.125). Insert into the workspace. Highlight the Define Training Testing Sample again, and once again insert Subset.

The Define Training Testing Sample node is highlighted, so the selected procedure will connect with the node. Place two of these subsets in the workspace, as in Figure G.126. (Remember to highlight the Define Training Testing node each time a subset node is selected.)

Right click on one Subset and rename as in Figure G.127. Right click on the other one and rename as Testing.

Then specify what the sample will comprise, as in Figures G.128 and G.129. Note that the quote marks are important.

The resulting workspace should look like the presentation in Figure G.130. Run each of the subset nodes to create the samples.

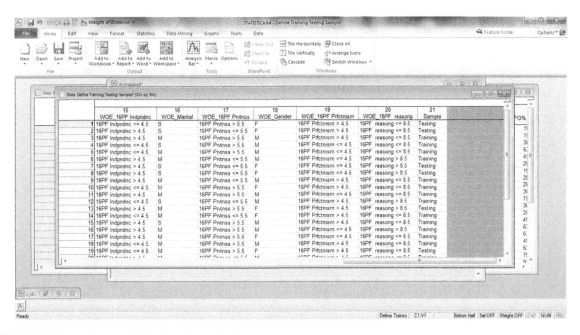

FIGURE G.124 Now we have an additional variable in the data.

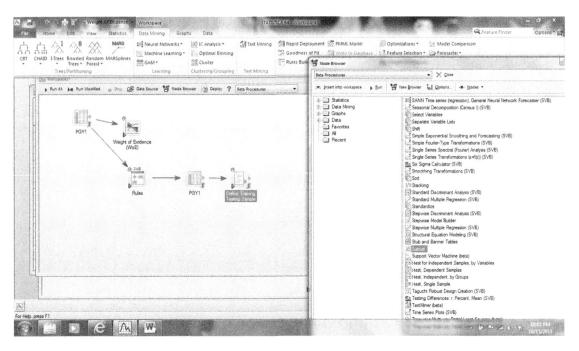

FIGURE G.125 Selecting subset. Be sure to follow the directions in the text!!

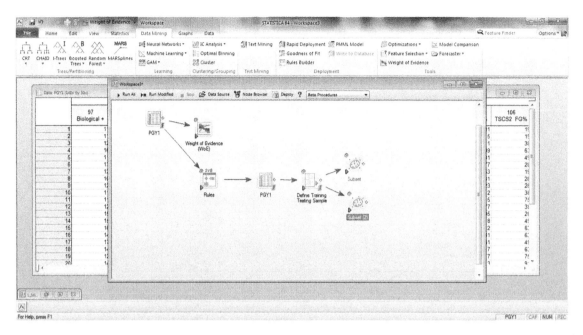

FIGURE G.126 The Define Training Testing Sample node is highlighted, so the selected procedure will connect with the node. Place two of these in the workspace.

FIGURE G.127 Right click on one Subset and rename. Do this for each.

FIGURE G.128 Specify what the sample comprises for "Training." Quote marks are necessary.

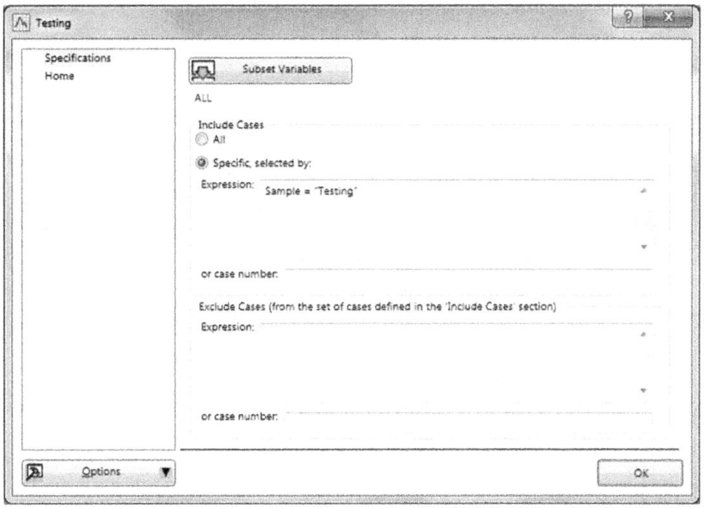

FIGURE G.129 Do it again for "Testing."

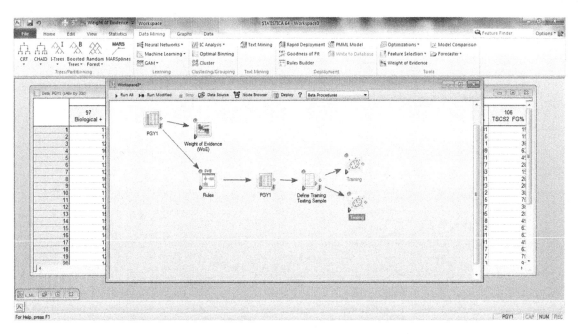

FIGURE G.130 Resulting Workspace.

Each subset was run in Figure G.131. Open each of the documents and note the separation of cases. If one clicks on the document symbol for each sample, we note that there are 20 cases in the Training sample and 10 cases in the Testing sample.

We next insert a stepwise model builder for the Training sample. *Highlight the Training subset sample.* Go to Statistics, Advanced Models, and then Stepwise Model Builder, as in Figure G.132. Note that the subset Training is highlighted while selecting Stepwise Model Builder, so that the stepwise model will attach to the Training subset sample.

Figure G.133 shows the result in the workspace.

Right click on the Stepwise Model Builder to edit the parameters as in Figure G.134.

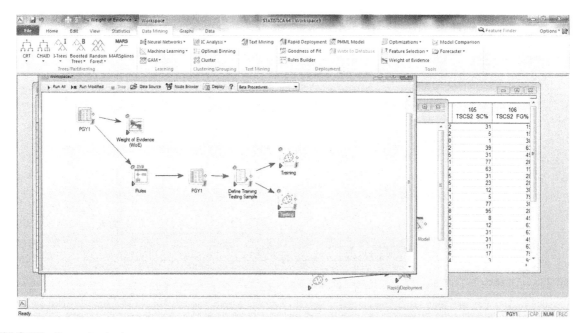

FIGURE G.131   Run each subset.

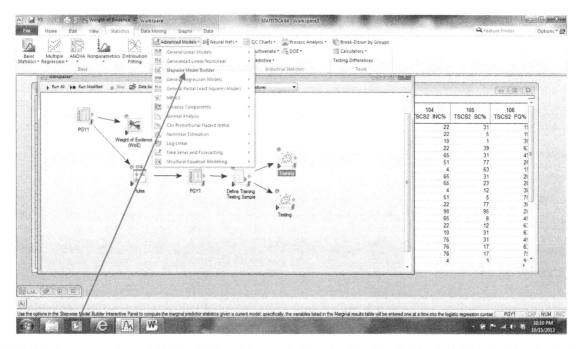

FIGURE G.132   Insert a stepwise model builder for the training sample. Note that the subset Training is highlighted while selecting Stepwise Model Builder.

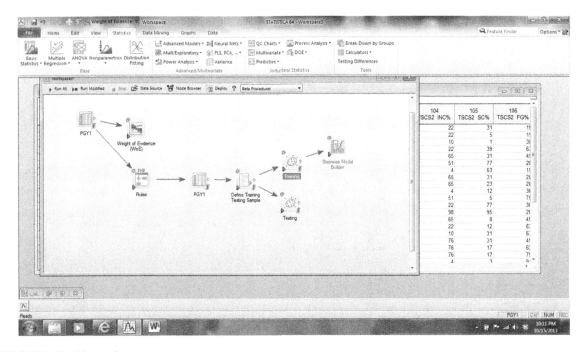

FIGURE G.133 Resulting workspace.

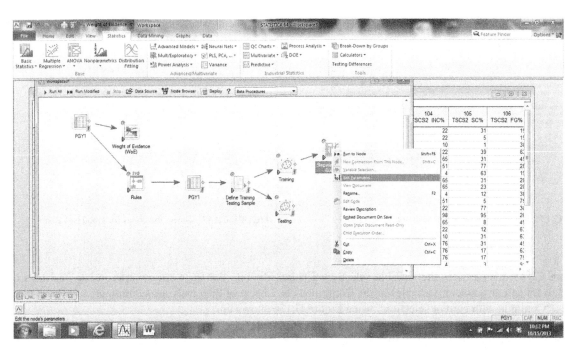

FIGURE G.134 Edit the parameters.

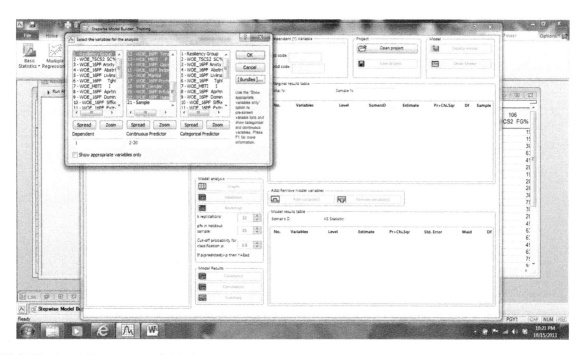

FIGURE G.135   In variable selection, unclick the box that says "Show appropriate variables only."

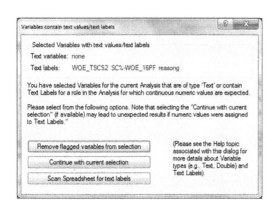

FIGURE G.136   Continue with current selection.

FIGURE G.137   Select the codes for Good and Bad.

Figure G.135 demonstrates the variable selection. Unclick the box that says "Show appropriate variables only," as we need to select our predictor variables in the Continuous box because they truly are continuous.

Click "Continue with current selection" when Figure G.136 shows up.

Again, select the codes for Good and Bad as in Figure G.137.

The resulting dialog box looks like that shown in Figure G.138.

Now, click on "Full sample" (under "Run marginal analysis"). Figure G.139 shows the result.

By clicking the Somer's D we can line up the variables by predictability and then add them into the model one by one. After each addition the model runs, and we see what next, if anything else, seems to be a potential good predictor. One can actually select anything that might seem potentially useful when examining the literature in the field. Figure G.140 shows what happened when we arranged by Somer's D. (We clicked Somer's D twice.)

Figure G.141 shows that we are about to add "Dominance" by highlighting the variable.

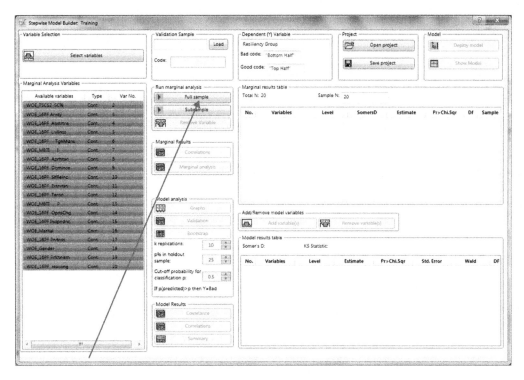

FIGURE G.138 Resulting dialog box. Click on "Full sample" (under "Run marginal analysis").

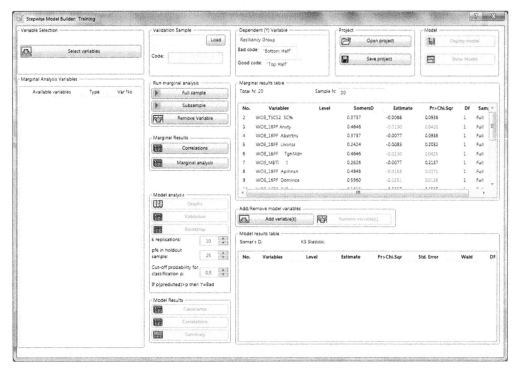

FIGURE G.139 Result

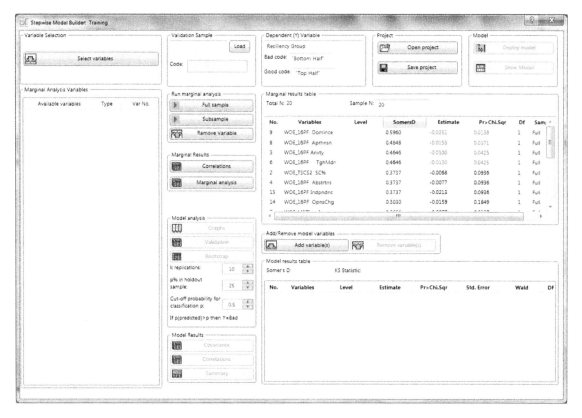

FIGURE G.140 Somer's D

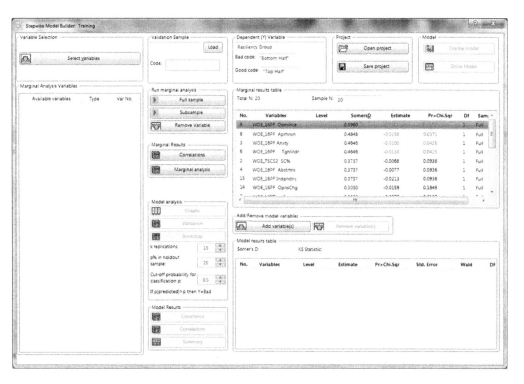

FIGURE G.141 About to add "Dominance"

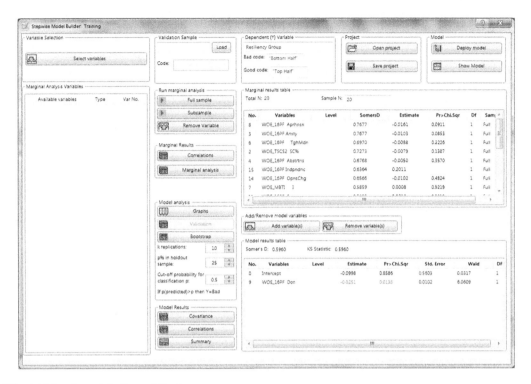

FIGURE G.142 Addition changed the Somers' D values.

Figure G.142 shows what happened to the model once we added the variable, as well as how the addition changed the Somer's D values of those variables remaining on the top portion.

Now, since we have added a significant predictor, the significance of the other variables has changed. We can add more if we like, however, and decided to add Variables 8, 3, 6, and 2 because they were the next ones on the list. After we added them, it appeared that a couple of others might be selected because of their Somer's D, so we did this and then stopped. Figure G.143 shows the variables we added.

Now, at this point, we are simply working with the Training data — and soon we will test our model on the training data.

Note that with this small sample, the model was able to predict 100% of both the top and the bottom half. This is not difficult when the sample is so small. Now, red X out of the stepwise node and select "Embed to workspace" as in Figure G.144.

One can also Delete All the warnings as in Figure G.145.

Run the node of the Stepwise Model Builder to achieve the PMML Model and Rapid Deployment in Figure G.146.

Note the PMML Model node and the Rapid Deployment node. Drag the Rapid Deployment node over to the Testing data as in Figure G.147.

Next, connect the Testing data to the Rapid Deployment node, which will apply the PMML code to the data. Figure G.148 shows the procedures we can view once the rapid deployment is run. We choose what we would like before running. This was found by right clicking on Rapid Deployment and editing the parameters.

For example, in Figure G.149, we selected Lift charts for the bottom half, and then Gains charts.

We can return to do others, but we'll go ahead and show these. Click OK and then run the Rapid Deployment node. The Reporting Documents appear in Figure G.150.

The Gains chart in Figure G.151 that our model predicted is better than not using a model for prediction.

In looking at the summary of the deployment, we see that the model accurately predicted 7 of the 10 cases in the testing group in Figure G.152.

For Figures G.153−G.155, Figure G.153 shows other selections when editing the parameters of the Rapid Deployment node. Again, the model is better than none.

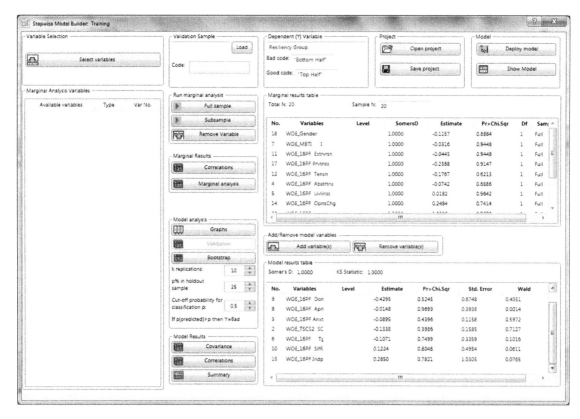

FIGURE G.143 Shows variables added.

FIGURE G.144 Embed to workspace.

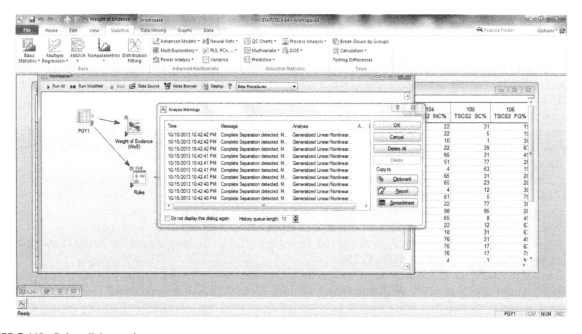

FIGURE G.145 Delete all the warning messages.

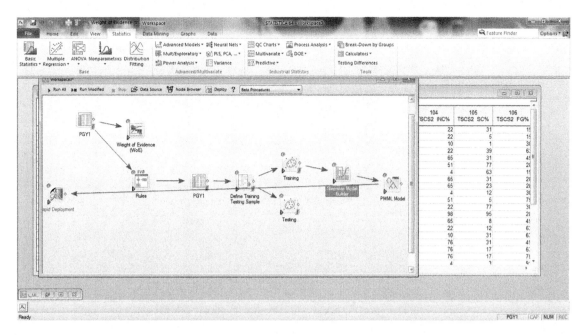

FIGURE G.146 Run the node of the Stepwise Model Builder.

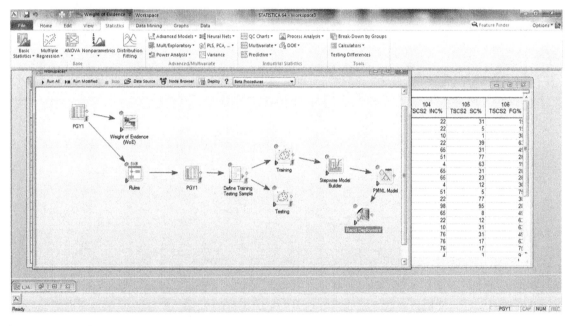

FIGURE G.147 Drag the Rapid Deployment node over to the Testing data.

FIGURE G.148 Procedures that can be viewed once the rapid deployment is run.

FIGURE G.149   Selected Lift charts for the bottom half, and then Gains charts.

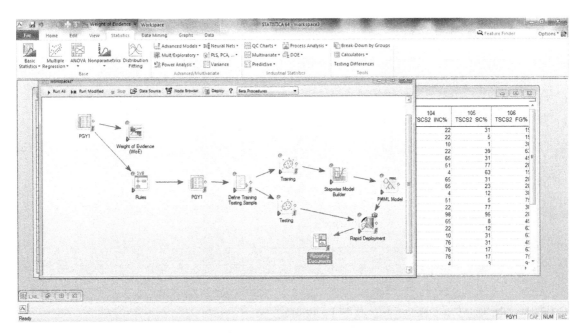

FIGURE G.150   After running Rapid Deployment node.

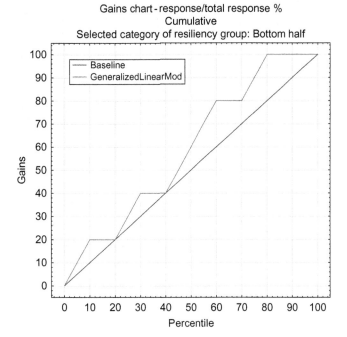

FIGURE G.151   Gains chart

	Summary of Deployment (Testing) FileNames:		
	Resiliency Group	GeneralizedLinearModelPred	GeneralizedLinearModelRes
1	Bottom Half	Bottom Half	Correct
2	Bottom Half	Bottom Half	Correct
7	Bottom Half	Bottom Half	Correct
8	Bottom Half	Top Half	Incorrect
13	Bottom Half	Bottom Half	Correct
19	Top Half	Top Half	Correct
21	Top Half	Bottom Half	Incorrect
25	Top Half	Bottom Half	Incorrect
27	Top Half	Top Half	Correct
28	Top Half	Top Half	Correct

FIGURE G.152   Accurately predicted 7 of the 10 cases in the testing group.

FIGURE G.153   Another selection.

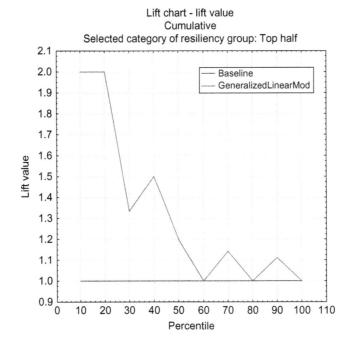

FIGURE G.154   Lift chart.

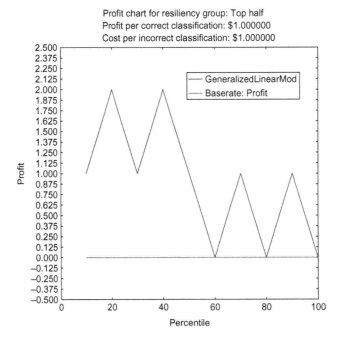

FIGURE G.155   Another selection

FIGURE G.A1   Go to file and create a new document.

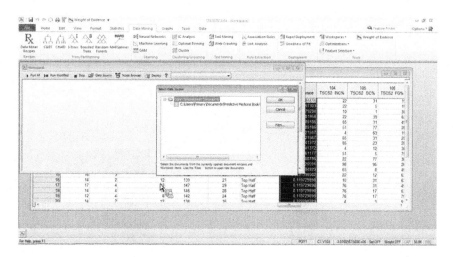

FIGURE G.A2   Go ahead and click on OK.

At this point, we have a model that predicts better than not having a model. A model does not have to predict at 100% to be useful. However, as we gain more data, and include better sets of variables, we will be able to improve our model and perhaps eventually be able to predict at 100%.

APPENDIX TO TUTORIAL G

Special Instructions for Those Who Installed Version 12 Over an Older Version of STATISTICA

If when you try to go to file and create a new document you get this (Figure G.A1):
   it has a slightly different configuration to the newest version. Go ahead and click on OK to get Figure G.A2.

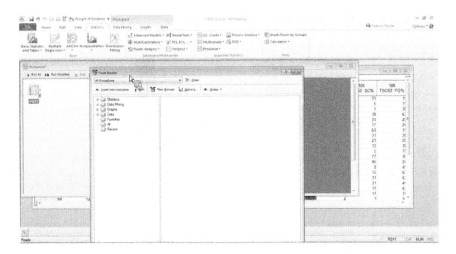

FIGURE G.A3 Connect the data set and click OK.

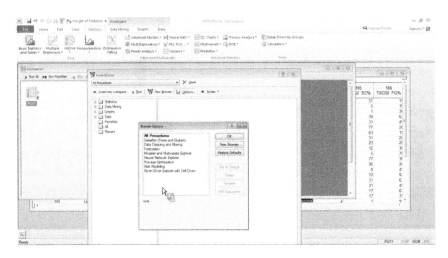

FIGURE G.A4 Click on Options and Restore Defaults.

Connect the data set and click OK. See Figure G.A3 with the Node Browser open in the workspace.

Click on Options and Restore Defaults in Figure G.A4.

Click Yes in Figure G.A5.

Figure G.A6 shows how the menu changes to the newer version.

Click on Restore defaults and OK. Then, in Figure G.A7, click on the red X.

Close this out and then create a new workspace as above in Figure G.92.

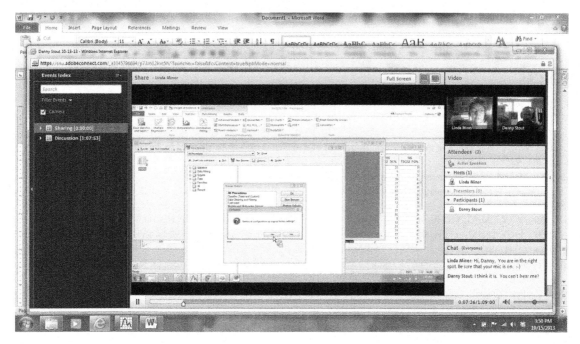

FIGURE G.A5   Click Yes.

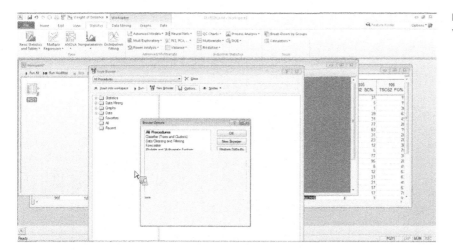

FIGURE G.A6   Menu changes to the newer version.

FIGURE G.A7   Click on Restore defaults and OK. Then, in Figure G.A7, click on the red X.

REFERENCES

Bolton, B., 1979. The Tennessee Self-Concept Scale and the Normal Personality Sphere (16PF). J. Pers. Assess. 43 (6), 608.

Catell, R.B., Saunders, D.R., Stice, G., 1957. Handbook for the Sixteen Personality Factor (Questionnaire). Institute for Personality and Ability Testing, Champaign, IL.

Fazeli, S., 2012. The exploring nature of the assessment instrument of five factors of personality traits in the current studies of personality. Asian Soc. Sci. 8 (2), 264–275.

Fitts, W.H., 1965. Manual for the Tennessee Self-Concept Scale. Counselor Recordings and Tests, Nashville, TN.

Lebovits, B.Z., Osteeld, A.M., 1970. Personality, defensiveness and educational achievement: II. The Cattell 16PR Questionnaire. J. Clin. Psychol. 26 (2), 183–188.

Li, Z., Bo, L., Hui, R., Yu-Fu, L., Yan, Z., 2013. The personality profile of excellent nurses in China: The 16PF. Contemp. Nurse. 43 (2), 219–224.

McCaulley, M.H., 1990. The Myers-Briggs type indicator: a measure for individuals and groups. Meas. Eval. Couns. Dev. (American Counseling Association). 22 (4), 181.

Myers, I.B., McCaulley, M.H., 1985. Manual: A Guide to the Development and Use of the Myers-Briggs Type Indicator. Consulting Psychologists Press, Palo Alto, CA.

NZCER (New Zealand Council for Educational Research), 2013. Tennessee Self-Concept Scale – Second Edition (TSCS-2). Last retrieved October 8, 2013, from <www.nzcer.org.nz/pts/tennessee-self-concept-scale-second-edition-tscs-2>.

Tutorial H

Medicare Enrollment Analysis Using Visual Data Mining

Samrat Majumdar, MSc

Chapter Outline

INTRODUCTION

This report provides an analysis of the Medicare Enrollment data for 2012, and highlights the area of focus to reduce cost and improve coverage. The Medicare Enrollment data set was prepared by collating various reports available at www.cms. gov/Research-Statistics-Data-and-Systems/Statistics-Trends-and-Reports/MedicareMedicaidStatSupp/2013.html.

MEDICARE ENROLLMENT DATA

The sample data file to be used in this analysis is MedicareEnrollment2012.sta, which contains state-wise various Medicare Enrollment related data as of July 1, 2012. The data set was prepared using CMS (Center of Medicare and Medicaid Services) reports on Medicare Enrollment 2013. Table H.1 describes the fields in MedicareEnrollment2012.sta.

There are a total of 51 instances (cases) in the data file.

Open the MedicareEnrollment2012.sta file in Data Miner Workspace. Select Data Miner − Workspaces − All Procedures. In the DM workspace, click on the Node Browser. Double click on "Multiple Copies of Data Source," as shown in Figure H.1.

Connect the MedicareEnrollment2012 data file node with the Multiple Copies of Data Source node by dragging the mouse. Double click on Multiple Copies of Data Source node and change the parameters as shown in Figure H.2.

Set the Number of copies to 6 and the Type of copy operation as Clone original datasource. Click OK to accept the parameter settings. Now click the Run button at the upper-left corner of the Data Miner workspace; alternatively, right click the Multiple Copies of Data Source node and select Run to Node.

To align the copies of the Data Source nodes, right click on Data Miner workspace and click on Align Icons. The copies of the Data Source node will be aligned as shown in Figure H.3.

FEATURE SELECTION AND ROOT CAUSE ANALYSIS

In this section we will use Feature Selection and Root Cause Analysis, available in STATISTICA Data Miner. Feature Selection and Root Cause Analysis are a good start for predicting or analyzing data which determine the most useful predictor variables in a data set.

Practical Predictive Analytics and Decisioning Systems for Medicine. DOI: http://dx.doi.org/10.1016/B978-0-12-411643-6.00024-7

TABLE H.1 Data Fields in MedicareEnrollment2012.sta Data Spreadsheet

Variable	Type	Description
Area of Residence	Categorical	US State
Region	Categorical	Region in which the State belongs
Total Population	Continuous	Total population of the state
State Buy Ins	Continuous	Medicare Enrollee count with StateBuyIn for low income group
All Others	Continuous	Medicare Enrollee count for non-StateBuyIn type
StateBuyIn %	Continuous	State BuyIn as percentage of total of (StateBuyIn and All Others) (This is a derived field for the purpose of data analysis)
StateBuyIn Level	Categorical	Derived level for StateBuyIn *Low*: If StateBuyIn % is less than 10 *Medium*: If StateBuyIn % is between 10 and 19 *High*: if StateBuyIn % is greater than or equal to 20 (This is a derived field for the purpose of data analysis)
Urban	Continuous	Medicare Enrollee count for urban population
Rural	Continuous	Medicare Enrollee count for rural population
Aged	Continuous	Medicare Enrollee count in Aged category
Disabled	Continuous	Medicare Enrollee count in Disabled category
% Aged	Continuous	Aged Medicare Enrollee as Percent of Total Resident Population
% Disabled	Continuous	Disabled Medicare Enrollee as Percent of Total Resident Population
Aged Without ESRD	Continuous	Aged Medicare Enrollee count without End Stage Renal Disease (ESRD)
Aged With ESRD	Continuous	Aged Medicare Enrollee count with End Stage Renal Disease (ESRD)
Disabled Without ESRD	Continuous	Disabled Medicare Enrollee count without End Stage Renal Disease (ESRD)
Disabled With ESRD	Continuous	Disabled Medicare Enrollee count with End Stage Renal Disease (ESRD)
ESRD Only	Continuous	End Stage Renal Disease (ESRD) only
FFS	Continuous	Fee For Service Medicare (Part A and Part B) enrollee count
MC	Continuous	Managed Care Medicare (Part A and Part B) enrollee count
FFS%	Continuous	FFS as percentage of (FFS + MC) (This is a derived field for the purpose of data analysis)

Double click on the first copy of the Data Source node and click the Variable button in the Edit Parameter window. Select the variables as shown in Figure H.4. Click OK.

Click on the Node Browser and then double click Feature Selection and Root Cause Analysis, as shown in Figure H.5.

The Feature Selection and Root Cause Analysis node will be added in the workspace. Double click on this node. Select the All Results option for the "Detail of computed results reported" list box and leave the rest of the options at their default setting (Figure H.6). Then click the OK button.

Right click the Feature Selection and Root Cause Analysis node and select Run to Node from the shortcut menu.

Next, right click the Feature Selection and Root Cause Analysis node and select Run to Node from the shortcut menu. You should now see two new result nodes displayed in your Data Miner workspace, as shown in Figure H.7.

View the reports by double clicking the Reporting Documents node (Figure H.8).

The histogram indicates that FFS, Rural, and Disabled with ESRD are the three top predictor variables for region-wise Medicare enrollment.

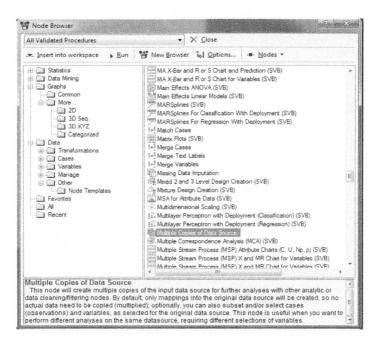

FIGURE H.1   The 'Node Browser' used in the data miner workspace.

FIGURE H.2   Dialog window in STATISTICA that allows a change in the number of copies of the data set, called a "clone process." This is useful when one wants to take the same data set through separate procedures in the workspace window of STATISTICA, which uses icons to represent entire analytic computation processes, data cleaning, or results tables.

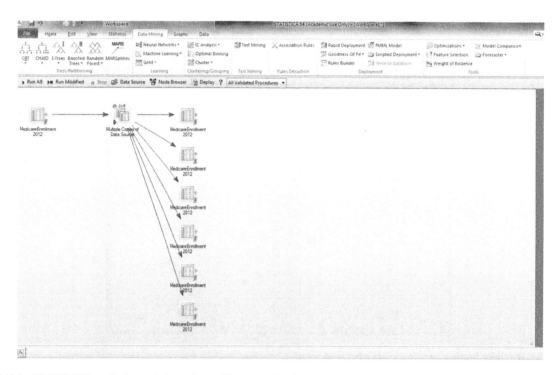

FIGURE H.3 STATISTICA predictive analytic workspace illustrating that the six "cloned" copies of the same data set are "in place" in the workspace; from here, various computations, data mining algorithms, and other processes (all represented by nodes − i.e., icons) can be connected to develop a complete "data analytic process."

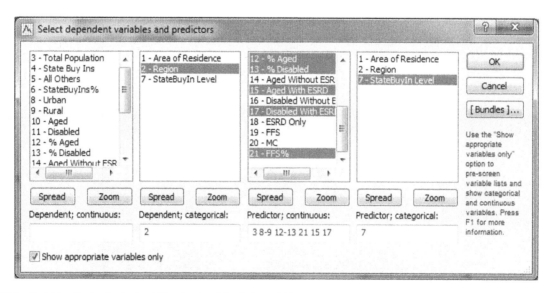

FIGURE H.4 Variable selection in the "variable selection dialog"; the variables can either be highlighted, *or* the number of the variable can be typed into the spaces at the bottom of each variable category, leaving one space between each variable, *or*, if a set of consecutive numbers, a "hyphen" can be used to set this group.

FIGURE H.5   Feature Selection is be chosen from this Node Browser dialog.

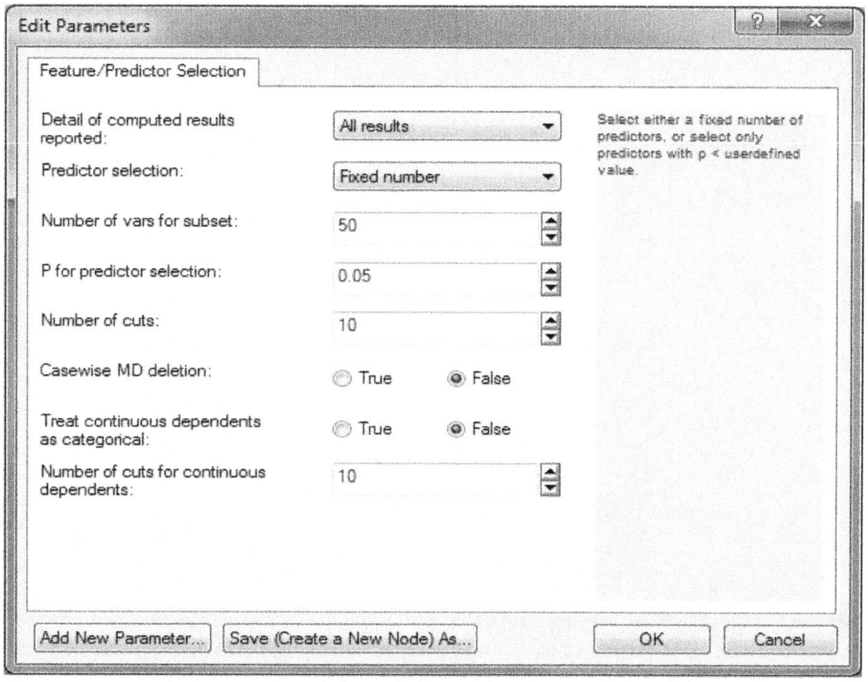

FIGURE H.6   The Edit Parameters dialog for the Feature Selection/Predictor Selection dialog.

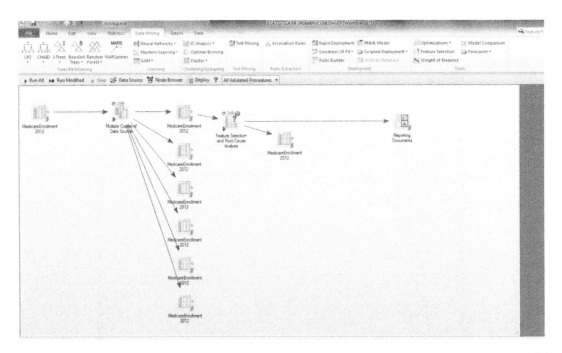

FIGURE H.7 A Result node is seen at the extreme right, above; this was produced when the Feature Selection node was "right clicked," and then Run to Node was selected from the flying menu.

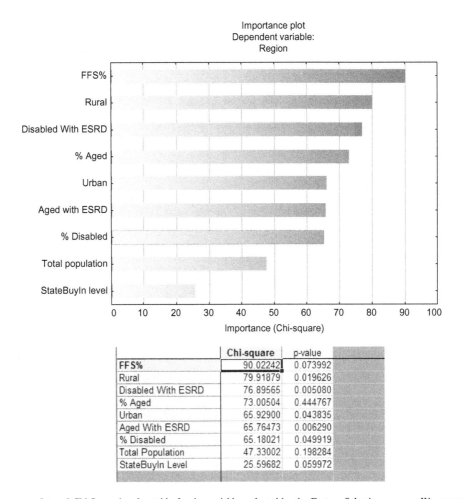

	Chi-square	p-value	
FFS%	90.02242	0.073992	
Rural	79.91879	0.019626	
Disabled With ESRD	76.89565	0.005080	
% Aged	73.00504	0.444767	
Urban	65.92900	0.043835	
Aged With ESRD	65.76473	0.006290	
% Disabled	65.18021	0.049919	
Total Population	47.33002	0.198284	
StateBuyIn Level	25.59682	0.059972	

FIGURE H.8 Importance plot and Chi-Square/p-value table for the variables selected by the Feature Selection process. We can see that the top seven variables all contribute in important ways to the "target," but that Total Population and StateBuyIn Level predictor variables are not that important. Since there is not a "clear" bend in the curve, individuals have to use their "domain/data knowledge" and "intuition" to select how many of these variables should be included in subsequent predictive analytic modeling. In fact, it may be necessary to try different sets/numbers of these predictors to come up with a "best exploratory" model. Sometimes, with too many predictors selected, the "noise" within the system reduces the accuracy scores; many times when this happens, a smaller set of the top predictor variables will have "less noise" and produce the best model.

2D MEAN PLOT ANALYSIS

In this section we will find the distribution pattern for some of the key fields using mean plot analysis.

In the DM workspace select the second copy of the Data Source node and then click on the Node Browser. Select 2D Means with Error Plots from the Graphs collection, as shown in Figure H.9.

Select FFS and MC as dependent variables and Region as a grouping variable, as shown in Figure H.10.

Right-click the 2D Means with Error Plots node and select Run to Node from the shortcut menu (Figure H.11).

To see the graph, double click on Reporting Documents. Figure H.12 shows the 2D mean plot generated, which indicates that the FFS (Fee-for-service) is high in the Mid-Atlantic region and East North Central region compared to other regions. (*Note*: One of the interpretations of this graph is that the CMS [Center of Medicare and Medicaid Services] needs to analyze further in those two regions to determine the reason for high FFS and derive the roadmap towards cost-effectiveness initiatives like Accountable Care Organization.)

Next we will investigate the influence of Area of Residence on Medicare Enrollment.

Select the third copy of the Data Source node and click on Node Browser. Again, select the 2D Means with Error Plots from the Graph collection. Select Urban and Rural as dependent variables, as shown in Figure H.13.

To see the graph, double click on Reporting Documents and select the right window. The graph plot is shown in Figure H.14.

The graph shows that Medicare enrollment is much higher in urban areas than in rural areas.

(*Note*: This graph can be useful to assess the provider network capacity planning to serve the Medicare population. The graph shows a good trend, as the number of providers is usually higher in urban areas compare to that in rural areas and hence can support large number of Medicare encounters. Insufficient provider network in a region is always a greater risk for emergency visits, causing more medical cost. The lesser number of enrollments in rural areas can be

FIGURE H.9   Selecting "2D Means with Error Plots" as the next process to use with the variables selected from the feature selection process.

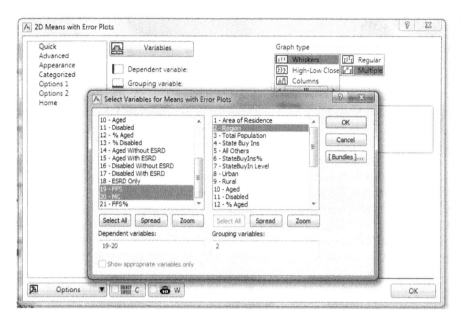

FIGURE H.10   Actual selection of variables for the Means with Error Plots computation.

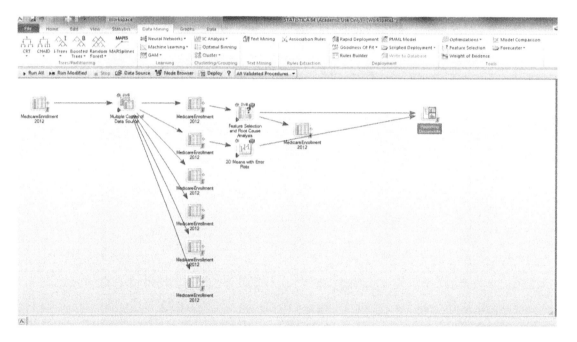

FIGURE H.11   Right clicking on the 2D Means with Error Plots node and then selecting Run to Node from the flying menu allows the computation to complete, putting the Results into the Results node at the farthest right-hand side.

useful in assessing the effectiveness of new cost-control initiatives, such as Telemedicine, which can bring good results for rural populations.)

Next we will analyze the distribution of the End Stage Renal Disease (ESRD) Medicare population in the United States. End stage renal disease is typically known as fifth stage chronic kidney disease, and Medicare insurance in the United States covers eligible patients who require dialysis or renal transplant.

Select the fourth copy of the Data File node and click on Node Browser. Again, select the 2D Means with Error Plots from the Graph collection. Now select the Aged With ESRD and Disabled With ESRD variables as dependent variables, and Region as a Grouping variable, as shown in Figure H.15.

Right-click the new 2D Means with Error Plots node and select Run to Node from the shortcut menu (Figure H.16).

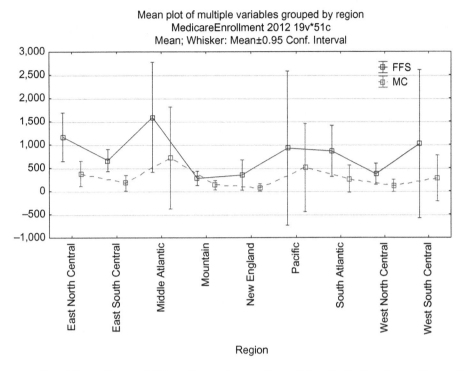

FIGURE H.12 Mean plot of multiple variables graphed by region; this is a specific result found in the Results node. One can "double click" on the Results node to bring up the entire "workbook" of results, and then click on the specific result(s) of interest.

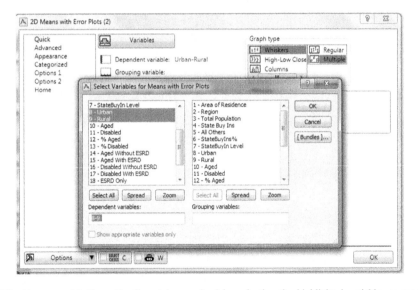

FIGURE H.13 Area of Residence vs. Medicare Enrollment is examined by selecting the highlighted variables as seen in this figure: Variable 8 = Urban, and Variable 9 = Rural.

To see the graph, double click on the Reporting Documents node. The report output is shown in Figure H.17. This mean plot shows that:

- The ESRD Medicare population is high in the Middle Atlantic zone. The Mountain and New England areas have a low mean for ESRD enrollment.
- The West South Central region has the highest range, compared to other regions.

(*Note*: This mean plot on ESRD can provide useful information for various health plans both for risk assessment and to frame the network structure to provide special services such as dialysis.)

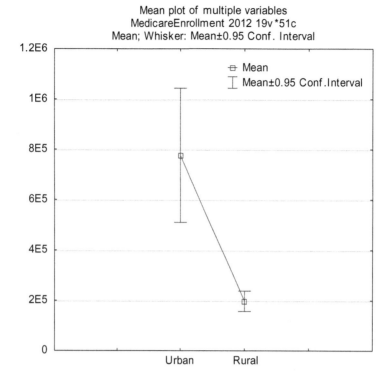

FIGURE H.14 Plot of Urban vs. Rural Medicare Enrollments; since the error bars do NOT overlap, but instead are completely separated, this shows a significance difference in enrollment between these two living areas.

FIGURE H.15 Using another of the cloned data sets, in the workspace, End Stage Renal Disease will be examined.

Next we will analyze the variable called StateBuyIn Level. State Buy In is a Medicare program created by Congress to help the low-income Medicare population. For the sake of our analysis, we have categorized the StateBuyIn Level into three categories:

- Low, when StateBuyIn % is less than 10
- Medium, when StateBuyIn % is between 10 and 19
- High, when StateBuyIn % is greater than or equal to 20.

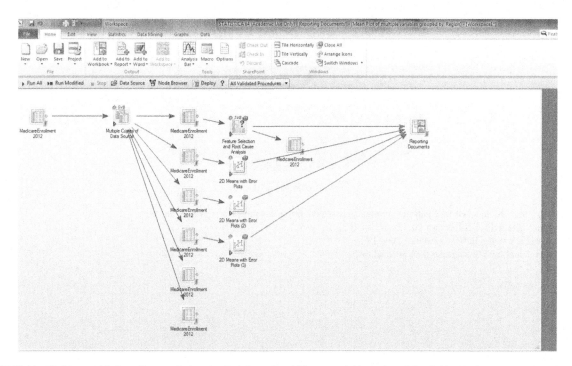

FIGURE H.16 2D Means with Error Bars applied to the End Stage Renal Disease variables; when right clicking on the icon and selecting Run to Node, the results were pushed up into the Results node at the upper right; from here one can double click on the Results node and select the graphs for End Stage Renal Disease.

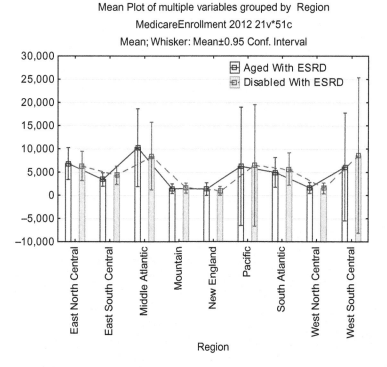

FIGURE H.17 End State Renal Disease distribution by region of country.

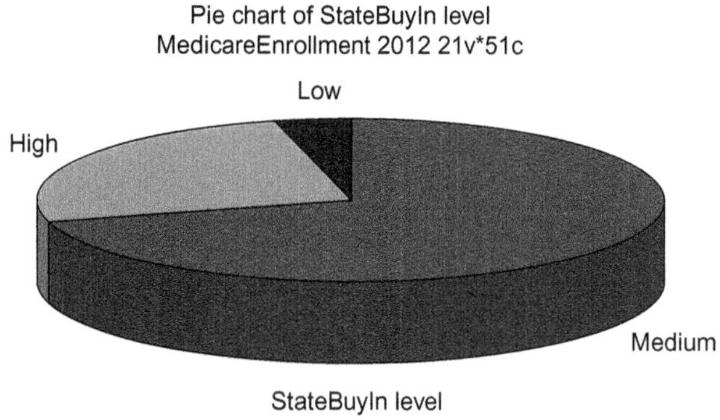

Pie chart of StateBuyIn level
MedicareEnrollment 2012 21v*51c

Low

High

Medium

StateBuyIn level

FIGURE H.18   StateBuyIn levels for Medicare enrollment, based on three categories: low, medium, and high.
- Low, when StateBuyIn % is less than 10
- Medium, when StateBuyIn % is between 10 and 19
- High, when StateBuyIn % is greater than or equal to 20.

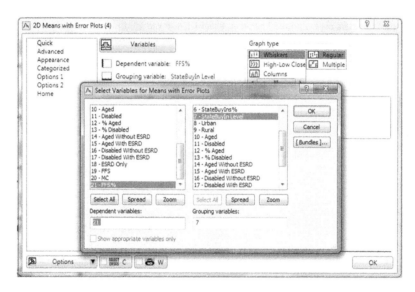

FIGURE H.19   Examining the relationship between FFS% and StateBuyIn Level.

First we will generate a pie chart for the StateBuyIn Level variable. Select the fourth data file node and click on Node Browser. Select the pie graph from the Graphs collection and then click OK. Next, double click the fourth copy of the Data File node and select the variable StateBuyIn Level as a Categorical predictor variable.

Right click the new 2D Pie Chart node and select Run to Node from the shortcut menu. Double click on the Report Documents to pull the pie chart on StateBuyIn Level, as shown in Figure H.18.

Figure H.18 shows that the Medium StateBuyIn Level (StateBuyIn % is between 10 and 19) is significantly high compared to the other two levels.

Next we will analyze the relationship between FFS% and StateBuyIn Level. First, select the sixth copy of the data file node and again select 2D Means with Error Plots from the Node Browser. Double click on the new 2D Means with Error Plots node, and select FFS% as dependent variable and StateBuyIn Level as the grouping variable (see Figure H.19).

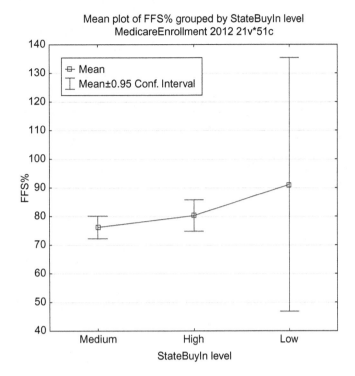

FIGURE H.20 Mean Plots comparing FFS% grouped by StateBuyIn Levels (buy in levels binned into three categories: High, Medium, and Low).

Right-click the new 2D Means with Error Plots node and select Run to Node from the shortcut menu. To see the graph, double click on the Reporting Documents node (Figure H.20).

The mean graph shows fee-for-service is low for a medium StateBuyIn level. As the medium level for StateBuyIn is high, as per the pie chart (Figure H.18), this may be a good trend for the States to control FFS related costs.

CONCLUSION

Visual data mining using graphical methods is a very useful technique in data mining projects, to find interesting patterns in the data set.

Tutorial I

Case Study: Detection of Stress-Induced Ischemia in Patients with Chest Pain After "Rule-Out ACS" Protocol

Sergii Alekseiev, MD and Ambria Harris, DO, with faculty advisors: Edward Rylander, MD, Frank Hamilton, MD, Linda A. Winters-Miner, PhD and Gary D. Miner, PhD

Chapter Outline

NOTE: Because it was not possible to completely de-identify the patients in the data set used in this study, this is presented as a case study without the data set provided; as a reader of this book you could create a hypothetical data set using the variables in this study, and then work through your own analysis following some of the procedures described below, in order to get an idea of how to do this type of study.

BACKGROUND

Every year, an estimated 5–10% of presentations to emergency departments, and up to a quarter of hospital admissions, are attributable to symptoms suggestive of acute coronary syndrome (Goodacre *et al.*, 2005). Most patients with symptoms suggestive of acute coronary syndromes undergo lengthy assessment, either in the emergency department or as hospital inpatients, even though 75–85% of these patients ultimately do not have a final diagnosis of acute coronary syndrome (Chase *et al.*, 2006; Pollack *et al.*, 2006). Prolonged assessment contributes to overcrowding in the hospital or department, physician duplication of effort, and clinical risk as patients are treated by different clinical staff (Goodacre *et al.*, 2005). This over-triage has enormous economic implications for the US healthcare system, estimated at $8 billion in annual costs (Fineberg *et al.*, 1984; Tosteson *et al.*, 1996).

On the other hand, studies have shown that between 2% and 5% of emergency department (ED) patients with chest pain who are sent home develop myocardial infarction (MI) within 30 days (Dagnone *et al.*, 2000; Pope *et al.*, 2000). In a prospective multicenter clinical trial, clinical data of all patients with chest pain or other symptoms suggesting acute cardiac ischemia who presented to the emergency departments of 10 US hospitals were analyzed (Pope *et al.*, 2000). Of 10,689 patients, 17% ultimately met the criteria for acute cardiac ischemia (8% had acute myocardial

Practical Predictive Analytics and Decisioning Systems for Medicine. DOI: http://dx.doi.org/10.1016/B978-0-12-411643-6.00025-9

infarction and 9% had unstable angina), 6% had stable angina, 21% had other cardiac problems, and 55% had non-cardiac problems. Among the 889 patients with acute myocardial infarction, 19 (2.1%) were mistakenly discharged from the emergency department (95% confidence interval [CI] 1.1−3.1%); among the 966 patients with unstable angina, 22 (2.3%) were mistakenly discharged (95% CI 1.3−3.2%). Multivariable analysis showed that patients who presented to the emergency department with acute cardiac ischemia were more likely not to be hospitalized if they were women less than 55 years old (odds ratio [OR] for discharge 6.7; 95% CI 1.4−32.5), were non-white (OR 2.2; 95% CI 1.1−4.3), reported shortness of breath as their chief symptom (OR 2.7; 95% CI 1.1−6.5), or had a normal or non-diagnostic electrocardiogram (OR 3.3; 95% CI 1.7−6.3). Patients with acute infarction were more likely not to be hospitalized if they were non-white (odds ratio for discharge 4.5; 95% CI 1.8−11.8) or had a normal or non-diagnostic electrocardiogram (OR 7.7; 95% CI 2.9−20.2) (Pope et al., 2000).

Unfortunately, no highly sensitive tools exist to detect acute coronary syndromes (ACS) in low-risk patients with chest pain (Swap and Nagurney, 2005). Although certain elements of the chest pain history are associated with increased or decreased likelihoods of a diagnosis of ACS or acute myocardial infarction (AMI), none of them alone or in combination identifies a group of patients that can be safely discharged without further diagnostic testing. Certain chest pain characteristics decrease the likelihood of ACS or AMI − namely, pain that is stabbing, pleuritic, positional, or reproducible by palpation (likelihood ratios [LRs] 0.2−0.3). Conversely, chest pain that radiates to one shoulder, or both shoulders or arms, or is precipitated by exertion is associated with LRs (2.3−4.7) that increase the likelihood of ACS. The chest pain history itself has not proven to be a powerful enough predictive tool to obviate the need for at least some diagnostic testing (Swap and Nagurney, 2005).

The belief that chest pain relief with nitroglycerin indicates the presence of active coronary artery disease is common. However, the data suggest that in a general population admitted for chest pain, relief of pain after nitroglycerin treatment does not predict active coronary artery disease and should not be used to guide diagnosis. In a prospective observational cohort study performed by Henrikson and colleagues, 459 consecutive patients with chest pain admitted through the emergency department received nitroglycerin from emergency services personnel or an emergency department nurse. Nitroglycerin relieved chest pain in 39% of patients (181 of 459). In patients with active coronary artery disease as the likely cause of their chest pain, 35% (49 of 141) had chest pain relief with nitroglycerin. In contrast, in patients without active coronary artery disease, 41% (113 of 275) had chest pain relief (p > 0.2). Four-month clinical outcomes were similar in patients with or without chest pain relief with nitroglycerin (p > 0.2) (Henrikson et al., 2003).

According to the recent report, currently available risk score models such as Goldman (Goldman et al., 1982, 1996), Thrombolysis in Myocardial Infarction (TIMI) (Antman et al., 2000), and Sanchis (Sanchis et al., 2005) lacked appropriate sensitivity to detect ACS for patients with acute chest pain (sensitivities 53%, 35%, and 41%, respectively) (Manini et al., 2009).

ECG and cardiac biomarkers are low-cost tools for identification of high-risk patients in need of intensive medical treatment; however, these tests are hampered by lack of sensitivity and are therefore insufficient for identifying all patients at high risk (Manini et al., 2009). In a retrospective literature review performed by Speake between 1976 and 1998, 10 papers were identified reporting the sensitivity of first EKG for diagnosis of ACS. These studies have shown that the first ECG is between 13% and 69% sensitive for AMI (Speake and Terry, 2001).

During the past two decades, troponins have been adopted as the preferred biomarker for the diagnosis of acute MI − a position reaffirmed in recent consensus guidelines (Thygesen et al., 2007). As part of this consensus for the preferred use of troponins for the diagnostic evaluation of the patient with suspected or proven acute coronary syndrome (ACS), the use of a troponin cut-point for acute MI that equals the 99th percentile in a healthy population has been endorsed, as long as the assay used delivers acceptable precision at this low threshold, because risk for adverse outcome (including death) has been demonstrated repeatedly in the context of values above this level (Morrow et al., 2001; Venge et al., 2002, 2009; James et al., 2004; Apple et al., 2008, 2009; Eggers et al., 2007, 2009). However, most commercial assays for troponin were inadequate to deliver such performance, because of either a limit of detection above that of reference populations, or unacceptable imprecision (by consensus, more than 10% variation from test to test) at low concentrations (Panteghini et al., 2004). Although recently developed high-sensitivity troponin assays may now achieve consensus guideline-recommended of 10% imprecision at this low reference limit, a degree of uncertainty regarding their clinical application exists, particularly with respect to the specificity of these tests for the clinical syndrome of acute MI. This is because they are able to detect even minor degrees of myocardial injury, even in the absence of ACS. Indeed, despite consensus regarding their adoption for clinical use, only preliminary data exist supporting the use of high-sensitivity troponin assays in populations of patients with chest pain and suspected ACS (Apple et al., 2008, 2009; Keller et al., 2009; Reichlin et al., 2009). Further, the term "highly sensitive" troponins still refers to sensitivities of 62−82.3% at admission, necessitating serial measurements (Januzzi et al., 2010; Keller et al., 2011).

Patients with negative cardiac enzymes and non-ischemic EKG present a diagnostic dilemma. Even in patients with "clear-cut alternative non-cardiac diagnosis," event rate at 30 days may be as high as 4% (death, MI, and revascularization) (Hollander et al., 2007). In patients with chest pain and no ST-segment changes or troponin elevation, the rate of death or MI at 1 year may be as high as 29.6%, depending on presenting risk factors (Sanchis et al., 2005). Patients with the presence of four out of the five following criteria are at the highest risk: chest pain score ≥ 10 points; more than two chest pain episodes over the past 24 hours; age ≥ 67 years; insulin dependent diabetes mellitus (this single criterion is equivalent to the presence of two other criteria); and prior history of percutaneous transluminal coronary angioplasty (Sanchis et al., 2005).

A reliable, reproducible, and more timely process for the identification of chest pain presentations that have a low short-term risk of a major adverse cardiac event is needed to facilitate earlier discharge (Hollander, 1999). Two major approaches have been implied to accomplish this purpose: accelerated diagnostic protocols, and imaging studies. In the ASPECT (Than et al., 2011) study, a 2-hour accelerated diagnostic protocol (ADP) was developed to assess patients presenting to the emergency department with chest pain symptoms suggestive of acute coronary syndrome. The predefined ADP under investigation was a combination of TIMI risk score of 0, no new ischemic changes on the initial ECG, and normal point-of-care biomarker panel (at 0–2 hours after arrival). All parameters had to be negative for the ADP to be considered negative (and thus for the patient to be identified as low risk). Of 3,582 consecutive patients, the ADP classified 352 (9.8%) patients as low risk and potentially suitable for early discharge. A major adverse cardiac event occurred in three (0.9%) of these patients, giving the ADP a sensitivity of 99.3%, a negative predictive value of 99.1%, and a specificity of 11.0% (Than et al., 2011). Similarly, the Chest Pain Choice Trial (Pierce et al., 2010) was aimed at developing a decision aid that communicates the short-term risk of ACS to patients with chest pain, non-ischemic EKG, and negative cardiac enzymes. The primary outcome of the trial measured was patient knowledge regarding their short-term risk for ACS, and the risks of radiation exposure. The impact of the decision aid on the admissions rate, rate of major adverse cardiac events, and economic costs and healthcare utilization was also evaluated. The Global Registry of Acute Coronary Events (GRACE) score (Lyon et al., 2007), the Thrombolysis in Myocardial Infarction (TIMI) risk score (Antman et al., 2000), and the computerized quantitative pretest probability calculator developed by Kline et al. (2009) were preselected as prospectively validated clinical prediction tools for the development of this decision aid. The decision aid included a 100-person pictograph depicting the pretest probability of acute coronary syndrome and available management options (observation unit admission and stress testing, or 24–72 hours outpatient follow-up). A total of 204 patients who were randomized to a decision aid or usual care were followed for 30 days. Compared with usual care patients (n = 103), decision aid patients (n = 101) decided less frequently to be admitted to the observation unit for stress testing (58% versus 77%; absolute difference, 19%; 95% CI 6–31%). There were no major adverse cardiac events after discharge in either group; however, the study was not powered to detect a difference in major adverse cardiac events between groups (Hess et al., 2012).

While the myocardial perfusion scan (MPS) seems to be the non-invasive imaging modality most often used by the IHI medicine team, other types of imaging are available and have been the subject of many studies to determine which offers the most accurate and cost-effective assessment of ACS. A 1-year cohort study of 265 patients by Pant and associates showed that, in one hospital alone, $600,000/year — the additive cost of the MPS studies — could have been saved if imaging had not been ordered in those with a low pretest probability (based on the Diamond & Forrester Score) (Pant et al., 2012). This same group (DFS <40%) showed MPS to have a positive predictive value of 22.7%, as opposed to 83.3% in those with high pretest probability (DFS >40%). In addition, $4.5 million was spent on admissions costs in those same low risk patients. In a prospective study by Kwong and associates, the use of cardiac MRI was analyzed among 161 patients presenting with chest pain to the ED. The sensitivity and specificity was determined to be 84% and 85%, respectively, and was also found to be of benefit in detecting those with troponin-negative unstable angina (Kwong et al., 2003). Compared to clinical parameters alone, MRI was found to be the strongest predictor used in the study for ACS. In an observational cohort study by Hoffman et al., CTA had a sensitivity of 100% (95% CI 98–100%) and a NPV of up to 100% (95% CI 89–100%) with a specificity for the presence of plaque or stenosis of 54% (CI 49–60%) and 87% (CI 83–90%) (Hoffman et al., 2009). Dobutamine stress echocardiography (DSE) is another non-invasive imaging option. In a prospective, double-blind, multicenter study involving 377 patients, the adverse cardiac event rate at 6-month follow-up was 8/26 (30.8%) in those with a positive DSE, but 14/351 (4.0%) in those with a negative DSE (p < 0.0001) (Bholasingh et al., 2003).

CASE STUDY

We conducted a retrospective chart review of patients that presented to the emergency department of St John Medical Center with a chief complaint of chest pain and were subsequently admitted by the In His Image (IHI) residency team to rule out acute coronary syndrome (ACS) (Figure I.1).

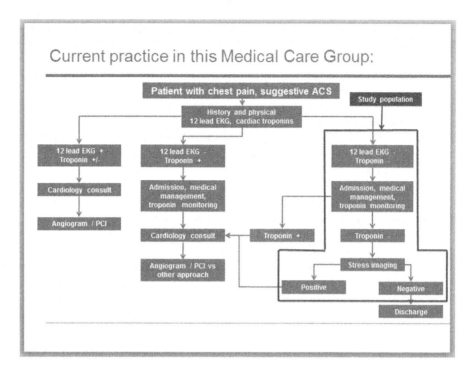

FIGURE I.1 Current practice in this medical care group.

Methods

Study Design

Inclusion criteria for the study were: (1) absence of EKG changes suggestive of ACS, such as ST segment deviation ≥ 2 mm, new bundle branch block, peaked T waves or q-waves; (2) negative results of two high sensitivity troponin assays 6 hours apart; (3) myocardial perfusion scan study results available prior to discharge. Exclusion criteria were: (1) presence of a clear-cut alternative diagnosis such as pneumonia; (2) evidence of acute coronary syndrome at any point during hospitalization.

Charts Selection

In order to determine eligible charts, the monthly discharge lists for the IHI team were reviewed for all patients admitted between June 2011 and April 2013. The in-hospital data of those whose admission indication was chest pain were then gathered directly from electronic charts in the EMR system.

Variables

Variables selected for statistical analysis were:

1. Age at the time of hospitalization. Additionally, all patients were stratified into two age groups: those 65 years and older, and those 67 years and older. The rationale for this stratification is described elsewhere (Antman *et al.*, 2000; Sanchis *et al.*, 2005).
2. Results of myocardial perfusion scan. These were stratified into two categories: "negative" and "positive." A negative result corresponds to no evidence of stress-induced ischemia on the tetrofosmin portion of the study, as concluded by the cardiologist. A positive result refers to either clear evidence of stress-induced ischemia or when the latter cannot be ruled out.
3. Gender male or female.
4. CATH lab report if available. Results were stratified as "positive" and "negative." A positive result refers to presence of coronary artery disease as evident by greater than 50% stenosis, as concluded by the cardiologist. A negative result corresponds to absence of coronary artery disease.

5. Risk factors for coronary artery disease, namely age 45 years and older for males and 55 years and older for females, cigarette smoking, hypertension (BP ≥ 140/90 or on antihypertensive medication), family history of premature CAD (in male first-degree relative <55 years, in female first-degree relative <65 yrs), low HDL cholesterol (<40 mg/dL), high LDL (≥160 mg/dL). All patients were stratified into two categories: those with three and more risk factors, and those with less than three risk factors.

6. Presence or absence of known CAD as documented in admission history and physical (H&P) or previous CATH lab report. Diabetes was considered as CAD equivalent.

7. Presence or absence of severe angina. Severe angina was defined as intensity of chest pain ≥ 10/10 at onset, as reported by the patient and documented in admission H&P. If no mention of chest pain severity was found in H&P, it was assumed to be non-severe (<10/10)

8. Aspirin use within the last 7 days (yes/no) as documented in H&P.

9. Presence of two and more anginal episodes within the last 24 hours (yes/no). If no mention of chest pain frequency was found in H&P, it was assumed that patient had one anginal episode.

10. Thrombolysis in myocardial infarction (TIMI) score for unstable angina or non-ST elevation myocardial infarction (see Antman *et al.*, 2000, for description of methodology).

11. Risk Score for Patients with Acute Chest Pain, NonoST-Segment Deviation, and Normal Troponin Concentrations (see Sanchis *et al.*, 2005, for methodology of calculation).

12. EKG findings stratified as "normal" and "abnormal". Abnormal findings included presence of any of the following: bundle branch blocks, atrioventricular block of any degree, atrial fibrillation/flutter, ST-T wave abnormality.

13. History of percutaneous coronary intervention (PCI) (yes or no).

14. History of diabetes (yes or no).

15. Age at the day of presentation in years.

16. Heart rate (HR). If the patient had a normal heart rate (60−100 bpm), then the first value on the day of presentation was recorded. If patient had an abnormal HR, then the highest or lowest abnormal value that day was recorded.

17. Systolic blood pressure. If patient had normal SBP (90−120), then first value on the day of presentation was recorded. If patient had abnormal SBP, then the highest or lowest abnormal value that day was recorded.

18. Creatinine level in mg/dL. The highest value on the day of presentation was recorded.

19. The Global Registry of Acute Coronary Events (GRACE) score (Lyon *et al.*, 2007).

20. Low- and high-density lipoprotein (LDL and HDL) levels within 3 months of presentation. Levels closest to presentation were recorded if more than one value was available within this period of time.

21. Hemoglobin A1C within 6 months of presentation. Levels closest to presentation were recorded if more than one value was available within this period of time.

22. Frequency of anginal episodes. Patients were stratified as those having more than two episodes within a 24-h period prior to presentation, and those with less than two episodes.

End Points

The primary end point of the study was the percentage of patients with positive MPS undergoing a percutaneous coronary intervention. The secondary end points were percentage of patients with chest pain, admitted to rule out ACS, who had positive MPS and a statistical model predicting MPS outcomes in these patients.

Statistical Analysis

The numerical data obtained in this study were analyzed using means (standard deviations) for continuous and frequencies for categorical variables. Correlations were assessed using non-parametric criteria. Prediction models were build utilizing modern predictive analytics. The following predictive algorithms were tested: Boosted Trees model (BTM), Neural Network model (NNM), Support Vector Machine (SVM) model, and Classification and Regression Trees (C&RT) model. The models were created on a training sample of patients, consisting of 75% of the patients from the main data set. Subsequently, models were assessed on a testing sample of patients consisting of 25% of patients from the main data set. Cross-validation was also used as a third, confirmatory validation of the model.

Results

General Overview and Study Stages

The study was performed in five key steps (see Figure I.2).

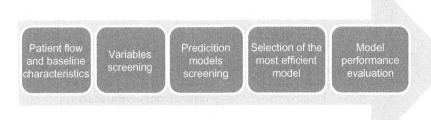

FIGURE I.2 Study stage sequence.

TABLE I.1 Analysis of Non-Negative MPS Outcomes That Did Not Result in Coronary Intervention

Outcomes	Number of cases	Comment
Inconclusive	9	**1** patient had recent positive CATH **2** patients had negative stress ECHO following MPS **1** patient had negative CT coronary angiogram following MPS **5** patients were clinically considered "safe" for discharge
Positive	7	**1** patient had second MPS study which was negative In **2** patients, cardiologist did not recommend further imaging In **2** patients, CATH was recommended but they refused the study **1** patient left the ward before MPS was read; further, he was lost for follow-up In **1** patient the reason for no further work-up was unclear

First, the patient's demographics, baseline clinical characteristics, and distribution according to the target outcome were summarized (Table I.1, Figure I.3).

Second, all variables (total of 22 – see Methods) were screened and ranked in order of importance for MPS outcome prediction (Table I.2). A set of 18 best predictors was selected. Third, various statistical prediction models were tested for accuracy, using variables obtained in Step 2. The most accurate model was selected for final analysis (Figure I.4). Table I.3 shows the variables that were omitted after the screening. Finally, the most efficient prediction models were tested for performance (Figure I.5).

Patient Characteristics and Flow in ACS "Rule Out" Algorithm (Step 1)

In total, 2,091 charts were screened and 243 cases identified as meeting inclusion criteria (see Figure I.3). The admission rate for patients undergoing work-up for ACS was 11.6%. Among the 243 cases, 102 charts were excluded due to the absence of stress testing prior to discharge, or for other reasons. Other reasons included readmissions for the same diagnosis, or stress testing other than MPS performed. A total of 141 patients had an MPS study prior to discharge and were included in our final analysis. Accordingly, 58% of all chest pain admissions underwent stress imaging with MPS modality. Positive or inconclusive results of MPS were found in 19 patients (13.4%), and negative results were found in 122 patients (86.5%). Of the 19 non-negative results, 10 (7%) were positive and 9 (6.4%) were inconclusive. Of the 10 patients with a positive MPS result, only 3 (2%) underwent invasive coronary angiogram and had percutaneous coronary intervention. *Out of all the myocardial perfusion studies ordered, only 2% led to coronary interventions.* Analysis of 16 cases with non-negative MPS results and no angiograms is presented in Table I.1. Most of these patients had an alternative imaging modality, such as stress echo or coronary CT.

Overall our study population consisted of predominantly males in their 50s, with more than three risk factors for CAD; nearly half of them had a history of CAD or diabetes (see Table I.2). Remarkably, in a subset of patients with positive MPS outcomes there was a significantly higher percentage of males with risk factors for CAD or known CAD than in the group with negative MPS results. Accordingly the mean TIMI score in the MPS + group was 2.2, vs 1.1 in the MPS − group (p < 0.0001).

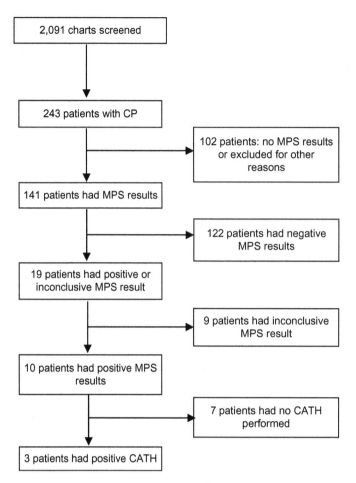

FIGURE I.3 Patient flowchart and MPS outcomes.

TABLE I.2 Baseline Clinical Characteristics of Patients with Different MPS Outcomes

Characteristic	Overall (n = 141)	MPS − (n = 122)	MPS + (n = 19)	p value	t test
Sex, male N (%)	67.0 (47.5)	53.0 (43.4)	14.0 (73.7)	0.015	2.46
Age, mean (SD)	55.0 (13.5)	54.2 (13.2)	60.5 (14.1)	0.056	−1.90
>3 risk factors for CAD, n (%)	71 (50.4)	53.0 (43.4)	18 (94.7)	0.0001	4.16
Known CAD, n (%)	41.0 (29.1)	30 (24.6)	11.0 (57.9)	0.0035	2.97
History of DM, n (%)	48.0 (34.0)	38.0 (31.1)	10.0 (52.6)	0.0679	1.84
History of PCA, n (%)	32.0 (22.7)	23.0 (19.0)	9 (47.3)	0.0245	2.3
TIMI score, mean (SD)	1.26 (1.13)	1.1 (1.07)	2.2 (1.08)	<0.0001	−4.15
SBP, mean (SD)	142 (31)	140 (29)	150 (40)	0.21	−1.27
LDL level, mean (SD)	99 (31)	102 (33)	84 (28)	0.07	1.82
HDL level, mean (SD)	39 (12)	39 (12)	35 (8)	0.09	1.34
Hemoglobin A1c, mean (SD)	7.1 (2.3)	7.3 (2.5)	6.7 (1.3)	0.42	0.82
SANCHES score, mean (SD)	0.94 (1.0)	0.86 (0.98)	1.42 (1.12)	0.02	−2.28

	Chi-square	p value
HR	19.17154	0.023773
A1c	16.71696	0.005069
LDL level	11.28281	0.186184
GRACE	10.94371	0.204909
> 3 CAD RF +/–	10.58156	0.001142
SBP	10.32700	0.242821
Creatinine	8.57498	0.127265
TIMI score	7.19101	0.126132
Age	6.63723	0.576229
H/O Diabetes yes/no	5.83282	0.015730
SANCHES	5.05054	0.168133
HDL	4.68586	0.698236
Sex	3.91966	0.047724
Killip class	3.89845	0.048331
EKG	3.84498	0.049895
Known CAD yes/no	2.73776	0.098002
H/O PCA yes/no	1.70083	0.192180
Age > 67 yes/no	0.58002	0.446306
ASA use past 7 days yes/no	0.50232	0.478483

FIGURE I.4 Best predictors of MPS outcomes based on Chi-square and p value.

TABLE I.3 Variables Omitted After Subjective Investigator Screening

Variables omitted	Reason
Heart rate	Significant variability between several measurements, common β-blocker use with CP "rule out ACS" diagnosis
Grace score	Unfamiliar to majority of providers, developed for patients with ACS
Creatinine level	Greatly impacted by presence of renal disease and in patients on dialysis
Killip class	All patients included into analysis had a score of 1
Age >67 years	Not significant Chi-square and p values
ASA use past 7 days	Not significant Chi-square and p values

	Variable Rank	Importance
> 3 CAD RF +/–	100	1.000000
H/O PCA yes/no	69	0.691395
A1c	66	0.664368
SBP	65	0.649668
HDL	48	0.484783
Age	48	0.475873
TIMI score	44	0.436043
Known CAD yes/no	42	0.420611
Sex	41	0.413618
LDL level	22	0.218893
>2 chest pain past 24 hrs yes/no	18	0.183808
SANCHES	12	0.120173
EKG	1	0.009570
H/O Diabetes yes/no	1	0.006150

FIGURE I.5 Final set of variables used in prediction modeling.

Variables Screening (Step 2)

The baseline 22 variables initially selected for analysis were screened and ranked based on the Chi-square and p values in order of importance for MPS outcome prediction (see Figure I.4). Further, this ranked list underwent subjective screening by investigators, and several variables were omitted from analysis for various reasons. In particular, the following variables were omitted: heart rate on presentation; GRACE score; Killip class; creatinine level; age >67 years; and history of ASA use over the last 7 days. Subjective reasons for omissions are displayed in Table I.3. The final list of variables used in prediction modeling is displayed in Figure I.5 and Figure I.6. The three most important variables based on the Chi-square value were level of hemoglobin A1c, presence of greater than three risk factors for coronary artery disease, and TIMI score. Similarly, based on the p value, the three most important predictors were the same; however, a history of PCA and the presence of known CAD were also strong predictors of MPS outcomes.

Only 30% of all patients included in the final analysis had a complete set of all variables, selected for prediction modeling (Table I.4). The most commonly missing variables were levels of hemoglobin A1c, LDL, and HDL. The percentages of patients with three, two, and one variables missing were 31, 12, and 27, respectively (see Table I.4).

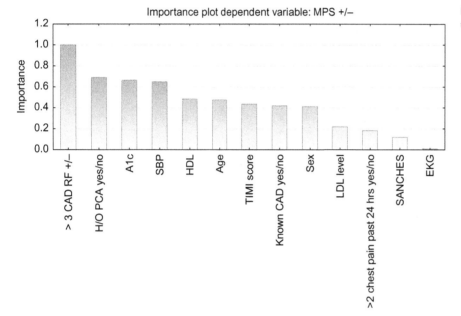

FIGURE I.6 Importance plot of variables used in prediction modeling.

TABLE I.4 Percentage of Patients with Missing Baseline Data

Patient category	Absolute number	Percentage of patients (%)
All variables present	43/141	30
Missing 3 variables	44/141	31
Missing 2 variables	16/141	12
Missing 1 variable	38/141	27
Missing A1c value	76/141	54
Missing LDL value	69/141	49
Missing HDL value	58/141	41

Prediction Models Screening (Step 3)

The following prediction models were screened for prediction accuracy: Boosted Trees model (BTM), Neural Network model (NNM), Support Vector Machine (SVM) model, and Classification and Regression Trees (C&RT) model.

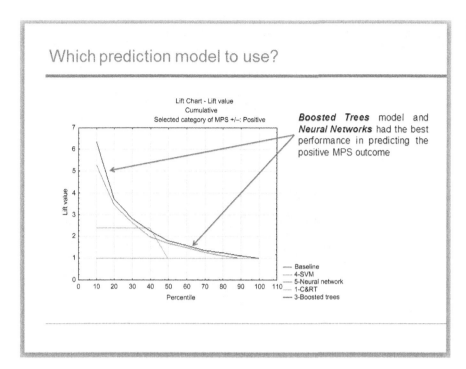

FIGURE I.7   Lift value of different models in predicting a positive MPS outcome.

TABLE I.5 Approximate Performance of Different Prediction Models on a Random Sample of Patients (n = 35)

Prediction model name	Estimated error rate (%) (n = 141)
Boosted Trees	6.38
Neural Networks	6.38
Superior Vector Machine	9.93
Classification and Regression Trees	30.5

Models screening was performed on a sub-sample of patients, called the "train sample," randomly selected from the main data set. Of these four models, BTM and NNM had the highest performance for predicting a positive MPS outcome (see Figure I.7). The error rate for these two models obtained on a training sample of patients was estimated at 6.38%. The SVM and the C&RT model had estimated error rates of 9.93 and 30.5 accordingly (see Table I.5).

Model Evaluation (Step 4)

Model performance was assessed on a training subset of patients, selected from the main data set. In total, 130 patients were included in the BT model evaluation analysis and 141 patients were included in neural network analysis.

Boosted Trees Model Performance

Of 130 cases included in BTM evaluation, 17 MPS outcomes were observed to be positive and 113 negative. Of 17 observed positive outcomes, BTM predicted them all correctly: no observed positive outcomes were predicted to be negative. This resulted in a sensitivity of 100% (95% CI 77−100) (see Table I.6). Of 113 negative observed outcomes, 73 were incorrectly predicted as positive. This resulted in a poor specificity of 35% (95% CI 27−45). Accordingly, the positive predicted and negative predicted values for this model were 18% (95% CI 12−29) and 100% (95% CI 89−100).

TABLE I.6 BTM Performance for Prediction of MPS Outcomes

Observed	Predicted positive	Predicted negative	
Positive	17	0	100% Sensitivity
Negative	73	40	35% Specificity
	19% PPV	100% NPV	(n = 130)

TABLE I.7 NNM Performance for Prediction of MPS Outcomes

Observed	Predicted positive	Predicted negative	
Positive	10	9	53% Sensitivity
Negative	0	122	100% Specificity
	100% PPV	93% NPV	(n = 141)

TABLE I.8 BTM and NNM Summary Performance for Prediction of MPS Outcomes

Parameters	Boosted trees	Neural networks
Sensitivity, % [95% CI]	100 [77−100]	53 [29−74]
Specificity, % [95% CI]	35 [27−45]	100 [96−100]
PPV, % [95% CI]	18 [12−29]	100 [66−100]
NPV, % [95% CI]	100 [89−100]	93 [87−97]
False positive rate % [95% CI]	81 [71−88]	0 [0−34]
False negative rate % [95% CI]	0 [0−10]	6 [3−13]
Positive result rate % [95% CI]	69 [60−76]	7 [4−13]
Negative result rate % [95% CI]	30 [23−40]	93 [87−96]

Neural Networks Model Performance

Out of 141 cases included in the NNM evaluation, 19 MPS outcomes were observed to be positive and 122 negative. Of the 19 positive outcomes, the model incorrectly predicted 9 as negative, which result in a sensitivity of 53% (95% CI 29−74) (see Table I.7). In contrast, out of 122 negative observed outcomes, the model correctly predicted all 122 of them as negative. This results in a specificity of 100% (95% CI 96−100). Accordingly, the positive predicted and negative predicted values for this model were 100% (95% CI 66−100) and 93% (95% CI 87−97). The summary of performance of two models is displayed in Table I.8.

Discussion

To our knowledge, this was the first study attempting to build a prediction model for stress imaging modality after "rule-out ACS" protocol. We also confirmed a previously made statement that patients with chest pain are often over-triaged (Pollack *et al.*, 2006; Chase *et al.*, 2006). In our study, only 19% of all MPS studies ordered in this subset of patients were positive or inconclusive, which is consistent with results previously obtained by Pant and Cook (Pant *et al.*, 2012), where the rates of positive MPS outcomes were 10−26% depending on a pretest probability. Similarly, in the same study the rate of revascularization procedures was 3%, which is consistent with the 2% rate obtained in our study. Given these data,

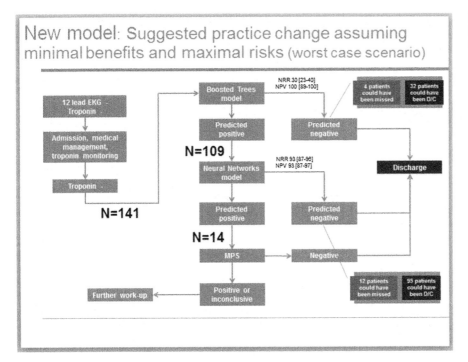

FIGURE I.8 New model: suggested practice change assuming minimal benefits and maximal risks (worst case scenario).

a fair question should be raised as to whether stress imaging, particularly MPS, should be ordered at all after ACS has been ruled out. It appears that only 2–3% of patients would benefit from the stress imaging approach. Thereby, not ordering the study at all would potentially result in missing 2% of treatable stable angina cases. The third option would be attempting to estimate the pretest probability and order MPS only in high-risk patients. Our model, if further validated, would potentially offer such an opportunity to a practicing clinician.

The sensitivity of a Boosted Trees model in our study was 100%, but it had a poor specificity of only 35%. In contrast, the Neural Networks model had a high specificity (100%) but poor sensitivity of 53%. The former model offers an excellent screening tool that could potentially eliminate unnecessary testing right away. The second model would be a good confirmatory test to select patients who definitely need stress imaging. Therefore, combining these two models could be a possible approach, previously adopted in other areas of medicine, where two tests (one with good sensitivity and another with high specificity) are being used to improve diagnostic yield (such as HIV testing with ELISA and Western Blot).

Utilization of our model would lead to tremendous resource saving. Negative results rates for Boosted Trees and Neural Networks models are 30% and 93%, respectively. This would allow discharge of 134 out of 141 patients without stress imaging, resulting in at least $87,000 in cost savings annually.

Our study has numerous limitations. The low sample size and low rate of positive MPS outcomes creates a problem with wide confidence intervals, which makes the study results less reproducible. Another important limitation is the high percentage of patients with missing baseline data. Only 30% of patients had a complete set of variables, required for predictive modeling. This creates a potential bias in prediction algorithms used by the models. Not surprisingly, the Boosted Trees model had the highest prediction accuracy, since it utilizes a high number of simple binary algorithms (205 in our study), each with weak prediction power (Figure I.8).

REFERENCES

Antman, E.M., Cohen, M., Bernink, P.J., McCabe, C.H., Horacek, T., Papuchis, G., et al., 2000. The TIMI risk score for unstable angina/non-ST elevation MI: a method for prognostication and therapeutic decision making. JAMA. 284 (7), 835–842.

Apple, F.S., Pearce, L.A., Smith, S.W., Kaczmarek, J.M., Murakami, M.M., 2009. Role of monitoring changes in sensitive cardiac troponin I assay results for early diagnosis of myocardial infarction and prediction of risk of adverse events. Clin. Chem. 55, 930–937.

Apple, F.S., Smith, S.W., Pearce, L.A., Ler, R., Murakami, M.M., 2008. Use of the Centaur TnI-Ultra assay for detection of myocardial infarction and adverse events in patients presenting with symptoms suggestive of acute coronary syndrome. Clin. Chem. 54, 723–728.

Bholasingh, R., Cornel, J.H., Kamp, O., van Straalen, J.P., Sanders, G.T., Tijssen, J.G., et al., 2003. Prognostic value of pre-discharge dobutamine stress echocardiography in chest pain patients with a negative cardiac troponin T. J. Am. Coll. Cardiol. 41, 596–602.

Chase, M., Robey, J.L., Zogby, K.E., Sease, K.L., Shofer, F.S., Hollander, J.E., et al., 2006. Prospective validation of the thrombolysis in myocardial infarction risk score in the emergency department chest pain population. Ann. Emerg. Med. 48, 252–259.

Dagnone, E., Collier, C., Pickett, W., Ali, N., Miller, M., Tod, D., et al., 2000. Chest pain with non-diagnostic electrocardiogram in the emergency department: a randomized controlled trial of two cardiac marker regimens. CMAJ. 162, 1561–1566.

Eggers, K.M., Jaffe, A.S., Lind, L., Venge, P., Lindahl, B., 2009. Value of cardiac troponin I cutoff concentrations below the 99th percentile for clinical decision-making. Clin. Chem. 55, 85–92.

Eggers, K.M., Lagerqvist, B., Venge, P., Wallentin, L., Lindahl, B., 2007. Persistent cardiac troponin I elevation in stabilized patients after an episode of acute coronary syndrome predicts long-term mortality. Circulation. 116, 1907–1914.

Fineberg, H.V., Scadden, D., Goldman, L., 1984. Care of patients with a low probability of acute myocardial infarction: cost effectiveness of alternatives to coronary-care unit admission. N. Engl. J. Med. 310, 1301–1307.

Goldman, L., Cook, E.F., Johnson, P.A., et al., 1996. Prediction of the need for intensive care in patients who come to the emergency department with acute chest pain. N. Engl. J. Med. 334, 1498–1504.

Goldman, L., Cook, E.F., Johnson, P.A, Brand, D.A., Rouan, G.W., Lee, T.H., 1982. A computer-derived protocol to aid in the diagnosis of emergency room patients with acute chest pain. N. Engl. J. Med. 307, 588–596.

Goodacre, S., Cross, E., Arnold, J., Angelini, K., Capewell, S., Nicholl, J., 2005. The health care burden of acute chest pain. Heart. 91, 229–230.

Henrikson, C.A., Howell, E.E., Bush, D.E., Miles, J.S., Meininger, G.R., Friedlander, T., et al., 2003. Chest pain relief by nitroglycerin does not predict active coronary artery disease. Ann. Intern. Med. 139, 979–986.

Hess, E.P., Knoedler, M.A., Shah, N.D., Kline, J.A., Breslin, M., Branda, M.E., et al., 2012. The chest pain choice decision aid: a randomized trial. Circ. Cardiovasc. Qual. Outcomes. 5 (3), 251–259.

Hoffman, U., Bamberg, F., Chae, C.U., Nichols, J.H., Rogers, I.S., Seneviratne, S.K., et al., 2009. Coronary computed tomography angiography for early triage of patients with acute chest pain. J. Am. Coll. Cardiol. 53, 1642–1650.

Hollander, J.E., 1999. The continuing search to identify the very-low-risk chest pain patient. Acad. Emerg. Med. 6, 979–981.

Hollander, J.E., Robey, J.L., Chase, M.R., Brown, A.M., Zogby, K.E., Shofer, F.S., 2007. Relationship between a clear-cut alternative non-cardiac diagnosis and 30-day outcome in emergency department patients with chest pain. Acad. Emerg. Med. 14, 210–215.

James, S.K., Lindahl, B., Armstrong, P., Califf, R., Simoons, M.L., Venge, P., et al., 2004. A rapid troponin I assay is not optimal for determination of troponin status and prediction of subsequent cardiac events at suspicion of unstable coronary syndromes. Int. J. Cardiol. 93, 113–120.

Januzzi Jr.J.L., Bamberg, F., Lee, H., Truong, Q.A., Nichols, J.H., Karakas, M., et al., 2010. High-sensitivity troponin T concentrations in acute chest pain patients evaluated with cardiac computed tomography. Circulation. 121, 1227–1234.

Keller, T., Zeller, T., Ojeda, F., Tzikas, S., Lillpopp, L., Sinning, C., et al., 2011. Serial changes in highly sensitive troponin I assay and early diagnosis of myocardial infarction. JAMA. 306 (24), 2684–2693.

Keller, T., Zeller, T., Peetz, D., Tzikas, S., Roth, A., Czyz, E., et al., 2009. Sensitive troponin assay in early diagnosis of acute myocardial infarction. N. Engl. J. Med. 361, 868–877.

Kline, J.A., Zeitouni, R.A., Hernandez-Nino, J., Jones, A.E., 2009. Randomized trial of computerized quantitative pretest probability in low-risk chest pain patients: effect on safety and resource use. Ann. Emerg. Med. 53 (6), 727–735.

Kwong, R.Y., Schussheim, A.E., Rekhraj, S., Aletras, A.H., Geller, N., Davis, J., et al., 2003. Detecting acute coronary syndrome in the emergency department with cardiac magnetic resonance imaging. J. Am. Heart Assoc. 107, 531–537.

Lyon, R., Morris, A.C., Caesar, D., Gray, S., Gray, A., 2007. Chest pain presenting to the emergency department – to stratify risk with GRACE or TIMI? Resuscitation. 74, 90–93.

Manini, A.F., Dannemann, N., Brown, D.F., Butler, J., Bamberg, F., Nagurney, J.T., et al., 2009. Limitations of risk score models in patients with acute chest pain. Am. J. Emerg. Med. 27, 43–48.

Morrow, D.A., Cannon, C.P., Rifai, N., Frey, M.J., Vicari, R., Lakkis, N., et al., 2001. Ability of minor elevations of troponins I and T to predict benefit from an early invasive strategy in patients with unstable angina and non-ST elevation myocardial infarction: results from a randomized trial. JAMA. 286, 2405–2412.

Pant, R., Cook, J., Gopalakrishnan, M., Urdininea, C., Syed, T., Rossell, G., et al., 2012. Rising health care cost in United States: Is defensive medicine the cause? Analysis in a chest pain rule-out cohort. J. Am. Coll. Cardiol. 59 (13), E1845.

Panteghini, M., Pagani, F., Yeo, K.T., Apple, F.S., Christenson, R.H., Dati, F., et al., 2004. Evaluation of imprecision for cardiactroponin assays at low-range concentrations. Clin. Chem. 50, 327–332.

Pierce, M.A., Hess, E.P., Kline, J.A., Shah, N.D., Breslin, M., Branda, M.E., et al., 2010. The Chest Pain Choice trial: a pilot randomized trial of a decision aid for patients with chest pain in the emergency department. Trials. 11, 57.

Pollack Jr.C.V., Sites, F.D., Shofer, F.S., Sease, K.L., Hollander, J.E., 2006. Application of the TIMI risk score for unstable angina and non-ST elevation acute coronary syndrome to an unselected emergency department chest pain population. Acad. Emerg. Med. 13, 13–18.

Pope, J.H., Aufderheide, T.P., Ruthazer, R., Woolard, R.H., Feldman, J.A., Beshansky, J.R., et al., 2000. Missed diagnoses of acute cardiac ischemia in the emergency department. N. Engl. J. Med. 342, 1163–1170.

Reichlin, T., Hochholzer, W., Bassetti, S., Steuer, S., Stelzig, C., Hartwiger, S., et al., 2009. Early diagnosis of myocardial infarction with sensitive cardiac troponin assays. N. Engl. J. Med. 361, 858–867.

Sanchis, J., Bodí, V., Núñez, J., Bertomeu-González, V., Gómez, C., Bosch, M.J., et al., 2005. New risk score for patients with acute chest pain, non-ST-segment deviation, and normal troponin concentrations. J. Am. Coll. Cardiol. 46 (3), 443–449.

Speake, D., Terry, P., 2001. Towards evidence based emergency medicine: best BETs from the Manchester Royal Infirmary: first ECG in chest pain. Emerg. Med. J. 18, 61–62.

Swap, C.J., Nagurney, J.T., 2005. Value and limitations of chest pain history in the evaluation of patients with suspected acute coronary syndromes. JAMA. 294, 2623–2629.

Than, M., Cullen, L., Reid, C.M., Lim, S.H., Aldous, S., Ardagh, M.W., et al., 2011. A 2-h diagnostic protocol to assess patients with chest pain symptoms in the Asia-Pacific region (ASPECT): a prospective observational validation study. Lancet. 377, 1077–1084.

Thygesen, K., Alpert, J.S., White, H.D.; Joint ESC/ACCF/AHA/WHF Task Force for the Redefinition of Myocardial Infarction, Jaffe AS, Apple FS, et al., 2007. Universal definition of myocardial infarction. Circulation. 116, 2634–2653.

Tosteson, A.N., Goldman, L., Udvarhelyi, I.S., Lee, T.H., 1996. Cost-effectiveness of a coronary care unit versus an intermediate care unit for emergency department patients with chest pain. Circulation. 94, 143–150.

Venge, P., Lagerqvist, B., Diderholm, E., Lindahl, B., Wallentin, L., 2002. Clinical performance of three cardiac troponin assays in patients with unstable coronary artery disease (a FRISC II substudy). Am. J. Cardiol. 89, 1035–1041.

Venge, P., James, S., Jansson, L., Lindahl, B., 2009. Clinical performance of two highly sensitive cardiac troponin I assays. Clin. Chem. 55, 109–116.

Tutorial J1

Predicting Survival or Mortality for Patients with Disseminated Intravascular Coagulation (DIC) and/or Critical Illnesses

Mahmood H. Khichi, MD, FAAP, Wanda P. Parsons, MBA, MHA and Linda A. Winters-Miner, PhD

Chapter Outline

DISSEMINATED INTRAVASCULAR COAGULATION IN CRITICALLY ILL PATIENTS

Disseminated intravascular coagulation (DIC) can accompany critical illnesses (Dressler, 2012). This study sought to predict outcomes for critically ill patients, many of whom also exhibited DIC conditions. We collected variables (through chart review) from patients when they first were admitted to the hospital in an effort to develop a prediction model for discharge from the hospital, or death. We reviewed the literature to determine those markers that normally accompany DIC.

DIC is a pathologic condition of system-wide hemorrhaging and clotting. Underlying conditions such as surgery, cancer, sepsis, and so on, can trigger inflammatory chemicals that cause micro-clots throughout the body (Dressler, 2004).

It seems a bit counterintuitive that clotting could cause bleeding. However, as the clotting increases, the clotting factor, fibrin, can become so otherwise engaged it is not available where it might be needed in wounds such as surgery sites, pick lines, IV lines, etc. Bleeding can therefore ensue as secondary to coagulopathology. The clots might also keep blood from vital organs, which can then begin to die. Extreme hemorrhaging and death is a real possibility with DIC.

The coagulopathology cascade is initiated in two ways: intrinsically and extrinsically (McCance *et al.*, 2010, p. 977). The intrinsic method, or contact activation pathway, generally starts with injury to the inside (endothelium) of the blood vessel, which then sends out negatively charged subendothelial substances. The extrinsic method, or the tissue factor (TF) pathway, starts with TF. The protein, CD142 (also called TF), can initiate the formation of thrombin. CD142 protein is found in leukocytes and the endothelium. Once the cascade begins it is difficult to stop, and soon the process is happening all over the body.

Practical Predictive Analytics and Decisioning Systems for Medicine. DOI: http://dx.doi.org/10.1016/B978-0-12-411643-6.00026-0

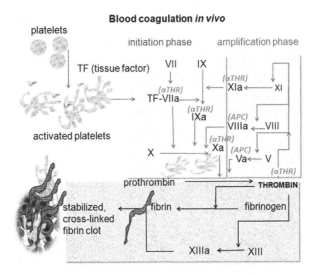

FIGURE J1.1   Blood coagulation in vivo. *Reproduced from Wikipedia (Dr. Graham Beards): http://en.wikipedia.org/wiki/File:Coagulation_in_vivo.png.*

Prothrombin or thrombin helps to make clots, and antithrombin helps to break down clots. Both are made in the liver. Thrombin converts fibrinogin into fibrin. There are also chemicals in the blood that break down clots: protein C, plasminogen, and antithrombin. If there is too much thrombin, then too much clotting occurs. For example, too much antithrombin (action increased by the use of heparin) can encourage bleeding.

Figure J1.1, from Wikipedia, illustrates the process of clot formation.

There are several ways in which the body reduces blood flow. Blood vessels constrict, clots form, or plugs form from platelets (Dressler, 2012). In simplistic terms, if the subendothelium of a blood vessel is damaged and exposed, then platelets start their action by changing their shape from disks to spheres. They then become sticky, clump, and plug the hole. If the hole is larger, platelets become more of a foundation for fibrin strands to knit more of a platform in an attempt to stop the bleeding. Furthermore, tissue that has been damaged produces tissue factor to stop the bleeding. Inflammation, caused by the trauma, induces cytokines, which serve to enhance coagulation. The problem is that the inflammatory response brings on white blood cells, vasodilation, and spreading of the inflammatory response down the line. As may be seen by the schematic in Figure J1.1, the processes of stopping up flow or of increasing flow are complicated, and if something goes awry in any of the links, clotting abnormalities can occur. In general, when the sequence gets out of control things do not go well.

Diagnosis of DIC

Many of the patients in this study either presented with a diagnosis of DIC or developed DIC during their stay. To diagnose and treat the disorder, many levels need to be monitored: blood pressure, platelet levels, creatinine, fibrinogen, electrolytes, aspartate aminotransferase, international normalized ratio, leukocytes, red blood cells, prothrombin time, etc. (Dressler, 2012) — basically, any measure of the dynamics of the blood, electrolytes, and gas exchanges (Franchini and Manzatob, 2004). We wanted to see which of the factors needed measuring immediately when patients were first admitted.

Dressler (2012, p. 53) constructed Table J1.1, which gives common considerations.

DIC is not something that can be diagnosed with static tests, however. There are many indicators, and some of those indicators need to be measured over time to observe changes. Therefore, diagnosis of the condition involves many indicators observed both subjectively (clinically) and objectively (laboratory tests). Levi *et al.* (2009) reported their meta-analysis of over 900 patients to give the most reported laboratory abnormalities. These were (most frequently mentioned first): "thrombocytopenia, elevated fibrin degradation products, prolonged PT, prolonged aPTT, and a low fibrinogen" (p. 26).

Levi *et al.* (2009) also reproduced the scoring system for diagnosing DIC developed by the International Society on Thrombosis and Hemostasis (ISTH). The scoring system was 91% sensitive and 97% specific for DIC. Figure J1.2 shows the system. The higher the score using this system, the greater the risk of death.

TABLE J1.1 Dressler's Table of Common Tests

Test	Purpose	Comments
Hemoglobin level and hematocrit	Measurement of red blood cells and oxygen-carrying capacity	Affected by fluid volume status
Platelet count	Numerical measurement of platelets present in plasma	Count does not indicate activity
International normalized ratio	General test of coagulation that monitors the tissue factor pathway and part of the common pathway	Used to monitor warfarin therapy
Activated partial thromboplastin time	General test of coagulation that monitors the tissue factor pathway and part of the common pathway	Used to monitor unfractionated heparin therapy
Anti-Xa activity assay	Measures the inhibition of factor Xa when antithrombin is added	Used for selected patients to monitor low molecular weight heparin therapy
Activated clotting time	Measures the time it takes for blood to clot after an activating agent is added	Used to monitor unfractionated heparin or bivalirudin activity
Fibrinogen level	Measures the quantity of fibrinogen	Used after bleeding and transfusion therapy
D-dimer level	A measurement of degraded fibrin released from a clot	Elevated in thromboembolic disease, disseminated intravascular coagulation, and other conditions

Based on information from Wheeler and Rice (2010).

Guideline

Table II. ISTH Diagnostic Scoring System for DIC.

Scoring system for overt DIC

   Risk assessment: Does the patient have an underlying disorder known to be associated with overt DIC?

   If yes: proceed

   If no: do not use this algorithm

Order global coagulation tests (PT, platelet count, fibrinogen, fibrin related marker)

Score the test results

- Platelet count ($>100 \times 10^9/l = 0$, $<100 \times 10^9/l = 1$, $<50 \times 10^9/l = 2$)
- Elevated fibrin marker (e.g. D-dimer, fibrin degradation products) (no increase = 0, moderate increase = 2, strong increase = 3)
- Prolonged PT (<3 s = 0, >3 but <6 s = 1, >6 s = 2)
- Fibrinogen level (>1 g/l = 0, <1 g/l = 1)

Calculate score:

   ≥ 5 compatible with overt DIC: repeat score daily

   <5 suggestive for non-overt DIC: repeat next 1–2 d

FIGURE J1.2   Guideline table from ISTH. *Reproduced from Levi et al. (2009, p. 28).*

The diagnosis cannot be set with only one time of testing, however, as DIC is a dynamic process. If the platelet count is low, for example, but stable, this could be an indication that the process is subsiding. Or on the other hand, the platelet count might be in the normal range, but descending over time, indicating pathology in coagulation. Labs along with clinical observations are required.

Etiologies

DIC is not a disease but rather a condition that is *secondary* to other disorders and diseases of the body. There are many illnesses that can activate the clotting cascade (McCance *et al.*, 2010).

- Shock can cause arterial hypotension, and thus clotting, so any time the blood starts slowing down or stopping (such as in thrombosis, problems with capillary walls, accumulation of leukocytes), or when there are low oxygen levels in the arteries (hypoxemia), it can cause clotting and low blood pH (acidemia) (McCance *et al.*, 2010, p. 1050).
- Reperfusion is associated with DIC (Takeda *et al.*, 1999; Armstead, 2006; Bush *et al.*, 2011). Armstead (2006) mentioned the effect of new blood bringing in more white cells, which then can cause inflammation. If blood volume reduces due to bleeding or transplantation, for example, organ tissues are deprived of oxygen. If blood volume is then increased, such as in transfusions, re-oxidation is the result. However, during the gap the inflammatory response can kick in and this can start the cascade, perhaps related to an immune reaction as well (Bush *et al.*, 2011).
- Other causes of DIC include sepsis or viral infections (Akinbiyi and Olatunbosun, 2004; Zabolotskikh *et al.*, 2006; Zenciroglu *et al.*, 2010) — any kind of pathogen that might hurt the lining of the blood vessels (endothelium), such as infection from using allogenic blood for transfusions (Woloszczuk-Gebicka, 2005), or malaria (Ghafoor *et al.*, 2010). Infections in mothers before giving birth can move to the baby, leading to DIC (Bryant *et al.*, 2004). Sepsis from any condition is a huge risk factor for DIC (Hopper and Bateman, 2005).
- Childbirth includes a number of circumstances in which DIC can occur. Besides infections that the mother might pass to the child, a baby that dies in the uterus can cause DIC in the mother (Erez *et al.*, 2009). If the mother develops a chorangioma in the placenta, low oxygen conditions as well as hydrops in the baby (from too much amniotic fluid) can cause DIC in the baby (Jones *et al.*, 1972). Amniotic fluid embolism (AFE) has been known to cause maternal DIC (Spiliopoulos *et al.*, 2009). When mothers breastfeed their babies or when the baby cannot take in liquids for some reason (such as not having the sucking response), dehydration can occur (hypernatremic dehydration) and lead to DIC, as can being rehydrated too quickly if dehydrated. Both can lead to sepsis and then DIC (Unal *et al.*, 2008). If the uterus does not contract well after childbirth (uterine atony) the mother can bleed uncontrollably, or chorioamnionitis (infection) can occur, and this may result in DIC (Akinbiyi and Olatunbosun, 2004; Bern, 2005). Akinbiyi and Olatunbosun (2004) also mentioned that halogenated anesthetics can cause atony. Interestingly, Dede *et al.* (2010) postulated that the use of dinoprostone for inducing labor might cause DIC after the labor is over. Antiphospholipid antibodies (aPLs) in mothers, such as in lupus, can give rise to stroke or renal thrombosis in babies (Boffa and Lachassinne, 2007).
- Various cancers and certainly leukemias are associated with DIC. Tumors can stimulate the growth of tissue factor, such as in prostate cancer (Bern, 2005; Guldbakke and Schanbacher, 2006).
- Cardiac surgery is another area for which DIC can be secondary (Sridhar *et al.*, 2004; Binder *et al.*, 2007; Besser and Klein, 2010).
- Postoperative bleeding occurs for many reasons, including prophylactic treatment with anticoagulants, thrombolytics or platelet inhibitors; prolonged procedures; age; and predisposing diseases (Rice, 2000; Dressler, 2004; 42nd National Congress of Society of Clinical Biochemistry and Clinical Molecular Biology, 2010).
- In neonates, protein C deficiency, an autosomal recessive condition, is often associated with DIC (Goldenberg and Manco-Johnson, 2008).
- Hung-Yang *et al.* (2007) conducted a predictive analytic analysis of 42 newborns with subgaleal hemorrhage (SGH). They compared good outcome with bad outcome and found that having been transferred from another hospital was associated with poor outcome, as were other indicators such as bleeding, skull fractures, intensive care admission, and longer stays.
- Leitner *et al.* (2010) found that DIC scores predicted poor outcomes and 1-year mortality levels for patients who suffered from venous thromboembolism. They used a DIC score based on the International Society of Thrombosis and Haemostasis (see Table J1.2) (Leitner *et al.*, 2010, p. 1478).
  However, higher scores were associated with worse outcomes.

TABLE J1.2 Definition of the Scoring System for Disseminated Intravascular Coagulation (DIC) as Suggested by the International Society of Thrombosis and Haemostasis

Points	0	1	2
Platelet count, g/L	>100	≥50	<50
D-dimer, µg/mL	<0.4		0.4−4.0
Fibrinogen, g/L	>1.0	≤1.0	
Prothrombin index, %	>70	40−70	<40

- Ören *et al.* (2005) looked at the records of over 5,000 children, finding 62 with DIC. They examined the underlying disorders and found that death was strongly associated with respiratory and cardiovascular problems. They did not find any predictive value in any laboratory tests. Multiorgan dysfunction syndrome (MODS) and acute respiratory distress syndrome (ARDS), along with other respiratory system and cardiovascular system dysfunctions, were most predictive of death.

Treatment of DIC

It is generally thought that antithrombin is decreased in plasma of DIC patients, and that the reduced antithrombin is an indicator of DIC (Asakura *et al.*, 2001). However, antithrombin levels are not always decreased for patients with DIC, as in the example of promyelocytic leukemia. Further, in that study, protein C was not decreased in the sample of 139 septic patients (Asakura *et al.*, 2001). Asakura *et al.* found no difference in antithrombin levels or in protein C levels between the DIC patients and the non-DIC patients. Therefore, at least for the septic patient, reduced activity of antithrombin does not seem to be a marker for DIC. Those two variables are usually indicators of severity of the disease, and so Asakura *et al.* turned this around to mean that DIC would not be a sufficient indicator of severity. Someone could have a poor prognosis and not have DIC.

Basically the treatment modalities in 2004 included getting more blood in as it was lost, providing anticoagulation factors, and inhibiting the formation of excess fibrin (Franchini & Manzatob, 2004). Anti-inflammatory cytokines have been used more recently. In a study by Sun *et al.* (2011), the prolonged prothrombin time (PT) was a marker for higher mortality in their traumatic brain-injured patients. Solvent/detergent-treated plasma was used for pediatric patients and led to better results in coagulation parameters (PT and APTT measures) (Chekrizova and Murphy, 2006).

Proactivity in DIC: Effectiveness of Prophylactic Measures

Prediction could be very important for both DIC and death in traumatic events, and for critically ill patients. Prophylactic measures are being studied by many researchers. Examples include the following.

- Stammers *et al.* (2000) tried prophylactic administration of fresh frozen plasma before operating on a neonate's heart. Evidently the operation was successful, but the baby died of a fungal infection a couple of weeks later.
- Ojala *et al.* (2005) performed prophylactic catheterization to prevent DIC during childbirth to prevent excessive postpartum bleeding.
- Early administration of therapy had a beneficial effect on children with leukemia in perhaps preventing DIC (dicentric chromosome DIC) (Pichler *et al.*, 2010).
- Choi *et al.* (1995) induced apoxia in mice, which all developed DIC. They were then able to prevent DIC by prophylactically administering platelet-activating factor.
- Callow *et al.* (2002) revised the prophylactic platelet transfusion (up to then) standard trigger with good results.
- Pahatouridis *et al.* (2010) used prophylactic low molecular weight heparin with good success in patients with traumatic brain injury.

PREDICTIVE ANALYTIC EXERCISE

This exercise was based on real data that were fictionalized to maintain anonymity. Values were standardized, and actual text values concerning initial diagnoses were grouped into 25 text categories in order that we might demonstrate text mining. We also artificially extended the data base so that all the procedures would all run for demonstration purposes. Any findings should not be interpreted as "real."

The Patients and Data

All critically ill pediatric patients admitted to the home hospital between January 2011 and March 2013 were included.

Excluded were hematology oncology patients with primary coagulopathy without critical illness affecting DIC parameters.

We collected the data but then "fictionalized" the data for this tutorial to maintain confidentiality. The actual data were reserved for further analysis.

The data file is DIC1.sta, which may be found on the disk. Open the data file and observe the variables that we used.

Examining the Data

First, we examined the continuous data in a gross fashion. The following are directions for the reader.

First, 3D graphs are made using the Batch (ByGroup) analysis (Figure J1.3).

Select 3D Sequential Graphs and Raw Data Plot as in Figure J1.4.

Next, click on Variables (Figure J1.5).

Click "Show appropriate variables only" to sort out the continuous variables (Figure J1.6) from the discrete variables. The appropriate variables for a surface graph are the continuous variables.

Click Select All and click OK. Next, click on "By variables" (Figure J1.7).

Select Variable 17 (see Figure J1.8).

Next, to select the type of graph, click on the General tab (Figure J1.9). Click Surface.

Grab the left bar and drag to the right so that the workbook area listing can be seen (Figure J1.10). Note where the peaks and valleys are across the cases.

Figure J1.11 shows the distribution of scores of the continuous variables across the discharged patients. Click on the title to revise.

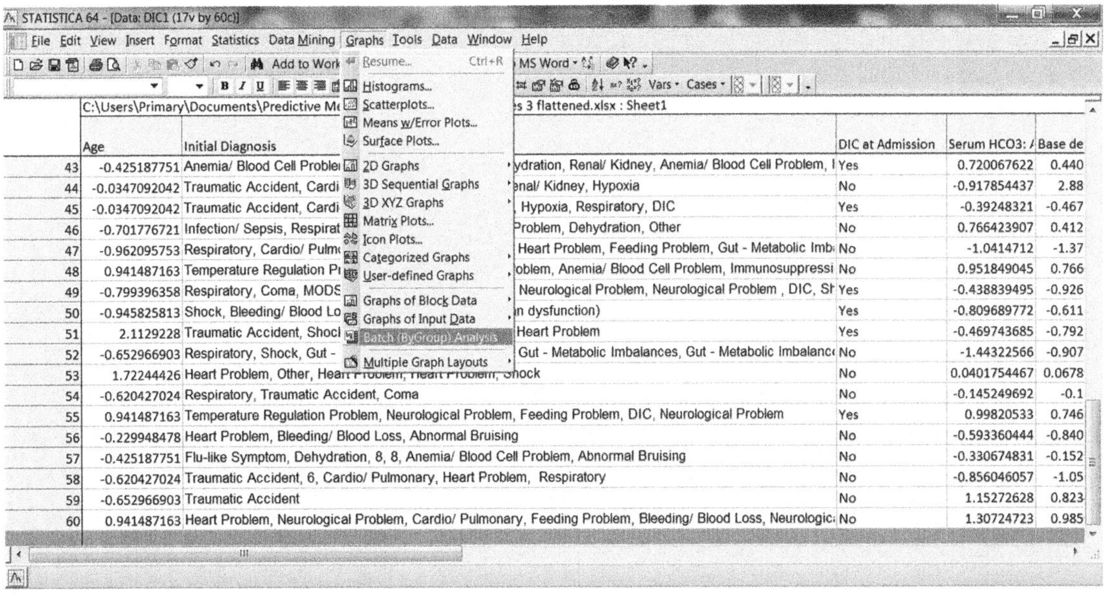

FIGURE J1.3   Location of By Group Analysis.

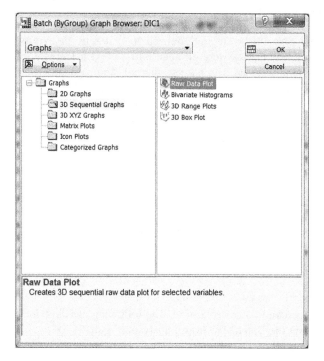

FIGURE J1.4 Select 3D Sequential Raw Data Plots.

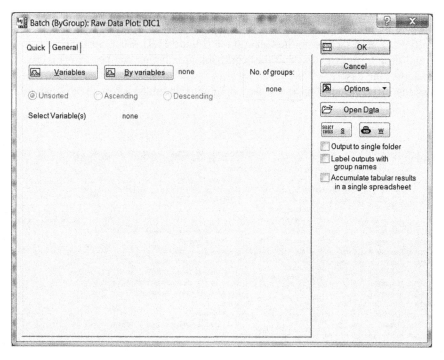

FIGURE J1.5 Select variables.

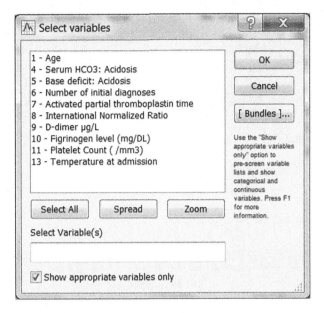

FIGURE J1.6 Click "Show appropriate variables only" Select All and click OK.

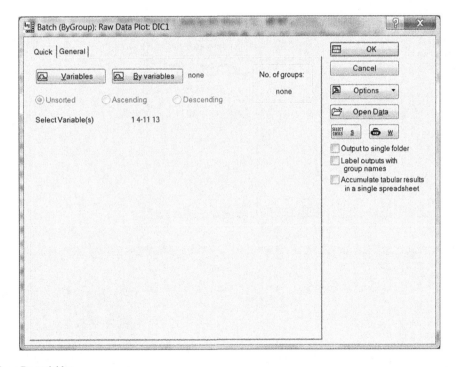

FIGURE J1.7 Click on By variables.

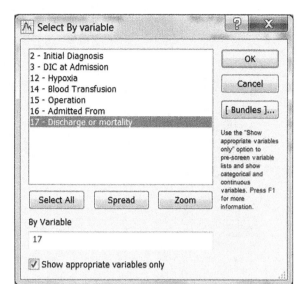

FIGURE J1.8   Select Discharge or Mortality.

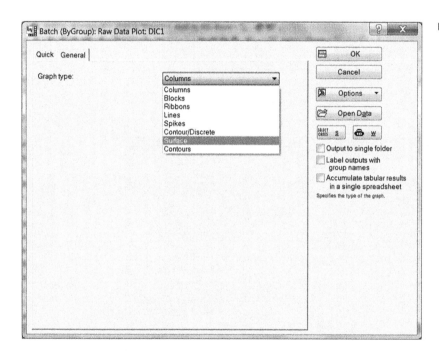

FIGURE J1.9   Select Surface.

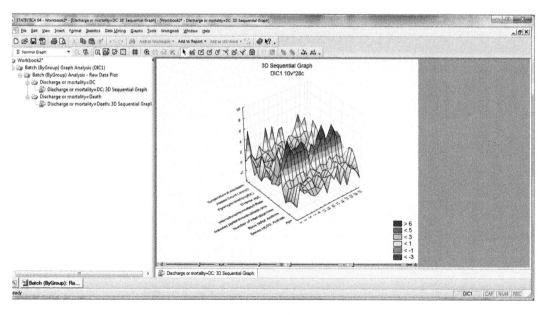

FIGURE J1.10
Overview of data.

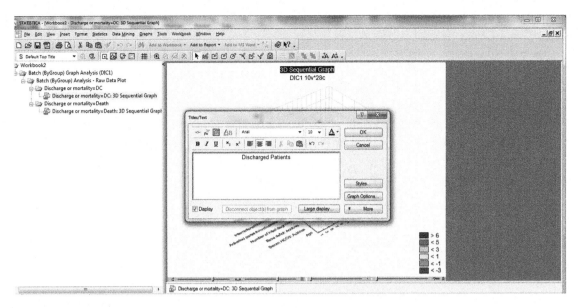

FIGURE J1.11   Can change the title.

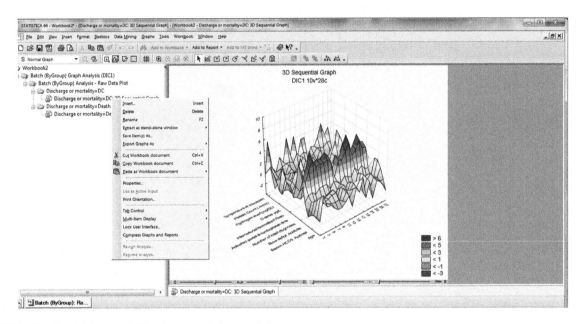

FIGURE J1.12   Right click on the left label and note that many choices are given.

Right click on the left label and note that many choices are given (Figure J1.12).

Click on Copy Workbook document, and the following may be pasted into a Word document or graphics program (Figure J1.13).

We can also see, as a comparison, the graph of the patients who died (Figure J1.14).

To get a better view of the graph, use the rotation button (Figure J1.15).

Figure J1.16 shows the rotation function. Click the "Analytic exploratory spin options" button and stop it when the view appears optimal for your purposes.

The manual slides at the bottom of the graph may also be used (Figure J1.17).

Looking at the groups side by side allows one to view the differences (Figure J1.18).

Many of the variables on the right appear to be higher on the z axis than on the left.

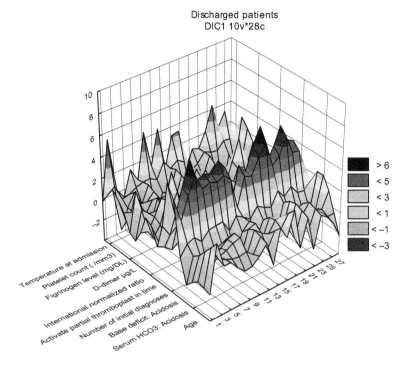

Discharged patients
DIC1 10v*28c

FIGURE J1.13 Discharged patients.

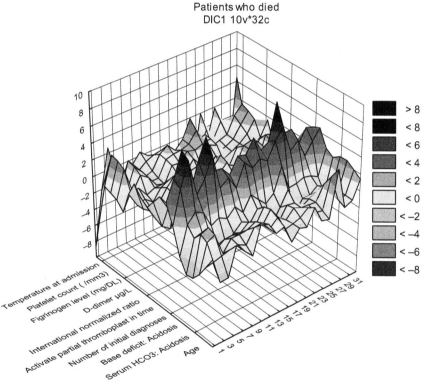

Patients who died
DIC1 10v*32c

FIGURE J1.14 Patients who died.

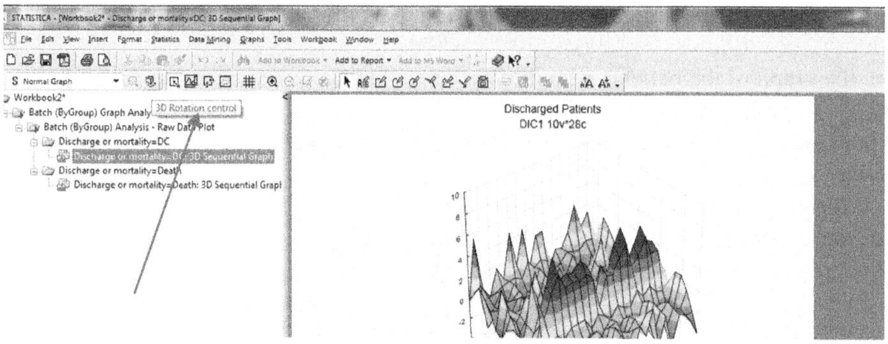

FIGURE J1.15 Can use the rotation button.

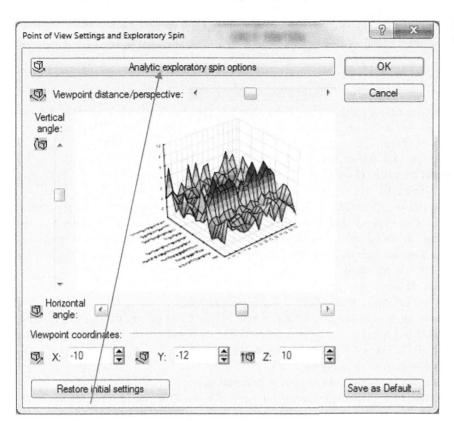

FIGURE J1.16 Click the Analytic exploratory spin.

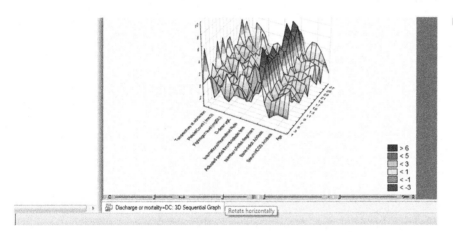

FIGURE J1.17 The image can be rotated.

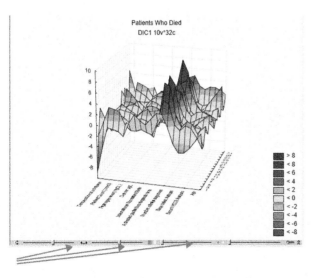

FIGURE J1.18 Manual slides at the bottom.

Data Mining Recipe

Next, to view predictive patterns, we ran the data mining recipe. If we detected possible worthwhile models, we then worked interactively with the best one. At this point we did not hold out any data or conduct any V-fold procedures. The reader may follow these steps to run a data mining recipe.

Click on Data Mining and the first option, Data Miner Recipes (Figure J1.19).

Click on "New" and on "Open/Connect data file" (Figures J1.20, J1.21).

Click on the data file (Figure J1.22). Click OK.

Next, click variables to select the ones to use. Note that if you click on the bottom left you can tell the program to show the appropriate variables only, as in Figure J1.23. Select the dependent variable (target) on the left side. Our target, Discharge or mortality, is categorical, so we select it. On the right-hand side are the predictors, both categorical and continuous. Select all but the target and the variable with the text (which will be saved until later). We did not select anything for the Testing sample, so leave that blank.

Click "Configure all steps" as in Figure J1.24.

Click on "Target variable," and then on "Discharge or mortality" (see Figure J1.25).

Click on Model Building and make sure all the models are clicked (Figure J1.26). Click on any that are not marked.

Note in Figure J1.26 that Random forest and Support Vector Machine (SVM) are not checked. Check them and then uncheck Configure all steps, as in Figure J1.27. The red Xs may be seen again.

Now, beside Next step, select Run to Completion as in Figure J1.28.

Now, just let the process run. It takes a few moments, and screens appear and disappear (see Figure J1.29.)

Pull the window over to the right so you can see what is contained in the workbook. First on the screen is the evaluation report of the various procedures tried. We see that the Boosted trees and Support Vector Machines seemed to predict the best, with only 3.33% error in them (Figure J1.30).

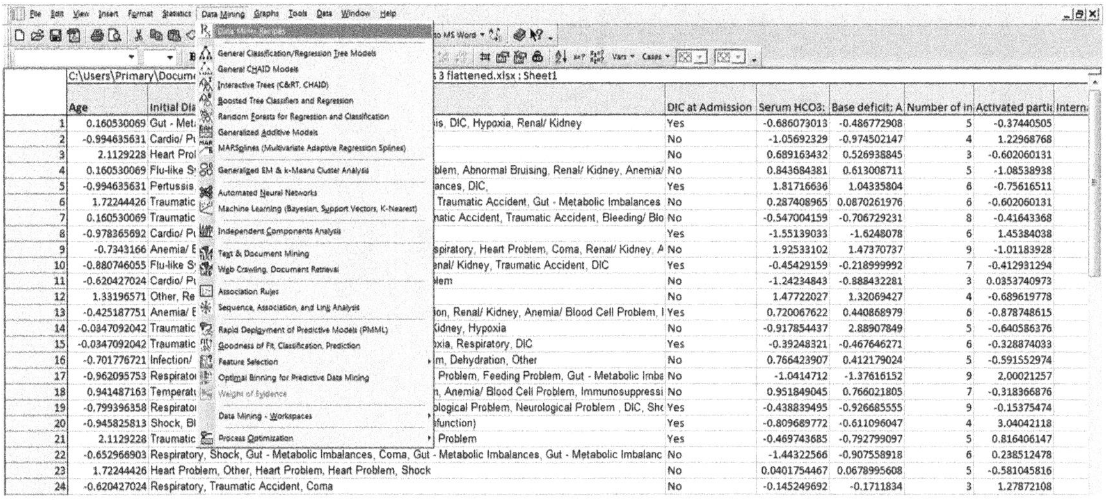

FIGURE J1.19   Click on Data Mining Recipe.

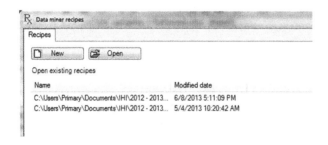

FIGURE J1.20   Select New.

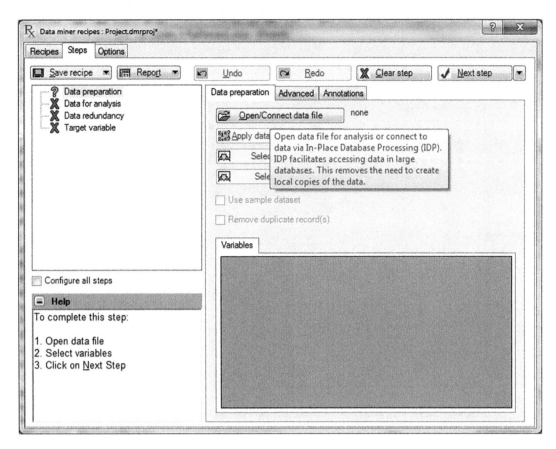

FIGURE J1.21   Open data file and connect.

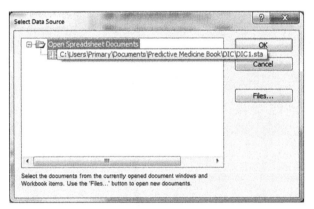

FIGURE J1.22   Click on data file and click OK.

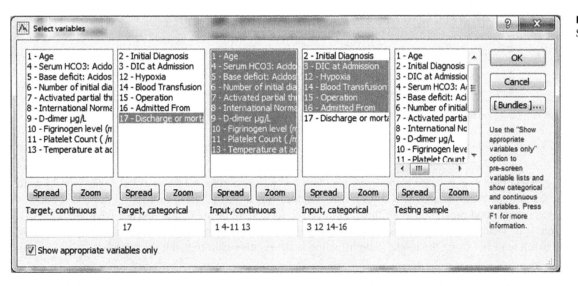

FIGURE J1.23
Select variables.

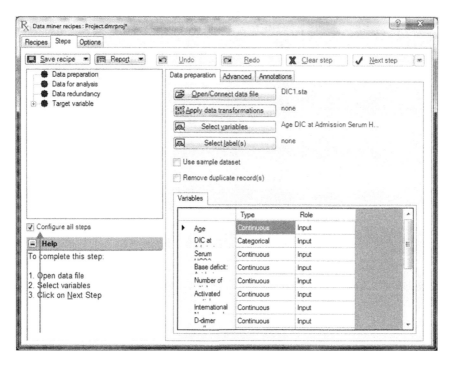

FIGURE J1.24   Click configure all steps.

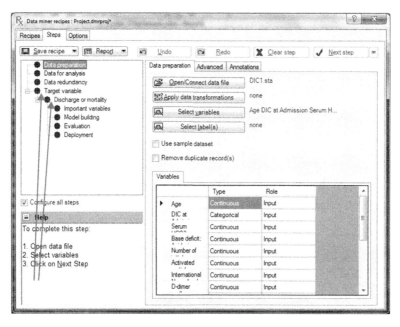

FIGURE J1.25   Click on "Target variable," and then on "Discharge or mortality".

One of these models might be best for working interactively, as our next step. Neural networks was next best, followed by Classification and regression trees (C&RT), and Random forest. All of these models on the surface look as though they might product good prediction algorithms. We need to look at all of the output and see what we find.

By clicking on a lift chart (Figure J1.31) we can see, graphically, the relative effectiveness of each of the models compared to the baseline of not using the model. The lift value is the relative gain in using the model.

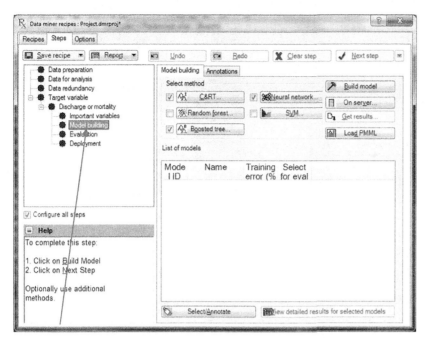

FIGURE J1.26 Click on Model Building.

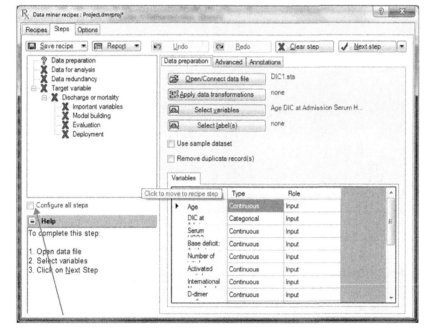

FIGURE J1.27 Uncheck configure all steps.

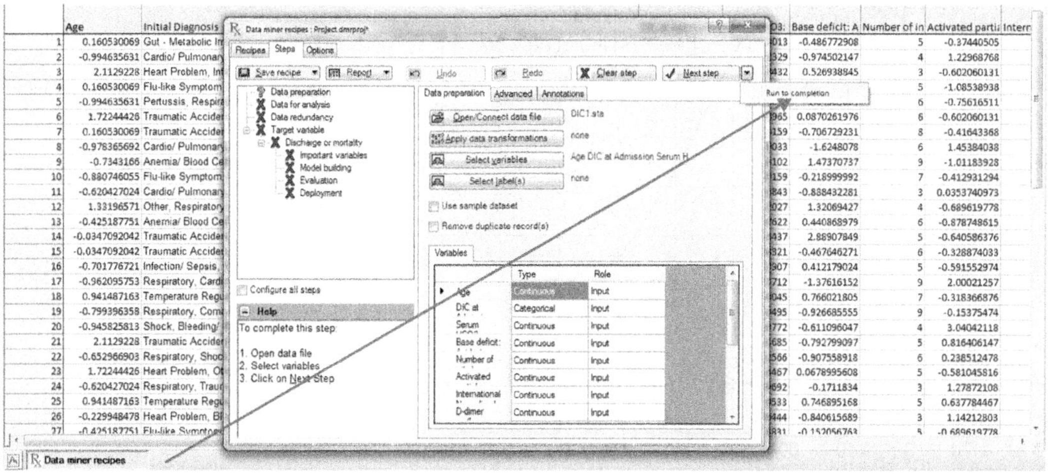

FIGURE J1.28 Click on Run to Completion.

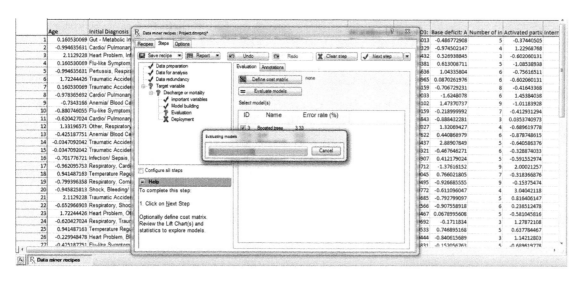

FIGURE J1.29
Let it run.

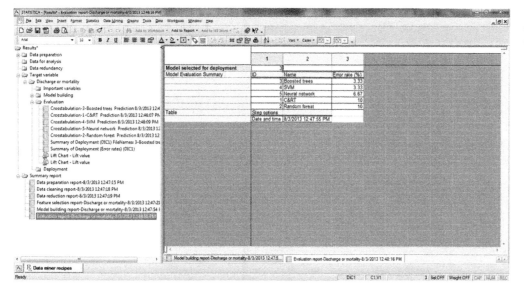

FIGURE J1.30 Output documents. Evaluation Summary.

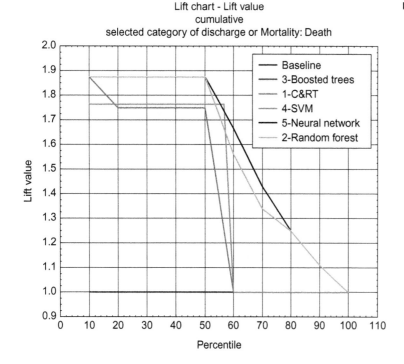

Lift chart - Lift value
cumulative
selected category of discharge or Mortality: Death

FIGURE J1.31 Lift Chart.

The baseline is at 1.0 and, as can be seen, all the models provided relative gain. It may not be the highest on a lift chart that turns out to be the best model to try. One has to look at all the components and then decide, given the problem in hand, what seems to be the best. So, next we look at the errors in the cross-tabulation tables (Figures J1.32—J1.36, below).

	Summary frequency table (Prediction) Table: Discharge or Mortality(2) x 3-Boosted trees Prediction(2)			
	Discharge or Mortality	3-Boosted trees prediction DC	3-Boosted trees prediction Death	Row totals
Count	DC	26	2	28
Column percent		100.00%	5.88%	
Row percent		92.86%	7.14%	
Total percent		43.33%	3.33%	46.67%
Count	Death	0	32	32
Column percent		0.00%	94.12%	
Row percent		0.00%	100.00%	
Total percent		0.00%	53.33%	53.33%
Count	All Grps	26	34	60
Total percent		43.33%	56.67%	

FIGURE   J1.32   Boosted   Trees   Cross Tabulation Table.

	Summary frequency table (Prediction) Table: Discharge or Mortality(2) x 1-C&RT Prediction(2)			
	Discharge or Mortality	1-C&RT prediction DC	1-C&RT prediction death	Row totals
Count	DC	26	2	28
Column percent		86.67%	6.67%	
Row percent		92.86%	7.14%	
Total percent		43.33%	3.33%	46.67%
Count	Death	4	28	32
Column percent		13.33%	93.33%	
Row percent		12.50%	87.50%	
Total percent		6.67%	46.67%	53.33%
Count	All Grps	30	30	60
Total percent		50.00%	50.00%	

FIGURE J1.33   C&RT Cross Tabulation Table.

	Summary frequency table (Prediction) Table: Discharge or Mortality(2) x 4-SVM Prediction(2)			
	Discharge or Mortality	4-SVM prediction DC	4-SVM prediction death	Row totals
Count	DC	26	2	28
Column percent		100.00%	5.88%	
Row percent		92.86%	7.14%	
Total percent		43.33%	3.33%	46.67%
Count	Death	0	32	32
Column percent		0.00%	94.12%	
Row percent		0.00%	100.00%	
Total percent		0.00%	53.33%	53.33%
Count	All Grps	26	34	60
Total percent		43.33%	56.67%	

FIGURE J1.34   SVM Cross Tabulation Table.

	Summary frequency table (Prediction) Table: Discharge or Mortality(2) x 5-Neural network Prediction(2)			
	Discharge or Mortality	5-Neural network prediction DC	5-Neural network prediction death	Row totals
Count	DC	24	4	28
Column percent		100.00%	11.11%	
Row percent		85.71%	14.29%	
Total percent		40.00%	6.67%	46.67%
Count	Death	0	32	32
Column percent		0.00%	88.89%	
Row percent		0.00%	100.00%	
Total percent		0.00%	53.33%	53.33%
Count	All Grps	24	36	60
Total percent		40.00%	60.00%	

FIGURE J1.35 Neural Network Cross Validation Table.

	Summary frequency table (Prediction) Table: Discharge or Mortality(2) x 2-Random forest Prediction(2)			
	Discharge or Mortality	2-Random forest prediction DC	2-Random forest prediction death	Row totals
Count	DC	28	0	28
Column percent		82.35%	0.00%	
Row percent		100.00%	0.00%	
Total percent		46.67%	0.00%	46.67%
Count	Death	6	26	32
Column percent		17.65%	100.00%	
Row percent		18.75%	81.25%	
Total percent		10.00%	43.33%	53.33%
Count	All Grps	34	26	60
Total percent		56.67%	43.33%	

FIGURE J1.36 Random Forest Cross Tabulation Table.

Boosted trees, Figure J1.32, was one of the two models with the least amount of error. To interpret these tables, one needs to look at the columns and rows. Of the 60 fabricated patients, 32 died and 28 lived to be discharged from the hospital. These are the "count" rows. The Boosted trees model predicted that 26 of the 28 discharged patients would be discharged. It predicted, incorrectly, that 2 would expire. Of the 32 patients that died, Boosted trees predicted all 32 would die. Therefore, its accuracy rate was 92.86% for the discharged patients and 100% for the patients that died.

For the Classification and regression trees model (Figure J1.33), the accuracy rate was not as good − 92.8% accurate predictions for those patients who were discharged, and 87.5% accuracy in predicting mortality. This means that the C&RT misclassified 7.14% of patients for death when they were actually discharged (false negative), and misclassified 12.5% of the patients who actually died into the discharged class (false positive). This was the model that predicted discharges for patients who died.

Figure J1.34 shows the SVM model, which had an overall error rate of only 3.33%, as did Boosted trees, and had the same percentages in its classification.

Figure J1.35 shows the Neural network model, with only 6.67% overall error rate.

Finally, Figure J1.36 shows that all of the discharges were correctly predicted, but not the deaths.

If a hospital were to use a decision model to try to predict who might be in danger of dying from DIC, then that model should not leave out any who might be in more danger. So, if a model underestimates the severity of threat, that model should not be used. Therefore, we probably would not use either C&RT or Random forest models for performing an interactive procedure.

Even though Neural networks did not misclassify any deaths, its accuracy rate was lower than that of the other two, so the decision for the predictor model likely would be either Boosted trees or SVM. SVM allows an easy V-fold alternative, and so we decided to use SVM.

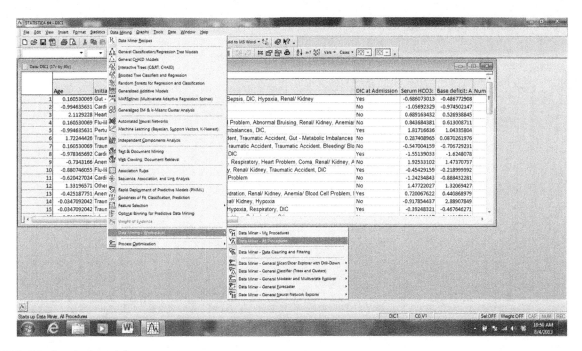

FIGURE J1.37   Start the data mining process.

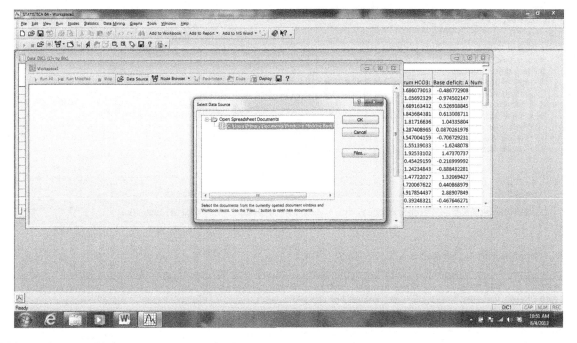

FIGURE J1.38   Open New Workspace.

SVM Model on the Fictionalized Data Set DIC1.Sta.

Feature Selection

We wanted to home in on the fewest variables possible to make the prediction, so our first task was to run a feature selection on the data to determine the possible best predictors. The instructions are as follows:

Open Data Mining – Workspace, Data Miner – All Procedures (Figure J1.37).
Connect the data source (Figure J1.38).

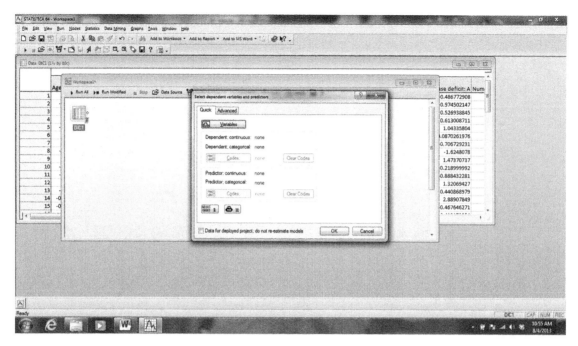

FIGURE J1.39   Get Data and Select Variables.

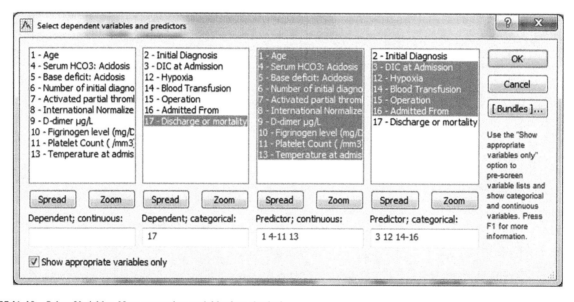

FIGURE J1.40   Select Variables. Note appropriate variables box checked.

Double click on the data file to select the variables (Figure J1.39).

Select the same variables as we did for the data miner recipe (Figure J1.40). Click OK and OK again.

Figure J1.41 shows the alternatives presented under the Node Browser tab. Click on Feature Selection under Tools, and see that Feature Selection shows up on the upper right. Either double click the upper right Feature Selection, or click it once and click "Insert into workspace."

Figure J1.42 shows the result. The module appears with an arrow connecting the data.

Right click on the module and "Edit Parameters" (Figure J1.43).

Change to "All results" and keep the defaults. Later, one could return and try the p values for Predictor selection (Figure J1.44).

Then click OK.

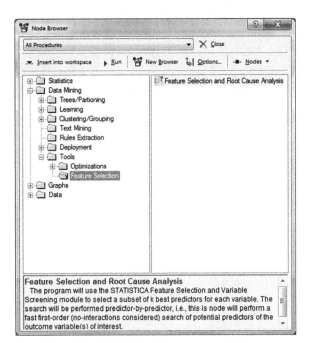

FIGURE J1.41 Add Feature Selection Module. Right-click on module and edit the parameters.

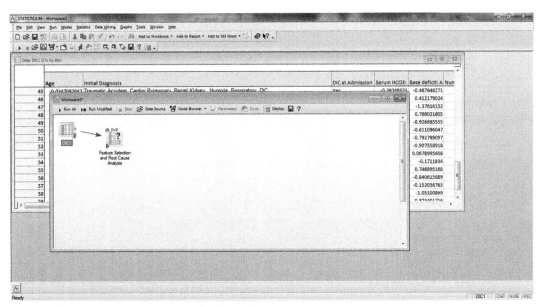

FIGURE J1.42 Resulting Workspace.

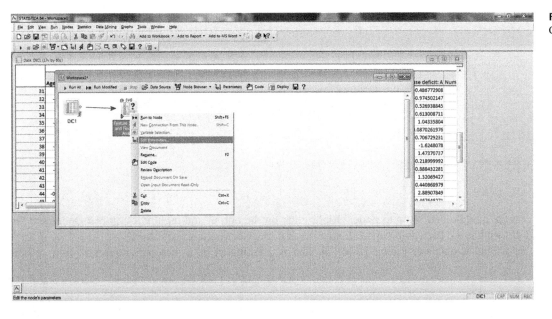

FIGURE J1.43 Change to "all results."

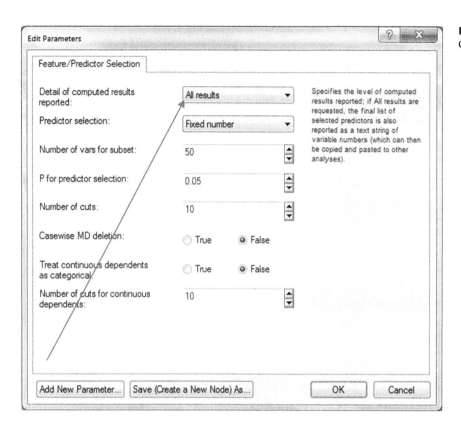

FIGURE J1.44 Keep all the other defaults. Click OK.

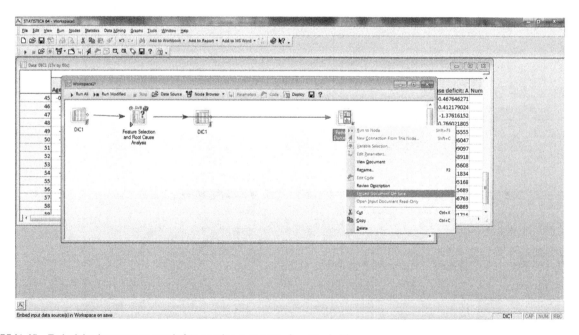

FIGURE J1.45 Embed the document on save before opening so as not to forget to do it!

Again, right click on the module and "Run to node." Right click on the output and highlight "Embed Document On Save," as in Figure J1.45, so that the file can be opened once the feature selection has been saved.

Double click the report and it opens to Figure J1.46. Up first is a listing of both the continuous and discrete best predictors.

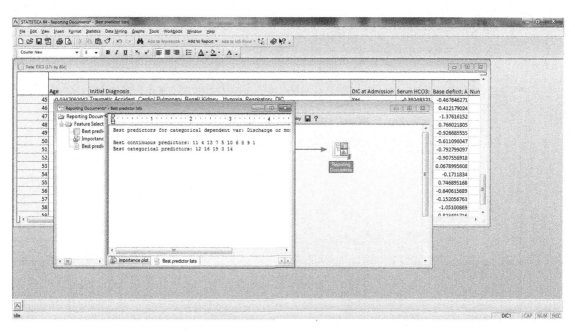

FIGURE J1.46   Open the documents. Best predictors shown.

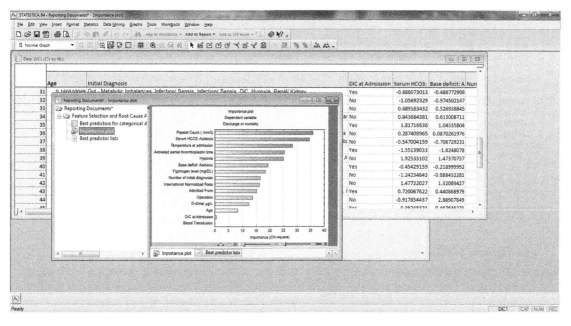

FIGURE J1.47   Importance Plot.

Move the window over a bit to see the workbook items. Click on the Importance plot, which shows the relative strengths in the predictors for "Discharge or mortality" (Figure J1.47).

Click on the top to find a listing of the p values for each of the predictors. (Figure J1.48). We highlighted the ones that had p values less than 0.05. These might be better predictors than the last four. We will use these top predictors in our SVM model.

In fact, it almost appears as though we could use the top seven predictors in terms of p value and decided to try those. Platelet Count, Serum HCO3, Temperature at admission, Activated partial thromboplastin time, Hypoxia, Base deficit, and Operation comprised variables 11, 4, 13, 7, 5,10, and 15, respectively.

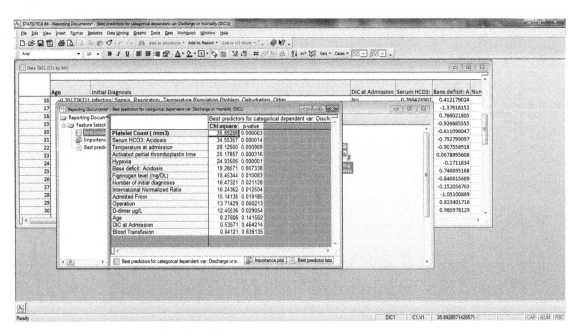

FIGURE J1.48   Best predictors with chi-square and P values.

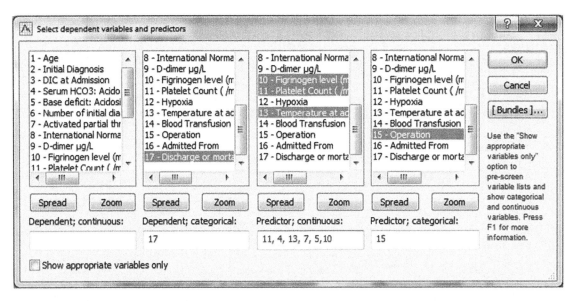

FIGURE J1.49   Use only the variables from the Feature Selection.

SVM Model 1 – Using Data Mining Space

First copy the data. Right click on the file, click Copy, and right click Paste. Select the variables, but this time use only the variables from the Feature Selection (Figure J1.49). Continue to use number 17 as the dependent categorical variable.

Go to the Node Browser again, click on Learning and Machine Learning. Support Vector Machine is the top one on the right (Figure J1.50).

The module appeared to the right of the data set with the arrow connected to the data (Figure J1.51).

Double click on the Support Vector Machine module to see the alternatives (Figure J1.52).

Click All results (Figure J1.53) and click OK on Cross-validation 1 (Figure J1.54).

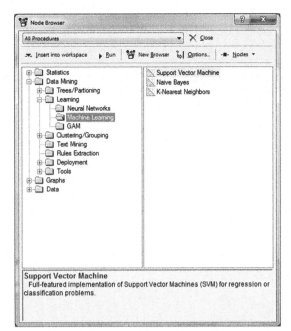

FIGURE J1.50 Opening Support Vector Machines (SVM).

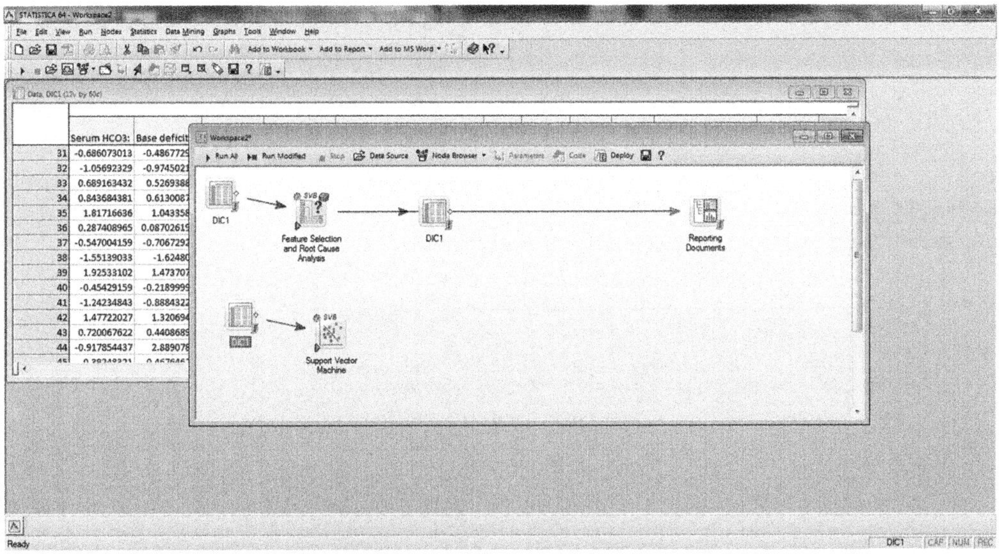

FIGURE J1.51 Copy the data and connect to the SVM module.

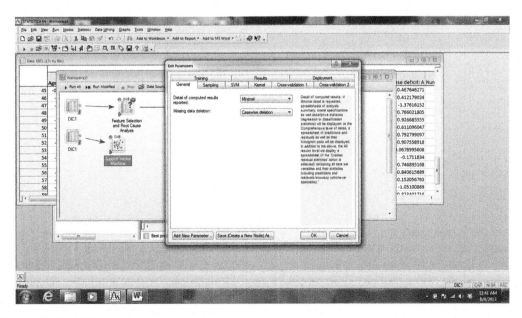

FIGURE J1.52 Support Vector Machine alternatives.

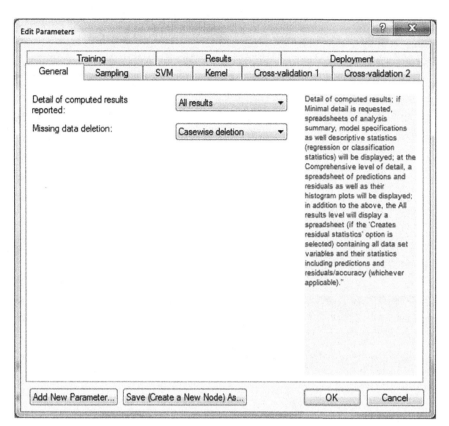

FIGURE J1.53 Click on all results.

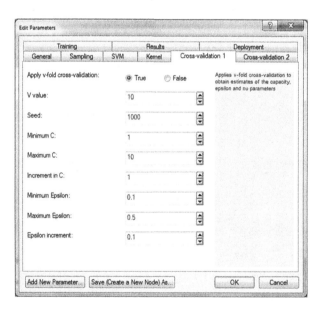

FIGURE J1.54 Click true on cross-validation 1.

Check under the Sampling tab and decide how large a random sample should be used for the training sample. Training and testing samples are a part of the SVM module. Because there are only 60 cases, we decided to use two-thirds for the training sample and one-third for the testing sample so we would have at least 20 cases for testing (Figure J1.55). This was just a guess, and the reader could try different percentages. Ideally, one would have a larger sample. At times it is necessary to start the process and then, over time, build up the data base so that learning can occur.

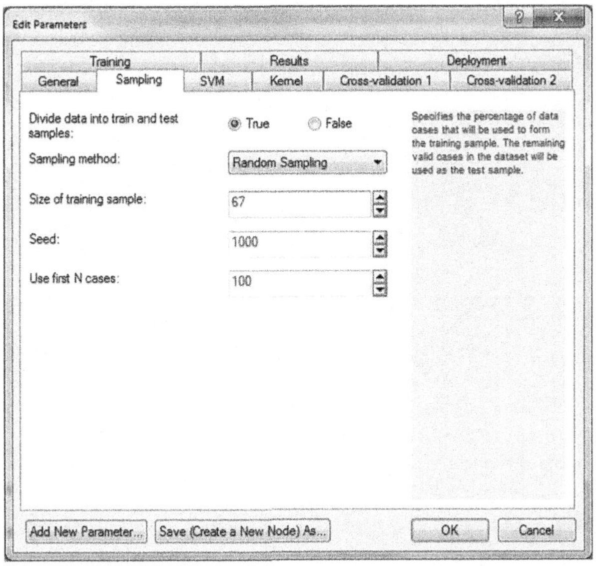

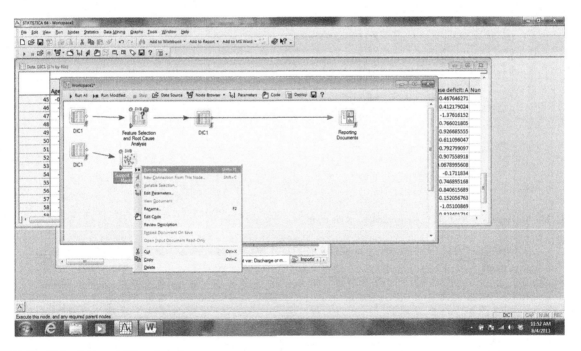

FIGURE J1.55   Sampling Tab.

FIGURE J1.56   Right click on module and run it.

Click OK and then right click on the module to run it (Figure J1.56).

The output goes to the Reporting Document already started (Figure J1.57).

The first screen is of the data set. Move the bar over to the right so the workbook entries may be viewed as in Figure J1.58.

Click on the classification summary and see the accuracy of this procedure in Figure J1.59.

Discharged was only 92% correct and Death was only 81% correct. Next, we will try the procedure interactively to see if the results are the same.

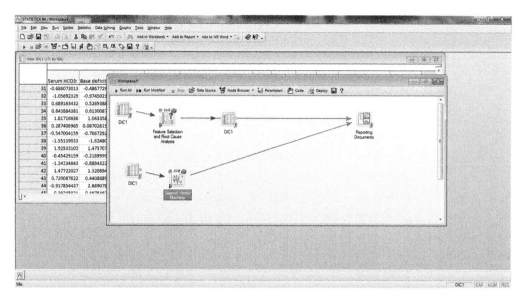

FIGURE J1.57 Output goes to the Reporting Document.

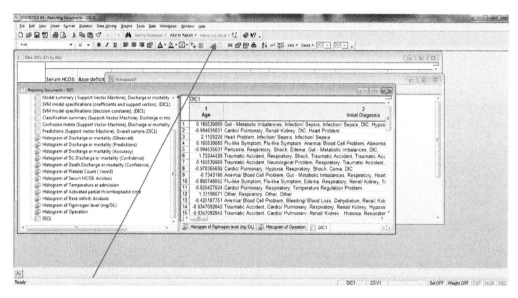

FIGURE J1.58 Moving bar to the right to see workbook entries easily.

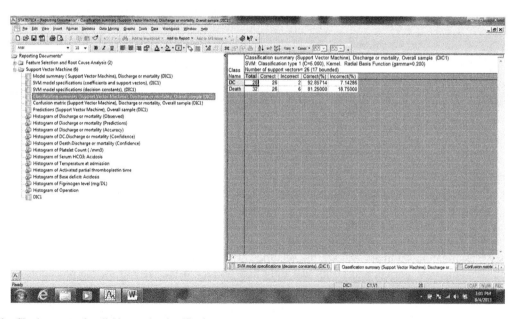

FIGURE J1.59 Check accuracy by clicking on the classification summary.

SVM Model 2 — Interactive Model

Go to Data Mining and Machine Learning (Figure J1.60).

Click on Support Vector Machine (Figure J1.61).

When the variables pop up, enter the exact variables as before (Figure J1.62).

Again, select 67% on the training sample and under Cross-validation select "Apply v-fold cross-validation" (Figure J1.63). Leave everything else on the default, and click OK.

The results of this analysis are in Figure J1.64 and they tell us that we have a fairly good prediction model.

Our model has an accuracy rate of about 85%. What is good about the model is that there is a basic match amongst the various ways of calculating the model — cross-validation accuracy of 82.5% is close to the training accuracy of 87.5% and the testing accuracy of 85%. With 86.667% overall accuracy, we have a good start on the prediction model. We would like to see if we can achieve even greater accuracy. We have not used the initial diagnoses yet (Variable 2). We will now demonstrate the use of text mining in an effort to improve our model.

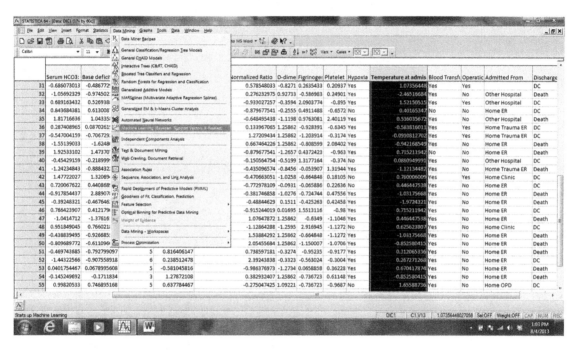

FIGURE J1.60   Go to Data Mining and Machine Learning.

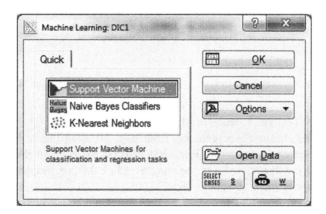

FIGURE J1.61   Click OK and then select variables.

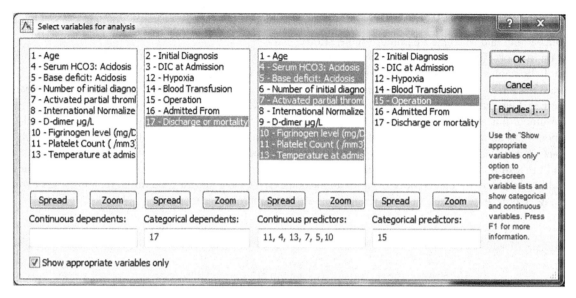

FIGURE J1.62 After selecting variables, click OK.

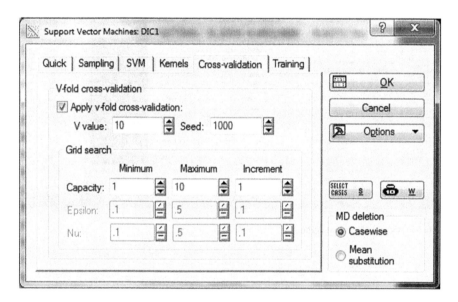

FIGURE J1.63 Apply V-fold cross-validation.

Text Mining

Go to Data Mining and click on "Text and Document Mining" to obtain Figure J1.65.

Click on the Advanced tab and change the percentages from 10 to 80, as in Figure J1.66.

Click on the Words tab and check to make sure EnglishStoplist.txt has been selected. This will eliminate any non-essential words (Figure J1.67). We will also add a few synonyms. Click the box beside Synonyms and Edit.

Figure J1.68 shows what happens when one clicks New.

In Figure J1.69 we connected cardio with pulmonary, so the two would be treated as one word.

First put in the Root (cardio), and then type pulmonary in the box beside Words. Click "Add new synonym." Click "Update synonyms" and OK. Click on the synonyms editor again and continue adding synonyms, as in Figure J1.70.

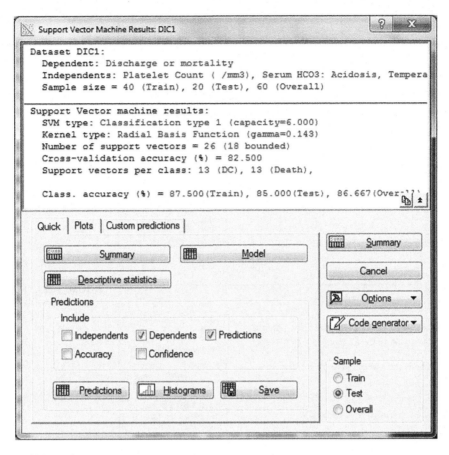

FIGURE J1.64   Results — fairly good.

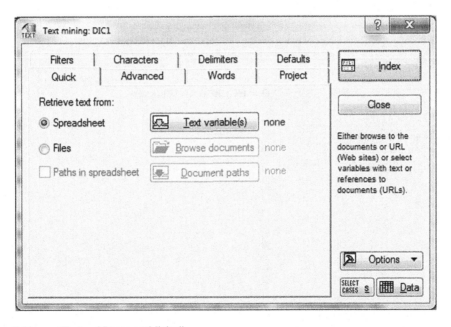

FIGURE J1.65   After clicking on "Text and Document Mining".

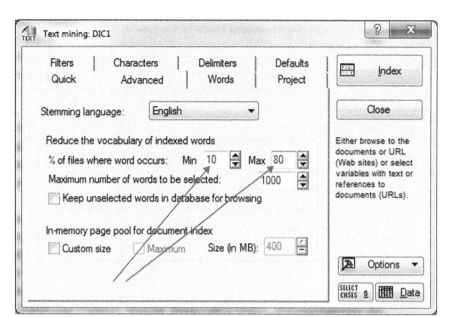

FIGURE J1.66 Change the percentages to from 10 to 80.

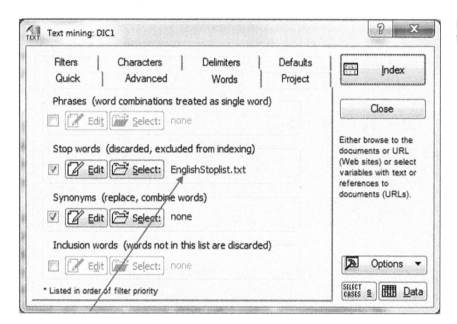

FIGURE J1.67 Make sure EnglishStoplist.txt is selected.

FIGURE J1.68 Click new.

FIGURE J1.69 Example: we connected cardio with pulmonary.

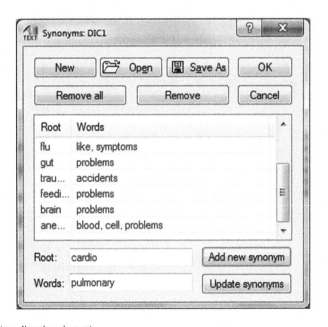

FIGURE J1.70 Adding synonyms (see directions in text).

After traumatic accidents were feeding (root), problems (Word); brain (root), problems (Words); anemia (root), blood, cell, problems (Words); Gut (root), metabolic, imbalances (Words). This listing can be saved in any spot you would like by clicking "Save As."

Next, we can select the variable to add into the text analysis (Figure J1.71). Add Variable 2 and then OK.

Now click on Index (Figure J1.72). If you already have an indexed file, a warning will appear that any old file will be removed (Figure J1.73). Click Yes to show the new file.

The words are counted and summarized as in Figure J1.74.

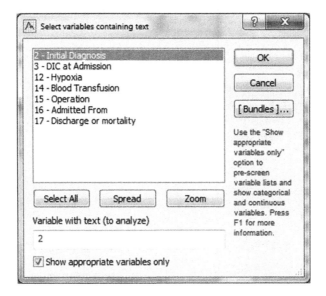

FIGURE J1.71 Add Variable 2 and then OK.

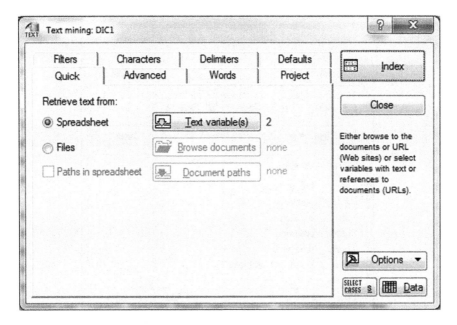

FIGURE J1.72 Click on Index.

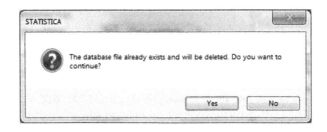

FIGURE J1.73 Choose yes.

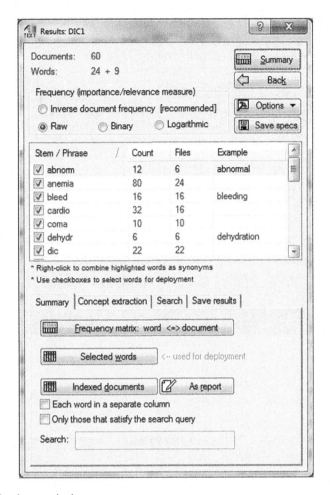

FIGURE J1.74 Words are counted and summarized.

In looking at the words, we tried to tie together words that meant about the same thing in the synonyms list but it appears that we missed the words "loss" and "flu and flu-like." We could return to the synonyms list and revise, or we could simply combine the related words. Highlight the words that need to go together, right click, and choose "Combine Words," as in Figure J1.75.

Then the program asks us to name the two words, as in Figure J1.76.

The final listing is shown in Figure J1.77(a).

Click on Summary and Selected words to see the 22 words that were deemed important by our criteria (Figure J1.77 (b)).

Next click on the Save results tab, as in Figure J1.78, and put 22 in the Amount box.

Next click on "Append empty variables," and Figure J1.79 tells us that the new variables have been added to the spreadsheet.

Click OK and then click on "Write back current results (to selected variables)" (see Figure J1.80).

Select the words on the left side and then the new variables on the right side, as seen in Figure J1.81.

Then click on the word Assign, to see Figure J1.82.

Next, click OK and the terms are added to the end of the data set.

If the variables are hiding the zeros, there will be a label in text labels (Figure J1.83(a)). You need to go in and eliminate those from the new variables. Just remove and go to the next variable until all are cleared, and then save to make the variables show the zeros (Figure J1.83(b)). Then they will be counted as continuous variables by the program.

To see if any of the new variables might have predictability, let's do a quick feature selection just on those new variables. Go to Data Mining and then Feature Selection in the pull down, as in Figure J1.84. Choose Feature Selection and Variable Screening.

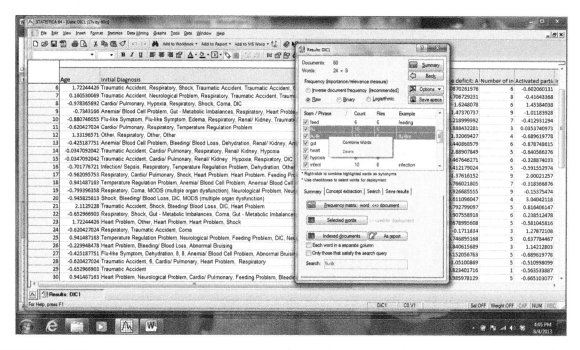

FIGURE J1.75   Combining synonyms.

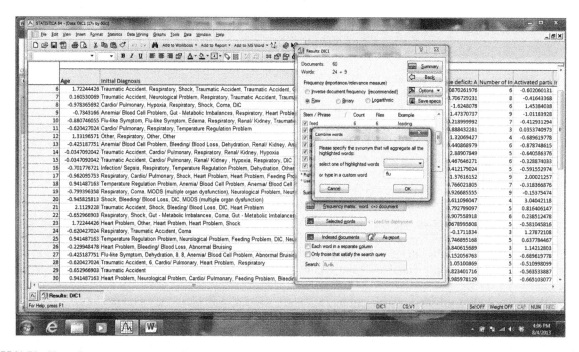

FIGURE J1.76   Name the two.

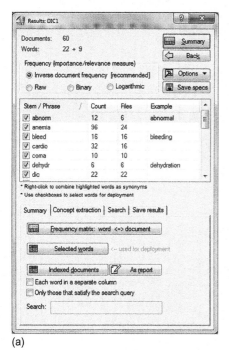

(a)

| Stem / Phras | Words summary (DIC1) | |
	Count	Number of documents
Abnorm	12	6
Anemia	96	24
Bleed	16	16
Cardio	32	16
Coma	10	10
Dehydr	6	6	d
Dic	22	22
Feed	6	6
Flu	20	6
Gut	48	12
Heart	96	36
Hypoxia	8	8
Infect	10	6
Kidney	16	16
Neurolog	14	8	n
Regul	8	8

(b)

FIGURE J1.77 Final Listing - Click on Summary and Selected words.

FIGURE J1.78 The 22 important words. Click on "Append empty variables".

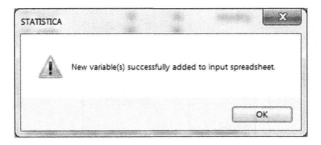

FIGURE J1.79   The new variables have been added.

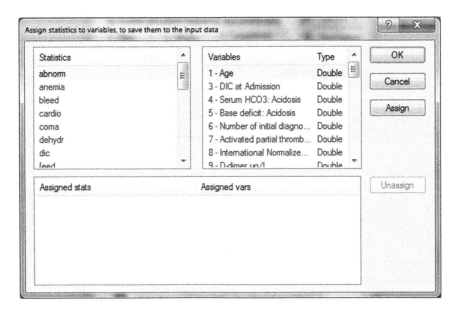

FIGURE J1.80   After clicking OK and then clicking on "Write back current results to selected variables" from figure J1.78.

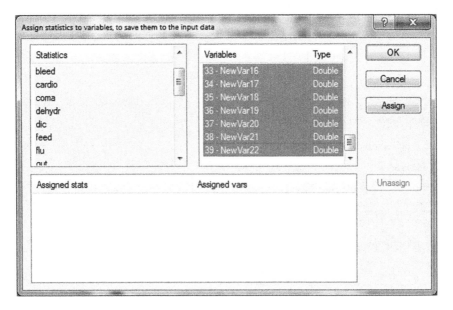

FIGURE J1.81   Select the words on the left side and then the new variables on the right side and then click assign.

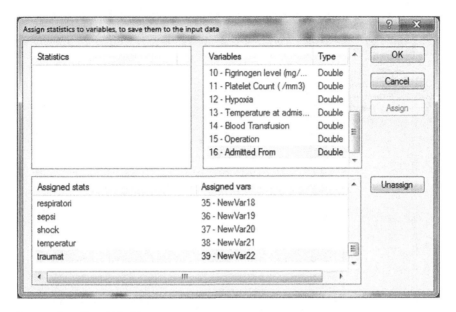

FIGURE J1.82 After clicking assign. Then click OK.

(a)   (b)

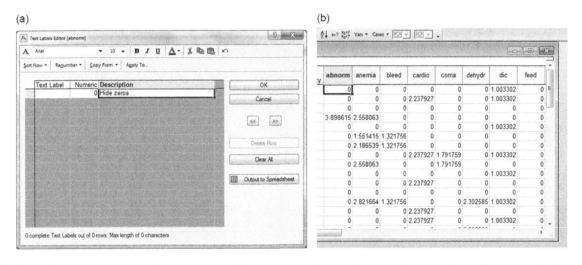

FIGURE J1.83 Hiding zeros in text labels. Remove the text label so the value is zero without a text label. Do this for all the new variables.

Choose all the new variables. It is hard to know why some are in the categorical column and some in the continuous column, but it won't matter. When the program doesn't like it, simply click on "Continue with current selection." See the variables in Figure J1.85.

Click OK and "Continue with current selection." Then click on the importance plot as in Figure J1.86.

Obviously, cardio/pulmonary was the most important variable; however, on examining the best predictors, p values in Figure J1.87 more seem important.

Perhaps the first eight are important. These are Variables 21, 23, 36, 30, 19, 39, 37. We will use them in our next SVM model.

At this point we can repeat the support vector machine analysis to see if the new information will add predictability. Go to Data Mining, Machine Learning, and Support Vector Machine. As in Figure J1.88, select the variables. Select the important ones from the first analysis, and add the important variables from the text mining.

Again, use cross-validation (click True on cross-validation) and change the percentage on the sampling tab to 67%. Click OK (Figure J1.89).

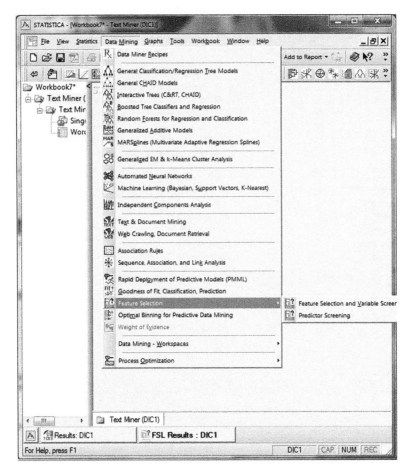

FIGURE J1.84   Select feature selection.

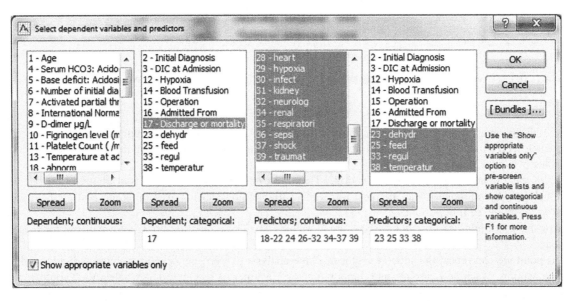

FIGURE J1.85   Variable Selection.

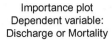

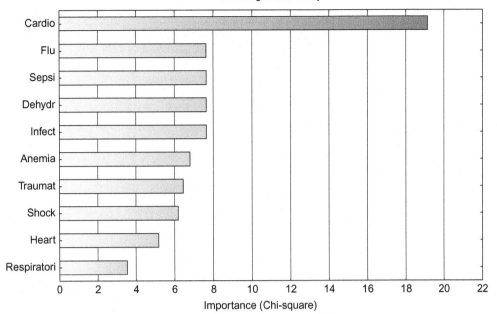

Importance plot
Dependent variable:
Discharge or Mortality

FIGURE J1.86 Importance Plot Cardio was the most predictive.

	Best predictors for categorical dependent var: Discharge or Mortality (DIC1)	
	Chi-square	p-value
Cardio	19.09091	0.000012
Flu	7.61905	0.005775
Sepsi	7.61905	0.005775
Dehydr	7.61905	0.005775
Infect	7.61905	0.005775
Anemia	6.77934	0.079274
Traumat	6.42857	0.040184
Shock	6.17347	0.012968
Heart	5.15625	0.271638
Respiratori	3.52041	0.172010

FIGURE J1.87 Chi-square values.

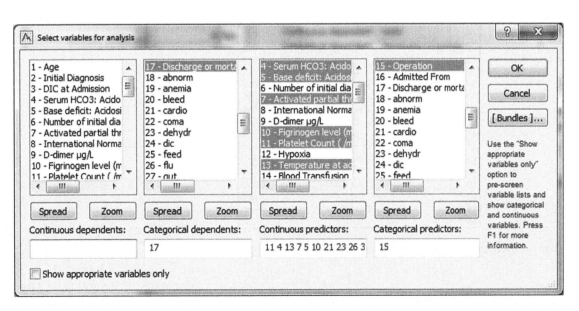

FIGURE J1.88 Selecting variables for SVM.

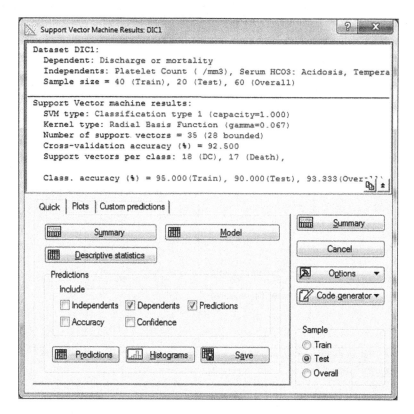

FIGURE J1.89 Output: good accuracy.

	Predictions (Support vector machine), Test sample (DIC1) SVM: Classification type 1 (C = 1.000), Kernel: Radial basis function (gamma = 0.067) Number of support vectors = 35 (28 bounded)	
Case Name	Discharge or Mortality dependent	Discharge or Mortality predicted
1	DC	DC
2	Death	Death
4	DC	DC
9	Death	DC
14	Death	Death
17	Death	Death
22	DC	Death
31	DC	DC
32	Death	Death
33	DC	DC
35	Death	Death
36	DC	DC
40	DC	DC
41	Death	Death
45	Death	Death
46	DC	DC
50	Death	Death
53	Death	Death
54	Death	Death
55	DC	DC

FIGURE J1.90 Our prediction in the testing sample, using the predictive algorithm, missed only once.

Success! The text from the initial diagnoses gave us a great prediction of about 92% consistently across training, texting and cross-validation. Our prediction in the testing sample, using the predictive algorithm, missed only once (see Figure J1.90).

CONCLUSION

We were able to fairly accurately predict between discharge and death for the fictionalized data (which are based upon real data). We were able to increase our predictability considerably (from 83% to 92%) by adding the text. We hope that the true data will yield results this beneficial if we are able to add more cases. Of course, the predictions may not hold true with additional, but different, patients. However, we will likely find that if we can develop a sound model that continually improves, it may be possible to avoid some deaths by increasing vigilance. Whether these findings will extrapolate to other hospitals it is impossible to say without further testing.

REFERENCES

42nd National Congress of the Italian Society of Clinical Biochemistry and Clinical Molecular Biology, Rome (Italy), 5—8 October 2010, 2010. Clin. Chem. Lab. Med. 48 (9), A183—A203.

Akinbiyi, A.A., Olatunbosun, O.A., 2004. Emergency obstetric hysterectomies (How many are potentially preventable?): a 28-year experience in Saskatoon. J. Gynecol. Surg. 20 (3), 81—87.

Armstead, W.M., 2006. Association between intravascular coagulopathy and outcome after traumatic brain injury. Neurol. India. 54 (4), 347—348.

Asakura, H., Ontachi, Y., Mizutani, T., Kato, M., Ito, T., Saito, M., et al., 2001. Decreased plasma activity of antithrombin or protein C is not due to consumption coagulopathy in septic patients with disseminated intravascular coagulation. Eur. J. Haematol. 67 (3), 170—175.

Bern, M.M., 2005. Coagulopathy, following medical therapy, for carcinoma of the prostate. Hematology. 10 (1), 65—68.

Besser, M.W., Klein, A.A., 2010. The coagulopathy of cardiopulmonary bypass. Crit. Rev. Clin. Lab. Sci. 47 (5/6), 197—212.

Binder, A.A., Endler, G.G., Müller, M.M., Mannhalter, C.C., Zenz, W.W., 2007. 4G4G genotype of the plasminogen activator inhibitor-1 promoter polymorphism associates with disseminated intravascular coagulation in children with systemic meningococcemia. J. Thromb. Haemost. 5 (10), 2049—2054.

Boffa, M.C., Lachassinne, E.E., 2007. Infant perinatal thrombosis and antiphospholipid antibodies: a review. Lupus. 16 (8), 634—641.

Bryant, P.A., Tingay, D., Dargaville, P.A., Starr, M., Curtis, N., 2004. Neonatal coxsackie B virus infection — a treatable disease? Eur. J. Pediatr. 163 (4/5), 223—228.

Bush, E.L., Barbas, A.S., Holzknecht, Z.E., Byrne, G.W., McGregor, C.G., Parker, W., et al., 2011. Coagulopathy in α-galactosyltransferase knockout pulmonary xenotransplants. Xenotransplantation. 18 (1), 6—13.

Callow, C.R., Swindell, R., Randall, W., Chopra, R., 2002. The frequency of bleeding complications in patients with haematological malignancy following the introduction of a stringent prophylactic platelet transfusion policy. Br. J. Haematol. 118 (2), 677—682.

Chekrizova, V.V., Murphy, W.G., 2006. Solvent-detergent plasma: use in neonatal patients, in adult and paediatric patients with liver disease and in obstetric and gynaecological emergencies. Transfus. Med. 16 (2), 85—91.

Choi, I.H., Ha, T.Y., Lee, D.G., Park, J.S., Lee, J.H., Park, Y.M., et al., 1995. Occurrence of disseminated intravascular coagulation (DIC) in active systemic anaphylaxis: role of platelet-activating factor. Clin. Exp. Immunol. 100 (3), 390—394.

Dede, H., Kandemir, O., Yalva, S., Karçaaltincaba, D., Kiykaç, S., 2010. Is dinoprostone safe? A report of three maternal deaths. J. Matern. Fetal Neonatal Med. 23 (6), 569—572.

Dressler, D.K., 2004. Coping with a coagulation crisis. Nursing. 34 (5), 58—62.

Dressler, D.K., 2012. Coagulopathy in the intensive care unit. Crit. Care Nurse. 32 (5), 48—60.

Erez, O., Gotsch, F., Mazaki-Tovi, S., Vaisbuch, E., Kusanovic, J., Kim, C., et al., 2009. Evidence of maternal platelet activation, excessive thrombin generation, and high amniotic fluid tissue factor immunoreactivity and functional activity in patients with fetal death. J. Matern. Fetal Neonatal Med. 22 (8), 672—687.

Franchini, M., Manzatob, F., 2004. Update on the treatment of disseminated intravascular coagulation. Hematology. 9 (2), 81—85.

Ghafoor, S., MacRae, E., Harding, K., Patel, G., 2010. Symmetrical peripheral digital gangrene following severe *Plasmodium falciparum* malaria-induced disseminated intravascular coagulopathy. Int. Wound J. 7 (5), 418—422.

Goldenberg, N.A., Manco-Johnson, M.J., 2008. Protein C deficiency. Haemophilia. 14 (6), 1214—1221.

Guldbakke, K.K., Schanbacher, C.F., 2006. Disseminated intravascular coagulation unmasked by Mohs micrographic surgery. Dermatol. Surg. 32 (5), 760—764.

Hopper, K., Bateman, S., 2005. An updated view of hemostasis: mechanisms of hemostatic dysfunction associated with sepsis. J. Vet. Emerg. Crit. Care. 15 (2), 83—91.

Hung-Yang, C., Chun-Chih, P., Hsin-An, K., Chyong-Hsin, H., Han-Yang, H., Jui-Hsing, C., 2007. Neonatal subgaleal hemorrhage: clinical presentation, treatment, and predictors of poor prognosis. Pediatr. Int. 49 (6), 903—907.

Jones, C.M., Rivers, R.A., Taghizadeh, A.A., 1972. Disseminated intravascular coagulation and fetal hydrops in a newborn infant in association with a chorangioma of placenta. Pediatrics. 50 (6), 901.

Leitner, J.M., Janata-Schwatzek, K.K., Spiel, A.O., Sterz, F.F., Laggner, A.N., Jilma, B.B., 2010. DIC score predicts mortality in massive clot coagulopathy as a result of extensive pulmonary embolism: reply to a rebuttal. J. Thromb. Haemost. 8 (7), 1658—1659.

Levi, M., Toh, C.H., Thachil, J., Watson, H.G., 2009. Guidelines for the diagnosis and management of disseminated intravascular coagulation. Br. J. Haematol. 145 (1), 24—33.

McCance, K.L., Huether, S.E., Brashers, V.L., Rote, N.S., 2010. Pathophysiology: The Biologic Basis for Disease in Adults and Children, sixth ed. Mosby, Elsevier, Maryland Heights, MS.

Ojala, K., Perälä, J., Kariniemi, J., Ranta, P., Raudaskoski, T., Tekay, A., 2005. Arterial embolization and prophylactic catheterization for the treatment for severe obstetric hemorrhage. Acta Obstet. Gynecol. Scand. 84 (11), 1075–1080.

Ören, H.H., Cingöz, I.I., Duman, M.M., Yîlmaz, S.S., Irken, G.G., 2005. Disseminated intravascular coagulation in pediatric patients: clinical and laboratory features and prognostic factors influencing the survival. Pediatr. Hematol. Oncol. 22 (8), 679–688.

Pahatouridis, D., Alexiou, G.A., Zigouris, A., Mihos, E., Drosos, D., Voulgaris, S., 2010. Coagulopathy in moderate head injury. The role of early administration of low molecular weight heparin. Brain Inj. 24 (10), 1189–1192.

Pichler, H., Möricke, A., Mann, G., Teigler-Schlegel, A., Niggli, F., Nebral, K., et al., 2010. Prognostic relevance of dic(9;20)(p11;q13) in childhood B-cell precursor acute lymphoblastic leukaemia treated with Berlin–Frankfurt–Münster (BFM) protocols containing an intensive induction and post-induction consolidation therapy. Br. J. Haematol. 149 (1), 93–100.

Rice, L.L., 2000. Surreptitious bleeding in surgery: a major challenge in coagulation. Clin. Lab. Haematol. 22, 17–20.

Spiliopoulos, M., Puri, I., Jain, N.J., Kruse, L., Mastrogiannis, D., Dandolu, V., 2009. Amniotic fluid embolism-risk factors, maternal and neonatal outcomes. J. Matern. Fetal Neonatal Med. 22 (5), 439–444.

Sridhar, A.V., Bulock, F., Hickey, M.St.J., Chikermane, A., Black, E., Currie, A., 2004. Papillary fibroelastoma of the tricuspid valve presenting as neonatal pulmonary haemorrhage. Acta Paediatr. 93 (9), 1254–1256.

Stammers, A.H., Rauch, E.D., Willett, L.D., Newberry, J.W., Duncan, K.F., 2000. Pre-operative coagulopathy management of a neonate with complex congenital heart disease: a case study. Perfusion. 15 (2), 161–168.

Sun, Y., Wang, J., Wu, X., Xi, C., Gai, Y., Liu, H., et al., 2011. Validating the incidence of coagulopathy and disseminated intravascular coagulation in patients with traumatic brain injury – analysis of 242 cases. Br. J. Neurosurg. 25 (3), 363–368.

Takeda, A., Morozumi, K., Uchida, K., Haba, T., Tominaga, Y., Yoshida, A., et al., 1999. Case study of paired cadaver renal allografts from the same donor: influence of local DIC kidney and concomitant acute rejection on early graft outcome. Clin. Transplant. 13 (Suppl. 1), 13–16.

Unal, S., Arhan, E., Kara, N., Uncu, N., Aliefendioğlu, D., 2008. Breast-feeding-associated hypernatremia: retrospective analysis of 169 term newborns. Pediatr. Int. 50 (1), 29–34.

Wheeler, A.P., Rice, T.W., 2010. Coagulopathy in critically ill patients: part 2. Chest. 137, 185–194.

Woloszczuk-Gebicka, B., 2005. How to limit allogenic blood transfusion in children. Pediatr. Anesth. 15 (11), 913–924.

Zabolotskikh, I.B., Sinkov, S.V., Averjanova, L.E., 2006. The clinical significance of hyperfibrinolysis in onset of disseminated intravascular coagulation syndrome. J. Thromb. Haemost. 4, 91.

Zenciroglu, A., Karagol, B., Ipek, M., Okumus, N., Yarali, N., Aydin, M., 2010. Neonatal purpura fulminans secondary to group B streptococcal infection. Pediatr. Hematol. Oncol. 27 (8), 620–625.

Tutorial J2

Decisioning for DIC

Mahmood H. Khichi, MD, FAAP, Wanda P. Parsons, MBA, MHA and Linda A. Winters-Miner

Chapter Outline

INTRODUCTION

This is the second part of the disseminated intravascular coagulation (DIC) tutorial. We used the data set we ended with in the first tutorial, "DIC1-orig-the one used in the tutorial originally.sta." Because the sample was so small we did not expect a significant finding at the end, but we were curious to see how the use of the added word variables would affect further analyses.

1. First, we ran a feature selection to get an overview.
2. Next, we tried weight of evidence (WoE).
3. Finally, we ran a couple of prediction techniques using the variable "Death or discharge" as the target variable, Boosted trees (because that procedure seemed to have the best lift chart in part 1), and C&RT to provide us with a visual plan of how one might be able to use individualized prediction for new cases, as part of the decisioning process.

FEATURE SELECTION

Open the File. To run feature selection, open New space, connect data as in Figure J2.1.

Select Beta procedures and then click OK. Figure J2.2 shows connecting the data.

Select variables as in Figure J2.3. Note that the new variables are also selected up to Variable 39.

Run the feature selection by clicking on the green arrow head. Figure J2.4 shows the output. You might want to embed the output by right clicking on the Reporting Documents, and clicking Embed. The Importance plot is shown in Figure J2.5.

Reviewing the probability chart in Figure J2.6 revealed that the first 22 best predictors seemed to have the strongest relationships to the target, and thus likely were the most predictive.

We repeated the feature selection with just the first 22 so that we could get an easy listing of the variable numbers (because they were all named, rather than numbered in the data file). (See Figures J2.7 and J2.8)

To change the way the graph looks to see all the variables, click on the labels for the Y axis. Find the "off" button and click it so the program will not skip values. Figure J2.9 demonstrates the process.

Figure J2.10 shows the graph with all the variable names.

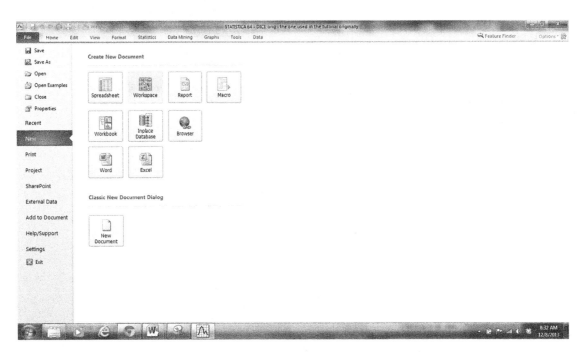

FIGURE J2.1 Open a new workspace.

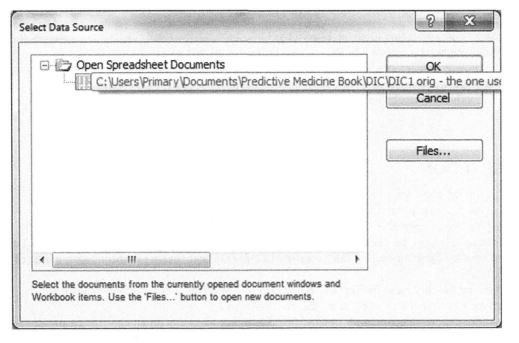

FIGURE J2.2 Place data into the workspace and open Feature Selection (under data mining tab).

Now, simply click on the "Best predictors for categorical dependent var" (i.e., best predictors for Death or discharge) as seen in Figure 12.10 and then selected in Figure 12.11 (not all variable numbers are seen in Figure 12.11, but all are there if one were to scroll over the list), which gives:

Best continuous predictors: 11 4 13 7 5 21 10 6 8 9 1 36 30 26 23 19 39 37
Best categorical predictors: 2 12 16 15

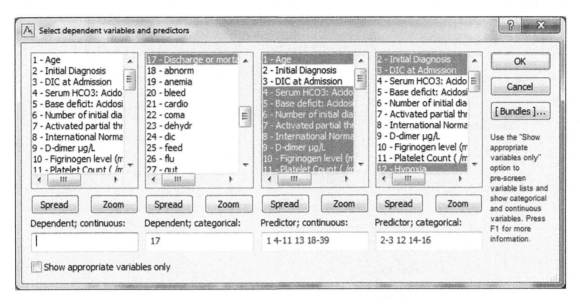

FIGURE J2.3   Variable Selection.

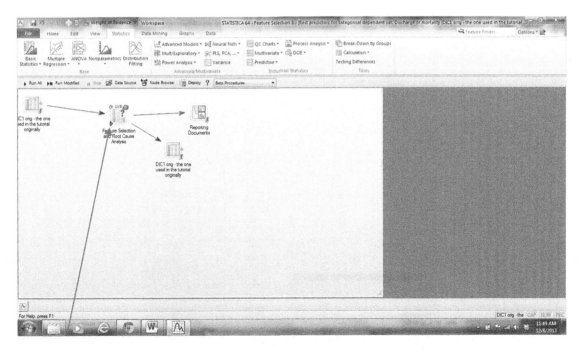

FIGURE J2.4   Click on green arrow to run module.

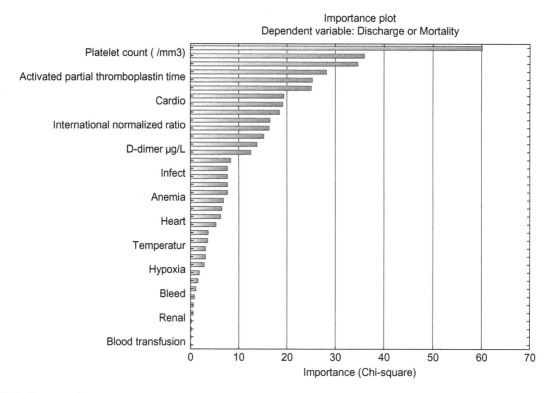

FIGURE J2.5 Importance Plot.

	Best predictors for categorical dependent var:		
	Chi-square	p-value	
Initial Diagnosis	60.00000	0.000618	
Platelet Count (/mm3)	35.89286	0.000003	
Serum HCO3: Acidosis	34.55357	0.000014	
Temperature at admission	28.12500	0.000909	
Activated partial thromboplastin time	25.17857	0.000316	
Hypoxia	24.93506	0.000001	
Base deficit: Acidosis	19.28571	0.007338	
cardio	19.09091	0.000012	
Figrinogen level (mg/DL)	18.45344	0.010083	
Number of initial diagnoses	16.47321	0.021128	
International Normalized Ratio	16.24362	0.012504	
Admitted From	15.14135	0.019185	
Operation	13.71429	0.000213	
D-dimer µg/L	12.45536	0.029054	
Age	8.27806	0.141562	
sepsi	7.61905	0.005775	
infect	7.61905	0.005775	
flu	7.61905	0.005775	
dehydr	7.61905	0.005775	
anemia	6.77934	0.079274	
traumat	6.42857	0.040184	
shock	6.17347	0.012968	
heart	5.15625	0.271638	
respiratori	3.52041	0.172010	
coma	3.42857	0.064078	
temperatur	2.97734	0.084438	
requl	2.97734	0.084438	

FIGURE J2.6 Best Predictors for Chi-Square Method.

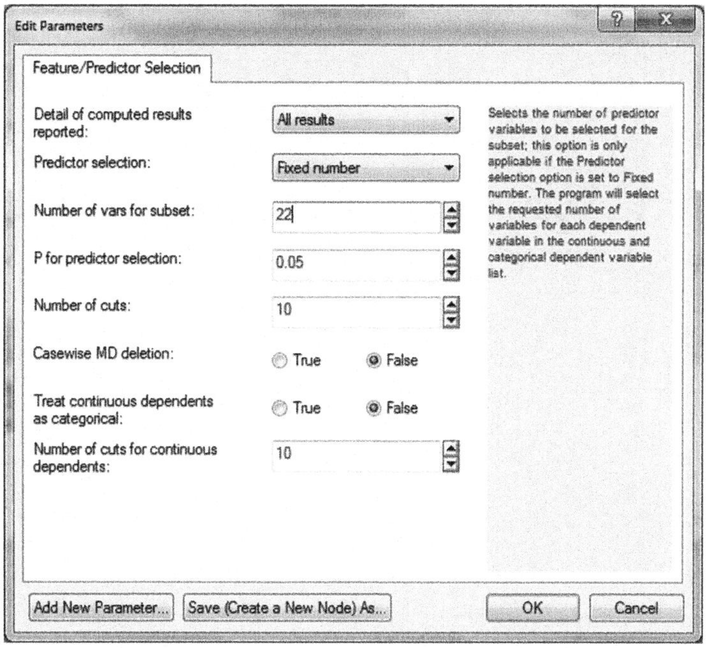

FIGURE J2.7   Feature Selection Repeated with First 22 Variables.

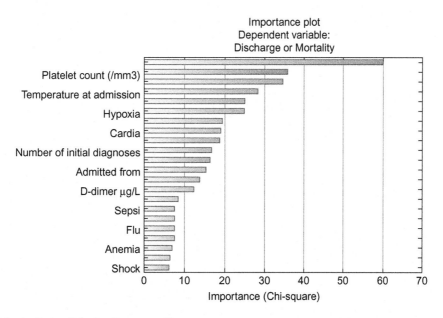

FIGURE J2.8   Output for the Feature Selection: Importance Plot.

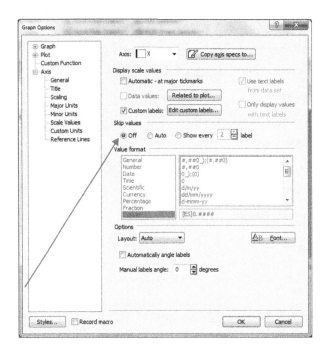

FIGURE J2.9 Skip Values off to see all the variable names.

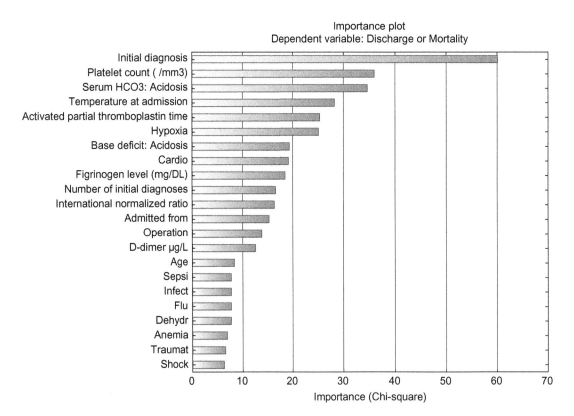

FIGURE J2.10 Result - now we see all the variable names.

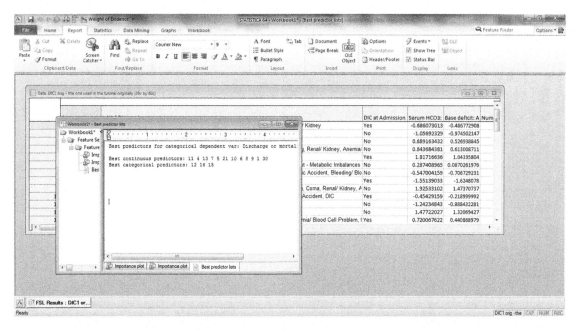

FIGURE J2.11   Best predictors for categorical dependent shows a listing of the variables that we can simply copy for further analysis.

WEIGHT OF EVIDENCE

We decided to use the 22 variables (see above) in the next analysis, which was Weight of Evidence (WoE). WoE bins the variables into intervals, and the intervals have "rules" attached to them. The WoE procedure provides boundaries for bins such that the interval is fairly homogeneous with respect to the risk of either dying or discharge. The program insures iteratively that there is the largest distance possible between those risk intervals. Discrete intervals can sometimes help in assigning future cases.

Open another workspace and bring in the data. Enter Weight of Evidence. Open it and select the variables (the 22 that seemed as though they might be important) in Figure J2.12.

The resulting workspace may be seen in Figure J2.13.

Next determine the "Good" and "Bad" codes, as in Figures J2.14 and J2.15 and compute groups.

In Figure J2.16, we see the default values for each of the variables.

The variable shown in Figure J2.16 is Base deficit: Acidosis. The group that is defined by the interval has many more bad outcomes than good outcomes. Note that the value of WoE is -137.056 using the default value. Unless there is some special reason, the default generally finds the best intervals for separating the good and bad outcomes. (The variables that were already 0 and 1 would not bin further and there was no analysis for them.)

When we click on the next variable, Serum HCO3: Acidosis, the WoE value is -181.24 with the proportion of bad -0.875. If we click on the interactions on the left side we produce the screen in Figure J2.17, which allows us to add interactions.

Custom split allows manipulation of the split if there is some reason to do this (Figure J2.18).

If we click on Rules we get the screen in Figure J2.19.

And if we click on Rules for all variables we get the screen in Figure J2.20.

Once we have everything as we like, click on the red exit box. We left everything as the defaults. When we click, the box in Figure J2.21 appears.

Embed to workspace, as in Figure J2.22.

Then Run to node as in Figure J2.23.

Connect the data to the new SVB Rules node in Figure J2.24.

Click on the gray gear symbol to edit the parameters as in Figure J2.25.

Click OK and then click on the green arrow head of the Rules node to generate the new data node, as in Figure J2.26.

If we open the data set (document on the lower right), we can see that the new variables have been added with the binning rules. Thus the continuous variables have become discrete (see Figure J2.27).

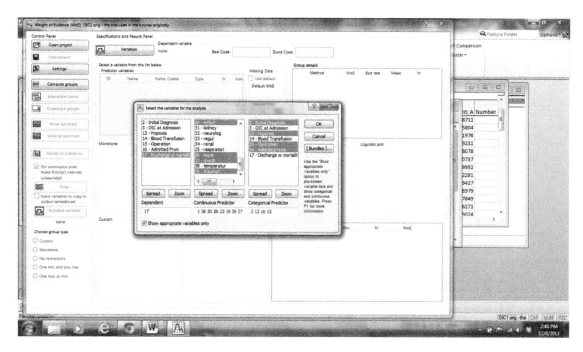

FIGURE J2.12 Open another workspace and bring in the data. Enter Weight of Evidence and then select variables.

FIGURE J2.13 Resulting Screen.

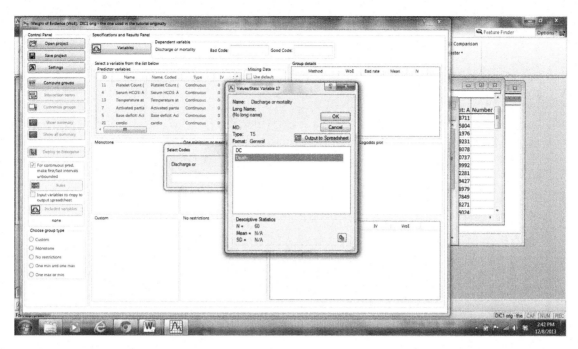

FIGURE J2.14   Select Bad Code and then Good Code.

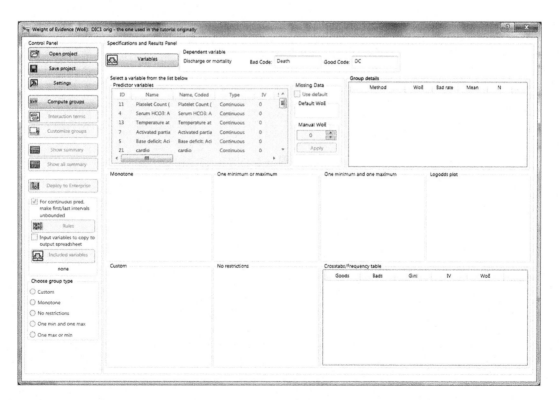

FIGURE J2.15   Compute groups.

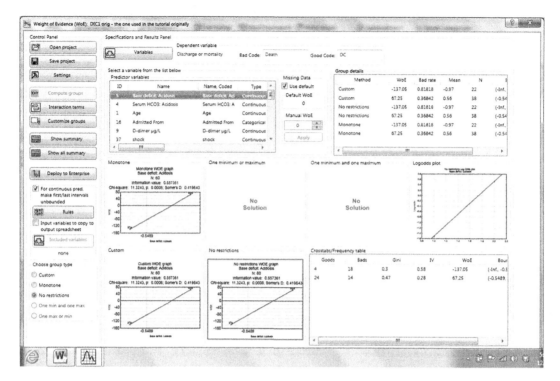

FIGURE J2.16   Default values for Base deficit: Acidosis.

FIGURE J2.17   Spot to Add Interactions.

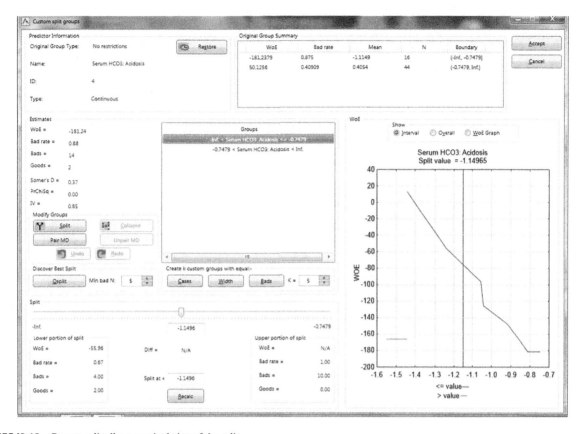

FIGURE J2.18 Custom split allows manipulation of the split.

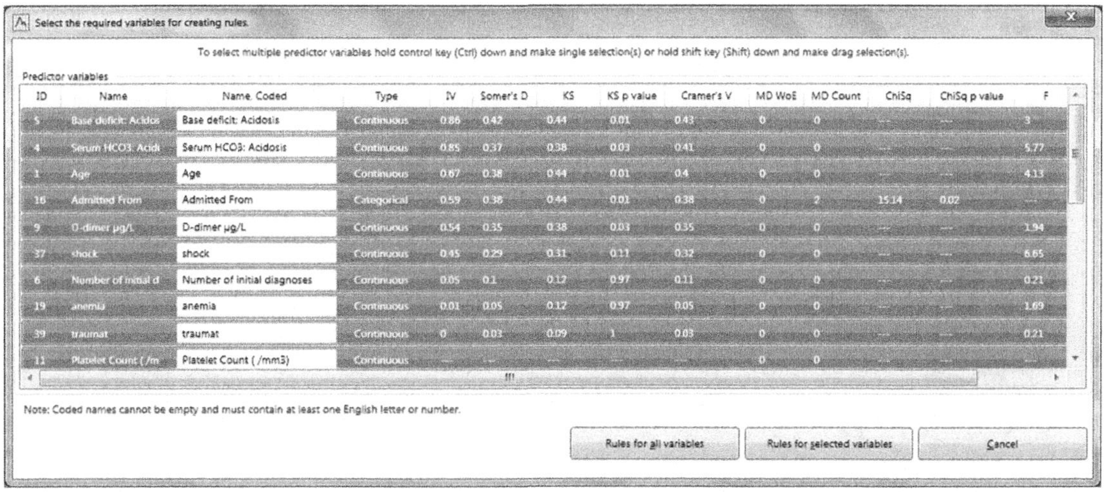

FIGURE J2.19 Clicking on "Rules."

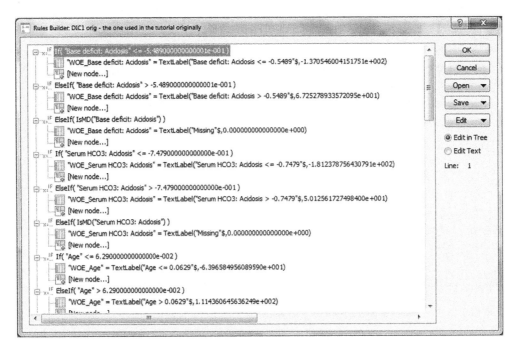

FIGURE J2.20 Clicking on Rules for all variables.

FIGURE J2.21 Result of clicking on red exit box. Click on Embed to workspace.

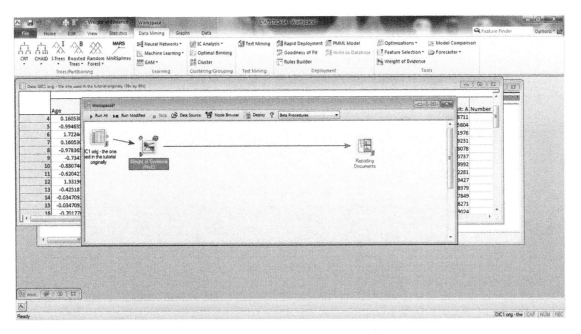

FIGURE J2.22 Result.

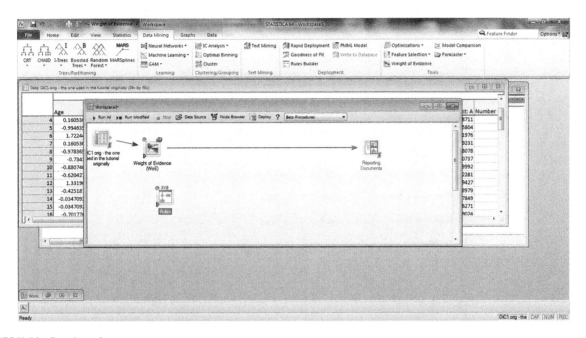

FIGURE J2.23   Run the node.

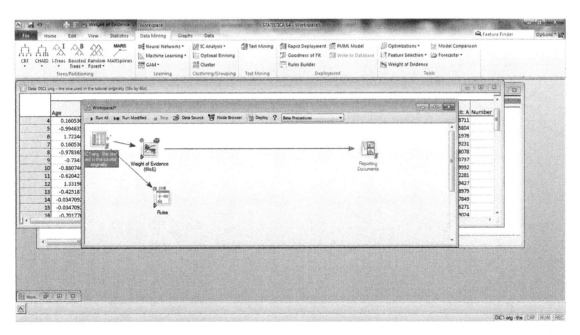

FIGURE J2.24   Connect the data to the new SVB Rules node.

FIGURE J2.25 Edit the parameters to match these.

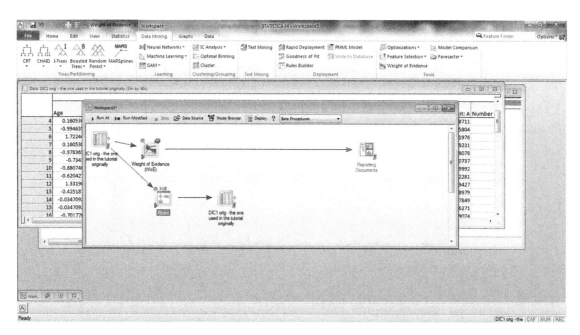

FIGURE J2.26 Click on green arrow of Rules node.

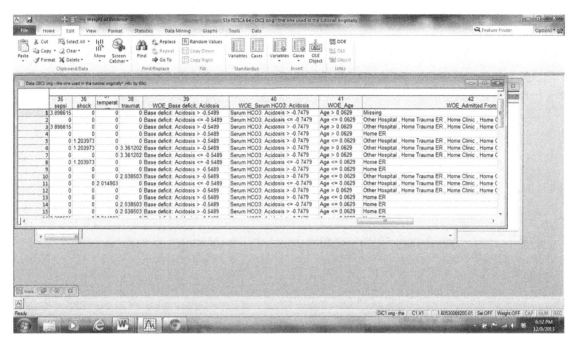

FIGURE J2.27   Continuous variables have become discrete.

DECISIONING/PREDICTIVE PROCEDURES

At this point we can run other analyses off of the new data set. Because earlier, in Tutorial J1, we noted that Boosted trees seemed to be most predictive model, we selected that analysis type for the next part. Highlight the data base and click on Boosted Trees, as in Figure J2.28.

We chose classification because our target was dichotomous. Double click on the node to bring up the dialog box in Figure J2.29.

Unclick "Show appropriate variables only" and click the new variables as Continuous. A warning will come up, but simply ignore it and click Proceed anyway (see Figure J2.30).

Under the Results tab, click on Classification and click the selections in Figure J2.31.

In the code generator, we unclicked all but PMML because our version of STATISTICA did not allow for other codes (See Figure J2.32).

Click OK and then run the node.

Figure J2.33 shows the workspace after running the node.

In the output of Figure J2.34, we can view the feature selection and compare it to the original one.

In both, Serum HCO3: Acidosis was a large predictor. It is possible that it would have been better to use interaction terms — for example, initial diagnosis. There was only one tree in the Boosted tree model. The lift chart showed that the prediction would be better than chance, though (see Figure J2.35). However, we tried another analysis to try to learn more. We realized that we no doubt needed more cases in addition.

Therefore, just to try another analysis, we used C&RT. Figure J2.36 shows the workspace.

Before running the node, we selected variables from the data set as in Figure J2.37.

On the node, when editing the parameters, we asked for All results and for a V-fold cross-validation.

The lift chart is not very good, as may be seen in Figure J2.38.

The tree graph looks very interesting, however (see Figure J2.39).

With such a chart, individual decisions would be possible, if the predictability were better. We plan to add many more cases to our data and repeat our analyses within the next year.

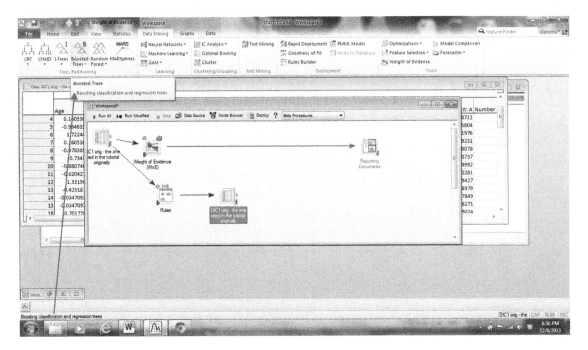

FIGURE J2.28 Adding Boosted Trees.

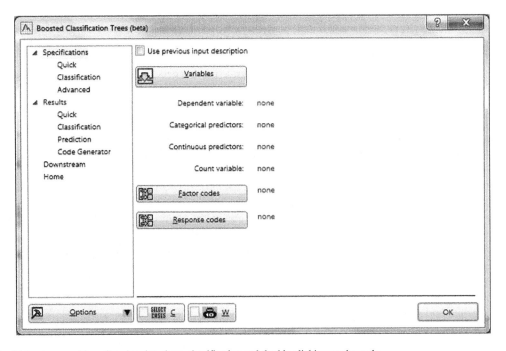

FIGURE J2.29 Dialog box resulting after choosing chose classification and double-clicking on the node.

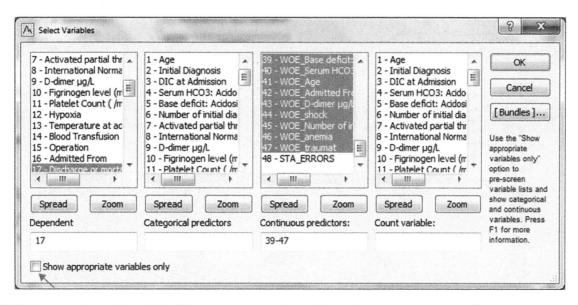

FIGURE J2.30 In selecting variables, Unclick "Show appropriate variables only" Ignore the warning message that will come up.

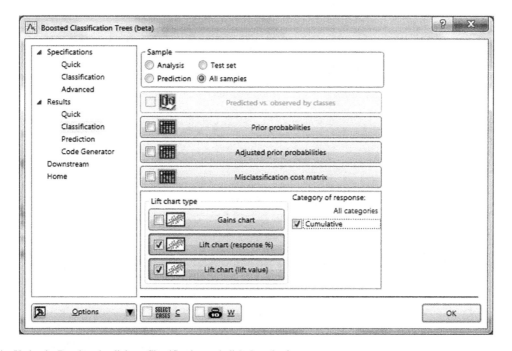

FIGURE J2.31 Under the Results tab, click on Classification and click the selections.

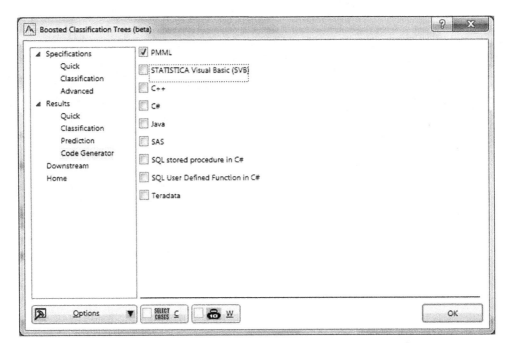

FIGURE J2.32 Because of my version of STATISTICA, I unclicked all but PMML.

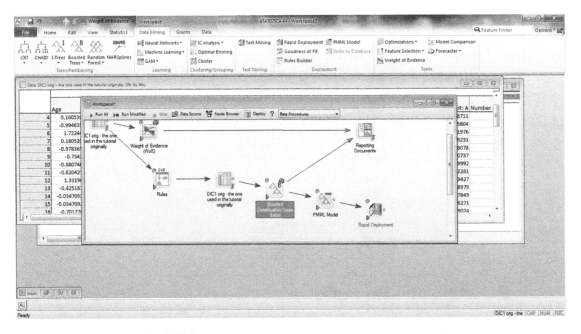

FIGURE J2.33 Workspace After Running the Node.

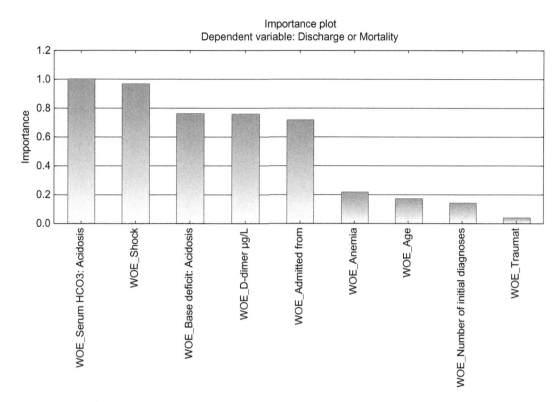

FIGURE J2.34   Compare this feature selection to the original one.

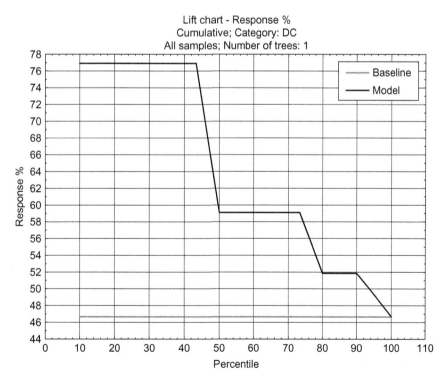

FIGURE J2.35   Lift Chart.

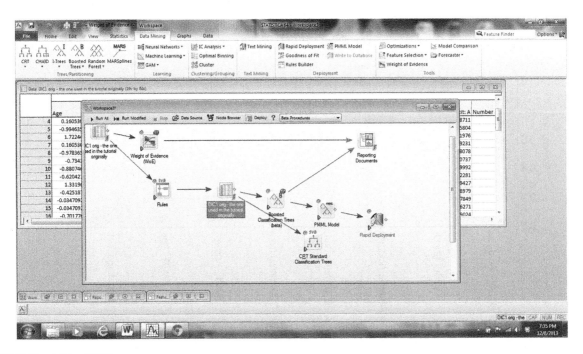

FIGURE J2.36 Adding C&RT.

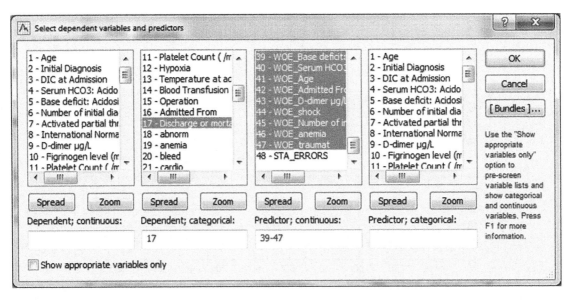

FIGURE J2.37 Select Variables.

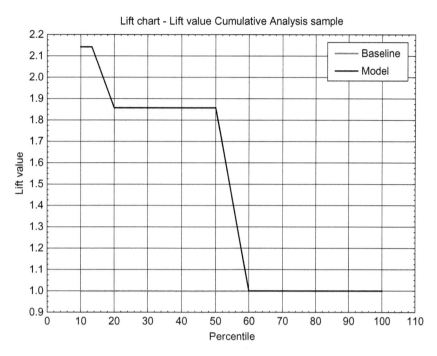

FIGURE J2.38   Lift Chart.

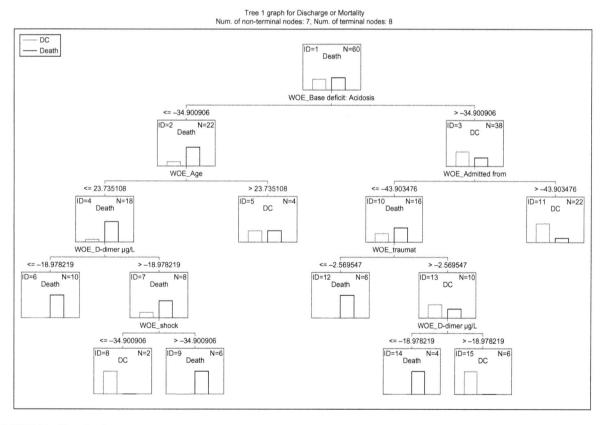

FIGURE J2.39   Tree Graph.

Tutorial K

Predicting Allergy Symptoms

Elizabeth Barancik, MS

Chapter Outline

INTRODUCTION

For this analysis, I considered the data allergycat.sta (see Figure K.1 below), which consist of 35 possible allergens and 3 measures of allergy symptoms: (1) Breathing Difficulty, (2) Watery Eyes, and (3) Fatigue. The three allergy symptoms are self-reported values from 1 to 100.

(*In order to view descriptions of each variable, go to the View tab, select Variable headers − Display long names.*)

Each predictor variable is a binary categorical variable, coded as follows:

- − 1 for no,
- 1 for yes, and
- 0 for when no data are recorded.

PROCEDURE

Ideally, the first step was to split the data into Training and Testing sets. However, I was unable to find any node for splitting data into these respective sets in my version of STATISTICA, although the node is addressed in the help manual within STATISTICA and online in StatSoft's Help, and is available in the current version of the software.

Next, I considered graphical representations of the three target variables to see if there was any time dependence, extreme skewedness of the data, or outliers.

The graphs in Figure K.2 show the target variables over time. The variables do not seem to be time dependent over the 40 recorded days (cases), so there is an argument against performing any temporal analysis at this time.

The histograms of the target variables (Figure K.3) show that the observations of each target variable are normally distributed.

While there are a few outliers, shown in Figure K.4, in the Watery Eyes and Breathing Difficulty data, they are not extreme enough for me to believe that they are errors or atypical enough readings to be thrown out.

All sets of graphs can be created using the Common section of the Graphs toolbar. Choose line graphs, histograms, and whisker plots, respectively, and select the three target variables (36−38) using the Variables button associated with each.

As there is relatively large number of possible predictor variables, it makes sense to use Feature Selection and Variable Screening; this picks the best possible predictors for each variable regardless of its relationship (e.g., linearity) to the predictor variables.

In the Data Mining tool bar, select the Tools section, then choose Feature Selection − Feature Selection, which brings up the Feature Selection and Variable Screening module. Select Variables 36−38 as continuous dependent variables, and all the other variables as categorical predictors (see Figure K.5). Press OK for the variable selection menu, and OK again for the Feature Selection menu. Then select Summary.

Practical Predictive Analytics and Decisioning Systems for Medicine. DOI: http://dx.doi.org/10.1016/B978-0-12-411643-6.00028-4

	1 ROOMTEMP	2 SLEEP	3 BREAKFST	4 ALCOHOL	5 RUN_OUTS	6 SHOWER	7 SWIMMING	8 NAP	9 SALAD	10 MEAT	11 DESERT	WI
1	-1	-1	1	-1	-1	1	1	-1	1	-1	1	
2	1	-1	-1	1	-1	-1	1	1	-1	1	-1	
3	-1	1	-1	-1	1	-1	-1	1	1	-1	1	
4	1	-1	1	-1	1	1	-1	-1	1	1	-1	
5	1	1	-1	1	-1	-1	1	-1	1	1	1	
6	1	1	1	-1	1	-1	-1	1	-1	-1	1	
7	-1	1	1	1	-1	1	-1	-1	1	-1	-1	
8	-1	1	1	1	1	1	1	-1	-1	1	1	
9	-1	-1	-1	1	1	1	-1	1	-1	1	1	
10	1	-1	-1	-1	1	1	1	-1	1	-1	-1	
11	1	1	-1	-1	-1	1	1	1	-1	1	-1	
12	1	1	1	-1	-1	-1	1	1	1	-1	1	
13	1	1	1	1	-1	-1	-1	1	1	1	-1	
14	1	1	1	1	1	-1	-1	-1	1	1	1	
15	-1	1	1	1	1	1	-1	-1	-1	1	1	

FIGURE K.1   The allergy data spreadsheet structure.

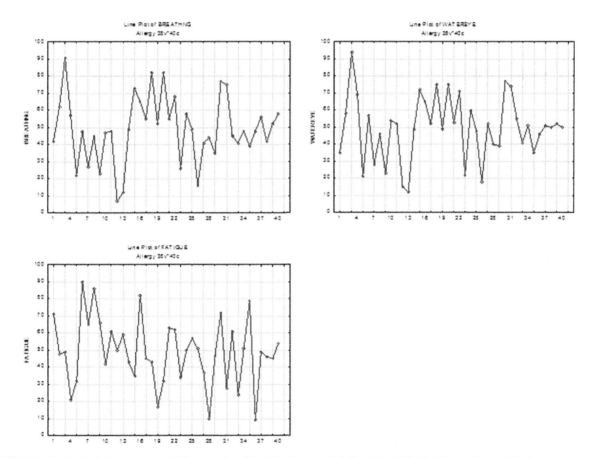

FIGURE K.2   Graphs of the three target variables over time. Clockwise from top left: Breathing Difficulty, Watery Eyes, and Fatigue.

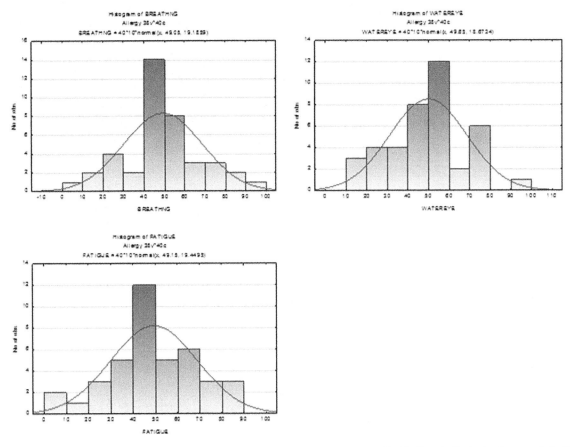

FIGURE K.3 Histograms of the three target variables, showing that they basically are normally distributed. Clockwise from top left: Breathing Difficulty, Watery eyes, and Fatigue.

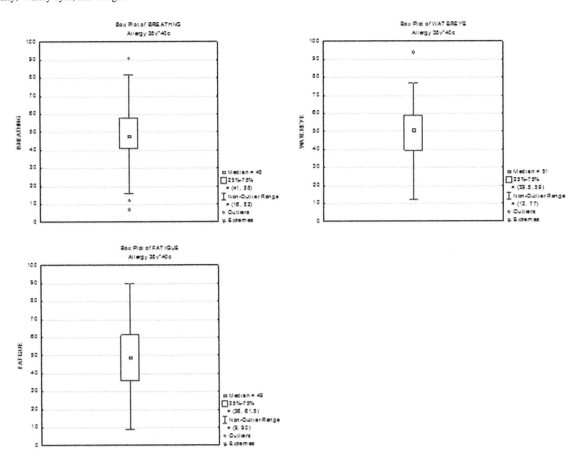

FIGURE K.4 There are a few outliers, but, from an understanding of the dataset, these do not appear to be atypical and thus were not discarded in this study. Box plots clockwise from top left: Breathing Difficulty, Watery eyes, and Fatigue.

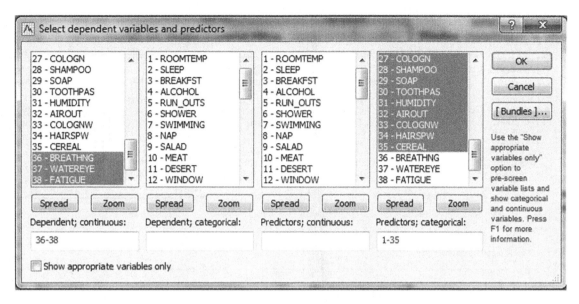

FIGURE K.5 Selecting variables for the analysis.

	Best predictors for continuous de	
	F-value	p-value
HUMIDITY	12.05423	0.000093
RUN_OUTS	4.94332	0.012512
AFTERSH	4.10269	0.024587
AIROUT	2.38382	0.106217
PETCAT	1.38468	0.263078
SOAP	0.11992	0.887337
HAIRSPW	0.11368	0.892852
ADRIAN	0.11368	0.892852
RELAX	0.11368	0.892852
COLOGN	0.10209	0.903199

	Best predictors for continuous de	
	F-value	p-value
HUMIDITY	11.50149	0.000130
RUN_OUTS	4.94351	0.012510
AFTERSH	4.35107	0.020087
AIROUT	1.97775	0.152741
PETCAT	1.56651	0.222304
NAP	0.14912	0.861982
ADRIAN	0.14912	0.861982
ALCOHOL	0.09124	0.913005
TOOTHPAS	0.05376	0.947731
COLOGN	0.04859	0.952628

	Best predictors for continuous de	
	F-value	p-value
HUMIDITY	10.46688	0.000250
RUN_OUTS	5.30755	0.009407
AIROUT	4.02640	0.026175
AFTERSH	3.10091	0.056878
PETCAT	0.98944	0.381405
PETDOC	0.12031	0.886992
RELAX	0.10451	0.901027
WINDOW	0.07005	0.932466
BOB	0.06402	0.938090
NEWSPAP	0.05280	0.948638

FIGURE K.6 Results of the Feature Selection of the "best" predictor variables from the data set.

The results of the summary are shown in Figure K.6, where we can see that the best predictors for Breathing Difficulty are Humidity, Running outside, and Using aftershave; the best predictors for Watery Eyes are also Humidity, Running outside, and Aftershave (the same as for Breathing Difficulty); the best predictors for Fatigue are Humidity, Running outside, and Airing out the bedroom before night.

While we could aggregate the three target variables into one "allergy variable" and regress this on the predictors, I suggest keeping the target variables distinct since the data already come disaggregated and because, in practice, each target variable may require a different response by the interested party (e.g., an inhaler for Breathing Difficulty, eye drops for Watery Eyes, and access to caffeine for Fatigue).

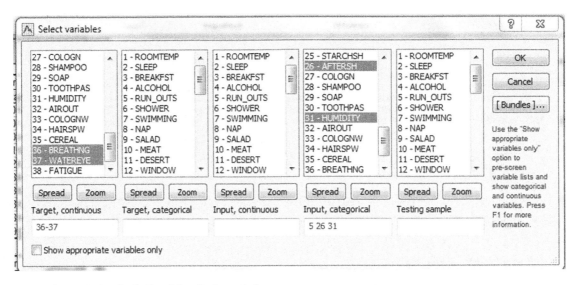

FIGURE K.7   Variable selection for the Data Miner Recipe analysis.

Model selected for deployment		1			
Model Evaluation Summary	ID		Name	Residual (mean square of residuals)	Correlation coefficient
		1	C&RT	468.25	0.2
		3	Neural network	24.98	0.06
		2	Boosted trees	6083.92	0.06
Table	Step options				
	Date and time		10/31/2013 9:00:54 PM		

FIGURE K.8   Data Miner Recipe results for target variable Breathing Difficulty.

Next, I ran a Data Miner Recipe on the target variables. Breathing Difficulty and Watery Eyes can be run together, since their predictor variables are the same. (See Figure K.7 for variable selection for this Data Miner Recipe analysis.)

First, consider Breathing Difficulty (see Figure K.8). The C&RT model had the highest correlation coefficient, although it was only 0.2. (*Note*: I was concerned that by deploying the model on the same data used to create it, I was letting in leaks from the future [see issue at the beginning of this chapter regarding being unable to find a node to split the data into Training and Testing sets]. However, if this was the case, I would expect a much better fitting model, so I'm not sure that I was actually allowing in such leaks.)

Figure K.9 shows the graph of the observations versus the values predicted by the C&RT model (along with the line of best fit, in blue). The model does not appear to be particularly predictive.

From the tree diagram in Figure K.10, we see that Humidity is the most sensitive predictor, and, if it is present, then Running outside is considered. If Humidity is not present, Use of aftershave is considered, followed by Running outside.

C&RT analysis seems to indicate that Humidity is the most significant predictor of allergic reactions, for this dataset; note that the FIRST SPLIT, in the ID = ! Box at the top, is due to HUMIDITY.

The correlation results for Watery Eyes (see Figure K.11) from the Data Miner Recipe were also unimpressive, with the best model, the C&RT model, having a correlation coefficient of only 0.14.

This low correlation is seen in the graph (Figure K.12) of the observed versus C&RT predicted values of Watery Eyes. The line of best fit is shown.

The Decision tree nodes were the same for Watery Eyes as for Breathing Difficulty.

Rather than continue to do a Data Miner Recipe for Fatigue, let's think about why the recipes were not particularly predictive. One reason could be that only extremely low or high target variable values are correlated with certain allergy conditions. If so, it might be better to use a definitional abstraction and turn the target variables into the categorical variables of low, medium, or high ratings.

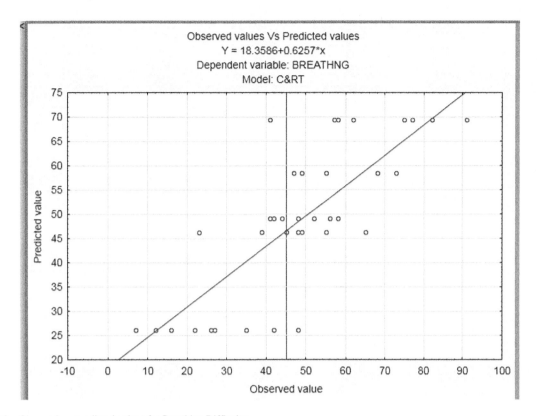

FIGURE K.9 Observed vs. predicted values for Breathing Difficulty.

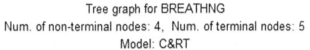
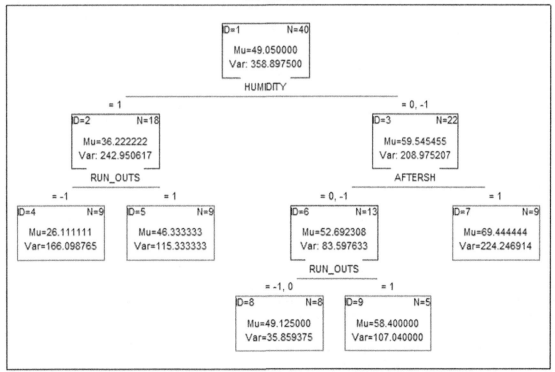

FIGURE K.10 Tree diagram for Breathing Difficulty.

		1	2	3	4
Model selected for deployment		1			
Model Evaluation Summary	ID		Name	Residual (mean square of residuals)	Correlation coefficient
		1	C&RT	490.24	0.14
		3	Neural network	13.67	0.04
		2	Boosted trees	5374.16	0.02
Table	Step options				
	Date and time		10/31/2013 9:40:56 PM		

FIGURE K.11   Data Miner Recipe correlation results for target variable Watery Eyes.

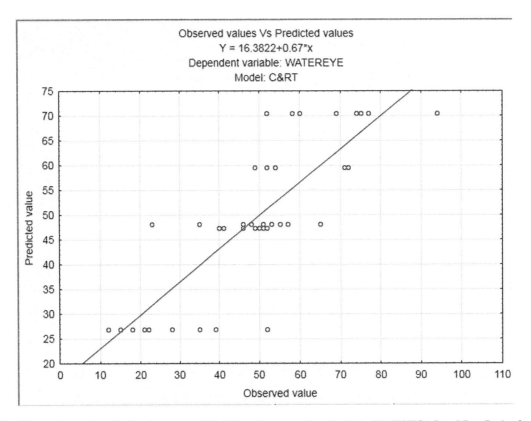

FIGURE K.12   Observed vs. predicted values for target variable Watery Eyes, as analyzed with the STATISTICA Data Miner Recipe format.

To explore this hypothesis about target variables, consider the most important predictor, Humidity (see Figure K.13).

While there are trends between Humidity and each target variable, the spread of the target variables around each Humidity rating (-1 or 1) overlap enough in the mid-range values that it may be better to predict a target variable range (such as each quartile, or a low, medium, high category) rather than the actual target variable value.

We have already seen the distributions of the target variables shown below, but now we are using the Statistics menu − Basic statistics − Graphical comparative summary display to view the quartiles of the data as well as other descriptive statistics, as shown in Figure K.14.

The fact that the descriptive statistics of the three target variables were so close (medians, means, quartiles, variances, etc.) led me to graph the three target variables over time to see if they were collinear, as shown in Figure K.15. From the plot of the target variables on the same timeline, it is clear that Breathing Difficulty and Watery Eyes are highly collinear, while Fatigue has a distinct trend from the other two variables. This is aligned with the Feature Selection module assigning Breathing Difficulty and Watery Eyes identical predictor variables.

From the graphs in Figure K.13, it is clear that the most predictive variable, Humidity, was more predictive at the extreme ratings of the target variables (very high or very low ratings). Therefore, I am going to divide the target

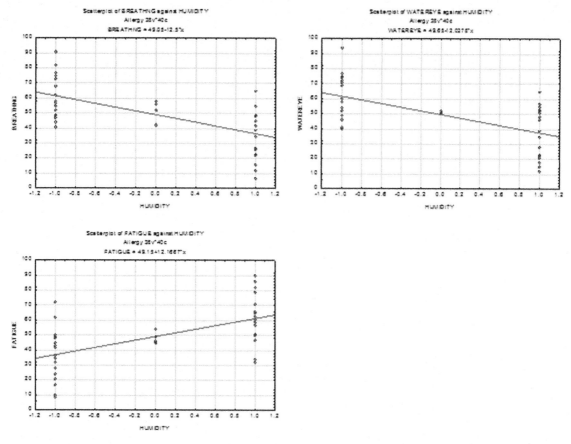

FIGURE K.13 Humidity distributions, as categories, among the three target variables. Humidity level is graphed on the horizontal axes. The vertical axes, clockwise from top left, are Breathing Difficulty, Watery Eyes, and Fatigue.

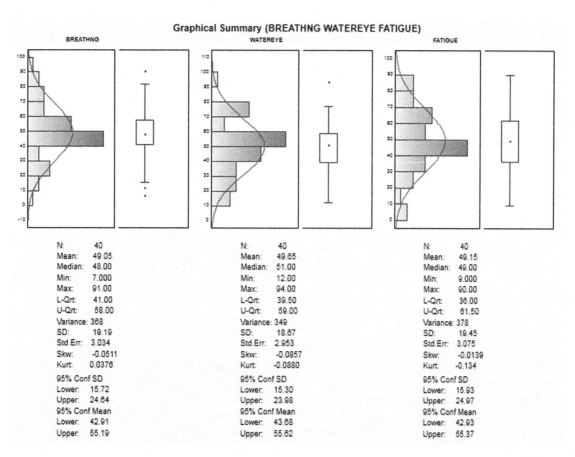

FIGURE K.14 Basic statistics from the BASIC STATS module in STATISTICA.

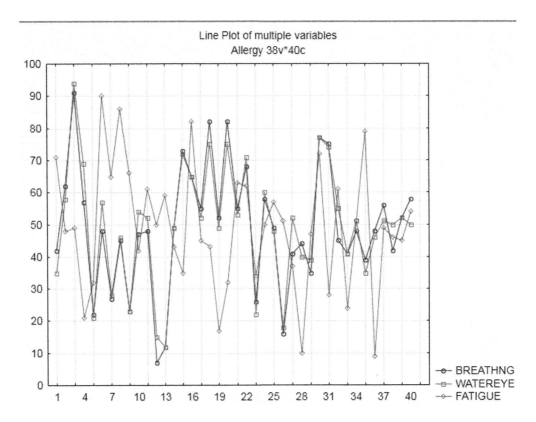

FIGURE K.15   The three target variables graphed over time to attempt to see if they were collinear.

36 BREATHNG	37 WATEREYE	38 FATIGUE	Cat_Brea thing	Cat_wate reye	Cat_fatig ue
42	35	71	low	low	high
62	58	48	high	med	med
91	94	49	high	high	med
57	69	21	med	high	low
22	21	32	low	low	low
48	57	90	med	med	high
27	28	65	low	low	high
45	46	86	med	med	high
23	23	66	low	low	high
47	54	42	med	med	low
48	52	61	med	med	high
7	15	50	low	low	med
12	12	59	low	low	med
49	49	43	med	med	med
73	72	35	high	high	low
65	65	82	high	high	high

FIGURE K.16   Binning of variables into categories.

variables into three categories, based on upper and lower quartiles. For the sake of ease of implementing the abstraction, I am going to use the bins of ratings equal to or below 40, ratings between 40 and 60, and ratings of 60 or above for target variables. These are the approximate Q1 and Q3 values for each of the predictor variables. I did the conversion using Excel formulas and then added the categories as Variables 39 through 41. I wanted to preserve the original ratings in the data, but it is important never to use Variables 36–38 to predict 39 through 41, or vice versa, as 39 through 41 are just abstractions of the first group. A snapshot of the target data is shown in Figure K.16.

	Best predictors for categorical de	
	Chi-square	p-value
HUMIDITY	13.54701	0.008890
RUN_OUTS	11.07787	0.025703
BOB	8.41880	0.077387
AIROUT	6.70940	0.152065
SOAP	6.59544	0.158875
PETCAT	6.48148	0.165961
AFTERSH	5.94967	0.202939
CEREAL	5.00000	0.287297
SHAMPOO	4.96201	0.291217
DESERT	4.96201	0.291217

	Best predictors for categorical de	
	Chi-square	p-value
HUMIDITY	18.46914	0.000999
RUN_OUTS	14.12346	0.006911
BOB ·	13.75309	0.008126
AFTERSH	11.16049	0.024818
DESERT	9.80247	0.043890
AIROUT	8.69136	0.069294
PETCAT	8.69136	0.069294
SWIMMING	7.90123	0.095264
STARCHSH	7.60494	0.107170
CEREAL	7.23457	0.124000

	Best predictors for categorical de	
	Chi-square	p-value
HUMIDITY	18.51852	0.000977
SALAD	14.07407	0.007062
RUN_OUTS	13.33333	0.009757
AIROUT	11.75926	0.019234
AFTERSH	11.75926	0.019234
SHOWER	11.01852	0.026357
JOHN	9.25926	0.054936
RELAX	9.25926	0.054936
PETDOC	9.25926	0.054936
TOOTHPAS	9.25926	0.054936

FIGURE K.17   Best Predictors obtained after using a Binning/Categorization technique with the data.

	1	2	3
Model selected for deployment	1		
Model Evaluation Summary	ID	Name	Error rate (%)
	1	C&RT	30
	3	Neural network	77.5
	2	Boosted trees	82.5
Table	Step options		
	Date and time	11/1/2013 12:28:02 AM	

FIGURE K.18   Model error rates for Breathing Difficulty.

When *Feature Selection* and *Variable Screening* are used to predict the categorical Variables 39−41, the predictors are as seen in Figure K.17.

The predictors for Breathing Difficulty are Humidity and Running outside; the predictors for Watery Eyes are Humidity, Running outside, Meeting with Bob, Aftershave, and Having dessert; the predictors for Fatigue are Humidity, Having a salad, Running outside, Airing out the bedroom, Using aftershave, and Showering.

Running a new Data Miner Recipe on Breathing Difficulty as a categorical variable gave the model error rates shown in Figure K.18.

Using binned (e.g., categorized) variables, the Data Miner Recipe was used for analysis again, this time obtaining higher accuracies. This makes a better "Predictive Model" than the use of the continuous data as in the earlier analysis.

The best model has 70% accuracy. This is not a sufficiently successful model (i.e., >95% accuracy) for my expectations, but does produce some lift.

Running a new Data Miner Recipe on the five predictor variables for Watery Eyes produced a C&RT model with 75% accuracy (see Figure K.19).

Lastly, running a new Data Miner Recipe on the six variables for the categorical variable Fatigue produced the error rates (the most predictive model has only a 57.5% accuracy), as shown in Figure K.20.

	1	2	3
Model selected for deployment	1		
Model Evaluation Summary	ID	Name	Error rate (%)
	1	C&RT	25
	2	Boosted trees	42.5
	3	Neural network	90
Table	Step options		
	Date and time	11/1/2013 12:41:16 AM	

FIGURE K.19 Data Miner Recipe modeling for Watery Eyes produced a 75% accuracy rate with C&RT.

	1	2	3
Model selected for deployment	1		
Model Evaluation Summary	ID	Name	Error rate (%)
	1	C&RT	42.5
	2	Boosted trees	52.5
	3	Neural network	90
Table	Step options		
	Date and time	11/1/2013 12:55:18 AM	

FIGURE K.20 Data Miner Recipe using six predictor variables for target variable Fatigue.

While none of the models was individually successful, each one did produce some lift for each category within each of the target variables.

(*Note*: There is a way to "automatically bin continuous data" within STATISTICA, to make the data behave as "categories"; if we had done this, the results may have been different. This "automatic binning" is explained in some of the other tutorials in this book, so we suggest to readers that this be tried with the above data, if they are interested.)

Tutorial L

Exploring Discrete Database Networks of TriCare Health Data Using R and Shiny

Matthew Wagner, PhD and Kenny Darrell, MS

Chapter Outline

NOTE: To do this tutorial you must also use the software component that is located on this book's Elsevier Companion Web page. The folder is called: "TUTORIAL L-DATABASE EXPLORATION"; this folder on the Companion Web page should contain the files shown in Figure L.1 (with the exception of the Word.doc file, the tutorial itself, which you are currently reading).

INTRODUCTION

Objective of This Tutorial

This tutorial will demonstrate capabilities developed in Shiny, an application using open source R, for exploration of databases, tables, and variable connections using network analysis to help frame analytic problems. The tool automates the data exploration process that is typically done by manual exploration of database schemas, databases, etc. This tool

Practical Predictive Analytics and Decisioning Systems for Medicine. DOI: http://dx.doi.org/10.1016/B978-0-12-411643-6.00029-6

FIGURE L.1   The folder "Tutorial L-Database Exploration" can be found on the Elsevier Companion Web page.

will reduce the amount of time it takes to explore databases and the possible connections between them. As a comparison, try to explore the data dictionary (*TRICARE Program MDR Data Dictionary*) without using this tool; you will quickly see the benefits of it and how they can be extrapolated to other data.

The tool used in this tutorial will be used to explore the data from two paradigms:

1. Posing a business problem or question
2. Using the data to frame a business question.

The data provided for this tutorial are from the *TRICARE Program MDR Data Dictionary*. TRICARE data "brings together the worldwide health care resources of the Uniformed Services and supplements this capability with network and non-network civilian health care professionals, institutions, pharmacies, and suppliers" (Evaluation of the TRICARE Program: Access, Cost, and Quality, 2013). *The TRICARE Program MDR Data Dictionary* contains data on the data systems, sources, and variables collected from several different systems. This aggregated file includes 95 databases and 76 sheets on "reference tables/appendices," with the databases and variable details. For this tutorial we will use the databases which include information on each individual database and the included variables. These data allow us to investigate the typical problems of exploring disparate and siloed databases and the associates between — a familiar problem in analytics and database aggregation.

This tutorial is purely an example of the tool's capabilities and utility in project definition and relational data exploration. It is generally applicable to any set of databases.

The Data

All data are from the TRICARE Data Dictionary.

General File Information
  1. Sheet Name — *Database reference name*
Database Information
  2. Database Name — *Database name*
  3. Common File Name (not used)
  4. Data Set Location (not used)
  5. Update Frequency — *Frequency at which the data are refreshed in the source data system*
  6. Source Location — *Data storage system*
  7. Description — *Detailed description of the database content or subject matter*

Variable Information

8. Data Element — *Variable name (English)*
9. Definition — *Detailed description of the data element*
10. Format — *Details on significant figures, numeric, character, etc.*
11. Position or SAS Variable — *Variable reference name (system)*
12. Values — *Possible values or conditions the variable takes*
13. Notes — *Extra comments on the data element*

About Database Structure and Network Analysis

Databases usually have a structure that allows different aspects of the data to be linked and joined to form different views for different purposes. This usually falls apart in larger contexts, though; as each system defines the mechanics about how its internal data can be merged, it is not very helpful regarding the growing number of silos that exist across a domain or agency. Some work can be done to alleviate this burden. A first step can be to recognize that disparate data were perhaps designed with common names; or you may actually have data from one database but the process undergone to obtain the data has destroyed any underlying schema, and you simply have a folder full of tables with no idea of how they are related. Either case leads to a daunting task of data fusion into a possible unknown territory.

Network analysis and graph data structures provide a great way to help in solving this problem of data relation and fusion. In a network we have edges and nodes; nodes are connected by edges, and in relation to the problem at hand a node is a variable in a table and a table is an edge. Thus, a node will have edges for each table it exists in, and these will link to other nodes that share similar tables. If you need to do some data analysis, you can create a network centered on your target node to see what information can be used as context in your analysis. You can also have a few pieces of data that may be a target and, through a network, learn how these pieces of information are linked, what neighboring data are required to join them, and what meaning this holds.

About Shiny

Shiny (Shiny Home Page) is an R package that enables the user to create interactive web applications based on R analytics. The application user can choose input parameters using friendly controls like sliders, dropdowns, and text fields to explore data, analytics, and visualizations. Some experience with R is necessary. No HTML or JavaScript knowledge is necessary.

Data Preparation

Data were downloaded from the TRICARE site as an Excel file and opened in Excel.

1. An Excel macro was used to create a table that lists all data elements (variables) in a single column for each database (data 1 and 8).
2. A second Excel macro was used to create a table that includes the database name, sheet name, description, source system, and update frequency (data 1, 2, 5—7).
3. A third Excel macro was used to generate a database that provides a description of all variables in the MDR (data 8—13).

Aggregating the data into these tables enables the user to start to look at and piece the data together so as to understand the information available in this tutorial.

Installing R and RStudio

R must be installed before running this application. Detailed instructions can be found at the R Home Page (www.r-project.org/) and RStudio Home Page (www.rstudio.com). This application was developed in R version 3.0.2.

Installing Shiny and Supporting Packages

The installation procedure will be performed with the provided Install.R file. R needs to be installed on the computer for this to execute.

1. In a Windows command prompt (terminal) window, set the directory to the location of the tutorial folder using *cd('file location path\Tutorial_L')*.
2. Use the *ls* command to make sure the working directory is active and the file Install.R is visible in the folder.
3. In the command prompt, type *Rscript Install.R* to execute the file.

Additional information about installing Shiny can be found at the Shiny Home Page (www.rstudio.com/shiny/).

Starting the Tutorial Application

1. Double click the file Tutorial L.Rproj, and it will start the RStudio program in the correct working directory of the tutorial.
2. The RStudio Window interface will appear (Figure L.2).
3. Install all necessary libraries for the application by typing source (*Setup.R*) at the R Console command line.
4. Initialize the working environment by loading the required libraries and data, and type source (*Init.R*) at the R Console command line.
5. At the R Console command line, type *runApp()* to start the Tutorial Application.
6. The Tutorial Application will open in your default Internet browser as a new window (Figure L.3).

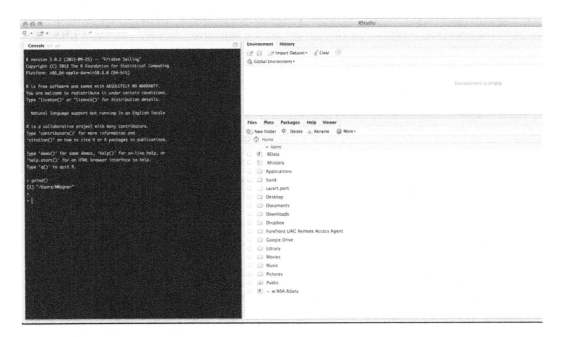

FIGURE L.2   RStudio console.

FIGURE L.3   Tutorial application.

Features and Functionality of the Tutorial Application

The Tutorial Application organizes and structures the exploration process of databases and their connectivity.

1. The *Select Table to Explore* pane (Figure L.4, highlighted box)
- Is used to select a database in the set of all available databases in the data dictionary.
- Describes the selected database.
- Identifies databases with no connections to other databases.
- Is always visible to the user.
2. *The Selected Database Description & Variables* tab (Figure L.4)
- Visualizes the database connections.
- Requires patience as the visualizations refresh and load, with 5- to 10-second waits for the visualizations to refresh.
- Provides multiple options for visualizations, weighting of connections, and layout options to change the views of the database connections.
  A connection denotes at least one variable in common.
3. The *Database Visualization* tab (Figure L.5)
- Visualizes the database connections.
  A connection denotes at least one variable in common.
- Requires patience as the visualizations refresh and load; wait 5–10 seconds for the visualizations to refresh.
- Provides multiple options for visualizations, weighting of connections, and layout options to change the views of the database connections.
  There are several options in the *Select Plot Type* menu, including:
  - Network (all connections):
    - A network plot of all databases and the selected database.
    - Provision of options for displaying the layout of the plot.
  - Network (selected node):
    - A network plot of the databases directly connected to the selected database.
    - First-degree connections – all databases with a direct variable link to the selected database.
    - First- and second-degree connections – all databases with a direct variable link to the selected database and all databases that are connected to the first-degree connections.

FIGURE L.4 Selected database description and variables.

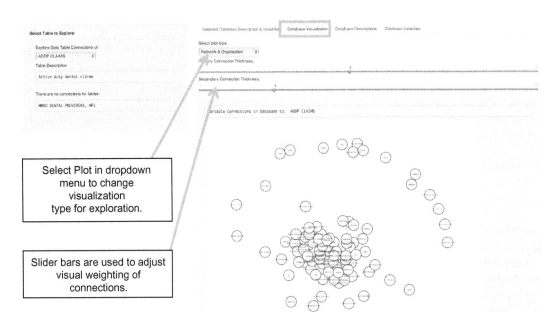

FIGURE L.5 Database Visualization tab.

FIGURE L.6 Database Description tab.

- First and second (direct) — same as first and second, but only displays databases with a direct link to the selected database.
- Provision of options for displaying the layout of the plot.
- Network (3D interactive):
  - A network plot of the databases directly connected to the selected database in an interactive 3D plot.

4. The *Database Description* tab (Figure L.6)

- Displays two tables that show all available information on the databases.
  - Database Name (Data.Set)
  - Number of Connections (Connections)
  - Description
  - Source System
  - Original Excel sheet name (Data.Sheet)
  - Number of Variables in Database
  - Update Frequency.

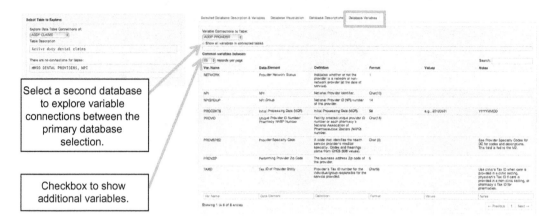

FIGURE L.7   Database Variables tab.

- Shows, in the top table, the information of the selected database.
- Shows, in the lower table, the information of all connected databases to the selected database.
- Provides tables that are sortable by column and searchable for text within any field.
5. The *Database Variables* tab (Figure L.7)
- Allows the user to select a second database to investigate connections by using the dropdown Variable Connections to Table.
- Displays two tables that show all available information on the variables within the selected databases, including the Data Variable Name (Var.Name), English Variable Name (Data.Element), Definition, Source System, Format, Values, Notes.
- Shows, in the top table, the information of the common database variables.
  - This includes direct variable matches such as IDs.
  - This includes variables that can provide "fuzzy" matches such as dates and names.
- Shows, in the lower table, the information of all connected databases to the selected database.
  - Appears if the "Show all variables in connected tables" box is checked. By default, it is not shown.
  - Shows variables in the connected table, selected in the Variable Connections to Table, that are not in common.
  - Allows the user to explore what information is contained in a connecting table that might provide utility during analytics.
  - Provides tables that are sortable by column and searchable for text within any field.

EXAMPLE I: BUSINESS-DRIVEN PROBLEM GENERATION – WHAT DO I WANT TO ASK OF MY DATA?

Every analyst is posed this question at the beginning of a project. Defining the business and analytics problem is imperative to setting up a successful project. This is not an easy task. Problem definition requires initial work in problem framing, data evaluation, and data exploration, with input from the business owners, subject matter experts, and analysts.

This business understanding phase of a project is never complete, and will evolve throughout a project as new data become available and new understanding of the data emerges. This is a highly iterative process, and there are many considerations to be aware of (see Wagner and Pilcher, 2013). By identifying and exploring available data and business problems, a detailed understanding of the workspace, goals, and success can be idealized. However, exploring and understanding relationships in the data is typically a manual and arduous task.

The CRISP-DM and Other Analytics Processes

Analytics can vastly improve the operations and efficiencies of a business. The CRISP-DM process (Figure L.8) made popular by IBM (Chapman *et al.*, n.d.) maps out an iterative process that begins with business understanding, proceeds with data analysis, and ends with business deployment. There is a highly iterative process between the business understanding, data understanding, and evaluation phases. This is the crux of the problem we wish to tackle.

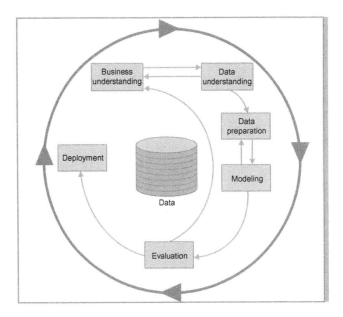

FIGURE L.8 The CRISP-DM process.

Business understanding, or problem definition, is the pivotal stage that can launch a successful project or lead to a dismal attempt. The ideals of a business and those of subject matter experts will always feed the problem, but the data availability and relationships will help to shape and define what can be accomplished. Understanding the data available, the content, and connections enables the analyst to perform meaningful analytics to deploy solutions to the stakeholder. Communication channels need to remain open between all stakeholders during the problem, data, and evaluation phases.

Completion of the problem definition steps, keeping the data in mind, might actually result in a database such as you may use in many others of these tutorials. Now you know how you get these nicely structured databases! Three mainstream methodologies of analytic and data mining projects (KDD, SEMMA, and CRISP-DM) are discussed and compared in Azevedo and Santos (2008). CRISP-DM is the only process that includes business understanding, while the other two methodologies focus on the analytics and data mining processes.

Exploring the Data

While complete, rich, and "perfect" data sets are desirable, the vast majority of data require aggregation, fusing, and/or fuzzy matching to paint only a partial picture. The data exploration and preprocessing steps should be adequately flexible to evaluate data sets with new and more complete information — a final (or textbook) data set is rarely created the first time around. Typically, several siloed, disparate, and analogous data sets are aggregated into a composite that is fused together on one of many data sets, including IDs or other relational information. *The ability to identify relationships and connections between databases can aid data exploration and facilitate business problem definition. Ultimately, an analyst can uncover what can be asked of the data and what data are needed to complete the picture.*

The Medical (Business) Problem

"Research has shown that more than 120 systemic diseases originate in the oral cavity" (Rudman *et al.*, 2010). Dr. Rudman and colleagues presented an article that articulates the need for integrated patient care records for both medical and oral health records to improve continuity of care, research, safety and cost. The fact that research has shown a distinct relationship between oral health and medical health provides a strong foundation to pursue what opportunities we might have with the TRICARE MDR database.

Our medical problem:

Integrating records of systemic and oral health would improve patient care. It would also open up a new frontier in health information management.

(Rudman *et al.*, 2010).

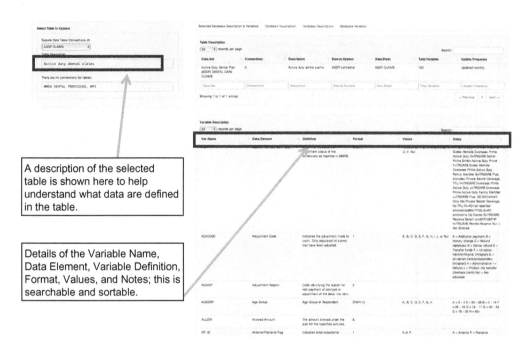

A description of the selected table is shown here to help understand what data are defined in the table.

Details of the Variable Name, Data Element, Variable Definition, Format, Values, and Notes; this is searchable and sortable.

FIGURE L.9 Opening screen of the application.

Our analytic problem:

What data are available in the MDR that connect both dental records and medical records together and that can inform on and provide a basis for analytic capabilities to improve provider care, outcomes, safety, and/or cost?

Now, we can start the Tutorial Application, or open the MDR Data Dictionary in Excel, and begin to look at the available data and the connections between these databases and databases. This exploration will provide an analyst with three main outcomes:

1. The databases and tables that contain pertinent information
2. The connections between the pertinent data that can link the information together to create a meaningful data set for exploitation
3. The data that are either unavailable in the present databases, or available but with no means available to connect the information together.

We can accomplish these goals through visual exploration of the databases and their connections, tabular format of the database information, and exploration of the variable connections and definitions.

Inspect the Selected Database – "What Do We Have?"

1. By default, the application will open to show the Selected Database Description and Variables tab for the first database ADDP CLAIMS (Figure L.9).
2. Select the Explore Database Connections window, and select the table for which you want to view a description and variables, as shown in Figure L.10. In this example we will explore the ADDP CLAIMS table first, since it is related to dental claims.
   a. Here it is possible to see all variables, and variable name, definition, format, values, and notes. This provides insight into the detail of the data contained in the database.
3. The Variable Description can be searched for terms relevant to our problem definition, as shown in Figure L.11, with the search term "dental." This search displays all descriptions or variable names that contain the word "dental."
   a. We see variables such as APPROVED, D_DTFREF, and QUADRANT, which define specific data related to the dental claim.
   b. By querying specific terms, it is possible to see which specific or related information fits our problem.
   c. Is this information useful to us, though? Might it be related to other databases that can help frame the problem definition and answer our business problem?

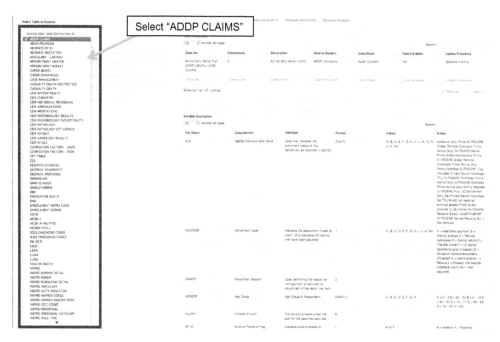

FIGURE L.10 Select database drop list.

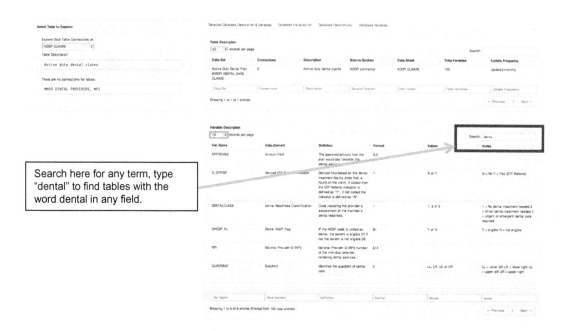

FIGURE L.11 Search capability in variables within ADDP database.

4. Spend some time exploring the database tables, descriptions, and variables in the tables. The more familiar you become with the databases, the more efficiently you can query and search the tables. Start to ask questions of the data:

a. What data do I need to answer my analytics and business problem?
b. What is available in different databases?
c. What variables are in the databases that contain useful information?
d. How might these databases be related? How can I exploit these relationships?

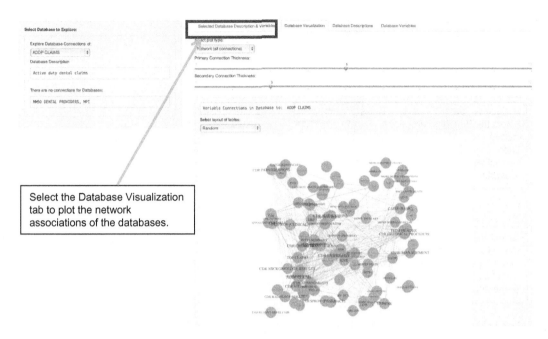

Select the Database Visualization tab to plot the network associations of the databases.

FIGURE L.12   ADDP database visualization and exploration.

Visual Exploration – "What Can We See?"

Visually exploring the data can help to identify underlying connections between databases of interest, such as the ADDP CLAIMS, and other available databases. Exploring both primary (first degree) and secondary (second degree) connections to the table of interest can help identify not only information that is available or useful to the problem definition but also how this information is related through the data. Let's explore.

1. With the database ADDP CLAIMS selected, click on the Database Visualization tab in the main tab panel, as shown in Figure L.12.
2. Select the Explore Database Connections window, and select the table for which you want to view a description and variables. In this example we will explore the ADDP CLAIMS table first, since it is related to dental claims.
3. By default, the application will show the Network plot of all connections in all of the databases that are being explored, including the selected database ADDP CLAIMS.
4. The Network plot has many parameters to control plot types, layout, and connection weighting to provide flexibility. Select the Plot Type dropdown menu to select "Network (all connections)" to show the network connection plots. This is a similar plot to the default, but provides some options in the layout of the plot. Choose the layout "Circle," as shown in Figure L.13.
5. Explore some of the different plot types and the ability they provide to explore the database relationships. Select the Plot Type dropdown menu to select "Network (primary node)" to show all databases that are connected to the selected database ADDP CLAIMS. It can be seen that there are far fewer databases shown, and it is much easier to identify which databases are connected directly to the ADDP CLAIMS database as in Figure L.14.
6. Select the Select Connections to Selected Node dropdown menu to select from the layout type of connections to be displayed, as shown in Figure L.15. The options are Primary connections, Primary + Secondary, and Primary + Secondary (direct only). Again, the plot changes and shows the Primary connections in light gray, and Secondary connections, connections to the databases that are directly connected to the ADDP CLAIMS database, are shown in dark gray. These Secondary connections can provide more information to the table of interest through variables in the intermediary (Primary connection) databases.
7. Again, the default view of the network isn't always insightful. By adjusting the thickness of the Primary and Secondary connections the connections become more visible for interpretation, as in Figure L.16. Slide the thickness bars for Primary and/or Secondary connections to view either as your primary interest of investigation. Set the Primary Connection Thickness to 10 and the Secondary Connection Thickness to 1. For instance, here we can see that some Secondary connections of tables we might explore are: OPT TABLE, ADDRESS (PITE), and HCPR.

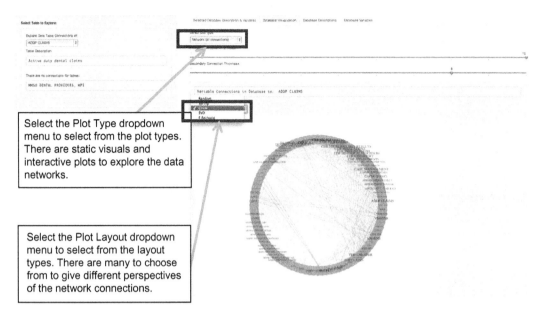

Select the Plot Type dropdown menu to select from the plot types. There are static visuals and interactive plots to explore the data networks.

Select the Plot Layout dropdown menu to select from the layout types. There are many to choose from to give different perspectives of the network connections.

FIGURE L.13   Select Plot Type and Plot Layout to change how the database connections are displayed in the network.

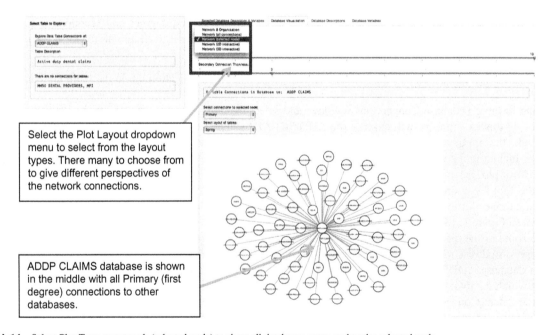

Select the Plot Layout dropdown menu to select from the layout types. There many to choose from to give different perspectives of the network connections.

ADDP CLAIMS database is shown in the middle with all Primary (first degree) connections to other databases.

FIGURE L.14   Select Plot Type as network (selected node) to show all databases connected to the selected node.

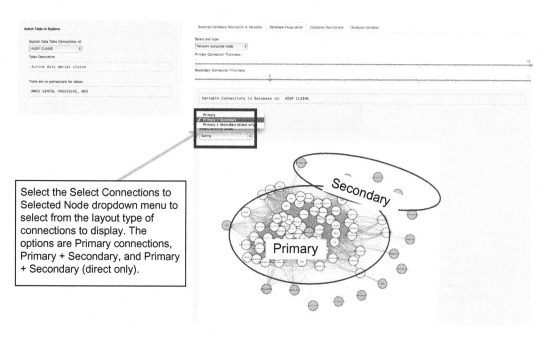

FIGURE L.15   Select the connections to be displayed in the network plot to show Primary and Secondary connections.

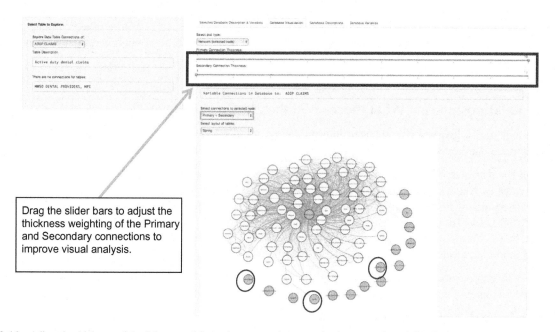

FIGURE L.16   Adjust the thickness of the Primary and Secondary connections to make the connections visible for interpretation.

8. Select the Select Connections to Selected Node dropdown menu to select the "Primary + Secondary (direct only)" connections shown in Figure L.17. ADDP CLAIMS is shown here in gray. Here, all connections between the primary databases connected directly to ADDP CLAIMS are shown. It is possible to see which databases are scarcely connected to others and which are very well connected. Through further exploration we can see which, if any, connections are feasible to connect the data. We can also see what the main contributing data sets might be; for example, DESPROV (CLINICAL), whereas TEDPR is not connected to any of the other Primary connections and might contain unique information pertinent to our problem.

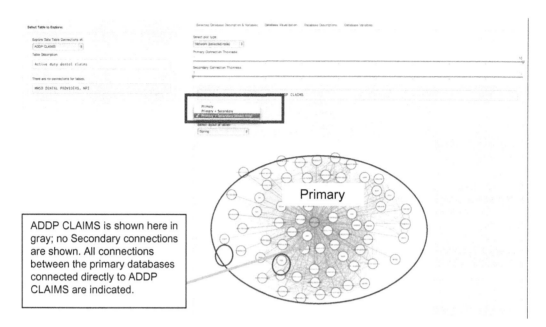

FIGURE L.17 Select the plot type to explore only the Primary and Secondary connections between all tables with primary connections to the selected ADDP CLAIMS table.

Spend some time exploring these relationships through the visualization panel. Explore other variables and start to see how the visualization can add value to the exploration process; however, it might not always get us to our end result and help to generate insightful questions of the databases available.

Database Relationships — "What Pieces of a Puzzle Do We Have?"

For now we will start to explore the tabulated information on the databases connected to ADDP CLAIMS to link both dental and medical data together — the main problem we seek to solve in this example.

1. Select the Database Descriptions tab (see Figure L.18).
2. In the Connected Databases & Details pane, type "dental" into the search panel and click Enter.
3. Review the results of the display to see that some of the tables which contain dental data are ADDP PROVIDER, DRF, MMSO DENTAL CLAIMS, and TDP CLAIMS.
4. Evaluate these tables by their description. We will explore both the variable connections between DRF, TDP CLAIMS, and our selected database, ADDP CLAIMS.

Next we will explore medical databases. With a little knowledge of the data dictionary, or insight from a subject matter expert, it is known that the CDR databases contain medical information.

1. Select the Database Descriptions tab (see Figure L.19).
2. In the Connected Databases & Details pane, type "CDR" into the search panel and click Enter.
3. Review the results of the display to see that some of the tables which contain medical data are CDR appointments, CDR Chemistry, CDR Historical Procedures, and eight other CDR databases.
4. Evaluate these tables by their description to explore further. We will explore both the variable connections between CDR CHEMISTRY and our selected database ADDP CLAIMS.

Through this example you have identified three databases with connections to the ADDP CLAIMS database that contain medical or dental data: DRF, TDP CLAIMS, and CDR CHEMISTRY. Continue to explore the database connections. If there is interest in a different primary database than ADDP CLAIMS, select it in the left pane. Then explore connections to another database. More time spent exploring and asking questions of the databases and data will lead to more insightful connections.

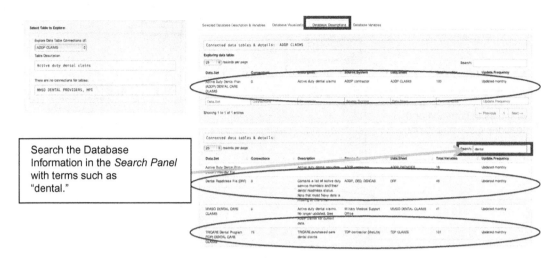

Search the Database Information in the *Search Panel* with terms such as "dental."

FIGURE L.18 ADDP database description and search of databases with "dental."

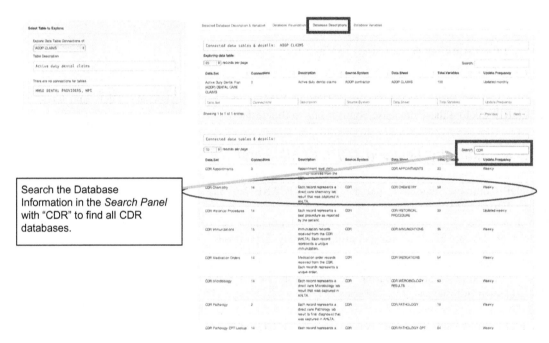

Search the Database Information in the *Search Panel* with "CDR" to find all CDR databases.

FIGURE L.19 ADDP database description and search of databases with "CDR."

Further evaluation of databases can take the form below; this could be an exercise for you on your own:

1. First-degree connections to ADDP CLAIMS: DESPROV (CLINICAL)
2. Second-degree connections of databases connected to ADDP CLAIMS: OPT TABLE, ADDRESS (PITE), and HCPR.
3. Other databases not explored though a connection to ADDP CLAIMS might contain unique information pertinent to our problem: TED-NI, TRICARE Encounter Data.

Variable Understanding and Connections — "How Can We Put the Pieces Together?"

Following exploration of the ADDP CLAIMS database, we are familiar with not only what the ADDP CLAIMS database is and what variables and data are in it, but also how it relates to other tables and the strength of these relationships.

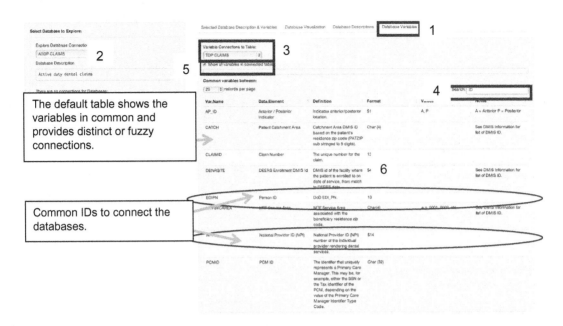

FIGURE L.20 ADDP and TDP CLAIMS connections.

Previously we found connections between ADDP CLAIMS and the TDP CLAIMS, DRF, and CDR CHEMISTRY databases. We will explore these database connections in this order.

Explore the Relationships Between ADDP CLAIMS and TDP CLAIMS

These two databases contain information on dental claims: the ADDP Active duty dental claims (ADDP CLAIMS) from the ADDP Contractor database, and the TDP TRICARE purchased care dental claims from a TDP Contractor (MetLife) (see Figure L.18).

The goal in this step is to investigate the variable relationships between the two databases to explore how they are related, and which data are available for gathering for analysis purposes.

1. Select the Database Variables tab (see Figure L.20).
   a. *Note*: At this point we are comparing the table in the Select Table to Explore pane (ADDP CLAIMS) with other tables selected in Database Variable pane (TDP).
2. Keep ADDP CLAIMS selected in the Explore Database Connections dropdown menu.
3. In the Variable Connections to Table pane, select "TDP CLAIMS."
   a. The default table shown shows the variables in common and provides distinct or fuzzy connections. Between these databases there are 75 common variables.
4. In the search field type "ID."
   a. It is possible to observe the common variables that serve as direct ID connections. These include the EDIPN (DEERS Person ID), NPI (National Provider ID), and SPONSSN (Sponsor Person ID). These are the variables we use to connect these tables.
5. In the Search pane, type "surface" to find all dental surface procedures that were performed, shown in Figure L.21.
6. Check the "Show all variables in connected tables" box to show all variables that are in both the ADDP CLAIMS and the TDP databases (see Figure L.22). There are 26 additional variables, not in common, in the TDP CLAIMS database.
7. With the "Show all variables in connected tables" checked, the other variables can be explored as shown in Figure L.22 by scrolling down the page.
   a. This table shows the variables that are not common and might add value to include in the analysis. There are 26 variables in this list.
   b. Investigate the variable names, elements, and definitions of the variables without a direct link in name in the table by scrolling up and down on the page.

FIGURE L.21   ADDP and TDP CLAIMS "surface" variables from dental records of TDP CLAIMS.

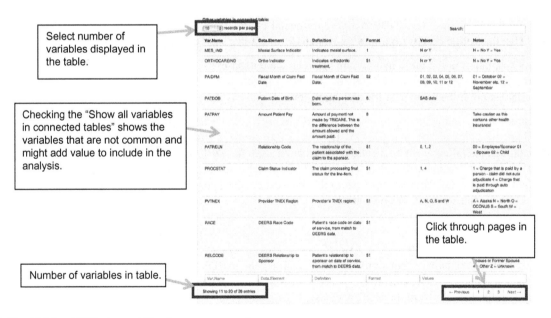

FIGURE L.22   ADDP and TDP other variables that are not connections.

    c. It is possible to observe the variables that we might want to use from either table that help answer or provide information to support our business problem. This can be done by browsing through the multiple pages in the table or by using a search term, as previously shown.

8. Click through the pages in the table and find the variables below.

a. A select few from these tables are: CLMFINDT (Claim Finalized Date) and DTF_DMISID (Dental Treatment Facility Code), ORTHOCAREIND (Ortho Indicator), TRMTTYPE (Treatment Type), and SPC (Provider Specialty).

    The common IDs we might use, moving forward, are: EDIPN (DEERS Person ID), NPI (National Provider ID), and SPONSSN (Sponsor Person ID). Some variables of interest might be: the surface indicators list, Ortho Code, Treatment Type, and Provider Specialty, and CLMFINDT (Claim Finalized Date).

FIGURE L.23   ADDP and DRF common variables.

Explore the Relationships Between ADDP CLAIMS and DRF

Repeat the same steps as in searching for relationships between ADDP CLAIMS and DRF. These two databases contain information on dental claims, the ADDP Active duty dental claims from the ADDP Contractor database, and the database Dental Readiness File (DRF) from multiple databases including ADDP, DED, DENCAS; see Figure L.23.

1. How many variables are in there in common between the databases?
2. What are common variables that are "IDs" or "fuzzy" connections?
3. What variables might be of interest for collection for our analysis database?

The common IDs we might use moving forward are: EDIPN (DEERS Person ID), NPI (National Provider ID), SPONSSN (Sponsor Person ID), and CLAIMID (Claim ID). Some of these are the same IDs to connect to the TDP CLAIMS database, and allow us to connect the information from the DRF with the same IDs. Some variables of interest might be DTF (Dental Treatment Facility) and BENCAT (Beneficiary Category). This isn't as interesting a connection, and you might not carry any variables forward to the analysis database, but this is the art of data exploration and we are able to quickly see what we need, or don't need.

Explore the Relationships Between ADDP CLAIMS and CDR CHEMISTRY

These two databases contain information on dental claims, the ADDP Active duty dental claims from the ADDP Contractor database and the CDR Chemistry database in which each record represents a direct care chemistry lab result that was captured in AHLTA from the CDR database. Now we are connecting medical lab results to the dental data.

1. Select the Database Variables tab (see Figure L.24).
   a. Note: At this point we are comparing the table in the Select Table to Explore pane (ADDP CLAIMS) with other tables selected in the Database Variable pane (CDR CHEMISTRY).
2. In the Variable Connections to Table pane, select "CDR CHEMISTRY."
   a. The default table shown shows the variables in common and provides distinct or fuzzy connections. Between these databases, there are 14 common variables.
3. In the search field type "ID."
   a. It is possible to observe the common variables that serve as direct ID connections. These are the DENSRITE (DEERS Enrollment DMIS ID), and SPONSSN (DEERS Enrollment DMIS ID).
4. Check the "Show all variables in connected tables" to show all variables that are in both the ADDP CLAIMS and CDR CHEMISTRY databases (see Figure L.24).
5. Investigate the variable names, elements and definitions of the variables without a direct link in name in the table by scrolling up and down the page (see Figures L.24, Figure L.25).

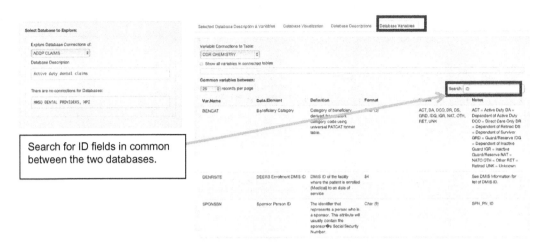

FIGURE L.24   ADDP and CDR CHEMISTRY common variables.

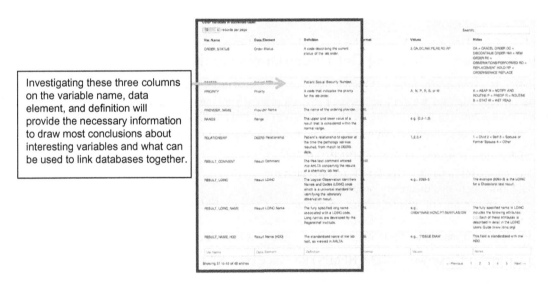

FIGURE L.25   ADDP and CDR CHEMISTRY other variables that are not connections.

6. With the "Show all variables in connected tables" checked, the other variables can be explored, as shown in Figure L.25.

  a. This table shows the variables that are not common and might add value, to include in the analysis. There are 48 variables in this list.

  b. It is possible to observe the variables that we might want to use from either table that help answer or provide information to support our business problem. This can be done by browsing through the multiple pages in the table, or by using a search term as previously shown.

7. Click through the pages in the table and find the variables below.

  a. A select few from these tables are: PROVIDER_NAME (Name of the Provider), RESULT_NAME_HDD (Result Name (HDD)).

8. In the Search pane, type "result" to find all variables that contain results of performed dental surface procedures.

  a. Figure L.26 shows a subset of these variables.

The common IDs we might use, moving forward, are: DENSRITE (DEERS Enrollment DMIS ID), and SPONSSN (DEERS Enrollment DMIS ID). Some variables of interest might be medical test results such as ABNORMAL_IND.

Var.Name	Data.Element	Definition
ABNORMAL_IND	Abnormal Indicator	A code that indicates the result value is outisde of the normal range.
ACCESS_SYSTEM_NCID	Accession System NCID	The HDD Numeric Concept Identifier (NCID) code, which is a number that represents a concept - in this case the Host platform sending the accession result data.
CDR_APPT_ID	CDR Appointment ID	CDR's version of a unique appt ID that represents the appointment record related to the pathology lab result.
DATE_RESULTED	Result Date	The date the results of the Microbiology test were provided.
HCDP	DEERS HCDP	The Health Care Delivery Program Plan Coverage Code that represents the plan coverage the beneficiary has at the time the pathology lab was resulted.
LAB_RESULT_NCID	Lab Result NCID	The HDD Numeric Concept Identifier (NCID) code, which is a number that represents a concept - in this case a type of lab result.

FIGURE L.26 A subset of variables.

Iterating the Process – "Refining Our Understanding of the Data?"

Data exploration is a time-consuming and highly iterative process. Through our previous step you found some databases that were useful and one that was not as useful for our problem statement. At this point it would be well advised to explore some connections to some of the databases we observed: TDP CLAIMS or CDR CHEMISTRY. Perform this exploration on your own, as in the previous steps. One useful connection might be CDR PATHOLOGY.

- What variables are of interest in CDR CHEMISTRY?
- What other databases is CDR CHEMISTRY connected to?
- Do visualizations help this discovery process?
- What are the descriptions of other databases connected to CDR CHEMISTRY?
- How are these other databases connected? With what variables?
- What additional information do these other databases allow us to connect to our current data?

  Possible connecting IDs between CDR CHEMISTRY and CDR PATHOLOGY are:

- LAB_ORDER_ID
- CDR_CINIC_ID
- CDR_PATIENT_ID

  Possible useful variables of the CDR PATHOLOGY database are:

- DATE_RESULTED
- FINAL_DX
- STATUS_ID

Understanding What Is Missing in the Data

When investigating a conglomerate of databases there are bound to be some data that have no connection to the rest. If we can identify these data then we can look for known data that might facilitate a connection. In the case of this tutorial there are two databases that have no connection to the others, the MPI and MMSO DENTAL PROVIDERS. An extension of this concept is looking for second degree and higher order connections of databases that can link data sets that aren't directly connected to a database of interest. In this case, there might be intermediary databases that are able to

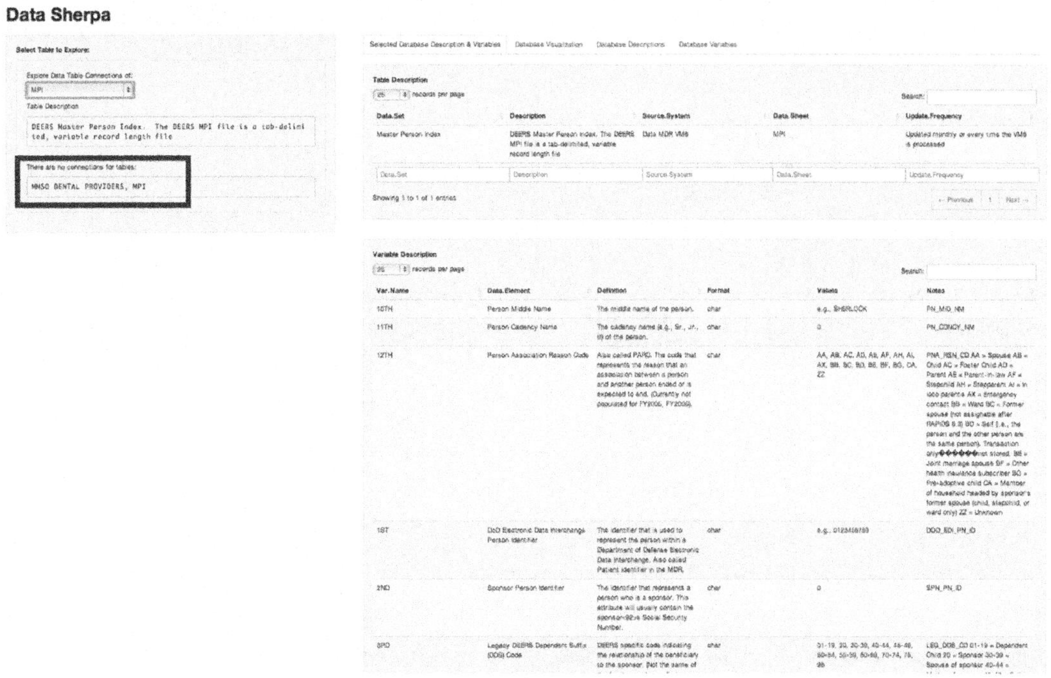

FIGURE L.27 Investigating the MPI data, which lack connections to other databases.

connect the important databases but add little value in content. To explore this concept, use the Database Visualization pane with the Network (selected node) plot, and the Primary and Secondary Connections option.

Explore the MPI database, shown in Figure L.27, to look for possible variables of interest, or variables that might have relationships with others we have seen. This is where experience, creativity, and knowledge of available data are paramount.

1. Select the "Selected Database Description & Variables" tab.
2. In the dropdown menu Explore Database Connections, select the MPI database.
3. Explore the table description and variables.

Conclusions — "Enough is Enough!"

This process of data gathering and evaluation can continue indefinitely. However, we have made some valuable connections between available dental and medical data. We can now start to create our analysis data set from each of the ADDP, CDR CHEMISTRY, DRF, and CDR Pathology databases. This resulting data set will enable us to perform analytics and investigate our business problem:

What data are available in the MDR that connect dental records and medical records together and that can inform on and provide a basis for analytic capabilities to improve provider care, outcomes, safety, and/or cost?

We now have data on dental claims, dental providers, patients, lab results, dental procedures, and pathology results. We have successfully connected disparate databases together for analytics (see Figure L.28), and we have compiled a list of data from these five databases that we will start to use for analytic purposes (Figure L.29).

Now you are well on your way to evaluating the possible relationships between medical diagnosis and lab results with those of dental observations and data around patients and provider care contained in the databases. The process of data exploration and gathering data is a highly iterative process, and is without doubt likely to develop successful analytics.

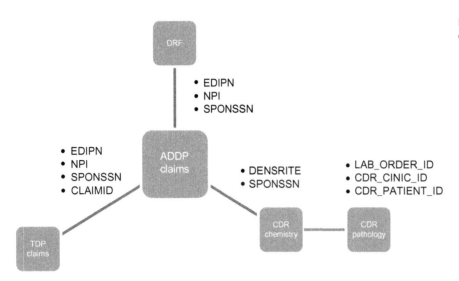

FIGURE L.28 Database connections and connection IDs.

Variable	Definition	Data Type	Database
DENTALCLASS	Dental Readiness Classification	Dental	ADDP PROVIDER
LAB_RESULT_NCID	Lab Result NCID	Medical	CDR CHEMISTRY
ABORMAL_IND	Abnormal Indicator	Medical	CDR CHEMISTRY
RESULT_NAME_HDD	Result Name (HDD)	Medical	CDR CHEMISTRY
PROVIDER_NAME	Name of the Provider	Provider	CDR CHEMISTRY
DATE_RESULTED	Result Date	Date	CDR PATHOLOGY
FINAL_DX	Final Diagnosis	Medical	CDR PATHOLOGY
STATUS_ID	Radiological Result Status	Medical	CDR PATHOLOGY
DTF	Dental Treatment Facility	Facility	DRF
BENCAT	Beneficiary Category	Patient	DRF
CLMFINDT	Claim Finalized Date	Dental	TDP CLAIMS
ORTHOCAREIND	Ortho Indicator	Dental	TDP CLAIMS
TRMTTYPE	Treatment Type	Dental	TDP CLAIMS
SPC	Provider Specialty	Dental	TDP CLAIMS
BUC_IND	Buccal Surface Indicator	Dental	TDP CLAIMS
DIS_IND	Distal Surface Indicator	Dental	TDP CLAIMS
FAC_IND	Facial Surface Indicator	Dental	TDP CLAIMS
INC_IND	Incisal Surface Indicator	Dental	TDP CLAIMS
LING_IND	Lingual Surface Indicator	Dental	TDP CLAIMS
MES_IND	Mesial Surface Indicator	Dental	TDP CLAIMS
OCCL_IND	Occlusal Surface Indicator	Dental	TDP CLAIMS

FIGURE L.29 Data variable aggregated from the five databases to provide a set of data for analytics.

EXAMPLE 2: DATA-DRIVEN PROBLEM GENERATION — "WHAT CAN MY DATA INFORM ME OF?"

The alternative approach to data exploration is that data are available and someone asks you what might be useful to their business. In this case, there is not much of a defined business or analytics problem. However, sense can be made of the data through exploration of the relationships and variables to paint a picture of what can be asked. The goal here is to evaluate the data purely from considering the questions:

- What data do I have available?
- What connections are in the databases?
- What information can provide a picture that can answer interesting problems for this stakeholder?

This latter question might be the hardest to reach a consensus on with a stakeholder. Nonetheless, with this application, and skills of defining business problems, you can generate the material needed to proceed with analytics:

1. Ideas for problem definition or problem framing.
2. A list of databases to which access and data are required.
3. The relationships and identifiers that will connect the databases.
4. A list of data variables from the databases that will be required to begin detailed exploration.
5. The ability to iterate this process with the stakeholder in mind.

This example is open ended and meant to be an exploration process. There is no correct answer, and there are no correct processes or steps to get to your final problem and data set, but always keep the stakeholder in mind. The idea here is to be curious and explore the data.

Exploration on Your Own . . .

Consider a stakeholder who has provided you with these data and indicated that they are having issues with their billing and claims group. This is all you have to go on at this point. How would you proceed?

Business and Analytic Project Ideas

Here are some initial questions you could seek to ask and explore:

1. Can we optimize some processes?
2. Can we find or use the current data to make connections to data that are more readily available, such as social media, or that can be obtained from other data sources?
3. Is there any event or state of being that it would be beneficial to know about in advance?
4. Can the data provide evidence of how business or processes really work, in cases that we might not understand?

Ready, Set, Explore!

Here is a hint on how to start. Identify a more specific problem around the stakeholder's comment. Then explore the databases from the Select Table to Explore dropdown menu and select any database that might fit the problem (see Figure L.30). Now, proceed with your exploration through the menu tabs as in the previous example, with your stakeholder in mind.

FIGURE L.30 Select a database to begin the exploration of a data-driven approach for the stakeholder's problem around billing and claims.

Come up with lists of:

1. Three to five databases you can connect (see Figure L.26)
2. The identifiers you can connect the databases with
3. A list of variables from these databases that might be useful for the problem you define for your stakeholder, based on your exploration (see Figure L.27).

A data-driven exploration of the data is now complete. This could be iterated several times with the stakeholder in mind. The final result is similar to that in Example 1, where you are now well on your way to evaluating the possible relationships between claims and billing data with analytics.

REFERENCES

Azevedo, A., Santos, M.F., 2008. KDD, SEMMA and CRISP-DM: A Parallel Overview. IADIS European Conference Data Mining, pp. 182–185.

Chapman, P., Khabaza, T., Shearer, C., n.d. CRISP-DM 1.0. Retrieved from <ftp://ftp.software.ibm.com/software/analytics/spss/support/Modeler/Documentation/14/UserManual/CRISP-DM.pdf>.

Evaluation of the TRICARE Program: Access, Cost, and Quality, 2013. Retrieved from <http://tricare.mil/tma/dhcape/program/downloads/TRICARE2013%2002_28_13%20v2.pdf>.

Rudman, W., Hart-Hester, S., Jones, W., Caputo, N., Madison, M., 2010. Integrating medical and dental records: a new frontier in health information management. J. AHIMA. 36–39.

Wagner, M.B., Pilcher, G., 2013. Association of Certified Fraud Examiners, Las Vegas, NV.

FURTHER READING

Guide for Data Researchers using MHS Data, n.d. Retrieved from <www.tricare.mil/tma/privacy/hrpp/downloads/Guide%20for%20DoD%20Researchers%20on%20Using%20MHS%20Data.pdf>.

MDR Functional Specifications, n.d. Retrieved from <http://tricare.mil/tma/dhcape/data/mdr.aspx>.

MDR Functional User Handbook, 2010. Retrieved from <http://www.tricare.mil/ocfo/_docs/MDR%20Functional%20User%20Guide%20V2.4(04-30-10).pdf>.

TRICARE MDR Data Dictionary, n.d. Retrieved from <http://tricare.mil/tma/dhcape/data/downloads/MDRDataDictionary.xlsx>.

Tutorial M

Schistosomiasis Data from WHO

Linda A. Winters-Miner, PhD

Chapter Outline

INTRODUCTION

One in thirty people worldwide has schistosomiasis (Jenkins-Holick and Kaul, 2013). Shockingly, this disease is one of the most prevalent on the face of the Earth, and very few people in the United States, or in any of the most developed countries, have even heard of it.

Jenkins-Holick and Kaul's (2013) epidemiologic article on schistosomiasis noted that it is a disease caused by parasites entering the bloodstream through the skin — typically, the feet. Schistosomiasis is carried by snails that live in and close to water. When people, or other animals, walk in infested water, the parasite seeks to enter. Children are especially susceptible to the disease as they often like to play in water. Women are also susceptible when washing clothes in infected water. The disease is endemic in many countries, such as in sub-Saharan Africa, South America, the Caribbean and Southeast Asia. Living in the host untreated, the parasite causes great damage to organs and can even lead to cancers.

Figure M.1 shows the stages of schistosomiasis shown in Jenkins-Holick and Kaul, 2013 (p. 165), which they found at the CDC (DPDx, 2009).

Children who are untreated often miss school, and growth may be retarded (Inyang-Etoh *et al.*, 2010). According to these authors (2010), some countries treat all school-age children prophylactically in an effort to stem the disease. Unfortunately, parents of affected children generally are financially unable to provide treatment, and many countries are not wealthy enough to initiate such national projects. Truly, this is a huge public health issue. Unfortunately, pharmaceutical companies have not made this disease a concern, even though it is endemic in the world, because the less developed nations are generally unable to pay for development of new drugs.

If the more developed countries such as the United States do not become concerned out of compassion, then they should do so out of self-interest. Travelers to those less developed countries are increasingly bringing the disease back with them (Pérignon *et al.*, 2007). The potential is there, although travelers bringing back the disease are often seen and, we hope, treated before they can urinate in streams. On the other hand, consider the possibility of someone returning to the United States and then going off on a fishing trip in the wilds. In the case described by Pérignon *et al.* (2007), the patient had vacationed with friends in Mali and had enjoyed a swim at a waterfall 4 weeks earlier. His symptoms were a rash on his lower limbs, itching, and a headache. (The most common symptom among males is blood

Practical Predictive Analytics and Decisioning Systems for Medicine. DOI: http://dx.doi.org/10.1016/B978-0-12-411643-6.00030-2

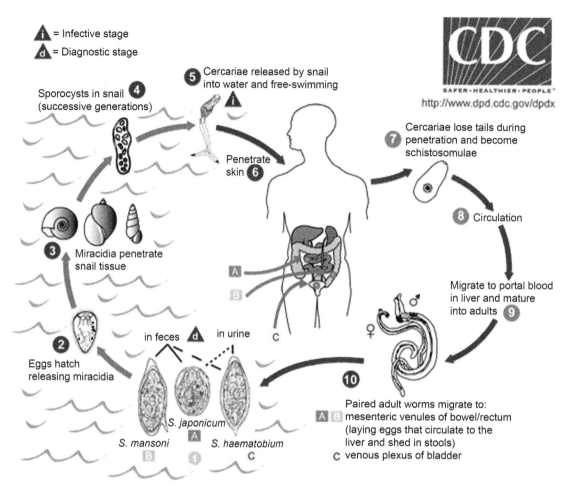

FIGURE M.1   The stages of schistosomiasis. *Figure from DPDx, Schistosomiasis, 2009.*

in the semen, as a matter of note.) This man was asymptomatic for 4 weeks after contracting the disease. Once the symptoms appeared he was treated twice with praziquantel (PZQ), a medication used by veterinarians for flatworms in animals and which is also being used in the stricken countries. PZQ has not been recommended for human use in the United States. PZQ is most effective against the adult eggs, and so generally is not effective when the eggs first enter the host. A second treatment is given about 2 months after the first dose to make sure that all the eggs that can hatch in the host have been eradicated. Frighteningly, there is evidence, according, to Pérignon *et al.*, that the infection is becoming resistant to PZQ.

Yaobi *et al.* (2007) reported on the effects of using preventive chemotherapy (with PZQ and albendazole, another drug that kills worms) in a Ugandan national control project for school-age children. They concluded that the preventive treatment was effective in reducing the prevalence of the disease. However, organisms mutate and find ways of surviving despite the poisons. Newer drugs and vaccines may not be developed by drug companies due to lack of funds to support such research, and this disease may remain one of the "neglected diseases" of the world − until our children start getting it.

THE TUTORIAL

The primary reason for this tutorial is to demonstrate data cleaning, which is about 90% of the work of any kind of data analysis. Data mining is labor intensive but extremely necessary for making good predictions. One needs to understand the structure and meaning of the data set. Generally, Excel or hand methods are used. STATISTICA's Data Health Check can be quite useful in aiding in the process and can speed up data cleaning, using less work. After cleaning the data, a few analyses were completed out of interest. The author wished to have some good data on the disease to be able to make good predictions, but they were not available. However, the data showed some interesting patterns.

Definitions for the tutorial from the WHO (2013) *website:*

- SAC = school-age children
- PC = preventive chemotherapy (agents such as the PZQ and albendazole above)
- World Regions: AFR = African countries; AMR = South America; EMR = Eastern Mediterranean; SEAR = Southeastern Asia; WPR = Western Pacific.

Also:

SAC population requiring PC for SCH annually − estimated number of SAC requiring PC for SCH annually according to the recommended strategy. Population requiring PC for SCH annually − estimated number of individuals requiring PC for SCH annually according to the recommended strategy. "Programme coverage" − proportion (%) of individuals treated as per programme target set. National coverage − proportion (%) of the population requiring PC for SCH annually in the country that has been treated.

(Located at the bottom of the WHO, 2013, data set).

and

Recommended strategy: To estimate the population requiring PC for SCH annually, the following model is used: High risk area − all school-age children and adults required PC. Moderate risk area − 50% of school-age children and 20% of adults to be treated. Low risk area − 33% of school-age children to be treated. This is equivalent to treating school-age children twice during their school years.

(Also located at the bottom of the WHO, 2013, data set).

Directions for the Tutorial

The first thing to be done is to hand clean the data. The second thing to be done is a demonstration of the use of STATISTICA's Data Health Check module for helping to clean and understand the data.

PART 1: CLEANING DATA AND USING FEATURE SELECTION AS A BEGINNING PREDICTIVE TECHNIQUE

The data were first placed into Excel (schistosomiasis data from WHO) and then the dashes (-) were eliminated by using the Find function and then replacing them with nothing. In this way, STATISTICA would interpret those cells as they should be − missing data. I opened the file in STATISTICA using the first row as the headers for columns. Next, in STATISTICA, for the column "Population requiring PC for SCh annually," the "No PC required" was replaced with a zero. It was assumed that if no PC was required, then the answer should be zero. This could be an erroneous assumption, but there was no further information at the website. The two cells that said "To be defined," in that same column, were simply removed. It seemed logical that the data would be missing, at the time of the data collection, if they were yet to be defined. Figure M.2 shows this process. In the Age column, "All" was put into the "SAC and Adult" category and "SAC 6-18" was changed to "SAC." The data were not weighted by population of the country, so only raw numbers were being considered.

Now, open the file Schistosomiasis data from WHO.sta. Create a new workspace by going to New and clicking on Workspace, as in Figure M.3, and then on All Beta Procedures.

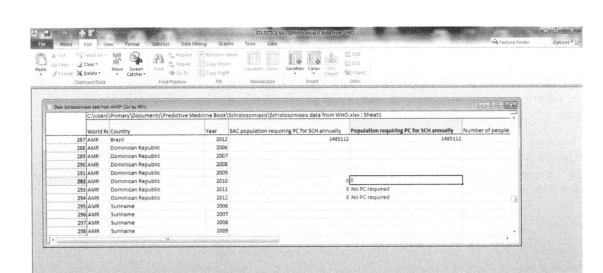

FIGURE M.2 Replacing No PC required with zeros.

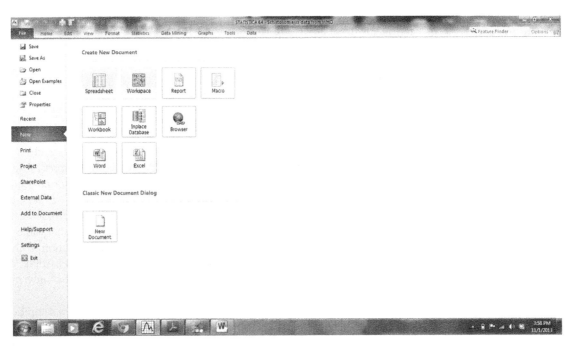

FIGURE M.3 Open a new workspace.

Figure M.4 shows connecting the data.

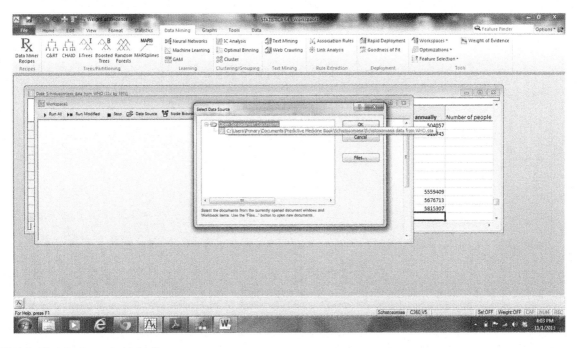

FIGURE M.4   Find the data and add the file.

With the data highlighted, go to Feature Selection and choose the first choice, Feature Selection, as in Figure M.5.

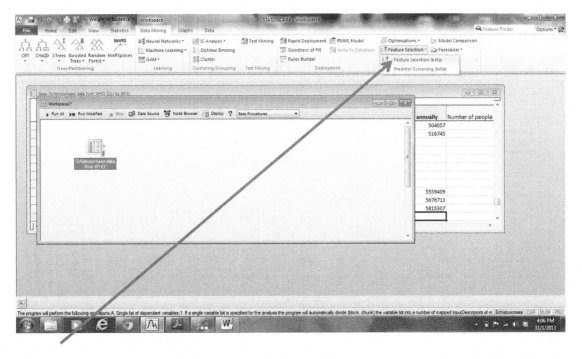

FIGURE M.5   Highlight the data and go to feature selection.

Figure M.6 shows clicking on the gear symbol to edit the parameters. Double clicking the node will do the same.

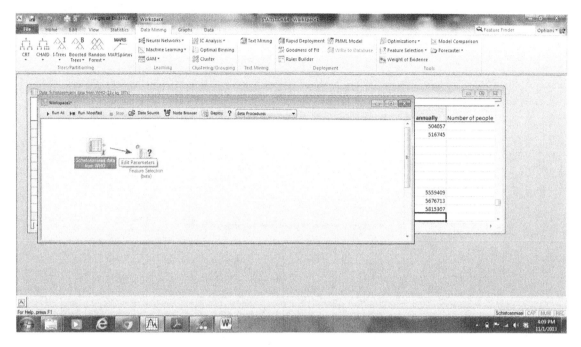

FIGURE M.6   Click the gear symbol or double click on the node to edit the parameters.

Select the variables as in Figure M.7. Note that "Show appropriate variables only" is checked. That helps in making selections.

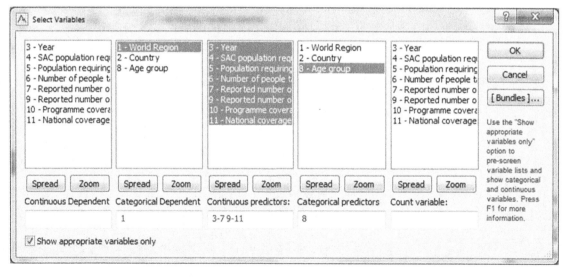

FIGURE M.7   Click on show appropriate variables only and then select the variables.

Click OK. The warning in Figure M.8 may come up, but Variables 4 and 5 are now continuous, so go ahead and continue with the current selection.

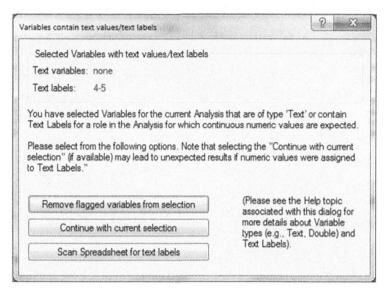

FIGURE M.8 Continue with current selection.

Click OK, then run the node using the green arrowhead, as in Figure M.9.

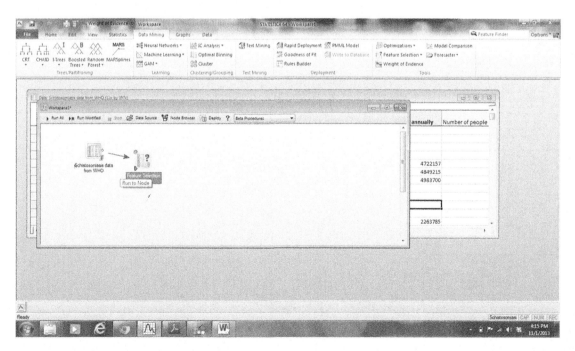

FIGURE M.9 Run the node.

Figure M.10 shows the Reporting Documents.

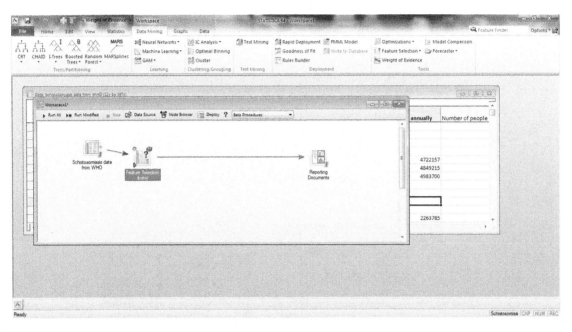

FIGURE M.10 Reporting Documents.

Click on the Reporting Documents to see the Best predictors and the Importance plot, plus the variable numbers of the Best predictors (Figure M.11).

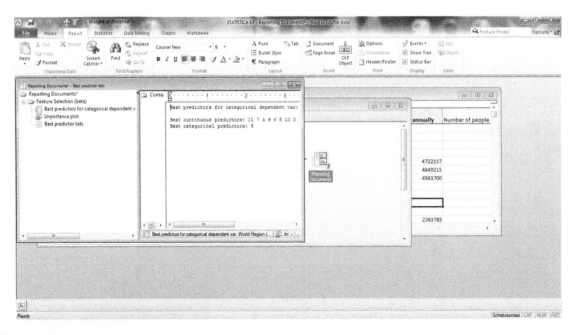

FIGURE M.11 Reporting Documents — Best Predictors.

Click on the Importance plot to view Figure M.12.

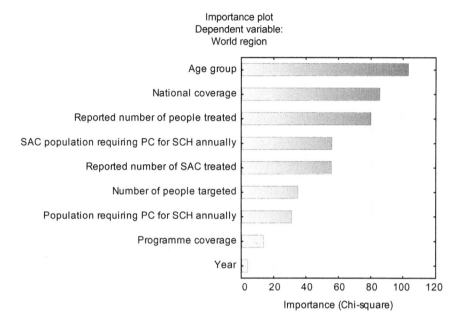

FIGURE M.12   Importance Plot.

The p values are shown in Figure M.13.

	Best predictors for categorical dependent v		
	Chi-square	p-value	
Age group	157.5465	0.000000	
National coverage	85.3024	0.000000	
Reported number of people treated	79.6332	0.000001	
SAC population requiring PC for SCH annually	55.6639	0.000255	
Reported number of SAC treated	55.4472	0.000061	
Number of people targeted	34.9034	0.028932	
Population requiring PC for SCH annually	30.8411	0.057324	
Programme coverage	13.6148	0.753836	
Year	4.0595	0.999998	

FIGURE M.13   Chi-Square P Values.

We can examine mean with error plots for these variables by conducting a GLM, ANOVA. Go to Statistics and click on General Linear Models, and then on One-way ANOVA, as in Figure M.14.

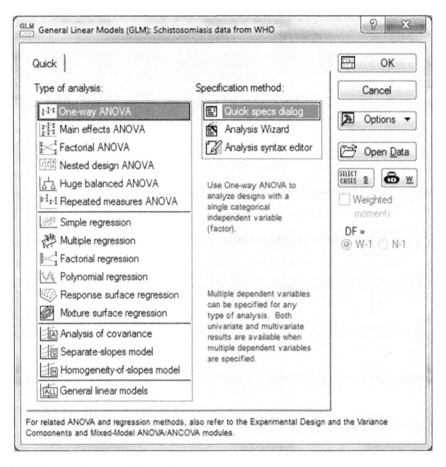

FIGURE M.14   Go to ANOVA to examine mean with error plots.

For variable selection we can use six continuous predictors, except for Variable 6, which is categorical (see Figure M.15).

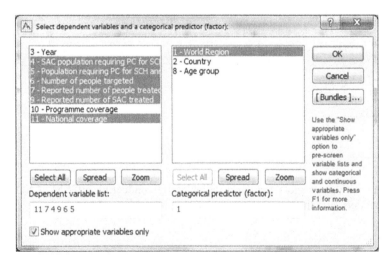

FIGURE M.15   Select best predictors as the dependent variables and World Region as the grouping variable.

Continue with the current selection and then click OK and OK again to see Figure M.16.

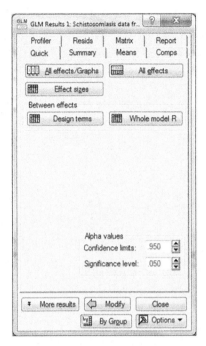

FIGURE M.16   Continue to see this. Click on all effects/Graphs.

Click on all variables and graphs to get Figure M.17.

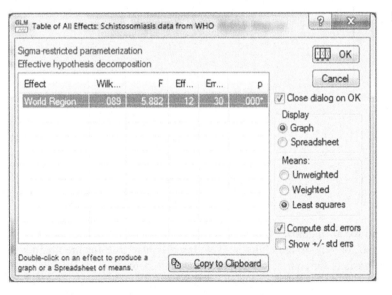

FIGURE M.17   Click OK.

Then click OK. Highlight all the variables in Figure M.18 to see them all at once. We may have to redo this and select only a few at a time.

FIGURE M.18 Select all variables to see all at once.

Figure M.19 shows the mean with error plot results.

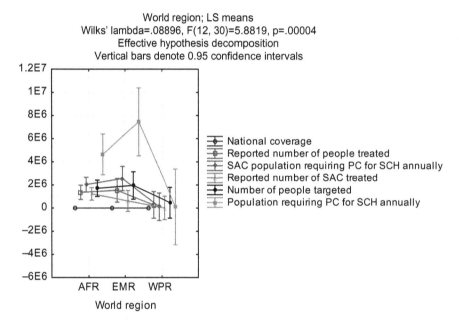

FIGURE M.19 Results.

It looks as though national coverage is the same for all regions. PCs are required more in the European and African regions than in the Western Pacific region, and also for school-age children. This trend is also true for the number of people targeted and the reported number of people treated. Of course, we do not know what percentage of the total population these numbers are. Determining percentages could also be very revealing. However, in terms of sheer numbers, it appears that perhaps the relative wealth of the regions could be a factor. According to Nations Online (2005), Eastern European nations earned about 6- to 16-fold more per capita than did the African nations.

To see a different variable predicted, let's look at predicting the age group. Repeat the Feature Selection steps, but now use Age groups as the dependent target. The arrow to the first feature selection can be deleted, as in Figure M.20.

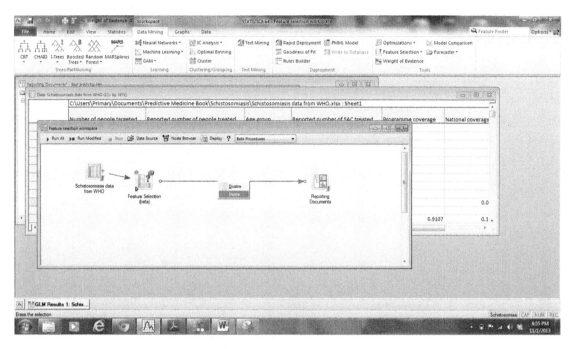

FIGURE M.20 Arrow Deleted.

Figure M.21 shows the importance plot.

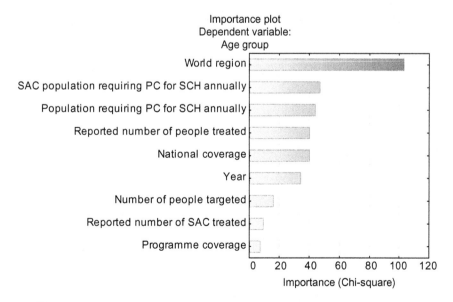

FIGURE M.21 Importance Plot.

Age group and Region seem highly related, so use a pie chart to show the relationship. Go to graphs, and batch by groups as in Figure M.22.

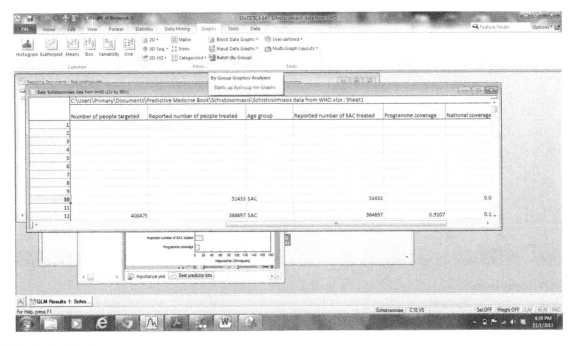

FIGURE M.22   Batch by Group.

Figure M.23 shows how to select the variables. Pick Age group as the variable to plot.

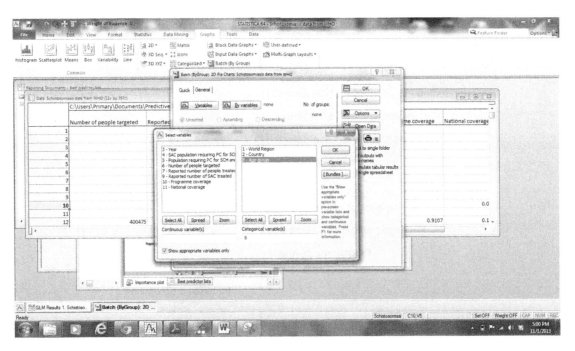

FIGURE M.23   Select Age Group.

Next, select Region as the by-group variable. Click OK (see Figure M.24).

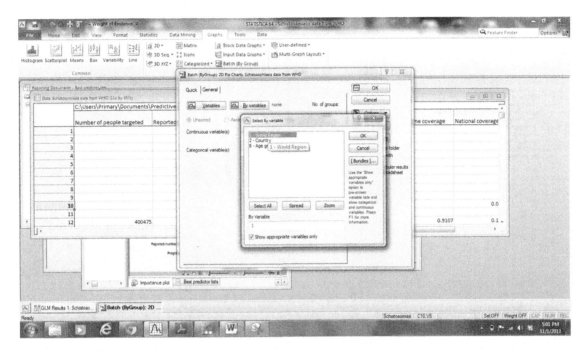

FIGURE M.24 Region is the By Group Variable.

Under the General tab, select "Text and percent," as in Figure M.25.

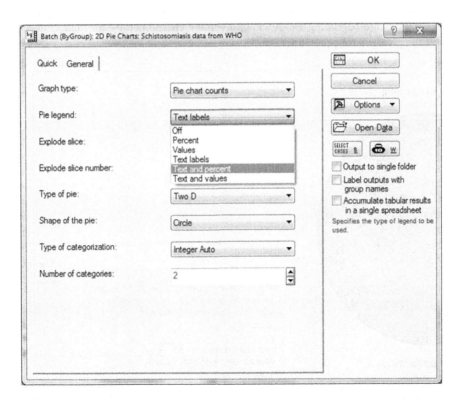

FIGURE M.25 Select Text and Percent.

Figure M.26 shows the pie chart workbook.

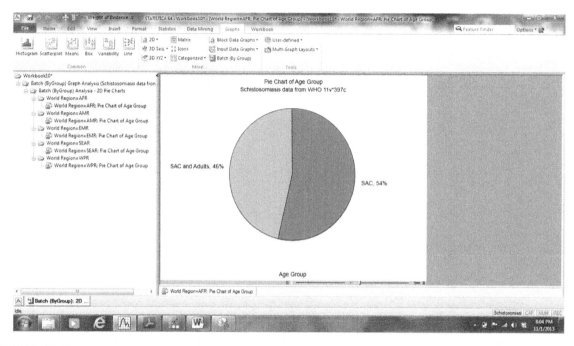

FIGURE M.26 Pie Chart.

Interpreting the graph above, about half of the countries in the African region were treating just school-age children and the other half were treating both adults and school-age children. In contrast, all the countries in the Western Pacific region were treating both children and adults, as may be seen in Figure M.27. The same was true in the South Eastern Asian region. One wonders at the reasons for this. It could be that in the African regions the situation has gotten so bad that, as with Uganda, countries are beginning nationwide preventive chemotherapy for their children.

Figure M.28 shows the p values for predicting age.

FIGURE M.27 Children and Adults.

	Best predictors for categorical depe	
	Chi-square	**p-value**
World Region	103.1010	0.000000
SAC population requiring PC for SCH annually	46.8569	0.003487
Population requiring PC for SCH annually	43.8862	0.001559
Reported number of people treated	40.1240	0.064465
National coverage	40.0899	0.020916
Year	34.2907	0.269362
Number of people targeted	15.9217	0.318178
Reported number of SAC treated	9.3139	0.810434
Programme coverage	7.3091	0.836530

FIGURE M.28 P Values for Predicting Age.

We could look at all the top predictors, but National coverage is one variable that is weighted by population, as it is the proportion (%) of the population requiring PC for SCH annually in the country that has been treated. One can use that variable to see if there are both age differences and regional differences. I ran two ANOVAs from the GLM module as above. Figure M.29 shows National coverage by region, and Figure M.30 shows the National coverage by Age.

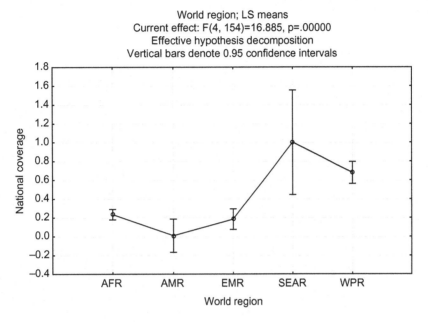

FIGURE M.29   National Coverage By Region.

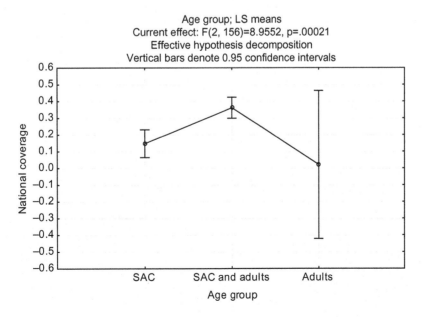

FIGURE M.30   National Coverage By Age.

The lowest percentages appear to be associated with the African and the American regions, whereas the highest percentages appear to be with the South East Asian and West Pacific regions.

National coverage percentages are smaller with the school-age children only versus the school-age children and adults group.

In predicting population requiring preventive chemotherapy for schistosomiasis, Figure M.31 shows the feature selection.

Only the country was a significant predictor. The raw numbers were not weighted by population, so this is not surprising. Figure M.32 shows the numbers by country.

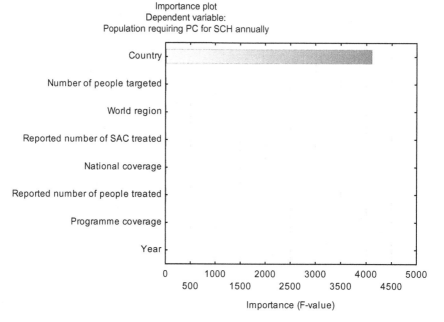

FIGURE M.31 Importance Plot.

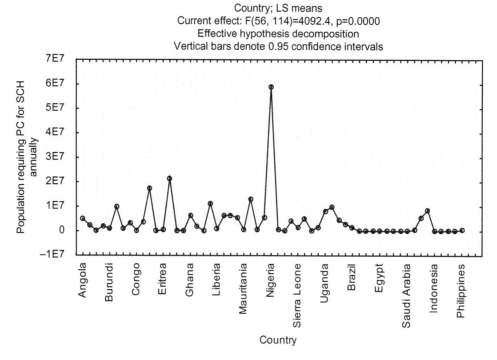

FIGURE M.32 Numbers by Country.

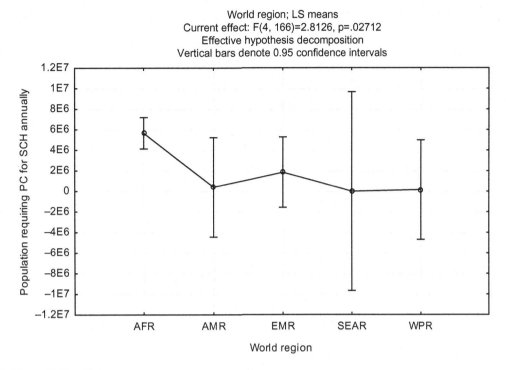

FIGURE M.33   Mean with Error Plot.

Nigeria, by far, required more treatment by preventive chemotherapy for schistosomiasis than did Uganda in 2005. However, Uganda seems to be higher than many other nations. Perhaps Nigeria has a smaller population than Uganda, but maybe Uganda started its program earlier and now can pull back. Or perhaps Uganda wanted to use the preventive chemotherapy but could not afford to. The situation may have changed by the time the project described by Yaobi *et al.* (2007) commenced.

Of the regions in Figure M.33, it appears that the African region had higher numbers than the other regions except for the Southeastern Asia region, which had a huge confidence interval.

I wish that I could have found more data on schistosomiasis; I would have expected more from such a prevalent disease.

PART 2: EXAMINING THE ORIGINAL DATA USING STATISTICA'S DATA HEALTH CHECK MODULE

To see what STATISTICA can do in helping to clean and understand the data and the data set's structure, open the Original WHO data from its Excel file as in Figure M.34. Open STATISTICA, go to Open, find the file to open, click on it, and then select "Import selected sheet to a Spreadsheet."

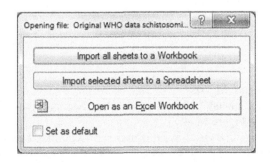

FIGURE M.34   Open Excel File.

Click OK in Figure M.35.

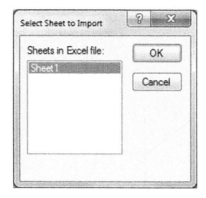

FIGURE M.35   Click OK.

Click OK again in Figure M.36. We want the case names in the first row.

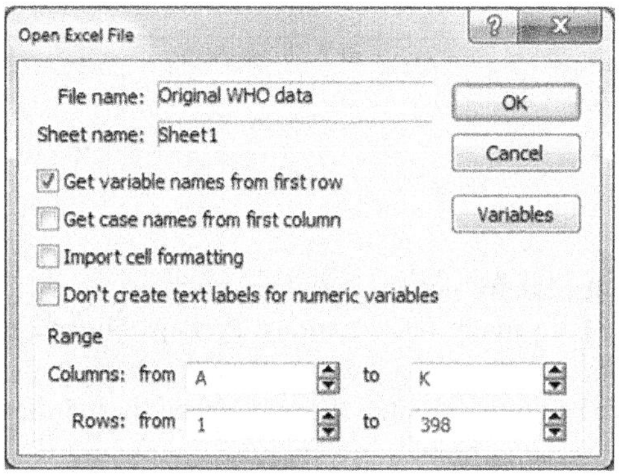

FIGURE M.36   Click OK again.

Click Import as Text Labels as in Figure M.37 and then OK.

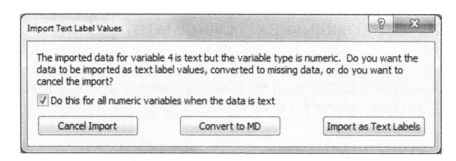

FIGURE M.37   Import as Text Labels.

Save the file as an .sta file (see Figure M.38).

Notice that the first variable is not named; create a name before beginning the Data Health Check process. Double click on the space that says Var1 as in Figure M.39.

Changed Var 1 to Region, and then click OK. Save this data set if you like. Leave it open for the next part.

Open a new workspace and connect the new dataset to it using the beta procedures (see steps at the beginning of this tutorial to review how to accomplish this task).

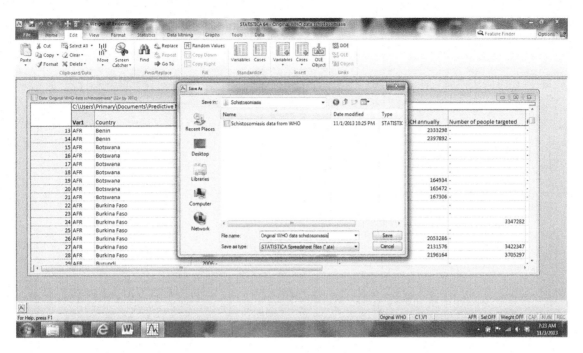

FIGURE M.38 Save as .sta file.

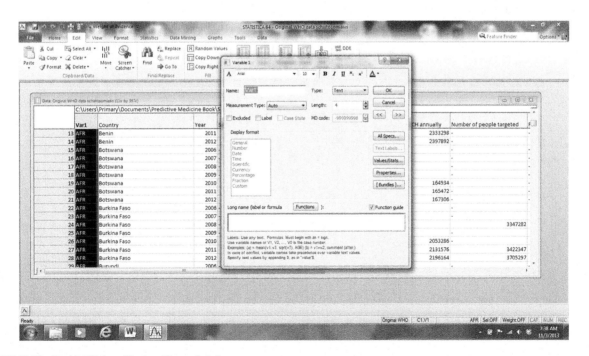

FIGURE M.39 Double Click on Var 1 to Change Label.

Highlight the dataset. Go to the node browser and select Data Health Check Summary as in Figure M.40.

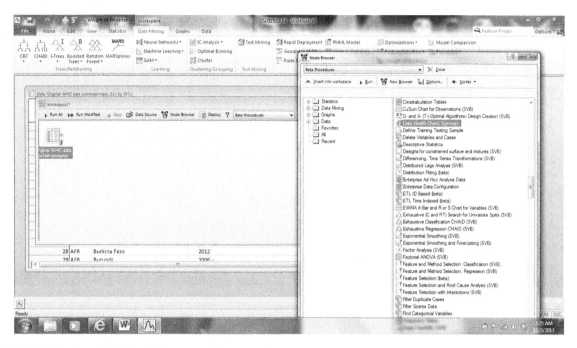

FIGURE M.40 Select Data Health Check Summary. Make sure your data are highlighted before selecting so the node will connect automatically.

Figure M.41 is the result.

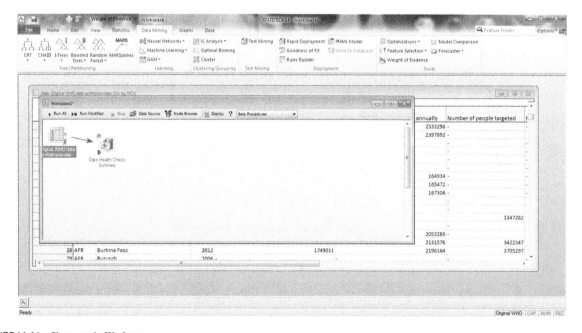

FIGURE M.41 Shows up in Workspace.

Double click on the Health Check node to see Figure M.42 (or click on the upper left-hand gear symbol on the node).

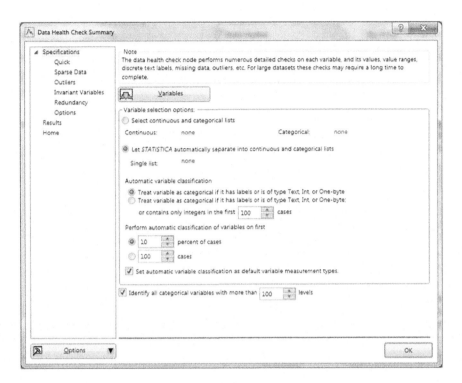

FIGURE M.42   Result of double clicking on the node.

Click on Variables and include all of them, as in Figure M.43.

FIGURE M.43   Select all the variables.

Click OK.

I wanted to click on each of the specifications using a different node for each in the workspace, in order to discover what each does. Figure M.42 shows the first one, the quick defaults. The Country variable has many, so I left the defaults as they were instead of changing the bottom default from 100 to something else.

I was curious to see what the program would do with the dashes. I opened the help file on STATISTICA to read what the default would do and Figure M.44 shows the output.

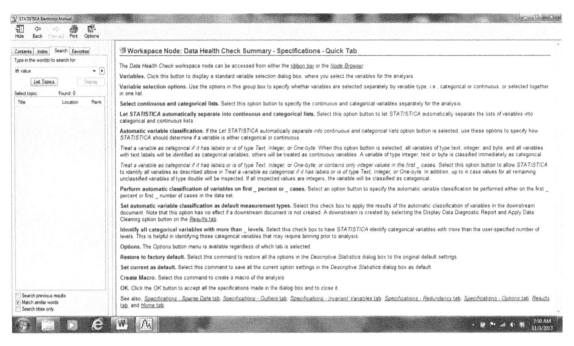

FIGURE M.44 Help File.

Back at the workspace, I clicked OK and ran the node. Figure M.45 shows the Reporting Documents and a summary of the cases.

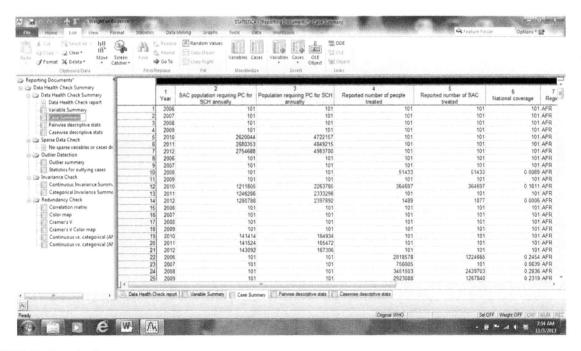

FIGURE M.45 Reporting Documents.

Figure M.46 shows the variable summary. The variable summary says there are 100% of the variables with data in them. I know that is not correct. I decide to remove the dashes manually and then retry. I generate a new workspace and enter the data without dashes (Original WHO data Schistosomiasis without dashes) and rerun the steps starting at Figure M.34.

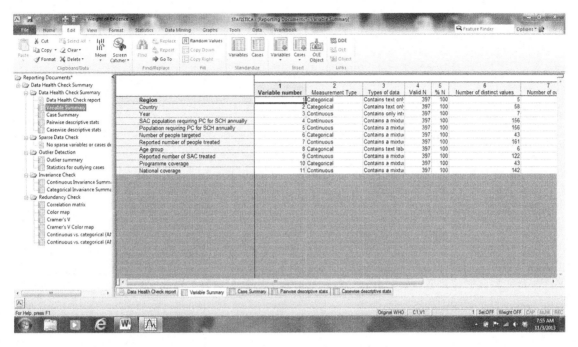

FIGURE M.46   Variable Summary.

Figure M.47 shows the new data set without dashes.

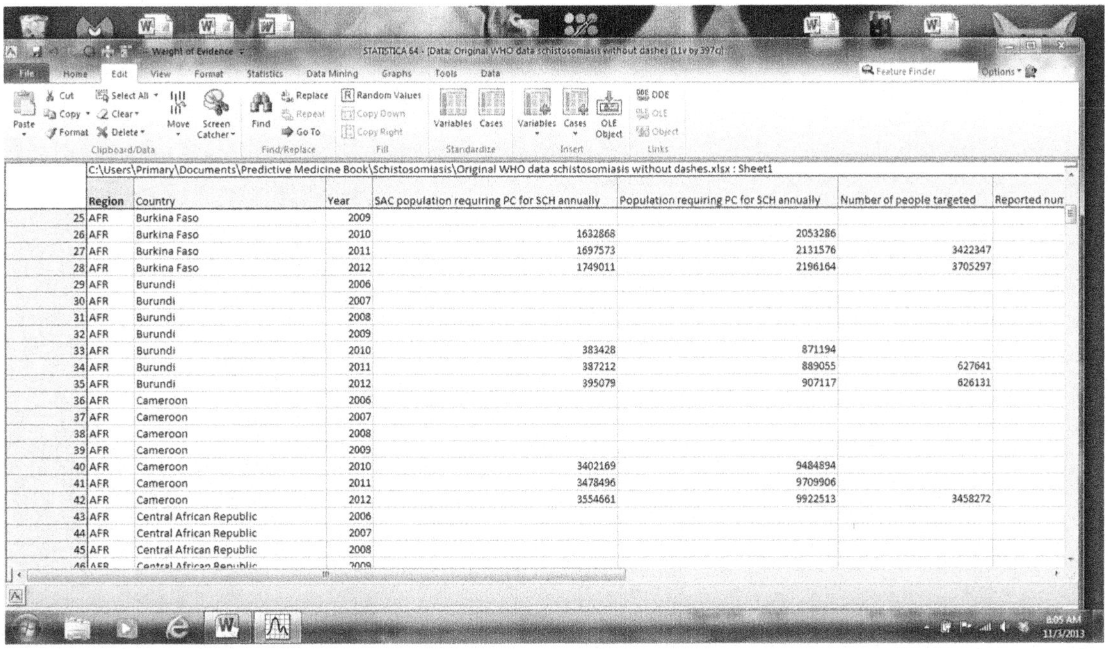

FIGURE M.47   New Data Set Without the Dashes.

Figure M.48 shows the Data Health Check Report.

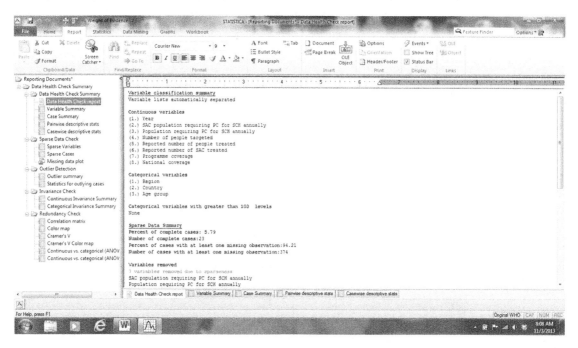

FIGURE M.48 Data Health Check Report.

The default program eliminated most of the variables, and all of the important variables. It seems we need to look further and try to manually adjust the program.

I renamed the reporting document and embedded it by right clicking to get those options. I eliminated the red arrow so I could try the next specification. Figure M.49 shows that I am ready to double click the node again to select the next specification.

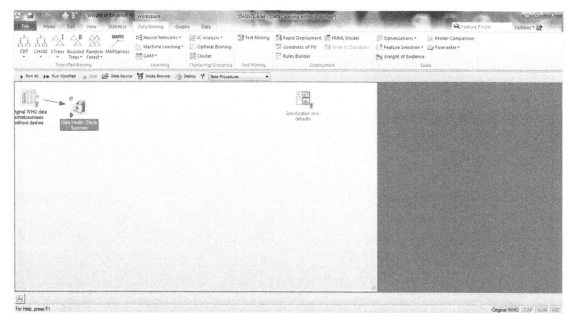

FIGURE M.49 Double click on node again to select the next specification.

Figure M.50 shows the explanation given in the STATISTICA help file.

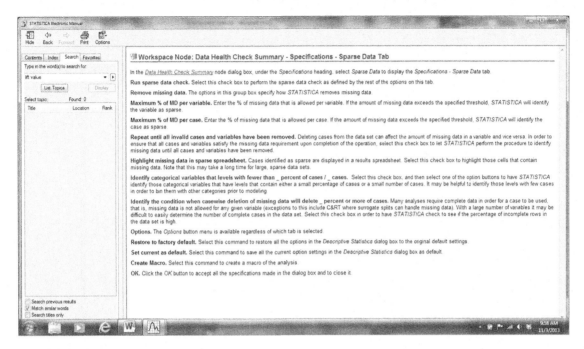

FIGURE M.50   Help File Explanation.

(One finds these explanations in windows by clicking on the question mark in the upper right hand corner.) Aha! Figure M.51 shows why the default eliminated most of the variables. They contained less than 10% in those seven variables.

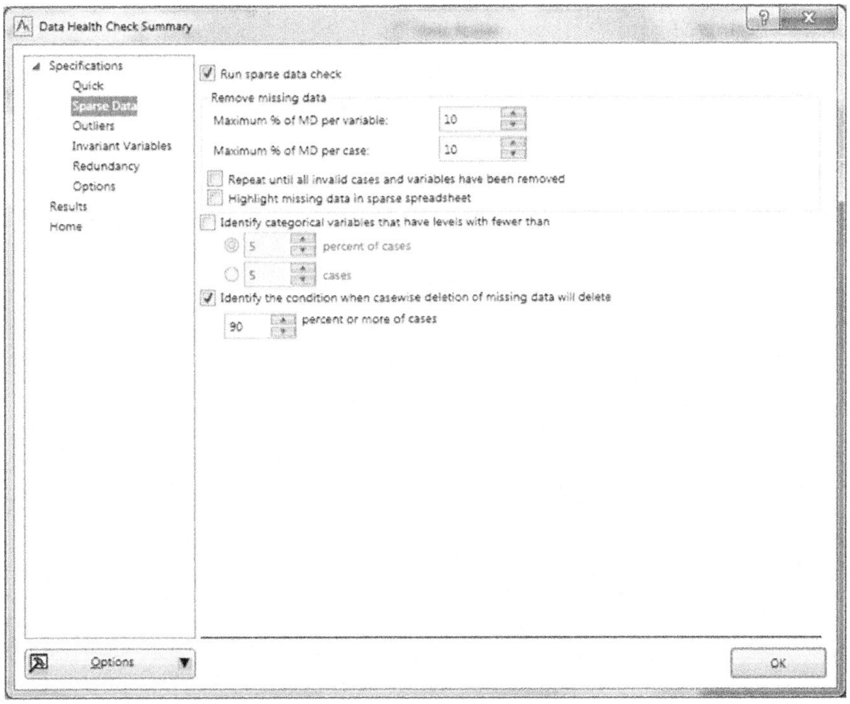

FIGURE M.51   Reason for Elimination.

We need to change these defaults so that we keep all our variables. However, cases can be removed if they have most of the data missing. Figure M.52 shows the new selections form.

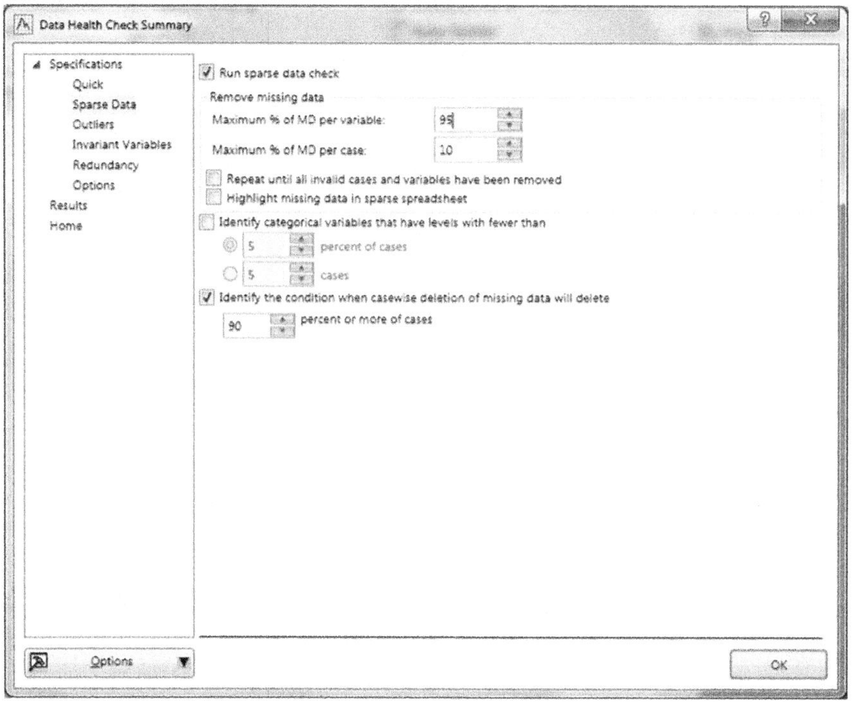

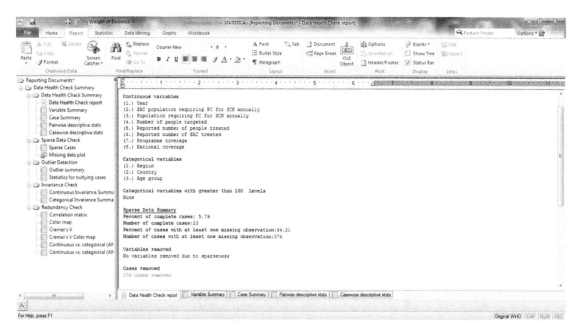

FIGURE M.52   Next Selections Form.

Now run the node to see the report. Note that I pulled the first output down and renamed the second one (plus embedded it so I could see it after saving). Ah, this is better. The Data Health Check Report removed no variables but did remove 370 cases (see Figure M.53).

FIGURE M.53   Removed 370 cases.

The Variable Summary also looks more accurate to the reality, as may be seen in Figure M.54.

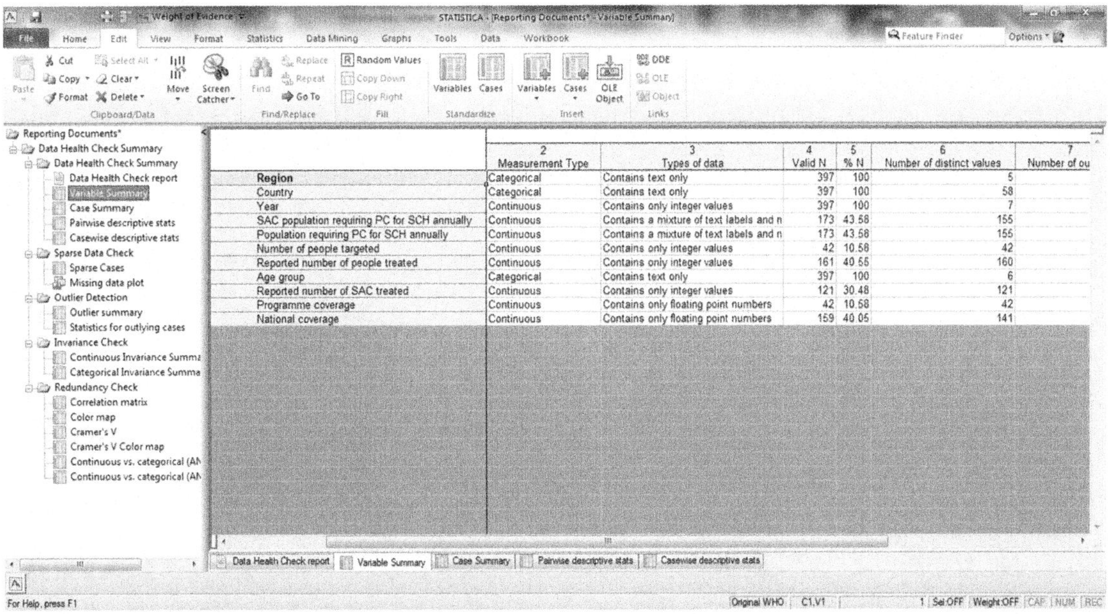

FIGURE M.54   Variable Summary.

In viewing the correlation matrix in Figure M.55 we see there are a couple of instances of collinearity.

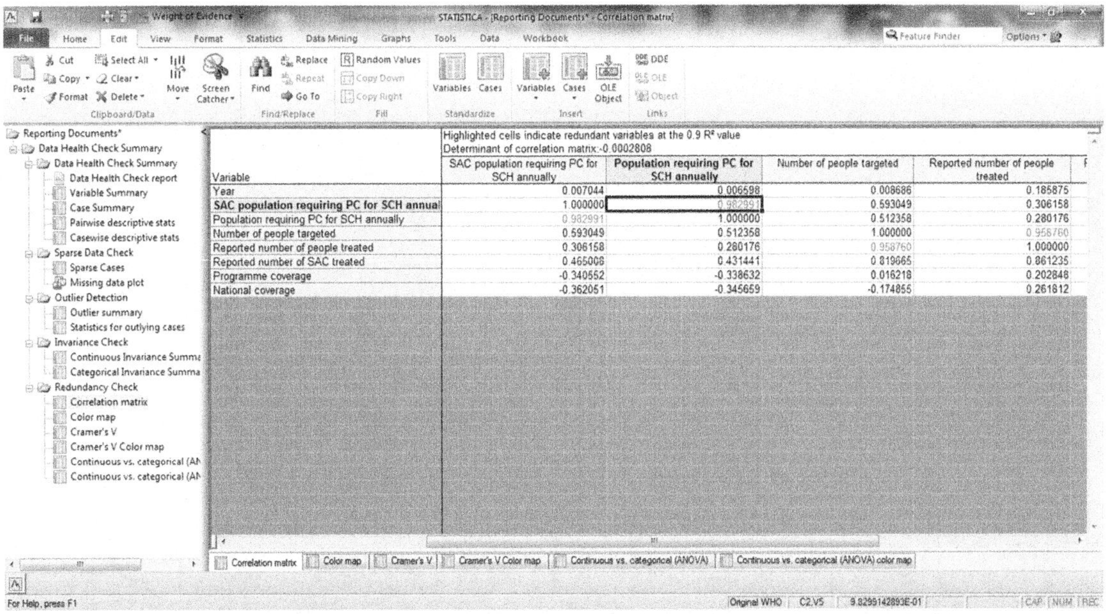

FIGURE M.55   Instances of collinearity in red.

The population requiring preventive chemotherapy for the population correlates 0.983 with the school-age children requiring such. In addition, the number of people targeted correlates 0.959 with the reported number of people treated. Pull Specification two to the bottom with number one, and delete the arrow as in Figure M.56. We can then see what will happen with Specification three.

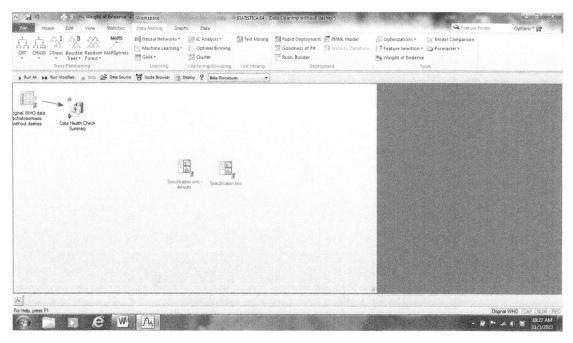

FIGURE M.56 Preparing for Specification Three.

By clicking on the question mark for the selection outliers, we find Figure M.57.

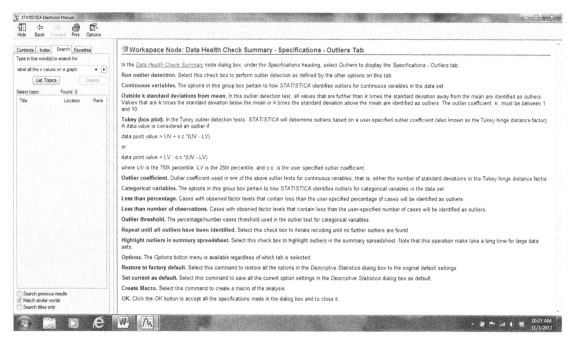

FIGURE M.57 Clicking on the question mark.

I really did not see anything that needed changing but, just for fun, I decided to click on the Tukey box and on showing the outliers, as in Figure M.58. By trying different choices in STATISTICA, one can learn many new things — or not. But it is fun to explore.

Click OK and run the new node. Embed, rename, and open the summary sheets.

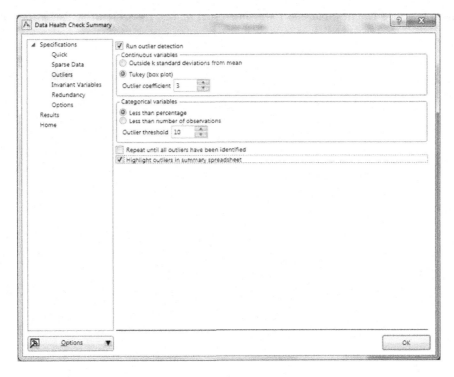

FIGURE M.58 Clicked on Tukey Box.

I ran down to the outlier summary to find confidence intervals given and highlighted cases. See Figure M.59 for the excitement.

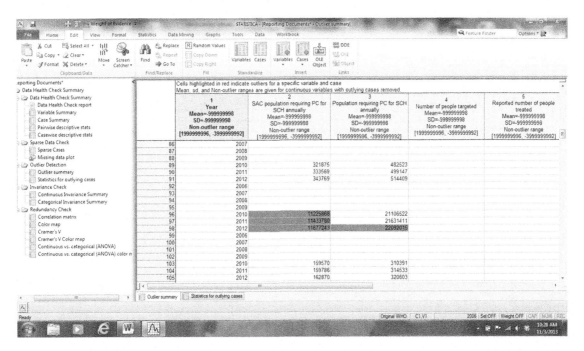

FIGURE M.59 Excitement Builds.

Nice. There are many nice features, but one I was interested in was the table of statistics for outlying cases as in Figure M.60.

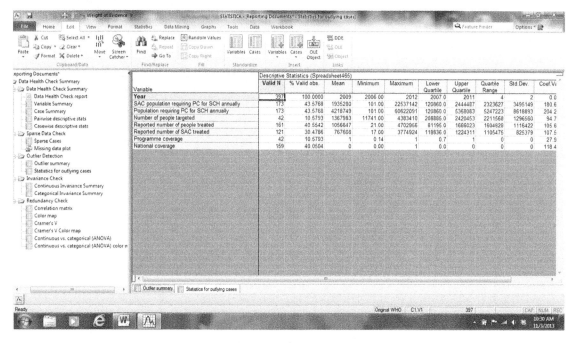

FIGURE M.60 Table of Statistics for Outlying Cases.

The next specification was the Invariant tab. Figure M.61 shows the explanation of the Invariant variables.

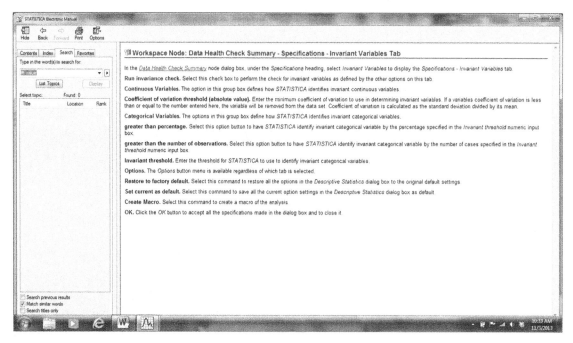

FIGURE M.61 Invariant Tab.

For continuous variables the default in Figure M.62 is given as 0.01 with the rule (equation) given in Figure M.59. The rule for categorical variables is seen in Figure M.63.

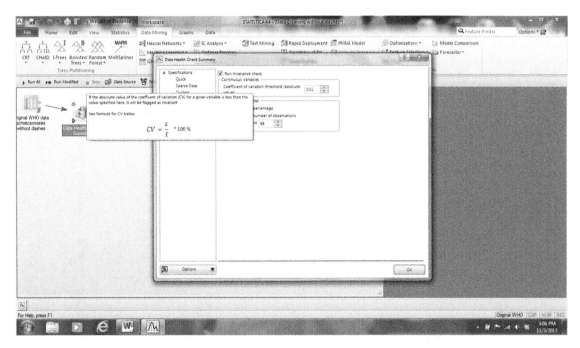

FIGURE M.62   Default is .01.

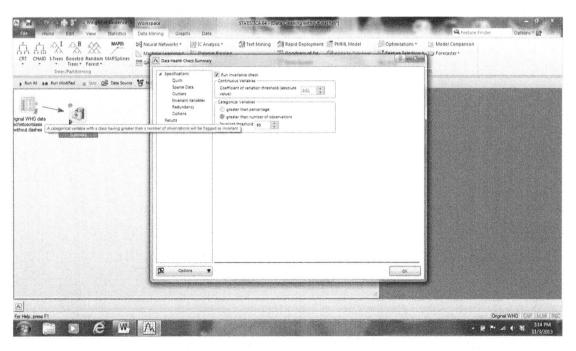

FIGURE M.63   Rule for Categorical Variables.

These defaults are fine, so I didn't change them. I went to the next specification for redundancy. This seemed obvious, as in Figure M.64. One could ask the program to remove the redundant variables, but I wanted to leave them in.

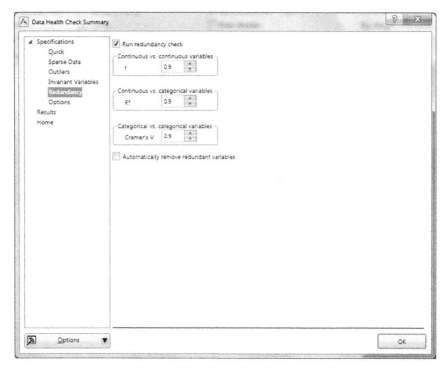

FIGURE M.64 Specification for Redundancy.

Figure M.65 shows that one can choose which of the specifications to run.

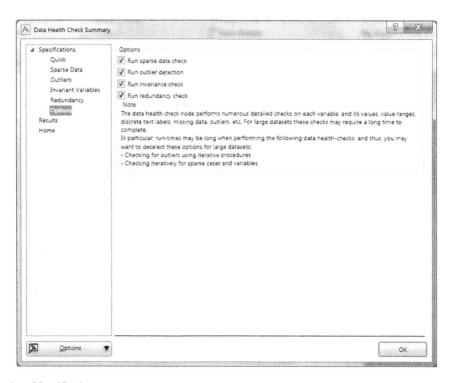

FIGURE M.65 Selection of Specifications.

And finally, in Figure M.66, one can decide on various output. I clicked OK and then ran the node to the final output.

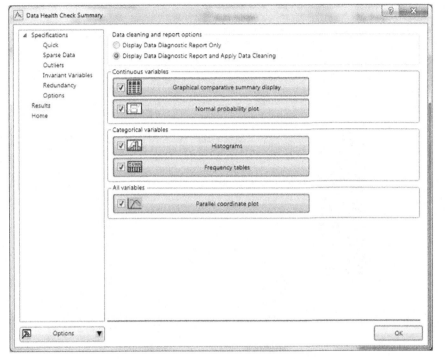

FIGURE M.66 Click OK to run.

I looked at the various histograms and noticed Figure M.67 for the Age variable.

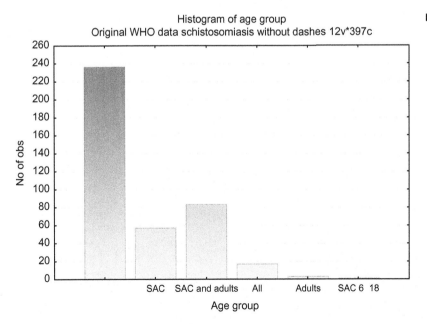

FIGURE M.67 Histogram of age group.

Here, the missing values were treated as a category. In hand-cleaning the variables, I had noticed this problem of copying in the dataset to STATISTICA. What I did by hand was copy the variable and then place the information in a new variable, removing the old one. If one double clicks on the problematic variable, the text labels cannot be examined (see Figure M.68).

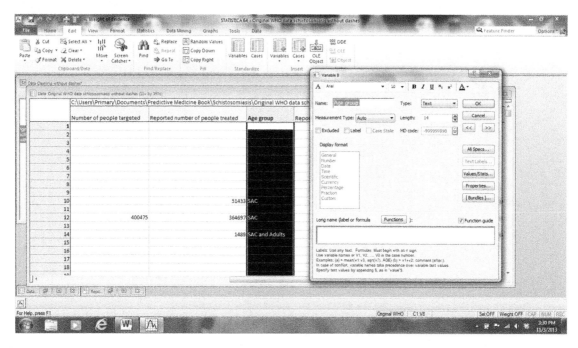

FIGURE M.68 Hand Cleaning Needed.

So, it seems that there should be some hand cleaning going on before using the Data Health Check node.

I deleted the arrow on the output, renamed it and then double clicked on the data. Figure M.69 shows what happened as I tried to formulate the new variable.

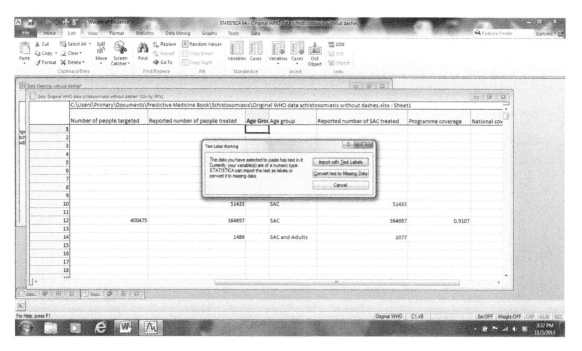

FIGURE M.69 Attempted to form a new variable.

As was seen before I started this tutorial, there are some overlapping labels in Figure M.70.

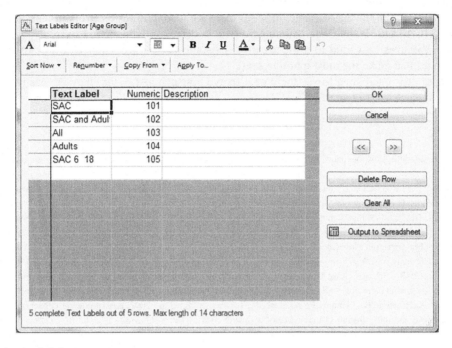

FIGURE M.70   Overlapping Labels.

So, I fixed them by hand so we had only SAC, SAC and Adults, and Adults. I ran the node once again. Now, in Figure M.71, Age is correct.

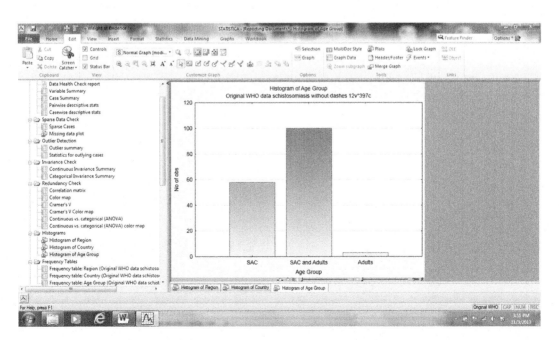

FIGURE M.71   After fixing, age is correct.

SOME THOUGHTS ON DATA CLEANING

- First, clean up what one knows will be problematic, such as dashes in Excel when there are missing data.
- Examine the variables, as in the age variable, to see if there are incongruities or errors in text labels.
- Use the STATISTICA Data Health Check Summary to aid in cleaning the data. For example, because it was evident that some of the variables co-varied to a great extent, it would not be necessary or even desirable to use all in a model. Use the ones that make the most intuitive sense.
- With all the output, it is interesting to see the data displayed in such a way that they are easily visualized and mistakes can be found, such as in Figure M.67.

REFERENCES

DPDx, 2009. Laboratory identification of parasites of public health concern: Schistosomiasis. Available at www.dpd.cdc.gov/dpdx/HTML/Schistosomiasis.htm.

Inyang-Etoh, P.C., Author, J.O., Eyo, A.O., Usanga, V.U., 2010. Self-diagnosis as a possible means of diagnosing urinary schistosomiasis among school children in an endemic community in Nigeria. Internet J. Trop. Med. 7 (1), 7.

Jenkins-Holick, D.S., Kaul, T.L., 2013. Schistosomiasis. Urol. Nurs. 33 (4), 163–170.

Nations Online (2005) National economic accounts for countries and regions around the world: Continents. http://www.nationsonline.org/oneworld/GNI_PPP_of_countries.htm (retrieved November 6, 2013).

Pérignon, A., Pelicot, M., Consigny, P., 2007. Genital schistosomiasis in a traveler coming back from Mali. J. Travel. Med. 14 (3), 197–199.

World Health Organization, 2013. Schistosomiasis: Countries × indicators. Available at: www.who.int/neglected_diseases/preventive_chemotherapy/sch/db/index.html?units = minimal&region = all&country = all&countries = all&year = all (retrieved October 27, 2013).

Yaobi, Z., Koukounari, A., Kabatereine, N., Fleming, F., Kazibwe, F., Tukahebwa, E., et al., 2007. Parasitological impact of 2-year preventive chemotherapy on schistosomiasis and soil-transmitted helminthiasis in Uganda. BMC Med. 5 (1), 27.

Tutorial N

The Poland Medical Bundle

Jacek Jakubowski, PhD, Michał Kusy, MSc and Grzegorz Migut, MSc

Chapter Outline

INTRODUCTION

Medical Bundle is an add-in to STATISTICA Advanced, providing a set of supplementary analytical tools dedicated for the medical field. It is not a part of a standard STATISTICA distribution.

Medical Bundle features are divided into three groups:

1. Data cleansing
2. Analyses
3. Additional analyses.

Data cleansing modules enable the user to define data correctness rules, to recode categorical data into dummy variables, and to manage missing data.

Analyses consist of three modules: *Meta-analysis and Meta-regression*, *ROC Curves*, and *Logistic Regression Wizard* (Figure N.1).

Medical Bundle is complemented with *Effect/Interrelation Measures*, *Post-hoc Test for Friedman ANOVA*, and *Bland-Altman Plot* features.

In the following sections a brief overview of the selected set of modules is presented (StatSoft Polska, 2013). All of the examples except "Meta-analysis and Meta-regression" will be based on a WCGS data set from the large epidemiological study, The Western Collaborative Group Study (Rosenman *et al.*, 1964) shows the relationship between coronary heart disease and certain diagnostic factors.

DATA VERIFICATION

To perform a data verification analysis, open the file WCGS_cleansing.sta and, on the Medical Bundle tab in the Data Cleansing group, select Data Verification to display the "Rules of data correctness" dialog. On the Rules of data

Practical Predictive Analytics and Decisioning Systems for Medicine. DOI: http://dx.doi.org/10.1016/B978-0-12-411643-6.00031-4

FIGURE N.1 Medical Bundle modules.

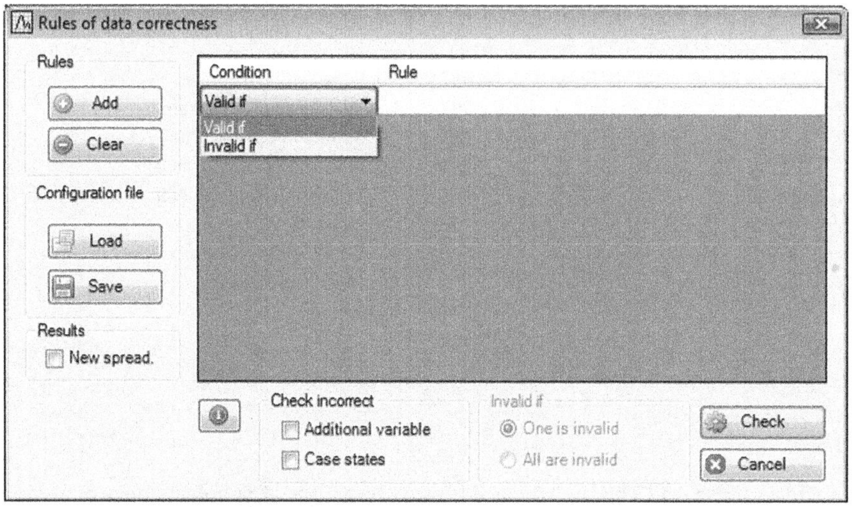

FIGURE N.2 The Rules of data correctness dialog.

correctness start-up panel (Figure N.2), click the Add button to add a new rule into the grid. In the Condition field we can define whether the new rule will have the form Valid if, or Invalid if. We can edit the body of the rule in the Rule field either manually or using the dedicated Rules editor dialog. To display the Rules editor, double click on the Rule field.

The Rules editor (Figure N.3) enables you to define data correctness rules conveniently. For example, let's assume that the incorrect cases are those for which the variables are: "*Smoking*" = "Yes" and "*Cigarettes*" = 0 or "*Smoking*" = "No" and "*Cigarettes*" > 0.

To insert a variable name (or a variable number) into the rule, double click on the appropriate cell of the data grid on the left side of the panel. Category names of selected variables are available in the data grid at the bottom of the window. Mathematical and logical operators are available by clicking on the corresponding buttons. Moreover, rules may include the same functions that are available in variable long name formulas.

After the rule is defined, click *Save* and go back to the *Rules of data correctness* dialog.

The user can define a set of new rules in the same way (Figure N.4). To check the correctness of the analyzed data set, click Check. For each defined rule a new variable will be created, informing the user if the given case is correct (value 1) or incorrect (value 0). If more than one rule is defined, the "Additional variable" option will create a "Correct" variable indicating the data correctness for all rules (Figure N.5). Moreover, the "Case states" option enables marking of incorrect cases with a special case state symbol.

The defined rules can be saved as a script file that can be loaded with another data set or used in selected STATISTICA modules (StatSoft Inc., 2013).

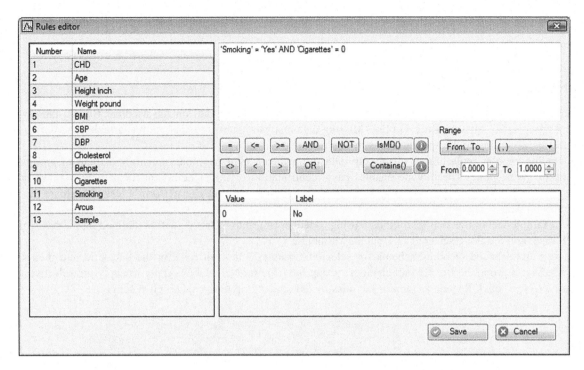

FIGURE N.3 The *Rules editor*.

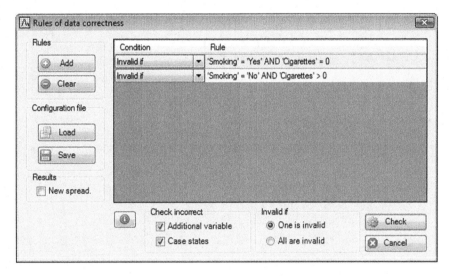

FIGURE N.4 Defined set of rules.

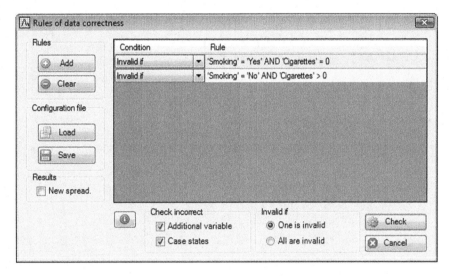

FIGURE N.5 Variables indicating the data correctness.

MISSING DATA ANALYSIS

To perform analysis of missing data, open the WCGS_cleansing.sta file and on the Medical Bundle tab in the Data Cleansing group select Missing Data. On the "Missing data analysis" start-up panel, click Variables and define the variables selection according to the specifications in Figure N.6.

The module enables replacement of missing data using mean, median, mode, mean or median in groups, nearest neighbors, or given value. The module enables easy identification of the same action for a number of variables and recording of specific schemes to the configuration file. In addition, the user can perform a test to evaluate the randomness of missing data.

In our example we will recode missing data using "Median in group." Groups will be defined on the basis of the categories Behpat and Smoking selected as grouping variables.

To assign the selected recoding schema for selected variables, mark all rows in the data grid and then select the option "Median in group" in the "Group changes" group box (Figure N.7). Click Apply to apply the selected action for marked rows. Next, click Recode to replace the missing data according to the specified schema.

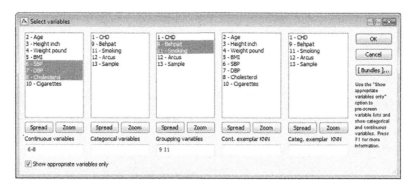

FIGURE N.6 Variables selection for the analysis of missing data in groups.

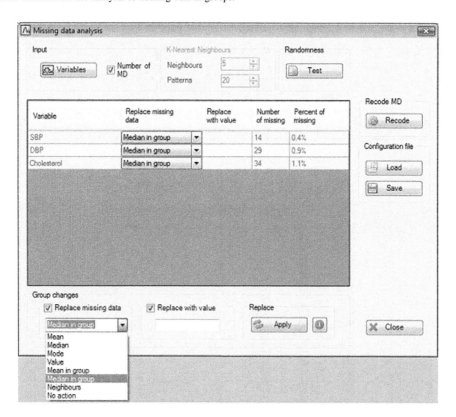

FIGURE N.7 Recoding missing data using "Median in group."

ROC CURVES

A ROC (receiver operating characteristic) curve is a tool often used in medical diagnostics to assess the accuracy of the continuous classifier in distinguishing classes of dichotomous dependent variable. ROC curves are based on two measures of prediction accuracy: Sensitivity and Specificity. The ROC curve is created by plotting Sensitivity (the true positive rate) over 1 − Specificity (the false positive rate).

AUC refers to the area under the (ROC) curve. This area varies from a low of 0 to a high of 1 (the entire area between the axes), and is widely used as a measure of predictive power of the analyzed predictor. In addition, the ROC curve is a very good tool to determine the optimal cut-off point considering the different costs of misclassification (Hanley and McNeil, 1982; Hanley and Hajian-Tilaki, 1997; Pencina *et al.*, 2007).

To perform the ROC analysis, open the WCGS.sta file and, on the Medical Bundle tab in the Analyses group, select ROC Analysis. On the ROC Analysis start-up panel, click Variables to display the "Select variables" dialog and select CHD as a dependent dichotomous variable, SBP and DBP as continuous predictors (Figure N.8).

In the "Code of marked level" group box, select Yes (persons with coronary heart disease). In the "Direction of impact on marked level" group box make sure that the both predictors are marked as Stimulant (Figure N.9).

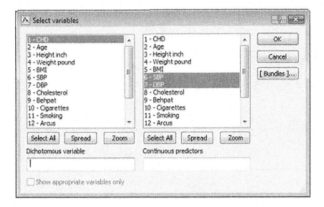

FIGURE N.8   Variables selection for the ROC analysis.

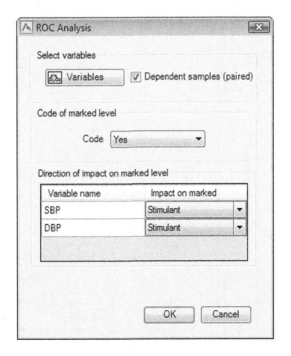

FIGURE N.9   The ROC Analysis dialog.

Confirm your choice by clicking OK and then display the ROC Results dialog (Figure N.10).

To display ROC graphs for selected predictors, click the ROC Graph button. You then obtain ROC graphs with suggested cut-off points and a graph in which curves for all predictors are plotted (Figure N.11).

We can select two methods of determining cut-off points: the *Youden Index* and the *Tangent method*. If we assume that misclassification costs are equal and the fraction of "marked" in the population is 0.5, then the tangent-based optimal cut-off point will be the one closest to the point with (0,1) coordinates. Changing the misclassification costs and the expected fraction of "marked" in the population will change the optimal cut-off point correspondingly.

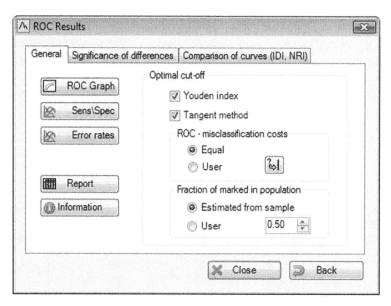

FIGURE N.10 The ROC Results dialog.

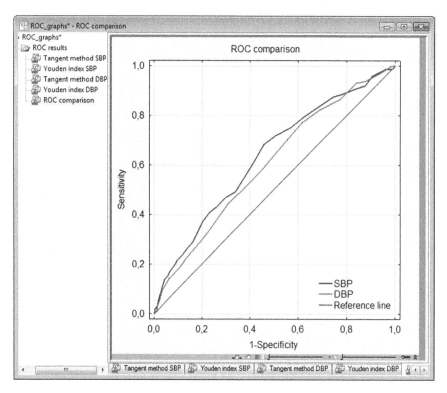

FIGURE N.11 Comparison of ROC curves.

After clicking the Report button on the General tab, you will find a workbook with report spreadsheets for selected predictors (Figure N.12). Each "ROC − report" spreadsheet contains a set of effect measures, such as Sensitivity, Specificity, Accuracy (ACC), Positive Predictive Value (PPV), Negative Predictive Value (NPV), False Positive Ratio, False Negative Ratio, Likelihood Ratio (LR), Error Rate, and Youden Index.

The ROC − results spreadsheet (Figure N.13) includes: AUC value, standard error of AUC, and a 95% confidence interval. AUC is treated as a synthetic goodness of fit measure indicating how well a given predictor can separate classes of dependent variable. The AUC value varies from a low of 0 to a high of 1 (the entire area between the axes). A value of 0.5 indicates the predictor has no ability to separate classes of dependent variable, while a value of 1 indicates perfect separation ability.

ROC analysis enables the assessment of the statistical significance of differences between AUC measures for selected predictors. To perform such an analysis, select DBP and SBP measures on the Significance of differences tab (Figure N.14). Next, click the Compare button to display the report with the results of the statistical test checking the significance of differences between areas.

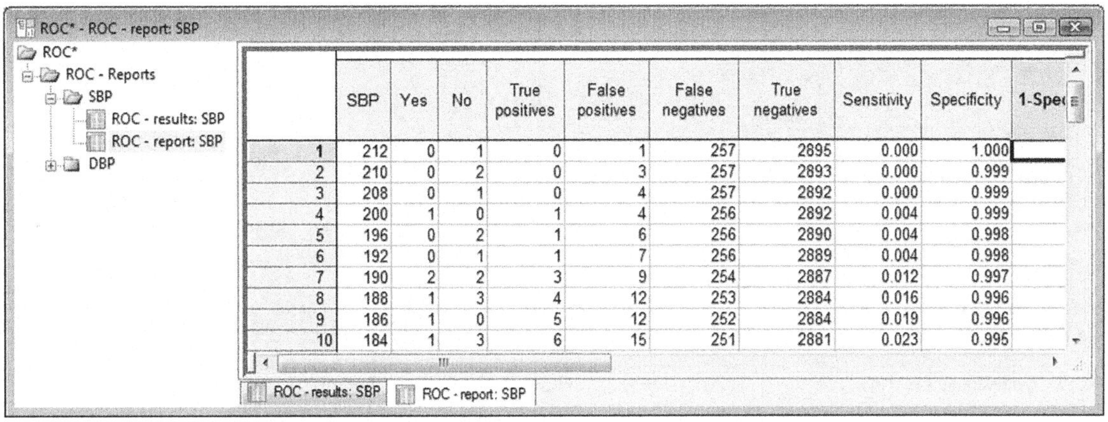

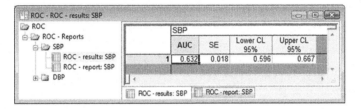

FIGURE N.12   "ROC − report" spreadsheet for selected predictor.

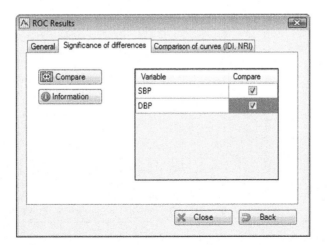

FIGURE N.13   "ROC − results" spreadsheet for selected predictor.

FIGURE N.14   The Significance of differences tab.

In this case, the p value equals 0.02, so we can assume that such AUCs differ significantly (Figure N.15).

In some cases the consequences of erroneous decisions based on a given diagnostic indicator are not equal. For example, in classifying patients into risk groups, treating a sick patient as a healthy one is a worse mistake than vice versa.

The criterion for selection of the optimal cut-off point can be changed on the General tab in the "Optimal cut-off point" group box. The user can change misclassification costs or enter expected fraction of "marked" in the population. By selecting User — Misclassification costs, we can enter values for each type of error and confirm the selection by clicking OK (Figure N.16).

To obtain an ROC curve with a cut-off point (Figure N.17), click the ROC Graph button.

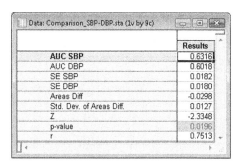

FIGURE N.15 Comparison of AUCs.

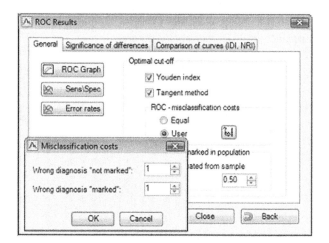

FIGURE N.16 Changing misclassification costs.

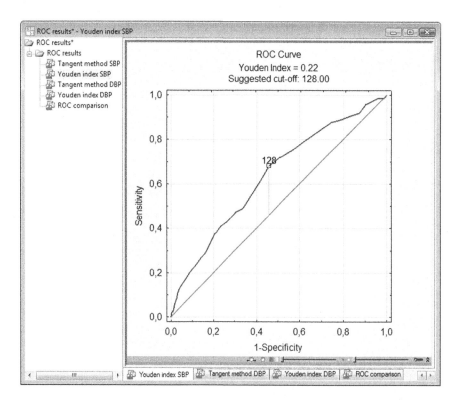

FIGURE N.17 ROC curve with a cut-off point.

Options on the "Comparison of curves (IDI, NRI)" tab (Figure N.18) allow you to compare curves using Net Reclassification Improvement (NRI) and Integrated Discrimination Improvement (IDI). Such measures are designed to compare ROC curves in cases when predictors are expressed in terms of likelihood — for example, the output of a logistic regression scoring model. To calculate NRI, you need to enter at least one cut-off point.

The ROC Curves module enables you to perform an analysis for several independent (unpaired) samples. For such a calculation, deselect "Dependent samples (paired)" in the ROC Analysis dialog. Click the Variables button to display the Select variables dialog and select CHD as a Dichotomous variable, Cholesterol as a Continuous predictor, and Smoking as a Grouping variable (Figure N.19).

Following the same steps as in the case of dependent samples, we obtain a graph comparing the ROC curves for specific groups (in this case, the groups Smoking = "Yes" and "Smoking" = "No") (Figure N.20).

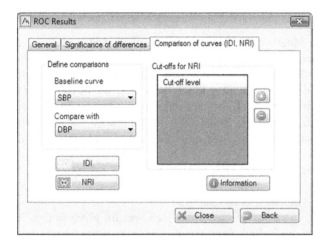

FIGURE N.18   The "Comparison of curves (IDI, NRI)" tab.

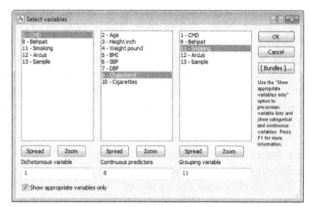

FIGURE N.19   Variables selection for independent samples.

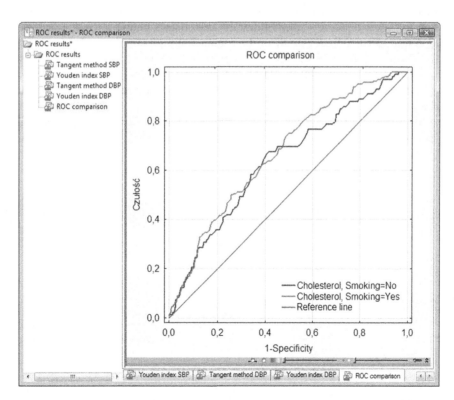

FIGURE N.20   Comparison of ROC curves for independent samples.

META-ANALYSIS AND META-REGRESSION

Study-Level Data Entry

Meta-analysis is used to evaluate the effect that is described by a number of publications. In systematic reviews researchers generally do not have access to the raw data, only to the conclusions of the study. Meta-analysis allows you to determine the overall effect on the basis of the studies' effects. Before conducting meta-analysis you need to enter study-level data. Data collected in systematic reviews are usually presented in various forms. The program allows you to enter the raw measures and already calculated effect sizes. The following is an example of a meta-analysis conducted in the Medical Bundle.

On the Medical Bundle tab in the Analyses group, click Meta-analysis and Meta-regression to display the Meta-analysis and Meta-regression dialog. Next, type your analysis name, e.g., "Analysis of treatment efficiency (1996−2008)," and groups compared (Treatment, Control). In order to enter raw measures, like a 2×2 table of outcomes, click the Measures button in the New group.

In the "Studies with raw measures" dialog, verify that the Measure is a 2×2 table and click Add in the "Single study" group. Now you can enter "Baker 1996" study outcomes (43 events out of 84 treated and 39 out of 81 patients in control group). After double clicking on the cell with the study name, you can use the 2×2 table dialog (Figure N.21). Enter the number of events and total number of cases, and the program will calculate the missing values.

You can also add some study characteristics, like year or type of study. To do this, click Edit in the Additional variables group. In the Additional variables dialog (Figure N.22), click the green $(+)$ button, select Variable type: Categorical and enter the variable name: Year. Click the OK button. Now you can enter the year of study (1996) in the Year column.

You can also import data from a STATISTICA spreadsheet. In STATISTICA, open the 2×2 Tables.sta data set from the example data sets. Next, in the "Studies with raw measures" dialog, click the Import button, select the 2×2 Tables.sta spreadsheet, and click OK. Seven new studies will be included in the analysis.

The "Studies with raw measures" dialog also enables you to calculate selected effect measures for given studies. To do this, select the chosen effect measure, or All measures, and click Save, in the Save to spreadsheet group (Figure N.23). After entering all studies with raw measures, click OK to return to the Meta-analysis and Meta-regression dialog.

Before entering studies with already calculated effect sizes, in the Meta-analysis and Meta-regression dialog change "Measure precision" on the Settings tab to 4. Next, click the Effect sizes button in New group. Select the Effect measure needed, e.g., OR (odds ratio), and click Add in the Single study group (Figure N.24). In the created row, enter Study: Owen, OR: 0.3333 and p: 0.1099. If the Automatic option in the Value calculation group is selected, the program will calculate missing values (in this case, standard error and confidence interval limits) on the basis of the data entered. The number of cases in the compared groups are N1: 22 for the treatment and N2: 25 for the control group. You can also enter the year of study (2005) in the Year column.

Now let's add the Morrow 2008 study which presents Cohen's d and p value, which equal, respectively, -0.0441 and 0.8099 for 74 patients in the treatment and 71 in the control group. Select "d (Cohen's)" in the Effect measure

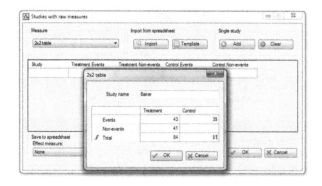

FIGURE N.21   The 2×2 table dialog.

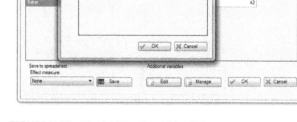

FIGURE N.22   The Additional variables dialog.

FIGURE N.23   Saving calculated measures to spreadsheet.

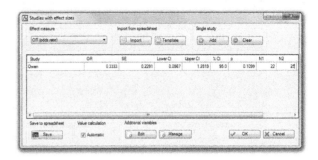

FIGURE N.24   Entering study with odds ratio.

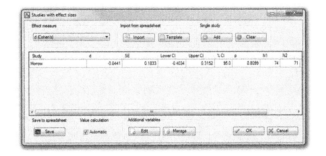

FIGURE N.25   Entering study with Cohen's d.

group, click Add in the Single study group, and enter the study's outcomes (Figure N.25) as in the previous example. After entering all studies, click OK to return to the Meta-analysis and Meta-regression dialog.

The program enables you to combine computations for effect sizes in different formats and convert some measures (e.g., odds ratio and Cohen's d) (Borenstein *et al.*, 2009; Higgins and Green, 2011). Meta-analysis will be performed on the set of studies presenting the selected effect measure or the outcome that can be converted to the selected effect measure. You can save studies included in meta-analysis as XML script. To do this, in the Meta-analysis and Meta-regression dialog, click the Save XML button. Previously saved XML files can be loaded to the Meta-analysis and Meta-regression module using the Load XML button.

Select the Analysis tab in the Meta-analysis and Meta-regression dialog and verify that the Effect measure is "OR (odds ratio)"; next, use the Settings tab to check meta-analysis model assumptions.

The module enables the user to perform meta-analysis for the fixed-effect and the random-effects models. The fixed-effect model assumes that studies are homogeneous and that observed variability of outcomes is a result of sampling error (Borenstein *et al.*, 2009; Higgins and Green, 2011). If you are considering the fixed-effect model, select "Fixed-effect" in the Model assumptions group (Figure N.26). Next, select the Studies tab.

The Studies tab presents results of the meta-analysis. After selecting "Include" in the Additional variable group, the program shows the given study characteristic, e.g., Year, in the grid. The summary odds ratio for the fixed-effect model is 0.6050 (0.4884, 0.7496), which is statistically significant (Figure N.27). As you can see, only three of the included studies are significant (using $\alpha = 0.05$).

The random-effects model corresponds to the situation when studies are heterogeneous and the real effect varies from study to study (Borenstein *et al.*, 2009; Higgins and Green, 2011). To show its results, select the Settings tab again and change "Model assumptions" to "Random-effects." Now the Studies tab presents the summary odds ratio for the random-effects model 0.6009 (0.4214, 0.8569), which is still significant, but the p value is slightly higher: p = 0.0049 (Figure N.28). You can see that the weights of studies have changed.

To create a spreadsheet with the meta-analysis outcomes, use the Analysis tab, select report type ("general" or "detailed") and click the Report button in the Meta-analysis group (Figure N.29).

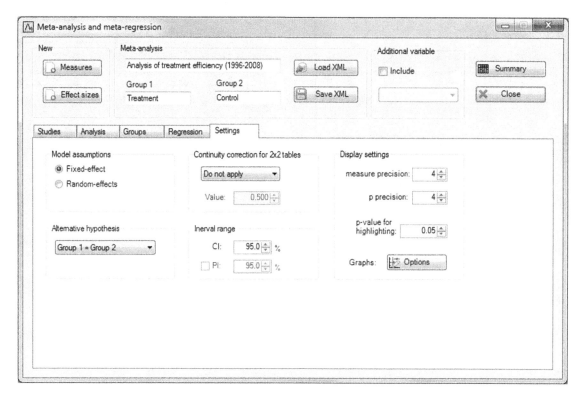

FIGURE N.26 "Model assumptions" on the Settings tab.

FIGURE N.27 Results of the fixed-effect model.

The general report presents results that you can see on the Studies tab. The detailed report (Figure N.30) includes additionally transformed measures, variability measures, weights used in the meta-analysis, and the number of cases in compared groups.

The results of the meta-analysis are very often presented in a forest plot. This shows the results and precision of individual studies, the dispersion of outcomes, and the summary effect. The outcomes are marked with squares proportional to the weights in the meta-analysis. To create a forest plot (Figure N.31), on the Analysis tab, click the "Forest

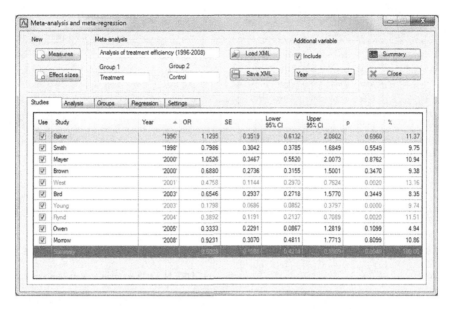

FIGURE N.28   Results of the random-effects model.

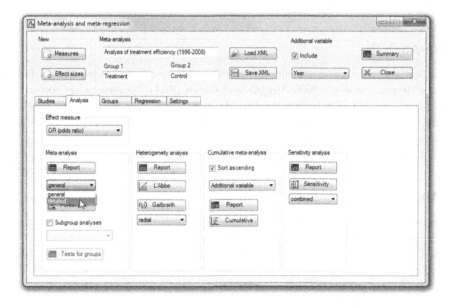

FIGURE N.29   The Analysis tab.

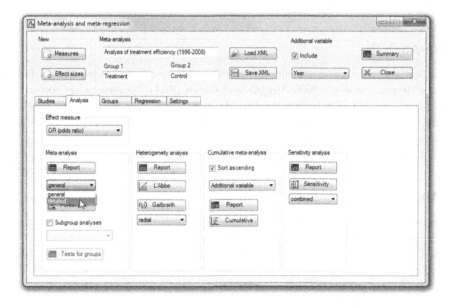

FIGURE N.30   Detailed report with the meta-analysis outcomes.

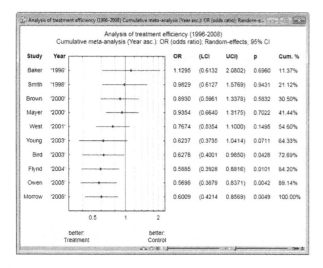

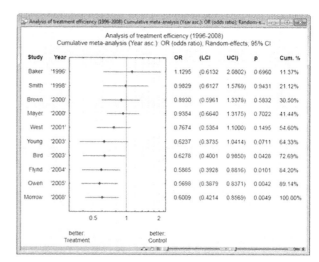

FIGURE N.31   Forest plot.

FIGURE N.32   Cumulative meta-analysis outcomes.

plot" button in the Meta-analysis group. Prior to plot creation, you can set forest plot options using the Options button in the Display settings group on the Settings tab.

Cumulative Meta-Analysis

The cumulative meta-analysis enables you to examine how the summary effect changes after including subsequent studies in the meta-analysis (Borenstein *et al.*, 2009; Higgins and Green, 2011). To sort studies you can use a specified measure or a given additional variable. Verify that the Include option and Year are selected in the Additional variable group in the Meta-analysis and Meta-regression dialog. To show how the conclusions shift over time, on the Analysis tab, select "Sort ascending" and "Additional variable" in the Cumulative meta-analysis group. After clicking Cumulative, you will get the plot presented in Figure N.32.

Heterogeneity Analysis

Meta-analysis can be used to estimate the effect size more accurately, if the effect is consistent across the studies, or to examine observed dispersion of studies outcomes (Borenstein *et al.*, 2009; Higgins and Green, 2011). To calculate the measures of heterogeneity on the Analysis tab, select "Report" in the Heterogeneity analysis group.

The p value is 0.0060 (Figure N.33), so we reject the null hypothesis that the studies share a common effect size. The estimated variance of true effects T^2 and its 95% confidence interval are, respectively, 0.1913 and (0.0348, 0.5037). The variance of true effects is about 61% of the dispersion observed.

Variability of studies outcomes can be seen in a forest plot. You can also use some dedicated plots, such as a L'Abbé plot (Higgins and Green, 2011), presenting less aggregated data (e.g., risks, odds, or means in the compared groups). To set L'Abbé plot options, use the Options button in the Display settings group on the Settings tab. Next, on

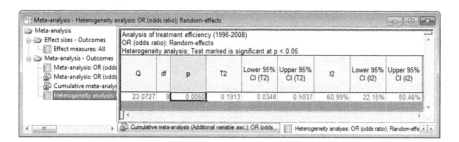

FIGURE N.33   Heterogeneity analysis outcomes.

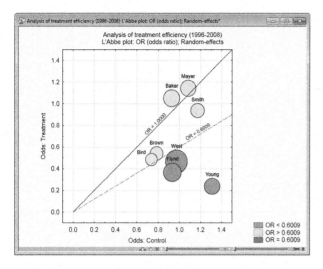

FIGURE N.34 L'Abbé plot.

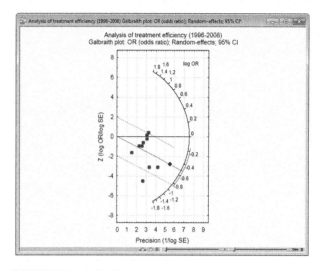

FIGURE N.35 Galbraith plot.

the Analysis tab, select "L'Abbé" in the Heterogeneity analysis group. The program will create a L'Abbé plot (Figure N.34) for eight studies for which you can determine the value of odds in treatment and control groups.

Another plot used in heterogeneity analysis, called a Galbraith plot (Higgins and Green, 2011), presents Z-statistics against precision for each study. The slope of the red line corresponds to the effect calculated in the meta-analysis. A Galbraith plot can be presented in a radial version, with an additional scale, where you can read the summary effect and its confidence interval.

To create a Galbraith plot (Figure N.35), click the Galbraith button in the Heterogeneity analysis group. Prior to plot creation, you can select graph type (simple or radial) and set some options using the Options button in the Display settings group on the Settings tab. If you want the precision to be based on the total variance of effects rather than the variance of true effects, before creating a graph select the Settings tab and change Model assumptions to Fixed-effect.

Subgroup Analyses

To check whether the effect variability is associated with certain studies' characteristics such as patient gender or type of treatment, you can carry out subgroup analyses (Borenstein *et al.*, 2009; Higgins and Green, 2011). Prior to the analyses, you define groups and assign individual studies to the specified groups. To do this, select the Groups tab (Figure N.36) and click Add in the Grouping group box. A new row will appear, in which you can enter the grouping name (e.g., Dose). Next, using the Add button under the Group grid, add three groups corresponding to 10 mg, 20 mg, and 30 mg doses. In the last step, assign studies to the appropriate groups. Select the 10 mg row in the Group grid and next, using the >> button, add the Baker, Mayer, and Morrow studies to this group. Similarly, assign the Smith, Brown, Bird, and Owen studies to the 20 mg group, and the West, Young, and Flynd studies to the 30 mg group.

Subgroup analyses options are available on the Analysis tab. Select "Subgroup analyses" in the Meta-analysis group, and choose the defined Dose grouping. The program will provide two new options on the Settings tab that enable you to calculate the variance of true effects in groups, separately or jointly. To calculate separate true variance, select "Random-effects, separate T2" in the Model assumptions group. The outcomes of subgroup analyses are presented on the Studies tab (Figure N.37). Different groups of studies and the corresponding results are marked with different colors.

Only the result of the 30 mg dose group was statistically significant, OR = 0.3425 (0.2019, 0.5810). The combined odds ratio calculated on the basis of outcomes in groups is 0.7028 (0.5486, 0.9004), and is also significant.

To create a categorized forest plot (Figure N.38), click the "Forest plot" button in the Meta-analysis group. Different groups of studies and the corresponding results are marked with different colors. Combined effect size is marked by a black diamond below the results of studies. To compare the mean effect across groups on the Analysis tab, select "Tests for groups" in the Meta-analysis group. The program will create a spreadsheet with Z-test results (when you compare two groups) and results of the test based on analysis of variance (Figure N.39). Comparing defined groups shows that the effect values differ substantially (p = 0.0032) across the groups.

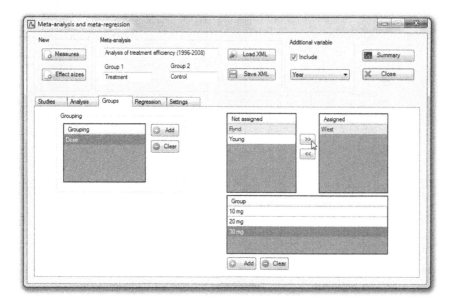

FIGURE N.36   The Groups tab.

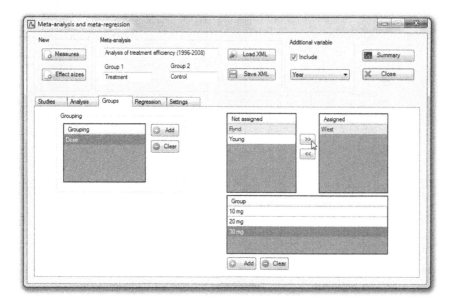

FIGURE N.37   Subgroup analyses outcomes.

Meta-Regression

Meta-regression is used to create a model describing the linear relationship between (both continuous and categorical) study-level covariates and the effect size (Hartung *et al.*, 2008; Borenstein *et al.*, 2009; Higgins and Green, 2011). If no predictors have been entered yet, you can add them now. In STATISTICA, open the Regression.sta data set containing study-level predictors. Select the Regression tab and click the Manage button in the Predictors group. Next click Edit in the Additional variables group. In the Additional variables dialog (Figure N.40) add Continuous, variable "Measurement" and "Categorical", variable "Group." Click the OK button. Two new columns, Measurement and Group, will be placed in the grid in the Manage additional variables dialog. You can enter predictor values manually or import data from a spreadsheet. Click the Import button, select the Regression.sta spreadsheet and click OK. Studies are identified by their names. Next, click the OK button to return to the Meta-analysis and Meta-regression dialog.

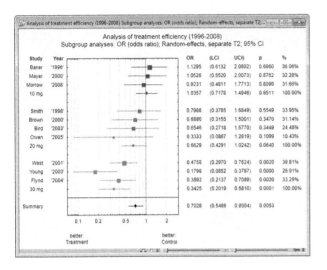

FIGURE N.38 Categorized forest plot.

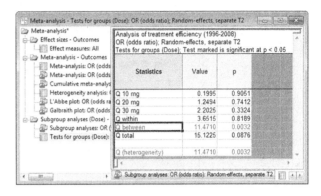

FIGURE N.39 Results of tests for groups.

FIGURE N.40 Defining predictors in the Additional variables dialog.

On the Regression tab you can select variables for analysis. Select "log OR (log odds ratio)" as the "Effect measure − dep. variable" and click Select in the Predictors group. Next, select continuous variable Measurement in the Meta-regression predictors dialog (Figure N.41) and click OK. A new column, Measurement, will be placed in the grid on the Regression tab. To create a meta-regression model, click the Report button in the Meta-regression group. The program will calculate the fixed-effect or the random-effects model depending on which option is selected in the "Model assumptions" group on the Settings tab.

The outcomes of the random-effects meta-regression model are presented in Figure N.42. The coefficient for the Measurement variable is −0.0147 and is statistically significant. This means that the effectiveness of therapy increases with the Measurement value. Note that the lower the odds ratio, the better the treatment effect.

The variance not explained by the model is 0.0226. Heterogeneity analysis shows that the estimated variance of true effects T^2 is 0.1913, which is about 61% of the dispersion observed. The R^2 index is about 88%, which means that the meta-regression model explains 88% of 61% of the dispersion observed.

The outcomes of the meta-regression model can be presented in a bubble plot (Figure N.43). To create such a plot, select "Bubble plot" in the Meta-regression group. The bubble plot shows, for each study, the value of the predictor Measurement on the horizontal axis and the effect measure "log OR" on the vertical axis. The area of each bubble indicates the weight of the corresponding study in the meta-regression model.

To include a categorical variable in the model, click "Select" in the Predictors group. Next, select the additional categorical variable "Group" in the Meta-regression predictors dialog, select a hidden level (e.g., A) and click OK. Now you can see codes of groups in the grid on the Regression tab. To select the type of categorical predictors coding, use the "Categorical variable" combo box. The options enable you to use "Reference coding," "Sigma restricted coding," or to treat the groups as "Strata." Select Reference coding. Next, click the Bubble plot button. When you select

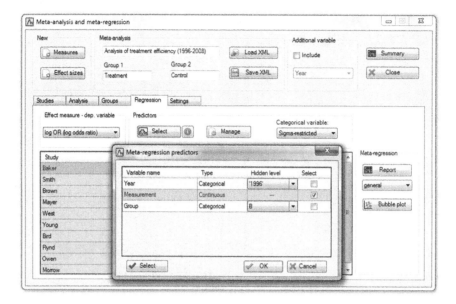

FIGURE N.41   Selection of meta-regression predictors.

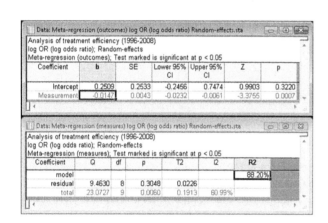

FIGURE N.42   Meta-regression outcomes.

FIGURE N.43   Bubble plot.

more than one predictor, the program will show the Variable values dialog in which you can set the values of variables not displayed on the two-dimensional plot. Use the default settings and click OK to create a categorized bubble plot (Figure N.44).

When you use the "Categorical variable: Strata" option, the program will calculate a meta-regression model separately for each group of studies.

Sensitivity Analysis

The module also contains sensitivity analysis features to show, for example, the impact of additional or excluded studies on the summary effect (Borenstein *et al.*, 2009; Higgins and Green, 2011). In STATISTICA, open the Additional.sta data set from the example data sets. This spreadsheet contains studies omitted in the meta-analysis due to their failure to meet some inclusion rules. To check how their exclusion affected the results of the analysis, first add them to the other studies. Click the Effect sizes button in the New group. In the Studies with effect sizes dialog, verify that the Effect measure is "OR (odds ratio)"; then click the Import button, select the Additional.sta spreadsheet and click OK (Figure N.45).

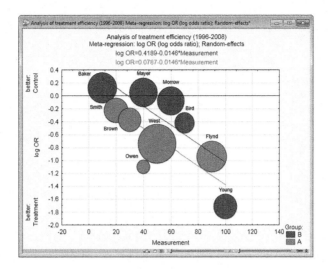

FIGURE N.44   Categorized bubble plot.

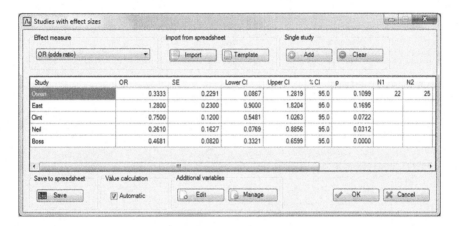

FIGURE N.45   Import of additional studies.

Click *OK* again to go back to the Meta-analysis and Meta-regression dialog. Using the Analysis tab, meta-analysis report, or a forest plot, you can check the summary effect for the extended set of studies (Figure N.46).

Sensitivity analysis can also assess how the summary effect will vary if given studies are excluded from the analysis. Select the Studies tab and uncheck the last four rows: Boss, Neil, Clint, and East. Each time the program will recalculate studies' weights and the summary effect.

By this means, you can check the summary effect and perform all presented analyses for any combination of studies (Figure N.47). The program also enables you to create a report with the impact of excluding each individual study. Select the Analysis tab and click the Sensitivity button on the Sensitivity analysis group. If you select the combined option, the program will create a graph showing the summary effect sensitivity and standard error change. Vertical dashed lines indicate the summary effect and its confidence interval for a complete set of studies.

The presented sensitivity plot (Figure N.48) shows that excluding the Young study, for example, from the meta-analysis will result in a substantial decrease of the summary effect, which, however, will remain statistically significant. In contrast, the meta-analysis is not very sensitive to the Bird study outcomes.

LOGISTIC REGRESSION WIZARD

Logistic Regression Wizard allows you to perform a complete step-by-step logistic regression analysis from the coding of variables, by examining the assumptions, the selection of variables for the evaluation of the model, and the residual analysis (Hosmer and Lemeshow, 2000; Vittinghoff *et al.*, 2005).

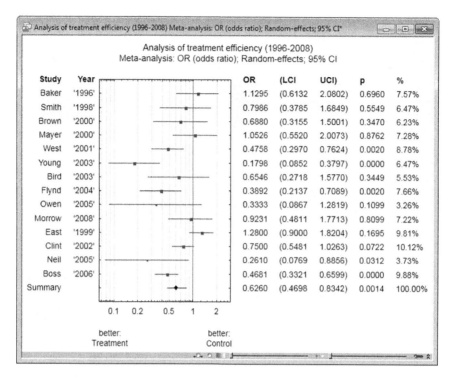

FIGURE N.46 Forest plot with additional studies.

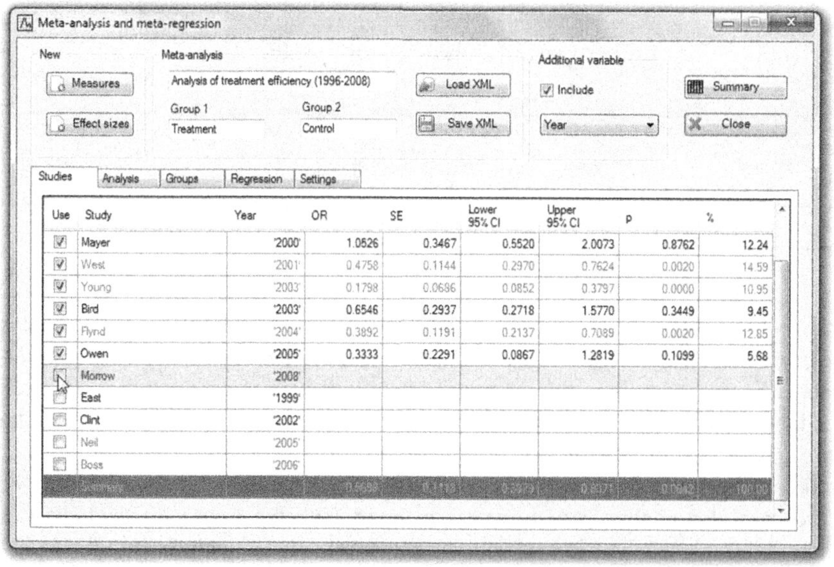

FIGURE N.47 Sensitivity analysis on the Studies tab.

To perform a Logistic regression analysis, open the WCGS.sta file (Figure N.49) and, on the Medical Bundle tab in the Analyses group, select Logistic Regression Wizard to display the Logistic regression step-by-step dialog. In this dialog, click the Variables button to display "Select variables" and select the variables according to the following screenshot (Figure N.50).

In our example, the CHD will be selected as a dependent variable: the value of Yes indicates coronary heart disease, No indicates no coronary heart disease. Other variables will act as the independent variables (predictors). Note that Behpat, Smoking, and Arcus are selected as categorical independent variables. Other predictors are selected as continuous.

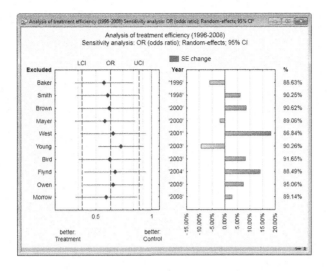

FIGURE N.48   Sensitivity plot.

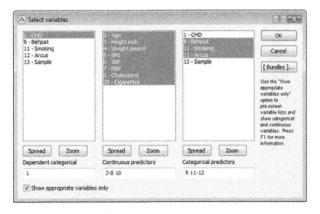

FIGURE N.49   The WCGS spreadsheet.

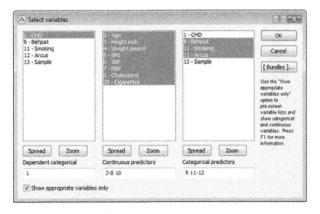

FIGURE N.50   Variables selection for the logistic regression model.

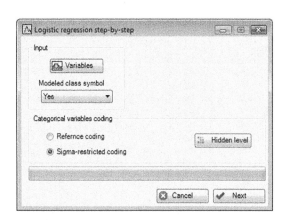

FIGURE N.51 The Logistic regression step-by-step dialog.

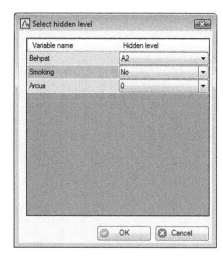

FIGURE N.52 Selection of reference levels.

The next step is to identify which level of the dependent variable will serve as the modeled class in analysis. The logistic regression module will recode this value to 1; the other class will be recoded to 0. To select the modeled class, click "Modeled class symbol" in the Input group box and choose the value Yes that indicates coronary heart disease (Figure N.51).

Because we have selected categorical predictors, we need to recode them into dummy variables. The next step is to select the recoding schema. In the "Coding of categorical dependent" group box, we can select Reference coding or Sigma restricted coding. When clicking the Hidden level button, you can indicate which values of selected categorical predictors will be treated as reference levels.

For the Behpat variable, select A2 as a reference level; for other variables, hidden levels remain unchanged (Figure N.52). Accept the selected reference levels by clicking OK.

Simple Regression Analysis

Click the Next button to calculate a simple logistic regression model separately for each of the selected predictors. Following this calculation, the Simple logistic regression dialog will be displayed.

On the General tab (Figure N.53), the list of selected predictors is displayed with the corresponding LR test results examining whether a simple model that contains a given predictor is significantly better than the model with the intercept only.

FIGURE N.53 Simple logistic regression — the General tab.

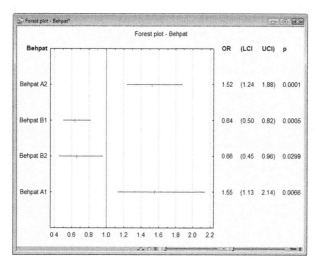

Effect	Hidden level	Estimate	Standard Error	Wald Stat.	Lower CL 95.0%	Upper CL 95.0%	p	Odds Ratio	OR CL -95%	OR CL +95%
Intercept	No	-2.448	0.067	1340.908	-2.579	-2.317	0.000	0.086	0.076	0.099
Smoking Yes	No	0.315	0.067	22.141	0.184	0.446	0.000	1.370	1.201	1.562

CHD - Parameter estimates (WCGS.sta)
Distribution : BINOMIAL, Link function: LOGIT
Modeled probability that CHD = Yes

FIGURE N.54 Simple logistic regression outcomes.

FIGURE N.55 Forest plot for categorical predictor.

You can see that for the variable "Height inch" the p value is 0.2867, which gives us no reason to reject the hypothesis of no significant impact of this variable on the analyzed outcome. You can then deselect the Include field corresponding to this variable to eliminate it from further analysis. In our example, leave this option unchanged.

After clicking the Estimates button, a set of simple analysis results for each of the selected predictors is displayed. Figure N.54 is a sample output spreadsheet for the Smoking variable, containing a selection of results such as estimates, odds ratios, confidence intervals, Wald statistics, and p value.

The Graphs button allows the user to display a forest plot for categorical predictors. The plot represents the values of the odds ratios calculated from the regression parameter estimates and the corresponding confidence intervals (Figure N.55). Thus, the researcher can clearly present the impact of individual parameters on the modeled outcome and their statistical significance.

Figure N.55 was prepared for the odds ratios relating to the estimates of regression parameters calculated for the Behpat variable. You can see that the values of odds ratios vary significantly from 1 (and thus the values of the regression parameter estimates vary significantly from 0). The confidence intervals do not overlap the value of 1.

Clicking the More button generates a spreadsheet with the results of LR and Wald tests for all single predictor models.

Linearity of Predictors

The uncritical assumption that the analyzed continuous predictors are linearly related to the dependent variable (actually the log odds of the dependent variable) can lead to biased values of the regression parameter estimates and incorrect inference about the influence of predictors on the analyzed outcome (Vittinghoff *et al.*, 2005).

To assess the linearity between continuous predictors and log odds of the dependent variable, click the Linearity button on the Predictor diagnostics tab (Figure N.56).

Assessment of linearity can be done using graphical data exploration. A sample scatter plot (Figure N.57) shows the log odds values (Y-axis) and the corresponding categorized SBP values (X-axis). For calculated points, you can fit a simple linear regression or use the LOWESS smoothing method.

FIGURE N.56   Simple logistic regression — the Predictor diagnostics tab.

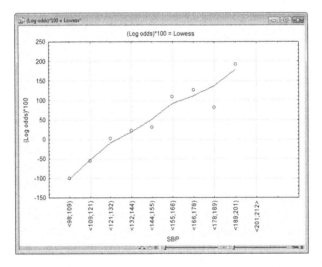

FIGURE N.57   Graphical assessment of linearity.

FIGURE N.58   Linearity test results.

Formally, we can assess the linearity of predictors using a statistical LR test to check whether adding the quadratic term of predictor to the single predictor model significantly improves the model quality (adding polynomial terms can also be useful). Figure N.58 shows the linearity test results for selected predictors. On this basis, we can conclude that there is no reason to reject the hypothesis of linear impact of analyzed variables on (log odds) CHD.

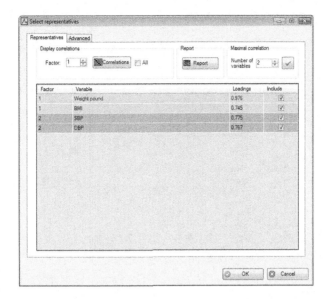

FIGURE N.59   The Select representatives dialog.

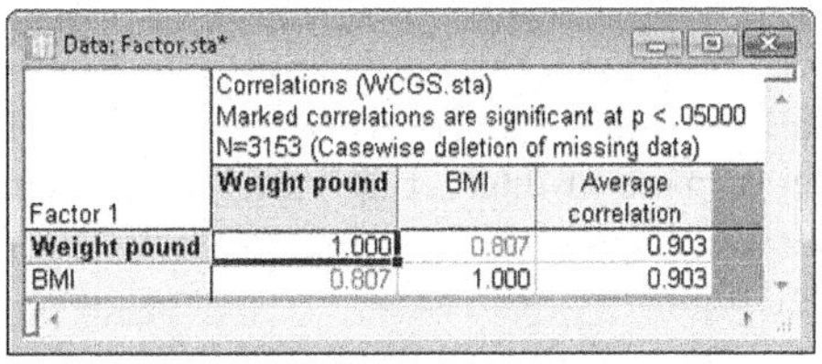

FIGURE N.60   The correlation matrix for bundle of variables.

Collinearity of Predictors

Highly correlated predictors used in the multiple regression do not contribute any new information to the model. Such variables unnecessarily complicate the model and usually lead to improper results. Collinearity leads to overestimation of standard errors of estimates, and hence to false assessment of the significance of the analyzed variables. In many cases it disables the calculation of the model (Hosmer and Lemeshow, 2000; Vittinghoff *et al.*, 2005). If two or more variables are highly correlated with each other, it is worth considering the selection of one only. To identify highly correlated variables, the user can analyze the correlation matrix. In a situation where the number of predictors exceeds 10, this analysis may be very time consuming; hence, a better approach is to use advanced statistical methods such as the principal components analysis for identifying bundles of highly correlated variables. To conduct such an analysis, click the Representatives button located in the Collinearity group box.

In the Select representatives dialog (Figure N.59) there are two distinguished groups of potentially correlated variables: "Weight pound" and "BMI," and "SBP" and "DBP." Now we can generate a correlation matrix for bundles of correlated variables. In Figure N.60, you can see the correlation matrix of variables included in the first bundle that appears after clicking the Correlations button. You can see a very strong correlation between the variables, allowing you to safely eliminate one of them. To remove variables, deselect the Include field in the rows corresponding to those variables. If a bundle of variables consists of more than two variables, the user can automatically select a certain number of representatives by clicking the blue tick.

After selection of representatives is complete, click the OK button to go back to the Simple logistic regression dialog. Eliminated variables are excluded from further analyses.

Interactions

Interaction between two predictors in a regression model means that the degree of association between each predictor and the outcome varies according to the levels of the other predictor (Hosmer and Lemeshow, 2000; Vittinghoff *et al.*,

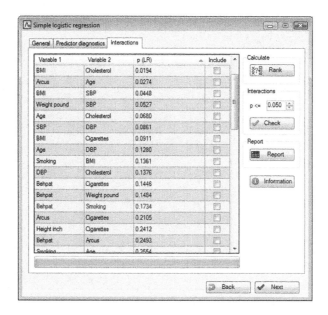

FIGURE N.61   Simple logistic regression − the Interactions tab.

2005). To perform identification of interaction, click the Interactions tab (Figure N.61) and then click the Rank button. This action will calculate the rank of all possible interactions between pairs of variables selected on the General tab. When the calculation is completed, a set of pairs of interacting variables and the p values for the LR test indicating the statistical significance of the interactions are displayed. Selecting the Include option for a given interaction will include that interaction in the multivariate model.

Building a Multivariate Model

Click the Next button in the Simple logistic regression dialog to display the "Logistic regression − multivariate model" dialog where we can determine the method of model building and its validation (Hosmer and Lemeshow, 2000; Vittinghoff *et al.*, 2005).

On the Model building tab (Figure N.62), you can specify the building method for the multivariate model. The All effects option will enter all selected variables and interactions into the regression model. The other options allow you to select predictors and interactions. Select the "Backward stepwise" method to reduce the initial number of selected predictors. On the Validation schema tab (Figure N.63) you can define the validation schema for the model. Please note that, based on the training set only, the predictive power of the model cannot be estimated. You need an external validation data set to assess how well such a model fits the problem. The Cross-validation option allows you to divide a data set into a learning and a validation set. The learning sample enables you to estimate the parameters of the model, and the validation sample enables you to estimate the predictive power of the model.Cross-validation is not an optimal

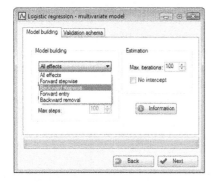

FIGURE N.62   The Model building tab.

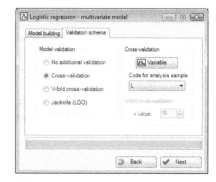

FIGURE N.63   The Validation schema tab.

FIGURE N.64 The "Multivariate logistic regression − results" dialog.

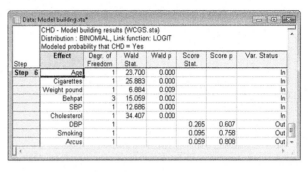

FIGURE N.65 Report with the model building process.

FIGURE N.66 The Fit measures tab.

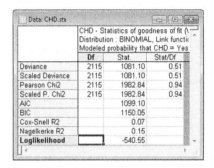

FIGURE N.67 Goodness of fit report.

strategy when your data set is relatively small. In such situations, excluding cases from the estimation process can substantially change the final model parameters. An error based on the validation sample also has a large variance that depends on the allocation of cases in the sample. You can validate a model built on the whole data set without using a validation sample, using either of the available options: V-fold cross-validation or Jacknife (LOO).

Because our data set is relatively large, select the "Cross-validation" radio button in the Model validation group box. In the Cross-validation group box, click the Variable button and select the Sample variable as the learning and validation set identifier. In the "Code for analysis sample" combo box, select L as the identifier of the learning set. Click Next to estimate and evaluate the multivariate regression model.

After the model is built, the Multivariate logistic regression − results dialog (Figure N.64) will be displayed. In the displayed dialog in the Model building group box, click the Report button to examine the process of elimination of predictors.

Based on the displayed report (Figure N.65), the user can see that only six variables are included in the model. Click the Estimates button to display a spreadsheet with model estimates and measures similar to those presented in the simple logistic regression analysis.

Model Evaluation

The next step of our analysis is model evaluation (Hosmer and Lemeshow, 2000; Vittinghoff *et al.*, 2005). The user can examine the results of the LR (Likelihood Ratio) and Wald tests. The quality of the model is evaluated using the pseudo R^2 measures, the AIC (Akaike Information Criterion), BIC (Bayesian Information Criterion), the Hosmer-Lemeshow test, and ROC curves.

Results of LR tests are available after clicking the LR tests button on the Regression results tab. Other measures can be obtained on the Fit measures tab (Figure N.66). After clicking the "Goodness of fit" button, the user obtains a set of fit measures. Note that AIC or BIC do not inform us directly about the quality of the model; we use them when we want to compare models and determine which of several models is the best. Figure N.67 shows an example of a goodness of fit report.

Data: HL.sta*

CHD - Goodness of Fit: Hosmer-Lemeshow Test (WCGS
Distribution : BINOMIAL, Link function: LOGIT
Hosmer Lemeshow = 6.2423, p value = 0.620112

Response	Group1	Group2	Group3	Group4	Group5
0: Observed	211	208	204	206	198
Expected	209	207	205	204	201
1: Observed	1	4	8	6	14
Expected	3	5	7	8	11
All Groups	212	212	212	212	212

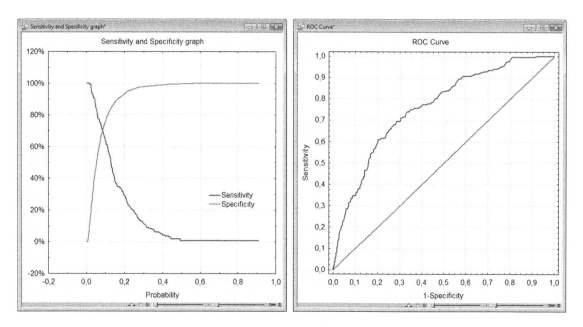

FIGURE N.68 Homer-Lemeshow test results.

FIGURE N.69 Sensitivity and specificity graph and a ROC curve.

Data: AUC.sta* (2v by 2c)

	1 AUC	2 SE
Learning sample	0.760	0.018
Validation sample	0.740	0.027

FIGURE N.70 Report with the AUCs.

Based on the Homer-Lemeshow test, p value = 0.6201 (Figure N.68), there is no reason to reject the hypothesis that our model fits well.

Click the ROC button on the same tab to display ROC curves for a learning and a validation sample. Among the available reports, there are graphs of sensitivity and specificity and a report containing a set of effect measures for each of the possible cut-off points (Figure N.69).

You can also examine a report containing information about the area under the ROC curve (AUC). Analysis of this area for the learning and validation samples shows that the model is not overfitted (Figure N.70). There is only a slight difference between the compared areas.

The value of the area under the ROC curve indicates that the model fits the data relatively well.

The last step of our analysis is to assess the residual and leverage values. For logistic regression, residual analysis is not as important as in the case of linear regression, but can be valuable when identifying some outlying cases or cases with immoderate impacts on the model.

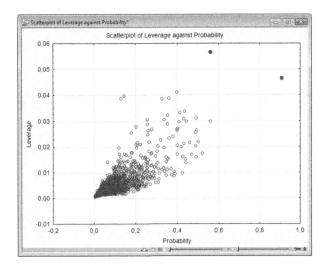

FIGURE N.71   Leverage points vs. probability.

   To display residuals, leverage points and related graphs, use the options available in the "Residuals and leverage" group box.

   Figure N.71 displays leverage points vs. probability. We can see that some points have stronger impacts on regression results than do the others. We can consider removing such points from the analysis, re-estimating the model, and then checking if the model estimates remain stable.

REFERENCES

Borenstein, M., Hedges, L.V., Higgins, J.P.T., Rothstein, H.R., 2009. Introduction to Meta-Analysis. John Wiley & Sons, New York, NY.

Hanley, J.A., Hajian-Tilaki, K.O., 1997. Sampling variability of nonparametric estimates of the areas under receiver operating characteristic curves: an update. Acad. Radiol. 4, 49–58.

Hanley, J.A., McNeil, B.J., 1982. The Meaning and use of the area under a Receiver Operating Characteristic (ROC) curve. Radiology. 143, 29–36.

Hartung, J., Knapp, G., Sinha, B.K., 2008. Statistical Meta-Analysis With Applications. John Wiley & Sons, New York, NY.

Higgins, J.P.T., Green, S. (Eds.), 2011. Cochrane Handbook for Systematic Reviews of Interventions Version 5.1.0 [updated March 2011]. The Cochrane Collaboration, London, UK.

Hosmer, D., Lemeshow, S., 2000. Applied Logistic Regression. 2nd ed. John Wiley & Sons, New York, NY.

Pencina, M.J., D'Agostino SrR.B., D'Agostino JrR.B., Vasan, R.S., 2007. Evaluating the added predictive ability of a new marker: From area under the ROC curve to reclassification and beyond. Stat. Med. 27, 157–172.

Rosenman, R.H., Friedman, M., Straus, R., Wurm, M., Kositchek, R., Hahn, W., et al., 1964. A predictive study of coronary heart disease: the Western Collaborative Group Study. JAMA. 189 (1), 15–22, 1964.

StatSoft Inc., 2013: STATISTICA (data analysis software system). Tulsa, OK.

StatSoft Polska, 2013. Medical Bundle Tutorial. Krakow, Poland.

Vittinghoff, E., Glidden, D.V., Shiboski, S.C., McCulloch, C.E., 2005. Regression Methods in Biostatistics. Springer-Verlag, New York, NY.

Tutorial O

Medical Advice Acceptance Prediction

Steve Petitt, MBA

Chapter Outline

INTRODUCTION

This tutorial will introduce you to using DMRecipe (DMR) with the Data Miner Workspace (DMW) application. The business goal of this project, described in this tutorial, is to find the best modeling algorithm that can be used to predict future purchase interest among a sample of hospital clinicians (surgeons, nurses, physician assistants) for a new medical device. The device will be called the infamous and universal Product X throughout this tutorial. Product X will be manufactured and marketed by a medical device company for the US hospital marketplace.

BACKGROUND

The clinicians were shown a written description and graphical depictions of the new product. Once they had carefully reviewed the information in the description, they were asked a series of rating and open-ended questions about their initial reaction (e.g., positive, negative) and their likelihood to want to use the new device if it came to market.

The target variable (also called the dependent variable) used in the analysis for this tutorial is a categorical variable that differentiates clinicians in the study that indicated that they would be *Highly Likely to Use Product X* from those that had a *Low Likelihood to Use* the new product.

- The two groups were formed by segmenting participants that indicated their *Likelihood to Use the New Product* on a 10-point scale (*0–10*, where *10 = Extremely Likely to Use*). Any clinicians with ratings of 8 or higher = *Highly Likely Users*, versus those below that rating = *Low Likelihood Users* of Product X.
- The target variable in the data set is the number 9, and is called "Code_Likely_Use_New_Prod."

A total of 38 predictor variables (also called *features* in data mining terminology) out of a data set of 56 variables were used against the target variable.

- The 38 variables were initially chosen based on using the domain knowledge from both the professional market research consultant/author of this tutorial, and internal "experts" of the company that sponsored the original study.

Note: The data used for this tutorial are only a subset of a larger database of information that was analyzed for and presented to the sponsoring company.

The tools used in this tutorial uncovered the variables that had the greatest strength in predicting a clinician's likely interest to want to use (or not use) Product X.

The 56 variables that comprise the data set are categorized by:

- *Demographics* — examples: Size of hospital, Number of surgical procedures performed per month
- *Satisfaction* with current product/devices

Practical Predictive Analytics and Decisioning Systems for Medicine. DOI: http://dx.doi.org/10.1016/B978-0-12-411643-6.00032-6

- *Reaction to new product concept* − examples: Initial reaction to product choice (very positive to very negative), Uniqueness of new product, Types of patients that new product would be used with, Likely to use the new product
- *Importance of factors used in current decision-making process* when deciding to acquire these types of products for hospital − examples: Product is technologically innovative, Sales reps are knowledgeable about products, Product is safe/prevents infections, Product is competitively priced
- *To what extent specific features/benefits of new product are liked* by participants − examples: Multiple pressure controls available within single medical device, Flexible integration into any other like device, Offering non-invasive control adjustments.

THE TUTORIAL

To begin with, we will examine our 38 potential predictor variables, and determine which are the most important in helping us to predict the target variable, by utilizing the Feature Selection tool.

The first thing to do is open up the initial Data Miner Workspace screen by clicking on the Data Mining tab. Next, go down and place the cursor on Data Mining − Workspaces among the choices that pop-up, then select Data Miner − All Procedures from the next menu that appears. Figure O.1 shows our initial Workspace screen.

Next, we select Data Source from the Data Miner Workspace menu, and then select and Open the data source, which is called "Medical Device X Implanted in Hospital Setting" in this tutorial (see Figure O.2).

We will then be asked to select the variables we wish to use from the data set. Some of the actual data set spreadsheet can be seen in the background of the "Select dependent variables and predictors" dialog window, as shown in Figure O.3.

Click on the Variables button, and the screen shown in Figure O.4 will appear. We will select the 39 variables (1 target plus 38 predictors) based on their value types − categorical or continuous.

- The variable names selected will become highlighted in blue and their corresponding variable numbers are shown in the boxes below the different variable type groups. (*Alternatively, you can input the variable numbers into the boxes if have you that information available and again the variable names will be highlighted in blue.*)

After variable selection, click OK and the window seen in Figure O.5 will appear; this summarizes our selection. Click OK again to return to the main Data Miner Workspace panel and an icon representing the data set is now embedded into the Data Acquisition section of the workspace.

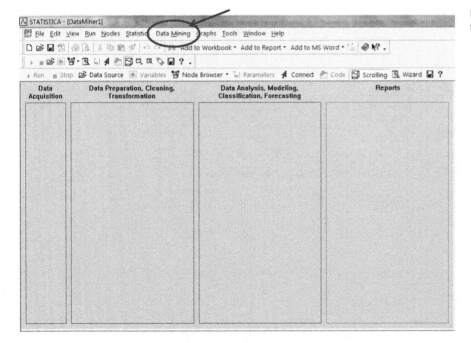

FIGURE O.1 Data Miner Workspace − the opening workspace screen.

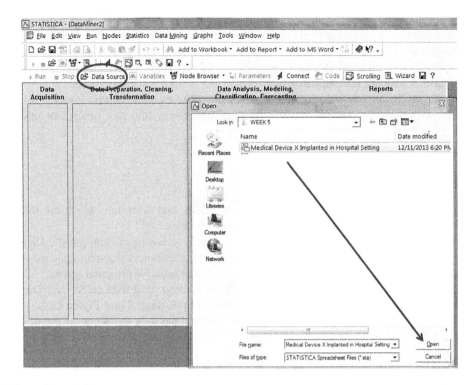

FIGURE O.2 Data Source file selection.

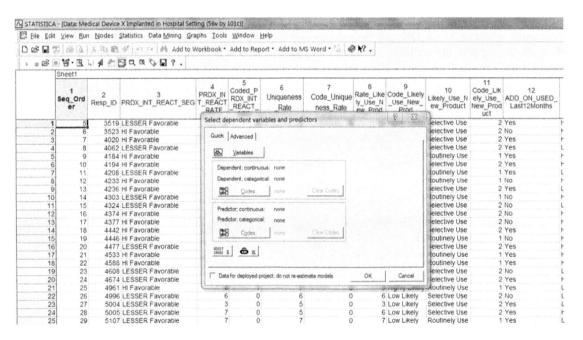

FIGURE O.3 Variables selection window.

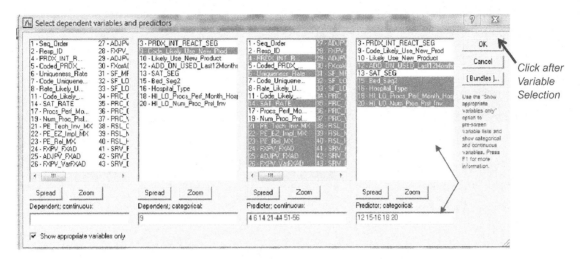

FIGURE O.4   Dialog window with variables selected.

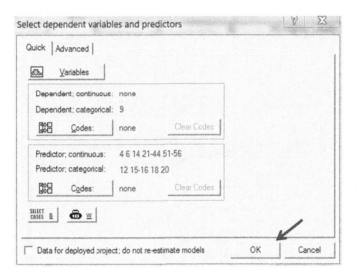

FIGURE O.5   Summary window of variable selections.

Next, we will use the Feature Selection tool to help us identify the predictor variables that have the strongest value in predicting our target variable no. 9 − which indicates if a clinician is going to be a *Highly Likely* or *Low Likelihood User* of Product X if it comes to market. Select the Node Browser button above the workspace panel (Figure O.6).

The Node Browser contains all of the different procedures available for data mining.

- The procedures (all 250 + of them) are categorized into three broad folders: Statistics, Data Mining, and Graphics.
- Open the Data Mining folder, look down the menu and select Feature Selection. Then select Feature Section and Root Cause Analysis in the right panel, and click on the Insert into workspace button (Figure O.7).

We can now see that the data source is automatically connected to the Feature Selection icon node that is now embedded into the Workspace in the Data Analysis, Modeling, Classification, Forecasting section (Figure O.8).

We will now run Feature Selection via the Data Miner Workspace. First we will look at some of the *settings* for Feature Selection.

- To open the parameter dialog, *right click* on the Feature Selection icon as noted in Figure O.8 and then select Edit Parameters; the window shown in Figure O.9 will appear.

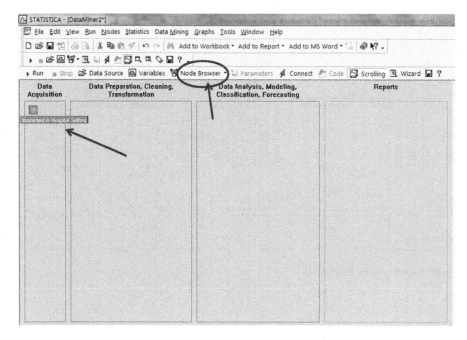

FIGURE O.6 Data Source icon in Data Acquisition section of workspace and Node Browser button.

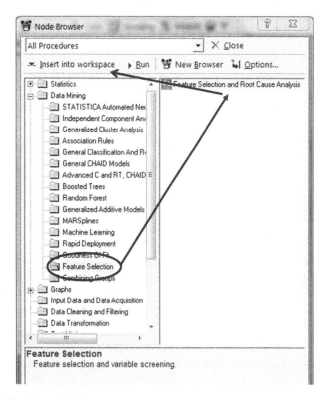

FIGURE O.7 Node Browser for finding Feature Selection.

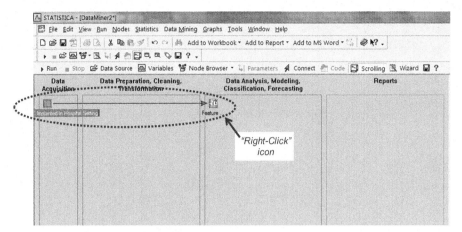

FIGURE O.8 Data Source and Feature.

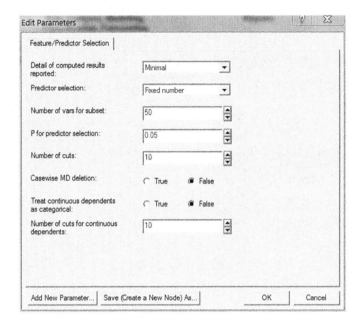

FIGURE O.9 Edit Parameters window from Feature Selection via workspace.

Now we will change a couple of the parameter options, as noted in Figure O.10. First, change the option for "Detail of computed results reported" to "All results."

- Next, change "Predictor selection" to "Based on p value" — this will identify the most important or most predictive variables that determine whether a clinician will *Likely Use (or Not Use) Product X*. In this case, all variables with p values that are <0.05 will be selected as the most important predictors.
- After these changes are made, click OK and you be returned to the Data Miner Workspace panel.

At this point, click the Run button found on the left and above the Data Acquisition section on workspace. This will execute the Feature Selection method. Once the Run is completed, two new *connected* icon nodes will be embedded within the workspace. One node is Generated Input Data that is connected with the Feature Selection icon within the Data Analysis, Modeling, Classification, Forecasting section, and the other is the Results Workbook found within the Reports section, as shown in Figure O.11.

We can review the Report Results by right-clicking the icon in the Reports section and then select View Document within the menu options.

- In Figure O.12 we can see an Importance plot showing that only eight variables had p values of <0.05 out of the 38 predictor variables.
- The plot depicts relative importance among the variables via Chi-square values. (However, the *order* of the variables is based on p values, which are shown in the Best Predictor report that is described next.)

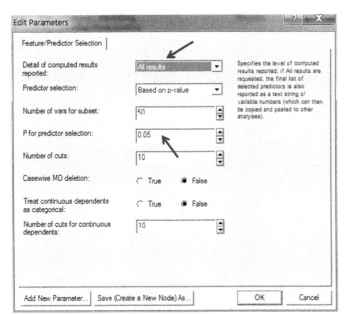

FIGURE O.10 Change some Parameters from Feature Selection.

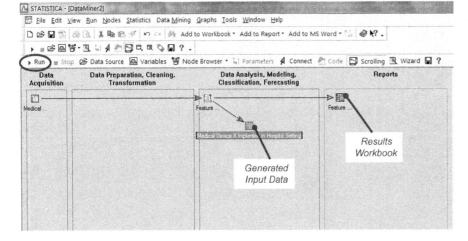

FIGURE O.11 Workspace after Feature Selection is run.

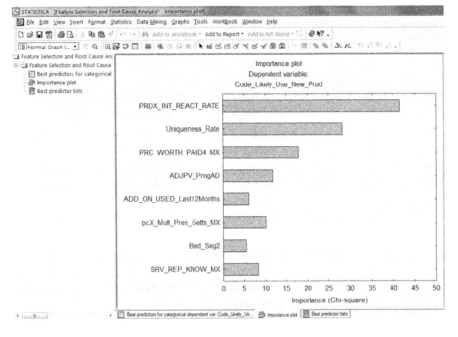

FIGURE O.12 Importance plot in Feature Selection Results.

TABLE O.1 Descriptors for the Eight Predictor Variables

1. *PRDX_INT_REACT_SEG*: Rating of initial reaction to written & graphically described new device concept *(1−10 Rating Scale, 10 = Very favorable)*

2. *Uniqueness_Rate*: Rating of how unique the features of Product X are compared to current products on market *(1−10 Rating, 10 = Extremely unique)*

3. *PRC_WORTH_PAID4_MX*: Importance weight used in decision-making process in terms of "The product is worth what paid for" *(Scale 0 to 100, 100 = Highest importance)*

4. *ADJPV_ProgAD*: Importance weight used in decision-making process in terms of "Wanting to use a product that offers adjustable pressure controls with an add-on programmable fluid controller" *(Scale 0 to 100, 100 = Highest importance)*

5. *ADD_ON_USED_Last12Months*: Used an add-on product feature in last 12 months *(Coded: Yes or No)*

6. *pcX_Mult_Pres_Setts_MX*: Weight given to how much a particular product feature/benefit is liked over other specified product features/benefits. This feature/benefit is "Multiple pressure controls available within single medical device" *(Scale 0 to 100, 100 = Highest importance)*

7. *Bed_Seg2*: Size of hospital that participant works at (Coded: Large vs Small)

8. *SRV_REP_KNOW_MX*: Importance weight used in decision-making process in terms of "Products are supported by knowledgeable sales rep" *(Scale 0 to 100, 100 = Highest importance)*

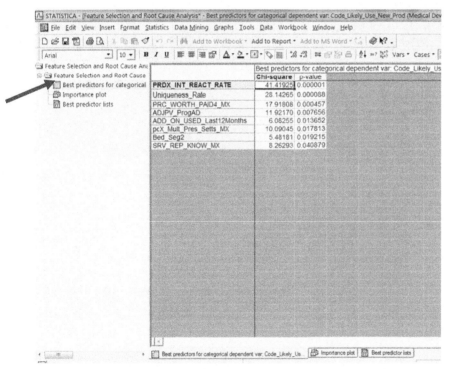

FIGURE O.13   Best predictor in Feature Selection Results.

Table O.1 shows decriptions for the eight predictor variables.

Let's look at a table showing these same variables and associated p values. Simply click on "Best predictor for categorical dependent var:" on the left panel to get the results shown in Figure O.13.

These two lists are extremely useful and will be used by us to select the variables to be utilized for the subsequent analyses that will be tested and reviewed within DMRecipe and its associated data mining algorithms.

Now we will access the Data Miner Recipe method by selecting "Data miner recipes" from the Data Mining menu. Once Data miner recipes (DMR) is selected, the following initial DMR window will open as shown in Figure O.14. Click the "New" button on the upper left of the window.

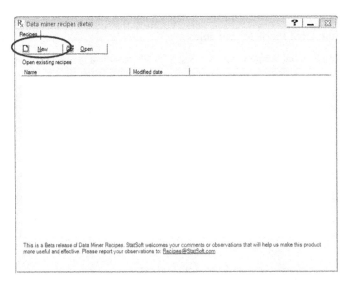

FIGURE O.14 DMRecipe – Data miner recipes initial window.

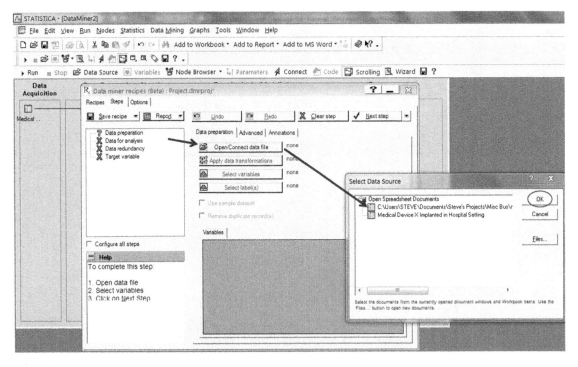

FIGURE O.15 DMRecipe selecting data set.

Next click on the Open/Connect data file button within the new DMR dialog window and then select the name of the data file as shown in Figure O.15. Click the OK button on the right of the Select Data Source window.

Now we will select the eight best predictor variables that were determined via Feature Selection. We will also select the target variable, Variable 9.

Click on the Select Variables button and then select the continuous and categorical variables as shown in Figure O.16. Then click OK on the right of the Select variables window.

Next, click the " + " sign that is next to "Target variable" in the tree hierarchy in the left pane. This will *expand* the tree below Target Variable, as shown in Figure O.17.

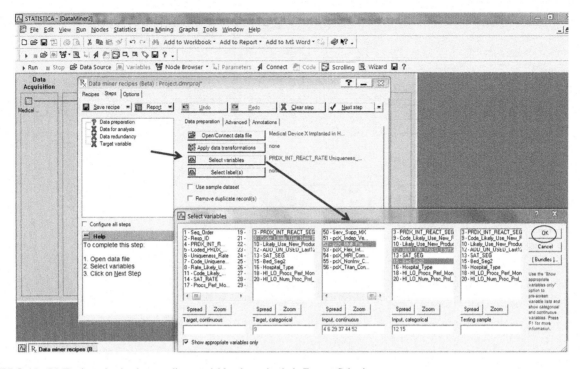

FIGURE O.16 DMRecipe selecting best predictor variables determined via Feature Selection.

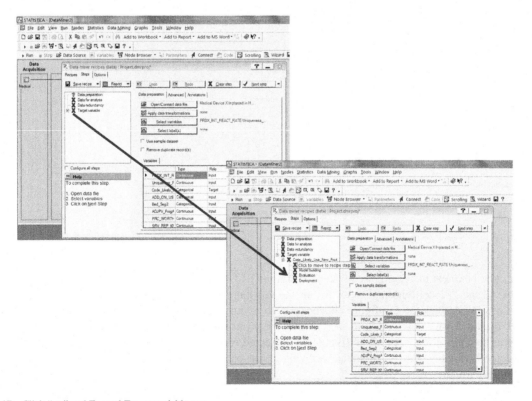

FIGURE O.17 Click " + " and Expand Target variable tree.

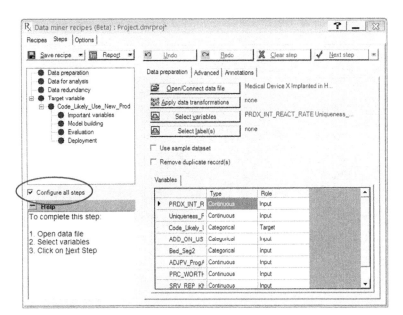

FIGURE O.18 Click checkbox next to Configure all steps.

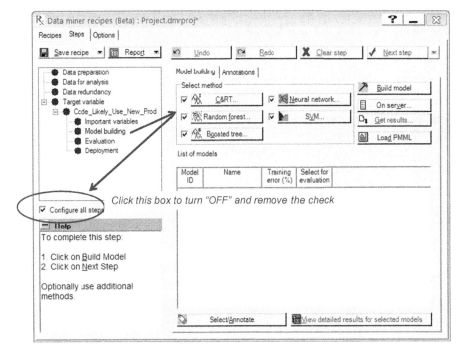

FIGURE O.19 Click all model building algorithms and remove check next to Configure all steps.

Now check the box next to "Configure all steps" (Figure O.18).

Next, click on the "Model building" selection in the left pane. Click all of boxes next to the five Model building algorithm options. Also, click the Configure all steps box to *remove* the check that is in the box (Figure O.19).

Now click on the down arrow button located in upper right of the DMRecipe dialog window (see Figure O.20) and then select "Run to completion." All of the five models selected will be running and processing results.

As DMRecipe is running, a series of status bars will appear on your screen. For this data set, the computations were completed within 2 minutes.

Once completed, a Summary workbook is generated that provides the data miner analyst several useful reports and charts that can be used to review and evaluate the relative performance of the predictive models that were run via DMRecipe (see Figure O.21).

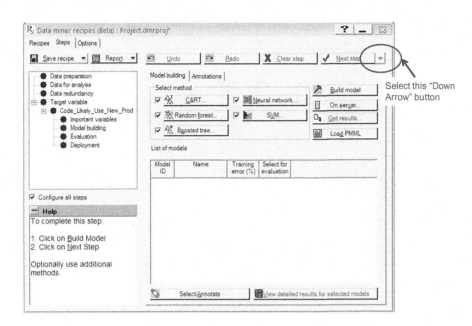

FIGURE O.20   Click down arrow button to Run models.

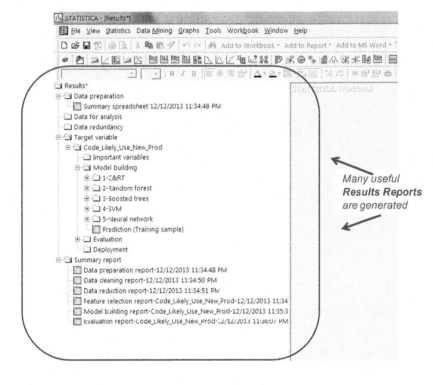

FIGURE O.21   Results reports generated in DMRecipe.

One of the easiest and most important reports generated is the Evaluation report comparing the error rates across the five algorithms, as shown in Figure O.22.

- The error rates actually reflect the accuracy rates of each model. Accuracy rates = (100% − error rate %).
- For example, the accuracy rate for the best model − SVM − is 91.9% (100% minus 8.91% error rate), which is followed by Boosted trees at 87.1%.

Another useful Output Report is the Lift chart. The values in the lift chart shown in Figure O.23 indicate how the five models predict a *Highly Likely User of Product X* better than the Baseline (i.e., no model).

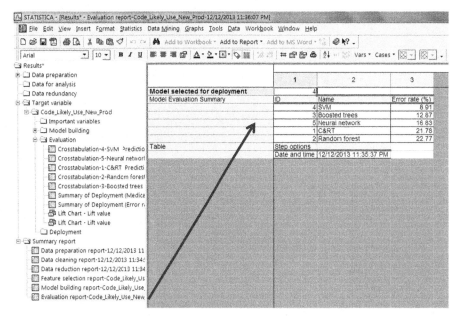

FIGURE O.22 DMRecipe Results workbook.

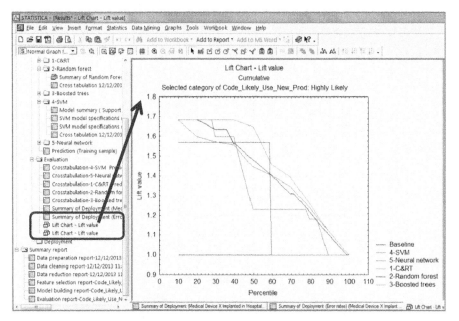

FIGURE O.23 Lift chart generated in DMRecipe summary workbook.

- All of the models create a noticeably strong Lift over the Baseline up to the 40 percentile. However, the Lift begins to drop across most of the models beyond that point.
- However, the Chart indicates that the SVM model predicts a steady and exceptionally strong lift over the Baseline across the first 6 deciles (60% of the cases) and drops to Baseline when predicting *Highly Likely Users of Product X.*

  Note: The results for *Likely Users* correspond to the fact that this segment does comprise almost 60% of the clinicians that indicated they would want to use the new product. Therefore the model appears to discriminate between these *Likely Users* across the entire population of cases in the data set (N = 101).
  - Although not shown here, a *similar* Lift Chart pattern was also generated with the SVM model for the *Low Likelihood Users* − which represent about 40% of the population in the data set.
  - The Lift chart for this clinician segment indicates a steady lift across these first four deciles − representing 40% of the clinicians that are *Not Likely* to be users of Product X.

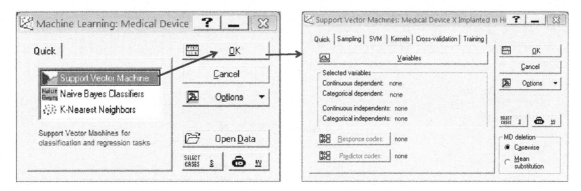

FIGURE O.24   Initial SVM dialog and Quick tab windows.

- Like the Lift chart pattern seen for *Highly Likely Users*, the SVM model drops to Baseline once it hits the 40th percentile.

Therefore, based on this analysis, the Support Vector Machine (SVM) model is the "*winner*." The model correctly predicts a clinician's *Likelihood to Want to Use Product X* with over 90% accuracy.

This is quite impressive, but we will now conduct some further validation of the SVM model through the Interactive SVM method. We will run the SVM model and get a V-fold cross-validation measure as a way to gauge and compare accuracy rates results across several test samples.

We will again use the *same* eight predictor variables against the same target variable, Variable 9.

To begin, open the Data Mining menu and select the Machine Learning (Bayesian, Support Vectors, Nearest Neighbor) option; the initial dialog window shown on the left of Figure O.24 will appear.

Click OK, since it automatically defaults to the Support Vector Machine option. Once clicked, the SVM Quick tab dialog window shown on the right of Figure O.24 will now appear. Next, click on the Variables button and that will open the Select Variables for Analysis window.

- As we did earlier, we will input the *best* continuous and categorical predictor variables that were determined via Feature Selection into the appropriate boxes.
- We will also input the target variable, Variable 9, into the "Categorical dependents" box (Figure O.25).

Now click OK on the Select variables for analysis window after the variables have been selected. The window shown in Figure O.26 will appear.

Next click on the Cross-validation tab and open it up to the window shown in Figure O.27.

- Place a check in the "Apply v-fold cross-validation" box. We will leave the V value to the default setting at 10 and change the Seed to 2806 (you may change this to whatever number you wish).
  - The V value of 10 means that 10 separate bootstrapping samples of our data set will be selected and a separate SVM analysis will be run for each of these samples.
  - The process will allow us to compare results and determine if we are getting the same (or nearly the same) results from the model across the different samples being tested.
- We will assess an accuracy score using this V-fold cross-validation procedure. This information will allow us to compare the training accuracy and testing accuracy rates to see if they are very similar.

Next we will open the Sampling tab. We change the "Size of training sample (%)" to 67 (and replace the default of 75) (Figure O.28).

- This % represents the proportion of our data set that will be used for the Training sample; the remaining 33% will be used as the Testing sample.
- The Seed was also changed to 8309 from its default setting (again, you may change this to any number you wish).
- We will leave all the values for the other tabs at their respective default settings.
- Now click OK, and all of the computations will commence.

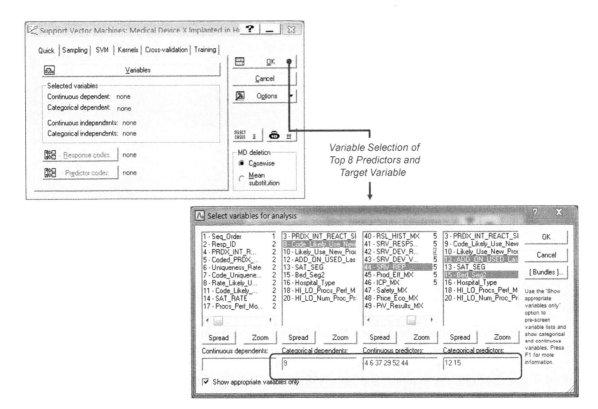

FIGURE O.25 SVM Quick tab dialog and Variable selection.

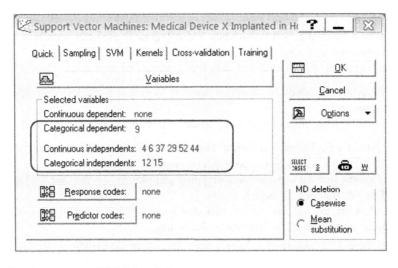

FIGURE O.26 Variables selected appear on the SVM dialog window.

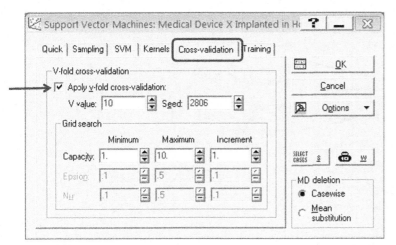

FIGURE O.27   Window after selecting Cross-validation tab.

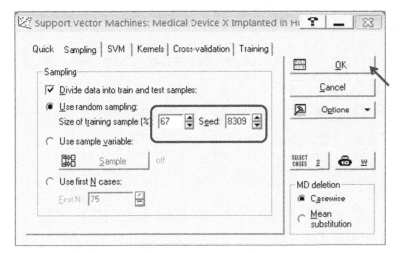

FIGURE O.28   Sampling tab with Sample % and Seed changed.

The Results are shown in Figure O.29. As you can see, the Train accuracy and Test accuracy are very close.

- Although the accuracy rates between the Training and Testing results are *comparable*, we would still like to see if we can tweak the model and find a *better* Overall accuracy rate — one that is closer to the results we obtained when we ran DMRecipe.
- In DMRecipe, the accuracy rate was 91.9% for SVM. The Overall accuracy rate is 82.2% under this initial Interactive SVM run.
- Close the Results window by click the white cross in the upper right corner.

You will now be returned to the SVM Quick tab dialog window as shown in Figure O.30.

Let's now click on the Kernels tab. The window shown in Figure O.31 will appear. Under Kernel type, check Polynomial in place of the default RBF option.

- Our data may follow a curve or non-linear pattern. A polynomial-based SVM model may capture this pattern from our data more effectively than linear options.
- Click OK to run the model again.

The new results are shown in Figure O.32. As you can see, the Train accuracy and Test accuracy rates have improved quite noticeably over our initial results. In addition, the Overall accuracy rate of 86.1% is closer to our DMRecipe result using the SVM model, which was 91.9%.

The Train and Test accuracy rates are reasonably close. This provides a strong indication that we have a good model.

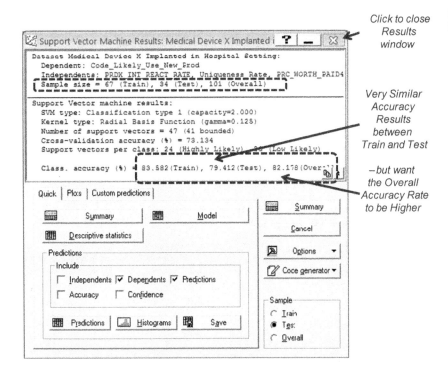

Click to close Results window

FIGURE O.29 Results for initial interactive SVM run.

Very Similar Accuracy Results between Train and Test

—but want the Overall Accuracy Rate to be Higher

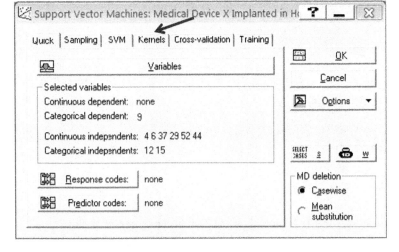

FIGURE O.30 Return to SVM Quick tab dialog window.

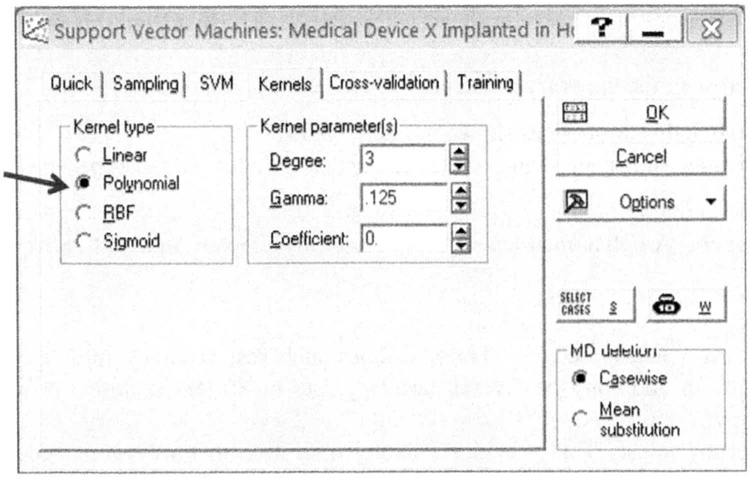

FIGURE O.31 Change Kernel type to polynomial.

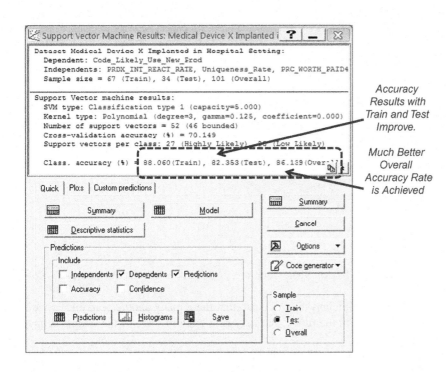

FIGURE O.32 Results for second interactive SVM run with Polynomial Kernel type.

Accuracy Results with Train and Test Improve.

Much Better Overall Accuracy Rate is Achieved

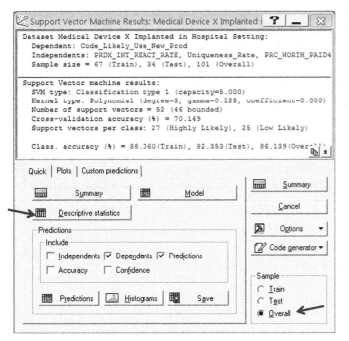

FIGURE O.33 Look at additional results for second interactive SVM.

Let's look at one more output report from these results.

First, select Overall in the Sample box located on bottom right. By selecting Overall we review the combined results from both the Training and Testing samples. Next, click the "Descriptive statistics" button, as shown in Figure O.33.

After the Descriptive statistics button is clicked, a Summary workbook will appear. Click on the report title Classification summary, and see the results shown in Figure O.34.

This report shows how well the predictive model performs at predicting the two outcomes for Product X — *Highly Likely to Use* versus *Low Likelihood to Use* among clinicians. The model does remarkably well at predicting clinicians that are *Highly Likely to Use* the new Product X.

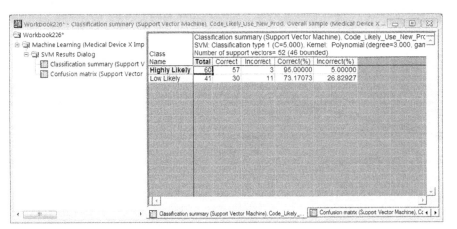

FIGURE O.34 Classification summary report for second interactive SVM.

- Of the 60 known *Likely Users*, the model predicted 57, or 95%, accurately. Likewise, the model predicted *Low Likelihood User* with 73.2% accuracy.
- This lower accuracy rate among the *Low Likelihood* clinicians may indicate that there many another variable or variables that could be considered and added to the model in the future that may help explain some of the unique behavior associated with this customer segment.
  - We would probably need to talk with some of the "experts" within the company designing Product X.
  - Their insights and knowledge about the product class and competitive environment may help us add and test additional variables across the various model algorithms.

Nevertheless, the overall model results does provide us a sense of satisfaction that were are predicting the *Most Likely Users* of new Product X with exceptional accuracy, and that we are still predicting *Unlikely Users* with much more considerable accuracy over simple random guessing (i.e., akin to "flipping a coin" and being right 50% of the time and wrong 50% of the time).

Obviously other factors will also impact the successful launch of a new product with clinicians that are beyond what the model can easily predict based on current information. Some factors that could aid or hinder success include regulatory changes from the FDA, new competitive products, technological changes, distribution issues, and promotional efforts put in place to create brand awareness, to name a few.

However, the approaches highlighted in this tutorial do indicate that developing a predictive model can offer this particular medical device company the ability to pinpoint potential future *Users of Product X* — thereby increasing and maximizing sales and customer targeting opportunities while minimizing promotional costs on customers that are *Not Likely Users (at least initially)* of the new product.

Tutorial P

Using Neural Network Analysis to Assist in Classifying Neuropsychological Data

Ronald Mellado Miller, Zachary W. Rupp, Amy Junghyun Lee, and John Meyers

INTRODUCTION

For this tutorial, the data file "combined rf 1b1.sta" is used. These data were originally analyzed in an article published in *Applied Neuropsychology*: *Adult* (Meyers *et al.*, 2014).

In order to create an algorithm through an artificial neural network (ANN), the "combined rf 1b1" data file is used. This file contains data on 246 individuals who were diagnosed with one of the following, PTSD, TBI, depression, anxiety, or post-concussion syndrome (PCS), including invalid or normal controls. In these data, those diagnoses are divided into the following four different groups: Malingering (invalid), PTSD, TBI, and Other (depression, anxiety, and PCS). The algorithm performs pattern analysis matching (PAM) functions which can analyze a patient's data and classify that patient into the most appropriate group.

EXAMINING THE DATA

Open Statistica with the "combined rf 1b1" data file (Figure P.1).

Click on the Statistics tab at the top (Figure P.2).

Click on Neural Nets (Figure P.3).

A new window will pop up, with SANN at the top. Click the button marked Classification, and then press OK (Figure P.4).

The window will then change (Figure P.5). Click on Variables.

A window (Figure P.6) will come up requesting variables for analysis. Input dependent variables as the "Categorical target" by either entering the number as 86 or clicking on Variable 86. Do the same for the independent variables under "Continuous inputs"; these are Variables 1−85. These variables represent data collected from the neuropsychological tests found in the Minnesota Multiphasic Personality Inventory, Second Edition, Restructured Form (MMPI-2-RF) and the Meyers Neuropsychological Battery (MNB). Once the variables have been selected, press "OK."

The SANN window will be visible again, but now with the selected variables. Now, click on the "Sampling (CNN and ANS)" tab (Figure P.7).

Set Train (%) to 80 and Validation (%) to 20 (Figure P.8). Use these same values to set the Subsampling percentages. Then click OK.

The window will change, showing you the screen in Figure P.9.

Set "Networks to train" to 200 (Figure P.10).

We also used the default weight decay parameters for both the hidden and output layers (Figure P.11).

Practical Predictive Analytics and Decisioning Systems for Medicine. DOI: http://dx.doi.org/10.1016/B978-0-12-411643-6.00033-8

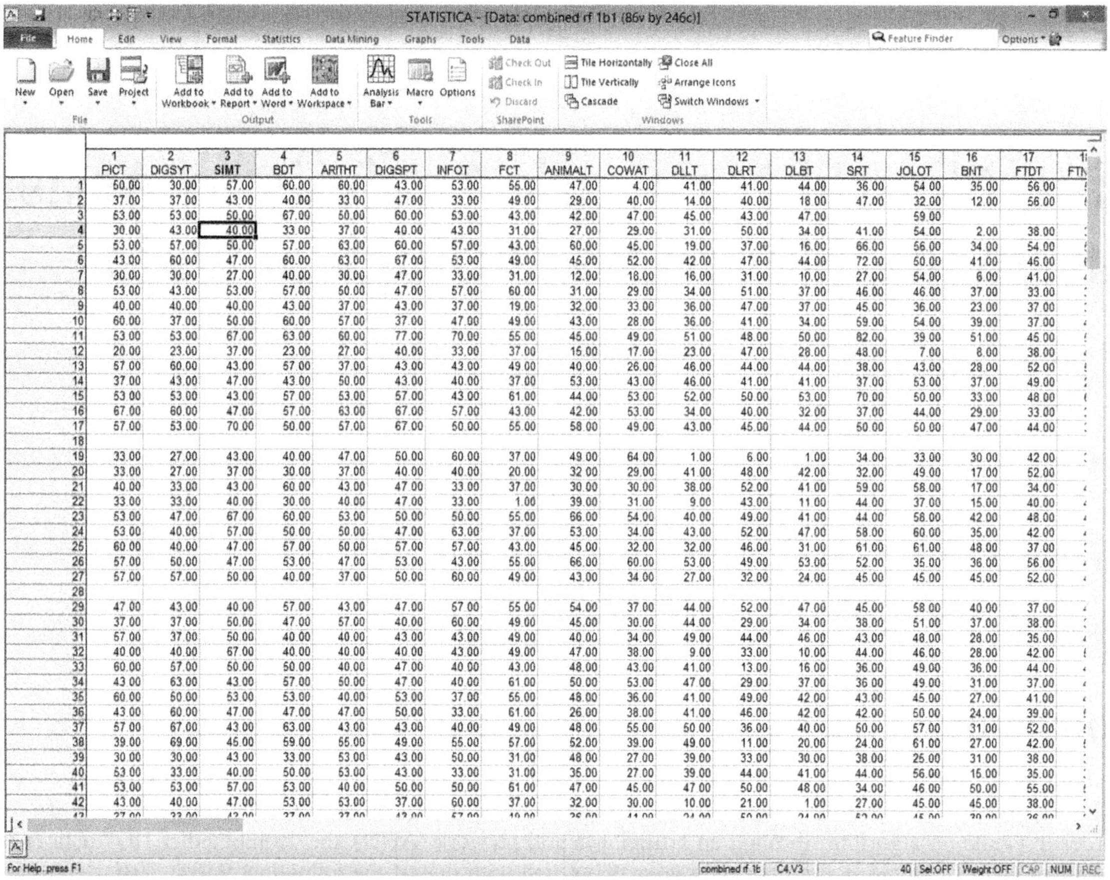

FIGURE P.1   Snapshot of part of the dataset showing format.

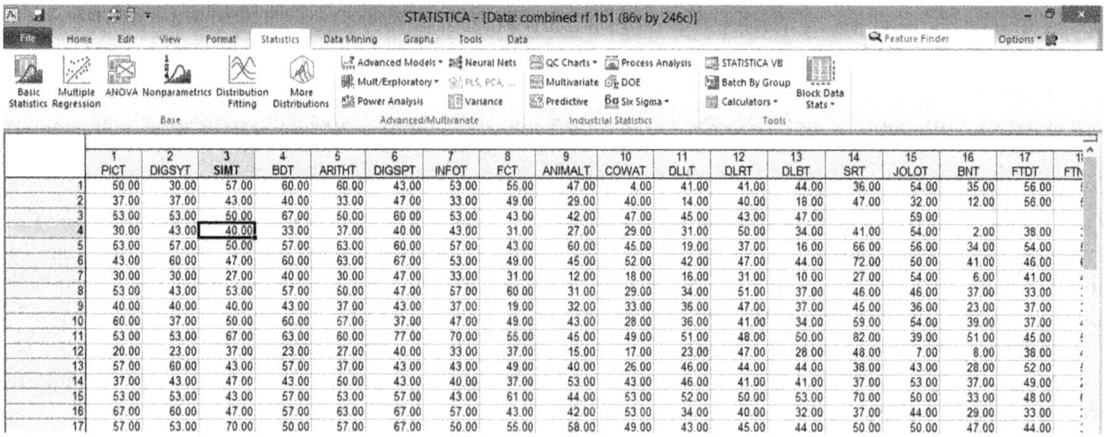

FIGURE P.2   Click on the 'Statistics' tab at the top to find the procedure needed.

STATISTICA - [Data: combined rf 1b1 (86v b

| | Home | Edit | View | Format | Statistics | Data Mining | Graphs | Tools | Data |

Multiple Regression | ANOVA | Nonparametrics | Distribution Fitting | More Distributions

Base

Advanced Models ▾ | Neural Nets | QC Charts ▾ | Process
Mult/Exploratory ▾ | PLS, PCA, ... | Multivariate | DOE
Power Analysis | Variance | Predictive | Six Sign

Advanced/Multivariate | Industrial Statistics

Neural Networks
Starts up Advanced Neural Networks

	1 PICT	2 DIGSYT	3 SIMT	4 BDT	5 ARITHT	6 DIGSPT	IN			T
1	50.00	30.00	57.00	60.00	60.00	43.00	53.00	55.00	47.00	4.00
2	37.00	37.00	43.00	40.00	33.00	47.00	33.00	49.00	29.00	40.00
3	53.00	53.00	50.00	67.00	50.00	60.00	53.00	43.00	42.00	47.00
4	30.00	43.00	40.00	33.00	37.00	40.00	43.00	31.00	27.00	29.00
5	53.00	57.00	50.00	57.00	63.00	60.00	57.00	43.00	60.00	45.00
6	43.00	60.00	47.00	60.00	63.00	67.00	53.00	49.00	45.00	52.00
7	30.00	30.00	27.00	40.00	30.00	47.00	33.00	31.00	12.00	18.00
8	53.00	43.00	53.00	57.00	50.00	47.00	57.00	60.00	31.00	29.00
9	40.00	40.00	40.00	43.00	37.00	43.00	37.00	19.00	32.00	33.00
10	60.00	37.00	50.00	60.00	57.00	37.00	47.00	49.00	43.00	28.00
11	53.00	53.00	67.00	63.00	60.00	77.00	70.00	55.00	45.00	49.00
12	20.00	23.00	37.00	23.00	27.00	40.00	33.00	37.00	15.00	17.00
13	57.00	60.00	43.00	57.00	37.00	43.00	43.00	49.00	40.00	26.00
14	37.00	43.00	47.00	43.00	50.00	43.00	40.00	37.00	53.00	43.00
15	53.00	53.00	43.00	57.00	53.00	57.00	43.00	61.00	44.00	53.00
16	67.00	60.00	47.00	57.00	63.00	67.00	57.00	43.00	42.00	53.00
17	57.00	53.00	70.00	50.00	57.00	67.00	50.00	55.00	58.00	49.00

FIGURE P.3   Neural Nets is selected (see top right of illustration above).

43.00	40.00	33.00	37.00	40.00	43.00	31.00	27.00	29.00	31.00	50.00	34.00	41.00
57.00	50.00	57.00	63.00	60.00	57.00	43.00	60.00	45.00	19.00	37.00	16.00	66.00
60.00	47.00	60.00	63.00	67.00	53.00	49.00	45.00	52.00	42.00	47.00	44.00	72.00
30.00	27.00	40.00	30.00	47.00	33.00	31.00	12.00	18.00	16.00	31.00	10.00	27.00
43.00	53.00	57.00	50.00	47.00	57.00	60.00	31.00	29.00	34.00	51.00	37.00	46.00

SANN - New Analysis/Deployment: combined rf 1b1

New analysis/Deployment

Deployment
○ Deploy models from previous analyses
Load network files

| File name | Net. ID | Net. name | Hidden act. | Output act. |

PMML file list

New analysis
● New analysis

- Regression
- Classification
- Time series (regression)
- Time series (classification)
- Cluster analysis

Select an analysis type from the list above to start a new analysis. To deploy models from previous analyses, use the deployment option.

OK
Cancel
Options ▾
Open Data

43.00	40.00	57.00	43.00	47.00	57.00	55.00	54.00	37.00	44.00	52.00	47.00	45.00
37.00	50.00	47.00	57.00	40.00	60.00	49.00	45.00	30.00	44.00	29.00	34.00	38.00
37.00	50.00	40.00	40.00	43.00	43.00	49.00	40.00	34.00	49.00	44.00	46.00	43.00
40.00	67.00	40.00	40.00	40.00	43.00	49.00	47.00	38.00	9.00	33.00	10.00	44.00
57.00	50.00	50.00	40.00	47.00	40.00	43.00	48.00	43.00	41.00	13.00	16.00	36.00

FIGURE P.4   Select classification, and then click OK.

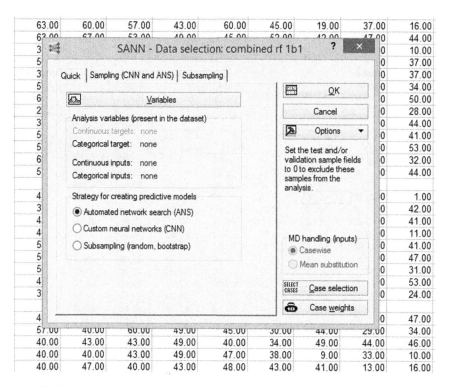

FIGURE P.5   Select the 'variables' button.

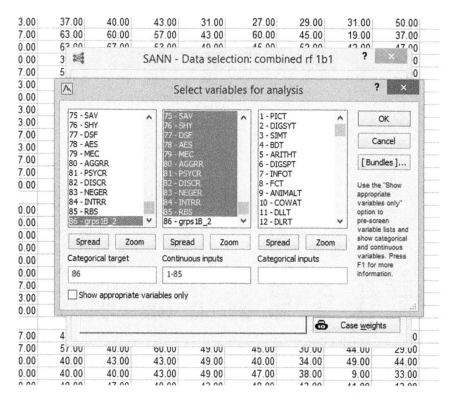

FIGURE P.6   Select variables, as illustrated above.

| 63.00 | 60.00 | 57.00 | 43.00 | 60.00 | 45.00 | 19.00 | 37.00 | 16. |

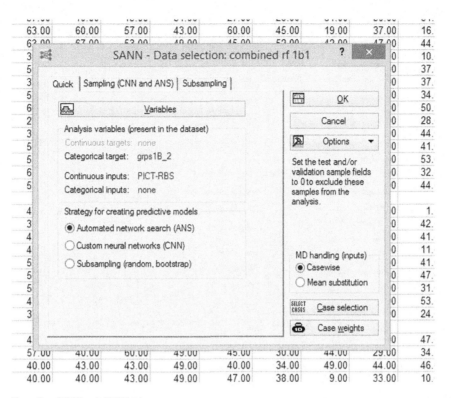

FIGURE P.7 Click on 'Sampling (CNN and ANS)' tab.

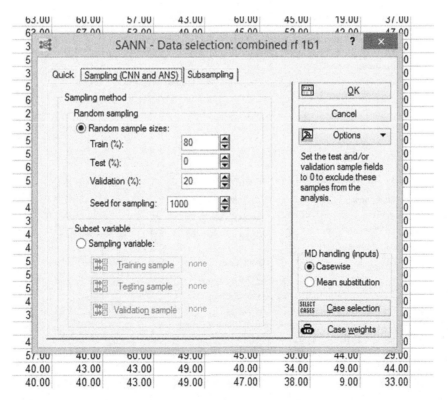

FIGURE P.8 Set Train to 80% and Validation to 20%.

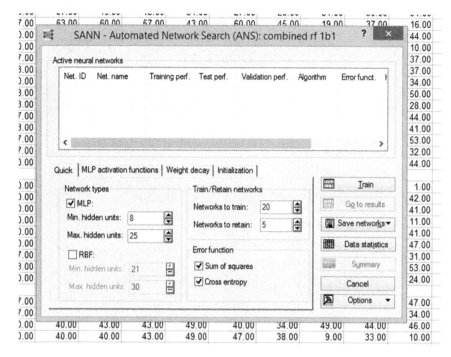

FIGURE P.9 The new screen that appears after performing the actions in Figure P.8 and clicking OK.

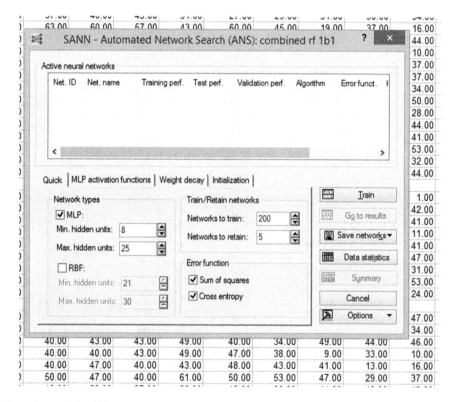

FIGURE P.10 Set 'Networks to train' to 200.

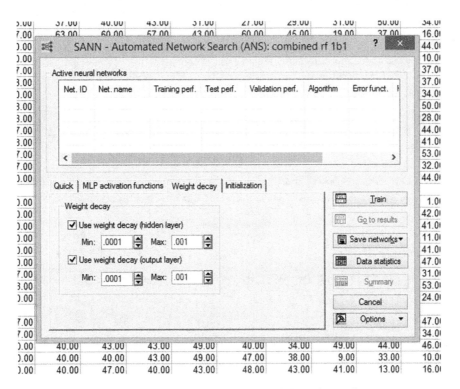

FIGURE P.11   The 'Weight decay' is left at the default, as shown here, for both the hidden and output layers.

Then click Train.

STATISTICA will now begin to build the neural network (Figure P.12).

Once the neural network is completed, the screen in Figure P.13 will appear. As neural networks capitalize on chance, these (and your) results may be different from those we originally published.

Click on "Save networks" and then on C/C++ (Figure P.14).

As shown in Figure P.15, at the top, under "Active neural networks," the best algorithms are listed. The higher the Validation performance and Training performance, the better the algorithm is. In this situation, Net. ID 3 (or in other words the third algorithm) is chosen because it has the highest validity. We also took the previously saved C++ file for this algorithm and made an executable file from it.

From now on, we will also be using the "100 subjectsb.sta" data file. It includes data on 100 individuals who were not part of the original data set.

Click on the Custom predictions tab, change the "Number of cases to predict" from 1 to 100, and then click on Custom inputs (Figure P.16).

The window in Figure P.17 will appear. At this point, copy the data for the 100 subjects and then paste them into the window. In our study we were able to simply use the C++ code, which was made into an executable file for this part of the study.

Once the 100 cases have been put in, click "OK" (Figure P.18).

The window shown in Figure P.19 will appear. At this point click on "Custom predictions."

This will then give you the group classifications according to the top five algorithms the neural network created (Figure P.20). So, in our case, we would examine the third algorithm to see what groups the neural network would classify the individuals into according to their data. The algorithm is able to classify them by inserting the data collected from their neuropsychological tests into the neural network that was trained using the 246 cases. Using the trained neural network, it is possible to derive whether or not a particular case should be classified as TBI, PTSD, MAL (malingerer), or OTHER.

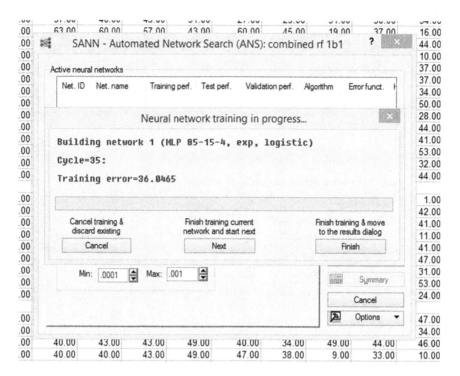

FIGURE P.12   STATISTICA is building the Neural Networks model.

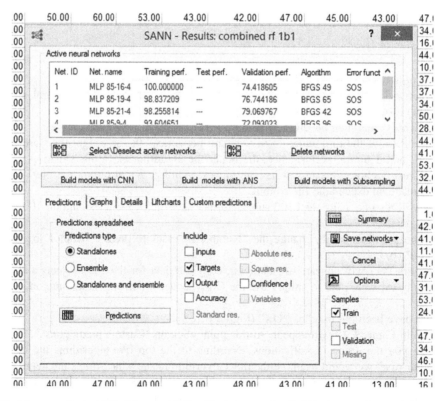

FIGURE P.13   Model building completed with the 5 best models listed in the top panel, called 'Active neural networks'.

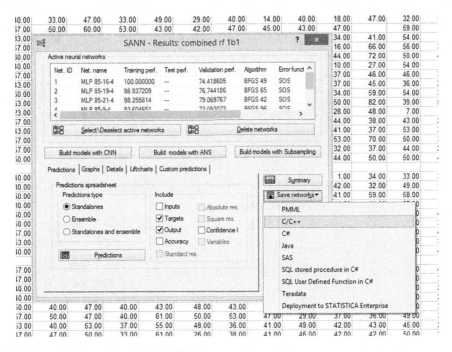

40.00	33.00	47.00	33.00	49.00	29.00	40.00	14.00	40.00	18.00	47.00	32.00
37.00	50.00	60.00	53.00	43.00	42.00	47.00	45.00	43.00	47.00		59.00
33.00									34.00	41.00	54.00
57.00									16.00	66.00	56.00
50.00									44.00	72.00	50.00
40.00									10.00	27.00	54.00
57.00									37.00	46.00	46.00
13.00									37.00	45.00	36.00
50.00									34.00	59.00	54.00
53.00									50.00	82.00	39.00
23.00									28.00	48.00	7.00
57.00									44.00	38.00	43.00
13.00									41.00	37.00	53.00
57.00									53.00	70.00	50.00
57.00									32.00	37.00	44.00
50.00									44.00	50.00	50.00
40.00											
30.00									1.00	34.00	33.00
50.00									42.00	32.00	49.00
30.00									41.00	59.00	58.00
50.00											
50.00											
57.00											
53.00											
40.00											
57.00											
17.00											
40.00											
40.00											
50.00	40.00	47.00	40.00	43.00	48.00	43.00					
57.00	50.00	47.00	40.00	61.00	50.00	53.00	47.00	29.00	37.00	36.00	49.00
53.00	40.00	53.00	37.00	55.00	48.00	36.00	41.00	49.00	42.00	43.00	45.00
17.00	47.00	50.00	33.00	61.00	26.00	38.00	41.00	46.00	42.00	42.00	50.00

FIGURE P.14   Click on 'Save networks', and then click on C/C++.

SANN - Results: combined rf 1b1   ?   ×

Active neural networks

Net. ID	Net. name	Training perf.	Test perf.	Validation perf.	Algorithm	Error funct
1	MLP 85-16-4	100.000000	---	74.418605	BFGS 49	SOS
2	MLP 85-19-4	98.837209	---	76.744186	BFGS 65	SOS
3	MLP 85-21-4	98.255814	---	79.069767	BFGS 42	SOS
4	MLP 85-9-4	93.604651	---	72.093023	BFGS 96	SOS

Select\Deselect active networks   Delete networks

FIGURE P.15   The best Neural Networks are shown in this box of the dialog.

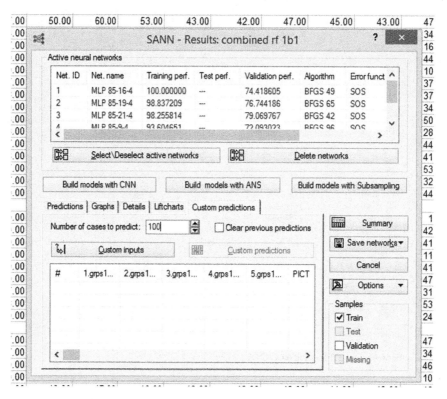

FIGURE P.16 Click on 'Custom predictors' tab (in center of above dialog), then change 'Number of cases to predict' from 1 to 100, and then click on 'Custom inputs'.

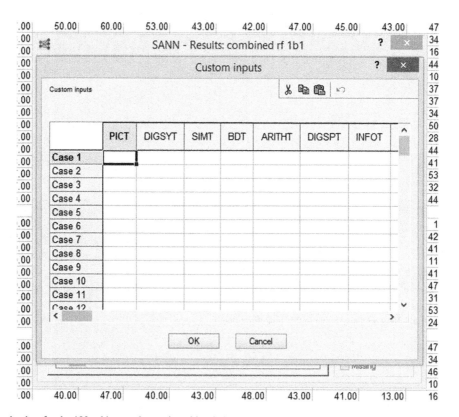

FIGURE P.17 Copy the data for the 100 subjects and paste into this window.

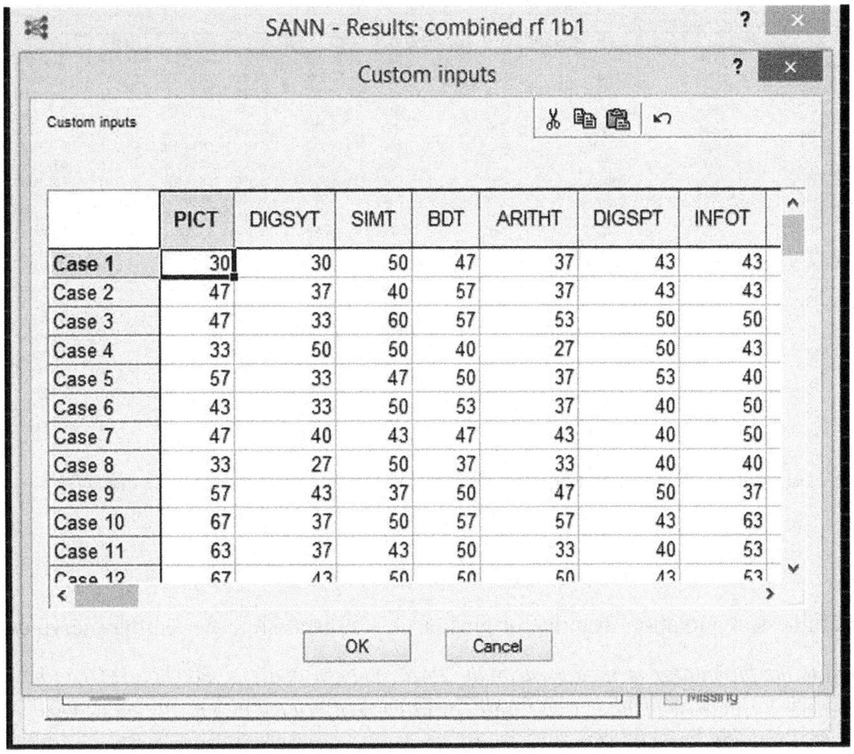

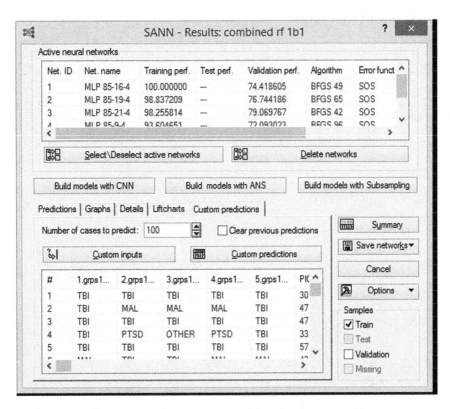

FIGURE P.18 After the data is pasted in (as illustrated above) click 'OK' to accept.

FIGURE P.19 Click 'Custom predictions' (middle to lower right in above dialog screen).

Custom predictions spreadsheet (combined rf 1b1)

Cases	1.grps1B_2_(t)	2.grps1B_2_(t)	3.grps1B_2_(t)	4.grps1B_2_(t)	5.grps1B_2_(t)	PICT	DIGSYT	SIMT	BDT	ARITHT	DIGSPT	INFOT
1	TBI	TBI	TBI	TBI	TBI	30.00000	30.00000	50.00000	47.00000	37.00000	43.00000	43.000
2	TBI	MAL	MAL	MAL	TBI	47.00000	37.00000	40.00000	57.00000	37.00000	43.00000	43.000
3	TBI	TBI	TBI	TBI	TBI	47.00000	33.00000	60.00000	57.00000	53.00000	50.00000	50.000
4	TBI	PTSD	OTHER	PTSD	TBI	33.00000	50.00000	50.00000	40.00000	27.00000	50.00000	43.000
5	TBI	TBI	TBI	TBI	TBI	57.00000	33.00000	47.00000	50.00000	37.00000	53.00000	40.000
6	MAL	TBI	TBI	MAL	MAL	43.00000	33.00000	50.00000	53.00000	37.00000	40.00000	50.000
7	TBI	TBI	TBI	TBI	TBI	47.00000	40.00000	43.00000	47.00000	43.00000	40.00000	50.000
8	TBI	TBI	OTHER	TBI	TBI	33.00000	27.00000	50.00000	37.00000	33.00000	40.00000	40.000
9	TBI	TBI	TBI	TBI	TBI	57.00000	43.00000	37.00000	50.00000	47.00000	50.00000	37.000
10	TBI	OTHER	OTHER	OTHER	TBI	67.00000	37.00000	50.00000	57.00000	57.00000	43.00000	63.000
11	TBI	TBI	TBI	TBI	TBI	63.00000	37.00000	43.00000	50.00000	33.00000	40.00000	53.000
12	TBI	TBI	TBI	TBI	TBI	67.00000	43.00000	50.00000	50.00000	50.00000	43.00000	53.000
13	OTHER	TBI	OTHER	OTHER	OTHER	67.00000	37.00000	43.00000	63.00000	57.00000	47.00000	50.000
14	TBI	OTHER	OTHER	TBI	TBI	47.00000	43.00000	57.00000	77.00000	67.00000	47.00000	60.000
15	TBI	TBI	TBI	TBI	TBI	43.00000	43.00000	50.00000	63.00000	50.00000	43.00000	50.000
16						43.00000	43.00000	50.00000	53.00000	50.00000	37.00000	37.000
17	OTHER	OTHER	OTHER	TBI	OTHER	43.00000	30.00000	33.00000	50.00000	40.00000	50.00000	37.000
18	TBI	TBI	TBI	TBI	TBI	57.00000	47.00000	50.00000	53.00000	60.00000	63.00000	47.000
19						53.00000	37.00000	47.00000	47.00000	37.00000	43.00000	50.000
20	TBI	TBI	TBI	TBI	TBI	43.00000	40.00000	50.00000	43.00000	50.00000	43.00000	53.000
21	TBI	TBI	TBI	OTHER	TBI	33.00000	37.00000	50.00000	53.00000	47.00000	43.00000	43.000
22	OTHER	TBI	TBI	OTHER	TBI	57.00000	47.00000	53.00000	50.00000	50.00000	57.00000	57.000

FIGURE P.20 The group classifications for the top five NN algorithms that the NN modeling produced are displayed.

In terms of its usefulness, a quotation from the original article's discussion section may serve us well here:

The question, "What is the formula or method used by the PAM [pattern analysis matching]?" can be asked; however, the answer is not an easy one for those unfamiliar with PAM. The formula, if printed in 8-point font is about 28 pages long, and is not a method that is easily usable by a clinician.

The results of this study indicate that a PAM is capable of making reliable classifications consistent with clinician judgment. Of course, the use of the PAM model does not remove ultimate diagnostic responsibility from the clinician. The PAM must be used in conjunction with clinical judgment; however, the use of the PAM model will help improve the consistency and accuracy of the clinician for the targeted diagnostic groups. The clinician could think of the PAM as a "second opinion" or as another factor to be included in clinical judgment. It seems clear that the PAM is a valuable clinical tool.

(Meyers *et al.*, 2014).

REFERENCE

Meyers, J.E., Miller, R.M., Tuita, A.R., 2014. Using pattern analysis matching to differentiate TBI and PTSD in a military sample. Appl. Neuropsychol. Adult. 21, 60–68.

Tutorial Q

Developing Interactive Decision Trees Using Inpatient Claims (with SAS Enterprise Miner)

Ralph Winters, BA, BS

Chapter Outline

ABOUT DECISION TREES

Decision trees are powerful and popular tools for classification and prediction. They enjoy popularity in the data science and healthcare communities since they can be presented visually, and can be explained in terms of a set of simple, logical, decision rules, which are easy to explain. The process of finding the optimal set of decision rules is referred to as *training* the data. This is accomplished by looking at each category of a tree (known as a *node)*, and then attempting to break (*split*) each category into two or more disparate groups. This methodology is not unlike playing the game Animal, Vegetable, Mineral, in which we try to develop a taxonomy for the data by defining the characteristics of the data and comparing them to one another.

Decision trees need historical outcome data, which are then trained to show the best decision path to take to achieve specified outcomes. The outcome variables are also known as the *target variables*.

In health care, the target variable can take on many values — for example, from whether or not a patient develops Parkinson's disease, to identifying which combination of symptoms can ultimately result in the highest payment

Practical Predictive Analytics and Decisioning Systems for Medicine. DOI: http://dx.doi.org/10.1016/B978-0-12-411643-6.00034-X

category for a health insurer. Other examples, such as identifying patients at high risk for certain medical conditions before major problems arise, are desirable goals, with a result being the offering of preventive healthcare services before adverse outcomes occur.

In the course of developing the decision rules, we set aside a separate set of data which is used as a control (or *validation*) data set. By applying the discovered decision rules to the validation data set, we assess the model in order to determine its power and stability.

In Enterprise Miner, trees can be developed in two ways. The first is the *automatic* mode. In this mode, the modeler first sets the parameters (which input variables are used, what the outcome variables are, how complex or simple the model is, etc.) and then the program automatically calculates the best decision tree model. This makes for quick model building. However, a major drawback is that there is less opportunity for manual knowledge and discovery. An automatic model has no real domain knowledge. Additionally, automatic models tend to steer modelers in certain directions. In the *interactive* mode, the modeler has more control over model construction through trial and error, and is more involved in the development of the model. In this tutorial we will show model development using both methods.

For those who need a refresher in decision tree terms, SAS has supplied a glossary (http://support.sas.com/documentation/cdl/en/emgsj/62040/HTML/default/viewer.htm#titlepage.htm).

ABOUT SAS© ENTERPRISE MINER

Enterprise Miner is SAS Institute's product for data mining across a variety of industries, including health care. It consists of a graphical user interface which allows for the development and assessment of models using building blocks. In addition to decision trees, Enterprise Miner can also build regression models, neural network models, and many others. It also encourages model building using a methodology referred to as SEMMA (www.sas.com/offices/europe/uk/technologies/analytics/datamining/miner/semma.html). The product runs under Windows, and is available in a desktop version as well. Enterprise Miner requires that base SAS and SAS/STAT be installed.

Versions of Enterprise Miner

This tutorial will assume that you are running Enterprise Miner version 6.2 in client/server mode. In this case, all projects are stored on the Enterprise Miner server. If you are unable to write to this location, ask your system administrator to configure the library location and access permission to the data.

If you are running Enterprise Miner in local or desktop mode, or if you are running another version of the software, your steps may be different and your results may vary slightly from the results in the tutorial. However, the overall methodology will be the same.

DATA FILE DESCRIPTION

The data used for this tutorial are from the BSA Inpatient Claims PUF file, which can be obtained from the Centers for Medicaid and Medicare Services(CMS) government site (www.cms.gov/Research-Statistics-Data-and-Systems/Statistics-Trends-and-Reports/BSAPUFS/index.html).

The tutorial sample file contains a 5% sample of 2008 Medicare inpatient claims (Table Q.1). This file has been enhanced by:

- The addition of English name descriptions for each of the codes in the file (all variables ending in _NM).
- Addition of the major diagnostic code name for each of the DRGs (Variable 14).
- Addition of the Service Intensity Weight (SIW variable 17), which was obtained via the NYS government site (www.health.ny.gov/faciliti + es/hospital/drg/).
- Purging observations with missing variables (NA) from the file.

The data have been aggregated by assigning a weight variable to each unique combination of variables in the file. For example, Variable 19, Wt, is a calculated variable which represents the number of claims for each combination of variables 1−17. drgcount (Variable 18) is calculated similarly. The purpose of these variables is to reduce the size of the analysis data set.

Target Variable

The target variable is the variable for which we desire a prediction. For this tutorial, the goal will be to predict the Payment category (Variable 13). CMS has ranked the payments for each claim into five equally spaced payment

TABLE Q.1 Tutorial Sample File*

		Import file list of variables		
#	Variable	Type	Len	Description
1	BENE_AGE_CAT_CD	Num	8	Beneficiary Age category code
2	BENE_AGE_CAT_CD_NM	Char	10	Beneficiary Age category name
3	BENE_SEX_IDENT_CD	Num	8	Beneficiary gender code
4	BENE_SEX_IDENT_CD_NM	Char	1	Beneficiary gender name
5	DrgDesc	Char	128	DRG Description
6	IP_CLM_BASE_DRG_CD	Num	8	Base DRG code
7	IP_CLM_BASE_DRG_CD_NM	Char	67	Base DRG Name
8	IP_CLM_DAYS_CD	Num	8	Inpatient days code
9	IP_CLM_DAYS_CD_NM	Char	14	Inpatient days category name
10	IP_CLM_ICD9_PRCDR_CD	Char	2	ICD9 primary procedure code
11	IP_CLM_ICD9_PRCDR_CD_NM	Char	30	ICD9 primary procedure name
12	IP_DRG_QUINT_PMT_AVG	Num	8	DRG quintile average payment amount
13	IP_DRG_QUINT_PMT_CD	Char	1	DRG quintile payment amount code
14	MDC	Char	3	Major Diagnosis Code
15	MdcDesc	Char	60	Major Diagnosis Code Description
16	MedSurg	Char	4	Medical or Surgical
17	SIW	Num	8	Service Intensity Weight
18	drgcount	Num	8	Number of unique DRGs (Calculated)
19	Wt	Num	8	Weight Factor (Calculated)

Disclaimer: This file has been constructed from merging data from several reliable public government sources. It is intended for demonstration purposes only.

categories (quintiles), with 1 being the lowest payment category for the claim type and 5 being the highest. The hospital administrator may be interested in seeing how payment categories break out, as expressed as a set of decision rules. This will help in allocating future resources.

CREATING A NEW PROJECT

Start Enterprise Miner. Begin by clicking New Project in the Welcome to Enterprise Miner window. Press "Next" after each instruction (Figure Q.1).

After the New Project has been created, notice that the right side of the window is blank (Figure Q.2). This is where we will construct diagrams which will contain process flows. Process flows are the building blocks for our model building, and consist of data sources, tasks, and outputs.

Start by creating a New Diagram, as outlined in Figure Q.3.

THE ENTERPRISE MINER TOOLBAR

The Enterprise Miner toolbar is located at the top left of the process flow diagram (Figures Q.2 and Figure Q.4), and this toolbar contains all of the modeling objects that we need. The modeling objects are located as a row of icons above each of the major modeling tasks. Click on one of the modeling tabs and you will see a new set of icons. Hover your mouse over each icon to see a brief description of each.

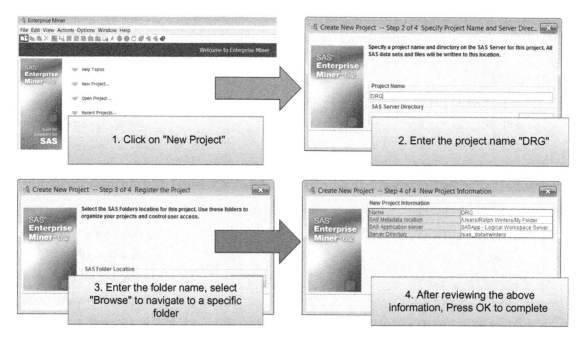

FIGURE Q.1 Creating a New Project.

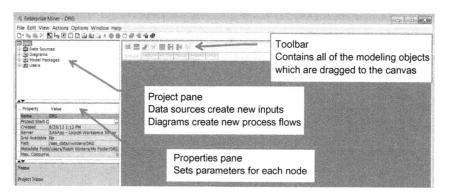

FIGURE Q.2 New Project created.

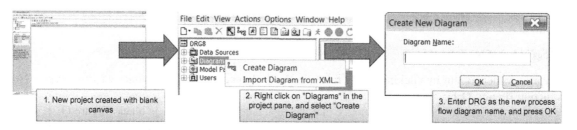

FIGURE Q.3 Creating a New Diagram.

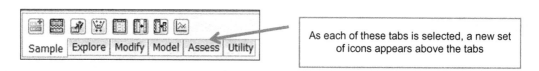

FIGURE Q.4 The Enterprise Miner toolbar.

The major modeling tasks are:

- **Sample**
- **Explore**
- **Modify**
- **Model**
- **Assess**.

These lead to the acronym SEMMA, which is an iterative methodology for data mining.

IMPORTING THE DATA FILE INTO SAS USING ENTERPRISE MINER

Refer to Figure Q.5.

- Download the sample data named "claims2.xpt" to your computer. Note the download location.
- From the Utility menu, drag a SAS Code node to a New Diagram.
- Select the SAS Code node and the Properties pane display will change. Select the Properties pane and click on the ellipsis (. . .) box to the right of the Code Editor line to open the Code Editor.
- The Training Code Window will appear. Type in the following code: proccimportinfile = "claims2.xpt" library = WORK; run;
- Make sure that the line containing "claims2.xpt" includes the correct path name within the double quotes that contains the downloaded sample file. For example, it can be something like "C:\Downloaded Files\claims2.xpt"
- Change the destination "library = " name to point to the library that will contain your Enterprise Miner Projects.
- Press the Run icon on the Training Code toolbar.
- You will receive a message in the Log that the dataset WT_BSA_INP_CLAIMS_NOMISS has been imported into the designated library (Figure Q.6).

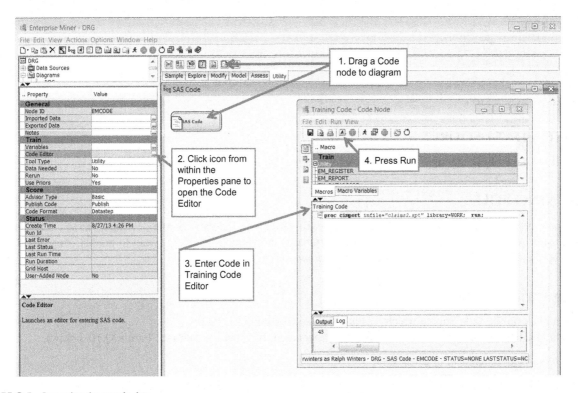

FIGURE Q.5   Importing the sample data.

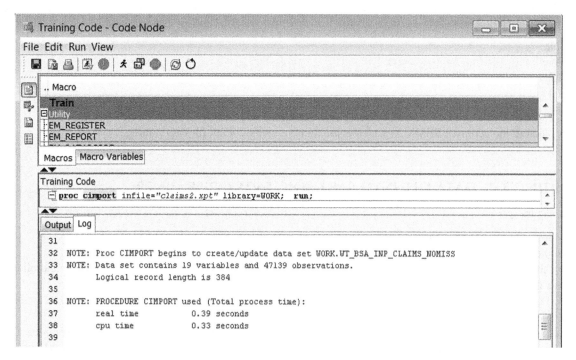

FIGURE Q.6   Code node.

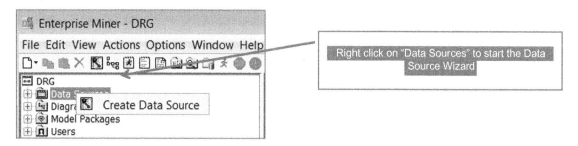

FIGURE Q.7   Create data source.

CREATE A DATA SOURCE

Now that we have physically imported some data, we can set up a data source (Figures Q.7, Q.8).

ASSIGNING ROLES

Before any model is run, we need to assign *roles* to each variable in the data. A role designates how a variable is used in the model. As previously mentioned, the target variable is the variable which we want to predict. Any other variable used to predict the target variable is referred to as an *input* variable.

Editing Variable Roles

1. Right click on the Data Source which was just created (Figure Q.9).
2. Select "Edit Variables"; the Edit Variable Roles assignment form will appear (see Figure Q.10, below).

   To change the assignment of a variable:

   Click on the "Role" column in the appropriate variable row (Figure Q.10)
   1. Assign IP_DRG_QUINT_PMT_CD as the Target Variable by clicking on the Down arrow in the "ROLE" column, and selecting "Target."
   2. Assign Variables 2, 4, 7, 9, 11, 15, and 16 as Input variables.

1. Select SAS Table as the data source, then press NEXT.

2. Enter the data set name which corresponds to the data set that we imported in Figure Q.6, line #32, and then press NEXT.

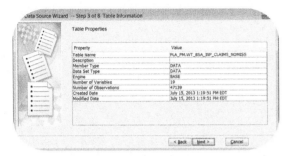

3. Verify that there are 47,139 rows and 19 variables, then press NEXT.

4. Choose the "Basic" Options, then press NEXT.

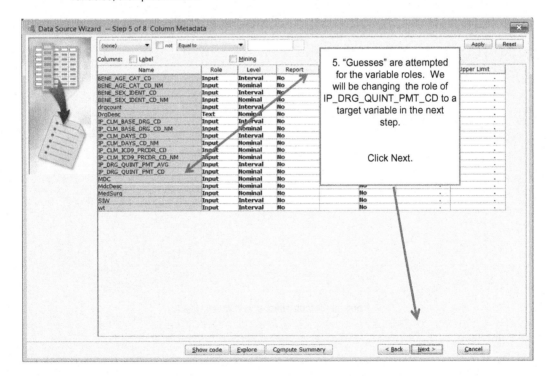

FIGURE Q.8   Setting up a data source.

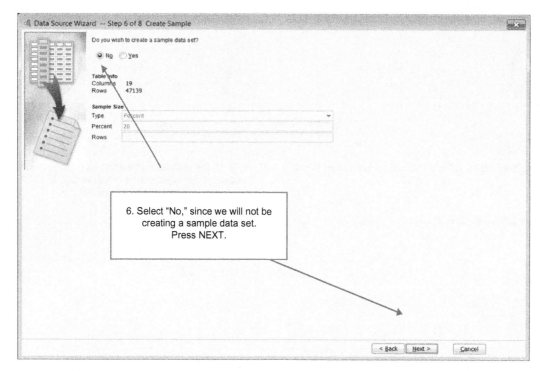

6. Select "No," since we will not be creating a sample data set.
Press NEXT.

7. Keep the default options, and press NEXT.

FIGURE Q.8 (Continued.)

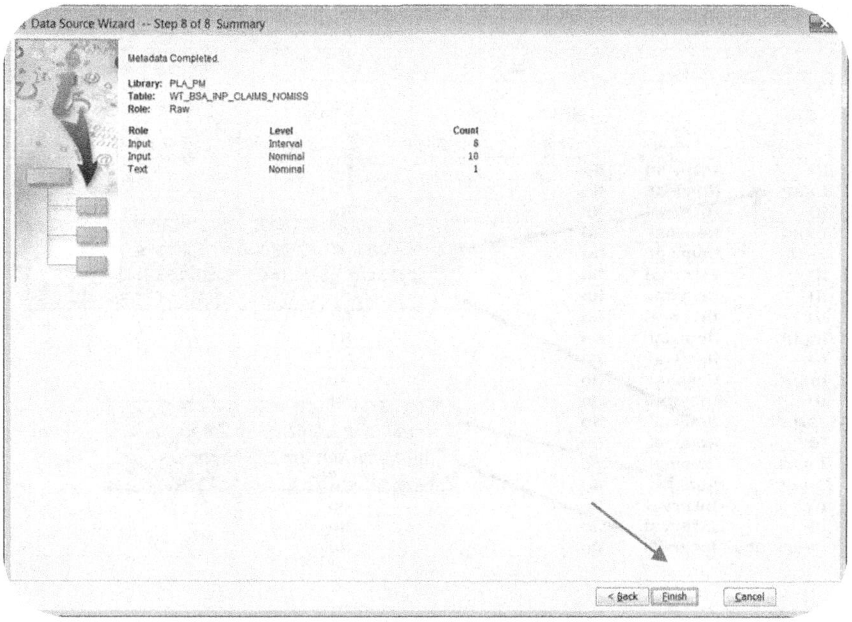

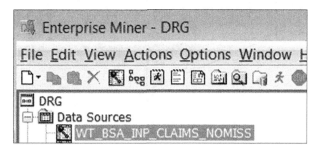

8. Press FINISH. A new Data Source will appear in the Project pane, under Data Sources (Figure Q.9).

FIGURE Q.8 (Continued.)

FIGURE Q.9 New data source created.

3. Assign wt as the Frequency Variable.
4. Assign all others to the ID Role.
5. Press the Apply button, then OK to exit.

ENTERPRISE MINER NODES

Predictive modeling in Enterprise Miner is performed by adding and connecting *nodes* to a diagram. A node is a task or process which accomplishes a particular piece of work, such as sampling the data, creating graphs, running a particular kind of model, or comparing and assessing a group of models.

READING A DATA SOURCE

Drag the Data Source that you have just set up to the process flow diagram (Figure Q.11).

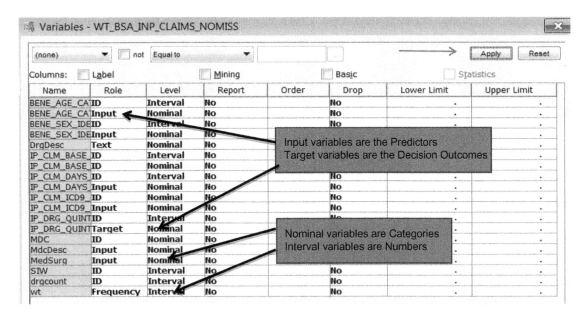

FIGURE Q.10 Edit variable roles.

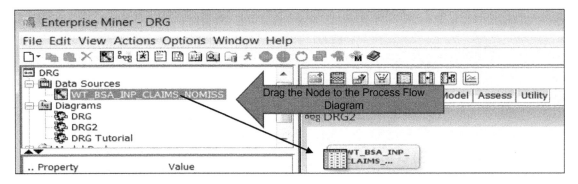

FIGURE Q.11 Reading a data source.

FIGURE Q.12 The 'StatExplore' button.

EXPLORING THE DATA

Let's explore the target variable and create some graphs.

1. Select the Explore tab in the Enterprise Miner Toolbar (Figure Q.12).
2. Drag the StatExplore node to the diagram.
3. Connect the StatExplore node to the input file by dragging the small gray rectangle to the right of the WT_BSA_INP_CLAIMS_NOMISS node to the StatExplore node. An arrow will appear which indicates that the nodes have been connected (Figure Q.13).

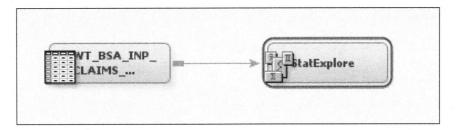

FIGURE Q.13   The StatExplore node placed in the workspace.

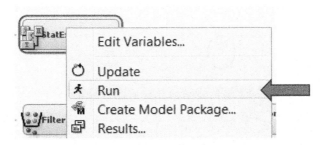

FIGURE Q.14   Click 'Run' for the StatExplore node.

FIGURE Q.15   When computations completed the symbol in the lower right corner turns into a check mark.

4. Right click on the StatExplore node, and select Run (Figure Q.14).
5. If prompted as to whether or not you want to "Run this path," choose "Yes." The node will turn green, and a star will appear in the bottom right corner of the node to indicate that it is running. It will turn into a check mark when it is completed (Figure Q.15).
6. After the Run Completion Dialog box appears, select Results. If it does not appear, right click on the StatExplore node again and select Results.
7. The results from StatExplore appear in Figure Q.16.

Three windows appear in the results window (see Figure Q.18 below):

1. The Chi-Square Plot, which measures the association between the input variables and the target variable. Higher values imply stronger associations.
2. The Variable Worth Chart, which arranges the predictive variables in order of importance.
3. The Results Output Window.

Charts 1 and 2 are in agreement. Both the Procedure Codes and the number of inpatient days have the highest bars, and are the most important predictors in determining the payment quintile.
To view the Chi-square statistics:

- Select the Chi-Square plot.
- Select Summary Statistics from the View menu.
- Select Cell Chi-Squares from the submenu (Figure Q.17).
- Figure Q.18 appears.

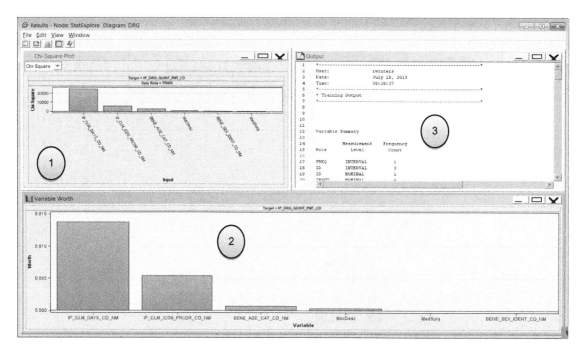

FIGURE Q.16   Results from StatExplore.

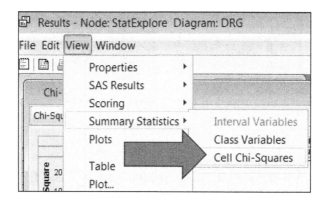

FIGURE Q.17   Selecting Cell Chi-Squares from the View Menu.

- Maximize the window, and then click on the Chi-Square column so the values are sorted in descending order.
- The rows at the top of the table show the categories with the highest association with the Target variable. (Column = "Target: Formatted Value").
- The highest associations are with the highest and lowest payment quintiles (1 = lowest and 5 = highest).
- Based upon this, we will only keep these extreme values in the model and filter out the mid-values 2, 3, and 4. We will create a model with only two outcome variables.

FILTERING THE DATA

1. Select the Sample tab from the Enterprise Miner toolbar (Figure Q.19).
2. Drag a Filter node to the diagram.
3. Connect the output of the StatExplore node to the Filter node (Figure Q.20).
4. Rearrange icons as needed (optional).
5. Select the Filter node; switch over to the Properties pane, and click on the ellipsis (. . .) in the Class Variables line (Figure Q.21).

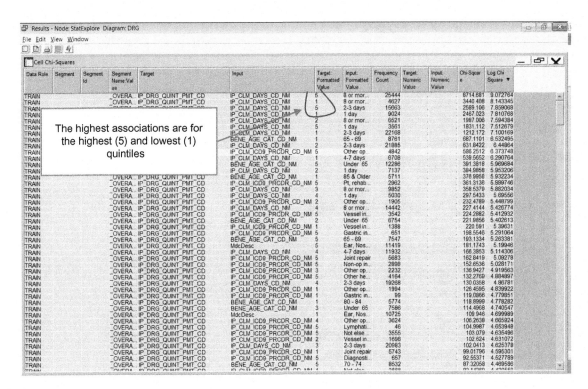

FIGURE Q.18   Cell summary Chi-square.

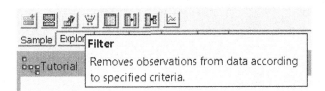

FIGURE Q.19   The sample tab in SAS-Enterprise Miner.

TIP: To "straighten out" icons display, right mouse click on any empty space on the Process Flow Diagram, select "Layout" and then choose Horizontal or Vertical Arrangement

FIGURE Q.20   Adding a filter mode.

The Interactive Class Filter appears (Figure Q.22).

1. Click Generate Summary to refresh the data. If another prompt box appears asking you if you want to continue, answer "Yes."
2. Explore each of the variables by clicking the variable in the name column, and observe the graph changing.
3. Select IP_DRG_QUINT_PMT_CD under the name column; the display shifts to show the distribution of payment codes.

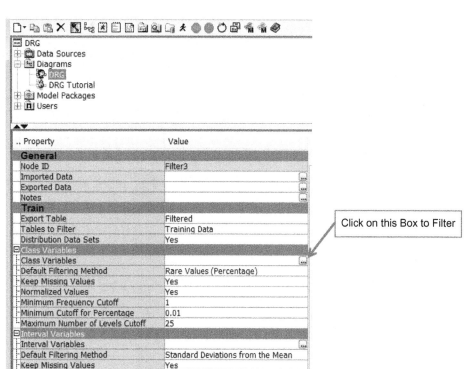

FIGURE Q.21 Properties pane for filtering.

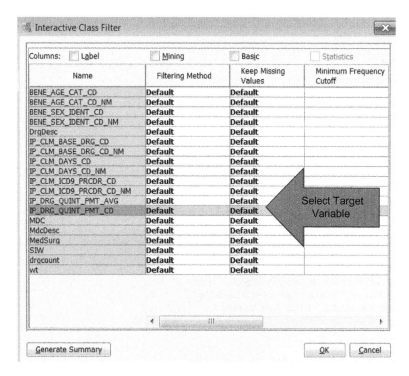

FIGURE Q.22 Interactive class filter.

4. Select "User Specified" under the "Filtering method" column (Figure Q.23). The display changes to show the frequencies for each of the five quintiles.
5. To exclude quintiles 2, 3, 4, *while holding down the CTRL key* select the bars corresponding to quintiles 2, 3, 4. Cross-lines will appear in each bar to indicate that they are excluded.

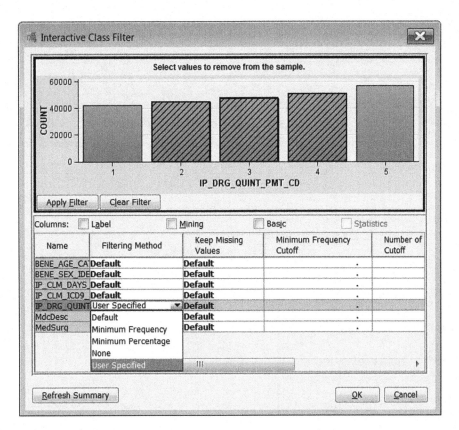

FIGURE Q.23 Filtering the quintiles.

6. Press "Apply Filter."
7. Press "OK" to exit the Interactive Class Filter and return to the diagram.
8. Right click on the Filter node, and select "Run." Answer "Yes" to any confirmation screens.

VIEWING FILTER RESULTS

After the data has been filtered, the Run Completed dialog box will appear. Select View Results. The display shows the breakdown of the excluded categories and the number of observations excluded (Figure Q.24).

PARTITIONING THE DATA

In model building, a separate validation sample is needed in order to verify that the training model is not biased. We will build a model based upon a 90% random sample of the original data, and we will reserve 10% of the data for validating the model. This is done via the Data Partition node.

Add a "Data Partition" Node

- Drag the Partition icon from the Sample tab in the toolbar and connect the output of the Filter node to the Data Partition node (Figure Q.25).
- Optional: arrange and straighten the data flow to Vertical − right click on any empty space in the flow diagram, and select Layout, and then Vertical Arrangement.

Set Values on the Properties Pane

- Set Partitioning Method to "Simple Random"
- Set Random Seed to 12345

Excluded Class Values							
Variable	Role	Level	Train Count	Train Percent	Label	Filter Method	Keep Missing Values
IP_DRG_QUINT_PMT_CD	TARGET	2	44741	18.47504	DRG qui...	MANUAL	Y
IP_DRG_QUINT_PMT_CD	TARGET	3	47408	19.57633	DRG qui...	MANUAL	Y
IP_DRG_QUINT_PMT_CD	TARGET	4	50672	20.92414	DRG qui...	MANUAL	Y

FIGURE Q.24   Excluded class values.

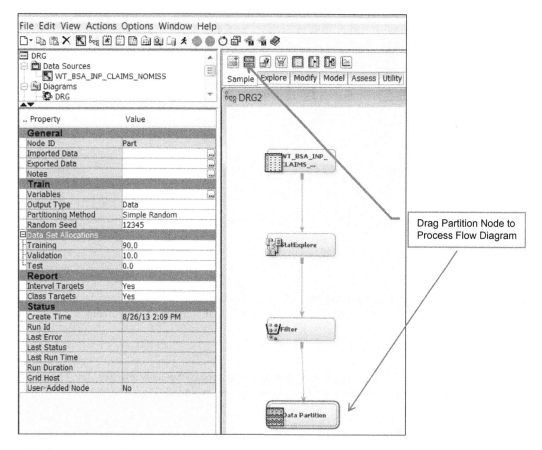

FIGURE Q.25   Adding a partition node.

- Set Training Percentage to 90.0
- Set Validation Percentage to 10.0
- Set Test Percentage to 0.0.

Run the Node

- Right click on the Data Partition node, and select Run.
- If prompted as to whether or not you want to run this node, choose "Yes."
- After the Run Completion Dialog box appears, select Results. The Results window (Figure Q.26) will display, indicating that the data have been allocated between the Training and Validation data sets. Note that "TRAIN" is approximately 90% of "DATA."
- When done, close the Results window ("X" in upper right) to return to the diagram.

Partition Summary – in Results Window

Type	Data Set	Number of Observations
DATA	EMWS.Filter3_TRAIN	19,365
TRAIN	EMWS.Part2_TRAIN	17,429
VALIDATE	EMWS.Part2_VALIDATE	1,936

Results Window from Data Partition Node – "DATA" has been split into two parts, "TRAIN" and "VALIDATE": 90% Train and 10% Validate

FIGURE Q.26 Results window.

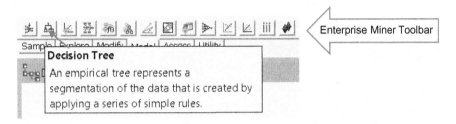

Enterprise Miner Toolbar

Decision Tree

An empirical tree represents a segmentation of the data that is created by applying a series of simple rules.

FIGURE Q.27 The Model tab is selected in this view.

DECISION TREE MODES

Now that we have prepared our data, we are ready to build our decision tree. Enterprise Miner enables you to build a decision tree in two different ways:

1. Automated mode – in this mode, the program decides the best optimal splitting criteria for you.
2. Interactive mode – in this mode, *you* decide which variable is used to split the node. You may choose the suggested choice, or override with the choice which you feel is more appropriate to the model that you wish to build.

Some experts recommend the interactive mode, rather than automated mode, in order to create stable models, since domain knowledge is incorporated into the selection process (www.palgrave-journals.com/jt/journal/v15/n3/full/5750045a.html).

You can also use a combination of the interactive and automated modes.

Node Splitting

Node splitting is the method by which each node of the tree is separated into multiple classes or outcomes. For example, a binary tree partitions each node into two parts – e.g., an outcome which is either fatal or not fatal. In recursive partitioning, a node is split multiple times over all of the *input* variables, and the best performing split is chosen. What is considered the "best" split may differ according to the algorithm selected. You can control the behavior of the algorithm by changing properties under the "splitting rule" (Figure Q.28, below)

Building the Interactive Tree

1. Drag a Decision Tree node from the selectable icons under the Model tab (Figure Q.27) to the diagram (Figure Q.28).
2. Connect the output of the Data Partition node to the Decision Tree node.
3. Select the Decision Tree node.
4. Select the Properties pane.
5. Set Maximum Branch = 30, Maximum Depth = 6, Minimum Category Size = 5, and Leaf Size = 1000.
6. Click on the ellipsis (...) under the Value column, within the Interactive property.

The Interactive Decision Tree opens containing only one node (Figure Q.29).

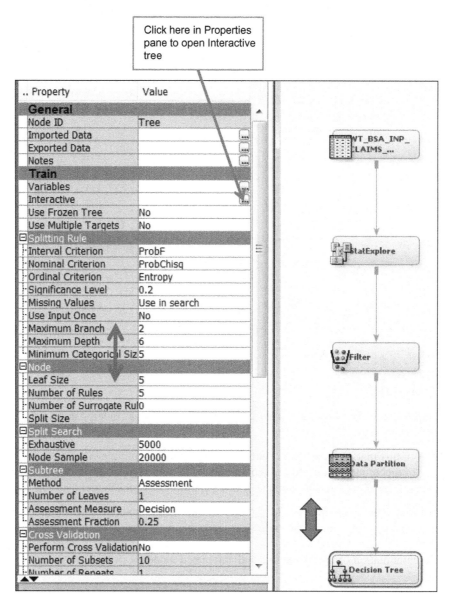

FIGURE Q.28 Adding a decision tree node.

Changing the Statistics Displayed in Each Node

Each column with the node shows the training and validation percentages classified by each category. It will also display in the bottom right pane when you select the node.

The nodes can be customized to show as few or as many statistics as desired. Right click on the background of the Tree View, and then select Node Statistics (Figure Q.30).

In our example each node contains the following statistics:

- Percentage per target level — the target levels are 1 (Lowest Payments), or 5 (Highest Payments).
- Number of observations per target level.
- Number of observations in a node.

Uncheck Node ID for now. Your display should match Figure Q.30. Press OK when done.

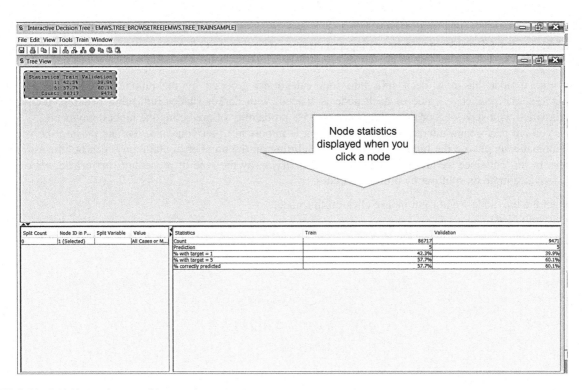

FIGURE Q.29 Initial interactive tree with one node.

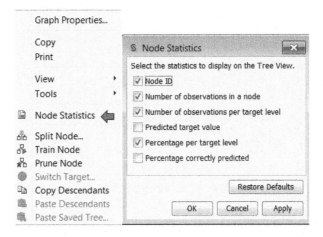

FIGURE Q.30 Selecting Node statistics.

Splitting a Single Node

Initially, the single node shows the existing breakdown of each category as it exists in the data. No prediction is reflected in the root node. To start predicting, we need to split the root node (Figure Q.31).

- Select the node and then right click on it.
- The Node menu will appear.
- Choose "Split Node" from the menu.
  A list of candidate split variables appears ordered by − Log (p). This formula is also known as the "logworth." The best split candidates are sorted in descending order, with the best splits at the top. As a rule of thumb, logworth values which are greater than 2 can be used to identify good split candidates. The Branches column will identify the

number of categories that will be produced as a result of the split. The highest ranking split candidate is IP_CLM_DAYS_CD_NM, the number of inpatient days stayed (Figure Q.32).
● Select the first variable at the top of the list and press OK.

The original node has now been split into four categories, grouped by the number of inpatient days stayed (Figure Q.33). The predictive value of each node is shaded, with darker shades indicating better predictive scores. Claims classified with stays of 8 or more days have an 85% probability of predicting the highest payments.

When you are performing interactive split analysis, it is important to let your *intuition* and *purpose* be your guide. Do not automatically choose the highest ranking split. Splitting on the number of claim days can be interesting, and is an obvious factor, but since we are more interested in classifying by the type of procedures performed, we can "redo" this split to concentrate on splitting by procedure codes.

1. Reselect the top Node 1 and right mouse click on this node.
2. Select "Split Node."
3. When the Split Node Menu appears, select the second variable (IP_CLM_ICD9_PRCD . . .), instead of the first.
4. Press OK.

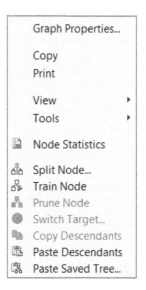

FIGURE Q.31 Splitting the root node.

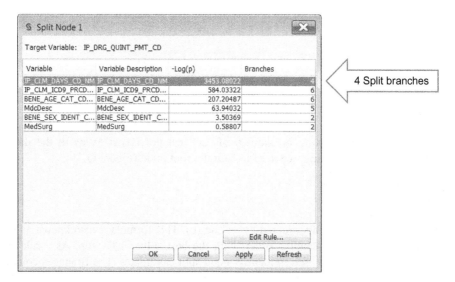

FIGURE Q.32 Split node menu.

Note: If you have a large number of splits, it is sometimes faster to prune the node first, and then split.

The decision tree is redrawn and the data have been split into six categories of procedure codes (Figure Q.34).

The first node has the best classification rate; 75% of all claims have been classified correctly in the highest payment category for this group. However, it is unclear what this category contains, since the display is trying to squeeze a lot of text into a small space.

To see the expanded text for this node:

1. Select the node starting with "VESSEL."
2. From the Tools menu bar, select Display Split Rule Text." The entire English rule displays in the pop-up box (Figure Q.35). Note that there are six distinct procedure codes listed in this node (Figure Q.36). However, that does

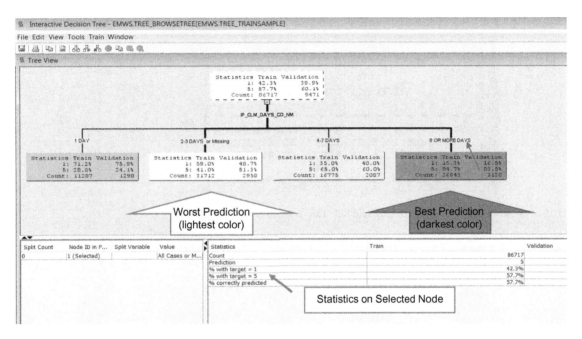

FIGURE Q.33   Split by inpatient number of claim days.

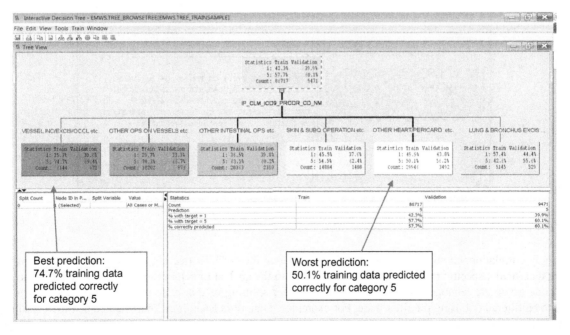

FIGURE Q.34   Split by procedure code.

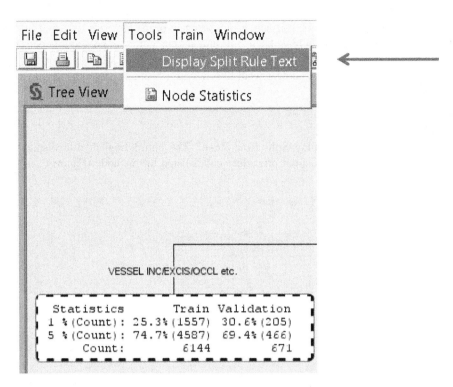

FIGURE Q.35   Pop-up box that shows when 'Display Split Rule Text' is selected.

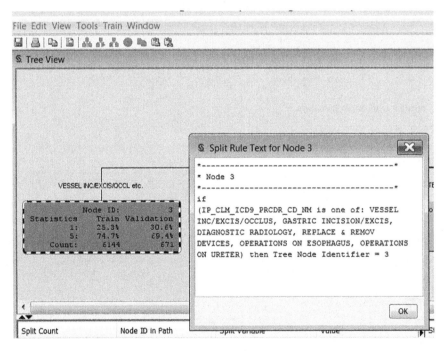

FIGURE Q.36   English rules.

not imply correlation among any of the specific procedures; the decision tree algorithm is simply grouping all categories that yield a specific result into one group. It is up to the analyst to determine whether or not the characteristics of a node group are homogeneous. If they are not, further splitting of that node may be desired, or categories may need to be filtered out using the filter node. For example, "Diagnosis Radiology" may be deemed too broad a group.

3. Press OK when done.

VESSEL INC/EXCIS/OCCL etc.

```
Statistics          Train  Validation
1 %(Count):  25.3%(1557)  30.6%(205)
5 %(Count):  74.7%(4587)  69.4%(466)
      Count:        6144         671
```

FIGURE Q.37   Classification into highest payer category.

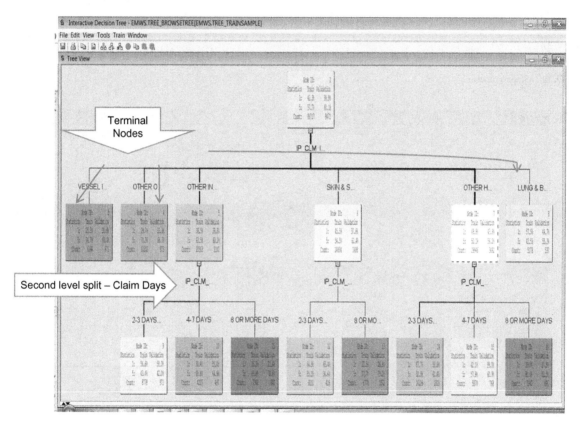

FIGURE Q.38   Splitting tree to the second level.

Terminal Nodes

A terminal node (or leaf) is a final branch on a tree path, and can no longer be split:

1. Select Node 3 (VESSEL INC/EXCIS/OCCL, etc.) and right click on the node.
2. The Node Menu will appear.
3. Note that you cannot choose "Split Node" from the menu, and it is grayed out.

The statistics for this node indicate that 75% of the data are classified into the highest payment quintile. An examination of the validation statistics corroborates this. Of the validation cases, 69% were also classified into the highest payer category (Figure Q.37).

Repeating this procedure over the other five nodes for the second-level branch (see "Splitting a single node", above) shows that there are two other terminal nodes. The other three nodes *can* be split, and for these we choose the first split criterion (Claim Days). This produces the tree shown in Figure Q.38.

ADJUSTING THE DECISION TREE DISPLAY

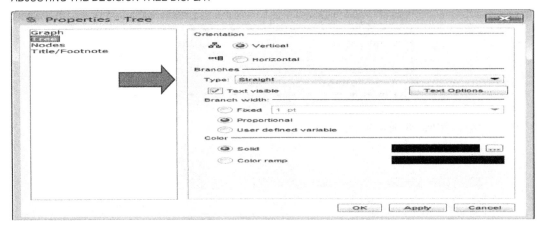

FIGURE Q.39   Graph properties.

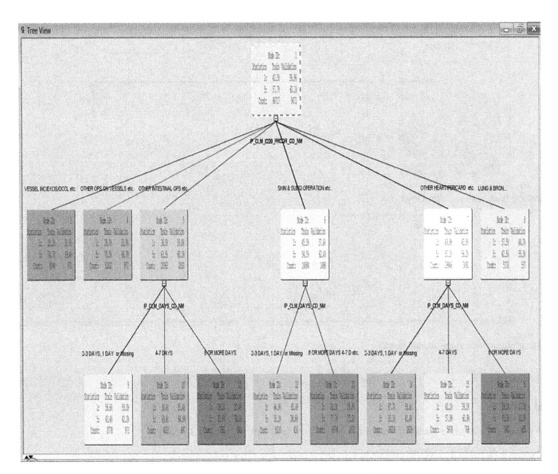

FIGURE Q.40   After "tweaking" graph properties.

Adjusting the Decision Tree Display

The resultant tree fits on one page; however, the text is too short to be able to read it. We can use the tree graph properties to fix this:

1. Right Click and select Graph Properties from anywhere on the Process Flow Diagram.
2. Change the "Branches Type" to "Straight" (Figure Q.39).

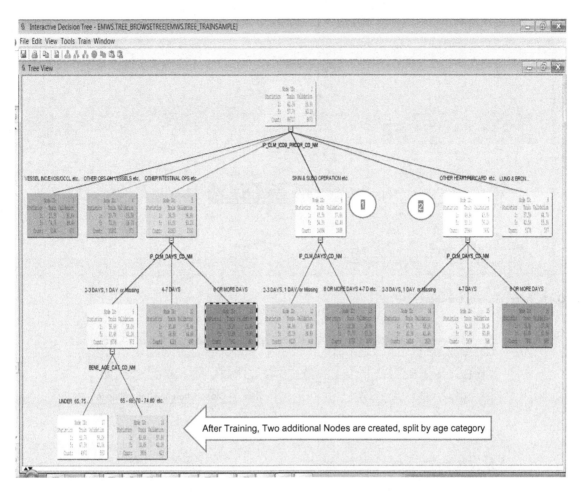

FIGURE Q.41 After training.

3. Press OK.
4. If the display still does not fit one one page, use the "View" menu (Right Mouse click), and set to "Fit to Page" (Figure Q.40).

Training the Remaining Nodes

Earlier, we discussed the difference between interactive and automatic modes. If we wanted to switch to automatic mode at this point and let the program choose the best splits, we could do so by "training" the branch.

1. Select the Node "1 Day, 2−3 Days, or Missing" (second bottom row) (Figure Q.41).
2. Right click on this mode, and click Train Node (instead of Split). The program automatically splits that node using the best criteria (BENE_AGE_CAT_CD_NM). No user choice is necessary in this case.
3. Examine all of the remaining nodes and verify that no other node can be split or trained.

Collapsing/Expanding Branches

Trees often get cluttered on a single display, so you may find it easier to view a tree by collapsing some of the child or descendent nodes

4. To collapse a branch, click on " − " at the bottom of any node, and all nodes underneath that node will collapse.
5. To expand a branch, click on " + " at the bottom of any node, and all nodes underneath that node will reappear.

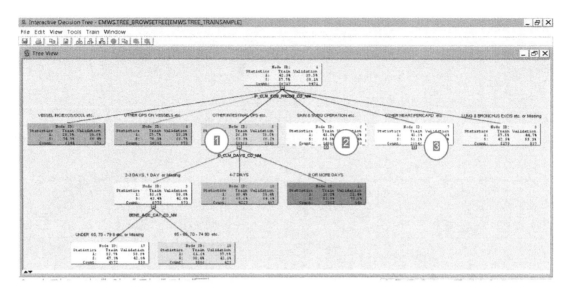

FIGURE Q.42   After collapsing branches.

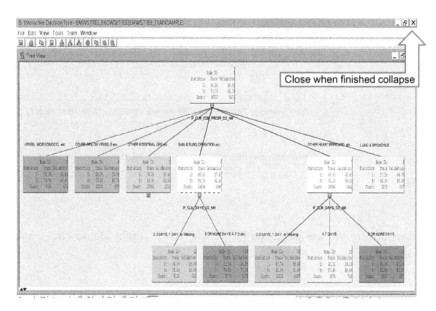

FIGURE Q.43   Right-handed tree.

In this way, we can easily display parts of a large tree. For example, to view the *left* branch of the tree, collapse two of the nodes of the right side of the tree by clicking on the " − " at the bottom of the node. This changes the box to a " + " to indicate all nodes underneath that node have been collapsed. Do this for the nodes marked 1 and 2 in Figure Q.41, above.

Next, view the right branch of the tree by collapsing "OTHER INTESTINAL OPS," and expand the nodes marked 2 and 3 in Figure Q.42. This results in an expanded "right-handed" tree (Figure Q.43).

At this point we are done with the interactive tree exploration, so click the "X" box of the top line to close the tree after responding "Yes" to "Do you want to save changes?" (Figure Q.44). You will then be returned to the flow diagram.

By default, each new Interactive Tree is named sequentially, Interactive Tree, Interactive Tree(1), Interactive Tree (2), etc. You may want to keep several versions of an interactive tree and give them meaningful names.

6. To give this version a name, right click on the Decision Tree node, select Rename, and rename the node to Procedure Code Tree. Then press OK (Figure Q.45).

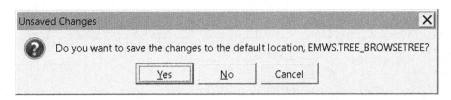

FIGURE Q.44 After clicking 'Yes', then click the 'X' box in the top line to close the tree and return to the flow diagram.

FIGURE Q.45 Renamed to procedure code tree.

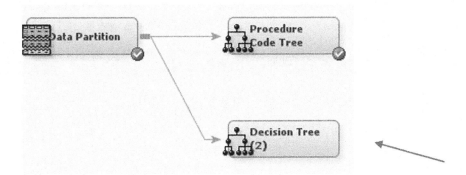

FIGURE Q.46 Connecting the Decision Tree node to the output of the Data Partition node.

Copying a Second Version of a Tree You Just Created

1. Drag a new Decision Tree node from the Enterprise Miner Toolbar to the Diagram.
2. Connect the Decision Tree node to the output of Data Partition (Figure Q.46).
3. Right click on the node that was just created and rename it "Pruned Tree."
4. Select the Decision Tree node.
5. Select the Properties pane.
6. Click on the ellipsis (...) under the Value column, within the Interactive property.
7. The interactive diagram will appear with the single root node displayed.
8. Right click on the diagram and select Paste Saved Tree (Figure Q.47).

A pop-up box will appear (Figure Q.48). Navigate to the folder "SAS Libraries/Emws" in the left pane (may be different in your installation) and select the file "Tree_browsetree" in the right pane. Press OK.

Pruning the Tree

Note that the entire tree that was saved in the previous example now appears. The Title bar indicates that the new tree has been created, and has a new name (Figure Q.49).

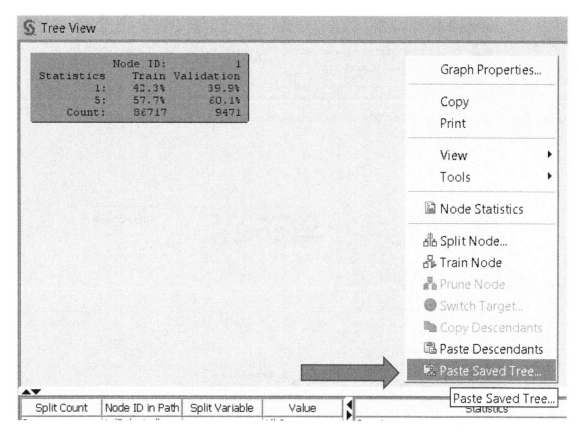

FIGURE Q.47   Selecting "Paste Saved Tree."

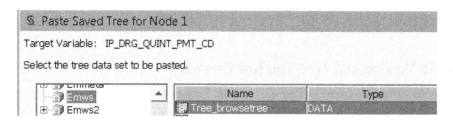

FIGURE Q.48   Selecting the tree to be pasted.

Pruning a tree involves eliminating node branches permanently. This is a bit different from "collapsing" a section of the tree, where the nodes still exist but are hidden from view. As we can see from Figure Q.49, the node marked "Other Heart/Pericard etc." has low predictive power, so it is a good candidate for elimination.

7. Select the node "Other Heart/Pericard etc."
8. Right click on this node and select Prune Node.
9. The three child nodes underneath the pruned nodes are removed from the tree permanently (Figure Q.50).
10. Close and save the current diagram by clicking the "X" in the upper righthand corner to return to the Process Flow (Figure Q.51).

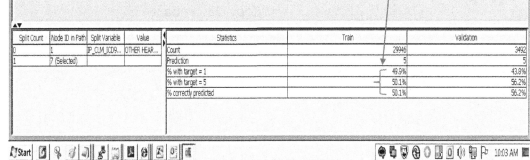

FIGURE Q.49   Identifying the section to be pruned.

Evaluating Performance of the Model

Enterprise Miner gives you many tools to enable you to evaluate the performance of your model.

11. Right click on the previous tree diagram "Procedure Code Tree" and select Results (Figure Q.52).

The decision tree results graphical output appears (Figure Q.53)

Description of Model Outputs

Tree Map

Decision trees can be quite complex and span several pages. The tree map represents a birds-eye view of the tree structure and helps you narrow down to specific sections of the tree.

12. The rightmost box in the second level of the tree map is a lighter shade, meaning the node has relatively low predictive power. Click on this box to select this node.

13. The Tree window repositions itself to the rightmost edge of the tree, and the selected node (LUNG & BRONCHUS) is outlined with dashes.

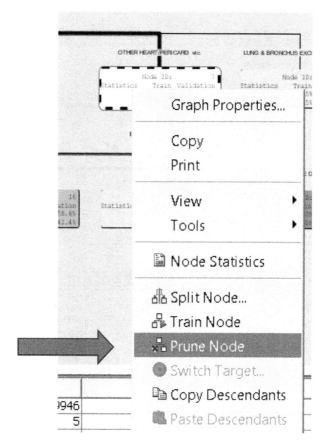

FIGURE Q.50   The menu selection used to 'Prune Nodes'.

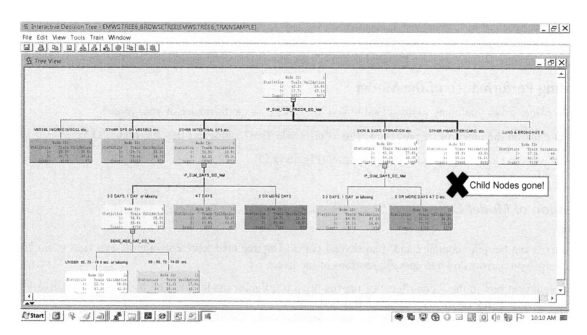

FIGURE Q.51   After pruning.

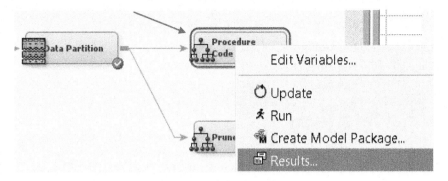

FIGURE Q.52 Right-click on 'Procedure Code Tree to get menu where Results can be selected.

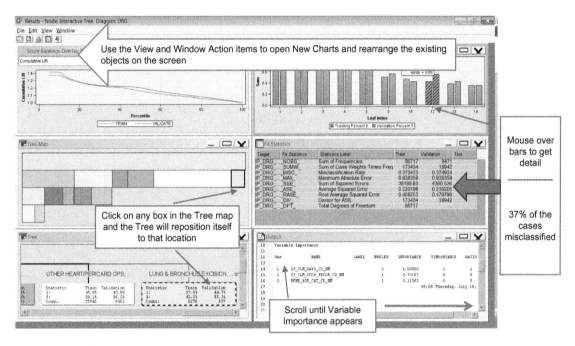

FIGURE Q.53 Decision tree model fit.

Note that there is an 11% difference between the training and validation predictions for this node. Large differences between training and validations percentages indicate poor fit.

14. Right click on this node and select Tools/Display English Rules from the context menu to see what procedures are contained in this node. Press OK when done.

Fit Statistics

The Fit Statistics window displays statistics which indicate the overall goodness of the model. One important measure of a model fit is the misclassification or error rate. The training model has an error rate of 37%, or, expressed in another way, a correct prediction rate of 63%. Equivalent statistics hold for the validation group, indicating that this is a stable overall model.

Classification Chart

The Classification chart displays a bar for each of the individual target outcome categories. It also colors each bar to display the percentage of correct and incorrect predictions for each category. It is related to the misclassification rate (shown as a double arrow in Figure Q.55 below), but breaks down the error rate by the specific outcomes.

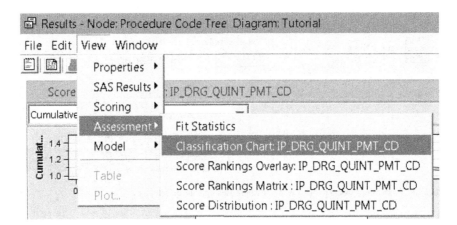

FIGURE Q.54 The Classification Chart is obtained by selecting View -> Assessment -> Classification Chart, as shown above.

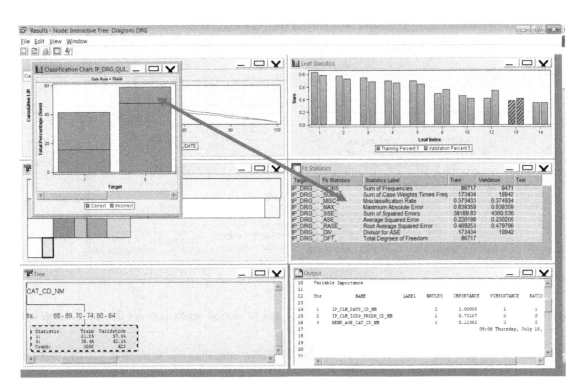

FIGURE Q.55 After adding a classification chart.

15. Click on Classification Chart by selecting View — Assessment — Classification from the main menu (Figure Q.54). It will superimpose itself over the other charts (Figure Q.55).

As displayed for our model, the classification chart indicates that it does a better job of predicting the higher paying category than it does the lower paying category. The sub-bar under the horizontal line of each of the two bars indicates the proportion of correct predictions.

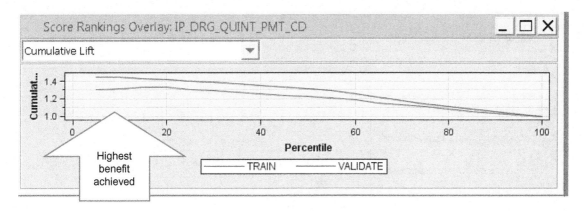

FIGURE Q.56 The Validation sample line (lower graph line above) compared to the Train sample line.

Cumulative Lift Chart

The Cumulative lift chart (positioned underneath the Classification chart) indicates the improvement of the model versus a random model for different cumulative percentages of the population. The outcomes are typically ranked by the highest probability of prediction, so that the highest lift (or benefit) of the model usually occurs at the initial percentiles of the file. This is important in health care since it enables you to measure the highest benefit of a model by scoring the highest predictions first.

The validation sample line tends to follow the training sample line, and is generally slightly lower scoring (Figure Q.56). Degradation of results on validation samples is normal. The lift score starts at ~1.4 for the top 10% of prediction scores, which indicates that it is roughly 40% better than a random model for the best performing nodes.

Leaf Statistics

This compares the statistics of the training group versus the control group for each leaf of the tree. Large variances between the training and validation bars for a leaf indicate that the leaf may be unstable and needs to be refined, or pruned from the tree. Large gaps between training and validation samples can also lead to uncovering problems in the underlying coding classification, such as medical coding errors.

Most of the training leaves are close to their validation counterparts, except perhaps for Leaf 12. Click on any bar in the Leaf Statistics, and the Tree pane will reposition to show the selected leaf.

Variable Importance

Select the Output window (Figure Q.55, bottom right pane), and scroll down until you locate the Variable Importance statistics. Each variable is ranked by Chi-square score, which indicates each variable's contribution toward a prediction.

Resizing the Charts

16. At any time, you may use the window controls in the upper right-hand corner of each chart to maximize, minimize, or close any windows you are interested in.
17. Use the Window/Tile or Window/Cascade option in the action window to redisplay and resize the windows you have already opened.
18. When you are done, close all of the model output windows, and then the Results window, to return to the process diagram.

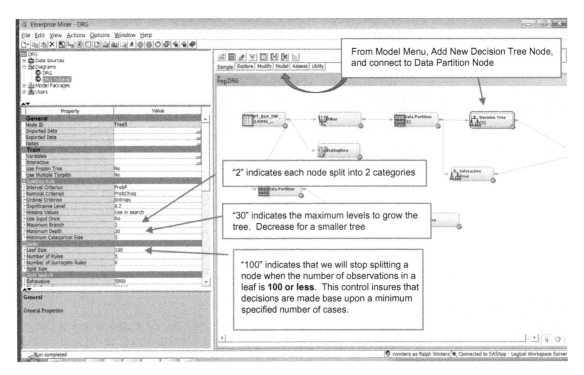

FIGURE Q.57 Setting decision tree properties for binary tree.

Building an Automatic Binary Tree as an Alternative Model

To compare an alternate model with the interactive model we've just built, we will build an "automatic" model using binary splits. However, binary splits will allow us to split each node into *only* two categories each.

19. Drag another Decision Tree icon to the process flow diagram and connect it to the output of the Data Partition node (Figure Q.57).
20. Right click on the node in the process flow diagram, choose "Rename," and name it "Automatic Binary Tree."
21. Select the Properties pane.
22. Set Maximum Branch = 2, Maximum Depth = 30, Minimum Category Size = 5, and Leaf Size = 100.
23. Right click on the New Decision Tree node and select Run.
24. After you receive a message that the run is completed, select Results.
25. After the Results window opens (see Figure Q.57, below), select and maximize the window for the Tree pane, and then follow the earlier procedure used to adjust the graph properties to make the display more readable (Adjusting the Decision Tree Display).

Model Results

The automatic model has chosen the Number of Claim Days as the best predictor, followed by Procedure code (Figure Q.58). It also included MDC (Major Diagnostic Classification) code as part of the model, which we did not use in the interactive building of the tree. We also instructed the model to go up to 30 levels deep; however, after 6 levels the automatic model could not improve. This could be because significant splits could no longer be found, or because a node was reduced to <100 observations, which we set as the minimum leaf size. In that case, the splitting would stop and that node would automatically become a terminal node.

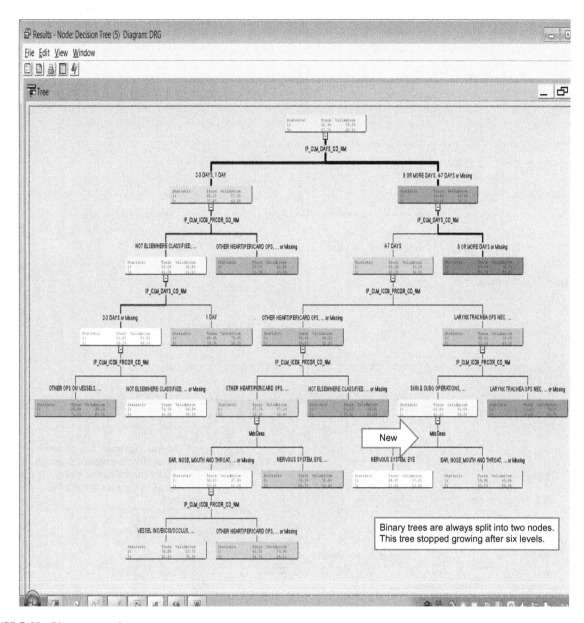

FIGURE Q.58 Binary tree results.

To see all of the English decision rules, for all of the nodes, Select View/Model/English Rules from the Menu Bar (Figure Q.59). Scroll down to see the entire list of all of the classification rules.

Close the results node by clicking on the "X" on the right side of the title bar (Figure Q.60).

Model Comparison

The model comparison node is useful when you have built many models and wish to compare the models' performance (Figure Q.61). To compare the automatic model to our interactively built models:

26. Drag a Model Comparison node from the Assess menu in the toolbar to the diagram (Figure Q.62).
27. Connect the three Tree nodes that have already been created to the input of the Model Comparison node.
28. Select the Model Comparison node, and then right click and select "Run."
29. After processing has been completed, select "Results."

FIGURE Q.59 English Rules.

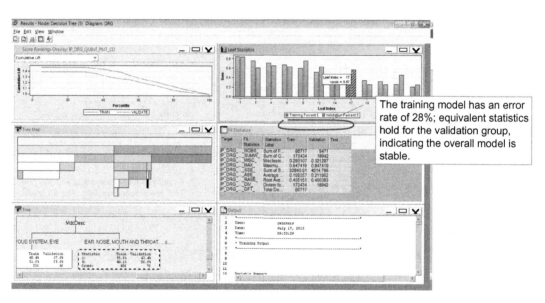

The training model has an error rate of 28%; equivalent statistics hold for the validation group, indicating the overall model is stable.

FIGURE Q.60 Results, alternate model.

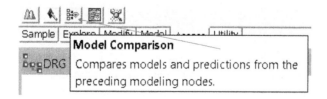

Model Comparison

Compares models and predictions from the preceding modeling nodes.

FIGURE Q.61 Model Comparison node is selected as indicated in above diagram.

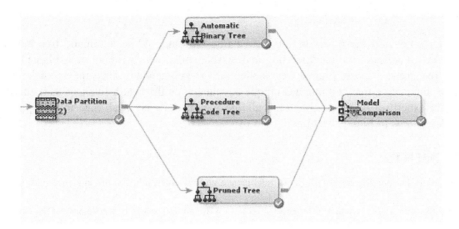

FIGURE Q.62 Model comparison.

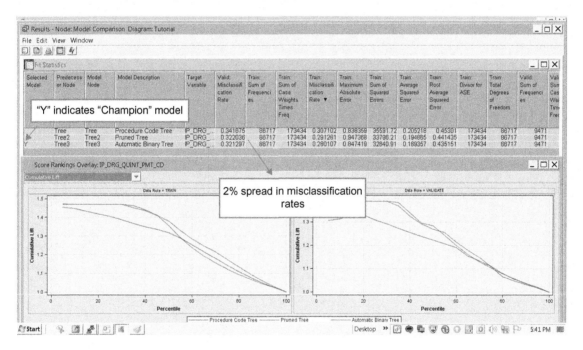

FIGURE Q.63 Performance Statistics for each model.

Fit Statistics

The Results window opens, and the Fit Statistics pane displays the performance statistics for each model (Figure Q.63). The Model Comparison node has selected the Automatic Binary Tree as the "champion" model. We can see that the automatic model has a lower misclassification rate than our interactively trained model using our the validation data set, although all of the misclassification rates are all very close and probably not significantly different. When performance statistics are close, it is usually better to go with a model that incorporates guided domain knowledge. In our example, we wished to explain the model in terms of Procedure codes, rather than Claim days, which had a slightly better misclassification rate. However, there is always a trade-off between ease of explanation and accuracy. By repeating the iterative model bulding process, it is possible to construct multiple models, all with different viewpoints, and then compare them to a baseline model.

CONCLUSION

In this tutorial we have covered the basics of interactive tree building. While automatic tree building can help you develop models quickly, it suffers from incorporating undesirable splits, which cannot be explained and can be difficult to remove. As the tree grows in size, pruned tree models are recommended, since they remove nonsensical "dead" branches from a tree. Interactive tree building has unique advantages in the health sciences as it encourages exploration and leverages domain expertise. As interactive tree building is not available in all data mining packages, I encourage you to explore its capabilities in Enterprise Miner.

ACKNOWLEDGMENTS

I would like to thank Matt Hudson, Director of Business Intelligence at EmblemHealth, for his guidance and encouragement with this tutorial.

SAS and all other SAS Institute Inc. product or service names are registered trademarks or trademarks of SAS Institute Inc. in the USA and other countries. ® indicates USA registration.

Tutorial R

Divining Healthcare Charges for Optimal Health Benefits Under the Affordable Care Act

Ken Yale, DDS, JD

Chapter Outline

INTRODUCTION

This tutorial takes you through a data set on hospital charges for an inpatient stay for heart failure, gathered from all the hospitals in the State of New York. The State of New York recently released all charge and cost data (the latter are estimated based on a formula) for all hospitals in the State of New York. With enormous changes taking place in healthcare insurance coverage and costs, this information may become very important in the future for consumers as they look for the best value (i.e., highest quality for the lowest charge) in caring for their health.

Health care is one of the most perplexing areas for price comparison. Over the years hospitals and physicians have charged a government mandated price, or negotiated prices with health insurance companies, or charged whatever the market would bear for those without health insurance. As a result, hospitals and physicians have learned to shift the cost of products and services around so the lower government mandated prices could be offset by charging more to insurance companies or persons without health insurance.

Because of this price shifting it has been almost impossible to determine how much you might pay for a procedure or visit to the hospital or doctor office, and there was little demand for the information because you might never see the charges or costs if your health insurance company handled all those issues. This situation could change in the near future. The Affordable Care Act, among other things, requires almost everyone to have health insurance coverage and be able to pay for the care they receive. Through employers, government benefit programs, and individual health insurance policies, most of the citizens of the United States are required by federal government law to purchase a health insurance policy. The new federal government requirement could make it more important than ever to better understand the amount you are charged and the quality measured for a service, and could increase demand for hospitals that provide higher-value products and services.

Here is some background on this growing demand for price comparison. The new, individual health insurance policies created by the Affordable Care Act come in three basic packages. The "Gold" covers richer packages with more benefits and lower payments every time you go to the hospital or see a physician (these payments are known as "copayments" or "copay"). The higher benefits and lower out-of-pocket copay means the plan is more expensive to purchase. Since payment of a monthly "premium" charge can be $800 or more (roughly the monthly cost of an expensive car payment), many people may decide they want to purchase a less expensive "Silver" or "Bronze" plan (if they purchase a

Practical Predictive Analytics and Decisioning Systems for Medicine. DOI: http://dx.doi.org/10.1016/B978-0-12-411643-6.00035-1

health insurance policy at all, as they can decide not to pay for the insurance, but rather get a federal government penalty for not buying health insurance coverage).

Silver and Bronze plans can have significantly less expensive upfront monthly premium payments, but in exchange for the less expensive monthly payment the plans have higher copayments and deductibles (the deductible is the annual amount that you have to pay before the insurance kicks in and starts paying anything). A person with health insurance coverage can have significant out-of-pocket costs when attending a hospital or doctor, and these costs can become very high before the deductible is met. As a result, knowing what a hospital or doctor charges for a product or service can be very important, and it is anticipated the demand for such information will grow as more people get health insurance coverage.

This tutorial looks at inpatient hospital charges, based on newly released information from the New York State Department of Health (https://health.data.ny.gov/Health/Hospital-Inpatient-Discharges-SPARCS-De-Identified/u4ud-w55t). The data set is 940 MB (almost a gigabyte), which might be difficult to download to your computer. Therefore, we went to the smaller Hospital Inpatient Cost Transparency data set (https://health.data.ny.gov/Health/Hospital-Inpatient-Cost-Transparency-Beginning-200/7dtz-qxmr), which is still relatively large at 61 MB, more than 380,000 rows of data on about 315 different procedures with variables in 14 columns. We then extracted the data set you see here — the charges and associated costs for the moderate "Heart Failure" procedure (also known as DRG 194, moderate severity) compiled for all hospitals in New York State. We could have used any of the 315 different procedures, and chose this because there were a couple of quality metrics associated with that DRG. To this extract we added back zip codes (which were in the original 940-MB data but removed in the 61-MB version), the ownership status of the individual hospitals (whether Publicly owned or Privately owned), their academic status (also known as "academic medical center," but here we use the simpler Training or Non-training hospital designation), and two proxies for quality — the AMI and HF process measures. The following is additional background information from the State of New York Department of Health:

Hospital Inpatient Cost Transparency: Beginning 2009

This data set contains information submitted by New York State Article 28 Hospitals as part of the New York Statewide Planning and Research Cooperative (SPARCS) and Institutional Cost Report (ICR) data submissions. The data set contains information on the volume of discharges, All Payer Refined Diagnosis Related Group (APR-DRG), the severity of illness level (SOI), medical or surgical classification, the median charge, median cost, average charge and average cost per discharge. When interpreting New York's data, it is important to keep in mind that variations in cost may be attributed to many factors. Some of these include overall volume, teaching hospital status, facility specific attributes, geographic region, and quality of care provided. For more information, check out: http://www.health.ny.gov/statistics/sparcs/

PRE-TUTORIAL BACKGROUND ON ORIGINAL DATA SET

The original Cost Transparency Data set had reported charges and costs for all procedures for the 3 years 2009, 2010, and 2011. Figure R.1 shows a screenshot of the original 61-MB data set.

Our initial view of the data used the Data tab, Filter function to determine if there were missing data (blanks) (Figure R.2). In addition, the Filter allows you to order the data alphabetically.

The initial review using the Filter showed very few blanks in the data, and sorting the hospital names alphabetically identified some hospitals that only reported for one or two years out of the three. Upon further investigation it turned out that those hospitals had closed, or did not do certain procedures, or did not do the procedure every year. In addition, the number of different procedures in the data set was very large, making it challenging to run a tutorial. As a result, we decided to extract the Heart Failure procedure (DRG 194) and, within DRG 194, the Moderate cases (Severity 2), which seemed to have data for most hospitals in the data set as well as a quality metric. We then removed the hospitals that had fewer than 3 years' data, including:

- Peninsula Hospital Center — closed
- Women and Children's Hospital of Buffalo — no 2010 data
- TLC Health Network Tri-County Memorial Hospital — only 2009 data
- SVCMC-St Vincents Manhattan — only 2009, 2010 data
- Sunnyview Hospital and Rehabilitation Center — only 2009 data
- North General Hospital — only 2009 data
- Long Island Jewish Schneider Children's Hospital Division — too few procedures (one in 2009, three in 2010, four in 2011).

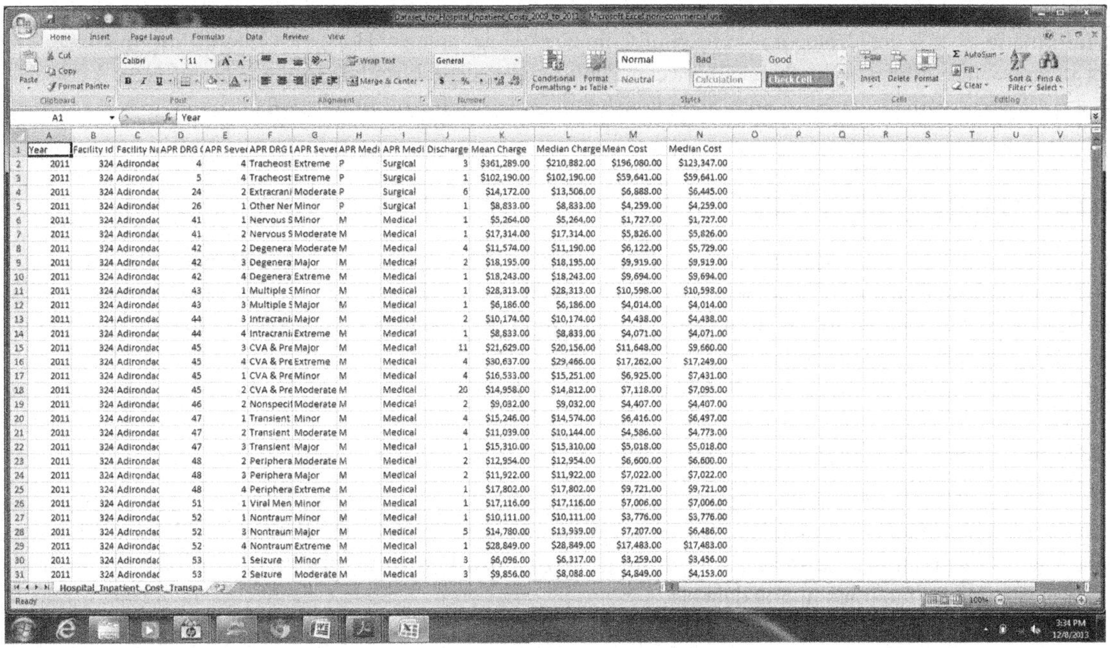

FIGURE R.1   View of the original Hospital Inpatient Cost Transparency dataset.

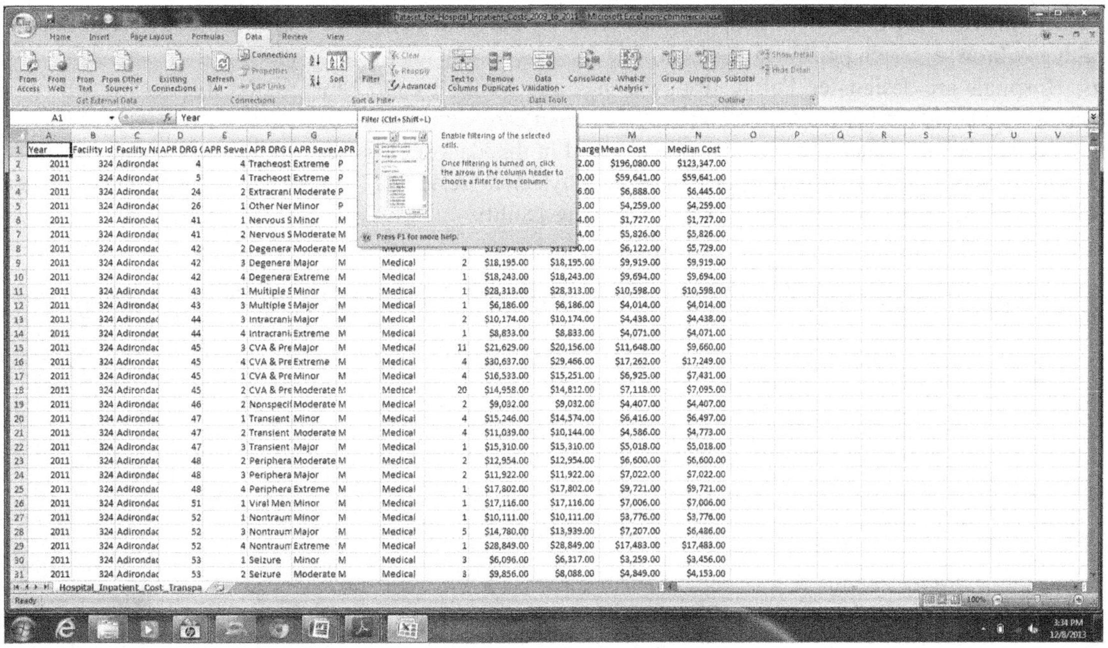

FIGURE R.2   Using the Filter function in Statistica.

Finally, we added information on training hospitals (also known as Academic Medical Centers) because these institutions generally advertise their university affiliation, giving the appearances of higher quality care (although the evidence for this is not settled), and it would be interesting to see if they cost more or less than other hospitals, and if they in fact have higher quality care. The information for training hospitals came from www.healthguideusa.org/teaching_hospitals_new_york.htm, and the Association of American Medical Colleges at www.aamc.org/members/coth/. We then added information on whether the hospital was government owned (Public) or privately owned (Private) by obtaining information from the New York City Department of Health & Human Services (http://home.nyc.gov/portal/site/nycgov/menuitem.12383c1cbb72dee6a62fa24601c789a0/), and the federal government Centers for Medicare and

Medicaid Services (CMS) Medicare Compare hospital database (https://data.medicare.gov/Hospital-Compare/Hospital-General-Information/v287-28n3?category = Hospital-Compare&view_name = Hospital-General-Information). These data would let us know the difference in charges between Public and Private hospitals in the State of New York. The Private hospitals are all non-profit, as the New York State legislature outlawed for-profit hospitals.

HOSPITAL CHARGE ANALYSIS

We first wanted to get familiar with the data, and see if there are simple relationships between the different variables associated with hospital charges. Once you open STATISTICA, import the data set labeled Hospital Inpatient Cost Transparency Tutorial by going to the Home tab, Open Icon, Open Document tab. Double click the file and it opens in the STATISTICA desktop (Figure R.3).

You can click "Import all sheets to a Workbook" (Figure R.4); in this case there is only one data sheet in the file (Figure R.4).

The data set contains the following variables (Figure R.5).

Facility ID: The identification number given to the facility by the State of New York — a unique code identifying a facility location certified to provide healthcare services under Article 28 of the Public Health Law. This number was assigned upon receiving a Certificate of Operation, and is also known as the Permanent Facility Identifier (PFI). There are 194 unique facilities in this data set.

Facility Name: This is the name of the facility where services were performed based on the Permanent Facility Identifier (PFI), as maintained by the New York State Department of Health Division of Health Facility Planning. Note that this field contains the Facility Name current to the update date of this record. It is not specific to the discharge year, and the names change as hospitals change ownership.

Zip Code: This is the zip code of the hospital as recorded by the New York State Department of Health (http://hospitals.nyhealth.gov/browse_search.php?form = ALL).

Status: Hospitals are designated Public from the lists maintained by the New York City Department of Health & Human Services, and the list maintained by the CMS Medicare Compare website.

AMC: This stands for "Academic Medical Center," and in this data set it is used to indicate whether the hospital is a training hospital, employing a significant number of physician "residents" in training and associated medical school faculties. The "N" indicates the hospital is not a training facility.

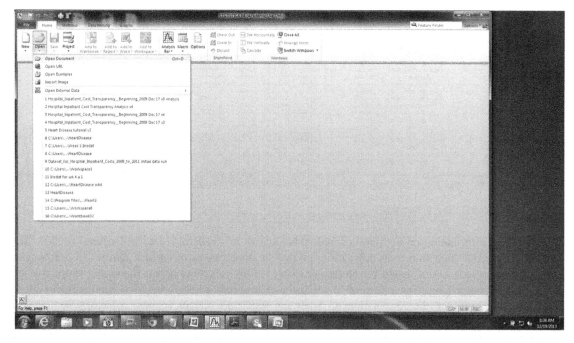

FIGURE R.3   The Open icon allows you to find and open the dataset.

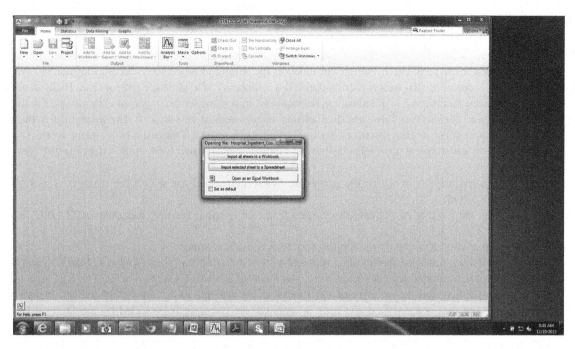

FIGURE R.4 Importing the dataset to a Workbook.

FIGURE R.5 View of the opened Hospital Inpatient Cost Transparency dataset file modified for this tutorial.

APR DRG: Diagnosis Related Groups (DRGs) are a patient classification system which associates the type of patients a hospital treats (i.e., its case mix) to the costs incurred by the hospital. There are currently three major versions of the DRG in use: basic DRGs, All Patient DRGs, and All Patient Refined DRGs. The basic DRGs are used by the Centers for Medicare and Medicaid Services (CMS) for hospital payment for Medicare beneficiaries. The All Patient DRGs (AP-DRGs) are an expansion of the basic DRGs to be more representative of non-Medicare populations, such as pediatric patients. The All Patient Refined DRGs (APR-DRG) incorporate severity of illness subclasses into the AP-DRGs

APR DRG Description: This is the name given to the particular APR DRG code. For example, DRG 194 is the code for Heart Failure.

APR Severity of Illness Code: The APR-DRGs have a severity of illness sub-code classification. According to the 3M, the organization that created the APR-DRGs, severity of illness is the "extent of physiologic decompensation or organ system loss of function." It is one of several factors used to define the complexity of a particular patient case. There are four severity of illness subclasses, numbered 1 to 4, indicating, respectively, minor, moderate, major, or extreme severity of illness.

APR Medical Surgical Code: Procedures are divided into either medical or surgical. The difference is that surgical procedures may require more intense resources, such as an operating room, anesthesia, or recovery room. The distinction between medical and surgical also helps define the clinical specialty involved. In this data set "M" designates a medical procedure.

Year: This is the calendar year in which the procedures were performed for which the Charges, Costs, and other information were reported.

Discharges: This is the number of patients discharged from the hospital for that particular APR-DRG in the year indicated.

Charge: This is the amount charged by the facility for the specific procedure.

Cost: Costs are estimates, based on facility data reported to the State of New York Statewide Planning and Research Cooperative. Costs are estimated for each procedure as a Ratio of Cost to Charges (RCC). The RCC are specific to the procedure, the facility, and the severity of the illness of the patient. RCCs are calculated and reported by the individual facility, and they are certified and may be audited. An example is provided by the State of New York: "For example, if hospital charge is $20,000 and the RCC is 50%, the estimated cost is $10,000."

AMI: The Acute Myocardial Infarction quality measure is a composite measure of the overall processes of care used to treat heart attack patients (for more information, see the National Quality Measures Clearinghouse AMI web page at www.qualitymeasures.ahrq.gov/content.aspx?id = 35572). In this data set, the number is out of a possible 100.

HF: The Heart Failure quality measure is a composite measure of the overall processes of care used to treat heart failure patients (for more information see the National Quality Measures Clearinghouse HF web page at www. qualitymeasures.ahrq.gov/content.aspx?id = 35573). In this data set, the number is out of a possible 100.

A note on the hospital performance measures AMI and HF. The measures included in the file are "screen scraped" from the quality tab of the New York State Department of Health hospital profile (see an example at http://hospitals. nyhealth.gov/browse_view.php?id = 208&p = quality&hpntoken = 1). In this data set are the composite measures for heart attack (AMI) and heart failure (HF), which we use as a proxy for quality. These are process measures, however, and not adjusted for the complications or difficulties of individual patients (also known as "risk adjustment"). For example, you can have an excellent process but a bad outcome. There are many other outcomes and quality measures that give a better indication of the quality of care. In addition, the data were based on content on the website in 2012, and the underlying data came from CMS Hospital Compare data submissions, which could have been measured some time before they appeared on the CMS website. More information may be found at http://hospitals.nyhealth.gov/faq.php.

Initial Data Exploration

To get a feel for the data, and perhaps discover some initial information, we are going to see how out-of-pocket charges vary with the different variables: location (Zip Code), ownership (Private or Government), academic status (T for training institution and N for not a training institution), and proxies for quality (AMI and HF). As a result, our dependent variable is Charges and the other variables are the predictor variables. We shall first explore the data graphically, looking for interesting relationships between variables.

Is There a Relationship Between Mean Charges and Status (Public or Private)?

We shall first create a means plot by going to the Graphs tab and clicking the Means button (Figure R.6).

Click on the Variables button; select Mean Charge as the continuous dependent variable, and Status as the grouping variable, then click OK and OK (Figure R.7).

It appears that Public hospitals, on average, charge slightly more than Private hospitals, with a very wide range of charges among Public hospitals and a much narrower range of charges among Private hospitals (Figure R.8). The wide range of charges looks unusual — one of those "That's odd ..." moments — and may require further exploration. Let's continue and see what else we find.

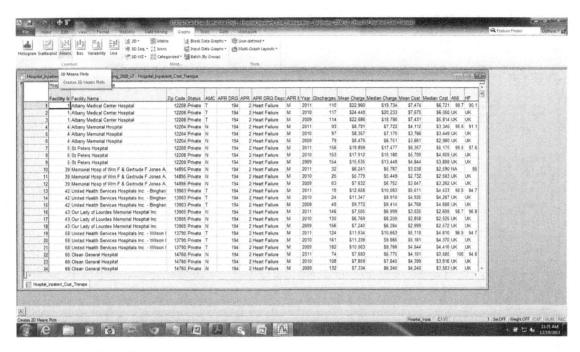

FIGURE R.6 Locating the Means Plot button in the Graphs tab.

FIGURE R.7 Selecting variables for the means plot.

Relationship of Charges to Location

A Scatterplot graph can help us look at the relationship between Mean Charges and Zip Code. Since the lower numbered zip codes in New York State happen to be in more populated eastern parts of the state, and higher number zip codes tend to be in more rural and western areas, it will be interesting to see if the charges follow a similar pattern. Go to the Graphs tab, Scatterplot button, and select Zip Code as the X variable and Mean Charges as the Y variable. Then click OK and OK (Figure R.9).

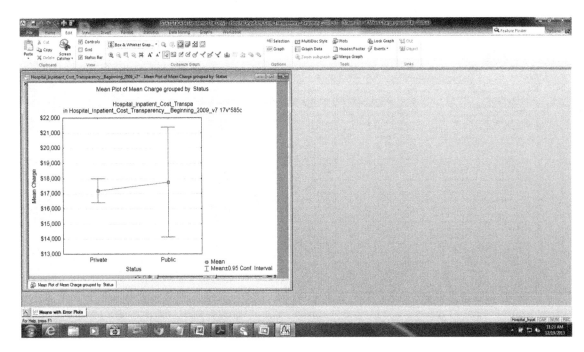

FIGURE R.8 Initial Private hospitals and Public hospitals means plot comparison.

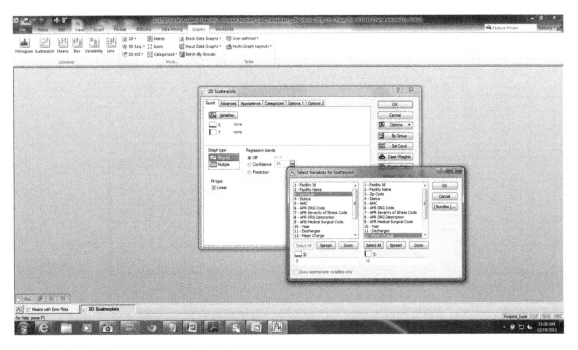

FIGURE R.9 Choosing variables to set up a scatterplot graph.

In the graph in Figure R.10 there appears to be a correlation between Zip Code and Mean Charges, but another interesting note is the outlier that appears around the $121,000 charge. This should be explored further, as it may have also been the cause for the wide range of charges identified for Public Hospitals.

One way to check for outliers is to use a Box Plot. Go to the Graphs tab, Histogram button, and choose Mean Charge for the Variable (Figure R.11).

And we can see in the graph, all charges are below $60,000, bar one charge above $120,000 (Figure R.12).

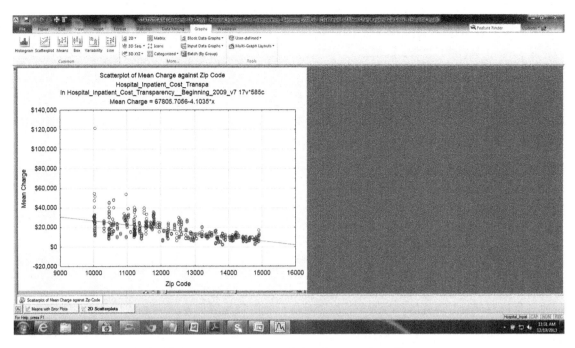

FIGURE R.10 Scatterplot showing relationship between mean charges and zip code — note the outlier.

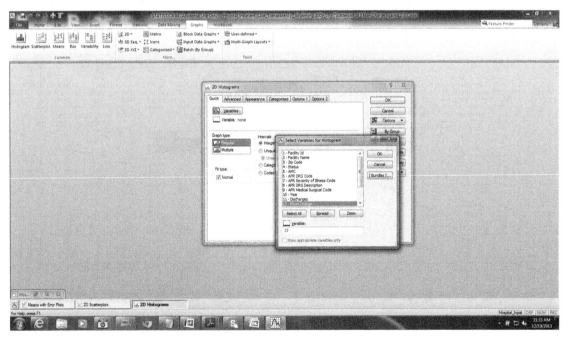

FIGURE R.11 Selecting a variable for a box plot histogram.

We find the outlier, and determine it is an abnormally high charge and the hospital has very few of these procedures. Few procedures could mean they do not normally handle these kinds of cases, or it is a mistake. Other reasons could be that, as a Public hospital, they have political pressures that create a unique situation. All of these are guesses, and the decision is to remove the outlier, as it skews the data. We remove all three rows (2009, 2010, and 2011 data) of the hospital (Figure R.13).

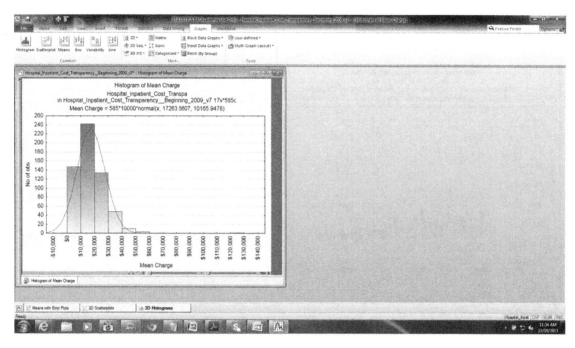

FIGURE R.12   Boxplot histogram showing distribution of variables and revealing an outlier.

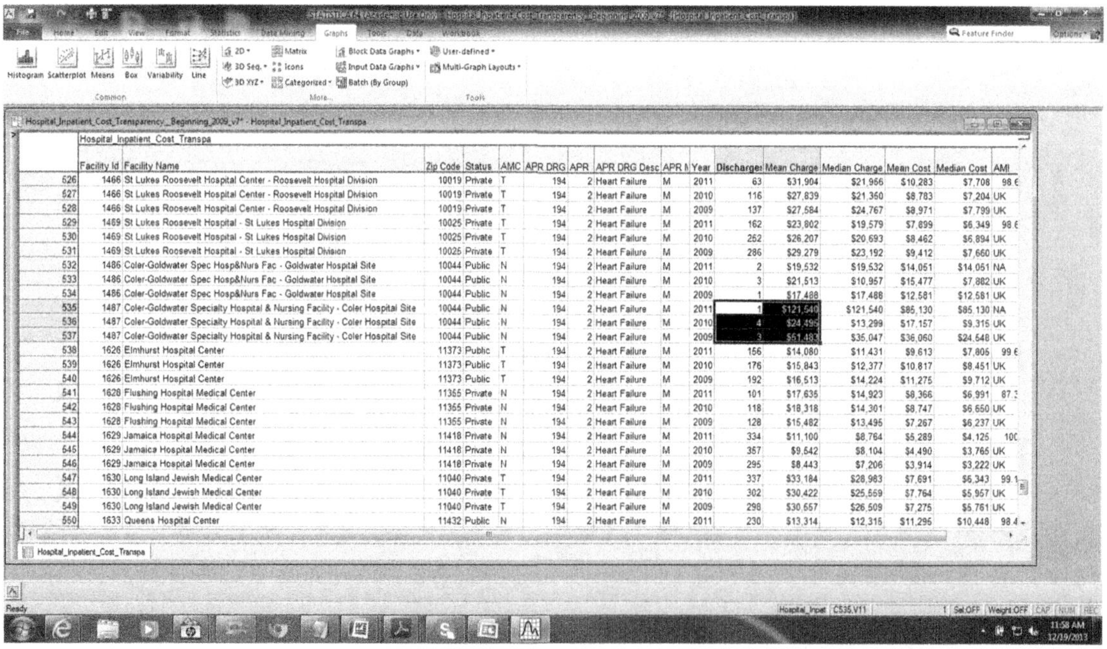

FIGURE R.13   Outliers located for removal from dataset.

With the outlier removed, we go back to the Histogram of Mean Charges and see a more even distribution of charges. It is interesting to note the charges are still skewed to the right (higher charges) but without the extreme outlier (Figure R.14).

We also run the Scatterplot again to view the relationship between Zip Code and Mean Charges, and see a more pronounced slope (Figure R.15).

With the outlier removed, we can go back to the Means analysis of the relationship between Mean Charges and Public or Private status by opening the previous analysis. We see lower overall charges by Public hospitals, but still a wide range of charges (Figure R.16).

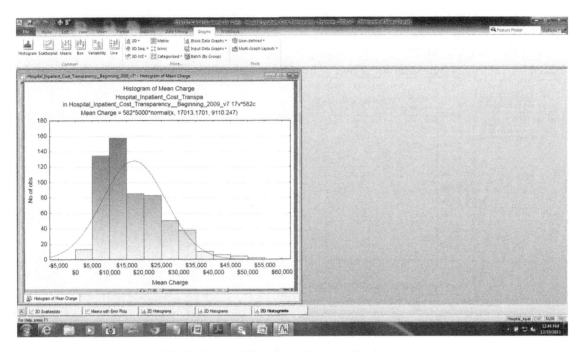

FIGURE R.14   Boxplot histogram showing distribution of variables after outlier removed.

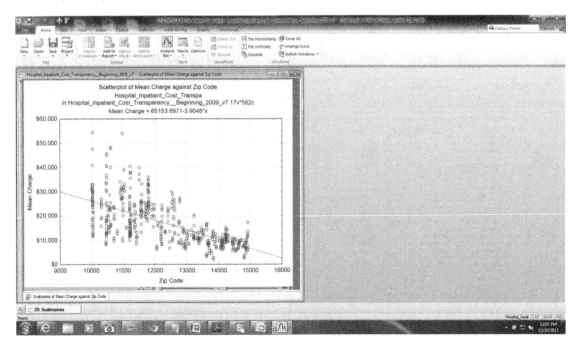

FIGURE R.15   New scatterplot after outlier removed showing relationship between mean charges and zip code.

We also want to see if there is a relationship between Mean Charges and Teaching status. To get a quick graphical view, we go to the Graph tab, Means button, and use Mean Charge as the continuous dependent variable and Teaching status as the grouping variable (Figure R.17).

Teaching hospitals appear to have higher charges (Figure R.18).

Since we're looking at the effect of Private versus Public hospitals, and Teaching versus Non-teaching hospitals, on Mean Charges, it might be important to explore the data some more and find out the proportions of Private to Public hospitals, and Teaching to Non-teaching hospitals. To view this, you go to the Graphs tab, Histogram button and use Status as the Variable to see how Private versus Public hospitals compare (Figure R.19).

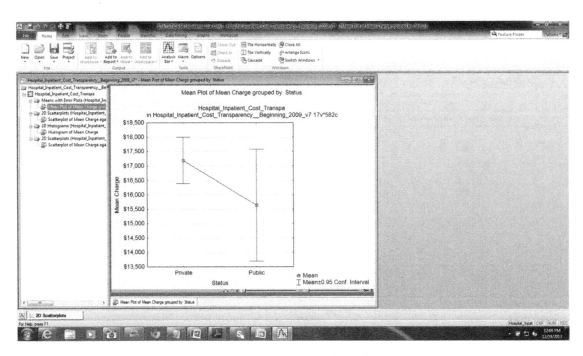

FIGURE R.16 New Private hospitals and Public hospitals means plot comparison after outlier removed.

FIGURE R.17 Setting up means plot, choosing variables.

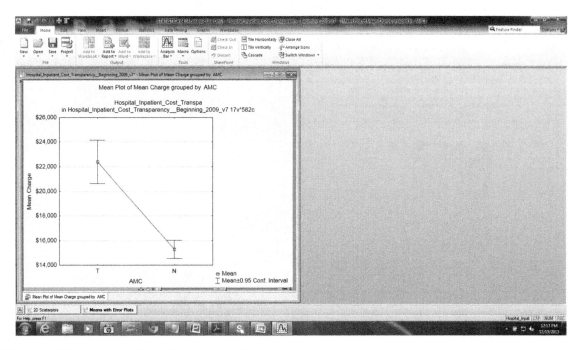

FIGURE R.18   Relationship between Mean Charges and teaching status.

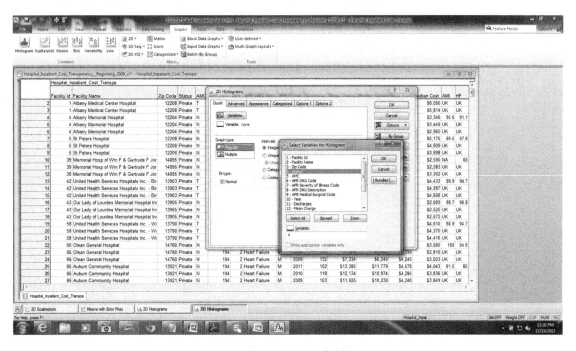

FIGURE R.19   Setting up box plot histogram, choosing variable Status (Private or Public).

Private hospitals outnumber public by more than five to one (Figure R.20).

To view Teaching versus Non-teaching hospitals, go to the Graph tab, Histogram button, and select AMC for the variable (Figure R.21).

The graph shows that about 33% of hospitals are labeled as Teaching (Figure R.22).

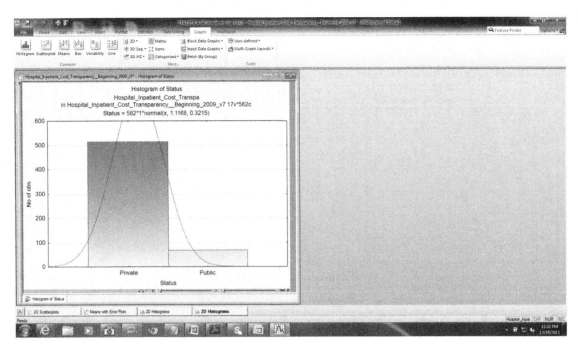

FIGURE R.20 Private hospitals compared to Public hospitals — numbers of hospitals in the state.

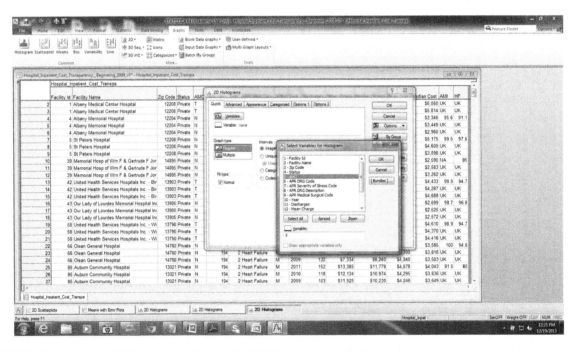

FIGURE R.21 Setting up box plot histogram, choosing variable AMC (teaching or non-teaching).

From our initial review of the data we have found Teaching hospitals charge more than Non-teaching hospitals; Public hospitals charge less than Private hospitals; and hospitals in and closer to New York City charge more than hospitals further away from New York City. Further analysis needs to be done to determine the relationship with quality of care, to assess whether the higher charging hospitals give higher quality care. These analyses shall be performed next.

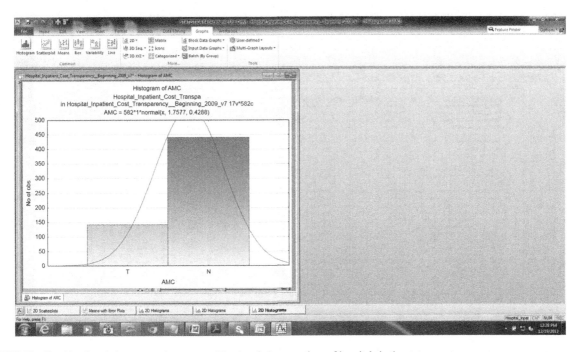

FIGURE R.22   Teaching hospitals compared to non-teaching hospitals — numbers of hospitals in the state.

QUALITY MATTERS

Now that we have a feel for the data, and see there are some correlations between the variables, we turn to the matter of quality. Charges might be higher because of more use of resources and better resulting quality. If this is the case, you might "get what you pay for" and may wish to pay for the better quality. On the other hand, if quality is not related to charges and we wish to go to the highest quality hospital at the lowest cost (the current definition of "value" in the healthcare ecosystem), then we would like to know how best to predict which hospital has the best value. This is where predictive analytics can assist. Here, we use a limited number of variables to simplify the example. To get a better understanding of the relationship between quality and cost requires many more quality measures, and is beyond the scope of this tutorial.

The metrics of quality in this tutorial data set include HF and AMI measures, which are required by CMS to be reported. These are surrogates rather than comprehensive measures of quality, as they are process (instead of outcomes) metrics and only use a small set of parameters. As CMS describes, HF "estimates a hospital-level risk-standardized mortality rate (RSMR), defined as death from any cause within 30 days after the index admission date, for patients discharged from the hospital with a principal diagnosis of heart failure (HF)" (www.qualitymeasures.ahrq.gov/content. aspx?id = 35573). The AMI measure is even further removed from the Heart Failure DRG, the subject of our inquiry. CMS states that AMI "estimates a hospital-level risk-standardized mortality rate (RSMS), defined as death from any cause within 30 days after the index admission date, for patients discharged from the hospital with a principal diagnosis of acute myocardial infarction (AMI)" (www.qualitymeasures.ahrq.gov/content.aspx?id = 35572). Nevertheless, the same hospital services treat both acute myocardial infarction and heart failure diagnosis groups — thus our inclusion in this tutorial as surrogates for quality. There are many other measures of quality that can be used, and the reader can see these measures at the National Quality Measures Clearinghouse (www.qualitymeasures.ahrq.gov/index.aspx). Additional measures used by the State of New York Department of Health can also be accessed at their website (http:// hospitals.nyhealth.gov/technotes.php).

The example we are going to run in this tutorial is a prediction of quality of care, as measured by the HF metric as the target variable. The predictor variables include Zip Code, Status (Private or Public), Discharges, and Mean Charge. All the variables listed, except Discharges, have been discussed previously, and some relationship seems to exist among them. The number of Discharges is included because the hypothesis is, the more procedures performed (here Discharges is a surrogate for the number of procedures) the better you get, and therefore the higher quality of care.

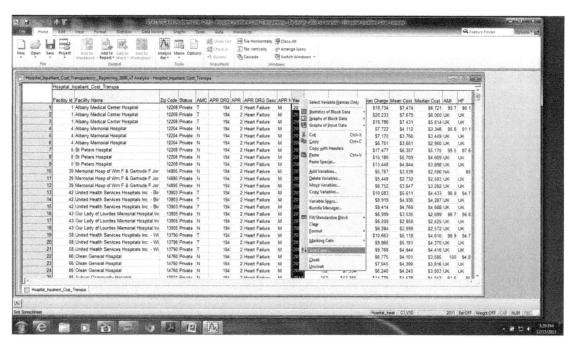

FIGURE R.23   Locating Sort Cases functionality in Statistica.

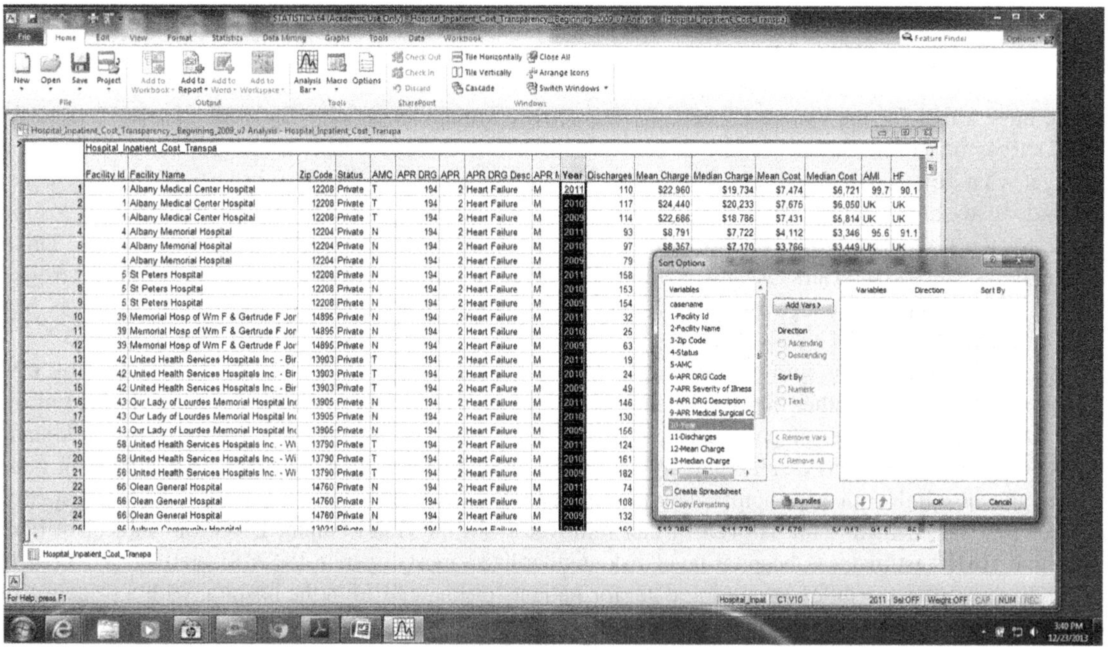

FIGURE R.24   Sorting by year to isolate observations (rows) with missing HF values.

We first look at the HF target variable, and see there are numerous missing numbers. This is because the measures were obtained only for 2011. To run the analysis we need to change or remove the missing variables. For the years 2009 and 2010 we are going to remove the cases, all of which have HF designated as UK (for unknown). First we go to the top of the Year variable, right click, and click on Sort Cases (Figure R.23).

The Sort Options dialog allows us to sort only by Year (Figure R.24).

When we click OK, we include the other variables by default (Figure R.25).

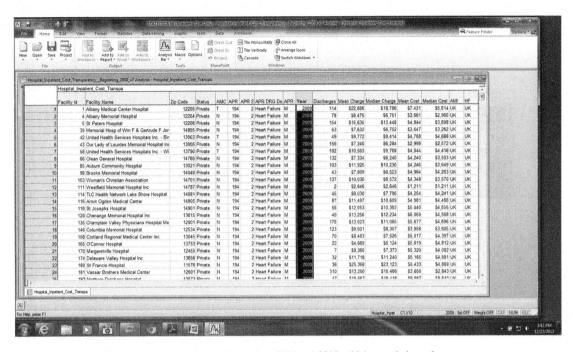

FIGURE R.25 Sorting by year allows you to isolate rows (cases) from 2009 and 2010, which are missing values.

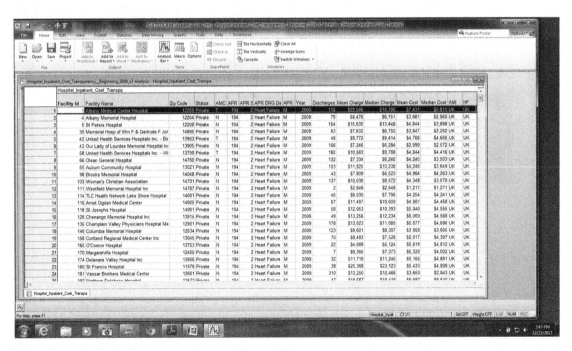

FIGURE R.26 Highlighting the 2009 and 2010 cases, starting from the top.

We then highlight the cases for 2009 (Figure R.26).

Scroll down to include all cases for 2009 and 2010, using the cursor to highlight and the Shift key to include all cases, and in the Edit tab click on the Delete button and Cases (Figure R.27).

You then see the dialog box that confirms the cases you wish to delete (Figure R.28).

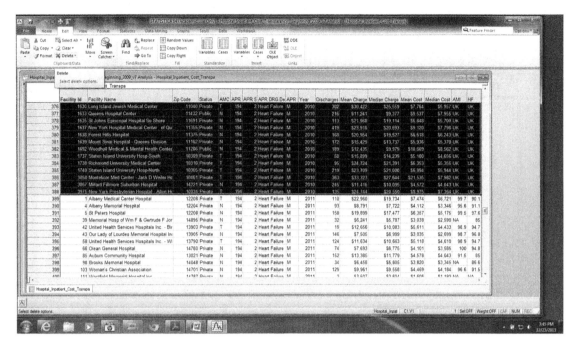

FIGURE R.27   All 2009 and 2010 rows (cases) highlighted, locating Delete button in Edit tab of Statistica.

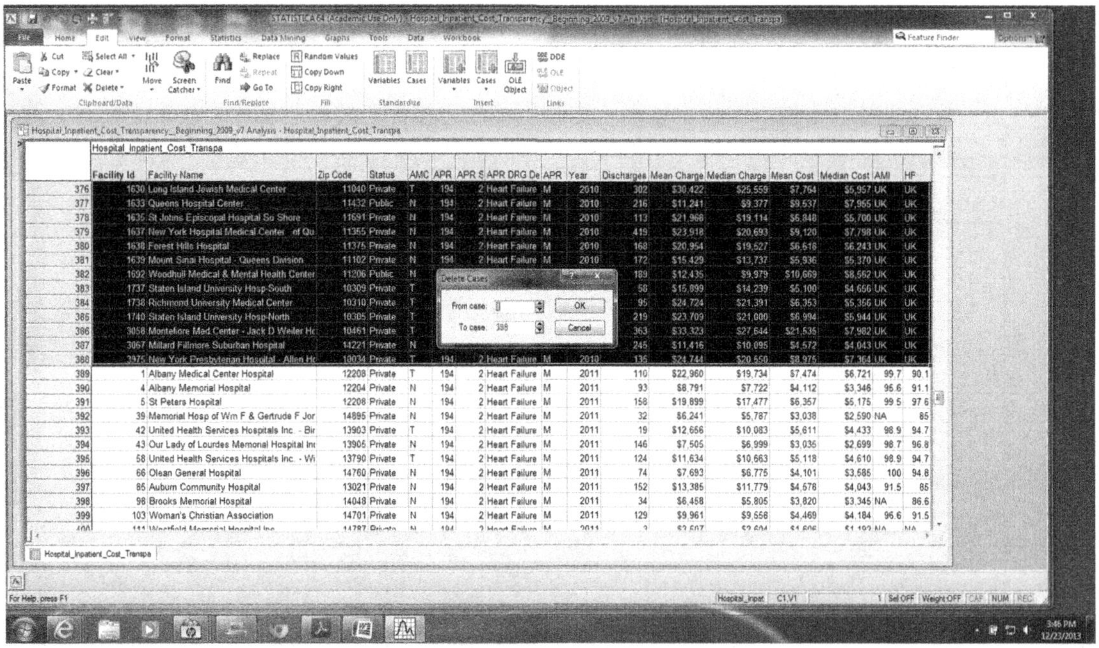

FIGURE R.28   Affirming cases to delete.

What is left is all the cases for 2011. Here, we are going to take all the missing numbers, designated by either 0 or NA for "Not Available," and substitute 94.5, which is the mean of the existing 169 values. We could also use the Mean imputation function, but since there are only 25 of 194 missing values we are going to simply change them to 94.5. To do this we highlight the column we wish to change, go to the Edit tab, Replace button, and either Replace All in the column or Find and Replace each cell (Figure R.29).

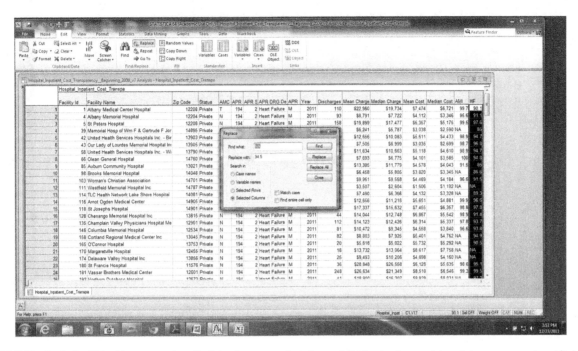

FIGURE R.29 Replacing NA with a mean value, all of the above steps show the work it takes to clean up data and steps necessary to get it right.

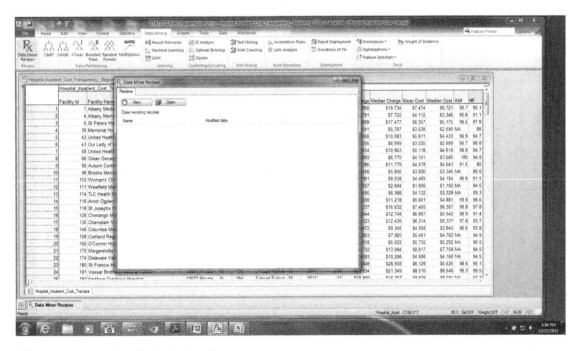

FIGURE R.30 Locating Data Miner Recipes in Statistica.

Next, we use the Data Miner Recipe application in the STATISTICA software. This will give us an initial feel for the data and possible predictive analytics we can use. First, go to the Data Mining tab and click the Data Miner Recipes button (Figure R.30).

Click the New button and the Data Miner Recipes application opens, and the Open/Connect data file button allows us to search for the appropriate data set (Figure R.31).

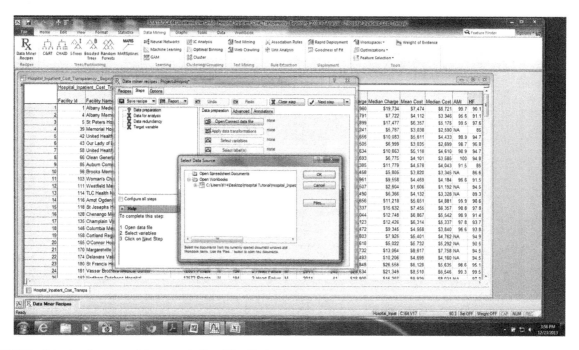

FIGURE R.31 Selecting the source of data to run in Data Miner Recipe.

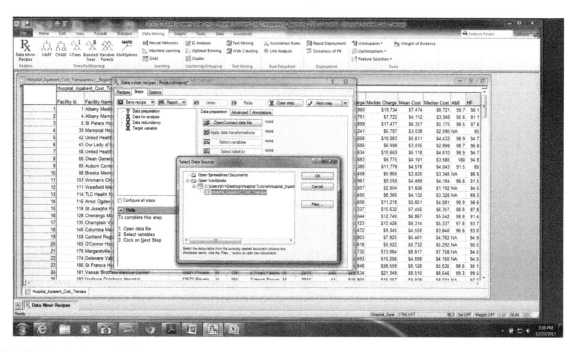

FIGURE R.32 Opening the specific dataset.

Here, we open the file to reveal the STATISTICA data set we plan to use (Figure R.32).

Clicking the OK button connects the data set to the software application. Then, clicking the Select Variables button opens the dialog box where we select our Target variable (HF) and Input variables (Zip Code, Discharges, Mean Charges, Status, and AMC). Individual variables can be selected by left clicking while you hold down the Ctrl button (Figure R.33).

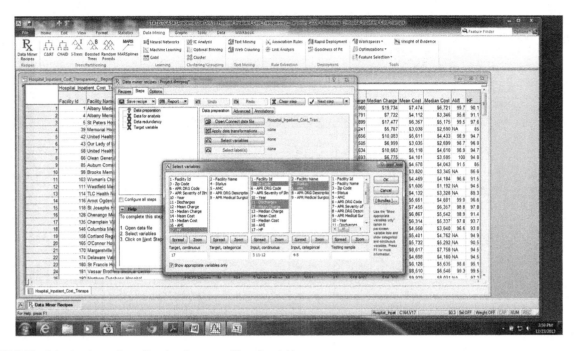

FIGURE R.33 Selecting the predictor (Input) and outcome (Target) variables.

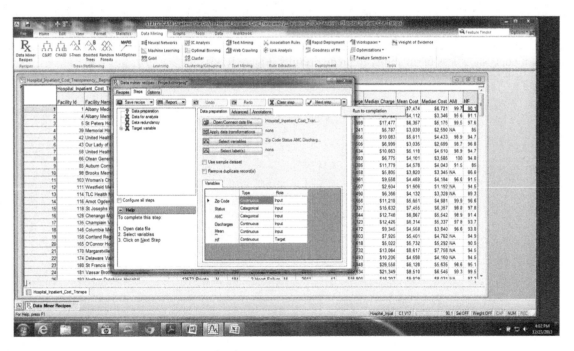

FIGURE R.34 Locating Run to Completion in the Next Step button.

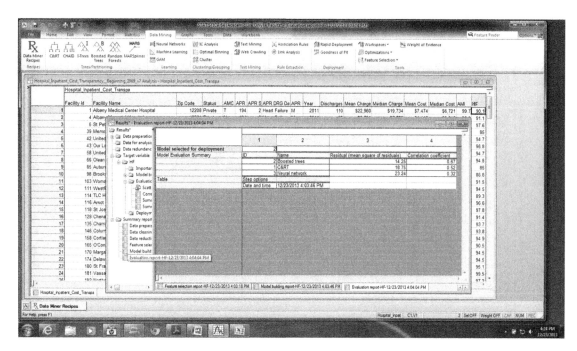

FIGURE R.35 Data Miner Recipe runs multiple models, here showing Boosted Trees giving the highest correlation coefficient.

After we click OK, we go to the Next step button drop-down arrow, find the Run to Completion button, and click it (Figure R.34).

Once the software finishes we see the results. The Boosted trees shows the greatest predictability, while the other three default models show less of an ability to predict results (Figure R.35).

Tutorial S

Availability of Hospital Beds for Newly Admitted Patients: The Impact of Environmental Services on Hospital Throughput

Michael Cook, PhD, CFM

Chapter Outline

INTRODUCTION

This tutorial is focused on hospital throughput, and specifically the impact EVS (Environmental Services) departments have on bed utilization. Bed utilization is a key component of throughput for all in-patient care hospitals. The goal is to have enough hospital beds available to meet the needs of newly admitted patients. A key constraint is the ability to quickly clean a room and make it ready for the next patient. This tutorial will focus on the impact of EVS and their ability to clean rooms to make them ready for the next patients. Central to EVS effectiveness is the ability to clean rooms within a required timeframe. At the moment a patient is discharged, the clock starts for the EVS department. The amount of time allotted to EVS for cleaning the rooms depends on the "bed priority" code assigned by the nurse entering it into the system. There are three codes used: STAT (45 minutes), NEXT (60 minutes), and NORMAL (120 minutes). Not meeting these timeframes impacts the throughput of the hospital. The data set for this tutorial represents over 1,600 discharge records for 1 month (January 2013), from a 352-bed hospital located in Southern California.

DATA EXTRACTION

We begin by extracting a file from electronic medical records. This file is brought into an Excel spreadsheet, where we begin some preliminary data transformation and then load it into STATISTICA for the analysis. One of the tasks we did in Excel was create some new variables. Figure S.1 provides an example of creating a new variable to combine the date field with the time field to make future calculations a little easier. We want to create a new variable that combines the date field with the associated time field. For example, we want to combine the date field "Bed is Cleaned Date" with the column "Bed is Cleaned Time" field to create one field to identify the date and time. This was done in .xlsx file (see Figure S.1).

Practical Predictive Analytics and Decisioning Systems for Medicine. DOI: http://dx.doi.org/10.1016/B978-0-12-411643-6.00036-3

Q	R	S	T	U	V	W	X	Y	Z	AA
Bed is	Bed is Clea	Next Ad	Next Admit	Bed	Discharg	Discharg	Total	Bed Turnaroui T		
1/3/2013	1:33:00 PM	1/18/2013	10:56:00 AM	NORMAL	22	69	47	21.443	=INT(Q486)+MOD(R486,1)	
									MOD(number, divisor)	

FIGURE S.1 Combine multiple fields to create a new variable.

RUNNING THE FEATURE SELECTION FOR THE EVS THROUGHPUT TUTORIAL DATA SET

Open the data set. Go to Data Mining, down to the bottom, Data Mining Workspace, and then Click on All Procedures. Your screen will look like the presentation in Figure S.2.

Click on Data Source and click on the EVS Throughput Tutorial Dataset file, and then on OK. The variable selection box will come up immediately (Figure S.3).

There are a couple of ways to approach this next step. For this tutorial, close the "Select dependent variables and predictors" box. Your screen will now look like the display in Figure S.4.

Now choose "Graphs" from the ribbon at the top (right next to the "Data Mining" tab you used before) (Figure S.5). Once you select Scatterplots, you'll have the display seen in Figure S.6.

Click OK; then select the variables Total Clean Time, Bed Priority, and Duration of Hospital stay (see Figure S.7).

If it wasn't evident during data preparation, it's evident now that there appear to be some non-valid results. We have negative times for Discharge to Bed is Clean results (Figure S.8). It's not feasible that a bed was cleaned and ready for a new admit before the current patient was even discharged. So, data cleaning is appropriate. It is important to notice that the results of the 3D scatterplot indicate that the Bed Priority is listed as NEXT, NORMAL, and STAT, but that is not the rank order. STAT is most important, then NEXT, then NORMAL.

To remove the rows with negative processing times, we select the Data tab on the top ribbon, and then Auto Filter. Click the down arrow in the Discharge Process Time variable and select the Custom option. In the Auto Filter Criteria dialog box, type in the Expression box V11 < = 0 and then press OK (Figures S.9, S.10).

When you hit OK, you should see the rows with negative or zero values in the Discharge Process Time column (Figure S.11).

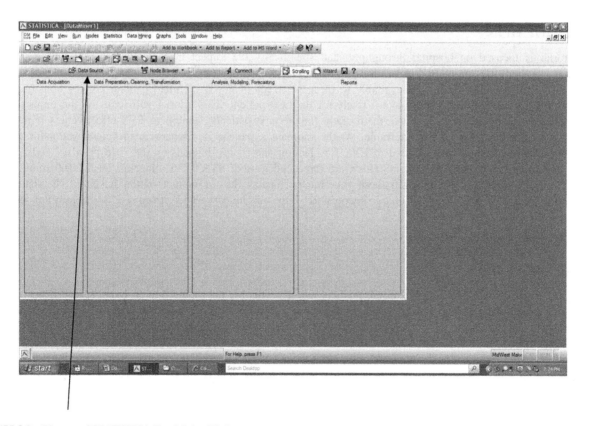

FIGURE S.2 Diagram of STATISTICA Data Mining Workspace.

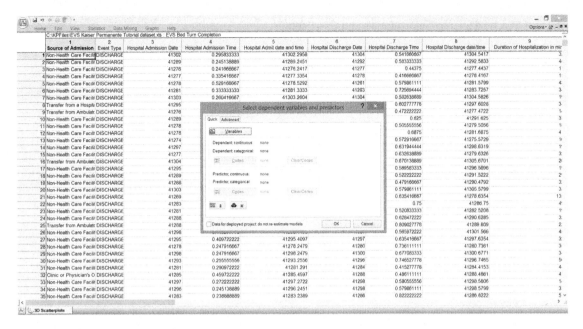

FIGURE S.3 Variable Selection Dialog Box.

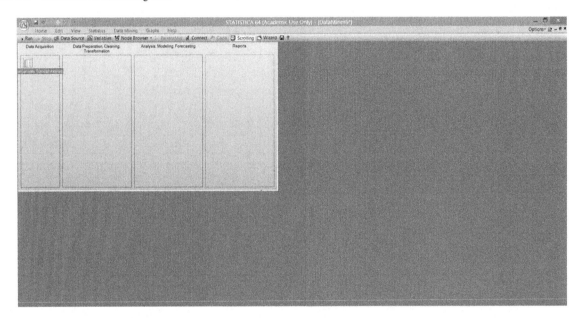

FIGURE S.4 Selecting the Data Set in DataMiner.

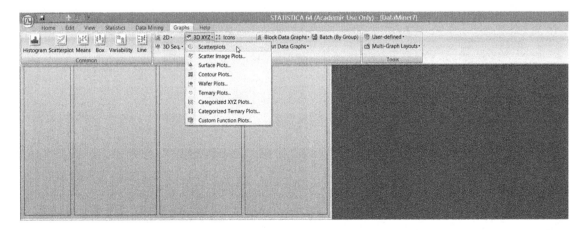

FIGURE S.5 Selecting the Graphical Output.

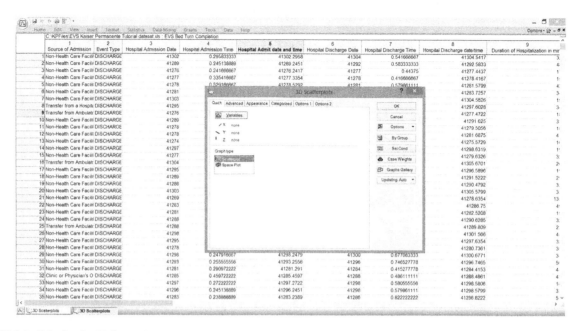

FIGURE S.6   Selecting the 3D Scatterplot.

FIGURE S.7   Selecting the Variables for the 3D Scatterplot.

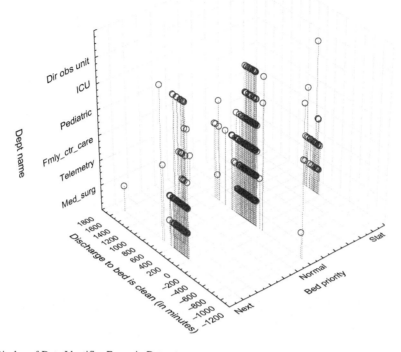

FIGURE S.8 Graphical Display of Data Identifies Errors in Dataset.

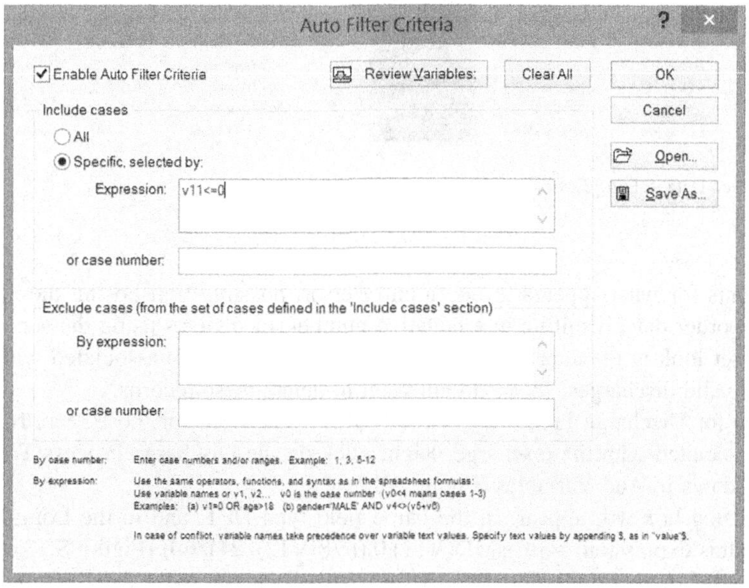

FIGURE S.9 Auto Filter Criteria — Expression Dialog Box.

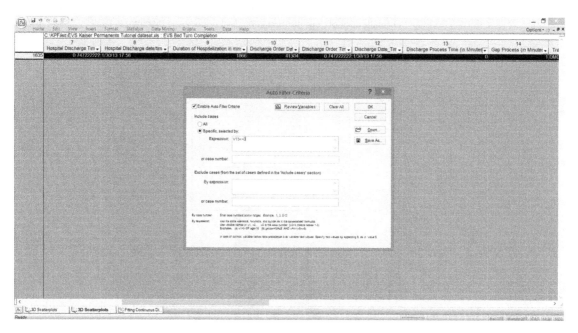

FIGURE S.10   Expression Dialog Box.

8 Discharge Order Date	9 Discharge Order Time	10 DisOrd_DT	11 Discharge Process Time (in Minutes)	12 Gap Process (in Minutes)	13 Dept Name	14 Transfer to Effective Date	15 Transfer to Effective Time
1/30/2013	6:05:00 PM	1/30/13 6:05 PM	-20	169	Med_Surg	1/30/2013	5:45:00 PM
1/24/2013	10:51:00 AM	1/24/13 10:51 AM	-1,293	1,440	Med_Surg	1/23/2013	1:18:00 PM
1/24/2013	10:51:00 AM	1/24/13 10:51 AM	-1,293	1,440	Med_Surg	1/23/2013	1:18:00 PM
1/31/2013	7:54:00 PM	1/31/13 7:54 PM	-24	24	Med_Surg	1/31/2013	7:30:00 PM
1/16/2013	6:50:00 PM	1/16/13 6:50 PM	-10	11	Telemetry	1/16/2013	6:40:00 PM
1/7/2013	2:23:00 PM	1/7/13 2:23 PM	-1,188	1,445	Med_Surg	1/6/2013	6:35:00 PM
1/11/2013	4:46:00 PM	1/11/13 4:46 PM	-1	20	Telemetry	1/11/2013	4:45:00 PM
1/8/2013	4:29:00 PM	1/8/13 4:29 PM	-9	68	Telemetry	1/8/2013	4:20:00 PM
1/9/2013	7:07:00 PM	1/9/13 7:07 PM	-12	17	Telemetry	1/9/2013	6:55:00 PM
1/12/2013	12:09:00 PM	1/12/13 12:09 PM	-89	273	Telemetry	1/12/2013	10:40:00 AM
1/18/2013	2:18:00 PM	1/18/13 2:18 PM	-6	8	Telemetry	1/18/2013	2:12:00 PM
1/25/2013	4:24:00 PM	1/25/13 4:24 PM	-69	126	Telemetry	1/25/2013	3:15:00 PM
1/27/2013	3:14:00 PM	1/27/13 3:14 PM	-1,286	1,443	Telemetry	1/26/2013	5:48:00 PM
1/30/2013	5:56:00 PM	1/30/13 5:56 PM	0	1	Dir Obs Unit	1/30/2013	5:56:00 PM

FIGURE S.11   Results of Filtered Data — Entry Errors Identified.

This procedure accounts for what appears to be an entry error, possibly transposing the actual discharge date with the physicians' discharge order date, resulting in a negative number, or perhaps using the same date and time, resulting in zeros. However, a closer look at the data reveals that not every discharge is associated with a physician's discharge order. These may still be valid discharges, so we do not want to delete these records.

Create a new variable for Discharge Processing Time (DPT), to account for those records that do not have a physician's discharge order associated with the discharge. Right click on the Discharge Process Time header in the variable name column, and scroll down to Add Variables (Figure S.12).

The Add Variables dialog box will appear. In the name field type DPT, and in the Long Name (label or functions with formulas) box, type this expression: = iif(isMD(V11),0,((V8-V12)*24)*60) (Figure S.13).

This formula states that if there are missing data (MD) in the discharge order date or time, then place a zero in the discharge processing time field. Otherwise, subtract the discharge order date and time from the actual hospital discharge date and time. Multiply by 24 to get hours, and then multiply by 60 to get discharge processing time in minutes.

STATISTICA 64 (Academic Use Only) - [Data: EVS Kaiser Permanente Tutorial dataset* (33v by 165c)]

Home   Edit   View   Insert   Format   Statistics   Data Mining   Graphs   Tools   Data   Help

C:\KPFiles\EVS Kaiser Permanente Tutorial dataset.xls : EVS Bed Turn Completion

	9 Duration of Hospitalization in mins	10 Discharge Order Date	11 Discharge Order Time	12 Discharge Date_Time	13 Discharge Process Time (in Minutes)	14 DI	15 (menu)	16 Transfer to Department Name	17 Transfer to Effective
186	1681			12/31/99 0:00			Select Variable Names Only	3 DMC 5EST DTL6	
187	3076	41300	0.389583333	1/26/13 9:21		349	Statistics of Block Data	0 DMC 4WST DMS4	
188	3431	41291	0.434027778	1/17/13 10:25		241	Graphs of Block Data	0 DMC 4WST DMS4	
189	8926	41296	0.339583333	1/22/13 8:09		141	Graphs of Input Data	7 DMC 4WST DMS4	
190	3435	41278	0.4875	1/4/13 11:42		275	Cut Ctrl+X	5 DMC 4WST DMS4	
191	2052	41296	0.43125	1/22/13 10:21		290	Copy Ctrl+C	1 DMC 5WST DMS5	
192	3137	41304	0.346527778	1/30/13 8:19		261	Copy with Headers	6 DMC 3FCE DOBX	
193	3212	41290	0.308333333	1/16/13 7:24		229	Paste Ctrl+V	1 DMC 5EST DTL6	
194	1909	41282	0.36875	1/8/13 8:51		470	Paste Special...	1 DMC 5EST DTL6	
195	3153	41289	0.345138889	1/15/13 8:17		403	Add Variables	0 DMC 3FCE DOBX	
196	5013	41285	0.354861111	1/11/13 8:31		629	Delete Variables...	0 DMC 5WST DMS5	
197	3293	41298	0.402083333	1/24/13 9:39		457	Move Variables...	0 DMC 4WST DMS4	
198	1824	41275	0.478472222	1/1/13 11:29		76	Copy Variables...	2 DMC 3FCE DOBX	
199	1865	41284	0.423611111	1/10/13 10:10		168	Variable Specs...	0 DMC 4WST DMS4	
200	2021	41298	0.50625	1/24/13 12:09		185	Bundle Manager...	0 DMC 4WST DMS4	
201	3188	41305	0.323611111	1/31/13 7:46		209	Fill/Standardize Block	8 DMC 3FCE DOBX	
202	2810	41290	0.321527778	1/16/13 7:43		817	Clear	7 DMC 3FCE DOBX	
203	3403	41298	0.457638889	1/24/13 10:59		151	Format	0 DMC 3FCE DOBX	
204	4675	41277	0.377777778	1/3/13 9:04		121	Marking Cells	0 DMC 4WST DMS4	
205	3289	41290	0.31875	1/16/13 7:39		231	Sort Cases...	8 DMC 3FCE DOBX	
206	1796	41282	0.513194444	1/8/13 12:19		138	Cloak	0 DMC 5EST DTL6	
207	4862	41285	0.448611111	1/11/13 10:46		243	Uncloak	0 DMC 4WST DMS4	
208	4723	41302	0.426388889	1/28/13 10:14		334		0 DMC 3FCE DOBX	
209	4824	41294	0.479861111	1/20/13 11:31		254		40 DMC 5WST DMS5	
210	1795	41283	0.347222222	1/9/13 8:20		200		14 DMC 5WST DMS5	
211	7642	41300	0.527083333	1/26/13 12:39		174		0 DMC 4WST DMS4	
212	3139	41292	0.521527778	1/18/13 12:31		64		4 DMC 3FCE DOBX	
213	1806	41296	0.624305556	1/22/13 14:59		53		5 DMC 5EST DTL6	
214	32618	41295	0.322222222	1/21/13 7:44		371		6 DMC 3FCE DOBX	
215	1697	41293	0.355555556	1/19/13 8:32		383		2 DMC 3FCE DOBX	
216	11930	41299	0.4	1/25/13 9:36		162		11 DMC 2DOU DME1	
217	3368	41286	0.427083333	1/12/13 10:15		195		132 DMC 4WST DMS4	
218	3279	41279	0.381944444	1/5/13 9:10		765		20 DMC 3FCE DOBX	
219	3956	41289	0.515277778	1/15/13 12:22		54		1 DMC 3FCE DOBX	
220	1915	41284	0.558333333	1/10/13 13:24		103		1 DMC 4WST DMS4	

3D Scatterplots   3D Scatterplots   Fitting Continuous Di...

FIGURE S.12   Adding New Variables in STATISTICA.

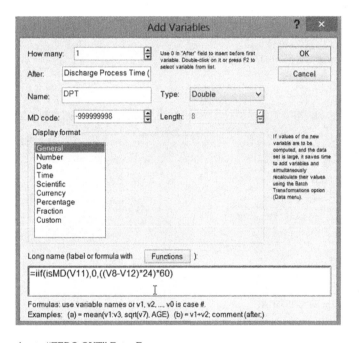

FIGURE S.13   Building the Expression to "ZERO OUT" Entry Errors.

Keep in mind that, depending how and where you create new variables, the field you actually select may be different than V11.

We will continue to clean up the data and add variables. For example, we still get negative numbers for "Discharge to Bed is Clean" and "Bed Turn."

We use the same process to create a new variable called "Time from Dis to Clean Bed" and in the Long name box this expression is input: $= iif(isMD(v24),median(v33),((Abs(v23-v8)*24)*60))$. This results in calculating the time between discharge from hospital and when the bed is ready for the next patient. This variable is a little different in that if there is no new patient admitted, there would be no value in this cell. So the decision was to take the median of the "Bed Turn" values.

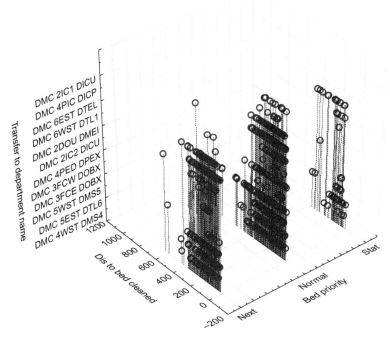

3D Scatterplot of transfer to department name against bed priority and
Dis to bed cleaned kaiser 33v*1651c

FIGURE S.14   New 3D Scatterplot After Entry Error Cleanup.

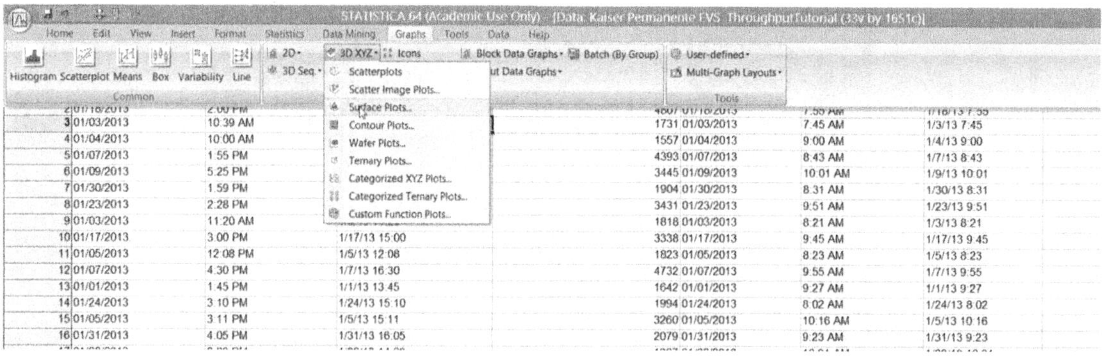

FIGURE S.15   Creating Surface Plot in STATISTICA.

Rerunning the 3D scatterplot from above (Figure S.8), we see a slightly clearer picture of the distribution of discharge times. By looking at the distribution, there appear to be a few clusters, and a few outliers as well (Figure S.14).

To get a surface plot, from main menu, select the Graphs tab, and then the 3D XYZ button (Figure S.15).

Click on the Variables tab, and then select your variables (Figure S.16).

This surface plot gives a somewhat different, but clearer, picture of the processing times. It appears that when discharge occurs between late evening and the early morning hours, the effective time (the time when all the documentation is complete) and the discharge processing time (the time when the patient is actually leaving hospital – the famous "wheelchair" ride) are pretty close together, meaning patients get out of the hospital more quickly when discharged in the morning. As it gets later into the afternoon and evening hours, the time between the doctor's order for discharge and the time the patient actually leaves the hospital increases.

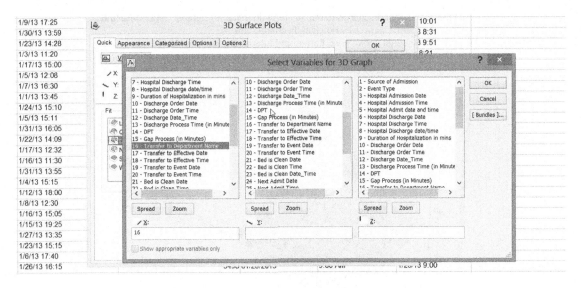

FIGURE S.16   3D Surface Plot Variable Selection.

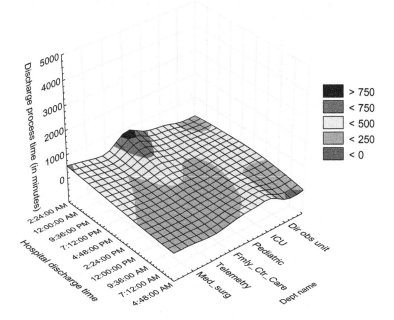

FIGURE S.17   3D Surface Plot for Discharge Processing Time Based on Hospital Time and Department Name.

As you might suspect, the plot indicates that the discharge processing time appears related to the type of nursing department as well as the time of the discharge event (Figure S.17).

Additionally, it is interesting to see if there appears to be a relationship between how long it takes between discharge time and cleaning the room, and if this is impacted by the department. The surface plot in Figure S.18 shows that there is quite a bit of variation by department and time.

When we want to see which variables have the largest impact, we can do a feature selection. On the main tabs, select the Data Mining tab, then Feature Selection on the far right (Figures S.19, S.20).

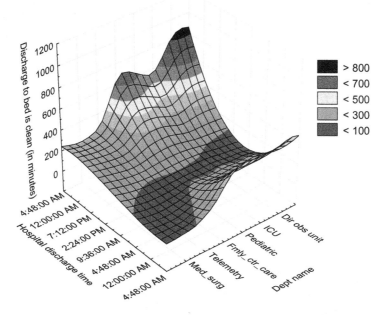

FIGURE S.18 3D Plot for Discharge Time to Clean Bed based on Hospital Discharge Time and Department Name.

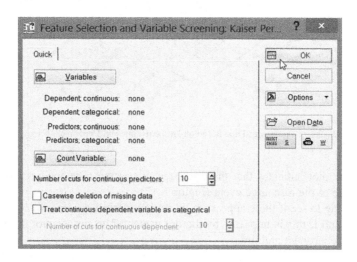

FIGURE S.19 Feature Selection in STATISTICA.

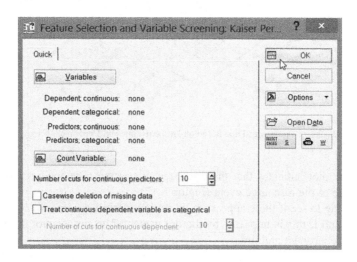

FIGURE S.20 Feature Selection and Variable Screening.

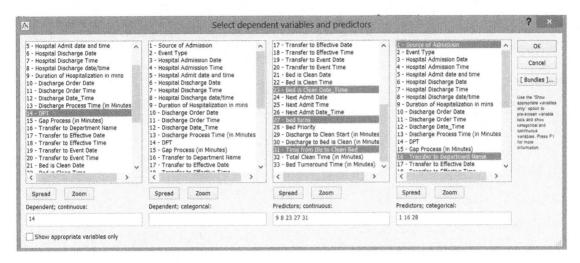

FIGURE S.21   Feature Selection – Dependent and Predictor Variables.

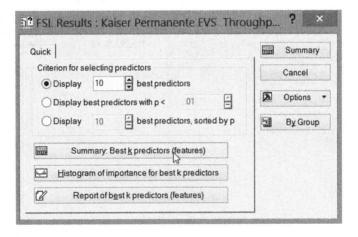

FIGURE S.22   Feature Selection Results – Summary: Best K Predictors.

Click on the Variables button and select DPT in the Dependent; continuous column. Then select Predictors; continuous (Bed is Clean Date_Time, bed turns, Discharge to Bed is Clean in minutes, etc.). Then select Transfer to Dept Name, Source of Admission, and Bed Priority in the Predictors; categorical column (Figures S.21).

From the Feature Selection Results, we will select the Summary: Best k predictors, and the Histogram of importance for best k predictors (Figure S.22).

It is clear from the graph (Figure S.23) that the department has the largest impact in determining the total discharge processing time. Although Discharge to Bed is Clean and Bed Turnaround are important for this study, they both occur after discharge and as such have little impact on discharge processing time, as indicated in this graph. If we rerun the graph to focus on EVS cleaning times, we would expect to see a somewhat different feature selection graph. We create a new variable, Hosp_Stay(in hours), to see if there is relationship between how long a patient was in the hospital and discharge processing times, as well as total cleaning time for EVS.

Once again, we will select a variable in the header of the spreadsheet, right click, and then scroll down to "Add Variables" (Figure S.24). In the dialog box, change the name to "Hosp_Stay(in hours)." In the "long name" dialog box, input this formula: = ((v7-v4)*24). This will compute the time between the admission date and the discharge date. I used the display format "number" with 0 decimals to show for how many hours a person was in the hospital.

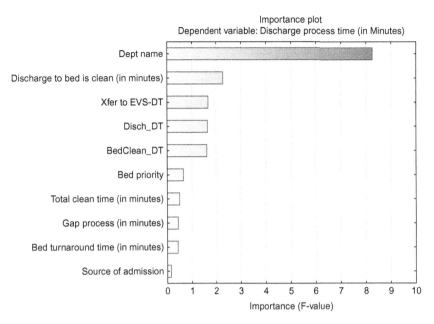

FIGURE S.23 Importance Plot — Discharge Processing Time.

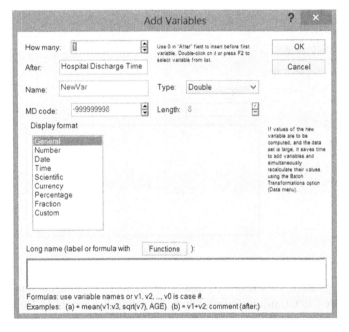

FIGURE S.24 Feature Selection — Adding Variables.

As we can see in Figure S.25, length of stay in the hospital becomes one of the more prominent items in the feature selection.

For the Total Clean Time in Minutes variable, go to Data Mining and Features Selection as before; then click on the Variables button, and select Total Clean Time (in Minutes) in the dependent, continuous column. Then select Next Admit Date_Time, Discharge to Clean Start (in Minutes), Discharge to Bed is Clean (in Minutes), Hospital Admit date and time, Hospital Discharge date/time, Duration of Hospitalization in mins, Bed is Clean Date_Time, and DPT in the Predictors Continuous column.

For the Categorical Predictors, select Bed Priority, Source of Admission column, and for Predictors Categorical select all four items. Once you've selected the variables, press OK, then OK on feature selection. You should have the FSL Results dialog box returned. Select the histogram of importance for best k predictors.

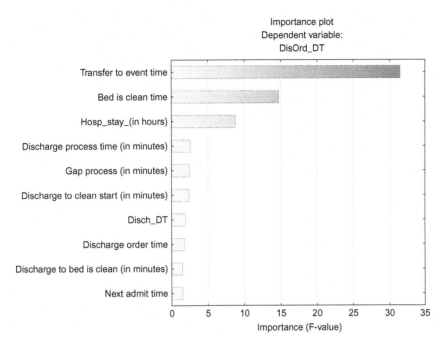

FIGURE S.25 Importance Plot − Dependent Variable: Discharge Order Time.

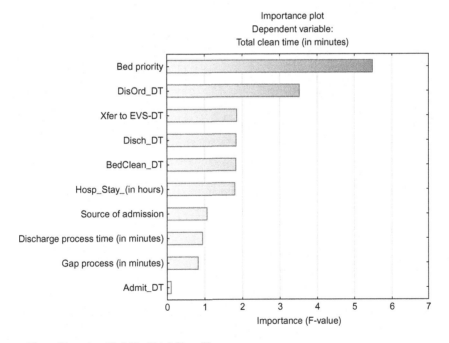

FIGURE S.26 Importance Plot − Dependent Variable: Total Clean Time.

The keys for how long it takes EVS to clean a room are the bed priority, discharge order date and time, when the room was transferred to EVS, and a few others (Figure S.26).

The importance plot (Figure S.27) indicates that the most significant factors are the time from discharge to clean bed, Bed Priority, Discharge Date and Time, and bed turns (which again means the time it takes to reassign the room to the next patient).

When we look at the Summary of key variables we see the F-Value as well as the p value associated with it (Figure S.28).

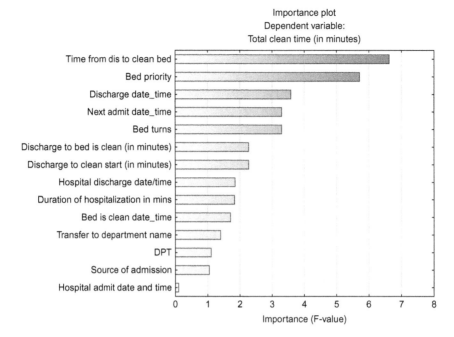

FIGURE S.27 Importance Plot – Dependent Variable: Total Clean Time.

	Best predictors for cc	
	F-value	p-value
Bed Priority	5.468955	0.004293
DisOrd_DT	3.522874	0.060704
Xfer to EVS-DT	1.851860	0.063666
Disch_DT	1.835370	0.066443
BedClean_DT	1.824706	0.068297
Hosp_Stay_(in hours)	1.797724	0.095946
Source of Admission	1.059139	0.385116
Discharge Process Time (in Minutes)	0.940972	0.464352
Gap Process (in Minutes)	0.822068	0.533839
Admit_DT	0.099150	0.752892

FIGURE S.28 Summary of Key Values: F and P Values.

Correlations (Spreadsheet2_(Recovered))
Marked correlations are significant at p < .05000
N=1626 (Casewise deletion of missing data)

Variable	Means	Std.Dev.	Hospital Discharge date/time	Duration of Hospitalization in mins	Discharge Date_Time	DPT	Bed is Clean Date_Time	Next Admit Date_Time	bed turns	Time from Dis to Clean Bed	Total Clean Time (in Minutes)
Hospital Discharge date/time	41291.10	8.679	1.000000	0.003134	0.006181	0.030350	0.999963	0.994133	-0.066833	0.008645	-0.048793
Duration of Hospitalization in mins	4977.10	6646.816	0.003134	1.000000	-0.036105	0.063592	0.003522	-0.000885	-0.040871	0.039106	0.056874
Discharge Date_Time	40376.76	6077.405	0.006181	-0.036105	1.000000	0.148412	0.005547	0.004671	-0.008189	-0.072168	-0.046176
DPT	219.49	222.629	0.030350	0.063592	0.148412	1.000000	0.030683	0.034370	0.033765	0.063727	-0.003756
Bed is Clean Date_Time	41291.20	8.678	0.999963	0.003522	0.005547	0.030683	1.000000	0.994183	-0.066709	0.015355	-0.047997
Next Admit Date_Time	41291.58	8.666	0.994133	-0.000885	0.004671	0.034370	0.994183	1.000000	0.041140	0.019410	-0.045585
bed turns	544.02	1347.068	-0.066833	-0.040871	-0.008189	0.033765	-0.066709	0.041140	1.000000	0.037373	0.022954
Time from Dis to Clean Bed	149.46	103.833	0.008645	0.039106	-0.072168	0.063727	0.015355	0.019410	0.037373	1.000000	0.067624
Total Clean Time (in Minutes)	36.44	24.246	-0.048793	0.056874	-0.046176	-0.003756	-0.047997	-0.045585	0.022954	0.067624	1.000000

FIGURE S.29 Correlation Matrix.

Reviewing the correlation matrix helps identify which variables are highly correlated with each other, and therefore should not be included together. For example, Next Admit date and time is highly correlated (0.999) with Hospital Discharge Date/Time (Figure S.29). These two variables may be explaining the same phenomenon, and should not both be used in the analysis.

Overall, it appears that the EVS department has a key role in assisting the hospital with throughput. Important factors in helping the success of the EVS department are Bed Priority, Hospital Discharge Date, Discharge Order Date and bed turns and are a focus for further study.

We would need to look at staffing levels, specialists on staff, and other factors to determine why afternoon discharges and specific departments increase the time to leave the hospital. Other key factors are the availability of EVS attendants to assist in cleaning the rooms and provide a quicker throughput.

Tutorial T

Predicting Vascular Thrombosis: Comparing Predictive Analytic Models and Building an Ensemble Model for "Best Prediction"

Magid Amer, MD, MBBCh, FRCS, FRCP, FACP, Danny W. Stout, PhD, and Gary D. Miner, PhD

Chapter Outline

INTRODUCTION

Venous thromboembolism (VTE) and cancer have been closely associated for over 150 years (Sack *et al.*, 1977). In patients with cancer, if they have VTE their prognosis is not as positive as someone without the syndrome (Sorensen *et al.*, 2000). Moreover, if patients have both cancer and VTE, their risk of bleeding following anticoagulant therapy is increased. Given this information it is not surprising that coagulation disorders in cancer patients have been an important issue in cancer management. In addition to this association, it has been shown that VTE in cancer patients is also associated with advanced disease, increased tumor cell burden, and immobilization due to tumor cachexia or hospitalization, as well as mechanical compression of veins by progressive tumor masses. Hence, VTE represents one of the most important causes of morbidity and mortality in cancer patients (Amer, 2013).

Since the overall prevalence of these clinical outcomes in cancer patient has been largely based on hospital-based statistics, medical insurance data, and retrospective studies, it would be insightful to have studies based upon other data using predictive analytics. This tutorial is an example of this type of effort.

TUTORIAL

Data were collected from a retrospective review of clinical data for patients with histologically confirmed cancer with an emphasis on cancer-related thrombosis. Of the data collected, of particular interest are age, race, gender, body mass index (BMI), how many packs of cigarettes per year the patient smokes (if any), type of atherosclerosis (if any), type of cancer, stage of cancer, factor V Leiden mutation, prothrombin G20210a gene mutation, MTHFR-A1298c gene mutation, and MTHFR-c677t gene mutation. A portion of the data is shown in Figure T.1.

An initial cursory review of the data shows that there appears to be a large amount of missing data. Therefore the Data Health Check node will be used to assess the implications of this missing data. With the data set open in STATISTICA, from the Home tab in the Output group select the button for Add to Workspace and click on Add to New Workspace; then save the workspace.

Practical Predictive Analytics and Decisioning Systems for Medicine. DOI: http://dx.doi.org/10.1016/B978-0-12-411643-6.00037-5

		1 DVT	2 Gender	3 Race	4 Age	5 BMI	6 Smoking-PKY	7 Atherosclerosis	8 Cancer_Gr1	9 Stage_Gr1	10 FVL	11 Prothrombin	12 MTHFR-A1298c	13 MTHFR-c677t	14 DVT_Genes
10		Thrombosis	Female	Caucasiar	87.3046	28.1635	10	Generalized	Breast	Stage-III					
11		Thrombosis	Female	Caucasiar	76.6188	23.9063	52	Generalized	Breast	Stage-IV					
12		Thrombosis	Female	Caucasiar	84.4189	24.9835	0	None	Gastrointes	Stage-IV					
13		Thrombosis	Female	Caucasiar	43.0691	21.6773	0	None	Gastrointes	Stage-IV					
14		Thrombosis	Male	Caucasiar	75.5483	33.6173	15	Cardiovasc	Gastrointes	Stage-IV					
15		Thrombosis	Female	Caucasiar	65.7906	29.7894	0	None	GU&GYN	Stage-IV					
16		Thrombosis	Female	Caucasiar	54.2396	21.342	0	None	GU&GYN	Stage-III					
17		Thrombosis	Male	Native-An	76.4736	26.8467	120	Generalized	GU&GYN	Stage-II					
18		Thrombosis	Female	Caucasiar	50.3381	40.722	0	None	GU&GYN	Stage-IV					
19		Thrombosis	Male	Caucasiar	49.076	31.4077	0	None	H&N	Stage-II					
20		Thrombosis	Male	Caucasiar	75.1047	27.9846	0	None	H&N	Stage-IV	1-Negati	1-Negative	2-Hetero	1-Negative	1-Gene
21		Thrombosis	Male	Caucasiar	49.7057	24.8197	0	None	H&N	Stage-III					
22		Thrombosis	Female	Caucasiar	74.7981	34.2209	75	Generalized	Hematologic	Stage-IV					
23		Thrombosis	Male	Caucasiar	62.4613	22.9926	10	Cardiovasc	Hepatobiliar	Stage-IV					
24		Thrombosis	Male	Caucasiar	75.4086	35.8321	30	Cardiovasc	Hepatobiliar	Stage-IV					
25		Thrombosis	Male	Caucasiar	62.7351	25.7662	65	Vascular	Lungs	Stage-IV	2-Hetero	1-Negative			1-Gene
26		Thrombosis	Female	Caucasiar	50.5352	21.0807	35	None	Lungs	Stage-IV	1-Negati	1-Negative	1-Negative	2-Hetero	1-Gene
27		Thrombosis	Female	Caucasiar	53.1389	30.6897	66	None	Lungs	Stage-III					
28		Thrombosis	Male	Caucasiar	46.9979	23.8519	38	None	Lungs	Stage-IV	1-Negati	1-Negative	1-Negative	2-Hetero	1-Gene
29		Thrombosis	Female	Caucasiar	68.4298	22.4766	0	Generalized	Breast	Stage-IV					
30		Thrombosis	Male	Caucasiar	22.538	24.1018	0	None	GU&GYN	Stage-IV					
31		Thrombosis	Female	Caucasiar	64.4654	36.8723	0	None	GU&GYN	Stage-IV	1-Negati	1-Negative	2-Hetero	1-Negative	1-Gene

FIGURE T.1 Data spreadsheet.

FIGURE T.2 Data set inserted into 'Data Miner Workspace' and 'Beta Procedures' selected in the node browser.

Verify that Beta Procedures are selected within the workspace as shown in Figure T.2. Click once on the node representing the data, and then from the Data tab in the Transformations click Data Health Check to add the Data Health Check node to the workspace. Since you clicked once on the data node, the Data Health Check node will automatically be connected to the data. If you do not select the data node first, you will need to manually connect the data to the analysis node by clicking on the small yellow diamond on the data node, holding down and drawing an arrow to the analysis node. Default settings for the Data Health Check node will be accepted, which will determine whether there are sparse data in variables or cases, whether there are outliers, whether there are invariant variables, and finally whether there are redundant variables. Also, they will determine which variables are continuous and which are categorical. At this point we are assessing implications of messy data, so we are not yet cleaning the data.

Edit the parameters of the Data Health Check node by clicking the gray cog icon at the upper left-hand corner of the node. From the Quick tab, click Select All variables (Figure T.3) and then click on OK on both the Variable selection dialog and also the Data Health Check node dialog. Run the Data Health Check node by clicking the green arrow head on the lower left-hand corner of the node.

Double click on the reporting documents node and then select the Data Health Check report. As shown in Figure T.4, currently, due to missing data, 1,799 cases will be removed; this is over 96% of the data set. Moreover, six variables will be removed due to sparseness.

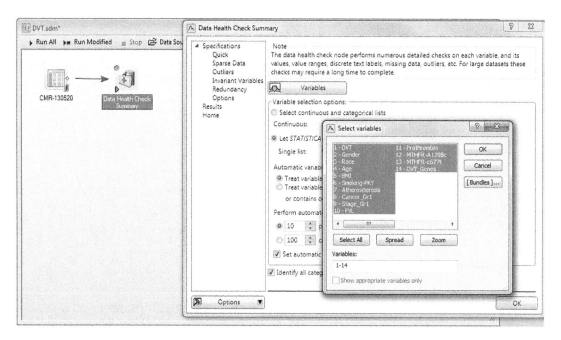

FIGURE T.3 Selecting variables for the 'Data Health Check Node'.

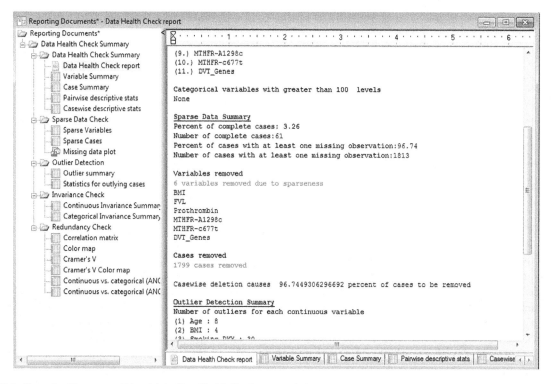

FIGURE T.4 Reporting Documents dialog for the Data Health Check report window.

In this case, so that we can investigate the possible implications of these variables in predicting DVT, we will impute missing data for the six variables indicated in the sparse data check. Click on the data node so that selected nodes will be automatically added to this node. From the Data tab, select the dropdown menu for Filter/Recode from the Transformations group and select Missing Data Imputation. Edit the parameters of the Missing Data Imputation node. Variables are selected as shown in Figure T.5.

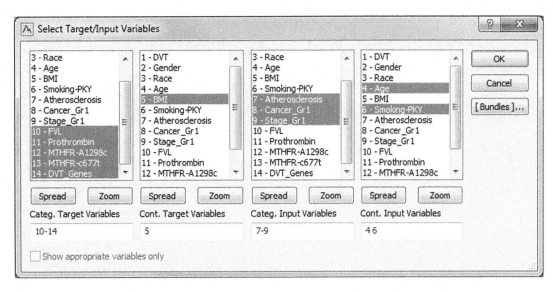

FIGURE T.5 Variable selection window.

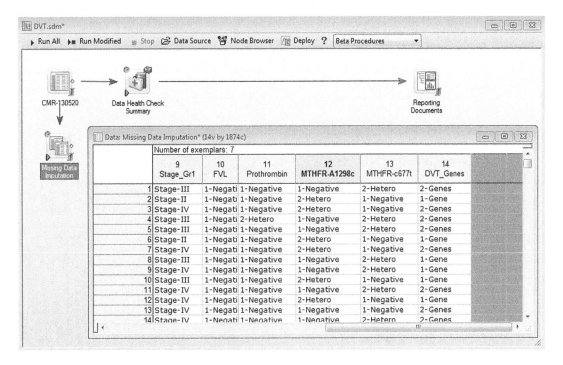

FIGURE T.6 Data imputation window, for missing data in the spreadsheet.

Accept these parameters and run the node. Once you run the Missing Data Imputation node, the background color of the node will turn from yellow to transparent. This lets you know that the procedure or analysis has completed. Click the document icon at the lower right-hand corner of the node to review the data after imputation. As you can see in Figure T.6, the missing data have been imputed using the k-Nearest Neighbor algorithm.

Close the spreadsheet with the imputed data. Now we will need to assess the imputed data using weight of evidence. This will be done so that we can logically explain when predicting the increasing or decreasing probability of VTE given a specific predictor. If we did not assess predictors using weight of evidence, we would be able to say that patients with a greater age are more likely to have VTE; however, we would not be able to say how much more likely

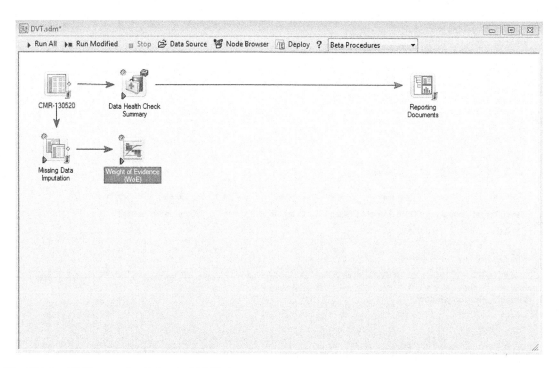

FIGURE T.7   Weight of Evidence node added to the DM Workspace.

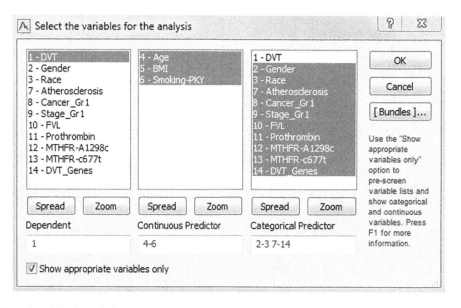

FIGURE T.8   Variables selected for the analysis.

those patients would be to have VTE. This is one of the reasons we will assess the predictors for weight of evidence. After binning a variable, which is the function of weight of evidence, if there are more cases with the undesired outcome, the weight of evidence value will be negative. If there are more cases with the desired outcome, the weight of evidence value will be positive.

From the Data Mining tab in the Tools group, click on WoE to add the Weight of Evidence node to the workspace. Make sure it is connected to the Missing Data Imputation node as shown in Figure T.7.

Edit the parameters of the Weight of Evidence node. Click on the Variables button and select variables, as shown in Figure T.8.

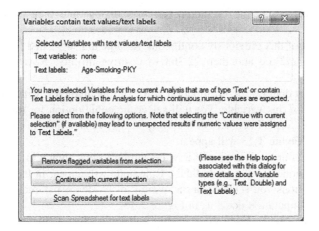

FIGURE T.9 Intermediate warning dialog that text values/text labels are in some of the variables; click on 'Continue with current selection'.

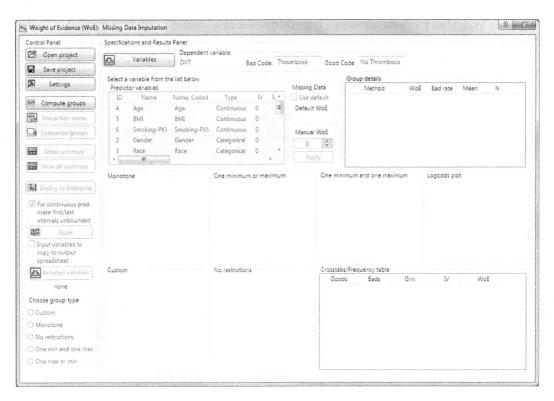

FIGURE T.10 Weight of Evidence Missing Data Imputation window.

STATISTICA will detect that there are text labels in some variables. In this case it will not adversely impact the analysis, so click "Continue with current selection," as shown in Figure T.9.

We need to specify the undesired (Bad) and desired (Good) outcomes for this analysis. In this instance, the Thrombosis level of Variable DVT will be Bad and the No Thrombosis level will be Good. In the Weight of Evidence dialog you will click in the boxes for Bad Code and Good Code to select these parameters, as shown in Figure T.10.

Click on the Compute Groups button to allow STATISTICA to suggest binning options for the available predictors chosen when selecting variables. Three binning options are possible, including Monotone, One minimum or maximum (curvilinear), or One minimum and one maximum (cubic). A No restrictions is also provided, as well as a Custom option where you can specify different groupings manually.

Now, click on the BMI Variable in the Predictor variables dialog, and then click the Monotone option as in Figure T.11.

You will see that three levels of this previously continuous variable are suggested for a monotone function: negative infinity to 20.7743, 20.7743 to 22.363, and then 22.363 to positive infinity. Now click on the cubic option as in Figure T.12.

This binning option more than doubles the information value of this predictor, with the information value representing the overall predictive power of this variable. We will select the cubic option for this variable. Leave all other variables at the settings suggested by STATISTICA. On the Weight of Evidence dialog, click the "x" at the top right-hand side of the dialog. The dialog in Figure T.13 will appear.

Select Embed to workspace. Your workspace will now be similar to that shown in Figure T.14.

Run the Weight of Evidence node. After you do this, a Rule node will appear in the workspace which will apply the Weight of Evidence recoding options you selected in the Weight of Evidence parameter selection process. Connect the Rules node to the Missing Data Imputation node, as in Figure T.15.

Edit the parameters of the Rules node. From the resulting Edit Parameters dialog, click Edit. A dialog similar to that shown in Figure T.16 will appear.

These rules will recode predictors using the Weight of Evidence codes you selected. As you can see in the first rule, if BMI is less than or equal to 20.7743 a new variable will be created, WOE_BMI, and any case with a BMI less than this will be given a Weight of Evidence value of 8.060. Of the five bins created for BMI, those with a BMI greater than 22.363 have more bad cases within the bin, resulting in a Weight of Evidence value of −8.179. This level of this predictor is more closely associated with cases where VTE is more common. Click OK. Since this node only recodes predictors, we need to carry over the dependent variable from the original data set. Click on the dialog Input variable to copy to result spreadsheet, and select DVT as in Figure T.17.

Click OK and then run the Rules node. Open the resulting spreadsheet. You will see what appear to be categorical codes representing the bins of the predictors, as in Figure T.18.

However, if you double click one of the variable headers and select Text Labels you will see the Weight of Evidence codes which underlie these labels. These are now continuous predictors with Weight of Evidence codes.

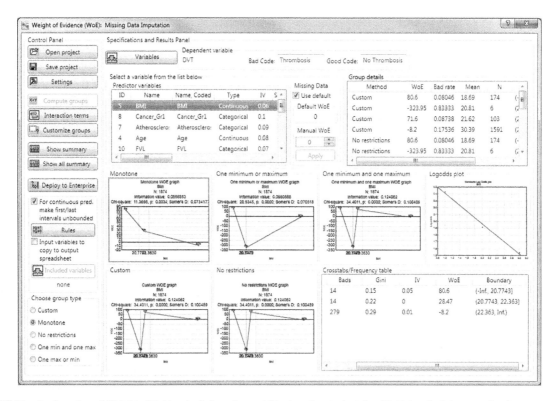

FIGURE T.11 Another view of Weight of Evidence window after variables have been selected and initial analysis has completed.

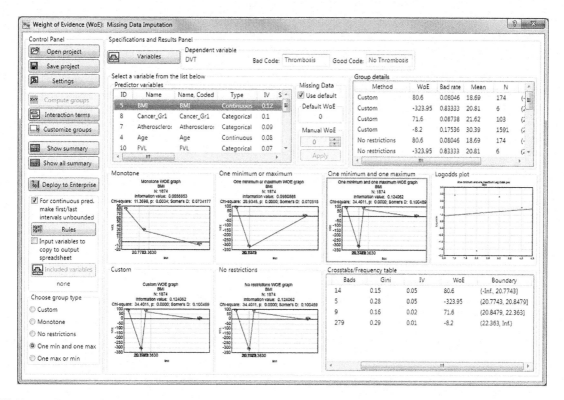

FIGURE T.12 Another view of Weight of Evidence window after 'One minimum and one maximum' model has been selected.

FIGURE T.13 Options for the model.

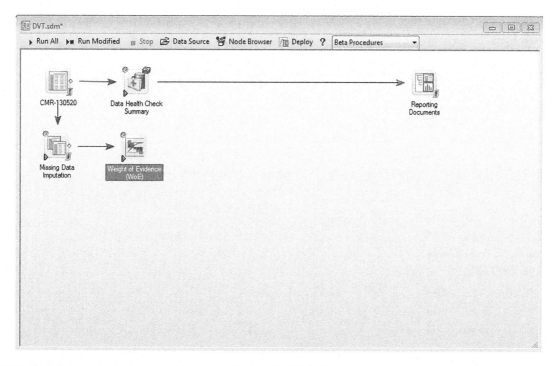

FIGURE T.14 DM Workspace look after "Embed to workspace" selected in Figure T.13.

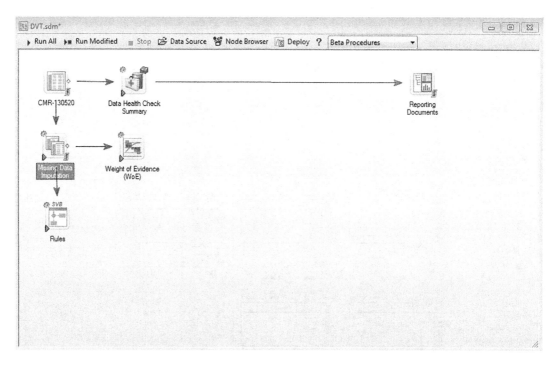

FIGURE T.15 After running the Weight of Evidence node, the recoding options will be embedded in a 'Rules node'; at this point connect the Missing Data Imputation node to the Rules node with an arrow.

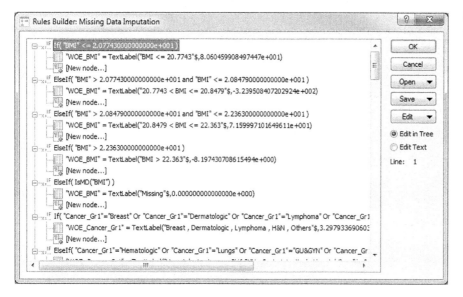

FIGURE T.16 This dialog will appear after clicking 'edit' on the 'rules node'.

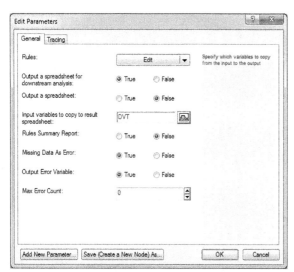

FIGURE T.17 Select DVT as shown here.

		1	2	3	
		DVT	WOE_BMI	WOE_Cancer_Gr1	
1	Thrombosis	BMI > 22.363	Breast , Dermatologic , Lymphoma , H&N , Others	Nor
2	Thrombosis	BMI > 22.363	Breast , Dermatologic , Lymphoma , H&N , Others	Nor
3	Thrombosis	BMI > 22.363	Hematologic , Lungs , GU&GYN , Gastrointestinal , Hepatobiliary	Ger
4	Thrombosis	BMI > 22.363	Breast , Dermatologic , Lymphoma , H&N , Others	Nor
5	Thrombosis	BMI > 22.363	Breast , Dermatologic , Lymphoma , H&N , Others	Nor
6	Thrombosis	BMI <= 20.7743	Breast , Dermatologic , Lymphoma , H&N , Others	Nor
7	Thrombosis	BMI > 22.363	Hematologic , Lungs , GU&GYN , Gastrointestinal , Hepatobiliary	Ger
8	Thrombosis	BMI > 22.363	Hematologic , Lungs , GU&GYN , Gastrointestinal , Hepatobiliary	Ger
9	Thrombosis	BMI > 22.363	Hematologic , Lungs , GU&GYN , Gastrointestinal , Hepatobiliary	Nor
10	Thrombosis	BMI > 22.363	Breast , Dermatologic , Lymphoma , H&N , Others	Ger

Data: Missing Data Imputation (14v by 1874c). Number of exemplars: 7.*

FIGURE T.18 The spreadsheet resulting from running the 'rules node'.

We will now attach three analysis nodes to the resulting data set from the Rules node so that we can compare the performance of these analyses. One will be Stepwise Model Builder, which will use logistic regression. One will be I-Trees, which will use the C&RT algorithm. Finally, we will use Boosted Trees. Stepwise Model Builder will be added from the Statistics tab, within the Advanced Models dropdown menu in the Advanced/Multivariate group, by clicking the icon for Stepwise Model Builder. The I-Trees node will be added from the Data Mining menu from the Trees/Partitioning group by activating the dropdown menu for I-Trees and selecting Advanced Classification Trees (CRT). Boosted Trees will be added also from the Data Mining tab from the Trees/Partitioning group by activating the dropdown menu under Boosted Trees and selecting the icon for Boosted Classification Trees. Your workspace will look similar to that in Figure T.19.

Edit the parameters of the Boosted Trees node. Click on the Variables button and for the Dependent variable select DVT. For Continuous predictors, select all available Weight of Evidence recoded predictors. If your dialog has the option for "Show appropriate variables only" selected, you will need to remove that selection as in Figure T.20.

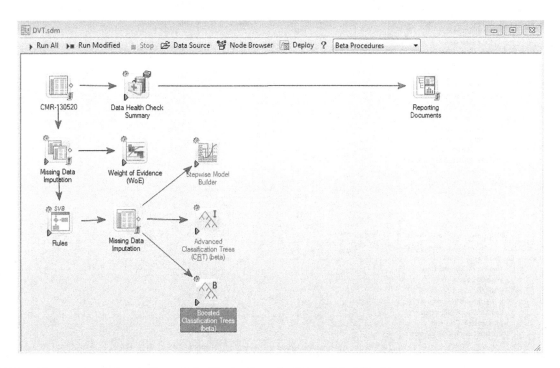

FIGURE T.19 After selecting the icon for Boosted Classification Trees, the dialog will look like this.

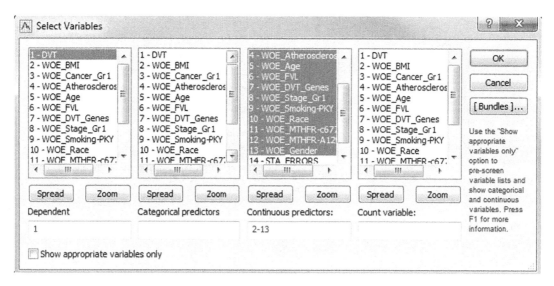

FIGURE T.20   If the 'Select Variables' window has the 'Show appropriate variables only' checked, this needs to be un-checked, as shown here.

You will receive a message that Selected variables have text labels, which is to be expected. Select the option for Continue with current selection. We will leave all settings for Boosted Trees at their default values for this comparison of models. Run the Boosted Trees node. This will generate a PMML model node which contains the model you have just developed. A Rapid Deployment node will also be generated, which we will use momentarily. At this time, you can also review the results for Boosted Trees by opening the Reporting Documents node. Do this now and select the option for Predictor importance, as in Figure T.21.

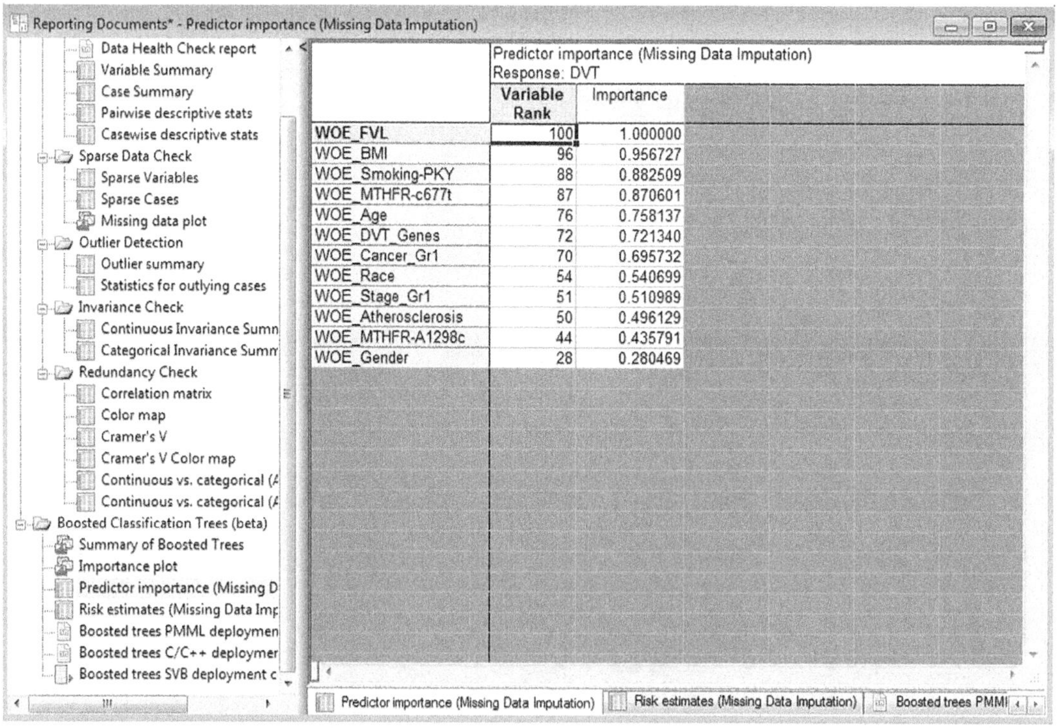

FIGURE T.21   Predictor variable importance listing, after running Boosted Trees.

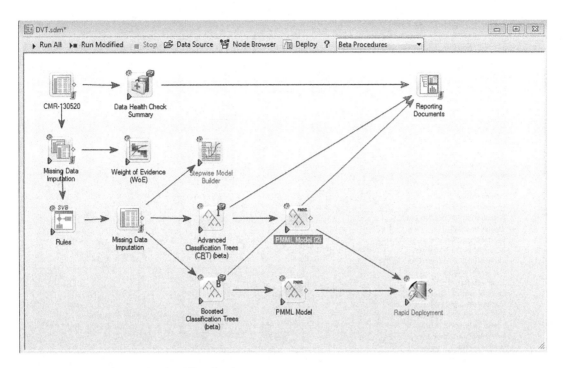

FIGURE T.22 DM Workspace after running the 'I-Trees' node.

From this we can see that FVL, BMI, and Smoking are the three most important variables for determining VTE in this population, using Boosted Trees. The least important are Atherosclerosis, MTHFR-A1298c, and Gender. Since Boosted Trees is a black box algorithm, reviewing the individual trees is not of primary interest.

Close the Reporting Documents and then edit the parameters of the I-Trees node. Select the same variables as we did for Boosted Trees, and also leave the remaining options at their default values. Run the I-Trees node. Your workspace will now appear similar to the one in Figure T.22.

Open the Reporting Documents and select the Predictor importance spreadsheet, as in Figure T.23.

You can see that the variables selected for I-Trees are very different from those selected for Boosted Trees. Also, we can now view the Tree Graph, which will allow us to see how the variables are related; this was not possible with the Boosted Trees model since it is a black box algorithm. A portion of this graph is shown in Figure T.24.

Look at Node ID 25 in the lower right-hand corner of the graph. We can see in this terminal node that if a case has Weight of Evidence codes for Cancer_Gr1, WOE_Age, WOE_Age, and WOE_Stage_Gr1, there will be a high predicted probability of not having thrombosis. Close the Reporting Documents.

We will now specify the model for logistic regression using the Stepwise Model Builder. Edit the parameters of the Stepwise Model Builder node. Select the variables as we did for the previous two analyses. We will now need to specify the Bad code and Good code as we did with the Weight of Evidence analysis, with Thrombosis being the Bad code and No Thrombosis being the Good code. The dialog will now appear as in Figure T.25.

We now need to make predictors available for the analysis. Click the button for Full sample. This will add each available predictor one at a time into a logistic regression model. The resulting dialog will appear as in Figure T.26.

You will see a Somer's D statistic as well as a level of significance in the column for Pr > Chi.Sqr. We will select in this first phase all predictors that are significant. You can hold down your Control key and select all those predictors that are red, indicating significance. Then click Add variable(s). This will add all the selected variables into the model and then re-estimate the remaining predictors for significance. Also, since you have added several predictors into a model, they will be assessed for significance within the final model and those statistics will be reported in the Model results table. Your dialog will appear similar to that in Figure T.27.

Add all significant predictors to the model then click the "x" at the top right-hand corner of the Stepwise Model Builder dialog as you did with the Weight of Evidence dialog. Similarly, select the option to Embed into workspace. Run the Stepwise Model Builder node. Your workspace will appear as in Figure T.28.

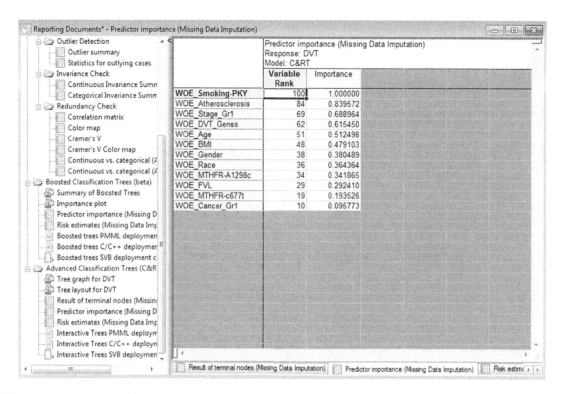

FIGURE T.23 Predictor importance for C&RT (I-Trees).

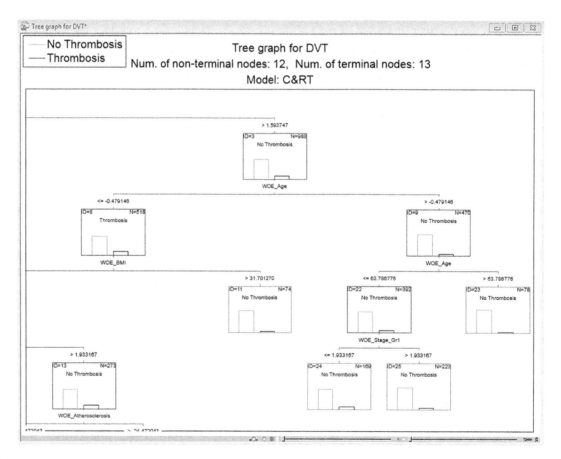

FIGURE T.24 Tree arrangement for DVT.

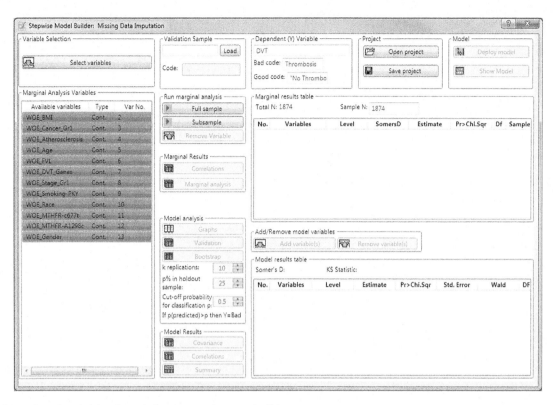

FIGURE T.25 Stepwise Model Builder window (see text for more details).

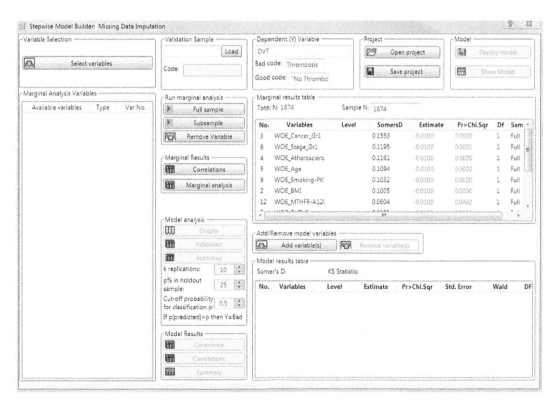

FIGURE T.26 Stepwise Model Builder window after variables have been added into it.

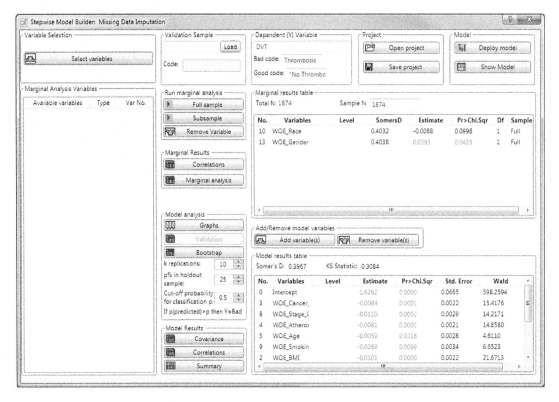

FIGURE T.27 Stepwise Model Builder window after modifying the variables.

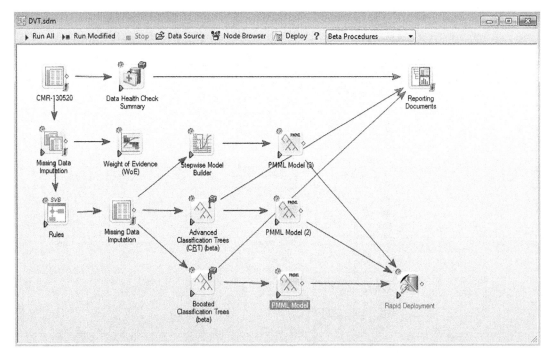

FIGURE T.28 DM Workspace appearance after the 'Stepwise Model Builder' has been computed.

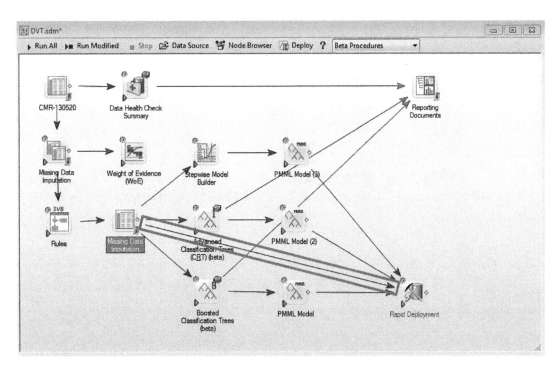

FIGURE T.29 Connecting the Downstream data node from the Rules node to the Rapid Deployment node.

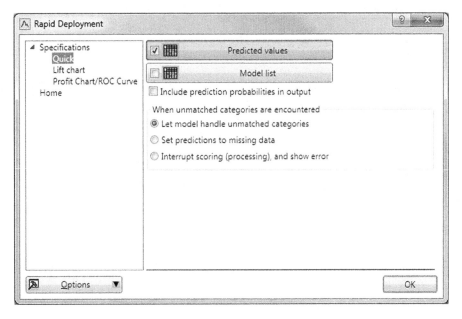

FIGURE T.30 Selecting parameters in the Rapid Deployment node.

Connect the downstream data node from the Rules node to the Rapid Deployment node as in Figure T.28. This allows the Rapid Deployment node to use the data that have been recoded by the Rules node. This will allow us to compare the performance of the three models we have developed. You can see the added connection in Figure T.29.

Edit the parameters of the Rapid Deployment node. Select the option for "Include prediction probabilities in output" from the Quick tab, as in Figure T.30.

On the Lift Chart tab, select Thrombosis as Category of response. Also, select the option for Lift chart (lift value) and verify that the option for Cumulative lift chart is selected. Your dialog will appear as in Figure T.31.

FIGURE T.31   Selecting more parameters in the Rapid Deployment node.

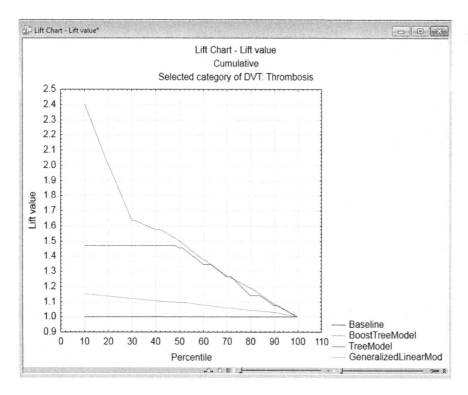

FIGURE T.32   Lift Chart from the Rapid Deployment Node (after computations).

Run the Rapid Deployment node and open the Reporting Documents node. Select the Lift chart generated in the folder for Rapid Deployment; this is shown in Figure T.32.

This lift chart shows that the Boosted Tree model outperforms all other models until the 60th percentile. What this means is that if all three models generate predicted probabilities for all cases, and we take the top 60th percentile according to predicted probability, Boosted Trees outperforms all other models.

Close the Reporting Documents dialog and open resulting output of the Rapid Deployment node by clicking on the document icon at the lower right-hand corner of the Rapid Deployment node. This will open the prediction output generated from each model, as in Figure T.33.

Data: Rapid Deployment

Summary of Deployment (Missing Data Imputation)
FileNames: ||

	DVT	BoostTreeModelPred	BoostTreeModelRes	TreeModelPred	TreeModelRes	GeneralizedLinearModelPred	GeneralizedLinearModelRes	Voted prediction
1	Thrombosis	No Thrombosis	Incorrect	Thrombosis	Correct	No Thrombosis	Incorrect	No Thrombosis
2	Thrombosis	No Thrombosis	Incorrect	No Thrombosis	Incorrect	No Thrombosis	Incorrect	No Thrombosis
3	Thrombosis	No Thrombosis	Incorrect	Thrombosis	Correct	No Thrombosis	Incorrect	No Thrombosis
4	Thrombosis	No Thrombosis	Incorrect	No Thrombosis	Incorrect	No Thrombosis	Incorrect	No Thrombosis
5	Thrombosis	No Thrombosis	Incorrect	Thrombosis	Correct	No Thrombosis	Incorrect	No Thrombosis
6	Thrombosis	No Thrombosis	Incorrect	No Thrombosis	Incorrect	No Thrombosis	Incorrect	No Thrombosis
7	Thrombosis	No Thrombosis	Incorrect	Thrombosis	Correct	No Thrombosis	Incorrect	No Thrombosis
8	Thrombosis	No Thrombosis	Incorrect	Thrombosis	Correct	No Thrombosis	Incorrect	No Thrombosis
9	Thrombosis	No Thrombosis	Incorrect	Thrombosis	Correct	No Thrombosis	Incorrect	No Thrombosis
10	Thrombosis	No Thrombosis	Incorrect	Thrombosis	Correct	No Thrombosis	Incorrect	No Thrombosis
11	Thrombosis	No Thrombosis	Incorrect	Thrombosis	Correct	No Thrombosis	Incorrect	No Thrombosis
12	Thrombosis	No Thrombosis	Incorrect	Thrombosis	Correct	No Thrombosis	Incorrect	No Thrombosis

FIGURE T.33 Prediction output generated for each model (see text for more details).

The last column of this spreadsheet shows the voted prediction of all three models. Each model is creating a prediction – either Thrombosis or No Thrombosis. And then, in essence, STATISTICA is taking a vote among those three predictions. The winning vote is the overall prediction from the ensemble. It has been found that, most often, ensembles will outperform a model performing individually.

REFERENCES

Amer, M.H., 2013. Cancer-associated thrombosis: clinical presentation and survival. Cancer Management and Research. 2013 (5), 165–178.

Sack JrG.H., Levin, J, Bell, WR., 1977. Trousseau's syndrome and other manifestations of chronic disseminated coagulopathy in patients with neoplasms: clinical, pathophysiologic, and therapeutic features. Medicine (Baltimore). 56 (1), 1–37.

Sorensen, H.T., Mellemkjaer, L., Olsen, J.H., Baron, J.A., 2000. Prognosis of cancers associated with venous thromboembolism. N. Engl. J. Med. 343 (25), 1846–1850.

Tutorial U

Predicting Breast Cancer Diagnosis Using Support Vector Machines

Haranath Varanasi

Chapter Outline

INTRODUCTION

Support vector machines (SVMs) are a set of related supervised learning methods that analyze data and recognize patterns, and are used for classification (machine learning) and regression analysis.

The goal of an SVM model is to predict which category a particular subject or individual belongs to, based on training set examples. In this tutorial we will carry out *feature selection* and *root cause analysis* to select predictors and then, using the SVM model, will predict the breast cancer diagnosis (benign or malignant) of a particular patient based upon information obtained by doctors through scanned images. The data set used is the Breast Cancer Wisconsin (Original) Data Set, and can be obtained from the UCI Machine learning library.

Data Description

The Wisconsin Breast Cancer Data Set comprises 699 patients with a total of 11 different variables. These variables will be used to create models that predict the diagnosis (benign or malignant) of a particular patient. The variables are:

1. Sample code number: ID number
2. Clump Thickness
3. Uniformity of Cell Size
4. Uniformity of Cell Shape
5. Marginal Adhesion
6. Single Epithelial Cell Size
7. Bare Nuclei
8. Bland Chromatin
9. Normal Nucleoli
10. Mitoses
11. Class: (2 for benign, 4 for malignant).

Practical Predictive Analytics and Decisioning Systems for Medicine. DOI: http://dx.doi.org/10.1016/B978-0-12-411643-6.00038-7

DATA ANALYSIS AND EXPLORATION

With these data the ID number will not be used and the categorical response is Diagnosis (2 for benign, 4 for malignant). This is a cleaned data set, so no cleaning is required. First we will run the feature selection process to select the best predictors to predict the target variable.

Feature Selection and Root Cause Analysis (Using Chi-square Method (Default)/p Value Method):

1. Go to Data Mining, then down to Data Mining Workspace, and click on All Procedures.
2. Click on Data Source and on the Breast-cancer-Wisconsin Data Set, then OK. The variable selection box will come up immediately.
3. Select Class (Variable 11) as a target variable which is categorical (with values 2 for benign, 4 for malignant) and the remaining variables (numbered 2 through 10) as predictors, excluding ID in the continuous category (shown in Figure U.1). This loads the data as shown in Figure U.2.
4. Click on Node Browser, and select Feature Selection and Root Cause Analysis (Figure U.3)
5. Right click on Feature Selection and Root Cause Analysis, and edit parameters.
   a. Edit parameters for running feature selection based on Chi-squares (Figure U.4).
   b. Edit parameters for running feature selection based on p values (Figure U.5).
6. Right click on Feature Selection and Root Cause Analysis, and click on Run to Node.
7. Click on Reporting Documents to view Results (Figures U.6, U.7, Tables U.1, U.2)
   As the p values of all predictors are 0 (zero) with both Chi-square and p-value methods, we might consider all to be predictors of class. Before we do that, let's examine data correlations more closely.
8. Open Data set, click on Multiple Regression, and select Variable 11 (Class) as the Dependent variable and Variables 2−10 as Independent variables; click OK, click the Advanced tab then select Descriptive Statistics (Figure U.8).
9. Open the Results book and have a look at the Correlations table and Scatterplots (Figure U.9 and Table U.3)

Using the Correlations scatterplots and Correlations matrix, we can conclude that the predictors are correlated with each other. As the p values of all predictors are zero and are correlated, we will consider all variables as predictors for modeling.

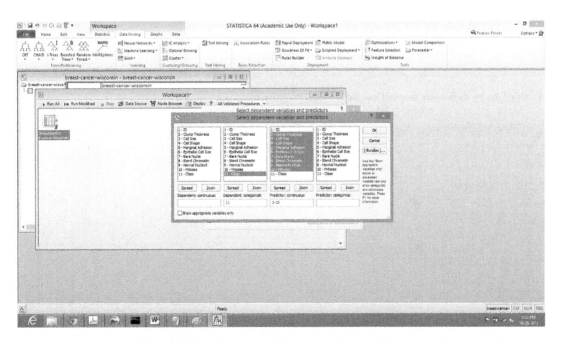

FIGURE U.1 Selecting variables in the STATISTICA workspace.

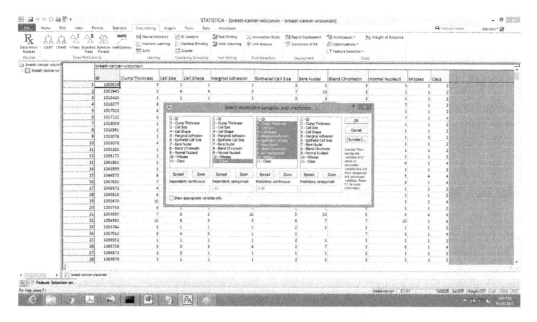

FIGURE U.2 Another view of the variable selection dialog, and the loaded data file in the background.

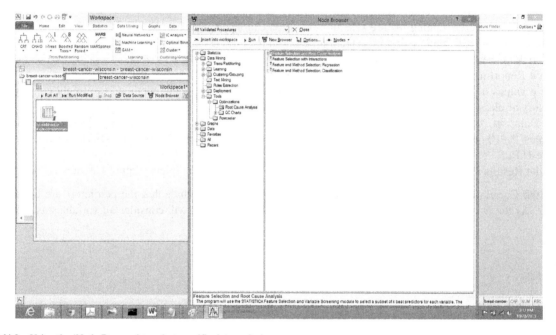

FIGURE U.3 Using the 'Node Browser' to select specific data analysis processes.

FIGURE U.4 The 'Edit Parameters' dialog for Feature Selection, selecting "Fixed Number" of predictors.

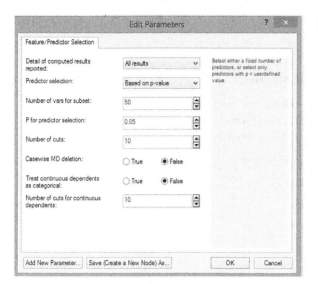

FIGURE U.5 The 'Edit Parameters' dialog for Feature Selection, selecting "Based on p-value" of predictors.

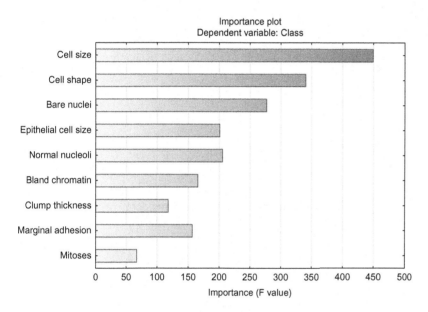

FIGURE U.6 Predictors Importance plot (p value).

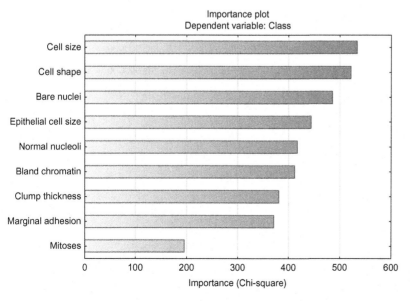

FIGURE U.7 Predictors Importance plot (Chi-square).

TABLE U.1 p Values Obtained Using Chi-Square Method

	Best predictors for categorical dependent var: Class (breast-cancer-wisconsin in breast-cancer-wisconsin)	
	Chi-square	p value
Cell Size	534.1405	0.00
Cell Shape	522.0482	0.00
Bare Nuclei	485.3459	0.00
Epithelial Cell Size	443.9259	0.00
Normal Nucleoli	417.2568	0.00
Bland Chromatin	411.7986	0.00
Clump Thickness	380.4005	0.00
Marginal Adhesion	370.7075	0.00
Mitoses	195.1930	0.00

TABLE U.2 p-Values Obtained Using p-Value Method

	Best predictors for continuous dependent var: Class (Spreadsheet in breast-cancer-wisconsin)	
	F value	p value
Cell Size	449.0604	0.000000
Cell Shape	340.2597	0.000000
Bare Nuclei	276.6565	0.000000
Epithelial Cell Size	200.7238	0.000000
Normal Nucleoli	205.2642	0.000000
Bland Chromatin	165.3686	0.000000
Clump Thickness	117.8626	0.000000
Marginal Adhesion	156.5069	0.000000
Mitoses	67.2202	0.000000

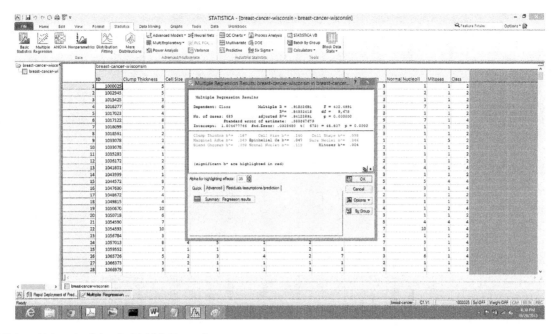

FIGURE U.8   Initial results dialog for Multiple Regression.

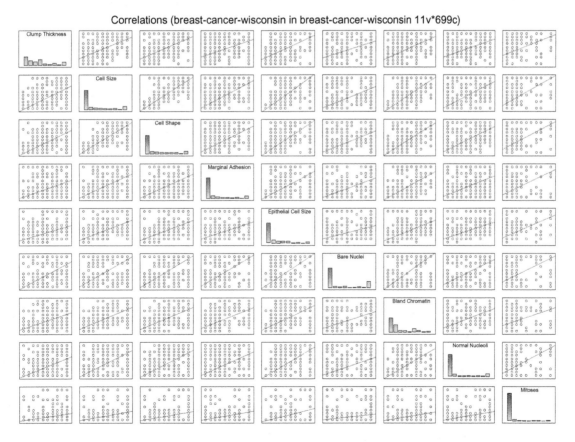

FIGURE U.9   Correlation scatterplots across predictors.

TABLE U.3 Correlation Table for Predictors

Variable	Correlations (breast-cancer-wisconsin in breast-cancer-wisconsin)									
	Clump thickness	Cell size	Cell shape	Marginal adhesion	Epithelial cell size	Bare nuclei	Bland chromatin	Normal nucleoli	Mitoses	Class
Clump Thickness	1.000000	0.642481	0.653470	0.487829	0.523596	0.593091	0.553742	0.534066	0.350957	0.714790
Cell Size	0.642481	1.000000	0.907228	0.706977	0.753544	0.691709	0.755559	0.719346	0.460755	0.820801
Cell Shape	0.653470	0.907228	1.000000	0.685948	0.722462	0.713878	0.735344	0.717963	0.441258	0.821891
Marginal Adhesion	0.487829	0.706977	0.685948	1.000000	0.594548	0.670648	0.668567	0.603121	0.418898	0.706294
Epithelial Cell Size	0.523596	0.753544	0.722462	0.594548	1.000000	0.585716	0.618128	0.628926	0.480583	0.690958
Bare Nuclei	0.593091	0.691709	0.713878	0.670648	0.585716	1.000000	0.680615	0.584280	0.339210	0.822696
Bland Chromatin	0.553742	0.755559	0.735344	0.668567	0.618128	0.680615	1.000000	0.665602	0.346011	0.758228
Normal Nucleoli	0.534066	0.719346	0.717963	0.603121	0.628926	0.584280	0.665602	1.000000	0.433757	0.718677
Mitoses	0.350957	0.460755	0.441258	0.418898	0.480583	0.339210	0.346011	0.433757	1.000000	0.423448
Class	0.714790	0.820801	0.821891	0.706294	0.690958	0.822696	0.758228	0.718677	0.423448	1.000000

MODELING USING SUPPORT VECTOR MACHINE WITH DEPLOYMENT

In these data the ID number will not be used and the categorical response is Diagnosis (2 for benign, 4 for malignant).

1. Click on All procedures in the Data mining tab (Figure U.10).
2. Now, click on Data Source and bring the Breast Cancer Data Set into the DM workspace (Figure U.11).

Categorical variables are those that contain information about some discrete quantity or characteristic describing the observations in the data file (e.g., Gender: Male or Female); continuous variables are measured on some continuous scale (e.g., Height, Weight, Cost).

Dependent variables are the ones we want to predict; they are also sometimes called outcome variables; predictor (independent) variables are those that we want to use for the prediction or classification (of categorical outcomes).

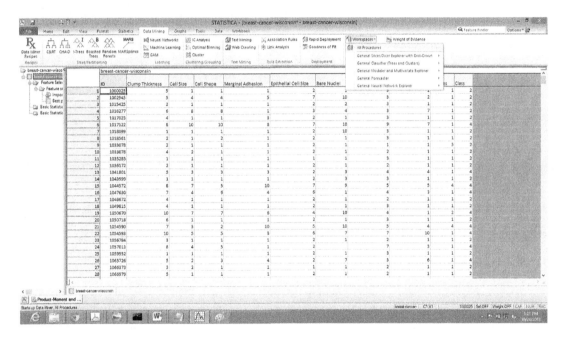

FIGURE U.10   Selecting All Procedures.

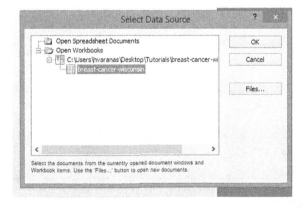

FIGURE U.11   Selecting Data Source.

3. Double click on input data (Breast cancer data) which is in the DM workspace, and click on Variables. Select Variable 11 (Class) in the "Dependent; categorical" section, and Variables 2−10 as predictor variables in the "Predictor; continuous category" (Figure U.12). Here we are trying to predict Class (2 for benign, 4 for malignant) using another variable (Cell information).
4. Click on the Node Browser and select Support Vector Machine with Deployment (Classification) and double click to bring it into the DM workspace.
5. Right click on "Support Vector Machine with Deployment" icon and Edit Parameters (Figure U.13)
6. Change details of computed results from "Minimal" to "All results" on the General tab (Figure U.14)

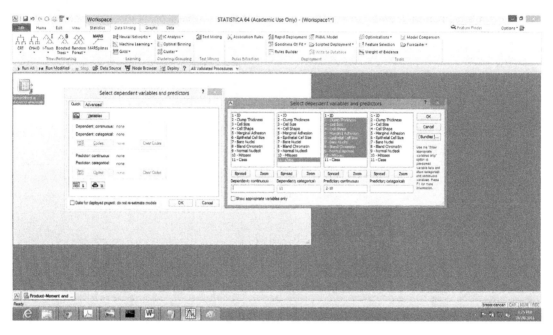

FIGURE U.12 Selecting variables dialog.

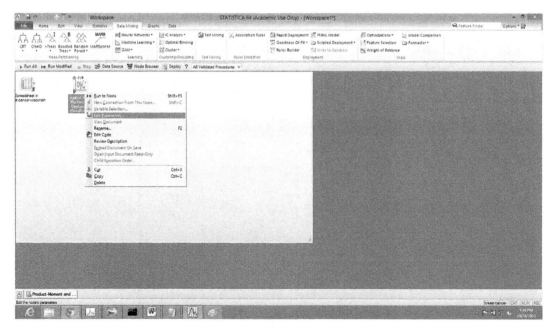

FIGURE U.13 By right-clicking on the Icon-Node the flying menu appears which includes 'Edit parameters'.

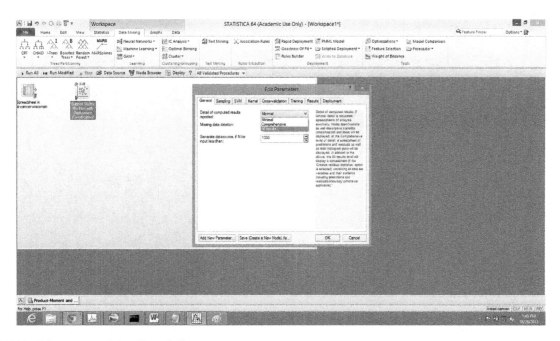

FIGURE U.14 Edit parameters dialog, General tab.

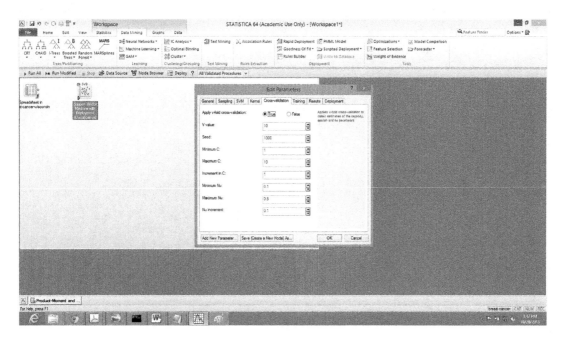

FIGURE U.15 Edit parameters dialog, Cross validation tab.

7. In the Cross-validation tab, select V-fold cross-validation (Figure U.15).
8. In the Deployment tab, check PMML/XML deployment so it will be outputted into a workbook (Figure U.16).
9. Leave the Sampling, SVM, Kernel, Training, and Results tabs alone (i.e., leave them at their "defaults").
10. Make a connection to the SVM node from our data set by right clicking the Data set icon and then clicking on Node (Connection from this Node) (Figure U.17).

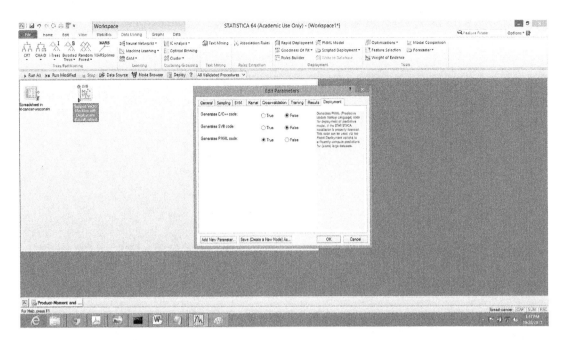

FIGURE U.16 Edit parameters dialog, Deployment tab.

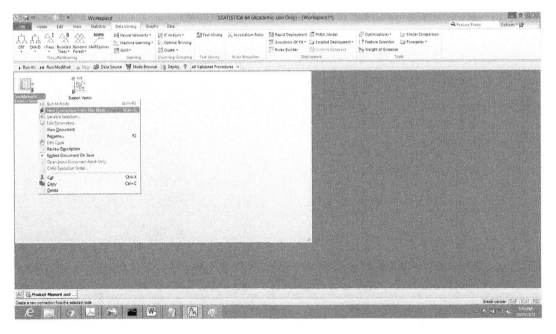

FIGURE U.17 Right clicking on the data set icon brings up this flying menu.

11. Right click on the SVM icon and click Run to Node to run the SVM model (Figure U.18).
12. Upon completion, there will be two more icons in the DM workspace. To view the results, right click on Results and click on View Document (Figure U.19; Tables U.4, U.5).
13. Right click on Support vector machine PMML deployment code, and save PMML xml file (Figure U.20).
14. Save as Breast_Cancer_SVM_PMML. We will use this file for rapid deployment and cross-validation on a different data set (Figure U.21).

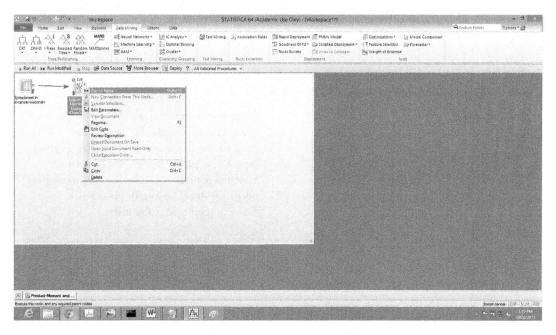

FIGURE U.18 Selecting 'Run to node' in the flying menu runs the computations up to and through this node.

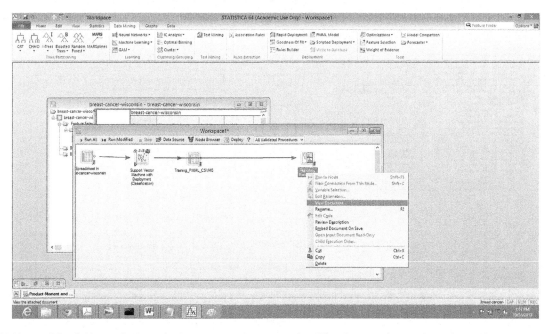

FIGURE U.19 By right-clicking on the Reporting Documents node one can select 'View Document' to see the results workbook.

TABLE U.4 Classification Summary (Support Vector Machine)

Class name	Classification summary (Support Vector Machine), Class, Overall sample (Spreadsheet in breast-cancer-wisconsin); SVM: Classification type 1 (C = 2.000); Kernel: Radial Basis Function (gamma = 0.200); Number of support vectors = 50 (40 bounded)				
	Total	Correct	Incorrect	Correct (%)	Incorrect (%)
2	444	432	12	97.29730	2.702703
4	239	232	7	97.07113	2.928870

TABLE U.5 Confusion Matrix (Support Vector Machine)

Class observed	Confusion matrix (Support Vector Machine), Class, Overall sample (Spreadsheet in breast-cancer-wisconsin); SVM: Classification type 1 (C = 2.000); Kernel: Radial Basis Function (gamma = 0.200); Number of support vectors = 50 (40 bounded) observed (rows) × predicted (columns)	
	2	4
2	432	12
4	7	232

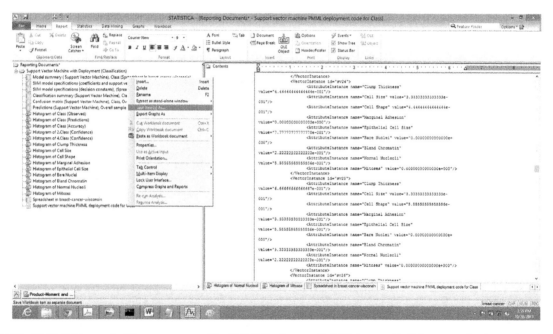

FIGURE U.20   Right-clicking on the "Support vector machine PMML Deployment Code" brings up this flying menu allowing saving of this code to another location.

RAPID DEPLOYMENT, CROSS-VALIDATING, AND PREDICTING ON DIFFERENT DATA

We will rapidly deploy the previously built SVM model and cross-validate using a different data set.

1. Open STATISTICA, and open the data set Breast_cancer_tut_test
2. From the Data Mining tab, click on Rapid Deployment (Figure U.22).
3. Click on "Variable selection via PMML" (selects predictors and target variable from PMML file) (Figure U.23).
4. Click on "Load models from disk" to select the data set (the data set on which you want to run the model) (Figure U.23).
5. Click OK. Upon completion, we will see the Result book (Figures U.24, U.25).

The SVM model predicted classes with 99.97 (100 − 0.03) accuracy, as shown in Table U.6.

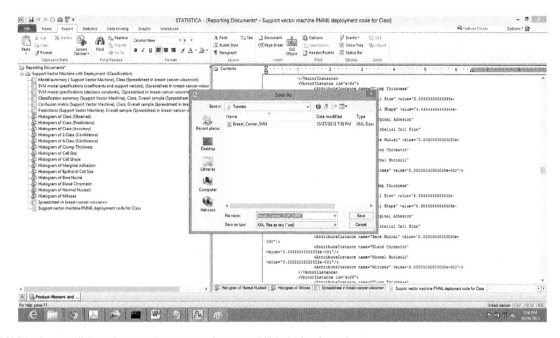

FIGURE U.21   Save As dialog, where the document can be renamed if desired and saved.

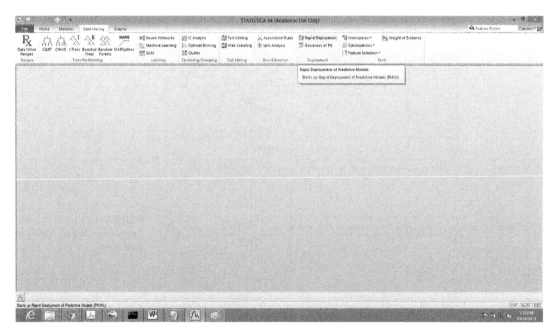

FIGURE U.22   Selecting the 'Rapid Deployment' module.

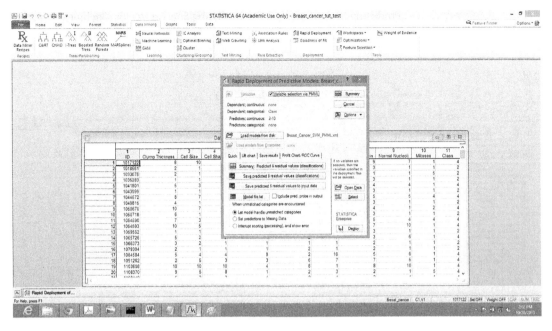

FIGURE U.23 The 'Rapid Deployment' module with the saved PMML (xml) model selected.

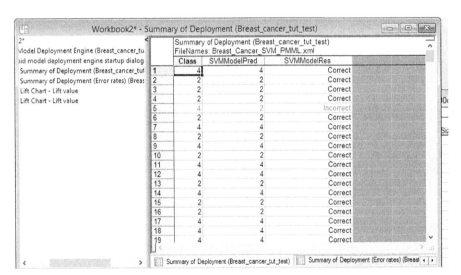

FIGURE U.24 Summary of the Rapid Deployment model's predictions of cases.

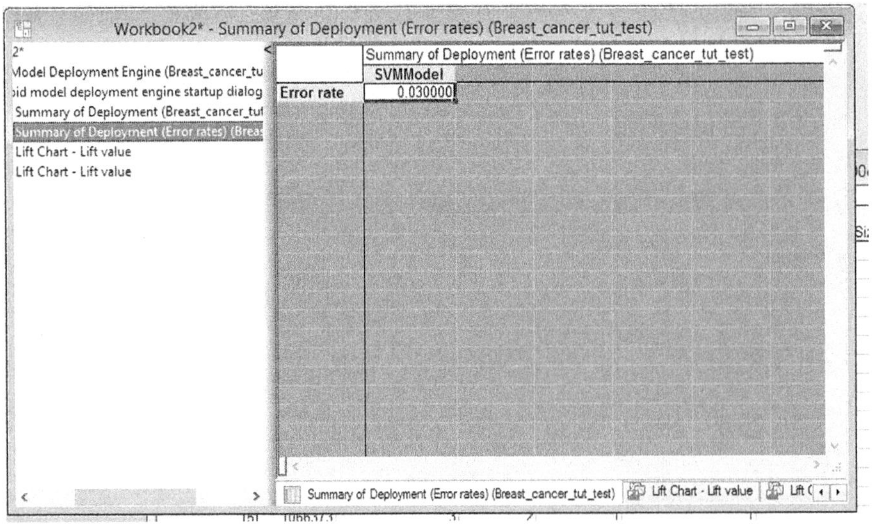

FIGURE U.25 The error rate spreadsheet from the Rapid Deployment results workbook.

TABLE U.6 Excerpt from Result Book Showing Prediction Accuracy

	Summary of deployment (Error rates) (Breast_cancer_tut_test)
	SVM Model
Error rate	0.030000

SUMMARY

In this tutorial, we have cleaned and run feature analysis to select predict variables. Upon noticing that all predictors had a zero p value (the lower the p value, the higher the significance of the predictor; in this case, all are equally valued), we further explored the data and analyzed correlations between the predictor variables. The correlation analysis also shows that all the predictors are highly correlated. Hence, we chose to give equal significance to all the predictors for SVM modeling. We also ran SVM modeling and saved a PMML XML file for rapid deployment and cross-validation, and then rapidly deployed the SVM model on different data and cross-validated our model.

DATA SET LOCATIONS

<http://archive.ics.uci.edu/ml/Datasets/Breast + Cancer + Wisconsin + %28Original%29>.
<http://archive.ics.uci.edu/ml/machine-learning-databases/breast-cancer-isconsin/wdbc.names>.
<https://courses.cs.washington.edu/courses/cse446/09wi/hw1/>.

Tutorial V

Heart Disease: Evaluating Variables That Might Have an Effect on Cholesterol Level (Using Recode of Variables Function)

Stephanie Moncada, MS

Chapter Outline

AIM

My aim was to evaluate what variables might have an effect on cholesterol level.

TUTORIAL STEPS

1. Click on data source to select the data set heart disease from the book's companion web page (filename: HEARTDISEASE with recode.sta). Then open a new workspace: Data Mining – Data Mining Workspaces – Data Miner – All procedures.
2. Next make multiple copies of the data set: click on Node Browser – Graphs – Input Data and Data Acquisition – Multiple copies of data source, and then double click on this node you just created. Select 7 copies (I like to have extra to play around with) and leave the other parameter as Clone Original Data Source; then click OK. Now click the Run button (upper left corner of the workspace).
3. Next is variables selection. Double-click the first data file copy of HeartDisease.sta appearing in the Data Preparation panel. Click on Variables. Select Cholesterol Level as your Dependent categorical variable. Select Adiposity as your predictor continuous variable. Select Blood Pressure Level, Tobacco Intake Level, Family History, Stress Level Type A, Obesity Level, Alcohol Intake Level, Age Range, and Coronary Heart Disease as your predictor categorical variables (Figure V.1).
4. Now that you have your variables, let's perform a feature selection. Click the Node Browser button. Open the Statistics folder, then Data Mining, and finally Feature Selection. Select the option appearing in the right-hand panel: Feature selection and root cause analysis. Select the All Results option for the Detail of Computed Results Reported list box, and leave the rest of the options at their default setting. Then click the OK button. Right-click the Feature Selection and Root Cause Analysis node, and select Run to Node from the shortcut menu. Right click on Feature selection and root cause analysis, and then select Embed document on Save. Double click to view, and click on Importance plot.

   From this importance plot, we can see that Adiposity may be the strongest predictor of Cholesterol Level, followed by Age Range and Obesity Level (Figure V.2).

Practical Predictive Analytics and Decisioning Systems for Medicine. DOI: http://dx.doi.org/10.1016/B978-0-12-411643-6.00039-9

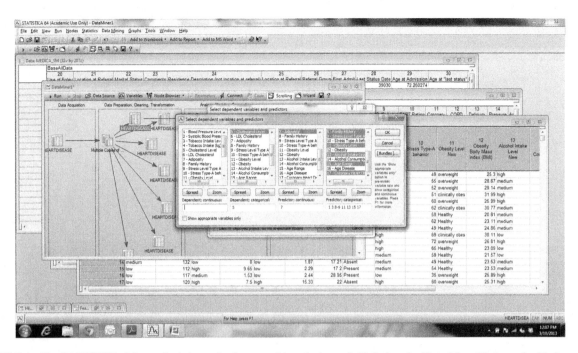

FIGURE V.1 The STATISTICA full set of windows: the data spreadsheet furtherest behind, then the 'Data Miner Workspace' with the top-most window the variable selection dialog.

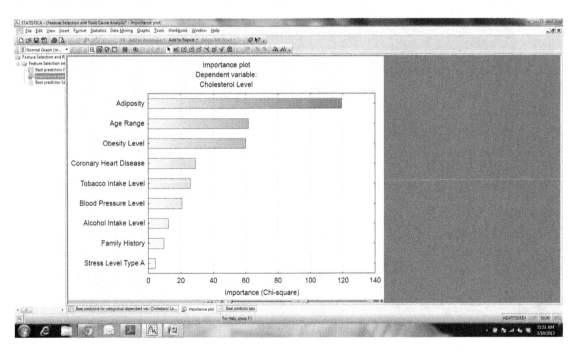

FIGURE V.2 Importance Plot indicating which predictor variables are the best ones to predict 'Cholesterol Level' which is the target variable.

5. Since Adiposity is a continuous variable, let's recode it to a categorical variable, since the variables we want to compare are all categorical. I performed a feature selection to help me recode my variable. Click on the Statistics menu, and then select Descriptive Statistics, click Frequency tables, select "adiposity levels of fat tissue" as the variable, and click on OK. You then get the table in Figure V.3.

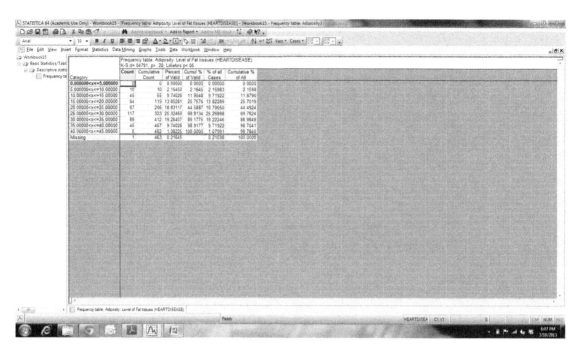

FIGURE V.3 Frequency table result.

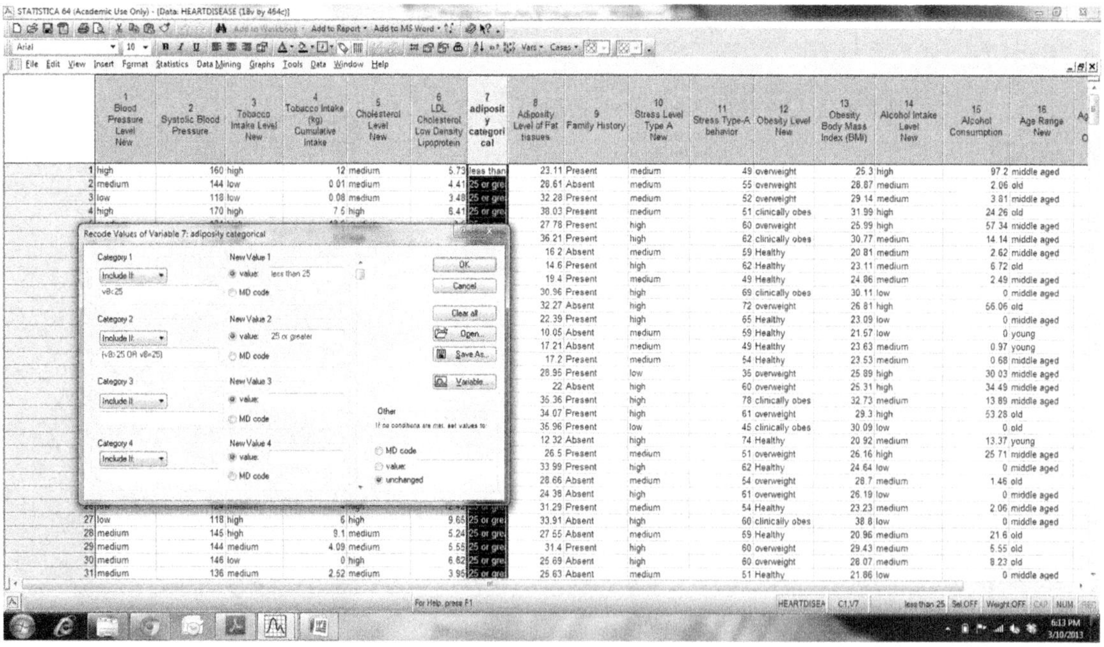

FIGURE V.4 Recode dialog window which allows recoding of selected variables.

I decided to make a cut-off of 25 and created two new values of "less than 25" or "greater than 25" (which includes 25). Insert a new variable and call it "adiposity categorical." Highlight the column for Adiposity and right click, click on Add Variable, set the type to Text and enter the name "adiposity categorical." Copy and paste all of the values from the original "adiposity levels of fat tissues" into your new variable column. Now you can recode, but still keep the original values. Highlight your new column and, under the Data menu, select Recode. See the screenshot in Figure V.4 for value criteria.

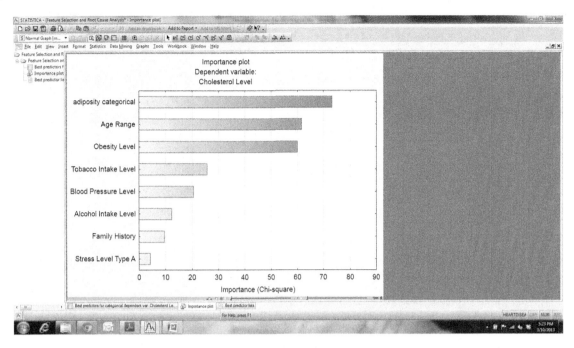

FIGURE V.5   Importance plot showing most important variables after recoding the adiposity variable from continuous to categorical.

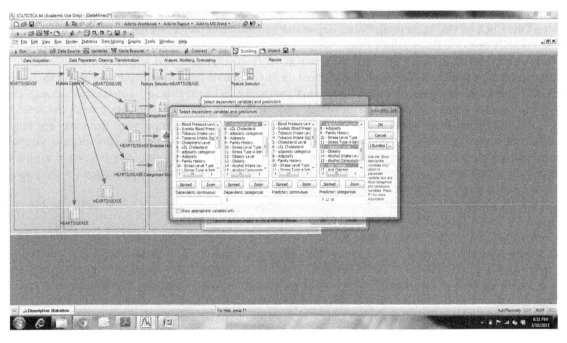

FIGURE V.6   Variable selection window showing selections after recoding.

6. Figure V.5 shows the second feature selection I ran, with the new variable "adiposity categorical." Follow the same steps as described earlier for running a feature selection.

   From this Importance plot, we can see that "adiposity categorical" may be the strongest predictor of Cholesterol Level, followed by Age Range and Obesity Level.

7. Now let's do a categorical histogram. Double click the data file node HeartDisease.sta to select the variables for Categorized Histograms. Click Variables. Select Cholesterol Level as the dependent categorical variable. Select "adiposity categorical," Obesity Level, and Age Range as the predictor categorical variables (Figure V.6).

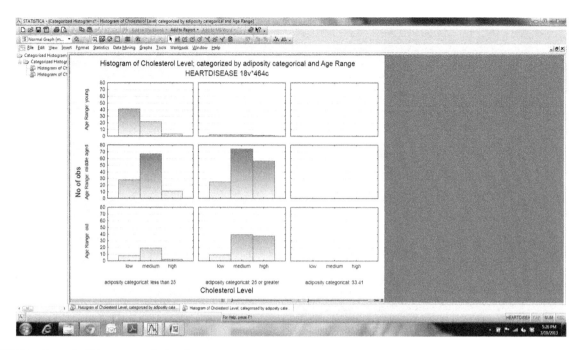

FIGURE V.7 Categorical histogram results based on age range.

Click on OK. Click on OK again in the Select dependent variables and predictors box.

Double-click Categorized Histograms to view the Edit Parameters dialog. Select fit off in the fit distribution. Leave all other settings and click OK. Right click the Categorized Histogram node and select Run to Node. Right click on the categorized histogram and click Embed document on Save. Double click the categorized histogram to view it.

Figure V.7 shows the histogram for Age Range and "adiposity categorical level" (dependent variable cholesterol level). You can see there is a difference in middle-aged folks who have an adiposity categorical level of 25 or greater; there are more folks who have medium or high cholesterol than compared to the same age range where fewer folks have high cholesterol when their adiposity categorical level is less than 25. This suggests that being middle aged and having adiposity categorical levels at 25 and above equates to more folks who have medium or high cholesterol. There is almost no difference in the bars in the graph in the top middle, meaning for the young an adiposity categorical level of 25 or greater doesn't much affect the cholesterol level.

Figure V.8 shows the histogram for obesity level and adiposity categorical level (dependent variable cholesterol level).

In this histogram we see that in the middle box of row 2 there is a big span between the bars on the graph, suggesting that those who are overweight and have an adiposity categorical of 25 or greater have more medium and high cholesterol levels. In this histogram in the first box of row 3, we see that those who are a healthy weight and have an adiposity categorical of less than 25 have fewer observations of high cholesterol, but similar observances of low and medium cholesterol.

8. Now let's try a Bivariate Histogram. Select a new copy of the HeartDisease.sta data set for auto connection. Click the Node Browser button to display the Node Browser dialog; click the Graphs folder and then 3D Sequential Graphs folder, and double click Bivariate Histograms to attach the node to the SDM workspace. Close the Node Browser.

Select cholesterol level as the dependent categorical variable. Select Adiposity, Age Range, and Obesity Level as the predictor categorical variables.

Figure V.9 shows the Cholesterol with Adiposity bivariate histogram.

This graph shows that there is a big difference in high cholesterol levels between those folks who had an adiposity level of 25 or less and those who had an adiposity level of 25 and greater. This suggests that those folks with an adiposity level of 25 and greater have more observations of high cholesterol. Those with a medium cholesterol level show little difference in the bar graphs, suggesting that the adiposity level is not a significant factor for medium-cholesterol folks.

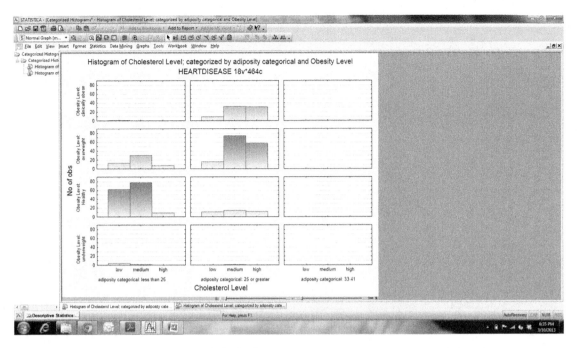

FIGURE V.8 Categorical histogram results based on obesity level.

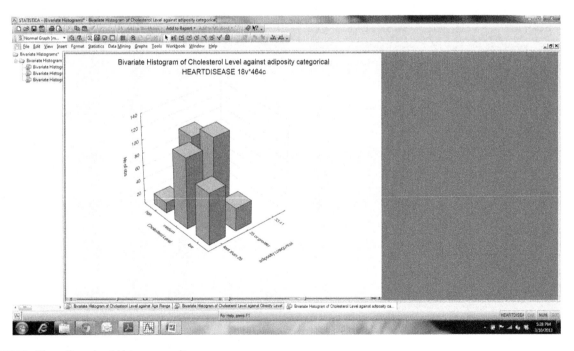

FIGURE V.9 Three-dimensional histogram results.

Figure V.10 shows the Cholesterol with Obesity Level bivariate histogram.
This graph suggests that obesity level of overweight has the most impact on cholesterol level, as suggested by the great difference between the bars.
Figure V.11 shows the bivariate for Cholesterol and Age Range histogram.
This graph suggests that middle age has the most impact on cholesterol level, as there is a big difference in between the bars on the graph.

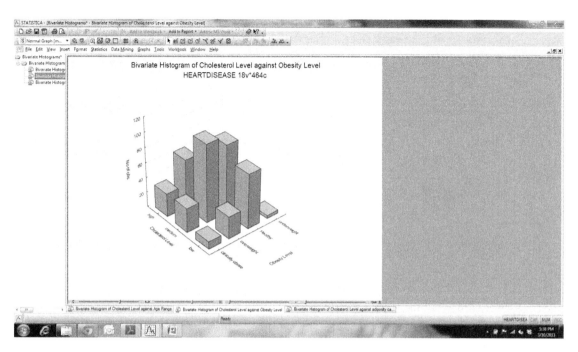

FIGURE V.10 Three-Dimensional histogram based on obesity level.

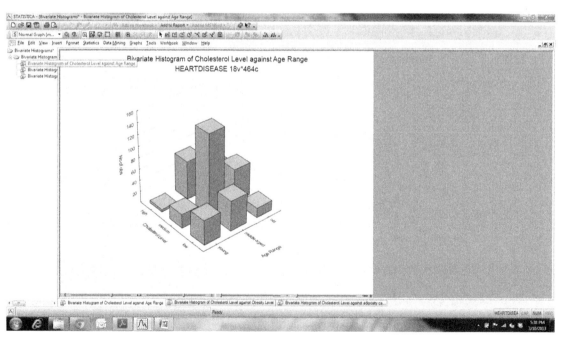

FIGURE V.11 Three-dimensional histogram results based on age range.

9. Now let's do a Categorized Box Plot. Select a new copy of the HeartDisease.sta data set for auto connection. Click the Node Browser button to display the Node Browser; click the Graphs folder and then the Categorized Graphs folder. Then double click Categorized Box Plots to attach the node to the SDM workspace. Close the Node Browser. Double click the HeartDisease.sta data file. Click on Variables. Select Cholesterol Level as the dependent categorical variable. Select "adiposity categorical," Obesity Level, and Age Range as the predictor categorical variables (Figure V.12).

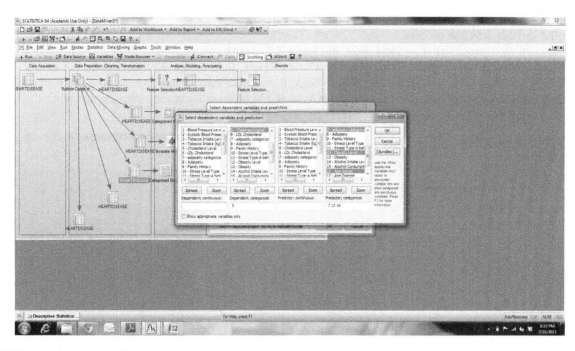

FIGURE V.12   Another analysis with adiposity, obesity level, and age range selected as predictor variables.

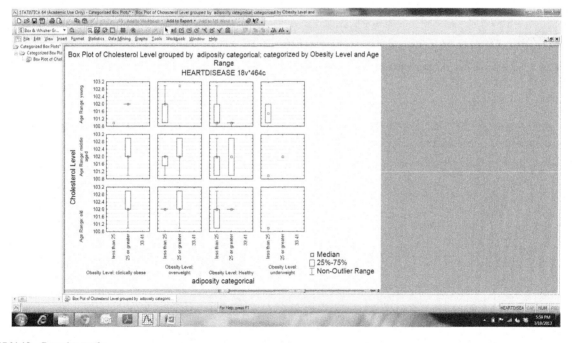

FIGURE V.13   Box plot results.

Click OK on the variable selection dialog and then on the Select Dependent Variables and Predictors dialog to complete the variable selection process.

Double-click the Categorized Box Plots node and select Whisker/Outliers tab from the Edit Parameters dialog. Set the Median Whisker Value option to Median Non-Outlier Range, and Median Whisker Coefficient to 1. Right click the Categorized Box Plots node and select Run to Node from the shortcut menu. Double click the workbook named Categorized Box Plot to review the results. Figures V.13 and V.14 show the results from the box plot.

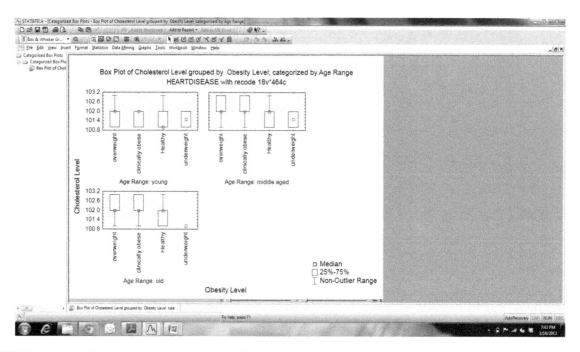

FIGURE V.14   Box plot with data grouped by obesity level and categorized by age range only.

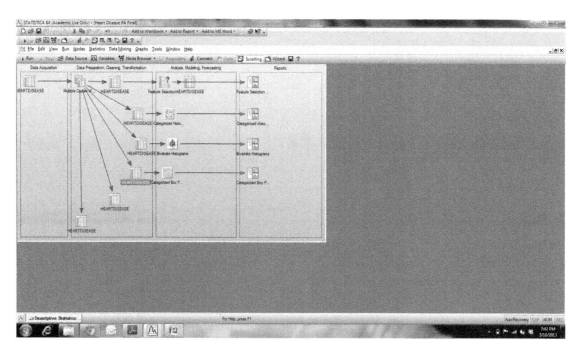

FIGURE V.15   Data Mining workspace.

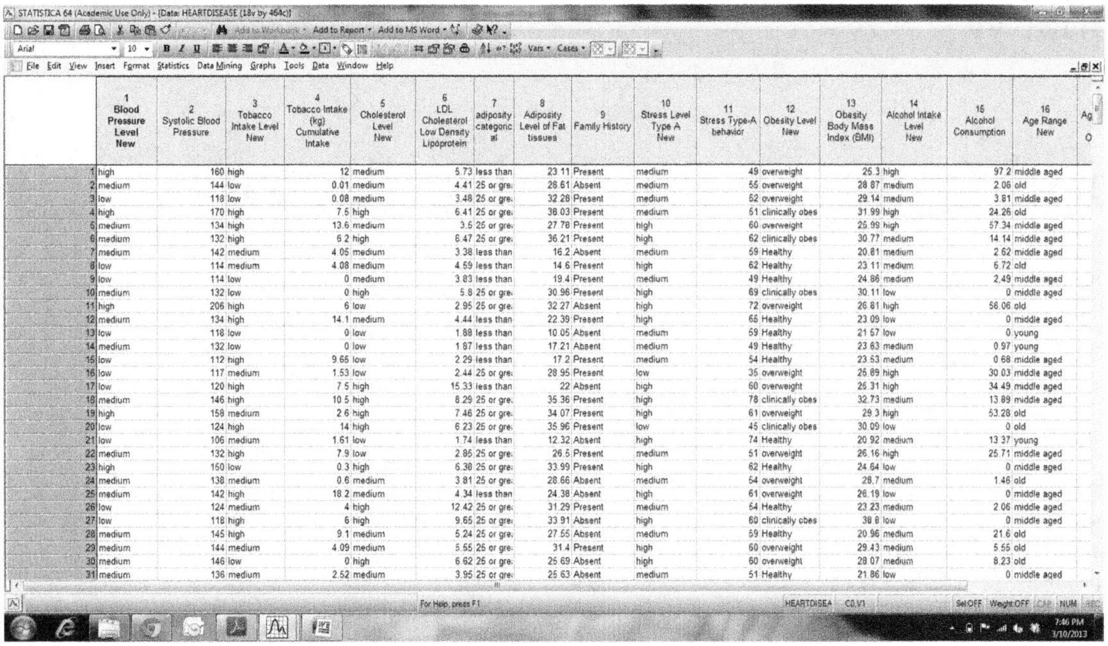

	1 Blood Pressure Level New	2 Systolic Blood Pressure	3 Tobacco Intake Level New	4 Tobacco Intake (kg) Cumulative Intake	5 Cholesterol Level New	6 LDL Cholesterol Low Density Lipoprotein	7 adiposity categorical	8 Adiposity Level of Fat tissues	9 Family History	10 Stress Level Type A New	11 Stress Type-A behavior	12 Obesity Level New	13 Obesity Body Mass Index (BMI)	14 Alcohol Intake Level New	15 Alcohol Consumption	16 Age Range New
1	high	160	high	12	medium	5.73	less than	23.11	Present	medium	49	overweight	25.3	high	97.2	middle aged
2	medium	144	low	0.01	medium	4.41	25 or gre	28.61	Absent	medium	55	overweight	28.87	medium	2.06	old
3	low	118	low	0.08	medium	3.48	25 or gre	32.28	Present	medium	52	overweight	29.14	medium	3.81	middle aged
4	high	170	high	7.5	high	6.41	25 or gre	38.03	Present	medium	51	clinically obes	31.99	high	24.26	old
5	medium	134	high	13.6	medium	3.5	25 or gre	27.78	Present	high	60	overweight	25.99	high	57.34	middle aged
6	medium	132	high	6.2	high	6.47	25 or gre	36.21	Present	high	62	clinically obes	30.77	medium	14.14	middle aged
7	medium	142	medium	4.05	medium	3.38	less than	16.2	Absent	medium	59	Healthy	20.81	medium	2.62	middle aged
8	low	114	medium	4.08	medium	4.59	less than	14.6	Present	high	62	Healthy	23.11	medium	6.72	old
9	low	114	low	0	medium	3.83	less than	19.4	Present	medium	49	Healthy	24.86	medium	2,49	middle aged
10	medium	132	low	0	high	5.8	25 or gre	30.96	Present	high	69	clinically obes	30.11	low	0	middle aged
11	high	206	high	6	low	2.95	25 or gre	32.27	Absent	high	72	overweight	26.81	high	56.06	old
12	medium	134	high	14.1	medium	4.44	less than	22.39	Present	high	65	Healthy	23.09	low	0	middle aged
13	low	118	low	0	low	1.88	less than	10.05	Absent	medium	59	Healthy	21.67	low	0	young
14	medium	132	low	0	low	1.87	less than	17.21	Absent	medium	49	Healthy	23.63	medium	0.97	young
15	low	112	high	9.65	low	2.29	less than	17.2	Present	medium	54	Healthy	23.53	medium	0.68	middle aged
16	low	117	medium	1.53	low	2.44	25 or gre	28.95	Present	low	35	overweight	25.89	high	30.03	middle aged
17	low	120	high	7.5	high	15.33	less than	22	Absent	high	60	overweight	25.31	high	34.49	middle aged
18	medium	146	high	10.5	high	8.29	25 or gre	35.36	Present	high	78	clinically obes	32.73	medium	13.89	middle aged
19	high	158	medium	2.6	high	7.46	25 or gre	34.07	Present	high	61	overweight	29.3	high	53.28	old
20	low	124	high	14	high	6.23	25 or gre	35.96	Present	low	45	clinically obes	30.09	low	0	old
21	low	106	medium	1.61	low	1.74	less than	12.32	Absent	high	74	Healthy	20.92	medium	13.37	young
22	medium	132	high	7.9	low	2.85	25 or gre	26.5	Present	medium	51	overweight	26.16	high	25.71	middle aged
23	high	150	low	0.3	high	6.38	25 or gre	33.99	Present	high	62	Healthy	24.64	low	0	middle aged
24	medium	138	medium	0.6	medium	3.81	25 or gre	28.66	Absent	medium	54	overweight	28.7	medium	1.46	old
25	medium	142	high	18.2	medium	4.34	less than	24.38	Absent	high	61	overweight	26.19	low	0	middle aged
26	low	124	medium	4	high	12.42	25 or gre	31.29	Present	medium	64	Healthy	23.23	medium	2.06	middle aged
27	low	118	high	6	high	9.65	25 or gre	33.91	Absent	high	60	clinically obes	38.8	low	0	middle aged
28	medium	145	high	9.1	medium	5.24	25 or gre	27.55	Absent	medium	59	Healthy	20.96	medium	21.6	old
29	medium	144	medium	4.09	medium	5.55	25 or gre	31.4	Present	high	60	overweight	29.43	medium	5.55	old
30	medium	146	low	0	high	6.62	25 or gre	25.69	Absent	high	60	overweight	28.07	medium	8.23	old
31	medium	136	medium	2.52	medium	3.95	25 or gre	25.63	Absent	medium	51	Healthy	21.86	low	0	middle aged

FIGURE V.16 The data set window showing the new variable 7 which was created for this study.

These graphs suggest that the middle-aged folks who are overweight or clinically obese have more cases of high cholesterol, and the same is true of the old age group, but not of the young age group.

Figure V.15 is my Data Mining workspace.
Figure V.16 is my data set; notice the new Variable 7 that was created.

Tutorial W

Blood Pressure Predictive Factors

Christopher D. Farrar, PhD

Chapter Outline

BACKGROUND

For this tutorial we're going to explore together a clinical application of data mining and predictive analytics.

Controlling blood pressure is a major health concern in the United States and in many parts of the world. Individuals who track their blood pressure on a frequent basis are often baffled by the wide variations in readings both within a day and over the course of days and months.

For this tutorial we will look at the blood pressure diary of one male Midwesterner. The data are real, but of course the subject is anonymous. His gender, age, height, weight, diet, etc., while certainly relevant for understanding blood pressure, are in fact not relevant to this exercise and will not be discussed.

We will attempt to identify explanatory patterns in the data. If we're successful, it may help this individual or his physician to understand what is driving the blood pressure readings.

We will not be developing a predictive model *per se*. Such a model would normally combine observations from thousands of subjects, and would take into account vastly more variables than we will be using. What we will be doing instead will be using data from our single subject to describe and explain the kinds of steps which need to be performed in the development of a predictive model.

Along the way we will be showing how many of the tools of data mining and predictive analytics can be used on a personal level to provide insight to individuals about their health, and perhaps a level of relief that observations which seem completely arbitrary may in fact not be quite so random.

Our subject has kept blood pressure records off and on for several years. One of our challenges in this project will be to deal with the sporadic nature of the observations and the incompleteness of the data.

Our analysis will consist of the following steps:

1. *Data review.* We'll look at the data to understand its structure and characteristics.
2. *Data preparation.* We'll fix deficiencies and irregularities in the data to make them ready for modeling.
3. *Importation.* We'll bring the data into STATISTICA 10.0 (Academic version) and convert it to a .sta file.
4. *Type validation.* We'll review the typing of the variables in STATISTICA to identify and correct any issues with data type that may have been introduced by the importation process.

Practical Predictive Analytics and Decisioning Systems for Medicine. DOI: http://dx.doi.org/10.1016/B978-0-12-411643-6.00040-5

5. *Analysis and pattern discovery.* We'll examine the results with some of the tools provided by STATISTICA and will attempt to develop useful insights.

Please note that this tutorial is not intended as an academically rigorous study. No publications are cited, and the terminology throughout is aimed at reasonably informed lay persons rather than at medical practitioners.

DATA REVIEW

Open the Excel spreadsheet named BP Tutorial.xlsx. Since this is a hands-on tutorial, it is a good idea to save a copy of the sheet under a new name. We'll save it as "BP Tutorial 1.xlsx" (Figure W.1).

Now examine the data on the tab labeled "Initial Data." Look carefully at the data and follow along with these observations:

- There are 506 cases organized chronologically. Dates are displayed in the format mm/dd/yy.
- The dates are discontinuous and the time periods are irregular. For example, the data jump directly from 05/23/09 to 09/29/09, then from 10/05/09 to 01/12/10.
- There is no discernible consistency in the time periods covered; we have 24 observations from 2009, 116 from 2010, 40 from 2011, 258 from 2012, and 68 from 2013.
- Pressure-related observations consist of the systolic pressure, the diastolic pressure, and the pulse. Observations were recorded 0, 1, 2, or 3 times per day (morning, mid-day, evening).
- The pressure readings can vary considerably during the course of a day. For example, look carefully at 10/03/09, a date for which we have three sets of readings. The systolic pressure from the morning reading was 151, from the midday reading it was 156, and from the evening reading it was 139.
- In addition we can see that the subject is evidently a runner, because on some days he has recorded miles run. We will assume that the days with no mileage recorded were days he did not run.

Date		Morning (M) Sys	Dia	Pulse	Mid-Day (MD) Sys	Dia	Pulse	Evening (E) Sys	Dia	Pulse	Miles Run
05/03/09	Sunday				124	75	55				
05/04/09	Monday							133	75	58	
05/05/09	Tuesday							122	68	54	4.0
05/06/09	Wednesday							122	67	61	
05/07/09	Thursday							117	73	54	4.0
05/08/09	Friday										
05/09/09	Saturday				119	67	64				
05/10/09	Sunday				138	77	56				
05/11/09	Monday							125	79	57	4.0
05/12/09	Tuesday										
05/13/09	Wednesday							126	79	54	4.0
05/18/09	Monday							127	77	51	
05/19/09	Tuesday							123	74	59	
05/20/09	Wednesday							129	77	55	
05/21/09	Thursday							123	70	70	
05/22/09	Friday							97	63	60	4.0
05/23/09	Saturday							110	92	68	4.0
09/29/09	Tuesday	129	74	71				138	75	77	
09/30/09	Wednesday							126	76	60	
10/01/09	Thursday							142	84	56	
10/02/09	Friday										
10/03/09	Saturday	151	76	57	156	87	58	139	77	65	
10/04/09	Sunday				141	86	64	143	79	59	
10/05/09	Monday	145	85	66							
01/12/10	Tuesday							159	79	69	
01/13/10	Wednesday	150	79	84							
01/14/10	Thursday							152	89	65	
01/15/10	Friday	125	68	85				135	82	61	
01/16/10	Saturday				130	70	62				
01/17/10	Sunday				145	77	58	147	90	50	

FIGURE W.1 BP Tutorial 1.xlsx worksheet.

DATA PREPARATION

All of the characteristics observed above could make the analysis problematic. In this data preparation phase we'll deal with them one by one.

We'll do the bulk of our preparation work in Excel. We will assume familiarity with basic Excel functionality and with the creation of formulas.

Discontinuity

First, we may want to smooth out the data in some fashion. Since we're dealing with time series information, it may be useful to know when readings are contiguous (one day following the next) and when they are not. With this in mind, let's mark each observation with either a 1 or a 0. The 1 will indicate to us that the observation is contiguous with the previous day's observation; the 0 will indicate that it is not. We can do this in Excel with date arithmetic.

First, type "Discontinuity" into cell M3 (Figure W.2). Next, we'll mark the first reading in the data set with a 1. For the second and subsequent observations we'll note whether the date of the current observation is equal to the date of the previous observation plus one day. If so we mark that observation with a 1, and if not we'll mark it with a 0. We'll use the "IF" function in Excel for this. Click in cell M5 and enter the formula as shown in Figure W.3.

Next, copy the formula down Column P to the end of the data set by grabbing the little handle in the lower right-hand corner of cell M5 and dragging it down to row 509. Your sheet will look like the display in Figure W.4.

Next we'll capture the number of contiguous days in each group of observations. First type "Contig Days" into cell N3. In the screenshots that follow, columns C through L have been hidden to improve clarity.

Begin by summing the discontinuity marks. Cell N5 is shown as an example (Figure W.5). Copy the formula down through row 509.

Your sheet will now look like the display in Figure W.6.

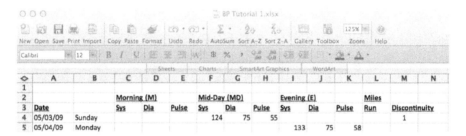

FIGURE W.2 Marking date discontinuities.

	K	L	M	N	O
		Miles			
	Pulse	**Run**	**Discontinuity**		
			1		
	58		=if(A5=A4+1, 1,0)		
	54	4.0			
	61				

FIGURE W.3 Marking Date Discontinuities.

Date Abstractions

The dates in Column A (above) above will be difficult for our modeling algorithms to handle because they're actually internal Excel numbers which are displayed as dates. As a result, and because we may want to examine seasonality in

FIGURE W.4 Marking Date Discontinuities.

Date		Morning (M) Sys	Dia	Pulse	Mid-Day (MD) Sys	Dia	Pulse	Evening (E) Sys	Dia	Pulse	Miles Run	Discontinuity
05/03/09	Sunday				124	75	55					1
05/04/09	Monday							133	75	58		1
05/05/09	Tuesday							122	68	54	4.0	1
05/06/09	Wednesday							122	67	61		1
05/07/09	Thursday							117	73	54	4.0	1
05/08/09	Friday											1
05/09/09	Saturday				119	67	64					1
05/10/09	Sunday				138	77	56					1
05/11/09	Monday							125	79	57	4.0	1
05/12/09	Tuesday											1
05/13/09	Wednesday							126	79	54	4.0	1
05/18/09	Monday							127	77	51		0
05/19/09	Tuesday							123	74	59		1
05/20/09	Wednesday							129	77	55		1
05/21/09	Thursday							123	70	70		1
05/22/09	Friday							97	63	60	4.0	1
05/23/09	Saturday							110	92	68	4.0	1
09/29/09	Tuesday	129	74	71				138	75	77		0
09/30/09	Wednesday							126	76	60		1
10/01/09	Thursday							142	84	56		1
10/02/09	Friday											1
10/03/09	Saturday	151	76	57	156	87	58	139	77	65		1
10/04/09	Sunday				141	86	64	143	79	59		1
10/05/09	Monday	145	85	66								1
01/12/10	Tuesday							159	79	69		0
01/13/10	Wednesday	150	79	84								1
01/14/10	Thursday							152	89	65		1
01/15/10	Friday	125	68	85				135	82	61		1
01/16/10	Saturday				130	70	62					1
01/17/10	Sunday				145	77	58	147	90	50		1

FIGURE W.5 Summing contiguous days.

Date		Disconti	Contig Days
05/03/09	Sunday	1	1
05/04/09	Monday	1	=IF(M5=0, 1, N4+1)
05/05/09	Tuesday	1	
05/06/09	Wednesday	1	
05/07/09	Thursday	1	

FIGURE W.6 Summing Contiguous Days.

Date		Disconti	Contig Days
05/03/09	Sunday	1	1
05/04/09	Monday	1	2
05/05/09	Tuesday	1	3
05/06/09	Wednesday	1	4
05/07/09	Thursday	1	5
05/08/09	Friday	1	6
05/09/09	Saturday	1	7
05/10/09	Sunday	1	8
05/11/09	Monday	1	9
05/12/09	Tuesday	1	10
05/13/09	Wednesday	1	11
05/18/09	Monday	0	1
05/19/09	Tuesday	1	2
05/20/09	Wednesday	1	3
05/21/09	Thursday	1	4

◇	A	B	M	N	O	P	Q	R
1								
2								
3	Date		Disconti	Contig D₂	Year	Month	Day	
4	05/03/09	Sunday	1		=YEAR(A4)			
5	05/04/09	Monday	1	2				
6	05/05/09	Tuesday	1	3				
7	05/06/09	Wednesday	1	4				
8	05/07/09	Thursday	1	5				

FIGURE W.7 Extracting year.

◇	A	B	M	N	O	P	Q	R
1								
2								
3	Date		Disconti	Contig D₂	Year	Month	Day	
4	05/03/09	Sunday	1	1	2009	5	3	
5	05/04/09	Monday	1	2	2009	5	4	
6	05/05/09	Tuesday	1	3	2009	5	5	
7	05/06/09	Wednesday	1	4	2009	5	6	
8	05/07/09	Thursday	1	5	2009	5	7	
9	05/08/09	Friday	1	6	2009	5	8	
10	05/09/09	Saturday	1	7	2009	5	9	
11	05/10/09	Sunday	1	8	2009	5	10	
12	05/11/09	Monday	1	9	2009	5	11	
13	05/12/09	Tuesday	1	10	2009	5	12	
14	05/13/09	Wednesday	1	11	2009	5	13	
15	05/18/09	Monday	0	1	2009	5	18	
16	05/19/09	Tuesday	1	2	2009	5	19	
17	05/20/09	Wednesday	1	3	2009	5	20	
18	05/21/09	Thursday	1	4	2009	5	21	
19	05/22/09	Friday	1	5	2009	5	22	
20	05/23/09	Saturday	1	6	2009	5	23	

FIGURE W.8 Extracting date.

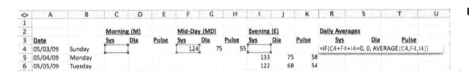

◇	A	B	C	D	E	F	G	H	I	J	K	R	S	T	U
1															
2			Morning (M)			Mid-Day (MD)			Evening (E)			Daily Averages			
3	Date		Sys	Dia	Pulse	Sys	Dia	Pulse	Sys	Dia	Pulse	Sys	Dia	Pulse	
4	05/03/09	Sunday				124	75	55				=IF(C4+F4+I4=0, 0, AVERAGE(C4,F4,I4))			
5	05/04/09	Monday							133	75	58				
6	05/05/09	Tuesday							122	68	54				

FIGURE W.9 Calculating averages.

our analysis, we will create three new fields to abstract, respectively, the year, the month, and the day, and we will store these as integer numbers.

First, enter Year, Month, and Day in cells O3, P3, and Q3, respectively (Figure W.7). Then, in cell O4, enter the formula for extracting the year from an Excel date field.

Copy cell O4 down through row 509. Next, use the Excel functions MONTH() and DAY() to abstract these values into cells P4 and Q4 respectively, and copy the cell through to the bottom of the worksheet (row 509).

Your sheet will now look as shown in Figure W.8.

Data Consolidation

As mentioned above, for some days we have no observations and for others we have one, two, or three. We'll deal with this by creating a new variable which will be an average daily value for each of these measurements. The days for which we have no observations will pose a special problem, since the calculation of an average for these days will result in division by zero. We'll handle these cases straight off by embedding the calculation of the average in an if-then-else formula which will filter out the division-by-zero cases and insert a 0 for them.

First, though, let's unhide columns C through L, and then hide columns L through Q. We won't be working with them for the moment. After this, enter Daily Averages in R2, and Sys, Dia, and Pulse in R3, S3, and T3, respectively (Figure W.9).

		Morning (M)			Mid-Day (MD)			Evening (E)			Daily Averages		
Date		Sys	Dia	Pulse	Sys	Dia	Pulse	Sys	Dia	Pulse	Sys	Dia	Pulse
05/03/09	Sunday				124	75	55				124	75	55
05/04/09	Monday							133	75	58	133	75	58
05/05/09	Tuesday							122	68	54	122	68	54
05/06/09	Wednesday							122	67	61	122	67	61
05/07/09	Thursday							117	73	54	117	73	54
05/08/09	Friday										0	0	0
05/09/09	Saturday				119	67	64				119	67	64
05/10/09	Sunday				138	77	56				138	77	56
05/11/09	Monday							125	79	57	125	79	57
05/12/09	Tuesday										0	0	0
05/13/09	Wednesday							126	79	54	126	79	54
05/18/09	Monday							127	77	51	127	77	51
05/19/09	Tuesday							123	74	59	123	74	59
05/20/09	Wednesday							129	77	55	129	77	55
05/21/09	Thursday							123	70	70	123	70	70
05/22/09	Friday							97	63	60	97	63	60

FIGURE W.10   Calculating Averages.

		Morning (M)			Mid-Day (MD)			Evening (E)			Daily Averages
Date		Sys	Dia	Pulse	Sys	Dia	Pulse	Sys	Dia	Pulse	Sys
05/03/09	Sunday				124	75	55				124
05/04/09	Monday							=IF(C5+F5+I5=0, R4, AVERAGE(C5,F5,I5))			
05/05/09	Tuesday							122	68	54	122
05/06/09	Wednesday							122	67	61	122

FIGURE W.11   Calculating Averages.

		Miles					Daily Averages			
Date		Run	Contig D;	Year	Month	Day	Sys	Dia	Pulse	Miles Last 5 Days
05/03/09	Sunday		1	2009	5	3	124	75	55	0.0
05/04/09	Monday		2	2009	5	4	133	75	58	0.0
05/05/09	Tuesday	4.0	3	2009	5	5	122	68	54	0.0
05/06/09	Wednesday		4	2009	5	6	122	67	61	0.0
05/07/09	Thursday	4.0	5	2009	5	7	117	73	54	=IF(N8<5, 0, SUM(L4:L8))
05/08/09	Friday		6	2009	5	8	117	73	54	

FIGURE W.12   Calculating running mileage.

Then, in cell R4, enter the formula " = IF(C4 + F4 + I4 = 0, 0, AVERAGE(C4,F4,I4))" as shown in Figure W.9. Copy this formula to the adjacent cells S4 and T4, then copy all three cells down through the entire data set. Your spreadsheet will appear as shown in Figure W.10.

Notice, though, that now we have 0s in rows 9, 13, 24, and many others. For this exercise we do not want 0s, representing missing values.

By examining the cases with missing readings, we can see that most (though not all) are for periods in which there are readings taken on adjacent days. That is, few of the 0 reading days fall after a chronological gap in the record keeping. We could replace these 0s with averages or medians, but given that the 0s are largely adjacent to days with actual readings, we will simply replace the 0s with the observations of the last previous day on which we have data.

Edit the formula in cell R5 to replace the "then" result of the if-then-else (0) with the value of the cell immediately above (Figure W.11). The edited formula will be " = IF(C5 + F5 + I5 = 0, R4, AVERAGE(C5,F5,I5))."

Then copy this revised formula to cells S5 and T5. Now copy all three cells (R5, S5, and T5) down through the complete data set. You should no longer have any 0 readings in these columns.

We have two more modifications to the data to make before we can start modeling. First, we will create a rolling sum of miles run. Next, we will import some climatological data to add to the analysis.

Rolling Sum of Running Data

One of the hypotheses we'll be interested in testing is that the total number of miles run over some period of time can have an effect on the blood pressure readings. In order to test this hypothesis we will need to derive a variable which will hold this information.

We're going to sum running mileage over a period of 5 days.

First, though, unhide columns L through Q, and then hide C through K. We won't be working with them. Hide column M, too; we won't need this either. Then type "Miles Last 5 Days" in cell U3 (Figure W.12).

Start by entering 0 in cells U4, U5, U6, and U7. Since our summing period is five days we won't be calculating values for these first four days. Next, look at the Contiguous Days field that we created in Column N. Whenever the value in Column N is 5 or more, we want to sum the running mileage for the previous 5 days.

The formula for cell U8 is " = IF(N8 < 5, 0, SUM(L4:L8))."

Copy this formula to the bottom of the spreadsheet.

Climate Data

One interesting hypothesis about blood pressure is that it may vary according to the seasons. In order to test this in our modeling, we will need to bring climatological information into the analysis.

Using Columbus, Ohio as a typical Midwestern location, we can find sources of climatological data on line. A Google search for "Columbus Ohio weather statistics" reveals that monthly temperatures for the area can be found at /www.weather.com/weather/wxclimatology/monthly/43210. Since the data may or may not be available at this site for the life of the current book, the information has been put in the tab labeled "Sheet 2" in your worksheet. Double click on this tab to rename it "Lookups." You'll see the data in Figure W.13.

Next, in cell V3 put the label "Avg Temp." Then, in cell V4, use the VLOOKUP() function to associate an average temperature with each month that we abstracted in Column S. The formula is " = VLOOKUP(P4, Lookups!$D$2:$H$13, 5, FALSE)." Be sure to include the dollar signs or the formula won't work properly when it's copied. Figure W.14 illustrates this step.

Copy the formula in cell V4 down through the spreadsheet.

Now we're almost ready to do some modeling. We need to convert the spreadsheet into a flat file with no Excel formulas.

D	E	F	G	H	I
Month		Avg High	Avg Low	Mean	Avg Precip
1	January	37	19	28	2.86
2	February	42	22	32	2.40
3	March	52	29	41	3.13
4	April	65	40	53	3.76
5	May	75	50	63	4.56
6	June	83	60	72	3.71
7	July	86	64	75	4.42
8	August	85	61	73	3.15
9	September	79	54	67	3.03
10	October	67	41	54	2.71
11	November	54	32	43	3.32
12	December	42	23	33	3.14

FIGURE W.13 Climate data.

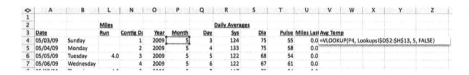

FIGURE W.14 Climate Data.

DATA IMPORTATION

The first step in getting the data ready for importation will be to convert the spreadsheet into a form compatible with the modeling algorithms of STATISTICA.

Step 1

Open a new blank spreadsheet and save it under the name "BP Modeling Data."

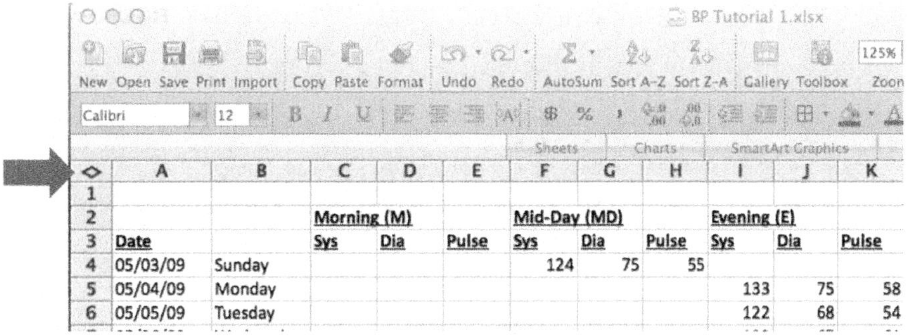

FIGURE W.15 Data importation.

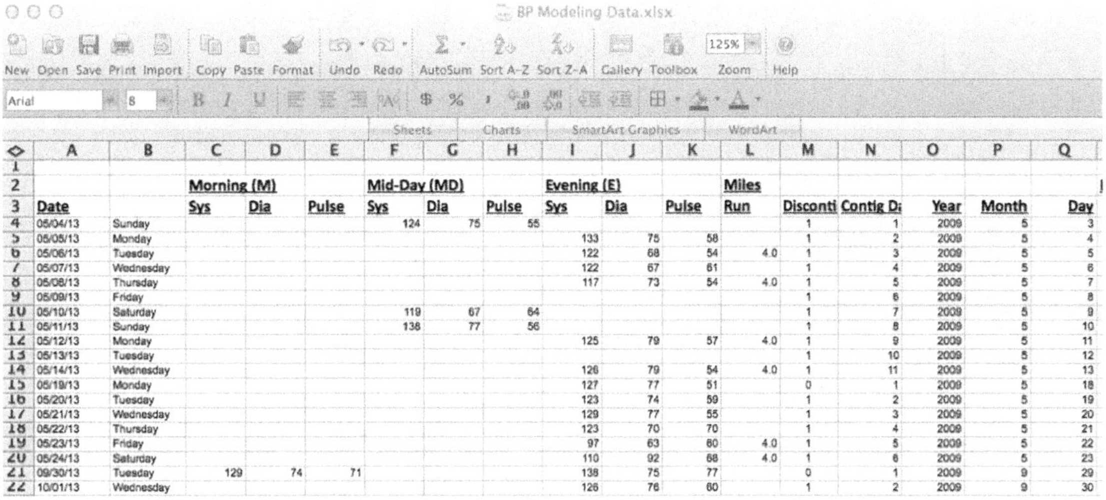

FIGURE W.16 Data Importation.

Next, unhide all the columns that were hidden the in the sheet "BP Tutorial 1.xlsx." Columns A through V will be populated with data. In "BP Tutorial 1" click on the diamond in the upper left, just above the numeral "1" of the first row (Figure W.15). This will select the entire sheet.

Next, use Command-C on a Mac (Control-C in Windows) to copy the sheet. Click on the diamond in your new sheet "BP Modeling Data" and use Command-V (Control-V) to paste the contents into the new sheet. Then in your new sheet (Modeling Data 1) click on the diamond again. Positioning your cursor within the body of the sheet, right click. Select Paste-Special and then Values (or VALU in some versions of Excel). This replaces all of the formulas in the original sheet with plain data values.

Your new sheet will look like the display in Figure W.16.

This will become more legible as we eliminate columns we don't need for modeling. Delete columns C through N. Next delete rows 1 and 2. Put the label "Weekday" in cell B1.

Your sheet will look like the display in Figure W.17. Make sure that the column headers are as shown.

Step 2

We're now ready to load our worksheet into STATISTICA.

Open STATISTICA and, from the File menu, select Open. Navigate to the spreadsheet BP Modeling Data and select it. The import dialog will appear (Figure W.18).

Click on "Import selected sheet to a Spreadsheet" and select Sheet1 in the dialog which appears (Figure W.19).

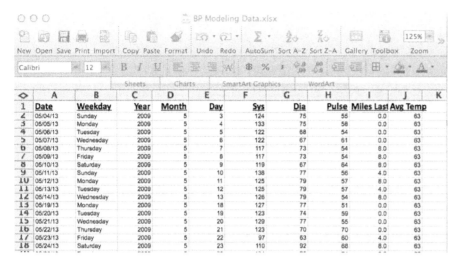

FIGURE W.17   Data Importation.

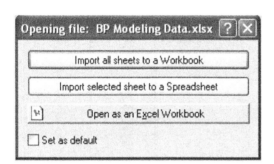

FIGURE W.18   Data importation – STATISTICA.

FIGURE W.19   Data Importation – STATISTICA.

In the "Open Excel File" dialog, make sure that "Get variable names from first row" is checked, and then click OK (Figure W.20).

If you get the dialog shown in Figure W.21, click on "Import as Text Labels."

Your screen will now appear as shown in Figure W.22.

Some of our file manipulations in Excel have fooled STATISTICA into thinking that there are 17 variables rather than the actual 10.

Select (empty) variables 11 through 17 by dragging through the headers. Then right-click and select Delete (Figure W.23).

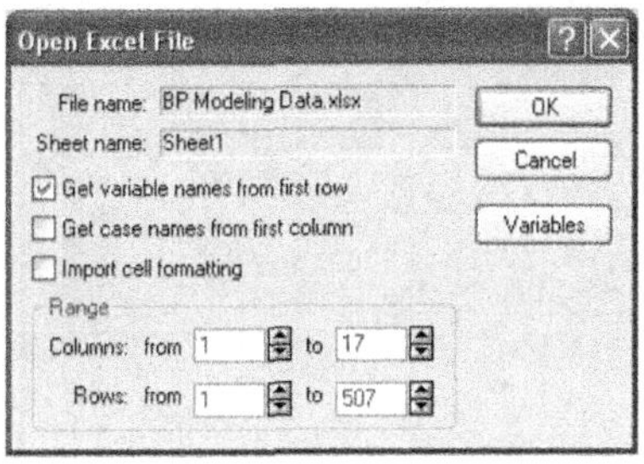

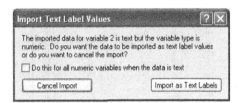

FIGURE W.20 Data Importation – STATISTICA.

Import Text Label Values

The imported data for variable 2 is text but the variable type is numeric. Do you want the data to be imported as text label values or do you want to cancel the import?

☐ Do this for all numeric variables when the data is text

| Cancel Import | Import as Text Labels |

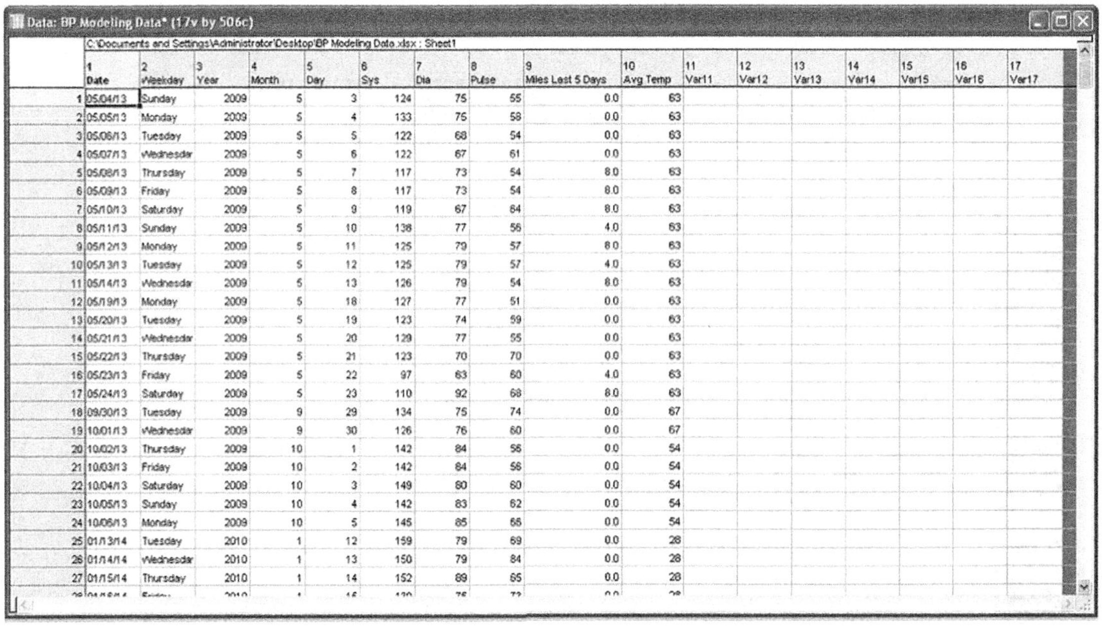

FIGURE W.21 Data Importation – STATISTICA.

Data: BP Modeling Data* (17v by 506c)

C:\Documents and Settings\Administrator\Desktop\BP Modeling Data.xlsx : Sheet1

	1 Date	2 Weekday	3 Year	4 Month	5 Day	6 Sys	7 Dia	8 Pulse	9 Miles Last 5 Days	10 Avg Temp	11 Var11	12 Var12	13 Var13	14 Var14	15 Var15	16 Var16	17 Var17
1	05/04/13	Sunday	2009	5	3	124	75	55	0.0	63							
2	05/05/13	Monday	2009	5	4	133	75	58	0.0	63							
3	05/06/13	Tuesday	2009	5	5	122	68	54	0.0	63							
4	05/07/13	Wednesday	2009	5	6	122	67	61	0.0	63							
5	05/08/13	Thursday	2009	5	7	117	73	54	8.0	63							
6	05/09/13	Friday	2009	5	8	117	73	54	8.0	63							
7	05/10/13	Saturday	2009	5	9	119	67	64	8.0	63							
8	05/11/13	Sunday	2009	5	10	138	77	56	4.0	63							
9	05/12/13	Monday	2009	5	11	125	79	57	8.0	63							
10	05/13/13	Tuesday	2009	5	12	125	79	57	4.0	63							
11	05/14/13	Wednesday	2009	5	13	126	79	54	8.0	63							
12	05/19/13	Monday	2009	5	18	127	77	51	0.0	63							
13	05/20/13	Tuesday	2009	5	19	123	74	59	0.0	63							
14	05/21/13	Wednesday	2009	5	20	129	77	55	0.0	63							
15	05/22/13	Thursday	2009	5	21	123	70	70	0.0	63							
16	05/23/13	Friday	2009	5	22	97	63	60	4.0	63							
17	05/24/13	Saturday	2009	5	23	110	92	68	8.0	63							
18	09/30/13	Tuesday	2009	9	29	134	75	74	0.0	67							
19	10/01/13	Wednesday	2009	9	30	126	76	60	0.0	67							
20	10/02/13	Thursday	2009	10	1	142	84	56	0.0	54							
21	10/03/13	Friday	2009	10	2	142	84	56	0.0	54							
22	10/04/13	Saturday	2009	10	3	149	80	60	0.0	54							
23	10/05/13	Sunday	2009	10	4	142	83	62	0.0	54							
24	10/06/13	Monday	2009	10	5	145	85	55	0.0	54							
25	01/13/14	Tuesday	2010	1	12	159	79	69	0.0	28							
26	01/14/14	Wednesday	2010	1	13	150	79	84	0.0	28							
27	01/15/14	Thursday	2010	1	14	152	89	95	0.0	28							
28	01/15/14	Friday	2010	1	15	139	75	73	0.0	28							

FIGURE W.22 Preparing STATISTICA sheet.

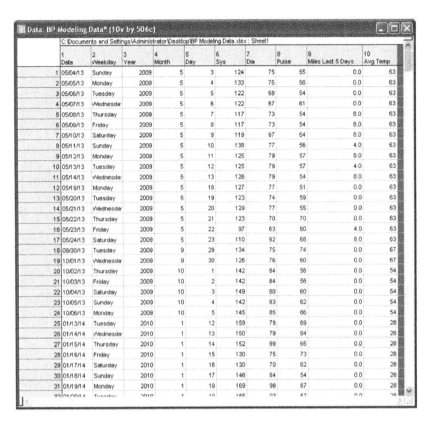

FIGURE W.23 Preparing STATISTICA Sheet.

VARIABLE TYPING

Now we want to be sure that our data are typed correctly. In the STATISTICA spreadsheet, double click on the column header for Date (Figure W.24).

Look at the type window in the upper right-hand corner. It should say "Double," as in the illustration. Double click on each column header in turn and make certain that the values in the type window are as indicated in Table W.1.

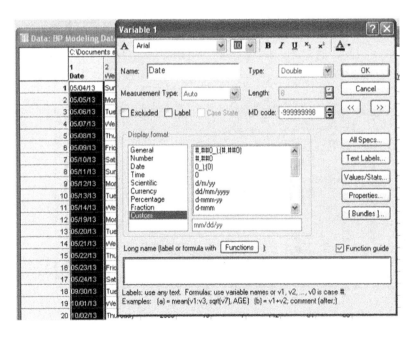

FIGURE W.24 Data typing.

TABLE W.1 Data Typing

Variable	Type	Change to
Date	Double	No change
Weekday	Double	Text
Year	Double	No change
Month	Double	No change
Day	Double	No change
Avg Sys	Double	No change
Avg Dia	Double	No change
Avg Pulse	Double	No change
Miles Last 5 Days	Double	No change
Avg Temp	Double	No change

PATTERN DISCOVERY

Descriptive Statistics

Next, let's get a feeling for some of the data.

With the spreadsheet foregrounded, select Statistics from the menu, and then Basic Statistics/Tables. A new dialog box will appear as in Figure W.25.

Click OK.

Select the variables for the analysis as shown in Figures W.26 and W.27.

After clicking OK, select Summary Statistics on the Descriptive Statistics dialog (Figure W.28).

The summary indicates that the mean systolic pressure is 134 but that there is relatively wide variation, with a standard deviation of 14.5 (Figure W.29).

Clicking on the Graphs 1 button (Figure W.28) yields three graphs, one for systolic pressure ("Sys"), one for diastolic pressure ("Dia"), and one for pulse ("Pulse"). If the graph for systolic pressure isn't visible, click on the tree branch "Summary: Sys" in the navigation pane (see Figure W.30).

FIGURE W.25 Statistics dialog.

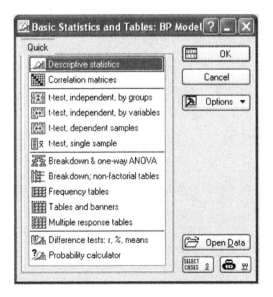

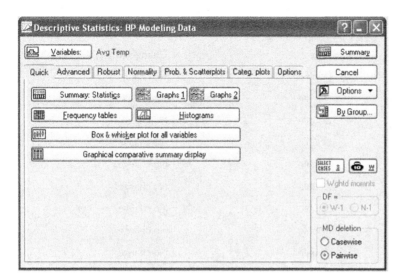

FIGURE W.26   Variable selection.

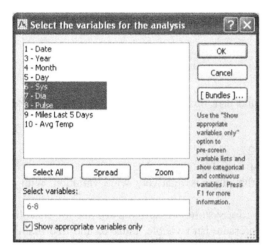

FIGURE W.27   Variable Selection.

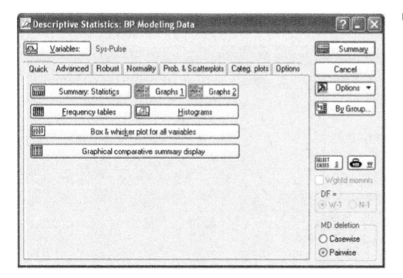

FIGURE W.28   Summary statistics.

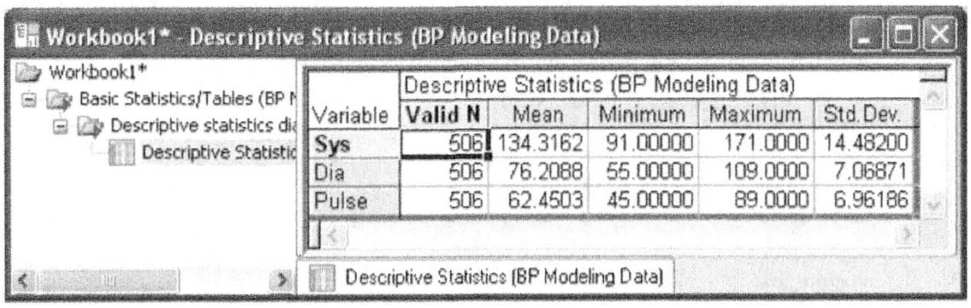

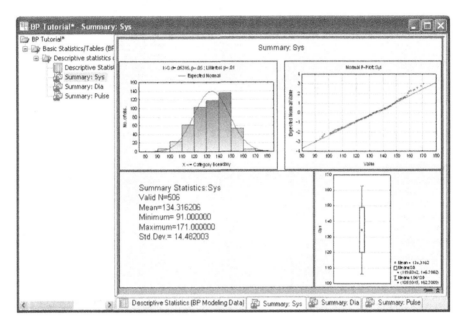

FIGURE W.29 Summary Statistics.

FIGURE W.30 Systolic pressure graph.

This graph indicates that the peak of the pressure distribution is shifted towards higher values than would be expected if the readings were normally distributed.

Next, click on the branch labeled "Summary: Dia" get the graph shown in Figure W.31.

These measurements are clearly more normally distributed than the measurements of systolic pressure, but notice the presence of two outliers at roughly 97 and 109, as indicated by the marks which are off the red line in the upper right-hand chart. In a predictive modeling analysis the records containing these measurements might be candidates for exclusion, meaning that the modeler might wish to leave them out of the data set used to train and evaluate the model. That judgment would be made based on subject matter expertise and experimentation – that is, comparing models built using the outliers against models built without them.

Next we'll try to determine the relative contributions of the variables Month, Miles Last 5 Days, and Avg Temp to the observed values of the variable Avg Sys.

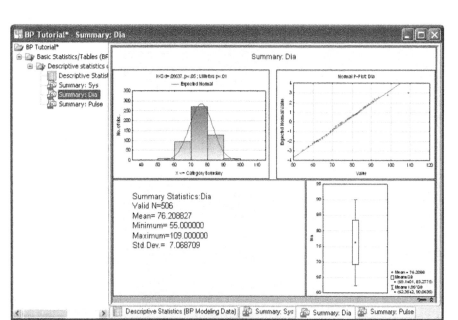

FIGURE W.31 Diastolic pressure graph.

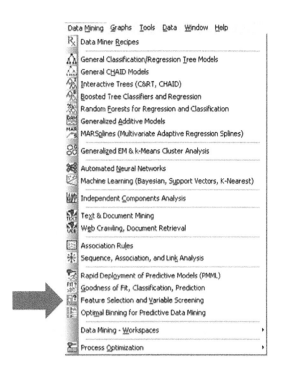

FIGURE W.32 Data mining menu.

Feature Selection

From The Data Mining menu select Feature Selection and Variable Screening (Figure W.32 — near the bottom of the menu).

From the Feature Selection and Variable Screening dialog (Figure W.33), click on Variables. This will bring up the dialog shown in Figure W.34. Select the variables shown and click OK; then click OK again in the Feature Selection dialog box. From the FSL Results dialog, click "Summary: Best k predictors (features)" (Figure W.35).

The results (Figure W.36) show that all three variables are highly predictive. The best predictor appears to be Avg Temp — the value obtained from the climatological data. However, Month is close behind, and Miles Last 5 Days, while not as strong a predictor as the other two, is also significant.

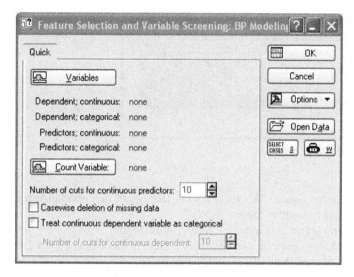

FIGURE W.33 Feature selection dialog.

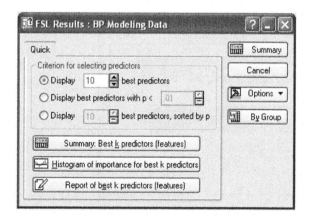

FIGURE W.34 Variable selection dialog.

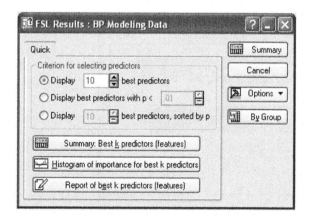

FIGURE W.35 FSL Results dialog.

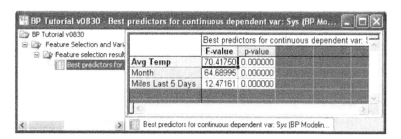

FIGURE W.36   Best predictors.

Pull up the FSL Results dialog again. This time select "Histogram of importance for best k predictors." That will display the same information, but visually (Figure W.37).

Now, from the Graphs menu select 2D Graphs − Scatterplots (Figure W.38).

From the 2D Scatterplots dialog, click on the Variables button. Select Miles Last 5 Days for the X variable and Avg Sys for the Y variable; click OK, and then OK again (Figure W.39).

The plot in Figure W.40 shows an interesting trend between miles run and average systolic pressure, though there is wide variation.

It is tempting to conclude that running lowers systolic blood pressure, but that conclusion is not warranted at this point because we haven't yet looked at the effect of seasonality. For example, it wouldn't be surprising to find out that the subject ran more during the warmer months of the year. We leave it as a further exercise for the reader to test this idea.

Now, generate a new scatterplot using Avg Temp as the X variable and Sys as the Y variable (Figure W.41).

Again, we see a clear trend with average systolic pressure decreasing when the average temperature is higher.

Finally, let's look at a scatterplot with Month as the X variable and Sys as the Y variable (Figure W.42).

Here we can, at first, barely discern a trend, but closer examination indicates that there seems to be a sinusoidal pattern to the data which can't be captured well with a linear regression. This pattern makes sense when we realize that month 1 is January and month 12 is December. With this understanding, it appears that the average systolic pressure is higher during the colder months of the year and lower during the warmer months. Because the calendar is cyclic, this shows up as a sinusoidal pattern.

There is still a great deal of variability evident in the systolic pressure readings, however. One reason may be that we used monthly temperatures, averaged over many years. Though beyond the scope of this tutorial, it would be an interesting research project to use the actual daily temperatures for the dates in question rather than multi-year averages.

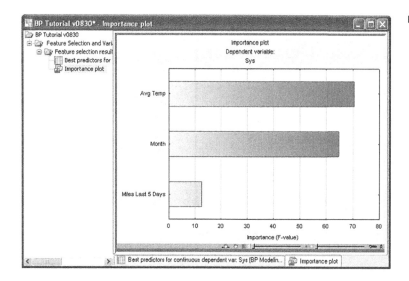

FIGURE W.37   Best predictors: histogram.

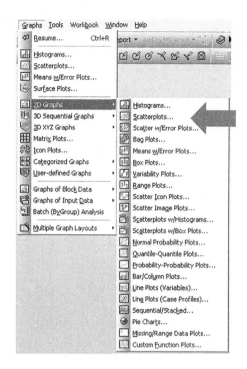

FIGURE W.38   Scatterplot.

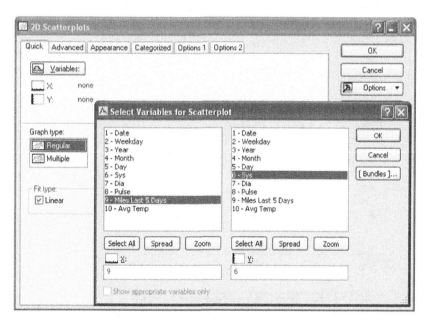

FIGURE W.39   Scatterplot.

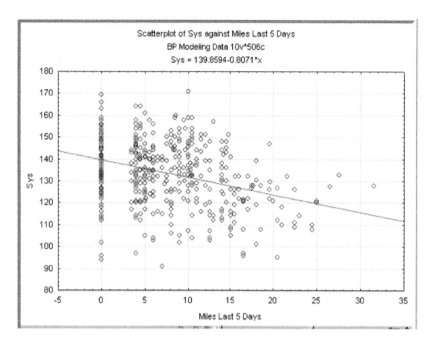

FIGURE W.40 Scatterplot: Sys vs. Miles Run.

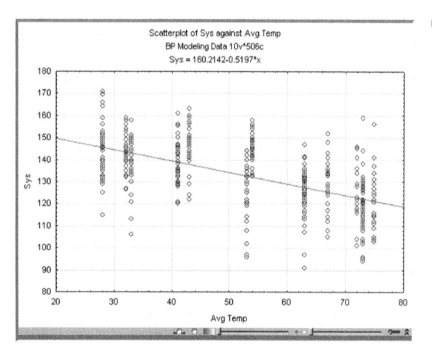

FIGURE W.41 Scatterplot: Avg Temp vs. Sys.

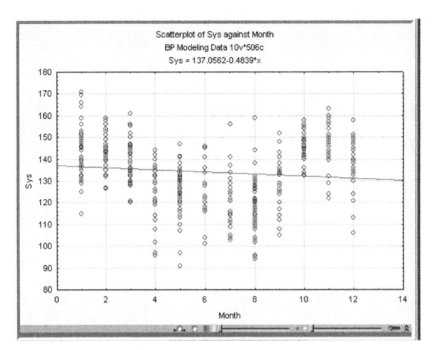

FIGURE W.42 Scatterplot: Month vs. Sys.

CONCLUSION

In this tutorial we have attempted to show how personal health observations, when analyzed with the tools of data mining and predictive analytics, can reveal unsuspected patterns and lead an individual to a greater understanding of his or her health. In doing this we have also exposed many of the processes which practitioners go through to develop their models.

As a postscript to this tutorial, we can say that this particular analysis offered surprises both for the subject and for his physician. The subject was surprised to find out that more running did not clearly lead to lower blood pressure. And both the subject and his physician were surprised at the clarity of the relationship between blood pressure and temperature.

We hope that this tutorial will encourage individuals to keep good records of health observations and that healthcare providers will see in this kind of analysis a new tool to use in supporting the wellness aspirations of the people in their care.

Tutorial X

Gene Search and the Related Risk Estimates: A Statistical Analysis of Prostate Cancer Data

Chamont Wang, PhD, Welling Howell, BS and Charlene Wang, BS

Chapter Outline

BACKGROUND AND THE BENCHMARK DATA

According to a 2013 report from the American Cancer Society, prostate cancer is the most common type of cancer in their top 10 list of cancers, with more than 238,000 new cases expected in the United States in 2013. The next most common cancers are breast cancer and lung cancer (www.cancer.org/research/cancerfactsfigures/cancerfactsfigures/cancer-facts-figures-2013, www.cancer.gov/cancertopics/types/prostate).

In this study, we will investigate a set of prostate cancer data to see whether statistical methods and machine-learning tools can help identify the genes that are related to this specific disease. The data comprises 102 patients (52 cancer, 50 normal) and 6,033 genes. The original data were collected and analyzed by a team of 15 scientists from a dozen institutions, including Harvard Medical School, Whitehead Institute/Massachusetts Institute of Technology, and Bristol-Myers Squibb Inc., Princeton (Singh *et al.*, 2002).

Efron and colleagues (Efron and Zhang, 2011; Efron, 2010, 2011) also discussed this set of data in the context of Benjamini-Hochberg FDR (false discovery rate) and Bayesian analysis. We are very grateful that Dr. Efron emailed us

Practical Predictive Analytics and Decisioning Systems for Medicine. DOI: http://dx.doi.org/10.1016/B978-0-12-411643-6.00041-7

the data he used in his papers. The data are in the Dap structure (http://fossies.org/dox/dap-3.8/classes.html) with a size of 11.5 MB. A glimpse of the data follows (here, we show only the first and the latter three lines of the file):

```
dap <-
structure(c(-0.930895161007995, -0.839996352777392, 0.0625080146627693,
-0.361593903716823, -1.12442739904722, -1.18049191810519, -1.09227619738030,
-1.14962414305984, -1.15750255953444, 0.219848844863316, 0.393209330689665,
.
.
.
-1.19168886655505, -0.96588562363763, 0.151368210227722, -0.910070480906474,
-0.574876515295521, -1.09407393877104, -1.19830036187316, -0.342059669784626,
-0.243874765058425, -0.707884483714245, -0.161796010537712), .Dim = c(6033L,
102L))
```

In order to facilitate the analysis that will be carried out by SAS, STATISTICA, R, and other software packages, we use the following SAS code to convert the Dap data:

To run the SAS code as is, the user needs to create a new folder called "Prostate_Cancer_data" in the C:drive, deposit the raw data in C:\Prostate_Cancer_data, and then run the above code in SAS Editor window. The output data file will be in the folder "C:\Prostate_Cancer_data," and will be called "dapout.sas7bdat."

After the conversion, there will be 102 rows, representing n = 102 patients in the study. The first column of the data will be "Target" (1 = cancer, 0 = normal patient), the second column will be "PatientID" and the remaining columns will be gene1−gene6033. One goal of the study is to find the genes that are related to the disease.

Due to the amount of the data and the intricate process of data conversion, it will take a few minutes to complete the run, so be patient.

VISUALIZATION (I): CATEGORIZED HISTOGRAMS AND MATRIX PLOTS

Efron (2010, Table 2) presented the top 10 genes via the Benjamini-Hochberg FDR: 610, 1720, 332, 364, 914, 3940, 4546, 1068, 579, 4331. In a later section, we will show how to use SAS to run FDR and pFDR (postive FDR) on the prostate cancer data. In addition, we will use other techniques, such as Lasso, Gradient Boosting, Random Forest, Decision Tree, and Support Vector Machines, to see whether they would select similar sets of genes as FDR. Furthermore, we will discuss prescreening, dimension reduction, and a number of other issues in the gene selection. In this section, we will use STATISTICA v12 to help visualize the expression levels of the selected genes.

To begin with, import the prostate cancer data into STATISTICA. Select Graph − Categorized Histograms, as in Figure X.1.

Due to the huge amount of data with 6,035 variables, we bundle the top 10 genes with the STATISTICA Variable Bundle Manager to help ease the subsequent analysis (Figure X.2).

Click on [top-10] for Variables, and "target" for X-Category, as shown in Figure X.3.

Click on OK to create 10 sets of side-by-side histograms. Figure X.4 shows the distribution of gene610 for the normal patients (target 0), and for the cancer patients (target 1).

The categorized histograms indicate considerable difference among the normal and cancer patients in the expression level of gene610. Later in the tutorial (under the Visualization (II) section) we will use this technique to compare the genes selected by other methods; and under Visualization (III) we will use categorized histograms to help decide the relevant and irrelevant genes in the hybrid models.

One assumption in the FDR procedure is that the predictors are statistically independent. The Matrix plot in Figure X.5 helps assess whether this assumption is reasonable.

On the diagonal of the Matrix plot are the uncategorized histograms of five genes in the Efron top 10 list. The histograms show that most of these variables are skewed to the right. The red lines in the scatterplots are LOWESS (locally weighted scatterplot smoothing) fits. The charts give support to the independent assumption of the FDR procedure. In addition, we tried categorized scatterplots, which seem to further confirm the independent assumption.

Note that statistical visualization is *not* a linear process. Instead, it should be part of statistical modeling and exploration. That is, after the examinations of modeling results, the second or third phase of visualization usually provides insights to the problem, as will be shown in subsequent discussions.

```
/* Save the data in the  floder: C:\Prostate_Cancer_data. File name:
Prostate_Cancer_data.txt */
%let dir=C:\Prostate_Cancer_data;
filename indap "&dir\Prostate_Cancer_data.txt";
libname outdap "&dir";
/* Read dap as is */
data outdap.dap1;
   infile indap length=reclen;
   input rec $varying1000. reclen;
run;
/* Clean the first two record and last two record by keeping only
valid data and removing data instruction */
data outdap.dap2;
set outdap.dap1;
if rec='dap <-' then delete;
else if index(rec,'(c(')>0 then rec=substr(rec,index(rec,'(c(')+3);
else if index(rec,'), .Dim = c')>0 then rec=substr(rec,1,index(rec,
'), .Dim = c')-1)||',';
else if rec='102L))' then delete;
run;
/* Separate each value by comma. So the output should have 615366
rows for 102 patients with 6033 genes */
/* x is character value; y is numeric value. Note: The value for y
has been truncated and rounded. */
/* Only 9 decimal points of y values were kept. This is done
automatically by SAS. */
/* add 1 column (variable): target. */
/* target=0 for the first 50 healthy people */
/* target=1 for the next 52 people - not healthy */
data outdap.dap3;
length x $25 y n patientID geneID target 8.;
set outdap.dap2;
retain n patientID geneID 0;
cnt=count(rec,',');
do i=1 to cnt;
   x=scan(rec,i,',');
   y=input(x,e15.);
   n=n+1;
   if mod(n,6033)=1 then do;
        geneID=0;
        patientID=patientID+1;
        end;
   geneID=geneID+1;
   if patientID <=50 then target=0;
   else target=1;
   output;
end;
run;
proc sort data=outdap.dap3 out=outdap.dap4;
by target patientID geneID;
run;
/* Make it 102 row * 6033 column. */
proc transpose data=outdap.dap4 out=outdap.dapout(drop=_NAME_)
prefix=gene;
   by target patientID     ;
   var y ;
   id geneID;
quit;
```

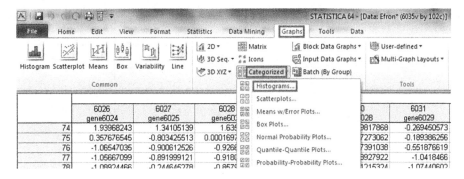

FIGURE X.1 Screenshot on how to create categorized histograms in STATISTICA.

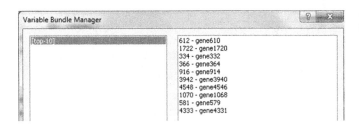

FIGURE X.2 Screenshot on how to use Variable Bundle Manager in STATISTICA.

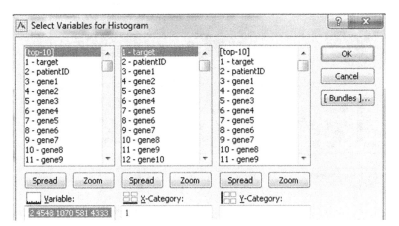

FIGURE X.3 Select Bundled Variables.

THE BENJAMINI-HOCHBERG FDR (FALSE DISCOVERY RATE)

Given 6,033 genes, one could conduct 6,033 t-tests on 6,033 null hypotheses, but then the Type I error would be totally out of control. Let m be the number of hypotheses that will be tested. The genius of the Benjamini-Hochberg paper is to sort the p values in $p_{(1)} \leq p_{(2)} \leq \ldots \leq p_{(m)}$ and let k be the largest J for which

$$p_{(j)} \leq \frac{j}{m} q^*$$

where q^* is a fixed number, and then reject all $H_{(j)}, j = 1, 2, \ldots, k$.

Benjamini and Hochberg's Theorem is that for independent test statistics and for any configuration of false null hypotheses, the above procedure controls the FDR at q^* (Benjamini and Hochberg, 1995).

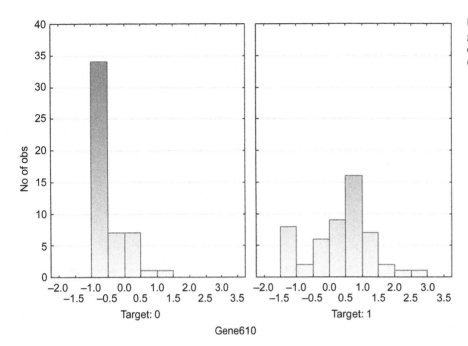

FIGURE X.4 Categorized histograms of gene610. The charts show a clear difference between normal (target 0) and cancer (target 1) patients.

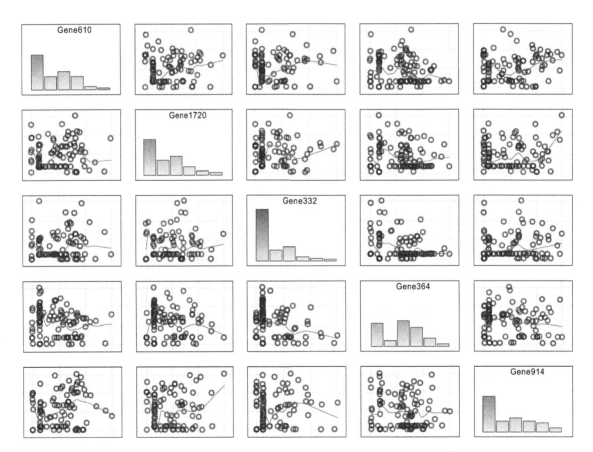

FIGURE X.5 Matrix plot and the LOWESS fits of the Efron top 5 genes. The charts give support to the independence assumption of the FDR procedure.

TABLE X.1 Consequences When Testing m Null Hypotheses (m = 6,033 in our Study)*

Hypothesis	Accept	Reject	Total
Null true	U	V	m_0
Alternative true	T	S	m_1
	W	R	m

R = number of hypotheses rejected; V = number of errors in the rejecting of the null hypotheses; T = number of errors in the accepting of the alternatives. R is an observable random variable; U, V, S, and T are unobservable random variables.

According to Efron (2010), the above result is "the second most striking theorem of post-war statistics." Efron (2010) and others indeed used this technique in the search for important genes. Consequently, a significant portion of this tutorial paper is devoted to the evaluation of this technique. A surprise to us is that the original intent of the technique was to control the false discovery rate, but the procedure helps reduce the irrelevant variables in the hybrid methods that will be discussed later in the tutorial, in the Hybrid Methods section.

Consider the test of m hypotheses as shown in Table X.1.

Benjamini and Hochberg (1995) established that

$$FDR = E\left(\frac{V}{R}|R>0\right) \quad P[R>0]$$

Storey and colleagues pointed out a number of weaknesses of FDR and considered the *positive false discovery rate* as follows (Storey, 2002; Storey *et al.*, 2004):

$$pFDR = E\left(\frac{V}{R}|R>0\right)$$

In addition, Storey *et al.* proposed a mechanism to estimate pFDR which would take advantage of more information in the data. Consequently, one would argue the new method is "more effective, flexible and powerful" (Storey, 2002). We indeed saw positive results in conference presentations, and hence include an evaluation of this method in the study.

The following SAS code produces FDR, pFDR, step-down Bonferroni p value, and the Sidak p value. The FDR column is sorted in ascending order:

```
proc multtest data = Sasuser.dapout holm sidak afdr pfdr(positive)
nopvalue noprint out=hello
(drop = _se_ _contrast_ _value_ _nval_ _test_);
 test mean (gene1 - gene6033);
 class target;
 contrast 'no yes' 0 1;
 run;
Proc Sort data = hello out=FDR;
 by afdr_p;
run;
```

If the cut-off of the adjusted p values is 5%, then FDR would select 21 genes. The following lists compare the Efron FDR top 10 and the SAS FDR top 12:

Efron top 10:   *610, 1720, 332, 364, 914, 3940, 4546,* 1068, 579, 4331

SAS FDR top 12:   *610, 1720, 332, 364, 914, 3940, 4546,* 579, 1068, 1089, 3647, 4331

The top seven genes of the two lists (in italics) are identical. The orders of #8 and #9 of the two lists are reversed, and #10 of the first list is #12 of the second list. In short, the two lists are slightly different, and the difference is probably not significant in the statistical sense and in biological applications (Figure X.6).

Note that if we set the cut-off at 5%, then FDR would select a total of 21 genes, the Bonferroni and Sidak methods would select only gene610 and gene1720, while pFDR would fail to select any.

	Variable	Raw p-value	Adaptive False Discovery Rate p-value	Stepdown Bonferroni p-value	Sidak p-value	Positive False Discovery Rate q-value
1	gene610	1.5440922E-7	0.000920279	0.0009315508	0.0009311172	0.0563783808
2	gene1720	1.576753E-6	0.004698724	0.0095109742	0.0094674572	0.0563783808
3	gene332	0.0000104473	0.0133949428	0.0629971611	0.0610835978	0.0563783808
4	gene364	9.3978035E-6	0.0133949428	0.0566781528	0.0551198782	0.0563783808
5	gene914	0.0000121025	0.0133949428	0.0729656994	0.0704126965	0.0563783808
6	gene3940	0.0000139439	0.0133949428	0.0840539966	0.0806830246	0.0563783808
7	gene4546	0.0000157323	0.0133949428	0.0948186645	0.0905486787	0.0563783808
8	gene579	0.0000329747	0.0186714842	0.1986726506	0.1804007095	0.0563783808
9	gene1068	0.0000267206	0.0186714842	0.161018159	0.1488844318	0.0563783808
10	gene1089	0.0000375905	0.0186714842	0.226407864	0.2029102781	0.0563783808
11	gene3647	0.0000375936	0.0186714842	0.226407864	0.2029249237	0.0563783808
12	gene4331	0.0000346483	0.0186714842	0.2087212246	0.1886345262	0.0563783808
13	gene1113	0.0000533727	0.024469325	0.3213569592	0.2753061758	0.0563783808
14	gene1077	0.000075249	0.0311141185	0.4529988838	0.3649135846	0.0563783808
15	gene1557	0.0000835278	0.0311141185	0.5026705103	0.3958570729	0.0563783808
16	gene4518	0.0000832527	0.0311141185	0.5010977984	0.3948532233	0.0563783808
17	gene3991	0.0001028849	0.0340663217	0.6189553438	0.4624515154	0.0563783808
18	gene4088	0.0000984289	0.0340663217	0.5922469191	0.4478033293	0.0563783808
19	gene3375	0.0001159808	0.0363813483	0.6976245616	0.5032919231	0.0563783808
20	gene4073	0.0001300652	0.0369137378	0.7820819477	0.5437590846	0.0563783808
21	gene4316	0.0001281441	0.0369137378	0.7706587133	0.5384398923	0.0563783808
22	gene735	0.0001906856	0.0516584555	1	0.6835264988	0.0563783808

FIGURE X.6 SAS outputs of the Raw p value, adaptive FDR p value, Bonferroni p value, Sidak p value, and pFDR q value.

PRESCREENING AND DIMENSION REDUCTION

Common tools such as regression, neural networks, and partial least squares (PLS) are often used to rank predictors and to select the top variables. The techniques often perform well with a dozen predictors, but do not really work for high-dimensional data with thousands of variables. Consequently, scientists often try to prune the variables by techniques such as R^2, χ^2, F-statistic, Nearest-Neighbor classifier, Decision Tree, Recursive Feature Elimination, Fisher's linear discriminant, or other techniques as discussed in Guyon *et al.* (2002). However, a cautionary note is that if the prescreening involves the binary target in the process, then it may distort the final results as shown in Hastie *et al.* (2009, p. 245). In this section, we present further evidence on how wrong the prescreening procedure can be.

Recall that the benchmark prostate cancer data were collected and analyzed by a team of 15 scientists from a dozen institutions, including Harvard Medical School, Whitehead Institute/Massachusetts Institute of Technology (MIT), and Bristol-Myers Squibb Inc., Princeton. As might be imagined, it is very expensive to conduct a microarray experiment of this magnitude, and it would be desirable to have more cost-effective alternatives. As a result, we frame a scenario as follows: a biologist who has limited budget collected only 10% of the samples as compared to the benchmark data set (i.e., there are only 10 patients in the sample). The biologist prescreened the 6,033 genes by a statistical variable selection technique, and then ran the PLS model with leave-one-out cross-validation, finding that the model can classify the validation data sets as cancer or normal with 100% prediction accuracy. In addition, the biologist used regression to double-check the PLS results and also obtained 100% prediction accuracy with the same genes as for the PLS model: gene1149, gene4201, and gene4780. Finally, the biologist double-checked the statistical results by examining the posterior probabilities as shown in Table X.2.

The posterior probabilities indicate that the model did extremely well classifying the data. This would represent an excellent finding for the biologist, especially considering that regression and PLS use different methodologies: regression is based on the maximum likelihood estimation of the parameters of the following equation:

$$\log\left(\frac{p}{1-p}\right) = a + b_1 x_1 + b_2 x_2 + \cdots + b_k x_k + \varepsilon,$$

while PLS is based on the extraction of latent variables from the covariance matrices of $X'X$ and $Y'X$.

Since the two methodologies are vastly different, the results appear to have reinforced each other in a significant manner. The scientist also noticed that PLS has been widely used in analytic chemistry (see, for example, Wold *et al.*,

TABLE X.2 PLS Posterior Probabilities of the 10 Patients Using Leave-One-Out Cross-Validation

Patient	Mean posterior probability	Cancer or Normal?
1	1	Cancer
2	1	Cancer
3	0.998	Cancer
4	0.995	Cancer
5	0.979	Cancer
6	0.011	Normal
7	0.007	Normal
8	0.005	Normal
9	0	Normal
10	0	Normal

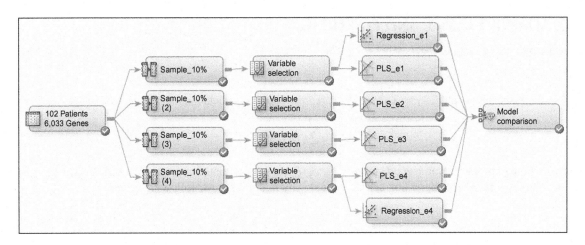

FIGURE X.7 Process flow of the PLS and regression models with 10% of the prostate cancer experiment sample. Here, four scientists used different samples to run their models. The first and the last scientists also used regression to double-check their PLS results.

2001) and other fields (see, for example, Vinzi *et al*., 2010), so the results are very encouraging and the 10% sample has the potential to cut research costs by 90%. If the results hold water, it would be great news for all researchers in this field of study.

But now the problem: three other imaginary scientists did the same experiment with a different 10% of the sample. The situation is depicted in the process flow shown in Figure X.7.

Now the miracle (see Table X.3): the four scientists all achieved 100% prediction accuracy but the genes they selected were vastly different.

In Table X.3 we also include the 10 genes that were selected by Efron (2010), which have very little in common with the other 4 sets of the genes. In summary, four scientists set out to collect data and use PLS to find the most important genes. In two of the four cases, the biologists even confirmed their PLS predictions using regression. Each of their models has a 100% prediction accuracy, but the genes they picked are vastly different. Which set of genes would you believe?

In sum, the 100% prediction accuracy actually misled our imaginary scientists to believe that a sample size of only 10 patients is sufficient to analyze the prostate cancer data set.

TABLE X.3 Four Different Runs of PLS Using Leave-One-Out Cross Validation*

Method	Prediction accuracy	Genes selected	Sample size	Seed
PLS-e1	100%	1149, 4201, 4780	10	12345
PLS-e2	100%	38, 476, 5585	10	23451
PLS-e3	100%	1352, 1751, 3560	10	34512
PLS-e4	100%	38, 1871	10	45123
Efron (2010)	n/a	610, 1720, 332, 364, 914, 3940, 4546, 1068, 579, 4331	102	n/a

All achieved 100% accuracy, but the genes the scientists selected were vastly different. Further, the genes selected by PLS have no overlap with the genes selected in the Efron (2010) study.

Prescreening that does not involve the binary target includes the shaving of the predictors based on the variance and other techniques of non-supervised learning. From the biological viewpoint, gene expression with small variability would indicate that the gene is stable and may be trimmed from the subsequent analysis. However, the threshold of the variability is not well established in the literature, and hence all results in this paper are obtained without any prescreening.

LASSO, ADAPTIVE LASSO, AND ELASTIC NET

Consider the binary regression model

$$Y_i = \alpha + S_i^T \beta + e_i, \quad i = 1,\ldots,n$$

where Y_i is the response variable, $X_i = (X_{i1}, \ldots, X_{ip})^T$ represents the p-dimensional centered covariates, i.e.,

$$\sum_{i=1}^n X_i = 0,$$

and where α is the constant parameter, $\beta_1 = (\beta_1, \ldots, \beta_p)T$ are the associated regression coefficients, and ε_i is the random error. The lasso penalized regression selects variables by minimizing the following criterion:

$$\sum_{i=1}^n (Y_i - \alpha - X_i^T \beta)^2 + \lambda \sum_{j=1}^p |\beta_j|$$

where $\lambda > 0$ is the shrinkage parameter. Fan and Li (2001) showed that the lasso method leads to estimators that may suffer an appreciable bias. Zou (2006) proposed the following adaptive lasso and showed that with a proper choice of λ_n and the weights $\hat{w}_j^{adl}$, the adaptive lasso enjoys the oracle properties:

$$Q^{adl} = \sum_{i=1}^n (y_i - \alpha - x_i^T \beta)^2 + \lambda_n \sum_{j=1}^p \hat{w}_j^{adl} |\beta_j|$$

In their applications of "robust sparse logistic regression" (i.e., penalized regression) on microarray data, Bootkrajang and Kabán (2013) asserted that "a vast literature demonstrates that sparsity-inducing regularization approaches are effective in such cases."

In SAS, Adaptive Lasso does not do well (see Biomarkers and Visualization (IV), below), and the Lasso via LARS (least angle regression) yielded more than 101 genes. The top 13 are displayed as follows:

Lasso top 13: *610, 1720, 332, 364*, 1068, 914, 3940, 1077, 579, 4331, 4518, 1089, 4546
Efron top 10: *610, 1720, 332, 364*, 914, 3940, 4546, 1068, 579, 4331

In short, the Efron top 10 genes are included in the Lasso top 13. To be more precise, the four italicized genes in the Lasso list are in the same order as those in the Efron top 10, and the six underlined genes in the Lasso list match the underlined genes in the Efron top 10.

A generalized version of Lasso is *Elastic Net*, which tries to minimize the following criterion:

$$\sum_{i=1}^{n} (Y_i - \alpha - X_i^T \beta)^2 + \lambda \sum_{j=1}^{p} |\beta_j|^{\gamma}.$$

When $\gamma = 2$, the process would render the *Ridge Regression* coefficients. In this study, we used Salford Systems GPS 7.0 to run Elastic Net with 10-fold cross-validation, and the model with the smallest misclassification rate is the Ridge Regression, which selected 122 genes with the top 15 being the following:

Ridge Regression top 15: 1082, 4315, 731, 4499, 2923, 3746, 1643, 78, 3712, 1090, 381, 1628, 5287, 1476, 5303
Efron top 10: 610, 1720, 332, 364, 914, 3940, 4546, 1068, 579, 4331

In short, the Efron top 10 are totally different from the Ridge Regression top 15. In fact, the Efron top 10 are ranked #112−121 by Salford Systems Ridge Regression. Very disconcerting indeed.

HOLD-OUT DATA AND OVER-FITTING

In predictive modeling, a common practice is to reserve a fraction of data for testing and cross-validation. This set of data is called the hold-out data, and is not used in the model-building process to prevent over-fitting and to avoid biased estimates of false positive rate, false negative rate, misclassification error, etc. In our use of Lasso and Adaptive Lasso, we followed this practice and deployed 10-fold cross-validation (10-fold CV) to gauge the misclassification rates. However, 10-fold CV reserved 10% of the original data for testing, and hence is probably a waste in gene search.

Recall that FDR does not use any hold-out data and does not involve misclassification rate (see, for example, Efron, 2010, Table 2). Similarly, one could argue that in gene search the misclassification rates are irrelevant, and hence the hold-out data would not be necessary. In our experiments, SVM selected similar genes with 10-fold and no hold-out with n = 102. Gradient Boosting (also known as TreeNet) also selects similar genes with or without 10-fold cross-validation. Nevertheless, we believe the practice of no hold-out may help identify the true genes in the use of other statistical methods, and should be used in conjunction with 10-fold CV and 90%−10% Training−Test split whenever possible. After all, no hold-out means more data in the model-building process, and we believe it should be checked before drawing the final conclusions. An illustration of this practice is shown in the Concluding Remarks to this tutorial.

PENALIZED SUPPORT VECTOR MACHINES

The SVM is a statistical classifier that separates two classes (Cancer vs. No cancer) by maximizing the margin between them. For non-separable data, the soft-margin SVM uses a slack variable to control an upper bound of the misclassification error. For cases where a linear separation via a hyper-plane is not feasible, the non-linear SVM uses a kernel to map the original data into a high-dimensional feature space. Common kernels include linear, polynomial, sigmoid, and radial basis function kernels.

Given an SVM algorithm, one can use forward selection, backward elimination, or stepwise procedures to help find the most important predictors. In addition, a penalty function can be used to screen out the unwanted variables. In this tutorial, we use the Smoothly Clipped Absolute Deviation penalty (SCAD penalty; Becker *et al*., 2009) as follows:

$$pen_{\lambda}(w) = \sum_{j=1}^{d} p_{\lambda}(w_j)$$

where the SCAD penalty function for each w_j is defined as

$$p_{\lambda}(w_j) = \begin{cases} \lambda|w_j| & \text{if } |w_j| \leq \lambda, \\ -\dfrac{(|w_j|^2 - 2a\lambda|w_j| + \lambda^2)}{2(a-1)} & \text{if } \lambda < |w_j| \leq a\lambda, \\ \dfrac{(a+1)\lambda^2}{2} & \text{if } |w_j| > a\lambda, \end{cases}$$

with tuning parameters $a > 2$ and $\lambda > 0$. Other details on the SCAD−SVM linear boundary and its optimal hyper-plane can be found in Becker *et al*. (2009).

For SCAD-SVM, we used svm.fs function in the penalizedSVM R package (the R code is included in Appendix B). The selected genes by penalizedSVM are listed as:

SVM top 12:   <u>364</u>, 3647, <u>610</u>, 3282, 3375, <u>1068</u>, 3585, 4396, 3269, 718, <u>1720</u>, <u>332</u>
Efron top 10:   <u>610</u>, <u>1720</u>, <u>332</u>, <u>364</u>, 914, 3940, 4546, <u>1068</u>, 579, 4331

The common genes of SVM and Efron top 10 are underlined.

CONFLICTING RESULTS FROM THE TREE METHODS

In this section, we discuss the conflicting results from the Tree Methods: Random Forest, Decision Tree (also known as CART, for Classification and Regression Trees), and Stochastic Gradient Boosting (a.k.a. TreeNet).

Decision Tree is one of the oldest and the most popular tools in data mining (Breiman *et al.*, 1983). The technique is well known for having a host of problems. For instance, Dwyer and Holte (2007) presented two vastly different trees grown from two subsets of data that differ in a single training example (n = 106 vs. n = 107). Changing a few observations can also substantially change the tree predictions (Friedman, 2006). The discrepancy widens when different researchers use different formulas (entropy reduction, Chi-squares, etc.) on different software platforms.

Random Forest and Stochastic Gradient Boosting are tree methods that were developed by various researchers to improve Decision Tree in the areas of predictive modeling and variable selection. In this section, we compare the genes that are selected by these three methods via Salford Systems SPM v7 where Stochastic Gradient Boosting is called *TreeNet*. The runs were executed without the use of hold-out data as explained in the section "Hold-out Data and Overfitting" above.

The right panel of Figure X.8 indicates that Random Forest selects a total of 4,103 predictors (out of 6,033). This huge number of variables would not help scientists to find the true genes.

In comparison, CART selects only 18 genes (out of 6,033), as shown in the right panel of Figure X.9.

TreeNet selected 279 genes (out of 6,033), as shown in the right panel of Figure X.10.

The top 12 genes of Random Forest, CART, and TreeNet are summarized as follows. In addition, we add the second group (Efron top 10, Lasso top 12, SVM top 12) for comparison:

TreeNet top 12:   *1627, 77, 5568, 571, 1147, 411, 1392, 1022, 1061, 820, 653, 576*
Random Forest: *1554, 1565, 1030, 284, 494, 2071, 2856, 2574, 5081, 1688, 594, 1346*
CART top 12:   *1627, 1353, 2327, 1696, 1143, 242, 160, 4583, 889, 1322, 1759, 812*
Efron top 10:   *610, 1720, 332, 364,* <u>*914*</u>*, 3940, 4546,* <u>*1068*</u>*, 579,* <u>*4331*</u>
Lasso top 12:   *610, 1720, 332, 364,* <u>*1068, 914*</u>*, 3940, 1077, 579,* <u>*4331*</u>*, 4518, 1089*
SVM top 12:   <u>364</u>*, 3647,* <u>610</u>*, 3282, 3375,* <u>1068</u>*, 3585, 4396, 3269, 718,* <u>1720</u>*,* <u>332</u>

The three lists of genes selected by the Tree methods literally have nothing in common. Furthermore, while the genes selected by SVM and Lasso are similar to the Efron top 10, the genes selected by the Tree methods are vastly different. In the next section, we will compare the categorized histograms of these two groups of methods. Later, we will discuss the hybrid methods in attempt to draw strengths from different techniques.

VISUALIZATION (II): LINEAR VS. NON-LINEAR MODELS

Among the Tree methods, Random Forest is not really a competitive tool for gene search when it selected 4,103 genes from a pool of 6,033. Furthermore, in our experiments with hold-out data, the misclassification rates of Random Forest are 47% or more, which is not much better than the blind bet. TreeNet (i.e., Gradient Boosting), on the other hand, performed very well in extensive scrutiny in Wang and Gevertz (2013). As a result, we will focus the discussions on Gradient Boosting. The theoretical aspect of Gradient Boosting is a beauty in itself, and is included in Appendix C.

As shown in the previous section, a big problem is that the genes selected by TreeNet and FDR are totally different. Consequently, in this section we set out to compare the categorized histograms of top genes selected by TreeNet and FDR. Recall that genes selected by FDR (t-tests), Lasso, and penalizedSVM are similar, and that these tools rely on linear techniques. In contrast, TreeNet is a tool to model the non-linear structure in the data. So the comparison is pitting non-linear technique against linear tools.

Figure X.11 shows four categorized histograms of the FDR top 10.

In these four cases, the differences of normal vs. cancer patients do not appear very significant. The histograms are also relatively symmetric.

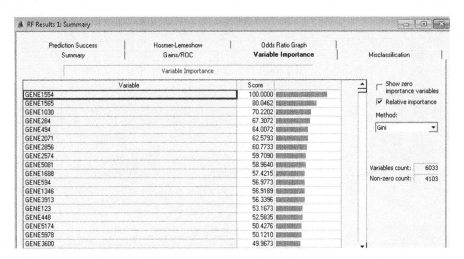

FIGURE X.8 4,103 genes are selected by Random Forest.

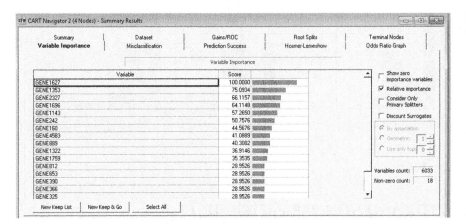

FIGURE X.9 18 genes are selected by CART.

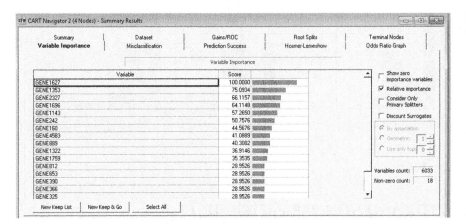

FIGURE X.10 279 genes are selected by TreeNet.

Figure X.11 shows that in gene364, gene914, gene3940, and gene4331, the differences of normal vs. cancer patients do not appear very dramatic. The histograms are also relatively symmetric. In contrast, Figure X.12 shows the top genes selected by TreeNet are all lop-sided to the left.

A natural question is: which set of the genes would be more relevant to the prostate cancer? The set from FDR or the set from TreeNet? The answer is surprisingly complicated − probably as complicated as the underlying biological mechanism that leads to the cancer. In the next section, we discuss this matter in more depth.

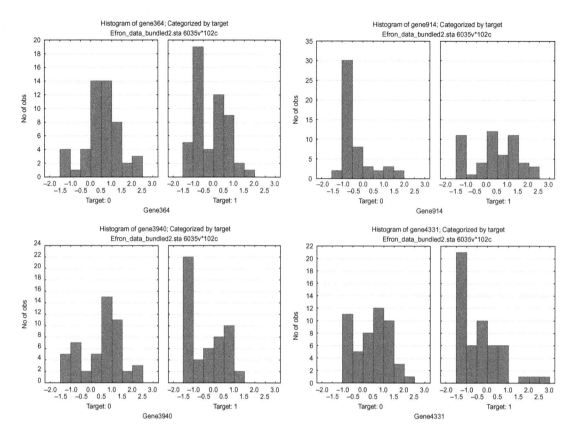

FIGURE X.11 Four categorized histograms of the FDR top 10.

THE BENJAMINI-HOCHBERG FDR AND NON-PARAMETRIC TESTS

Recall that SAS FDR is based on the t-test, but the lopsided histograms in Figure X.12 indicate that the t-test is probably not the best tool to deal with the differences between normal and cancer patients. As a result, we set out to use the Kolmogorov-Smirnov (KS) test to rank the 6,033 genes (the R code of the Kolmogorov-Smirnov test is in Appendix D to this tutorial). A comparison of the KS top 20 genes with the TreeNet top 12 is as follows:

TreeNet: <u>1627</u>, <u>77</u>, **5568**, <u>571</u>, <u>1147</u>, 411, <u>1392</u>, <u>1022</u>, <u>1061</u>, **820**, <u>653</u>, <u>576</u>
KS top 20:   411, <u>1627</u>, <u>77</u>, <u>1392</u>, <u>571</u>, <u>1147</u>, <u>1022</u>, 902, 37, <u>653</u>, 614, 808, 1554, 739, <u>1061</u>, 406, 897, 979, <u>576</u>, 657

The comparison shows that most of TreeNet top 12 are in the Kolmogorov-Smirnov top 20. The only exceptions are gene5568 and gene820 (in bold).

A caution is that Kolmogorov-Smirnov test is often not very sensitive in establishing distances between two distributions. As a result, the Anderson-Darling (AD) test is often used to compare the differences between two distributions. The following table compares the top 20 genes selected by Anderson-Darling as opposed to the top 12 of TreeNet:

TreeNet top 12:   <u>1627</u>, <u>77</u>, **5568**, <u>571</u>, <u>1147</u>, 411, <u>1392</u>, <u>1022</u>, 1061, 820, 653, 576
AD top 20:   411, 610, 452, <u>1627</u>, **5568**, <u>77</u>, 1720, 739, 579, 4552, 37, 370, 81, <u>1392</u>, 902, <u>571</u>, <u>1022</u>, 2, <u>1147</u>, 614

The comparison shows the following: (1) Four genes in TreeNet are not in the Anderson-Darling list: 1061, 820, 653, 576; (2) gene5568 is in the TreeNet list but not in the KS list, and yet it is in the AD list; (3) gene820 is in the TreeNet list but not in the KS list and not in the AD list; (4) all genes in the TreeNet list are covered by the union of KS or AD, with the exception of gene820.

In short, SAS FDR is based on the linear t-tests while TreeNet is a non-linear tool that selects genes closer to the Kolmogorov-Smirnov and Anderson-Darling non-parametric tests. Consequently, it requires more work to decide the merits and potential pitfalls of these methods.

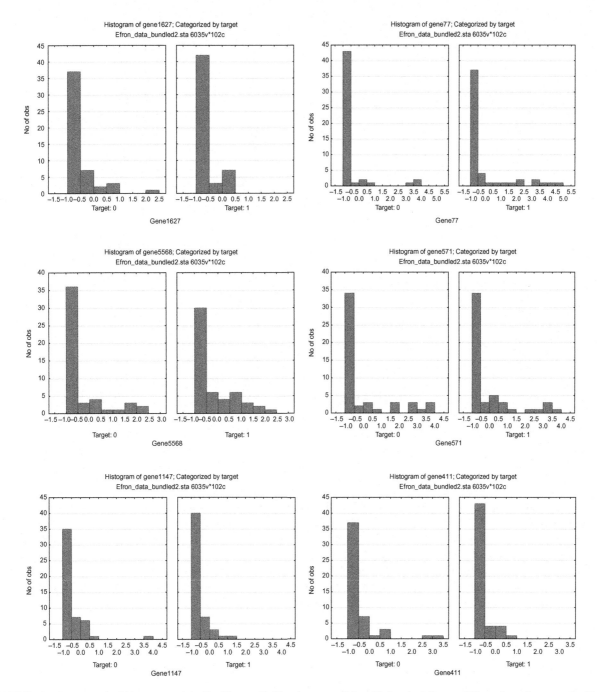

FIGURE X.12   Ten categorized histograms of the TreeNet top 10. The charts are all lop-sided to the left, very different from the categorized histograms of FDR genes as shown in Figure X.10.

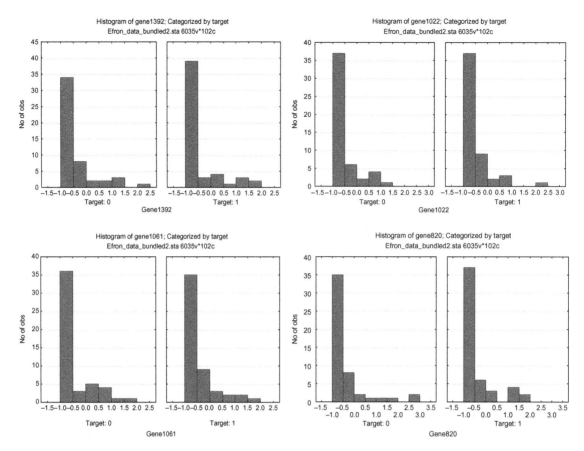

FIGURE X.12 Continued

Note that both KS and AD are based on empirical distribution functions. In many applications, the rank-based methods may be preferred. Figure X.13 gives the Mann-Whitney-Wilcoxon tests of the top genes selected by both FDR and TreeNet.

Figure X.13 reveals that genes selected by FDR are *sometimes* better than those selected by TreeNet *and vice versa*. For example, on the top of Figure X.13 is gene411, which is on the TreeNet list but not in the FDR top 10, while the second in Figure X.13 is gene610, which is in the FDR list but not in the TreeNet top 12.

In short, no tool is universally better and hence hybrid methods may be needed. This observation is consistent with the results from extensive computer simulations in Wang and Gevertz (2013).

HYBRID METHODS

In this section we discuss hybrid methods that may provide a better tool for gene search. The discussions will focus on two types of hybrids: Sequential Hybrids and Eclectic Hybrids.

Sequential Hybrids

In this case, a statistical tool (or tools) is used to prescreen the variables and then another tool (or tools) is used to determine the final set of genes. For example, Osborne *et al.* (1998) advise using Lasso to do the initial selection which, according to Zhao and Yu (2006), can be loosely justified by the asymptotic results of Knight and Fu (2000). Consequently, one may attempt to use the following Lasso–Gradient Boosting hybrid: use Lasso for prescreening, and then Gradient Boosting for final selection. Similarly, one may attempt to use Gradient Boosting (or other methods) *repeatedly* to trim the predictors in a sequential manner. However, as pointed out in Hastie *et al.* (2009, p. 245) and in the section on Prescreening, above, prescreening with supervised learning might distort the model performance, and both Lasso and Gradient Boosting are methods for supervised learning. Consequently, in this tutorial we avoid this kind of sequential hybrid.

| variable | Mann-Whitney U Test (w/ continuity correction) (Efron_data_bundled2.sta) By variable target Marked tests are significant at p <.05000 | | | | | | | | | |
	Rank Sum Group 1	Rank Sum Group 2	U	Z	p-value	Z adjusted	p-value	Valid N Group 1	Valid N Group 2	2*1sided exact p
gene411	3298.000	1955.000	577.0000	4.83641	0.000001	4.83641	0.000001	50	52	0.000001
gene610	1889.000	3364.000	614.0000	-4.58873	0.000004	-4.58873	0.000004	50	52	0.000002
gene1720	1907.000	3346.000	632.0000	-4.46824	0.000008	-4.46824	0.000008	50	52	0.000004
gene4331	3242.000	2011.000	633.0000	4.46155	0.000008	4.46155	0.000008	50	52	0.000004
gene3940	3209.000	2044.000	666.0000	4.24065	0.000022	4.24065	0.000022	50	52	0.000014
gene579	1955.000	3298.000	680.0000	-4.14693	0.000034	-4.14693	0.000034	50	52	0.000022
gene5568	1964.000	3289.000	689.0000	-4.08668	0.000044	-4.08668	0.000044	50	52	0.000029
gene364	3178.000	2075.000	697.0000	4.03313	0.000055	4.03313	0.000055	50	52	0.000039
gene1147	3175.000	2078.000	700.0000	4.01305	0.000060	4.01305	0.000060	50	52	0.000042
gene4546	3174.000	2079.000	701.0000	4.00636	0.000062	4.00636	0.000062	50	52	0.000043
gene1392	3152.000	2101.000	723.0000	3.85909	0.000114	3.85909	0.000114	50	52	0.000084
gene1627	2014.000	3239.000	739.0000	-3.75198	0.000175	-3.75198	0.000175	50	52	0.000134
gene571	3119.000	2134.000	756.0000	3.63819	0.000275	3.63819	0.000275	50	52	0.000218
gene576	3118.000	2135.000	757.0000	3.63149	0.000282	3.63149	0.000262	50	52	0.000224
gene1022	3105.000	2148.000	770.0000	3.54447	0.000393	3.54447	0.000393	50	52	0.000320
gene1068	2053.000	3200.000	778.0000	-3.49092	0.000481	-3.49092	0.000481	50	52	0.000397
gene914	2058.000	3195.000	783.0000	-3.45745	0.000545	-3.45745	0.000545	50	52	0.000454
gene1061	2063.000	3190.000	788.0000	-3.42398	0.000617	-3.42398	0.000617	50	52	0.000518
gene77	3071.000	2182.000	804.0000	3.31687	0.000910	3.31687	0.000910	50	52	0.000783
gene653	2091.000	3162.000	816.0000	-3.23655	0.001210	-3.23655	0.001210	50	52	0.001058
gene820	3029.000	2224.000	846.0000	3.03573	0.002400	3.03573	0.002400	50	52	0.002176
gene332	2184.000	3069.000	909.0000	-2.61400	0.008949	-2.61400	0.008949	50	52	0.008554

FIGURE X.13   Mann-Whitney-Wilcoxon tests of the top genes selected by both FDR and TreeNet.

On the other hand, prescreening via non-supervised learning would not distort the model performance. One method is to trim out the variables with small variability in gene expression, but the threshold of the variability is not well-established in literature; hence, this method is not used in this tutorial.

Eclectic Hybrids

In this case, multiple tools are used, with each tool selecting a set of genes; the *union* of the sets is then reported. In the case of the FDR−TreeNet hybrid, if we select the top 10 genes from each, the union will result in 20 genes. And if we add other tools such as Lasso and SVM, then the number of genes in the union may quickly balloon.

Among all the tools we have used, it is inevitable that irrelevant variables are included in the process of gene search. Theoretically, certain hybrid indexes may help determine the size of the final set of the genes and the number of irrelevant variables. In our case, the hybrid uses the union of the set of genes identified by each statistical method, and a sensible hybrid index would be *the ratio of the size of the intersection compared to the size of the union.*

For instance, a hybrid index of 1 would mean the multiple methods selected all the same variables, whereas a hybrid index of 0 would mean not one variable was selected by the statistical tools. Intuitively, the closer the hybrid index is to 1, the more confident we can be that all the relevant variables have been selected. That said, we have seen counterexamples to this, and hence the distribution and the theoretical property of this hybrid index will be postponed for future investigation.

In the next section, we will use a combination of visualization and the Mann-Whitney test to simultaneously help trim the irrelevant genes and find other important genes.

VISUALIZATION (III): SEEING CAN BE DECEIVING

Given a set of high-dimensional data with 6,033 genes, such as the benchmark prostate cancer data, it would be a challenge to inspect the data with eyeball examinations. However, we found that it is helpful actually to plot the data to compare the probability distributions of normal and cancer patients. For instance, the categorized histograms of gene2 and gene332 indicate pronounced differences between the normal and cancer patients, as shown in Figure X.14.

Note that gene2 is *neither* in the Efron top 10 list (610, 1720, 332, 364, 914, 3940, 4546, 1068, 579, 4331), *nor* in the TreeNet top 12 list. In comparison, gene364 and gene3940 are in the Efron top 10 list but the categorized histograms of these two genes show little difference between normal and cancer patients (Figure X.15).

In short, biologists may want to do two things: (1) add gene2 in the hybrid model, and (2) leave gene364 and gene3940 in the irrelevant (or semi-irrelevant) pool. However, the Mann-Whitney tests below indicate the following:

1. Adding gene2 may be a good idea.
2. However, leaving out gene3940 and gene364 may not be so.

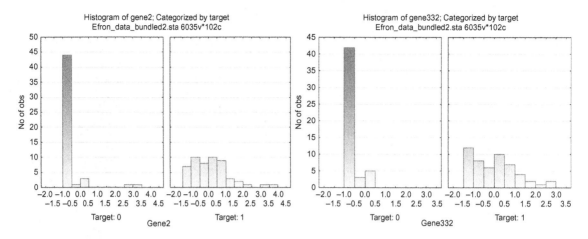

FIGURE X.14 The categorized histograms of gene2 and gene332 indicate pronounced differences between the normal and cancer patients — but seeing can be deceiving.

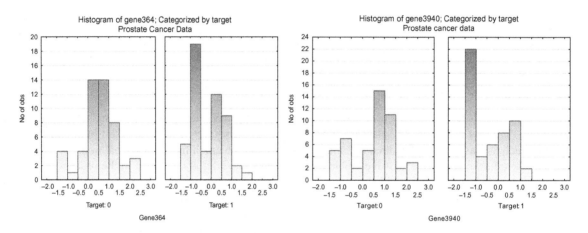

FIGURE X.15 Gene364 and gene3940 are in the Efron top 10, but the categorized histograms of these two genes show little difference between normal and cancer patients — but again, seeing can be deceiving.

3. The right panel of Figure X.14 indicates that gene332 is probably as important as gene2, but the Mann-Whitney tests below do not really support this conclusion.

In Figures X.14 and X.15, gene2 and gene332 appear more important than gene364 and gene3940, but the Wilcoxon ranking is the opposite (Figure X.16).

In short, visualization is a useful tool in the selection of gene2 (which is actually #18 on the Anderson-Darling list), but it is less than reliable on the rejection of gene364 and gene3940.

On the other hand, gene332 is an oddball: its categorized histograms are so lopsided that almost everyone would include this gene in the top list, yet its actual ranking (among the 6,033 genes) is far below the top 20 list in the Kolmogorov-Smirnov and Anderson-Darling rankings.

A conservative approach would be to include all genes that are selected by visualization and statistical tools, but then this would render many irrelevant genes. In contrast, a bold approach would be to exclude gene364 and gene3940, whose categorized histograms are very similar.

Our feeling is to go conservative for the very reason that if an important gene is missed in the exploratory stage, then it will be missed in the subsequent biological investigations.

variable	Mann-Whitney U Test (w/ continuity correction) (Efron_data_bundled2.sta) By variable target Marked tests are significant at p <.05000									
	Rank Sum Group 1	Rank Sum Group 2	U	Z	p-value	Z adjusted	p-value	Valid N Group 1	Valid N Group 2	2*1sided exact p
gene411	3298.000	1955.000	577.0000	4.83641	0.000001	4.83641	0.000001	50	52	0.000001
gene610	1889.000	3364.000	614.0000	-4.58873	0.000004	-4.58873	0.000004	50	52	0.000002
gene1720	1907.000	3346.000	632.0000	-4.46824	0.000008	-4.46824	0.000008	50	52	0.000004
gene4331	3242.000	2011.000	633.0000	4.46155	0.000008	4.46155	0.000008	50	52	0.000004
gene3940	3209.000	2044.000	666.0000	4.24065	0.000022	4.24065	0.000022	50	52	0.000014
gene579	1955.000	3298.000	680.0000	-4.14693	0.000034	-4.14693	0.000034	50	52	0.000022
gene5568	1964.000	3289.000	689.0000	-4.08668	0.000044	-4.08668	0.000044	50	52	0.000029
gene364	3178.000	2075.000	697.0000	4.03313	0.000055	4.03313	0.000055	50	52	0.000038
gene1147	3175.000	2078.000	700.0000	4.01305	0.000060	4.01305	0.000060	50	52	0.000042
gene4546	3174.000	2079.000	701.0000	4.00636	0.000062	4.00636	0.000062	50	52	0.000043
gene1392	3152.000	2101.000	723.0000	3.85909	0.000114	3.85909	0.000114	50	52	0.000084
gene2	2010.000	3243.000	735.0000	-3.77876	0.000158	-3.77876	0.000158	50	52	0.000119
gene1627	2014.000	3239.000	739.0000	-3.75198	0.000175	-3.75198	0.000175	50	52	0.000134
gene571	3119.000	2134.000	756.0000	3.63819	0.000275	3.63819	0.000275	50	52	0.000218
gene576	3118.000	2135.000	757.0000	3.63149	0.000282	3.63149	0.000282	50	52	0.000224
gene1022	3105.000	2148.000	770.0000	3.54447	0.000393	3.54447	0.000393	50	52	0.000320
gene1068	2053.000	3200.000	778.0000	-3.49092	0.000481	-3.49092	0.000481	50	52	0.000397
gene914	2058.000	3195.000	783.0000	-3.45745	0.000545	-3.45745	0.000545	50	52	0.000454
gene1061	2063.000	3190.000	788.0000	-3.42398	0.000617	-3.42398	0.000617	50	52	0.000518
gene77	3071.000	2182.000	804.0000	3.31687	0.000910	3.31687	0.000910	50	52	0.000783
gene653	2091.000	3162.000	816.0000	-3.23655	0.001210	-3.23655	0.001210	50	52	0.001058
gene820	3029.000	2224.000	846.0000	3.03573	0.002400	3.03573	0.002400	50	52	0.002176
gene332	2184.000	3069.000	909.0000	-2.61400	0.008949	-2.61400	0.008949	50	52	0.008554

FIGURE X.16 Wilcoxon tests.

BIOMARKERS AND VISUALIZATION (IV)

The statistical analysis of the prostate cancer data as shown in the preceding sections indicates that the current dataset and tools would not give a definitive answer on the exact genes that are the causes of the disease. In this section, we turn to a less lofty goal of finding the biomarkers in the sense of determining whether a small set of genes can tell us the risk of getting the disease.

In five different runs with random seeds (training data: 90%, test data: 10%), the Lasso test error rates are as follows: 0.0833, 0.25, 0.17, 0.18, 0.33; i.e., the average error rate is about 23%, which is not very encouraging. In addition, more than 100 genes are selected by the model. It is doubtful that this result would be helpful for biological applications.

Recall that Lasso is a popular tool in bioinformatics (Bootkrajang and Kabán, 2013 and the references therein). The poor performance of Lasso in this study is not a surprise to us; it is the same in extensive simulation studies of Wang and Gevertz (2013), and it has been observed by others: for example, in a recent study, Huang *et al*. (2012) found that Lasso "selects 17 genes out of 30 and 435 markers out of 532, failing to shed light on the most important genetic markers." This is also compatible with the findings of Zhao and Yu (2006) where Lasso picked wrong genes in a number of important settings.

The misclassification rate of TreeNet (with 10-fold cross-validation) is 3/102 = 3%; i.e., the accuracy of the model is 97%. This is great for predictive modeling. Now the bad news: TreeNet used a total of 277 predictors in the model, and it would be an embarrassment for a statistician to present this result to his or her biology colleagues.

Random Forest is even worse, with misclassification rates at 47% or more. This tool appears to have advantages in certain applications, but for gene search or risk estimates, we don't find it appealing.

CART is much better. With 10-fold cross-validation, it selected only 18 genes which would be more manageable for biologists. The accuracy is 87.3%, not as high as the 97% from TreeNet, but with a small sample of n = 102 patients, the model should be considered as a success or at least moderately useful.

Note that CART uses Gini index in the tree split. Out of curiosity, we compared the Chi-squares for tree split. To this end, we used SAS Enterprise Miner Decision Tree and the results yielded a few surprises. In short, we tried no hold-out, 10-fold CV, and 90%−10% split for training and test datasets.

In each of these settings SAS Decision Tree selected only three or two genes, as shown in Table X.4.

Table X.4 contains results from 12 Tree models: no hold-out, 10-fold CV, and 10 other Trees with a 90%−10% split for training and test data sets. The reason for 10 additional Trees is because SAS-EM 10-fold CV gives an error rate for the training data but not for the test data. Consequently, we were forced to use 10 additional Trees to gauge the error rate for the test data. (Theoretically, in the 10-fold CV the algorithm can keep track of the error rate in each fold and finally lump together the cases that were misclassified for the calculation of the overall error rate. Salford Systems does this for their TreeNet and CART, but SAS does not do this in their 10-fold CV.)

TABLE X.4 SAS Decision Trees*

SAS Tree	1	2	3	4	5	6	7	8	9	10	Average error
Error rate	17%	8%	0%	0%	8%	33%	27%	8%	8%	25%	13.6%
Genes	1627	1627	1627	1627	*5568*	**1392**	**1392**	1627	1627	1627	
	1322	1322	2327	2327	**1061**	**5604**	**5604**	2327	*5568*		
		143	1322	1322	**1126**				**1388**		

In-sample (or SAS 10-fold): 1627, 1322, 2327

Ten Trees with 90%−10% split for training−testing are shown in the main part of the table. SAS 10-fold CV and no hold-out models selected the same genes (1627, 1322, 2327), as shown in the last row, which are then used as the benchmark to see whether 10 other Trees would select the same genes. The union of the genes selected by the 12 Trees has 10 elements (1627, 1322, 2327, 143, 5568, 1061, 1126, 1392, 5604, 1388), there Tree6 and Tree7 have very high error rates and the genes selected may not be very useful.

Table X.4 shows the following:

1. Each of the 12 Trees selected only 3 or 2 genes in the model.
2. Their 10-fold CV and no hold-out models selected the same genes (1627, 1322, 2327) as shown in the last row, which is then used as the benchmark to see whether 10 other Trees would select the same genes.
3. The error rates of the models ranged from 0% to 33%, with the average at 13.6%. Hence the overall accuracy is 86.4%, very close to the 87.3% of CART.
4. In the table, there are 10 genes (in bold) that are different from the benchmarks. Altogether, the 12 Trees rendered 10 different genes (1627, 1322, 2327, 143, 5568, 1061, 1126, 1392, 5604, 1388), where Tree6 and Tree7 have very high error rates and the genes selected may not be very useful.
5. Instead of running 12 Trees, if we run more Trees the accuracy probably will remain but the list of genes probably will grow.
6. We tried 80%−20% splits and the results were similar, with some deterioration of accuracy, as expected.
7. The 10 different genes in the table match with 4 genes in the TreeNet list (underlined) and are totally different from the Efron top 10:

Efron top 10:	**610**, **1720**, **332**, **364**, **914**, **3940**, **4546**, **1068**, **579**, **4331**
SAS Tree (10 genes):	**1627**, **2327**, **1322**, **143**, **5568**, **1061**, **1126**, **1392**, **5604**, **1388**
TreeNet top 12:	**1627**, **77**, **5568**, **571**, **1147**, **411**, **1392**, **1022**, **1061**, **820**, **653**, **576**

Figure X.17 is produced by SAS Tree4 (see Table X.4). The Tree used 90% of the data for training and then 10% for validation, as shown in the first node of the Tree Diagram.

After one split via gene1627, the left node produced a perfect prediction, while the right node needed further splitting. The second split used gene2327, and the left node is perfect. The final split used gene1322, and the bottom nodes are perfect in the validation data. Quite a remarkable feat.

In additional, this Tree diagram is identical to those by the 10-fold Tree and the no hold-out Trees. It is rather convincing that these three genes (gene1627, gene1322, gene2327) are useful at least for prediction purposes, although they are completely missing from the Efron top 10 and the Lasso top 15 lists.

Furthermore, the latter two of this set (gene1322, gene2327) are not in the KS, AD, Wilcoxon, or TreeNet lists. It is a very peculiar phenomenon, and we suspect that the Efron data are probably standardized, which may be one of the sources of the conflicting results.

In the above section on Conflicting Results, we quoted different studies saying that the Tree model is not stable and may suffer from different problems. The above Tree diagram and Table X.4 show that, despite its documented shortcomings, the Tree is a valuable method and should be used in conjunction with other statistical tools in gene search and biomarker studies.

In conclusion, we report that in 12 runs of the SAS Decision Tree, a total of 10 genes would render a prediction accuracy of 86.4%. All other models would need more than 100 genes in their prediction, and hence would not be helpful.

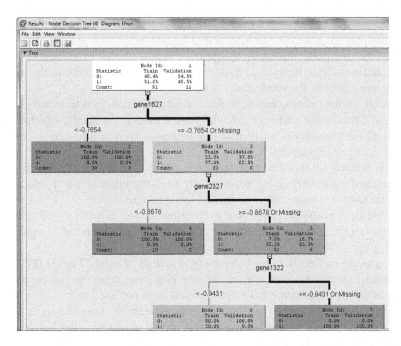

FIGURE X.17   SAS Decision Tree. In three splits, the prediction accuracies of the end nodes of the validation data are all 100% — very remarkable indeed.

CONCLUDING REMARKS AND THE LIMITATIONS OF STATISTICAL ANALYSIS OF GENE DATA

In this study, we focused on the benchmark prostate cancer data that was collected and analyzed by a team of 15 scientists from a dozen institutions including Harvard Medical School, Whitehead Institute/Massachusetts Institute of Technology, and Bristol-Myers Squibb Inc., Princeton (Singh *et al.*, 2002). The data were further discussed in Efron (2008, 2010) in a cross-over of Gaussian framework and Benjamini-Hochberg FDR (false discovery rate).

Our study found that the genes selected by Lasso and linear penalizedSVM are very similar to the top 10 genes (where the same genes are emboldened, or underlined):

Efron top 10:   **610**, **1720**, **332**, **364**, 914, 3940, 4546, **1068**, 579, 4331
Lasso top 13:   **610**, **1720**, **332**, **364**, **1068**, 914, 3940, 1077, 579, **4331**, 4518, 1089, **4546**
SVM top 12:   **364**, 3647, 610, 3282, 3375, 1068, 3585, 4396, 3269, 718, 1720, 332

On the other hand, Tree methods (Random Forest, CART, TreeNet) selected totally different genes from the above list. Nevertheless, the genes selected by TreeNet are similar to those of the non-parametric tests of Kolmogorov-Smirnov (KS) and Anderson-Darling (AD):

TreeNet top 12:   **1627**, **77**, **5568**, **571**, **1147**, **411**, **1392**, **1022**, 1061, 820, 653, 576
KS top 20:   411, 1627, 77, 1392, 571, 1147, 1022, 902, 37, 653, 614, 808, 1554, 739, 1061, 406, 897, 979, 576, 657
AD top 20:   **411**, 610, 452, **1627**, **5568**, 77, 1720, 739, 579, 4552, 37, 370, 81, **1392**, 902, **571**, **1022**, 2, **1147**, 614, 245

In addition, we used visualization techniques such as categorized histograms to help identify the variables that are important (e.g., gene2) and that are semi-important (e.g., gene332). This is somewhat subjective, so we used Anderson-Darling to cross-check the relevance of the genes.

An eclectic hybrid that combines the strengths of FDR, TreeNet, and Visualization appears feasible, and may provide a better model than each of the above methods. However, the hybrid may contain too many irrelevant genes, and additional work is needed to address this thorny issue.

In our study we also discussed the issues of biomarkers and the related risk estimates. To this end, the above methods are less than satisfactory. For example, the accuracy of Lasso is 77% with more than 100 genes in the model, the accuracy of TreeNet is 97% with 279 genes in the model, and FDR, KS, and AD do not provide risk estimates at all.

On the other hand, we found the Decision Tree to be an acceptable tool which rendered a total of 10 biomarkers with an average of 86% accuracy in 10 different runs. However, a concern with this approach is that, of the 10 biomarkers, 7 are not in the top lists of the above methods (FDR, Lasso, SVM, TreeNet, KS, and AD).

In short, the biomarkers from SAS Decision Tree may be useful for prediction purposes regarding whether a person with a specific gene profile may get a specific disease with a certain risk — but most of these biomarkers (70% in our Tree example) may not be the true genes that cause the disease. That is, the identification of biomarkers and the search for important genes are fundamentally different and must be treated as such. A tired cliché is that correlation is not causation, but in gene search, the distinction is subtle and can be easily blurred.

In biological gene search, an important question is: how reliable are statistical tests and modeling techniques in the variables selection process? Specifically, one may ask whether the models are stable, whether they are consistent, and, as stated in Mongan *et al.* (2010), whether it is true that "the increased level of algorithmic complexity does not always translate to improved biological understanding."

Similarly, Efron (2008) pointed out that the prostate cancer data set has low power, and if the study were re-run the list of important genes selected could very likely differ greatly from the original list of selected variables. Sadly, what Efron said appears to be the norm for most studies in modern gene searches.

In short, the current statistical methods cannot give a definitive answer to what set of genes is causing the disease. This may be disappointing to certain statistics users, but this conclusion is expected — otherwise, the authors of this paper might have already gotten a Nobel Prize.

Given the benchmark prostate cancer data, our hybrid would include at least 23 genes (FDR top 10, TreeNet top 12, and gene2 from Visualization). At this moment, we are not sure how many irrelevant genes are included in this set, and we do not know whether other important genes have been left out from our list.

One way to improve the statistical power of gene search is to increase the sample size. It is conceivable that sample size at n = 102 patients is probably too small and that a hybrid method would be better for n = 300.

When microarray and other technologies were new, even data sets with n = 100 would have been incredibly large and prohibitively expensive, which casts doubt on the usefulness of sample-size analysis of n ≥ 300. However, due to the declining costs of high-throughput biological technology, the collection and analysis of larger samples is now feasible (Pool *et al.*, 2010).

Furthermore, in the study of COMT genetic variation by Funke *et al.* (2005), a sample of 861 (394 Caucasian cases and 467 controls) was used, while a sample of 779 students was reported in a different study. In yet another example, Lettre *et al.* (2011) used n = 8,090 patients in the study of genome-wide association of coronary heart disease and its risk factors. We believe sample sizes at these magnitudes, coupled with the use of hybrid methods, would be more realistic in finding the important genes.

APPENDICES

Appendix A: Efron 2010, Top 10 Genes

Table X.A1 shows the top 10 genes, those with largest values of $|z_i|$, in the prostate study and their corresponding effect size estimates $\hat{\mu}_i$.

TABLE X.A1 Top 10 Genes

	Gene	z-value	$\hat{\mu}_i = \hat{E}\{\mu_i|z_i\}$
1	610	5.29	4.11
2	1720	4.83	3.65
3	332	4.47	3.24
4	364	−4.42	−3.57
5	914	4.40	3.16
6	3940	−4.33	−3.52
7	4546	−4.29	−3.47
8	1068	4.25	2.99
9	579	4.19	2.92
10	4331	−4.14	−3.30

Appendix B: The R Code for penalizedSVM, svm.fs Function Usage

```
"oneTrial" <- function(thisTrial,selGenes,E) {
 # WARNING - new seed set for EVERY ATTEMPT (LoopNr) -
 # re-seeding in hopes of find a solution which avoids known penalizedSVM
error
 # set seed from the clock to one of 99,999 values
 # using seconds from Sys.time() and elapsed milliseconds from proc.time()
 whSeed = floor(
 ( ( (as.numeric(Sys.time()) %% 1000) + proc.time()[3] %% 1) * 1000) %% 10000
)
 cat("\n#-#-#-# USING Seed Value of: ",whSeed , " for trial = ",thisTrial, "
#-#-#\n")

 bounds=t(data.frame(log2lambda1=c(-10, 10)))
 colnames(bounds) = c("lower", "upper")
 scad = NULL

 scad =svm.fs(x=selGenes, y=E, fs.method="scad", bounds=bounds,
 cross.outer= 10, grid.search = "interval", maxIter = 100,
 inner.val.method = "cv", cross.inner= 10, maxevals=500,
 seed=whSeed, parms.coding = "log2", show="none", verbose=FALSE )

 return(scad)
}


##########################################################################
# package containing the svm functions we'll use - also loads many other
packages
library(penalizedSVM)
##########################################################################
# use FILE / change dir to set working directory
setwd("c:/jobs/4_chamont/efronData") ### CHANGE THIS ###
# File CONTAINS: patientID in column 1, genes in 2 - 6034, 0/1 target in 6035
#08/02/2013 03:32 PM 4,723,233 efron102target080213.RData
load(file="efron102target080213.RData") # returns the data.frame
"efron102target"

 nPtnts = dim(efron102target)[1]
 nGenes = dim(efron102target)[2] - 2 # drop patientID and target columns

 # convert disease state from 0/1 variable to a no/yes FACTOR
 # dummy-coded 0/1 answer
 state = efron102target[,6035] ### to select Efron 0/1 target value
 stateName = "target"
 E = ifelse(state==1,+1,-1)

 table(E,state)
# pull all BUT the respID in column 1 and 0/1 classification variable in
column nGenes+2
 selGenes = as.matrix(efron102target[,-c(1,6035)],ncol=nGenes,nrow=nPtnts )

 colnames(selGenes) = colnames(efron102target)[-c(1,6035)]

 pdf(file=NULL) ## DUMB WAY to supress any plotting attempts!!
# loop for a maximum of 30 attempts to re-seed and get past penalizedSVM
Lapack error
 for(trial in 1:30) {

 thisScad = try( oneTrial(trial, selGenes, E) )

 #*#*# go around AGAIN, IF we failed, else break out of trial loop
 if(class(thisScad)=="try-error") { next } else { break }
```

```
} # end trial loop
### CHANGE THIS ###
goodWorkspace = "inSamplePenSVM.RData"
cat("\n#-#-# Results for: ",goodWorkspace,"\n")

# Report the results for the FIRST successful seed used in
# svm.fs function of penalizedSVM package
cat("scad final model - Full Sample Results:\n")

# in-sample prediction of disease state
scad.train<-predict.penSVM(thisScad, selGenes, newdata.labels=E)
cat("IN-Sample Confusion Matrix")
print( scad.train$tab )

nGenesFound = length(thisScad$model$fit.info$model$model$w)
cat("IN-Sample Model: Selected Gene Weights for",nGenesFound,"genes \n")
print(thisScad$model$fit.info$model$model$w)

cat( "IN-Sample Model: Intercept Term")
print(thisScad$model$fit.info$model$model$b )

# SAVE THIS WORKSPACE for further analysis
save.image(goodWorkspace)
```

Appendix C: Stochastic Gradient Boosting

Stochastic Gradient Boosting is one of our favorite tools in predictive modeling and variable selection. The method can be traced back to Schapire (1990), Freund (1995), and Freund and Schapire (1996). The algorithm was taken to new levels in other papers by Friedman (2001, 2006), Friedman *et al.*, (2000), Friedman and Popescu (2005), and Hastie *et al.* (2001, 2009).

Mathematically speaking, a Boosted Tree is a linear combination of Decision Trees:

$$T = \sum_{m}^{M} {}_{1} a_m T_m \tag{1}$$

where a_m is a constant and T_m is a Decision Tree with k nodes. In the extreme case where $m = 1$, a Boosted Tree would be a simple decision tree, but the performance of a single tree tends not to be competitive in predictions even with a large number of nodes. The main idea of a Boosted Tree is to combine hundreds or thousands of small, non-competitive trees and allow the averaging effect to work its wonder. The number of nodes can be as small as 2 and rarely exceeds 8 or 10.

Specifically, in the first stage ($m = 1$), a small tree is built. In the second iteration, another small tree is built on the residuals (or pseudo-residuals) of the first tree, and then the process repeats itself until the model reaches its full potential. In each iteration, the residuals from the previous model reveal information about where the model failed most, and the next stage of the model tries to improve upon these failures. This incremental process is called *boosting* in the machine learning community.

For the *j*-th iteration, let k_j be the number of nodes in the small tree that will be added to the model. In theory, it may be desired to use different k_j for different trees, but in practice the same *k* for all trees appears to perform adequately. The common setting of *k* is 6. If $k = 2$, the Boosted Tree would render an additive effects model, assuming *no interactions* among the predictors. On the other hand, if $k > 2$, then the Boosted Tree would model interactions among $(k - 1)$ variables.

The key for the gradient boosting to succeed is the *shrinkage* parameter ν (learning rate) in the modification of equation (1) as follows:

$$\sum_{m=1}^{J-1} a_m T_m + \nu * a_J T_J, \quad 0 < \nu < 1 \tag{2}$$

where $J = 2, \ldots, m$. In practice, the learning rate can be as small as $0 < \nu < 0.1$ and hence is called *shrinkage* in statistical literature. In other words, at each step, the contribution to the estimated best model is reduced by a shrinkage factor $0 < \nu < 1$. Empirical evidence showed dramatic improvement of all boosting methods, but the reason for its success was a mystery until the publications of Hastie *et al.* (2001) and Efron *et al.*, (2004). A concise explanation of the shrinkage effect can be found in Friedman (2006).

Furthermore, at each iteration, a sample of the training data is drawn to build a tree and to compute the model update for the current iteration. This scheme is a radical departure from other data mining tools such as Neural Networks or Support Vector Machines. Using a sample of the training data naturally *increases* the variability of each base learner at each iteration, but the advantage is the reduced correlation between these estimates at different iterations. The linear combination of hundreds or thousands of small trees produces an averaging effect that overwhelms the increased variability of each tree and leads to the ultimately reduced model variability.

In practice, of 6,033 genes, gradient boosting can easily trim out about 5,800 of them, but that still leave 200 genes or so in the model. In our investigation, we set a threshold of 12 and checked to see whether the top genes are in the small pool − i.e., if the important genes are not included in the top 12, then the model is deemed a failure. Here we are being conservative − only picking 12 genes because whatever works on a computer will work less well in the lab.

Appendix D: The R Code for Kolmogorov-Smirnov, Mann-Whitney, and Anderson-Darling Tests

```
library(adk) # for ADK test function
# use FILE / change dir to set working directory
setwd("c:/jobs/4_chamont/efronData") ### CHANGE THIS ###
#@#@# HAS 0/1 target in column 6035
#@#@# respID in column 1, genes in 2 - 6034, 0/1 target in 6035
#08/02/2013 03:32 PM 4,723,233 efron102target080213.RData
load(file="efron102target080213.RData") ## WARNING - fetches data.frame
"efron102target"
selGeneNames =
c("gene0610","gene1720","gene0364","gene0332","gene0914","gene3940",
 "gene4546","gene1068","gene0579","gene4331","gene1089","gene3647")
selGenes = efron102target[,c(selGeneNames,"target")]
t_Dis = selGenes[,13]==1 # flag of Diseased states of "target" variable

# do all 12 genes below and create 12 row data.frame (testrpt)
for(gene in 1:12 ) {
 normAvg = mean(selGenes[!t_Dis,gene]); dis_Avg = mean(selGenes[t_Dis,gene])

 # perform Man-Whitney Wilcoxon, Kolomogorov-S and Anderson-Darling tests
 MwWresult = wilcox.test(selGenes[,gene]~target, data=selGenes)
 KSresult = ks.test(selGenes[!t_Dis,gene],selGenes[t_Dis,gene])
 ADresult = adk.test(selGenes[!t_Dis,gene], selGenes[t_Dis,gene])
 # pick non-tied pValue or tied pValue if some (very few) ties are found
 ADpValue = ifelse(ADresult$n.ties==0,ADresult$adk[1,2] ,ADresult$adk[2,2] )
 # build testrpt data frame
 if(gene==1) {
 testsrpt = data.frame(selGeneNames[gene], normAvg, dis_Avg,
 MwWresult$p.value, KSresult$p.value, ADpValue)
 colnames(testsrpt) = c("Gene","NormAvg","Dis_Avg",
 "Wilcoxon_pValue","KS_pValue","AD_pValue")
 } else {
 newRow = data.frame(selGeneNames[gene], normAvg, dis_Avg,
 MwWresult$p.value, KSresult$p.value, ADpValue)
 colnames(newRow) = colnames(testsrpt)
 testsrpt = rbind(testsrpt,newRow)
 }

 }
write.csv(testsrpt,file="test12n.csv")
```

REFERENCES

Becker, N., Werft, W., Toedt, G., Lichter, P., Benner, A., 2009. PenalizedSVM: a R-package for feature selection SVM classification. Bioinformatics. 25 (13), 1711−1712.

Benjamini, Y., Hochberg, Y., 1995. Controlling the false discovery rate: a practical and powerful approach to multiple testing. J. R. Stat. Soc. B. 57, 289−300.

Bootkrajang, J., Kabán, A., 2013. Classification of mislabelled microarrays using robust sparse logistic regression. Bioinformatics. 29 (7), 870−877.

Breiman, L., Friedman, J.H., Olshen, R.A., Stone, C.J., 1983. Classification and Regression Trees. Chapman & Hall/CRC, New York, NY.

Dwyer, K., Holte, R., 2007. Decision tree instability and active learning. Proceedings of the 18th European Conference on Machine Learning (ECML/PKDD'07), Springer LNAI 4701, pp. 128−139.

Efron, B., 2008. Microarrays, empirical Bayes and the two-groups model. Stat. Sci. 23, 1−22.

Efron, B., 2010. The future of indirect evidence. Stat. Sci. 25, 145−157.

Efron, B., 2011. The bootstrap and Markov chain Monte Carlo. J. Biopharm. Statist. 21, 1052−1062. Available from: http://dx.doi.org/doi:10.1080/10543406.2011.607736.

Efron, B., Zhang, N., 2011. False discovery rates and copy number variation. Biometrika. 98, 251−271.

Efron, B., Hastie, T., Johnstone, I., Tibshirani, R., 2004. Least angle regression. Ann. Stat. 32, 407−499.

Fan, J., Li, R., 2001. Variable selection via nonconcave penalized likelihood and its oracle properties. J. Am. Stat. Assoc. 96, 1438−1460.

Freund, Y., 1995. Boosting a weak learning algorithm by majority. Inf. Comput. 121, 256−285.

Freund, Y., Schapire, R.E., 1996. Experiments with a new boosting algorithm. Machine Learning: Proceedings of the Thirteenth International Conference. Morgan Kaufman, San Francisco, CA, pp. 148−156.

Friedman, J.H., 2001. Greedy function approximation: a gradient boosting machine. Ann. Stat. 29, 1189−1232.

Friedman, J.H., 2006. Recent advances in predictive (machine) learning. J. Classif. 23, 175−197.

Friedman, J.H., Popescu, B.E., 2005. Uncovering interaction effects. Presented in the Second International Salford Systems Data Mining Conference, New York and Barcelona, 2005.

Friedman, J.H., Hastie, T., Tibshirani, R., 2000. Additive logistic regression: a statistical view of boosting (with discussion). Ann. Stat. 28, 337−407.

Funke, B., Malhotra, A.K., Finn, C.T., Plocik, A.M., Lake, S.L., Lencz, T., et al., 2005. COMT genetic variation confers risk for psychotic and affective disorders: a case control study. Behav. Brain Funct. 1, 1−19.

Guyon, I., Weston, J., Barnhill, S., Vapnik, V., 2002. Gene selection for cancer classification using support vector machines. Mach. Learn. 46, 389−422.

Hastie, T., Friedman, J.H., Tibshirani, R., 2001. The Elements of Statistical Learning. Springer-Verlag, New York.

Hastie, T., Friedman, J.H., Tibshirani, R., 2009. The Elements of Statistical Learning. second ed. Springer-Verlag, New York.

Huang, J., Breheny, P., Ma, S., 2012. A selective review of group selection in high dimensional models. Stat. Sci. 27 (4), 481−499.

Knight, K., Fu, W.J., 2000. Asymptotics for Lasso-type estimators. Ann. Stat. 28, 1356−1378.

Lettre, G., Palmer, C.D., Young, T., Ejebe, K.G., Allayee, H., Benjamin, E.J., et al., 2011. Genome-wide association study of coronary heart disease and its risk factors in 8,090 African Americans: The NHLBI CARE Project. PLOS Genet. 7 (2), e1001300.

Mongan, M.A., Dunn IIR.T., Vonderfecht, S., Everds, N., Chen, G., Su, C., et al., 2010. A novel statistical algorithm for gene expression analysis helps differentiate pregnane X receptor-dependent and independent mechanisms of toxicity. PLOS ONE. 5 (12), e15595.

Osborne, M.R., Presnell, B., Turlach, B.A., 1998. Knot selection for regression splines via the Lasso. Comput. Sci. Stat. 30, 44−49.

Pool, J.E., Hellmann, I., Jensen, J.D., Nielsen, R., 2010. Population genetic inference from genomic sequence variation. Genome Res. 20, 291−300.

Schapire, R.E., 1990. The strength of weak learnability. Mach. Learn. 5, 197−227.

Singh, D., Febbo, P.G., Ross, K., Jackson, D.G., Manola, J., Ladd, C., et al., 2002. Gene expression correlates of clinical prostate cancer behavior. Cancer Cell. 1, 203−209.

Storey, J.D., 2002. A direct approach to false discovery rates. JRSS-B. 64, 479−498.

Storey, J.D., Taylor, J.E., Siegmund, D., 2004. Strong control, conservative point estimation, and simultaneous conservative consistency of false discovery rates: a unified approach. JRSS-B. 66, 187−205.

Vinzi, V.E., Chin, W.W., Henseler, J., Wang, H. (Eds.), 2010. Handbook of Partial Least Squares. Springer, New York, NY.

Wang, C., Gevertz, J., 2013. Finding important genes from high-dimensional data: a novel investigation of variable selection techniques. In the process of journal review.

Wold, S., Sjöström, M., Eriksson, L., 2001. PLS-regression: a basic tool of chemometrics. Chemometr. Intell. Lab. Syst. 58, 109−130.

Zhao, P., Yu, B., 2006. On model selection consistency of lasso. J. Mach. Learn. Res. 7, 2541−2563.

Zou, H., 2006. The adaptive lasso and its oracle properties. J. Am. Stat. Assoc. 101 (476), 1418−1429.

Tutorial Y

Ovarian Cancer Prediction via Proteomic Mass Spectrometry

Chamont Wang, PhD, Charlene Wang, BS, and Welling Howell, BS

Chapter Outline

BACKGROUND AND THE DATA

Mass spectrometry is an analytical procedure that is used to determine the composition of chemical compounds. Mass spectra of cancer data can be used to create a profile of a disease, and this profile can be used to classify a patient as having cancer or not. The data are stored into files containing the mass-to-charge ratio and the intensity values. A quantity called the *m/z ratio* is formed by dividing the mass number of the ion (*m*) by its charge number (*z*), and will be used in this study.

In our investigation, the data are obtained from the US National Institute of Health, National Cancer Institute, at www.cancer.gov/. The data are available for free download at http://home.ccr.cancer.gov/ncifdaproteomics/ OvarianCD_PostQAQC.zip. The original data set comprises 216 patients (95 normal and 121 cancer patients) and 368,749 predictors. For each individual, there are two columns of the data: the first column is the proteomic mass spectrum (m/z ratio ranging from 699.991 to 11999.983), and is identical in all files. The second column is the intensity of the m/z ratio.

DATA PREPROCESSING (I) AND DYNAMIC BINNING

The number of variables in the raw data is very large and data preprocessing, including dynamic binning, was used to lump the predictors before the testing of any models. Dynamic binning is a process for the following tasks: to standardize the maximum intensity values of the spectra through a normalization method; to align the spectrograms; to correct for the baseline; and to assign similar peaks to a common reference vector, reducing the number of reference peaks while minimizing losses in resolution.

Practical Predictive Analytics and Decisioning Systems for Medicine. DOI: http://dx.doi.org/10.1016/B978-0-12-411643-6.00042-9

The original data are stored in216 files with 368,749 predictors in each file. The following SAS code is used to merge adjacent spectra by assigning similar compounds to the same spectrum without minimizing peak resolution:

```
%letM_Z_ratio_first=699.991;
data cancer1;
infile"C:\OvarianCD_PostQAQC\OvarianCD_PostQAQC\Cancer\daf-0603.txt"delimiter
= '09'xtruncoverDSDlrecl=50 ;
inputM_Z_ratio Intensity;
lengthmz_bin$8. ;
retain k 1count_Intensitysum_Intensitycurrent_bin_sizenext_bin_size0 ;

ifM_Z_ratio=.and Intensity =.thendelete; /* drop the records if both fields
are blank */
mz_bin='BIN'||strip(k);
count_Intensity=count_Intensity+1;
sum_Intensity=sum(sum_Intensity, Intensity);
mean_Intensity=sum_Intensity/count_Intensity;
current_bin_size = &M_Z_ratio_first.+K*.28+K*(K-1)*.000371 ;
next_bin_size= &M_Z_ratio_first.+(K+1)*.28+(K+1)*K*.000371 ;

ifnext_bin_size>M_Z_ratio>=current_bin_sizethendo;
k=k+1;
mz_bin='BIN'||strip(k);
count_Intensity=1;
sum_Intensity=Intensity;
mean_Intensity=sum_Intensity/count_Intensity;
current_bin_size = &M_Z_ratio_first.+K*.28+K*(K-1)*.000371 ;
next_bin_size= &M_Z_ratio_first.+(K+1)*.28+(K+1)*K*.000371 ;
end;
run;
procsortdata=cancer1;
by k count_Intensity;
run;
data cancer1bin(keep=mz_binmean_Intensity);
set cancer1;
by k count_Intensity;
iflast.k=1 ;
run;
/* Change path to root dirctory for input file under which two folders:
cancer and normal should be created */
/* Change sasloc to location for output SAS dataset under which one folder
'sasdata' should be created */
%let path=C:\cwang\wang\20131215;   /* input root dirctory */
%letsasloc=C:\cwang\wang\20131215\sasdata; /* output location */
%let target1=cancer;
%let target0=normal;
%letM_Z_ratio_first=699.991; /* used for bin size calculation */
libnamecan_nor"&sasloc.";
/* mean_cancer_nameslist contain all mean cancer Intensity field name from
mean_cancer1 to mean_cancerxxx */
/* mean_normal_nameslist contain all mean normal Intensity field name from
mean_normal1 to mean_normalxxx */
%globalmean_cancer_nameslistmean_normal_nameslist ;
/* read each source file to create SAS data and append them together */
%macroprocess_file(type, fname, fnum);
%put&type;
%put&fname;
%put&fnum;
/* Read one file. each file has two fields: 1. M_Z_ratio 2. Intensity */
/* 1. Assign bin_size = &M_Z_ratio_first.+K*.28+K*(K-1)*.000371 */
/* 2. Assing Mean_Intensity_&type._&fnum.: the average Intensity in each
bin_size */
/* type is either cancer or normal; fnum is the file numeber under cancer or
normal folder */
datameantemp ;
infile"&path.\&type.\&fname." delimiter = '09'xtruncover DSD lrecl=50 ;
inputM_Z_ratio Intensity;
retain k 1count_Intensitysum_Intensity0 ;
lengthmz_bin$8. ;
ifM_Z_ratio=.and Intensity =.then delete; /* drop the records if both fields
are blank */
      mz_bin='BIN'||strip(k);
      count_Intensity=count_Intensity+1;
      sum_Intensity=sum(sum_Intensity, Intensity);
      mean_Intensity=sum_Intensity/count_Intensity;
      bin_size = &M_Z_ratio_first.+K*.28+K*(K-1)*.000371;
```

```sas
/* when M_Z_ratio is between the current bin_size and next bin_size, increase
the bin -- k */
if&M_Z_ratio_first.+(K+1)*.28+(K+1)*K*.000371>M_Z_ratio>=bin_size then do;
k=k+1;
count_Intensity=1;
sum_Intensity=Intensity;
end;
run;
/* output only mz_bin and mean intensity */
procsql;
create table mean&fnum.as
select mz_bin, max(mean_Intensity) as mean_&type.&fnum.
frommeantemp
group by mz_bin;
quit;
/* Hold the first mean intensity */
%if&fnum=1%then%do;
datamean_&type.;
      setmean&fnum. ;
      run;
%end;
/* merge each mean intensity with the previous one by matching mz_bin */
%else%do;
      procsql;
      create table mean_&type.as
            selecta.*, b.mean_&type.&fnum.
            from mean_&type._1 a, mean&fnum.b
                  wherea.mz_bin =b.mz_bin ;
      quit;
%end;
/* Hold the mean intensity for the next loop to merge */
data mean_&type._1;
setmean_&type.;
run;
%mendprocess_file;
/* read the specified folder and get a list of txt FILE */
/* execute Macro %process_file for each file */
/* Transpose the table */
%macrofilelist(type);
data&type.list (keep=filename count);
length filename $40.;
retain count 0;
rc=filename("CURRENT","%nrbquote(&path)\%nrbquote(&type)");
did=dopen("CURRENT");
filecnt=dnum(did);
doi=1 to filecnt;
      filename=dread(did,i);
      if index(filename,'bak')= 0 and index(filename,'ZIP')= 0 then do;
            count+1;
            callsymput('filename'||compress(put(count,8.)), filename);
            output;
      end;
end;
  callsymput('totfile',left(trim(put(count,8.))));
  rc=dclose(did);
  run;
  %if&totfile>0%then%do;
      %dofnum=1%to&totfile ;
      %process_file(&type, &&filename&fnum, &fnum)
      %end;
  %end;
  proc contents data=mean_&type.out=mean_&type._name(keep=name);
  run;
  procsql;
      select compress(name)
      into: mean_&type._nameslist
      separated by ' '
      frommean_&type._name
      where index(upcase(name), 'MEAN') >0;
  quit;
  %put&&mean_&type._nameslist;
  %mend;
  /* process files in cancer folder*/
  %filelist(&target1);
  /* process files in normal folder*/
```

```
%filelist(&target0);
/* keep records where mz_bin exists in both cancer and normal */
procsql;
      createtablecan_nor.mean_canceras
      select1as target, a.*
      frommean_cancer a, mean_normal b
      wherea.mz_bin =b.mz_bin
      orderbymz_bin;
quit;
procsql;
      createtablecan_nor.mean_normalas
      select0as target, b.*
      frommean_cancer a, mean_normal b
      wherea.mz_bin =b.mz_bin
      orderbymz_bin;
quit;
/* Transpose cancer */
proctransposedata=can_nor.mean_cancerout=can_nor.mean_cancer_tranname=bin_cat
egoryprefix=bin;
by target;
var&mean_cancer_nameslist ;
idlabelmz_bin;
quit;
/* Transpose normal */
proctransposedata=can_nor.mean_normalout=can_nor.mean_normal_tranname=bin_cat
egoryprefix=bin;
by target;
var&mean_normal_nameslist ;
idlabelmz_bin;
quit;
datacan_nor.mean_all;
setcan_nor.mean_cancer_tran
      can_nor.mean_normal_tran ;
run;
quit;
```

The SAS code can be copied and pasted in the SAS Editor to process the data, but the user needs to change the path as designated in the third line of the code (or store the raw data in the specified folder):

```
infile"C:\OvarianCD_PostQAQC\OvarianCD_PostQAQC\Cancer\daf-0603.txt".
```

In the code, the green parts such as

```
/* drop the records if both fields are blank */
```

are comments to the specific portions of the code. In the middle of the code, the following formula is used for the bin size:

```
bin_size = M_Z_ratio_first.+K*.28+K*(K-1)*.000371; k = 1 to 5,155;
```

In the raw data, the range of the m/z ratio is $11999.983 - 699.991 \cong 11300$. The above formula grouped the 368,749 m/z ratios into 5,155 bins of increasing length. The process reduced the raw data from 1.16 GB to 9.3 MB in SAS data format.

The new data can be plotted to display the difference between the serum samples of a patient and of a healthy individual, as in Figure Y.1.

The images in Figure Y.1 show that, to the human eye, there is almost no distinction between the two mass spectra. Only when the images are overlapped is there some indication of dissimilarity between the two. Figure Y.2 displays the overlap of the individual spectra to aid in this visualization.

This image underlines the difficulty of cancer detection and the need for other methods of diagnosis. Note that ovarian cancer has the highest fatality rate of gynecological cancers, and is generally not detected early due to the unspecific symptoms of the disease. It has been estimated in a study (Pavlik *et al.*, 2009) that an ultrasound can detect malignant ovarian cancer with a sensitivity of 73.3% compared to detection by symptoms alone, which is only 20%. In the next section, we will use machine-learning tools to see whether proteomic mass spectrometry data can help improve the prediction accuracy.

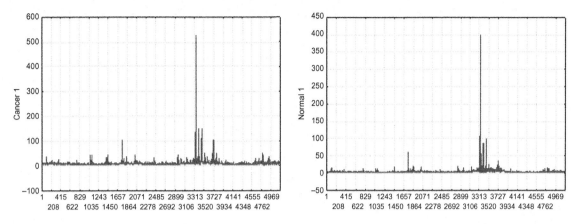

FIGURE Y.1 Mass spectra using 5,155 bins of a cancer patient (left) and a healthy subject (right).

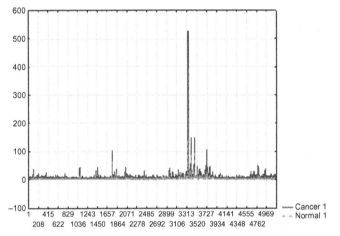

FIGURE Y.2 Comparison of cancer (blue) and healthy participants (red).

PREDICTION ACCURACIES OF COMPETING MODELS

In this section we illustrate the use of SAS Enterprise Miner 7.1 for binary classification of the ovarian cancer data (detailed steps to set-up the process flow in Figure Y.3 can be found in the *Handbook of Statistical Analysis and Data Mining Applications* (Nisbet *et al.*, 2009, pp. 419–425).

In Figure Y.3 the first node contains the data with 216 rows in binary code (1 = cancer, 0 = normal patients) and 5,155 predictors. The second node partitions the data into Training (55%), Validation (15%), and Test (30%). The

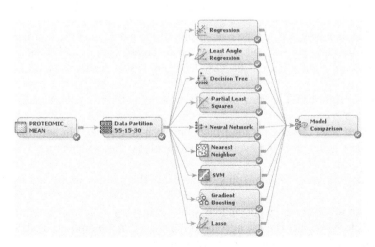

FIGURE Y.3 SAS process flow for predictive modeling. The first node contains the data. The second node partitions the data. The third layer contains the models in the order of perceived popularity: Logistic Regression, Least Angle Regression, Decision Tree, etc.

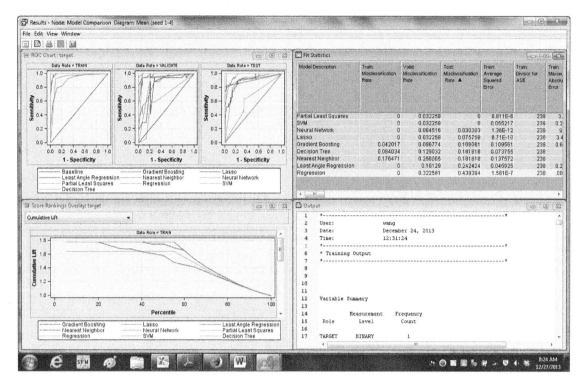

FIGURE Y.4 Comparison of the nine models in Figure Y.3.

Model Description	Train: Misclassification Rate	Valid: Misclassification Rate	Test: Misclassification Rate ▲
Partial Least Squares	0	0.032258	0
SVM	0	0.032258	0
Neural Network	0	0.064516	0.030303
Lasso	0	0.032258	0.075758
Gradient Boosting	0.042017	0.096774	0.106061
Decision Tree	0.084034	0.129032	0.181818
Nearest Neighbor	0.176471	0.258065	0.181818
Least Angle Regression	0	0.16129	0.242424
Regression	0	0.322581	0.439394

FIGURE Y.5 Comparison of the "Misclassification Rates" of the Training, Validation, and Test (hold-out) data sets. The ranking of the models is sorted in the last column. PLS (partial least squares) and SVM appear to be the best among all models for this specific data set.

training data are used to build the model, the validation data help prevent the over-fitting of the model, and the test data (also known as hold-out data) are free from the model-building process and are used for the comparison of the models.

After execution of the process flow (see Figure Y.3), right click on the "Model Comparison" node to view the results (Figure Y.4).

Zoom in on the "Fit Statistics" window on the upper right panel to view the results (sorted by the last column "Test Misclassification Rate" in ascending order) (see Figure Y.5).

Figure Y.5 shows that both PLS and SVM achieved zero misclassification rates on the hold-out data. In addition, Neural Network and Lasso are also doing well, at least better than the eyeball examination as shown in Figure Y.3. Other models are less than satisfactory.

Table Y.1 shows the Prediction Accuracies with five different random splits of the data. The models are ranked by the Mean column, in descending order.

Table Y.1 indicates that SVM is the best model in all five runs with random splits, achieving 100% accuracy in three of five runs − very impressive indeed. PLS is a close second. The Mean column indicates that the top four models are clearly better than the eyeball examination in Figure Y.3 or the Pavlik *et al.* (2009) study.

TABLE Y.1 Prediction Accuracies of the Top Six Models with Five Different Random Seeds*

	Prediction accuracy (Hold-out data)						
Model	Seed 1	Seed 2	Seed 3	Seed 4	Seed 5	Mean	SD
SVM	100.0%	95.5%	100.0%	100.0%	97.0%	98.5%	2.1%
Partial Least Squares	100.0%	95.5%	100.0%	98.5%	95.5%	97.9%	2.3%
Neural Network	97.0%	88.1%	100.0%	95.5%	95.5%	95.2%	4.4%
Lasso	92.4%	89.5%	100.0%	92.4%	92.5%	93.4%	3.9%
Gradient Boosting	89.4%	82.1%	89.4%	87.9%	82.1%	86.2%	3.8%
Decision Tree	81.8%	79.1%	87.9%	86.4%	82.1%	83.5%	3.6%

*The models are ranked by the Mean column, in descending order.

In Table Y.1, the high accuracies in the first few rows (especially the SVM perfect runs and the 98.5% mean accuracy) prompted us to use other tools for a cross-check. The results are as follows:

- R penalized SVM: 97.4%
- Salford Systems GPS (Generalized Path Seeker)/Generalized Lasso: 97.2%
- Salford Systems TreeNet (a.k.a., Gradient Boosting): 94%

The results of R penalized SVM (97.4%) and Salford Systems GPS (97.2%) indicate that the high accuracies in the top models in Table Y.1 are solid and should generalize well in other studies of ovarian cancer diagnosis via proteomic mass spectrometry data.

FALSE POSITIVE, FALSE NEGATIVE, AND THE ROC INDEX

In cancer diagnosis, a *false negative* (FN) incorrectly identifies a sick person as healthy. This is arguably more serious than a *false positive* (FP), which incorrectly identifies a healthy person as being ill. In practice, a statistical quantity called *Sensitivity* is defined to capture the model's ability to identify positive results, while another quantity, called *Specificity*, is related to the negative results (here, TP = True Positive and TN = True Negative):

$$\text{Sensitivity} = \frac{TP}{FN + TP} = \frac{TP}{P}$$

$$\text{Specificity} = \frac{TN}{TN + FP} \frac{TN}{N}$$

Note that

$$1 - \text{Sensitivity} = \frac{FN}{FN + TP} = \frac{FN}{P},$$

which is the *Rate of False Negative* among all positives; while

$$1 - \text{Specificity} = \frac{FP}{TN + FP} = \frac{FP}{N},$$

is the *Rate of False Positive* among all negatives. The ROC charts in Figure Y.6 are plots of Sensitivity vs. 1 − Specificity at different cut-off probabilities for the top three models (SVM, PLS, and Neural Network) in Table Y.1.

The left panel says that the three models did perfect prediction on the Training data. In the middle panel (Validation data), the upper left-hand corner says that one of the models is not doing that well, and the third panel says that the three models did not perform the same on the Hold-out data.

In Figure Y.7, a close look of the ROC curves of the Test data reveals further detail. The figure indicates that, for the Hold-out data, SVM has an edge against other models.

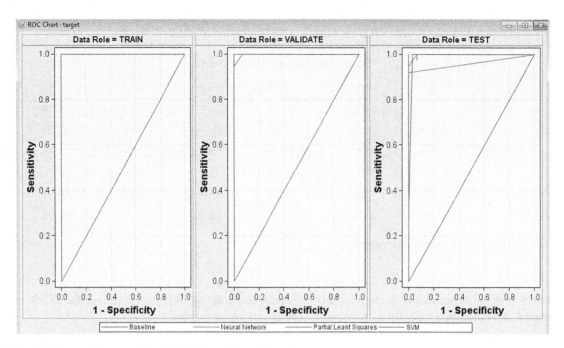

FIGURE Y.6 ROC charts of the top models: SVM, PLS, and Neural Network.

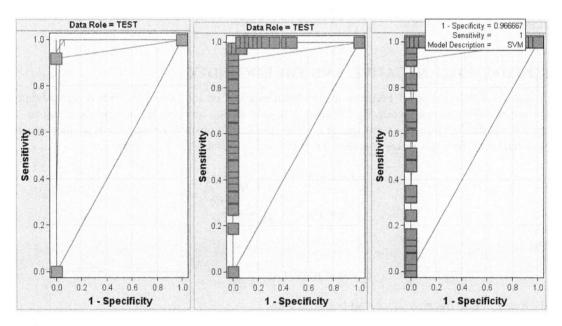

FIGURE Y.7 A comparison of the ROC charts for the hold-out data: Neural Network (left), PLS (middle) and SVM (right).

In literature, scientists often calculate AUC (Area under the Curve), a.k.a. the ROC index, and then rank the models by the AUC values. In a 2009 article in *Machine Learning*, Professor David Hand wrote a very long article with complicated mathematics to criticize this practice and concluded that "it is as if one measured person A's height using a ruler calibrated in inches and person B's using one calibrated in centimetres, and decided who was the taller by merely comparing the numbers . . . This is clearly nonsensical . . . This is absurd."

We basically agree with Professor Hand's conclusion. Note that the consequences of a False Negative would be a lot more severe than that of a False Positive. In other words, it is a more serious mistake if a patient is misdiagnosed as healthy when he or she actually has cancer, than if a patient is misdiagnosed as having cancer when he or she is in fact healthy.

The asymmetry of the FP and FN casts doubt on the comparison of the areas under the curves, especially when the curves cross each other. Sadly, though, the AUC is still being widely used in the data mining community, even long after the publication of the Hand (2009) article, and we urge readers of this tutorial to take heed of this problem.

Nevertheless, the ROC curves are sometimes useful in the selection and screening of the models, as shown in Figure Y.7. The problem is more the area under the curve, and less the curve itself.

In short, both Figure Y.7 and Table Y.1 indicate that SVM is the best model, and hence it will be used to predict the probability of cancer in the next section.

PROBABILITY OF CANCER

Figure Y.8 shows an SAS process flow to calculate the probability of cancer for each patient (here we use Seed-2, the worst scenario of the five SVM experiments [see Table Y.1]; hold-out error rate = 4.5%).

In Figure Y.8, the Input Data node contains the data that will be used for scoring purposes. Click on the node to activate the Property Panel and then change the Role of the Input Data node from Raw to Score, as shown in Figure Y.9.

Furthermore, right click on the Input Data node and select Edit Variable to change the role of Target variable from Target to Rejected (Figure Y.10).

Next, right click on the SAS Code node to activate the Property Panel and then click on the little button on the right of Code Editor, as in Figure Y.11.

In the Code Editor window, type in the following SAS code:

```
DataCancer_SVM_Pr (keep = Patient_ID P_Target1 Target);
Set&EM_Import_Score;
Patient_ID = _N_;
Run;
ProcSort;
BYdescending P_Target1;
run;
Procprint;
VarPatient_ID P_Target1 Target;
run;
```

FIGURE Y.8 SAS process flow for the calculation of cancer probability.

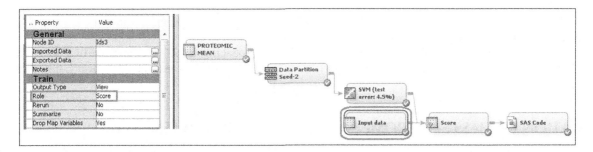

FIGURE Y.9 SAS process for Scoring Data.

FIGURE Y.10 SAS Input Data for Scoring.

Name	Role	Level
target	Rejected	Binary
category	Rejected	Nominal
bin100	Input	Interval
bin1000	Input	Interval
bin1001	Input	Interval
bin1002	Input	Interval
bin1003	Input	Interval

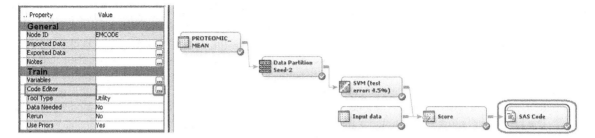

FIGURE Y.11 SAS Code Editor for Scoring Data.

TABLE Y.2 Probabilities of Cancer

Obs	Patient ID	P_target1
1	102	0.92821
2	11	0.90341
3	12	0.89831
4	16	0.89024
5	10	0.87231
6	83	0.87206
7	93	0.86170
8	108	0.85196
9	90	0.85161
10	121	0.84869

Run the code to see P_target1 (the probabilities of cancer) and the corresponding Patient ID in descending order. The top 10 are displayed in Table Y.2.

Table Y.2 shows that Patient #102 is at the highest risk, with probability at 92.8%, followed by Patient #11 with probability at 90.3%, and so on. The default threshold is 50%: if the probability is less than the cut-off, then the patient will be classified as being healthy.

LIMITATION OF MASS SPECTROMETRY AND DATA PREPROCESSING (II)

Recall that in five independent runs SVM scored three perfect runs, and its average prediction accuracy is 98.5% (see Table Y.2). This is good news for the ovarian cancer diagnosis. However, the same technology does not appear to be that great when applied to breast cancer data, as shown in the Hand (2008) paper in *Statistical Applications in Genetics and Molecular Biology*. The paper summarizes the results of an international competition on "Breast Cancer Diagnosis from Proteomic Mass Spectrometry Data." The Training data consist of 117 patients and 116 healthy volunteers with m/z ratios in 11,205 bins. The hold-out data consist of equal numbers of cancer and normal subjects, with 39 in each

TABLE Y.3 Classification Results for the Hold-out Data (n = 78)

Method	TN	FN	FP	TP	Accuracy	Sensitivity	Specificity
1	30	4	9	35	83%	0.897	0.769
2	23	10	16	29	67%	0.744	0.590
3	30	6	9	33	81%	0.846	0.769
4	19	5	20	34	68%	0.872	0.487
5	32	8	7	31	81%	0.795	0.821
6	32	8	7	31	81%	0.795	0.821
7	29	8	10	31	77%	0.795	0.769
8	32	12	7	27	76%	0.692	0.821
9	28	3	11	36	82%	0.923	0.718
10	37	13	2	26	81%	0.667	0.949
11	30	14	9	25	71%	0.641	0.769

TABLE Y.4 Classification Results for the Training Data (n = 233)*

Method	TN	FN	FP	TP	Accuracy	Sensitivity	Specificity
1	66	14	11	62	89%	0.816	0.857
2	66	10	11	66	91%	0.868	0.857
3	69	13	8	63	91%	0.829	0.896
4	65	7	12	69	92%	0.908	0.844
5	66	14	11	62	89%	0.816	0.857
6	69	9	8	67	93%	0.882	0.896
7	69	8	8	68	93%	0.895	0.896
8	76	8	1	68	96%	0.895	0.987
9	67	14	10	62	90%	0.816	0.870
10	71	8	6	68	94%	0.922	0.895

*The paper by Hand (2008, p. 11) contains the information only for Method-1 to Method-10 for the training data. Method-8 has the highest prediction accuracy.

category. There were 11 competition submissions that used various data preprocessing techniques (including the use of principal component analysis to bundle the variables) or no preprocessing at all. Two of the statistical models used the variants of SVM technology. Their prediction results on the hold-out data are shown in Table Y.3 (n = 78).

Table Y.3 shows that the prediction accuracies of the 11 competition entries are less than satisfactory as compared to the ovarian cancer prediction. Professor Hand (2008) mentioned that a potential complicating factor in the model evaluations was that the data for the training set were obtained from two plates, and the data for the hold-out set were from a third plate. Table Y.4 shows the competition results from the training data (n = 233):

In Table Y.4, the accuracy of Method #8 is close to that of SVM ovarian cancer prediction, but this method performed poorly on the hold-out data (accuracy = 76%, Table Y.3) as compared to Methods #1 and #9 that used the same data.

We were curious whether our models could do better, and tried to obtain the data from the journal editor and the competition organizer, but the replies were that the data sets were commercially copyrighted during the competition and are no longer available for academic research or for any further evaluations of statistical methods.

In short, proteomic mass spectrometry can be very useful in ovarian cancer prediction and perhaps in many other applications as well, but for breast cancer prediction the same technology may not be as reliable as other types of applications.

Potential improvements may be possible via further data preprocessing of the breast cancer data. For example, the original data probably have about 368,749 m/z ratios, like the ovarian cancer data, and the Hand (2008) paper did not give the details on how the data were grouped into 11,205 bins.

Note that there are different ways to preprocess the data − equal length of the bins, dynamic length, etc. − and a goal would be to make the m/z ratios as similar to each other in the same bin. Consequently, one may set a threshold of the Standard Deviation and then bundle the adjacent m/z ratios into the bins so that their Standard Deviations are within the threshold.

For the ovarian cancer data, the prediction accuracy is already at 98.5% and any further work probably will not help. But for the breast cancer and other experiments, additional efforts on data preprocessing may be worthwhile (note that Tutorial U in this book is the breast cancer tutorial).

VARIABLE SELECTION AND GENE SEARCH

In a *Nature* review article, Aebersold and Mann (2003) used a number of case studies to illustrate the role of proteomic mass spectrometry as a tool for molecular and cellular biology and for the field of systems biology. The potential applications include the study of protein−protein interactions via affinity-based isolations on a small and proteome-wide scale, the mapping of numerous organelles, the concurrent description of the malaria parasite genome and proteome, and the generation of quantitative protein profiles from diverse species. In addition, the authors mentioned the potential use of mass spectrometry to identify and to quantify thousands of proteins from complex samples.

After the seminar paper of Aebersold and Mann (2003), there have been new developments in the applications of this technology which include the identification of serum markers of specific diseases. In this section, we will limit our discussion on the feasibility of using proteomic mass spectrometry in the search for important markers associated with the bins that are most influential in the statistical models. Specifically, we will discuss whether the given data can be used to identify the top 10 variables (out of 5,155) in ovarian cancer prediction. Table Y.5 summarizes the results of our investigation (where five different colors are used to highlight the same variables that are selected by different models).

TABLE Y.5 Top 10 Predictors Selected by Various Methods*

	Model (accuracy)	Selected variables
1	R-SVM (97.4%)	354, 383, 3873, 3991, 3998, 4010, 4024, 4052, 4175, 4255
2	PLS (97.9%)	250, 2762, 2836, 2837, 3781, 3782, 4259, 4355, 5085, 5084
3	Neural Network (95.2%)	250, 594, 2162, 2721, 2762, 4174, 4175, 4252, 4258, 5103
4	Lasso (93.4%)	239, 373, 516, 3086, 3245, 3506, 4052, 4175, 4259, 4612
5	TreeNet (94%)	354, 383, 2762, 3713, 3779, 3782, 3980, 3982, 4254, 4255
6	FDR	300, 354, 383, 385, 666, 4014, 4020, 4021, 4025, 4037

Some variables are selected by different models as indicated by the colored code, but not a single predictor is used by all methods. Overall, the models selected very different variables.

Comments and a few words of caution on Table Y.5:

1. SAS-SVM does not produce any information on variable importance, so we used R penalized SVM and report the variables with the highest weights in Table Y.5.
2. SAS-PLS has high prediction accuracy at 97.9% (averaged over five runs), and the top 10 predictors are reported in Table Y.5. However, in the SAS Variable Selection window (see Appendix A), none of the top predictors of PLS is really more important than other variables in the model. Hence the user of this model needs to be cautious in the final judgment on selection of the top variables.
3. SAS Neural Network uses three hidden nodes with the associated weights in the following manner: H3 (27.58), H2 (-9.28), H1 (-4.12). We were lucky to find that the weights for the predictors linked to H3 are the highest, and hence these predictors are chosen to be in the list. In general, the extraction of top variables from a neural network is very tricky or plain impossible; hence extra caution is needed in attempts to do so.
4. SAS default Penalized Regression uses an algorithm via Least Angle Regressions (LARS), as introduced by Efron *et al.* (2004), but for this specific data set LARS does not do well (hold-out error rate = 24%, Figure Y.5). In SAS, two other options are Lasso and Adaptive Lasso. The latter option does not work at all for this data set.
5. SAS gradient boosting does not do well for this data set (hold-out error rate = 11%, Figure Y.5). Salford Systems TreeNet does better, and its results are displayed in Table Y.5.
6. The last row of Table Y.5 uses the technique of False Discovery Rate (FDR) as introduced by Benjamini-Hochberg (1995). The process involves the calculation of 5,155 t-tests and then uses a clever algorithm to control the FDR. According to Efron (2010), the main theorem in the Benjamini-Hochberg paper is "the second most striking theorem of post-war statistics," and our experience indicates that this technique is worth the effort of inclusion in the variable selection process. The following SAS code can be used for this purpose:

```
procmulttestdata = Sasuser.proteomic_meanholmsidakafdrpfdr(positive)
nopvaluenoprintout=hello
(drop = _se_ _contrast_ _value_ _nval_ _test_);
testmean (bin1 - bin5155);
class target;
contrast'no yes'01;
run;
ProcSortdata = hello out=FDR;
byafdr_p;
run;
```

Copy and paste the code in SAS editor. Click on Run and then the FDR results will show up in the SAS Work library (see Appendix B).

Taken together, Table Y.5 indicates that the models selected very different variables; while some variables are selected by certain models, not a single predictor is used by all methods. Consequently, in the search for biomarkers, one may have to take the *union* of the sets of the top variables from reliable models. It is conceivable that the union would result in more variables than a scientist could manage, but, given the current technology and the small sample size (n = 216), this is probably all we can hope for.

As a related note, in a recent *New York Times* article Peikoff (2013) found that in her DNA tests of psoriasis (an immune system disorder), one lab reported a risk of 20.2% while another lab reported a risk of only 2% (www.nytimes.com/2013/12/31/science/i-had-my-dna-picture-taken-with-varying-results.html?hp&_r = 0). Peikoff (2013) reported a number of similar cases and quipped that the first test result would make her worried, while the second would make her relieved.

It seems we can do better in the statistical predictions of ovarian cancer via proteomic mass spectrometry, especially in the case where an average of 98.5% prediction accuracy was achieved by SAS-SVM in five different runs. However, the search for the most important biomarkers remains elusive, and more research efforts will be needed to improve the performance of predictive science in this important matter.

APPENDICES A–C

Appendix A: The Top 10 Variables Selected by SAS-PLS

In five different runs with random seeds, SAS-PLS achieved the following accuracies: 100%, 95.5%, 100%, 98.5%, and 95.5% (average = 97.9%, SD = 2.3%) and there are two perfect runs. However, as shown in the right-hand three columns of Figure Y.A1, none of the top variables is really more important than others in the model.

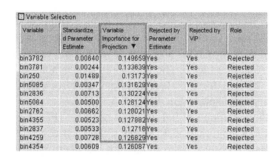

FIGURE Y.A1 Variable Selection.

Appendix B: The Top 10 Variables Selected by Benjamini-Hochberg FDR

See Figure Y.A2.

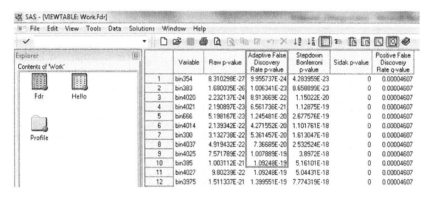

FIGURE Y.A2 Top 10 variables.

Appendix C: R Code for the Penalized SVM

```
"oneTrial" <- function(trial,selGenes,E) {
### Interval search ####
 ################################################################
# WARNING - new seed set for EVERY RUN -
 # set seed from the clock to one of 99,999 values
 # using seconds from Sys.time() and elapsed milliseconds
# fromproc.time()
whSeed = floor( ( ( (as.numeric(Sys.time()) %% 1000)
 + proc.time()[3] %% 1) * 1000) %% 10000 )
cat("\n#-#-#-# USING Seed Value of: ",whSeed ,
" for trial = ",trial," #-#-#\n")
################################################################
seed<- whSeed
bounds=t(data.frame(log2lambda1=c(-10,10)))
colnames(bounds)<-c("lower","upper")
scad = NULL
scad=svm.fs(x=selGenes,y=E,fs.method="scad",bounds=bounds,
cross.outer= 10,grid.search = "interval",maxIter = 100,
inner.val.method = "cv",cross.inner= 10,maxevals=500,
seed=seed,parms.coding="log2",
show="none",verbose=FALSE )
return(scad)
}
################################################################
# this script used for 216 patient data data converted from
# cancer_means.sas7bdat to
# .rdata format with Circle Systems Stat/Transfer ~7AM 12/21/13
################################################################
# package containing the svm functions we'll use (loads others)
library(penalizedSVM)
# package containing function kfold for stratified validation
library(dismo)
################################################################
# POSSIBLE CHANGE lines are marked: ### CHANGE THIS
################################################################
# use FILE / change dir to set working directory
setwd("c:/jobs/4_chamont/Chapter2a") ### CHANGE THIS ###
load(file="cancer_mean.rdata") ### CHANGE THIS ###
cNames = colnames(cancer_mean)
dim(cancer_mean)
# document some of cancer_mean data frame (first/last 8 "bins")
head(cancer_mean[,1:10])
tail(cancer_mean[,1:10])
# cancer (1) and normal (0) patient counts
table(cancer_mean[,1])
#IF re-start is needed after a fewrun OK ### CHANGE THIS ###
nStartTrials = 1
nTrials = 2 ### CHANGE THIS ###
maxLoops = 15 # reach this maxLoops value ### CHANGE THIS ###
nPtnts = dim(cancer_mean)[1]
nGenes = dim(cancer_mean)[2]-2 # drop off first 2 columns
# convert disease state from 0/1 variable to a no/yes FACTOR
# dummy-coded 0/1 answer
state = cancer_mean[,1] ### target is 0=normal,1=cancer
# factor with A==0 as "no" and A==1 as "yes"
F = factor(state,level=c(0,1),labels=c("no","yes"))
# effects-code with A==0 as -1 and A==1 as +1
E = ifelse(state==1,+1,-1)
# compare new "E" factor frequency with original 0/1 "state"
table(E,state)
# number of k-fold validation samples
# (each will be "held out" and remainder used)
nKfold = 10 ### CHANGE THIS ###
# prepare save data frames as NULL or NA so we can record results
saveTrainTbl = NULL
saveTestTbl = NULL
```

```
saveTestTbl = NULL
saveWvalues = NULL
saveBvalues = NULL
saveTrial = rep(NA,nTrials*nKfold)
saveGrp =rep(NA,nTrials*nKfold)
##################################################################
# run for nTrials (set above)
##################################################################
selGenes =as.matrix(cancer_mean[,-c(1:2)],
ncol=nGenes,nrow=nPtnts )
cancer_mean = NULL # wipe outdata.frame to save space
pdf(file=NULL) ## DUMB WAY to suppress plotting attempts!!
for(trial in nStartTrials:nTrials) {
kGroup = kfold(selGenes,nKfold,F)
print(addmargins( table(F,kGroup) ) )
for(grp in 1:nKfold) {
# THE data rows to be used in the TEST dataset
testFlag = kGroup==grp
for(loopNumber in 1:maxLoops) {
 runTimeData1 = proc.time()
 # try is a wrapper to allow error-recovery.
 # pass all selGenes AND E rows that are NOT testFlag
thisScad = try( oneTrial(trial,selGenes[!testFlag,],
E[!testFlag]) )
 runTimeData2 = proc.time()
runTimeData = runTimeData2 - runTimeData1
#*#*# go around AGAIN,we failed in oneTrial
if(class(thisScad)=="try-error") next
cat("scad final model for trial=",trial,
" and kFoldGroup=",grp," Train Results:\n")
scad.train<-predict.penSVM(thisScad,
selGenes[!testFlag,],newdata.labels=E[!testFlag])
print(scad.train$tab )
 # try to PREDICT the TEST SET using the model just
 # built from the non-test set
cat(" -- and Test Results:\n")
scad.test<-predict.penSVM(thisScad,
selGenes[testFlag,],newdata.labels=E[testFlag])
print(scad.test$tab )
# if there is no saveTrainTbl - initialize save areas
if(is.null(saveTrainTbl)) {
saveTrainTbl = scad.train$tab
saveTestTbl = scad.test$tab
saveWvalues = scad.train$model$w
saveBvalues = scad.train$model$b
saveSlot = 0
saveTrial[saveSlot] = trial
saveGrp[saveSlot] = grp
 } else {
# there WAS a saveTrainTbl - rbind this trial's results
saveTrainTbl = rbind(saveTrainTbl,scad.train$tab)
saveTestTbl = rbind(saveTestTbl,scad.test$tab)
saveWvalues = rbind(saveWvalues,scad.train$model$w)
saveBvalues = rbind(saveBvalues,scad.train$model$b)
saveSlot = saveSlot + 1
saveTrial[saveSlot] = trial
saveGrp[saveSlot] = grp
 }
# myNow is a time-stamp for UNIQUE file names
myNow = format(Sys.time(),"%m%d%y_%H%M%S")
grpNrStr = sprintf("%02d_",grp)
 ### CHANGE THIS ###
goodWorkspace = paste("trial6f_t",trial,"KF",
grpNrStr,myNow,".RData",sep="")
# SAVE THE ENTIRE WORKSPACE for post-processing
```

```
save.image(goodWorkspace)
 ### CHANGE THIS ###
cat("\n#-#-# Results for: trial = ",trial,
" Kfold Group=",grp,"\n")
# show final predictor set and their weights (w)
print(thisScad$model$fit.info$model$model$w )
# show final model intercept (b)
print(thisScad$model$fit.info$model$model$b )
# display all we've learned in this trial on CRT
flush.console()
break()# SUCCESSFULLY completed this trial exit loop
 } # end of loopNumber loop trying to compute thisScad
flush.console()
 } # end trials loop
} # end k-fold group loop
#################################################################
# (R code to sumarize 20 10-fold runs of penalized SVM)
#################################################################
# read in multiple (20) trial result saved workspaces and for
# 10-fold tests and report on each of the 20 x 10 = 100
# trials,showingTRain and TeST confusion matricies
# (no "Predicted" no; no "Predicted" yes.....)
setwd("c:/jobs/4_chamont/Chapter2a") ### CHANGE THIS ###
confusionCols = c("TRNnoPno","TRNnoPyes","TRNyesPno",
"TRNyesPyes","TSTnoPno","TSTnoPyes","TSTyesPno","TSTyesPyes")
# N.B.table2Genes is over-written with same values by every
# "load()" command in the fNr loop below
# BEST bestGenesBest (most often modeled) 45 genes based in
# presence in 200 models (20 10-fold reps)
table2Genes =
c("bin46","bin49","bin354","bin383","bin546","bin594","bin2577","bin2636","bin
2704","bin3868","bin3873","bin3879","bin3986","bin3990","bin3991","bin3993","b
in3994","bin3995","bin3998","bin4005","bin4010","bin4013","bin4022","bin4023",
"bin4025","bin4026","bin4036","bin4052","bin4053",
"bin4056","bin4062","bin4109","bin4114","bin4118","bin4119",
"bin4175","bin4176","bin4230","bin4231","bin4254","bin4259","bin4309","bin4350
","bin4714","bin4715") ### CHANGE THIS ###
table2G_Nr = c(46,49,354,383,546,594,2577,2636,2704,3868,3873,3879,3986,
3990,3991,3993,3994,3995,3998,4005,4010,4013,4022,4023,4025,
4026,4036,4052,4053,4056,4062,4109,4114,4118,4119,4175,4176,
4230,4231,4254,4259,4309,4350,4714,4715) ### CHANGE THIS ###
table2G_Nr
# list of 10-fold RData files (20 10-fold runs 10%/90% split)
# output of Windows dir /od trial*.rdata>kFoldPenSVM20runs6f.lst
# with file text-edited to include ONLY directory row on line 1 # and complete
file-name rows (drop 4 other lines from top of
# kFoldPenSVM20runsf.lst AND last 2 lines at bottom of file)
# note skip=1 to skip first row of Windows dir /od command
 ### CHANGE THIS ###
rdataFiles = read.table(file="kFoldPenSVM20runs6f.lst",skip=1,
stringsAsFactors=FALSE)
nRData = dim(rdataFiles)[1]
head(rdataFiles)
tail(rdataFiles)
# string vector of EVERY gene used in ANY of 200 models
allKFnames = NULL
# data.frame to receive rowinfo
kFoldResults = NULL
for(fNr in 1:nRData) {
load(rdataFiles[fNr,5])
matTrainTbl = matrix(unlist(scad.train$tab),
ncol=4,byrow=TRUE)
matTestTbl = matrix(unlist(scad.test$tab),ncol=4,byrow=TRUE)
 # the names of all genes for the TRAINING sample model
kFoldNames = names(thisScad$model$w)
allKFnames = c(allKFnames,kFoldNames)
```

```
NkFoldNames = length(kFoldNames)
foundGenes = NULL
nFound = 0
for(c in 1:length(table2Genes)) {
if(table2Genes[c] %in% kFoldNames) {
foundGenes = paste(foundGenes,
table2Genes[c],collapse="+")
nFound = nFound + 1
 }
 }
rowInfo = data.frame(matTrainTbl,matTestTbl,
NkFoldNames,nFound,foundGenes)
names(rowInfo) = c(confusionCols,"nKfoldVars",
"nMatchBest20","matchedGenes")
kFoldResults = rbind(kFoldResults,rowInfo)
}
### CHANGE THIS ###
write.csv(kFoldResults,file="kFoldResults36.csv")
summary(kFoldResults)
head(kFoldResults)
# frequency count of times each gene was in a model
tblAllKFnames = table(allKFnames)
str(tblAllKFnames)
### CHANGE THIS ###
# frequently selected genes (in more than 174 of the 200 models
goodGenesSel = tblAllKFnames>174
tblAllKFnames[goodGenesSel]
```

REFERENCES

Aebersold, R., Mann, M., 2003. Mass spectrometry-based proteomics. Nature. 422, 198–207.

Benjamini, Y., Hochberg, Y., 1995. Controlling the false discovery rate: a practical and powerful approach to multiple testing. J. R. Stat. Soc. B. 57, 289–300.

Efron, B., Hastie, T., Johnstone, I., Tibshirani, R., 2004. Least Angle Regression. Ann. Stat. 32, 407–499.

Efron, B., 2010. The future of indirect evidence. Stat. Sci. 25, 145–157.

Hand, D.J., 2008. Breast cancer diagnosis from proteomic mass spectrometry data: a comparative evaluation. Stat. Appl. Genet. Mol. Biol. 7 (2), Art. 15.

Hand, D.J., 2009. Measuring classifier performance: a coherent alternative to the area under the ROC curve. Mach. Learn. 77, 103–123.

Nisbet, R., Elder, J., Miner, G., 2009. Handbook of Statistical Analysis and Data Mining Applications. Academic Press/Elsevier, New York, NY.

Pavlik, E.J., Saunders, B.A., Doran, S, McHugh, K.W., Ueland, F.R., Desimone, C.P., et al., 2009. The search for meaning – symptoms and transvaginal sonography screening for ovarian cancer: predicting malignancy. Cancer. 115 (16), 3689–3698.

Peikoff, K., 2013. I Had My DNA Picture Taken, With Varying Results. The New York Times, <www.nytimes.com/2013/12/31/science/i-had-my-dna-picture-taken-with-varying-results.html?hp&_r = 0>.

Tutorial Z

Influence of Stent Vendor Representatives in the Catheterization Lab

Brian J. Smith and Linda A. Winters-Miner, PhD

Chapter Outline

INTRODUCTION AND REVIEW OF THE LITERATURE

In today's medical environment, hospitals have to become more conscious about cost. They must stay in budget if they want to remain viable. Choices of the physician might depend on the presence of vendor representatives (reps). Even if those choices do not affect patient care, they could affect the compliancy of the contract that the hospital has with a vendor and thus increase supply costs. If this study shows that the physicians or some of the physicians had been influenced, whether aware or not, then it may be worth looking at restricting access of vendor representatives in the catheterization lab.

Every year medical costs increase in the United States. The cost of health care as a percentage of the gross domestic product (GDP) in 1960 was 5%; in 2008 it was 17%; and it is projected to be 20% by the year 2018. Many factors have contributed to the increases in medical costs, and some are more significant than others. New technology, including new procedures, drugs, and devices, has been estimated to account for between 38% and 65% of the healthcare cost growth (Social Security Advisory Board, 2009). From 2003 to 2005 the average hospital's medical supply cost increased by 40%, rising from US$36 million to $50.5 million during that 2-year span. These supply costs represented as much as 31% of the total cost per case for hospitals. Physician preference items (PPIs), such as orthopedic implants, mechanical devices used for surgery, and implantable devices such as pacemakers and defibrillators sold by cardiac industry representatives, accounted for up to 61% of the cost of medical supplies for hospitals (Montgomery and Schneller, 2007).

Physicians and the medical industry have had a good longstanding working relationship in the United States. Since the 1970s, the medical industry—physician relationship has given the world an overwhelming array of life-saving medicines and medical devices (Nakayama, 2010). Entrepreneurial physicians have translated their innovated ideas into life-improving and life-saving devices by working with the biotechnology companies and academic researchers (Stossel and Stell, 2011). Industry has needed physicians to enroll patients in clinical trials and to test prototype inventions. Research physicians have worked collaboratively with industry, and have been deserving of appropriate compensation for their part in the research and development (Nakayama, 2010).

Physicians have been the ones to decide which PPIs they want to use, based on their own experience with the devices, the particular need of the patient, and comfort level that they have with the companies and their representatives (Montgomery and Schneller, 2007). The cost of PPIs has been taken on by the hospital in its treatment of the patient. The price of the devices may not have been known by the physician, as many manufacturers have demanded a secrecy

Practical Predictive Analytics and Decisioning Systems for Medicine. DOI: http://dx.doi.org/10.1016/B978-0-12-411643-6.00043-0

clause in their contracts with the hospitals. The secrecy in those contracts affected nearly 60% of the $112 billion cost of all medical devices used in 2007, and the device industry's returns to shareholder doubled that of the pharmaceutical industry in that same year. This lack of transparency has compounded the problems of cost for hospitals. Hospitals had no idea what the average market price was for some devices, and this prevented them from making better informed judgments when they negotiated the cost of those devices. This has led to a wide range of prices paid across the country for any one of many PPIs. A survey conducted by the Integrated Healthcare Association (IHA) showed that a particular hip implant device used by different hospitals ranged in price from $2,300 to $7,300 (Lerner *et al.*, 2008).

This lack of transparency has also put the physicians and the hospitals on different goal paths. The vendors of these PPIs targeted their sales not to the hospital but to physicians, and the physicians then told their hospitals which device they wanted. Because the physicians were unaware that there was such significant price disparity between similar products, they then appeared to be insensitive to the cost of the device selected (Lerner *et al.*, 2008).

What a hospital bills its payers doesn't reflect what they receive in payment. Most insurance carriers follow the lead of Medicare. Medicare's reimbursement to a hospital has been based on the diagnosis related group (DRG). This per-case payment was designed to cover all the services, including devices, provided by the hospital in its treatment of a patient. Generally, device prices have gone up, while the DRGs by Medicare have decreased in many instances (Montgomery and Schneller, 2007). Physicians, historically, have had the ability to bill separately from the hospital for their services, thus being unaffected by narrowing margins. The physicians were not directly challenged, like the hospitals were, to perform the same procedures as before but to utilize fewer hospital supplies.

The medical device industry and their representatives have commanded the making, supplying, and distributing of PPIs. These suppliers have also provided the knowledge about their products, and training on their usage, and given on-site technical help in the hospital setting. Vendor companies have also spent millions of dollars per year supporting their representatives so that they can have some influence in the cardiac catherization lab (Kern, 2009). The problem is that when reps visit and give help, they can also influence what devices the physicians prefer to order.

Most hospitals have utilized third-party services that help them to monitor when they have vendor reps in their buildings. Major monitoring services include Vendormate and Reptrax, to name but two. Vendor reps had to sign into these monitoring services' kiosk when they visited a hospital, and were then issued a temporary name tag with the name of the department they were allowed into. These systems also tracked their departure time. Systems like these made it easier and more effective for hospitals to enact their own existing policies regarding vendors (Traynor, 2009).

The original study that led to this tutorial examined specific hypotheses related to compliance with contracts and the possible influence of presence of the reps. This tutorial represents our effort to conduct some exploratory analyses on the data to further substantiate what was suspected, to identify additional hypotheses, and to provide a pattern for readers who might wish to explore data using predictive analytic techniques. The data have been partially fictionalized, so the reader should not draw conclusions from the results. In addition, the study was purely exploratory.

DEFINITION OF TERMS

- *Bare Metal Stent (BMS)*: Representative was helping with type of coronary stent that had no drug coating.
- *Drug Eluting Stent (DES)*: Representative was helping with the type of stent that was coated with a drug that slowly released the drug to block the growth of tissue inside the vessel.

METHOD OF GATHERING DATA

The data were adapted and partially fictionalized from an earlier study in which data were retrieved from two different computer tracking systems. The first system was from Reptrax, a web-driven software service that has assisted in the credentialing and tracking of medical vendor representatives for hospitals all across the United States. By using Reptrax, all visits by all the vendor representatives of each of the companies whose product usage was being tracked for the study were downloaded and recorded. Each visit by each vendor's representative was then entered into an Excel spreadsheet separating each visit by company and by date. These data were tracked from January 1, 2012 through December 31, 2012. Any visit by one of the three companies being tracked was considered a presence in the cath lab.

The second tracking system was Xper Inventory Coordinator. This system recorded all data, including supplies used, for every procedure performed in the cath lab that was studied. A report was run for each month of the calendar year that displayed every coronary intervention procedure for each day of the month. The report showed which physician performed the procedure and which coronary industry representatives were utilized.

The study only included coronary stents that were actually deployed, and coronary stents that were opened for the case but not utilized for whatever reason. Not considered was the scenario whereby one company's stent was tried but did not cross the lesion, so was not deployed, and was removed and replaced by a stent from a different company which did cross the lesion and was deployed. In this case, the second stent was counted on the survey but the first stent was not.

The data were then reformulated into the present stents.sta. The reformulation was as follows. First, the Rep Present data included the first instance of the rep being present in the cath lab and the next instance of order, as we suspected that the influence was longer than the specific time. We actually suspected a longer interval of influence, but only included the presence plus the next order period. If a different rep was in the next order spot, we used "both"; if two reps were there, we also used "both." After determining those "influence" periods, we considered only the instances in which there were actual orders. Weeks in which there were no orders were removed. The resulting data file was called stents.sta.

EXPLORATORY ANALYSIS

Open the data file stents.sta. The entries include eight surgeons (A—H), the instances per month that the data were collected, the company the stents were purchased from, the totals for each type of stent for the collection period, and whether or not an industry representative visited the cath lab. Reps could sell either type of stent; however, we collected data on the type that they represented by visit, allowing us to divide the data by type being represented/used (hence DES Rep present or BMS Rep present, Both or None). We will call them BMS Rep or DES Rep herein.

A screenshot of the data may be seen in Figure Z.1.

We wanted to see if we could predict the sales of the two types of stents from the other variables. We first conducted a feature selection to see which variables might be the most important. The directions are as follows.

First go to the Data Mining drop box and click on Feature Selection. Choose "Feature Selection and Variable screening" as in Figure Z.2.

Figure Z.3 shows the resulting dialog box.

Click on variables and enter them. Figure Z.4 shows that we selected Variables 5 and 6 as the dependent variables because they were our variables of interest. They also were continuous. Note that the check mark places the variables in their appropriate box, whether continuous or categorical. We chose as the predictors Variables 1—4. We wanted to predict the stent sales.

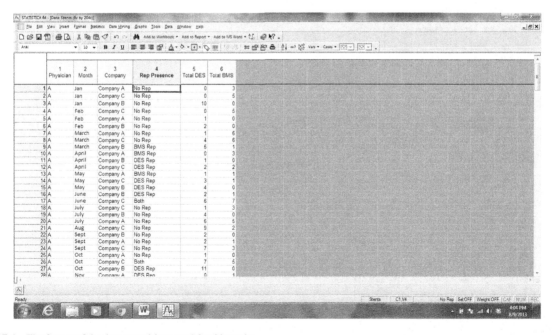

FIGURE Z.1   The format of the data spreadsheet used for this study.

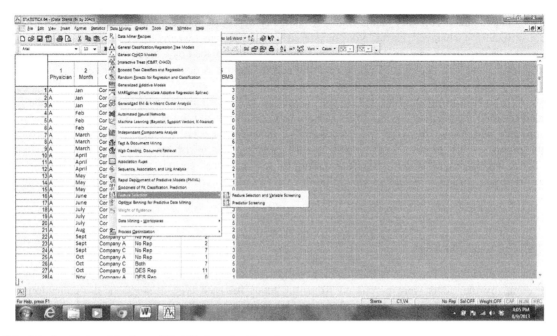

FIGURE Z.2 Selecting 'Feature Selection and Variable Screening' from the menu.

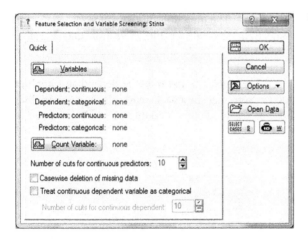

FIGURE Z.3 Resulting Dialog Box.

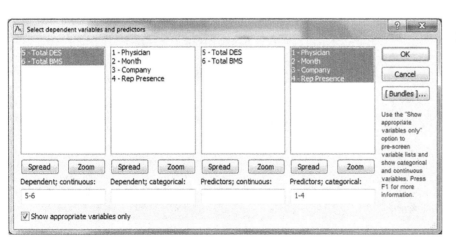

FIGURE Z.4 Select Variables 5 and 6 as Dependent Variables.

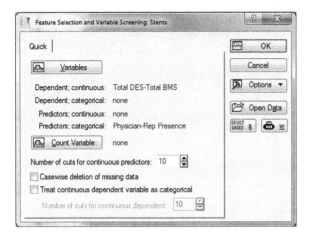

FIGURE Z.5 The Feature Selection and Variable Screening dialog window now shows that the variables have been selected.

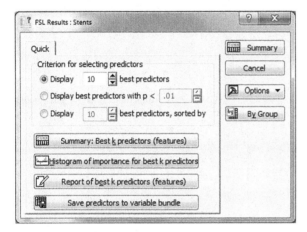

FIGURE Z.6 Feature Selection Results Dialog.

Best predictors for continuous dependent var: Total DES (stents)		
	F-value	p-value
Company	23.50332	0.000000
Rep presence	7.71236	0.000067
Physician	3.85557	0.000593
Month	0.75858	0.680939

FIGURE Z.7 Best predictor variables results for the target variable 'Total DES'.

Best predictors for continuous dependent var: Total BMS (stents)		
	F-value	p-value
Company	34.32800	0.000000
Physician	5.51736	0.000008
Rep presence	3.44840	0.017641
Month	0.53798	0.875759

FIGURE Z.8 Best predictors results spreadsheet for the target variable 'Total BMS'.

Click OK (Figure Z.5) and then OK again.

Figure Z.6 shows the Feature Selection results dialog.

Click first on "Summary: best k predictors (features)" to get Figures Z.7 and Z.8.

In both cases, it appears as though Month is not a good predictor but the others may be. We can also see the relationships by viewing the Importance plots in Figures Z.9 and Z.10.

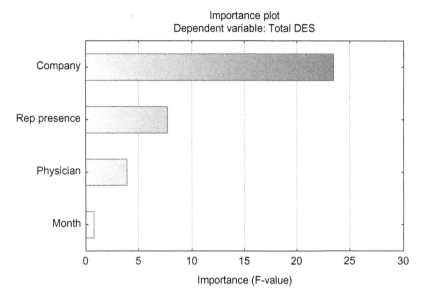

FIGURE Z.9 Importance plot showing best predictors for target 'Total DES'.

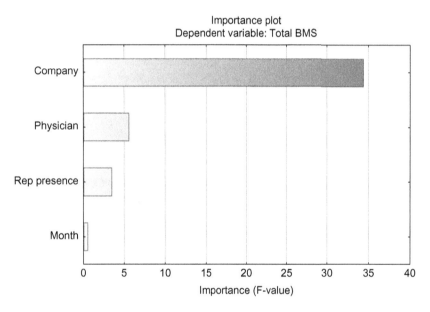

FIGURE Z.10 Importance plot for best predictors for target 'Total BMS'.

Pull up the Results dialog box again, Figure Z.6, and click on "Histogram of importance for best k predictors" to create Figures Z.9 and Z.10.

At this point, conduct a data mining recipe for predicting sales for both DES and BMS.

Go to Data Mining and click on the first heading, Data Miner Recipes, as in Figure Z.11.

When the box in Figure Z.12 emerges, click on New.

The Data Miner Recipes dialog box will look like the display in Figure Z.13.

Click on Open/Connect data file.

Now click on the data file to connect the data to the program (Figure Z.14) and click OK. The program will go back to the Data Miner Recipes dialog box (Figure Z.15).

Click on Select variables and select the ones that we determined might be important (Figure Z.16).

Click OK. Now, in Figure Z.17, click the box to Configure all steps.

The red Xs will turn to purple circles. Click on the box beside Target variable. See Figure Z.18.

There, you will see both Total DES and Total BMS. Click on each, one at a time, as in Figure Z.19.

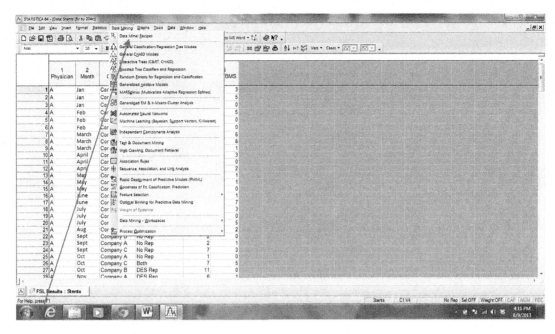

FIGURE Z.11 Get Data Mining Recipes.

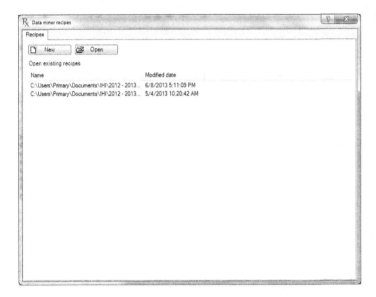

FIGURE Z.12 The initial 'Data Miner Recipe' window.

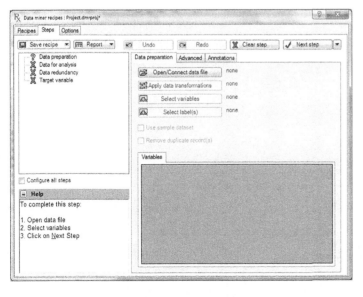

FIGURE Z.13 The Data Miner Recipe window as it appears after one selects 'New' recipe.

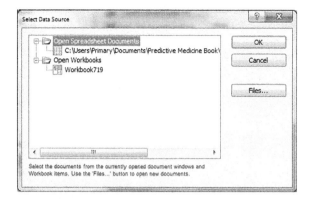

FIGURE Z.14   The 'Select Data Source' window for the Data Miner Recipe.

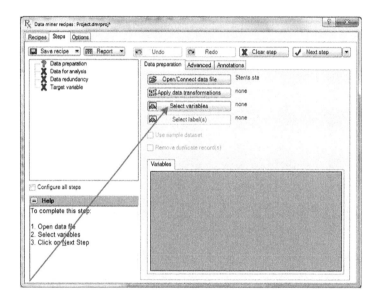

FIGURE Z.15   The Data Miner Recipe window as it appears following selection of the data spreadsheet.

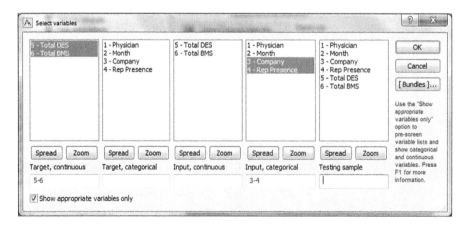

FIGURE Z.16   Selecting the variables in the DMRecipe (Data Miner Recipe) format.

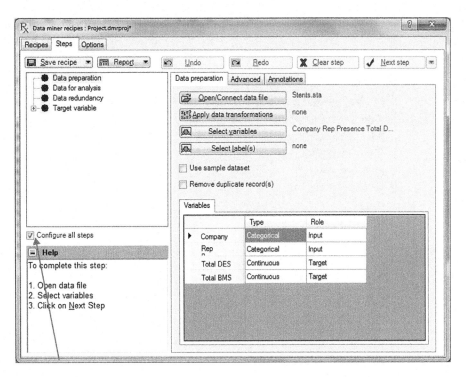

FIGURE Z.17   Click Configure all steps and Xs turn purple/blue.

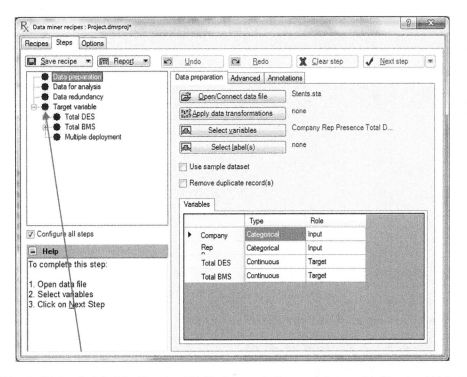

FIGURE Z.18   Clicking the " + " to the left of the 'Target variable' in the menu in the upper left causes this 'Target variable' category to expand.

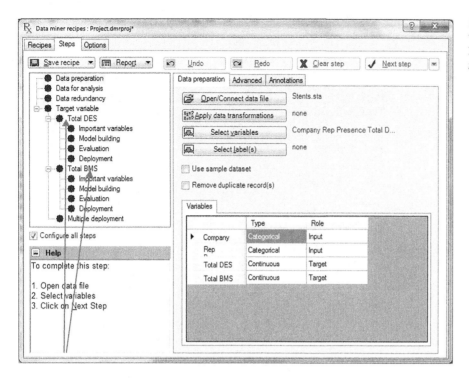

FIGURE Z.19 And further clicking the "+" in the boxes to the left of 'Total DES' and 'Total BMS' causes these categories to also further expand.

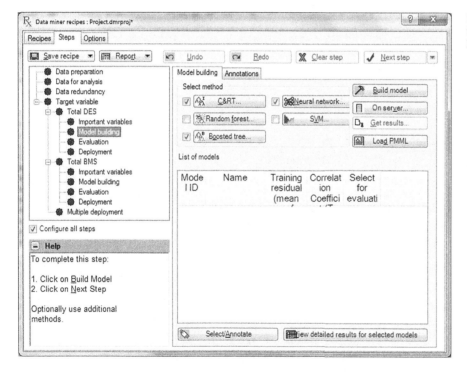

FIGURE Z.20 Note default procedures that will run. You may choose Random Forests and SVM as well for each.

Next, click on Model building and make sure that all methods are checked. Figure Z.20 shows that Random forest and SVM have not been checked. Not all will run, depending on the data, but click them anyway so if they can run they will. Now complete the above steps for BMS as well.

Figure Z.20 shows the default setting for DES.

Figure Z.21 shows that the BMS has been completed as well.

Now unclick the Configure all steps button and the red Xs will reappear (see Figure Z.22).

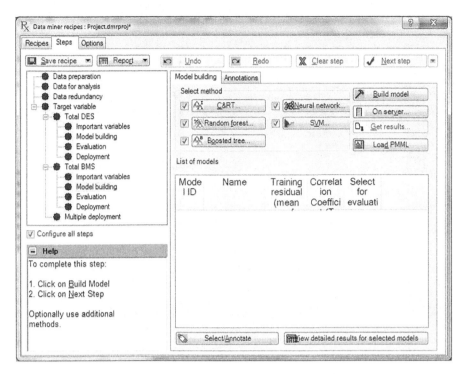

FIGURE Z.21 This figure shows the BMS with all selected.

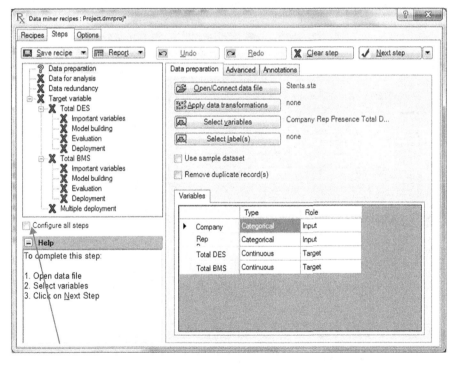

FIGURE Z.22 Unclick Configure all steps and red Xs reappear.

Go to the upper right-hand corner and click on Run to completion (Figure Z.23).

Wait until the program does its thing (Figure Z.24).

Figure Z.25 shows the Results workbook.

Pull the edge of the top screen to the right to see what is behind as in Figure Z.26.

It looks as though the Classification and Regressions Trees (C&RT) is the best prediction model with a correlation of 0.55 (if we had been predicting discrete variables, then we would have seen an error percentage). The correlation is

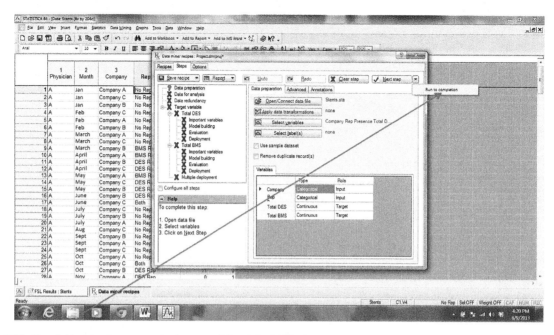

FIGURE Z.23 By clicking the down arrow in the upper right of the DMRecipe window, a 'run to completion' selection pops up; when this is selected the entire predictive analytic computations will be automatically run to completion.

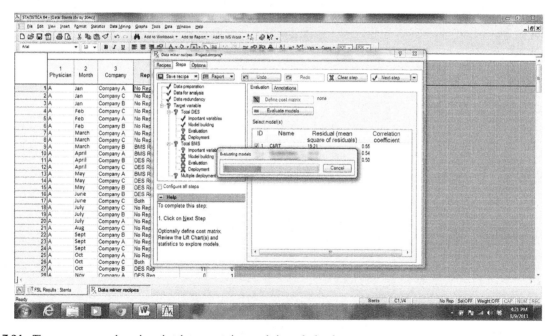

FIGURE Z.24 The green progress bars show that the computations are being calculated.

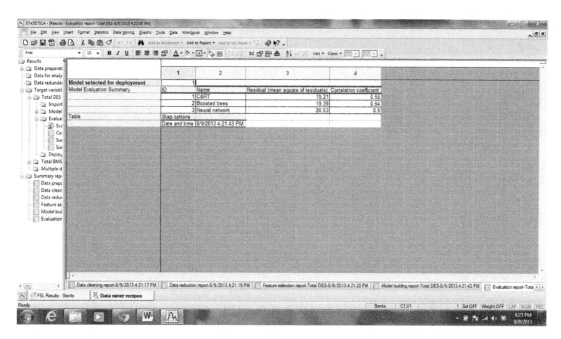

FIGURE Z.25   After a few minutes (or longer, if a very large dataset) the final summary result becomes the top screen showing which algorithm performed best; the one with the highest correlation coefficient is deemd 'best'.

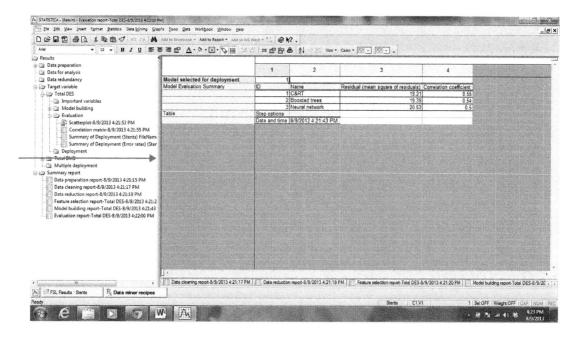

FIGURE Z.26   The C&RT (i.e. 'trees') algorithm has the highest correlation coefficient; however it is about the same as Boosted Trees. Pull edge over so you can see underneath.

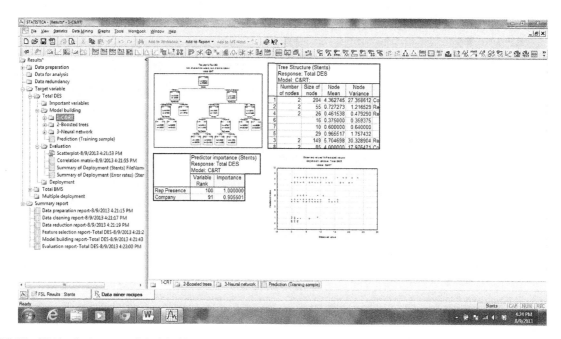

FIGURE Z.27 Clicking back on one of the left side menu results items, we can get different results dialogs; here we see one for the 'Trees' for the DES target.

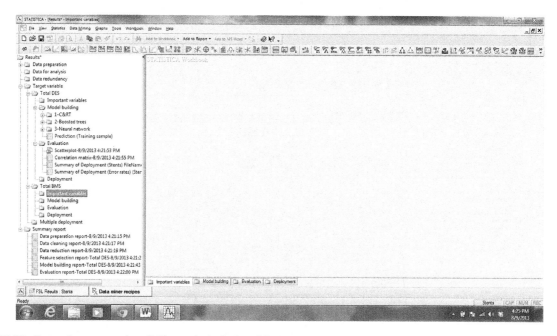

FIGURE Z.28 Screen that appears when clicking on the beginning of the BMS target result dialogs.

not particularly high, so we really do not have a great model. However, this model may help us to find some possible patterns and perhaps some hypotheses that we could test.

First, click on each of the folders under Target variable. The first one is Total DES. Click on it and then on the C&RT, as in Figure Z.27.

Next, click on the folder for Total BMS. It appears that there is nothing in that folder but other empty folders. It seemed as though both variables were being analyzed, but we might have to analyze the BMS separately (Figure Z.28).

None of the folders opens to anything. So, we'll return to the DES where we have output.

DRUG ELUTING STENT OUTPUT

Click on the Tree graph so we can see some of the possible relationships in Figure Z.29.

The first break is for company and then after that, the presence of the rep. At the first node, or split, Company A is split from Company B and C. The mean number of orders for DES is given in the boxes. Looking under Company A, the rep or both reps conditions led to a greater mean number of stents than when either the DES rep or the BMS rep was there.

Looking under Company C and B, the first split under those companies was with the presence of the rep. Both of the DES reps led to a higher mean, whereas BMS rep or no rep led to a lower mean.

Returning to the workbook output, click on Predictor importance as in Figure Z.30.

We see that the most important predictor was the presence of the rep (Figure Z.31).

We ran a quick ANOVA of DES orders versus the variable Rep Presence, and found an interesting pattern. Go to Statistics, ANOVA (Figure Z.32), and then One Way ANOVA (Figure Z.33).

Select the variables as in Figure Z.34.

Enter Total DES on the dependent variable side and Rep Presence on the categorical (predictor) side. Click OK and then OK again. Figure Z.35 shows the resulting dialog box.

Click on All effects/Graphs, which produces Figure Z.36.

Note the p value of 0.000. Of course we are only searching for possible patterns, so we do not focus unduly on the p value! Click OK to see the graph in Figure Z.37.

One certainly wonders if the DES sales reps are getting more orders because of the presence of the rep. There is no overlap between the confidence interval around the DES rep and BMS rep or No rep for mean number of DES stent orders. There was overlap between DES rep and Both, which again might have been the presence of the DES rep.

At this point we decided to run a data miner recipe on BMS as the target. We repeated the steps above to find out.

Go to Data Mining, Data Miner Recipes, and click New. Again, select the data set as in Figure Z.38.

Click the Data file and then OK. Next, in the dialog box for Figure Z.39, click on Variables.

Try Total BMS as the dependent continuous variable and Physician, Company, and Rep Presence as the three independent variables (Figure Z.40).

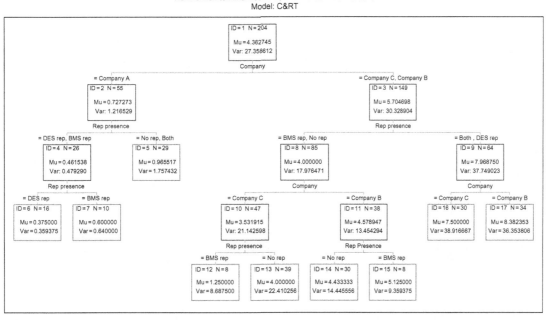

FIGURE Z.29 The Tree graph for the DES target.

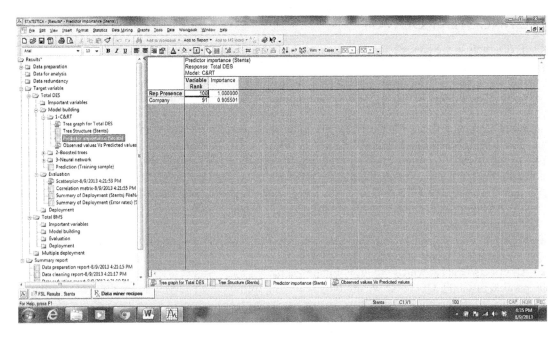

FIGURE Z.30   Predictor Importance.

	Predictor importance (stents) Response: Total DES Model: C&RT	
	Variable Rank	Importance
Rep Presence	100	1.000000
Company	91	0 905501

FIGURE Z.31   The predictor variable importance for target DES using the C&RT model.

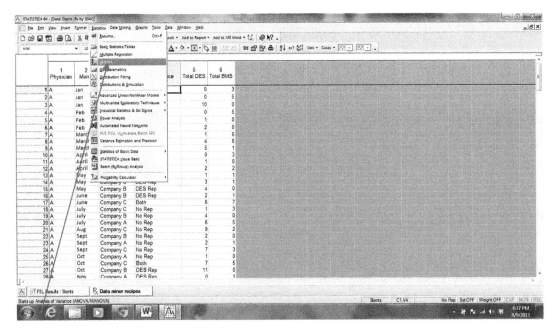

FIGURE Z.32   Selecting ANOVA module form the 'Statistics' pull down menu.

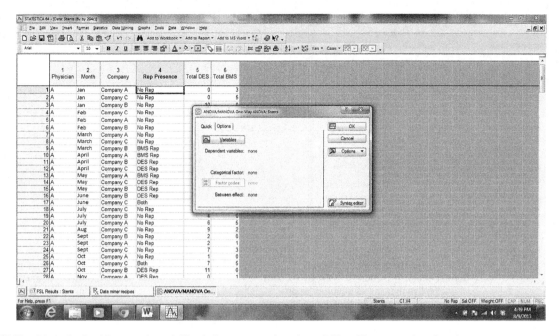

FIGURE Z.33 After selecting 'One way Anova' this window appears where the variables of interest can be selected.

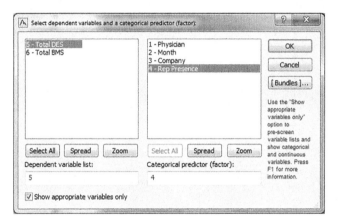

FIGURE Z.34 Variables selected for the one way Anova.

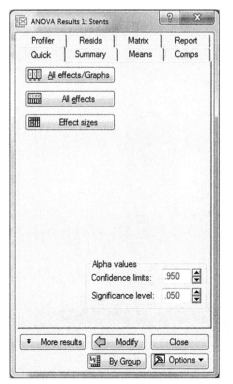

FIGURE Z.35 Results dialog for the One way Anova.

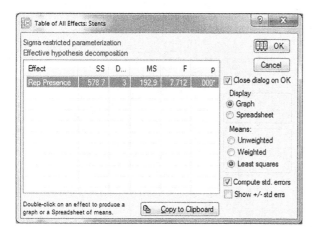

FIGURE Z.36 Looking at the 'Table of Effects' one can select the radio-button Graph and the Least squares method, and select OK to produce a graph.

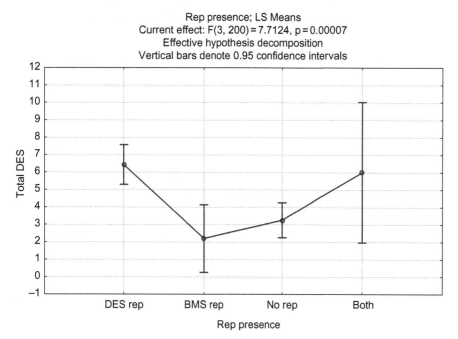

FIGURE Z.37 Graph resulting from breaking down whether or not a representative of the stent company was present.

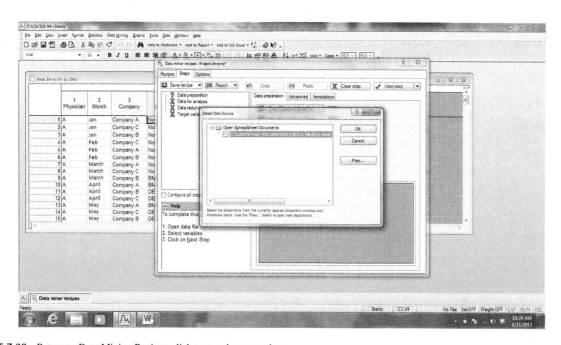

FIGURE Z.38 Return to Data Mining Recipes, click new and connect data.

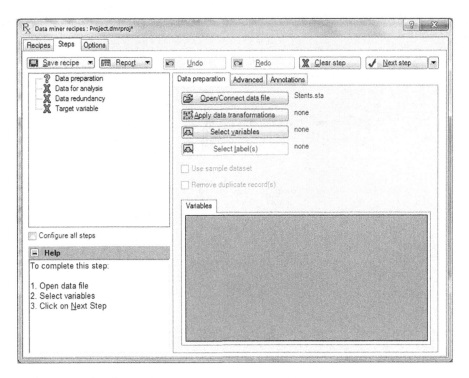

FIGURE Z.39   Stents.sta data source selected.

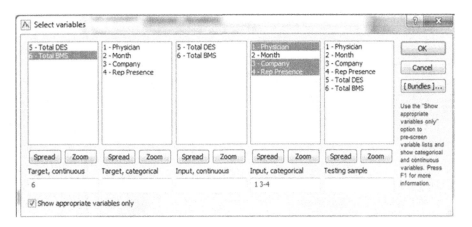

FIGURE Z.40   Set target as BMS this time.

Click OK. Next, click Configure all steps, click on the purple target variable, then on Total BMS, and finally on Model building (Figure Z.41). Random forest will probably not work, but go ahead and click it anyway along with the SVM module. Why not? If it runs, it might give us more information.

Uncheck Configure all steps, and then, in the upper right, in the arrow box beside Next step, click Run to completion (Figure Z.42).

As suspected, Random forest would not run. We continued. Surprise! The model ran and C&RT had a value of 0.86! (see Figure Z.43 for evaluation of the models).

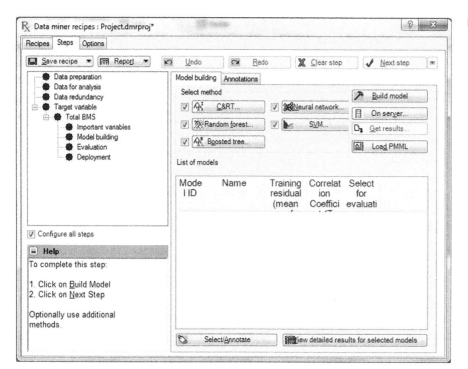

FIGURE Z.41 Configure all steps.

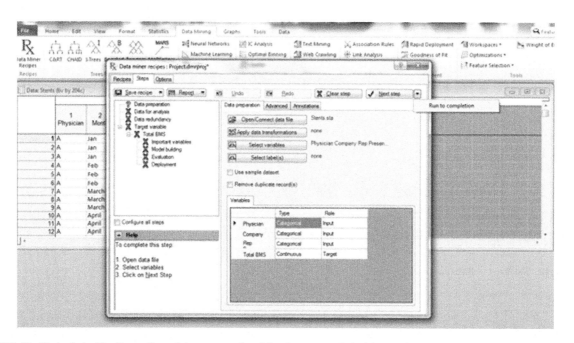

FIGURE Z.42 Uncheck the 'Configure all steps', icons turn red, and then 'run to completion' (upper right corner down arrow selection).

	1	2	3	4
Model selected for deployment	1			
Model Evaluation Summary	ID	Name	Residual (mean square of residuals)	Correlation coefficient
	1	C&RT	2.73	0.86
	3	Boosted trees	3.09	0.85
	5	Neural network	3.05	0.85
	4	SVM	11.47	0.77
Table	Step options			
	Date and time	7/13/2014 5:35:57 PM		

FIGURE Z.43 Evaluation of Models. Note that C&RT was best model for BMS.

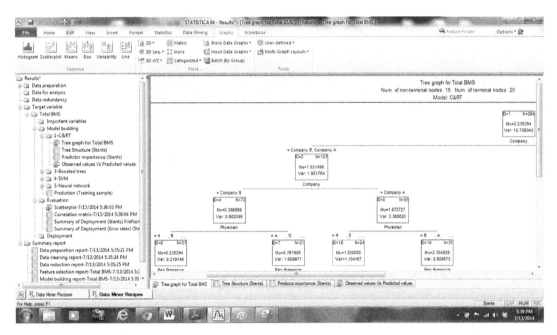

FIGURE Z.44 View Trees.

We opened the trees from Figure Z.44, which resulted in Figure Z.45.

Interestingly, for the BMS, it seemed that overall the physician was the most important predictor, as Figure Z.46 reveals but Company made the first split on the trees.

Again, we looked at the Reps in the OR relative to the BMS and found this relationship in Figure Z.47.

The BMS stent also seemed to be purchased more when the BMS rep was present.

To view both together, we did a Means with Errors plot. Go to Graphs and Means with Errors plots, as in Figure Z.48.

Select Multiple (Figure Z.49).

Then select the variables (Figure Z.50). For the dependent variables, select the sales for DES and BMS, and for the independent variable, select Rep Presence. Click OK and then click OK again.

Figure Z.51 shows the resulting graph.

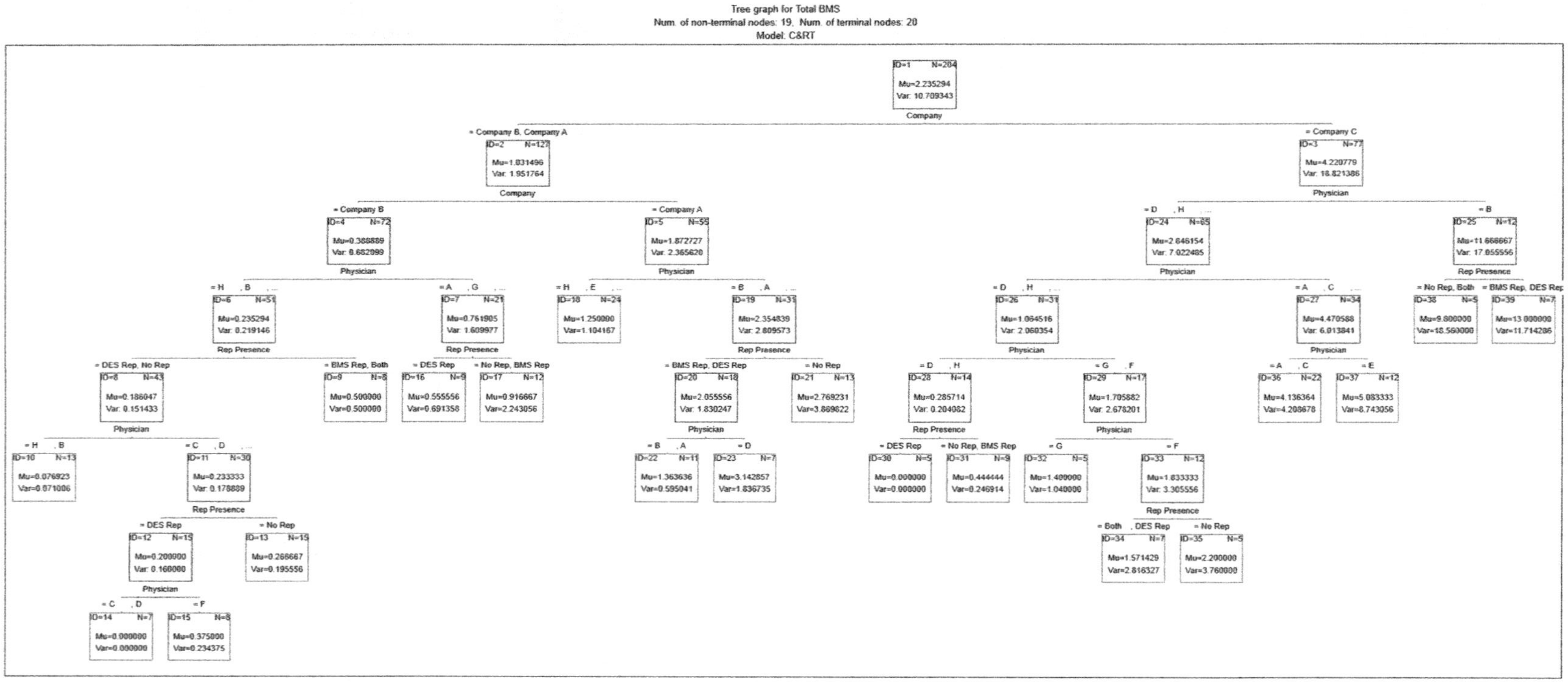

Tree graph for Total BMS
Num. of non-terminal nodes: 19. Num. of terminal nodes: 20
Model: C&RT

FIGURE Z.45 Tree Graph.

Predictor importance (Stents) Response: Total BMS Model: C&RT		
	Variable Rank	Importance
Physician	100	1.000000
Company	42	0.422243
Rep Presence	28	0.276328

FIGURE Z.46 Physician seemed to be the most important variable.

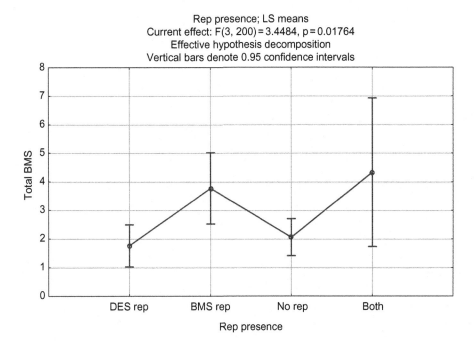

FIGURE Z.47 Graphical Relationship.

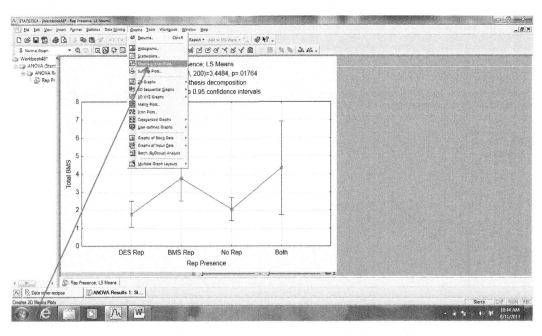

FIGURE Z.48 Go to graphs and then Means with Errors plots.

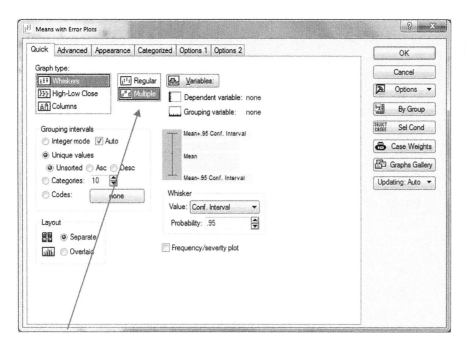

FIGURE Z.49 Means with Error Plots graph options dialogs where various parameters can be adjusted.

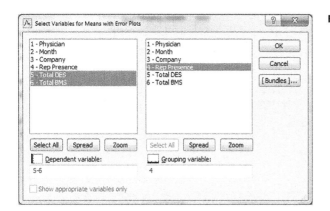

FIGURE Z.50 Variables selected for the Means with Error Plots graph.

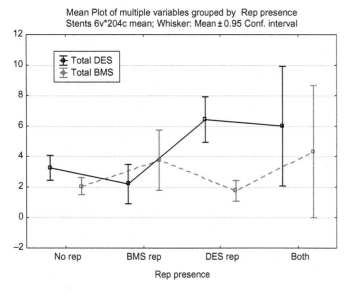

FIGURE Z.51 Multiple plots comparing 'Total DES' vs 'Total BMS'.

CONCLUSION

Although we could not state anything definitively with this exploratory analysis, it has certainly addressed the question of whether having a stent representative in the catheterization lab influences choices, and allows us to hypothesize that having such an industry representative present likely does influence the physician. When looking at the data and seeing that, after a rep has been in several operations, suddenly a particular stent is purchased, it is interesting. Perhaps the physician is learning new techniques and prefers the stent because it works better. However, in the data there were several instances of stent purchases going back and forth between two types of stents after industry representatives had visited. We suspect it might be worthwhile tracking such events on a regular basis. It might be thought that reps should be banned from the catheterization lab. Data could be tracked after such a ban and compared to the present data.

REFERENCES

Kern, M., 2009. Working with industry representatives and conflicts of interest in the Cath Lab. Cathlab Dig. 17 (11), 4–6.

Lerner, J., Fox, D., Nelson, T., Reiss, J., 2008. The consequence of secret prices: the politics of physician preference items. Health Aff. 27 (6), 1560–1565.

Montgomery, K., Schneller, E.S., 2007. Hospitals' strategies for orchestrating selection of physician preference items. Milbank Q. 85, 307–335.

Nakayama, D.K., 2010. In defense of industry-physician relationships. Am. Surg. 76 (9), 987–994.

Social Security Advisory Board, 2009. (September). The Unsustainable Cost of Health Care [Finance Report]. Retrieved from Social Security Advisory Board website: <http://ssab.gov>.

Stossel, T.P., Stell, L.K., 2011. Time to "walk the walk" about industry ties to enhance health. Nat. Med. 17 (4), 437–438.

Traynor, K., 2009. Some hospitals outsourcing vendor compliance. Am. J. Health Syst. Pharm. 66 (6), 524–526.

Prologue to Part 3

In Part 3 of this book you will find chapters on the use of advanced predictive analytics in healthcare delivery, administration, and medical research, including some real-world examples of the use of predictive analytics in medical clinics and hospital settings. These include deployment of a predictive analytic model resulting in decisioning done in real time, even in the operating room during surgery, and to the point of deciding what is the next step in the care of a particular patient.

Specific topics in Part 3 include: nursing informatics; the rapidly growing use of mobile devices to provide medical data to the patient and doctor for, in some cases, instant decisions; medical fraud in claims reimbursement; a thorough discussion of what a decisioning platform is all about; a discussion of IBM-Watson; and examples from real-world healthcare facilities. These include the University of Iowa Department of Surgery, which offers a demo-project of cutting-edge medical care decisioning that affects the patient positively, and, finally, a fully functioning cutting-edge IT medical informatics model from the Military Institute of Medicine (MIM) in Warsaw, Poland, and the Regional *Specialist Hospital in Wroclaw, Poland, in* a project *named TeleMedNet*.

This Part 3 includes the final chapter, Chapter 26, which speculates on what the future holds for global medicine.

Part 3

Practical Solutions and Advanced Topics in Administration and Delivery of Health Care Including Practical Predictive Analytics for Medicine

Chapter 16

Predictive Analytics in Nursing Informatics

PREAMBLE

From the beginning of medical treatment in our civilization, the prevailing view was that medicine was a "noble" art practiced by the physician, rather than a science pursued by the learned. That view began to change in the mid-1800s, instigated not by a physician but by a nurse – Florence Nightingale. She said: "To understand God's thoughts we must study statistics, for these are the measure of His purpose" (Cook, 1942). Florence Nightingale transformed nursing from an occupation of poor women to the noble profession it is today, and initiated the study of medical data with statistical visualizations (polar diagrams). Modern nursing informatics, as presented in this chapter, follows in her footsteps.

INTRODUCTION

The intention of this chapter is to inspire the nurse informatician with the possibilities of predictive analytics in nursing informatics, and examples of current research projects. There is endless potential in this field for effectively using predictive analytics and data mining. This chapter is not meant to be a complete assessment of the possibilities, or to describe all the areas in which PA can be used, but rather to be a guide with examples to stimulate the mind. Readers should not limit themselves to the topics discussed in this chapter but realize that any other topics described within the chapters in this book hold possibilities for nursing research. Reading Chapter 3 of this book, on Biomedical Informatics, in conjunction with this chapter will give the reader a better background on how to tackle predictive analytics projects.

Nurses are a vital part of the medical system, outnumbering any other positions in the healthcare field and functioning on the front line of health care. It is the nurses who have the most constant contact with patients and relay vital information to physicians that often determine patient outcome. They are the ones who most often interact with patient monitoring devices, administer the medications, and provide the monitoring that is prescribed. They also serve outside the hospital in patients' homes and in care facilities, allowing health care to extend its reach outside the hospital. Because of the vital role of nurses and the growing role of technology in this field, nursing informatics has a critical role as part of the future of healthcare predictive analytics.

Nursing informatics is a distinct specialty within nursing that has recently seen significant growth. The term was first introduced in 1976 by Scholes and Barber, when computers themselves were in their infancy. They described the potential of computers to contribute to service, education, and research in nursing. It makes sense that nurses would be early adopters of technology, as they were on the frontline of using technology to help patients, and played critical roles in determining its usability and maximizing its potential for patient care. The most recent definition of nursing informatics by the International Medical Informatics Association is as follows: "Nursing Informatics science and practice integrates nursing, its information and knowledge and their management with information and communication technologies to promote the health of people, families and communities world wide." This definition was updated at the group's meeting in Helsinki, Finland, in 2009 (Moen and Mæland Knudsen, 2013).

In 2013 The Nursing Informatics International Research Network (NIIRN) put together a survey of the top priorities in nursing informatics. The NIIRN is a group of experts who are collaborating on the development of internationally relevant research programs for nursing informatics (Dowding *et al.*, 2013). Their survey resulted in the following as the top five priorities.

1. The development of electronic information systems that can provide real-time feedback to nurses about their practices/healthcare delivery to improve safety.
2. Evaluation of the impact of HIT systems for nursing care (e.g., EHR) on outcomes for patients (safer care, better patient outcomes).
3. The development of decision support systems specific to nursing practice decisions.
4. Investigation of the impact of HIT systems for nursing care (e.g., EHR) on nurses' work practices and workflow.
5. The design and management of nursing information databases for use in patient management, clinical records and research.

All five of these topics can be improved or addressed with predictive analytics. With the first priority, predictive algorithms can monitor nursing and patient data in real time, predicting impending events and notifying nurses, thus allowing them to take the appropriate interventions before a problem occurs. The second priority involves evaluation of the former. The third priority could involve incorporating predictive algorithms into the decision support system, giving probabilities of outcomes and allowing nurses to make more informed decisions. The fourth involves designing intelligent interfaces that predict your next move, allowing for a more seamless workflow. The fifth is a critical element in developing databases that can be mined to build predictive analytics models.

NURSING INFORMATICS

The following headings define some of the areas that come under the umbrella of nursing informatics.

Patient Education

Education is one of the critical roles played by nurses. Nurses often do most of the patient education before a patient leaves the hospital. This is a huge responsibility, as giving proper education can have a tremendous impact on a patient's health and affect whether or not they will be readmitted to the hospital. Nurses are required to know and provide education about a number of topics, catering to an individual's understanding, education, background, and resources, which can have wide variability. It is therefore important to know how to deliver the appropriate education in the right context to the right individual. Through the use of intelligent systems we can better cater to the individual patient. An important part of this process is understanding which patients are likely to fail, and for what reason they are likely to fail. Using asthma as an example, asthma admissions are significant drivers of admissions to pediatric hospitals, particularly during seasons when asthma is more prevalent. Many young people end up returning to the hospital because of lack of understanding of how to properly manage their asthma, and others end up in the ICU because of misunderstandings regarding the treatment of asthma. A large part of the problem in this case is an incomplete understanding of the asthma action plan. If this is the case, steps should be taken to direct interventions and education to patients before they leave the hospital. Another point of failure may be access to medication; if this is predicted to be a problem, then appropriate follow-up can be arranged to ensure a patient's medical needs are being met outside the hospital. Diabetes is another disease with considerable impact that is a growing problem, with similar characteristics that can be approached in the same way. In both cases the psychosocial element must also be taken into account, considering the patients' view of their disease and the importance they place on using the medication and maintaining their health. Many young people in particular have a hard time dealing with and understanding chronic disease, and often fail to comply with medications. Early identification of these high-risk individuals may allow targeted intervention. Using predictive analytics we can target potential failures with targeted education and early interventions that will come across at the appropriate comprehension level to achieve the best possible outcomes and prevent readmission. These measures have the potential for saving substantial healthcare dollars.

Supporting Nurses' Work

Nurses spend considerable time with information systems, logging patient events and measurements. Particularly in an ICU setting, this can be very burdensome, and their observations and recordings are critical for patient care. Monitoring of ICU nurses found that while nurses were performing common tasks, critical information was often inaccessible, difficult to see at a distance, or located on multiple monitoring devices – current devices at the ICU bedside do not adequately support a nurse's information-gathering activities (Koch *et al.*, 2012).

Therefore, it is critical that information systems and devices allow for easy, quick, and accurate ways to input and access information. Streamlining these processes can make for more efficient care and decreased error. Part of this process is predicting need and what is to be logged per patient in an intelligent way. A patient with a heart condition, for example, might need very different monitoring and a different interface than a patient with a viral respiratory illness. Bypassing unneeded screens and presenting the user only with the screens needed for the current scenario may increase the efficiency of nurses, allowing them to spend more time on their most important task – caring for the patient.

The evaluation of a display prototype which combined information from multiple sources – dependent on the patient's condition and the current nursing task – found that nurses were able to perform tasks significantly faster and had a better awareness of the patient's condition (Koch *et al.*, 2013).

Predicting the Patient's Future Development

Nurses are keen observers of their patients, and there is rarely anyone who knows the patient better. The number of patients that nurses have been watching for hours, with similar conditions, is unparalleled, and the observations of an experienced nurse should be considered paramount in patient care. Experienced nurses may be able to detect an event or outcome in a patient before physiological signs are present (Collins *et al.*, 2013). The ability to qualify and quantify these observations into a predictive model could allow intervention before a bad outcome occurs. There will need to be considerable research into patient cues, perhaps even taking parents' and friends' observations into account to build a model. With medicine in its current state, even if a nurse approaches a physician with these concerns the physician may not act without objective measures to work from. Building such models could better inform the physician and improve patient outcomes. With readily available information to project future patient development, ICU nurses were shown to significantly better predict the future development of the patients and the treatment (Koch *et al.*, 2013).

Patient Monitoring Data

The amount of data which is automatically collected on patients increases with advances in technology, and we capture a large amount of data today that is largely overlooked but has tremendous data mining potential. This is particularly true of the critical care setting, where constant monitoring takes place. This constant stream of data is largely untapped and is a goldmine for predictive analytics. As domain experts on inpatient monitoring data, nursing informatics researchers are in an ideal position to build predictive models based on this data and to transform the existing and previously untapped information into important tools to improve patient care (Berger and Berger, 2004). Showing the predicted mean arterial blood pressure to nurses – derived from clinical parameters – demonstrated that nurses in experimental settings more accurately titrated vasoactive drugs (Görges *et al.*, 2010).

Home Nursing and Nursing Homes

A patient's encounter with nurses does not always end when he or she leaves the hospital. This is especially true in the critical care setting with newborns and the elderly, where they are usually discharged with follow-up nursing visits at their home, or follow-up visits to nursing homes. The home nurse is responsible for assessing the patient's condition and ability to thrive outside the hospital. This presents nurses with many different challenges in making sure that the patient can maintain his or her own health at home. This not only encompasses watching vitals and directly intervening, but also includes an assessment of patients' ability to function in the home setting and ensure they have the appropriate care and services to maintain their health. Nurses will often be faced with the dilemma of directing patients back to the hospital, or providing additional services for their care. Existing approaches include identifying scenarios which require additional attention, such as increased risk of mortality (Sharifi *et al.*, 2012), or predicting the recovery from acute brain injury (Oh and Seo, 2013). However, such approaches are currently far from being used in common clinical settings. This area provides great opportunity for predictive analytics, with a myriad of different outcomes to be predicted depending on diagnosis and setting. If it is possible to predict what will happen to a patient in a given a scenario, or even present a probability, it make the decision-making for the nurses much easier, avoiding unnecessary admissions while at the same time preventing morbidity and mortality from not directing care to the hospital when it is required.

Telemedicine

Nurses are now expanding their area of practice with telemedicine, also called telenursing. They can now monitor patients from home, decreasing travel time and expense and allowing them to outreach to areas where nursing care is sparse or where specialized nursing care is unavailable. In addition, this allows monitoring of more patients and allows experienced nurses to assist those with less experience, particularly in the ICU setting (Williams *et al.*, 2012). Predictive analytics systems can monitor continuing streams of data and help notify nurses remotely of upcoming adverse events, allowing nurses to tele-monitor multiple patients simultaneously with alerts to any impending events.

Triaging Patients

Nurses face significant challenges triaging patients in busy emergency departments. The status or score they assign the patient determines the urgency for and level of care they receive. Assessing acuity incorrectly can cause significant morbidity and possibly even death if a patient does not get the appropriate level of care at the right time. By mining data from busy ERs and building predictive models we may be able to create real-time scoring tools that can be used as an adjunct to nurses' experience. This could allow for more quick and accurate assignment of acuity level scores and improvement in patient outcomes.

Furthermore, patients who can safely be discharged need to be identified, in order for hospitals to provide care for as many patients as possible by increasing the availability of hospital beds for new patients. As such, approaches try to identify discharge ability (Cuthbert *et al.*, 2011) or discharge destination (van der Zwaluw *et al.*, 2011).

Preventing Inpatient Morbidity

While physicians shoulder the primary burden of providing the correct treatment of the primary condition, nurses are responsible for monitoring and handling many of the adverse events that occur related to the hospitalization. They are experts at monitoring patients for occurrences such as bedsores, dehydration, constipation, falls, rashes, and infections. As they see every day the variables that contribute to these events in the hospital, it only makes sense that they would be most qualified to build predictive models to anticipate and prevent these occurrences. Data mining techniques have been used to identify predictors that can be used to guide ulcer interventions (Lee *et al.*, 2012), and many other applications of this technology are possible.

Patient Comfort and Satisfaction

The opinion of the hospital that people (patients and family members) leave with can often be directly related to the nursing care the patient has received. Even if they have the best physicians, patients may not have a high level of satisfaction if the nurses who provide patients with care and comfort are not performing well. It is often hard to satisfy all patients, as they will all have different needs and some may find too much assistance overbearing and interfering while others may need a higher level of attention. Mining patient survey data in relation to nursing providers' data and interventions may provide predictive models of patients' needs and contribute to higher patient satisfaction. Some work has been done using data mining and predictive methods to custom tailor patient distraction during hospital procedures to meet patients' and parents' needs (Hanrahan *et al.*, 2012); similar work can be expanded into other areas of patient comfort and satisfaction.

Staffing

Appropriate staffing of nurses leads to better patient outcomes both in morbidity and in mortality. However, with rising healthcare costs these needs must be balanced so that staffing is adequate but not excessive in a way that unnecessarily increases healthcare costs. It is not only critical that the correct number of staff are available, but also that the experience level of the staff is appropriate to optimize patient care. It has been theorized that, using data mining, we could build models that could predict staffing needs, and models have been constructed that show promise of prediction of hospital burden (Hyun et al., 2008; Harper, 2012). This is an area of need in health care that can save considerable costs and frustration; such models of staffing needs are being developed (Harper, 2012).

Patient Hand-Offs

Patient hand-offs are a critical part of medicine, and essential to nursing. The information provided during hand-offs serves as the basis for patient care for the next shift. This serves as a potential area to predict the most important aspects for hand-off, and in addition the data from patient hand-offs over time may be predictive of a patient's trajectory and need for further intervention. The data from hand-offs contain considerable nursing knowledge, and would be very useful for mining and for improving patient care (Matney et al., 2014; see also Staggers and Blaz, 2013).

Approach to Projects

Nurses do more of the daily monitoring of patients and have more contact with them, which gives them a distinct advantage in visualizing the changes that take place with a patient in regard to different clinical variables and occurrences. This unique situation gives them an unparalleled ability to use data mining and build predictive models for improving patient care and the affordability of health care. The possibilities mentioned in this chapter are only a drop in the ocean regarding what is possible with predictive analytics in nursing, and there is no reason why the scope of nursing informatics could not encompass the majority of the topics covered in Chapter 3 of this book. It is recommended that readers also read Chapter 3 regarding in particular the step-by-step approach to embarking on a predictive analytics project. Nursing informatics is a vast, virtually untapped field from the perspective of predictive analytics, and full of endless potential.

There are other areas that we could discuss in more detail, but we will leave this chapter by just listing some of these; readers who have a greater interest can then search these areas out further:

- Alerting
- Financial Management
- Automated Care Plans
- Patient Classification
- Nursing Workload
- Unit Staffing
- Risk Identification.

POSTSCRIPT

If nurses and their service mediated by informatics is one of the unifying influences in a hospital, the integration of mobile health devices is one of the most disruptive. Even highly skilled people can fall victim to the notion that "we've always done it this way." This disruptive influence, however, can be harnessed to significantly enhance the means to capture new kinds of information in new ways. Chapter 17 describes some these exciting new ways for care of patients, which may transform the way medicine is practiced in the future.

REFERENCES

Berger, A.M., Berger, C.R., 2004. Data mining as a tool for research and knowledge development in nursing. Comput. Inform. Nurs. 22 (3), 123–131.

Collins, S.A., Cato, K., Albers, D., Scott, K., Stetson, PD, Bakken, S, Vawdrey, D.K., 2013. Relationship between nursing documentation and patients' mortality. Am. J. Crit. Care. 22 (4), 306–313.

Cook, S.E., 1942. The Life of Florence Nightingale. MacMillan & Co. Ltd, London.

Cuthbert, J.P., Corrigan, J.D., Harrison-Felix, C., Coronado, V., Dijkers, M.P., Heinemann, A.W., et al., 2011. Factors that predict acute hospitalization discharge disposition for adults with moderate to severe traumatic brain injury. Arch. Phys. Med. Rehabil. 92 (5), 721−730.

Dowding, D.W., Currie, L.M., Borycki, E., Clamp, S., Favela, J., Fitzpatrick, G., et al., 2013. International priorities for research in nursing informatics for patient care. Stud. Health Technol. Inform. 192, 372−376.

Görges, M., Westenskow, D.R., Kück, K., Orr, J.A., 2010. A tool predicting future mean arterial blood pressure values improves the titration of vasoactive drugs. J. Clin. Monit. Comput. 24 (3), 223−235.

Hanrahan, K., McCarthy, A.M., Kleiber, C., Ataman, K., Street, W.N., Zimmerman, M.B., et al., 2012. Building a computer program to support children, parents, and distraction during healthcare procedures. Comput. Inform. Nurs. 30 (10), 554−561.

Harper, E.M., 2012. Staffing based on evidence: can health information technology make it possible? Nurs. Econ. 30 (5), 262−267, 281.

Hyun, S., Bakken, S., Douglas, K., Stone, P.W., 2008. Evidence-based staffing: potential roles for informatics. Nurs. Econ. 26 (3), 151−158, 173.

Koch, S.H., Weir, C., Haar, M., Staggers, N., Agutter, J., Görges, M., et al., 2012. Intensive care unit nurses' information needs and recommendations for integrated displays to improve nurses' situation awareness. J. Am. Med. Inform. Assoc. 19 (4), 583−590.

Koch, S.H., Weir, C., Westenskow, D., Gondan, M., Agutter, J., Haar, M., et al., 2013. Evaluation of the effect of information integration in displays for ICU nurses on situation awareness and task completion time: a prospective randomized controlled study. Int. J. Med. Inform. 82 (8), 665−675.

Lee, T.T., Lin, K.C., Mills, M.E., Kuo, Y.H., 2012. Factors related to the prevention and management of pressure ulcers. Comput. Inform. Nurs. 30 (9), 489−495.

Matney, S.A., Maddox, L.J., Staggers, N., 2014. Nurses as knowledge workers: is there evidence of knowledge in patient handoffs? West. J. Nurs. Res. 36 (2), 171−190.

Moen, A., Mæland Knudsen, L.M., 2013. Nursing informatics: decades of contribution to health informatics. Healthc. Inform. Res. 19 (2), 86−92.

Oh, H.S., Seo, W.S., 2013. Development of a decision tree analysis model that predicts recovery from acute brain injury. Jpn. J. Nurs. Sci. 10 (1), 89−97.

Scholes, M., Barber, B., 1976. The role of computers in nursing. Nurs. Mirror Midwives J. 143 (13), 46−48.

Sharifi, F., Ghaderpanahi, M., Fakhrzadeh, H., Mirarefin, M., Badamchizadeh, Z., Tajalizadekhoob, Y., et al., 2012. Older people's mortality index: development of a practical model for prediction of mortality in nursing homes (Kahrizak Elderly Study). Geriatr. Gerontol. Int. 12 (1), 36−45.

Staggers, N., Blaz, J., 2013. Research on nursing handoffs for medical and surgical settings: an integrative review. J. Adv. Nurs. 69 (2), 1365−2648.

van der Zwaluw, C.S., Valentijn, S.A., Nieuwenhuis-Mark, R., Rasquin, S.M., van Heugten, C.M., 2011. Cognitive functioning in the acute phase poststroke: a predictor of discharge destination? J. Stroke Cerebrovasc. Dis. 20 (6), 549−555.

Williams, L.M., Hubbard, K.E., Daye, O., Barden, C., 2012. Telenursing in the intensive care unit: transforming nursing practice. Crit. Care Nurs. 32 (6), 62−69.

Chapter 17

The Predictive Potential of Connected Digital Health

Chapter Outline

Practical Predictive Analytics and Decisioning Systems for Medicine. DOI: http://dx.doi.org/10.1016/B978-0-12-411643-6.00045-4

PREAMBLE

Buying things used to be location-specific; that is, you went to a "brick-and-mortar" establishment to purchase them. The retail business domain is in the midst of turmoil associated with a significant change in this business model, instigated by online retailers such as Amazon.com. In 2013, the number of online purchases eclipsed those in a specific location for the first time in history. Online banking and financial services (i.e., investment management) has become the predominant medium for doing business in the financial world. The question posed by this chapter is: Are we at the beginning of a similar revolution in mobile health care? The answer provided by this chapter is: Yes. The evidence for this revolution, the dimensions of it, and the vast potential of predictive analytics in the practice of it are among the issues discussed in this chapter. Hold on to your hat; a mobile future is coming.

Mobile connected health devices and applications are proving to be one of the most disruptive forces within health care — but this disruption is moving health care in new, exciting directions. These "bring your own device" technologies are generally smaller, faster, better, and cheaper than many traditional products. They enable democratization of health care, with the patient performing more self-diagnostics and self-care with adequate levels of safety, security, and satisfaction. With the development of a healthcare-centered democracy, we have seen an explosion in the volume and velocity of patient-generated data. This development has become a driving force in the connection of digital health records to each other, and to diagnosis and treatment practitioners. The volume of patient-generated data and their digital format provide hints that point to the promise and potential of what predictive analytics will be able to do if we can harness this torrent of bits and bytes. Unfortunately, many people are sounding warnings and declaring an unwillingness to participate in what appears to be a revolution in the practice of medicine. The clinical community has been especially wary. In order to support and promote this digital transformation in health care, we must understand initially why the clinical community has these reservations. Then, we must describe and demonstrate the power of the type of predictive analytics emerging from these new mobile and connected technologies, and apply the teachings from other industries that have already withstood and survived this data tsunami. Finally, we must show how this process is likely to unfold, and the value it can deliver.

WHY DON'T CLINICIANS EMBRACE DIGITAL CONSUMER CONNECTIONS?

Most consumers, medical device and pharmaceutical companies, and many other healthcare IT professionals assume that clinicians want more data and embrace the accelerating data explosion. They believe that more data will lead to further analysis and greater insights, as well as more personalized and individualized care; more data will transform medicine from an anecdotal practice to one providing more accurate and precise predictions. Greater accuracy in predictions will promote correct diagnosis and treatment; greater precision will enable the application of this practice to much finer levels of distinction. These two factors, working together, will encourage the development of a more analytical medical practice. Greater availability of data and associated analytical techniques will enable the emergence of new analytics-based medicine, in a manner similar to that in other business domains (e.g., Retail, Travel, Energy, Media, Banking & Finance, and e-Commerce). Greater accuracy and precision of predictions in medicine will enable providers to deliver four key predicting capabilities that answer the key questions necessary for the radical transformation of the cost, quality, and access to care we so desperately seek:

1. Who is at risk for future healthcare problems?
2. When and where will such a problem occur?
3. What is the best solution to prevent, intervene in, or ameliorate the problem?
4. How long does a mitigation strategy need to remain in place?

So, why isn't the medical profession running to embrace the future of precision medicine?

Our research reveals that clinicians have seven primary reservations regarding the value and potential of patient-generated data that result from mobile sensors, devices, and applications, and which are becoming the key to the application of big data analytics for creating predictive capabilities.

The huge potential of analytical medicine begs the question: Why aren't medical professionals anxious to embrace the future of it? Based on discussions with many medical professionals, we suggest seven primary barriers to the adoption of analytical medicine. These barriers can be expressed in the form of questions.

What are the seven reservations? They are as follows:

1. What do I do with the data?
2. Who says that the data are valuable?

3. What new liabilities emerge from precision and probabilistic medicine?
4. How cumbersome and difficult are new data collection solutions?
5. How do the devices and apps integrate and interoperate?
6. How do you maintain privacy and security with mobile consumer engagement?
7. How and when will clinicians get paid for participating in mobile health?

1. What Do I Do with the Data?

No Training

This is not a trivial question. No medical school has trained, or currently trains, doctors on the sources and uses of patient-generated data. There are only a handful of continuing medical education (CME) courses that address mobile health technologies and their uses. Without training, we cannot expect physicians and other clinicians to know what to do with this new data source.

No Time

Many medical device companies assume that if they provide the data to clinicians, the clinicians will be able to shift through them, analyze them, and develop insights and understanding that could improve patient care. But the business model of a medical practice does not allow for this type of analytical activity. The average physician has 2,500 patients, sees 30 or more patients a day, and spends 5−10 minutes with each patient during a visit. In extreme cases, a physician may see as many as 90 patients a day and rely on a scribe for recording and data entry. Until recently, all patient data were in paper form and therefore not easily accessible for analysis and manipulation. We have never created a medical model to enable, allow, and reward this type of analytical rigor.

No Money

Perhaps most importantly, the current business model has no revenue source tied to detailed analytics, and consequently the practice has no analyst role such as we see in many other industries, where junior talent uses spreadsheets to do rigorous data analytics to create insights that generate more revenues. In other industries, the analyst role provides an apprentice-like training of staff in the fundamentals required for future management. But this is neither how medical practice has emerged, nor how it is compensated. Although the Accreditation Council for Graduate Medical Education (ACGME) has mandated a data project focused on quality improvement tied to re-credentialing, the analysis process is not standardized, and there is no financial remuneration directly tied to its completion.

No Space

None of the electronic health record (EHR) formats offered currently in the market is designed to accept and integrate standardized patient-generated data. Consequently, even if a clinician wanted to gather and use the data, there is no existing technology to do this effectively. Although this practice is not technologically difficult to accomplish, it was never anticipated; therefore, it was not included in the design format of EHR applications. Although there may be ways of including these practices in a limited way, these "band-aid" approaches make it difficult to store and retrieve data for use in the practice of medicine. Until this information is integrated into the clinical workflow in a meaningful way, it will provide little value.

2. Who Says That the Data Are Valuable?

Useful Data

The underlying assumption is that these data are valuable. This may be true for some data, but it may not be true for much other data. Most data in most industries pertain to normal situations, and may support few insights and changes in behavior and action. However, it is the body of exceptional data that may highlight dangers, inflections, transitions, and warnings which may provide useful insights and value. As a result, many clinicians are skeptical of the value of normative data. An answer-oriented medical record with predictive responses may be a better strategy to follow than filling up EHRs with mountains of normal patient data.

Scientific Method

Physicians are trained as scientists and, by nature, they are skeptical of claims that do not follow the scientific method for drawing conclusions. The FDA follows this process in approving drugs and devices. CMS (Centers for Medicare and Medicaid Services) and other payers are applying this approach increasingly in their definitions and declarations of evidenced-based medicine. Responsible clinicians want to see long-term longitudinal, double-blinded, and randomized controlled studies, which demonstrate that mobile health technologies provide appropriate clinical outcomes and reductions in healthcare costs with improved access to care. To date, there have been very few studies like these. The evidence is still forthcoming.

Long Timeframe

In the pharmaceutical and medical device industries, the level of scientific rigor and FDA processing requires 3–10 years to move a new drug or device into the market. Yet the mobile health and consumer connected technology market is less than 10 years old. It is unlikely to provide the traditional type of scientific analysis necessary to meet the standards of traditional medicine.

Peer Review

The peer review process is the gold standard in medicine used to validate new technologies in health care, and it adds 3–5 years to the time it takes to disseminate new knowledge. As many as a dozen years are required after that before an established best practice emerges, though peer reviewed research can be applied regularly and practiced across the medical field.

Accelerated Learning

This new field of health care is less than 10 years old, and it is changing at an exponential pace each year. The relatively slow-paced research methods of the past cannot keep pace with the accelerating rate of innovation happening at present. Some of the studies published in 2013 that looked back at mobile health solutions during the previous decade suggested that mobile health applications were not necessarily safe, effective, and efficient (Tomlinson *et al.*, 2013). A detailed analysis of these studies, however, suggested that most of the applications they reviewed were part of research that pre-dated the launch of the iPhone in 2007 and other ubiquitous Web devices, and the avalanche of apps that followed. So, one might ask, what type of relevance has such a study in today's world?

3. What New Liabilities Emerge from Precision and Probabilistic Medicine?

Litigation Risk

The US healthcare industry is the most litigious in the world. It is estimated that malpractice insurance and claims add 1% (*Wall Street Journal*, 2009) in direct costs to the system, and add an additional 26–34% (Jackson Healthcare, n.d.) in the form of unnecessary tests and procedures where physicians must practice defensive medicine to avoid malpractice claims. The US rate of cesarean births is 50% higher than the average in Europe (Darkins *et al.*, 2008), largely to mitigate the liability associated with perinatal complications. The fear is that new data would provide litigious attorneys with additional fodder for law suits.

Data Quality

The advent of a plethora of new data types coming from patient treatments exposes clinicians to many kinds of new risks. These risks post new questions:

1. Did the patient collect data appropriately?
2. Was it actually the patient's data, or did the patient allow another family member to use the device?
3. Did the patient fudge the figures in order to cause the clinician to think he or she was compliant and within range?

Clinicians may not have a problem with collecting and warehousing data collected by their staff in their clinical environment, but are highly skeptical of doing the same with data collected by patients at home.

Data Vigilance

Most of the data gathered are rather normal in character, with only occasional aberrations. Therefore, the challenge is to find the "signal" amid a lot of "noise" (un-useful data). This process requires constant vigilance and active monitoring of detailed data inputs. The absence of this constant and detailed information today insulates the clinicians from risk. Many unknown health risks may be related to data that are not measured. Clinicians fear that, with the volumes of new patient-generated data, they will be held accountable for not predicting risky outcomes. Data vigilance places unrealistic expectations on the physician. How can a physician comb through the mountains of anticipated data generated to identify indicators of adverse events?

Probabilistic Predictions

Analysis is at the heart of the promise of precision medicine. Clinicians should be able to mine big data repositories and make predictions that lead to measuring probabilities of what can happen, how to mitigate it, and how to manage it. The legal precedence for this analysis is uncertain. Clinicians are justifiably more comfortable making decisions without all this information and without applying probabilities to big data analytics, because to them professional opinion matters more than raw data. But once we move to precision medicine, the numbers tell the story and take a lot of the professional judgment out of the process. How will juries react? For example, will a physician experience decreased liability risk if they prescribe a drug or perform a procedure that has a 98% chance of success for patients with a unique genomic profile, presenting unique symptoms, and a specific history? Or will the jury find fault since there was a 2% chance that the physician's actions could lead to harm? The new black box warnings from the FDA often deal with fairly low risk levels. The physician response has been largely to avoid prescribing these medications if an acceptable alternative exists.

Transparency Risks

It is ironic that, from a liability perspective, clinicians prefer the world of today that lacks the new scientific rigor promised by big data and transparency. Once hospitals start collecting quality measures, many more quality errors and problems appear as systems are subjected to greater analysis. While measuring these risks may lead to reducing adverse events, in the near term the improved transparency will show dramatic "perceived" increased risk to the healthcare system. In fact the risk is the same; it is now just revealed, as opposed to being invisible or unknown, as it was in the past.

Creation of Hypochondriacs

With this greater transparency, there is a concern that patients will use and misuse this information to become "worried worts," or even hypochondriacs. Clinicians are not sure that patients can handle the unfiltered truth regarding healthcare risks, especially with an abundance of new data and information. Will they become overly concerned about their health and increase their demands on the healthcare system? Will they take actions that will actually put them at greater risks than if they had not been aware of the risks to begin with?

4. How Cumbersome and Difficult Are New Data Collection Solutions?

Various approaches can be followed to generate new data for healthcare solutions.

Lack of Solutions

Too often, technology vendors create products and services but not solutions. They often provide their technologies to providers, and expect the clinicians individually to figure out where and how they are useful. The provider has to then determine which is the best technology, create the integration and interoperability of the various disparate parts, bundle all this into a solution, and deploy, manage, and maintain the various pieces of technology. Especially in information technology-rich applications, this is more than most clinicians want to, or can, do.

Mimic of the Drug Industry Business Model

When it comes to deploying consumer and patient-oriented mobile health devices and applications, the clinicians want a business model that is as simple as that provided by the drug industry. For example, imagine if the business model of a pharmaceutical company were to invent new drugs, patent them, and then sell a chemistry set to doctors, provide the license to the patented formula to them, and then wish them luck in making as much as they wanted for their patients.

Such a business model would never have enabled the emergence of a multibillion dollar industry. What the drug industry has done is create solutions for specific diseases that are simple and elegant. All the physician has to do is write a prescription for the drug. Almost magically, the rest of the process of supply chain management, retailing, fulfilling, and refilling is taken care of by others without the physician having to raise a finger. Clinicians want this same simple and elegant process for mobile consumer health technology solutions. They want simply to write a prescription and have all the deployment, installation, maintenance, management, call center follow-up, customer service, and refurbishment done by someone else.

Vetting Applications

Clinicians need help in selecting the best solution to prescribe. Initially, their minds are full of questions. Of the nearly 20,000 mobile health applications and devices, which ones are best in class? How do you select the right one to prescribe? What are the criteria for selection? Who has done the rating and ranking? This is where organizations like Happtique have been able to step in and provide the peer review process in evaluating these applications and establishing private label app stores for provider networks where their patients and clinicians can go to find and download the apps that have been pre-approved to address specific needs.

Outsourced Monitoring

Once the patient has the application and device, clinicians need to understand how engaged they need to be in the active monitoring of the patient information. In most cases, the clinician doesn't really want to see a patient's daily glucometer, weight, blood pressure, heart rate, temperature, pulse-oximetry, nutrition, activity, exercise, mood, sleep, or other measures that are now part of the consumer health revolution. Most of these data for most of the patients most of the time are normal and not very interesting or useful. A clinician may want them monitored, but by someone else who will identify aberrations and then attempt to identify the cause and develop corrective actions without practicing medicine. Reminding the patient to do something the physician already has instructed them to do is part of this monitoring. Still, when none of the interventions produces the desired result, the physician is notified.

Business Models

In surveys done by PwC on barriers to adoption of mobile health solutions, one of the gaps cited most commonly is the lack of successful business models. Innovators and entrepreneurs experiment continually to invent new business models that will address the various barriers and provide solutions that address the "five Cs" of a value proposition:

- Cost — how does the offering reduce the administrative, operating, or clinical costs of care?
- Convenience — how does the offering decrease time, eliminate the need to travel for a visit, or make it easier to address healthcare needs?
- Confidence — how does the offering improve quality, increase adherence, or change behaviors among patient, clinician, family members, and others?
- Compensation — how does the clinician make money by providing this offering; is it through new services, a higher reimbursement level, better margins, or higher patient volumes?
- Character — what is the branding, style, and design of the offering, and how do these make you feel and think about its use and application?

5. How Do the Devices and Apps Integrate and Interoperate?

Getting systems to integrate and work together is crucial for developing and using these systems to address the complexity of issues in any medical outcome.

Closed Systems

One of the greatest frustrations among clinicians comes from the closed business model strategy that medical device companies create to force the providers to lock in to a specific vendor's solution set. They create apps and devices that only integrate and interoperate with those made by a single vendor, or those that are part of the vendor's narrow and tightly controlled business ecosystem. This increases costs for the provider, decreases flexibility, and forces clinicians to remain with a solution long after it has become obsolete due to new technology.

Open Systems

Providers in health care want the same thing enjoyed by consumers in consumer electronics and the computer industry − open access. A relatively open architecture enables a variety of choice among similar technologies that can interoperate with products from many vendors. A closed system locks users into specific technologies via the proprietary tools and interfaces of specific vendors. Such closed systems do not integrate or interoperate well with other systems.

Workflow Integration

In addition, the providers want solutions that have been designed with the patient and clinician in mind, which are seamlessly integrated into the lifestyle and workflow of the user. They require minimal disruption of integration and interoperability. These tools are expected to cause these disruptions only when implementing changes which can lead to significant improvements in outcomes and performance. For example, Apple and Google pioneered new touch-screen navigation practices that required some time and effort to learn and get used to − but these new practices eliminated the need for keyboards, stylus, and other tools required previously to interact with a computer or smartphone screen. The benefit of such a disruption in use has far outweighed the cost of integration disruption while implementing it.

Data Freedom

Too often, medical technology vendors have viewed the data created by the devices as belonging to them. Providers have also viewed patient data that the clinician collects as belonging to the clinician, not the patient. What this has done is create data silos with incomplete data held by many different organizations and individuals that is not shared in a useful way. Currently, there is a movement towards patient ownership of data related to their health, combined with a more open and integrated approach to collection and sharing of these data. The birth of health information exchanges is evidence of patient ownership and broad-based sharing of this information to the patient's advantage. Key to this type of open sharing are standards for interoperability among devices, applications, and healthcare systems.

6. How Do You Maintain Privacy and Security with Mobile Consumer Engagement?

Some Safeguards are in Place

In surveys on consumer health privacy and security, we find that consumers are not as concerned about these issues as HIPAA might lead you to believe. Patients are happy to share their personal health information as long as they make the decision about who benefits from it. This benefit may be related to them personally, to someone else, or to a cause they believe in. Sharing of health information is not the issue; it is who it is shared with that matters. Consumers are comfortable with the safeguards for data security and privacy adopted in other industries, such as banking, to protect their healthcare information.

Risks are Low

Consumers are very concerned about inappropriate sharing of information that could embarrass them, impact their employment, or challenge their healthcare coverage and services. During the past few years, Congress has passed laws that protect consumers from untoward actions by employers or insurance companies based upon genetic or other health information. In addition, patients and consumers do not bear any personal financial liability if their healthcare identity is stolen and used to create fraudulent charges. This means that the one remaining issue of privacy and security concerns revelations of healthcare procedures or highly personal issues (e.g., HIV, pregnancy, cosmetic surgery), which can have significant impacts on other aspects of their lives (such as employment).

Follow the Money

Of general concern is that the risk of inadvertent or malicious exposure increases as more of this information is converted from written format in files of a physician's office to digital format in office computers and personal monitoring devices. Our most sensitive financial information, our financial identity, is protected with appropriate privacy and security, as that entire industry moves to mobile access and applications. Perhaps health care can follow a similar model with similar or enhanced results?

7. How and When Will Clinicians Get Paid for Participating in Mobile Health?

It's More Than Money

This barrier is not placed last on the list because it is of least importance, but because too often it is viewed as being the most important concern. The thinking often goes, "If only payers paid doctors to participate in mobile health plans, then they and their patients would readily adopt it." However, as the previous six points have highlighted, clinicians have many other barriers to overcome in the adoption of mobile health, and merely paying for them to adopt this new practice of medicine does not address the others.

Money Matters

Some may argue that if payment were available, then clinicians would become more proficient in addressing these barriers in order to expedite the payment for new practices based upon mobile technologies. This argument appears to be logically sound and has precedence in other areas of medicine, but it obscures issues of timing, process, and sequencing.

PROMISE AND PROBLEMS OF SHIFTING TO MOBILE HEALTH TECHNOLOGY

Shifting to Mobile Health Technology May Not Lead to Additional Revenue

Payers don't want to pay for the old way of practicing medicine plus additional payments for a new mobile practice. The new approach seems like nothing more than an incremental cost on top of the existing system. Payers want to move to mobile health because of its promise to decrease the total cost of care for patients. Such a rationale suggests that they would expect to pay much less to clinicians for providing services the old way, and also less for providing them through the new mobile approach. This "lose−lose" proposition would create a virtual incentive for clinicians to abandon the traditional way of providing care with the lowest reimbursement and moving to the new mobile care paradigm that, while paying less than that with the previous approach, would pay more than the traditional alternatives. Under this assumption, the only way that a clinician could make the same amount of money would be by increasing volumes and/or changing the payer mix of patients and procedures − something that clinicians are not excited to do.

Mobile Disruption

Mobile health technology is one of the most disruptive forces in medicine. It disrupts the current incumbent business models and payment structures, and powers the creative destruction of Schumpeter's innovation cycle (see Figures 17.1−17.3 to get a better understanding of Schumpeter's concept).

This means that most of today's clinicians will not readily embrace this new painful and difficult change that forces them to transform the way they service patients and earn a living. For this reason, new market entrants, like Walmart, Walgreens, and CVS, enter the primary care area by leveraging new business models and mobile technology to deliver a more attractive value proposition to payers and patients.

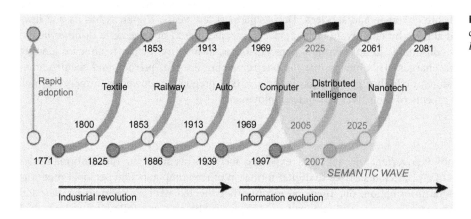

FIGURE 17.1 Schumpeter's innovation cycle. *Source: Norman Poire, Merrill Lynch, based on Joseph Schumpeter.*

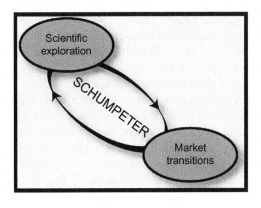

FIGURE 17.2 Schumpeter's innovation cycle.

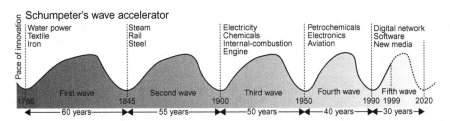

FIGURE **17.3** Schumpeter's innovation cycle.

Consumer Health

Healthcare reforms can force patients increasingly to become consumers so that they have more "skin in the game" by paying higher deductibles and using Health Savings Accounts. As consumers, patients care more about outcomes, costs, and the value they receive from their providers. This new vigilance forces providers to measure quality and patient satisfaction in order to attract and retain customers. Consumers want to have the same purchasing experience using mobile technology in health care that they have in travel, media, and online shopping.

Outcomes Matter

Payers, whether they be employers, insurance companies, governments or consumers, want to know if they are receiving what they paid for. They want quantifiable outcomes that are tied to the value they receive. This has a ripple effect so that it applies to not only providers but also to pharmaceutical and medical technology companies. Part of the power of mobile is the ability to capture patient and consumer data associated with their health activities and outcomes that supports the need for validating value. This approach is requiring providers and others in the healthcare ecosystem to find ways to harness mobile sensors, devices, and smartphones to capture information that will be critical to their future payment.

WHAT CAN WE LEARN FROM THE VA ABOUT THE POTENTIAL OF PREDICTIONS?

In the United States, no organization has shown a more powerful commitment to mobile health adoption and analytics than the Department of Veterans Affairs (the VA). The VA is the second largest government department after the Department of Defense, and manages a $100Bn budget with 300,000 employees. Half of the budget and nearly all the employees are part of the Veterans Health Administration (VHA), which delivers health benefits and services to 8.3 million patients per year (of which 5.3 million are unique patients) through 152 medical centers and 1,400 community clinics. Being an early and rapid adopter of mobile health solutions, the VHA represents half of the 300,000 chronic disease remote patient-monitoring patients in the USA. It has awarded contracts for $1.4Bn to technology vendors for devices and services, and has published the most comprehensive studies on the costs and benefits of deploying mobile health and remote patient monitoring across multiple chronic diseases, geographies, and socio-demographics.

The VHA has grown its telehealth and remote patient monitoring from an initial program of 2,000 patients in 2003, to over 150,000 in 2012. It provides services primarily to men between the ages of 50 and 90 years of age, with specific disease programs addressing diabetes (48%), hypertension (40%), CHF (25%), COPD (12%), and mental health ($\sim$5%). Two-thirds of these patients had a single condition, while the remainder had two or more conditions to be treated. Half of these were in distinctly rural locations, 30% were in urban ones, and the remainder in semi-rural areas. About 90% of patients who were offered this form of care eagerly accepted the increased convenience and control they experienced in their care, which generated a level of 86% patient satisfaction for these services (Darkins *et al.*, 2008).

The annual cost to deploy these programs is $1,600 per patient per year, compared to over $13,000 for traditional home-based care and over $77,000 for nursing home care. The key economic benefit from the cost avoidance associated with telehealth and mobile health remote monitoring services has led to a 25% reduction in the number of bed days of care and a 19% reduction in hospital admissions. The benefits are not the same among all disease conditions, because solutions differ by type of disease and level of acuteness. (*Note*: acuity is synonymous with acuteness in medical circles, but in society at large, acuity refers to a visual characteristic.) For example, the reduction in hospitalization for mental health patients exceeds 40%, while reductions for CHF (congestive heart failure) and hypertension range from 25% to 30%, and for diabetes and COPD average about 20%.

Cost−benefit analyses by the VHA have determined that an investment of $1,600 per patient per annum in its program can enable a call center nurse or social worker to use analytics to predict and prevent expensive emergency department visits and hospitalizations, which can cost in excess of $16,000 per patient per event. The VHA determined that this $1,600 investment decreases average costs by over $6,500 per year, averaged across its entire population, producing an ROI of 4:1. Cost savings were even greater for the patient segment of "frequent flyers" − the 5% of patients that represent 30% of the costs.

The VHA's unparalleled success with its telehealth program has led the UK's National Health System to specifically reference the VHA's work as the example they wish to follow in their 3millionlives and Whole Systems Demonstrator projects to address similar fundamental challenges, including:

1. More patients − a rapidly aging population needing greater healthcare services;
2. Fewer healthcare professionals − shortages of healthcare professionals and an inability to deliver the same type of care to a larger population without a transformation in the practice of medicine
3. Insufficient healthcare facilities − shortage of hospital or institutional facilities and budget constraints for building more
4. Budget shortages − few resources to finance healthcare services like those provided in the past, and
5. A complex adaptive system − deploying transformational change in a complex system among diverse, semi-independent, and autonomous agents (doctors, hospitals, patients, etc.).

Dr. Adam Darkins (Chief Consultant for Telehealth Services at the VHA) has pointed out that the VHA (and indeed all healthcare systems in the world) have the same challenges, although the VHA began to experience them and address them earlier than most (author's interview with Dr. Darkins, March 24, 2011). He points out that nothing short of a revolution in the delivery of care will enable us to address these issues. The connected technologies we have and deploy through mobile health can enable us to change workflow, medical practice, and healthcare economics. Now, we can move most of future health care associated with prevention and chronic disease management into the home, where a patient's vital signs and activity are monitored by call-center health professionals using sophisticated analytics to predict and prevent medical mishaps. He observed that acute episodes that require hospitalization will continue to occur, but treatment of these acute episodes comprises 75% of our healthcare costs associated with chronic disease management, and most hospitals were not designed to manage such a high volume of these diseases. The support infrastructure in most hospitals is inappropriate for managing most of the costs of our healthcare systems; therefore, a new model of healthcare delivery is needed. This new model is a home-based mobile system that is more consumer-centric and harnesses the cooperative power of patients and family members. VHA experience has shown that these mobile home-based systems of health care can improve the quality of outcomes, increase patient satisfaction, and function simultaneously to decrease costs significantly.

Dr. Darkins maintains that the VHA's impressive achievements have been hard won, and they required significant rethinking of the approach to health care in a large system. He sees the VHA as a complex adaptive system that cannot be forced to adopt these new medical practices purely through command and control measures. As a student of complexity theory, he has designed the VHA's system in a way that enables the emergence of new practices across the system in an organic manner by providing key enablers to support the transformation of the system. The VHA has found that offering merely to pay providers for offering these services does not assure that providers will deliver them. These enablers must address the seven barriers described, which are common among the VHA and all other provider systems.

Only after addressing the seven barriers to the adoption of analytical medicine (discussed above) was the VHA able to engage 150,000 patients with a mobile health system, and achieve the impressive clinical and financial outcomes cited above. This success set the stage for continued mobile health adoption and innovations, which include the following initiatives:

1. Issuing and running IT Innovation Challenges and selecting the top 26 best IT innovations
2. Enabling clinicians to use mobile devices in all VHA facilities
3. Partnering with the Continua Health Alliance to promote standards for mobile health interoperability
4. Providing cloud-based services for clinician collaboration
5. Opening the VHA app store for clinicians and patients to download mobile apps
6. A new diabetes mobile health remote patient monitoring program
7. Purchasing 100,000 iPads
8. Issuing a new study showing that remote monitoring decreased mortality by 45%
9. Launching a new telepsychiatry program
10. Local press releases by regional VHA providers indicating cost and clinical benefits of mobile health
11. Eliminating co-pays for mobile health services
12. Launching an iPhone EHR app
13. Launching home (mobile health care?) as the hospital program
14. Upgrading wifi capabilities.

Dr. Darkins believes that other public and private healthcare systems can learn a lot from the VHA's experience. He observed that when they began their remote monitoring programs in 2005, and gained early success, many people said, "If the VHA can do this, then any one can do this." In the interim, other programs have "stubbed their toes" trying to replicate the VHA system. The common sentiment has changed to say that "only the VHA could do something like this." He disagrees with both statements. He believes that there is no choice of whether or not to adopt a mobile health design — it is a requirement for future survival. He believes that all healthcare systems can learn from the VHA and become successful in developing such programs, if they apply the enablers to overcome the barriers. By doing so, access to and quality of service will improve, while costs decline.

WHAT CAN WE LEARN FROM FINANCIAL SERVICES REGARDING DIGITAL TRANSFORMATION?

Health care has notoriously been 5–15 years behind other industries in adopting information technology. This delay has resulted in healthcare services being less efficient, less effective, and less safe than services in most other industries. As a late adopter, health care can learn from the mistakes of other industries as it charts the course of its own digital transformation. In particular, the financial services industry can provide many lessons that can benefit the healthcare industry as it moves forward in this transformation.

It is amazing that you can use an ATM card to get money from a machine anywhere in the world. We have the ability to access online our checking and savings accounts at a bank, and our insurance, mutual funds, stocks, mortgages, credit cards, and car loans, without ever going to a physical location. Some of this interaction can be done even on your smartphone with considerable safety and security.

The promise of these future benefits of mobile health care raises several questions:

1. Can health care really function like that?
2. Can healthcare information be stored online and accessed through a consumer portal like banks provide?
3. Can healthcare services be provided online?
4. Will mobile personal healthcare apps become available to allow access to all required healthcare services as easily as can be done with mobile banking?

Before jumping to any conclusions in the answers to these questions for health care, it is necessary to understand some of the history of how our digital financial services industry has emerged during the past half century.

The Rise of Mobile Financial Services

At the dawn of the information technology (IT) revolution in the early 1970s, banks began investing heavily in IT to provide the necessary security, standardization, and efficiencies required by government regulations for their operations.

At the same time, banks noticed that their clients were moving abroad and engaging in more international business, which required cash management and treasury functions in multiple currencies and locations around the world. Initial attempts to follow these clients and provide these services led to the development of point solutions with individual banks. Each bank would create a direct IT link, or digital pipe, with every other bank to share data and information about money transfers, deposits, and other financial services. Banks quickly realized that they couldn't afford to have direct and individual digital pipes into every bank in the process chain. To decrease costs and improve security a consortium of large banks created the Society for Worldwide Interbank Financial Telecommunication (SWIFT), charged with providing a common infrastructure, messaging, standards, and protocols for transferring money around the world. Today, SWIFT has 9,000 members and transacts over $2 trillion every day (SWIFT, n.d.).

Twenty years later, banking in most countries was still a very local business — much like health care is today. In the United States, banks were national in name only; interstate banking transactions were awkward. In some states, such as Iowa, banking transactions could not cross county lines, let alone state boundaries. In the 1970s, banks provided three primary services: (1) they provided checking accounts; (2) they provided savings accounts; and (3) they lent out your money to businesses for commercial loans. No banks provided the array of financial services you can get today. Through two decades of changes in federal regulations, many mergers and innovation among banks, savings and loan institutions, insurance companies, brokerage firms, and mortgage companies developed the financial supermarkets that provide the complex array of products and services available today.

In the 1980s and early 1990s, banks extended this common IT infrastructure to enable the emergence of a global ATM system. The ATM system started with individual banks providing their own devices and then partnering with neighboring banks in their local market to share ATM infrastructure. This partnering grew into regional systems like NYCE in New York City, multi-regional systems like Cirrus on the East Coast, and then national ATM systems. Today we have global ATM networks that can dispense cash in any currency using credit, debit, and smart cards in hundreds of countries.

Here are a few key insights into the digital financial transformation we need to understand before we can figure out what we can learn from banking to apply to our emerging digital healthcare system.

1. It has taken a long time — financial digital transformation has taken nearly five decades
2. Follow the customer — banks followed their customer's global migration and demands with digital financial services that customers were willing to pay for eventually, but which were largely free at first
3. It was transparent — no government set the standards for bank digital information interoperability; banks created these systems organically through cooperation and partnership to solve a common need
4. Financial information is simple — while there is a very large volume of digital financial transactions, the information itself is quite simple to describe as debits, credits, in various currencies, interest rates, sizes, maturity, and other financial services
5. Comprehensive relationship — nearly every financial transaction is captured by your bank, even cash purchases in stores being reflected in patterns of cash withdrawals.

How Do These Five Insights from the Digitization of the Financial Services Industry Inform Our Views About the Digitization of Healthcare Information?

Timing of Digital Transformation

Prior to the 2009 American Recovery Act (ARA), less than 20% of physicians, hospitals, and other healthcare providers had digital healthcare information systems. As a result of the $20 billion in net rewards and penalties associated with the adoption of electronic health records, adoption was expected to exceed 44% by 2012 — triple the level seen in 2009 (Charles et al., 2013). According to the Robert Wood Johnson Foundation, this figure topped out at 42% by the end of 2012 (Mathematica Policy Research et al., 2013). In essence, the healthcare industry is where the banking industry was over 40 years ago. Even if health care moves at three times the pace of financial services in leveraging digital information, it could take a decade before we see the type of data sharing common between banks. The difference in health care, though, is the rapid timetable for conversion to digital format required by the Affordable Care Act (ACA). This impetus may shorten the development time considerably.

Local Customer Pull

Health care is perhaps the most regional and local of all industries. Few people will travel long distances to get care, and they rarely need their healthcare information beyond the boundaries of their local community. There is virtually no pull by the consumer or healthcare providers to share information across state or country borders, like we have seen in banking. This localization is why efforts to create state-wide health information exchanges (HIEs) or national digital healthcare information sharing systems may not be sustainable. The HIEs that focus on local and regional markets have gained some traction, and have succeeded because they follow the patients, but larger systems have few takers. In addition, private systems have been more successful than public systems because the organizations sponsoring them have a strong value proposition associated with decreasing costs, improving access, and increasing quality.

Emerging Dominance

With the focus of the ACA on creating accountable care organizations (ACOs), we have seen significant consolidation among providers and between providers and payers across the country. This consolidation has led to significant dominance among these organizations in geographic markets, where there may be only three or four choices of healthcare provider systems. At this time a competitive market does not exist in healthcare services like it does in financial services, where no US bank has more than a 10% market share. The lack of market dominance and power in banking, forces banks to cooperate and share information. With dominant market positions emerging across all healthcare markets, providers are less willing to share information, and they view sharing as a competitive threat rather than an advantage.

Healthcare Digital Complexity

For every patient encounter a health provider will use several five-digit ICD-9 codes, of which there are presently over 15,000, to describe what was diagnosed; the USA will be moving to ICD-10 in the next few years. ICD-10 will require providers to use 68,000 seven-digit codes to describe the same diagnosis tree but in more detail. Then, a health provider must select one of the 68,000 ICD codes and one of over 8,800 CPT codes (an additional five-digit code) to justify reimbursement for providing services to treat health problems. Financial transactions are much simpler: banks need only about 20 different parameters to describe financial transactions, versus thousands for health care. In addition, EHRs include significant clinical comments and annotations from clinicians in non-structured data, which are notoriously difficult to mine and use in analytical systems. This complexity has created an entire industry focused just on coding, scrubbing codes, and rejecting and paying claims. The difficulty in creating transactionally relevant information in health care is without precedent.

Digital Data Capture

Until recently, patients had almost *no* digital healthcare information. With the adoption of EHRs, infrequent physician and hospital visits will produce digital data records of pulse, heart rate, weight, blood pressure, temperature, and other medical measures. However, this information is only captured once or a few times a year. This schedule would not create a very useful banking report, if transactions could be conducted only by a personal visit to the bank and only received information from these in-person visits. Just as your bank captures all your financial transactions every day with no requirement to visit your bank, we need the ability to capture all our health information on a daily basis without going to the doctor. We need to capture and create digital information daily from such things as diet, activity, vital signs, medical information, and other daily functions. Capturing daily digital information is the starting point.

So what does all this mean for the future of digital health technology? The following drivers should lead to the digital transformation of the healthcare industry.

- Consumers will drive the emergence of digital healthcare delivery over the next 10 years, as they become forced to manage more of the financial risks and consequences of their healthcare decisions. We see this emerging with high-deductible health savings accounts, increasing co-pays, and employers moving from-defined benefit to defined contribution in health plan design. In addition, we see the emergence of health insurance exchanges that enable greater choice, but which also have caused some employers to exit the self-insured employer market.
- Mobile devices will enable consumers to generate a large amount of digital information, on a daily basis, from home. The emergence of a wide variety of mobile sensors and devices is beginning to generate large bodies of personal health data, both actively and passively, for both traditional healthcare measures and new ones. This explosion of data will do in health care what it has done in other industries; it will open novel insights into better ways to improve health in multiple dimensions. Data stored in such large amounts are termed "Big Data."
- Big-Data analytics will provide the tools to transform consumer behavior, payer economics, and care delivery. As Big Data has enabled retailers to transform their supply chains, it has powered the predictive retail capabilities in

e-commerce, and enabled auto manufacturers to predict future failures and mitigate those risks; it will do the same in health care. Big Data will enable the prediction and prevention of events that would otherwise increase costs, decrease healthcare outcomes, and limit access to care.

SUMMARY AND RECOMMENDATIONS

Any discussion of mobile health care can generate excitement about the new technology that enables it. This technology alone, however, will not change the world. As we look at the adoption of any revolutionary product over time, we see that there is a long lag between its introduction and any transformation caused by it. This lag occurs because the workflow and practices that existed before the introduction of the new technology must be transformed in order for the new technology to take effect. It took 100 years for the steam engine to become the dominant technology of its day, resulting in the restructuring of society into a system of large industrial centers. In the electric power industry, it took 50 years to modularize production by using small decentralized motors rather than a single large one used in steam power. It took about 20 years for computers to transform information management from centralized processing to the individual computer on a desktop.

It appears that the introduction of each new paradigm decreases the transformation time by half. For that reason, we would expect it might take only a decade for mobile technologies to transform all aspects of society, including health care.

Clearly, there are substantial barriers to overcome, but none is insurmountable. The success in the VA healthcare system has shown that all of these barriers can be addressed in a way that leads to broad-based adoption. And the financial services industry, though different in many ways, provides a good roadmap for the digital transformation that health care must accomplish in order to address its many challenges and requirements in the future.

POSTSCRIPT

Online tax preparation has been a boon for many people; you use Turbo-Tax to prepare your tax return, and file it electronically with the IRS. What a blessing it is for us to be able to do the very complex job of completing our own tax returns. But this capability is also becoming a bane to our government. Fraudsters can use Turbo-Tax to submit bogus tax returns for people whose identity has been stolen online. This type of fraud amounted to about $4 billion in 2011, and it is expected to explode to about $24 billion/year by 2017 (Anonymous, 2014). Chapter 18 describes the coming onslaught of mobile health device data. Could the extensive criminal activity associated with Turbo-Tax fraud morph into mobile health claim fraud in the future? Chapter 19 explores the answer to this question, and some of the broader dimensions of healthcare fraud in America.

REFERENCES

Anonymous, 2014. Bloomberg Businessweek January 13, 2014: 52–56

Charles, D., King, J., Patel, V., Furukawa, M.F., 2013. Adoption of Electronic Health Record Systems among US Non-federal Acute Care Hospitals: 2008–2012. ONC Data Brief No. 9, March 2013. Available at: <www.healthit.gov/sites/default/files/oncdatabrief9final.pdf>.

Darkins, A., Ryan, P., Kobb, R., Foster, L., Edmonson, E., Wakefield, B., et al., 2008. Care Coordination/Home Telehealth: the systematic implementation of health informatics, home telehealth, and disease management to support the care of veteran patients with chronic conditions. Telemed. J. E. Health. 14 (10), 1118–1126.

Jackson Healthcare, n.d. A Costly Defense: Physicians Sound Off on the High Price of Defensive Medicine in the US. Available at: <www.jacksonhealthcare.com/media/8968/defensivemedicine_ebook_final.pdf>.

Mathematica Policy Research, Harvard School of Public Health, Robert Wood Johnson Foundation, 2013. In: DesRoches, C.M., Painter, M.W., Jha, A.K. (Eds.), Health Information Technology in the United States: Better Information Systems for Better Care. Robert Wood Johnson Foundation, Princeton, NJ.

SWIFT, n.d. Swift History, 40 Years. Available at: <www.swift.com/about_swift/company_information/swift_history>.

Tomlinson, M., Rotheram-Borus, M.J., Swartz, L., Tsai, A.C., 2013. Scaling up mHealth: where is the evidence? PLoS Med. Feb 12, 2013. Available at: <www.plosmedicine.org/article/info:doi/10.1371/journal.pmed.1001382>.

Wall Street Journal, 2009. "Tangible and Unseen Health Care Costs", Sep 3, 2009. Available at: <http://online.wsj.com/article/SB125193312967181349.html?mod = djemHL>.

Chapter 18

Healthcare Fraud

Chapter Outline

PREAMBLE

Chapter 18 begins with a discussion of about $700 billion of "improper" medical payments, of which it is estimated that about 20% (about $150 billion) is due to fraud. Therefore, the answer to the question posed at the end of the last chapter is, Yes. Fraud is a major problem in medical payments. Chapter 18 describes various types of medical payment fraud, some challenges in fraud detection in medical payments, and some analytical methods for detecting it.

INTRODUCTION

It is estimated that annual healthcare system expenditures in the United States are approaching $3 trillion (CMS, n.d., a). An examination of the breakdown of healthcare industry costs shows that over 60% result from: hospital care

Practical Predictive Analytics and Decisioning Systems for Medicine. DOI: http://dx.doi.org/10.1016/B978-0-12-411643-6.00046-6

(30%), physician care (20%), and prescription medications (10%). However, it should be noted that, given the enormous level of expenditures, costs associated with services that represent even a relatively small proportion of total costs, such as durable medical equipment (1.5%), amount to billions of dollars of revenue (∼$50 billion) (CMS, n.d., a).

Given the vast amounts of money in play and the high volume transactions, healthcare revenue is an attractive and target-rich environment for those looking to employ fraudulent means to skim money from the system. The sheer volume and velocity of healthcare transactions poses a commensurate challenge to efforts to prevent and detect fraud.

There is another more fundamental attribute of the healthcare payment system that makes it innately attractive and well suited for fraudulent activities. The US healthcare payment system, a complex one involving interactions among the US Government, large private insurers, large providers, durable medical equipment providers, pharmaceutical companies, physicians, a multitude of ancillary heathcare providers, and of course patients, is predominantly a third-party payer system. The percentage of adults in the United States who have some form of health insurance has declined in recent years, but most use a third-party payer model, including seniors (through Medicare) and children (through federal and state benefit programs). In the third-party payer model, some entity distinct from the recipient of health care, be that entity a government program or private insurer, is responsible for paying some or all of the cost of services and medicines provided to the recipient. The payer may be a government entity such as Medicare that is mandated to provide payment. Alternatively, it may be a private insurer that pays part or all of a provider's charges in exchange for the payment of insurance plan premiums by an individual insured or, more commonly, by an employer's group health insurance plan.

As in all cases where the payer is not the recipient of services, stakeholder incentives may become warped. Providers become incentivized to maximize fee-for-service billables, and intermediaries are incentivized to maximize administrative costs. Moreover, the recipients of services become de-incentivized to ensure efficient service at reasonable cost, and incentivized to become involved in fraudulent schemes.

The resulting excessive or outright improper payments, sometimes referred to as "leakage" (Evans, 2013), are commonly broken down into three categories: waste, abuse, and fraud. It is estimated that $600−850 billion dollars annually are lost to leakage in the healthcare system. Medicare costs taxpayers in excess of 500 billion dollars annually (Annual Report, 2010, p. 5), and Medicaid costs another $400 billion (Henry J. Kaiser Family Foundation, 2012), and it is estimated that 30% of that total results from leakage (*The Sentinel*, 2012). (The federally funded Medicare and Medicaid programs were enacted in 1965; coverage for prescriptions was added in 2003 [CMS, n.d., b]. Medicare was formed to provide coverage for seniors aged over 65 [CMS, 2010, p. 7], and Medicaid provides coverage for low income persons. Unlike Medicare, which is a purely federal program, Medicaid is a joint federal/state entitlement program.)

Waste and abuse falls into the grayer area of negligence and other forms of inadvertent overcharges; fraud, the focus of this chapter, consists of those instances of overbilling that result from intentional deceptive acts. The benchmark of outright fraud is the intention to deceive the payer as to the nature or existence of services for which payment is made.

Given the breadth and scope of health care, and the activities engaged in by organizations to prevent, detect, and prosecute it, this chapter can serve only as a brief introduction to the topic.

LEAKAGE DUE TO FRAUD

Because of its covert nature, there are no hard numbers on the amount of leakage due to fraud. However, one estimate that gives some insight into the magnitude of leakage from fraud puts the total between $125 billion and $175 billion annually (Reuters, 2009). Although it is thought that the largest segment of fraud in the healthcare system is associated with federal Medicare and Medicaid program billing, private health insurers are also victims of fraud.

DEFINITION OF FRAUD IN THE HEALTHCARE CONTEXT

Fraud in the context of health care can generally be defined as knowingly and willfully executing or attempting to execute a scheme "to defraud any healthcare benefit program or to obtain by means of false or fraudulent pretenses, representations, or promises any of the money or property owned by ... any healthcare benefit program" (Rudman *et al.*, 2009).

The varieties of fraud in health care are myriad. Much of the fraudulent activity in health care can be broken down into four main categories: fraud perpetrated by a provider; fraud perpetrated by a patient subscriber; fraud perpetrated by third parties; and fraud perpetrated by agents/brokers. Although the list below references individual actors, many of these fraudulent activities can be, and are, carried out by organized groups of criminals.

Fraud Perpetrated by a Provider

Billing for Services Not Provided

Conceptually one of the simplest methods to commit fraud, healthcare providers can simply bill for services to covered patients for services that were simply never rendered. Generally, patients are unaware of the submission of claims. Insurers have implemented concurrent statement-of-service statements (to provider as well as insured) to deter this type of fraud.

Billing for Low Value or Unwarranted Services, and Incorrect Reporting of Diagnoses or Procedures to Maximize Payments

In this form of fraud, providers provide services that are unwarranted, of little value, or performed by unqualified staff, but submit claims for legitimate treatment. Alternatively, the provider performs services not eligible for coverage but disguises the services using covered service treatment codes. The separate provider/patient statement-of-service described above is less effective against this type of fraud because patients may not take note of billing details in statements where they actually did attend a provider's facilities.

Treatment Upcoding and Code Unbundling

Treatment in US health care is apportioned according to a system of codes. The Centers for Medicare & Medicaid Services issues an elaborate system of codes, which is known as the Healthcare Common Procedure Coding System (HCPCS) (CMS, n.d., c).

Commonly, a provider submits treatment codes for services eligible for greater reimbursement than legitimately entitled, or fraudulently "unbundles" specifically aggregated treatment codes into separate component treatment codes to obtain greater reimbursement.

Misrepresentation of Dates or Descriptions of Services to Create Additional Eligible Charges

Insurers, including Medicare and Medicaid, place frequency restrictions on payment for some services. Providers submit fraudulent claims for services by altering the dates of service to fall outside these restrictions.

Fraud Perpetrated by a Patient Subscriber

Selling or Lending Covered Healthcare Identity to Others

The subscriber provides another person for receipt of healthcare coverage who impersonates the subscriber.

Fraudulent Enrollment in a HealthCare Plan

The subscriber mistakes or omits factual information that would preclude coverage.

Schemes to Fraudulently Obtain Prescription Medication

The subscriber obtains prescriptions by fabricating a medical condition, or obtains multiple prescriptions from different physicians, often with the intention of reselling medications on the black market. In addition, organized criminal groups may create service company "fronts" to secure access to medical facilities to obtain prescription pads (see *The Inquirer*, 2011).

Fraud Perpetrated by Third Parties

Individuals as well as criminal groups use many of these fraudulent schemes by illegally obtaining the medical identity of innocent third parties or accomplices (see, for example, CAIF, n.d.).

Fraud Perpetrated by Agents/Brokers

In addition, perpetrators fraudulently create fictional companies that pretend to employ people who then become covered under an employer group medical plan. Often the scheme involves "employees" with extensive medical needs that dramatically increase the amount of claims beyond what the insurer reasonably expected (see, for example, *New York Daily News*, 1995).

STATUTES AND REGULATIONS INTENDED TO PREVENT, DETECT, AND PROSECUTE FRAUD

There are a number of specific federal statutes employed to curtail healthcare fraud using both criminal and civil penalties (see, for example, 42 U.S.C. §§ 1320a−7, 1320c−5; 42 C.F.R. pts. 1001 and 1002; Statute: 42 U.S.C. § 1320a−7a; 42 C.F.R. pt. 1003; 18 U.S.C. §§ 1347, 1349 (HIPAA) [HEAT, n.d.]). The most significant criminal statutes include the Health Care Fraud Statute (18 USC § 1347), which reads:

(a) Whoever knowingly and willfully executes, or attempts to execute, a scheme or artifice −

    (1) to defraud any health care benefit program; or

    (2) to obtain, by means of false or fraudulent pretenses, representations, or promises, any of the money or property owned by, or under the custody or control of, any health care benefit program,

    in connection with the delivery of or payment for health care benefits, items, or services, shall be fined under this title or imprisoned not more than 10 years, or both. If the violation results in serious bodily injury (as defined in section 1365 of this title), such person shall be fined under this title or imprisoned not more than 20 years, or both; and if the violation results in death, such person shall be fined under this title, or imprisoned for any term of years or for life, or both.

    (b) With respect to violations of this section, a person need not have actual knowledge of this section or specific intent to commit a violation of this section.

(www.law.cornell.edu/uscode/text/18/1347)

More recently these charges have been coupled with charges of federal wire and mail fraud, which are broadly construed criminal statutes (Mintz Levin, 2012).

In addition, there are two statutes that create criminal culpability for conduct related to bribery in healthcare services: the Anti-Kickback Statute (see, for example, 42 U.S.C. § 1320a−7(b)) which broadly criminalizes provider referrals based in exchange for remuneration; and the Foreign Corrupt Practices Act (15 U.S.C. §§ 78dd−1, *et seq.*) (FCPA), which prohibits payment to any foreign officials or enumerated related entities any remuneration in exchange for obtaining or retaining business (which, although not specifically enacted to address healthcare fraud, has increasingly been used by the federal government to prosecute healthcare industry companies operating internationally). The FCPA in particular has been the criminal statute underlying some of the largest healthcare settlement fines in recent history, particularly in the pharmaceuticals industry (see, for example, Korkor and Saleem, 2012).

The federal government has also effectively employed the False Claims Act (31 U.S.C. §§ 3729−3733) to root out fraud in healthcare organizations that transact business with the federal government. The False Claims Act power derives from its *qui tam* provision which enables private individuals to bring whistleblower lawsuits on behalf of the United States Government that allege fraud related to the submission of claims for payment to the government.

Moreover, there are civil penalties and the possibility of being disqualified from doing Medicare- and Medicaid-related work (Staman, 2013).

MAJOR AGENCIES INVOLVED IN HEALTHCARE ANTI-FRAUD EFFORTS

There are number of federal agencies and task forces mandated to deter fraud, including the Office of the Inspector General; US Department of Health and Human Services; Federal Bureau of Investigation; Internal Revenue Service; Department of Justice; and United States Attorney's Office.

In addition, under the Affordable Care Act, the Centers for Medicare & Medicaid Services (CMS) contracts with private entities, known as Recovery Audit Contractors (RACs), that are tasked with identifying Medicare fraud.

Moreover, there are numerous state agencies that investigate healthcare fraud, including various states' Office of the Attorney General and state-level Medicaid Inspectors General.

Private insurers also maintain fraud departments, often referred to as Special Investigation Units (SIUs).

CHALLENGES THAT FACE ANTI-FRAUD EFFORTS

Challenges may be traditional or emerging.

Traditional Challenges

Non-Certainty of Detection

Some forms of fraud, such as credit card fraud, will generally be detected at some point in time. Many forms of healthcare fraud, because of the existence of a third-party insurer, may never be detected. The fact that many instances of healthcare fraud go undetected means that it is difficult to quantify accurately the extent of the problem. Also, as discussed below, it makes the use of supervised learning analytical models more challenging.

Overlapping Patchwork of Enforcement

The complex quilt of discrete federal and state law enforcement agencies, as well as regulators tasked with curtailing fraud in health care, does not lend itself to efficiency, although there have been efforts made to address this problem through interagency coordination — see, for example, the Health Care Fraud Prevention and Enforcement Action Team (HEAT), a joint enforcement by the Department of Health and Human Services and Department of Justice (DHHS and DOJ, n.d.). In some instances, multiple agencies may act upon information that has been received about possible fraudulent activity, and wasting of precious investigative resources. Alternatively, agencies may refer tips to other agencies without any one taking responsibility for an investigation. Finally, all organizations tend to develop a territorial dynamic when dealing with other agencies that share their mandate, which can inhibit investigations — unwittingly or otherwise.

Budget

In both the public and private arenas, budget constraints make effective fraud-fighting a significant challenge. The extent of fraud is often not quantifiable, and any organizational budget allocated to combat it has an equally uncertain return on investment. Because fraud managers often cannot measure directly their effect on revenue, it is difficult to build a traditionally persuasive business case for expenditures.

Size of Industry

In terms of transactions, revenue, operational stakeholders, statutes, and regulations, the healthcare industry presents an intimidating system in which to be tasked with policing fraud. Conversely, fraudsters can skim substantial amounts of money from the system without creating obvious fraud signals, by maintaining fraudulent activity below the level of easy detection.

Organized Crime Efforts

Sophisticated criminal organizations can make fraud detection even more difficult. Their efforts at fraud can often be more subtle, and can involve people inside healthcare organizations. Therefore, they can skim significant revenue without being detected.

Privacy Statutes and Data Sharing

Investigators, in particular non-federal entities, must often contend with federal limitations on data disclosure and/or sharing.

Emerging Challenges

Big Data

As the volume and velocity of healthcare data increase, the challenge of detecting signals that indicate fraud becomes increasingly difficult among the noise. Medical documentation is becoming more complex, creating disparate information sources and systems. In addition, much of the information related to the provisioning of health care is stored in unstructured data — a more challenging data source to mine than structured data.

TRADITIONAL MEANS OF DETECTION

Investigators have traditionally worked in a reactive fashion. Employees of government programs or individual insurance companies notice something amiss, and refer the matter to investigators. Sometimes law enforcement investigators become aware of fraudulent activity in healthcare transactions through informants or cooperating defendants. In addition, fraudulent transactions have been detected as a result of healthcare or accounting audits.

Limitations of Traditional Means of Detection

Reactive Detection

Traditional detection methods have often relied upon reports of healthcare fraud from healthcare providers, patients, or unrelated law enforcement operations. In addition, transactional records would be examined by subject matter experts to identify patterns that might indicate fraudulent activity. Obviously, these methods are entirely reactive and can offer little or no help in recognizing emerging fraudulent behavior.

Ad hoc Investigations

Traditionally, fraud investigations have been done in isolation. Investigators would go from case to case, and little effort was made to "connect the dots" or to systematically determine from the cases factors that could be generalized to better recognize emerging problems.

Traditional Detection Systems

Many traditional detection systems rely on the experience of subject matter experts to create rule sets that flag transactions based upon known patterns of fraud. There are obvious limitations to these approaches. First, these systems are only effective in detecting established fraud techniques. Second, the better fraudsters do not remain static in the face of anti-fraud initiatives, and adjust to the perception of detection. In addition, some investigative programs rely on reactive audits of transactions, which are labor intensive and can only examine a very small proportion of transactions.

Inability to Effectively Triage Investigations

Reactive detection methods present little opportunity to gauge the significance of suspected fraudulent behavior. Moreover, fraud detection systems must be "tuned" between mutually antagonistic objectives: the desire to detect as much fraud as possible, and the need to avoid overwhelming under-resourced investigation units with insignificant and incorrect flags.

Inability to Incorporate Unstructured Information

Fraud detection systems have traditionally relied on transactional data as inputs to detection systems. However, in many situations unstructured data (medical documents, healthcare forms, emails, etc.) provide much greater insight into the nature of healthcare services. The challenge in analyzing unstructured data is to formulate structured information from text that can then be incorporated into analytical processes.

THE EMERGENCE OF BIG DATA IN HEALTHCARE INVESTIGATIONS

ACA Anti-Fraud Provisions

The Patient Protection and Affordable Care Act (ACA), also known as "the Affordable Care Act," is a broad healthcare reform law that was enacted in 2010. The Affordable Care Act will likely have a significant impact on fraudulent activity as well as efforts to curb fraud (see, for example, Kracov and Ogrosky, 2010). As part of its mandate, the law sets forth an array of incentives and approaches to prevent, detect, prosecute, and otherwise reduce occurrences of fraud in the government Medicare and Medicaid systems, as well as in private insurance. These include greater fraud fighting resources; enhanced screening procedures; harsher penalties; and, most significantly for the purposes of this chapter, data sharing. The data-sharing component contemplates complete aggregation of healthcare data involving federal insurance programs (Health Benefits, n.d.).

The ACA also expands the role of RACs. States are now required to contract with specialized companies that are tasked with identifying overpayments in the healthcare system; central to the RAC programs is an anti-fraud plan (CMS, 2011).

ANALYTICAL ANTI-FRAUD APPROACHES

More often now, healthcare fraud investigators employ a variety of methods to combat fraud, including traditional rule-based filters as well as sophisticated data analytical techniques. Used in combination, these techniques allow investigators to better detect fraudulent activity, as well as to triage incidents by likely loss level.

Anomaly Detection

Anomaly detection systems define "normal" bands of behavior in healthcare transactions and flag transactions that lie outside their boundaries. Anomaly detection systems include a variety of outlier detection methods, from traditional manually derived business rules that require continual tuning to sophisticated neural networks that can intrinsically adapt to changing behavior patterns.

Text Analytics

Text analysis involves the use of natural language processing and artificial intelligence to extract information and insight from traditionally out-of-reach unstructured information. Techniques include entity extraction, word and phrase extraction, concept clustering, and document classification against existing defined categories of information.

Supervised Learning Techniques and Predictive Analytics

Advanced predictive analytics enables fraud investigators to use historical fraud data to "train" sophisticated mathematical models which can identify subtle non-trivial patterns in data that indicate fraudulent activity. Supervised learning approaches rely on significant input from subject matter experts in the many areas of healthcare fraud where detection is uncertain and therefore the historical set of fraudulent examples is sparse.

Link Analysis

Link analysis is a method to "connect" entity information in structured data as well as extracted information from unstructured sources. The resulting visual presentation allows investigators to see non-obvious but potentially significant connections among seemingly unassociated people and organizations. Link analysis is particularly useful in connecting people and organizations that may represent an organized fraud ring.

Combined Analytical Techniques

Healthcare fraud analytics is best implemented when all sources of data are available to be analyzed for valuable insight. For example, the "best" truth is often available when transactional healthcare data analysis can be combined with output from an analysis of associated healthcare provider data.

THE FUTURE OF HEALTHCARE ANTI-FRAUD EFFORTS

Health care is currently in a state of significant flux, and this instability will almost certainly have an impact on anti-fraud efforts. For example, implementation of the Affordable Care Act provides enhanced mechanisms and better resources to address fraud (NHCAA, 2010).

Changes in the universally used healthcare billing code system will likely present new opportunities for novel fraudulent schemes related to healthcare billing (Nigam and Vadlamani, 2012).

In addition, the expansion of electronic health records will present challenges to the integrity and security of health information (Clearwater Compliance, n.d.)

The almost certain increase in the healthcare industry's substantial revenues as well as the changing operational and regulatory terrain in which it operates, combined with constrained resources available to combat fraud, indicates that analytics will play an increasingly significant role in the fight against fraud.

ANTI-FRAUD ORGANIZATIONS

There are several associations focused on fraud in the healthcare and insurance industries that provide information about fraud generally as well as the use of analytics to prevent and detect it, including:

- National Health Care Anti-Fraud Association (NHCAA) (www.nhcaa.org)
- Global Health Care Anti-Fraud Network (www.ghcan.org)
- Coalition Against Insurance Fraud (www.insurancefraud.org/index.htm#.UooxCMRwofU).

POSTSCRIPT

Many challenges (such as medical payment "leakage" and fraud) face us in our medical system. The greatest among these challenges involve the administrative operations of our medical and healthcare organizations. In order to take advantage of other than the simplest of analytical solutions in their operations, these organizations must change the way they work with their data. Most managers have been trained to think in terms of operational and financial efficiencies, of doing things over the short and medium term. The reason for this focus is that most medical and healthcare organizations are private, and must answer to their owners and stockholders, most of whom have a relatively near horizon of interest. The enablement of predictive analytics will require significant investment of time and money. The ACA has mandated much of this change; therefore, this expenditure can be justified to stockholders. The incorporation of predictive analytics into the administrative operations of these organizations, however, requires an ever greater change — in the way they "think" about their data. Chapter 19 discusses some the conceptual challenges facing these organizations as they move toward the incorporation of predictive analytics into their administrative operations.

REFERENCES

Annual Report, 2010. 2010 Annual Report of the Boards of Trustees of The Federal Hospital Insurance and Federal Supplementary Medical Insurance Trust Funds. CMS, Washington, DC.

CAIF (Coalition Against Insurance Fraud), n.d. Medical Identity Theft. CAIF, Washington, DC. Available at: <www.insurancefraud.org/scam-alerts-medical-id-theft.htm#.UmqC6vlwofU>.

Clearwater Compliance, n.d. About HIPAA (Health Insurance Portability and Accountability Act). Available at: <http://abouthipaa.com/wp-content/uploads/Information-security-and-privacy-in-healthcare_Current-State-of-Research.pdf, http://www.healthcareitnews.com/news/providers-respond-holder-sebelius-troubling-indications-ehr-fraud>.

CMS (Centers for Medicare and Medicaid Services), n.d., a. National Health Expenditure Projections 2011–2021. CMS, Baltimore, MD. Available at: <www.cms.gov/Research-Statistics-Data-and-Systems/Statistics-Trends-and-Reports/NationalHealthExpendData/Downloads/Proj2011PDF.pdf>.

CMS, n.d., b. History. CMS, Baltimore, MD. Available at:<www.cms.gov/About-CMS/Agency-Information/History/index.html?redirect = /history>.

CMS, n.d., c. HCPCS – General Information: What's New. CMS, Baltimore, MD. Available at: <www.cms.gov/Medicare/Coding/MedHCPCSGenInfo/index.html?redirect = /MedHCPCSGenInfo>.

CMS, 2010. Brief Summaries of Medicare & Medicaid Title XVIII and Title XIX of The Social Security Act as of November 1, 2010. CMS, Washington, DC. Available at: <www.cms.gov/Research-Statistics-Data-and-Systems/Statistics-Trends-and-Reports/MedicareProgramRatesStats/downloads/MedicareMedicaidSummaries2010.pdf>.

CMS, 2011. Frequently Asked Questions: Section 6411(a) of the Affordable Care Act, December 2011. CMS, Baltimore, MD. Available at: <www.cms.gov/Medicare-Medicaid-Coordination/Fraud-Prevention/MedicaidIntegrityProgram/Downloads/Medicaid_RAC_FAQ.pdf>.

DHHS, DOJ, n.d. HEAT Task Force. Health Care Fraud Prevention and Enforcement Action Team (HEAT). US Department of Health and Human Services and US Department of Justice, Washington, DC. Available at: <www.stopmedicarefraud.gov/aboutfraud/heattaskforce/index.html>.

Evans, J., 2013. Payment Policy Optimization: Blending Analytics with Rules to Prevent Wasteful, Abusive and Fraudulent Healthcare Spending. McKesson Health Solutions, Newton, MA. Available at: <www.nhcaa.org/media/21834/whitepaper_paymentpolicyoptimization.pdf>.

Health Benefits, n.d. Summary of Anti-Fraud Provisions in the Affordable Care Act. Prepared for the National Consumer Protection Technical Resource Center, Waterloo, IA. Available at: <www.smpresource.org/Content/NavigationMenu/ConsumerProtection/HealthCareReform/Anti-Fraud_Provisions_in_Health_Care_Reform.docx>.

HEAT (Health Care Fraud Prevention and Enforcement Action Team), n.d. Federal Health Care Fraud and Abuse Laws. Available at: <http://oig.hhs.gov/compliance/provider-compliance-training/files/HandoutLegalCitations508.pdf>.

Henry J. Kaiser Family Foundation, 2012. Total Medicaid Spending. Henry J. Kaiser Family Foundation, Menlo Park, CA. Available at: <http://kff.org/medicaid/state-indicator/total-medicaid-spending>.

The Inquirer, 2011. Norristown Man Charged with Stealing Prescription Pads, Keeping Aligators [sic]. The Inquirer, August 20, 2011. Available at: <http://articles.philly.com/2011-08-20/news/29909519_1_fake-prescriptions-pit-bull-fraudulent-prescriptions>.

Korkor, S., Saleem, N., 2012. Enforcement of the Foreign Corrupt Practices Act in the Healthcare Industry and Foreign Bribery's Adverse Consequences for Patients. Available at: <http://moritzlaw.osu.edu/students/groups/oslj/files/2013/04/Furthermore.KorkorandSaleem.pdf>.

Kracov, D.A., Ogrosky, K., 2010. The Impact of the Patient Protection and Affordable Care Act on Fraud Prevention and Enforcement. Arnold & Porter LLP, Washington, DC. Available at: <www.arnoldporter.com/resources/documents/Arnold%26PorterLLP_ABA_Ogrosky_Kracov_2010. pdf>.

Mintz Levin, 2012. Health Care Enforcement Defence. Boston, MA. Available at: <www.mintz.com/newsletter/2012/Advisories/1791-0412-NAT-HCED/1791-0412-NAT-HCED_index.pdf>.

New York Daily News, 1995. Empire Nets 82 m B'klyn Pair Sued in Insure Scam. New York Daily News, June 21, 1995. Available at: <www.nydailynews. com/archives/money/empire-nets-82m-b-klyn-pair-sued-insure-scam-article-1.682000>.

NHCAA (National Health Care Anti-Fraud Association), 2010. Combating Health Care Fraud in a Post-Reform World: Seven Guiding Principles for Policymakers. NHCAANational Health Care Anti-Fraud Association), 2010, New York, NY. Available at: <www.nhcaa.org/media/5994/ whitepaper_oct10.pdf>.

Nigam, S., Vadlamani, S., 2012. An Innocent Mistake or Intentional Deceit? How ICD-10 is blurring the line in Healthcare Fraud Detection. Jvion Whitepaper Series No. 7. Available at: <www.jvion.com/pdf/ICD10_Fraud_Final.pdf>.

Reuters, 2009. Waste in the US Healthcare System Pegged at $700 Billion in Report From Thomson Reuters. Reuters, October 26, 2009. Available at: <www.reuters.com/article/2009/10/26/idUS78128+26-Oct-2009+PRN20091026>.

Rudman, W.J., Eberhardt, J.S., Pierce, W., Hart-Hester, S., 2009. Healthcare fraud and abuse. Perspect. Health Inf. Manag. 6, 1g.

The Sentinel, 2012. Medicare/Medicaid Improper Payments Exceed $64 Billion a Year. The Sentinel, May 2012. Available at: <www.smpresource. org/docs/The_Sentinel_May2012_HBABCs_Fraud_Estimates.pdf>.

Staman, J., 2013. Health Care Fraud and Abuse Laws Affecting Medicare and Medicaid: An Overview. CRS Report for Congress, Washington, DC. Available at: <www.fas.org/sgp/crs/misc/RS22743.pdf>.

Chapter 19

Challenges for Healthcare Administration and Delivery: Integrating Predictive and Prescriptive Modeling into Personalized Health Care

PREAMBLE

This chapter describes 13 challenges that we face in efforts to integrate predictive analytics into health care. These challenges are associated with the following issues and questions.

1. A new infrastructure must be created for health care.
2. Who will pay for gene sequencing?
3. Who will regulate the predictive models?
4. What effects will predictions have?
5. Does the ability to predict someone's health outcome change their behavior?
6. Legal liability exposure will increase.
7. Many specimens for "omics" analysis are not acquired easily.
8. The technology requires further refinement to be effective.
9. Genetic counselors might be needed.
10. There are many scientific disciplines involved with personalized predictive medicine.
11. Is health care a right?
12. Health care delivery must be "right sized" to match intended recipients.
13. Physicians can make mistakes while filling out death certificates.

CHALLENGES

We face many challenges as we integrate predictive modeling into personalized health care. Some of these challenges raise questions for which we don't have answers at present.

Challenge 1

A new infrastructure must be created for health care. As personalized medicine based on individual characteristics becomes the norm, healthcare providers and pharmacists must be educated about these measures and how to

Practical Predictive Analytics and Decisioning Systems for Medicine. DOI: http://dx.doi.org/10.1016/B978-0-12-411643-6.00047-8

prescribe for and manage patients in a less standard manner. This transition will require also additional education in the use of complicated tools to help manage this information. The structure of electronic medical record (EMR) systems in their present configuration cannot incorporate or manage even genetic information, let alone integrate all the other variables such as metabolomics, epigenetics, and transcriptomics.

Challenge 2

Who will pay for gene sequencing of every individual for healthcare purposes? Granted, the cost of genotyping is declining rapidly, but is still relatively expensive, and even patients with significant genetic features and disabilities often have difficulty getting insurance companies to pay for testing. Considering the difficulties in gaining approval for testing of sick people, it is hard to imagine convincing insurance companies to pay for a relatively expensive test on an otherwise healthy individual. One argument for these tests might be that the genetic information could save money through preventative care. The problem with using that argument is that it opens up the possibility that insurance companies might raise prices or deny coverage based on genetic information.

Challenge 3

Who will regulate predictive models that directly affect patient care? How will these models be tested for clinical use? The possibility of FDA regulation for these models is a consideration, but it raises some serious concerns. If the FDA becomes involved with predictive modeling, will the costs of testing and regulation drive up the prices? Probably it will. In addition, can we expect the FDA to be able to interpret and integrate predictive modeling properly in their deliberations? Probably we cannot, at least in the near future.

Serious questions are raised already about the regulation of genetic testing, in the wake of new offerings by many companies to provide genetic testing services directly to consumers. These and many other questions regarding genetic testing remain open, as we enter this era of predictive medicine.

Challenge 4

What effects will predictions of health outcome have on an individual's mental health and general overall daily anxiety levels? Knowing that there is a certain probability of developing a debilitating disease could have a significant impact on an individual's mental state. Patient response to genetic risk assessments is highly variable, depending on disease and a number of other issues. Strategies have been developed to present this information effectively, but more research is needed in this area as it develops (Lautenbach et al., 2013).

Challenge 5

Does the ability to predict someone's health outcome change their behavior? For years, it has been known that the effects of smoking have caused cancer and cardiovascular disease, and it contributes to a myriad of other diseases. Yet people continue to smoke. Diet and exercise can also reduce your health burden significantly on a number of different fronts, yet the rate of obesity continues to rise in America. Millions of people smoke, millions are overweight, and millions of people have high cholesterol. Regardless of the many warnings in schools and the media that these practices are associated with high risks of serious diseases, many people continue the practices. Even though we are constantly bombarded about the benefits of healthy diet and exercise, yet we continue to get fatter, and continue to maintain unhealthy diets. Early evidence from studies in this area suggest that genetic risk has a minimal effect on behavior, and has questionable effectiveness in motivating changes in behavior (Henrickson et al., 2009). Based on this information, significant effort must be made to create plans for effective interventions, in order for personalized medicine to be effective in its truest form. Despite the possibility that people may not change their behavior, predicting risk does give the physician an advantage for prescribing the proper medications for people on the edge of disorders, such as diabetes or hypertension. Strong predictions by these models might induce the physician to prescribe drugs earlier than otherwise. Currently, we do not have information to determine when or how genetic risk information might motivate healthy behavior. Identifying the settings in which genetic risk can motivate healthy behavior, and identifying which people are likely to respond to this information, are important goals for predictive analytics (Henrickson et al., 2009).

Challenge 6

With the possibility of building clinical risk prediction models also comes the possibility of legal liability. There has been little if any litigation that addresses the use of risk prediction models. However, as they become more widely used, the prospect of a legal liability and lawsuits will only increase. There is, however, an existing body of litigation on family history and genetics that would have some relevance to the use of risk prediction models. The possibility of a "bad prediction" is a legal concept that presents some difficulty, and it is very problematic to judge its significance at this early stage of the implementation of predictive analytic risk models. Outside of blatant misuse or absolute failure to use a required risk prediction model, there is very little legal guidance to avoid the risk for medical liability (Black et al., 2012).

Challenge 7

Many of the biological (body) specimens that are required for full "omics" analysis are not acquired easily. More effective and less invasive methods of gathering this information will be required to get a good assessment of the "omics" of the body. For example, requiring a brain biopsy and undergoing general anesthesia at every check-up is not a likely possibility considering the risk, time, and cost involved, yet some markers of neurological disease using today's technology would require this information.

Challenge 8

The technology required for personalized medicine is certainly not perfect, and many refinements and further developments are needed. For example, despite the hype about the value of whole genome and whole exome sequencing, these tests still have an error rate above 1%. This might not sound like much, but when you consider the billions of nucleotides involved, this 1% error rate becomes quite significant in its effect on diagnosis and treatments.... Significant improvements have been made recently in computing ability and Big Data storage capacities, but we are still not where we need to be to process the huge amount of information these new "omics" technologies can provide. For example, data on just 200 patients can consume petabytes (a million gigabytes, or 1,000 terabytes) of data storage (Chen *et al.*, 2012; Chen and Snyder, 2013).

Challenge 9

It is likely that the implementation of iPOP (integrated personalized omics profiling) into daily practice will modify the role of the physician, and require the added services of genetic counselors to assist patients in making their medical choices. Consideration must be given for creating a model for this type of interaction, and for determining how this process will fit into our healthcare delivery and reimbursement systems.

Challenge 10

The scientific disciplines covered by personalized predictive medicine are numerous, and the tremendous amount of data and computing power required to employ them is unprecedented. New devices and techniques must be developed to collect and analyze these data. The complete implementation of personalized predictive medicine will require the concerted work of teams of scientists and engineers from many fields, along with assistance from ethical and legal professionals to develop guidelines for implementing this technology. The task is daunting, but also very exciting.

Challenge 11

We must determine as a society if we wish to think of health care as a right. Do we want to guarantee all citizens decent and affordable health care, regardless of social status, pre-existing conditions, lifestyle, and age? Do we provide expensive treatment to those in their 90s? To those who are in a permanent coma with little likelihood of recovery? To those who are long unemployed or have an addiction? If so, how is such a healthcare system funded?

Challenge 12

My most important challenge would be to "right size" healthcare delivery for the intended recipient — 80-year-old men do not need coverage for pregnancy related complications; 23-week preterm infants do not need prostate exams. HIS (hospital information systems) and CPOE (computerized physician order entry) must be designed for the right age, size, and sex.

Challenge 13

Another challenge is the inaccuracy of death-certificate completion by physicians, which is particularly important for population health stats ... which affects public health policy, insurance rates, research focus, pharmaceutical development, etc. Studies have indicated that there is disagreement regarding autopsy findings and/or chart notes in up to 25–30% of cases. Completing the certificate can be a laborious and time-consuming task, establishing a chain of causation to the final event causing the patient's demise. So, as with coding, for the sake of time the physician may again often choose a more general diagnosis rather than reviewing the medical record in detail.

POSTSCRIPT

How we approach these (and other similar) challenges may determine our success in integrating predictive analytics in health care and medicine. It is incumbent upon healthcare managers to address these issues and answer these questions *before* they develop into road blocks. These road blocks may cause healthcare administrators to paint themselves into a corner in the process of implementing predictive analytics, and find themselves in a position where they realize that they "can't get there from here."

REFERENCES

Black, L., Knoppers, B.M., Avard, D., Simard, J., 2012. Legal liability and the uncertain nature of risk prediction: the case of breast cancer risk prediction models. Public Health Genomics. 15 (6), 335–340.

Chen, R., Snyder, M., 2013. Promise of personalized omics to precision medicine. Wiley Interdiscip. Rev. Syst. Biol. Med. 5 (1), 73–82.

Chen, R., Mias, G.I., Li-Pook-Than, J., Jiang, L., Lam, H.Y., Chen, R., et al., 2012. Personal omics profiling reveals dynamic molecular and medical phenotypes. Cell. 148 (6), 1293–1307.

Henrikson, N.B., Bowen, D., Burke, W., 2009. Does genomic risk information motivate people to change their behavior? Genome Med. 1 (4), 37.

Lautenbach, D.M., Christensen, K.D., Sparks, J.A., Green, R.C., 2013. Communicating genetic risk information for common disorders in the era of genomic medicine. Annu. Rev. Genomics Hum. Genet. 14, 491–513.

Chapter 20

Challenges of Medical Research for the Remainder of the 21st Century

Chapter Outline

PREAMBLE

A number of challenges also face medical researchers. This chapter presents seven challenges which must be addressed before a tight link can be forged between the laboratory and the treatment clinic. Many research results and insights that appear very promising in the research laboratory cannot be implemented in the clinic, because the conditions are not the same, or the sets of individuals considered by each are not compatible (e.g., non-smokers vs the general population).

CHALLENGES

We face many challenges as we design research to answer the medical questions facing us both now and in the future. Some of these challenges raise questions for which we don't have answers at present.

Challenge 1

The first challenge is getting the "best datasets." PCORI, the new National Patient Centered Outcomes Research Institute, has making "National networks of medical data" one of its primary goals; the success of this will depend on cooperation from both academic and non-profit and for-profit organizations in sharing this data so that scientific medical researchers can use it to produce new knowledge.

Challenge 2

The majority of health outcomes analysis of Medicare data is based on in-hospital data. The reason is that such data are much easier to conjoin with individual patient records as well as with episodes of disease or disability and treatment. Outpatient health data have been notoriously difficult to track since they are collected at various sites which typically do not share records. In order to better assess the efficacy of outpatient disease episodes and treatment, ways must be developed to create and store patient-level inpatient and outpatient episode data.

Challenge 3

Accurate frontline data capture (i.e., clinic, hospital bedside) is particularly problematic. The patient's condition is "described" by the ICD codes chosen by the clinician. Higher-level, non-specific codes are frequently chosen for the sake of time. EMRs have not made this necessarily any easier, even though there may be built in coding assistance — it still requires more steps than using a more generic code which may be memorized or chosen from the patient's problem list. For example, 250.00 is the code for type 2 diabetes under good control.

Practical Predictive Analytics and Decisioning Systems for Medicine. DOI: http://dx.doi.org/10.1016/B978-0-12-411643-6.00048-X

This code is commonly used even though we know that the vast majority of diabetics are not controlled and have one or more complications. Code 250.02 is type 2 diabetes not controlled but with no complications. For each body system affected by the diabetes (kidneys, peripheral nerves, cardiovascular, eyes, etc.) there is a specific fourth and fifth digit with an accompanying "buddy code" from the particular system involved. And this is just for diabetes! Also, for the majority of patients seen, the diagnostic code does not affect reimbursement. (In Medicare Advantage Plans [HMOs, Health Maintenance Organizations], the insurance company is capitated [paid on a per member per month basis] based on the severity of illness of the member [higher SI factor = higher payment] so there is a financial incentive for more accurate coding.) So as long as the doctors function as data entry clerks this is not likely to change. Perhaps new technologies, like "natural language processing," will help solve this dilemma ... (as one author commented on this "challenge," "Excellent! Yes, like we all want doctors to be "data entry clerks," in the wee hours of the night! I wonder if the EMR creators include all types of physicians? PCPs would have to learn the most. How many codes are there for ICD-10? Is it 140,000? And the old one was 20,000? Watson will have to be the clerk!").

Challenge 4

The fourth challenge is the development of new antibiotics, especially for Gram-negative infections, and methods for reducing the approval time (in keeping with continued safety concerns).

Challenge 5

A further issue is the development of innovative methods for treatment of infections and other diagnoses — genetic considerations and biomarkers, for example, to target treatments to individual patients. Such targeting will involve research into diagnostic procedures/tests more specific to medical conditions.

Challenge 6

Another problem is that of obtaining good data for analysis, considering the non-communication between EMRs and HIPAA as it stands. Chapter 13 suggests that informed consent could be obtained as patients enter clinics and hospitals — but what if they don't consent? How will researchers be able to get data that are valid and reliable for making the predictions, especially moving prospectively? Many data will be needed for good predictions, and from all people.

Challenge 7

As Nephi Walton stated in Chapter 13, paying for genome research will be a challenge, but payments in general will also be a problem until we work out the Affordable Care Act. The United States pays about $8,200 per person per year, and our nearest neighbor in terms of amount paid is Norway, at $5,388. Many other countries have more efficient healthcare delivery systems than that of the USA. These countries also have lower percentages of GNP going to health care. How we morph will be a big issue for health care and, therefore, predictive research in the next 10 years.

POSTSCRIPT

Specific "challenges" aside, the three main processes that are essential for efficient and accurate personalized healthcare delivery are:

1. Quality control — Six Sigma
2. Modern predictive analytics, which has as its core data mining and text mining statistical learning theory algorithms
3. Use of both the quality control and predictive analytics in a "decisioning system" framework.

Predictive analytics applications and decisioning systems are the main topics of the remaining chapters in this book.

Chapter 21

Introduction to the Cornerstone Chapters of this Book, Chapters 22–25: The "Three Processes" – Quality Control, Predictive Analytics, and Decisioning

Chapter Outline

PREAMBLE

This chapter simply introduces the ideas of predictive analytics and decisioning systems as the remaining components in developing both accurate and cost-effective healthcare delivery.

INTRODUCTION

The three major processes emphasized in this book that are needed and essential for obtaining both accuracy in diagnosis and treatment, and cost effectiveness in medicine, are:

1. *Quality control/Six Sigma* for "effective/efficient" medical care delivery ("the First Process").
2. *Predictive analytics* to make "accurate" models for diagnosis and treatment delivery ("the Second Process").
3. *Decisioning systems* delivery of health care ("the Third Process"), which is needed to allow "good use" of the predictive analytics such that we can go to the "Fourth Process," which is just emerging: *Prescriptive analytics.*

If you, the reader, want to get a better idea of prescriptive analytics, you might go to the forum discussion that one of this book's authors initiated during the early part of 2014, on Analytic Bridge (www.analyticbridge.com/forum/topics/prescriptive-analytics-the-new-kid-on-the-data-scientist-block?xg_source = activity):

Prescriptive Analytics . . . The "new kid" on the "Data Scientist Block" . . .

We are beginning to see a NEW TERM being used by data scientists; previously there were two main terms to describe different aspects of data analysis:
- Descriptive Analytics
- Predictive Analytics
  BUT NOW:
- PRESCRIPTIVE ANALYTICS . . . .
  is starting to pop up, here and there. It was discussed recently here: http://www.informationweek.com/big-data/big-data-analytics/big-data . . .

Posted byGary D. Miner, PhD on January 8, 2014 at 1:22 pm in Healthcare Datamining

---

Chapters 22–25 describe processes and medical examples using all three of these "processes" in addition to other aspects of data analysis: descriptive analytics; Six Sigma and quality control; predictive analytics; and decisioning. Chapter 25 describes IBM Watson Healthcare, for clinical decision support, which is one method of utilizing predictive methods leading to decisions. Some of the chapters (Chapter 22) and also some tutorials (Tutorial D, for example) show as the end result a "prescription" of how to treat an individual patient, which leads into prescriptive analytics AND what is currently becoming "personalized," "person-centered," and even "person-directed" medicine.

Chapter 22 describes decisioning systems for the ultimate in predictive analytics and real-time decision-making as the *"Third Process"* to bring quality and cost-effectiveness to medical care delivery.

Chapter 23 describes a currently "real-world," working, effective predictive analytics and decisioning system at the Military Institute of Medicine and associated hospitals of Poland. (Poland, as with so much of Europe and other industrialized nations, is ahead of the USA in efficient, cost-effective, healthcare delivery that serves all of the country's population.)

Chapter 24 describes another "real-world" working decisioning system coupled with predictive analytics in a real hospital setting in the USA, at a surgery unit currently functioning within the University of Iowa Hospitals, written by the medical doctor who heads this system.

And Chapter 25 presents a description of IBM Watson Healthcare, written by the medical doctor who heads the medical care delivery systems for IBM Research.

TRADITIONAL STATISTICS VS DATA MINING VS PREDICTIVE ANALYTICS

Data Analytic formats probably can be described best by comparing the following methods, all needed at some point in the "Data Scientist's" toolbox:

- *Descriptive* statistics (based on traditional "Frequentist" Fischerian statistics)
- Descriptive graphical *visualization* of data (generally based on traditional statistics)
- *Traditional* Fischerian (Central Limit Theorem) statistics, versus:
- *Data mining* modern "Statistical Learning Theory" algorithms, versus:
- *Predictive analytics* ... and:
- *Prescriptive analytics* ...

There are minimally four ways "Data Scientists" can analyze data today:

1. Old-fashioned 20th century p-value "frequentist statistics," which for the most part look at "means" of populations (just what we do not want for personalized medicine – which requires predictions for the *individual*).
2. Use of DA (discriminant analysis) and LR (logistic regression) to get at *individual scored* predictions – i.e., lower-level personalized data analysis, which will generally give the lowest, least powerful scores compared to points 3 and 4, below. (*These two are exceptions among the "traditional methods" because they make predictions for the individual.*)
3. Logistic regression (LR) modified by "standardization," so to speak, with WoE (weight of evidence). This is needed by certain organizations that are "regulated" industries and have to give a set of rules for each score/each decision made; these have more power, thus giving more reliable predictions (compared to using DA and LR in the "traditional format"). (*Note*: this third group is included in the domain of predictive analytics, but 1 and 2 above, although useful for visualizing data trends, are not generally defined as being the core part of the field of predictive analytics.)
4. Data mining algorithms (from statistical learning theory methods) that do not need to meet the assumptions of "traditional statistics" but instead learn from the data and can understand any crazy type of curvilinear distribution. *Generally these methods find the highest accuracy scores* (or predictions) from the same data that may be barely touched by 20th century Fischerian statistics, or at the best give "predictions for means of populations or sub-populations (groups)" but not for the individual.

In summary, generally today predictive analytics is thought to include only the modern statistical learning theory, plus weighted regression methods, plus discriminant analysis and logistic regression. Thus, much of Fischerian statistics are becoming "outdated" for medicine as today there are much better ways to analyze data.

The final bottom-line criterion must be this: Does the data analysis work and predict for the *individual*, or for the group? True predictive analytics can do both at the same time; traditional statistics cannot do both but only work at the population level – and not even that is done well in most circumstances, because the assumptions of traditional

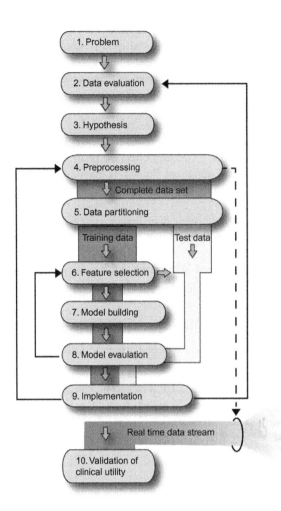

FIGURE 21.1 The Real Time Data Stream shown in the lower right of this illustration is where the predictive analytic models are being applied to the individual patient. © *2013, Nephi Walton, MD.*

statistics (which are dependent on the Central Limit Theorem) are usually not met with life science data (and in fact most "real world data"). All kinds of variations of the Generalized Model can be done to attempt to take care of some of these things, but it is a lot of work, it is important that the operator really knows what he or she is doing statistically, and the results are generally inferior to what can be done with true predictive analytics.

Some data scientists, coming from the traditional 20th century statistical domain, may argue that statistical modeling and testing versus predictive modeling via general approximators is not really related to the nomothetic/idiographic distinction of how one conducts science and/or modeling and prediction. Prediction of individuals (every person is unique – *idiographic science*) or groups (every person is like every other person – *nomothetic science*) can be done using any modeling tool the data scientist desires. It is just a matter of how many models the scientist is willing to build, or capable of building, if agreeing that the goal is one model per person, to find out exactly what works for Jo [hn] Jones (should Jo[hn] Jones get sick).

However, what this book is all about is data analysis that most efficiently and most accurately predicts what is best for the individual person (patient). The process for this was presented in Chapter 3, and we repeat it here in Figure 21.1 because it is so crucial.

The model shown in Figure 21.1, with a decisioning process added, is where it is at today ... the place where medicine and healthcare delivery are evolving to in order to treat the individual with accuracy, instead of guesswork. We live in a different age today; Bayesian data analysis methods are again coming into use in the 21st century – the past century was an "anomaly" in data science.

Another way of describing the controversy between traditional 20th century Fischerian statistics and modern predictive analytic data analysis is to use the term *Global Learning* (i.e., a population-based learning where means of the population and corresponding t-tests, p values, and other stats of traditional statistics are used) vs. *Individual Statistical Learning Theory* methods (i.e., the case-by-case learning approach of data mining algorithms). This distinction is important for the main message of this book, which is personalized and person-centered health care. This distinction is also important for CER (Comparative Effectiveness Research) and HTE (Heterogeneous Treatment Effect), in which some scientists are intent on looking at groups of people (groups classified by age, sex, etc.) but for which the ultimate goal is to look at individuals. CER and HTE will be discussed more thoroughly in Chapter 26: 21st Century Healthcare and Wellness: Getting the Health Care Delivery System That Meets Global Needs.

POSTSCRIPT

The next chapter, Chapter 22, provides the theoretical and practical background to the Second and Third Processes that are needed for effective healthcare delivery: predictive analytics coupled with decisioning systems. Chapters 23–25 will then provide some practical, working examples of the application of the three essential processes needed for 21st century healthcare administration, delivery, and medical research.

Chapter 22

The Nature of Insight from Data and Implications for Automated Decisioning: Predictive and Prescriptive Models, Decisions, and Actions

PREAMBLE

The foundations of the general challenges facing implementation of predictive analytics in medicine and health care have been presented in theory and in practice (the tutorials). In Chapter 22, we move to the next phase of the predictive analytics operation – combining the various hardware and software elements into an automated decision-making system. These "decisioning" systems are the goal – the "Holy Grail" of predictive analytics. Individual algorithms and methodologies should not be viewed as ends in themselves, but as means to an end – the predictive analytics systems that receive input data, conduct necessary data preparation operations, train the appropriate modeling algorithms, and output the decisions themselves – not just some information that can be used by subjective humans to make decisions.

OVERVIEW

Data mining and predictive modeling methods have transformed numerous industries and altered day-to-day life in remarkable ways. As you search for specific products such as laptops on the Internet, your clicking experience at various websites can be customized automatically to this specific product type. As you peruse various online sellers of laptops, the particular specifications and interests of your searches can be broadcast to all online merchants, who customize their offerings to present to you exactly what you are looking for.

Practical Predictive Analytics and Decisioning Systems for Medicine. DOI: http://dx.doi.org/10.1016/B978-0-12-411643-6.00050-8

Functionally, these systems can:

- Retrieve automatically the relevant information to predict future behavior or outcomes
- Create customized predictions about the propensity for specific decisions, behaviors, or outcomes
- Provide suggestions to guide best next actions.

Such capabilities can deliver tremendous value in healthcare domains, and offer promise to improve the efficacy of information and guidance provided to patients after medical procedures or hospitalization.

Imagine a system that can monitor all processes and actions during hospitalization and at the point of discharge. It can also provide post-discharge data captured during follow-up visits, to generate relevant guidance about likely next outcomes, best next actions and treatments, and accurate predictions about readmission to expensive emergency care, and can offer ways to prevent this. Today, these methods and technologies exist in various industries for creating such a system, including facilities to maintain, update, and validate it to support critical decision-making processes.

The purpose of this chapter is to review the building blocks required to create an effective automated *decisioning* system — a system that will process all available relevant information to make accurate predictions about likely outcomes, and provide *prescriptions* for best next actions, and treatments. Before reviewing the technical aspects of such a system, however, a review is necessary to present a philosophical and research-based justification for why and how such systems can be effective, and how they can mimic the information processing operations of experienced expert medical practitioners. It is often the case that these practitioners can generate decisions of far superior quality, compared to those generated by simple rules and standard operating procedures.

In summary, this chapter will describe not only *how* an effective decisioning and prescriptive modeling platform can and should be built to improve healthcare delivery, but also *why* such systems can automate expertise usually only available from long-term, highly competent practitioners, who cannot devote equal attention and consideration to all patients and relevant medical decision-making.

THE NATURE OF INSIGHT AND EXPERTISE

In many ways, experts do not (consciously) "know" what they are doing. At first this may seem to be an odd comment, but in fact day-to-day observation is consistent with this statement. For example, an expert violinist cannot write a manual about, or convey through verbal instruction to others, how to play the violin. Expert fishermen cannot verbalize easily the rules that allow those unfamiliar with a specific lake or part of the ocean to be equally successful.

In practically all highly skilled professions — including, and in particular, medical professions — a critical part of the training is an extended internship (or practicum) that provides trainees with a rich and diverse environment and various structured and unstructured learning experiences.

Procedural and Declarative Knowledge

In cognitive psychology, the distinction between *declarative* and *procedural* knowledge describes the difference between the things we know and can verbalize explicitly as rules (*declarative* knowledge), and the things we know how to do or judge intuitively (*procedural* knowledge) (see, for example, Lewicki, 1986a,b; Lewicki *et al.*, 1992). The knowledge of the alphabet is declarative, we can recite it. However, knowledge of how we judge distances intuitively, determine if we find another person interesting or attractive, or decide quickly that "something is not right" with the medical profile of a patient, is not easily verbalized, and is procedural in nature: we know *do* it, but cannot describe *how it is done*.

Lewicki and colleagues (Lewicki, 1986a; Lewicki *et al.*, 1992) have accumulated a large amount of evidence demonstrating that much of the knowledge that experts use to make effective and efficient decisions is not only procedural in nature and not accessible to conscious scrutiny, but also never *was* accessible to conscious awareness in the first place.

Non-Conscious Acquisition of Knowledge

In short, Lewicki and others have demonstrated, over a wide range of human experiences and expertise, that exposure to complex and rich stimuli, consisting of large numbers of sensory inputs and high-order interactions between the presence or absence of specific features, will stimulate the acquisition of complex procedural knowledge without the learners' conscious awareness. Hence the acquisition of such knowledge is best characterized as *non-conscious* information acquisition and processing. For example, when humans look at sequences of abstract pictures, faces, or tracking targets over seemingly random locations on the screen, carefully calibrated measures of procedural knowledge (e.g., based on response times) will reflect the acquisition of knowledge about complex covariations and rules inferred from the rich and complex stimuli.

The Nature of the "Non-Conscious"

It is important to note at this point that the notion of "non-conscious" here is quite different from the commonly used "unconscious" in the psychoanalytic tradition. This research is about information processing, and the mechanism that enables humans to extract common co-occurrences of features and interactions between features from extremely complex experiences (stimuli). These low-level cognitive (learning) mechanisms are the building blocks from which complex knowledge and expertise is built. The notion of "non-consciousness" here pertains to the fact that the respective expertise is almost entirely *procedural* in nature, rather than *declarative*. Hence, experts cannot verbalize or consciously scrutinize how rapid decisions, choices, and predictions are made in the presence of very complex stimuli – but they can make those decisions and predictions with remarkable accuracy. Conscious reasoning, it appears, rather is reserved for explicit problem solving in the presence of novel situations or detailed evaluations – for example, when solving math problems, or thinking about a strategy for success.

Conclusion: Expertise and the Application of Pattern Recognition Methods

The conclusions from this research are highly relevant for understanding how large amounts of high-dimensional information, consisting of complex interactions between numerous parameters, can be derived efficiently through systematic exposure to relevant stimuli and exemplars. Specifically:

- It appears that knowledge about complex interactions and relationships in rich stimuli are the result of the repeated application of simple covariation-learning algorithms that detect co-occurrences between certain stimuli and combine them into complex interactions and knowledge.
- In human experts most of this knowledge is procedural in nature, not declarative; in short, experienced experts can be effective and efficient decision-makers, but are poor at verbalizing *how* those decisions were made.
- When the covariations and repeated patterns in the rich stimulus field change, so that previously acquired procedural knowledge is no longer applicable, experts are slow to recognize this and are often confused and reluctant to let go of "old habits."

Human expertise and effective decision-making can be remarkable in many ways:

- It is capable of leveraging "Big Data" – i.e., it is remarkably capable with respect to the amount of information and stored knowledge that is used.
- It is capable of coping with high-velocity data – i.e., it is very fast, with respect to the speed with which information is synthesized into effective accurate decisions.
- It is very efficient, with respect to how little energy our brain requires to process vast amounts of information and make near-instant decisions.

From the perspective of the analytic approach, these capabilities are accomplished through the repeated application of simple learning algorithms to rich and complex stimuli to identify repeated patterns that allow for accurate expectations and predictions regarding future events and outcomes. This approach is quite different from statistical hypothesizing and significance testing. These differences will be highlighted in the next section.

STATISTICAL ANALYSIS VS PATTERN RECOGNITION

There is a fundamental difference in approaches to data analysis between statistical hypothesis testing and pragmatic predictive modeling and data mining, or learning-from-the-data. This difference has been pointed out by numerous authors familiar with both approaches, such as the classic paper by Breiman (2001) on *Statistical modeling: The two cultures* (see also Nisbet *et al.*, 2009; Miner *et al.*, 2012).

Fitting *a priori* Models

In traditional clinical research, statistical data analysis methods have been applied widely to build predictive models. A common example of such a method is a multiple linear regression model which is fitted to the data, following the form

$$y = b_0 + b_1 * x_1 + \ldots b_n * x_n + \varepsilon,$$

where y is some variable or outcome that is to be predicted (e.g., propensity for hospital readmission after discharge), x_1 through x_n are predictor variables, b_0 through b_n are coefficients of the linear prediction model, and ε is the error variability that cannot be accounted for by the prediction model.

In general (and without going into details about the theory of statistical inference), the approach for building such models is to estimate the parameters of the model from a subsample of cases and then to perform statistical significance tests to decide if the model parameters and predictions from the model are more accurate than some baseline (usually random) expectation.

The general approach to modeling is that a set of *a priori* expectations regarding possible functional relationships between predictors and outcomes are tested for statistical significance (i.e., an outcome that is highly unlikely to have been observed in the sample by chance alone). If found to be significant, it is concluded that the respective relationships thus hold in the population at large. So, fundamentally, statistical modeling is about hypothesis testing, and the rejection or acceptance of *a priori* hypotheses about the data, and how important outcomes can be predicted from available inputs (predictor variables).

Pattern Recognition: Data are the Model

Modern data mining, machine learning, or predictive analytics approaches are different. In these approaches, no *a priori* hypotheses are tested, but instead the goal of the analysis is to extract from the data set repeated patterns and relationships that are useful in the prediction of future outcomes. Thus, this approach closely resembles how expertise and procedural knowledge are acquired by human experts when interacting with complex and rich (sensory) inputs.

Data are the Model

Suppose that some important outcome — such as hospital readmission — was 100% predictable from a set of input variables, measured accurately and reliably (without error). In that case, given a data set of historical experience with other patients, a prediction about hospital readmission would be easy to make. Simply find, for each patient to be discharged, the one or more most similar patients with respect to the available inputs; the prediction then would be the outcome based on those similar cases. This example is illustrated in the simplified graph shown in Figure 22.1.

It is assumed in Figure 22.1 that there are three relevant predictors. Furthermore, in the historical data, existing patients based on observed outcomes were assigned to either *Low*, *Moderate*, or *High Risk* groups. How should a new patient, as shown in Figure 22.1, be predicted? It would make sense to assign this patient to the *High Risk* group, as shown in Figure 22.2.

The *New Patient* in Figure 22.2 is closest to other patients in the historical data that were classified as *High Risk*, with respect to three important *Predictors* of risk. Therefore, the *New Patient* will be assigned to the *High Risk* group.

The method of assigning new observations to the most likely outcome among the nearest "neighbors" in the space defined by the predictors is a well-known and effective data mining algorithm: k-Nearest Neighbors.

During the "learning" process of this algorithm, the task is to find a good subset of representative and informative exemplars with respect to important predictor variables. The prediction simply is to assign a new observation to the similar "neighbors."

Pattern Recognition Via General Approximators

In predictive modeling, unlike in statistical analyses, no *a priori* hypotheses or functional relationships are tested with the data. Instead, simple learning algorithms capable of approximating any kind of relationship in the data are applied to extract the repeated and consistent patterns across all of the data, which are relevant and useful for the prediction of important outcomes. Therefore, such algorithms are also called *general approximators*.

To reiterate, this general approach is most similar to what we know about the mechanism by which the human cognitive system learns and acquires knowledge of patterns from diverse and rich sensory inputs with remarkable efficiency, even when those repeated patterns are very complex.

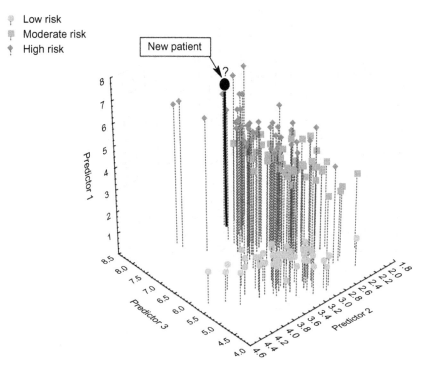

FIGURE 22.1 Predicting a new patient from similar patients.

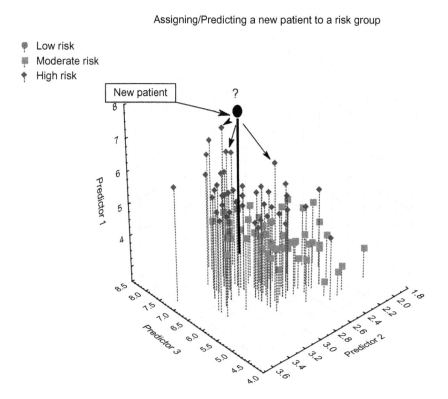

FIGURE 22.2 Predicting a new patient using k-Nearest Neighbors.

The algorithms of data mining and predictive modeling are explained briefly elsewhere in this book (see Chapter 15, *Prediction in Medicine — the Data Mining Algorithms of Predictive Analytics*). All of the most powerful and effective predictive modeling algorithms will apply pattern recognition methods to approximate the repeated patterns in data.

These algorithms have revolutionized risk modeling and prediction, fraud detection, and demand forecasting, to name only a few of the domains where data mining and predictive modeling are common. These algorithms will also transform the way patient outcomes are modeled and predicted, and how best next-action plans with respect to treatment regimens will be determined.

Pattern Recognition and Declarative Knowledge: Interpretability of Results

To summarize, in statistical modeling, *a priori* model-based expectations about relationships in the data are tested using statistical methods; in data mining and predictive modeling, pattern recognition algorithms are applied to extract repeated relationships and patterns from the data, to enable accurate prediction.

One of the common criticisms and often barriers to the adoption of data mining techniques is that they are "black boxes." For example, neural networks or the k-Nearest Neighbor method described earlier may yield very accurate predictions regarding hospital readmission, but provide little information about *why* a patient is likely to be readmitted. In order to provide actionable information regarding effective treatments and the best next-action, it is important that prediction models also provide insights into what to do or change to affect an outcome.

Statistical Models, and Reason Scores

Using statistical modeling — for example, linear regression models — simplifies the task of identifying the important predictors driving outcomes. Those predictors associated with the largest parameters in the respective prediction model are the ones that are most important in driving the outcomes, and, using statistical and mathematical reasoning alone, it is possible to determine why a specific outcome is predicted to occur, and hence help to determine what could be done about it.

For example, suppose you had a linear equation, in a simple linear model, which predicted the likelihood of hospital readmission based on numerous predictors. Given the specific values for the predictor variables, for each patient it will be obvious which predictor variable and specific value contributes most to the expectation of elevated readmission risk. If blood pressure is an important predictor variable in the linear prediction equation and a patient shows elevated blood pressure, then it is clear and apparent that steps should be taken to lower blood pressure in order to lower the risk of hospital readmission.

Thus, statistical models are usually more easily interpretable, providing useful *reason scores* for why a particular predicted value was computed, and what to do to change it.

Pattern Recognition Algorithms and Reason Scores

It is true that some of the methods and algorithms used for data mining and predictive modeling are complex, yielding complex predictions. Not unlike human expertise, as discussed earlier, it can be difficult to derive declarative knowledge from even highly accurate procedural knowledge contained in a repeated pattern extracted via general approximators.

What-if, and Reason Scores as Derivatives

"Reason scores" are a way to explain the prediction of analytic models and to identify the root causes driving specific prediction. The term emerged in the risk scoring domain, where a final score is computed as the sum of reason scores from multiple predictors (see, for example, Siddiqi, 2006). In general, and regardless of the prediction model, reason scores are computed as first-order partial derivatives of the parameter under consideration (e.g., partial derivative for hospital readmission probability with respect to parameter *Patient Age*). Thus, these scores address the question of by how much the outcome variable of interest will change if the value of a specific predictor variable changes or is changed.

It should be noted that the parameter estimates of linear regression models such as logistic regression models also describe a *slope* and thus derivative. Therefore, the interpretation of simpler statistical regression is derived from the same information — how much the respective outcome variable of interest will change when the values in a specific predictor variable change.

TABLE 22.1 Characteristics of a Patient

Parameter name	Value	Parameter name	Value
APGAR_SCORE	6	APGAR_BMI	35
AGE	83	HMB_WI60DAYS	13.8
RBC_TRANSF	1200	LAST_HMB	9.6
EBL	1500	WND_CLASS	20-Clean Contaminated
ASA	3	surgeon_id	33

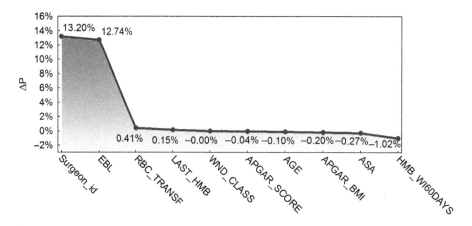

FIGURE 22.3   Reason scores for a specific prediction based on derivatives for important predictors, as shown in Table 22.1.

For example, consider the following case (Hill *et al.*, 2013). Shown in Table 22.1 are the values of important predictors for a patient predicted to have an elevated risk for hospital readmission.

To compute reason scores for this patient's risk profile, based on (numeric) derivatives, one can use "what-if" analyses, running slightly different values than those actually observed through the respective prediction model. In fact, this is the basic approach for computing numeric derivatives for the prediction function of risk.

Using the approach (numerical differentiation computed via "what-if"), Figure 22.3 shows that two major contributing factors for the risk prediction are *surgeon_id* and *EBL*.

Therefore, while general predictive models can possibly be complex, identifying the specific reasons (*drivers*) of a specific prediction is relatively straightforward, and is consistent with the way that inferences are typically drawn from statistical prediction models.

PREDICTIVE MODELING AND PRESCRIPTIVE MODELS

The previous discussion provides an overview of the cognitive algorithms that allow human experts to develop their expertise through interactions with complex stimuli, from which they learn the repeated patterns. Many of the most robust and accurate algorithms of predictive modeling implement a similar approach, by applying general learning algorithms in order to extract repeated patterns from data. However, human experts do more than just predict: they often make critical decisions.

So while accurate predictions of patient health outcomes resulting from a certain treatment are important, actual decisions must be made in real-world applications about what to do next and what *not* to do. In the predictive modeling and data analysis domain, this is the difference between *predictive models* (what is likely to happen) and *prescriptive models* (what is the best suggested course of action; see, for example, Evans and Lindner, 2012). An effective useful system that will improve the quality of day-to-day decisions made in any business (including hospitals and all healthcare-related activities) should provide actionable information and suggestions, and not just predictions or predicted probabilities. Human experts do not simply predict probabilities or outcomes; they can make high quality optimized decisions automatically to improve outcomes.

Therefore, what is needed is a prescriptive analytics system that incorporates advanced predictive modeling.

Rules, Conditional Scoring Logic, Action Plans

To complete a system that will not only make predictions based on models but also return actionable advice and information about available alternatives, it is necessary to integrate the predictions from models with rules and logic in order to arrive at optimal decisions. For example, rules may be applied to compare the expected benefits and risks of different courses of action, based on multiple predictive models for different outcomes and risks. In that manner, possible alternative decisions can be compared and ranked, and, based on the optimal decision and outcome, or specific documentation, can be retrieved to guide the next steps.

An Example System: The STATISTICA Enterprise Decisioning Platform®

Figure 22.4 shows the different components of the STATISTICA Enterprise Decisioning Platform (StatSoft, 2013), for delivering predictions and suggested best next-action *prescriptions*. It consists of the following components.

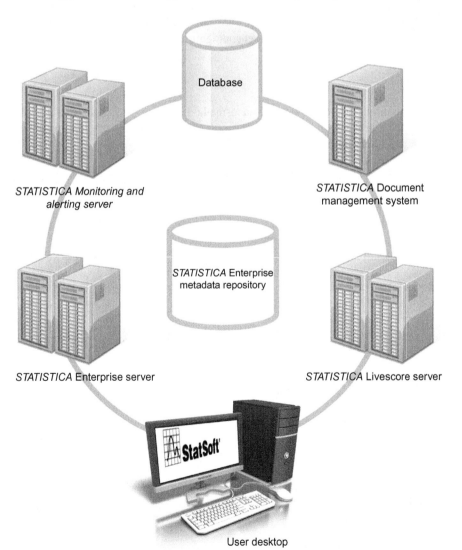

FIGURE 22.4 The STATISTICA Enterprise Decisioning Platform®.

STATISTICA Enterprise Metadata Repository
Metadata, and Control

A capable system for predictive and prescriptive modeling to support a large organization like a hospital not only needs to provide the relevant analytic algorithms and methods, but also must manage relevant metadata such as settings, configurations, analysis templates, models, workflows, and user accounts. There are many reasons why creating, storing, and sometimes versioning of the metadata can be important.

- The protection of patient privacy is of utmost importance in an effective and acceptable analytics platform; it is also a legal requirement — HIPAA and similar regulations require protection of the data. Secure storage of user accounts and roles is important to assure access control and data security. For instance, data analysts may be provided with access to only a limited set of information in the data set and be restricted from viewing patient identities; user sessions can be logged; analysis roles can be separated in a way that permits data preparation and data analysis to be performed by different user groups.
- Typically, analytical models deal with the same or similar structures of the data made available to researchers and analysts. To serve this broad access, the data access templates or configurations should be stored and backed up in a metadata repository, so that the specific data that were used in a study can be used to repeat the same analysis. This metadata repository can be useful for data audit operations, and it permits version control, logging of improvements, and the addition of new predictor variables.
- Likewise, all analyses and reports should be managed as templates to minimize *ad hoc* modeling and permit the repeat of specific analytic workflows and approaches identified as best practices. When analytic approaches and workflows are stored as metadata, experience of what works and what does not work can be institutionalized and separated from individual analysts and *ad hoc* analytic sessions, thus encouraging the standardization of these best practices.

Prediction Models, and Rules

The STATISTICA Decisioning system contains numerous user interfaces and methods for building predictive models, including automated methods that apply model templates and yield a best (most accurate) model or combination of models (model ensembles) without requiring any interventions by analysts.

The basic analytic process is summarized in Figure 22.5.

Prediction models are built following data access templates (*Data Acquisition*) using various predictive modeling algorithms and methods, yielding a best model or best ensemble of models that "vote" to derive a prediction (for categorical outputs) or average outcomes (for continuous number outcomes).

The predictions from models are combined with rules. Rules can describe pre-scoring segmentation — for example, which specific models are applicable to which group of specific patients, or post-scoring ("policy") rules — for example, how to combine known risk factors and predictions about various dimensions of risk into a single best next-action recommendation.

Model Management refers to the activities for validating and documenting the prediction models, as well as the approval process that is typically guided by SOPs (standard operating procedures). Depending on the specific

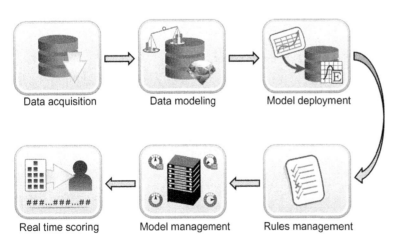

FIGURE 22.5 Analytic process in STATISTICA Enterprise Decisioning Platform®.

Data acquisition Data modeling Model deployment

Real time scoring Model management Rules management

application, the platform can be configured to enforce specific policies with respect to who can approve models (not the person[s] who built them), and how they must be documented to permit subsequent audits to replicate properly the process governing how specific models were built and how specific results were obtained.

Real-Time Scoring is the final step that occurs when models are put into a production environment. This step provides critical information and recommendations in a real-time environment (e.g., to support day-to-day evaluations of hospital patients).

STATISTICA Enterprise Server for Batch Scoring

In Figure 22.5, the component labeled STATISTICA Enterprise is the server where regular batch scoring happens. Batch scoring means that there are regularly scheduled scoring runs, in which predictions (e.g., complete risk profiles and alerts) are written back to the patient profiles in the database. Also, standard reports and other scheduled or *ad hoc* analytics are performed on that server.

STATISTICA Live Score Server for Real-Time Scoring

"Real-time" scoring refers to applications where predictions and recommendations must be computed as the data are gathered — in real time. For example, a patient may answer a few questions during an admission interview, and those narratives can be processed immediately and submitted to prediction models to return instant recommendations and risk profiles. In the STATISTICA Decisioning Platform, these computations are performed in the STATISTICA Live Score server(s), which are optimized for preparing data (e.g., applying a text mining model), scoring multiple models and rules, and returning multiple recommendations within milliseconds to the system or user. Note that the same models and decisioning flows (models and rules) can be used for batch, as well as real-time, scoring.

Monitoring and Alerting Server

The Monitoring and Alerting server is the sentinel watching the data and the model performance, to alert analysts that models should be updated (or re-calibrated), or, alternatively, to trigger automated model updates in a fully automated system. There are two "conditions" that must be monitored, to assess that a specific prediction model or set of models need to be updated.

First, the accuracy of models must be monitored. For example, based on the most recent available data, the system will track the error rate in the predictions (e.g., the percentage of patients with a low readmission risk who actually *were* readmitted). There are well-known and highly effective statistical procedures that can detect not only simple outliers and deviations, but also trend reversals or slight shifts. For example, they can detect when the prediction slowly becomes inaccurate (models become "stale") but *before* it becomes so inaccurate as to be no longer useful.

The second piece of information to monitor is the distribution of input values to the model predictions. This is also sometimes called *population stability*. The concern in focus here is that if the distribution of values in the critical inputs is different from that observed when the models were built, then it is likely that "something" has changed on the input side of the modeling equations.

For example, suppose that the models were built for patients with a median age of 45 years. However, a major university expansion or influx of young people to a new employer in the region changes that median age to 30 years. It is advisable in that case to update (recalibrate) the relevant prediction models where *Age* is an important predictor, in order to capture and reflect in the prediction models any specific relationships that are applicable only to younger patients. Put another way, models built and validated for patients aged 45 years or older may or may not be accurate when predicting risk for patients aged 25 years or younger.

Document Management System for Version Control of Models, Model Management

Finally, a critical component of the system is the Document Management System, which imposes version control and audit logs onto all data connections and models, as well as all activities in the system. This system also implements approval processes and other requirements typical of such systems, to ensure regulatory compliance.

It is a general trend across all industries and applications of data analysis technologies that consumers are demanding more transparency, quality, and oversight, particularly in the application of predictive modeling methods. For example, this is the case in food, pharmaceutical, and medical device manufacturing, which is regulated by the US FDA and similar international bodies; this is also true in banking, insurance, etc.

These increasing demands require that the system must keep track of what was done by whom, when, and why; who approved models; who used models; and other activities related to models, so that all aspects of the analytic and scoring process can be audited by independent reviewers. These demands require also that that the process of how models are built and approved is transparent and safe. For example, a common requirement is that "no one person or group of persons can commit a crime." This principle applies also to analytical model building, meaning that one person cannot build, test, and validate a model properly alone. The outflow of this principle is that those who build models or generate analytic results cannot approve those models or related reports. Instead, any model or analytic report that is created must be approved and signed (e.g., via electronic signature) via an independent and different *reviewer* role. Afterward, the approved material cannot be altered in any way, other than by superseding it with subsequent approved models and reports (and backing up the previous information for auditing purposes).

The STATISTICA Document Management System is fully integrated into the overall Decisioning Platform and enables approval processes, version control, and audit trails, so that nothing happens in the system without leaving a record of who did what, when, and why. In some ways this piece of the system is perhaps the most important one, because even if an analytic platform can produce highly accurate predictions, it will fail if it does not guarantee that there is full transparency and integrity with respect to the fair and impartial application of prediction models that does not discriminate or result in favoritism.

SUMMARY

This chapter consists of two major parts.

The first part discusses how human complex decision-making and expertise is the result of mostly non-conscious learning from diverse exemplars, which is organized to derive repeated patterns that allow for better-than-random prediction of future outcomes, and the identification of factors responsible for those outcomes. Modern predictive modeling methods and systems are functionally very similar to how human expertise is acquired, and the implementation of such systems to improve the effectiveness of healthcare delivery holds enormous promise.

The second part of this chapter discusses the functional aspects of a complete system, and identifies the key requirements to ensure the effectiveness and integrity of such systems. Specifically, it is critical that prediction models can be integrated with rules logic to deliver actual recommendations rather than just prediction probabilities, or some other evaluation metric. In addition, the complete system must support features to support regulatory compliance, such as audit logs, electronic signatures, version control, and approval processes. The integrity and trustworthiness of the prediction system is critical for acceptance both by healthcare practitioners and by patients alike, and hence are major factors determining the success or failure of an implementation of such a system.

POSTSCRIPT

Chapter 22 functions to get to the question: How can we do it? In other words, what are the specific components of such an integrated decisioning system, and how can we orchestrate them to produce appropriate decisions that are accurate and specific to the patients? Chapter 23 describes an example of how such a predictive analytics decisioning system was built in Poland.

REFERENCES

Breiman, L., 2001. Statistical modeling: the two cultures. Stat. Sci. 16 (3), 199–231.

Evans, J.R., Lindner, C.H., 2012. Business analytics: the next frontier for decision sciences. Decision Line. 43, 12.

Hill, T., Rastunkov, V., Cromwell, J.W., 2013. Predictive and Prescriptive Analytics for Optimal Decisioning: Hospital Readmission Risk Mitigation. Paper presented at the 2013 IEEE International Conference on Healthcare Informatics (ICHI), Philadelphia, PA.

Lewicki, P., 1986a. Nonconscious Social Information Processing. Academic Press, New York, NY.

Lewicki, P., 1986b. Processing information about covariations that cannot be articulated. J. Exp. Psychol. Learn. Mem. Cogn. 12, 135–146.

Lewicki, P., Hill, T., Czyzewska, M., 1992. Nonconscious acquisition of information. Am. Psychol. 47, 796–801.

Miner, G., Elder, J., Hill, T., Nisbet, R., Delen, D., Fast, A., 2012. Practical Text Mining and Statistical Analysis for Non-structured Text Data Applications. Elsevier, Cambridge, MA.

Nisbet, R., Elder, J., Miner, G., 2009. Handbook of Statistical Analysis and Data Mining Applications. Elsevier, Cambridge, MA.

Siddiqi, N., 2006. Credit Risk Scorecards: Developing and Implementing Intelligent Credit Scoring. Wiley & Sons, New York, NY.

StatSoft, 2013. STATISTICA Enterprise Decisioning Platform®. StatSoft, Tulsa.

Chapter 23

Platform for Data Integration and Analysis, and Publishing Medical Knowledge as Done in a Large Hospital

PREAMBLE

The Military Institute of Medicine in Poland had a problem. They wanted to build a predictive analytics decisioning system, but realized that it had to be designed as a whole system – they could not just cobble together some existing parts and resources. They designed the entire system from scratch, including standardized data access from a variety of sources, data preparation, and data analysis to guide medical diagnosis and treatment. This chapter describes how they did it.

INTRODUCTION

Between 2010 and 2012 the Military Institute of Medicine (MIM) in Warsaw, Poland and the Regional Specialist Hospital in Wroclaw, Poland conceived, framed, and carried out a large medical diagnostics, research infrastructure, and analysis project named "TeleMedNet" (full name: "TeleMedNet – medical and scientific diagnostic platform"). The project was funded by the European Union's "Innovative Economy" program, and by the Polish government.

The primary goals of the TeleMedNet project were to create a reliable IT infrastructure using the latest technologies to provide validated clinical data, and to support managers and scientific researchers in innovative scientific research in various fields of medicine. These goals have been achieved through:

1. creating an IT infrastructure and a group of applications for the collection and storage of data
2. building a platform for integrating and sharing collected data, data analysis, and medical knowledge to be published (referred to as the Platform)
3. providing safe and permanent access to the IT infrastructure
4. extending databases of medical procedure costs
5. creating an integrated infrastructure for establishing a means of communication among scientists.

Practical Predictive Analytics and Decisioning Systems for Medicine. DOI: http://dx.doi.org/10.1016/B978-0-12-411643-6.00051-X

Building the platform (item 2 in the list above) refers to the part of the project commissioned to StatSoft Polska. The primary component of the platform is the Medical Research Environment (MRE), which is the main subject of this chapter.

The MIM and the Regional Specialist Hospital in Wroclaw are large, top-ranked hospitals in Poland, serving as clinics; they employ a large academic staff and conduct extensive research programs. The project was led by MIM and based to a large extent on MIM's infrastructure.

StatSoft is a global provider of data analysis integrated solutions and the creator of the STATISTICA platform. Its Polish office, StatSoft Polska, has been operating for 19 years and employs a qualified and experienced staff of data analysts, developers, and database programmers.

FUNCTIONS AND APPLICATIONS OF THE PLATFORM

The integrated platform for collecting and publishing medical knowledge was designed to be used in three primary fields of application:

1. Hospital management
2. Financial clearing with the Polish National Health Fund (NHF)
3. Scientific research.

These three activities are performed by the three groups of Platform users, respectively:

1. Top-level hospital and clinic managers, along with the heads of various hospital units
2. The Department of Medical Services Sales and Analysis, which deals with the NHF
3. Researchers, scientists, and physicians.

Hospital management obtains the best and most current knowledge about key aspects of the hospital units, physicians' performance indicators, usage of resources (beds, physicians), changes in demand for services, and so forth. This knowledge permits the optimization of performance processes of individuals, and for the hospital as a whole.

The majority of hospital income is derived from the Clearing House of the National Health Fund. Regular receipt of reliable information, delivered automatically in a single standardized format, enables:

- optimization of contracts through early warning of limit excess (services provided by a hospital beyond the limits specified in a contract are not reimbursed by the NHF [National Health Fund, 2012a])
- adjustment of the size of future contracts to the actual demand for services
- detection of any clearing house irregularities on time.

The implementation of the Platform imposed the process of data verification and improved all data collection procedures in the hospital. Additional processes for data validation were implemented at early stages to eliminate inconsistencies in data entry.

The Platform enables avoidance or minimization of the risks associated with:

- inappropriate interpretation of incoming information
- contradictory information received from several sources or not at the right time.

Research scientists and physicians have access to large amounts of high quality information crucial for their research work, which was formerly unavailable, because the system can select almost any type of patient information, medical procedures, and laboratory tests, and data analyses can be conducted which were not even considered previously.

PLATFORM COMPONENTS AND ARCHITECTURE

The Platform for data integration, analysis, and publication of medical knowledge (Figure 23.1) consists of the following functional components:

- *Medical Data Warehouse* (STATMED) — an integrated central database containing all the data for the Platform stored in relational and multidimensional online analytical processing (OLAP) data structures. The Medical Data Warehouse was implemented in order to optimize queries for both reporting and analysis.

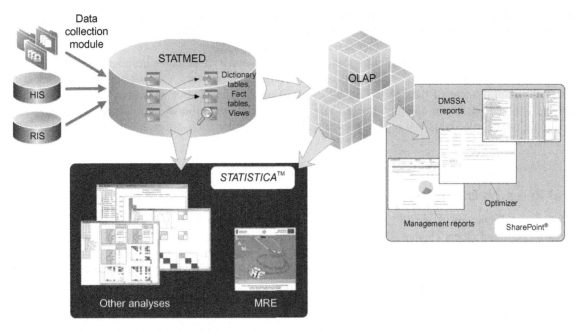

FIGURE 23.1 The Platform for data integration, analysis, and publishing of medical knowledge (Platform).

- *Data Collection Module* − responsible for data collection from external data sources (e.g., Hospital Information System, Radiology Information System, Laboratory Information System), and data cleansing and integration, transforming source data into the form most suitable for further analysis and storage in the Medical Data Warehouse.
- *STATISTICA software* − an environment for statistical analyses.
- *Medical Research Environment and Wizard (MRE)* − STATISTICA add-on. Along with STATISTICA, it creates a platform supporting data analysis. It also provides an environment that enables researchers to define a data extract from the Medical Data Warehouse and submit it in optimal form for further analysis in STATISTICA.
- *Management Portal* (management reports) − a set of dedicated reports including the key performance indicators (KPIs) of individual hospital units, and the entire hospital, to support managerial decision-making.
- *Reports for NHF contract monitoring and clearance* − a set of reports used in the planning and optimization of the hospital with regard to payments from the National Health Fund.
- *Optimizer* − a component improving the economical effectiveness of patient hospitalization by analyzing and indicating optimal Diagnosis Related Groups (DRGs) (DRG is a healthcare services billing method, used by the National Health Fund, which assumes that certain groups of patients require similar treatment [National Health Fund, 2012b]).

Data Warehouse and OLAP

The Medical Data Warehouse STATMED is a central component containing all the data from various data sources. It is also a dedicated tool for optimized analytical and reporting queries. OLAP cubes were prepared in the data warehouse to enable easy browsing of hospital performance indicators by different headings and levels of detail.

Data Collection Module

The Platform uses a variety of heterogeneous data sources, updated with variable frequency. The scope of data includes:

- Hospital administrative information (structure, beds, physician schedules, etc.)
- Patient data (stays, diagnosis, treatments, lab and medical tests, medications, etc.)
- A list of diseases and medical procedures
- A list of limits for medical procedures
- Contracts with the National Health Fund.

The sources of these data are various databases, including the Hospital Information System (HIS), Radiological Information System (RIS), and Laboratory Information System (LIS) databases stored in the Sybase and Microsoft SQL Server, as well as contracts and parameter files stored as XML or CSV files.

Procedures of cleansing and integrating of source data implemented in this module assure appropriate quality and coherence of data. Verification and validation of incoming data prevents inconsistent and invalid data entry. It enforces the improvement of data collection by the existing data acquisition systems. The above guarantees that the Platform is based on certain and high quality information. Single data format and consistency of data stored in a warehouse and used for analyses and reports prevents improper interpretation of results and contradictory information delivery.

Medical Research Environment – Overview

Medical Research Environment and Wizard (MRE) is a platform providing medical information collected by the hospital for researchers and others (Figure 23.2). It is a consistent base of information (Medical Data Warehouse) about patients and their treatments, covering the entire hospital over the long term.

MRE Data Warehouse can contain data collected automatically from medical systems such as HIS, RIS, LIS, and others, as well as individual research results.

MRE Wizard is an add-on to STATISTICA, with the aim of downloading and preparing data from various medical systems in order to perform appropriate analysis (StatSoft Inc., 2012).

A single patient episode may consist of the number of stays, diagnoses, and dozens of treatments and performed tests, as well as medicines taken, diet, infections on the wards, etc. (*Note*: a "stay" is the course of treatment of the patient within a single ward; each "episode" consists of at least one stay. A patient episode [hospitalization] is treatment of the patient within a single hospital admission. Platform records a patient episode as a list of all diagnosed diseases, performed medical procedures and tests for a single patient within the same hospital admission, in all wards.)

All of these items may be important for researchers. In addition, it may be interesting to look at the medical data in many ways – in one case the subject of the research may be a patient, in another a single diagnosis or medical procedure, and in still another, a test or group of tests such as blood tests along with all relevant results. MRE is a program that systematizes the process of filtering, selecting, and conducting preliminary analysis of the data.

The MRE environment has been developed as a Wizard interface that guides the user step-by-step in preparing the data for analysis.

These are the steps for the Wizard interface:

1. *Data filtering* – MRE Wizard enables the researcher to specify the range of data that he is interested in analyzing, in a flexible and convenient way
2. *Column selection* – this specifies which information concerning patients' medical treatment should be included
3. *Spreadsheet layout* – the Wizard enables specification of one of several predefined STATISTICA spreadsheet layouts into which data will be retrieved

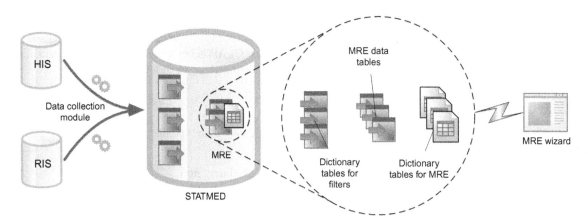

FIGURE 23.2 Medical Research Environment (MRE).

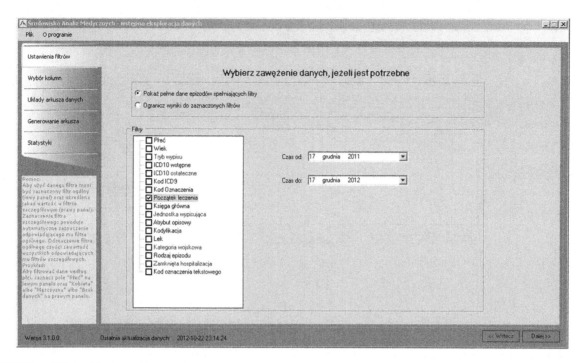

FIGURE 23.3   MRE data filtering.

4. *Spreadsheet generator* − at this stage the researcher can run data cleansing based on specific rules, and/or replace missing data
5. *Statistics* − the last step enables the researcher to make a preliminary review of the data, using a range of predefined statistics automatically executed for the variables in the spreadsheet.

MRE − Data Filtering

At this stage the researcher is able to filter the desired range of data. A list of available filters used in the Wizard and the filtering scheme is defined in the dictionary, which can be customized at the database level without interfering with the other layers of the system. For example, a user might select the following filters (among many others): admission and discharge date, gender, age, ICD-10 diagnoses, ICD-9 procedures, tests, medicines taken (Figure 23.3).

MRE − Column Selection

At this stage it is possible to select objects of the patient treatment to be transferred to a STATISTICA spreadsheet. For example, an initial diagnosis code might be selected, along with a final diagnosis code, test results (a specific test with its unit and tolerance limits), and text descriptions of the test results or medicines taken (Figure 23.4). Currently, there are about 60 objects grouped thematically into 9 data fields.

MRE − Spreadsheet Layout

Subsequently, the researcher can select one of the predefined spreadsheet layouts. The layout is determined by the level of aggregation: specifically, the type and range of data represented by a single row. Layouts are defined by patient episode, single test, any diagnosis, and tests performed on a given day of the episode (Figure 23.5).

In addition, the layout and content of the columns is determined by the aggregation method of other objects. The researcher can display various statistics (frequency, data code, average, maximum, minimum, median, first and last values, etc.). For example, the layout of the spreadsheet can be specified to show data in a sheet on a single episode level, and, in the adjacent columns, to display codes of all tests and the values of the first and the last tests during the episode.

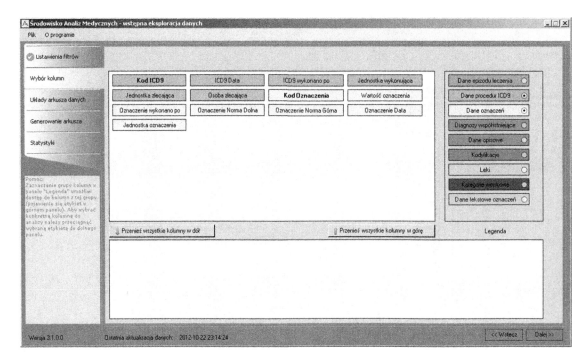

FIGURE 23.4   MRE column selection.

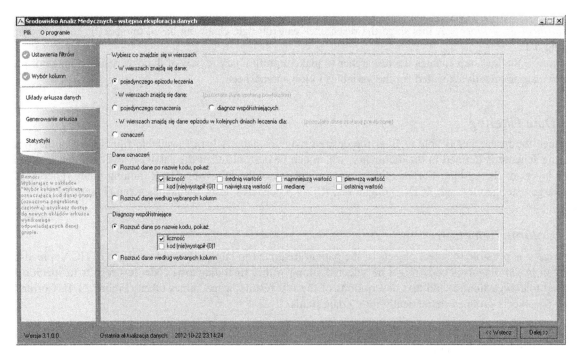

FIGURE 23.5   MRE spreadsheet layout.

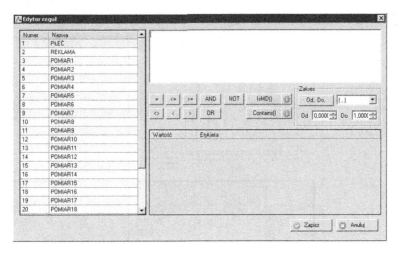

FIGURE 23.6 Validation Rules Editor of the MRE Spreadsheet generator.

MRE – Spreadsheet Generator

The next step of the analysis is transferring data to STATISTICA and running initial data cleansing.

As part of initial data cleansing, many validation rules can be applied to detect potential problems and to replace missing data before performing further analysis. The volume of data may be large, so manual detection of lines that do not meet researcher rules might be very time consuming, or impossible. Data validation rules can be specified using predefined tools, such as the Validation Rules Editor (Figure 23.6).

The Wizard enables replacement of missing data with the intuitive values of the mean, the median, the mode, the group mean and group median, Nearest Neighbors, or a constant value.

MRE – Statistics

The last step in the MRE Wizard is the generation of automated summaries and preliminary analyses of variables – even hundreds of variables, if necessary. With the results of these analyses, a researcher can pre-evaluate the nature and quality of the data and automatically identify interesting cases stored in the data warehouse.

Using predefined macros, the user can quickly create summaries such as frequency tables, histograms, box-and-whisker plots and more advanced analysis results (Hill and Lewicki, 2006; Nisbet *et al.*, 2009; StatSoft Inc., 2012; see also Tutorial N: The Poland Medical Bundle).

After the appropriate data have been selected in the previous steps, the user can perform analyses of laboratory and medical test results performed through subsequent days of hospitalization, as well as study the significance and validity of tests on certain days of hospitalization. Several statistics, graphs, matrices, and maps are plotted (Figure 23.7) for each selected ICD-10 diagnosis.

Another feature is correlation analysis for test results. Again, summaries in the form of tables and graphs are presented for each selected ICD-10 diagnosis (Figure 23.8).

Management Portal

Management Portal was designed to allow easy viewing of summaries and indicators relevant to hospital management. The data presented relate to different areas of the medical center, including the queue of patients waiting for treatment, occupancy of beds in wards, and monitoring of physicians' working hours related to mortality rates on the wards. These reports provide convenient and fast access to both current and historical data.

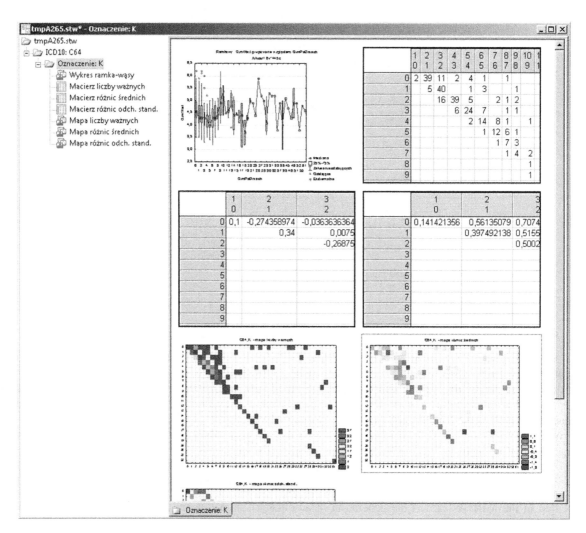

FIGURE 23.7 Sample screenshot of output graphs and matrices in an MRE report.

The following list presents some examples of available reports.

- *In-hospital mortality rate* — a report used to study hospital mortality, one of the key indicators of the quality of the hospital and particular hospital units
- *Number of patients according to ICD-10* — a report for viewing the number of patients with different diagnoses, gender, place of residence, and time range
- *Indicators of average treatment duration* — a report used to study selected quality indicators of the hospital and individual cost centers involving average duration of treatment
- *Medical advice per hour* — used to examine the quality of physicians' work, the hospital, and particular cost centers on the basis of admissions of patients to the hospital
- *Services year to year* — report of the operating efficiency of the hospital and individual cost centers in the current year compared to the previous year
- *Forecasts* — present data for the last 3 months, and forecast 3 months ahead for:
  - projections of the number of patients expected in the future, for planning purposes
  - the number of vacant beds
  - the number of beds occupied
  - the percentage of occupied beds in each hospital unit.

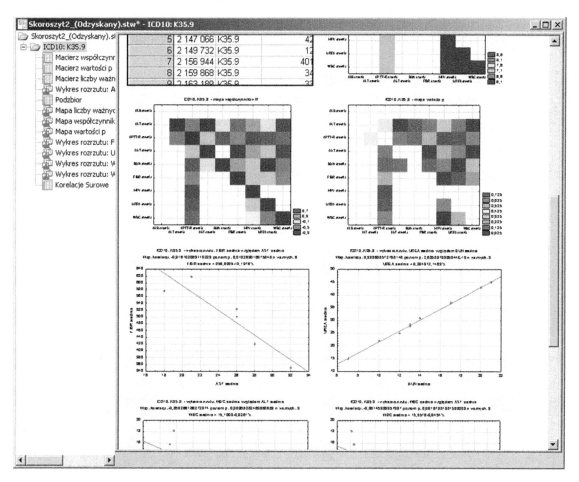

FIGURE 23.8   Sample screenshot of data plots in an MRE report.

The reports are viewed by the end users in a web browser. Appropriate panels enable the specification of data ranges and data exploration, and are exported to Excel, STATISTICA, etc. Figure 23.9 shows an example of such a panel.

All data in the reports are presented in several ways, depending on the level and nature of data aggregation. The central part of the report is a data table for reviewing data — for example, for individual cost centers, diagnoses from the ICD-10 list, or medical procedures from the ICD-9 list which can be divided further into categories such as patient gender or address. Appropriate sets of resulting graphs can be displayed, according to the type of report (including administration region breakdowns, as shown in Figure 23.10).

Reports for NHF Contract Monitoring and Clearance

The information presented in the reports is used to monitor hospital activity, mainly within the framework of clearing with the NHF. These reports include the following.

- *Average time of treatment* — details about the number of beds for each cost center, the length of a patient's hospital stay (including particular costs of hospitalization and branches of the NHF which were assigned to the patient), and the percentage of occupied beds together with average time of treatment.
- *Hospitalizations* — details of admissions, discharges, treatment, and summarized number of patients in terms of defined groups of patients (including particular costs of hospitalization and NHF branches to which the patient was assigned during hospitalization).

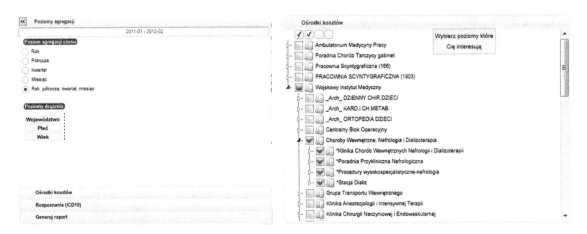

FIGURE 23.9 Management Portal interface, data specification, and exploration panel.

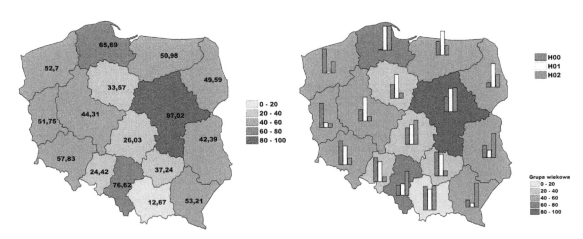

FIGURE 23.10 *STATISTICA Maps* add-in output within a Management Portal.

- *NHF contract fulfillment* – details of services performed within contracts with the National Health Fund and the summarized value of services by contracts, months, and products (groups of services) included in the contracts. In addition, the corresponding indicators used for dealing with the NHF are calculated.
- *Primary value of the contracts* – details of the value of products (groups of services) resulting from contracts signed with the NHF. Data are arranged in order to compare both monthly and annual changes in the values of individual contracts, in relation to all groups of services contained in the contracts.
- *NHF contract plan* – details of contract ranges (groups of services), including particular cost centers responsible for a particular range. The report also presents a simulation of contract fulfillment, and a template to compare fulfillment with the initial plan.

The generation of each report consists of three main steps:

1. Download appropriate raw data from the medical database for the period specified by the user.
2. Aggregate the data at the appropriate levels.
3. Submit an Excel report containing the aggregated results.

Report templates and the periodic reports on which they are based are regularly published on the Microsoft SharePoint Platform on a MIM internal network.

Optimizer

The cost of a patient's stay is optimized by a program indicating the most cost-effective DRG group he or she is to be assigned, based on the course of treatment.

Optimizer creates a list of any potential DRG groups ranked by cost effectiveness, with additional information on all of the conditions required but not yet met for application of a particular DRG group (National Health Fund, 2012b).

CONCLUSIONS

TeleMedNet was a large IT project carried out by the Military Institute of Medicine in Warsaw. It was devoted primarily to the creation of an IT infrastructure and to the organization of a comprehensive system for acquiring and storing data about patients. Data were made available for both medical research and financial/economic analysis.

The data, acquired and organized within other parts of the project, were made available for data analysis by the concluding component of the project, which was developed by StatSoft Polska. The Medical Research Environment extracts a large amount of data from various sources and places it at the researcher's fingertips, ready to be analyzed by the STATISTICA software, which is the final analytical environment for the system.

The key to the success of the project was the clear understanding of both the clinical hospital data sources and the needs of researchers and hospital managers.

POSTSCRIPT

The Platform appeared to work for the Polish Military Institute of Medicine, but the creation of such a decisioning system in the United States was a much more challenging operation. The US legal landscape is far more complicated than that in Poland. Also, the medical establishment in the USA serves as much more diverse and extensive population than exists in Poland. Some of these additional challenges, along with some suggested solutions, are presented in Chapter 24.

REFERENCES

Hill, T., Lewicki, P., 2006. Statistics Methods and Applications: A Comprehensive Reference for Science, Industry, and Data Mining. StatSoft Inc, Tulsa, OK.

National Health Fund, 2012a. Conditions of Reimbursing of Cost of Services by NHF [in Polish]. NHF, Warsaw, Poland. Available at: <www.nfz.gov.pl>.

National Health Fund, 2012b. Algorithms and Necessary Conditions of Assignment to DRG Groups [in Polish]. NHF, Warsaw, Poland. Available at: <www.nfz.gov.pl>.

Nisbet, R., Elder, J., Miner, G., 2009. Handbook of Statistical Analysis & Data Mining Applications. Burlington, MA.

StatSoft Inc., 2012. STATISTICA (Data Analysis Software System). StatSoft Inc, Tulsa, OK.

Chapter 24

Decisioning Systems (Platforms) Coupled With Predictive Analytics in a Real Hospital Setting — A Model for the World

PREAMBLE

The vast complexity of the medical establishment in the USA, and the very conservative approach of its practitioners, requires a significant cultural change before predictive analytics decisioning systems will catch on in America. Chapter 24 relates necessary culture changes to specific elements of medical decisioning systems, and proposes how some of these changes can be implemented while still maintaining the "healing touch" of the physician.

INTRODUCTION

Fundamental changes to the financial incentives that the healthcare industry operates under are happening. The movement towards risk-adjusted, value-based compensation has given delivery systems the motivation to fundamentally change the delivery of patient care. Healthcare delivery systems that provide higher quality care at lower cost are more likely to survive the coming changes.

In line with this, our hospital began a service excellence initiative to improve the experiences of our patients. During a presentation related to this initiative, a consultant speaker showed a particularly good example of anticipating customer needs. We were shown a photograph of a main street in Disneyland packed with hundreds of people. The speaker pointed out that the streets and sidewalks were perfectly clean of trash and debris. The reason for this finding was that at the time Disneyland had first opened its doors, decades ago, an observation was made: "People will walk no more than 30 paces to throw refuse into a garbage can. If the distance is greater than that, they will throw it on the ground." This observation resulted in the placement of garbage cans no further than 30 paces away from most areas in the park, creating an environment that is clean despite throngs of people. This is an extraordinarily simple but elegant example of how anticipating a customer's needs can improve operational effectiveness and efficiency.

Practical Predictive Analytics and Decisioning Systems for Medicine. DOI: http://dx.doi.org/10.1016/B978-0-12-411643-6.00052-1

Hospital units are more complex (and less amusing) than amusement parks, but, similar to such a park, each individual on the unit has differing expertise and knowledge important for anticipating patient needs. Healthcare providers are also remarkably poor at anticipating patient needs:

- In 2011, physicians at University of California, San Francisco, demonstrated that physicians, case managers, and nurses were able to predict patients' need for unplanned readmissions no better than a coin toss (Allaudeen *et al.*, 2011).
- In February 2013, researchers at the International Stroke Conference presented data showing that physicians were accurate 16.9% of the time in predicting key outcomes for stroke, while the accuracy of a predictive analytic model for the same outcomes was 90% (Saposnik *et al.*, 2013).
- In April 2013, investigators at the European Society for Radiotherapy and Oncology showed that mathematical models perform better than doctors at predicting responses to cancer treatment (Oberije *et al.*, 2013).

With these mounting data, it became important for us to begin to use the best of what physicians and other health providers had to offer and combine it with the best of data science to achieve our goals. The complexity present on a surgical unit meant that anticipating patient needs would likely involve complex modeling and require a method of consistently and reliably presenting the output of these models, as well as the rules that would be applied based upon the output of these models, to the right staff at the right time. Just as importantly, the staff would need to engage with such a system and base their subsequent actions on insight gained from this modeling.

With these understandings, we set out to move our surgical unit to one that offers uncompromising patient care through an analytics driven approach. By *anticipating* patients needs rather than *responding to* patients' needs, our hope was that this pilot program would serve to lead the hospital in achieving the levels of safety, effectiveness, and efficiency needed to survive the coming changes in health care. This chapter is not written from the perspective of someone with decades of experience in predictive analytics, but from that of a clinician with an appreciation for decisioning platforms who has spent 3 years coming to know how to use such a system in a real-world clinical environment. The hope is that the paragraphs and pages that follow will expedite readers through the critical steps in using such a platform in their own environment.

The Steps in Setting the Stage for a Decisioning Platform

1. Get support from information technology and hospital leadership
2. Create an analytical culture
3. Define the outcomes that you want to improve
4. Identify the clinical decisions that are being made
5. Define the resources requiring management
6. Determine what data you have access to and what data you need access to.

SETTING THE STAGE FOR A DECISIONING PLATFORM

Getting Support from Information Technology and Hospital Leadership

Our observation of numerous hospitals and their patient care units, and our own experience, led us to believe that deployment of a clinical decisioning platform will involve barriers including technology, policy, and local culture. In many cases, the use of decision support tools may be driven by hospital leadership, in which case communicating with the appropriate leadership about the needs for your group or unit could be sufficient. In other cases, the hospital leadership may not understand the concepts, the language, or the value of decisioning platforms. Here, education of hospital leadership will be a critical step for success. A strategy for garnering interest and engagement from senior hospital leadership, which we used successfully, is as follows:

- Identify an outcome that is currently of high institutional interest and focus (length-of-stay, readmissions, patient falls, nosocomial infections, etc.). Choose an outcome for which outcome data are available to you.
- Use available information technology and/or quality assurance resources to obtain data on the patient population of interest that are helpful in modeling the chosen outcome. Use variables that are available in real time if you're interested in models that can be used in real time.
- Using standard predictive analytics techniques, develop some models that provide clinically useful predictive power on test data. Start small, with intent to scale.

- Present the modeling data at a meeting of the hospital clinical leadership team, and use the presentation as a venue for teaching them about decisioning platforms.
- Request analytical and IT resources for a small pilot project for formally developing and validating additional models for a decisioning platform.
- Once you have a set of clinically valuable models, make the financial case with your models for funding a decisioning platform managed by the hospital enterprise.

The best pathway in other environments may be different.

Creating an Analytical Culture (Or, Have You Ever Tried to Tell a Surgeon He's Doing Things Wrong?)

The author serves as medical director of a 40-bed surgical unit at the University of Iowa Hospitals and Clinics. This unit provides world-class care for patients from several surgical service lines, including colorectal, trauma, bariatric, minimally invasive, general, and vascular surgery. It is a complex environment, with wide variation in patient acuity, care plans, and surgical practices. Like all academic medical centers our mission includes training the next generation of physicians, and so each service line has residents which rotate in and out every month, thus increasing the complexity by not having static teams that develop familiarity with one another's strengths, weaknesses, and processes. In addition to the complex environment, the decision-making ranges from routine to highly complex.

In implementing a decisioning platform, we understood that our goal was to use an analytics driven approach to develop the best processes and improve their reliability, rather than focusing on specific personnel and errors they make that may contribute to poor outcomes. Our assumption was that all team members wanted to perform well, but processes were not designed to optimize this.

We had often observed new initiatives that threaten provider autonomy to be unsuccessful without the provider's engagement and understanding. This was particularly true of surgeons, who had highly invested in the protocols and beliefs that had followed most of them from their training. We felt that employing a decisioning platform, without having employees engaged in analytical thinking, would fail.

It was fortuitous that we were to be involved in another initiative: the Comprehensive Unit-Based Safety Program (CUSP). This program is designed to improve hospital safety by focusing on changing culture in a structured way through engaging the frontline staff. Much has been written about this program, and the most famous demonstration of its ability to improve safety in a significant and sustainable way is the Keystone Project for reducing Central Line-Associated Blood Stream Infections (CLABSI) (Pronovost *et al.*, 2006). The critical part of this program is in developing a culture in which the frontline staff (doctors, nurses, social workers, discharge planners, environmental services) ask this set of questions as part of their daily routine:

- How will the next patient be harmed?
- What will you do to prevent the next patient from being harmed?
- How do you know that risks were reduced?

While these questions focus on safety, they could easily be changed to "How will the next patient be dissatisfied?" or "How will the next patient have an outcome other than what we desire?" Importantly, by incorporating such questions into everyday routine, frontline staff anticipate problems and develop an analytical mindset to determine if risk exists and if it's been reduced. With this system in place the analytical process is no longer something that exists only at the level of the senior hospital leadership, with changes to be handed down to the staff. It is likely hard for those without experience in frontline health care to understand how this isn't a part of the culture, and understanding this culture is beyond the scope of this chapter.

The fact that CUSP has demonstrated numerous successes in improving patient safety through teaching this analytical method in healthcare organizations like ours gave us hope that it was relevant for preparing our staff for a decisioning platform. Our unit has been actively involved in CUSP methodology since October 2012, and our safety measures have markedly improved as a result. We believe that incorporation of analytical thinking into the daily routine is an important reason for this improvement. The staff can now easily see how a decisioning system can make their own processes simpler and more reliable while remaining transparent and focused on processes rather than individuals.

Defining the Outcomes Targets

Ultimately, the reason to deploy a decisioning system is to improve some form of outcome. Our initial exercise to determine what outcome improvements we would pilot was based on two factors: (1) current institutional priorities with regard to quality, safety, and efficiency, and (2) those adverse events that were most significant to our unique patient population. Determining institutional priorities should require no more than a conversation with senior hospital leadership. They will likely be grateful that you are asking, or shocked that you aren't already aware.

Most hospitals maintain a safety reporting system for the purpose of tracking adverse events such as falls, medication errors, and unexpected deaths. This is a rich source of data for defining what your priorities should be with respect to patient safety. To determine the adverse events most significant in our population, we performed an analysis of our hospital's safety reporting system over an arbitrarily chosen 6-month time interval. Adverse events were ranked by severity and frequency. By reviewing these data, we could determine where to focus our energy. Based upon the above priorities, our initial outcome improvements were to be centered on (1) unplanned hospital readmissions, and (2) patient falls.

Defining the Clinical Decisions

A decisioning platform will allow routine, repeated clinical decisions to be made through an analytics driven process. The rules engine within such a platform will need to know what decisions are to be made and what the possible responses are. Defining the decisions to be made and the potential responses can only be accomplished by engaging clinicians with a thorough understanding of the patient population being managed in the process of system development.

In the case of readmission, decisions being made during hospitalization that may influence the outcome involve answering the following questions:

- When does the patient get discharged?
- Will the patient have a follow-up visit?
- When will the patient have a follow-up visit?
- With whom will the patient have follow-up?
- Will the patient be discharged to home or a facility?
- Will the patient have home health care or a visiting nurse ordered?
- What subsequent laboratory and/or imaging will the patient need after discharge, and who is responsible for following up on these?
- Will the patient need nutritional supplementation?
- What potential problems do we counsel the patient about?
- Who will the patient call if he or she has a problem after discharge?

In many cases, hospital service lines will have clinical pathways that spell out their practices with regard to each of these questions. While these pathways are not dynamic and responsive to differences in patients, they may serve as a starting point for determining the current clinical decisions that are being made.

Our advice to those embarking on deploying a decisioning platform is to start with a small hospital service or unit with well-defined protocols that have been developed by staff physicians through a cooperative process. This will be the easiest group of physicians to work with for deploying a decisioning platform. A quick victory in deploying a system with a small, cooperative team will provide momentum for moving forward with increasingly complex and perhaps divided areas.

Define the Resources That Need to be Managed

If there were no resources that could be varied in response to patient needs and predicted outcomes, there would be no need for a decisioning platform. In modern health care, however, there is no shortage of expensive, invasive, or high-resource interventions that can be applied to patients. In GI surgery, we routinely offer patients outpatient clinic visits, laboratory studies, imaging studies, medications, wound-care regimens, nutritional therapies, home healthcare visits, long-term inpatient care, and physical therapy, to name just a few. In addition, hospitals frequently staff their units at levels that are managed in a way that is reactive to patient acuity and census, rather than anticipatory. These are the resources that need to be managed and applied via an analytics driven approach to maximize good outcomes, and minimize patient risks and expenses.

Determine What Data You Have Access to

The decision management system is fundamentally an information system, and must have access to enterprise data. In our case, these data include the electronic health record (EHR), billing and claims data, admission and transfer data, and registry data such as data from the National Surgical Quality Improvement Project (NSQIP) and University HealthSystem Consortium (UHC).

External Data

We have observed that determining what data are accessible is complex in large systems. Frequently, siloed groups within an organization are submitting registry data to outside entities. The surgery department is submitting NSQIP data, transplant registry data are being submitted by the transplant center, bariatric surgery center-of-excellence data are being submitted by that section, and pediatric data are being submitted by yet another internal entity. These registries can be a rich source of outcome data, and what outcomes you wish to track will help you to decide what registry data you need access to. Because business associate agreements (BAAs) need to be executed prior to sharing of hospital data externally, we have found the hospital compliance office to be an excellent source for understanding what data are being submitted to registries.

EHR Data

There are approximately 737 EHR systems available at the time of this writing (ehrscope.com). The availability of EHR data to a decisioning platform will depend on the specific EHR system, and should be an important part of the EHR purchasing decision. Readers must seek help in understanding how data can be moved out of their specific EHR and into a database suitable for use with a decisioning platform. Other factors that are critical include the time cycle for which data in the EHR are available. In some cases, clinical data available for modeling and decisioning will be from 1 day old to 1 week old. For real-time decisioning, processes to move data out of the EHR in a more rapid cycle could be critical.

As an example, Epic EHR is in use at the University of Iowa. Epic EHR data are maintained in a hierarchical database that is not suitable for using with industry analytics tools. The Epic Clarity application allows for copying EHR data into a relational database, which is then available to industry business intelligence, and analytic tools through structured query language (SQL) queries. These data are moved out of the EHR and into Epic Clarity each night, so the most recent data available for decisioning could be up to 24 hours old. An additional function of Epic is the Reporting Workbench function, which allows a real-time query of EHR data to be scheduled and executed in real time, and the output is written to a delimited data file on the network. Unfortunately, these real-time queries begin to run poorly if large quantities of data are requested.

We use each of these data transfer processes to our advantage, through extract, transfer, and load processes (ETL) that bring these together. Small amounts of rapidly changing data (vital signs, blood counts, nursing assessments, bed transfers) can be queried on time cycles of minutes to hours using Reporting Workbench and combined by ETL with other slowly changing data (demographics, pathology, radiology, billing) from Epic Clarity into our data mart.

DEPLOYING THE DECISION MANAGEMENT SYSTEM

Decision Management System Tools

The fundamental characteristics of a decisioning system have been discussed in previous chapters. For the purposes of deployment of a system in our unique clinical setting, we first determined, using a restrictive set of characteristics, what our system needed to do for us. The decisioning platform for GI Surgery at the University of Iowa would have the following characteristics:

- It integrates with our current enterprise software systems.
- It is built around the repeated, clinical decisions that can be made from analysis of clinical, enterprise, and external data.
- It transparently exposes the clinical rules that will be applied to our patients.
- It uses our historical data to predict risks and opportunities.
- It learns, improves, and optimizes itself over time.

After evaluating commercial and open-source products, we chose to partner with and use the Decisioning Platform from StatSoft Inc. This particular product was advantageous to us in that clinicians with great intuition about processes

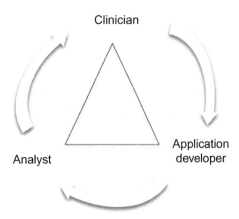

FIGURE 24.1 The triad of a clinician, data analyst, and application developer is critical to success.

could develop predictive models in a familiar spreadsheet and point-and-click environment, rather than learning to code in R or another proprietary language. The rules engine that applies clinical and business rules maintains these separately from the modeling components, and is very transparent.

In our environment, as outlined above, ETL processes are used to bring EHR and other data into our clinical data mart in different time-cycles. This data mart is a large set of tables in the Microsoft SQL Server. It is maintained and backed up behind our hospital's secure firewall by our Health Care Information Systems group. The ETL processes are designed and scheduled by a senior application developer who works side by side with the clinicians.

Decision Management Process

We firmly believe that the triad of a clinician, data analyst, and application developer who work together regularly is critical to success (Figure 24.1). Understanding and prioritizing clinical problems, creating data acquisition and data quality assurance strategies, and applying decisioning algorithms in a meaningful way becomes an intensely iterative process requiring the full talents of each of these individuals.

In addition to such a triad working on this continuously, we have enlisted the help of human factors engineers in the design of the dashboards and reports that clinicians are exposed to, as we did not wish to create "warning fatigue." Warning fatigue is a phenomenon where decision-makers are exposed to too much information continuously, creating a situation where they ignore the warnings that they are receiving.

Decision Management System Workflow Example

Our readmission modeling workflow is an example of a workflow for decision management deployment in a clinical setting. For developing and deploying predictive models to the decisioning platform, we use the CRISP-DM methodology (Figure 24.2). Our initial modeling goal was to predict which of our surgical patients would require unplanned readmission within 30 days of discharge, so that high-risk patients could have their outpatient follow-up intensity increased in hopes of mitigating the need for readmission.

First, we carefully sought to understand what readmission data were available to us. Readmission data are not found in the EHR in real time for obvious reasons. Readmission within 30 days is the most commonly used metric for readmission in surgical patients. For our particular surgical population, the most reliable data at our disposal were from the National Surgical Quality Improvement Project (NSQIP). NSQIP readmission data is available to us in 3-month cycles, and is loaded into our data warehouse at these intervals through an ETL process. Readmissions are matched with the surgical log for each associated encounter.

Next, we sought to understand which variables present in our EHR were available at the time our patients were in the hospital. It is critical to distinguish this, because much administrative data for an encounter is entered by coding specialists many days or weeks after the patient has been discharged, and thus wouldn't be available for real-time use during a patient's hospital stay. To our dismay, we determined that some data which could be important, such as our patients' diagnoses and the procedures that were performed, weren't available as discretely encoded data during the hospital stay. They were contained within unstructured operative reports or progress notes until these were interpreted by coding specialists following discharge. For this reason, they were eliminated from consideration for use in real time.

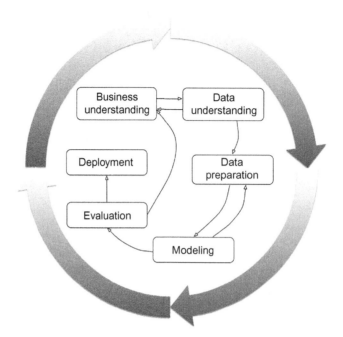

FIGURE 24.2 The CRISP-DM methodology.

Our intention is eventually, in the future, to text-mine these unstructured data sources. We initially identified 12 variables or transformations of variables that were present on most of our patients. These included such things as patient factors (age, gender, ethnicity, home zip code, body mass index, ASA score), procedure factors (surgical Apgar score, surgeon identity, estimated blood loss, transfusion volume), and laboratory studies (preoperative hemoglobin level and last hemoglobin level measured prior to discharge).

With our readmission outcome data and predictor variables now in the data warehouse, we proceeded with data preparation. Missing data replacement strategies were designed, skewed continuous data was normalized, and cases with numerous missing values were removed.

The readmission rate for our population was 16% over the course of 375 encounters. We screened several modeling algorithms for performance on our data. Our goal was to retain only models that had a c-statistic greater than 0.7 (our definition of a model with good discrimination). We used Naive Bayes (NB), Logistic Regression (LR), Support Vector Machine (SVM), Random Forest (RF), Neural Networks (NN), and Classification and Regression Trees (CARTs). Initial performance of most of the models was poor due to the significant class imbalance present in our readmission classifier. To overcome this, we used an oversampling strategy that resulted in 45% of our training data set being positive for readmission. With this sampling strategy in place, the discrimination of our models ranged from 0.59 (RF) to 0.97 (NB). Our NB model had a sensitivity of 0.67 and specificity of 100%. This model was chosen for subsequent deployment.

At the time of this writing, our model has been deployed to our decisioning platform and rules for the timing of follow-up appointments have been entered into the rules engine. Readmission risk-scoring information is displayed on the unit census dashboard so that clinician, discharge navigator, social workers, and all other staff involved in the discharge process are able to view it. The follow-up rules, based upon readmission risk, are now used for determining follow-up appointment timing, and may be over-ridden by the faculty clinicians. We are currently collecting data to determine the effect of this analytics driven discharge process on outcomes.

CONCLUSION

The healing touch and technical skills of surgeons and physicians need to be combined with the powerful predictive capabilities of data science at the bedside. In the right hands, this will result in compassionate and uncompromising care that is truly personalized and appropriate for each patient.

We have demonstrated the technical feasibility of accomplishing this through the use of cultural change and a decisioning platform, and outlined the approach that was taken to get there. It is still early in our own experience, and we have yet to demonstrate our outcomes in terms of patient satisfaction, outcomes, and efficiency, but the models we have created have been validated as powerful real-time predictive tools. By improving and building upon this approach, we hope that our readers can enhance the care of their patients who present with endless numbers of complex problems every day.

POSTSCRIPT

Here we have seen how the healing touches of the surgeon can be combined with accurate predictive analytics and decisioning to provide both safer and more accurate treatment for the patient. In the next chapter, Chapter 25, this same basic idea is applied to diagnosis and decisioning using another type of artificial intelligent health care system that has been developed in recent years, the IBM Watson for Healthcare application.

REFERENCES

Allaudeen, N., Schnipper, J.L., Orav, E.J., Wachter, R.M., Vidyarthi, A.R., 2011. Inability of providers to predict unplanned readmissions. J. Gen. Intern. Med. 26 (7), 771−776.

Oberije, C., Nalbantov, G., Dekker, A., Reymen, B., Baardwijk van, A., Wanders, D., et al., 2013. A prospective study to compare doctor versus model predictions for outcome in lung cancer patients: pick the winner! Eur. Soc. Radiother. Oncol. Geneva, Switzerland.

Pronovost, P., Needham, D., Berenholtz, S., Sinopoli, D., Chu, H., Cosgrove, S., et al., 2006. An intervention to decrease catheter-related bloodstream infections in the ICU. N. Engl. J. Med. 355 (26), 2725−2732.

Saposnik, G., Cote, R., Mamdani, M., Raptis, S., Thorpe, K.E., Fang, J., et al., 2013. How Reliably Do Clinicians Predict Stroke Outcomes? Results from the JURaSSiC (Clinician JUdgment vs. Risk Score to predict Stroke outComes) randomized trial. International Stroke Conference. Honolulu, HI.

Chapter 25

IBM Watson for Clinical Decision Support

Chapter Outline

PREAMBLE

One approach to the design of a medical decisioning system is to avoid making specific decisions, but rather scan through the hugely voluminous structured (databases) and unstructured (text) data sources, and present a list of evidence-based alternatives. These alternatives can be submitted to the most sophisticated non-linear analytical processing system in the universe: the minds of the physicians charged with providing the right diagnosis and treatment for the right patient at the right time. Chapter 25 describes an early attempt to use the IBM Watson computer (winner of the TV contest show, *Jeopardy!*) to create such a tool, which in the hands of the physician is a very sophisticated extension of his or her own brain.

INTRODUCTION

Disappointment with the current state of health care is a global issue. Many countries and health policy organizations desire to improve healthcare outcomes while simultaneously controlling costs. While many current healthcare systems can provide extraordinary services, health care is still plagued by errors, waste, and the adverse effect of flawed decisions. It is estimated that between 21% and 47% (averaging 34%) of what we spend on health care in the USA provides no value (Berwick and Hackbarth, 2012). "Failure of Care Delivery," including the lack of adoption of known best care, and overtreatment (providing care that cannot possibly help) contribute to waste (Berwick and Hackbarth, 2012). Addressing issues such as the failure of care delivery and overtreatment could improve health outcomes and help control costs. Personalized or precision health care is a concept that could improve care delivery, reduce overtreatment, and limit unnecessary costs.

PERSONALIZED HEALTH CARE AND CLINICAL DECISION SUPPORT

The objective of personalized health care includes making decisions that are more likely to be beneficial for the individual patient. It requires a deep understanding of the patient, along with the ability to collect, analyze, and use information germane to the patient to make an evidence-supported decision. Clinical decision support tools can help with that objective. The amount of information that can be available for clinical decision support is overwhelming, and qualifies as "Big Data." Big Data are not amenable to the traditional programmatic computing that most of us learned. Among other attributes, Big Data are marked by ambiguous and inconsistent information. Cognitive computing is data-centric, using statistical analysis to help deal with inconsistency and unreliability, whereas programmatic computing was processor-centric, using fixed programming.

Practical Predictive Analytics and Decisioning Systems for Medicine. DOI: http://dx.doi.org/10.1016/B978-0-12-411643-6.00053-3

Clinical decision support can be divided into two broad categories. One is data-driven decision support, which uses information stored in sources such as electronic health records to help draw inferences about a patient. The second is knowledge-driven, using existing published or other text-like (unstructured, natural language) medical information. Keeping current with medical literature is challenging. Most physicians have fewer than 3−5 hours a week to read, and usually read just a few journals that are specific for their practices (Williamson *et al.*, 1989). However, there are many journals for each practice area, and important information may appear in publications other than those usually read. In addition, reading an article does not mean we will remember everything we read. In the year 2010 alone, the National Library of Medicine in the United States catalogued 699,000 articles (NLM, 2012). The volume of printed material is increasing annually. A tool that can help us to understand the nature of a decision before us (such as a diagnosis or a therapeutic choice), collect specific information about the patient, and then review thousands of articles and offer options based on that information, for us to consider when we make a decision, would be very helpful.

Imagine that you are sitting in your office, pondering a decision. You are fairly comfortable with your knowledge, but perhaps are not sure that you have all the most recent data. You go next door to your colleague, whom you know to be a voracious speed-reader, and discuss your problem with her. She comes back to your office a few minutes later and says that she has just read 100,000 articles and has identified five areas that you might want to consider when making your decision. A system that would provide that kind of support could be very valuable. Until recently, analyzing and using unstructured information had not been very productive. Natural language-processing tools were able to recognize words, but they didn't truly understand the full meaning of documents.

IBM Watson technology was developed to "understand" the meaning of English language documents − not just recognize the words. It demonstrated that ability by successfully playing the game *Jeopardy!*™ and defeating the two reigning champions. Watson understood the *Jeopardy!* stimulus, which was an answer requiring a question in response. Watson then analyzed as many as 200 million pages of text in 3 seconds to learn enough to compose an appropriate question. Watson learned how to play *Jeopardy!* through machine learning. It was given thousands of *Jeopardy!* clues and asked to respond with an answer. Watson was then "told" whether it was correct or not, and adjusted its algorithms in response to improve its performance.

IBM WATSON AND MEDICAL DECISION-MAKING

Watson is now being developed to help medical professionals with their medical decision-making by extracting information from large volumes of data, including medical literature that are relevant to the patient and the decision at hand. In health care, however, Watson would not provide a single answer, such as the only therapy. When playing *Jeopardy!*, Watson actually created a long list of possible responses, and then evaluated the appropriateness of each response to narrow down to likely responses. The rules of the game, however, required that Watson provide only a single answer. There is no such restriction in health care. Watson will provide a prioritized list of evidence-based potential treatment options for the decision-maker to consider, rather than providing a single answer. IBM is currently working with the Memorial Sloan-Kettering Cancer Center, Wellpoint, Inc. and the MD Anderson Cancer Center to develop Watson applications for use by clinicians for decision support in cancer treatment.

In providing those options, Watson performs three cognitive computing tasks. First, Watson analyzes the patient's electronic health record in its natural language form. Watson then analyzes content from many documents, and returns treatment options. Second, Watson is a discovery tool, giving access to extracts from the historical medical record and the documents used to generate the treatment options. Third, Watson is a decision support tool. It learns through repetition what kinds of information are important in making certain decisions. If it is not given that information, Watson will indicate this. When Watson gets the additional information, it can generate updated options and may indicate what other information could be relevant. Just as Watson improved its performance in *Jeopardy!* with feedback about its response, it also is expected to learn from your feedback about the treatment options that you selected. It uses this feedback to improve its decision support capability.

In addition to providing insight from large volumes of literature, Watson's cognitive processes help overcome some limitations of human reasoning, such as the *availability heuristic*. The availability heuristic states that a person is heavily influenced by recent events − for example, a clinician misses a rare diagnosis, and thus will consider that rare diagnosis to be more likely than actually occurs. "The availability heuristic is a mental shortcut that occurs when people make judgments about the probability of events by how easy it is to think of examples" (Wikipedia, n.d.). Second, since Watson can request missing information, it helps remind you about information you may have forgotten to obtain. Third, trying to extract all the important information from a voluminous record can be frustrating and difficult. Watson helps with this process as well.

This last capability is proving especially important for addressing the challenge of leveraging the unstructured information in an electronic health record. Much of the most relevant and useful information in the health record is contained in the clinical notes, which are entered by the healthcare provider after each patient encounter. The aggregate collection of clinical notes in a longitudinal health record maintained over several years can easily exceed thousands of pages of text. Watson can analyze this text, identify information that has been determined to be important, connect that information with structured elements in the health record, and provide the user with direct and relevant access to that information. One specific use case for this analysis is automatic generation and maintenance of the problem list – the list of the current, key health issues that have been determined to be important for a healthcare provider to be aware of when treating the patient.

The IBM Research Watson team is conducting research to develop methods that can explore the relationships among the clinical data contained in electronic health records in a project called WatsonPaths. The current goal is to improve Watson's ability to answer typical medical questions. It is being used as an educational tool for medical students. WatsonPaths is intended to deal with more complex scenarios associated with a typical diagnostic question. This technology will be designed to have the ability to analyze a paragraph describing the patient's problem, decompose the problem into the relevant factors, and connect those factors to potential diagnoses along relevant relationships and intermediate results. The factors can include the current symptoms, signs, labs, and other relevant pieces of information from the patient's medical history. The relationships might be simple associations, or they might be specific to the type of the current factor – for example, exploring causal relationships between diseases and symptoms. The goal is to build a graph that connects all of the factors to potential diagnoses, possibly traversing several intermediate results.

Beyond the ability to deal with complex scenarios, there are two other key aspects of the WatsonPaths approach. The first is the explanatory power of the approach. Relationships and intermediate results proposed by WatsonPaths is supported by evidence from the underlying corpus of relevant medical literature, providing an intelligible explanation of how the input factors connect to the final potential diagnoses for explanatory purposes. This capability leverages Watson's core ability to support answers with evidence from the underlying literature.

The second key aspect is the user interaction model. The WatsonPaths approach enables the creation of a collaborative tool that can suggest complex connections between input factors and potential diagnoses by analyzing a massive corpus of medical literature, as well as integrate suggestions and feedback from the user. The system leverages the user's knowledge and expertise to enhance or correct the graph, while simultaneously integrating relevant information that would otherwise be trapped in the vast medical literature. IBM is exploring the potential of this approach with the Cleveland Clinic, working with physicians, faculty, and students at the Cleveland Clinic Lerner College of Medicine to evaluate WatsonPaths as a collaborative learning tool for medicine.

Thus, Watson and WatsonPaths brings us closer to the goal of evidence-supported decision-making by helping us better use healthcare literature and leverage information typically buried and trapped in the health record.

POSTSCRIPT

In the preceding chapters and tutorials, the authors have introduced the readers to: (1) background medical information such as "Meaningful Use," HIMSS, EMR (electronic medical records), JCAHO (an accrediting agency for health care), Gene Informatics, and associated topics including the Lean Hospital Movement which involves quality control and Six Sigma; (2) modern data analysis methods, including data mining, text mining, and predictive analytics with decisioning systems; and (3) numerous practical step-by-step tutorials and case studies where you, the reader, can rapidly learn how to do these analyses yourself. This completes the book, with one exception: in the next and final chapter, Chapter 26, the authors discuss some leading phenomena currently happening at the cutting edge of medicine and health care, and also make some speculative predictions on what to expect in the next 3–20 years.

REFERENCES

Berwick, D., Hackbarth, A., 2012. Eliminating waste in us health care. JAMA. 307 (14), 1513–1516.

NLM, 2012. The Library and Book Trade Almanac on NLM 2011. National Library of Medicine, Bethesda, MD. Available at: <www.nlm.nih.gov/pubs/staffpubs/od/ocpl/library_booktrade_almanac_2012.html> (last accessed 17.10.12).

Wikipedia, n.d. Availability Heuristic. Available at <http://en.wikipedia.org/wiki/Availability_heuristic> (last accessed 20.10.13).

Williamson, J.W., German, P.S., Weiss, R., Skinner, E.A., Bowes IIIF., 1989. Health science information management and continuing education of physicians. A survey of US primary care practitioners and their opinion leaders. Ann. Intern. Med. 110 (2), 151–160.

Chapter 26

21st Century Health Care and Wellness: Getting the Health Care Delivery System That Meets Global Needs

Cost-Effective, Evidence Based, Meaningful Use Perfected, and Effective Delivery for a New "Personalized Prescriptive Medicine" Resulting from Rapid Decisions Derived from Accurate Predictive Analytics Models

Chapter Outline

INTRODUCTION

What is the value of the book you have just read? Minimally, your reading should have provided a framework and focus for the future in the following:

1. Gaining new insights into disease pathways and progression
2. Understanding the effectiveness of interventions
3. Discovering "new knowledge" and the "real cause(s)" of diseases
4. Speeding the pace of science
5. Moving towards personalized medicine — even patient-directed medicine.

Practical Predictive Analytics and Decisioning Systems for Medicine. DOI: http://dx.doi.org/10.1016/B978-0-12-411643-6.00054-5

Overview

This chapter attempts to summarize much of the preceding book and also focuses the reader on the future. There will be dramatic changes and improvements in the field of health care and wellness within the next 6 years: a new 21st century high-technology health care and wellness movement will shake the existing healthcare industry and institutions. By 2020, we expect that the healthcare industry will be reorganized into patient-centered wellness and medical teams supported by digital and mobile health technologies. By 2020 the first comprehensive health and wellness sensors and predictive analytics hardware tools will be common, embedded in eye glasses, clothing, architecture, facilities, and nanotechnologies in the human body. Our 21st century wellness movement will be focused on real-time analytics and feedback to achieve peak wellness through optimal nutrition, exercise, stress reduction, and measurements of continuous human health improvements and medical treatments, when needed. By 2020, science-based personalized medicine and wellness will become the standard: most (if not all) wellness and medical treatments will be based upon individual genome studies combined with a full array of digital health information with real-time analytics guiding individuals and medical support teams.

BACKGROUND AND NEED FOR CHANGE

We started this book in its initial chapters (see particularly Chapter 2) with the need for changes in healthcare delivery, and especially the need for predictive analytics in medicine. We restate that need for change and point to the fact that change is happening already.

To reiterate, in a recent online guide (AMA, 2013, p. 2) for medical doctors who are considering joining ACOs (Accountable Care Organizations), the American Medical Association (AMA) set out the business case for why the existing medical fee for service model must change in the United States. In that document it was said:

> "In 2008, health care expenditures in the US exceeded $2.3 trillion with costs per resident at $7,631 per year" (Henry J. Kaiser Family Foundation, n.d., cited in AMA, 2013). One other source gave the amount as $7,538 (Henry J. Kaiser Family Foundation, 2011, Exhibit 4A).
>
> "In 2009, the percentage of gross domestic product (GDP) spent on health care was 17.3 percent. In 2008, it was 16.2 percent, making the increase to 17.3 percent in 2009 the largest one-year increase since 1960 (Truffer *et al.*, 2010, cited in AMA, 2013, p. 2).
>
> "The country closest to the United States in health care expenditures is Germany, where 11.1 percent of its GDP is spent on health care" (Truffer *et al.*, 2010 cited in AMA, 2013).

The United States has poor health outcomes compared with other developed countries: the effectiveness of healthcare delivery, despite the high costs, is far less than in other advanced economies. One of the primary needs to help correct this is the application of predictive analytics and decisioning, as eloquently stated by Dr. David Dimas of the University of California, Irvine (personal communications, 2012 and 2013):

> ***The Importance of Predictive Analytics in Healthcare:*** *Current practice in healthcare is often based on more traditional statistical analysis (p-value), which can lead to treating a person as a "mean" of a population. An individual's demographics, health history, comorbid conditions and genetics may cause him to react differently to a particular drug or treatment. As a result, predictive analytics applied to medical data can help develop treatments that are more in tune with the individual patient.*
>
> (David Dimas, PhD).

Dr. Dimas, trained as an engineer, and seeing the value of predictive analytics, established one of the first graduate extension Predictive Analytics Certificate Programs in the USA. A course in Predictive Analytics for Healthcare & Medical Research will be added to this program, projected for 2014. The need for people to be trained in predictive analytics is so great that this program has a waiting list of students — and the students are not only the "young twenties" generation; there are also MD and PhD holders and seasoned IT professionals with 20 years of experience taking this program. This speaks to the perceived need in our society for people trained in this field.

LEARNING OBJECTIVES

- To learn how Predictive Analytics and Digital & Mobile Health will change health care, and what these changes mean for your health and organization.
- To recognize the necessary steps a healthcare organization must undertake to successfully harness the power of analytics, digital, and mobile technologies.
- To understand emerging trends and best practices for the use and adoption of mobile technology, and particularly predictive analytics coupled with decisioning.

TRENDS IMPACTING HEALTHCARE INDUSTRIES

Peter Drucker (2006) advised his students, when planning their careers in non-profits and business, to focus on the perceived major trends in society and the domain of interest, and in fact to consider major trends in all their strategic planning. We can see many of the major trends in medicine today based upon technology roadmaps and demographics that will impact 21st century health care:

- Electronic medical record (EMR) systems, Health Information Exchanges (HIEs), and health and wellness applications — making all forms of health digital data available.
- Big Data, use of large patient databases with patient-identifying information removed, combined with predictive analytics to guide effective decisions.
- Expansion of EMR systems and tools leading to consolidations of providers and payers; some hospital health systems are creating health insurance plans of their own.
- Finally, a growth of interest in scientific research support for clinical effectiveness: global movements towards comparative effectiveness research (CER) and heterogeneous treatment effects research (HTE) to guide decision-makers and healthcare providers regarding the scientific merit of clinical treatments.

A major trend in health systems in advanced economies is to remove the marketing and hype surrounding healthcare treatments and drug effectiveness, and move to scientific studies of clinical effectiveness that specifically target individuals and individual outcomes. Many examples of such scientific studies have been given in the previous chapters, such as that of the University of Pittsburg Medical Center (UPMC) reducing its readmissions dramatically by use of predictive analytics instead of techniques that regress to the mean (Mace, 2013). They were able to develop an algorithm based on "eight combinations of answers" to 5 questions on a 24-question survey, to target individuals who "were going to run about 300% more expensive than people who don't hit those rules" (Mace, 2013, para. 7).

Many of the developed world's national healthcare systems use a structured process to synthesize scientific studies; many use comparative effectiveness research (CER) and heterogeneous treatment effect research (HTE) to help determine optimal courses of care and improve science-based medical treatments that have been proven to be effective. CER compares the benefits and harms of alternative methods to prevent, diagnose, and treat a clinical condition and monitor care; and HTE looks at different "groupings" of individuals based on genetics and other parameters that separate them into distinct groups; the focus is on methods to improve the delivery of care, including the effectiveness of drug treatments and dosage, for the individual patient.

In 2010, the Patient Protection and Affordable Care Act established the Patient-Centered Outcomes Research Institute (PCORI, 2014a), a non-profit organization, to conduct research to provide information about the best available evidence to help patients and their healthcare providers make more informed decisions. PCORI has focused on comparative effectiveness research and heterogeneous treatment effects, and is building a national infrastructure to conduct CER and HTE research (PCORI, 2014b). PCORI's targeted grants are helping to build this CER and HTE national infrastructure, and contribute to the overall PCORI Mission and Vision (PCORI, 2014a):

Mission of PCORI

The Patient-Centered Outcomes Research Institute (PCORI) helps people make informed health care decisions, and improves health care delivery and outcomes, by producing and promoting high integrity, evidence-based information that comes from research guided by patients, caregivers and the broader health care community.

(PCORI, 2014a, para. 1).

Vision of PCORI

Patients and the public have the information they need to make decisions that reflect their desired health outcomes.

(PCORI, 2014a, para. 2).

Obviously, PCORI emphasized the importance of patients in all aspects of their medical care. The addition of Steven Clauser, PhD, MPA, as the Director of Improving Healthcare Systems emphasizes PCORI's commitment to patient-centered outcome research that encourages "self-management of their care" (PCORI, 2013, para. 2). The role of patient had shifted from passively receiving care to interactive involvement. Patient-directed medical care (see Chapter 14 in this book) is recognized as vital.

EXISTING AND EMERGING HEALTHCARE ORGANIZATIONS

The existing healthcare industry consists of three major groups:

- *payers* — health insurance firms or non-profits or governmental agencies
- *providers* — hospitals and medical practices
- *life science firms* — firms that manufacture medical devices, and pharmaceutical and biotechnology firms that manufacture drugs and other medicines.

Given grave concerns by both the general public and employers and employees in the United States regarding high healthcare costs and poor quality, citizens have called for reforms and new legislation. Passage of the Affordable Care Act in 2010 has greatly impacted the regulation and delivery of health care in the United States. Government incentives have helped move provider organizations to electronic health record (EHR) systems and other forms of digital data.

Most if not all groups in the healthcare industry now have a focus on innovation and the use of analytics and scientific research to improve healthcare delivery. Some health systems are both payers and providers, such as Kaiser Permanente, which includes a HMO Health Insurance division and a health system of more than 40 large hospitals and integrated medical clinics and medical practices. Kaiser has invested heavily in its administrative, clinical, and data warehousing systems, reportedly investing more than $4 billion in its Epic clinical system, patient-provider portal, and a series of data warehousing systems, including a large Teradata clinical data warehouse for longitudinal data on its 8 million patients.

The University of Pittsburgh Medical Center (UPMC, 2014) has established a regional health system and health insurance plans, and has started to offer health services internationally:

With more than 3,200 physicians, 20 hospitals, and a myriad of community-based facilities and outpatient programs serving 29 counties in western Pennsylvania, UPMC is the leading provider of health care services in the region.

(UPMC, 2014, para. 1).

Through advisory services, infrastructure consultation, and clinical management, UPMC is helping to transform health care throughout communities in:

- Ireland: Cancer centers and a full-service hospital
- Italy: Transplantation, radiotherapy, and biotechnology centers
- United Kingdom: Information technology and cancer care
- Kazakhstan: Oncology center consults
- Singapore: Transplantation and clinical management
- China: Pathology consults and health care collaboration
- Japan: Education in primary care and family medicine.

(UMPC, para. 4).

Working with the Carnegie Mellon University, Software Engineering Institute (SEI) teams, and major technology partners, UPMC has announced a $100 million initiative to build a state-of-the-art predictive analytics data warehousing system, to develop new models of affordable, effective, patient-focused health care:

PITTSBURGH, Oct. 1, 2012 *— What if a doctor could easily predict which treatment would be most effective and least toxic for an individual breast cancer patient, based on her genetic and clinical information? What if an intelligent electronic medical record could flag patients at risk for kidney failure, based on subtle changes in lab results? Or what if physicians could tell* *from the medical records of a large population of patients when the next outbreak of flu might occur and have the right kind and quantity of vaccine ready?*

These are just a few of the scenarios behind UPMC's five-year, $100 million investment in a sophisticated enterprise analytics effort that will foster personalized medicine. Together with technology partners Oracle, IBM, Informatica and dbMotion, UPMC today announced that it intends to create a best-in-class data warehouse that brings together clinical, financial, administrative, genomic and other information that today is difficult to integrate and analyze. Advanced analytic and predictive modeling applications for clinical and financial decision-making are expected to produce better patient outcomes, enhanced research capabilities, continual quality improvements across UPMC, and reduced costs.

With predictive analytics fully integrated with a decision support platform, hospital teams can quickly summarize and analyze patient information for the entire medical team, including doctors, nurses, specialists and other staff, so quick and informed decisions can be made.

(UPMC, 2012).

HEALTH START-UPS AND ESTABLISHED TECHNOLOGY FIRMS CONTRIBUTING TO HEALTH CARE

Both large corporations that have been around for a long time and many new small technology firms are contributing to the revolution in Big Data innovations in health care, including the following established companies:

- IBM, Oracle, and Teradata, supplying core database software and hardware
- DELL-StatSoft (STATISTICA Data Miner & Decisioning)
- IBM (SPSS — i.e., IBM-MODELER formerly known as Clementine)
- SAS (SAS Enterprise Miner)
- SAP-KXEN, providing predictive analytics software.

In March of 2014, Dell acquired StatSoft STATISTICA in order to better supply all types of support for data analysis, from hardware to software to consulting services to cloud storage — i.e., true "end-to-end" solutions where everything, from computers to servers to tablets to cloud to smart phones and any other e-communication formats yet to be developed, seamlessly communicates among all formats. (This seamless communication is one of the big problems within EMR systems and between EMRs and other medical data sources, as pointed out in the early chapters of this book). Predictive analytics for health care was a priority in that acquisition, providing the final major missing link in Big Data science analytics to fully enable this end-to-end solution for medicine.

As the authors of this book write the final chapter in late May of 2014, we see an interesting phenomenon reminiscent of the Silicon Valley "bubble" of the 1990s: many MDs are leaving their practice or CMO (Chief Medical Officer) positions in major companies to start their own small "start-up" companies. These start-ups are pursuing various medical technology advanced products and processes, including mobile, genetic, and other avenues. Apparently venture capital is flowing into these start-ups, meaning that investors see a potential market. Only the best of these products and processes will likely prevail. One of this book's authors (Gary Miner) predicts that within a short period of time (years) this bubble will burst, just like the Silicon Valley bubble burst several years ago, and then the best of these will become part of our routine healthcare procedures, making health care more cost-effective and individualized.

There are many examples that could be cited, but for the purposes of this book, those below should give you, the reader, an idea of what is going on in this area of technology — healthcare start-up endeavors.

IBM Watson

IBM's Watson machine, which is an integrated hardware and software process, won its initial fame on the TV show *Jeopardy!*, beating the leading human champions. Watson has started to use its natural language capabilities, hypothesis generation, and evidence-based learning to support medical professionals and organizations.

The Memorial Sloan-Kettering Cancer Center (MSKCC) is the world's oldest and largest private cancer center. MSKCC has partnered with IBM to put IBM Watson to work fighting cancer. Beginning with breast and lung cancers, MSKCC and IBM are using Watson to consolidate clinical expertise, molecular and genomic data, and its repository of cancer case histories to create evidence-based solutions. Physicians can use Watson to assist in diagnosing and treating cancer patients. Watson supports medical terminology by design by extending Watson's natural language processing capabilities and data mining of patient data, such as family histories available in digital EMR records. Watson

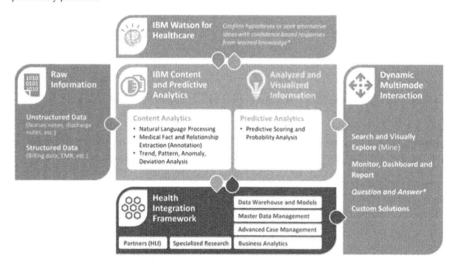

FIGURE 26.1 Multiple Analytic Services.
Reproduced from IBM (2012, p. 4).

incorporates treatment guidelines, electronic medical record (EMR) data, and doctors' and nurses' notes. Further, Watson can include research and clinical studies, journal articles, and patient information into the data available for analysis. Watson's natural language processing capabilities enable the system to leverage unstructured data. Watson can include genomic data and other insights to provide individualized, confidence-scored recommendations to physicians (Memorial Sloan-Kettering Cancer Center, 2013).

According to IBM, "IBM Advanced Care Insights enables care providers to apply predictive and similarity analytics to confirm what is suspect, discover new information, flag what is being missed and anticipate change" (IBM, 2014) (Figure 26.1).

New Technology and 21st Century Health Care: Health Start-Up Firms

Rock Health is a health start-up firm incubator that operates in San Francisco and Boston (Rock Health, 2013). Rock Health helps chosen start-up companies by providing office space, technology, and advertising to potential investors. New York, San Diego, Austin, and other areas have many health start-ups. Often, digital health start-ups use crowd funding platforms such as Kickstarter, Indiegogo, Fundable, and Medstartr.

In 2013, Rock Health featured a list of 236 health start-up firms on its website (Rock Health, 2013). Many of the 236 health start-ups were part of the "Quantify Yourself" movement: health and wellness digital tracking devices and cloud software that incorporate analytics or predictive analytics.

Building the *Star Trek* Tricorder

Remember the TV and movie series *Star Trek*, and how Dr. "Bones" McCoy used a tricorder device to help diagnose all medical problems?

In 2012, the X Prize Foundation announced a long-term, worldwide contest in which $10 million would be awarded to the three teams that produced the best "tricorder type" device for detecting and monitoring a variety of diseases and conditions. Teams registered in 2013, and were to show their devices and test results in early 2014. By the summer of 2013, the Qualcomm Tricorder X Prize had drawn hundreds of competitor teams. In 2014, the original 300 teams had been whittled down to 10 (Dvorsky, 2014; see also Figure 26.2).

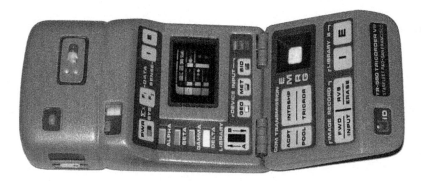

FIGURE 26.2 Tricorder. *Reproduced from Dvorsky (2014).*

According to the contest website, the Qualcomm Tricorder X Prize would provide $7 million to the winning team and prize monies to the second- and third-placed teams:

The Qualcomm Tricorder XPRIZE is a $10 million global competition to stimulate innovation and integration of precision diagnostic technologies, making reliable health diagnoses available directly to "health consumers" in their homes ...

Advances in fields such as artificial intelligence, wireless sensing, imaging diagnostics, lab-on-a-chip, and molecular biology will enable better choices in when, where, and how individuals receive care, thus making healthcare more convenient, affordable, and accessible. The winner will be the team whose technology most accurately diagnoses a set of diseases independent of a healthcare professional or facility, and that provides the best consumer user experience with their device.

(Qualcomm, 2014, paras 2 and 3).

The winning tricorder device was to be a tool capable of capturing key health metrics that lead to diagnosing a set of 15 diseases; among the core set of screens and diseases that had to be diagnosed were the following:

1. Anemia
2. Urinary tract infection, lower
3. Diabetes, type 2
4. Atrial fibrillation
5. Stroke
6. Foodborne illness
7. Shingles
8. Melanoma
9. Strep throat
10. Cholesterol screen
11. HIV screen
12. Osteoporosis
13. Absence of condition.

The Vital Signs Set Tricorder requirements included the following:

1. Blood pressure
2. Electrocardiography (heart rate/variability)
3. Body temperature
4. Respiratory rate
5. Oxygen Saturation.

The winning tricorder device was to collect large volumes of data from various sources, from ongoing measurements of health data, using wireless sensors, and imaging technologies. Further, the tricorder was to use portable, non-invasive laboratory test replacements. Of the 300 teams, several leading medical sensor technology companies registered to join the contest to win the tricorder prize monies. For example, 10 teams of firms registered from the San Diego area.

FIGURE 26.3   Scanadu Scout Tricorder. *Reproduced from Dvorsky (2014).*

In this competition, teams were to leverage technology innovation in areas such as artificial intelligence and wireless sensing. Much like the medical tricorder of *Star Trek* fame, doctors, nurses, and individual/ patients can use the tricorder devices and a smart phone to make preliminary medical diagnoses independent of a physician or healthcare provider. The goal of the competition is to drive development of devices that will give consumers access to their state of health using the new devices connected to smart phones to share data in the cloud.

The 10 teams that were left were each working to improve medical care by taking the devices to the home and to the patients themselves. Diagnoses can be made regardless of the location of the individual (Dvorsky, 2014). Our future doctors could be robots! And predictive analytics should be at the center of those processes.

Team Scanadu's Scout™ is a $150 device that in 2014 was considered a front runner among the 10 entrants left in the contest (Dvorsky, 2014; see also Figure 26.3). The team was able to raise over $1 million by June 2013, and was then able to construct its Scout device that could gather key health metrics in under 10 seconds by holding it to one's temple, recording vitals such as heart rate, blood pressure, temperature, heart activity, and oxygenation (Stenovec, 2013). Scanadu uses Bluetooth technology to upload information to a smart phone.

> *Project ScanaFlo is a low-cost device that uses the smart-phone as a urine analysis tool. For pregnant women, Project ScanaFlo will be the first portable device to provide health data throughout the duration of a pregnancy.*
>
> *Project ScanaFlu is a low-cost tool that uses the smart-phone as a reader to assess cold-like symptoms. By testing saliva, the disposable cartridge can provide early detection for flu-like symptoms and Strep A, Influenza A, Influenza B, and other respiratory diseases.*
>
> (Scanadu, 2013).

Wearable Computers for Doctors

Google glasses were emerging in 2013–2014, and seemed a novelty. However, some physicians used them as they performed operations or interviewed their patients. The physician could be operating and intermittently glance at the patient's charts or the patient's results from tests (Hay, 2013).

Explorys

Based in Cleveland, Explorys is a Cleveland Clinic spin-off company, founded in 2009, that leverages Big Data to support clinical decisions. Explorys provides turnkey solutions for clinical integration, at-risk population management, cost of care measurement, and pay-for-performance solutions. Explorys' solutions help clinicians analyze data from multiple clinical and administrative sources. Data mining can guide physicians to the personalized treatment plan called for by each patient's unique case: analytic tools can show variations among patients and treatments influencing health outcomes. Several major hospital and health systems have joined to share clinical data; Explorys has created one of the largest clinical databases with predictive analytic, data mining, and other analytic tools available to support clinical decisions (Explorys, 2014).

*Explorys' healthcare customers include some of the most prominent healthcare systems in the United States, together account-ing for over $45 billion in care. With over **100** billion clinical, financial, and operational data elements, spanning **40** million patients, **200** hospitals, and over **100,000** providers, Explorys' secure cloud-computing platform is being used by **14** major integrated healthcare systems to identify patterns in diseases, treatments, and outcomes. Our network includes Cleveland Clinic, Trinity Health, St Joseph Health System, Catholic Health Partners, and many others with patients in all 50 states.*

(Cleveland Biomedical Job Fair, 2014).

TECHNOLOGY TRENDS THAT IMPACT HEALTH AND WELLNESS

Current Trends Outside Healthcare Facilities

There is an increasing use of smart phones and tablets by clinicians and patients. Even a report back in 2011 (Boulos *et al.*, 2011, para. 33) stated:

According to a recent video report by Mobile Future, a Washington, DC, broad-based coalition of businesses and non-profit organizations, there has been a massive increase in the numbers of consumer smart phone apps (applications) downloaded over the past two years, with figures going up from 300 million apps downloaded in 2009 to five billion in 2010.

The eCAALYX Example

As stated by Boulos *et al.* (2011, para. 11):

The eCAALYX Mobile Application is being developed under the scope of the eCAALYX EU-funded project (Enhanced Complete Ambient Assisted Living Experiment, 2009–2012) which aims at building a remote monitoring system targeting older people with multiple chronic diseases. Patients, carers and clinicians' involvement is extensive throughout the prototype design, deployment and testing, and clinical trial phases of the project. The main functionality of the eCAALYX Mobile Platform is to act as a seamless "informed" intermediary between the wearable health sensors (in a "smart garment") used by the older person and the health professionals' Internet site, by reporting to the latter (but also to the patients) alerts and measurements obtained from sensors and the geographic location (via smart phone GPS) of the user. Additionally, the mobile platform is also able to reason with the raw sensor data to identify higher level information, including easy-to-detect anomalies such as tachycardia and signs of respiratory infections, based on established medical knowledge. A user interface is also provided, which allows the user to evaluate the most recent medical details obtained from sensors, perform new measurements, and communicate with the caretakers.

Usability becomes a key issue for the group of individuals (patients) that are the target group for using eCAALYX, since this group may be an older population that is not necessarily familiar with using technology and may have physical impairments such as poorer eyesight and dementia. With that in mind, the eCAALYX mobile platform is designed to be as transparent as possible for the user.

Other e-items in this "outside of healthcare facilities" category but within at least the partial control of patients include:

- Mobile health and social media — patients can (and are) form(ing) groups (support groups) based on either risk profiles or chronic diseases
- Mobile patient management with social components
- Digital health sensors and tracking — health sensors can be put into buildings, homes, bathrooms, and other places to keep track of a patient's symptoms
- Wearable computing machines, such as Google Glasses
- In-body sensors — i.e., either ingested or implantable computerized devices.

TRENDS AND EXPECTATIONS FOR THE FUTURE OF HEALTH IT AND ANALYTICS

The following "predictions" are based on the authors' own "intuition" and from readings on eHealth and mHealth in various references, including the following: Wicklund (2014), in HIMSS mHealthNews; HIMSS14 (2014); HIMSS Analytics (2014); HIMSS Healthcare Global (2014); and HIMSS Transforming Health Through IT (2014).

The Next 4 Years — by-2018 Predictions

- More than 90% of US hospitals and larger medical practices will be using EMR systems with advanced analytics and predictive analytics.
- More than 70% of US doctors will be working in organizations that charge fees based on other than fee-for-service models; ACOs (accountable care organizations) and HMOs will become the dominant model for health care in the USA. Integrated delivery organizations will use advanced Health IT systems with predictive analytics.
- New types of professional models for health care will emerge, such as Wal-Mart delivery of drop-in medical care; we will see rapid growth of comprehensive health plans with shared risk, and "medical tourism" with patients traveling to high quality overseas centers of excellence at lower costs.
- Globally, millions upon millions of patients will be remotely monitored (telehealth).
- Predictive analytics will combine with health IT systems, digital and mobile, and with comprehensive genome services studies on all high-risk patients and those with chronic diseases to create fully personalized medicine; personalized drug therapy will improve outcomes and reduce patient safety risks.

The Next 9 Years — by-2023 Predictions

Articles concerning changes in medicine are appearing daily in the popular press. For example, in one recent *Wall Street Journal* edition (Chernova, 2014; Marcus, 2014) there were two such articles. The first discussed baby clothing that can track vital signs of infants (Chernova, 2014); the second concerned the efforts of physicians currently tracking and analyzing patient data from routine check-ups (Marcus, 2014) that help to personalize advice given to patients, such as whether or not a sore throat is likely to be strep or whether the patient can simply stay home with chicken soup. Technological devices such as implants, data tracking tattoos, and nanotechnology are springing up like weeds (Hotz, 2014).

By 2023:

- Fully operational tricorder, non-invasive devices to help medical staff identify potential illness factors will be in use, including medical detector devices.
- Sensors embedded in clothing and architecture, and bathroom devices, will continuously monitor health risks and send alerts; monitoring will focus on the development of pre-cancer formations that may require early treatment; heart and stroke monitoring will reach an advanced state.
- Advances in health care, nutrition, and fitness, and health and wellness tracking and alerts, will boost life spans; many citizens will move to more vegetarian diets many days of the week, as well as taking moderate exercise such as averaging 30 minutes of walking daily.
- More than 80–90% of the population in advanced economies will have smart phones within 10 years; all will be using mobile medical or fitness applications.
- More than 90% of patients and doctors in advanced economies will be using health and wellness smart phone applications to maintain and improve their health and fitness. Advanced Patient & Provider portals will link health IT systems and mobile solutions.
- Patients will become more informed consumers of medical care, and more actively involved in their own health care, including using personalized predictive analytics.
- Google Glass and/or similar types of wearable computers will be used in all aspects of the delivery of medical care.

Some of the items listed above are happening already. For example, the Scanadu Scout™ (discussed earlier in this chapter), a sensor that measures various vital body functions such as heart rate, was initially released to a handful of people on March 31, 2014. This device is produced by a company on the NASA Ames Research Park Campus in Mountain View, California. The initial batch had some "bugs" and went back to the drawing board, but an updated version is expected to be released soon. Importantly, this means that Scanadu is bringing to life a vision, shared by the company, its backers, and people/patient supporters, of a

health environment where each individual person is empowered through knowledge of their own health. People interested can become test volunteers during the full development of this device.

(Scanadu, 2014).

CONCLUSIONS AND SUMMARY OF IMPORTANT CONCEPTS PRESENTED IN THIS BOOK

The evolution of data analytics, and what are the best practices for accuracy in 2014, include:

- Bayesian data analysis, which was used for centuries prior to Fischerian Central Limit Theory statistics of the 20th century (for more detail, see Nisbet *et al.*, 2009)
- Traditional p-value Fischerian statistics (population mean ... group mean ... central limit theory based)
- Data mining (statistical learning theory algorithms — mostly machine learning/artificial intelligence based, and also some clustering and "rules based" methods)
- Predictive analytics, which is "broader" than data mining, including some DA (discriminant analysis), LR (logistic regression), and WoE-LR (weight of evidence combined with logistic regression); and the data mining algorithms, especially the statistical learning algorithms, but including CART, CHAID, K-E-means clustering, interactive trees, boosted trees, MARSplines, neural networks, Bayesian analysis, support vector machines, k-Nearest Neighbors analysis, association rules, SAL (Sequence, Association, and Link Analysis), and independent components analysis, among others)

The potential accuracy of a "predictive model" tends to increase as one goes from the lowest level with DA and LR, next to WoE-LR, and then finally to the "true" machine learning methods, as illustrated in Figure 26.4.

The model in Figure 26.4 does not mean that any specific data set will only get the best predictive analytic model by using the AI—machine learning algorithms, as some data sets, especially if the data are clearly linear (but this rarely happens with medical data), may get highest accuracy models using DA and LR. However, in general, for most data sets, in our experience, the best models with the highest "accuracy scores" are obtained by using the true statistical learning theory modern algorithms.

Another way of describing this is to use the term "global learning" (i.e., a population-based learning where means of the population and corresponding t-tests, p values, and other traditional statistics are used) vs. "individual statistical learning theory" methods (i.e., the case-by-case learning approach of data mining algorithms). This distinction is important for the main message of this book, which is "personalized" and "person-centered" health care. This distinction is also important for CER (comparative effectiveness research) and HTE (heterogeneous treatment effects), in which some scientists are intent on looking at "groups" of people (groups classified by age, sex, etc.) but for which the ultimate goal is to look at "individuals" — individuals that are genetically distinct, thus a finer grouping than that obtained by just looking at age, sex, and similarly classified groups.

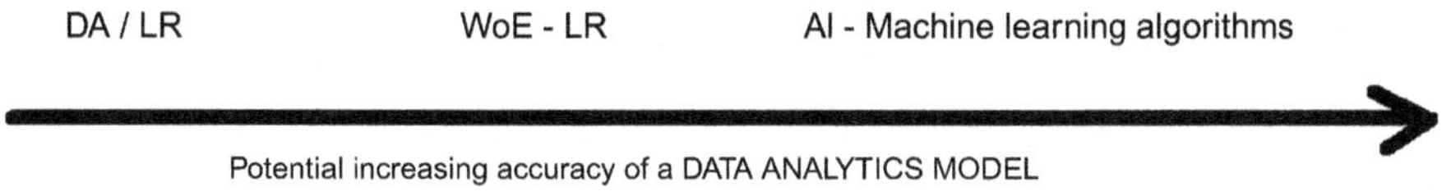

DA / LR   WoE - LR   AI - Machine learning algorithms

Potential increasing accuracy of a DATA ANALYTICS MODEL

FIGURE 26.4 Potential increasing accuracy of a data analytics model.

Technology for the Elderly

Consider this statistic: "In 2010, the total direct medical costs of fall injuries for people 65 and older, adjusted for inflation, was $30 billion" (CDC, 2014, para. 7). That same site predicted that, unless things change, the figure in 2020, using 2012 dollar values, will be a whopping $67.7 billion. One-third of adults over age 65 fall each year. The monetary costs are only a part of the issue — there is also the matter of pain and suffering, and of income lost, family duties increasing to take care of the older member, and permanent losses that can result. Falls are a big problem in our country.

Technologies already present are helping the elderly stay in their homes, and many medical scientists are beginning to find ways of collecting day-to-day data to use in predictive analytic individualized medicine (Wang, 2014). For example, Skubic *et al.* (2009) have been collecting data on stride length and speed of stride among residents of elderly apartments. They have been using 3D sensors, and with the data are developing a prediction model for falls.

Demiris *et al.* (2008) installed various monitoring devices in nine seniors' living quarters, validating the devices with independent observations, and found that the devices were accurate, accepted, and not considered intrusive by the residents after the initial phase of getting used to the devices. The authors did point out ethical concerns about privacy and control as the users learn to rely on automation. However, as if in answer, the residents reported they felt more of a sense of control over their lives and often wanted to see their data, reinforcing the concept that patients, if given the chance, would really like to become more involved in research.

Predictive analytic techniques and projects can significantly impact the quality of lives of seniors and help reduce healthcare costs.

Technology for Rural Areas

This is an area alluded to earlier in this chapter where mobile sensing devices were discussed. However, a specific example that came to our attention recently was the use of mobile phone technology for doing eye exams in rural Africa, where previously many people were going blind because of lack of access to eye doctors and eye clinics.

In March 2014, Andrew Bastawrous, an eye surgeon and inventor, and a TED Fellow, filmed a description of this technology currently used in Kenya, Africa. It is called "Peek," and is based on a smart phone that is given to community health workers who travel out to the field. In these rural areas this phone takes "snapshots" of a person's inner eye conditions and sends it back to the diagnosing doctor at the clinic. Difficult cases can even be evaluated at major eye centers around the world, communicating the best diagnosis and treatment plan rapidly back to the health worker in the field.

Currently, around the world, over 80 million people are blind. Most of this blindness occurs in underserved areas like Kenya. Most of this blindness is also easily preventable. So here, in this current development in Africa, we see not only a cost-effective solution, but also a saving of sight for potentially millions of people (Bastawrous, 2014; see also Box 26.1).

Box 26.1

We encourage the reader to watch the following video (http://www.ted.com/talks/andrew_bastawrous_get_your_next_eye_exam_on_a_smartphone?utm_campaign=&awesm=on.ted.com_quBe&utm_source=facebook.com&utm_medium=on. ted.com-facebook-share&utm_content=awesm-publisher) as it demonstrates what is going on in mobile health technology in a much better way than we can put down here in words.

The Kenyan example is of special interest to one of the authors of this book, who had an eye condition that could eventually result in blindness. The author spent 18 months going to 5 different eye clinics, getting different diagnoses, but more concerning were the treatment plans (which were different at each facility). At the fifth, with the "renowned real expert," the author was told that "this is a 'no brainer,' there is only one thing to do first"! Thus, the author finally had to take things into his own hands, Google, do research, and discover for himself what was the "best treatment plan" (it turned out that this fifth expert was right; the "no brainer" treatment was the first of five possible treatments, the least invasive, simplest, and least costly, and it in itself would also be "diagnostic" − if it worked we would know the cause of the condition; if it did *not* work, then we knew that the cause was different and would move on to the number two treatment). *Five different and conflicting medical opinions before a good "right" answer!* If this author had taken some of the earlier "treatment plans" presented it would have been absolutely the wrong thing to do. Additionally, eye pressure checks were needed frequently (every 2 weeks) during this period for safely monitoring the condition, involving considerable time and expense in attending the eye clinic. The author kept wondering, "Why is there not a 'smart contact lens' that can do this monitoring, sending continuous readings to the clinic?" If the author had had the smart phone mobile device current being used in Africa, he would have probably saved 17 of those 18 months of searching among different clinics, arrived at the "right answer" much faster, and received treatment earlier … all at considerably less medical cost!

This example illustrates first-hand how "fragmented" our medical knowledge is in the US Health Care Delivery System, and what needs to be done to rectify the problems:

- *If* predictive analytic models had been developed, the correct diagnosis could have been made on the first eye clinic visit.
- *If* the professional readers of this book work toward the goals presented therein, then we will have this cost-effective, accurate diagnosis and treatment in health care in the future.

Final Concluding Statements

This book has provided a background for predictive analytics; methodologies for predictive analytics; and examples of predictive analytics. It has also gone beyond that to the next step: decisioning systems that lead to action. *In today's world, data comprise the new gold.* Acquiring appropriate data has become the supreme challenge to efforts at prediction. Those who are able to obtain permission to use the data have the best chance of producing individualized models, and generally those individuals likely are those closest to the data, such as physicians, medical groups, and teaching hospitals. It does no good if those data are unavailable, however, even if they are structured in EMRs that allow communication between departments and institutions. Patients are the closest to the data, but HIPAA generally stands in the way between the data and the research. Voluntary permission for one's data to be used in research could be given in one of the many forms that new patients fill out. National groups such as PCORI can aid in joining patient data to researchers that need them. New IRB practices could include generalized informed consent to cover research both within and between institutions. New predictive techniques of analysis are imperative to the goal of individualizing practice, and reliance upon the older methodologies must be combined with newer techniques to produce better outcomes, which constitute the prize.

In addition to the "futuristic ideas" discussed in this book, we have presented *three phases* in the development of accurate, non-error, cost-effective health care:

- *Phase I* – Quality control/Six Sigma applied to medicine
- *Phase II* – Predictive analytics applied to medicine
- *Phase III* – Automatic decisioning systems applied to medicine.

Will there be a fourth phase? Yes, most likely there will be – and that will probably be the topic of our next book!

REFERENCES

AMA, 2013. ACOs and Other Options: A "how-to" Manual for Physicians Navigating a Post-Health Reform World. Fourth ed. Practice Management Center. American Medical Association, Chicago, IL. Available at: <www.acponline.org/running_practice/delivery_and_payment_models/aco/physician_howto_manual.pdf>.

Bastawrous, A., 2014 TED: Get your next eye exam on a smartphone. Available at: <www.ted.com/talks/andrew_bastawrous_get_your_next_eye_exam_on_a_smartphone?utm_campaign=&awesm=on.ted.com_quBe&utm_source=facebook.com&utm_medium=on.ted.com-facebook-share&utm_content=awesm-publisher>.

Boulos, M.N.K., Wheeler, S., Tavares, C., Jones, R., 2011. How smartphones are changing the face of mobile and participatory healthcare: an overview, with example from eCAALYX. Biomed. Eng. Online. 10, 24. Available at: <www.ncbi.nlm.nih.gov/pmc/articles/PMC3080339>.

CDC (Centers for Disease Control and Prevention), 2014. Costs of Falls Among Older Adults. CDC, Atlanta, GA. Available at: <www.cdc.gov/homeandrecreationalsafety/falls/fallcost.html> (last retrieved June 5, 2014).

Chernova, Y., 2014. Oh, Baby. Wearables track infants' vital signs. Wall Street J. 263 (111), B1.

Demiris, G., Oliver, D., Dickey, G., Skubic, M., Rantz, M., 2008. Findings from a participatory evaluation of a smart home application for older adults. Technol. Health Care. 16 (2), 111–118.

Drucker, P.F., 2006. What executives should remember. Harv. Bus. Rev. 84 (2), 144–152.

Dvorsky, G., 2014. Meet the teams who are building the world's first tricorder. Available at: io9.com/meet-the-teams-who-are-building-the-worlds-first-medic-1543000639.

Explorys, 2014. About Us: Who We Are. Explorys, Cleveland, OH. Available at: <www.explorys.com/about-us/who-we-are>.

Hay, T., 2013. Google glass could become a fixture in the operating room. Wall Street J. August 12, 2013. Available at: <http://blogs.wsj.com/venturecapital/2013/08/12/google-glass-could-become-a-fixture-in-the-operating-room>.

HIMSS Analytics, 2014. Healthcare IT News. HIMSS, Chicago, IL. Available at: <www.healthcareitnews.com/directory/himss-analytics>.

HIMSS Healthcare Global, 2014. HIMSS 2014 Uncovers 5 New mHealth Trends. HIMSS, Chicago, IL. Available at: <www.healthcareglobal.com/healthcare_technology/himss-2014-uncovers-5-new-mhealth-trends>.

HIMSS Transforming Health Through IT, 2014. Five Emerging Trends for State Public Policy & Mobile Health IT. HIMSS, Chicago, IL. Available at: <www.himss.org/ResourceLibrary/NewsDetail.aspx?ItemNumber=29708&navItemNumber=18600>.

HIMSS14, 2014. 7 Trends Healthcare Experts Anticipate in 2014. HIMSS, Chicago, IL. Available at: <www.himssconference.org/GenInfo/NewsDetail.aspx?ItemNumber=26634>.

Hotz, R.L., 2014. A future where bionics track your health. Wall Street J. 263 (93), D2.

IBM, 2012. Solutions for Healthcare: IBM Content and Predictive Analytics for Healthcare. Available at: <http://public.dhe.ibm.com/common/ssi/ecm/en/zzb03009usen/ZZB03009USEN.pdf>.

IBM, 2014. Analytics gives care providers new insights to improve individual outcomes. Available at: <www.upmc.com/media/newsreleases/2012/pages/upmc-personalized-medicine-investment.aspx> (last retrieved May 17, 2014).

Kaiser Family Foundation, n.d. Health Care Costs. Available at: <www.kaiseredu.org/Issue-Modules/US-Health-Care-Costs/Background-Brief.aspx>.

Kaiser Family Foundation, 2011. Snapshots: Health Care Spending in the United States & Selected OECD Countries, Exhibit 4A. Available at: <http://kff.org/health-costs/issue-brief/snapshots-health-care-spending-in-the-united-states-selected-oecd-countries> (last retrieved May 16, 2014).

Mace, S., 2013. Readmissions drop like a rock with predictive modeling. Predictive Analytics Times. October 30, 2013. Available at: <www.predictiveanalyticsworld.com/patimes/readmissions-drop-like-a-rock-with-predictive-modeling>.

Marcus, A.D., 2014. A hidden data treasure trove in routine checkups. Wall Street J. 263 (111), D1.

Memorial Sloan-Kettering Cancer Center, 2013. IBM Watson helps fight cancer with evidence-based diagnosis and treatment suggestions. Available at: <www.03.ibm.com/innovation/us/watson/pdf/MSK_Case_Study_IMC14794.pdf>.

Nisbet, R., Elder, J., Miner, G., 2009. Handbook of Statistical Analysis and Data Mining Applications. Elsevier, New York, NY.

PCORI, 2013. Steven Clauser to Join PCORI as Improving Healthcare Systems Program Director. PCORI, Washington, DC. Available at: <www. pcori.org/2013/steven-clauser-to-join-pcori-as-improving-healthcare-systems-program-director> (3 December 2013).

PCORI, 2014a. About Us. PCORI, Washington, DC. Available at: <http://pcori.org/about-us/mission-and-vision> (last retrieved May 17, 2014).

PCORI, 2014b. Improving Our National Infrastructure to Conduct Comparative Effectiveness Research. PCORI, Washington, DC. Available at: <http://pcori.org/funding-opportunities/improving-our-national-infrastructure-to-conduct-comparative-effectiveness-research>.

Qualcomm, 2014. Qualcomm Tricorder Prize. X Prize Foundation, Culver City, CA. Available at: <www.qualcommtricorderxprize.org/competition-details/overview>.

Rock Health, 2013. Digital Health Startup list. Available at: <http://rockhealth.com/resources/digital-health-startup-list>.

Scanadu, 2013. Scanadu Secures $10.5 Million in Series A Funding From Relay Ventures, Tony Hsieh and Jerry Yang. Press Releases, Scanadu, Mountain View, CA. Available at: <www.scanadu.com/pr> (November 11, 2013).

Scanadu, 2014. Bloomberg Businessweek – Kickstarter Lures Startups Seeking Guinea Pigs Over Cash. Scanadu Scout: Progress and Scanathon. Scanadu, Mountain View, CA. Available at: <www.scanadu.com/blog/>.

Skubic, M., Alexander, G., Popescu, M., Rantz, M., Keller, J., 2009. A smart home application to eldercare: current status and lessons learned. Technol. Health Care. 17 (3), 183−201.

Stenovec, T., 2013. Scanudu Scout, medical tricorder, passes $1 million on Indiegogo, but doesn't need the money. Huffington Post. June 20, 2013. Available at: <www.huffingtonpost.com/2013/06/20/scanadu-scout_n_3468894.html>.

Truffer, C.J., Keehan, S., Smith, S., Cylus, J., Sisko, A., Poisal, J.A., et al., 2010. Health spending projections through 2019: the recession's impact continues. Health Aff. 29 (3), 522−529.

UPMC (University of Pittsburgh Medical Center), 2012. UPMC Fosters "Personalized Medicine" with $100 Million Investment in Sophisticated Data Warehouse and Analytics. Available at: <www.upmc.com/media/newsreleases/2012/pages/upmc-personalized-medicine-investment.aspx>.

UPMC, 2014. About UMPC. UPMC, Pittsburgh, PA. Available at: <www.upmc.com/about/partners/icsd/locations/Pages/default.aspx> (last retrieved May 16, 2014).

Wang, S.S., 2014. New technologies to help seniors age in place. Wall Street J. D2, June 3, 2014.

Wicklund, E., 2014. Editor, mHealthNews; 7 mHealth Trends at HIMSS 14. mHealthNews, March 12, 2014. Available at: <www.mhealthnews.com/news/7-mhealth-trends-himss14>.

BIBLIOGRAPHY

Additional books that discuss in further detail the needs of healthcare both in the USA and globally:

Agus, D.B., 2011. The End of Illness. Free Press, New York, NY.

Berry, L.L., Seltman, K.D., 2008. Management Lessons from Mayo Clinic. McGraw Hill, New York, NY.

Boult, C., Giddens, J., Frey, K., Reider, L., Novak, T., 2009. Guided Care: A New Nurse−Physician Partnership in Chronic Care. Springer, New York, NY.

Brawley, O.W., Goldberg, P., 2011. How We Do Harm: A Doctor Breaks Ranks about Being Sick in America. St Martin's Press, New York, NY.

Carey, R.G., Lloyd, R.C., 2001. Measuring Quality Improvement in Healthcare: A Guide to Statistical Process Control Applications. ASQ (American Society for Quality) Quality Press, Milwaukee, WI.

Clifton, G.L., 2009. Flatlined: Resuscitating American Medicine. Rutgers University Press, New Brunswick, NJ.

Duncan, I., 2011. Healthcare Risk Adjustment and Predictive Modeling. ACTEX Publications, Winsted, CT.

Gawande, A., 2010. The Checklist Manifesto: How to Get Things Right. Picador (Henry Holt and Company), New York, NY.

Goldhill, D., 2013. Catastrophic Care: How American Health Care Killed my Father And How We Can Fix It. Alfred A. Knopf, New York, NY.

Kudyba, S.P. (Ed.), 2010. Healthcare Informatics: Improving Efficiency and Productivity. CRC Press, Boca Raton, FL.

Makary, M., 2012. Unaccountable: What Hospitals Won't Tell You and How Transparency Can Revolutionize Health Care. Bloomsbury Press, New York, NY.

Pronovost, P., Vohr, E., 2010. Safe Patients. Smart Hospitals: How One Doctor's Checklist Can Help Us Change Health Care from the Inside Out. Plume, New York, NY.

Reid, T.R., 2010. The Healing of America: A Global Quest for Better, Cheaper, and Fairer Health Care. Penguin, New York, NY.

Sheehan, B., 2013. Doctored. Jeff Hays Films, Sandy, UT. Available at: <www.doctoredthemovie.com/>.

Topol, E., 2012. The Creative Destruction of Medicine: How the Digital Revolution Will Create Better Health Care. Basic Books, New York, NY.

Weinberg, J.E., 2010. Teaching Medicine: A Researcher's Quest to Understand Health Care. Oxford University Press, New York, NY.

Index

Note: Page numbers followed by "*f*" and "*t*" refer to figures and tables, respectively.

CPSIA information can be obtained
at www.ICGtesting.com
Printed in the USA
LVOW05s2016061217

558084LV00027B/5/P